INTRODUCTION

We are delighted that you have decided to use the *Collins Polish Dictionary* and hope that you will enjoy using it at home, on holiday, or at work.

This introduction gives you a few tips on how to get the most out of your dictionary, not simply from its comprehensive wordlist, but also from the information provided in each entry. This will help you to read and understand modern Polish, as well as communicate and express yourself in the language.

USING THE DICTIONARY

A wealth of information is presented in the dictionary, using various typefaces, sizes of type, symbols, abbreviations, and brackets. The various conventions and symbols used are explained in the following sections.

HEADWORDS

The words you look up in a dictionary – 'headwords' – are listed alphabetically. The headwords appearing at the top of each page indicate the first word (if it appears on a left-hand page) and last word (if it appears on a right-hand page) dealt with on the page in question. Common expressions in which the headword is used are shown in bold roman type, for example:

jealous ['dʒɛləs] *adj* zazdrosny; **to be ~ of sb/sth** być zazdrosnym o kogoś/coś

TRANSLATIONS

Headword translations are given in ordinary type. You will often find other words in *italics* in brackets before the translations – these offer synonyms or suggested contexts or subject fields in which the headword might appear, for example:

landing ['lændɪŋ] *n* **1** (*on stairs*) podest **2** (*Aviat*) lądowanie

KEY WORDS

Special status is given to certain Polish and English words which are considered 'key' words in each language. They may, for example, occur very frequently or have several types of usage (eg **get, have, mieć**). The layout of the entry helps you to distinguish different parts of speech and meanings. Further helpful information is provided in brackets and *italics*.

GRAMMATICAL INFORMATION

Parts of speech are given in abbreviated form after the inflected forms of the headword on the Polish-English side, and after the phonetic spellings on the English-Polish side of the dictionary. Genders of Polish nouns are indicated as follows: *m* for masculine nouns, *f* for feminine nouns, and *nt* for neuter nouns. Plural is shown with the abbreviation *pl*.

Information about the inflected forms of headwords (verb conjugations, cases, irregular plurals and so on) is given in brackets immediately after the headword on the Polish-English side of the dictionary. The first letter of the inflection corresponds to the point where the ending adds onto the main form, for example:

fot|ka (**-ki**, **-ki**; *dat sg* **-ce**; *gen pl* **-ek**) *f* (*fotografia*) snap

We have shown genitive and plural information for all nouns, and other cases only where they are irregular. Verb conjugations have also been shown for all verbs. Polish translations of adjectives have been given in the masculine as the default, as have translations of phrases which use the first person singular.

The second person singular has been translated into Polish using the formal *pan/pani* construction, unless otherwise indicated.

We have shown which cases follow particular parts of speech. Where there is no information about case, it can be assumed that the accusative case is used.

Finally, the perfective aspect of each verb has been shown at the imperfective headword, where it exists. In phrases, verbs have been shown with both aspects where they both work in the context. Where there is no information about the aspect of a verb, it can be assumed that it only works in that context in the imperfective, and therefore does not need to be marked.

For more information on Polish irregular forms, see pages xii–xxi.

SKRÓTY		ABBREVIATIONS
skrót	*abbr*	abbreviation
biernik	*acc*	accusative
przymiotnik	*adj*	adjective
administracja	*Admin*	administration
przysłówek	*adv*	adverb
rolnictwo	*Agr*	agriculture
anatomia	*Anat*	anatomy
architektura	*Archit*	architecture
astrologia	*Astrol*	astrology
astronomia	*Astron*	astonomy
motoryzacja	*Aut*	automobiles
czasownik posiłkowy	*aux verb*	auxiliary verb
lotnictwo	*Aviat*	aviation
biologia	*Bio*	biology
botanika	*Bot*	botany
język angielski brytyjski	*Brit*	British English
budownictwo	*Bud*	construction
chemia	*Chem*	chemistry
kino	*Cine*	cinema
handel i biznes	*Comm*	business
stopień wyższy	*compar*	comparative
komputery	*Comput*	computing
spójnik	*conj*	conjunction
budownictwo	*Constr*	construction
kulinaria	*Culin*	cookery
celownik	*dat*	dative
przedimek określony	*def art*	definite article
zdrobnienie	*dimin*	diminutive
dosłowny	*dosł*	literal
drukarstwo	*Druk*	printing
ekonomia	*Econ, Ekon*	economics
elektronika	*Elec, Elektr*	electronics
szczególnie	*esp*	especially
i temu podobne	*etc*	et cetera
wykrzyknienie	*excl*	exclamation
rodzaj żeński	*f*	feminine
w przenośnym znaczeniu	*fig*	figurative
finanse	*Fin*	finance
fizyka	*Fiz*	physics
fotografia	*Fot*	photography
ogólnie rzecz biorąc	*gen*	generally
dopełniacz	*gen*	genitive
geografia	*Geo*	geography
geologia	*Geol*	geology
geometria	*Geom*	geometry
historia	*Hist*	history
aspekt niedokonany	*impf*	imperfective
wyraz nieodmienny	*ind*	indeclinable
przedimek nieokreślony	*indef art*	indefinite article
nieformalny	*inf*	informal
obraźliwy	*inf!*	offensive
bezokolicznik	*infin*	infinitive
narzędnik	*inst*	instrumental
niezmienny	*inv*	invariable
nieregularny	*irreg*	irregular
językoznawstwo	*Jęz*	linguistics
prawniczy	*Jur*	law
informatyka, komputery	*Komput*	computing
kulinaria	*Kulin*	cookery
język	*Ling*	language
literatura	*Lit*	literature
dosłowny	*lit*	literal
miejscownik	*loc*	locative

Collins
POLISH
DICTIONARY
ESSENTIAL EDITION

Published by Collins
An imprint of HarperCollins Publishers
Westerhill Road
Bishopbriggs
Glasgow G64 2QT

First Edition 2019

10 9 8 7 6 5 4 3 2 1

ISBN 978-0-00-827064-3

www.collinsdictionary.com

Typeset by Davidson Publishing Solutions, Glasgow

Printed and bound by CPI Group (UK) Ltd, Croydon, CR0 4YY

A catalogue record for this book is available from the British Library.

If you would like to comment on any aspect of this book, please contact us at the given address or online.
E-mail: dictionaries@harpercollins.co.uk
facebook.com/collinsdictionary
@collinsdict

Acknowledgements
We would like to thank those authors and publishers who kindly gave permission for copyright material to be used in the Collins Corpus. We would also like to thank Times Newspapers Ltd for providing valuable data.

SPIS TREŚCI

CONTENTS

WPROWADZENIE

Cieszymy się, że wybraliście Państwo nasz słownik Collins Polish Dictionary, i mamy nadzieję, że z przyjemnością będziecie z niego korzystać w domu, w podróży i w pracy.

W niniejszym wprowadzeniu podajemy kilka wskazówek, jak najlepiej korzystać ze słownika – nie tylko z samych jego haseł, lecz również z informacji znajdujących się przy każdym z nich. Pomoże to Państwu nie tylko lepiej czytać i rozumieć współczesny język angielski, ale również skutecznie w nim się porozumiewać.

JAK KORZYSTAĆ ZE SŁOWNIKA

Wiele informacji jest przekazanych w słowniku za pomocą różnego rodzaju czcionek, skrótów oraz nawiasów. Użyte oznaczenia i symbole wyjaśnione są poniżej.

WYRAZY HASŁOWE

Wyrazy hasłowe, czyli słowa, których szukacie Państwo w słowniku, są ułożone alfabetycznie. U góry każdej strony znaleźć można pierwszy (na stronie lewej) i ostatni wyraz hasłowy (na stronie prawej) pojawiający się na danej stronie.

Popularne zwroty, w których użyty jest wyraz hasłowy, zapisane są wytłuszczonym drukiem, na przykład:

da|ta (**-ty**, **-ty**; *dat & loc sg* **-cie**) *f* (*termin*) date; **~ urodzenia** date of birth

ZNACZENIA

Znaczenia wyrazów hasłowych podane są zwykłą czcionką. Często napotkacie Państwo również słowa pisane *kursywą* w nawiasach przed tłumaczeniami – są one po to, aby podawać synonimy, sugerowane konteksty albo pola znaczeniowe, w których słowo hasłowe może wystąpić, na przykład:

drama|t (**-tu**, **-ty**; *loc sg* **-cie**) *m* **1** (*Lit*) drama **2** (*nieszczęście*) tragedy

SŁOWA KLUCZOWE

Specjalną rangę otrzymały niektóre polskie bądź angielskie słowa, które potraktowane zostały jako „słowa kluczowe". Mogą one na przykład często występować w danym języku albo też mieć wiele różnych zastosowań (na przyktad **mieć, get, have**). Układ graficzny hasła ma za zadanie pomóc Państwu w odpowiednim rozpoznaniu części mowy i znaczeń. Dalszej pomocy udzielić mogą informacje zawarte w nawiasach bądź pisane *kursywą*.

INFORMACJE GRAMATYCZNE

Części mowy oznaczone są za pomocą skrótów (na przyktad: *adj*, *conj*). Znaleźć je można po informacji o końcówkach fleksyjnych wyrazu hasłowego (w części polsko-angielskiej) lub po transkrypcji fonetycznej (w części angielsko-polskiej). Rodzaje polskich rzeczowników oznaczone są następująco: *m* dla rzeczowników rodzaju męskiego, *f* dla rodzaju żeńskiego, a *nt* dla rodzaju nijakiego. Liczba mnoga jest oznaczona skrótem *pl*.

Informacja odnośnie odmiany wyrazów hasłowych (koniugacje czasowników, przypadki, nieregularne formy liczby mnogiej itp.) podana jest w nawiasach zaraz po wyrazie hasłowym.

lie[1] [laɪ] (*pt* **lay**, *pp* **lain**) *vi* leżeć

Końcówki dopełniacza oraz liczby mnogiej podane zostały dla wszystkich rzeczowników zamieszczonych w słowniku, końcówki pozostałych przypadków tylko wtedy, gdy są one nieregularne.

Formy koniugacji czasowników zostały podane tylko w przypadku nieregularnej ich odmiany. Jeśli chodzi o polskie tłumaczenia przymiotników, podane one są w rodzaju męskim, zaś tłumaczenia zwrotów domyślnie używają pierwszej osoby liczby pojedynczej.

W przypadku czasowników oba aspekty (niedokonany/dokonany) podane są tam, gdzie występują obie formy. Tam, gdzie nie ma żadnej informacji o aspekcie czasownika, należy przyjąć, iż posiada on tylko formę niedokonaną.

lotnictwo	*Lot*	aviation
rodzaj męski	*m*	masculine
matematyka	*Mat, Math*	mathematics
medycyna	*Med*	medicine
meteorologia	*Meteo, Meteor*	meteorology
rodzaj męski/rodzaj żeński	*m/f*	masculine/feminine
wojskowy	*Mil*	military
motoryzacja	*Mot*	motoring
muzyka	*Mus, Muz*	music
mitologia	*Myth*	mythology
rzeczownik	*n*	noun
żeglarstwo	*Naut*	sailing
mianownik	*nom*	nominative
rodzaj męski nieosobowy	*non-vir*	non-virile
rodzaj nijaki	*nt*	neuter
liczba	*num*	number
staromodny	*o.f.*	old-fashioned
siebie, się, sobie, sobą,	*o.s.*	oneself
parlament	*Parl*	parliament
partykuła	*part*	particle
aspekt dokonany	*pf*	perfective
fotografia	*Phot*	photography
fizyka	*Phys*	physics
fizjologia	*Physiol*	physiology
pejoratywny	*pej*	pejorative
liczba mnoga	*pl*	plural
polityka	*Pol*	politics
potoczny	*pot*	informal
obraźliwy	*pot!*	offensive
imiesłów przeszły	*pp*	past participle
przyimek	*prep*	preposition
zaimek	*pron*	pronoun
przenośny	*przen*	figurative
psychologia	*Psych*	psychology
czas przeszły	*pt*	past tense
radio	*Rad*	radio
koleje	*Rail*	railways
religia	*Rel*	religion
rolnictwo	*Rol*	agriculture
ktoś	*sb*	somebody
nauka	*Sci*	science
szkolnictwo	*Scol, Szkol*	schooling
liczba pojedyncza	*sg*	singular
socjologia	*Sociol*	sociology
coś	*sth*	something
stopień najwyższy	*superl*	superlative
technologia	*Tech*	technology
telekomunikacja	*Tel*	telecommunications
teatr	*Teatr, Theat*	theatre
telewizja	*TV*	television
typografia	*Typ*	typography
uniwersytet	*Univ, Uniw*	university
język angielski amerykański	*US*	American English
zazwyczaj	*usu*	usually
czasownik	*vb*	verb
czasownik nieprzechodni	*vi*	intransitive verb
rodzaj męskoosobowy	*vir*	virile
wołacz	*voc*	vocative
czasownik przechodni	*vt*	transitive verb
czasownik złożony (nierozdzielny)	*vt fus*	phrasal verb (where the particle is inseparable)
wojskowość	*Wojsk*	military
zoologia	*Zool*	zoology
żegluga	*Zegl*	nautical
znak towarowy zastrzeżony	®	registered trademark
poprzedza ekwiwalent kulturowy	≈	introduces a cultural equivalent

POLISH PRONUNCIATION

Generally, every letter in Polish corresponds to one sound and, apart from ch, cz, sz, dz, dź, dż, and rz, every letter is pronounced separately.

VOWELS

The pronunciation of Polish vowels resembles that of Spanish or Italian. Every vowel is pronounced and there is no variation in their sound as in English.

hat	a	*matka*
best	e	*gest, tekst*
seek	i	*blisko*
slot	o	*Polska, most*
goose, loo	u = ó	*student, ból*
grim	y	*syn, pytam*

NASAL VOWELS

song	ą	*mądry, książka*
Tom	ąb, ąp	*ząb, gąbka*
ten, Bengali	ę	*często, więcej*
them	ęb, ęp	*gęba, sęp*
net	final ę	*uczę się*

CONSONANTS

Most Polish consonants are pronounced just as in English. A few are pronounced differently:

guts, lots	c	*co, nic*
hill, horse	ch = h	*chyba, hotel*
much, church	cz	*wieczór, cześć*
cheese	ć = ci	*rozumieć, cię*
goods	dz	*bardzo, dzwon*
Jimmy, jeans	dź = dzi	*dźwięk, dziś*
jungle, gentlemen	dż	*dżungla, dżentelmen*
yellow	j	*jeden, maj*
window, wow	ł	*ładny, miło*
onion	ń = ni	*Gdańsk, do widzenia*
"rolling r"	r	*proszę, dobra*
sure	ś, si	*dziś, dzisiaj*
mash, show	sz	*paszport, masz*
Victoria	w	*Wiktoria, piwo*
garage, pleasure	ż = rz	*garaż, dobrze*
Rhodesia	ź = zi	*źle, zielony*

VOICED AND UNVOICED CONSONANTS

Some consonants become unvoiced in certain positions in a word, i.e. at the end of a word and before or after a voiceless consonant:

chleb	pronounced	[chlep]
jabłko	pronounced	[yapko]
wódka	pronounced	[vootka]
ogród	pronounced	[ogrut]
róg	pronounced	[ruk]
lew	pronounced	[lef]
wszystko	pronounced	[fshystko]
wyraz	pronounced	[wyras]
weź	pronounced	[vesh]
wódz	pronounced	[voots]
Łódź	pronounced	[Wootch]
też	pronounced	[tesh]
brydż	pronounced	[brych]

WYMOWA ANGIELSKA

ENGLISH PRONUNCIATION

SPÓŁGŁOSKI		CONSONANTS
Polska	[p]	*puppy*
bilet	[b]	*baby*
tutaj, tenis	[t]	*tent*
dom	[d]	*daddy*
korek, kawa	[k]	*cork, kiss, chord*
gag, gazeta	[g]	*gag, guess*
sklep, masło	[s]	*so, rice, kiss*
kuzyn, zero	[z]	*cousin, buzz*
szok, szelest	[ʃ]	*sheep, sugar*
ważny, beż	[ʒ]	*pleasure, beige*
czerwony, czas	[tʃ]	*church*
dżem, dżungla	[dʒ]	*judge, general*
farma, fotel	[f]	*farm, raffle*
Warszawa, woda	[v]	*very, rev*
wymawia się jak "s" z językiem między zębami	[θ]	*thin, maths*
wymawia się jak "z" z językiem między zębami	[ð]	*that, other*
list, lato	[l]	*little, ball*
brak polskiego odpowiednika, wymawiać jak polskie "r"	[R]	
retrofleksyjne "r"	[r]	*rat, rare*
mama, minuta	[m]	*mummy, comb*
noga, mina	[n]	*no, ran*
Bank (wymowa z niemym "k")	[ŋ]	*singing, bank*
hotel, wiecha	[h]	*hat, reheat*
jeden, Maja	[j]	*yet*
łaska, łoskot	[w]	*wall, bewail*
loch	[x]	*loch*

NB. Zestawienie niektórych par angielskich samogłosek i ich polskich odpowiedników odzwierciedla tylko ich częściowe podobieństwo brzmieniowe.

NB. The pairing of some vowel sounds only indicates approximate equivalence.

SAMOGŁOSKI		VOWELS
list	iː	*heel, bead*
syn.	ɪ	*hit, pity*
tekst, prezent	ɛ	*set, tent*
otwarte "e"	æ	*bat, apple*
Ala, mały, kasa	ɑː	*after, car, calm*
fanfary	ʌ	*fun, cousin*
samogłoska centralna nieakcentowana	ə	*over, above*
długa samogłoska centralna	əː	*fern, work*
potok, grosz	ɔ	*wash, pot*
korek, lotnisko	ɔː	*born, cork*
gust, bufet	u	*full, soot*
długie "u" z zakrąglonymi wargami	uː	*boot, crew*
myśl	ɪ	*lynch*

DYFTONGI		DIPHTHONGS
połączenie	ɪə	*beer, pier*
połączenie	ɛə	*tear, fair*
lejce,	eɪ	*date, place, day*
maj, kraj	aɪ	*life, buy, cry*
mały	au	*owl, foul, now*
ołtarz	əu	*low, no*
moje	ɔɪ	*boil, boy, oil*
połączenie	uə	*poor, tour*

Poprawną wymowę wyrazu hasłowego podajemy w nawiasach kwadratowych, umieszczonych po danym słowie.

ANGIELSKIE CZASOWNIKI NIEREGULARNE

present	pt	pp
arise	arose	arisen
awake	awoke	awoken
be (am, is, are; being)	was, were	been
bear	bore	born(e)
beat	beat	beaten
begin	began	begun
bend	bent	bent
bet	bet, betted	bet, betted
bid *(at auction)*	bid	bid
bind	bound	bound
bite	bit	bitten
bleed	bled	bled
blow	blew	blown
break	broke	broken
breed	bred	bred
bring	brought	brought
build	built	built
burn	burnt, burned	burnt, burned
burst	burst	burst
buy	bought	bought
can	could	(been able)
cast	cast	cast
catch	caught	caught
choose	chose	chosen
cling	clung	clung
come	came	come
cost	cost	cost
creep	crept	crept
cut	cut	cut
deal	dealt	dealt
dig	dug	dug
do (does)	did	done
draw	drew	drawn
dream	dreamed, dreamt	dreamed, dreamt
drink	drank	drunk
drive	drove	driven
eat	ate	eaten
fall	fell	fallen
feed	fed	fed
feel	felt	felt
fight	fought	fought
find	found	found
fling	flung	flung
fly	flew	flown
forbid	forbad(e)	forbidden
forecast	forecast	forecast
forget	forgot	forgotten
forgive	forgave	forgiven
freeze	froze	frozen
get	got	got, *(US)* gotten
give	gave	given
go (goes)	went	gone
grind	ground	ground
grow	grew	grown
hang	hung	hung
hang *(execute)*	hanged	hanged

present	pt	pp
have	had	had
hear	heard	heard
hide	hid	hidden
hit	hit	hit
hold	held	held
hurt	hurt	hurt
keep	kept	kept
kneel	knelt, kneeled	knelt, kneeled
know	knew	known
lay	laid	laid
lead	led	led
lean	leant, leaned	leant, leaned
leap	leapt, leaped	leapt, leaped
learn	learnt, learned	learnt, learned
leave	left	left
lend	lent	lent
let	let	let
lie (lying)	lay	lain
light	lit, lighted	lit, lighted
lose	lost	lost
make	made	made
may	might	–
mean	meant	meant
meet	met	met
mistake	mistook	mistaken
mow	mowed	mown, mowed
must	(had to)	(had to)
pay	paid	paid
put	put	put
quit	quit, quitted	quit, quitted
read	read	read
rid	rid	rid
ride	rode	ridden
ring	rang	rung
rise	rose	risen
run	ran	run
saw	sawed	sawed, sawn
say	said	said
see	saw	seen
sell	sold	sold
send	sent	sent
set	set	set
sew	sewed	sewn
shake	shook	shaken
shear	sheared	shorn, sheared
shed	shed	shed
shine	shone	shone
shoot	shot	shot
show	showed	shown
shrink	shrank	shrunk
shut	shut	shut
sing	sang	sung
sink	sank	sunk
sit	sat	sat

present	pt	pp
sleep	slept	slept
slide	slid	slid
sling	slung	slung
slit	slit	slit
smell	smelt, smelled	smelt, smelled
sow	sowed	sown, sowed
speak	spoke	spoken
speed	sped, speeded	sped, speeded
spell	spelt, spelled	spelt, spelled
spend	spent	spent
spill	spilt, spilled	spilt, spilled
spin	spun	spun
spit	spat	spat
spoil	spoiled, spoilt	spoiled, spoilt
spread	spread	spread
spring	sprang	sprung
stand	stood	stood
steal	stole	stolen
stick	stuck	stuck
sting	stung	stung
stink	stank	stunk
stride	strode	stridden
strike	struck	struck
swear	swore	sworn
sweep	swept	swept
swell	swelled	swollen, swelled
swim	swam	swum
swing	swung	swung
take	took	taken
teach	taught	taught
tear	tore	torn
tell	told	told
think	thought	thought
throw	threw	thrown
thrust	thrust	thrust
tread	trod	trodden
wake	woke, waked	woken, waked
wear	wore	worn
weave	wove	woven
weep	wept	wept
win	won	won
wind	wound	wound
wring	wrung	wrung
write	wrote	written

TABLES OF POLISH IRREGULAR FORMS

NUMERALS

CARDINAL NUMERALS

The number 1 has three forms: **jeden** (*m*); **jedna** (*f*); **jedno** (*nt*) and declines like an adjective.

	m	*f*	*nt*
nom	jeden	jedna	jedno
gen	jednego	jednej	jednego
dat	jednemu	jednej	jednemu
acc	jeden, jednego	jedną	jedno
inst	jednym	jedną	jednym
loc	jednym	jednej	jednym

2 (**dwa**) declines as follows:

	vir	*non-vir nt*	*f*
nom	dwaj	dwa	dwie
gen	dwóch, dwu	dwóch, dwu	dwóch, dwu
dat	dwóm, dwu, dwom	dwóm, dwu, dwom	dwóm, dwu, dwom
acc	dwóch	dwa	dwie
inst	dwoma	dwoma	dwoma, dwiema
loc	dwóch, dwu	dwóch, dwu	dwóch, dwu

3 and 4 follow the same pattern:

	vir	*non-vir*
nom	czterej	cztery
gen	czterech	czterech
dat	czterem	czterem
acc	czterech	cztery
inst	czterema	czterema
loc	czterech	czterech

5, 6, 7, 8, 9 and 10 follow this pattern:

	vir	*non-vir*
nom	pięciu	pięć
gen	pięciu	pięciu
dat	pięciu	pięciu
acc	pięciu	pięć
inst	pięciu, pięcioma	pięciu, pięcioma
loc	pięciu	pięciu

11, 13, 14, 15, 16, 17, 18 and 19 follow this pattern:

	vir	*non-vir*
nom	jedenastu	jedenaście
gen	jedenastu	jedenastu
dat	jedenastu	jedenastu
acc	jedenastu	jedenaście
inst	jedenastu, jedenastoma	jedenastu, jedenastoma
loc	jedenastu	jedenastu

The stem 'dwa' declines in numbers 12 and 20.

	vir	*non-vir*
nom	dwunastu	dwanaście
gen	dwunastu	dwunastu
dat	dwunastu	dwunastu
acc	dwunastu	dwanaście
inst	dwunastu, dwunastoma	dwunastu, dwunastoma
loc	dwunastu	dwunastu

20 declines as follows. 30 and 40 decline in the same way as 20.

	vir	*non-vir*
nom	dwudziestu	dwadzieścia
gen	dwudziestu	dwudziestu
dat	dwudziestu	dwudziestu
acc	dwudziestu	dwadzieścia
inst	dwudziestu, dwudziestoma	dwudziestu, dwudziestoma
loc	dwudziestu	dwudziestu

50, 60, 70, 80 and 90 follow this pattern:

	vir	*non-vir*
nom	pięćdziesięciu	pięćdziesiąt
gen	pięćdziesięciu	pięćdziesiąt
dat	pięćdziesięciu	pięćdziesięciu
acc	pięćdziesięciu	pięćdziesiąt
inst	pięćdziesięciu, pięćdziesięcioma	pięćdziesięciu, pięćdziesięcioma
loc	pięćdziesięciu	pięćdziesięciu

100 and 200 decline as follows:

	vir	*non-vir*
nom, acc	stu	sto
gen, dat, loc	stu	stu
inst	stoma	stoma

	vir	*non-vir*
nom, acc	dwustu	dwieście
gen, dat, loc	dwustu	dwustu
inst	dwustoma	dwustoma

300 and 400 decline as follows:

	vir	*non-vir*
nom, acc	trzystu	trzysta
gen, dat, loc	trzystu	trzystu
inst	trzystoma	trzystoma

500, 600, 700, 800 and 900 follow this pattern:

	vir	*non-vir*
nom, acc	pięciuset	pięćset
gen, dat, loc, inst	pięciuset	pięciuset

1000 declines as follows:

	sg	*pl*
nom	tysiąc	tysiące
gen	tysiąca	tysięcy
dat	tysiącowi	tysiącom
acc	tysiąc	tysiące
inst	tysiącem	tysiącami
loc	tysiącu	tysiącach

COLLECTIVE NUMERALS

Collective numerals refer to mixed gender groups.

The numbers **dwoje** (2), **troje** (3), **czworo** (4), **pięcioro** (5), **sześcioro** (6), **siedmioro** (7), **ośmioro** (8), **dziewięcioro** (9), **dziesięcioro** (10), **jedenaścioro** (11), **dwanaścioro** (12) decline as follows. Each numeral takes the case shown in the table.

nom	dwoje	czworo	pięcioro	*+gen*
gen	dwojga	czworga	pięciorga	*+gen*
dat	dwojgu	czworgu	pięciorgu	*+dat*
acc	dwoje	czworo	pięcioro	*+gen*
inst	dwojgiem	czworgiem	pięciorgiem	*+gen*
loc	dwojgu	czworgu	pięciorgu	*+loc*

PRONOUNS

PERSONAL PRONOUNS

Singular

nom	ja	ty	on *(m)*	ona *(f)*	ono *(nt)*
gen	mnie	ciebie, cię	jego, niego, go	jej, niej	jego, niego, go
dat	mnie, mi	tobie, ci	jemu, niemu, mu	jej, niej	jemu, niemu, mu
acc	mnie	ciebie, cię	jego, niego, go	ją, nią	je, nie
inst	mną	tobą	nim	nią	nim
loc	mnie	tobie	nim	niej	nim

Plural

nom	my	wy	oni *(vir)*	one *(non-vir)*
gen	nas	was	ich, nich	ich, nich
dat	nam	wam	im, nim	im, nim
acc	nas	was	ich, nich	je, nie
inst	nami	wami	nimi	nimi
loc	nas	was	nich	nich

pan/pani

	m sg	*f sg*	*m pl*	*f pl*	*m & f pl*
nom	pan	pani	panowie	panie	państwo
gen	pana	pani	panów	pań	państwa
dat	panu	pani	panom	paniom	państwu
acc	pana	panią	panów	panie	państwa
inst	panem	panią	panami	paniami	państwem
loc	panu	pani	panach	paniach	państwu
voc	pan	pani	panowie	panie	państwo

POSSESSIVE PRONOUNS

mój, **swój** and **twój** decline as follows:

Singular

	m	*f*	*nt*	*vir pl*	*non-vir pl*
nom	mój	moja	moje	moi	moje
gen	mojego	mojej	mojego	moich	moich
dat	mojemu	mojej	mojemu	moim	moim
acc	mój, mojego	moją	moje	moich	moje
inst	moim	moją	moim	moimi	moimi
loc	moim	mojej	moim	moich	moich

wasz follows the same pattern as **nasz**:

Singular

	m	*f*	*nt*	*vir pl*	*non-vir pl*
nom	nasz	nasza	nasze	nasi	nasze
gen	naszego	naszej	naszego	naszych	naszych
dat	naszemu	naszej	naszemu	naszym	naszym
acc	nasz, naszego	naszą	nasz, naszego	naszych	nasze
inst	naszym	naszą	naszym	naszymi	naszymi
loc	naszym	naszej	naszym	naszymi	naszych

The following do not decline:

its, his	jego
her, hers	jej
their, theirs	ich
your, yours (*polite m sg*)	pana
your, yours (*polite f sg*)	pani

INTERROGATIVE PRONOUNS

kto/co

nom	kto	co
gen	kogo	czego
dat	komu	czemu
acc	kogo	co
inst	kim	czym
loc	kim	czym

REFLEXIVE PRONOUNS

nom	—
gen, acc	siebie, się
dat, loc	sobie
inst	sobą

RELATIVE PRONOUNS

czyj

	m	*f*	*nt*	*vir pl*	*non-vir pl*
nom	czyj	czyja	czyje	czyi	czyje
gen	czyjego	czyjej	czyjego	czyich	czyich
dat	czyjemu	czyjej	czyjemu	czyim	czyim
acc	czyj, czyjego	czyją	czyje	czyich	czyje
inst	czyim	czyją	czyim	czyimi	czyimi
loc	czyim	czyjej	czyim	czyich	czyich

jaki follows the same pattern as **który**:

	m	*f*	*nt*	*vir pl*	*non-vir pl*
nom	który	która	które	którzy	które
gen	którego	której	którego	których	których
dat	któremu	której	któremu	którym	którym
acc	który, którego	którą	które	których	które
inst	którym	którą	którym	którymi	którymi
loc	którym	której	którym	których	których

DEMONSTRATIVE PRONOUNS

	m	*f*	*nt*	*vir pl*	*non-vir pl*
nom	ten	ta	to	ci	te
gen	tego	tej	tego	tych	tych
dat	temu	tej	temu	tym	tym
acc	ten, tego	tę	to	tych	te
inst	tym	tą	tym	tymi	tymi
loc	tym	tej	tym	tych	tych

NOUNS

Masculine

	animate			
	singular	*plural (irreg)*	*singular*	*plural (irreg)*
nom	mąż	mężowie	człowiek	ludzie
gen	męża	mężów	człowieka	ludzi
dat	mężowi	mężom	człowiekowi	ludziom
acc	męża	mężów	człowieka	ludzi
inst	mężem	mężami	człowiekiem	ludźmi
loc	mężu	mężach	człowieku	ludziach
voc	mężu	mężowie	człowieku	ludzie

	inanimate			
	singular	*plural*	*singular*	*plural*
nom	sklep	sklepy	stół	stoły
gen	sklepu	sklepów	stołu	stołów
dat	sklepowi	sklepom	stołowi	stołom
acc	sklep	sklepy	stół	stoły
inst	sklepem	sklepami	stołem	stołami
loc	sklepie	sklepach	stole	stołach
voc	sklep	sklepy	stole	stoły

Feminine

	singular	*plural*	*singular*	*plural*
nom	kobieta	kobiety	noga	nogi
gen	kobiety	kobiet	nogi	nóg
dat	kobiecie	kobietom	nodze	nogom
acc	kobietę	kobiety	nogę	nogi
inst	kobietą	kobietami	nogą	nogami
loc	kobiecie	kobietach	nodze	nogach
voc	kobieto	kobiety	nogo	nogi

Neuter

	singular	*plural*	*singular*	*plural*
nom	miasto	miasta	dziecko	dzieci
gen	miasta	miast	dziecka	dzieci
dat	miastu	miastom	dziecku	dzieciom
acc	miasto	miasta	dziecko	dzieci
inst	miastem	miastami	dzieckiem	dziećmi
loc	mieście	miastach	dziecku	dzieciach
voc	miasto	miasta	dziecko	dzieci

	singular	*plural*
nom	imię	imiona
gen	imienia	imion
dat	imieniu	imionom
acc	imię	imiona
inst	imieniem	imionami
loc	imieniu	imionach
voc	imię	imiona

ADJECTIVES

	m	*f*	*nt*	*vir pl*	*non-vir pl*
nom	dobry	dobra	dobre	dobrzy	dobre
gen	dobrego	dobrej	dobrego	dobrych	dobrych
dat	dobremu	dobrej	dobremu	dobrym	dobrym
acc	dobry, dobrego	dobrą	dobre	dobrych	dobre
inst	dobrym	dobrą	dobrym	dobrymi	dobrymi
loc	dobrym	dobrej	dobrym	dobrych	dobrych
voc	dobry	dobra	dobre	dobrzy	dobre

VERB CONJUGATIONS

First Conjugation

pisać to write

PRESENT

(ja)	piszę
(ty)	piszesz
(on)	pisze
(ona)	pisze
(ono)	pisze
(my)	piszemy
(wy)	piszecie
(oni)	piszą
(one)	piszą

PAST

(ja)	pisałem/pisałam
(ty)	pisałeś/pisałaś
(on)	pisał
(ona)	pisała
(ono)	pisało
(my)	pisaliśmy/pisałyśmy
(wy)	pisaliście/pisałyście
(oni)	pisali
(one)	pisały

IMPERATIVE

(ja)	—
(ty)	pisz
(on, ona, ono)	niech pisze
(my)	piszmy
(wy)	piszcie
(oni, one)	niech piszą

FUTURE

The way the future tense is formed depends on whether you are using an imperfective or a perfective verb.

Perfective: Conjugate the verb as if it were the present tense.

powiedzieć (*to say*)
powiem ci później – I will tell you later

Imperfective: Use the verb **być** (*to be*) in its future form, followed either by the infinitive or the third person past form of the verb.

być (future form) + infinitive
or
być (future form) + past form

będę pisać – I will write
będzie czytał – he will read
będą zaczynali – they will begin

Second Conjugation

płacić to pay

PRESENT

(ja)	płacę
(ty)	płacisz
(on)	płaci
(ona)	płaci
(ono)	płaci
(my)	płacimy
(wy)	płacicie
(oni)	płacą
(one)	płacą

PAST

(ja)	płaciłem/płaciłam
(ty)	płaciłeś/płaciłeś
(on)	płacił
(ona)	płaciła
(ono)	płaciło
(my)	płaciliśmy/płaciłyśmy
(wy)	płaciliście/płaciłyście
(oni)	płacili
(one)	płaciły

IMPERATIVE

(ja)	—
(ty)	płać
(on, ona, ono)	niech płaci
(my)	płaćmy
(wy)	płaćcie
(oni, one)	niech płacą

FUTURE

See First Conjugation

Third Conjugation

czytać to read

PRESENT		PAST	
(ja)	czytam	(ja)	czytałem/czytałam
(ty)	czytasz	(ty)	czytałeś/czytałaś
(on)	czyta	(on)	czytał
(ona)	czyta	(ona)	czytała
(ono)	czyta	(ono)	czytało
(my)	czytamy	(my)	czytaliśmy/czytałyśmy
(wy)	czytacie	(wy)	czytaliście/czytałyście
(oni)	czytają	(oni)	czytali
(one)	czytają	(one)	czytały

IMPERATIVE		FUTURE
(ja)	—	See First Conjugation
(ty)	czytaj	
(on, ona, ono)	niech czyta	
(my)	czytajmy	
(wy)	czytajcie	
(oni, one)	niech czytają	

Fourth Conjugation

wiedzieć to know

PRESENT		PAST	
(ja)	wiem	(ja)	wiedziałem/wiedziałam
(ty)	wiesz	(ty)	wiedziałeś/wiedziałaś
(on)	wie	(on)	wiedział
(ona)	wie	(ona)	wiedziała
(ono)	wie	(ono)	wiedziało
(my)	wiemy	(my)	wiedzieliśmy/wiedziałyśmy
(wy)	wiecie	(wy)	wiedzieliście/wiedziałyście
(oni)	wiedzą	(oni)	wiedzieli
(one)	wiedzą	(one)	wiedziały

IMPERATIVE		FUTURE
(ja)	—	See First Conjugation
(ty)	wiedz	
(on, ona, ono)	niech wie	
(my)	wiedzmy	
(wy)	wiedzcie	
(oni, one)	niech wiedzą	

IRREGULAR VERBS

być to be

PRESENT		PAST	
(ja)	jestem	(ja)	byłem/byłam
(ty)	jesteś	(ty)	byłeś/byłaś
(on)	jest	(on)	był
(ona)	jest	(ona)	była
(ono)	jest	(ono)	było
(my)	jesteśmy	(my)	byliśmy/byłyśmy
(wy)	jesteście	(wy)	byliście/byłyście
(oni)	są	(oni)	byli
(one)	są	(one)	były

IMPERATIVE		FUTURE	
(ja)	—	(ja)	będę
(ty)	bądź	(ty)	będziesz
(on, ona, ono)	niech będzie	(on, ona, ono)	będzie
(my)	bądźmy	(my)	będziemy
(wy)	bądźcie	(wy)	będziecie
(oni, one)	niech będą	(oni, one)	będą

---

iść to go

PRESENT		PAST	
(ja)	idę	(ja)	szedłem/szłam
(ty)	idziesz	(ty)	szedłeś/szłaś
(on)	idzie	(on)	szedł
(ona)	idzie	(ona)	szła
(ono)	idzie	(ono)	szło
(my)	idziemy	(my)	szliśmy/szłyśmy
(wy)	idziecie	(wy)	szliście/szłyście
(oni)	idą	(oni)	szli
(one)	idą	(one)	szły

IMPERATIVE		FUTURE	
(ja)	—	See First Conjugation	
(ty)	idź		
(on, ona, ono)	niech idzie		
(my)	idźmy		
(wy)	idźcie		
(oni, one)	niech idą		

mieć to have

PRESENT		PAST	
(ja)	mam	(ja)	miałem/miałam
(ty)	masz	(ty)	miałeś/miałaś
(on)	ma	(on)	miał
(ona)	ma	(ona)	miała
(ono)	ma	(ono)	miało
(my)	mamy	(my)	mieliśmy/miałyśmy
(wy)	macie	(wy)	mieliście/miałyście
(oni)	mają	(oni)	mieli
(one)	mają	(one)	miały

IMPERATIVE		FUTURE
(ja)	—	See First Conjugation
(ty)	miej	
(on, ona, ono)	niech ma	
(my)	miejmy	
(wy)	miejcie	
(oni, one)	niech mają	

---

móc to be able to

PRESENT		PAST	
(ja)	mogę	(ja)	mogłem/mogłam
(ty)	możesz	(ty)	mogłeś/mogłaś
(on)	może	(on)	mógł
(ona)	może	(ona)	mogła
(ono)	może	(ono)	mogło
(my)	możemy	(my)	mogliśmy/mogłyśmy
(wy)	możecie	(wy)	mogliście/mogłyście
(oni)	mogą	(oni)	mogli
(one)	mogą	(one)	mogły

IMPERATIVE

not used

FUTURE

See First Conjugation

LICZEBNIKI GŁÓWNE		CARDINAL NUMBERS
jeden	1	one
dwa	2	two
trzy	3	three
cztery	4	four
pięć	5	five
sześć	6	six
siedem	7	seven
osiem	8	eight
dziewięć	9	nine
dziesięć	10	ten
jedenaście	11	eleven
dwanaście	12	twelve
trzynaście	13	thirteen
czternaście	14	fourteen
piętnaście	15	fifteen
szesnaście	16	sixteen
siedemnaście	17	seventeen
osiemnaście	18	eighteen
dziewiętnaście	19	nineteen
dwadzieścia	20	twenty
dwadzieścia jeden	21	twenty-one
dwadzieścia dwa	22	twenty-two
trzydzieści	30	thirty
czterdzieści	40	forty
pięćdziesiąt	50	fifty
sześćdziesiąt	60	sixty
siedemdziesiąt	70	seventy
osiemdziesiąt	80	eighty
dziewięćdziesiąt	90	ninety
sto	100	a hundred
sto jeden	101	a hundred and one
dwieście	200	two hundred
trzysta	300	three hundred
czterysta	400	four hundred
pięćset	500	five hundred
sześćset	600	six hundred
siedemset	700	seven hundred
osiemset	800	eight hundred
dziewięćset	900	nine hundred
tysiąc	1000	a thousand
milion	1000000	a million

LICZEBNIKI PORZĄDKOWE		ORDINAL NUMBERS
pierwszy	**1st**	first
drugi	**2nd**	second
trzeci	**3rd**	third
czwarty	**4th**	fourth
piąty	**5th**	fifth
szósty	**6th**	sixth
siódmy	**7th**	seventh
ósmy	**8th**	eighth
dziewiąty	**9th**	ninth
dziesiąty	**10th**	tenth
jedenasty	**11th**	eleventh
dwunasty	**12th**	twelfth
trzynasty	**13th**	thirteenth
czternasty	**14th**	fourteenth
piętnasty	**15th**	fifteenth
szesnasty	**16th**	sixteenth
siedemnasty	**17th**	seventeenth
osiemnasty	**18th**	eighteenth
dziewiętnasty	**19th**	nineteenth
dwudziesty	**20th**	twentieth
dwudziesty pierwszy	**21st**	twenty-first
dwudziesty drugi	**22nd**	twenty-second
trzydziesty	**30th**	thirtieth
czterdziesty	**40th**	fortieth
pięćdziesiąty	**50th**	fiftieth
sześćdziesiąty	**60th**	sixtieth
siedemdziesiąty	**70th**	seventieth
osiemdziesiąty	**80th**	eightieth
dziewięćdziesiąty	**90th**	ninetieth
setny	**100th**	hundredth
sto pierwszy	**101st**	hundred-and-first
tysięczny	**1000th**	thousandth

CZAS / TIME

CZAS	TIME
Która godzina?	*What time is it?*
Jest ...	*It's ...*
północ/pierwsza (w nocy)	midnight/one o'clock (in the morning), one (a.m.)
pięć po pierwszej/dziesięć po pierwszej	five past (*Brit*) *lub* after one (*US*)/ten past (*Brit*) *lub* after (*US*) one
kwadrans po pierwszej, dwadzieścia po pierwszej	quarter/twenty past (*Brit*) *lub* after (*US*) one
pierwsza piętnaście	one fifteen
wpół do drugiej, pierwsza trzydzieści	half past one, one thirty
za dwadzieścia pięć druga, pierwsza trzydzieści pięć	twenty-five to two, one thirty-five
za dwadzieścia druga	twenty to two, one forty
za kwadrans druga	a quarter to two
(godzina) dwunasta, południe	twelve o'clock, midday, noon
za dziesięć druga, pierwsza pięćdziesiąt	ten to two, one fifty
(godzina) druga po południu/czternasta	two o'clock (in the afternoon), two (p.m.)
(godzina) siódma (wieczorem)/dziewiętnasta	seven o'clock (in the evening), seven (p.m.)
O której godzinie?	*At what time?*
o północy	at midnight
o siódmej	at seven o'clock
o pierwszej	at one o'clock
za dwadzieścia minut	in twenty minutes
dziesięć minut temu	ten minutes ago

DATA / DATE

DATA	DATE
dziś	today
jutro	tomorrow
pojutrze	the day after tomorrow
wczoraj	yesterday
przedwczoraj	the day before yesterday
w przeddzień, poprzedniego dnia	the day before, the previous day
następnego dnia	the next *lub* following day
rano	morning
wieczór	evening
dziś rano/wieczorem	this morning/evening
dziś po południu	this afternoon
wczoraj rano/wieczorem	yesterday morning/evening
jutro rano/wieczorem	tomorrow morning/evening
podczas sobotniej nocy	during Saturday night
w sobotę	on Saturday
w soboty	on Saturdays
w każdą sobotę	every Saturday
w ostatnią/następną sobotę	last/next Saturday
od tej soboty za tydzień	a week on Saturday
od tej soboty za dwa tygodnie	a fortnight *lub* two weeks on Saturday
od poniedziałku do soboty	from Monday to Saturday
każdego dnia	every day
raz w tygodniu/miesiącu	once a week/month
dwa razy w tygodniu	twice a week
tydzień temu	a week ago
dwa tygodnie temu	a fortnight *lub* two weeks ago
zeszłego roku	last year
za dwa dni, w ciągu dwóch dni	in two days
za tydzień	in a week
za dwa tygodnie	in a fortnight *lub* two weeks
w przyszłym/następnym miesiącu	next month
w przyszłym/następnym roku	next year
Jaki dziś mamy dzień?	*What day is it?*
1/24 października 2019	the 1st/24th of October 2019, October the 1st/24th 2019
w 2022	in 2022
w dwa tysiące szóstym roku	in 2006
44 rok przed Chrystusem/44 rok przed naszą erą	44 BC
14 rok po Chrystusie/14 rok naszej ery	14 AD
w dziewiętnastym wieku	in the nineteenth century
w latach dziewięćdziesiątych	in the nineties

Polsko – Angielski

Polish – English

ABC *nt inv* ABC
abecad|ło (**-ła, -ła**; *loc sg* **-le**; *gen pl* **-eł**) *nt* **1** alphabet **2** (*przen: podwaliny*) the basics *pl*
abonamen|t (**-tu, -ty**; *loc sg* **-cie**) *m* **1** (*dla telewizji*) subscription **2** (*w telekomunikacji*) standing charges *pl*
abonen|t (**-ta, -ci**; *loc sg* **-cie**) *m* subscriber
abonent|ka (**-ki, -ki**; *dat sg & loc sg* **-ce**; *gen pl* **-ek**) *f* subscriber
aborcj|a (**-i, -e**; *gen pl* **-i**) *f* abortion; **dokonywać** (**dokonać** *pf*) **aborcji** to have an abortion
absencj|a (**-i, -e**; *gen pl* **-i**) *f* **1** (*nieobecność: w szkole, w pracy*) absence **2** (*stała*) absenteeism; **usprawiedliwiona/ nieusprawiedliwiona ~** excused/ unexcused absence
absolutnie *adv* absolutely
absolwen|t (**-ta, -ci**; *loc sg* **-cie**) *m* graduate; **zjazd ~ów** class reunion
absolwent|ka (**-ki, -ki**; *dat sg & loc sg* **-ce**; *gen pl* **-ek**) *f* graduate
abstynen|t (**-ta, -ci**; *loc sg* **-cie**) *m* teetotaller (*Brit*), teetotaler (*US*)
abstynent|ka (**-ki, -ki**; *dat sg & loc sg* **-ce**; *gen pl* **-ek**) *f* teetotaller (*Brit*), teetotaler (*US*)
absurdalny *adj* (*pomysł*) absurd
aby *conj* (so as) to; **pojechał do Francji, ~ nauczyć się francuskiego** he went to France to learn French; **~ nie przestraszyć psa** so as not to frighten the dog
ach *excl* oh
adidas|y (**-ów**) *pl* trainers (*Brit*), sneakers (*US*)
administracj|a (**-i, -e**; *gen pl* **-i**) *f* **1** (*w zarządzaniu*) administration **2** (*funkcja kierownicza*) management **3** (*organ władzy*) administration; **~ rządowa/lokalna** central government/local government
administracyjny *adj* **1** (*podział*) administrative **2** (*zarządzający*) managing **3** (*Prawo*): **sąd ~** *court with special jurisdiction in the area of administrative law*
administrato|r (**-ra, -rzy**; *loc sg* **-rze**) *m* **1** (*zarządca*) administrator **2** (*w zarządzaniu*) manager; **~ budynku** property manager
adopcj|a (**-i, -e**; *gen pl* **-i**) *f* adoption
adopt|ować (**-uję, -ujesz**; *pf* **za-**) *vt* to adopt; **~ dziecko** to adopt a child
ador|ować (**-uję, -ujesz**) *vt* (*dziewczynę*) to adore
adre|s (**-su, -sy**; *loc sg* **-sie**) *m* address; **~ odbiorcy/nadawcy** recipient's/sender's address; **podawać** (**podać** *pf*) **~ korespondencyjny** to give a contact address
adresa|t (**-ta, -ci**; *loc sg* **-cie**) *m* addressee; **~ nieznany** addressee unknown
adres|ować (**-uję, -ujesz**; *pf* **za-**) *vt* (*list*) to address
adwen|t (**-tu, -ty**; *loc sg* **-cie**) *m* Advent
adwoka|t (**-ta, -ci**; *loc sg* **-cie**) *m* barrister (*Brit*), attorney (*US*)
aerobi|k (**-ku**; *inst sg* **-kiem**) *m* aerobics; **uprawiać ~** to do aerobics
aerozo|l (**-lu, -le**; *gen pl* **-li**) *m* aerosol; **w ~u** in aerosol form
afe|ra (**-ry, -ry**; *dat sg & loc sg* **-rze**) *f* scandal; **~ gospodarcza** swindle
Afry|ka (**-ki**; *dat sg* **-ce**) *f* Africa
afrykański *adj* African
agencj|a (**-i, -e**; *gen pl* **-i**) *f* (*biuro*) agency; **~ turystyczna** travel agency; **~ towarzyska** escort agency

agen|t (**-ta, -ci**; *loc sg* **-cie**) *m* **1** (*szpieg*) agent **2** (*przedstawiciel*) rep; **~ ubezpieczeniowy** insurance agent
agent|ka (**-ki, -ki**; *dat sg & loc sg* **-ce**; *gen pl* **-ek**) *f* **1** agent **2** rep
agraf|ka (**-ki, -ki**; *dat sg & loc sg* **-ce**; *gen pl* **-ek**) *f* safety pin
agresj|a (**-i, -e**; *gen pl* **-i**) *f* aggression; **~ wobec** *+gen* hostility to
agre|st (**-stu, -sty**; *loc sg* **-ście**) *m* gooseberry
agresywny *adj* (*człowiek, zachowanie, zwierzę*) aggressive
aha *excl* **1** (*zgadzanie*) uh-huh **2** (*przypomnienie sobie*) oh **3** (*rozumienie*) ah
AIDS *abbr* AIDS (= *acquired immune deficiency syndrome*); **chory na ~** suffering with AIDS
akademi|a (**-i, -e**; *gen pl* **-i**) *f* **1** (*uczelnia*) academy **2** (*spotkanie*) ceremony; **~ dla uczczenia rocznicy** anniversary celebration ceremony; **Polska A~ Nauk** Polish Academy of Sciences; **~ Teatralna** drama school
akademicki *adj* (*dyskusja*) academic; **dom ~** hall(s *pl*) of residence (*Brit*), dormitory (*US*); **rok ~** the academic year
akademi|k (**-ka, -ki**; *inst sg* **-kiem**) *m* (*pot: na uniwersytecie*) hall (*Brit*), dorm (*US*)
akapi|t (**-tu, -ty**; *loc sg* **-cie**) *m* paragraph; **zaczynać** (**zacząć** *pf*) **od nowego ~u** to begin with a new paragraph
akcen|t (**-tu, -ty**; *loc sg* **-cie**) *m* **1** (*w językoznawstwie*) stress **2** (*sposób wymiawiania*) accent **3** (*symbol*) accent (mark) **4** (*podkreślenie*) emphasis **5** (*w muzyce*) emphasis
akcent|ować (**-uję, -ujesz**; *pf* **za-**) *vt* **1** (*w językoznawstwie*) to stress **2** (*przen*) to emphasize
akceptacj|a (**-i, -e**; *gen pl* **-i**) *f* **1** (*prezentu*) acceptance **2** (*propozycji*) approval
akcept|ować (**-uję, -ujesz**; *pf* **za-**) *vt* **1** (*prezent*) to accept **2** (*decyzję*) to approve of
akcj|a (**-i, -e**; *gen pl* **-i**) *f* **1** (*wojskowa*) campaign **2** (*działanie*) action **3** (*w powieści*) plot **4** (*Fin*) share; **spadek/wzrost cen akcji na giełdzie** a fall/rise in the share's market price; **~ zbrojna** military action
akcyz|a (**-y, -y**; *dat sg* **-ie**) *f* excise
ak|t (**-tu, -ty**; *loc sg* **-cie**) *m* **1** act **2** (*uroczystość*) ceremony **3** (*w sztuce*) nude **4** (*nom pl* **-ta** *lub* **-ty**) (*zaświadczenie*) certificate; **akta** (*gen pl* **akt**) *pl* **1** (*dokumenty*) files **2** (*zbiór dokumentów na jakiś temat*) dossier; **~ urodzenia** birth certificate
akto|r (**-ra, -rzy**; *loc sg* **-rze**) *m* actor
aktor|ka (**-ki, -ki**; *dat sg & loc sg* **-ce**; *gen pl* **-ek**) *f* actress
aktów|ka (**-ki, -ki**; *dat sg & loc sg* **-ce**; *gen pl* **-ek**) *f* briefcase
aktualiz|ować (**-uję, -ujesz**; *pf* **z-**) *vt* (*dane*) to update
aktualnie *adv* (*obecnie*) currently
aktualny *adj* current; **aktualne zagadnienia** current affairs
aktywi|sta (**-sty, -ści**; *dat sg & loc sg* **-ście**) *m decl like f in sg* activist; **~ organizacji ekologicznej** green activist
aktywist|ka (**-ki, -ki**; *dat sg & loc sg* **-ce**; *gen pl* **-ek**) *f* activist
aktywnoś|ć (**-ci**) *f* activity; **~ fizyczna** physical activity
aktywny *adj* (*działacz*) active
akumulato|r (**-ra, -ry**; *loc sg* **-rze**) *m* (*w motoryzacji*) battery
akurat *adv* **1** (*dokładnie*) exactly **2** (*właśnie w tym momencie*) at this *lub* that very moment; **~ kiedy wychodził, zadzwonił telefon** the very moment he left the phone rang
akwari|um (**-um, -a**; *gen pl* **-ów**) *nt* aquarium
alar|m (**-mu, -my**; *loc sg* **-mie**) *m* **1** alarm **2** (*stan gotowości*) alert **3** (*pot: urządzenie*) alarm system **4** (*w muzeum*) anti-theft system; **~ pożarowy** fire alarm; **fałszywy ~** a false alarm
alarm|ować (**-uję, -ujesz**; *pf* **za-**) *vt* **1** (*informować o zagrożeniu*) to alert **2** (*przestraszyć*) to alarm
alarmowy *adj* (*sygnał*) alarm
albo *conj* or; **~ ... ~ ...** either ... or ...
ale *conj* but ▷ *part*: **~ deszcz!** that's some rain!; **~ jaja!** (*pot!*) well, I never!

ale|ja (**-i, -je**; *gen pl* **-i**) *f* **1** (*droga*) alley **2** (*ulica*) avenue
alergi|a (**-i, -e**; *gen pl* **-i**) *f* allergy; **mieć alergię na coś** to be allergic to sth
alergiczny *adj* (*Med*) allergic
alfabe|t (**-tu, -ty**; *loc sg* **-cie**) *m* alphabet
alfabetyczny *adj* alphabetical; **ułożyć** (**układać** *pf*) **coś w porządku ~m** to arrange sth in alphabetical order
alkohol (**-u, -e**; *gen pl* **-i** *lub* **-ów**) *m* **1** (*napój alkoholowy*) alcohol **2** (*Chem*): **~ przemysłowy** industrial alcohol
alkoholicz|ka (**-ki, -ki**; *dat sg & loc sg* **-ce**; *gen pl* **-ek**) *f* alcoholic
alkoholi|k (**-ka, -cy**; *inst sg* **-kiem**) *m* alcoholic
alkoholiz|m (**-mu**; *loc sg* **-mie**) *m* alcoholism
alpini|sta (**-sty, -ści**; *dat sg & loc sg* **-ście**) *m decl like f in sg* mountaineer
alpinist|ka (**-ki, -ki**; *dat sg & loc sg* **-ce**; *gen pl* **-ek**) *f* mountaineer
alpiniz|m (**-mu**; *loc sg* **-mie**) *m* mountaineering
Alp|y (-) *pl* the Alps
alternaty|wa (**-wy, -wy**; *dat sg & loc sg* **-wie**) *f* alternative
alternatywny *adj* (*styl życia, metoda, plan*) alternative
aluminium *nt inv* aluminium (*Brit*), aluminum (*US*)
amato|r (**-ra, -rzy**; *loc sg* **-rze**) *m* **1** (*nie zawodowiec*) amateur **2** (*zwolennik*) enthusiast **3** (*Sport*) amateur; **~ dobrego jedzenia** gourmet
amator|ka (**-ki, -ki**; *dat sg & loc sg* **-ce**; *gen pl* **-ek**) *f* amateur
amatorski *adj* **1** (*niezawodowy: pej*) amateurish **2** (*nieprofesjonalny*) amateur; **teatr ~** amateur dramatics
ambasa|da (**-dy, -dy**; *dat sg & loc sg* **-dzie**) *f* embassy
ambasado|r (**-ra, -rzy** *lub* **-rowie**; *loc sg* **-rze**) *m* ambassador; **~ dobrej woli** good will ambassador
ambicj|a (**-i, -e**; *gen pl* **-i**) *f* **1** (*dążenie*) ambition **2** (*pycha*) self-respect
ambitny *adj* ambitious
ambulatori|um (**-um, -a**; *gen pl* **-ów**) *nt* outpatient clinic
ambulatoryjny *adj*: **leczenie ambulatoryjne** outpatient treatment
Amery|ka (**-ki, -ki**; *dat sg* **-ce**) *f* America; **~ Łacińska** Latin America
Ameryka|nin (**-nina, -nie**; *loc sg* **-ninie**; *gen pl* **-nów**) *m* American
Amerykan|ka (**-ki, -ki**; *dat sg* **-ce**; *gen pl* **-ek**) *f* American
amerykański *adj* American
amfiteat|r (**-ru, -ry**; *loc sg* **-rze**) *m* amphitheatre (*Brit*), amphitheater (*US*)
amputacj|a (**-i, -e**; *gen pl* **-i**) *f* amputation
amput|ować (**-uję, -ujesz**) *vt impf/pf* to amputate
analfabe|ta (**-ty, -ci**; *dat sg & loc sg* **-cie**) *m decl like f in sg* illiterate person
analfabet|ka (**-ki, -ki**; *dat sg & loc sg* **-ce**; *gen pl* **-ek**) *f* illiterate person
anali|za (**-zy, -zy**; *dat sg & loc sg* **-zie**) *f* **1** (*Med*) test **2** (*Chem*) analysis
analiz|ować (**-uję, -ujesz**; *pf* **z-**) *vt* to analyse (*Brit*), to analyze (*US*)
anana|s (**-sa, -sy**; *loc sg* **-sie**) *m* pineapple
andrzej|ki (**-ek**) *pl* *St Andrew's Day*

ANDRZEJKI

St Andrew's Day (30 November) is celebrated in the evening of 29 November, and is referred to as **andrzejki**. Games are organized for young people and some tell fortunes by, for example, pouring hot wax into water. The congealed wax forms various shapes, which supposedly tell the fortune of the person who poured the wax.

anegdo|ta (**-ty, -ty**; *loc sg* **-cie**) *f* anecdote
anemi|a (**-i**) *f* anaemia (*Brit*), anemia (*US*)
Angiel|ka (**-ki, -ki**; *dat sg* **-ce**; *gen pl* **-ek**) *f* Englishwoman
angielski *adj* English ▷ *m decl like adj* English; **mówić po angielsku** to speak English

angi|na (**-ny**; *loc sg* **-nie**) *f* throat infection
Angli|a (**-i**) *f* England
Angli|k (**-ka, -cy**; *inst sg* **-kiem**) *m* Englishman
anglikański *adj* Anglican; **Kościół A~** the Church of England
ani *conj*: **~ ... ~ ...** neither ... nor ...; (*z innym wyrazem przeczącym*) either ... or ... ▷ *part* **1** not a (single) **2** (*z innym wyrazem przeczącym*) a (single); **~ be ~ me** not a single word; **~ trochę** not even a little bit; **~ jeden** not a single one, none
animowany *adj*: **film ~** (*TV*) cartoon
ani|oł (**-oła, -ołowie** *lub* **-oły**; *loc sg* **-ele**) *m* angel
ankie|ta (**-ty, -ty**; *dat sg & loc sg* **-cie**) *f* **1** (*badanie opinii*) survey **2** (*formularz*) questionnaire; **wypełniać** (**wypełnić** *pf*) **ankietę** to fill out a questionnaire
anonimowy *adj* (*list, utwór*) anonymous
Antarkty|ka (**-ki**; *dat sg* **-ce**) *f* the Antarctic
ante|na (**-ny, -ny**; *dat sg & loc sg* **-nie**) *f* aerial (*Brit*), antenna (*US*); **zakładać** (**założyć** *pf*) **antenę satelitarną** to install a satellite dish
antropologi|a (**-i**) *f* anthropology
antybioty|k (**-ku, -ki**; *inst sg* **-kiem**) *m* antibiotic; **brać** (**wziąć** *pf*) **~** to take an antibiotic
antykoncepcj|a (**-i**) *f* contraception
antykoncepcyjny *adj*: **środek ~** contraceptive
antysemi|ta (**-ty, -ci**; *dat sg & loc sg* **-cie**) *m decl like f in sg* anti-Semite
antysemit|ka (**-ki, -ki**; *dat sg & loc sg* **-ce**; *gen pl* **-ek**) *f* anti-Semite
antysemityz|m (**-mu**; *loc sg* **-mie**) *m* anti-Semitism
antywirusowy *adj* (*Komput*) antivirus; **program ~** antivirus program
anul|ować (**-uję, -ujesz**) *vt impf/pf* **1** (*rezerwację*) to cancel **2** (*małżeństwo*) to annul
apara|t (**-tu, -ty**; *loc sg* **-cie**) *m* (*naukowy*) apparatus; **~ fotograficzny** camera; **~ telefoniczny** telephone
apartamen|t (**-tu, -ty**; *loc sg* **-cie**) *m* **1** (*mieszkanie w luksusowym bloku*) apartment **2** (*w hotelu*) suite
apel (**-u, -e**; *gen pl* **-i** *lub* **-ów**) *m* **1** (*wezwanie*) appeal **2** (*Wojsk*) assembly; **~ poranny** morning assembly
apetyczny *adj* appetizing
apety|t (**-tu, -ty**; *loc sg* **-cie**) *m* appetite
aplikacj|a (**-i, -e**; *dat sg* **-i**) *f* app
aplik|ować (**-uję, -ujesz**; *pf* **za-**) *vt* +*dat* **1** (*lek*) to administer **2** (*makijaż, kosmetyk*) to apply
aproba|ta (**-ty**; *dat sg & loc sg* **-cie**) *f* approval; **okazywać** (**okazać** *pf*) **aprobatę** to show one's approval
aprob|ować (**-uję, -ujesz**; *pf* **za-**) *vt* (*pomysł*) to approve of
apteczk|ka (**-ki, -ki**; *dat sg & loc sg* **-ce**; *gen pl* **-ek**) *f* medicine cabinet; **~ samochodowa** first-aid kit
apte|ka (**-ki, -ki**; *dat sg & loc sg* **-ce**) *f* pharmacy
aptekar|ka (**-ki, -ki**; *dat sg & loc sg* **-ce**; *gen pl* **-ek**) *f* pharmacist
apteka|rz (**-rza, -rze**; *gen pl* **-rzy**) *m* pharmacist
arbu|z (**-za, -zy**; *loc sg* **-zie**) *m* watermelon
archeolo|g (**-ga, -dzy** *lub* **-gowie**; *inst sg* **-giem**) *m* archaeologist (*Brit*), archeologist (*US*)
archeologi|a (**-i**) *f* archaeology (*Brit*), archeology (*US*); **~ śródziemnomorska** Mediterranean archaeology
archeologiczny *adj* archaeological (*Brit*), archeological (*US*); **wykopaliska archeologiczne** archaeological excavations
architek|t (**-ta, -ci**; *loc sg* **-cie**) *m* architect
architektu|ra (**-ry**; *dat sg & loc sg* **-rze**) *f* architecture
archiwalny *adj* archival
archiw|um (**-um, -a**; *gen pl* **-ów**) *nt inv in sg* archive
arcydzie|ło (**-ła, -ła**; *loc sg* **-le**) *nt* masterpiece
aresz|t (**-tu, -ty**; *loc sg* **-cie**) *m* **1** (*pozbawienie wolności osobistej*) arrest **2** (*pomieszczenie*) jail;

zatrzymywać (**zatrzymać** *pf*) **kogoś w areszcie** to keep sb in custody
areszt|ować (**-uję, -ujesz**; *pf also* **za-**) *vt impf/pf* to arrest; **jest pan aresztowany** you're under arrest
Argenty|na (**-ny**; *dat sg* **-nie**) *f* Argentina
argumen|t (**-tu, -ty**; *loc sg* **-cie**) *m* argument
arkusz (**-a, -e**; *gen pl* **-y**) *m* sheet; **~ kalkulacyjny** spreadsheet
armi|a (**-i, -e**; *gen pl* **-i**) *f* army; **powoływać** (**powołać** *pf*) **do armii** to call up for military service
arogancki *adj* arrogant
artyku|ł (**-łu, -ły**; *loc sg* **-le**) *m* article; **~y spożywcze** groceries
arty|sta (**-sty, -ści**; *dat sg & loc sg* **-ście**) *m decl like f in sg* **1** artist **2** (*pot: Teatr*) actor; **~ malarz** painter
artyst|ka (**-ki, -ki**; *dat sg & loc sg* **-ce**; *gen pl* **-ek**) *f* **1** artist **2** (*pot: Teatr*) actress
artystyczny *adj* artistic
arystokracj|a (**-i**) *f* aristocracy
arystokra|ta (**-ty, -ci**; *loc sg* **-cie**) *m decl like f in sg* aristocrat
arystokrat|ka *f* (**-ki, -ki**; *dat sg & loc sg* **-ce**; *gen pl* **-ek**) *f* aristocrat
as (**asa, asy**; *loc sg* **asie**) *m* ace; **as kier/karo/pik/trefl** ace of hearts/diamonds/spades/clubs; **mieć asa w rękawie** to have an ace up one's sleeve
aspiry|na (**-ny, -ny**; *loc sg* **-nie**) *f* aspirin
asysten|t (**-ta, -ci**; *loc sg* **-cie**) *m* assistant
asystent|ka (**-ki, -ki**; *dat sg & loc sg* **-ce**; *gen pl* **-ek**) *f* assistant
asyst|ować (**-uję, -ujesz**) *vi*: **~ komuś** (*towarzyszyć*) to accompany sb; (*współdziałać*) to assist sb
ata|k (**-ku, -ki**; *inst sg* **-kiem**) *m* attack; **dostawać** (**dostać** *pf*) **~u nerwowego** to get an attack of nerves
atak|ować (**-uję, -ujesz**; *pf* **za-**) *vt* to attack
atlantycki *adj* Atlantic; **Ocean A~** the Atlantic (Ocean)
Atlantyk (**-ku**; *inst sg* **-kiem**) *m* the Atlantic
atla|s (**-su, -sy**; *loc sg* **-sie**) *m* atlas; **~ samochodowy** road atlas
atmosfe|ra (**-ry, -ry**; *loc sg* **-rze**) *f* (*przen*) atmosphere; **stwarzać** (**stworzyć** *pf*) **przyjazną atmosferę** to create a welcoming atmosphere
atrakcyjny *adj* (*wygląd*) attractive
atramen|t (**-tu, -ty**; *loc sg* **-cie**) *m* ink; **~ sympatyczny** invisible ink
atu|t (**-tu, -ty**; *loc sg* **-cie**) *m* trump (card); **mieć niezaprzeczalne ~y** to have definite advantages
audycj|a (**-i, -e**; *gen pl* **-i**) *f* (radio) programme
Australi|a (**-i**) *m* Australia
Australijczy|k (**-ka, -cy**; *inst sg* **-kiem**) *m* Australian
Australij|ka (**-ki, -ki**; *dat sg & loc sg* **-ce**; *gen pl* **-ek**) *f* Australian
australijski *adj* Australian
Austri|a (**-i**) *f* Austria
austriacki *adj* Austrian
autentyczny *adj* (*document*) authentic
au|to (**-ta, -ta**; *loc sg* **-cie**) *nt* car
autobiografi|a (**-i, -e**; *gen pl* **-i**) *f* autobiography
autobu|s (**-su, -sy**; *loc sg* **-sie**) *m* (*w mieście*) bus
autobusowy *adj* bus; **przystanek ~** bus stop; **dworzec ~** bus station
autoka|r (**-ru, -ry**; *loc sg* **-rze**) *m* coach
automa|t (**-tu, -ty**; *loc sg* **-cie**) *m* (*telefoniczny*) public telephone
automatyczny *adj* automatic; **sekretarka automatyczna** answering machine
auto|r (**-ra, -rzy**; *loc sg* **-rze**) *m* author
autor|ka (**-ki, -ki**; *dat sg & loc sg* **-ce**; *gen pl* **-ek**) *f* author
autorski *adj* author's; **prawa ~e** author's rights; **wieczór ~** meet-the-author event
autoryte|t (**-tu, -ty**; *loc sg* **-cie**) *m* **1** authority **2** (*uznanie*) prestige; **mieć ~** to enjoy respect
autosto|p (**-pu**; *loc sg* **-pie**) *m* hitch-hiking; **jechać** (**pojechać** *pf*) **~em** to hitch-hike
autostopowicz (**-a, -e**) *m* hitch-hiker

autostopowicz|ka (**-ki, -ki**; *dat sg & loc sg* **-ce**; *gen pl* **-ek**) *f* hitch-hiker

autostra|da (**-dy, -dy**; *dat sg & loc sg* **-dzie**) *f* motorway (*Brit*), freeway (*US*)

awan|s (**-su, -se** *lub* **-sy**; *loc sg* **-sie**) *m* promotion; **otrzymywać (otrzymać** *pf*) **~** to get promoted

awans|ować (**-uję, -ujesz**) *vt impf/pf* to promote ▷ *vi* to be promoted

awantu|ra (**-ry, -ry**; *dat sg & loc sg* **-rze**) *f* disturbance; **wszczynać (wszcząć** *pf*) **awanturę** to start a fight

awantur|ować się (**-uję, -ujesz**) *vr* to cause a disturbance

awari|a (**-i, -e**; *gen pl* **-i**) *f* breakdown; **~ sieci elektrycznej** power failure

awi|zo (**-za, -za**; *loc sg* **-zie**; *gen pl* **-zów**) *nt* advice note

Azj|a (**-i**) *m* Asia

azjatycki *adj* Asian

azyl (**-u, -e**) *m* (*Pol*) (political) asylum; **udzielać (udzielić) komuś ~u** to grant sb asylum

b

ba|ba (**-by, -by**; *dat sg & loc sg* **-bie**) *f* (*pot: pej: starsza pani*) biddy; **~ Wielkanocna** Easter cake

bab|cia (**-ci, -cie**; *gen pl* **-ci** *lub* **-ć**) *f* **1** grandma **2** (*pot: starsza kobieta*) old woman

bać się (**boję się, boisz się**; *impf* **bój się**) *vr* to be afraid; **~ kogoś/czegoś** to be afraid of sb/sth; **~ o przyszłość** to be worried about the future; **nie bój się, na pewno jej się uda** don't worry, she's bound to succeed

bad|acz (**-a, -e**; *gen pl* **-y**) *m* **1** (*uczony*) researcher **2** (*poszukiwacz*) explorer

badacz|ka (**-ki, -ki**; *dat & loc sg* **-ce**; *gen pl* **-ek**) *f* researcher

bad|ać (**-am, -asz**; *pf* **z-**) *vt* **1** (*przedmiot*) to study **2** (*stan zdrowia*) to test **3** (*u lekarza*) to examine

bada|nie (**-nia, -nia**; *gen pl* **-ń**) *nt* **1** test **2** (*Med*) examination; **badania** *pl* research; **~ moczu** urine test

badawczy *adj* **1** (*praca*) research **2** (*przenikliwy*) scrutinizing

bagaż (**-u, -e**; *gen pl* **-y**) *m* luggage (*Brit*), baggage (*US*); **~ podręczny** hand baggage

bagażni|k (**-ka, -ki**; *inst sg* **-kiem**) *m* **1** (*Mot*) boot (*Brit*), trunk (*US*) **2** (*na dachu samochodu*) roof rack **3** (*na rowerze*) carrier

baje|r (**-ru, -ry**; *dat sg & loc sg* **-rze**) *m*: **wstawiać (wstawić** *pf*) **komuś ~** to tell sb a cock and bull story; **bez żadnych ~ów** with no frills

baj|ka (**-ki, -ki**; *dat sg & loc sg* **-ce**; *gen pl* **-ek**) *f* **1** fairy tale **2** (*Lit*) fable; **opowiadać o czymś bajki** (*przen*) to tell tales about sth
bajkowy *adj* (*niezwykłej urody*) fabulous
ba|k (**-ku, -ki**; *inst sg* **-kiem**) *m* (fuel) tank; **napełniać** (**napełnić** *pf*) **~** to fill up (a fuel tank)
bakali|e (**-i**) *pl* (*Kulin*) dried fruit and nuts; **ciasto z bakaliami** rich fruit cake
bakłaża|n (**-na** *lub* **-nu, -ny**; *loc sg* **-nie**) *m* aubergine (*Brit*), eggplant (*US*)
bakteri|a (**-i, -e**; *gen pl* **-i**) *f* germ; **bakterie** *pl* bacteria *pl*
bakteriobójczy *adj* antiseptic; **środek ~** antiseptic
bal (**-u, -e**; *gen pl* **-ów**) *m* (*zabawa taneczna*) ball; **~ maskowy** masked (*Brit*) *lub* costume (*US*) ball
balero|n (**-nu, -ny**; *loc sg* **-nie**) *m* smoked ham
bale|t (**-tu, -ty**; *loc sg* **-cie**) *m* ballet
balko|n (**-nu, -ny**; *loc sg* **-nie**) *m* balcony
balo|n (**-nu, -ny**; *loc sg* **-nie**) *m* balloon; **robił z niego ~a** he took him for a ride (*pot*)
balsa|m (**-mu, -my**; *loc sg* **-mie**) *m* balm; **twoje słowa są dla mnie jak ~** your words are music to my ears
bałaga|n (**-nu**; *loc sg* **-nie**) *m* mess
bałaga|nić (**-nię, -nisz**; *impf* **-ń**; *pf* **na-**) *vi* to make a mess
Bałkan|y (**-ów**) *m pl* the Balkans
bałtycki *adj* (*państwo, region*) Baltic; **Morze B~e** the Baltic (Sea)
Bałty|k (**-ku**; *inst sg* **-kiem**) *m* the Baltic (Sea)
bałwa|n (**-na, -ny**; *loc sg* **-nie**) *m* **1** (*śniegowy*) snowman **2** (*morski*) breaker; **robić** (**zrobić** *pf*) **z kogoś ~a** (*pot*) to make a fool of sb
bana|n (**-na, -ny**; *loc sg* **-nie**) *m* banana
ban|da (**-dy, -dy**; *dat sg & loc sg* **-dzie**) *f* gang
bandaż (**-a, -e**; *gen pl* **-y**) *m* (*elastyczny*) bandage
bandaż|ować (**-uję, -ujesz**; *pf* **o-** *lub* **za-**) *vt* to bandage
bandy|ta (**-ty, -ci**; *dat sg & loc sg* **-cie**) *m decl like f in sg* bandit
ban|k (**-ku, -ki**; *inst sg* **-kiem**) *m* bank; **~ krwi/szpiku** blood/marrow bank; **masz to u mnie jak w ~u!** (*pot*) it's in the bag!
bankno|t (**-tu, -ty**; *loc sg* **-cie**) *m* (bank)note (*Brit*), bill (*US*); **~ dziesięciozłotowy** a 10-zloty note
bankoma|t (**-tu, -ty**; *loc sg* **-cie**) *m* cash machine, ATM
ba|r (**-ru, -ry**; *loc sg* **-rze**) *m* **1** (*kawowy, mleczny*) café **2** (*stołówka*) cafeteria; **~ samoobsługowy** self-service restaurant
bara|n (**-na, -ny**; *loc sg* **-nie**) *m* **1** ram **2** (*dureń*) idiot **3** (*Astrol*): **B~** Aries; **jak stado ~ów** (*przen*) like a flock of sheep
barani|na (**-ny**; *dat sg & loc sg* **-nie**) *f* mutton
bardziej *adv comp od* **bardzo** more; **~ sprawny** more effective; **im więcej pracował, tym ~ miał dość** the more he worked, the more fed up he was; **coraz ~** more and more
bardzo *adv* **1** (*szczególnie*) very **2** (*mocno*) very much; **~ coś lubić** to love sth very much; **~ dobry** very good; (*w uniwersytecie*) ≈ first; **tak ~ mi go brak** I miss him so much; **za ~ się męczy** he is working too hard; **~ dziękuję** thank you very much; **~ przepraszam za jej zachowanie** I'm very sorry about her behaviour (*Brit*) *lub* behavior (*US*)
bar|k (**-ku, -ki**; *inst sg* **-kiem**) *m* shoulder; **jest szeroki w ~ach** he is broad-shouldered
barma|n (**-na, -ni**; *loc sg* **-nie**) *m* barman (*Brit*), bartender (*US*)
barman|ka (**-ki, -ki**; *dat sg & loc sg* **-ce**; *gen pl* **-ek**) *f* barmaid

BAR MLECZNY

Bar mleczny is a Polish type of a fast-food restaurant. Its name comes from the large number of dairy and vegetarian dishes on the menu and relative lack of meat dishes. **Bary mleczne** were first set up during the **PRL** and are characterised by low prices.

barszcz (**-u, -e**; *gen pl* **-y**) *m* beetroot soup

BARSZCZ

Barszcz is a soup made from beetroot, one of the specialities of Central European cuisine. **Barszcz biały**, otherwise known as **żur**, is also popular in Poland. This is made with flour, sausage, milk and vinegar.

bar|wa (**-wy, -wy**; *dat sg & loc sg* **-wie**) *f* (*kolor*) colour (*Brit*), color (*US*); **feria barw** a riot of colour
barwny *adj* **1** (*różnobarwny*) colourful (*Brit*), colorful (*US*) **2** (*kolorowy*) colour (*Brit*), color (*US*) **3** (*zajmujący*) vivid
base|n (**-nu, -ny**; *loc sg* **-nie**) *m* **1** (*zbiornik na wodę*) basin **2** (*pływalnia*) (swimming) pool; **~ kryty/otwarty** covered/open-air swimming pool
bateri|a (**-i, -e**; *gen pl* **-i**) *f* battery
bato|n (**-nu, -ny**; *loc sg* **-nie**) *m* (*czekoladowy*) bar (*of chocolate*)
baweł|na (**-ny**; *dat sg & loc sg* **-nie**) *f* cotton
bawełniany *adj* cotton
ba|wić (**-wię, -wisz**; *pf* **u-**) *vt* to entertain; **~ się** *vr* **1** (*grać*) to play **2** (*uprzyjemniać sobie czas*) to have a good time; **~ się z kimś w kotka i myszkę** to play cat and mouse with sb; **baw się dobrze!** have a good time!
baza|r (**-ru, -ry**; *loc sg* **-rze**) *m* bazaar
bąb|el (**-la, -le**; *gen pl* **-li**) *m* **1** (*odcisk*) blister **2** (*pęcherzyk na wodzie*) bubble
becz|ka (**-ki, -ki**; *dat sg & loc sg* **-ce**; *gen pl* **-ek**) *f* barrel; **jeść** (**zjeść** *pf*) **z kimś beczkę soli** to go back a long way with sb
bek|ać (**-am, -asz**; *pf* **-nąć**) *vi* (*pot*) to burp
beko|n (**-nu, -ny**; *loc sg* **-nie**) *m* bacon
Belgi|a (**-i**) *f* Belgium
belgijski *adj* Belgian
benzy|na (**-ny**; *dat sg & loc sg* **-nie**) *f* petrol (*Brit*), gas(oline) (*US*); **~ bezołowiowa** lead-free petrol
benzynowy *adj* (*stacja, zapalniczka*) petrol (*Brit*) *lub* gas (*US*) station
bere|t (**-tu, -ty**; *loc sg* **-cie**) *m* beret
besti|a (**-i, -e**; *gen pl* **-i**) *f* beast
bestialski *adj* bestial; **bestialska zbrodnia** brutal crime
beto|n (**-nu, -ny**; *loc sg* **-nie**) *m* concrete; **~ partyjny** (*pot*) party hardliners
betoniar|ka (**-ki, -ki**; *dat sg & loc sg* **-ce**; *gen pl* **-ek**) *f* concrete mixer
beton|ować (**-uję, -ujesz**) *vt* to concrete
bez *prep +gen* without; **~ celu** aimless; **~ sensu** pointless; **mówił ~ ładu i składu** he rambled on
bezalkoholowy *adj* **1** (*napój*) non-alcoholic **2** (*płyn kosmetyczny*) alcohol-free; **napoje bezalkoholowe** soft drinks
bezbarwny *adj* colourless (*Brit*), colorless (*US*)
bezbolesny *adj* painless
bezbronny *adj* **1** (*bezsilny*) helpless **2** (*nie stawiający oporu*) defenceless (*Brit*), defenseless (*US*)
bezcenny *adj* **1** (*nieoceniony*) invaluable **2** (*skarb*) priceless
bezcłowy *adj* duty-free; **strefa bezcłowa** duty-free zone
bezczelny *adj* insolent
bezdomny *adj* homeless; **bezdomni** *pl* the homeless
bezkofeinowy *adj* decaffeinated
beznadziejny *adj* (*sprawa, sytuacja*) hopeless
bezokoliczni|k (**-ka, -ki**; *inst sg* **-kiem**) *m* infinitive
bezpieczeńst|wo (**-wa**; *loc sg* **-wie**) *nt* security; **~ i higiena pracy** (*bhp*) health and safety at work
bezpieczni|k (**-ka, -ki**; *inst sg* **-kiem**) *m* (*urządzenie elektryczne*) fuse (*Brit*), fuze (*US*)
bezpieczny *adj* **1** (*pewny*) secure **2** (*nie stwarzający zagrożenia*) safe
bezpłatnie *adv* free of charge
bezpłatny *adj* **1** (*darmowy*) free **2** (*bez wynagrodzenia*) unpaid
bezpłodnoś|ć (**-ci**) *f* infertility
bezpłodny *adj* **1** infertile **2** (*przen*) sterile
bezprzewodowa *adj* contactless

bezpośredni *adj* (*pociąg, trasa, odpowiedź*) direct
bezroboci|e (**-a**) *nt* unemployment
bezrobotny *adj* unemployed ▷ *m decl like adj* unemployed person; **bezrobotni** *pl* the unemployed
bezsennoś|ć (**-ci**) *f* insomnia
beztłuszczowy *adj* fat-free
beżowy *adj* beige
będę, będzie *itd. vb zob.* **być**
białacz|ka (**-ki, -ki**; *dat sg & loc sg* **-ce**) *f* leukaemia (*Brit*), leukemia (*US*)
biał|ko (**-ka, -ka**; *inst sg* **-kiem**; *gen pl* **-ek**) *nt* **1** (*Kulin*) (egg)white **2** (*Bio*) protein **3** (*oka*) white
Białoru|ś (**-si**) *f* Belarus
biały *adj* white ▷ *m decl like adj* white person; **biali** *pl* the whites *pl*; **w ~ dzień** in broad daylight; **białe mięso** white meat; **biała kawa** white coffee
Bibli|a (**-i, -e**; *gen pl* **-i**) *f* the Bible
bibliote|ka (**-ki, -ki**; *dat sg & loc sg* **-ce**) *f* **1** library **2** (*półka na książki*) bookcase
bibliotekar|ka (**-ki, -ki**; *dat sg & loc sg* **-ce**; *gen pl* **-ek**) *f* librarian
bibliotekarz (**-a, -e**; *gen pl* **-y**) *m* librarian
bi|ć (**-ję, -jesz**) *vt* **1** (*osobę*) to hit **2** (*pf* **u-**) (*zabijać: w rzeźni*) to slaughter ▷ *vi* (*serce*) to beat; **~ się** *vr* to fight; **~ na alarm** to raise the alarm; **bije go na głowę w matematyce** he beats him hands down in maths
bie|c (**-gnę, -gniesz**; *impf* **-gnij**; *pt* **-gł**) *vi* to run; **czas biegnie bardzo szybko** time passes very quickly
bie|da (**-dy**; *dat sg & loc sg* **-dzie**) *f* **1** (*brak pieniędzy*) poverty **2** (*problem: przen*) trouble; **~ aż piszczy** dire poverty
biedny *adj* poor; **~ jak mysz kościelna** as poor as a church mouse
bie|g (**-gu, -gi**; *inst sg* **-giem**) *m* **1** run **2** (*ciąg wydarzeń*) course **3** (*w samochodzie*) gear; **skrzynia ~ów** gearbox
biega|ć (**-am, -asz**) *vi* **1** to run **2** (*amatorsko*) to jog
biegle *adv* (*mówić, pisać*) fluently; **mówić ~ po francusku** to speak fluent French
bieg|nąć (**-nę, -niesz**; *pt* **-ł**) *vb* = **biec**
biegun|ka (**-ki, -ki**; *dat sg & loc sg* **-ce**; *gen pl* **-ek**) *f* diarrhoea (*Brit*), diarrhea (*US*)
bieli|zna (**-zny**; *dat sg & loc sg* **-źnie**) *f* **1** (*poszwa*) (bed) linen **2** (*majtki, stanik*) underwear
biernie *adv* passively
bierni|k (**-ka, -ki**; *inst sg* **-kiem**) *m* (*przypadek gramatyczny*) accusative
bieżący *adj* **1** (*rachunek w banku*) current **2** (*okres*) current **3** (*woda*) running
bigo|s (**-su, -sy**; *loc sg* **-sie**) *m* *typical Polish dish consisting of wild mushrooms, sauerkraut and sausage*

BIGOS

Bigos is a traditional Polish dish, made from sauerkraut and sausage as well as various other ingredients, including wild mushrooms, prunes, and onion.

bilar|d (**-du, -dy**; *loc sg* **-dzie**) *m* billiards *sg*
bile|t (**-tu, -ty**; *loc sg* **-cie**) *m* ticket
biletowy *adj*: **kasa biletowa** (*kasa na dworcu*) ticket office; (*kasa w teatrze*) box office
bilio|n (**-na, -ny**; *loc sg* **-nie**) *m* trillion
bilo|n (**-nu**; *loc sg* **-nie**) *m* (loose) change
bimb|er (**-ru**; *loc sg* **-rze**) *m* (*pot*) bootleg vodka, ≈ moonshine (*US*); **pędzić ~** to brew moonshine
biod|ro (**-ra, -ra**; *loc sg* **-rze**; *gen pl* **-er**) *nt* hip; **ona ma smukłe biodra** she has slender hips
biologi|a (**-i**) *f* biology
bisku|p (**-pa, -pi**; *loc sg* **-pie**) *m* bishop
biszkop|t (**-tu, -ty**; *loc sg* **-cie**) *m* **1** (*lekkie ciasto*) sponge cake **2** (*ciastko*) biscuit (*Brit*), cookie (*US*)
bit|wa (**-wy, -wy**; *dat sg & loc sg* **-wie**) *f* (*bój*) battle
biur|ko (**-ka, -ka**; *inst sg* **-kiem**; *gen pl* **-ek**) *nt* desk
biu|ro (**-ra, -ra**; *loc sg* **-rze**) *nt* **1** (*miejsce pracy*) office **2** (*urząd*) office, bureau; **~ rzeczy znalezionych** lost

property (office) (*Brit*), lost-and-found (office) (*US*)

biuro|wiec (**-wca, -wce**) *m* office building

biu|st (**-stu, -sty**; *loc sg* **-ście**) *m* **1** (*kobiecy*) breasts *pl*, bosom **2** (*popiersie*) bust

biustonosz (**-a, -e**; *gen pl* **-y**) *m* bra

biwa|k (**-ku, -ki**; *inst sg* **-kiem**) *m* bivouac

bizne|s (**-su, -sy**; *loc sg* **-sie**) *m* (*interes*) business

biznesme|n (**-na, -ni**; *loc sg* **-nie**) *m* businessman

biżuteri|a (**-i**; *gen pl* **-i**) *f* jewellery (*Brit*), jewelry (*US*); **nosić biżuterię** to wear jewellery

blady *adj* pale; **~ świt** early hours

blas|k (**-ku, -ki**; *inst sg* **-kiem**) *m* **1** (*złota*) glitter **2** (*promieni słońca*) glare **3** (*poświata*) glow

bled|nąć (**-nę, -niesz**; *impf* **-nij**; *pf* **z-**) *vi* to go pale; **zbladł ze strachu** he went white with fear

bliski *adj* **1** (*niedaleki*) near **2** (*znajomy*) close **3** (*krewny*) close **4** (*relacja*) close **5** (*przyszłość*) near ▷ *m decl like adj* relative; **bliscy** *pl* relatives *pl*; **~ rozpaczy** close to despair; **być ~m prawdy** to be close to the truth; **z bliska** at close range; **B~ Wschód** the Middle East

blisko *adv* **1** (*niedaleko*) close **2** (*niedługo*) near **3** (*prawie*) almost ▷ *prep +gen* close to, near (to)

bli|zna (**-zny, -zny**; *dat sg & loc sg* **-źnie**) *f* scar

bliźniacz|ka (**-ki, -ki**; *dat sg & loc sg* **-ce**; *gen pl* **-ek**) *f* twin (sister)

bliźnia|k (**-ka, -ki**; *inst sg* **-kiem**) *m* **1** (*bliźnię*) twin **2** (*szeregowiec: pot*) semidetached house

Bliźnięta *pl* (*Astrol*) Gemini

bliżej *adv comp od* **blisko**

bliższy *adj comp od* **bliski**; (*sprecyzowany*) specific

bloger (**-a, -zy**; *dat sg* **-owi**) *m* blogger

bloger|ka (**-ki, -ki**; *dat sg* **-ce**) *f* blogger

blo|k (**-ku, -ki**; *inst sg* **-kiem**) *m* **1** (*kształt*) block **2** (*budynek mieszkalny*) block of flats (*Brit*), apartment house (*US*) **3** (*notatnik*) writing pad **4** (*partyjny*) bloc **5** (*startowy*) (starting) block

blond *adj*: **włosy ~** blonde hair

blondy|n (**-na, -ni**; *loc sg* **-nie**) *m* blond, blonde (*esp Brit*)

blondyn|ka (**-ki, -ki**; *dat sg & loc sg* **-ce**; *dat pl* **-ek**) *f* blonde

blu|za (**-zy, -zy**; *dat sg & loc sg* **-zie**) *f* (*dresowa*) sweatshirt

bluz|ka (**-ki, -ki**; *dat sg & loc sg* **-ce**; *gen pl* **-ek**) *f* blouse

bł|ąd (**-ędu, -ędy**; *loc sg* **-ędzie**) *m* **1** (*omyłka*) mistake **2** (*usterka*) fault; **robić (zrobić** *pf*) **~ ortograficzny** to make a spelling mistake; **jesteś w błędzie** you are wrong; **nie popełniaj błędów** don't make any mistakes

błą|dzić (**-dzę, -dzisz**; *impf* **-dź**) *vi* **1** (*szukać celu*) to wander round in circles **2** (*wykonywać niewłaściwie*) to make a mistake

błękitny *adj* blue

bło|na (**-ny, -ny**; *dat sg & loc sg* **-nie**) *f* membrane; **~ śluzowa** mucous membrane; **~ dziewicza** hymen

bło|to (**-ta, -ta**; *loc sg* **-cie**) *nt* mud

błyskawic|a (**-y, -e**) *f* lightning; **informacje rozeszły się lotem błyskawicy** the news spread like wildfire

błyskawicznie *adv* **1** (*bardzo szybko*) in a flash **2** (*natychmiastowo*) instantly

bm. *abbr* (= *bieżącego miesiąca*) (of) the current month

bo *conj* **1** (*ponieważ*) because **2** (*w przeciwnym razie*) or (else); **pospiesz się, bo nie zdążysz** hurry up, or you'll be late

bochen|ek (**-ka, -ki**; *inst sg* **-kiem**) *m* loaf

bocia|n (**-na, -ny**; *loc sg* **-nie**) *m* stork; **on nadal wierzy w ~y** he still believes that the stork brings babies

BOCIANY

Bocian biały (the White Stork) is an integral part of the Polish landscape, particularly in the north-eastern part of the country. Every year Poland hosts approximately one quarter of the world's stork population. Numerous beliefs, traditions and proverbs are connected with the stork.

oczek (**-ku, -ki**; *inst sg* **-kiem**) *m* bacon

oczny *adj* (*wejście*) side

ogaty *adj* **1** rich **2** (*majętny*) wealthy; **bogaci** *pl* the wealthy; **jego życie było bogate w wydarzenia** he led an eventful life

ohater (**-ra, -rowie** *lub* **-rzy**; *loc sg* **-rze**) *m* (*narodowy, powieści*) hero

ohaterka (**-ki, -ki**; *dat sg & loc sg* **-ce**; *gen pl* **-ek**) *f* (*filmu*) heroine

ohaterski *adj* (*czyn*) heroic

ohaterstwo (**-wa**; *loc sg* **-wie**) *nt* (*odwaga*) heroism

oisko (**-ka, -ka**; *inst sg* **-kiem**) *nt* sports field

ok (**-ku, -ki**; *inst sg* **-kiem**) *m* side; **sklep jest pod ~iem** the shop is nearby; **omijać ~iem** to sidestep; **odsunął się na ~** he moved aside; **cały wieczór zrywał ~i ze śmiechu** he split his sides laughing all evening; **przez całą noc przewracał się z ~u na ~** he tossed and turned all night

oks (**-su**; *loc sg* **-sie**) *m* (*pięściarstwo*) boxing

okser (**-ra**; *loc sg* **-rze**) *m* **1** (*nom pl* **-rzy**) (*pięściarz*) boxer **2** (*nom pl* **-ry**) (*rasa psa*) boxer

olec (**-ca, -ce**) *m* **1** (*w technice*) pin **2** (*z gwintem*) bolt

oleć (**-i**) *vi* to hurt; **boli mnie głowa** I've got a headache; **boli mnie, że tak o nim myślisz** it hurts me that you think of him this way

olesny *adj* **1** painful **2** (*uszkodzenie nogi, ręki*) sore

omba (**-by, -by**; *dat sg & loc sg* **-bie**) *f* (*ładunek wybuchowy*) bomb; **ale ~!** (*pot*) sensational!

ombka (**-ki, -ki**; *dat sg & loc sg* **-ce**; *gen pl* **-ek**) *f* (*na choince*) bauble

ombonierka (**-ki, -ki**; *dat sg & loc sg* **-ce**; *gen pl* **-ek**) *f* chocolate box

ól (**-u, -e**; *dat sg* **-owi**) *m* **1** (*nogi, ręki, pleców*) pain **2** (*przen: kłopot*) distress; **odczuwać ~ głowy** to have a headache; **cierpieć na ~ zęba** to have toothache; **~ gardła** a sore throat; **skarżyć się na ~ brzucha** to complain of stomach ache

Bośnia (**-i**) *f* Bosnia

br. *abbr* (= *bieżącego roku*) (of) the current year

brać (**biorę, bierzesz**; *pf* **wziąć**) *vt* **1** to take **2** (*pieniądze*) to get **3** (*prysznic*) to take **4** (*przykład*) to follow; **~ (za~ *pf*) się do czegoś** to set about doing sth; **skąd się bierze twój upór?** where does your stubbornness come from?

brak¹ (**-ku**; *inst sg* **-kiem**) *m* lack; **braki** *pl* (*usterki*) defects

brak² *inv*: **~ mi 300 złotych** I'm short of 300 zlotys; **ciągle ~ mi mojej matki** I miss my mother; **~ mi słów** I'm lost for words

brakować (**-uje**) *vi* to lack; **Ewie brakuje Adama** Ewa misses Adam; **kogo dziś brakuje na lekcji?** who is missing from the class today?; **tylko tego brakowało!** that's all we needed!

brama (**-my, -my**; *dat sg & loc sg* **-mie**) *f* gate(way)

bramka (**-ki, -ki**; *dat sg & loc sg* **-ce**; *gen pl* **-ek**) *f* **1** (*drzwiczki*) gate **2** (*gol*) goal

bramkarz (**-a, -e**; *gen pl* **-y**) *m* **1** (*w piłkę nożną*) goalkeeper **2** (*w nocnym lokalu*) bouncer

brat (**-ta, -cia**; *dat sg* **-tu**; *loc sg* **-cie**; *gen pl* **-ci**; *dat pl* **-ciom**; *inst pl* **-ćmi**; *loc pl* **-ciach**) *m* **1** brother **2** (*Rel*) friar; **~ przyrodni** stepbrother, half-brother

bratanek (**-ka, -kowie**; *inst sg* **-kiem**) *m* nephew (*brother's son*)

bratanica (**-y, -e**) *f* niece (*brother's daughter*)

bratowa (**-ej, -e**) *f decl like adj* sister-in-law

Brazylia (**-i**) *f* Brazil

brąz (**-zu, -zy**; *loc sg* **-zie**) *m* **1** (*kolor*) brown **2** (*metal*) bronze

brązowy *adj* **1** brown **2** (*wykonany z brązu*) bronze

brew (**-wi, -wi**; *gen pl* **-wi**) *f* eyebrow; **marszczyć (zmarszczyć *pf*) brwi** to frown; **spoglądać (spojrzeć *pf*) spod brwi (na kogoś)** to look disapprovingly (at sb)

br|oda (**-ody, -ody**; *dat sg & loc sg* **-odzie**; *gen pl* **-ód**) *f* **1** (*dolna część twarzy*) chin **2** (*zarost na twarzy*) beard; **pluć sobie w brodę** to kick o.s.
brokuł (**-a** *lub* **-u, -y**; *gen pl* **-ów**) *m* broccoli
bro|nić (**-nię, -nisz**; *imp* **-ń**; *pf* **o-**) *vt +gen* **1** to defend **2** (*ochraniać*) to guard **3** (*pf* **za-**) (*zakazywać*) to forbid; **~ się** *vr* (*przed kimś, zarzutami*) to defend o.s.
bru|d (**-du, -dy**; *loc sg* **-dzie**) *m* dirt; **prać** (*impf*) **publicznie swoje ~y** (*przen*) to wash one's dirty laundry in public

BRUDERSZAFT

Bruderszaft, also colloquially referred to as **brudzio**, is a kind of ceremonial move to first-name terms. Two people simultaneously raise their glasses in a toast, link arms and empty their glasses in one gulp. They then kiss each other on the cheeks and say their first names. From this moment on they can be on first name terms with each another.

brudno *adv*: **jest tu bardzo ~** it's very dirty here; **najpierw napisz to na ~** first write a rough version
brudny *adj* dirty, filthy
brunatny *adj* dark brown
brune|t (**-ta, -ci**; *loc sg* **-cie**) *m* dark-haired man
brunet|ka (**-ki, -ki**; *dat sg & loc sg* **-ce**; *gen pl* **-ek**) *f* dark-haired woman
Brytyjczy|k (**-ka, -cy**; *loc sg* **-kiem**) *m* Briton; **Brytyjczycy** *pl* the British
Brytyj|ka (**-ki, -ki**; *dat sg* **-ce**; *gen pl* **-ek**) *f* Briton
brytyjski *adj* British
brze|g (**-gu, -gi**; *inst sg* **-giem**) *m* **1** (*o rzecze*) bank **2** (*o jeziorze*) shore **3** (*o morzu*) shore **4** (*krawędź*) brink **5** (*piaszczysty*) beach **6** (*szklanki*) brim **7** (*kant*) edge
brzoskwi|nia (**-ni, -nie**; *gen pl* **-ń**) *f* peach
brzuch (**-a, -y**) *m* stomach, belly (*pot*); **wiercić komuś dziurę w ~u** (*przen*) to pester sb
brzydki *adj* **1** (*nieestetyczny*) ugly **2** (*działanie*) dirty
brzydko *adv* **1** (*nieładnie*) ugly **2** (*rysować*) terribly **3** (*czynić*) meanly
budo|wa (**-wy, -wy**; *dat sg & loc sg* **-wie**) *f* **1** (*budowanie: kościół*) building **2** (*konstrukcja*) construction **3** (*kształt*) structure **4** (*fizjonomia*) build
bud|ować (**-uję, -ujesz**; *pf* **z-** *lub* **wy-**) *vt* **1** (*blok*) to build **2** (*maszynę*) to construct; **w przyszłym roku będziemy się ~** we will build next year
budowl|a (**-i, -e**; *gen pl* **-i**) *f* **1** (*dom, wieżowiec*) building **2** (*konstrukcja*) structure
budownict|wo (**-wa**; *loc sg* **-wie**) *nt* construction industry
budyn|ek (**-ku, -ki**; *inst sg* **-kiem**) *m* building
bu|dzić (**-dzę, -dzisz**; *impf* **-dź**) *vt* (*pf* **z-** *lub* **o-**) **1** (*osobę*) to wake (up) **2** (*pf* **wz-**) (*strach*) to arouse; **~ się** (*pf* **o-**) *vr* to wake (up); **efekty badań budzą nadzieję** the test results give reason to hope
budzi|k (**-ka, -ki**; *inst sg* **-kiem**) *m* alarm clock; **nastawiać** (**nastawić** *pf*) **~** to set an alarm clock
bufe|t (**-tu, -ty**; *loc sg* **-cie**) *m* buffet; **zimny ~** cold buffet
bukie|t (**-tu, -ty**; *loc sg* **-cie**) *m* bouquet
bulio|n (**-nu, -ny**; *loc sg* **-nie**) *m* consommé
Bułgari|a (**-i**) *f* Bulgaria
buł|ka (**-ki, -ki**; *dat sg & loc sg* **-ce**; *gen pl* **-ek**) *f* **1** roll **2** (*drożdżówka*) bun
bura|k (**-ka, -ki**; *inst sg* **-kiem**) *m* beet; **ale z niego ~!** (*przen: pej*) what a bumpkin!
burz|a (**-y, -e**) *f* (*Meteo*) (thunder) storm
burz|yć (**-ę, -ysz**; *pf* **z-**) *vt* **1** (*dom*) to demolish **2** (*spokój*) to destroy
bu|t (**-ta, -ty**; *loc sg* **-cie**) *m* **1** shoe **2** (*z cholewami*) boot; **no to umarł w ~ach!** (*pot*) it's too late; there's nothing more we can do
butel|ka (**-ki, -ki**; *dat sg & loc sg* **-ce**; *gen pl* **-ek**) *f* bottle
buti|k (**-ku, -ki**; *inst sg* **-kiem**) *m* boutique

bu|zia (**-zi, -zie**; *gen pl* **-zi** *lub* **-ź**) (*pot*) *f* **1** (*usta*) mouth **2** (*twarz*) face; **wycierać sobie kimś buzię** to mouth off about sb
być (**jestem, jesteś**; *1 pl* **jesteśmy**; *2 pl* **jesteście**; *3 pl* **są**; *impf* **bądź**; *pt* **był, była, byli**; *1 sg fut* **będę**; *2 sg fut* **będziesz**) *vi* to be; **jestem!** here!; **jestem autobusem** I've come by bus; **jest chłodno** it's cold; **jest mi niedobrze** I feel sick; **będę krzyczeć** I'll scream; **ta książka była napisana w 1967 roku** this book was written in 1967; **~ może** maybe; **może ~** it will do
by|k (**-ka, -ki**; *inst sg* **-kiem**) *m* **1** bull **2** (*Astrol*): **B~** Taurus; **tylko nie narób ~ów** (*pot*: *przen*) just don't make mistakes
były *adj* (*mąż, ambasador*) former
by|t (**-tu, -ty**; *loc sg* **-cie**) *m* **1** (*życie*) existence **2** (*istnienie*) being
bzdu|ra (**-ry, -ry**; *dat sg & loc sg* **-rze**) *f* nonsense; **pleść bzdury** to talk nonsense

C

ca|l (**-la, -le**; *gen pl* **-li**) *m* inch
całkiem *adv* **1** (*zupełnie*) entirely **2** (*dość*) quite; **jest ~ szalony** he is completely crazy; **ciasto jest ~ smaczne** the cake tastes pretty good
całkowicie *adv* completely
całkowity *adj* **1** (*ciemność*) total **2** (*wartość*) total **3** (*w matematyce*: *liczba*) integer
całodobowy *adj* twenty-four-hour; **sklep ~** twenty-four-hour store
całodzienny *adj* all-day; **całodzienne wyżywienie** full board
całonocny *adj* all-night
cał|ować (**-uję, -ujesz**; *pf* **po-**) *vt* to kiss; **~ się** *vr* to kiss
cały *adj* whole; **~ czas** all the time; **~ tydzień** all week (long); **cała okolica** the whole district; **cała nuta** (*Muz*) semibreve (*Brit*), whole note (*US*); **~mi godzinami** for hours on end; **całą parą** full steam ahead
cdn. *abbr* (= *ciąg dalszy nastąpi*) to be continued
CD-ROM (**-u, -y**; *dat sg & loc sg* **-ie**) *m* CD-ROM
cebu|la (**-li, -le**) *f* onion; **ubierać** (**ubrać** *pf*) **się na cebulę** (*przen*) to wear plenty of layers
ce|cha (**-chy, -chy**; *dat sg & loc sg* **-sze**) *f* feature; **~ ujemna/ dodatnia** negative/positive characteristic; **~ dziedziczna** inherited characteristic
ce|gła (**-gły, -gły**; *dat sg & loc sg* **-gle**; *gen pl* **-gieł**) *f* brick

cel (**-u, -e**) *m* **1** (*działania*) purpose **2** (*wyprawy*) destination **3** (*punkt w środku tarczy*) target; **chybiać** (**chybić** *pf*) **~u** to miss the target; **osiągać** (**osiągnąć** *pf*) **~** to achieve one's objective; **~ uświęca środki** the end justifies the means

ce|la (**-li, -le**) *f* cell

celni|k (**-ka, -cy**; *inst sg* **-kiem**) *m* customs officer

celny *adj* **1** (*rzut*) accurate **2** (*udany, zręczny*) relevant **3** (*urząd celny*) customs

cel|ować (**-uję, -ujesz**; *pf* **wy-**) *vi* to take aim; **~ do kogoś z pistoletu** to aim a pistol at sb

celowo *adv* (*umyślnie*) deliberately

celowni|k (**-ka, -ki**; *inst sg* **-kiem**) *m* (*przypadek gramatyczny*) dative

ce|na (**-ny, -ny**; *dat sg & loc sg* **-nie**) *f* (*hurtowa/detaliczna*) price; **~ okazyjna/fabryczna/sugerowana** bargain/factory/recommended price

ce|nić (**-nię, -nisz**; *imp* **-ń**) *vt* (*poważać*) to value; **~ kogoś/coś** to appreciate sb/sth; **on się wysoko ceni** he thinks highly of himself

cenni|k (**-ka, -ki**; *inst sg* **-kiem**) *m* price list

cenny *adj* (*wartościowy*) valuable

centra|la (**-li, -le**; *gen pl* **-li** *lub* **-l**) *f* **1** (*telefoniczna*) (telephone) exchange **2** (*banku, firmy*) head office

centralny *adj* (*położony w środku*) central; **centralne ogrzewanie** central heating

centr|um (**-um, -a**; *gen pl* **-ów**) *nt inv in sg* (*środek*) centre (*Brit*), center (*US*); **~ miasta** town *lub* city centre (*Brit*), downtown (*US*); **~ handlowe** shopping centre (*Brit*), mall (*US*); **znajdować** (**znaleźć** *pf*) **się w ~ uwagi** to find o.s. the centre of attention

centymet|r (**-ra, -ry**; *loc sg* **-rze**) *m* **1** centimetre (*Brit*), centimeter (*US*) **2** (*centymetr: do mierzenia*) tape measure

cenzu|ra (**-ry**; *dat sg & loc sg* **-rze**) *f* censorship; **~ represyjna** repressive censorship

cer|kiew (**-kwi, -kwie**; *gen pl* **-kwi**) *f* Orthodox church

certyfika|t (**-tu, -ty**; *loc sg* **-cie**) *m* (*jakości, bezpieczeństwa*) certificate

cesarst|wo (**-wa, -wa**; *loc sg* **-wie**) *nt* empire

cesarz (**-a, -e**; *gen pl* **-y**) *m* emperor

cha|m (**-ma, -my**; *loc sg* **-mie**) *m* (*pot!*) lout; **robić** (**zrobić** *pf*) **coś na ~a** (*pot!*) to do sth in a slapdash way

chamski *adj* (*pej: niekulturalny*) boorish

chaotyczny *adj* (*rozmowa, działanie*) chaotic

charakte|r (**-ru, -ry**; *loc sg* **-rze**) *m* **1** (*osoby*) character **2** (*rzeczy, zjawiska*) nature; **w ~ze** *+gen* in the capacity of; **człowiek z ~em/ bez ~u** a person of character/of no character; **~ pisma** handwriting

charakterystyczny *adj*: **~ (dla** *+gen*) typical (of)

charakterysty|ka (**-ki, -ki**; *dat sg & loc sg* **-ce**) *f* (*osoby, dzieła*) profile

chcieć (**chcę, chcesz**) *vt* to want

chciwy *adj* greedy

chemi|a (**-i**) *f* chemistry

chemiczny *adj* (*skład, analiza*) chemical

chemi|k (**-ka, -cy**; *inst sg* **-kiem**) *m* **1** (*specjalista*) chemist **2** (*Szkol*) chemistry teacher

chę|ć (**-ci, -ci**) *f* desire; **~ do działania** a desire to be active; **zrobię to z miłą chęcią** I'll be glad to do that

chętnie *adv* eagerly

chętny *adj* eager

Chile *nt inv* Chile

Chi|ny (**-n**) *pl* China

chiński *adj* Chinese; **Chińska Republika Ludowa** the People's Republic of China

chips|y (**-ów**) *pl* crisps (*Brit*), chips (*US*)

chirur|g (**-ga, -dzy**; *inst sg* **-giem**) *m* surgeon

chirurgi|a (**-i**) *f* surgery

chle|b (**-ba, -by**; *loc sg* **-bie**) *m* bread; **przeciętny zjadacz ~a** (*przen*) the average person

chłodno *adv* (*traktować kogoś*) coolly; **dziś było ~** it was chilly today; **nagle zrobiło się ~** it got cold all of a sudden

chłodny *adj* cool

chłopa|k (**-ka, -cy**; *inst sg* **-kiem**) *m* **1** boy **2** (*sympatia*) boyfriend
chło|piec (**-pca, -pcy**; *dat sg & loc sg* **-pcu**) *m* **1** boy **2** (*narzeczony*) boyfriend; **~ do bicia** (*przen*) whipping boy
chmu|ra (**-ry, -ry**; *dat sg & loc sg* **-rze**) *f* cloud; **drapacz chmur** skyscraper
chmurz|yć się (**-ę, -ysz**; *pf* **za-**) *vr* **1** (*marszczyć czoło*) to frown **2** to cloud over
choć *conj* = **chociaż**
chociaż *conj* though, although
cho|dzić (**-dzę, -dzisz**; *imp* **-dź**) *vi* **1** (*spacerować*) to walk **2** (*uczęszczać*) to go **3** (*działać*) to work; **~ z kimś** (*pot*) to go out with sb; **chodźmy do kina** let's go to the cinema; **o co chodzi?** what's the problem?; **chodzi o to, że...** the thing is...

CHODZIĆ/IŚĆ/PÓJŚĆ

Chodzić, iść and **pójść** are all verbs of motion meaning "to go" (on foot), but they have different implications. With the perfective verb – **pójść** – the emphasis is on the act of going to and arriving at the destination, whereas with the imperfective verbs – **chodzić** and **iść** – the focus is more on the act of going itself and it is not made clear whether the subject arrives at the destination or not. **Chodzić** is also used to describe habitual activities and **iść** is used to describe going to or from a particular point on one occasion.

choin|ka (**-ki, -ki**; *dat sg & loc sg* **-ce**; *gen pl* **-ek**) *f* **1** (*drzewo w lesie*) spruce **2** (*drzewo iglaste z bombkami*) Christmas tree
chole|ra (**-ry**; *dat sg & loc sg* **-rze**) *f* **1** (*choroba*) cholera **2** (*wulgaryzm*): **~!** shit! (*pot!*); **do jasnej cholery!** (*pot!*) for Christ's sake! (*pot!*)
chomi|k (**-ka, -ki**; *inst sg* **-kiem**) *m* hamster
chor|oba (**-oby, -oby**; *dat sg & loc sg* **-obie**; *gen pl* **-ób**) *f* disease; (*słabość*) illness; **zamknięte z powodu choroby** closed because of illness
chor|ować (**-uję, -ujesz**) *vi* to be ill, to be sick (*esp US*); **~ (za~** *pf*) **obłożnie** to be confined to bed; **~ (za~** *pf*) **na anginę** to have a throat infection; **~ (za~** *pf*) **z przepracowania** to make o.s. ill from overwork
Chorwacj|a (**-i**) *f* Croatia
chory *adj* **1** (*osoba*) sick **2** (*obolały*) sore **3** (*oko*) bad **4** (*zwierzę*) sick ▷ *m decl like adj* **1** (*człowiek, który choruje*) sick person **2** (*pacjent*) patient; **śmiertelnie/ciężko ~** terminally/ seriously ill
chow|ać (**-am, -asz**) *vt* **1** (*pf* **s-**) (*kłaść*) to put (*somewhere*) **2** (*pf* **s-**) (*odłożyć*) to put away **3** (*pf* **s-**) (*w ukryciu*) to hide **4** (*mieć: tajemnicę, sekret*) to keep **5** (*pf* **po-**) (*grzebać*) to bury; **~ się** (*pf* **s-**) *vr* (*ukryć się*) to hide
Chrystu|s (**-sa**; *loc sg* **-sie**) *m* Christ; **Jezus ~** Jesus Christ
chrz|est (**-tu, -ty**; *loc sg* **-cie**) *m* **1** (*nadanie imienia w kościele*) christening **2** (*statku*) naming ceremony
chrześcija|nin (**-nina, -nie**; *loc sg* **-ninie**) *m* Christian
chrześcijański *adj* Christian
chrześcijańst|wo (**-wa**; *loc sg* **-wie**) *nt* Christianity
chud|nąć (**-nę, -niesz**; *imp* **-nij**; *pf* **s-**) *vi* to slim down
chudy *adj* **1** (*o osobie*) thin **2** (*o mięsie*) lean; **~ jak patyk** as thin as a rake
chuliga|n (**-na, -ni**; *loc sg* **-nie**) *m* (*łobuz: pej*) yob
chustecz|ka (**-ki, -ki**; *dat sg & loc sg* **-ce**; *gen pl* **-ek**) *f* (*do nosa*) handkerchief; **~ higieniczna** tissue
chwa|lić (**-lę, -lisz**; *pf* **po-**) *vt* (*mówić z aprobatą o kimś*) to praise; **~ się** *vr*: **~ (po~** *pf*) **się** (*+loc*) to brag (about); **nie chwaląc się jestem najlepszy** with all due modesty, I'm the best
chwi|la (**-li, -le**) *f* moment, instant; **poczekaj na mnie chwilę!** wait a moment!; **~ mi pada** from time to time it rains; **co ~ budzi się** every now and then he wakes up; **lada ~ może przyjść** he could be here any moment; **za chwilę pójdę** I'll go in a minute

chwy|cić (**-cę, -cisz**; *imp* **-ć**) *vb pf od* **chwytać**
chwyt|ać (**-am, -asz**) *vb* to catch, to capture
chyba *part* probably ▷ *conj*: **~ że** unless; **~ tak/~ nie** I think so/I don't think so
ci|ało (**-ała, -ała**; *loc sg* **-ele**) *nt* body; **przybierać** (**przybrać** *pf*) **na ciele** to put on weight
cia|sny *adj* **1** tight **2** (*pomieszczenie*) cramped
ciast|ko (**-ka, -ka**; *inst sg* **-kiem**; *gen pl* **-ek**) *nt* cake
ci|asto (**-asta, -asta**; *loc sg* **-eście**) *nt* **1** (*masa*) dough **2** (*wypiek z ciasta*) cake
ciąć (**tnę, tniesz**; *imp* **tnij**) *vt* (*narzędziem z ostrzem*) to cut
ciągle *adv* **1** (*wciąż, nadal*) still **2** (*nieprzerwanie*) all the time; **on ~ jeszcze choruje** he is still a sick man
ciąg|nąć (**-nę, -niesz**; *imp* **-nij**; *pf* **po-**) *vt* (*wlec*) **1** to pull **2** (*w loterii*) to draw ▷ *vi* (*kontynuować wypowiedź*) to continue; **~ się** *vr* **1** (*o brzegu, trasie*) to extend, to stretch **2** (*o rozmowie*) to drag on
cicho *adv* **1** quietly **2** (*bez głosu*) silently; **mówić ~** to speak quietly; **~!** quiet!
cichy *adj* **1** (*ulica*) quiet **2** (*dźwięk*) low; **wszedł po cichu** he came in quietly
ciecz (**-y, -e**; *gen pl* **-y**) *f* liquid
ciekawost|ka (**-ki, -ki**; *dat sg & loc sg* **-ce**; *gen pl* **-ek**) *f* **1** (*osobliwość*) curiosity **2** (*przyrodnicza, historyczna*) interesting fact
ciekawoś|ć (**-ci**) *f* curiosity; **~ to pierwszy stopień do piekła** curiosity killed the cat
ciekawy *adj* **1** (*zajmujący*) interesting **2** (*wykazujący zainteresowanie*) curious
cielęci|na (**-ny**; *dat sg & loc sg* **-nie**) *f* veal
ciem|no (**-na**; *loc sg* **-nie**) *nt* dark ▷ *adv* dark; **w ~** on spec; **iść** (**pójść** *pf*) **na randkę w ~** to go on a blind date; **robi się ~** it's getting dark
ciemnoś|ć (**-ci, -ci**; *dat sg & loc sg* **-ci**) *f* darkness; **egipskie ciemności** pitch darkness
ciemny *adj* **1** (*kolor*) dark **2** (*pomieszczenie*) dark **3** (*pieczywo*) brown **4** (*nierozgarnięty*) dim
cie|nki *adj* thin
cie|ń (**-nia, -nie**; *gen pl* **-ni**) *m* **1** (*człowieka, domu*) shadow **2** (*miejsce osłonięte od słońca*) shade; **pozostawać** (**pozostać** *pf*) **w cieniu** to remain in the background; **~ do powiek** eyeshadow
ciep|ło (**-ła**; *loc sg* **-le**) *nt* **1** warmth **2** (*w fizyce*) heat ▷ *adv*: **było ~** it was warm; **jest mi ~** I'm warm
ciepły *adj* warm; **ciepłe kluchy** (*pot*) wimp
ciesz|yć (**-ę, -ysz**; *pf* **u-**) *vt* to delight; **~ się** *vr*: **~ się** (**z** *+gen*) to be pleased (with); **cieszę się na nasze spotkanie** I'm looking forward to seeing you; **~ się powodzeniem** to be popular
cię *pron gen, acc sg od* **ty**
cio|cia (**-ci, -cie**; *gen pl* **-ć**) *f* (*pot*) auntie
ciot|ka (**-ki, -ki**; *dat sg & loc sg* **-ce**; *gen pl* **-ek**) *f* aunt
cisz|a (**-y**) *f* silence; **~ przed burzą** the calm before the storm
ciszej *adv comp od* **cicho**
ciśnie|nie (**-nia, -nia**; *gen pl* **-ń**) *nt* pressure; **mierzyć** (**zmierzyć** *pf*) **komuś ~ krwi** to take sb's blood pressure
cm *abbr* (*= centymetr*) cm
cmentarz (**-a, -e**; *gen pl* **-y**) *m* **1** (*komunalny, wojskowy*) cemetery **2** (*przykościelny*) graveyard

SŁOWO KLUCZOWE

co *pron* **1** (*w pytaniu*) what; **co to jest?** what is that?; **co to za film?** what film is this?
2 (*w zdaniach względnych*): **mówił o tych, co odeszli** he talked about those who were no longer with us; **udało mu się, co nas zaskoczyło** he managed it, which surprised us
3 (*w równoważnikach zdań*): **rób, co chcesz** do what you want; **nie ma co narzekać** there's no use complaining
4 (*w zdaniach wykrzyknikowych*): **co za pomysł!** what a thought!

▷ *part* **1** (*wzmacniająco*): **co najmniej** at least; **co najwyżej** at the most; **co gorsza** what's worse; **co prawda** as a matter of fact; **nie ma za co** you're welcome, don't mention it
2: **co drugi/trzeci raz** every second/third; **co poniedziałek/tydzień/rok** every Monday/week/year
3 (*odnośnie*): **co do** +*gen* as for; **wszyscy co do jednego wyszli** to a man, they went out

c.o. *abbr* (= *centralne ogrzewanie*) central heating
codziennie *adv* every day
codzienny *adj* **1** (*spacer*) daily, everyday **2** (*gazeta*) daily **3** (*zajęcia*) everyday
cof|ać (**-am, -asz**; *pf* **-nąć**) *vt* **1**: **~ swoje słowa** to take back one's words **2** (*pojazd*) to reverse **3** (*zegar*) to put back **4** (*wojska*) to withdraw; **~ się** *vr* **1** (*usuwać się w tył*) to draw back **2** (*ustępować*) to retreat, to pull back
coraz *adv*: **~ lepiej** better and better
coś *pron* **1** (*w zdaniach twierdzących*) something **2** (*w zdaniach pytajnych*) anything; **robić** (**zrobić** *pf*) **~ innego** to do something else; **~ ciekawego** something interesting; **~ do czytania** something to read
cór|ka (**-ki, -ki**; *dat sg & loc sg* **-ce**; *gen pl* **-ek**) *f* daughter
crowdfunding (**-u, -i**; *dat sg* **-owi**) *m* crowdfunding
cuch|nąć (**-nę, -niesz**; *imp* **-nij**) *vi* to stink
cudowny *adj* **1** (*siła*) miraculous **2** (*pomysł, obraz*) wonderful
cudzozie|miec (**-mca, -mcy**) *m* (*obcokrajowiec*) foreigner
cudzoziem|ka (**-ki, -ki**; *dat sg & loc sg* **-ce**; *gen pl* **-ek**) *f* foreigner
cudzoziemski *adj* foreign; **~ akcent** a foreign accent
cudzy *adj* somebody else's
cu|kier (**-kru**; *loc sg* **-krze**) *m* (*puder, w kostkach*) sugar
cukier|ek (**-ka, -ki**; *inst sg* **-kiem**) *m* (*orzechowy, owocowy*) sweet (*Brit*), candy (*US*)
cukier|nia (**-ni, -nie**; *gen pl* **-ni** *lub* **-ń**) *f* pastry shop
cukrzyc|a (**-y**) *f* (*choroba*) diabetes
cyberprzemoc (**-y, -e**; *dat sg* **-y**) *m* cyberbullying
cyf|ra (**-ry, -ry**; *dat sg & loc sg* **-rze**) *f* figure; **cyfry arabskie/rzymskie** Arabic/Roman numerals
Cyga|n (**-na, -nie**; *loc sg* **-nie**) *m* gypsy
Cygan|ka (**-ki, -ki**; *dat sg & loc sg* **-ce**; *gen pl* **-ek**) *f* gypsy
Cyp|r (**-ru**; *loc sg* **-rze**) *m* (*Geo*) Cyprus
cyr|k (**-ku, -ki**; *inst sg* **-kiem**) *m* circus; **urządzać** (**urządzić** *pf*) **~** (*pot*) to make a fuss
cytry|na (**-ny, -ny**; *dat sg & loc sg* **-nie**) *f* lemon; **herbata z cytryną** tea with lemon
cywilizacj|a (**-i, -e**; *gen pl* **-i**) *f* civilization
cywilny *adj* **1** (*nie odnoszący się do wojska*) civil **2** (*strój niewojskowy*) ordinary; **stan ~** marital status; **ślub ~** civil marriage ceremony
czadowy *adj* (*pot*) funky
czajni|k (**-ka, -ki**; *inst sg* **-kiem**) *m* kettle
czap|ka (**-ki, -ki**; *dat sg & loc sg* **-ce**; *gen pl* **-ek**) *f* **1** hat **2** (*nakrycie głowy z daszkiem*) cap; **czapki z głów!** hats off!
czap|la (**-li, -le**; *gen pl* **-li**) *f* heron
czarny *adj* **1** (*barwa*) black **2** (*smutny: obraz, pogląd*) black; **czarna lista** blacklist; **podawać** (**podać** *pf*) **czarną polewkę** (*przen*) to discourage someone's advances; **~ rynek** black market; **czarna porzeczka** blackcurrant; **czarno na białym** (*przen*) in black and white
czarterowy *adj* (*lot, samolot*) charter
cza|s (**-su**; *loc sg* **-sie**) *m* **1** time **2** (*nom pl* **-sy**) (*odcinek czasu*) period **3** (*nom pl* **-sy**) (*w językoznawstwie*) tense; **dawne/dobre/złe ~y** old/good/bad/ times; **zabijać** (**zabić** *pf*) **~** (*przen*) to kill time; **to tylko kwestia ~u** it's only a matter of time; **najwyższy ~** it is high time; **na ~** on time; **od ~u do ~u** from time to time
czasami *adv* sometimes
czasem *adv* (*czasami*) sometimes
czasopi|smo (**-sma, -sma**; *loc sg* **-śmie**) *nt* (*dla dzieci, kobiet*) periodical

czasowni|k (**-ka, -ki**; *inst sg* **-kiem**) *m* (*w językoznawstwie*) verb; **~ dokonany/niedokonany** perfective/imperfective verb; **~ przechodni/nieprzechodni** transitive/intransitive verb

czasowy *adj* **1** (*tymczasowy*) temporary **2** (*odnoszący się do czasu*) temporal

czasz|ka (**-ki, -ki**; *dat sg & loc sg* **-ce**; *gen pl* **-ek**) *f* skull

cza|t (**-tu, -ty**; *dat sg & loc sg* **-cie**) *m* (*Komput*) (online) chat

czcion|ka (**-ki, -ki**; *dat sg & loc sg* **-ce**; *gen pl* **-ek**) *f* **1** (*w drukarstwie*) type **2** (*w komputerze*) font

Czech|y (**-**) *pl* the Czech Republic

czego *pron gen od* **co**

czegoś *pron gen od* **coś**

cze|k (**-ku, -ki**; *inst sg* **-kiem**) *m* cheque (*Brit*), check (*US*); **wypisywać** (**wypisać** *pf*) **~ na sumę 100 złotych** to write a cheque for 100 złotys; **płacić** (**zapłacić** *pf*) **~iem** to pay by cheque

czek|ać (**-am, -asz**) *vi*: **~ na** to wait for

czekola|da (**-dy, -dy**; *dat sg & loc sg* **-dzie**) *f* chocolate; **tabliczka czekolady** a bar of chocolate

czekolad|ka (**-ki, -ki**; *dat sg & loc sg* **-ce**; *gen pl* **-ek**) *f* (a) chocolate; **pudełko czekoladek** a box of chocolates

czekoladowy *adj* (*cukierek, batonik*) chocolate

czemu *pron dat od* **co**; **~?** (*pot*) how come?

czereś|nia (**-ni, -nie**; *gen pl* **-ni**) *f* **1** (*owoc z drzewa*) cherry **2** (*drzewo*) cherry tree

czerwiec (**-wca, -wce**) *m* June

czer|wony *adj* (*barwa*) red ▷ *m decl like adj* (*pot, pej*: *komunista*) Red; **~ jak burak** (*przen*) red as a beetroot; **~ Krzyż** Red Cross

cze|sać (**-szę, -szesz**; *pf* **u-**) *vt* **1** (*siebie*) to brush **2** (*układać fryzurę*) to style; **~ się** *vr* **1** (*grzebieniem*) to comb one's hair **2** (*szczotką*) to brush one's hair

czeski *adj* Czech; **Republika Czeska** the Czech Republic

czesn|e (**-ego**) *nt decl like adj* (*Szkol, Uniw*) tuition (fee)

cześć (**czci**) *f* (*uznanie*: *książk*) reverence ▷ *excl*: **~!** (*pot*: *witaj!*) hi!; (*pot*: *do zobaczenia!*) see you!; **człowiek bez czci i wiary** a total scoundrel; **przyjęcie na ~ kogoś/czegoś** a reception in honour (*Brit*) *lub* honor (*US*) of sb/sth

częś|ć (**-ci, -cią**) *f* (*domu, urządzenia, ciała*) part

czę|sto *adv* often, frequently

częsty *adj* common, frequent

człon|ek (**-ka**; *inst sg* **-kiem**) *m* **1** (*nom pl* **-kowie**) (*partii, stowarzyszenia*) member **2** (*nom pl* **-ki**) (*ręka, noga*) limb **3** (*też*: **~ męski**) penis

człowie|k (**-ka, ludzie**; *inst sg* **-kiem**; *gen pl* **ludzi**; *dat pl* **ludziom**; *inst pl* **ludźmi**; *loc pl* **ludziach**) *m* **1** human being **2** (*osoba płci męskiej*) man **3** (*bezosobowo*) one, you; **~ nie wie, co powiedzieć** one doesn't know what to say; *zob. też* **ludzie**

cz|oło (**-oła, -oła**; *dat sg & loc sg* **-ołu**; *loc sg* **-ole**; *gen pl* **-ół**) *nt* **1** forehead **2** (*loc sg* **-ele**) (*część z przodu*) front; **puknij się w ~!** (*pot*: *przen*) you're crazy!

czosn|ek (**-ku, -ki**; *inst sg* **-kiem**) *m* garlic

czterdziest|ka (**-ki, -ki**; *dat sg & loc sg* **-ce**; *gen pl* **-ek**) *f* forty; **ona jest po czterdziestce** she is in her forties

czterdziesty *num* fortieth; **~ pierwszy** forty-first

czterdzieści *num* forty

czternasty *num* fourteenth

czternaście *num* fourteen

cztery *num* four

czterysta *num* four hundred

czu|ć (**-ję, -jesz**; *pf* **po-**) *vt* **1** to feel **2** (*woń*) to smell; **~ się** *vr*: **~ się dobrze/źle** to feel well/unwell; **czułem, że...** I felt that...; **jak się dziś czujesz?** how are you feeling today?

czule *adv* (*witać, przytulać*) affectionately

czu|ły *adj* **1** (*serdeczny*) affectionate **2** (*wyczulony*): **~ (na)** sensitive (to) **3** (*punkt, miejsce*) sensitive; **to jego ~ punkt** that's a sore point with him

czwartek (**-ku, -ki**; *inst sg* **-kiem**) *m* Thursday; **Wielki C~** (*Rel*) Maundy Thursday; **tłusty ~** *the last Thursday before Lent*

czwarty *num* fourth; **spotkajmy się o czwartej** let's meet at four; **jedna czwarta** a quarter

 **SŁOWO KLUCZOWE**

czy *part* **1** (*w pytaniach*): **czy znasz tę dziewczynę?** do you know this girl?; **czy byłeś kiedyś w Polsce?** have you ever been to Poland?; **czy mogę wyjść?** can I go?; **czy ja wiem?** (*pot*) how would I know?
2 (*w zdaniach podrzędnych*) if, whether; **nie wiem, czy to ma sens** I don't know if this makes sense; **zapytaj ją, czy go lubi** ask her if she loves him
▷ *conj* or; **wódka czy piwo?** vodka or beer?

czyj *pron* whose; **~ to dom?** whose house is this?

czyli *part* (*zatem*) in other words; **~ nie będziesz mógł dzisiaj przyjść?** in other words you won't be able to come today?

czynnoś|ć (**-ci, -ci**) *f* (*działalność*) activity; **czynności** *pl* (*działanie w urzędzie*) measures

czynny *adj* **1** active **2** (*urząd*) open **3** (*winda, toaleta*) working; **strona czynna** the active (voice)

czynsz (**-u, -e**; *gen pl* **-ów**) *m* (*stała opłata mieszkaniowa*) rent

czy|sto *adv* **1** (*bez brudu*) clean(ly) **2** (*wyraźnie*) clear(ly) **3** (*grać*) in tune **4** (*wyłącznie*) purely; **sprawa ~ osobista** a purely personal matter

czysty *adj* **1** (*nie brudny*) clean **2** (*bez dodatków*) pure **3** (*pot: wariactwo*) sheer **4** (*pot: nie łamiący prawa*) clean; **mieć czyste sumienie** to have a clear conscience

czy|ścić (**-szczę, -ścisz**; *impf* **-ść**; *pf* **wy-**) *vt* to clean; **czyści mnie** (*pot: przen*) I've got diarrhoea (*Brit*) *lub* diarrhea (*US*)

czyt|ać (**-am, -asz**; *pf* **prze-**) *vt/vi* to read; **zawsze czyta od deski do deski** he reads everything from cover to cover

czytel|nia (**-ni, -nie**; *gen pl* **-ni**) *f* reading room

czytelni|k (**-ka, -cy**; *inst sg* **-kiem**) *m* reader

czytelny *adj* legible; **~ podpis** a legible signature

czytnik e-booków (**-a, -i**; *dat sg* **-owi**) *m* e-reader

ćwicze|nie (**-nia, -nia**; *gen pl* **-ń**) *nt* **1** (*trening*) practice **2** (*w szkole, fizyczne*) exercise; **ćwiczenia** *pl* (*na uniwersytecie*) classes *pl*

ćwicz|yć (**-ę, -ysz**) *vt* **1** (*trenować*) to practise (*Brit*), to practice (*US*) **2** (*pf* **wy-**) (*kształcić: człowieka*) to train **3** (*pamięć, umysł*) to train **4** (*pf* **wy-**) to exercise ▷ *vi* **1** to practise (*Brit*), to practice (*US*) **2** (*wykonywać ćwiczenia fizyczne*) to exercise

d

dach (**-u, -y**) *m* (*budynku, samochodu*) roof

dać (**dam, dasz**; *3 pl* **dadzą**) *vt pf od* **dawać**

dalej *adv comp od* **daleko 1** (*w odległym miejscu*) farther **2** (*w przyszłości*) further; **i tak ~** and so forth

daleko *adv* far; **jak ~ jest stąd do kina?** how far is it from here to the cinema?

dalszy *adj comp od* **daleki 1** (*w odległym miejscu, w następnej kolejności*) farther **2** (*w przyszłości*) further; **dopełnienie dalsze** (*Jęz*) indirect object; **ciąg ~ nastąpi** to be continued

da|ma (**-my, -my**; *dat & loc sg* **-mie**) *f* **1** (*kobieta*) lady **2** (*w grze w karty, w szachach*) queen

damski *adj* **1** (*fryzjer*) ladies'; (*odzież*) women's **2** (*składający się z kobiet*) female

dan|e (**-ych**) *pl* (*informacje*) data

Dani|a (**-i**) *f* Denmark

da|nie (**-nia, -nia**; *gen pl* **-ń**) *nt* **1** (*mięsne, jarskie*) dish **2** (*część obiadu*) course; **drugie ~** main course

da|r (**-ru, -ry**; *loc sg* **-rze**) *m* (*prezent, zdolność*) gift

darmowy *adj* (*bezpłatny*) free

da|ta (**-ty, -ty**; *dat & loc sg* **-cie**) *f* (*termin*) date; **~ urodzenia** date of birth

da|wać (**-ję, -jesz**; *pf* **dać**) *vt* (*prezent, pozwolenie, pracę*) to give; **~ (dać** *pf***) komuś coś** to give sb sth; **daj mi**

spokój leave me alone; **daj mi znać** let me know; **to się da zrobić** it can be done

dawno *adv* **1** (*w odległych czasach*): **~ (temu)** long ago **2** (*od długiego czasu*) for a long time; **już ~ jej nie widziałam** it's been a long time since I saw her

dawny *adj* **1** (*były, poprzedni*) former **2** (*stary, zabytkowy*) ancient **3** (*czasy, znajomy*) old; **od dawna** for a long time

db|ać (**-am, -asz**; *pf* **za-**) *vi*: **~ (za~** *pf*) **o kogoś/coś** to look after sb/sth; **nie ~** (*impf*) **o coś** to be unconcerned about sth

debiu|t (**-tu, -ty**; *loc sg* **-cie**) *m* (*aktorski, literacki*) debut

decyd|ować (**-uję, -ujesz**) *vi*: **~ (z~** *pf*) **(o czymś)** (*postanawiać coś*) to decide (on sth); **~ (za~** *pf*) **(o czymś)** (*mieć wpływ na coś*) to determine (sth); **~ się** (*pf* **z-**) *vr* **1** (*dokonywać wyboru*) to make up one's mind **2** (*rozstrzygać czyjś los*) to be determined; **~ (z~** *pf*) **się na coś** to opt for sth

decyzj|a (**-i, -e**; *gen pl, dat & loc sg* **-i**) *f* (*postanowienie*) decision; **podejmować (podjąć** *pf*) **decyzję** to make a decision

definicj|a (**-i, -e**; *gen pl, dat & loc sg* **-i**) *f* (*wyrażenia, znaczenia*) definition

deklar|ować (**-uję, -ujesz**; *pf* **za-**) *vt* **1** (*obwieszczać*) to declare **2** (*zobowiązywać się*) to pledge; **~ się** (*pf* **z-**) *vr*: **~ (z~** *pf*) **się za czymś** to declare o.s. in favour (*Brit*) *lub* favor (*US*) of sth; **~ (z~** *pf*) **się przeciw czemuś** to declare o.s. against sth

deklinacj|a (**-i, -e**; *gen pl, dat & loc sg* **-i**) *f* (*Jęz*) declension

dekol|t (**-tu, -ty**; *loc sg* **-cie**) *m* **1** (*w bluzce*) neckline **2** (*niezasłonięte piersi*) cleavage; **koszulka z ~em** low-cut top

dekoracj|a (**-i, -e**; *gen pl, dat & loc sg* **-i**) *f* **1** (*ozdoba*) decoration **2** (*w teatrze lub filmie*) scenery

delfi|n (**-na, -ny**; *loc sg* **-nie**) *m* (*Zool*) dolphin

delikates|y (**-ów**) *pl* **1** (*sklep z jedzeniem*) delicatessen *sg* **2** (*wykwintne jedzenie*) delicacies

delikatnie *adv* **1** (*wrażliwie, z taktem*) gently **2** (*nieintensywnie*) delicately

delikatny *adj* **1** (*wrażliwy, taktowny*) gentle **2** (*o drobnej budowie*) delicate **3** (*nieintensywny, przyjemny*) soft **4** (*o zapachu*) mild **5** (*zdrowie*) delicate **6** (*drażliwy, wymagający ostrożności*) sensitive

demokracj|a (**-i, -e**; *gen pl, dat & loc sg* **-i**) *f* (*sposób rządzenia*) democracy

demon (**-a, -y**) *m* demon

demonstr|ować (**-uję, -ujesz**; *pf* **za-**) *vt* (*nowe produkty*) to demonstrate ▷ *vi* (*protestować*) to demonstrate

denerw|ować (**-uję, -ujesz**; *pf* **z-**) *vt* (*działać na nerwy*) to irritate, to annoy; **~ się** (*pf* **z-**) *vr* **1** (*być stale niespokojnym*) to be nervous **2** (*być rozdrażnionym w danej chwili*) to be irritated **3** (*martwić się*) to be anxious; **~ się czymś** to be nervous about sth; **on mnie denerwuje** he gets on my nerves

denerwujący *adj* (*irytujący*) irritating, annoying

denty|sta (**-sty, -ści**; *dat & loc sg* **-ście**) *m decl like f in sg* (*Med*) dentist

dentystyczny *adj* **1** (*o gabinecie, fotelu*) dentist's **2** (*o zabiegu*) dental

departamen|t (**-tu, -ty**; *loc sg* **-cie**) *m* (*w ministerstwie*) department

depozy|t (**-tu, -ty**; *loc sg* **-cie**) *m* (*w banku*) deposit

dep|tać (**-czę, -czesz**; *pf* **po-**) *vt* (*przygniatać, łamać*) to trample (on); **„nie ~ trawnika"** "keep off the grass"

dese|r (**-ru, -ry**; *loc sg* **-rze**) *m* (*Kulin*) dessert; **na ~ są lody** for dessert there is ice cream

des|ka (**-ki, -ki**; *dat & loc sg* **-ce**; *gen pl* **-ek**) *f* **1** (*gruba, do krojenia*) board **2** (*wąska, płaska*) plank **3** (*snowboardowa*) snowboard; **deski** *pl* (*pot: narty*) skis; **~ do prasowania** ironing board

deszcz (**-u, -e**) *m* **1** (*opady*) rain **2** (*duża ilość czegoś*) floods *pl*; **pada ulewny ~** it is pouring; **~ obelg** a torrent of abuse

deszczowy *adj* (*dzień, pogoda*) rainy

dezodoran|t (**-tu, -ty**; *loc sg* **-cie**) *m* (*higiena osobista*) deodorant; **~ w kulce** roll-on deodorant

diab|eł (**-ła**, **-ły** *lub* **-li**; *dat sg* **-łu**; *loc sg* **-le**) *m* (*szatan*) devil; **idź do diabła!** go to hell!
dialo|g (**-gu**, **-gi**; *inst sg* **-giem**) *m* (*konwersacja*) dialogue (*Brit*), dialog (*US*)
die|ta (**-ty**, **-ty**; *dat & loc sg* **-cie**) *f* (*styl odżywiania*) diet; **diety** *pl* (*pokrycie kosztów podróży służbowej*) expenses; **być na diecie** to be on a diet
dietetyczny *adj* **1** (*np. reżim*) dietary **2** (*potrawa*) diet **3** (*niskokaloryczny*) diet
dla *prep +gen* **1** (*przeznaczenie, cel*) for **2** (*względem*) to; **ta wiadomość jest ~ ciebie** this message is for you; **była to ~ niego wielka niespodzianka** it was a big surprise for him; **przyjazny ~ środowiska** environmentally friendly; **~ przyjemności** for pleasure
dlaczego *adv, conj* why; **~ to zrobiłeś?** why did you do that?
dlatego *conj* **1** (*więc*) so, therefore **2** (*z tej przyczyny*) that's why; **było jej zimno, ~ założyła sweter** she was cold, so she put on a jumper; **pojechał taksówką, ~ że nie chciał się spóźnić** he took a taxi because he didn't want to be late
dłu|g (**-gu**, **-gi**; *inst sg* **-giem**) *m* debt
dłu|gi *adj* (*film, lekcja, podróż*) long
dłu|go *adv* **1** (*trwać, rozmawiać*) long **2** (*iść, podróżować*) far; **jak ~ czekałeś?** how long did you wait?; **na jak ~ przyjechałeś do Anglii?** how long are you in Britain for?
długopi|s (**-su**, **-sy**; *loc sg* **-sie**) *m* ballpoint (pen)
długoś|ć (**-ci**, **-ci**; *gen pl, dat & loc sg* **-ci**) *f* (*odległość, czas trwania*) length; **~ geograficzna** longitude; **szlak spacerowy o długości sześciu kilometrów** a 6km route for walkers
dłużej *adv comp od* **długo**
dmuch|ać (**-am**, **-asz**; *pf* **-nąć**) *vi* (*na gorącą zupę*) to blow
dno (**dna**, **dna**; *loc sg* **dnie**; *gen pl* **den**) *nt* **1** (*butelki*) bottom **2** (*rzeki*) bed **3** (*przen: beznadziejnej jakości*) depths

SŁOWO KLUCZOWE

do *prep +gen* **1** (*w stronę*) to; **jadę do Polski** I'm going to Poland; **idę do teatru/pubu** I'm going to the theatre/the pub; **jadę do dziadka** I'm going to my granddad's (place); **chodźmy do domu** let's go home
2 (*do środka*) into; **do torby/kieszeni/portfela** into a bag/pocket/wallet; **wejść do biura** to walk into the office
3 (*do jakiegoś punktu, miejsca*) to; **odprowadź ją do samochodu** see her to the car; **podejdź do okna** come up to the window
4 (*dopóki*) till, until; **zostanę do soboty** I'll stay until Saturday; **zrobię to do poniedziałku** I'll do it by Monday; **(w)pół do czwartej** half past three; **do jutra!** see you tomorrow!; **do widzenia/zobaczenia!** see you!
5 (*o górnej granicy czegoś*) up to; **czas oczekiwania wynosi do 2 tygodni** the waiting time is up to 2 weeks
6 (*dla wyrażenia przeznaczenia*): **do czego to jest?** what is it for?; **płyn do mycia naczyń** washing-up liquid; **pasta do zębów** toothpaste; **coś do czytania** something to read

doba (**doby**, **doby**; *dat & loc sg* **dobie**; *gen pl* **dób**) *f* **1** (*24 godziny*) day (and night) **2** (*przen: okres, era*) age; **(przez) całą dobę** day and night
dobranoc *inv*: **~!** good night!
dob|ro (**-ra**, **-ra**; *loc sg* **-rze**; *gen pl* **dóbr**) *nt* (*wartość, pożytek*) good; **dobra** *pl* **1** (*o towarach*) goods *pl* **2** (*o majątku*) property *sg*
dobroczynnoś|ć (**-ci**) *f* (*niesienie pomocy*) charity
dobry *adj* **1** (*prawidłowy, moralny, smaczny, grzeczny*) good **2** (*życzliwy*) kind ▷ *m decl like adj* **1** (*w szkole: ocena*) ≈ B **2** (*w uniwersytecie*) ≈ 2:1; **on jest ~ z fizyki** he's good at physics; **~ wieczór!** good evening!; **dobra!** (*pot*) OK!
dobrze *adv* well; **~ się bawić** to have a good time; **~!** OK!; **~ znany** well-known

dobyt|ek (**-ku**; *inst sg* **-kiem**) *m* (*człowieka*) belongings *pl*
dochodze|nie (**-nia, -nia**; *gen pl* **-ń**) *nt* (*policyjny*) investigation
doch|ód (**-odu, -ody**; *loc sg* **-odzie**) *m* **1** (*pensja*) income **2** (*państwa z podatków*) revenue
dod|ać (**-am, -asz**; *imp* **-aj**) *vb pf od* **dodawać**
dodat|ek (**-ku, -ki**; *inst sg* **-kiem**) *m* **1** (*w gazecie*) supplement **2** (*do pensji*) bonus **3** (*Kulin*) additive; (*do drugiego dania*) side dish; **na ~** *lub* **w dodatku** as well
dodatkowy *adj* **1** (*informacja, praca, połączenie*) additional **2** (*opłata*) extra
doda|wać (**-ję, -jesz**; *pf* **dodać**) *vt* (*nadziei*) to add; **~ do znajomych** to friend (*on social media*)
doj|azd (**-azdu, -azdy**; *loc sg* **-eździe**) *m* **1** (*droga prowadząca do garażu itp.*) access **2** (*podróż do pracy*) commute
dojrza|ły *adj* **1** (*o osobie, alkoholu, decyzji*) mature **2** (*o zbożu, owocu*) ripe **3** (*o serze*) mature
dojrz|eć (**-eję, -ejesz**) *vb pf od* **dojrzewać**
dojrzew|ać (**-am, -asz**; *pf* **dojrzeć**) *vi* **1** (*o osobie, alkoholu, zamierzeniach, uczuciach*) to mature **2** (*do zbiorów*) to ripen **3** (*Kulin*) to mature
dojrzewani|e (**-a**) *nt* (*stawanie się dorosłym*) adolescence; **~ płciowe** puberty
dokąd *pron* where (to); **nie wiem, ~ poszedł** I don't know where he went; **nie miał ~ pojechać** he had nowhere to go
dokład|ka (**-ki, -ki**; *dat & loc sg* **-ce**; *gen pl* **-ek**) *f* (*pot: obiadu, deseru*) seconds *pl*
dokładnie *adv* (*precyzyjnie*) precisely
dokładny *adj* **1** accurate **2** (*o czasie*) exact **3** (*osoba*) meticulous
dokoła *adv* (*ze wszystkich stron*) (all) (a)round ▷ *prep +gen* (*wokół*) (a) round
dokon|ać (**-am, -asz**) *vb pf od* **dokonywać**
dokon|ywać (**-uję, -ujesz**; *pf* **-ać**) *vt +gen* **1** (*zrobić*) to accomplish **2** (*zbrodni*) to commit; **~ się** *vr* (*mieć miejsce*) to take place; **~** (**dokonać** *pf*) **cudów** to work wonders
dokto|r (**-ra, -rzy**; *loc sg* **-rze**) *m* (*lekarz*) doctor
doktora|t (**-tu, -ty**; *loc sg* **-cie**) *m* **1** (*stopień naukowy*) doctorate, PhD **2** (*dysertacja*) doctoral thesis
doktorski *adj*: **praca doktorska** doctoral thesis
dokumen|t (**-tu, -ty**; *loc sg* **-cie**) *m* (*urzędowy, komputerowy*) document; **dokumenty** *pl* (*dowód potwierdzający tożsamość*) means *sg* of identification
dola|r (**-ra, -ry**; *loc sg* **-rze**) *m* (*waluta*) dollar
doli|na (**-ny, -ny**; *dat & loc sg* **-nie**) *f* (*Geo*) valley
dolny *adj* **1** (*część ciała*) lower **2** (*szuflada, półka*) bottom **3** (*granica wieku*) minimum
dom (**-u, -y**) *m* **1** (*o budynku*) house **2** (*o mieszkaniu, rodzinie*) home **3** (*o gospodarstwie domowym*) household; **~ studencki** hall of residence (*Brit*), dormitory (*US*); **w ~u** at home; **iść** (**pójść** *pf*) **do ~u** to go home
domofo|n (**-nu, -ny**; *loc sg* **-nie**) *m* (*urządzenie przy drzwiach wejściowych*) intercom
domowy *adj* **1** (*dotyczący domu*) home **2** (*zrobiony w domu*) home-made **3** (*o zwierzętach*) domestic; **praca domowa** homework
domyśl|ać się (**-am, -asz**; *pf* **-ić**) *vr +gen* to guess
donicz|ka (**-ki, -ki**; *dat & loc sg* **-ce**; *gen pl* **-ek**) *f* (*do kwiatów*) flowerpot
dookoła *adv, prep* = **dokoła**
dopełniacz (**-a, -e**; *gen pl* **-y**) *m* (*przypadek gramatyczny*) genitive
dopełnie|nie (**-nia, -nia**; *gen pl* **-ń**) *nt* (*część zdania*) object; **~ dalsze/bliższe** indirect/direct object
dorosły *adj* (*osoba, zwierzę*) adult ▷ *m decl like adj* (*dorosła osoba*) adult; **dorośli** *pl* adults *pl*
dorsz (**-a, -e**; *gen pl* **-y**) *m* (*ryba*) cod
doskonale *adv* (*wspaniale*) perfectly; **~!** (*pot*) outstanding!
doskonal|ić (**-ę, -isz**; *pf* **u-**) *vt* (*umiejętności, technikę*) to improve; **~ się** (*pf* **u-**) *vr*: **~** (**u~** *pf*) **się** (**w czymś**)

(*śpiewie, sporcie, nauce*) to improve (in sth)

doskonały *adj* **1** (*perfekcyjny*) perfect **2** (*wspaniały*) splendid **3** (*zupełny*) absolute

dosłownie *adv* **1** (*w dosłownym znaczeniu*) literally **2** (*przetłumaczyć, zacytować*) word for word

dosłowny *adj* (*znaczenie, cytat*) literal

dosta|ć (**-nę, -niesz**; *imp* **-ń**) *vb pf od* **dostawać**

dostarcz|ać (**-am, -asz**; *pf* **-yć**) *vt* (*przynosić, przywozić*) to deliver; **~ komuś czegoś** to provide sb with sth; **~** (**dostarczyć** *pf*) **coś komuś** to deliver sth to sb

dosta|wa (**-wy, -wy**; *dat & loc sg* **-wie**) *f* **1** (*towaru, listu*) delivery **2** (*prądu, gazu*) supply **3** (*dostarczone towary*) supplies *pl*

dost|awać (**-aję, -ajesz**; *imp* **-awaj**; *pf* **-ać**) *vt* **1** (*list, nagrodę, awans*) to get **2** (*zawału*) to have ▷ *vi* (*być bitym*) to get beaten up; **~ się** *vr*: **~** (**dostać** *pf*) **się do niewoli** to be taken prisoner; **~** (**dostać** *pf*) **się na studia** to be accepted for university; **dostać** (*pf*) **się w czyjeś ręce** to fall into sb's hands

dostosow|ywać (**-uję, -ujesz**; *pf* **-ać**) *vt*: **~ coś do czegoś** to adjust sth to sth; **~ się** *vr*: **~ się do** *+gen* (*do potrzeb, sytuacji*) to adjust to; (*do reguł, zasad*) to conform to

dosyć, dość *adv* **1** (*dostatecznie dużo*) enough **2** (*całkiem*) fairly **3** (*raczej*) rather; **mam tego ~!** I've had enough!; **~ długi** long enough; **mieć ~ czegoś** to be fed up with sth

doświadczony *adj* (*alpinista*) experienced

dotąd *adv* **1** (*do danego miejsca: niedaleko*) this far **2** (*do dalszego miejsca*) that far **3** (*do tej pory, dotychczas*) so far

dotk|nąć (**-nę, -niesz**; *imp* **-nij**) *vb pf od* **dotykać**

dotyk|ać (**-am, -asz**; *pf* **dotknąć**) *vt +gen* **1** (*mieć punkt styczny*) to touch **2** (*palcem, ręką*) to feel **3** (*dosięgać: nogami pedałów*) to reach **4** (*kwestii*) to touch on **5** (*o pechu, dolegliwości*) to afflict

dowci|p (**-pu, -py**; *loc sg* **-pie**) *m* **1** (*śmieszna historia*) joke **2** (*bystrość umysłu*) wit

dow|odzić (**-odzę, -odzisz**; *imp* **-ódź**; *pf* **dowieść**) *vt +gen* **1** (*podawać dowody*) to establish **2** (*wykazywać np. prawdziwość czegoś*) to establish **3** (*stanowić dowód czegoś*) to prove ▷ *vi* (*argumentować*) to argue

dowolny *adj* **1** (*którykolwiek*) any **2** (*fakultatywny*) discretionary **3** (*tłumaczenie, styl sportowy*) free

dow|ód (**-odu, -ody**; *loc sg* **-odzie**) *m* **1** (*okoliczność lub rzecz potwierdzająca coś*) evidence **2** (*wdzięczności, szacunku, przyjaźni*) token **3** (*Mat*) proof **4** (*wpłaty, odbioru*) receipt; **~ osobisty** form of identification

DOWÓD OSOBISTY

Dowód osobisty is a mandatory identity card. It contains basic personal details, including the holder's permanent address. It is a plastic card the size of a business card.

dowódc|a (**-y, -y**) *m decl like f in sg* (*Wojsk*) commander

dozorc|a (**-y, -y**) *m decl like f in sg* **1** (*osoba utrzymująca porządek w budynku*) caretaker (Brit), janitor **2** (*osoba pilnująca kogoś lub czegoś*) guard

dół (**dołu, doły**; *loc sg* **dole**) *m* **1** (*zagłębienie w ziemi*) pit **2** (*dolna część*) bottom **3** (*w budynku, domu*) downstairs; **iść** (**zejść** *pf*) **na ~** to go downstairs; **na dole** at the bottom

drabi|na (**-ny, -ny**; *dat & loc sg* **-nie**) *f* **1** (*duża, ze szczeblami*) ladder **2** (*mała, ze stopniami*) stepladder

drama|t (**-tu, -ty**; *loc sg* **-cie**) *m* **1** (Lit) drama **2** (*nieszczęście*) tragedy

dra|pać (**-pię, -piesz**) *vt* (*pf* **po-**) (*paznokciami, narzędziami*) to scratch ▷ *vi* **1** (*o kurzu*) to be an irritant **2** (*o swetrze itp.*) to be itchy; **~ się** (*pf* **po-**) *vr* (*skrobać się*) to scratch (o.s.)

drażnić (**-nię, -nisz**; *imp* **-nij**) *vt* **1** (*o kurzu, dymie*) to irritate **2** (*wywoływać negatywne emocje*) to annoy; **~ się** *vr*: **~ się z kimś** to tease sb

dre|s (**-su, -sy**; *loc sg* **-sie**) *m* (*strój sportowy*) tracksuit
dreszcz (**-u, -e**; *gen pl* **-y**) *m* (*z zimna, ze strachu*) shiver; **mieć ~e** to be shivering
drewniany *adj* wooden; **instrumenty drewniane** (*Muz*) woodwind instruments
dre|wno (**-wna, -wna**; *loc sg* **-wnie**; *gen pl* **-wien**) *nt* **1** (*surowiec*) wood **2** (*polano*) piece of wood
dręcz|yć (**-ę, -ysz**) *vt* (*o wyrzutach sumienia, pytaniu*) to torment
drin|k (**-ka, -ki**; *inst sg* **-kiem**) *m* (*pot: napój alkoholowy*) drink
drobiaz|g (**-gu, -gi**; *inst sg* **-giem**) *m* **1** (*mały przedmiot*) knick-knack **2** (*nieistotna sprawa*) trifle
drobiazgowy *adj* (*analiza, osoba*) meticulous
drobny *adj* **1** (*o małych rozmiarach*) small **2** (*mało ważny*) petty **3** (*delikatny*) slight **4** (*piasek, sól*) fine
dr|oga (**-ogi, -ogi**; *dat & loc sg* **-odze**; *gen pl* **-óg**) *f* **1** (*ulica*) road **2** (*szlak komunikacyjny*) route **3** (*kierunek podróży*) way **4** (*podróż, wędrówka*) journey **5** (*długość trasy między dwoma punktami*) distance **6** (*metoda działania*) way; **drogą lądową/morską** by land/sea; **swoją drogą...** still,...; **po drodze** on the way
drogeri|a (**-i, -e**; *gen pl, dat & loc sg* **-i**) *f* (*sklep*) ≈ chemist's (*Brit*), ≈ drugstore (*US*)
dro|gi *adj* **1** (*o wysokiej cenie*) expensive **2** (*bliski uczuciowo*) dear
dro|go *adv* **1** (*sprzedawać*) at a high price **2** (*płacić za coś*) a lot
drogocenny *adj* valuable
drogowy *adj* (*prace, znaki*) road; **kodeks ~** ≈ Highway Code (*Brit*); **wypadek ~** traffic accident
drożdżów|ka (**-ki, -ki**; *dat & loc sg* **-ce**; *gen pl* **-ek**) *f* (*słodka bułka*) sweet bun
dr|ób (**-obiu**) *m* (*Kulin*) poultry
drugi *num decl like adj* **1** (*po pierwszym*) second **2** (*strona, koniec itp.*) the other; **z ~ej strony...** on the other hand...; **druga klasa** (*kolejowa*) second class; (*Szkol*) second year of primary school (*Brit*), second grade (*US*); **~ maja** the second of May; **po ~e,...** second(ly),...; **druga wojna światowa** the Second World War; **~e śniadanie** (*o posiłku*) midmorning snack; (*kanapki*) packed lunch (*Brit*), box *lub* bag lunch (*US*); **~ od góry** second from the top; **co ~ dzień** every other day; **jest (godzina) druga** it's two (o'clock)
dru|k (**-ku**; *inst sg* **-kiem**) *m* **1** (*proces*) printing **2** (*czcionka*) type **3** (*odbitka*) print **4** (*formularz*) form; **druki** *pl* (*materiały drukowane*) printed matter *sg*
drukar|ka (**-ki, -ki**; *dat & loc sg* **-ce**; *gen pl* **-ek**) *f* (*Tech: Komput*) printer
druk|ować (**-uję, -ujesz**; *pf* **wy-**) *vt* **1** (*dokument z komputera*) to print **2** (*gazety, książki*) to publish
drukowany *adj* (*tekst, informator*) printed; **pisać ~mi literami** to print
dru|t (**-tu, -ty**; *loc sg* **-cie**) *m* **1** (*pręt, przewód*) wire **2** (*do robienia swetrów*) knitting needle; **robić szalik na ~ach** to knit a scarf
druży|na (**-ny, -ny**; *dat & loc sg* **-nie**) *f* **1** (*sportowa*) team **2** (*w wojsku*) squad; **~ harcerska** scout troop
dr|wić (**-wię, -wisz**; *imp* **-wij**; *pf* **za-**) *vi*: **~ (z** *+gen*) (*śmiać się z kogoś*) to sneer (at)
drzem|ka (**-ki, -ki**; *dat & loc sg* **-ce**; *gen pl* **-ek**) *f* (*krótki sen*) nap
drze|wo (**-wa, -wa**; *loc sg* **-wie**) *nt* **1** (*Bot*) tree **2** (*materiał budowlany*) wood **3** (*na opał*) firewood
drzwi (**-**) *pl* (*wejściowe, do pokoju*) door
duch (**-a, -y**) *m* **1** (*nastrój, usposobienie, odwaga*) spirit **2** (*bezcielesna istota*) ghost; **w ~u** inwardly
du|ma (**-my**; *dat & loc sg* **-mie**) *f* (*poczucie zadowolenia, godności*) pride
dumny *adj*: **~ (z** *+gen*) (*zadowolony, z poczuciem godności*) proud (of)
du|pa (**-py, -py**; *dat & loc sg* **-pie**) *f* **1** (*pot!: pośladki*) arse (*Brit*), ass (*US*) **2** (*pot!: niezaradna osoba*) arsehole (*Brit*), asshole (*US*)
duszny *adj* (*bez powietrza*) oppressive
dużo *pron* (*osób, książek*) a lot ▷ *adv* (*coś robić*) a lot; **~** *+gen* a lot of
duży *adj* **1** (*dom, samochód, zysk*) big **2** (*niezwykły, poważny*) great **3** (*dorosła

osoba) grown-up **4** (*szansa*) good; **duże litery** capital letters; **~ palec** (*u ręki*) thumb; (*u nogi*) big toe

DVD *nt inv* DVD; **odtwarzacz ~** DVD player

dwa *m/nt num* two; **~ kwiaty/lwy/krzesła** two flowers/lions/chairs; **co ~ dni/miesiące/lata** every other day/month/year; **~ razy** twice

dwadzieścia *num decl like adj* twenty

dwaj *num zob.* **dwa**

dwanaście *num decl like adj* twelve

dwie *f num decl like adj* two; **~ dziewczyny/butelki/gazety** two girls/bottles/newspapers

dwieście *num decl like adj* two hundred

dwo|rzec (**-rca, -rce**) *m* (*miejsce przyjazdu i odjazdu środków transportu*) station; **~ autobusowy** bus station; **~ kolejowy** railway (*Brit*) *lub* railroad (*US*) station; **~ centralny** central station

dwóch *num zob.* **dwa**

dw|ór (**-oru, -ory**; *loc sg* **-orze**) *m* **1** (*przy zamku królewskim*) court **2** (*duży dom, majątek ziemski*) manor **3** (*teren na zewnątrz domu*) outside; **wyjść na ~** to go outside

dwudziest|ka (**-ki, -ki**; *dat & loc sg* **-ce**; *gen pl* **-ek**) *f* twenty

dwudziestoletni *adj* **1** (*plan, wojna*) twenty-year **2** (*chłopak, dziewczyna*) twenty-year-old

dwudziesty *num decl like adj* twentieth

dwujęzyczny *adj* (*słownik, osoba*) bilingual

dwunast|ka (**-ki, -ki**; *dat & loc sg* **-ce**; *gen pl* **-ek**) *f* twelve

dwunasty *num decl like adj* twelfth; **o dwunastej** (*godzinie*) at twelve (o'clock); **jest dwunasta** (*godzina*) it's twelve (o'clock)

dwuosobowy *adj* **1** (*dla dwóch osób*) double **2** (*składający się z dwóch osób*) two-person

dwupokojowy *adj* (*mieszkanie*) two-room

dwuznaczny *adj* **1** (*mający dwa możliwe wytłumaczenia*) ambiguous **2** (*z ukrytą aluzją*) suggestive

dy|cha (**-chy, -chy**; *dat & loc sg* **-sze**) *f* (*banknot: pot*) tenner

dykt|ować (**-uję, -ujesz**; *pf* **po-**) *vt* to dictate

dy|m (**-mu, -my**; *loc sg* **-mie**) *m* (*z papierosa*) smoke

dynamiczny *adj* (*żywiołowy, prężny*) dynamic

dynasti|a (**-i, -e**; *gen pl, dat & loc sg* **-i**) *f* (*ród*) dynasty

dyplo|m (**-mu, -my**; *loc sg* **-mie**) *m* (*dokument*) diploma

dyr. *abbr* (= *dyrektor*) Mgr (= *manager*)

dyrekcj|a (**-i, -e**; *gen pl* **-i**) *f* (*zarząd*) management

dyrekto|r (**-ra, -rzy** *lub* **-rowie**; *loc sg* **-rze**) *m* **1** (*zakładu pracy*) manager **2** (*Szkol*) head teacher (*Brit*), principal (*US*)

dyskiet|ka (**-ki, -ki**; *dat & loc sg* **-ce**; *gen pl* **-ek**) *f* (*Komput*) (floppy) disk

dyskot|eka (**-eki, -eki**; *dat & loc sg* **-ece**; *gen pl* **-ek**) *f* (*zabawa*) disco(theque)

dyskusj|a (**-i, -e**; *gen pl, dat & loc sg* **-i**) *f*: **~ o** *+loc* (*omówienie, rozmowa*) discussion about

dyskut|ować (**-uję, -ujesz**; *pf* **prze-**) *vt*: **~ nad** *lub* **o czymś** (*omawiać, rozmawiać*) to discuss sth ▷ *vi* (*prowadzić debatę*) to debate

dyskwalifik|ować (**-uję, -ujesz**; *pf* **z-**) *vt* (*zawodnika*) to disqualify

dyspon|ować (**-uję, -ujesz**; *imp* **-uj**; *pf* **za-**) *vt*: **~ czasem** to have time on one's hands; **~ gotówką** to have spare cash

dywa|n (**-nu, -ny**; *loc sg* **-nie**) *m* (*tkanina na podłodze*) carpet

dyżu|r (**-ru, -ry**; *loc sg* **-rze**) *m* (*lekarza*) surgery hours *pl*; **być na ~ze** (*strażak*) to be on call

dyżurny *adj* **1** (*pracownik pełniący dyżur*) on duty **2** (*często używany, np. argument*) tried-and-tested

dzban|ek (**-ka, -ki**; *inst sg* **-kiem**) *m* (*naczynie*) jug (*Brit*), pitcher (*US*); **~ do kawy** coffee pot; **~ do herbaty** teapot; **~ do wody** water jug

dziać się (**dzieje**) *vr* (*wydarzać się*) to happen; **co tam się dzieje?** what's going on there?; **co się z nim dzieje?** what's the matter with him?

dziad|ek (**-ka, -kowie**; *inst sg* **-kiem**) *m* **1** (*krewny*) grandfather **2** (*starszy*

mężczyzna) old man; **dziadkowie** *pl* grandparents *pl*; **~ do orzechów** nutcracker
dział|ać (**-am, -asz**) *vt* (*robić coś*) to bring about ▷ *vi* **1** (*w czyimś imieniu, w jakiejś sprawie*) to act **2** (*o lekach*) to have an effect **3** (*o prawie, regułach*) to operate **4** (*o urządzeniach*) to work; **~ cuda** to work wonders
działalnoś|ć (**-ci**) *f* (*działanie, zajęcie*) activity
działa|nie (**-nia, -nia**; *gen pl* **-ń**) *nt* **1** (*podjęte kroki*) action **2** (*urządzeń, maszyn itp.*) operation **3** (*leków itp.*) effect **4** (*zadanie matematyczne*) operation
dział|ka (**-ki, -ki**; *dat sg* **-ce**; *gen pl* **-ek**) *f* **1** (*parcela pod ogródek*) plot **2** (*ogródek warzywny*) allotment **3** (*dom*) holiday cottage (*in the country*) **4** (*pot: zakres obowiązków*) department **5** (*pot: porcja narkotyków*) fix **6** (*pot: udział w zysku*) cut
dzieci *n pl* = **dziecko**
dziecięcy *adj* **1** (*przeznaczony dla dzieci*) children's **2** (*śmiech*) child's **3** (*zachowujący się jak dziecko*) childish
dziecinny *adj* **1** (*przeznaczony dla dziecka*) child's **2** (*zachowujący się jak dziecko*) childish; **pokój ~** nursery; **wózek ~** pram (*Brit*), baby carriage (*US*)
dziecińst|wo (**-wa**; *loc sg* **-wie**) *nt* (*wczesny okres życia*) childhood
dzie|cko (**-cka, -ci**; *inst sg* **-ckiem**; *gen pl* **-ci**) *nt* child; **mieć ~** to have a baby
dziedzic (**-a, -e**) *m* heir
dziedziczny *adj* (*choroba, tytuł, posiadłość*) hereditary
dziedzicz|yć (**-ę, -ysz**; *pf* **odziedziczyć**) *vt* (*majątek, bogactwo*) to inherit
dzieka|n (**-na, -ni**; *loc sg* **-nie**) *m* (*Uniw*) dean
dziekana|t (**-tu, -ty**; *loc sg* **-cie**) *m* (*Uniw*) faculty office
dzieleni|e (**-a**) *nt* (*w matematyce*) division
dziel|ić (**-ę, -isz**; *pf* **po-**) *vt* **1** (*Mat*) to divide **2** (*pf* **roz-**) (*dawać coś innym*) to share out **3** (*stanowić granicę, podział*) to separate **4** (*wspólnie korzystać z mieszkania, kuchni*) to share; **~ się** *vr* to divide; **cztery dzieli się przez dwa** four is divisible by two; **~ (po~** *pf*) **się czymś z kimś** to share sth with sb
dzielnic|a (**-y, -e**) *f* **1** (*w mieście*) district, quarter **2** (*w kraju*) region
dzielny *adj* **1** (*odważny*) brave **2** (*umiejący sobie radzić*) resourceful
dziennie *adv* (*co dzień*) daily; **osiem godzin ~** eight hours a day
dziennikar|ka (**-ki, -ki**; *dat & loc sg* **-ce**; *gen pl* **-ek**) *f* (*radiowa, telewizyjna*) journalist
dziennikarst|wo (**-wa**; *loc sg* **-wie**) *nt* (*śledcze, sportowe, ekonomiczne*) journalism
dziennikarz (**-a, -e**; *gen pl* **-y**) *m* (*radiowy, telewizyjny*) journalist
dzienny *adj* **1** (*edukacja, telewizja*) daytime **2** (*o zwierzętach*) diurnal **3** (*zysk, wydanie gazety*) daily
dzień (**dnia, dni** *lub* **dnie**) *m* **1** (*nie noc*) day **2** (*cała doba*) day (including night) **3** (*wyznaczony termin*) date; **~ dobry!** (*rano*) good morning!; (*po południu*) good afternoon!
dziesiąt|ka (**-ki, -ki**; *dat & loc sg* **-ce**; *gen pl* **-ek**) *f* ten
dziesiąty *num decl like adj* tenth
dziesięć *num* ten
dziewczy|na (**-ny, -ny**; *dat & loc sg* **-nie**) *f* **1** (*o młodej kobiecie*) girl **2** (*o sympatii*) girlfriend
dziewczyn|ka (**-ki, -ki**; *dat & loc sg* **-ce**; *gen pl* **-ek**) *f* (*mała dziewczyna*) young girl
dziewiąt|ka (**-ki, -ki**; *dat & loc sg* **-ce**; *gen pl* **-ek**) *f* nine
dziewiąty *num decl like adj* ninth
dziewięć *num* nine
dziewięćdziesiąt *num* ninety
dziewięćdziesiąty *num decl like adj* ninetieth
dziewięćset *num* nine hundred
dziewiętnasty *num decl like adj* nineteenth
dziewiętnaście *num* nineteen
dzięk|ować (**-uję, -ujesz**; *pf* **po-**) *vi*: **dziękuję (bardzo)!** thank you (very much)!; **~ komuś (za coś)** to thank sb (for sth)
dziki *adj* **1** (*nieoswojony, pierwotny, niedostępny, niepohamowany*) wild **2** (*niecywilizowany*) savage

3 (*agresywny*) fierce **4** (*nieśmiały*) unsociable **5** (*nielegalny*) illegal
dzisiaj, dziś *adv* **1** (*w dniu bieżącym*) today **2** (*w bieżącym okresie*) nowadays; **którego ~ mamy?** what date is it today?; **~ rano/wieczorem** this morning/evening; **~ w nocy** tonight; **od ~** starting today
dzisiejszy *adj* **1** (*dotyczący bieżącego dnia*) today's **2** (*dotyczący bieżącego okresu*) present-day
dziś *adv* = **dzisiaj**; **od ~** from now on
dziwny *adj* (*dziwaczny*) strange; **nic dziwnego, że...** (it's) no wonder that...
dzwo|n (**-nu, -ny**; *loc sg* **-nie**) *m* (*kościelny*) bell; **dzwony** *pl* (*o spodniach*) flares
dzwon|ek (**-ka, -ki**; *inst sg* **-kiem**) *m* **1** (*mechanizm*) bell **2** (*do drzwi*) doorbell **3** (*dźwięk*) ring **4** (*roślina*) bluebell
dzwo|nić (**-nię, -nisz**; *imp* **-ń**; *pf* **za-**) *vi +inst* **1** (*dzwonkiem*) to ring **2** (*czymś metalowym*) to make a clattering noise with **3** (*czymś szklanym*) to clink **4** (*pot: zatelefonować*): **~** (**za~** *pf*) **do kogoś** to give sb a ring (*Brit*), to give sb a call (*US*)
dźwię|k (**-ku, -ki**; *inst sg* **-kiem**) *m* **1** (*brzmienie*) sound **2** (*w muzyce*) tone
dźwig|ać (**-am, -asz**) *vt* (*pf* **-nąć**) **1** (*podnieść*) to lift **2** (*nosić*) to carry
dże|m (**-mu, -my**; *loc sg* **-mie**) *m* (*Kulin*) jam
dżentelme|n (**-na, -ni**; *loc sg* **-nie**) *m* gentleman
dżin|s (**-su**; *loc sg* **-sie**) *m* (*tkanina*) denim; **dżinsy** *pl* **1** denims **2** (*spodnie*) jeans
dżinsowy *adj* denim

edukacj|a (**-i**) *f* (*dobra, wyższa, solidna*) education
efek|t (**-tu, -ty**; *loc sg* **-cie**) *m* **1** (*rezultat: doskonały, marny*) effect **2** (*wrażenie: dobre, doskonałe, świetne*) impression; **~ cieplarniany** greenhouse effect; **~y specjalne** special effects; **nasze wysiłki dały dobry ~** our efforts have been successful
efektowny *adj* **1** (*wygląd, makijaż, fryzura*) striking **2** (*aktorka*) glamorous
efektywny *adj* (*praca, pracownik, czas pracy*) effective
Egip|t (**-tu**; *loc sg* **-cie**) *m* Egypt
egoi|sta (**-sty, -ści**; *dat sg & loc sg* **-ście**) *m decl like f in sg* (*nieznośny, prawdziwy, okropny*) egotist
egoiz|m (**-mu**; *loc sg* **-mie**) *m* selfishness
egz. *abbr* (= *egzemplarz*) copy
egzami|n (**-nu, -ny**; *loc sg* **-nie**) *m* (*trudny, ciężki, ważny*) exam(ination); **~ poszedł mu jak z płatka** he sailed through the exam; **~ dojrzałości** school-leaving exam, ≈ A-levels *pl* (*Brit*); **~ na prawo jazdy** driving test; **zdawać** (*impf*) **~** to take an examination; **zdać** (*pf*) **~** to pass an examination; **nie zdać** (*pf*) **~u** to fail an examination
egzamin|ować (**-uję, -ujesz**; *pf* **prze-**) *vt*: **~ kogoś (z czegoś)** to examine sb (in sth)
egzemplarz (**-a, -e**; *gen pl* **-y**) *m* **1** (*książki, listu, gazety: rzadki*) copy

2 (*o zwierzęciu*) specimen; **niezły z niego ~!** (*pot: pej*) he's quite a character!
egzotyczny *adj* (*kraj, roślina, danie*) exotic
ekonomi|a (**-i**) *f* **1** (*Uniw*) economics **2** (*gospodarka: chwiejna, silna*) economy; **~ od paru lat znów nabiera tempa** for a year or two the economy has been growing more rapidly again
ekonomiczny *adj* **1** (*klimat*) economic **2** (*oszczędny*) economical
ekonomi|sta (**-sty, -ści**; *dat sg & loc sg* **-ście**) *m decl like f in sg* economist
ekra|n (**-nu, -ny**; *loc sg* **-nie**) *m* screen; **gwiazda ~u** film star
eksmit|ować (**-uję, -ujesz**; *pf* **wy-**) *vt* to evict; **nakaz eksmisji** eviction notice
ekspedien|t (**-ta, -ci**; *loc sg* **-cie**) *m* (*uprzejmy, uśmiechnięty, pomocny*) shop assistant
ekspedient|ka (**-ki, -ki**; *dat sg & loc sg* **-ce**; *gen pl* **-ek**) *f* shop assistant
eksper|t (**-ta, -ci**; *loc sg* **-cie**) *m* (*słynny, znany*) expert; **światowej sławy ~** world authority
eksperymen|t (**-tu, -ty**; *loc sg* **-cie**) *m* (*chemiczny, naukowy, genetyczny*) experiment
eksperyment|ować (**-uję, -ujesz**) *vi*: **~** (**na** *+inst*) to experiment (on)
ekspon|ować (**-uję, -ujesz**; *pf* **wy-**) *vt* **1** (*wystawiać sztukę*) to display **2** (*wysuwać na widzialne miejsce*) to emphasize; **ta fryzura ładnie eksponuje kształt jej twarzy** this hairstyle nicely complements the shape of her face; **wystawa eksponuje osiągnięcia uczniów naszej szkoły** the exhibition showcases what our school's pupils have achieved
ekspor|t (**-tu**; *loc sg* **-cie**) *m* export; **nadwyżka ~u** export surplus
ekspre|s (**-su, -sy**; *loc sg* **-sie**) *m* **1** (*pociąg pośpieszna*) express (train) **2** (*maszyna do kawy*) coffee machine; **kawa z ~u** filter coffee
elastyczny *adj* **1** (*sprężysty: materiał*) elastic **2** (*przen: człowiek, natura, czas pracy*) flexible
elegancj|a (**-i**) *f* elegance
elegancki *adj* (*człowiek, zachowanie, ubiór*) elegant
elektroniczny *adj* **1** electronic **2** (*zegarek*) quartz-crystal
elektroni|ka (**-ki**; *dat sg & loc sg* **-ce**) *f* (*Uniw*) electronics
elektrycznoś|ć (**-ci**) *f* electricity
elektryczny *adj* **1** (*prąd, światło*) electric **2** (*usterka, urządzenie*) electrical; **krzesło elektryczne** electric chair
elektry|k (**-ka, -cy**; *inst sg* **-kiem**) *m* (*znajomy, solidny*) electrician
elemen|t (**-tu, -ty**; *loc sg* **-cie**) *m* **1** (*część*) component **2** (*grupa ludzi: podejrzany, społeczny*) element (*pej*); **elementy** *pl* (*podstawy*) basics; **tej okolicy trzeba unikać; tu spotyka się lokalny ~** this is an area to be avoided; it is a hang-out for local criminals
elimin|ować (**-uję, -ujesz**; *pf* **wy-**) *vt* (*ekipę, drużynę, kandydata*) to eliminate; **jego zgłoszenie zostało wyeliminowane po egzaminie wstępnym** he didn't get beyond the entrance exam
e-mail (**-a, -e**; *loc sg* **-u**; *gen pl* **-i**) *m* email
emancypacj|a (**-i**) *f* (*wyzwolenie*) emancipation; **~ kobiet** the emancipation of women
emery|t (**-ta, -ci**; *loc sg* **-cie**) *m* (*rencista*) (old-age) pensioner
emeryt|ka (**-ki, -ki**; *dat sg & loc sg* **-ce**; *gen pl* **-ek**) *f* (*rencistka*) (old-age) pensioner
emerytu|ra (**-ry, -ry**; *dat sg & loc sg* **-rze**) *f* **1** (*zasłużona, wysoka, skromna*) (old-age) pension **2** (*okres*) retirement
emigracj|a (**-i, -e**; *gen pl* **-i**) *f* (*zarobkowa, polityczna, powojenna*) emigration; **fala emigracji** wave of emigration
emigracyjny *adj* emigration; **rząd ~** government in exile; **przepisy emigracyjne** emigration regulations; **urząd ~** emigration office
emigran|t (**-ta, -ci**; *loc sg* **-cie**) *m* **1** emigrant **2** (*Pol*) émigré

emigr|ować (**-uję, -ujesz**; *pf* **wy-**) *vi* to emigrate; **~ za chlebem** to go and work abroad
emocjonalny *adj* (*ból, przeżycie, chwila*) emotional
emotikon (**-a, -y**; *dat sg* **-owi**) *m* emoji
encyklopedi|a (**-i, -e**; *gen pl* **-i**) *f* (*wiedzy, roślin, dla dzieci*) encyclop(a)edia
energetyczny *adj* energy; **przemysł ~** energy industry; **sektor ~** the energy sector; **surowiec ~** source of energy
energi|a (**-i**) *f* energy; **~ słoneczna/atomowa** solar/atomic power
entuzjastyczny *adj* (*odbiór, ocena, recenzja*) enthusiastic
e-papieros (**-a, -y**; *dat sg* **-owi**) *m* e-cigarette
epidemi|a (**-i, -e**; *gen pl* **-i**) *f* epidemic
epilepsj|a (**-i**) *f* (*padaczka*) epilepsy; **cierpieć na epilepsję** to suffer from epilepsy
epo|ka (**-ki, -ki**; *dat sg & loc sg* **-ce**) *f* **1** epoch **2** (*kamienia*) age
era (**ery, ery**; *dat sg & loc sg* **erze**) *f* era; **przed naszą erą** BC; **naszej ery** AD
erotyczny *adj* (*taniec, film*) erotic
esej (**-u, -e**) *m* (*filozoficzny, literacki*) essay
Estoni|a (**-i**) *f* Estonia
eta|p (**-pu, -py**; *loc sg* **-pie**) *m* (*faza: ważny, decydujący*) stage
eta|t (**-tu, -ty**; *loc sg* **-cie**) *m* (*stanowisko*) job; **wolny ~** vacancy; **na pół ~u** part-time; **na pełen ~** full-time
ety|ka (**-ki**; *dat sg & loc sg* **-ce**) *f* **1** (*pracy, postępowania*) ethics *pl* **2** (*filozofia moralności*) ethics *sg*
euro *nt inv* euro
Euro|pa (**-py**; *dat sg* **-pie**) *f* Europe
europejski *adj* European
ewentualnie *adv, conj* **1** (*albo*) alternatively **2** (*w razie czego*) perhaps

fabry|ka (**-ki, -ki**; *dat & loc sg* **-ce**) *f* (*zakład pracy*) factory
face|t (**-ta, -ci**; *loc sg* **-cie**) *m* (*mężczyzna: pot*) bloke (*Brit*), guy
fachowy *adj* **1** (*specjalistyczny*) specialist **2** (*rada*) professional **3** (*z kwalifikacjami*) skilled
fajerwerk (**-u, -i**; *gen pl* **-ów**) *m* (*sztuczny ogień*) firework; **pokaz ~ów** firework display
fajnie *adv* (*pot: świetnie, super*) great
fajny *adj* (*pot: świetny, super*) great
fak|t (**-tu, -ty**; *loc sg* **-cie**) *m* (*niezbity, suchy*) fact; **literatura ~u** non-fiction; **suche ~y** plain facts
faktu|ra (**-ry, -ry**; *dat & loc sg* **-rze**) *f* **1** (*rachunek*) invoice **2** (*materiału*) texture
faktycznie *adv* **1** actually **2** (*rzeczywiście, istotnie*) in fact
fa|la (**-li, -le**; *dat & loc sg* **-li**) *f* (*morska, włosów*) wave
falsyfika|t (**-tu, -ty**; *loc sg* **-cie**) *m* forgery
fałsz (**-u, -e**) *m* (*kłamstwo*) falsehood
fałszerst|wo (**-wa, -wa**; *loc sg* **-wie**) *nt* forgery
fałsz|ować (**-uję, -ujesz**; *pf* **s-**) *vt* **1** to forge **2** (*przen: przedstawiać nieprawdę*) to falsify ▷ *vi* (*Muz*) to be out of tune
fałszywie *adv* **1** (*kłamliwie*) falsely **2** (*nieszczerze*) insincerely **3** (*Muz*) out of tune

fałszywy *adj* **1** (*banknot, dzieło sztuki*) counterfeit **2** (*dokument*) forged **3** (*dowód, wniosek*) false **4** (*uśmiech, skromność*) insincere **5** (*Muz*) out of tune

fa|n (**-na, -ni**; *loc sg* **-nie**) *m* (*wielbiciel, sympatyk: pot*) fan

fantastyczny *adj* (*wspaniały, baśniowy*) fantastic; **film ~** a fantasy film

fantazj|ować (**-uję, -ujesz**) *vi* to fantasize

far|ba (**-by, -by**; *dat & loc sg* **-bie**) *f* **1** (*malarska*) paint **2** (*do drukarki*) ink **3** (*do farbowania*) dye

farb|ować (**-uję, -ujesz**) *vt* (*pf* **u-** *lub* **po-**) (*ubranie, włosy*) to dye ▷ *vi* (*o tkaninie: puścić kolor*) to run

fartuch (**-a, -y**) *m* **1** (*kucharza*) apron **2** (*lekarza*) gown

fascynujący *adj* (*urzekający*) fascinating

faso|la (**-li, -le**; *gen pl & loc sg* **-li**) *f* (*Kulin*) bean(s *pl*)

faszyz|m (**-mu**; *loc sg* **-mie**) *m* (*Pol*) fascism

faul|ować (**-uję, -ujesz**; *pf* **s-**) *vt* (*w piłkę nożną*) to foul

faworki *pl crispy ribbons of pastry, deep-fried and sprinkled with powdered sugar, traditionally eaten on the last Thursday before Lent*

feri|e (**-i**) *pl* **1** (*zimowe*) break **2** (*letnie*) holiday(s *pl*) (*Brit*), vacation *sg* (*US*)

festiwa|l (**-lu, -le**; *gen pl* **-li** *lub* **-lów**) *m* (*filmowy, muzyczny*) festival

festy|n (**-nu, -ny**; *loc sg* **-nie**) *m* (*odpustowy*) gala

figu|ra (**-ry, -ry**; *dat & loc sg* **-rze**) *f* **1** (*sylwetka*) figure **2** (*w szachach*) piece **3** (*w kartach*) face card

fikcj|a (**-i, -e**; *gen pl & loc sg* **-i**) *f* (*Lit: coś wymyślonego*) fiction

fikcyjny *adj* **1** (*Lit*) fictional **2** (*adres, małżeństwo*) fictitious

Filipin|y (**-**) *pl* the Philippines

filiżan|ka (**-ki, -ki**; *dat & loc sg* **-ce**; *gen pl* **-ek**) *f* **1** (*o naczyniu*) cup **2** (*o zawartości*) cupful; **~ herbaty/kawy** a cup of tea/coffee

fil|m (**-mu, -my**; *loc sg* **-mie**) *m* **1** (*utwór*) film (*Brit*), movie (*US*) **2 ~ fabularny** (feature) film; **~ dokumentalny** documentary (film); **kręcić** (**nakręcić** *pf*) **~** to make a film

film|ować (**-uję, -ujesz**; *pf* **s-**) *vt* **1** (*robić zdjęcia*) to film **2** (*ekranizować*) to make into a film

filmowy *adj* (*reżyser, festiwal, magazyn*) film (*Brit*), movie (*US*); **przemysł ~** film (*Brit*) *lub* movie (*US*) industry

filologi|a (**-i, -e**; *gen pl & loc sg* **-i**) *f* (*nauka*) philology; **student filologii francuskiej** a student of French (studies)

filozo|f (**-fa, -fowie**; *loc sg* **-fie**) *m* (*uczony*) philosopher

filozofi|a (**-i, -e**; *gen pl & loc sg* **-i**) *f* (*nauka, zasada, idea*) philosophy

filt|r (**-ru** *lub* **-ra, -ry**; *loc sg* **-rze**) *m* (*urządzenie*) filter; **~ do wody** water filter; **krem z ~em przeciwsłonecznym** sunscreen

fina|ł (**-łu, -ły**; *loc sg* **-le**) *m* **1** (*filmu itp.*) ending **2** (*zawodów sportowych*) final **3** (*Muz*) finale

finałowy *adj* **1** (*zawodów sportowych*) final **2** (*Muz*): **scena finałowa** finale

finansowy *adj* (*rok, rozliczenie*) financial

finisz|ować (**-uję, -ujesz**) *vi* (*peleton, bieg*) to put on a spurt (*in a race*)

Finlandi|a (**-i**) *f* Finland

fioletowy *adj* (*kolor*) purple

firan|ka (**-ki, -ki**; *dat & loc sg* **-ce**; *gen pl* **-ek**) *f* (*przejrzysta zasłona na okno*) net curtain

fir|ma (**-my, -my**; *dat & loc sg* **-mie**) *f* **1** (*mała*) firm, business **2** (*duża*) company

fizy|k (**-ka, -cy**; *inst sg* **-kiem**) *m* **1** (*naukowiec*) physicist **2** (*Szkol*) physics teacher

fizy|ka (**-ki**; *dat & loc sg* **-ce**) *f* (*nauka*) physics

fla|ga (**-gi, -gi**; *dat & loc sg* **-dze**) *f* (*państwowa*) flag

fle|t (**-tu, -ty**; *loc sg* **-cie**) *m* (*Muz*) flute; **~ prosty** recorder

flirt|ować (**-uję, -ujesz**) *vi*: **~** (**z** *+inst*) to flirt (with)

fontan|na (**-ny, -ny**; *dat & loc sg* **-nie**) *f* (*budowla; tryskająca woda*) fountain

for|ma (**-my, -my**; *dat & loc sg* **-mie**) *f* **1** (*kształt*) form **2** (*do wypieków*) baking tin **3** (*matryca, odlew*) mould (*Brit*), mold (*US*); **być w złej/ dobrej formie** to be in bad/good shape

formalnoś|ć (**-ci, -ci**; *gen pl & dat, loc sg* **-ci**) *f* (*urzędowa, prawna*) formality

formalny *adj* (*język, list*) formal

formularz (**-a, -e**; *gen pl* **-y**) *m* form; **wypełniać** (**wypełnić** *pf*) **~** to fill in (*Brit*) *lub* out (*US*) a form

for|sa (**-sy**; *dat & loc sg* **-sie**) *f* (*pieniądze: pot*) dough, dosh

fortepia|n (**-nu, -ny**; *loc sg* **-nie**) *m* (*Muz*) (grand) piano

for|um (**-um, -a**) *m* (online) forum

fotel (**-a** *lub* **-u, -e**; *gen pl* **-i**) *m* (*mebel*) armchair; **~ na biegunach** rocking chair

fot|ka (**-ki, -ki**; *dat sg* **-ce**; *gen pl* **-ek**) *f* (*fotografia*) snap

fotogra|f (**-fa, -fowie**; *loc sg* **-fie**) *m* (*osoba*) photographer

fotografi|a (**-i**) *f* **1** (*sztuka, technika*) photography **2** (*nom pl* **-e**; *gen pl, dat & loc sg* **-i**) (*zdjęcie*) photo(graph)

fotograf|ować (**-uję, -ujesz**; *pf* **s-**) *vt* (*robić zdjęcia*) to photograph

fragmen|t (**-tu, -ty**; *loc sg* **-cie**) *m* (*kawałek*) fragment

Francj|a (**-i**) *f* France

francuski *adj* French

fruw|ać (**-am, -asz**) *vi* (*latać*) to fly

fryt|ki (**-ek**) *pl* (*Kulin*) chips *pl* (*Brit*), (French) fries *pl* (*US*)

fryzje|r (**-ra, -rzy**; *loc sg* **-rze**) *m* **1** (*damski*) hairdresser **2** (*dla mężczyzn*) barber

fryzjer|ka (**-ki, -ki**; *dat & loc sg* **-ce**; *gen pl* **-ek**) *f* (*osoba*) hairdresser

fryzu|ra (**-ry, -ry**; *dat & loc sg* **-rze**) *f* (*uczesanie*) haircut, hairstyle

fund|ować (**-uję, -ujesz**) *vt* **1** (*pf* **za-**) (*stawiać*): **~** (**za~** *pf*) **komuś coś** to treat sb to sth **2** (*pf* **u-**) to found, to establish

funkcj|a (**-i, -e**; *gen pl, dat & loc sg* **-i**) *f* function

fun|t (**-ta, -ty**; *loc sg* **-cie**) *m* (*pieniądz, jednostka wagi*) pound; **~ szterling** (pound) sterling

futbol (**-u**) *m* (*piłka nożna*) football (*Brit*), soccer (*US*); **~ amerykański** American football (*Brit*), football (*US*)

fut|ro (**-ra, -ra**; *loc sg* **-rze**; *gen pl* **-er**) *nt* **1** (*na zwierzęciu*) fur **2** (*ubranie*) fur coat

g

gabine|t (**-tu, -ty**; *loc sg* **-cie**) *m* **1** (*w mieszkaniu*) study **2** (*w miejscu pracy*) office **3** (*w przychodni*) surgery (*Brit*), office (*US*) **4** (*Rada Ministrów*) Cabinet
ga|d (**-da, -dy**; *loc sg* **-dzie**) *m* (*w zoologii*) reptile
gad|ać (**-am, -asz**) *vi* (*pot: mówić*) to chatter; **~ co ślina na język przyniesie** to talk a load of rubbish
gadu|ła (**-ły, -ły**; *dat sg & loc sg* **-le**) *m/f decl like f* (*pot: osoba dużo mówiąca*) chatterbox
ga|j (**-ju, -je**; *gen pl* **-i**) *m* grove
gajo|wy (**-wego, -wi**) *m decl like adj* (*leśniczy*) forester
galaret|ka (**-ki, -ki**; *dat sg & loc sg* **-ce**; *gen pl* **-ek**) *f* jelly
galeri|a (**-i, -e**; *gen pl* **-i**) *f* gallery; **~ sztuki współczesnej** gallery of modern art
gał|ąź (**-ęzi, -ęzie**; *gen pl* **-ęzi**; *inst pl* **-ęziami** *lub* **-ęźmi**) *f* branch; **~ przemysłu** branch of industry
gangste|r (**-ra, -rzy**; *loc sg* **-rze**) *m* gangster
garbaty *adj* **1** (*o człowieku*) hunchbacked **2** (*o nosie*) hooked
gar|bić się (**-bię, -bisz**; *pf* **z-**) *vr* (*pochylać się*) to stoop
gar|dzić (**-dzę, -dzisz**; *impf* **-dź**; *pf* **wz-**) *vt*: **~** *+inst* to despise
garn|ek (**-ka, -ki**; *inst sg* **-kiem**) *m* (*Kulin*) pot
garnitu|r (**-ru, -ry**; *loc sg* **-rze**) *m* (*marynarka i spodnie*) suit
garson|ka (**-ki, -ki**; *dat sg & loc sg* **-ce**; *gen pl* **-ek**) *f* (*garnitur dla kobiet*) suit
ga|sić (**-szę, -sisz**; *imp* **-ś**; *pf* **z-**) *vt* **1** (*pożar*) to put out **2** (*niedopałek*) to put out **3** (*urządzenie elektryczne*) to switch off **4** (*nadzieję*) to kill **5** (*pf* **u-**) (*zaspokajać pragnienie*) to quench
ga|snąć (**-snę, -śniesz**; *impf* **-śnij**; *pf* **z-**) *vi* **1** (*o płomieniu*) to go out **2** (*o motorze*) to stall **3** (*o uczuciach*) to fade; **jej gwiazda zgasła już dawno** her star faded years ago
gastronomi|a (**-i**) *f* **1** (*sztuka gotowania*) gastronomy **2** (*prowadzenie restauracji*) catering industry
gaśnic|a (**-y, -e**) *f* fire extinguisher
gatun|ek (**-ku, -ki**; *inst sg* **-kiem**) *m* **1** (*odmiana*) kind **2** (*w biologii*) species **3** (*wartość*) quality; **być w pierwszym gatunku** to be top quality; **romans to ~ literacki** the love story is a literary genre
ga|z (**-zu, -zy**; *loc sg* **-zie**) *m* **1** (*w naukach przyrodniczych*) gas **2** (*w motoryzacji*) accelerator (*Brit*), gas pedal (*US*) **3** (*pot: instalacja gazowa*) gas fittings *pl*; **gazy** *n pl* (*wiatry*) wind *sg*; **on ciągle jest na ~ie** (*pot: podpity*) he's always drunk
gaze|ta (**-ty, -ty**; *dat sg & loc sg* **-cie**) *f* (*codzienna, brukowa*) newspaper
gazomierz (**-a, -e**; *gen pl* **-y**) *m* gas meter
gazowy *adj* **1** (*butla, licznik*) gas **2** (*rodzaj opatrunku*) gauze
gąb|ka (**-ki, -ki**; *dat sg & loc sg* **-ce**; *gen pl* **-ek**) *f* sponge; **on ma umysł chłonny jak ~** he has a brain like a sponge
gąsienic|a (**-y, -e**) *f* **1** caterpillar **2** (*w traktorze*) caterpillar tread

 **SŁOWO KLUCZOWE**

gdy *conj* **1** (*kiedy*) when, as; **ściemniało się, gdy nagle zatrzymał się i krzyknął do nas** it was getting dark when he suddenly stopped and shouted to us; **podczas gdy** ((*wtedy*) *kiedy*) while **2** (*natomiast*) whereas; **gdy tylko**

zrozumiał, odszedł he left as soon as he understood
3 (*jeżeli*) when; **gdy będziesz chciał wyjść, zamknij drzwi** when you want to leave, close the door

gdyby *conj* if; **~ś to zrozumiał, zdałbyś egzamin** if you'd understood that, you'd have passed the exam

SŁOWO KLUCZOWE

gdzie *pron* **1** (*w pytaniach*) where; **gdzie on teraz jest?** where is he now?
2 (*w zdaniach podrzędnych*) where; **nie wiem, gdzie ona mieszka** I don't know where she lives
3 (*w zdaniach względnych*) where; **wszedł do pokoju, gdzie było ciemno** he went into the room where it was dark
4: **nie miał gdzie usiąć** he had nowhere to sit; **byle gdzie** anywhere

gdziekolwiek *pron* anywhere
gdzieniegdzie *adv* here and there
gdzieś *adv* somewhere
gej (**-a, -e**) *m* (*osoba homoseksualna*) gay
gejowski *adj* (*homoseksualny*) gay
generacj|a (**-i, -e**; *gen pl* **-i**) *f* (*młodsza, starsza*) generation
generalny *adj* **1** (*porządki, przegląd*) general **2**: **Sekretarz G~** Secretary General **3** (*w teatrze*): **próba generalna** dress rehearsal
genera|ł (**-ła, -łowie**; *loc sg* **-le**) *m* (*Wojsko*) general
genialny *adj* (*bardzo zdolny*) brilliant
genitali|a (**-ów**) *pl* genitals
gen|za (**-zy**; *dat sg & loc sg* **-zie**) *f* (*pochodzenie*) origin
geografi|a (**-i**) *f* (*fizyczna, historyczna*) geography
geograficzny *adj* (*atlas, odkrycie*) geographic(al)
geologi|a (**-i**) *f* geology
geometri|a (**-i**) *f* geometry
germanisty|ka (**-ki**; *dat sg & loc sg* **-ce**) *f* (*nauka o kulturze niemieckiej*) German studies
ge|st (**-stu, -sty**; *loc sg* **-ście**) *m* (*pusty, teatralny*) gesture
gestykul|ować (**-uję, -ujesz**) *vi* to gesticulate
get|to (**-ta, -ta**; *loc sg* **-cie**) *nt* ghetto
gę|ś (**-si, -si**) *f* goose; **a niech cię ~ kopnie** (*przen*) stuff you then
gieł|da (**-dy, -dy**; *dat sg & loc sg* **-dzie**) *f* (*papierów wartościowych, pracy*) exchange
gigantyczny *adj* (*ogromny*) gigantic
gimnasty|ka (**-ki**; *dat sg & loc sg* **-ce**) *f* (*poranna, artystyczna*) gymnastics
gimnastyk|ować (**-uję, -ujesz**) *vt* to exercise; **~ się** *vr* **1** to exercise **2** (*starać się*) to exert o.s.; **gimnastykuje się, aby mu starczyło pieniędzy** he struggles to make ends meet

GIMNAZJUM

Gimnazjum is the name for a compulsory three-year secondary school, for students aged 13 to 16.

ginekolo|g (**-ga, -dzy** *lub* **-gowie**; *inst sg* **-giem**) *m* gynaecologist (*Brit*), gynecologist (*US*)
gip|s (**-su**; *loc sg* **-sie**) *m* (*murarski*) plaster; **mieć rękę w ~ie** to have one's arm in plaster
gita|ra (**-ry, -ry**; *dat sg & loc sg* **-rze**) *f* (*elektryczna, klasyczna*) guitar
gitarzy|sta (**-sty, -ści**; *dat sg & loc sg* **-ście**) *m decl like f in sg* guitarist
gitarzyst|ka (**-ki, -ki**; *dat sg & loc sg* **-ce**) *f* guitarist
gli|na (**-ny, -ny**; *dat sg & loc sg* **-nie**) *f* (*skała*) clay ▷ *m decl like adj* (*pot: policjant*) cop; **z innej gliny** (*przen*) from a different mould (*Brit*) *lub* mold (*US*)
gliniarz (**-a, -e**; *gen pl* **-y**) *m* (*pot: policjant*) cop
gluko|za (**-zy**; *dat sg & loc sg* **-zie**) *f* glucose
gładki *adj* **1** (*cera, materiał*) smooth **2** (*trasa*) smooth **3** (*sierść*) sleek **4** (*bez wzoru*) plain
gładko *adv* (*równo*) smoothly; **~ ogolony** clean-shaven; **~ mu poszedł egzamin** his exam went smoothly

gładz|ić (**-ę, -isz**; *pf* **u-**) *vt* to stroke
głębia *f* depth
głęboki *adj* **1** deep **2** (*pochylenie się*) low **3** (*dekolt*) low-cut **4** (*doniosły*) profound **5** (*uczucia*) strong; **zapadł w ~ sen** he fell into a deep sleep
głęboko *adv* **1** (*zanurzyć się*) deep **2** (*zadać ranę*) deeply
głodny *adj* hungry; **opowiadać głodne kawałki** to talk nonsense
gło|s (**-su, -sy**; *loc sg* **-sie**) *m* **1** voice **2** (*prawo wypowiedzi*) say **3** (*podczas wyborów*) vote; **podnosić** (**podnieść** *pf*) **~ na kogoś** to raise one's voice to sb; **mówić na ~** to speak out loud; **krzyczeć** (**krzyknąć** *pf*) **na cały ~** to shout at the top of one's voice; **oddawać** (**oddać** *pf*) **~ na partię** to vote for the party
głos|ka (**-ki, -ki**; *dat sg & loc sg* **-ce**; *gen pl* **-ek**) *f* (*w językoznawstwie*) sound
głos|ować (**-uję, -ujesz**; *pf* **za-**) *vi* (*na partię, za zmianami*) to vote
głosowa|nie (**-nia, -nia**; *gen pl* **-ń**) *nt* (*tajne, jawne*) vote
głośno *adv* loudly; **myśleć ~** to think out loud
głośny *adj* **1** (*donośny*) loud **2** (*hałas*) noisy **3** (*znany*) famous
gł|owa (**-owy, -owy**; *dat sg & loc sg* **-owie**; *gen pl* **-ów**) *f* **1** head **2** (*pot: mózg*) brain; **dochód na głowę** income per capita; **mieć dach nad głową** to have a roof over one's head; **od stóp do głów** from top to toe; **mieć głowę nie od parady** to have one's head screwed on; **tracić** (**stracić** *pf*) **głowę** to lose one's head; **przyszło mi dziś do głowy, że...** it occurred to me today that...
głównie *adv* mainly
główny *adj* **1** (*problem, ulica*) main **2** (*księgowy*) head **3** (*aktor, aktorka*) lead; **główna wygrana** star prize; **Kraków G~** Cracow Central
głuchy *adj* **1** (*niesłyszący*) deaf **2** (*bez dźwięku*) hollow
głupi *adj* (*pot*) **1** (*ograniczony*) foolish **2** (*nieistotny*) silly **3** (*niezdarny*) awkward
głupo|ta (**-ty**; *dat sg & loc sg* **-cie**) *f* (*brak rozumu*) foolishness
głupst|wo (**-wa, -wa**; *loc sg* **-wie**) *nt* **1** foolish thing **2** (*brednia*) nonsense **3** (*drobnostka*) trifle
gmach (**-u, -y**) *m* (*ogromny budynek*) edifice
gmi|na (**-ny, -ny**; *dat sg & loc sg* **-nie**) *f* commune; **izba Gmin** House of Commons; **urząd gminny** *local government office*
gniazd|ko (**-ka, -ka**; *inst sg* **-kiem**; *gen pl* **-ek**) *nt* (*Elektr*) socket (*Brit*), outlet (*US*)
gni|azdo (**-azda, -azda**; *loc sg* **-eździe**) *nt* nest; **~ rodzinne** the family nest
gnić (**gniję, gnijesz**; *impf* **gnij**; *pf* **z-**) *vi* to rot; **~ w łóżku** (*pot: przen*) to lie in one's pit
gnie|w (**-wu**; *loc sg* **-wie**) *m* anger; **wpadać** (**wpaść** *pf*) **w ~** to fly into a rage; **powściągać** (**powściągnąć** *pf*) **~** to keep one's temper
gniew|ać (**-am, -asz**; *pf* **roz-**) *vt* to anger; **~ się** *vr* to be angry; **~ się na** to be angry at; **od dawna gniewa się z ciocią** he has been angry with his aunt for a long time
godz. *abbr* (*= godzina*) hr.
godzi|na (**-ny, -ny**; *dat sg & loc sg* **-nie**) *f* hour; **jest ~ ósma** it's eight o'clock; **półtorej godziny** an hour and a half; **czekał (całymi) ~mi** he waited for hours (on end); **która (jest) ~?** what time is it?
go|ić (**-ję, -isz**) *vi* to heal; **rana szybko się goi** the wound is healing quickly
go|l (**-la, -le**; *gen pl* **-li**) *m* goal; **Adam strzelił ~a** Adam scored a goal
gol|f (*loc sg* **-fie**) *m* **1** (*gen sg* **-fa**) (*gra*) golf **2** (*gen sg* **-fu**; *nom pl* **-fy**) (*sweter z przylegającym wysokim kołnierzem*) turtle-necked sweater
golić (**golę, golisz**; *impf* **gol**; *pf* **o-**) *vt* to shave; **~ się** *vr* to shave
goł|ąb (**-ębia, -ębie**; *gen pl* **-ębi**) *m* (*pocztowy, pokoju*) pigeon
goły *adj* **1** (*bez ubrania*) naked **2** (*bez zawartości*) bare **3** (*pot: bez grosza*) broke; **widzieć ~m okiem** to see with the naked eye; **spać pod ~m niebem** to sleep in the open air

gor|ąco (**-ąca**) *nt* (*skwar*) heat ▷ *adv* **1** (*ciepło*) hot **2** (*przen: przywitać, pożegnać*) warmly; **jest mi ~** I'm hot; **danie na ~** hot meal

gor|ący *adj* **1** (*klimat, kraj*) hot **2** (*list*) urgent **3** (*zwolennik, fan*) fervent; **~ czas/okres** hectic time/period; **łapać** (**złapać** *pf*) **kogoś na ~m uczynku** to catch sb red-handed

gorącz|ka (**-ki, -ki**; *dat sg & loc sg* **-ce**) *f* (*wysoka temperatura*) fever

gorszy *adj comp od* **zły** worse

gorzej *adv comp od* **źle** worse

gorzki *adj* **1** (*smak*) bitter **2** (*napój*) unsweetened

gospodarczy *adj* (*rozwój, polityka*) economic

gospodar|ka (**-ki, -ki**; *dat sg & loc sg* **-ce**; *gen pl* **-ek**) *f* (*rynkowa, komunalna*) economy

gospodarz (**-a, -e**; *gen pl* **-y**) *m* **1** (*na wsi*) farmer **2** (*w domu*) host **3** (*właściciel domu*) landlord

gospody|ni (**-ni, -nie**; *gen pl* **-ń**) *f* **1** (*w domu*) hostess **2** (*właścicielka mieszkania*) landlady **3** (*na wsi*) farmer's wife

go|ścić (**-szczę, -ścisz**; *impf* **-ść**) *vt* (*pf* **u-**) **1** (*częstować*) to entertain **2** (*w hotelu*) to accommodate ▷ *vi*: **~ (u kogoś)** to stay (at sb's place); **ciocia gości u nas od czwartku** auntie has been staying with us since Thursday

gościnnoś|ć (**-ci**) *f* (*serdeczność wobec gości*) hospitality

gościnny *adj* **1** (*o człowieku*) hospitable **2** (*pokój*) guest

goś|ć (**-cia, -cie**; *gen pl* **-ci**; *inst pl* **-ćmi**) *m* **1** (*przyjezdny*) guest **2** (*wczasowicz*) guest **3** (*pot: mężczyzna*) guy, bloke (*Brit*)

got|ować (**-uję, -ujesz**) *vt* **1** (*pf* **u-**) (*obiad*) to cook **2** (*pf* **u-**) (*warzywa*) to boil **3** (*pf* **za-**) (*płyn*) to boil; **~ się** *vr* **1** (*pf* **u-**) (*o obiedzie*) to cook **2** (*pf* **u-**) (*o warzywach*) to boil **3** (*pf* **za-**) (*o płynie*) to boil

gotowany *adj* boiled

gotowy *adj* **1** (*ukończony*) finished **2** (*obiad*) ready **3** (*zrobiony fabrycznie*) ready-made **4** (*ubranie seryjne w sklepie*) ready-to-wear

gotów|ka (**-ki**; *dat sg & loc sg* **-ce**) *f* cash; **kupować** (**kupić** *pf*) **coś za gotówkę** to buy sth for cash; **płacić** (**zapłacić** *pf*) **gotówką** to pay in cash

gó|ra (**-ry, -ry**; *dat sg & loc sg* **-rze**) *f* **1** (*lodowa*) mountain **2** (*bluzka*) top **3** (*piętro w domu*) upstairs **4** (*śmieci*) heap; **w ~ch** in the mountains; **obiecywać** (**obiecać** *pf*) **złote góry** to promise the earth; **ona mieszka na górze** she lives upstairs; **on chodzi do szkoły pod górę** he walks uphill to school; **do góry nogami** upside down; **ceny poszły w górę** the prices have gone up; **płacić/dziękować z góry** to pay/thank in advance

górni|k (**-ka, -cy**; *inst sg* **-kiem**) *m* miner

górzysty *adj* (*teren, okolica*) hilly

gó|wno (**-wna, -wna**; *loc sg* **-wnie**; *gen pl* **-wien**) *nt* (*pot!*) shit; **~ mnie to obchodzi** (*pot!*) I don't give a shit about this (*pot!*)

gra (**gry, gry**; *dat sg & loc sg* **grze**; *gen pl* **gier**) *f* **1** game **2** (*na scenie*) acting **3** (*przen: pozorowanie*) act

gracz (**-a, -e**; *gen pl* **-y**) *m* (*zręczny, nałogowy*) player

gr|ać (**-am, -asz**; *pf* **za-**) *vt, vi* to play; **~ na pianinie** to play the piano; **~ w szachy** to play chess; **wiesz, że grasz mi na nerwach?** you know you're getting on my nerves?; **coś grają w kinie w środę?** is there anything on at the cinema on Wednesday?

gra|m (**-ma, -my**; *loc sg* **-mie**) *m* gram(me)

gramaty|ka (**-ki, -ki**; *dat sg & loc sg* **-ce**) *f* **1** (*reguły języka*) grammar **2** (*książka do nauki*) grammar (book)

granic|a (**-y, -e**) *f* **1** (*międzypaństwowa*) border **2** (*między miastami*) boundary, limit(s *pl*) (*US*) **3** (*limit*) limit; **mieszkać za granicą** to live abroad; **jechać** (**pojechać** *pf*) **za granicę** to go abroad

granicz|yć (**-ę, -ysz**) *vi*: **~ z** *+inst* (*dzielić granicę*) to border on

grani|t (**-tu, -ty**; *loc sg* **-cie**) *m* (*skała, złoża*) granite

gratis *adv inv* (*obiad, usługa*) free (of charge)

gratul|ować (**-uję, -ujesz**; *pf* **po-**) *vi*: **~ (komuś czegoś)** to congratulate (sb on sth); **gratulował nam zwycięstwa** he congratulated us on our victory
Grecj|a (**-i**) *f* Greece
grecki *adj* **1** Greek **2** (*sztuka*) Grecian
grill (**-a, -e**; *gen pl* **-ów**) *m* barbecue; **mięso pieczone na ~u** meat cooked on the barbecue
groch (**-u**) *m* **1** (*roślina*) pea **2** (*zbiór*) peas *pl*; **grochy** *pl* (*wzór*) polka dots
grochów|ka (**-ki, -ki**; *dat sg & loc sg* **-ce**; *gen pl* **-ek**) *f* pea soup
groma|dzić (**-dzę, -dzisz**; *imp* **-dź**; *pf* **z-**) *vt* to accumulate; **~ się** *vr* (*o osobach, o rzeczach*) to gather
grosz (**-a, -e**; *gen pl* **-y**) *m* grosz (*Polish monetary unit equal to 1/100 zloty*); **kupować** (**kupić** *pf*) **za ~e** to buy dirt-cheap; **nie śmierdzieć ~em** to be skint
gr|ozić (**-ożę, -ozisz**; *impf* **-óź**) *vi* **1** (*zastraszać*) to threaten **2** (*stwarzać zagrożenie*) to be imminent
gr|oźba (**-oźby, -oźby**; *dat sg & loc sg* **-oźbie**; *gen pl* **-óźb**) *f* threat
groźny *adj* **1** (*zachowanie, zjawisko*) dangerous **2** (*gest*) threatening
gruba|s (**-sa, -sy**; *loc sg* **-sie**) *m* (*pot*) fatty
gruby *adj* **1** (*książka*) thick **2** (*osoba*) fat; **to była gruba przesada!** (*pot*) that was a gross exaggeration!
gru|pa (**-py, -py**; *dat sg & loc sg* **-pie**) *f* **1** group **2** (*kiść, kępka*) cluster; **ma grupę krwi AB Rh +** he is blood group AB Rh +
grusz|ka (**-ki, -ki**; *dat sg & loc sg* **-ce**; *gen pl* **-ek**) *f* **1** (*drzewo*) pear tree **2** (*owoc*) pear; **obiecywać** (**obiecać** *pf*) **gruszki na wierzbie** to promise the moon on a stick
gruziński *adj* Georgian
Gruzj|a (**-i**) *f* Georgia
gruźlic|a (**-y**) *f* (*w medycynie*) TB
gry|pa (**-py**; *dat sg & loc sg* **-pie**) *f* influenza, flu (*pot*)
gry|źć (**-zę, -ziesz**; *imp* **-ź**; *pt* **-zł, -zła, -źli**) *vt* **1** to bite **2** (*gnat*) to gnaw ▷ *vi* **1** (*dym*) to sting **2** (*wełna*) to itch; **~ się** *vr* **1** (*o zwierzętach*) to fight **2** (*o barwach, wzorach*) to clash
grz|ać (**-eję, -ejesz**) *vt* **1** (*pf* **za-**) (*zupę*) to heat **2** (*pf* **o-**) (*dłonie*) to warm ▷ *vi* **1** (*słońce*) to beat down **2** (*grzejnik*) to be hot; **~ się** *vr* **1** (*w promieniach słońca*) to bask **2** (*przy kaloryferze*) to warm o.s. **3** (*podnosić temperaturę*) to heat up
grzeb|ać (**-ię, -iesz**) to bury; **~ się** *vr* (*pot*) to take a long time getting ready; **~ zmarłych** to bury the deceased
grzebie|ń (**-nia, -nie**; *gen pl* **-ni**) *m* **1** comb **2** (*u koguta*) crest
grzech (**-u, -y**) *m* sin; **popełniać** (**popełnić** *pf*) **~** to sin
grzeczny *adj* **1** (*człowiek*) polite **2** (*dobrze wychowany*) good
grzejni|k (**-ka, -ki**; *inst sg* **-kiem**) *m* radiator; **~ elektryczny** electric heater
grzesz|yć (**-ę, -ysz**; *pf* **z-**) *vi* to sin; **nie ~ mądrością** to be a bit soft in the head
grzy|wna (**-wny, -wny**; *dat sg & loc sg* **-wnie**; *gen pl* **-wien**) *f* fine; **płacić** (**zapłacić** *pf*) **grzywnę za** to pay a fine for
gu|bić (**-bię, -bisz**; *pf* **z-**) *vt* to lose; **~ się** *vr* **1** (*w drodze*) to lose one's way **2** (*o rzeczach*) to get lost
gu|ma (**-my, -my**; *dat sg & loc sg* **-mie**) *f* (*wyrób kauczukowy*) rubber; **~ do żucia** chewing gum; **złapał gumę na drodze** (*pot*) he got a flat tyre (*Brit*) *lub* tire (*US*) on the way
gum|ować (**-uję, -ujesz**) *vt* to erase
gustowny *adj* tasteful
gu|z (**-za, -zy**; *loc sg* **-zie**) *m* **1** (*obrzmiałe stłuczenie*) bump **2** (*w medycynie*) tumour (*Brit*), tumor (*US*); **nabijać** (**nabić** *pf*) **sobie ~a** to bump one's head
gwał|cić (**-cę, -cisz**; *impf* **-ć**) *vt* **1** (*pf* **z-**) (*zmuszać do stosunku seksualnego*) to rape **2** (*pf* **po-**) (*łamać prawo*) to violate
gwał|t (**-tu, -ty**; *dat sg & loc sg* **-cie**) *m* **1** (*akt przemocy*) violence **2** (*na osobie*) rape
gwarancj|a (**-i, -e**; *gen pl* **-i**) *f* guarantee; **na gwarancji** under guarantee

gwarant|ować (**-uję, -ujesz**; *pf* **za-**) *vt* (*bezpieczeństwo, zysk*) to guarantee
gwi|azda (**-azdy, -azdy**; *dat sg & loc sg* **-eździe**) *f* **1** star **2** (*przen: osobistość*) celebrity; **~ filmowa** film (*Brit*) *lub* movie (*US*) star
gwiazdo|r (**-ra, -rzy**; *loc sg* **-rze**) *m* (*filmowy*) film (*Brit*) *lub* movie (*US*) star
gwi|zdać (**-żdżę, -żdżesz**; *pf* **-zdnąć**) *vi* **1** to whistle **2** (*o syrenie*) to whine **3** (*podczas występu*) to boo; **gwiżdżę na to** (*pot*) I couldn't care less about that

ha|k (**-ka, -ki**; *inst sg* **-kiem**) *m* (*przyrząd*) hook
halo *excl* (*i przez telefon*) hello
hała|s (**-su, -sy**; *loc sg* **-sie**) *m* **1** (*głośny dźwięk*) noise **2** (*rozgłos*) noise; **robić** (**narobić** *pf*) **~u** (*przen*) to make a fuss
hałas|ować (**-uję, -ujesz**) *vi* (*głośno się zachowywać*) to make a noise
hałaśliwy *adj* (*sąsiad, uczeń*) noisy
hamburge|r (**-ra, -ry**; *dat sg* **-rze**) *m* (*Kulin*) hamburger
ham|ować (**-uję, -ujesz**) *vt* **1** (*pf* **po-**; *pf* **za-**) (*powstrzymywać, utrudniać*) to slow down **2** (*pf* **po-**) (*śmiech, łzy*) to hold back ▷ *vi* (*pf* **za-**) (*zmniejszać prędkość*) to brake; **~ się** (*pf* **po-**) *vr* to hold o.s. back; *zob. też* **zahamować**
hamul|ec (**-ca, -ce**) *m* (*urządzenie*) brake; **~ ręczny** handbrake (*Brit*), parking brake (*US*); **~ bezpieczeństwa** communication cord (*Brit*), emergency brake (*US*)
hand|el (**-lu**) *m* (*Ekon*) trade, commerce
handl|ować (**-uję, -ujesz**) *vi* *+inst* **1** (*produktami*) to trade in **2** (*narkotykami*) to deal in
handlo|wiec (**-wca, -wcy**) *m* salesman
handlowy *adj* (*umowa, działalność, izba*) trade; **szkoła handlowa** business school; **centrum handlowe** shopping centre (*Brit*), mall (*US*)
hań|ba (**-by**; *dat & loc sg* **-bie**) *f* (*wstyd, ujma*) dishonour (*Brit*), dishonor (*US*)

harcerz (**-a, -e**; *gen pl* **-y**) *m* (*członek organizacji młodzieżowej*) scout
harmoni|a (**-i**) *f* (*zgoda*) harmony
ha|sło (**-sła, -sła**; *loc sg* **-śle**; *gen pl* **-seł**) *nt* **1** (*Pol*) watchword **2** (*do działania*) signal **3** (*Komput*) password **4** (*w encyklopedii*) entry

HEJNAŁ MARIACKI

Hejnał Mariacki is the bugle call played every hour from the tower of the Mariacki Church in Kraków. Legend has it that its melody is interrupted to commemorate an event from the Tatar raids in the 13th century, when the bugle call was played to alert the city to an attack. One of the arrows shot by the Tatars pierced the bugle player's neck before he finished the call. Every day the bugle call is broadcast throughout Poland on Polish radio.

helikopte|r (**-ra, -ry**; *loc sg* **-rze**) *m* (*Lot*) helicopter
herba|ta (**-ty, -ty**; *dat & loc sg* **-cie**) *f* (*Kulin*) tea
herbatni|k (**-ka, -ki**; *inst sg* **-kiem**) *m* (*ciastko*) biscuit
heroi|na (**-ny**; *dat sg* **-nie**) *f* heroin
Himalaj|e (**-ów**) *pl* (*Geo*) the Himalayas
hinduski *adj* Hindu
hipermarke|t (**-tu, -ty**; *dat & loc sg* **-cie**) *m* hypermarket
hipote|ka (**-ki, -ki**; *dat & loc sg* **-ce**) *f* **1** (*Fin*) collateral **2** (*księga wieczysta*) mortgage deed; **brać** (**wziąć** *pf*) **pożyczkę pod hipotekę** to take out a secured loan
hipotetyczny *adj* (*prawdopodobny*) hypothetical
histori|a (**-i, -e**; *gen pl & dat, loc sg* **-i**) *f* **1** (*dzieje*) history **2** (*opowiadanie*) story
historyczny *adj* **1** (*dotyczący przeszłości*) historical **2** (*istotny*) historic **3** (*zabytki, budynki*) historic
history|k (**-ka, -cy**; *inst sg* **-kiem**) *m* **1** (*naukowiec*) historian **2** (*Szkol*) history teacher
Hiszpani|a (**-i**) *f* Spain
hiszpański *adj* Spanish
HIV *abbr* HIV
hobby *nt inv* (*zainteresowanie*) hobby
hokej (**-a**) *m* (*sport*): **~ na trawie** hockey (*Brit*), field hockey (*US*); **~ na lodzie** ice hockey
Holandi|a (**-i**) *f* the Netherlands
holenderski *adj* Dutch
homoseksuali|sta (**-sty, -ści**; *dat & loc sg* **-ście**) *m decl like f in sg* (*osoba*) homosexual
hono|r (**-ru**; *loc sg* **-rze**) *m* (*godność, zaszczyt*) honour (*Brit*), honor (*US*); **honory** *pl* (*hołd*): **oddawać** (**oddać** *pf*) **~y** to salute; **słowo ~u** word of hono(u)r
hormo|n (**-nu, -ny**; *loc sg* **-nie**) *m* (*Bio*) hormone
horosko|p (**-pu, -py**; *loc sg* **-pie**) *m* horoscope
horro|r (**-ru, -ry**; *loc sg* **-rze**) *m* **1** (*gatunek filmu*) horror (movie) **2** (*pot: groźna sytuacja*) horror
hot-do|g (**-ga, -gi**; *inst sg* **-giem**) *m* (*Kulin*) hot dog
hotel (**-u, -e**; *gen pl* **-i**) *m* (*luksusowy, tani*) hotel; **zatrzymywać** (**zatrzymać** *pf*) **się w ~u** to stay in a hotel
hu|k (**-ku, -ki**; *inst sg* **-kiem**) *m* **1** (*wybuchu*) bang **2** (*wody*) rumble **3** (*w czasie burzy*) roll **4** (*duża ilość*): **~** *+gen* loads of; **z ~iem** (*zamknąć się*) with a bang
humo|r (**-ru**; *loc sg* **-rze**) *m* **1** (*komiczna scena, sytuacja*) humour (*Brit*), humor (*US*) **2** (*stan usposobienia*) mood; **poczucie ~u** sense of humo(u)r
hura!, hurra! *excl* hurrah!
huraga|n (**-nu, -ny**; *loc sg* **-nie**) *m* (*porywisty wiatr*) hurricane
hurtow|nia (**-ni, -nie**; *gen pl & dat, loc sg* **-ni**) *f* **1** (*o przedsiębiorstwie*) wholesalers *pl* **2** (*o magazynie*) (wholesale) warehouse
hutni|k (**-ka, -cy**; *inst sg* **-kiem**) *m* (*stali, żelaza*) steelworker
hydrauli|k (**-ka, -cy**; *inst sg* **-kiem**) *m* (*robotnik wykonujący prace wodnokanalizacyjne*) plumber

ich *pron gen pl od* **oni, one** ▷ *possessive pron* **1** (*z rzeczownikiem*) their **2** (*bez rzeczownika*) theirs; **nie ma ~** they are not here; **zadzwoniłem do n~** I phoned them; **to jest ~ dom** this is their house; **~ znajomy** a friend of theirs; **ten dom jest ~** this house is theirs

ide|a (**-i, -e**; *gen pl & dat, loc sg* **-i**) *f* (*pomysł, koncepcja*) idea

idealny *adj* **1** (*perfekcyjny*) perfect **2** (*nierzeczywisty*) ideal

idea|ł (**-łu, -ły**; *loc sg* **-le**) *m* (*wzór doskonałości*) ideal; **~ studenta** the ideal student

identyczny *adj* (*taki sam*) identical

identyfik|ować (**-uję, -ujesz**; *pf* **z-**) *vt* (*rozpoznawać*) to identify; **~ się** *vr*: **~ się z kimś/czymś** (*utożsamiać się*) to identify with sb/sth

ideologi|a (**-i, -e**; *gen pl & dat, loc sg* **-i**) *f* (*system poglądów*) ideology

idio|ta (**-ty, -ci**; *dat & loc sg* **-cie**) *m decl like f in sg* (*pot: głupek*) idiot

idiot|ka (**-ki, -ki**; *dat & loc sg* **-ce**; *gen pl* **-ek**) *f* (*pot: głupek*) idiot

idol (**-a, -e**; *gen pl* **-i**) *m* (*bożyszcz*) idol

idziesz *itd. vb zob.* **iść**

igła (**igły, igły**; *dat & loc sg* **igle**; *gen pl* **igieł**) *f* (*narzędzie, Bot*) needle

ignor|ować (**-uję, -ujesz**; *pf* **z-**) *vt* (*lekceważyć*) to ignore

ikonka (**-ki, -ki**; *dat sg* **-ce**) *f* (*komputerowy*) icon

SŁOWO KLUCZOWE

ile *pron +gen* **1** (*z rzeczownikami policzalnymi*) how many; **ile kobiet/sióstr?** how many women/sisters?; **ilu chłopców/braci?** how many boys/brothers?; **ile on ma lat?** how old is he?; **ile razy?** how many times?
2 (*w zdaniach względnych: z rzeczownikami policzalnymi*) as many; (*z rzeczownikami niepoliczalnymi*) as much; **jedz, ile chcesz** eat as much as you want
3 (*z rzeczownikami niepoliczalnymi*) how much; **ile soku/ryżu/kawy?** how much juice/rice/coffee?; **ile czasu?** how long?; **ile kosztuje ta bluzka?** how much is this blouse?
4: **ile jedzenia!** what a lot of food!

ileś *pron +gen* (*non-vir*) some, a number of

iloś|ć (**-ci, -ci**; *gen pl & dat, loc sg* **-ci**) *f* (*liczba, wielkość*) amount, quantity

ilustracj|a (**-i, -e**; *gen pl & dat, loc sg* **-i**) *f* (*przykład, rysunek*) illustration

iluś *pron +gen* (*vir*) some, a number of

im *pron dat pl od* **oni, one** (to) them ▷ *adv*: **im prędzej, tym lepiej** the sooner the better; **nie ufam im** I don't trust them; **daj im tę książkę** give them the book

im. *abbr* (*= imienia*): **uniwersytet ~ Adama Mickiewicza** Adam Mickiewicz University

imienin|y (**-**) *pl* (*uroczystość*) name day *sg*

IMIENINY

Imieniny is the popular Polish custom of celebrating the name day of one's patron saint. **Imieniny** are celebrated like birthdays – the person celebrating is given presents and good wishes.

imi|ę (**-enia, -ona**) *nt* **1** (*nazwa*) name **2** (*pierwsze imię*) first name **3** (*honor*) reputation; **szkoła imienia Tadeusza Kościuszki** Tadeusz Kosciuszko School; **jak masz na ~?** (*pot*) what's your name?; **w czyimś**

imieniu on (*Brit*) *lub* in (*US*) behalf of sb; **w ~ Ojca i Syna, i Ducha Świętego** in the name of the Father, the Son and the Holy Spirit
imigracj|a (**-i, -e**; *gen pl & dat, loc sg* **-i**) *f* (*proces, ludzie*) immigration
imigran|t (**-ta, -ci**; *loc sg* **-cie**) *m* (*osoba*) immigrant
imigr|ować (**-uję, -ujesz**) *vi* to immigrate
imit|ować (**-uję, -ujesz**) *vt* (*naśladować*) to imitate
impon|ować (**-uję, -ujesz**; *pf* **za-**) *vi* (*wzbudzać podziw*): **~ komuś (czymś)** to impress sb (with sth)
impor|t (**-tu**; *loc sg* **-cie**) *m* (*Ekon*) import
import|ować (**-uję, -ujesz**) *vt* (*towary, surowce*) to import
impre|za (**-zy, -zy**; *dat & loc sg* **-zie**) *f* **1** (*kulturalna*) event **2** (*pot: towarzyska*) party
imprez|ować (**-uję, -ujesz**) *vi* to party
impulsywny *adj* (*popędliwy*) impulsive
inaczej *adv* **1** (*odmiennie*) differently **2** (*w konsekwencji*) otherwise, or (else); **tak czy ~** one way or another
indek|s (**-su, -sy**; *loc sg* **-sie**) *m* **1** (*skorowidz*) index **2** (*studenta*) *student record book*
Indi|e (**-i**) *pl* India
indyjski *adj* (*Geo*) Indian; **Ocean I~** the Indian Ocean
indy|k (**-ka, -ki**; *inst sg* **-kiem**) *m* (*drób*) turkey
indywidualny *adj* individual
infekcj|a (**-i, -e**; *gen pl & dat, loc sg* **-i**) *f* (*zakażenie*) infection
informacj|a (**-i, -e**; *gen pl & dat, loc sg* **-i**) *f* **1** (*o wiadomości*) piece of information **2** (*o danych*) information **3** (*o biurze*) information office (*Brit*) *lub* bureau (*US*); **~ turystyczna** tourist information centre (*Brit*) *lub* center (*US*)
informatycz|ka (**-ki, -ki**; *dat & loc sg* **-ce**; *gen pl* **-ek**) *f* computer scientist
informaty|k (**-ka, -cy**; *inst sg* **-kiem**) *m* (*specjalista komputerowy*) computer scientist
informaty|ka (**-ki**; *dat sg* **-ce**) *f* (*technologia, nauka*) computer science
inform|ować (**-uję, -ujesz**; *pf* **po-**) *vt*: **~ kogoś (o czymś)** (*powiadamiać*) to inform sb (of sth); **~ się** *vr* (*zasięgać informacji*): **~ się o czymś** to inquire about sth
inhalacj|a (**-i, -e**; *gen pl & dat, loc sg* **-i**) *f* (*zabieg leczniczy*) inhalation
inicja|ł (**-łu, -ły**; *loc sg* **-le**) *m* (*początkowa litera*) initial
inny *pron* **1** (*nie ten, nie taki*) another **2** (*różny*) other, different ▷ *m decl like adj* (*pot: człowiek*) another man; **inni** *pl* (the) others *pl*; **coś innego** something else
inspekto|r (**-ra, -rzy** *lub* **-rowie**; *loc sg* **-rze**) *m* (*kontroler*) inspector
inspektor|ka (**-ki, -ki**; *dat & loc sg* **-ce**; *gen pl* **-ek**) *f* inspector
inspir|ować (**-uję, -ujesz**; *pf* **za-**) *vt* (*artystę, dziecko*) to inspire
instrukcj|a (**-i, -e**; *gen pl & dat, loc sg* **-i**) *f* (*wskazówka*) instruction; **~ obsługi** instructions *pl* (for use)
instrumen|t (**-tu, -ty**; *loc sg* **-cie**) *m* (*przyrząd, narzędzie*) instrument
instynk|t (**-tu, -ty**; *loc sg* **-cie**) *m* (*przetrwania*) instinct
insuli|na (**-ny**; *dat & loc sg* **-nie**) *f* (*Med*) insulin
intelektuali|sta (**-sty, -ści**; *dat & loc sg* **-ście**) *m decl like f in sg* (*wykształcona osoba*) intellectual
intelektualist|ka (**-ki, -ki**; *dat & loc sg* **-ce**; *gen pl* **-ek**) *f* intellectual
inteligencj|a (**-i**) *f* **1** (*umysł*) intelligence **2** (*grupa społeczna*) intelligentsia
inteligentny *adj* (*pomysł, odpowiedź*) intelligent
intensywny *adj* **1** (*uczenie się, szukanie*) intensive **2** (*kolor*) intense
intere|s (**-su, -sy**; *loc sg* **-sie**) *m* **1** (*pożytek, zysk*) interest **2** (*sprawa, przedsiębiorstwo*) business **3** (*przedsięwzięcie*) deal
interes|ować (**-uję, -ujesz**; *pf* **za-**) *vt* (*wzbudzać chęć poznania*) to interest; **~ się** *vr*: **~ się** *+inst* (*być zaciekawionym*) to be interested in
interesujący *adj* (*zajmujący, absorbujący*) interesting
interna|t (**-tu, -ty**; *loc sg* **-cie**) *m* (*miejsce zamieszkania uczniów*)

(school) dormitory; **szkoła z ~em** boarding school
interne|t (**-tu, -cie**) *m* the internet
interni|sta (**-sty, -ści**; *dat & loc sg* **-ście**) *m decl like f in sg (lekarz)* internist
internist|ka (**-ki, -ki**; *dat & loc sg* **-ce**; *gen pl* **-ek**) *f* internist
interpretacj|a (**-i, -e**; *gen pl & dat, loc sg* **-i**) *f (wyjaśnienie)* interpretation
interpunkcj|a (**-i**; *dat & loc sg* **-i**) *f (zasady pisowni)* punctuation
interweni|ować (**-uję, -ujesz**) *vi (w jakiejś sprawie)* to intervene
intymny *adj (prywatny, osobisty)* intimate
inwali|da (**-dy, -dzi**; *dat & loc sg* **-dzie**) *m decl like f in sg (osoba niepełnosprawna)* person with a disability
inwalid|ka (**-ki, -ki**; *dat & loc sg* **-ce**; *gen pl* **-ek**) *f* person with a disability
inwest|ować (**-uję, -ujesz**; *pf* **za-**) *vt* to invest ▷ *vi*: **~ w** *(pieniądze, czas, energię)* to invest in
inwestycj|a (**-i, -e**; *gen pl & dat, loc sg* **-i**) *f* investment
inż. *abbr (= inżynier)* engineer
inżynie|r (**-ra, -rowie**; *loc sg* **-rze**) *m (osoba)* engineer
inżynier|ka (**-ki, -ki**; *dat & loc sg* **-ce**; *pl* **-ek**) *f* engineer
Ira|k (**-ku**; *inst sg* **-kiem**) *m* Iraq
Ira|n (**-nu**; *loc sg* **-nie**) *m* Iran
Irlandczy|k (**-ka, -cy**; *inst sg* **-kiem**) *m* Irishman
Irlandi|a (**-i**) *f* Ireland; **~ Północna** Northern Ireland
Irland|ka (**-ki, -ki**; *dat sg* **-ce**; *gen pl* **-ek**) *f* Irishwoman
irlandzki *adj* Irish
ironi|a (**-i**; *dat & loc sg* **-i**) *f (losu, sytuacji, komentarza)* irony
ironiczny *adj (sarkastyczny, kąśliwy)* ironic
iryt|ować (**-uję, -ujesz**; *pf* **z-**) *vt (drażnić, denerwować)* to irritate; **~ się** *vr*: **~ się czymś** *(denerwować się)* to get annoyed at sth
isla|m (**-mu**; *loc sg* **-mie**) *m (Rel)* Islam
islamski *adj (kraj)* Islamic
Islandi|a (**-i**) *f* Iceland
ist|nieć (**-nieję, -niejesz**) *vi (egzystować)* to exist; **~ od** *+gen...* to have existed since...
isto|ta (**-ty, -ty**; *dat & loc sg* **-cie**) *f* **1** *(Bio)* creature **2** *(sens)* essence; **~ ludzka** human being; **w istocie** in fact
istotnie *adv* **1** *(prawdziwie)* indeed **2** *(całkowicie)* essentially, fundamentally **3** *(w ważny sposób)* significantly
istotny *adj* **1** *(prawdziwy)* real **2** *(całkowity)* essential **3** *(ważny)* significant
iść (**idę, idziesz**) *vi* to go; **~ piechotą** to go on foot; **~ w Internet** to go viral

CHODZIĆ/IŚĆ/PÓJŚĆ

Chodzić, iść and **pójść** are all verbs of motion meaning "to go" (on foot), but they have different implications. With the perfective verb – **pójść** – the emphasis is on the act of going to and arriving at the destination, whereas with the imperfective verbs – **chodzić** and **iść** – the focus is more on the act of going itself and it is not made clear whether the subject arrives at the destination or not.

itd. *abbr (= i tak dalej)* etc.
itp. *abbr (= i tym podobne lub podobnie)* etc.
izolat|ka (**-ki, -ki**; *dat & loc sg* **-ce**; *gen pl* **-ek**) *f (oddział w szpitalu)* isolation ward
izol|ować (**-uję, -ujesz**) *vt* **1** *(pf* **od-**) *(ludzi)* to isolate **2** *(pf* **za-**) *(okno)* to insulate
iż *conj (książk) od* **że** that
Izrael (**-a**) *m* Israel

ja *pron* I ▷ *nt inv* **1** (*jako podmiot zdania*) I **2** (*jako podmiot lub dopełnienie w zdaniu*) I **3** (*osobiście*) self; **ja też lubię lody** I like ice cream too; **mój brat i ja** my brother and I; **niższy niż ja** shorter than me; **ja sam to zrobię** I'll do it myself

jabł|ko (**-ka, -ka**; *inst sg* **-kiem**; *gen pl* **-ek**) *nt* (*owoc*) apple

jadal|nia (**-ni, -nie**; *gen pl & dat, loc sg* **-ni**) *f* dining room

jadalny *adj* (*rośliny*) edible ▷ *m decl like adj* (*miejsce*) dining room

jadę *itd. vb zob.* **jechać**

jadł *itd. vb zob.* **jeść**

jadłospi|s (**-su, -sy**; *loc sg* **-sie**) *m* (*spis dań*) menu

jaj|ko (**-ka, -ka**; *inst sg* **-kiem**; *gen pl* **-ek**) *nt* (*Kulin*) egg; **~ sadzone** fried egg

jaj|o (**-a, -a**) *nt* egg

 **SŁOWO KLUCZOWE**

jak *pron* **1** (*zaimek pytajny*) how; **jak daleko?** how far?; **jak się masz?** (*familiar sg*) how are you?; **jak smakuje zupa?** is the soup good?; **jak on wygląda?** what does he look like?

2 (*zaimek względny*) as, like; **zrobił, jak chciałem** he did as I wanted; **wiesz, jak to napisać?** do you know how to write that?; **nie wiemy, jak wygląda nowe mieszkanie** we don't know what the new flat looks like

3 (*opisując nasilenie*): **jak wspaniale!** how wonderful!

▷ *conj* **1** (*porównując*) as; **tak przystojny jak ja** as handsome as me; **za młody jak na dyrektora** too young to be a director; **tak jak...** just like...

2 (*kiedy*) when; **jak skończysz, idź do domu** go home when you finish; **widziałem go, jak przechodził przez ulicę** I saw him crossing the street

3 (*jeżeli*) if; **jak chcesz, możemy pójść na spacer** we can go for a walk if you like; **jak nie ten, to tamten** if not this one, then that one

▷ *part*: **jak najszybciej** as soon as possible; **jak gdyby** as if

 **SŁOWO KLUCZOWE**

jaki *pron decl like adj* **1** (*wprowadzając pytanie ogólne*) what; **jakie lody lubisz?** what ice cream do you like?; **jaki to język?** what language is that?

2 (*dokonując wyboru z podanych opcji*) which; **jakie chcesz piwo: małe czy duże?** which would you prefer, a pint or a half?

3 (*przed przymiotnikiem*) how; **jaka ona jest piękna!** how beautiful she is!

4 (*przed rzeczownikiem*) what; **jaki piękny dom!** what a beautiful house!

jakiś (*f* **jakaś**; *nt* **jakieś**) *pron* **1** some **2** (*nieco, trochę*) a little bit; **~ student pytał o ciebie** some student was asking about you; **wróci za jakąś godzinę** he'll be back in an hour or so; **był ~ markotny** he was a little bit glum

jako *conj* (*w charakterze kogoś/czegoś*) as; **ja ~ były prezydent...** as a former chairman, I...; **~ tako** (*nieźle*) so-so

jakoś|ć (**-ci**; *dat & loc sg* **-ci**) *f* (*towaru, życia*) quality

Japoni|a (**-i**) *f* Japan

japoński *adj* Japanese

JARMARK

Jarmark is a fair, taking place on set dates in towns and villages. A traditional **jarmark** is a combination of trade and entertainment in a festive atmosphere. Efforts are made to preserve this tradition, for example in Gdańsk, where, every summer, "Jarmark Dominikański" is organized with great pomp and ceremony.

jarski *adj* (*bezmięsny*) vegetarian
jasno *adv* **1** (*wyjaśniać, pisać*) clearly **2** (*błyszczeć, ubierać się*) brightly
jasny *adj* **1** (*pokój, spojrzenie, żarówka*) bright **2** (*włosy*) blonde **3** (*o kolorze*) light **4** (*skóra*) pale **5** (*zrozumiały*) clear; **czy to jest jasne?** is that clear?
jawny *adj* **1** (*spotkanie, proces*) public **2** (*podziw, żal, niechęć*) open **3** (*kłamstwo*) blatant
jaz|da (**-dy, -dy**; *dat & loc sg* **jeździe**) *f* **1** (*samochodem*) drive; (*autobusem*) journey; (*motocyklem, rowerem*) ride **2** (*ruch samochodu*) driving; (*ruch motocykla, roweru*) riding; **~ konna** horse riding; **~ na nartach** skiing; **prawo jazdy** driving licence (*Brit*), driver's license (*US*); **rozkład jazdy** timetable (*Brit*), schedule (*US*)
ją *pron acc od* **ona**
je *pron* **1** *acc sg od* **ono 2** *acc pl od* **one**
jechać (**jadę, jedziesz**; *imp* **jedź**; *pf* **po-**) *vi* **1** (*na wakacje, do innych krajów, do pracy*) to go **2** (*na motocyklu, koniu*) to ride **3** (*prowadzić samochód*) to drive **4** (*o środkach lokomocji: kursować*) to run; **~ na nartach** to ski; **~ (po~** *pf*) **za granicę** to go abroad
jeden *decl like adj num* (*cyfra*) one ▷ *adj* **1** (*los, charakter*) one **2** (*jakiś*) a; **jedna druga** one half; **jeszcze ~** one more; **z jednej strony... z drugiej strony...** on the one hand... on the other hand...; **ani ~** not a single one
jedenasty *num decl like adj* eleventh
jedenaście *num decl like adj* eleven
jednak *conj* (*ale*) but, yet
jednakowy *adj* **1** (*równy*) equal **2** (*taki sam, identyczny*) identical
jedno *pron* **1** one thing **2** (*jedność, wszystko*) one **3** (*ta sama rzecz*) one and the same; **~ jest pewne** one thing is for certain
jednocześnie *adv* (*w tym samym czasie*) simultaneously
jednodniowy *adj* **1** (*seminarium, wyjazd*) one-day **2** (*zarost, pisklę*) one-day-old
jednoosobowy *adj* **1** (*firma*) one-man **2** (*pokój, łóżko*) single
jednost|ka (**-ki, -ki**; *dat & loc sg* **-ce**; *gen pl* **-ek**) *f* **1** (*pojedyncza osoba*) individual **2** (*przy pomiarach*) unit
jednoś|ć (**-ci**; *dat & loc sg* **-ci**) *f* **1** (*spójność, zgoda*) unity **2** (*bycie całością*) whole
jedyna|k (**-ka, -cy**; *inst sg* **-kiem**) *m* only child
jedynie *adv* **1** (*wyłącznie*) only **2** (*zaledwie*) merely
jedyn|ka (**-ki, -ki**; *dat sg* **-ce**; *gen pl* **-ek**) *f* **1** (*cyfra*) one **2** (*nr autobusu/domu, stacja radiowa*) one **3** (*ocena w szkole*) ≈ F
jedyny *adj* **1** (*kraj, gatunek*) only **2** (*umiłowany*) dearest; **~ w swoim rodzaju** unique
jedzeni|e (**-a**) *nt* **1** (*pokarm*) food **2** (*konsumowanie*) eating
jego *pron gen od* **on, ono**
jej *pron gen od* **ona**
jemu *pron dat od* **on, ono**
jesie|ń (**-ni, -nie**; *gen pl & dat, loc sg* **-ni**) *f* (*pora roku*) autumn (*Brit*), fall (*US*)
jest *itd. vb zob.* **być**
jeszcze *part* **1** (*nadal*) still **2** (*już*) still **3** (*w przeczeniu*) yet **4** (*nawet; w porównaniu*) even **5** (*ponadto, więcej*) more; **mamy ~ godzinę** we still have an hour; **~ przed miesiącem się nie znaliśmy** only a month ago we had not even met; **spotkali się ~ na studiach** they met whilst they were still students; **~ nie zadzwonił** he hasn't called yet; **~ droższy** even more expensive; **dziś jest ~ cieplej niż wczoraj** it's even warmer today than it was yesterday; **coś ~?** anything else?; **~ raz** one more time; **poczekaj ~ parę minut** wait another few minutes; **~ jeden przykład** one more example
jeść (**jem, jesz**; *3 pl* **jedzą**; *imp* **jedz**; *pt* **jadł, jedli**; *pf* **z-**) *vt* (*spożywać*) to eat; **~ (z~** *pf*) **śniadanie/kanapkę** to have

breakfast/a sandwich; **chce mi się ~** I'm hungry

jeśli *conj* (*jeżeli, pod warunkiem*) if; **~ chcesz, pójdziemy do kina** we can go to the cinema if you want; **~ nie teraz, to kiedy?** if not now, then when?; **~ nie przestanie padać, zostaniemy w domu** if it doesn't stop raining we'll stay at home

jezio|ro (**-ra, -ra**; *loc sg* **-rze**) *nt* (*Geo*) lake

je|ździć (**-żdżę, -ździsz**; *imp* **-źdź**) *vi* **1** (*na wakacje, do innych krajów, do pracy*) to go **2** (*na motocyklu, rowerze*) to ride **3** (*prowadzić samochód*) to drive **4** (*być pasażerem w samochodzie*) to ride **5** (*o środkach lokomocji: kursować*) to run; **czym jeździsz do pracy?** (*familiar sg*) how do you get to work?; **~ na nartach** to ski

jeżeli *conj* if; *zob. też* **jeśli**

języ|k (**-ka, -ki**; *inst sg* **-kiem**) *m* **1** (*obcy, literacki, ciała, programowania*) language **2** (*organ mowy*) tongue; **~ ojczysty** mother tongue

jogur|t (**-tu, -ty**; *loc sg* **-cie**) *m* (*Kulin*) yoghurt

jubile|r (**-ra, -rzy**; *loc sg* **-rze**) *m* **1** (*osoba*) jeweller (*Brit*), jeweler (*US*) **2** (*sklep*) jeweller's (*Brit*), jeweler's (*US*)

Jugosławi|a (**-i**) *f*: **Republiki byłej Jugosławii** the former Yugoslavia

jury *nt inv* (*komisja sędziowska*) jury

jut|ro (**-ra**; *loc sg* **-rze**) *nt* (*następny dzień*) tomorrow ▷ *adv* (*następnego dnia*) tomorrow; **do jutra!** see you tomorrow!; **~ rano** tomorrow morning

jutrzejszy *adj* (*lekcja, gazeta, spotkanie*) tomorrow's

JUWENALIA

Juwenalia is a student event that takes place every year in May or June in university cities. **Juwenalia** lasts up to ten days, during which a wide range of sporting events are organized by students for students.

już *adv* **1** (*twierdząco*) already **2** (*pytająco*) yet **3** (*w przeczeniach*) any more; **~ to zrobiliśmy** we've already done it; **czy skończyła ~ czytać tę gazetę?** has she finished reading that newspaper yet?; **ona ~ tutaj nie mieszka** she no longer lives here

k

kab|el (**-la, -le**; *gen pl* **-li**) *m* (*telefoniczny, elektryczny*) cable
kabi|na (**-ny, -ny**; *dat sg & loc sg* **-nie**) *f* **1** (*w pojeździe mechanicznym*) cabin **2** (*w łazience*) cubicle **3** (*telefoniczna*) booth
kac (**-a**) *m* hangover
kacz|ka (**-ki, -ki**; *dat sg & loc sg* **-ce**; *gen pl* **-ek**) *f* duck
kaja|k (**-ku, -ki**) *m* canoe
kakao *nt inv* (*nasiona, napój*) cocoa
kalafio|r (**-ra, -ry**; *loc sg* **-rze**) *m* cauliflower
kalecz|yć (**-ę, -ysz**; *pf* **s-**) *vt* **1** to cut **2** (*przen: mowę: robiąc błędy w języku*) to murder; **~ się** *vr* to cut o.s.; **~** (**s~** *pf*) **się w nogę** to cut one's leg
kale|ka (**-ki, -ki**; *dat sg & loc sg* **-ce**) *m/f decl like f* person with a disability; **~ życiowy** lame duck
kalendarz (**-a, -e**; *gen pl* **-y**) *m* (*ścienny, juliański*) calendar
kalkulato|r (**-ra, -ry**; *loc sg* **-rze**) *m* calculator
kaloryfe|r (**-ra, -ry**; *loc sg* **-rze**) *m* radiator
kame|ra (**-ry, -ry**; *loc sg* **-rze**) *f* camera; **~ wideo** video camera; **~ samochodowa** dashcam
kamienic|a (**-y, -e**) *f* (*czynszowa, ośmiopiętrowa*) tenement (house)
kamienny *adj* **1** (*mur*) stone **2** (*wyraz twarzy*) stony **3** (*sen*) deep; **wydobywać** (**wydobyć** *pf*) **węgiel ~** to mine coal
kamie|ń (**-nia, -nie**; *gen pl* **-ni**) *m* **1** stone **2** (*Tech: panewka, w zegarku*) jewel **3** (*w zapalniczce*) flint; **~ szlachetny** gem(stone); **~ żółciowy** gallstone; **~ nazębny** tartar; **śpi jak ~** he is sleeping like a log; **~ spadł mu z serca** (*przen*) it was a load off his mind
kamizel|ka (**-ki, -ki**; *dat sg & loc sg* **-ce**; *gen pl* **-ek**) *f* waistcoat (*Brit*), vest (*US*); **policjant ma kamizelkę kuloodporną** the policeman has a bullet-proof vest; **mieć na sobie kamizelkę ratunkową** to wear a life jacket
kamy|k (**-ka, -ki**; *inst sg* **-kiem**) *m* pebble; **wrzucać** (**wrzucić** *pf*) **~ do czyjegoś ogródka** (*przen*) to provoke sb
Kana|da (**-dy**; *loc sg* **-dzie**) *f* Canada
kanadyjski *adj* Canadian
Kanadyjczy|k (**-ka, -cy**; *inst sg* **-kiem**) *m* Canadian
Kanadyj|ka (**-ki, -ki**; *dat sg* **-ce**; *gen pl* **-ek**) *f* Canadian
kana|ł (**-łu, -ły**; *loc sg* **-le**) *m* **1** (*wodny*) ditch **2** (*rów odprowadzający nieczystości*) sewer **3** (*w telewizji, na morzu*) channel **4** (*droga łącząca dwa morza*) canal
kana|pa (**-py, -py**; *dat sg & loc sg* **-pie**) *f* (*mebel do spania, do siedzenia*) sofa
kanap|ka (**-ki, -ki**; *dat sg & loc sg* **-ce**; *gen pl* **-ek**) *f* (*z serem, z masłem*) sandwich
kancelari|a (**-i, -e**; *gen pl* **-i**) *f* office; **~ adwokacka** chambers *pl* (*Brit*); **K~ Prezesa Rady Ministrów** Prime Minister's Office
kandyda|t (**-ta, -ci**; *loc sg* **-cie**) *m* candidate; **jest dobrym ~em na męża** he is good husband material
kandyd|ować (**-uję, -ujesz**) *vi*: **~ (do parlamentu)** to stand (for Parliament) (*Brit*), to run (for Congress) (*US*)
kangu|r (**-ra, -ry**; *loc sg* **-rze**) *m* kangaroo
kanto|r (**-ra, -ry**; *loc sg* **-rze**) *m* (*wymiany walut*) bureau de change
kapelusz (**-a, -e**; *gen pl* **-y**) *m* **1** (*góralski, męski*) hat **2** (*u grzyba*) cap

kapitalistyczny *adj* (*ustrój, kraj*) capitalist

kapitaliz|m (**-mu**; *loc sg* **-mie**) *m* capitalism; **~ z ludzką twarzą** capitalism with a human face

kaplic|a (**-y, -e**) *f* chapel

kapła|n (**-na, -ni**; *loc sg* **-nie**) *m* (*w kościele*) priest

kapu|sta (**-sty**; *dat sg & loc sg* **-ście**) *f* **1** cabbage **2** (*kiszona lub kwaszona*) sauerkraut **3** (*włoska*) savoy (cabbage); **groch z kapustą** (*przen*) hodgepodge

kapuśnia|k[1] (**-ku, -ki**) *m* cabbage soup

kapuśnia|k[2] (**-ka, -ki**; *inst sg* **-kiem**) *m* (*drobny deszcz*) drizzle

ka|ra (**-ry, -ry**; *dat sg & loc sg* **-rze**) *f* **1** (*cielesna, dotkliwa*) punishment **2** (*urzędowa, pieniężna*) fine; **~ śmierci** capital punishment

karabi|n (**-nu, -ny**; *loc sg* **-nie**) *m* rifle; **strzelać** (**strzelić** *pf*) **z ~u maszynowego** to fire a machine gun

ka|rać (**-rzę, -rzesz**; *pf* **u-**) *vt* **1** to punish **2** (*urzędowo*) to penalize

kardiolo|g (**-ga, -dzy** *lub* **-gowie**; *inst sg* **-giem**) *m* (*lekarz specjalista*) cardiologist

karet|ka (**-ki, -ki**; *dat sg & loc sg* **-ce**; *gen pl* **-ek**) *f* (*pogotowia, szpitalna*) ambulance

karie|ra (**-ry, -ry**; *dat sg & loc sg* **-rze**) *f* (*praca zawodowa*) career

kar|k (**-ku, -ki**; *inst sg* **-kiem**) *m* nape of the neck; **ona ma głowę na ~u** she has her head screwed on; **nadstawiać** (**nadstawić** *pf*) **~u** to stick one's neck out

kar|mić (**-mię, -misz**) *vt* (*żywić*) (*pf* **na-**) **1** to feed **2** (*niemowlę piersią*) to breast-feed **3** (*niemowlę butelką*) to bottle-feed; **~ się** *vr* (*o zwierzętach*): **~ się (czymś)** to feed (on sth)

karnawa|ł (**-łu, -ły**; *loc sg* **-le**) *m* carnival

karne|t (**-tu, -ty**; *loc sg* **-cie**) *m* **1** (*na występy artystyczne*) subscription card **2** (*na komunikację*) book of tickets

kar|p (**-pia, -pie**; *gen pl* **-pi**) *m* (*Zool, Kulin*: *smażony, w galarecie*) carp

Karpat|y (**-**) *pl* the Carpathian Mountains

kar|ta (**-ty, -ty**; *dat sg & loc sg* **-cie**) *f* **1** (*w zeszycie*) sheet **2** (*w książce*) page **3** (*walet, król*) (playing) card **4** (*jadłospis*) menu; **~ kredytowa** credit card; **~ płatnicza** cash card; **~ gwarancyjna** guarantee slip; **~ do biblioteki** library card; **~ telefoniczna** phonecard; **~ pocztowa** postcard; **domek z kart** (*przen*) house of cards

kart|ka (**-ki, -ki**; *dat sg & loc sg* **-ce**; *gen pl* **-ek**) *f* **1** (*w zeszycie*) sheet **2** (*w książce*) page **3** (*żywieniowa*) ration card; **~ widokówka** postcard

kartof|el (**-la, -le**; *gen pl* **-li**) *m* (*gotowany, w mundurku*) potato

kartot|eka (**-eki, -eki**; *dat sg & loc sg* **-ece**; *gen pl* **-ek**) *f* **1** (*katalog kartkowy*) card index **2** (*karty z danymi*) files *pl*

ka|sa (**-sy, -sy**; *dat sg & loc sg* **-sie**) *f* **1** (*sklepowa*) cash desk **2** (*w supermarkecie*) checkout **3** (*w centrum handlowym*) till **4** (*w kinie, teatrze*) box office **5** (*okienko na dworcu*) ticket office **6** (*pieniądze państwa*) treasury **7** (*sejf*) safe

kase|ta (**-ty, -ty**; *dat sg & loc sg* **-cie**) *f* **1** (*taśma z nagraniem*) cassette **2** (*w fotografii*) cartridge

kasje|r (**-ra, -rzy**; *loc sg* **-rze**) *m* **1** (*sklep*) cashier **2** (*kino, teatr*) box-office clerk **3** (*bank*) teller **4** (*dworzec*) ticket clerk

kasjer|ka (**-ki, -ki**; *dat sg & loc sg* **-ce**; *gen pl* **-ek**) *f* **1** (*sklep*) cashier **2** (*kino, teatr*) box-office clerk **3** (*bank*) teller **4** (*dworzec*) ticket clerk

kasz|a (**-y, -e**) *f* **1** (*produkt spożywczy*) groats *pl* **2** (*potrawa*) porridge; **~ gryczana/jęczmienna** buckwheat/barley; **jeść** (**zjeść** *pf*) **kogoś w kaszy** to walk all over sb

kaszan|ka (**-ki, -ki**; *dat sg & loc sg* **-ce**; *gen pl* **-ek**) *f* black pudding (*Brit*), blood sausage (*US*)

kasz|el (**-lu**) *m* (*suchy, mokry*) cough; **dostawać** (**dostać** *pf*) **atak kaszlu** to have a coughing fit

kaszl|eć (**-ę, -esz**; *pf* **-nąć**) *vi* to cough

katakliz|m (**-mu, -my**; *loc sg* **-mie**) *m* (*powódź, trzęsienie ziemi*) disaster

katalo|g (**-gu, -gi**; *inst sg* **-giem**) *m* catalogue (*Brit*), catalog (*US*);

~ alfabetyczny/rzeczowy catalogue arranged alphabetically/by subject
kata|r (**-ru, -ry**; *loc sg* **-rze**) *m* catarrh; **on ma ~** he has a runny nose; **~ sienny** hay fever
katastro|fa (**-fy, -fy**; *dat sg & loc sg* **-fie**) *f* **1** (*motoryzacyjna*) accident **2** (*powietrzna*) (plane) crash **3** (*tragedia*) catastrophe
kated|ra (**-ry, -ry**; *dat sg & loc sg* **-rze**) *f* **1** (*główny kościół*) cathedral **2** (*pulpit wykładowcy*) teacher's desk **3** (*na uniwersytecie: jednostka administracyjna*) department **4** (*stanowisko profesora*) chair
kategori|a (**-i, -e**; *gen pl* **-i**) *f* (*klasa*) category
katolicki *adj* (*kościół, wiara*) (Roman) Catholic
katolicyz|m (**-mu**; *loc sg* **-mie**) *m* (Roman) Catholicism
katolicz|ka (**-ki, -ki**; *loc sg* **-ce**; *gen pl* **-ek**) *f* (Roman) Catholic
katoli|k (**-ka, -cy**; *inst sg* **-kiem**) *m* (Roman) Catholic
ka|wa (**-wy**; *dat sg & loc sg* **-wie**) *f* **1** (*drzewo*) coffee plant **2** (*ziarna*) coffee (beans *pl*) **3** (*czarna, z mlekiem*) coffee **4** (*nom pl* **-wy**) (*porcja napoju*) a (cup of) coffee
kawale|r (**-ra, -rowie** *lub* **-rzy**; *loc sg* **-rze**) *m* **1** (*mężczyzna bez żony*) bachelor **2** (*młody mężczyzna*) youth; **stary ~** confirmed bachelor
kawaler|ka (**-ki, -ki**; *dat sg & loc sg* **-ce**; *gen pl* **-ek**) *f* (*mieszkanie jednopokojowe*) one-room flat (*Brit*) *lub* apartment (*US*)
kawa|ł (**-łu, -ły**; *loc sg* **-le**) *m* **1** (*znaczna część*) chunk **2** (*żart*) joke **3** (*figiel*) trick; **powiedzieć** (**opowiedzieć** *pf*) **pieprzny ~** to tell a dirty joke
kawał|ek (**-ka, -ki**; *inst sg* **-kiem**) *m* (*fragment całości*) piece; **grać** (**zagrać** *pf*) **~** to play a piece; **ciężki ~ chleba** a hard-earned crust
kawiar|nia (**-ni, -nie**; *gen pl* **-ni** *or* **-ń**) *f* café
ka|zać (**-żę, -żesz**) *vi impf/pf*: **~ komuś coś zrobić** to tell sb to do sth; **kazał mi odpowiedzieć na pytanie** he told me to answer the question
każdy *pron decl like adj* **1** every **2** (*każdy człowiek*) everybody **3** (*z wymienionych przedmiotów*) each; **każdego dnia/roku** every day/year; **o każdej porze dnia** any time of the day; **ma rację za ~m razem** he is right every time; **w ~m razie trzeba tam pójść** in any case, we should go there; **~ z nas umie pływać** each one of us knows how to swim; **mamy prezent dla każdego z was** we have a present for each of you
ką|pać (**-pię, -piesz**; *pf* **wy-**) *vt* to bath (*Brit*), to bathe (*US*); **~ się** *vr* **1** (*w wannie*) to have a bath, to bathe (*US*) **2** (*w basenie*) to swim; **~ się w promieniach słońca** to sunbathe
kąpiel (**-i, -e**; *gen pl* **-i**) *f* **1** (*w wannie*) bath **2** (*w basenie*) swim; **brać** (**wziąć** *pf*) **~** to have a bath
kąpielów|ki (**-ek**) *pl* swimming trunks
ką|t (**-ta, -ty**; *loc sg* **-cie**) *m* **1** (*Mat*) angle **2** (*róg*) corner **3** (*pot: lokum*) pad
kciu|k (**-ka, -ki**; *inst sg* **-kiem**) *m* thumb; **trzymam za ciebie ~i** (*przen*) I'm keeping my fingers crossed for you
keczu|p (**-pu**; *loc sg* **-pie**) *m* (*sos pomidorowy*) ketchup
kefi|r (**-ru**; *loc sg* **-rze**) *m fermented milk drink popular in Eastern European countries*
kelne|r (**-ra, -rzy**; *loc sg* **-rze**) *m* waiter
kelner|ka (**-ki, -ki**; *dat sg & loc sg* **-ce**; *gen pl* **-ek**) *f* waitress
kempin|g (**-gu, -gi**; *inst sg* **-giem**) *m* campsite (*Brit*), camping ground (*US*)
kg *abbr* (= *kilogram*) kg
kibic (**-a, -e**) *m* **1** (*widz sportowy*) supporter **2** (*fan sportu: Sport*) fan
kibic|ować (**-uję, -ujesz**) *vi* to support; **kibicuje naszej drużynie od lat** he has supported our team for years
kich|ać (**-am, -asz**; *pf* **-nąć**) *vi* to sneeze; **kicham na problemy** (*przen*) I couldn't care less about the problems
kiedy *pron* when ▷ *conj* **1** when **2** (*podczas gdy*) while; **~ przyjdziesz?** when will you arrive?; **od ~ pracujesz?** since when have you

been working?; **pójdziemy ~ bądź** we can go at any time; **zrobimy to ~ indziej** we'll do it some other time; **~ tylko będę miał okazję** whenever I have a chance; **~ tylko wstałem, on wyszedł** as soon as I got up, he went out
kiedykolwiek *adv* **1** (*nieważne kiedy*) whenever **2** (*w pytaniach*) ever; **czy byłaś ~ w Londynie?** have you ever been to London?
kielisz|ek (**-ka, -ki**; *inst sg* **-kiem**) *m* **1** (*do alkoholu*) glass **2** (*do jajek*) (egg) cup; **stuknijmy się kieliszkami!** let's clink glasses!
kiełba|sa (**-sy, -sy**; *loc sg* **-sie**) *f* sausage
kier|ować (**-uję, -ujesz**) *vt* **1** (*pf* **s-**) (*wysłać*) to refer **2** (*słowa*) to direct **3** (*reflektor, lunetę*) to aim **4** (*wzrok*) to direct **5** (*donos*) to file ▷ *vi +inst* **1** (*pojazdem mechanicznym*) to drive **2** (*sterować*) to steer **3** (*zarządzać*) to manage; **~ się** (*pf* **s-**) *vr*: **~ się do** *+gen* to head towards; **~ się sercem** to be governed by one's emotions
kierowc|a (**-y, -y**) *m decl like f in sg* **1** driver **2** (*limuzyny*) chauffeur
kierownic|a (**-y, -e**) *f* **1** (*w samochodzie*) (steering) wheel **2** (*w rowerze*) handlebars *pl*
kierowni|k (**-ka, -cy**; *inst sg* **-kiem**) *m* (*biura, firmy*) manager
kierun|ek (**-ku, -ki**) *m* **1** (*trasy*) direction **2** (*w literaturze*) trend **3** (*na wyższej uczelni*) subject (*Brit*), major (*US*); **w kierunku Warszawy** towards Warsaw; **w tym samym kierunku** in the same direction
ki|j (**-ja, -je**; *gen pl* **-jów**) *m* stick; **~ bilardowy** cue; **~ golfowy** (golf) club; **bez ~a nie podchodź** stay well away from him/her/them
kilka *num* several
kilo *nt inv* kilo
kilogra|m (**-ma, -my**; *loc sg* **-mie**) *m* kilogram(me), kilo; **29 złotych za ~** 29 zlotys a *lub* per kilo
kilomet|r (**-ra, -ry**; *loc sg* **-rze**) *m* kilometre (*Brit*), kilometer (*US*); **90 ~ów na godzinę** 90 kilometres an hour; **w odległości pięciu ~ów** five kilometres away
kim *pron inst, loc od* **kto**; **z ~ się spotkałeś?** who did you meet?
kimś *pron inst, loc od* **ktoś**
ki|no (**-na, -na**; *loc sg* **-nie**) *nt* **1** (*obiekt*) cinema (*Brit*), (movie) theater (*US*) **2** (*rodzaj sztuki*) the cinema (*Brit*), the movies *pl* (*US*); **iść** (**pójść** *pf*) **do kina** to go to the cinema; **co grają dziś w kinie?** what's on at the cinema today?
kios|k (**-ku, -ki**; *inst sg* **-kiem**) *m* (*z gazetami, z biletami*) kiosk
kiszony *adj* (*ogórek*) pickled; **kiszona kapusta** sauerkraut
klap|ki (**-ek**) *pl* (*buty*) flip-flops *pl*
kla|sa (**-sy, -sy**; *dat sg & loc sg* **-sie**) *f* **1** class **2** (*w szkole*) class **3** (*pomieszczenie w szkole*) classroom **4** (*rocznik uczniów*) form (*Brit*), grade (*US*); **miejsca w pierwszej/drugiej klasie** seats in first/second class
klasów|ka (**-ki, -ki**; *dat sg & loc sg* **-ce**; *gen pl* **-ek**) *f* test; **dostawać** (**dostać** *pf*) **piątkę z klasówki** to get top marks in the class test
klasyfik|ować (**-uję, -ujesz**; *pf* **s-**) *vt* to classify
klaszto|r (**-ru, -ry**; *loc sg* **-rze**) *m* **1** (*dla zakonników*) monastery **2** (*dla zakonnic*) convent; **wstępować** (**wstąpić** *pf*) **do ~u** to enter a monastery/convent
klawiatu|ra (**-ry, -ry**; *dat sg & loc sg* **-rze**) *f* (*komputera, fortepianu*) keyboard
klej (**-u, -e**) *m* (*roślinny, stolarski*) glue
klien|t (**-ta, -ci**; *loc sg* **-cie**) *m* **1** (*kupujący*) customer **2** (*interesant*) client
klient|ka (**-ki, -ki**; *dat sg & loc sg* **-ce**; *gen pl* **-ek**) *f* **1** (*kupująca*) customer **2** (*interesantka*) client
klima|t (**-tu**; *loc sg* **-cie**) *m* (*nom pl* **-ty**) (*zwrotnikowy, łagodny*) climate
klimatyzacj|a (**-i**) *f* air conditioning
klimatyzowany *adj* (*samochód, pomieszczenie*) air-conditioned
klini|ka (**-ki, -ki**; *dat sg & loc sg* **-ce**) *f* clinic
klisz|a (**-y, -e**) *f* (*w fotografii*) film
klu|b (**-bu, -by**; *loc sg* **-bie**) *m* (*nocny, sportowy*) club; **~ studencki** students' union

klucz (**-a, -e**; *gen pl* **-y**) *m* **1** (*do zamykania i otwierania zamka*) key **2** (*w muzyce*) clef **3** (*w technice*) spanner (*Brit*), wrench (*US*); **dobra dieta to ~ do zdrowia** a good diet is the key to good health; **zamykać (zamknąć** *pf*) **coś na ~** to lock sth

klus|ka (**-ki, -ki**; *dat sg & loc sg* **-ce**; *gen pl* **-ek**) *f* dumpling; **mieć kluski w gębie** (*przen*) to mumble

kła|mać (**-mię, -miesz**; *pf* **s-**) *vi* to lie; **on zawsze kłamie jak najęty** he always tells bare-faced lies

kłamc|a (**-y, -y**) *m decl like f in sg* liar

kłamst|wo (**-wa, -wa**; *loc sg* **-wie**) *nt* lie

kłani|ać się (**-am, -asz**; *pf* **ukłonić**) *vr* **1** (*schylać się*) to bow **2** (*kiwnąć głową*) to nod **3** (*przen*) to say hello

kła|ść (**-dę, -dziesz**; *imp* **-dź**; *pt* **-dł**; *pf* **położyć**) *vt* **1** (*na półce, na półkę*) to put **2** (*do kieszeni*) to put **3** (*układać*) to lay; **~ się** *vr* **1** (*na wersalce*) to lie down **2** (*iść spać*) to go to bed; **~ coś do głowy komuś** to put something in sb's head

kłopo|t (**-tu, -ty**; *loc sg* **-cie**) *m* (*domowy, finansowy*) problem; **kłopoty** *pl* trouble; **w szkole ma ciągle ~y** he's always having problems at school; **on znów wpadł w ~y** he's in trouble again

kłopotliwy *adj* **1** (*przysparzający kłopotu*) inconvenient **2** (*cisza, pytanie*) embarrassing

kłó|cić się (**-cę, -cisz**; *imp* **-ć**; *pf* **po-**) *vr* (*spierać się*) to quarrel

kłót|nia (**-ni, -nie**; *gen pl* **-ni**) *f* (*spór*) quarrel

kobiecy *adj* **1** (*urok*) feminine **2** (*narządy*) female **3** (*powieść, dolegliwość*) women's

kobie|ta (**-ty, -ty**; *dat sg & loc sg* **-cie**) *f* woman; **~ lekkich obyczajów** loose woman

koch|ać (**-am, -asz**) *vt* (*z całego serca, namiętnie*) to love; **~ się** *vr* to love each other; **kochają się dwa razy dziennie** they make love twice a day; **kocha się w niej od lat** he has been in love with her for years

kochany *adj* dear

ko|d (**-du, -dy**; *loc sg* **-dzie**) *m* code; **podaj mi swój ~ pocztowy** give me your postcode (*Brit*) *lub* zip code (*US*)

kodek|s (**-su, -sy**; *loc sg* **-sie**) *m* (*cywilny, handlowy*) code; **~ drogowy** rules of the road, ≈ Highway Code (*Brit*)

kogo *pron gen, acc od* **kto**; **~ brakuje?** who's absent?; **~ widziałeś?** who(m) did you meet?; **ktoś, ~ znam** someone I know

kogoś *pron gen, acc od* **ktoś**

koko|s (**-su** *lub* **-sa, -sy**; *loc sg* **-sie**) *m* coconut

kolacj|a (**-i, -e**; *gen pl* **-i**) *f* **1** supper **2** (*wystawna, uroczysta*) dinner

kola|no (**-na, -na**; *loc sg* **-nie**) *nt* knee; **przeprosił na kolanach** he begged forgiveness on bended knees; **dziecko siedzi na kolanach u mamy** the child sits on his mother's lap; **stał w wodzie po kolana** he was standing knee-deep in water

kolarst|wo (**-wa**; *loc sg* **-wie**) *nt* cycling

kolczy|k (**-ka, -ki**; *inst sg* **-kiem**) *m* earring

kole|ga (**-gi, -dzy**; *dat sg & loc sg* **-dze**) *m decl like f in sg* **1** friend **2** (*w szkole*) school friend **3** (*w pracy*) colleague

kole|j (**-i, -je**; *gen pl* **-i**) *f* **1** (*pociągi*) railway (*Brit*), railroad (*US*) **2** (*środek transportu*) rail **3** (*jeden po drugim*) turn; **jechał ~ą do Warszawy** he took the train to Warsaw; **jego ~** *lub* **~ na niego** (it's) his turn; **po kolei** in turn

kolej|ka (**-ki, -ki**; *dat sg & loc sg* **-ce**; *gen pl* **-ek**) *f* **1** (*podmiejska, na krótkich trasach*) local train **2** (*zabawka elektryczna*) model railway (*Brit*) *lub* railroad (*US*) **3** (*wyznaczone miejsce, w szeregu*) turn **4** (*ogonek*) queue (*Brit*), line (*US*)

kolejno *adv* in turn

kolejny *adj* **1** (*jeden po drugim*) next **2** (*sąsiadujący*) consecutive **3** (*jeszcze jeden*) another

kolekcj|a (**-i, -e**; *gen pl* **-i**) *f* (*monet, obrazów*) collection

koleżan|ka (**-ki, -ki**; *dat sg & loc sg* **-ce**; *gen pl* **-ek**) *f* **1** friend **2** (*w szkole*) school friend **3** (*w pracy*) colleague

koleżeński *adj* (*relacja, osoba*) friendly
kolę|da (**-dy, -dy**; *dat sg & loc sg* **-dzie**) *f* (Christmas) carol
kolo|r (**-ru, -ry**; *loc sg* **-rze**) *m* **1** (*barwa: jasny, intensywny*) colour (*Brit*), color (*US*) **2** (*karo, pik*) suit; **jaki ~ mają te spodnie?** what colour are these trousers?; **jakiego ~u jest ta bluzka?** what colour is this blouse?
kolorowy *adj* **1** (*barwny*) colour (*Brit*), color (*US*) **2** (*różnorodny*) colourful (*Brit*), colorful (*US*)
kołd|ra (**-ry, -ry**; *dat sg & loc sg* **-rze**; *gen pl* **-er**) *f* quilt
ko|ło (**-ła, -ła**; *loc sg* **-le**; *gen pl* **kół**) *nt* **1** (*okrąg*) circle **2** (*w matematyce*) circle **3** (*w samochodzie*) wheel ▷ *prep +gen* (*niedaleko*) by, next to; **jeździć w ~** to go round in circles
kołysan|ka (**-ki, -ki**; *dat sg & loc sg* **-ce**; *gen pl* **-ek**) *f* lullaby
kołys|ka (**-ki, -ki**; *dat sg & loc sg* **-ce**; *gen pl* **-ek**) *f* cradle; **taki był od kołyski** he's been like that since he was a baby
komedi|a (**-i, -e**; *gen pl* **-i**) *f* **1** (*gatunek w sztuce*) comedy **2** (*przen: obłuda*) game
komen|da (**-dy, -dy**; *dat sg & loc sg* **-dzie**) *f* command; **~ policji** headquarters
komentarz (**-a, -e**; *gen pl* **-y**) *m* **1** commentary **2** (*uwaga*) comment; **odmawiać** (**odmówić** *pf*) **~a** to make no comment
komentato|r (**-ra, -rzy**; *loc sg* **-rze**) *m* commentator
koment|ować (**-uję, -ujesz**; *pf* **s-**) *vt* **1** (*robić uwagi*) to comment on **2** (*relacjonować: w sporcie*) to commentate on
komercyjny *adj* (*sukces, film*) commercial
komfortowy *adj* **1** (*łóżko, sytuacja*) comfortable **2** (*apartament*) luxury
komi|k (**-ka, -cy**; *inst sg* **-kiem**) *m* **1** (*artysta sceniczny*) comic actor **2** (*satyryk*) comedian
komik|s (**-su, -sy**; *loc sg* **-sie**) *m* **1** (*w gazecie*) strip cartoon **2** (*książka*) comic
komi|n (**-na, -ny**; *loc sg* **-nie**) *m* **1** chimney **2** (*w fabryce*) chimney **3** (*lokomotywy*) funnel
komin|ek (**-ka, -ki**; *inst sg* **-kiem**) *m* fireplace
komisaria|t (**-tu, -ty**; *loc sg* **-cie**) *m* (*też:* **~ policji**) police station
komisj|a (**-i, -e**; *gen pl* **-i**) *f* **1** (*śledcza, dyscyplinarna*) committee **2** (*rewizyjna*) board
komite|t (**-tu, -ty**; *loc sg* **-cie**) *m* (*organizacyjny, powitalny*) committee; **~ rodzicielski** ≈ parent-teacher association, ≈ PTA
komo|da (**-dy, -dy**; *dat sg & loc sg* **-dzie**) *f* chest of drawers
komór|ka (**-ki, -ki**; *dat sg & loc sg* **-ce**; *gen pl* **-ek**) *f* **1** (*w biologii*) cell **2** (*pot: telefon*) mobile (*Brit*), cellphone (*US*)
komórkowy *adj* cellular
komplek|s (**-su, -sy**; *loc sg* **-sie**) *m* (*budynków, niższości*) complex
komplemen|t (**-tu, -ty**; *loc sg* **-cie**) *m* compliment
komple|t (**-tu, -ty**; *loc sg* **-cie**) *m* **1** (*zestaw*) set **2** (*ubrań*) suit **3** (*na widowni*) full house **4** (*w samolocie*) full complement of passengers
kompletny *adj* **1** (*zbiór*) complete **2** (*absurd, pomyłka*) total
komplik|ować (**-uję, -ujesz**; *pf* **s-**) *vt* to complicate; **~ się** *vr* to become more complicated
kompo|t (**-tu, -ty**; *loc sg* **-cie**) *m* (*napój z owoców*) stewed fruit
kompromi|s (**-su, -sy**; *loc sg* **-sie**) *m* compromise
kompute|r (**-ra, -ry**; *loc sg* **-rze**) *m* (*osobisty, stacjonarny*) computer
komputerowy *adj* computer
komu *pron dat od* **kto**; **~ to zabrałeś?** who did you take that from?
komuni|a (**-i, -e**; *gen pl* **-i**) *f* communion; **przystępować** (**przystąpić** *pf*) **do Pierwszej Komunii (Świętej)** ≈ to receive one's first (Holy) Communion
komunikacj|a (**-i**) *f* **1** (*miejska, morska*) transport (*Brit*), transportation (*US*) **2** (*międzyludzka*) communication
komunika|t (**-tu, -ty**; *loc sg* **-cie**) *m* **1** (*wiadomość*) communiqué **2** (*ogłoszenie*) announcement

komunik|ować się (-uję, -ujesz) *vr* **1** (*między ludźmi*) to communicate **2** (*kontaktować się*) to keep in touch (with one another)
komuni|sta (-sty, -ści; *dat sg & loc sg* **-ście**) *m decl like f in sg* communist
komunistyczny *adj* (*ustrój, kraj*) communist
komuniz|m (-mu; *loc sg* **-mie**) *m* communism
komuś *pron dat sg od* **ktoś**
koncentr|ować (-uję, -ujesz; *pf* **s-**) *vt* (*gromadzić*) to concentrate
koncepcj|a (-i, -e; *gen pl* **-i**) *f* (*projekt*) conception
koncer|t (-tu, -ty; *loc sg* **-cie**) *m* **1** (*symfoniczny, kameralny*) concert **2** (*utwór instrumentalny*) concerto
kondycj|a (-i) *f* (*forma*) fitness
konfitur|y (-) *pl* conserve *sg*
konflik|t (-tu, -ty; *loc sg* **-cie**) *m* (*spór*) conflict
kongre|s (-su, -sy; *loc sg* **-sie**) *m* (*zjazd partii, organizacji*) congress; **K~ Stanów Zjednoczonych** the U.S. Congress
ko|niec (-ńca, -ńce) *m* **1** end **2** (*w ołówku*) point; **do samego końca** to the bitter end; **liczyć (policzyć** *pf*) **od końca** to count (off) in reverse order; **na końcu języka miałem pytanie** the question was on the tip of my tongue; **w końcu się nam udało** we succeeded in the end; **potrafi związać ~ z końcem** (*przen*) he can make ends meet
koniecznie *adv* absolutely
koniecznoś|ć (-ci) *f* (*potrzeba*) necessity
konieczny *adj* (*niezbędny*) necessary
konkretny *adj* **1** (*wypowiedź*) accurate **2** (*pytanie, sytuacja*) specific **3** (*osoba*) matter-of-fact
konkurencj|a (-i) *f* **1** (*rywalizacja*) competition **2** (*nom pl* **-e**; *gen pl* **-i**) (*rozgrywka sportowa*) event
konkuren|t (-ta, -ci; *loc sg* **-cie**) *m* rival
konkur|ować (-uję, -ujesz) *vi*: **~ z** *+inst* to compete with
konkur|s (-su, -sy; *loc sg* **-sie**) *m* (*piękności, poetycki*) contest
konsekwentny *adj* consistent
konserwacj|a (-i) *f* **1** (*dzieł sztuki*) conservation **2** (*urządzeń mechanicznych*) maintenance
konserwatywny *adj* (*pogląd, partia*) conservative
konserwatyz|m (-mu; *loc sg* **-mie**) *m* conservatism
konserwowy *adj* **1** (*Kulin: mięso*) tinned (*Brit*), canned (*US*) **2** (*ogórek*) pickled
konsula|t (-tu, -ty; *loc sg* **-cie**) *m* consulate
konsumen|t (-ta, -ci; *loc sg* **-cie**) *m* consumer
konsum|ować (-uję, -ujesz; *pf* **s-**) *vt* (*jeść, używać*) to consume
konsumpcj|a (-i) *f* (*jedzenie, używanie*) consumption
kontak|t (-tu, -ty; *loc sg* **-cie**) *m* **1** (*relacja osobista*) contact **2** (*gniazdko elektryczne*) socket (*Brit*), outlet (*US*) **3** (*w instalacji elektrycznej: pot*) switch
kontakt|ować (-uję, -ujesz; *pf* **s-**) *vt*: **~ kogoś z kimś** to put sb in touch with sb; **~ się** *vr*: **~ się (z kimś)** to be in touch (with sb); **często kontaktuje się z rodzicami** he is in regular contact with his parents
kontek|st (-stu, -sty; *loc sg* **-ście**) *m* (*sytuacji, wydarzenia*) context
kon|to (-ta, -ta; *loc sg* **-cie**) *nt* (*bankowe, osobiste*) account; **zakładać (założyć** *pf*) **~ w banku** to open a bank account
kontrak|t (-tu, -ty; *loc sg* **-cie**) *m* (*umowa*) contract
kontra|st (-stu, -sty; *loc sg* **-ście**) *m* (*przeciwieństwo*) contrast
kontrol|a (-i) *f* **1** (*sprawowanie nadzoru*) control **2** (*nom pl* **-e**; *gen pl* **-i**) (*zbadanie*) check **3** (*badanie okresowe*) check-up
kontrole|r (-ra, -rzy; *loc sg* **-rze**) *m* ticket inspector
kontrol|ować (-uję, -ujesz; *pf* **s-**) *vt* (*sprawdzać*) to control; **~ się** *vr* **1** (*panować nad sobą*) to control o.s. **2** (*sprawdzać się wzajemnie*) to check one another
kontuzj|a (-i, -e; *gen pl* **-i**) *f* (*sportowa, nogi*) (minor) injury
kontynen|t (-tu, -ty; *loc sg* **-cie**) *m* (*europejski, amerykański*) continent

kontynu|ować (**-uję, -ujesz**) *vt* to continue
konwencj|a (**-i, -e**; *gen pl* **-i**) *f* (*sposób, styl*) convention
konwencjonalny *adj* **1** (*sposób, transport*) conventional **2** (*gest, rozmowa*) polite
ko|ń (**-nia, -nie**; *gen pl* **-ni**; *inst pl* **-ńmi**) *m* horse; **policjant na koniu** mounted police officer; **silnik o mocy 75 koni mechanicznych** a 75-horsepower engine; **znamy się jak łyse konie** we know each other inside out
końcowy *adj* (*przystanek, rezultat*) final
końców|ka (**-ki, -ki**; *dat sg & loc sg* **-ce**; *gen pl* **-ek**) *f* ending
kończ|yć (**-ę, -ysz**) *vt* **1** (*pf* **s-**) (*rozmowę*) to end **2** (*pf* **s-**) (*obiad, zadanie*) to finish **3** (*pf* **u-**) (*szkołę wyższą*) to graduate from **4** (*pf* **u-** *lub* **s-**) (*szkolenie*) to finish ▷ *vi* to finish; **~ się** *vr* (*pf* **s-**) (*o wycinku czasu*) to end; **kończy nam się chleb** we are running out of bread; **~ nad czymś pracować** to finish working on sth
kooperacj|a (**-i, -e**; *gen pl* **-i**) *f* (*współpraca*) co-operation
koordyn|ować (**-uję, -ujesz**; *pf* **s-**) *vt* (*zamierzenia, działania*) to co-ordinate
ko|pać (**-pię, -piesz**) *vt* **1** (*pf* **-pnąć**) (*piłkę, przeciwnika*) to kick **2** (*pf* **wy-**) (*w ziemi*) to dig ▷ *vi* (*uderzać nogą: osobę, przedmiot*) to kick
kopal|nia (**-ni, -nie**; *gen pl* **-ni**) *f* (*soli, węgla*) mine
koper|ta (**-ty, -ty**; *dat sg & loc sg* **-cie**) *f* (*na korespondencję*) envelope
kopi|a (**-i, -e**; *gen pl* **-i**) *f* **1** (*nie oryginał*) reproduction **2** (*odbitka*) copy
kopi|ować (**-uję, -ujesz**) *vt* **1** (*pf* **s-**) (*dokumenty, obrazy*) to copy **2** (*pf* **prze-**) (*w informatyce*) to copy
kop|nąć (**-nę, -niesz**; *imp* **-nij**) *vb pf od* **kopać**
Kora|n (**-nu**; *loc sg* **-nie**) *m* (*święta księga islamu*) the Koran
kor|ek (**-ka, -ki**; *inst sg* **-kiem**) *m* **1** (*do butelki*) cork **2** (*nom pl* **-ki**) (*do zlewu*) plug **3** (*pot: w instalacji elektrycznej: bezpiecznik*) fuse (Brit), fuze (US) **4** (*na drodze*) traffic jam
korepetycj|e (**-i**) *pl* (*z matematyki*) private lessons
korespondencj|a (**-i**) *f* **1** (*wysyłanie i otrzymywanie listów*) correspondence **2** (*listy, pocztówki*) post (Brit), mail (US) **3** (*nom pl* **-e**; *gen pl* **-i**) (*artykuł*) report
korespond|ować (**-uję, -ujesz**) *vi*: **~ z** *+inst* to correspond with
korkocią|g (**-gu, -gi**; *inst sg* **-giem**) *m* **1** (*do otwierania butelek*) corkscrew **2** (*w lotnictwie*) spin
koro|na (**-ny, -ny**; *loc sg* **-nie**) *f* crown; **zrób to, a ~ ci z głowy nie spadnie** it wouldn't hurt you to do it
korupcj|a (**-i**) *f* (*branie, dawanie łapówek*) corruption
koryg|ować (**-uję, -ujesz**; *pf* **s-**) *vt* (*naprawiać*) to correct
korytarz (**-a, -e**; *gen pl* **-y**) *m* (*w budynku*) corridor
korze|ń (**-nia, -nie**; *gen pl* **-ni**) *m* root; **korzenie** *pl* **1** (*genealogia, początki*) roots **2** (*przyprawy*) spice(s *pl*)
korzyst|ać (**-am, -asz**; *pf* **s-**) *vi*: **~ z czegoś** (*z urządzenia, pomieszczenia*) to use sth; (*z przysługujących praw*) to exercise sth; **~ z okoliczności** to take advantage of the circumstances
korzystny *adj* **1** (*przynoszący zyski*) profitable **2** (*wpływ, okoliczności*) auspicious
korzyś|ć (**-ci, -ci**; *gen pl* **-ci**) *f* **1** (*osobista*) advantage **2** (*finansowa*) benefit
kosmetyczny *adj* (*zabieg, preparat*) cosmetic; **gabinet ~** beauty salon *lub* parlor (US)
kosmety|k (**-ku, -ki**; *inst sg* **-kiem**) *m* (*upiększający, naturalny*) cosmetic
kosmonau|ta (**-ty, -ci**; *loc sg* **-cie**) *m decl like f in sg* **1** astronaut **2** (*rosyjski*) cosmonaut
kosmopoli|ta (**-ty, -ci**; *dat sg & loc sg* **-cie**) *m decl like f in sg* (*osoba*) cosmopolitan
kosmo|s (**-su**; *loc sg* **-sie**) *m* **1** (*przestrzeń pozaziemska*) (outer) space **2** (*wszechświat*) cosmos
kostiu|m (**-mu, -my**; *loc sg* **-mie**) *m* **1** (*żakiet i spódnica*) suit **2** (*dla aktora*) costume; **~ kąpielowy** swimming costume

kosz (**-a, -e**; *gen pl* **-y** *lub* **-ów**) *m* (*wiklinowy, z kwiatami*) basket; **mecz ~a** (*pot*) basketball game; **~ na śmieci** dustbin (*Brit*), garbage can (*US*)

koszma|r (**-ru, -ry**; *loc sg* **-rze**) *m* (*zły sen, tragedia*) nightmare

koszmarny *adj* (*sen, sytuacja*) nightmarish

kosz|t (**-tu, -ty**; *loc sg* **-cie**) *m* (*w gospodarce*) cost; **koszty** *pl* **1** (*społeczne, zdrowotne*) costs **2** (*wydana suma pieniędzy*) expenses; **robić** (**zrobić** *pf*) **coś ~em czegoś/kogoś** (*przen*) to do something at the cost of sth/at sb's expense

kosztory|s (**-su, -sy**; *loc sg* **-sie**) *m* (*plan wydatków*) estimate (of costs)

koszt|ować (**-uję, -ujesz**) *vt* **1** (*o produkcie*) to cost **2** (*pf* **s-**) (*o jedzeniu, napojach*) to try

kosztowny *adj* (*prezent, zabawa*) expensive

koszul|a (**-i, -e**) *f* (*z krótkimi, długimi rękawami*) shirt; **~ nocna** nightdress

koszul|ka (**-ki, -ki**; *dat sg & loc sg* **-ce**; *gen pl* **-ek**) *f* (*bawełniana, sportowa*) T-shirt

koszy|k (**-ka, -ki**; *inst sg* **-kiem**) *m dimin od* **kosz**

koszyków|ka (**-ki**; *dat sg & loc sg* **-ce**) *f* basketball

koś|ciół (**-cioła, -cioły**; *loc sg* **-ciele**) *m* **1** (*budowla*) church **2** (*instytucja*) Church; **Głowa Kościoła** Head of the Church

koś|ć (**-ci, -ci**; *gen pl* **-ci**) *f* **1** (*człowieka, zwierzęcia*) bone **2** (*w komputerze*) chip; **kości** *pl* (*gra*) dice; **wieża z kości słoniowej** ivory tower; **spadek był kością niezgody między nimi** the inheritance was a bone of contention between them

ko|t (**-ta, -ty**; *loc sg* **-cie**) *m* cat; **oni ciągle drą ze sobą ~y** (*przen*) they are still at loggerheads

kotle|t (**-ta, -ty**; *loc sg* **-cie**) *m* (*schabowy, smażony*) chop

ko|za (**-zy, -zy**; *dat sg & loc sg* **-zie**; *gen pl* **kóz**) *f* goat

ko|zioł (**-zła, -zły**; *loc sg* **-źle**) *m* billy-goat

Koziroż|ec (**-ca, -ce**) *m* (*Astrol*) Capricorn; **Zwrotnik Koziorożca** Tropic of Capricorn

kożuch (**-a, -y**) *m* **1** (*skóra owcy*) sheepskin **2** (*ciepłe ubranie*) sheepskin coat **3** (*gęsta warstwa na mleku*) skin

kół|ko (**-ka, -ka**; *inst sg* **-kiem**) *nt dimin od* **koło 1** (*rzecz*) ring **2** (*zakreślenie*) circle **3** (*organizacja*) circle; **w ~** (*chodzić*) round in circles; (*mówić*) endlessly

kradzież (**-y, -e**; *gen pl* **-y**) *f* theft; **popełniać** (**popełnić** *pf*) **~** to steal

kraj (**-u, -e**) *m* (*państwo, ojczyzna*) country; **w ~u** at home; **odwiedzać** (**odwiedzić** *pf*) **ciepłe ~e** to travel to warmer climes; **wiadomości z ~u i ze świata** domestic and international news

krajobra|z (**-zu, -zy**; *loc sg* **-zie**) *m* (*nizinny, górski*) scenery

kraker|s (**-sa, -sy**; *loc sg* **-sie**) *m* cracker

Krak|ów (**-owa**; *loc sg* **-owie**) *m* Cracow

kra|n (**-nu, -ny**; *loc sg* **-nie**) *m* (*z wodą*) tap, faucet (*US*)

kra|ść (**-dnę, -dniesz**; *imp* **-dnij**; *pf* **u-**) *vt* to steal; **ukradł mi portfel** he stole my wallet

kra|ta (**-ty, -ty**; *dat sg & loc sg* **-cie**) *f* **1** (*zabezpieczenie*) grating **2** (*na materiale*) check **3** (*w więzieniu*) bars *pl*; **za kradzież dostał się za kraty** he went to prison for theft

krat|ka (**-ki, -ki**; *dat sg & loc sg* **-ce**; *gen pl* **-ek**) *f dimin od* **krata**; (*puste miejsce w formularzu*) blank; **w kratkę** (*materiał*) checked; **chodzi do szkoły w kratkę** (*pot*) he goes to school on and off

kraul (**-a**) *m* (*styl pływacki*) crawl

krawa|t (**-ta** *lub* **-tu, -ty**; *loc sg* **-cie**) *m* tie

krawco|wa (**-wej, -we**) *f decl like adj* dressmaker

krawę|dź (**-dzi, -dzie**; *gen pl* **-dzi**) *f* (*skraj*) edge

krawężni|k (**-ka, -ki**; *inst sg* **-kiem**) *m* kerb (*Brit*), curb (*US*)

kra|wiec (**-wca, -wcy**) *m* **1** (*dla mężczyzn*) tailor **2** (*dla kobiet*) dressmaker

krawiect|wo (**-wa**; *loc sg* **-wie**) *nt* **1** (*dla kobiet*) dressmaking **2** (*dla mężczyzn*) tailoring

kr|ąg (**-ęgu, -ęgi**; *inst sg* **-ęgiem**) *m* **1** (*figura geometryczna*) circle **2** (*przen: przyjaciół*) circle **3** (*przen: badań*) area
krąże|nie (**-nia**) *nt* (*obieg*) circulation
krąż|yć (**-ę, -ysz**) *vi* **1** (*o ptaku*) to circle **2** (*o krwi*) to circulate **3** (*o rzeczy*) to be passed around **4** (*po orbicie*) to rotate
kreacj|a (**-i, -e**; *gen pl* **-i**) *f* (*elegancki strój*) outfit
kre|da (**-dy, -dy**; *dat sg & loc sg* **-dzie**) *f* (*do tablicy*) chalk
kred|ka (**-ki, -ki**; *dat sg & loc sg* **-ce**; *gen pl* **-ek**) *f* **1** crayon **2** (*do rysowania*) coloured (*Brit*) *lub* colored (*US*) pencil; **~ do ust** lipstick
kredy|t (**-tu, -ty**; *loc sg* **-cie**) *m* (*hipoteczny, inwestycyjny*) credit; **tracić** (**stracić** *pf*) **u kogoś ~** (*przen*) to lose favour (*Brit*) *lub* favor (*US*) with sb
kre|m (**-mu, -my**; *loc sg* **-mie**) *m* (*czekoladowy, waniliowy*) cream; **~ do rąk/stóp** hand/foot cream
kremowy *adj* cream
kres|ka (**-ki, -ki**; *dat sg & loc sg* **-ce**; *gen pl* **-ek**) *f* **1** (*prosta linia*) line **2** (*myślnik*) dash **3** (*łącznik*) hyphen **4** (*nad, pod wyrazem*) diacritical mark **5** (*pozioma linia na termometrze*) mark
kreskówk|ka (**-ki, -ki**; *dat sg & loc sg* **-ce**; *gen pl* **-ek**) *f* (*gatunek filmowy*) cartoon
kreśl|ić (**-ę, -isz**) *vt* **1** (*szkicować*) to draw **2** (*słowa*) to cross out
kr|ew (**-wi**) *f* blood; **grupa krwi** blood group; **to bohater z krwi i kości** he's every inch a hero; **~ odpłynęła mu z twarzy** the blood drained from his face; **zbrodnia z zimną krwią** a crime committed in cold blood
krewet|ka (**-ki, -ki**; *dat sg & loc sg* **-ce**; *gen pl* **-ek**) *f* prawn
krewn|a (**-ej**) *f decl like adj* relative
krew|ny (**-nego, -ni**) *m decl like adj* relative
kręc|cić (**-cę, -cisz**; *imp* **-ć**) *vt* **1** (*włosy w loki*) to curl **2** (*o wąsach*) to twirl **3** (*mieszać składniki*) to mix; **~ się** *vr* **1** (*wirować*) to spin **2** (*na siedzeniu*) to squirm; **~** (**po~** *pf*) **głową z niedowierzaniem** to shake one's head in disbelief; **~ film w Polsce** to shoot a film (*Brit*) *lub* movie (*US*) in Poland; **łza kręci mi się w oku** it brings a tear to my eye; **kręci mu się w głowie** his head is spinning
kręgosłu|p (**-pa, -py**; *loc sg* **-pie**) *m* spine; **~ moralny** (*przen*) moral backbone; **to człowiek bez ~a** (*przen*) he's a spineless individual
krępy *adj* stocky
kr|oić (**-oję, -oisz**; *imp* **-ój**) *vt* **1** (*pf* **u-**) (*na kawałki*) to cut **2** (*pf* **s-**) (*ubranie*) to tailor; **~** (**po~** *pf*) **coś w kostkę/w paski** to dice sth/cut sth in strips; **kroi mi się podwyżka** (*przen*) I'm due a (pay) rise (*Brit*) *lub* raise (*US*)
kro|k (**-ku, -ki**; *inst sg* **-kiem**) *m* **1** (*do przodu, do tyłu*) step **2** (*przen: przedsięwzięcie*) measure **3** (*krocze*) crotch; **co ~ ich spotykam** I meet them at every turn; **robić coś ~ po ~u** to do sth step by step; **o ~ stąd jest nasz dom** our house is (just) a step away; **muszę podjąć ~i w celu zmiany pracy** I must make an effort to get a new job
krokodyl (**-a, -e**; *gen pl* **-i**) *m* crocodile
krom|ka (**-ki, -ki**; *dat sg & loc sg* **-ce**; *gen pl* **-ek**) *f* (*chleba*) slice (of bread)
krop|ka (**-ki, -ki**; *dat sg & loc sg* **-ce**; *gen pl* **-ek**) *f* **1** (*punkt*) dot **2** (*znak na końcu zdania*) full stop (*Brit*), period (*US*); **czas postawić kropkę nad i** (*przen*) it's time to spell it out; **znów znalazł się w kropce** he found himself once again put on the spot
kropl|a (**-i, -e**; *gen pl* **-i**) *f* drop; **krople** *pl* (*żołądkowe, do oczu*) drops; **~ w morzu** (*przen*) a drop in the ocean
kroplów|ka (**-ki, -ki**; *dat sg & loc sg* **-ce**; *gen pl* **-ek**) *f* (*w medycynie*) drip; **dwa dni leżał pod kroplówką** he was on a drip for two days
kro|sta (**-sty, -sty**; *loc sg* **-ście**) *f* pimple
kr|owa (**-owy, -owy**; *dat sg & loc sg* **-owie**; *gen pl* **-ów**) *f* cow
król (**-a**) *m* **1** (*nom pl* **-owie**) (*dziedziczny, elekcyjny*) king **2** (*nom pl* **-e**) (*figura w szachach, kartach*) king; **Święto Trzech K~i** (*uroczystość religijna*) Epiphany

królest|wo (**-wa, -wa**; *loc sg* **-wie**) *nt* kingdom
królewicz (**-a, -e**) *m* (*syn króla*) prince
króle|wna (**-wny, -wny**; *dat sg & loc sg* **-wnie**; *gen pl* **-wien**) *f* (*córka króla*) princess
królewski *adj* (*zamek, dwór*) royal
króli|k (**-ka, -ki**; *inst sg* **-kiem**) *m* rabbit; **nie jestem ~iem doświadczalnym** I'm not a guinea pig
królo|wa (**-wej, -we**) *f decl like adj* queen
król|ować (**-uję, -ujesz**) *vi* (*rządzić*) to reign
krótki *adj* **1** (*fryzura, ubranie*) short **2** (*zdawkowy*) brief; **~e spodnie** *lub* **spodenki** shorts; **to się uda tylko na krótką metę** (*przen*) that will only be successful in the short term
krótko *adv* **1** (*o włosach*) short **2** (*o wypowiedzi*) briefly; **~ mówiąc, on ma rację** in short, he's right
krótkometrażowy *adj* (*o filmie*) short
krótkowidz (**-a, -e**) *m*: **być ~em** to be near-sighted *lub* short-sighted
kruchy *adj* **1** (*delikatny*) fragile **2** (*bułka*) crisp **3** (*cielęcina*) tender **4** (*przen*) fragile
kru|k (**-ka, -ki**; *inst sg* **-kiem**) *m* (*ptak*) raven
krupni|k (**-ku, -ki**; *inst sg* **-kiem**) *m* barley soup
krwoto|k (**-ku, -ki**; *inst sg* **-kiem**) *m* (*wewnętrzny, z nosa*) bleeding
krykie|t (**-ta**; *loc sg* **-cie**) *m* (*gra*) cricket
Kry|m (**-mu**; *loc sg* **-mie**) *m* the Crimea
kryminali|sta (**-sty, -ści**; *dat sg & loc sg* **-ście**) *m decl like f in sg* (*przestępca*) criminal
kryminalny *adj* (*więzień, policja*) criminal; **film ~** detective film (*Brit*) *lub* movie (*US*)
krymina|ł (**-łu, -ły**; *loc sg* **-le**) *m* **1** (*powieść*) detective novel **2** (*film*) detective film (*Brit*) *lub* movie (*US*)
kryszta|ł (**-łu, -ły**; *loc sg* **-le**) *m* **1** (*skała*) crystal **2** (*szkło*) crystal (glass) **3** (*produkt*) crystal vase
kryształowy *adj* crystal; **to ~ człowiek** he's an honest man
kryty|k (**-ka, -cy**; *inst sg* **-kiem**) *m* (*filmowy, teatralny*) critic
kryty|ka (**-ki**; *dat sg & loc sg* **-ce**; *nom pl* **-ki**) *f* **1** (*wypowiedź oceniająca*) criticism **2** (*filmowa, teatralna*) review
krytyk|ować (**-uję, -ujesz**; *pf* **s-**) *vt* (*oceniać negatywnie*) to criticize
kryzy|s (**-su, -sy**; *loc sg* **-sie**) *m* crisis
kryzysowy *adj* crisis
krza|k (**-ka** *lub* **-ku, -ki**; *inst sg* **-kiem**) *m* bush; **krzaki** *pl* shrubbery *sg*
krze|sło (**-sła, -sła**; *loc sg* **-śle**; *gen pl* **-seł**) *nt* (*drewniane, elektryczne*) chair
krztu|sić się (**-szę, -sisz**; *imp* **-ś**) *vr* to choke
krzy|czeć (**-czę, -czysz**; *pf* **-knąć**) *vi* to shout; **nie krzycz na nią** don't shout at her
krzy|k (**-ku, -ki**; *inst sg* **-kiem**) *m* shout; **i już po ~u** (*przen*) all done
krzyk|nąć (**-nę, -niesz**; *imp* **-nij**) *vb pf od* **krzyczeć**
krzyw|da (**-dy, -dy**; *dat sg & loc sg* **-dzie**) *f* (*fizyczna, moralna*) harm; **wyrządził jej krzywdę** he hurt her
krzyw|dzić (**-dzę, -dzisz**; *imp* **-dź**; *pf* **s-**) *vt* to harm
krzywy *adj* **1** (*nie prosty*) crooked **2** (*o nogach*) knock-kneed **3** (*o powierzchni*) uneven; **patrzy na niego ~m okiem** (*przen*) she is frowning at him
krzyż (**-a, -e**; *gen pl* **-y**) *m* **1** (*rzecz*) cross **2** (*Anat: w okolicach miednicy*) lower back; **Czerwony K~** Red Cross; **przyszło parę osób na ~** (*pot*) only a handful of people turned up
krzyżów|ka (**-ki, -ki**; *dat sg & loc sg* **-ce**; *gen pl* **-ek**) *f* **1** (*zagadka*) crossword (puzzle) **2** (*Bio*) hybrid
krzyży|k (**-ka, -ki**; *inst sg* **-kiem**) *m dimin od* **krzyż**; (*w muzyce*) sharp; **ma piąty ~ na karku** he's in his fifties
ksero *nt inv* **1** (*pot: maszyna robiąca kopie*) photocopier **2** (*pot: kopia*) photocopy
kserokopi|a (**-i, -e**; *gen pl* **-i**) *f* photocopy
kser|ować (**-uję, -ujesz**; *pf* **s-**) *vt* (*robić kopie*) to photocopy

ksiądz (**księdza, księża**; *voc sg* **księże**; *gen pl* **księży**; *inst pl* **księżmi**) *m* priest

książę (**księcia, książęta**; *gen pl* **książąt**) *m* **1** (*tytuł szlachecki*) duke **2** (*syn króla, królowej*) prince

książ|ka (**-ki, -ki**; *dat sg & loc sg* **-ce**; *gen pl* **-ek**) *f* (*dla dzieci, z obrazkami*) book; **~ dla dzieci** a children's book; **~ telefoniczna** phone book

książkowy *adj* **1** (*publikacja*) in book form **2** (*styl*) bookish

księgar|nia (**-ni, -nie**; *gen pl* **-ń**) *f* bookshop (*Brit*), bookstore (*US*)

księgo|wa (**-wej, -we**) *f decl like adj* accountant

księgowoś|ć (**-ci**) *f* **1** (*rachunkowość*) accounting **2** (*dział firmy*) accounts department

księgo|wy (**-wego, -wi**) *m decl like adj* accountant

księżnicz|ka (**-ki, -ki**; *dat sg & loc sg* **-ce**; *gen pl* **-ek**) *f* princess

księżyc (**-a, -e**) *m* moon

kształ|cić (**-cę, -cisz**; *imp* **-ć**; *pf* **wy-**) *vt* **1** (*w szkole*) to educate **2** (*charakter*) to form; **~ się** *vr*: **~ się (na inżyniera)** to train (to be an engineer); **podróże kształcą** travel broadens the mind

kształ|t (**-tu, -ty**; *loc sg* **-cie**) *m* shape; **ma bujne, kobiece ~y** she has voluptuous, feminine curves; **w kształcie piłki** shaped like a ball

kształt|ować (**-uję, -ujesz**; *pf* **u-**) *vt* to shape; **~ się** *vr* to develop

SŁOWO KLUCZOWE

kto *pron* **1** (*w zdaniach pytajnych*) who; **kto to (jest)?** who is it?; **kto przyjdzie?** who's coming?
2 (*w zdaniach podrzędnych*) who; **sprawdź, kto wyszedł** see who has left; **ten, kto go spotka** whoever meets him
3: **nieważne, kto przyjedzie** it doesn't matter who comes

ktokolwiek *pron* **1** (*nieważne kto*) anyone **2** (*ten, kto*) whoever; **~ z nas** any one of us; **~ widział...** whoever saw...

ktoś *pron* (*w zdaniach orzekających*) someone; (*w zdaniach pytających*) anyone; **czy widziałeś kogoś?** did you see anybody *lub* anyone?; **ona myśli, że jest naprawdę kimś** she thinks she's really somebody; **~ inny przyjdzie** someone else is coming; **~, kogo nie widziałem** someone I didn't see

którędy *pron* which way

SŁOWO KLUCZOWE

który *pron decl like adj* **1** (*w zdaniach pytajnych*) which; **którą gazetę chcesz?** which paper do you want?; **którego dzisiaj mamy?** what's the date today?; **która jest godzina?** what time is it?, what's the time?; **który z was to zna?** which one of you knows?
2 (*w zdaniach podrzędnych*): **człowiek, którego znasz...** the man (that) you know...; **nie wiem, którą z nich wybrać** I don't know which to choose; **ludzie, z którymi mieszkam** the people (that) I live with; **dziewczyna, z której mamą rozmawiałem** the girl whose mother I was talking to

kub|ek (**-ka, -ki**; *inst sg* **-kiem**) *m* mug

kub|eł (**-ła, -ły**; *loc sg* **-le**) *m* **1** (*plastikowy, aluminiowy*) bucket **2** (*kosz na śmieci*) bin (*Brit*), trash can (*US*)

kuchar|ka (**-ki, -ki**; *dat sg & loc sg* **-ce**; *gen pl* **-ek**) *f* cook

kucharski *adj*: **książka kucharska** cookbook

kucharz (**-a, -e**; *gen pl* **-y**) *m* cook, chef

kuchen|ka (**-ki, -ki**; *dat sg & loc sg* **-ce**; *gen pl* **-ek**) *f* **1** (*gazowa, elektryczna*) cooker **2** (*też*: **~ turystyczna**) camping stove; **~ mikrofalowa** microwave (oven)

kuchenny *adj* (*zestaw, mebel*) kitchen

kuch|nia (**-ni, -nie**; *gen pl* **-ni**) *f* **1** (*miejsce w domu*) kitchen **2** (*sztuka kulinarna*) cuisine **3** (*przyrządzanie potraw*) cooking

kuf|el (**-la, -le**; *gen pl* **-li**) *m* **1** (*do piwa*) (beer) mug **2** (*ilość płynu*) ≈ pint (of beer)

kul|a (**-i, -e**) *f* **1** (*rzecz*) ball **2** (*w geometrii: bryła*) sphere **3** (*nabój*) bullet; **chodzić o kuli/~ch** to walk on crutches; **~ ziemska** the globe

kulisty *adj* (*kształt*) spherical

kultu|ra (**-ry, -ry**; *dat sg & loc sg* **-rze**) *f* (*narodowa, starożytna*) culture; **dom kultury** ≈ community centre (*Brit*) *lub* center (*US*)

kulturalny *adj* **1** (*dorobek, wydarzenie*) cultural **2** (*osoba*) well-mannered, cultured

kulturowy *adj* (*krąg*) cultural

kump|el (**-la, -le**; *gen pl* **-li**) *m* (*pot*) mate

ku|pić (**-pię, -pisz**) *vb pf od* **kupować**

kupny *adj* (shop-) bought (*Brit*), store-bought (*US*)

ku|pować (**-puję, -pujesz**; *pf* **-pić**) *vt* to buy

kupując|y (**-ego, -y**) *m decl like adj* buyer

ku|ra (**-ry, -ry**; *loc sg* **-rze**) *f* hen; **ale z niej ~ domowa** (*pej*) she's such a homebody; **ten interes to ~ znosząca złote jaja** this business is a sure-fire winner

kuracj|a (**-i, -e**; *gen pl* **-i**) *f* (*odchudzająca, zdrowotna*) treatment

kurcza|k (**-ka, -ki**; *inst sg* **-kiem**) *m* chicken

kur|s (**-su, -sy**; *loc sg* **-sie**) *m* **1** (*autobusem, taksówką*) journey **2** (*Żegl: kierunek*) course **3** (*wymiany walut*) (exchange) rate **4** (*cena na giełdzie*) price **5** (*w szkole, na uniwersytecie*) course

kurt|ka (**-ki, -ki**; *dat sg & loc sg* **-ce**; *gen pl* **-ek**) *f* jacket

kur|wa (**-wy, -wy**; *dat sg & loc sg* **-wie**; *gen pl* **-ew**) *f* (*pot!: prostytutka*) whore (*pot!*)

kuzy|n (**-na, -ni**; *loc sg* **-nie**) *m* cousin

kuzyn|ka (**-ki, -ki**; *dat sg & loc sg* **-ce**; *gen pl* **-ek**) *f* cousin

kwadran|s (**-sa, -se**; *loc sg* **-sie**) *m* quarter (*of an hour*); **~ po czwartej** a quarter past (*Brit*) *lub* after (*US*) four; **za ~ ósma** a quarter to eight; **~ akademicki** *15 minute period at the start of each lecture during which the lecture must begin*

kwadra|t (**-tu, -ty**; *loc sg* **-cie**) *m* **1** (*figura geometryczna*) square **2** (*potęga*): **sześć do ~u** six squared; **dureń do ~u** (*pot: pej*) a complete idiot

kwadratowy *adj* square

kwarantan|na (**-ny, -ny**; *dat sg & loc sg* **-nie**) *f* quarantine

kwa|s (**-su, -sy**; *loc sg* **-sie**) *m* acid

kwaśny *adj* sour; **mleko jest już kwaśne** the milk's gone off; **~ deszcz** acid rain

kwiaciar|nia (**-ni, -nie**; *gen pl* **-ni**) *f* florist('s)

kwia|t (**-tu, -ty**; *loc sg* **kwiecie**) *m* **1** (*ogrodowy*) flower **2** (*na drzewie*) blossom **3** (*doniczkowy*) plant

kwie|cień (**-tnia, -tnie**; *gen pl* **-tni**) *m* April

kwit|nąć (**-nie**) *vi* **1** (*kwiaty*) to bloom **2** (*drzewa*) to blossom; **jego życie towarzyskie kwitnie od lat** he has had a busy social life for years

kwo|ta (**-ty, -ty**; *dat sg & loc sg* **-cie**) *f* (*suma pieniędzy*) sum; **~ 200 złotych** the sum of 200 zlotys

l

laboratori|um (**-um, -a**; *gen pl* **-ów**) *nt inv in sg* (*językowe, chemiczne*) lab

lać (**leję, lejesz**) *vt* **1** (*wodę*) to pour **2** (*pf* **z-**) (*pot: bić człowieka*) to belt ▷ *vi* **1** (*o ulewnym deszczu*) to pour **2** (*pot!: sikać*) to piss (*pot!*); **leję na to!** (*pot!*) I don't give a damn!; **~ się** *vr* **1** (*o płynie*) to flow **2** (*pot: w bijatyce*) to fight

lakie|r (**-ru, -ry**; *loc sg* **-rze**) *m* (*do malowania powierzchni*) varnish; **malować** (**pomalować** *pf*) **paznokcie ~em do paznokci** to varnish one's nails; **niestety nie ma ~u do włosów** sorry, we don't have any hair spray

lakier|ować (**-uję, -ujesz**; *pf* **po-**) *vt* **1** (*paznokcie*) to varnish **2** (*drewno*) to varnish **3** (*karoserię*) to paint

lal|ka (**-ki, -ki**; *dat sg & loc sg* **-ce**; *gen pl* **-ek**) *f* **1** (*dla dzieci*) doll **2** (*w teatrze*) puppet

lament|ować (**-uję, -ujesz**) *vi* (*użalać się*) to lament

lam|pa (**-py, -py**; *dat sg & loc sg* **-pie**) *f* **1** (*wisząca, naftowa*) lamp **2** (*w elektronice*) valve (*Brit*), (vacuum) tube (*US*); **~ błyskowa** (*Fot*) flash; **~ jarzeniowa** fluorescent light

lapto|p (**-pa, -py**; *loc sg* **-pie**) *m* laptop

laryngolo|g (**-ga, -gowie** *lub* **-dzy**; *inst sg* **-giem**) *m* ear, nose and throat specialist

la|s (**-su, -sy**; *loc sg* **lesie**) *m* **1** (*rozległy*) forest **2** (*niewielki*) wood **3** (*przen: chorągwi, rąk*) forest; **jestem całkiem w lesie z robotą** (*pot: przen*) I am well behind schedule with work

las|ka (**-ki, -ki**; *dat sg & loc sg* **-ce**; *gen pl* **-ek**) *f* **1** walking stick **2** (*pot: atrakcyjna dziewczyna*) chick; **kuleje i musi chodzić o lasce** he has a limp and needs to walk with a stick

lat|a (**-**) *pl* **1** years *pl* **2** (*określenie wieku*) age; **~ pięćdziesiąte/sześćdziesiąte** the fifties/the sixties; **pracuje już od wielu lat** he has been working for many years; **miało to miejsce przed laty** it happened years ago; **ile masz lat?** (*familiar sg*) how old are you?; **mam 20 lat** I'm 20 years old; **sto lat!** many happy returns!; *zob. też* **rok**

lat|ać (**-am, -asz**) *vi +inst* **1** (*samolotem*) to fly **2** (*pot: być zabieganym*) to run; **od tygodnia latam z wywieszonym jęzorem** I've been run ragged for a week

latar|ka (**-ki, -ki**; *dat sg & loc sg* **-ce**; *gen pl* **-ek**) *f* torch (*Brit*), flashlight (*US*)

latar|nia (**-ni, -nie**; *gen pl* **-ni**) *f* (*na ulicy*) street lamp; **~ morska** (*Żegl*) lighthouse; **latarnie lotniskowe** (*Aviat*) landing lights

la|to (**-ta, -ta**; *loc sg* **lecie**) *nt* summer; **wakacje są latem** *lub* **w lecie** the holidays are in the summer

laurea|t (**-ta, -ci**; *loc sg* **-cie**) *m* (*zdobywca nagrody*) laureate

laureat|ka (**-ki, -ki**; *dat sg & loc sg* **-ce**; *gen pl* **-ek**) *f* (*zdobywczyni nagrody*) laureate

ląd|d (**-du, -dy**; *loc sg* **-dzie**) *m* land; **stały ~** mainland, dry land

ląd|ować (**-uję, -ujesz**; *pf* **wy-**) *vi* (*znaleźć się na ziemi*) to land

lądowa|nie (**-nia, -nia**; *gen pl* **-ń**) *nt* (*samolotu*) landing

lądowy *adj* **1** (*formacja wojskowa*) ground **2** (*zwierzęta, rośliny*) terrestrial **3** (*granica państwa*) land **4** (*Geo: klimat*) continental **5** (*komunikacja*) overland; **inżynieria lądowa** civil engineering

le|cieć (**-cę, -cisz**; *impf* **-ć**) *vi* **1** (*pf* **po-**) (*owad, samolot*) to fly **2** (*pf* **po-**) (*o cieczy*) to flow **3** (*pf* **z-**) (*spadać*) to fall (down) **4** (*pf* **po-**) (*pot: szybko biec*) to fly **5** (*pot: program w radiu, telewizji*) to be on
lecz *conj* but
leczeni|e (**-a**) *nt* (*kuracja*) treatment
lecznic|a (**-y, -e**) *f* (*weterynaryjna, dla ludzi*) clinic
lecz|yć (**-ę, -ysz**; *pf* **wy-**) *vt* **1** (*pacjenta*) to treat **2** (*przy pomocy lekarstwa*) to cure; **~ się** *vr* to get treatment
legalnie *adv* legally
legalny *adj* legal
legen|da (**-dy, -dy**; *dat sg & loc sg* **-dzie**) *f* legend; **jego czyn przejdzie do legendy** his deed will become legendary
legitymacj|a (**-i, -e**; *gen pl* **-i**) *f* **1** (*do identyfikacji*) ID **2** (*dowód członkostwa*) membership card
le|k (**-ku, -ki**; *inst sg* **-kiem**) *m* medicine
lekar|ka (**-ki, -ki**; *dat sg & loc sg* **-ce**; *gen pl* **-ek**) *f* doctor
lekarski *adj* **1** (*wizyta, przychodnia*) doctor's **2** (*recepta, zalecenie*) doctor's **3** (*badanie*) medical; **dostał zwolnienie ~e na 2 dni** he got 2 days' sick leave
lekarst|wo (**-wa, -wa**; *loc sg* **-wie**) *nt* **1** medicine **2** (*przen: środek przeciw problemom duchowym*) remedy; **nie było jedzenia ani na ~** there was absolutely no food
lekarz (**-a, -e**; *gen pl* **-y**) *m* doctor
lekcj|a (**-i, -e**; *gen pl* **-i**) *f* lesson; **lekcje** *pl* (*praca domowa*): **odrabiać** (**odrobić** *pf*) **lekcje** to do (one's) homework; **~ fizyki/ polskiego** physics/Polish class
lekki *adj* **1** (*mało ważący*) light **2** (*nieznaczny*) slight **3** (*mało wyczuwalny*) faint
lekko *adv* **1** lightly **2** (*nieznacznie: unosić się, posuwać*) slightly; **~ licząc, wydał 200 złotych** he spent at least 200 zlotys
lekkomyślnie *adv* recklessly
lekkomyślny *adj* reckless
le|nić się (**-nię, -nisz**; *imp* **-ń**) *vr* to sit around idle
lenist|wo (**-wa**; *loc sg* **-wie**) *nt* laziness; **oddawać** (**oddać** *pf*) **się słodkiemu lenistwu** to laze about
le|ń (**-nia, -nie**; *gen pl* **-ni** *lub* **-niów**) *m* layabout; **ale z niego śmierdzący ~!** (*pot*) what a shirker!
lepiej *adv comp od* **dobrze** better; **coraz ~ pracował** he worked better and better; **im prędzej to zrobisz, tym ~** the sooner you do it, the better; **~ już pójdę** I'd better go now
lepszy *adj comp od* **dobry** better; **wziął z sobą pierwszy ~ parasol** (*pot*) he took any old umbrella
lesbij|ka (**-ki, -ki**; *dat sg & loc sg* **-ce**; *gen pl* **-ek**) *f* lesbian
lesie *n zob.* **las**
letni *adj* **1** (*wypoczynek, strój*) summer **2** (*o napojach: nie gorący*) lukewarm; **przestawiać** (**przestawić** *pf*) **zegarek na czas ~** to put the clocks forward
letniskowy *adj* (*domek, kurort*) holiday
lew (**lwa, lwy**; *loc sg* **lwie**) *m* **1** (*zwierzę*) lion **2** (*Astrol*): **L~** Leo
lewicowy *adj* (*polityk, poglądy*) left-wing
lewo *adv*: **w** *lub* **na ~** (to the) left; **na prawo i ~** all over the place; **na ~** (*pot: prowadzić interesy*) on the quiet
lewy *adj* **1** (*noga, strona*) left **2** (*spodnia strona tkaniny*) reverse **3** (*pot: o dokumentach: nieprawdziwy*) dodgy; **~ pas** (*na drodze*) left lane
leż|eć (**-ę, -ysz**; *pt* **-ał**) *vi* **1** to lie **2** (*o stroju: pasować*) to fit; **jest chory i musi ~ w łóżku** he is ill and must stay in bed; **całe dnie leży do góry brzuchem** (*pot*) he lies around all day
lę|k (**-ku, -ki**; *inst sg* **-kiem**) *m* (*strach*) anxiety; **cierpieć na ~ przestrzeni/ wysokości** to be afraid of open spaces/heights
lęk|ać się (**-am, -asz**) *vr* +*gen* (*bać się*) to fear
lice|um (**-um, -a**; *gen pl* **-ów**) *nt inv in sg* secondary school (*Brit*), high school (*US*); **~ zawodowe** vocational

school; **~ ogólnokształcące** ≈ grammar school (*Brit*), ≈ high school (*US*)

LICEUM

Liceum is a type of secondary school. At present there are some **licea** which teach a general curriculum (humanities, mathematics and science) as well as those **licea** which are more focused on providing training for specific professions. Graduates of both **licea** can take the **matura**.

licyt|ować (**-uję, -ujesz**) *vt* **1** (*pf* **z-**) (*przedmioty na aukcji*) to auction **2** (*pf* **za-**) (*podczas gry w karty*) to bid
licz|ba (**-by, -by**; *dat sg & loc sg* **-bie**) *f* **1** number **2** (*w językoznawstwie*): **~ pojedyncza/mnoga** singular/ plural
liczebni|k (**-ka, -ki**; *inst sg* **-kiem**) *m* (*główny, porządkowy*) number
licznie *adv* (*pojawić się, przyjść*) in large numbers
liczni|k (**-ka, -ki**; *inst sg* **-kiem**) *m* (*urządzenie do mierzenia*) meter
liczny *adj* (*rodzina, obowiązek*) numerous
licz|yć (**-ę, -ysz**) *vt* (*pf* **po-**) to count ▷ *vi* (*pf* **po-**) **1** (*wykonywać działania matematyczne*) to calculate **2** (*dawać wynik*): **klasa liczy 15 osób** there are 15 in the class **3** (*o oczekiwaniach*): **~ na** to count on; **liczę na was** I am counting on you
lide|r (**-ra, -rzy**; *loc sg* **-rze**) *m* (*przywódca*) leader
liftin|g (**-gu, -gi**; *inst sg* **-giem**) *m* facelift
likwid|ować (**-uję, -ujesz**; *pf* **z-**) *vt* **1** (*biedę, dolegliwość*) to eliminate **2** (*przedsiębiorstwo: zamykać*) to liquidate
limi|t (**-tu, -ty**; *loc sg* **-cie**) *m* limit
li|na (**-ny, -ny**; *dat sg & loc sg* **-nie**) *f* rope
lin|ka (**-ki, -ki**; *dat sg & loc sg* **-ce**; *gen pl* **-ek**) *f* line; **~ holownicza** (*Żegl, Aut*) towrope
li|piec (**-pca, -pce**) *m* July
li|s (**-sa, -sy**; *loc sg* **-sie**) *m* fox; **on jest chytry jak ~** he is as sly as a fox; **uważaj, to farbowany ~** (*przen*) look out, it's a con
li|st (**-stu, -sty**; *loc sg* **-ście**) *m* (*miłosny, oficjalny*) letter; **~ zwykły** surface-mail letter; **~ lotniczy** airmail letter; **mamy ~ polecony dla pana** we have a recorded-delivery letter for you; **poprosił o ~ polecający** he asked for a letter of recommendation
li|sta (**-sty, -sty**; *dat sg & loc sg* **-ście**) *f* (*spis przedmiotów, osób*) list; **~ przebojów** (*spis utworów*) the charts *pl*; **sprawdzać** (**sprawdzić** *pf*) **listę obecności** to take the register
listonosz (**-a, -e**; *gen pl* **-y**) *m* postman (*Brit*), mailman (*US*)
listopa|d (**-da, -dy**; *loc sg* **-dzie**) *m* November
liś|ć (**-cia, -cie**; *gen pl* **-ci**; *inst pl* **-ćmi**) *m* leaf
lite|ra (**-ry, -ry**; *loc sg* **-rze**) *f* letter; **pisać** (**napisać** *pf*) **wielką** *lub* **dużą/ małą literą** to write in upper case/ lower case letters; **litery drukowane** printed characters
literatu|ra (**-ry, -ry**; *dat sg & loc sg* **-rze**) *f* (*fachowa, historyczna*) literature; **~ piękna** belles-lettres
lit|r (**-ra, -ry**; *loc sg* **-rze**) *m* litre (*Brit*), liter (*US*)
Lit|wa (**-wy**; *loc sg* **-wie**) *f* Lithuania
li|zać (**-żę, -żesz**; *pf* **-znąć**) *vt* to lick
liza|k (**-ka, -ki**; *inst sg* **-kiem**) *m* lollipop
lodowis|ko (**-ka, -ka**; *inst sg* **-kiem**) *nt* skating *lub* ice rink
lodów|ka (**-ki, -ki**; *dat sg & loc sg* **-ce**; *gen pl* **-ek**) *f* fridge (*Brit*), refrigerator
lod|y (**-ów**) *pl* (*owocowe, czekoladowe*) ice cream *sg*
logiczny *adj* (*błąd, argument*) logical
login (**-u, -y**; *loc sg* **-ie**) *m* (*Komput*) login
lokal (**-u, -e**; *gen pl* **-i** *lub* **-ów**) *m* **1** (*pomieszczenie*) premises *pl* **2** (*gastronomiczny*) restaurant; **bawili się w nocnych ~ach** they went clubbing
lokato|r (**-ra, -rzy**; *loc sg* **-rze**) *m* (*mieszkaniec*) occupant; **dziki ~** squatter

Londy|n (**-nu**; *loc sg* **-nie**) *m* London
lo|s (**-su, -sy**; *loc sg* **-sie**) *m* **1** (*droga życiowa*) lot **2** (*przeznaczenie*) fate **3** (*kupon na loterii*) (lottery) ticket; **zrządzenie ~u** bad fortune; **to prawdziwa ironia ~u!** (*przen*) an ironic twist of fate!
lo|t (**-tu, -ty**; *loc sg* **-cie**) *m* (*ptaka, samolotu*) flight
lotnict|wo (**-wa**; *loc sg* **-wie**) *nt* **1** (*pasażerskie*) aviation **2** (*formacja wojskowa*) air force
lotniczy *adj* (*transport, terminal*) air; **linia lotnicza** airline
lotnis|ko (**-ka, -ka**; *inst sg* **-kiem**) *nt* **1** (*dla pasażerów*) airport **2** (*miejsce do lądowania*) airfield
lód (**lodu, lody**; *loc sg* **lodzie**) *m* ice; **jesteś zimny jak ~** you're as cold as ice; **ma pieniędzy jak lodu** (*pot*) he is rolling in money; *zob. też* **lody**
lś|nić (**-nię, -nisz**; *imp* **-nij**) *vi* to glisten
lub *conj* or; **~ też** or else
lubiany *adj* popular
lu|bić (**-bię, -bisz**) *vt* to like; **~ coś robić** to like doing sth *lub* to do sth; **lubi biegać** he likes running; **~ się** *vr* to like one another; **lubią się od dziecka** they've been friends since childhood
ludnoś|ć (**-ci**) *f* (*miasta, kraju*) population
ludowy *adj* **1** (*sztuka, ubiór*) folk **2** (*Pol: ustrój państwa*) people's
lu|dzie (**-dzi**; *inst pl* **-dźmi**) *pl* people; *zob. też* **człowiek**
ludzki *adj* **1** (*charakter, stworzenie*) human **2** (*stosunek do innych*) humane; **musisz traktować go po ludzku** you've got to treat him humanely
ludzkoś|ć (**-ci**) *f* humanity
luksusowy *adj* (*dom, strój*) luxury
luster|ko (**-ka, -ka**; *inst sg* **-kiem**; *gen pl* **-ek**) *nt* **1** mirror **2** (*wsteczne w samochodzie*) rear-view mirror **3** (*boczne w samochodzie*) wing (*Brit*) *lub* outside (*US*) mirror
lust|ro (**-ra, -ra**; *loc sg* **-rze**; *gen pl* **-er**) *nt* mirror; **co wieczór pije do lustra** he drinks alone every night
lut|y (**-ego, -e**) *m decl like adj* February
luźny *adj* **1** (*marynarka, spódnica*) loose(-fitting) **2** (*w książce: kartka*) loose **3** (*przen: niepoważny: opinia*) casual **4** (*niezobowiązujący: relacja*) casual **5** (*pot: poufały: rozmowa*) casual
lżej *adv comp od* **lekko**
lżejszy *adj comp od* **lekki**

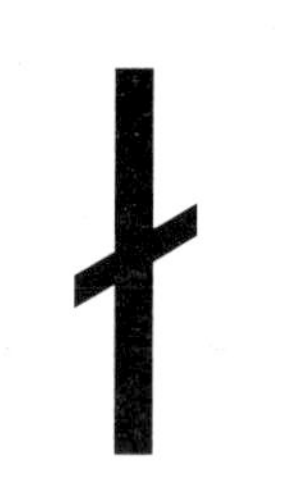

łaci|na (**-ny**; *dat sg & loc sg* **-nie**) *f* Latin; **~ kuchenna** (*pot: przen*) swear words
łaciński *adj* (*alfabet, język*) Latin
ładnie *adv* (*wyglądać, zachowywać się*) nicely; **to ciasto ~ pachnie** that cake smells nice
ładny *adj* **1** (*kobieta*) pretty **2** (*widok*) nice
ład|ować (**-uję, -ujesz**) *vt* **1** (*pf* **za-**) (*towar*) to load **2** (*pf* **na-**) (*baterię*) to charge
ładun|ek (**-ku, -ki**; *inst sg* **-kiem**) *m* **1** load **2** (*towary na statku, w samolocie*) cargo **3** (*wybuchowy*) charge **4** (*elektryczny*) charge
łagodnie *adv* **1** (*z sympatią*) softly **2** (*delikatnie*) gently
łagodny *adj* **1** (*spokojny*) gentle **2** (*delikatny*) mild **3** (*efekt działania*) mild
łag|odzić (**-odzę, -odzisz**; *imp* **-odź** *lub* **-ódź**; *pf* **z-** *lub* **za-**) *vt* **1** (*smutek, rozpacz*) to soothe **2** (*mękę*) to alleviate **3** (*kłótnię*) to moderate
ła|mać (**-mię, -miesz**; *pf* **z-**) *vt* **1** (*nogę, przepisy*) to break **2** (*pokonywać: opór, przeszkody*) to overcome; **~ się** *vr* (*o gałęzi*) to break; **powiedział to łamiącym się głosem** he said it in a faltering voice; **przed deszczem zawsze łamie mnie w kościach** my bones always ache before it rains
łańcuch (**-a, -y**) *m* chain; **~ górski** (*Geo*) mountain range
łańcusz|ek (**-ka, -ki**; *inst sg* **-kiem**) *m* **1** *dimin od* **łańcuch** **2** (*fragment biżuterii*) chain
ła|pać (**-pię, -piesz**; *pf* **z-**) *vt* to catch; **proszę nie ~ mnie za słowa** please stop interrupting me
łapów|ka (**-ki, -ki**; *dat sg & loc sg* **-ce**; *gen pl* **-ek**) *f* bribe
łapu-capu *adv*: **na ~** in a mad rush; **robić coś na ~** to do sth quickly and carelessly
łaskawy *adj* (*przychylny*) favourable (*Brit*), favorable (*US*)
łat|ać (**-am, -asz**; *pf* **za-**) *vt* (*dziurę, spodnie*) to patch
łatwo *adv* easily; **ta uwaga była ~ zrozumiała** that point of view was easy to understand
łatwopalny *adj* (*materiał, płyn*) flammable
łatwowierny *adj* (*człowiek*) gullible
łatwy *adj* (*nieskomplikowany, jasny*) easy
ła|wa (**-wy, -wy**; *dat sg & loc sg* **-wie**) *f* **1** (*miejsce do siedzenia*) bench **2** (*niski stół*) coffee table **3** (*ława przysięgłych: w sądzie*) jury box; **zasiąść na ławie oskarżonych** to be in the dock; **powiedział wszystko kawa na ławę** he put all his cards on the table
ław|ka (**-ki, -ki**; *dat sg & loc sg* **-ce**; *gen pl* **-ek**) *f* **1** (*na zewnątrz*) bench **2** (*w klasie*) desk; **~ kościelna** a pew
łazien|ka (**-ki, -ki**; *dat sg & loc sg* **-ce**; *gen pl* **-ek**) *f* bathroom
łącznie *adv* (*wraz z*): **~ z** *+inst* including; **to należy pisać ~** that should be written as one word
łącz|yć (**-ę, -ysz**; *pf* **po-**) *vt* **1** (*składniki, części, kolory, funkcje*) to combine **2** (*poprzez komunikację*) to connect; **~ się** *vr* **1** (*stykać się: o częściach*) to be joined **2** (*o dłoniach, gałęziach*) to meet **3** (*o trasach*) to merge; **proszę czekać, już łączę!** hold on, I'm putting you through!
łą|ka (**-ki, -ki**; *dat sg & loc sg* **-ce**) *f* meadow
łobu|z (**-za, -zy**; *loc sg* **-zie**) *m* **1** (*niegrzeczny chłopiec*) yob (*Brit*), punk (*US*) **2** (*osoba podła*) rat
ło|kieć (**-kci, -kcie**; *gen pl* **-kci**) *m* elbow; **rozpychać się łokciami** to elbow one's way

łopa|ta (**-ty, -ty**; *dat sg & loc sg* **-cie**) *f* shovel
łoso|ś (**-sia, -sie**; *gen pl* **-si**) *m* salmon
Łot|wa (**-wy**; *dat sg* **-wie**) *f* Latvia
ło|wić (**-wię, -wisz**; *imp* **łów**; *pf* **z-**) *vt* **1** (*polować*) to hunt **2** (*łapać ryby, zwierzynę*) to catch; **~ ryby** to fish
łódź (**łodzi, łodzie**; *gen pl* **łodzi**) *f* boat; **~ podwodna** submarine; **~ ratownicza** lifeboat
łóż|ko (**-ka, -ka**; *inst sg* **-kiem**; *gen pl* **-ek**) *nt* bed
łupież (**-u**) *m* dandruff
łyd|ka (**-ki, -ki**; *dat sg & loc sg* **-ce**; *gen pl* **-ek**) *f* calf
ły|k (**-ku, -ki**; *inst sg* **-kiem**) *m* (*wody, powietrza*) gulp
łyk|ać (**-am, -asz**; *pf* **-nąć**) *vt* (*kęs jedzenia, napój*) to swallow
łyk|nąć (**-nę, -niesz**; *imp* **-nij**) *vb pf od* **łykać**
łysi|eć (**-eję, -ejesz**; *pf* **wy-**) *vi* to go bald
łysi|na (**-ny, -ny**; *loc sg* **-nie**) *f* **1** (*miejsce bez włosów*) bald patch **2** (*na głowie*) baldness
łysy *adj* (*o człowieku, o terenie*) bald
łyżecz|ka (**-ki, -ki**; *dat sg & loc sg* **-ce**; *gen pl* **-ek**) *f* **1** teaspoon **2** (*pojemność*) teaspoonful
łyż|ka (**-ki, -ki**; *dat sg & loc sg* **-ce**; *gen pl* **-ek**) *f* **1** spoon **2** (*pojemność*) spoonful; **~ wazowa** ladle; **~ stołowa cukru** a tablespoon of sugar; **~ do butów** shoehorn
łyż|wa (**-wy, -wy**; *dat sg & loc sg* **-wie**; *gen pl* **-ew**) *f* skate; **pójść na łyżwy** to go skating
łza (**łzy, łzy**; *dat sg & loc sg* **łzie**; *gen pl* **łez**) *f* tear; **on jest czysty jak ~** he's as pure as the driven snow

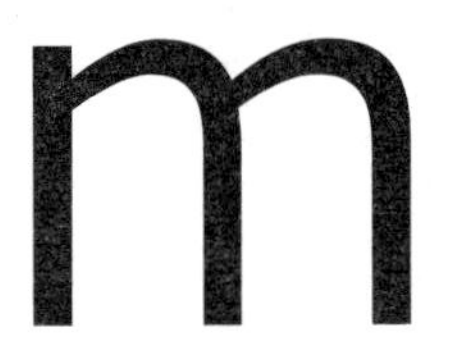

Macedoni|a (**-i**) *f* Macedonia
mach|ać (**-am, -asz**; *pf* **-nąć**) *vi* **1** (*chorągiewką*) to wave **2** (*o psie*) to wag **3** (*o ptaku*) to flap **4** (*wywijać szablą*) to brandish
macierzyński *adj* **1** (*Bio: instynkt*) maternal **2** (*uczucie*) motherly; **brać** (**wziąć** *pf*) **urlop ~** to be on maternity leave
macierzyńst|wo (**-wa**; *loc sg* **-wie**) *nt* motherhood
maco|cha (**-chy, -chy**; *dat sg & loc sg* **-sze**) *f* stepmother
magazy|n (**-nu, -ny**; *loc sg* **-nie**) *m* **1** (*budowla*) warehouse **2** (*miejsce do przechowywania rzeczy*) storeroom **3** (*miesięcznik, tygodnik*) magazine
magi|a (**-i, -e**; *gen pl* **-i**) *f* magic; **to jest dla mnie czarną magią** it's all Greek to me
magiczny *adj* **1** (*przyrząd, zaklęcie*) magic **2** (*moc*) magical
magist|er (**-ra, -rzy** *lub* **-rowie**; *loc sg* **-rze**) *m* **1** (*matematyki, biologii*) Master of Science **2** (*historii, filozofii*) Master of Arts
magisterski *adj* master's (degree); **egzamin ~** finals
magne|s (**-su**; *loc sg* **-sie**) *m* magnet
magnetofo|n (**-nu, -ny**; *loc sg* **-nie**) *m* tape recorder; **odtwarzać** (**odtworzyć** *pf*) **muzykę z ~u** to play music from a tape
magnetowi|d (**-du, -dy**; *loc sg* **-dzie**) *m* (*wideo*) VCR

maho|ń (**-niu, -nie**; *gen pl* **-ni** *lub* **-niów**) *m* (*drzewo, kolor*) mahogany; **meble z mahoniu** mahogany furniture
maj (**-a, -e**) *m* May; **Święto Pierwszego M~a** May Day; **Święto Trzeciego M~a** Third of May Holiday (*Polish national holiday*)
mają *vb zob.* **mieć**
mająt|ek (**-ku**; *inst sg* **-kiem**) *m* **1** (*dobytek*) property **2** (*wielki dorobek pieniężny*) fortune **3** (*posiadłość*) estate; **~ ruchomy/ nieruchomy** personal property/real estate
majone|z (**-zu, -zy**; *loc sg* **-zie**) *m* mayonnaise
majo|r (**-ra, -rowie** *lub* **-rzy**; *loc sg* **-rze**) *m* (*Wojsk*) major
majów|ka (**-ki, -ki**; *dat sg & loc sg* **-ce**; *gen pl* **-ek**) *f* (*wycieczka za miasto*) picnic
majst|er (**-ra, -rowie** *lub* **-rzy**; *loc sg* **-rze**) *m* **1** (*nadzorca na budowie, w fabryce*) foreman **2** (*szewc, zegarmistrz*) master
majstr|ować (**-uję, -ujesz**) *vi*: **~ przy czymś** (*pot*) to interfere with sth; **nie majstruj przy radiu** stop fiddling about with the radio
majt|ki (**-ek**) *pl* **1** (*dla kobiet*) panties **2** (*dla mężczyzn*) briefs
makaro|n (**-nu, -ny**; *loc sg* **-nie**) *m* (*nitki, rurki*) pasta
makijaż (**-u, -e**; *gen pl* **-y** *lub* **-ów**) *m* make-up; **robić** (**zrobić** *pf*) **sobie ~** to make o.s. up; **zrobiła sobie wyzywający ~** her make-up was outrageous
maksymalny *adj* maximum
malar|ka (**-ki, -ki**; *dat sg & loc sg* **-ce**; *gen pl* **-ek**) *f* painter
malarst|wo (**-wa**; *loc sg* **-wie**) *nt* **1** (*rodzaj sztuki*) painting **2** (*zbiór obrazów*) paintings *pl*
malarz (**-a, -e**; *gen pl* **-y**) *m* (*artysta*) painter
mal|eć (**-eję, -ejesz**; *pf* **z-**) *vi* **1** (*popularność*) to diminish **2** (*temperatura*) to decrease
mali|na (**-ny, -ny**; *dat sg & loc sg* **-nie**) *f* raspberry; **nie daj się wpuścić w maliny!** (*pot*) don't let yourself get taken in!
mal|ować (**-uję, -ujesz**) *vt* **1** (*pf* **po-**) (*powierzchnię farbą*) to paint **2** (*pf* **wy-**) (*pokój*) to decorate, to paint **3** (*pf* **na-**) (*dzieło sztuki*) to paint; **~ się** *vr* (*robić makijaż*) to apply one's make-up; **„świeżo malowane"** "wet paint"
maltret|ować (**-uję, -ujesz**; *pf* **z-**) *vt* (*dręczyć*) to abuse; **~ fizycznie/ psychicznie** to abuse physically/ psychologically
małoduszny *adj* (*podły*) mean
Małopols|ka (**-ki**; *dat sg & loc sg* **-ce**) *f a province in southern Poland whose capital is Cracow*
małostkowy *adj* (*przejmujący się drobnostkami*) petty
mał|pa (**-py, -py**; *dat sg & loc sg* **-pie**) *f* **1** (*zwierzę*) monkey **2** (*człekokształtna*) ape **3** (*Komput*) @ sign
mały *adj* **1** (*niewielkiego rozmiaru*) small **2** (*dom, przestrzeń*) little **3** (*o dziecku*) small **4** (*o literze*) lower-case
małżeński *adj* **1** (*o pożyciu*) married **2** (*kryzys, obowiązek*) marital; **zawierać** (**zawrzeć** *pf*) **związek ~** to enter the state of matrimony
małżeńst|wo (**-wa, -wa**; *loc sg* **-wie**) *nt* **1** (*związek formalny*) marriage **2** (*mąż i żona*) (married) couple **3** (*sakrament*) matrimony; **~ mieszane** mixed marriage
małżon|ek (**-ka, -kowie**; *inst sg* **-kiem**) *m* (*mąż*) husband; **małżonkowie** *pl* (*mąż i żona*) husband and wife
małżon|ka (**-ki, -ki**; *dat sg & loc sg* **-ce**; *gen pl* **-ek**) *f* (*żona*) wife
mam *vb zob.* **mieć**
ma|ma (**-my, -my**; *dat sg & loc sg* **-mie**) *f* (*pot: matka*) mum
maminsyn|ek (**-ka, -kowie** *lub* **-ki**; *inst sg* **-kiem**) *m* (*pej*) mummy's boy
mamy *vb zob.* **mieć**
manifestacj|a (**-i, -e**; *gen pl* **-i**) *f* **1** (*wyraz*) expression **2** (*protest społeczny*) demonstration
manifest|ować (**-uję, -ujesz**; *pf* **za-**) *vi* (*brać udział w demonstracji*) to demonstrate
manipul|ować (**-uję, -ujesz**) *vi +inst* (*uczuciami, faktami*) to manipulate

mańku|t (**-ta, -ci**; *loc sg* **-cie**) *m* left-hander; **on jest ~em** (*pej*) he's left-handed
ma|pa (**-py, -py**; *loc sg* **-pie**) *f* map; **~ samochodowa Europy** road map of Europe
march|ew (**-wi, -wie**; *gen pl* **-wi**) *f* carrot
margary|na (**-ny, -ny**; *dat sg & loc sg* **-nie**) *f* margarine
marmola|da (**-dy, -dy**; *dat sg & loc sg* **-dzie**) *f* preserve
marmu|r (**-ru, -ry**; *loc sg* **-rze**) *m* marble
marn|ować (**-uję, -ujesz**; *pf* **z-**) *vt* (*czas, pieniądze*) to waste; **~ się** *vr* to be wasted
marny *adj* **1** (*nieznaczny*) paltry **2** (*kiepski, słaby*) poor; **wysiłki poszły na marne** the efforts went to waste
marsz (**-u, -e**) *m* march; **~ do szkoły!** (*pot*) off to school with you!
marszcz|yć (**-ę, -ysz**; *pf* **z-**) *vt* **1** (*twarz*) to wrinkle **2** (*ubranie*) to gather; **~ się** *vr* **1** (*na twarzy*) to wrinkle **2** (*o tkaninie*) to crease
mart|wić (**-wię, -wisz**; *pf* **z-**) *vt* to upset; **~ się** *vr* to worry; **martwię się twoim zdrowiem** I'm worried about your health; **martwię się o ciebie** I'm concerned about you; **nie martw się już tym!** don't worry about it any more!
martwy *adj* dead; **ten obraz to martwa natura** this painting is a still life
maru|dzić (**-dzę, -dzisz**; *imp* **-dź**) *vi* (*narzekać*) to whine
marynar|ka (**-ki**; *dat sg & loc sg* **-ce**; *nom pl* **-ki**; *gen pl* **-ek**) *f* **1** (*strój*) jacket **2** (*formacja wojskowa*) navy; **~ dwurzędowa/jednorzędowa** a double-/single-breasted jacket
marynarz (**-a, -e**; *gen pl* **-y**) *m* **1** (*członek załogi na statku*) seaman **2** (*Wojsk*) sailor
ma|rzec (**-rca, -rce**) *m* March
marze|nie (**-nia, -nia**; *gen pl* **-ń**) *nt* dream; **~ senne** dream
marz|nąć (**-nę, -niesz**; *imp* **-nij**) *vi* **1** (*pf* **z-**) (*o osobie*) to freeze **2** (*pf* **za-**) (*o pogodzie*) to freeze
marz|yć (**-ę, -ysz**) *vi* to (day)dream; **~ o** *+loc* to dream of; **~ o niebieskich migdałach** to daydream
ma|sa (**-sy, -sy**; *dat sg & loc sg* **-sie**) *f* mass; **ale z ciebie ciemna ~** (*pot*: *pej*) you really are an idiot; **masy** *pl* (*zwykli ludzie*) the masses
mas|ka (**-ki, -ki**; *dat sg & loc sg* **-ce**; *gen pl* **-ek**) *f* **1** mask **2** (*w samochodzie*) bonnet (Brit), hood (US)
mask|ować (**-uję, -ujesz**; *pf* **za-**) *vt* **1** (*ukrywać*) to camouflage **2** (*uczucia*: *przen*) to mask; **~ się** *vr* to put on a facade
ma|sło (**-sła**; *loc sg* **-śle**) *nt* (*orzechowe, kakaowe*) butter; **wszystko idzie jak po maśle** everything is going swimmingly
mas|ować (**-uję, -ujesz**; *pf* **po-**) *vt* to massage
mass-medi|a (**-ów**) *pl* the (mass) media
masz *vb zob.* **mieć**
maszy|na (**-ny, -ny**; *dat sg & loc sg* **-nie**) *f* (*urządzenie*) machine; **~ do szycia** sewing machine; **mam w domu starą maszynę do pisania** I have an old typewriter at home
maszynopi|s (**-su, -sy**; *loc sg* **-sie**) *m* typescript
maszynowy *adj* **1** (*odnoszący się do maszyny*) machine **2** (*zrobiony maszyną*) machine-made; **broń maszynowa** machine gun
maś|ć (**-ci, -ci**; *gen pl* **-ci**) *f* **1** (*lekarstwo*) ointment **2** (*ubarwienie konia*) colour (Brit), color (US); **aktywiści wszelkiej maści** activists of every description
matematyczny *adj* (*działanie*) mathematical
matematy|ka (**-ki**; *dat sg & loc sg* **-ce**) *f* **1** mathematics **2** (*w szkole*) maths (Brit), math (US)
matera|c (**-ca, -ce**; *gen pl* **-cy** *lub* **-ców**) *m* (*sprężynowy, dmuchany*) mattress
materialny *adj* **1** (*dobra kultury*) material **2** (*trudności, położenie*) financial
materia|ł (**-łu, -ły**; *loc sg* **-le**) *m* **1** (*tworzywo sztuczne*) material

2 (*jedwab, bawełna*) fabric; **~ wybuchowy** explosives *pl*
mat|ka (**-ki, -ki**; *dat sg & loc sg* **-ce**; *gen pl* **-ek**) *f* **1** (*rodzona*) mother **2**: **~ chrzestna** (*Rel*) godmother; **M~ Boska** the Virgin Mary
matowy *adj* **1** (*nieprzezroczysty*) frosted **2** (*barwa głosu*) dull **3** (*zdjęcie*) mat(t)
matrymonialny *adj* matrimonial; **biuro matrymonialne** marriage bureau; **ogłoszenie matrymonialne** lonely-hearts ad
matu|ra (**-ry, -ry**; *dat sg & loc sg* **-rze**) *f* (*egzamin dojrzałości*) ≈ A-levels (*Brit*), ≈ high school finals (*US*); **zdać** (*pf*) **maturę** ≈ to pass one's A-Levels (*Brit*), ≈ to graduate (*US*)

MATURA

Matura is the exam taken at the end of secondary school and is compulsory for those students who wish to study at university. It is also referred to as "the maturity exam" as it is usually taken at the age of seventeen or eighteen. See also **liceum**.

Mazur|y (-) *pl a region in north-eastern Poland, famous for its great lakes*
mądroś|ć (**-ci, -ci**; *gen pl* **-ci**) *f* wisdom; **cechuje go ~ życiowa** he has a lot of common sense
mąd|ry *adj* wise
mądrz|eć (**-eję, -ejesz**; *pf* **z-**) *vi* to grow wise
mądrz|yć się (**-ę, -ysz**) *vr* (*pot*) to talk pretentious rubbish
mą|ka (**-ki, -ki**; *dat sg & loc sg* **-ce**) *f* flour; **z tej mąki chleba nie będzie** (*przen*) it's a waste of effort
mąż (**męża, mężowie**) *m* husband; **wychodzić** (**wyjść** *pf*) **za ~** to get married (*about a woman*); **to prawdziwy ~ stanu** he is a true statesman
mdl|eć (**-eję, -ejesz**; *pf* **ze-**) *vi* to faint
mdły *adj* **1** (*bez wyrazu*) bland **2** (*powodujący mdłości*) nauseating
meb|el (**-la, -le**) *m* piece of furniture; **meble** (*gen pl* **-li**) *pl* (*kuchenne, do salonu*) furniture
mebl|ować (**-uję, -ujesz**; *pf* **u-**) *vt* (*pokój, mieszkanie*) to furnish
mecena|s (**-sa, -si** *lub* **-sowie**; *loc sg* **-sie**) *m* **1** (*sztuki*) patron **2** (*adwokat*) lawyer
mechaniczny *adj* **1** mechanical **2** (*pojazd*) motor
mechani|k (**-ka, -cy**) *m* mechanic
mechaniz|m (**-mu, -my**; *loc sg* **-mie**) *m* **1** (*w maszynie*) mechanism **2** (*społeczny, historii*) mechanics
mecz (**-u, -e**) *m* (*piłkarski, tenisowy*) match
medal (**-u, -e**; *gen pl* **-i**) *m* medal; **zdałeś egzamin na ~** you have passed the exam with flying colours
medi|a (**-ów**) *pl* **1** (*elektroniczne, drukowane*) media **2** (*woda, prąd*) utilities; **~ społecznościowe** social media
medycy|na (**-ny**; *dat sg & loc sg* **-nie**) *f* (*nauka*) medicine
medyczny *adj* (*personel, wydział*) medical; **studia medyczne** medicine
medytacj|a (**-i, -e**; *gen pl* **-i**) *f* meditation
Meksy|k (**-ku**; *inst sg* **-kiem**) *m* Mexico
melancholi|a (**-i**) *f* melancholy; **wpadać** (**wpaść** *pf*) **w melancholię** to get depressed
melancholijny *adj* (*charakter, nastrój*) melancholy
meld|ować (**-uję, -ujesz**; *pf* **za-**) *vt* **1** to report; **~ się** *vr* **1** (*Wojsk: na stanowisku*) to report **2** (*jako mieszkaniec*) to register; **~ o** *+loc* to report
melodi|a (**-i, -e**; *gen pl* **-i**) *f* melody
melo|n (**-na, -ny**; *loc sg* **-nie**) *m* melon
mem (**-a, -y**; *dat sg* **-owi**) *m* meme
menedże|r (**-ra, -rowie**; *loc sg* **-rze**) *m* (*kierownik*) manager
menstruacj|a (**-i, -e**; *gen pl* **-i**) *f* (*miesiączka*) menstruation
menu *nt inv* (*karta dań*) menu
merytoryczny *adj* substantive; **książka zawiera wiele błędów ~ch**

the book contains many factual errors
me|ta (**-ty, -ty**; *dat sg & loc sg* **-cie**) *f* finishing line; **to się nie uda na dłuższą/krótszą metę** this is unlikely to succeed in the long/short term
metaboliz|m (**-mu**; *loc sg* **-mie**) *m* metabolism
metafo|ra (**-ry, -ry**; *dat sg & loc sg* **-rze**) *f* (*przenośnia*) metaphor
metal (**-u, -e**; *gen pl* **-i**) *m* (*kolorowy, szlachetny*) metal
metalowy *adj* (*przedmiot*) metal
met|ka (**-ki, -ki**; *dat sg & loc sg* **-ce**; *gen pl* **-ek**) *f* **1** (*naklejana na produkcie*) label **2** (*przywieszana na bagażu*) tag
meto|da (**-dy, -dy**; *dat sg & loc sg* **-dzie**) *f* (*badawcza, poznawcza*) method
metodyczny *adj* **1** (*planowy*) methodical **2** (*związany z metodą*) methodological
met|r (**-ra, -ry**; *loc sg* **-rze**) *m* metre (*Brit*), meter (*US*); **pokój ma 20 ~ów kwadratowych** the room is 20 square metres
met|ro (**-ra**; *loc sg* **-rze**) *nt* (*Rail*) underground (*Brit*), subway (*US*)
metryczny *adj* (*system*) metric
me|wa (**-wy, -wy**; *dat sg & loc sg* **-wie**) *f* seagull
męcz|yć (**-ę, -ysz**) *vt* **1** (*pf* **z-**) (*powodować wyczerpanie*) to tire out **2** (*maltretować*) to harass **3** (*dokuczać*) to bother; **~ się** *vr* **1** (*pf* **z-**) (*odczuwać wyczerpanie*) to tire **2** (*odczuwać cierpienie*) to suffer; **on męczy się nad pracą domową** he is toiling over his homework
mę|ka (**-ki, -ki**; *dat sg & loc sg* **-ce**; *gen pl* **mąk**) *f* **1** (*tortura fizyczna*) torture **2** (*cierpienie psychiczne*) torment
męski *adj* **1** (*ubranie*) men's **2** (*zachowanie*) manly; **rodzaj ~** masculine (gender)
męskoosobowy *adj*: **rodzaj ~** (*w językoznawstwie*) virile gender
męskoś|ć (**-ci**) *f* (*zbiór cech męskich*) masculinity
mężat|ka (**-ki, -ki**; *dat sg & loc sg* **-ce**; *gen pl* **-ek**) *f* (*żona*) married woman
mężczy|zna (**-zny, -źni**; *dat sg & loc sg* **-źnie**; *gen pl* **-zn**) *m decl like f in sg* man
mglisty *adj* **1** (*pogoda*) foggy **2** (*niewyraźny*) hazy **3** (*niekonkretny*) indistinct
mg|ła (**-ły, -ły**; *dat sg & loc sg* **-le**; *gen pl* **mgieł**) *f* **1** (*zawiesista*) fog **2** (*przeciętna*) mist **3** (*delikatna*) haze
mgr *abbr* (= *magister*) **1** (*historii, filozofii*) ≈ MA (= *Master of Arts*) **2** (*biologii, matematyki*) ≈ MSc (= *Master of Science*)
mianowni|k (**-ka, -ki**; *inst sg* **-kiem**) *m* **1** (*przypadek gramatyczny*) nominative **2** (*w matematyce*) denominator
mia|ra (**-ry, -ry**; *dat sg & loc sg* **mierze**) *f* **1** (*wielkość*) measure **2** (*ubrania*) size **3** (*umiar*) moderation; **w dużej mierze zależy to od ciebie** it depends on you to a great extent
miastecz|ko (**-ka, -ka**; *gen pl* **-ek**; *inst sg* **-kiem**) *nt* (small) town; **~ uniwersyteckie** university campus; **wesołe ~** funfair (*Brit*), amusement park (*US*)
miast|o (**-a, -a**; *loc sg* **mieście**) *nt* **1** (*średniej wielkości*) town **2** (*wielkie*) city; **iść (pójść** *pf*) **do centrum miasta** to go (in)to town (*Brit*), to go downtown (*US*)
miażdż|yć (**-ę, -ysz**; *pf* **z-**) *vt* (*zgniatać*) to crush
miąższ (**-u**) *m* (*owocowy*) pulp, flesh

SŁOWO KLUCZOWE

mieć (**mam, masz**; *imp* **miej**; *pt* **miał, mieli**) *vt* **1** (*posiadać na własność*) to have; **mam nowy samochód** I have a new car; **czy masz dużą kolekcję muzyki?** do you have a large music collection?; **mieć na sobie spodnie** to be wearing trousers (*Brit*) *lub* pants (*US*)
2 (*katar, kłopoty*) to have; **mam trudności ze znalezieniem pracy** I am having difficulty finding a job; **czy masz pojęcie, ile to kosztuje?** do you have any idea how much it costs?; **rano ma zawroty głowy** in

the morning he feels dizzy; **mieć coś do kogoś** to have sth against sb
3 (*z różnymi dopełnieniami*) to have; **przedstawienie będzie mieć miejsce w czwartek** the performance will take place on Thursday; **masz (jeszcze) dużo czasu!** take your time!; **mam ochotę na ciastko** I feel like a cake
4 (*dla wyrażenia powinności*) to be supposed to; **masz się uczyć** you're supposed to be studying
5 (*dla wyrażenia zamiaru*) to be going to; **ona ma przyjść we wtorek** she's going to come on Tuesday
6 (*forma zaprzeczona czasownika być*): **nie ma** (*liczba pojedyncza*) there is none
7: **nie ma** (*liczba mnoga*) there are no; **nie ma pieniędzy** there's no money; **nie ma chleba** there is no bread; **nie ma co o tym myśleć** there's no use thinking about it; **nie ma się czemu więcej dziwić** (there's) no wonder; **nie ma za co!** don't mention it!; **cudów nie ma** (*pot*) that's the way the cookie crumbles!
mieć się *vr*: **jak się masz?** how are you?; **mieć się za** to take o.s. to be; **ma się za niezłą aktorkę** she considers herself to be a decent actress

mie|dź (**-dzi**) *f* (*metal*) copper
miejsc|e (**-a, -a**) *nt* **1** (*przestrzeń*) space **2** (*fragment przestrzeni*) place **3** (*usytuowanie*) position **4** (*miejscowość*) place **5** (*w pensjonacie*) vacancy **6** (*w pociągu*) seat **7** (*paragraf w tekście*) passage **8** (*w hierarchii*) position; **musimy dojechać do miejsca przeznaczenia** we must reach our destination; **proszę podać ~ zamieszkania** please give your place of residence; **na miejscu czeka na nas obiad** dinner will be waiting for us when we arrive; **spotkanie ma ~ w sali numer...** the meeting is taking place in room number...; **na twoim miejscu obraziłabym się** if I were you, I would be offended; **miejscami masz rację** you are partially right; **z miejsca odrzucam twoją propozycję** I am rejecting your proposal out of hand
miejscowni|k (**-ka, -ki**; *inst sg* **-kiem**) *m* (*przypadek gramatyczny*) locative
miejscowoś|ć (**-ci, -ci**; *gen pl* **-ci**) *f* place; **~ turystyczna** tourist destination
miejscowy *adj* (*gazeta, zwyczaj*) local
miejscówk|ka (**-ki, -ki**; *dat sg & loc sg* **-ce**; *gen pl* **-ek**) *f* (*w pociągu*) seat reservation
miejski *adj* (*transport*) urban
mielone (**-go**) *nt decl like adj* (*mięso*) mince (*Brit*), ground beef (*US*)
mielony *adj* **1** (*kawa, mąka*) ground **2** (*mięso*) minced ▷ *m decl like adj*: **kotlet ~** ≈ meat patty, hamburger
mieni|e (**-a**) *nt* (*prywatne, państwowe*) property
mierz|yć (**-ę, -ysz**; *pf* **z-**) *vt* (*robić pomiar*) to measure ▷ *vi*: **~** (**wy~** *pf*) **(do kogoś/czegoś)** to aim (at sb/sth); **~ w tarczę** to aim at a target; **on mierzy wszystkich własną miarą** he judges everyone by his own standards
miesi|ąc (**-ąca, -ące**; *gen pl* **-ęcy**) *m* (*część roku*) month; **miodowy ~** honeymoon
miesiącz|ka (**-ki, -ki**; *dat sg & loc sg* **-ce**; *gen pl* **-ek**) *f* (*menstruacja*) period
miesięczni|k (**-ka, -ki**; *inst sg* **-kiem**) *m* (*gazeta*) monthly
miesięczny *adj* (*dochód, rozliczenie*) monthly
miesz|ać (**-am, -asz**) *vt* **1** (*pf* **wy-** *lub* **za-**) (*rozrabiać składniki*) to stir **2** (*pf* **z-**) (*łączyć składniki*) to mix **3** (*pf* **w-**) (*wplątywać w sprawę*) to involve **4** (*pf* **po-**) (*mylić fakty, osoby*) to confuse; **~ się** *vr* **1** (*łączyć się*) to mix **2** (*ingerować*) to meddle; **nie mieszaj się w ich sprawy** don't stick your nose into their business; **ostatnio wszystko mi się miesza** recently I have been getting things all mixed up
mieszani|na (**-ny, -ny**; *dat sg & loc sg* **-nie**) *f* (*substancja*) mixture
mieszan|ka (**-ki, -ki**; *dat sg & loc sg* **-ce**; *gen pl* **-ek**) *f* (*substancja*) mixture
mieszany *adj* (*małżeństwo, emocje*) mixed

mieszk|ać (-am, -asz) *vi* **1** (*być zameldowanym*) to live **2** (*przebywać chwilowo*) to stay
mieszkalny *adj* (*część miasta*) residential
mieszka|nie (-nia, -nia; *gen pl* **-ń**) *nt* (*jednopokojowe, dwupokojowe*) flat (*Brit*), apartment (*US*)
mieszka|niec (-ńca, -ńcy) *m* **1** (*w domu*) occupant **2** (*w mieście*) inhabitant **3** (*w państwie*) resident
między *prep +loc* **1** (*pomiędzy dwoma obiektami, osobami*) between **2** (*wśród ludzi, przedmiotów*) among **3** (*dla określenia przedziału czasu*) between ▷ *prep +inst* between; **~ (godziną) ósmą a dziewiątą** between eight and nine o'clock; **~ nami mówiąc, masz rację** just between you and me, I think you are right; **załatwcie to ~ sobą** sort it out between yourselves; **~ innymi czyta książki** he reads books among other things
międzymiastowy *adj* **1** (*komunikacja*) intercity **2** (*rozmowa telefoniczna*) long-distance
międzynarodowy *adj* (*umowa, festiwal*) international
miękki *adj* soft; **masz ~e serce** you are too soft with people
miękko *adv* (*chodzić, mówić*) softly; **jajko na ~** soft-boiled egg
mię|sień (-śnia, -śnie; *gen pl* **-śni**) *m* muscle
mięsny *adj* meat; **sklep ~** butcher's (shop)
mię|so (-sa, -sa; *loc sg* **-sie**) *nt* meat; **~ wieprzowe/wołowe/drobiowe** pork/beef/poultry
miętowy *adj* (*cukierek, smak*) mint
mig|ać (-am, -asz; *pf* **-nąć**) *vi +inst* (*światłami*) to flash
migre|na (-ny; *dat sg & loc sg* **-nie**) *f* migraine; **cierpieć na migrenę** to suffer from migraine
mij|ać (-am, -asz; *pf* **minąć**) *vt* to pass ▷ *vi* to pass; **~ się** *vr* **1** (*wymijać się: w przeciwnych kierunkach*) to pass (each other) **2** (*nie rozumieć się*) to differ (in opinion)
Mikołaj (-a, -e) *m* (*też*: **Święty ~**) Father Christmas (*Brit*), Santa (Claus); **mikołajki** St Nicholas's Day
mikrofalów|ka (-ki, -ki; *dat sg & loc sg* **-ce**; *gen pl* **-ek**) *f* (*pot: kuchenka mikrofalowa*) microwave
mil|a (-i, -e) *f* mile
milczący *adj* (*człowiek*) silent
milcz|eć (-ę, -ysz) *vi* to remain silent; **milczał jak zaklęty** he was as quiet as a mouse
milczeni|e (-a) *nt* silence; **~m pominął zdradę** he kept silent about his betrayal
miliar|d (-da, -dy; *loc sg* **-dzie**) *m* billion
milimet|r (-ra, -ry; *loc sg* **-rze**) *m* millimetre (*Brit*), millimeter (*US*)
milio|n (-na, -ny; *loc sg* **-nie**) *m* million
milione|r (-ra, -rzy; *loc sg* **-rze**) *m* millionaire
militarny *adj* (*akcja*) military
miło *adv* **1** (*spędzać czas, rozmawiać*) pleasantly **2** (*życzliwie*) kindly; **~ mi (pana/panią) poznać** pleased to meet you; **to bardzo ~ z państwa strony/pani strony** that's very kind of you
miłosny *adj* (*zawód,podbój*) amorous
miłoś|ć (-ci, -ci; *gen pl* **-ci**) *f* (*odwzajemniona, bez wzajemności*) love; **na ~ boską!** (*pot*) for God's sake!
miłośni|k (-ka, -cy; *inst sg* **-kiem**) *m* (*amator*) enthusiast
miły *adj* nice; **bądź tak ~ i przyjdź tu** be so kind and come over here
mimo *prep +gen* in spite of; **~ wszystko udało się** in spite of everything, it worked out; **~ woli opuścił pokój** he left the room against his will; **~ że** *lub* **iż padało, wyszliśmy** even though it was raining, we headed out
m.in. *abbr* (= *między innymi*) among other things
mi|na (-ny, -ny; *dat sg & loc sg* **-nie**) *f* **1** (*na twarzy*) facial expression **2** (*przeciwpiechotna, lądowa*) mine
mi|nąć (-nę, -niesz; *imp* **-ń**) *vb pf od* **mijać**
minimalnie *adv* **1** (*nieznacznie*) minimally **2** (*ledwo*) narrowly
minimalny *adj* minimal

minim|um (**-um, -a**; *gen pl* **-ów**) *nt inv in sg* minimum ▷ *adv* (*co najmniej*) at least
miniony *adj* **1** (*epoka*) past **2** (*rok, tydzień*) last
minist|er (**-ra, -rowie**; *loc sg* **-rze**) *m* (*sekretarz stanu*) government minister (*Brit*), Secretary (*US*); **M~ Spraw Zagranicznych** foreign minister, ≈ Foreign Secretary (*Brit*), ≈ Secretary of State (*US*); **M~ Spraw Wewnętrznych** minister of the interior, ≈ Home Secretary (*Brit*), ≈ Secretary of the Interior (*US*); **~ bez teki** (*członek rządu, nie kierujący ministerstwem*) minister without portfolio; **posiedzenie rady ministrów** cabinet meeting
ministerst|wo (**-wa, -wa**; *loc sg* **-wie**) *nt* department of state; **M~ Spraw Wewnętrznych** ministry of the interior, ≈ Home Office (*Brit*), ≈ Department of the Interior (*US*); **M~ Spraw Zagranicznych** ministry of foreign affairs, ≈ Foreign (and Commonwealth) Office (*Brit*), ≈ Department of State (*US*)
minu|s (**-sa, -sy**; *loc sg* **-sie**) *m* minus; **plus ~** more or less; **jestem na ~ie** I'm in debt
minusowy *adj* **1** (*temperatura poniżej zera*) subzero **2** (*wynik, bilans*) negative
minu|ta (**-ty, -ty**; *dat sg & loc sg* **-cie**) *f* minute; **za parę minut** in a couple of minutes
miot|ła (**-ły, -ły**; *dat sg & loc sg* **-le**; *gen pl* **-eł**) *f* (*do sprzątania*) broom
miód (**miodu**; *loc sg* **miodzie**) *m* **1** honey **2** (*pitny*) mead
mis|ka (**-ki, -ki**; *dat sg & loc sg* **-ce**; *gen pl* **-ek**) *f* bowl
mistrz (**-a, -owie**) *m* **1** (*radzący sobie doskonale w czymś*) master **2** (*sportowy*) champion
mistrzost|wo (**-wa, -wa**; *loc sg* **-wie**) *nt* **1** (*biegłość*) mastery **2** (*sportowe*) championship; **mistrzostwa świata** world championships
mistrzowski *adj* **1** (*osiągnięcie*) brilliant **2** (*drużyna*) title-holding
mistrzy|ni (**-ni, -nie**; *dat sg & loc sg* **-ni**; *gen pl* **-ń**) *f* champion
mistyczny *adj* (*poezja, rytuał*) mystic(al)
mistyfikacj|a (**-i, -e**; *gen pl* **-i**) *f* mystification
mi|ś (**-sia, -sie**) *m* (*pot*) **1** (*niedźwiedź*) (little) bear **2** (*pluszowy*) teddy (bear)
mi|t (**-tu, -ty**; *loc sg* **-cie**) *m* myth
mitologi|a (**-i, -e**; *gen pl* **-i**) *f* (*grecka, słowiańska*) mythology
mityczny *adj* (*postać, opowieść*) mythical
mizeri|a (**-i, -e**; *gen pl* **-i**) *f* (*potrawa*) cucumber salad
mizerny *adj* **1** (*źle wyglądający*) sickly **2** (*kiepski*) miserable
mleczar|nia (**-ni, -nie**; *gen pl* **-ni** *lub* **-ń**) *f* dairy (*factory*)
mleczny *adj* **1** (*napój, zupa*) milky **2** (*gruczoł*) mammary **3** (*nieprzezroczysty*) frosted; **Droga Mleczna** the Milky Way
mle|ko (**-ka**) *nt* milk; **~ zsiadłe** (*Kulin*) sour milk; **~ w proszku** (*Kulin*) powdered milk
młod|e (**-ych**) *pl decl like adj* (*Zool*) young *pl*
młodociany *adj* (*przestępca*) juvenile ▷ *m decl like adj* juvenile
młodoś|ć (**-ci**) *f* youth; **przeżywać** (**przeżyć** *pf*) **drugą ~** to experience a second youth
młodszy *adj comp od* **młody**
młody *adj* **1** young **2** (*o ziemniakach*) new; **pan ~** (bride)groom; **panna młoda** bride; **młoda para** *lub* **młodzi** (*przed przysięgą*) bride and groom; (*po przysiędze*) newlyweds
młodzie|niec (**-ńca, -ńcy**) *m* (*młody mężczyzna*) youth
młodzież (**-y**) *f* youth
młodzieżowy *adj* (*zespół, obóz*) youth
młot|ek (**-ka, -ki**; *inst sg* **-kiem**) *m* **1** hammer **2** (*z drewna*) mallet
mły|n (**-na, -ny**; *loc sg* **-nie**) *m* mill; **ale dziś był ~ w pracy** (*pot: przen*) it's been nose to the grindstone today at work
mną *pron inst od* **ja** me; **chodź ze ~** come with me
mni|ch (**-cha, -si**) *m* monk
mnie *pron gen, dat, acc, loc od* **ja** me; **myśl o ~** think about me

mniej *adv comp od* **mało** **1** (*o przedmiotach*) fewer **2** (*o czasie*) less; **ten film jest ~ interesujący** this film is less interesting; **~ więcej to mam na myśli** that is more or less what I have in mind

mniejszoś|ć (**-ci, -ci**; *gen pl* **-ci**) *f* (*seksualna, etniczna*) minority

mniejszy *adj comp od* **mały**; **mniejsza o to** *lub* **mniejsza z tym, kto wydał rozkaz** never mind who gave the order

mnoże|nie (**-nia, -nia**; *gen pl* **-ń**) *nt* (*działanie matematyczne*) multiplication; **tabliczka/znak mnożenia** multiplication table/sign

mnoż|yć (**-ę, -ysz**; *imp* **mnóż**; *pf* **po-**) *vt* (*w matematyce*) to multiply; **~ się** *vr* (*zwiększać ilość*) to increase

moc (**-y, -e**; *gen pl* **-y**) *f* power

mocarst|wo (**-wa, -wa**; *loc sg* **-wie**) *nt* (*Pol*) superpower

mocno *adv* **1** (*przyciskać*) firmly **2** (*bić*) hard **3** (*przykręcać*) tightly **4** (*pragnąć*) very much **5** (*pachnieć*) strongly; (*zaskoczony*) very; **wczoraj ~ wiało** it was very windy yesterday; **~ spała** she was deeply asleep

mocny *adj* **1** strong **2** (*solidny*) firm, tight **3** (*mechanizm*) powerful

mocz (**-u**) *m* urine

mocz|yć (**-ę, -ysz**; *pf* **z-**) *vt* to moisten; **~ się** *vr* to wet o.s.

mo|da (**-dy, -dy**; *loc sg* **-dzie**; *gen pl* **mód**) *f* fashion; **szary jest w modzie** grey (*Brit*) *lub* gray (*US*) is in fashion; **mini wyszło z mody** mini skirts have gone out of fashion

model (*nom pl* **-e**) *m* **1** (*gen sg* **-u**; *gen pl* **-i**) (*samolotu, silnika*) model **2** (*gen sg* **-a**; *gen pl* **-i**) (*na wybiegu*) model

model|ka (**-ki, -ki**; *dat sg & loc sg* **-ce**; *gen pl* **-ek**) *f* (*kobieta na wybiegu*) model

modl|ić się (**-ę, -isz**; *imp* **módl**) *vr* to pray

modlit|wa (**-wy, -wy**; *dat sg & loc sg* **-wie**) *f* prayer; **odmawiać** (**odmówić** *pf*) **modlitwę** to say one's prayers

modny *adj* fashionable

mogę *itd. vb zob.* **móc**

moi *itd. pron zob.* **mój**

moja, moje *itd. pron zob.* **mój**

mok|nąć (**-nę, -niesz**; *imp* **-nij**; *pt* **mókł**; *pf* **z-**) *vi* (*na deszczu*) to get wet (*in the rain*)

mokro *adv*: **jest dziś bardzo ~** it is very wet today

mokry *adj* wet

molest|ować (**-uję, -ujesz**) *vt* **1** to harass **2** (*wykorzystać seksualnie*) to molest

momen|t (**-tu, -ty**; *loc sg* **-cie**) *m* (*chwila*) moment; **czekaj na ~!** wait a minute!; **w tym momencie nie mogłem skłamać** at that moment I couldn't lie; **w pewnym momencie** at one point

momentalny *adj* (*natychmiastowy*) instant

MON *abbr* (= *Ministerstwo Obrony Narodowej*) ≈ MoD (*Brit*), ≈ DOD (*US*)

monarchi|a (**-i, -e**; *gen pl* **-i**) *f* (*konstytucyjna, dziedziczna*) monarchy

mone|ta (**-ty, -ty**; *dat sg & loc sg* **-cie**) *f* coin

monito|r (**-ra, -ry**; *loc sg* **-rze**) *m* (*komputera, telewizora*) monitor

mont|ować (**-uję, -ujesz**) *vt* **1** (*pf* **z-**) (*meble*) to assemble **2** (*pf* **za-**) (*urządzenie elektryczne*) to install **3** (*pf* **z-**) (*pot*: *Pol*: *grupę*) to put together **4** (*pf* **z-**) (*Cine, TV*) to edit

moralnoś|ć (**-ci**) *f* morality; **podwójna ~** double standards *pl*

moralny *adj* (*czyn, człowiek*) moral

morderc|a (**-y, -y**) *m decl like f in sg* murderer

morderczy *adj* (*instynkt*) murderous

morderst|wo (**-wa**; *loc sg* **-wie**) *nt* murder

mord|ować (**-uję, -ujesz**; *pf* **za-**) *vt* (*odbierać komuś życie*) to murder

morel|a (**-i, -e**; *gen pl* **-i**) *f* **1** (*Kulin*: *owoc*) apricot **2** (*Bot*: *drzewo*) apricot (tree)

morski *adj* **1** (*transport*) sea **2** (*przemysł*) maritime **3** (*akademia*) maritime; **Gdańsk to stary port ~** Gdańsk is an ancient seaport; **choroba morska** seasickness; **katastrofa morska** disaster at sea; **świnka morska** guinea pig

morz|e (**-a, -a**; *gen pl* **mórz**) *nt* (*Bałtyckie, Śródziemne*) sea; **nad ~m** (*niedaleko morza*) by the sea; (*spędzać*

wakacje) at the seaside; **wysokość nad poziomem morza** height above sea level; **poniżej poziomu morza** below sea level; **jechać (pojechać** *pf*) **nad ~** to go to the seaside
mo|st (-stu, -sty; *loc sg* **-ście**) *m* bridge; **powiem ci to prosto z ~u** I'll tell it to you like it is
motel (-u, -e; *gen pl* **-i**) *m* motel
motocykl (-a, -e; *gen pl* **-i**) *m* motorcycle
motyl (-a, -e; *gen pl* **-i**) *m* butterfly
motywacj|a (-i, -e; *gen pl* **-i**) *f* (*uzasadnienie postępowania*) motivation
motyw|ować (-uję, -ujesz; *pf* **u-**) *vt* **1** (*wspierać*) to motivate **2** (*tłumaczyć*) to justify
mo|wa (-wy; *dat sg & loc sg* **-wie**) *f* **1** (*obca, rodzima*) language **2** (*umiejętność mówienia*) speech **3** (*nom pl* **-wy**; *gen pl* **mów**) (*powitalna, na konferencji*) speech; **nie ma mowy!** (*pot*) that's out of the question!; **część mowy** (*w językoznawstwie*) part of speech; **~ zależna/niezależna** (*w językoznawstwie*) reported/direct speech
może *inv* perhaps; **być ~** maybe; **~ być** it will do; **~ coś zjemy?** perhaps we'll get a bite to eat?; **~ byśmy poszli do kina?** how about we go to the cinema?
możesz *itd. vb zob.* **móc**
możliwoś|ć (-ci, -ci; *gen pl* **-ci**) *f* **1** possibility **2** (*okazja*) opportunity; **możliwości** *pl* capabilities; **zrobimy to w miarę możliwości** we'll do it as well as possible
możliwy *adj* **1** (*wyobrażalny*) conceivable **2** (*realny*) feasible **3** (*pot: wystarczająco dobry*) passable; **możliwe, że przyjdzie jutro** it is likely that he will come tomorrow; **zrobię to, o ile to możliwe** I'll do it as far as it's possible; **~ do uniknięcia/rozpoznania** avoidable/recognizable
można *inv*: **~ stwierdzić, że masz rację** one *lub* you might say that you are indeed right; **~ już jeść** you may eat now; **nie ~ tego oddać** this cannot be returned; **nie ~ tak robić** you must not do that; **czy ~ usiąść?** can I sit down?

SŁOWO KLUCZOWE

móc (mogę, możesz; *pt* **mógł, mogła, mogli**) *vi* **1** (*być w stanie*) to be able; **czy możesz to przeczytać?** can *lub* could you read this?; **nie będę mógł wam pomóc** I shall not be able to help you; **szkoda, że nie możesz z nami pójść** it is a pity that you can't come with us; **gdybym tylko mógł, to bym poszedł** if only I could, then I would go
2 (*mieć zgodę*): **móc coś zrobić** to be allowed to do sth; **czy mogę przyjść później?** may I come later?; **czy mógłbym rozmawiać z Kasią?** could I speak to Kasia, please?
3 (*wyrażenie prawdopodobieństwa*): **on może nie przyjść** he might not come; **gdzie może być życie pozaziemskie?** where can there be extraterrestrial life?; **mogła o tym zapomnieć** she may have forgotten; **mogli nas zabić!** they could have killed us!
4 (*w prośbach*): **czy mógłbyś zamknąć drzwi?** could you close the door?
5 (*dla wyrażenia niezadowolenia*): **mogłeś mnie uprzedzić** you might have warned me

mój *possessive pron* **1** (*z rzeczownikiem*) my **2** (*bez rzeczownika*) mine; **to są moje rzeczy** these are my things; **te rzeczy są moje** these things are mine
mó|wić (-wię, -wisz) *vt* **1** (*coś*) to say **2** (*opowiadać*) to tell ▷ *vi* **1** (*wygłosić przemówienie*) to speak **2** (*prowadzić rozmowę*) to talk; **on mówi, że masz rację** he says that you're right; **mówił mi, że się uda** he told me that it would work out; **~ po włosku/hiszpańsku** to speak Italian/Spanish; **nie mówiąc (już) o** *+loc* not to mention; **prawdę mówiąc nie interesuje mnie to** to tell the truth, it doesn't interest me

mózg (**-u, -i**) *m* **1** brain **2** (*osoba bardzo inteligentna: przen*) mastermind
mp3 *nt inv* mp3
mp4 *nt inv* mp4
mroczny *adj* (*sekret, nastrój*) dark
mro|k (**-ku, -ki**; *inst sg* **-kiem**) *m* (*ciemność*) darkness
mro|zić (**-żę, -zisz**; *imp* **-ź**) *vt* **1** (*oziębiać*) to chill **2** (*o zamrażarce*) to freeze
mroźny *adj* (*dzień, pogoda*) frosty
mrożon|ki (**-ek**) *pl* frozen foods
mrożony *adj* (*mięso, produkty*) frozen; **kawa mrożona** iced coffee
mrów|ka (**-ki, -ki**; *dat sg & loc sg* **-ce**; *gen pl* **-ek**) *f* ant
mr|óz (**-ozu, -ozy**; *loc sg* **-ozie**) *m* frost; **7 stopni mrozu** 7 degrees below (zero)
MSW *abbr* = **Ministerstwo Spraw Wewnętrznych**
MSZ *abbr* = **Ministerstwo Spraw Zagranicznych**
msz|a (**-y, -e**; *gen pl* **-y**) *f* (*Rel: w intencji, poranna*) mass
mścić się (**mszczę, mścisz**; *imp* **mścij**; *pf* **ze-**) *vr*: **~ (na kimś)** to take revenge (on sb); **~ za krzywdę** to revenge o.s. for a wrong suffered
mu *pron dat od* **on, ono**
mu|cha (**-chy, -chy**; *dat sg & loc sg* **-sze**) *f* **1** (*owad*) fly **2** (*element męskiego stroju*) bow tie
multimedi|a (**-ów**) *pl* multimedia
multimedialny *adj* multimedia
mundu|r (**-ru, -ry**; *loc sg* **-rze**) *m* (*służbowy, wojskowy*) uniform
mu|r (**-ru, -ry**; *loc sg* **-rze**) *m* wall; **~em stanęła za nim** she stood firmly behind him; **na ~ beton** (*pot*) for sure
mur|ować (**-uję, -ujesz**; *pf* **wy-**) *vt* to build ▷ *vi* to lay bricks
murowany *adj* **1** (*ściana: z cegieł*) brick **2** (*z kamienia*) stone; **~ sukces** a dead cert (*pot*)
murzyński *adj* (*kultura, getto*) black

SŁOWO KLUCZOWE

mu|sieć (**-szę, -sisz**) *vi* **1** (*wyrażenie konieczność*): **czy muszę złożyć depozyt pieniężny, aby grać?** do I have to pay a deposit to be allowed to play?; **nie musisz nas pytać** you don't need to ask us
2 (*wyrażenie zobowiązania*): **musimy zapewnić ochronę środowiska naturalnego** we have to ensure the protection of the natural environment; **czy musisz tam jechać?** do you have to go there?; **nie musiałeś tego robić** you need not have done it; **musiała mu to wyznać** she must have told him

muszę *itd. vb zob.* **musieć**
musztar|da (**-dy**; *dat sg & loc sg* **-dzie**) *f* mustard
muze|um (**-um, -a**; *gen pl* **-ów**) *nt inv in sg* (*zbiór eksponatów*) museum
muzułma|nin (**-nina, -nie**; *loc sg* **-ninie**; *gen pl* **-nów**) *m* Muslim
muzułmański *adj* (*państwo, tradycja*) Muslim
muzyczny *adj* musical
muzy|k (**-ka, -cy**; *inst sg* **-kiem**) *m* musician
muzy|ka (**-ki**; *dat sg & loc sg* **-ce**) *f* music
my *pron* we; **halo, to my** hello, it's us
myci|e (**-a**) *nt* **1** (*czynność*) washing **2** (*naczyń*) washing-up
my|ć (**-ję, -jesz**; *pf* **u-**) *vt* **1** (*ciało, samochód*) to wash **2** (*wannę*) to clean **3** (*zęby*) to brush; **~ się** *vr* to wash (o.s.); **ręka rękę myje** you scratch my back and I'll scratch yours
myd|ło (**-ła, -ła**; *loc sg* **-le**; *gen pl* **-eł**) *nt* soap
myj|nia (**-ni, -nie**; *gen pl* **-ni**) *f*: **~ (samochodowa)** car wash
myl|ić (**-ę, -isz**) *vt* **1** (*pf* **po-**) (*osoby, fakty*) to confuse **2** (*pf* **z-**) (*wprowadzać w błąd*) to mislead; **~ się** *vr* (*robić błędy*) to make mistakes; **jesteś w błędzie** you are mistaken
mysz (**-y, -y**; *gen pl* **-y**) *f* **1** mouse **2** (*komputerowa*) mouse (*for computer*); **myszy** *pl* mice
myśl (**-i, -i**; *gen pl* **-i**) *f* thought; **mam coś innego na ~i** I have something else in mind; **tego nie miałem na ~i** I didn't mean that; **złota ~** words of wisdom
myślący *adj* intelligent

myśl|eć (**-ę, -isz**; *pt* **-ał, -eli**) *vi* to think; **~ o czymś** (*zastanawiać się nad czymś*) to think about sth; **~ o kimś** (*troszczyć się*) to think of sb; **myślę, że tak/nie** I think so/I don't think so
myśleni|e (**-a**) *nt* (*proces intelektualny*) thinking
myśliwski *adj* (*pies, strój*) hunting; **samolot ~** fighter (plane)
myśli|wy (**-wego, -wi**) *m decl like adj* hunter
mż|yć (**-y**) *vi*: **mży** (*o deszczu*) it's drizzling

SŁOWO KLUCZOWE

na *prep +loc* (*miejsce*) on; **na stole/drzwiach/ścianie** on the table/door/wall; **na Słowacji/ Śląsku** in Slovakia/Silesia; **wakacje na wsi** holidays in the country; **firma szuka ludzi na Wschodzie** the firm is looking for people in the East; **na Kubie** in Cuba; **na morzu** at sea; **na niebie** in the sky; **na naszej ulicy** in (*Brit*) *lub* on (*US*) our street; **na uniwersytecie/zajęciach** at the university/in class
▷ *prep +acc* **1** (*wskazywanie kierunku*) to; **na salę operacyjną** to the operating theatre; **na Słowację/Majorkę** to Slovakia/Majorca; **na wschód/północ** east/north; **wpadałam na niego przypadkowo** I bumped into him by accident
2 (*odcinek czasu*): **na cztery dni** for four days; **na dziesięć minut przed** *+inst* ten minutes before
3 (*wyznaczanie terminu*): **na środę** for Wednesday; **na szóstą** (*wykonać coś*) by six o'clock; (*przybyć*) at six o'clock
4 (*wydarzenie*): **na obiad** for lunch; **na jesień** for autumn (*Brit*) *lub* fall (*US*)
5 (*sposób*): **na kilogramy/litry** by the kilogram/the litre (*Brit*) *lub* liter (*US*); **na czyjś koszt** at sb's expense; **na raty** on hire purchase (*Brit*) *lub* instalment plan (*US*); **jajko na miękko** soft-boiled egg

6 (*z jakiejś przyczyny*): **na czyjeś zaproszenie** at sb's invitation; **chory na gruźlicę** ill *lub* sick (*US*) with TB
7 (*tempo*): **tysiąc litrów na godzinę** a thousand litres (*Brit*) *lub* liters (*US*) per hour; **dwa razy na dzień** twice a day
8 (*rezultat*): **kroić** (**pokroić** *pf*) **coś na plasterki** to cut sth into slices; **malować** (**pomalować** *pf*) **coś na żółto** to paint sth yellow
9 (*przeznaczenie*): **szafka na buty** shoe cupboard; **kosz na śmieci** dustbin (*Brit*), garbage can (*US*); **przerwa na herbatę** tea break
10 (*cel*): **wyjść** (*pf*) **na spacer** to go for a walk; **jechać na wakacje** to go on holiday (*Brit*) *lub* vacation (*US*); **iść na lekcję/koncert** to go to class/ to a concert

nabia|ł (**-łu**; *loc sg* **-le**) *m* (*mleko, ser, jajka*) dairy products *pl*
nabier|ać (**-am, -asz**; *pf* **nabrać**) *vt*: **~** *+gen* (*pożywienia*) to take in; (*prędkości*) to gather; (*masy*) to gain; **~ biegłości w czymś** to acquire facility with sth; **~ kogoś** (*pot*: *robić żarty*) to pull sb's leg; (*pot*: *okłamywać*) to deceive sb
na|być (**-będę, -będziesz**; *imp* **-bądź**) *vb pf od* **nabywać**
na|bywać (**-bywam, -bywasz**; *imp* **-bywaj**) *vt* to purchase
nachalny *adj* (*pej*: *natarczywy*) pushy
nachyl|ać się (**-am, -asz**) *vr* **1** (*pf* **-ić**) (*o osobie*) to bend down **2** (*o krzywiźnie terenu*) to slope
naciąg|ać (**-am, -asz**; *pf* **-nąć**) *vt* **1** (*naprężać*) to tighten **2** (*cięciwę łuku*) to draw **3** (*ubierać*) to pull on **4** (*nadwerężać mięsień*) to pull
nacin|ać (**-am, -asz**; *pf* **naciąć**) *vt*: **~ coś** (*skórę, powierzchnię przedmiotu*) to make an incision into sth
nacis|kać (**-kam, -kasz**; *pf* **-nąć**) *vt* to press; **naciskał mnie, żebym przyszła** he was pressuring me into coming
naci|snąć (**-snę, -śniesz**; *imp* **-śnij**) *vb pf od* **naciskać**
nacjonali|sta (**-sty, -ści**; *dat sg* **-ście**) *m decl like f in sg* (*Pol*) nationalist
nacjonalistyczny *adj* (*partia, poglądy*: *Pol*) nationalist
nacjonaliz|m (**-mu**; *loc sg* **-mie**) *m* (*Pol*) nationalism
naczelni|k (**-ka, -cy**; *inst sg* **-kiem**) *m* **1** (*dowódca*) chief **2** (*w więzieniu*) governor **3** (*oddziału*) head
naczy|nie (**-nia, -nia**; *gen pl* **-ń**) *nt* **1** (*talerz, miska*) dish **2** (*drewniany, gliniany*) vessel; **naczynia** *pl* dishes *pl*; **~ krwionośne** (*Anat*) blood vessel; **zmywać** (**pozmywać** *pf*) **naczynia** to do the washing-up

SŁOWO KLUCZOWE

nad *prep +inst* (*wyznaczający miejsce*)
1 (*powyżej*) above; **nad stołem/ górami** over the table/mountains
2 (*mieć przewagę, władzę*) over
3 (*niedaleko*): **nad Tamizą** by the Thames; **nad Morzem Północnym** by the North Sea; **nad ranem** at dawn
4 (*na jakiś temat*): **nad czym pracujesz?** what are you working on?
▷ *prep +acc* (*wyznaczający kierunek*): **nad jezioro** to the lake

nadajni|k (**-ka, -ki**; *inst sg* **-kiem**) *m* (*Tel*) transmitter
nad|awać (**-aję, -ajesz**; *pf* **-ać**) *vt* **1** (*w radiu, telewizji*) to broadcast **2** (*sygnał dźwiękowy*) to transmit **3** (*przesyłkę na poczcie*) to send, to mail (*US*); **~ się** *vr*: **~ się (do czegoś)** to be suitable (for sth); **to nie nadaje się do spania** this isn't fit for sleeping in/on
nadawc|a (**-y, -y**) *m decl like f in sg* (*listu, wiadomości*) sender
nadąż|ać (**-am, -asz**; *pf* **-yć**) *vi*: **nie ~ (z czymś)** to be unable to keep up (with sth); **nie nadążam z pracą** I can't keep up with the workload; **nie nadążałem za nimi** I could not keep up with them
nadbagaż (**-u, -e**; *gen pl* **-y**) *m* (*Aviat*) excess baggage
nadcho|dzić (**-dzę, -dzisz**; *imp* **-dź**; *pf* **nadejść**) *vi* **1** (*o osobie, o wydarzeniu*) to come **2** (*o informacji, przesyłce*) to arrive

nadciąg|ać (**-am, -asz**; *pf* **-nąć**) *vi* (*o burzy, wydarzeniu*) to approach
nadciśnie|nie (**-nia**) *nt* (*choroba*) hypertension
nadej|ść (**-dę, -dziesz**; *imp* **-dź**) *vb pf od* **nadchodzić**
nade|słać (**-ślę, -ślesz**; *imp* **-ślij**) *vb pf od* **nadsyłać**
nadgarst|ek (**-ka, -ki**; *inst sg* **-kiem**) *m* (*Anat*) wrist
nadgodzin|y (**-**) *pl* overtime
nadgorliwy *adj* (*urzędnik*) officious
nadjeżdż|ać (**-am, -asz**; *pf* **nadjechać**) *vi* (*o osobie, o pojeździe*) to arrive
nadmia|r (**-ru**; *loc sg* **-rze**) *m* excess; **alkohol w ~ze szkodzi** excessive alcohol consumption is harmful
nadobowiązkowy *adj* (*zajęcia*) optional
nadpła|ta (**-ty, -ty**; *dat sg* **-cie**) *f* overpayment; **~ wynosi dziesięć złotych** the overpayment amounts to 10 zlotys
nadprzyrodzony *adj* (*siła, zjawisko*) supernatural
nadrabi|ać (**-am, -asz**; *pf* **nadrobić**) *vt* to make good; **~ straty** to recoup one's losses
nadro|bić (**-bię, -bisz**; *imp* **nadrób**) *vb pf od* **nadrabiać**
nadsył|ać (**-am, -asz**; *pf* **nadesłać**) *vt* to send
nadoży|cie (**-cia, -cia**; *gen pl* **-ć**) *nt* misuse
nadużyw|ać (**-am, -asz**; *pf* **nadużyć**) *vt +gen* to abuse
nadwa|ga (**-gi**; *dat sg* **-dze**) *f* excess weight; **mam lekką nadwagę** I'm a little overweight
nadziej|a (**-i, -e**; *gen pl* **-i**) *f* hope; **mam nadzieję, że przyjdziesz** I hope that you will come; **mam nadzieję, że zwyciężymy** I hope that we win
nadzie|nie (**-nia, -nia**; *gen pl* **-ń**) *nt* **1** (*w wypiekach, słodyczach*) filling **2** (*w kurczaku, indyku*) stuffing
nadz|ór (**-oru**; *loc sg* **-orze**) *m* (*nad pracą, osobą*) supervision
naf|ta (**-ty**; *dat sg* **-cie**) *f* **1** (*Aviat*) kerosene **2** (*pot: ropa naftowa*) oil
naftowy *adj* **1** (*wydobycie*) oil **2** (*lampa, ogrzewanie*) paraffin; **ropa naftowa** petroleum, oil
nagi *adj* **1** (*osoba bez ubrania*) naked, nude **2** (*bez dodatków*) plain
nagin|ać (**-am, -asz**; *pf* **nagiąć**) *vt* to bend
naglący *adj* urgent
nagle *adv* **1** (*raptem*) suddenly **2** (*bez uprzedzenia*) unexpectedly
nagłów|ek (**-ka, -ki**; *inst sg* **-kiem**) *m* **1** (*w artykule*) heading **2** (*w gazecie*) headline **3** (*na papeterii*) letterhead
nagły *adj* **1** (*przyjazd, spotkanie*) sudden **2** (*wymagający szybkiej reakcji*) urgent; **w ~m wypadku należy zadzwonić na numer 112** in case of emergency, ring 112
nago *adv* in the nude
nagoś|ć (**-ci**) *f* nudity
nagradz|ać (**-am, -asz**; *pf* **nagrodzić**) *vt* (*za zwycięstwo, medalem*) to reward
nagra|nie (**-nia, -nia**; *gen pl* **-ń**) *nt* (*muzyczne, filmowe*) recording
nagro|da (**-dy, -dy**; *loc sg* **-dzie**; *gen pl* **nagród**) *f* **1** (*w konkursie*) prize **2** (*za osiągnięcia*) reward **3** (*dawana przez stowarzyszenie*) award; **~ Nobla** the Nobel prize
nagr|odzić (**-odzę, -odzisz**; *imp* **-odź** *lub* **-ódź**) *vb pf od* **nagradzać**
nagryw|ać (**-am, -asz**; *pf* **nagrać**) *vt* to record
naiwny *adj* naive; **pierwsza naiwna** ingénue
najbardziej *adv superl od* **bardzo**; **jak ~!** by all means!
najbliższy *adj superl od* **bliski**; **przyjdę w ~m czasie** I will come very soon
najdalej *adv superl od* **daleko**
naj|eść się (**-em, -esz**; *3 pl* **-edzą**; *imp* **-edz**; *pt* **-adł, -adła, -edli**) *vr pf* to eat one's fill; **najadł się do syta** he had had enough to eat
najgorszy *adj superl od* **zły**; **w ~m wypadku** *lub* **razie przyjdziemy jutro** if the worst comes to the worst, we'll come tomorrow
najgorzej *adv superl od* **źle**; **nie jest z nami ~** we're not doing too badly
najlepiej *adv superl od* **dobrze**

najlepszy *adj superl od* **dobry**; **w ~m wypadku pojedziemy razem** the best-case scenario is that we would go together; **najlepsze, co możesz zrobić, to...** the best thing you can do is...

najmniej *adv superl od* **mało**; **~ problemów** the least problems; **~ osób/towarów** the fewest people/ goods; **co ~ 5 osób zostało rannych** at least five people were injured

najmniejszy *adj superl od* **mały**; **on zawsze idzie po linii najmniejszego oporu** he always takes the line of least resistance

najnowszy *adj superl od* **nowy**

najpierw *adv* to begin with

najpóźniej *adv superl od* **późno**; **~ w niedzielę** on Sunday at the (very) latest

najstarszy *adj superl od* **stary**

najwięcej *adv superl od* **dużo, wiele**

najwyżej *adv superl od* **wysoko**; **~ cztery** four at the (very) most

najwyższy *adj superl od* **wysoki**; **~ czas, żeby przeprosił** it's high time he apologized; **sąd N~** ≈ the High Court (*Brit*), ≈ the Supreme Court (*US*); **najwyższe piętro** the top floor

nakar|mić (-mię, -misz) *vb pf od* **karmić**

naka|z (-zu, -zy; *loc sg* **-zie)** *m* **1** order **2** (*w prawie: eksmisji, konfiskaty*) warrant

nakaz|ywać (-uję, -ujesz; *pf* **-ać)** *vt* to order; **nakazuję ci przestać mówić** I order you to stop talking!; **lekarz nakazał mi dietę** the doctor put me on a diet

nakle|jać (-jam, -jasz; *pf* **-ić)** *vt* (*naklejki, plakaty*) to stick

naklej|ka (-ki, -ki; *dat sg* **-ce**; *gen pl* **-ek)** *f* **1** (*na produkcie*) label **2** (*z nazwiskiem, obrazkiem*) sticker

nakła|d (-du, -dy; *loc sg* **-dzie)** *m* (*publikacji*) edition; **nakłady** *pl* (*Fin*) expenditure *sg*; **~ książki jest wyczerpany** the book is out of print; **ponosić (ponieść** *pf*) **znaczne ~y finansowe** to incur considerable costs

nakry|cie (-cia, -cia; *gen pl* **-ć)** *nt* **1** covering **2** (*sztućce, naczynia*) place setting; **~ głowy** headgear; **podaj ~ na trzy osoby** set the table for three

nakry|ć (-ję, -jesz) *vt pf od* **nakrywać**; (*pot: przestępcę*) to nail; **nakryli go na gorącym uczynku** they caught him red-handed

nakryw|ać (-am, -asz; *pf* **nakryć)** *vt* to cover; **nakryła dziecko kocem** she covered the child with a blanket

nal|ać (-eję, -ejesz) *vb pf od* **nalewać**

naleg|ać (-am, -asz) *vi*: **~ na coś** to insist on sth; **nalegam, abyś to przeczytał** I insist that you read this

naleśni|k (-ka, -ki; *inst sg* **-kiem)** *m* (*Kulin*) pancake (*Brit*), crepe (*US*)

nalew|ać (-am, -asz; *pf* **nalać)** *vt* (*napełniać płynem naczynie*) to pour (out)

należ|eć (-ę, -ysz) *vi*: **~ do** *+gen* to belong to; **~ się** *vr*: **ile się należy?** what do I owe you?; **należy to oddać** it's necessary to return it; **należy mi się pięć złotych** I am owed 5 zlotys; **to mi się od nich należy** I am entitled to this from them

należnoś|ć (-ci, -ci; *gen pl* **-ci)** *f* amount payable; **musimy uiścić ~ za te usługi** we have to settle the bill for these services

nałogo|wiec (-wca, -wcy) *m* (*osoba uzależniona*) addict

nałogowy *adj* **1** (*alkoholik*) confirmed **2** (*hazardzista*) problem

nał|óg (-ogu, -ogi; *inst pl* **-ogiem)** *m* **1** (*szkodliwy nawyk*) habit **2** (*zależność od substancji*) addiction

nam *pron dat od* **my**

nami *pron inst od* **my**; **chodź z ~** come with us

namiętnoś|ć (-ci, -ci; *gen pl* **-ci)** *f* passion

namiętny *adj* **1** (*kochanek*) passionate **2** (*kinoman*) avid

namio|t (-tu, -ty; *loc sg* **-cie)** *m* tent

namó|wić (-wię, -wisz) *vt pf*: **namówił mnie na kupno samochodu** he talked me into buying a car

naokoło *prep +gen* round ▷ *adv* (all) around

napa|d (-du, -dy; *loc sg* **-dzie)** *m* **1** (*akt agresji*) assault **2** (*bólu, płaczu*) fit

napa|dać (**-dnę, -dniesz**; *pf* **napaść**) *vt* to attack
napastni|k (**-ka, -cy**; *inst sg* **-kiem**) *m* **1** (*osoba atakująca*) assailant **2** (*piłkarz*) striker
napaś|ć[1] (**-ci, -ci**; *gen pl* **-ci**) *f* (*akt fizycznej agresji*) assault
napa|ść[2] (**-dnę, -dniesz**; *imp* **-dnij**) *vb pf od* **napadać**
napeł|niać (**-niam, -niasz**; *pf* **-nić**) *vt* (*naczynie, pojemnik*) to fill
napeł|nić (**-nię, -nisz**; *imp* **-nij**) *vb pf od* **napełniać**
napi|ć się (**-ję, -jesz**) *vr pf* (*wody, alkoholu*) to have a drink
napię|cie (**-cia, -cia**; *gen pl* **-ć**) *nt* **1** (*elektryczne*) voltage **2** (*mięśni*) tension **3** (*emocjonalne*) tension
napięty *adj* **1** (*plan dnia*) full **2** (*sytuacja, emocje*) tense
napi|s (**-su, -sy**; *loc sg* **-sie**) *m* notice; **napisy** *pl* (Cine) **1** (*czołówka*) the credits **2** (*dialogowe*) subtitles
napi|sać (**-szę, -szesz**; *imp* **-sz**) *vb pf od* **pisać**
napiw|ek (**-ku, -ki**; *inst sg* **-kiem**) *m* (*w restauracji, w hotelu*) tip
nap|ój (**-oju, -oje**; *gen pl* **-ojów**) *m* drink
napra|wa (**-wy, -wy**; *dat sg* **-wie**) *f* repair; **samochód jest w naprawie** the car is being repaired
naprawdę *adv* really; **~ to powiedział?** did he really say that?
napra|wiać (**-wiam, -wiasz**; *pf* **-wić**) *vt* **1** (*likwidować wady*) to repair **2** (*przen: likwidować negatywne skutki*) to put right **3** (*brak*) to compensate for
naprzód *adv* forward
naraz *adv* **1** (*raptem*) all of a sudden **2** (*w tym samym czasie*) at the same time; **nie (mówcie) wszyscy ~!** don't all talk at the same time!
narciarst|wo (**-wa**; *loc sg* **-wie**) *nt* skiing
narciarz (**-a, -e**; *gen pl* **-y**) *m* skier
nareszcie *adv* at (long) last
narkoma|n (**-na, -ni**; *loc sg* **-nie**) *m* drug addict
narkomani|a (**-i**) *f* drug addiction
narkoty|k (**-ku, -ki**; *inst sg* **-kiem**) *m* (*substancja odurzająca*) drug
narko|za (**-zy, -zy**; *dat sg* **-zie**) *f* (*w medycynie*) anaesthesia (*Brit*), anesthesia (*US*); **być pod narkozą** to be under anaesthetic (*Brit*) *lub* anesthetic (*US*)
narodowoś|ć (**-ci, -ci**; *gen pl* **-ci**) *f* (*polska, francuska*) nationality
narodowy *adj* national
narodze|nie (**-nia, -nia**; *gen pl* **-ń**) *nt* birth; **Boże N~** Christmas
nar|odzić się (**-odzę, -odzisz**; *imp* **-ódź**) *vr* to come into being
nar|ód (**-odu, -ody**; *loc sg* **-odzie**) *m* **1** (*społeczność*) nation **2** (*mieszkańcy kraju*) people; **Organizacja Narodów Zjednoczonych** the United Nations
narys|ować (**-uję, -ujesz**) *vb pf od* **rysować**
narzą|d (**-du, -dy**; *loc sg* **-dzie**) *m* (*wewnętrzny, władzy*) organ
narzeczon|a (**-ej, -e**) *f decl like adj* fiancée
narzecz|ony (**-onego, -eni**) *m decl like adj* fiancé; **narzeczeni** *pl* the engaged couple
narzek|ać (**-am, -asz**) *vi* to complain; **nigdy nie narzekał na brak pieniędzy** he never complained about being short of money
narzę|dzie (**-dzia, -dzia**; *gen pl* **-dzi**) *nt* **1** (*instalatorskie, stolarskie*) tool **2** (*elektrotechniczne*) instrument
nas *pron gen, acc, loc od* **my**; **nie ma ~ w pracy** we're out (at the moment); **mówią o ~** they're talking about us; **idą bez ~** they're going without us
nasenny *adj*: **lek ~** sleeping pill
nasi *pron zob.* **nasz**
nasi|ać się (**-a**; *pf* **-ić**) *vr* (*zwiększać prędkość, intensywność*) to intensify
nastawie|nie (**-nia**) *nt* attitude; **~ do życia** attitude to life; **przyjechał z ~m, że wygra** he came with the expectation of winning
nastą|pić (**-pię, -pisz**; *impf* **następować**) *vi* to follow; **nastąpił psu na ogon** he stepped on the dog's tail
następc|a (**-y, -y**) *m decl like f in sg* successor
następnie *adv* next
następny *adj* next; **następnego dnia** the next *lub* following day;

~ **proszę!** next, please!; **~m razem uważaj co mówisz!** next time, mind what you say!
nastę|powa ć (**-puję, -pujesz**) *vb* to follow
nastolat|ek (**-ka, -ki**; *inst sg* **-kiem**) *m* teenager
nastr|ój (**-oju, -oje**) *m* **1** (*samopoczucie psychiczne*) mood **2** (*atmosfera*) atmosphere; **jestem dziś w dobrym/złym nastroju** I'm in a good/bad mood today
nasu|nąć (**-nę, -niesz**; *imp* **-ń**) *vb pf od* **nasuwać**
nasuw|ać (**-am, -asz**; *pf* **nasunąć**) *vt*: **nasunął kaptur na głowę** he pulled his hood over his head; **~ się** *vr* (*o pomyśle*) to come to mind; **nasunęło mi się to na myśl** it crossed my mind
nasz *possessive pron* **1** (*przed rzeczownikiem*) our **2** (*bez rzeczownika*) ours; **to jest ~ dom** this is our house; **ten dom jest ~** this house is ours
naszyjni|k (**-ka, -ki**; *inst sg* **-kiem**) *m* necklace
naślad|ować (**-uję, -ujesz**) *vt* **1** (*kopiować*) to copy **2** (*imitować*) to imitate
naśladowc|a (**-y, -y**) *m decl like f in sg* imitator
naśmiew|ać się (**-am, -asz**) *vr* to ridicule; **inne dzieci ciągle się z niego naśmiewały** the other children always made fun of him
natchnie|nie (**-nia, -nia**; *gen pl* **-ń**) *nt* (*inspiracja*) inspiration
natk|nąć się (**-nę, -niesz**; *imp* **-nij**) *vb pf od* **natykać się**
natomiast *adv* however
natrętny *adj* obtrusive; **prześladują go natrętne myśli** he is tormented by obsessional ideas
natrys|k (**-ku, -ki**; *inst sg* **-kiem**) *m* (*prysznic*) shower
natu|ra (**-ry**; *loc sg* **-rze**) *f* nature; **ten obraz to martwa ~** this picture is a still life
naturalnie *adv* naturally
naturalny *adj* natural; **jest naturalną blondyką** she's a natural blonde
natychmiast *adv* immediately, instantly
natychmiastowy *adj* immediate, instant
natyk|ać się (**-am, -asz**; *pf* **natknąć**) *vr*: **~ na kogoś/coś** to bump into sb/sth
naucz|ać (**-am, -asz**) *vt*: **~ dzieci języków obcych** to teach children foreign languages, to teach foreign languages to children; **poświęca się nauczaniu młodzieży** he is dedicated to teaching young people
nauczyciel (**-a, -e**; *gen pl* **-i**) *m* teacher; **~ polskiego/chemii** Polish/chemistry teacher
nauczyciel|ka (**-ki, -ki**; *dat sg* **-ce**; *gen pl* **-ek**) *f* teacher
naucz|yć (**-ę, -ysz**) *vb pf od* **uczyć**
nau|ka (**-ki, -ki**; *dat sg* **-ce**) *f* **1** (*dziedzina wiedzy*) science **2** (*edukacja*) study **3** (*morał*) lesson; **~ jazdy** (*kurs*) driving lessons *pl*
nauko|wiec (**-wca, -wcy**) *m* **1** scholar **2** (*fizyki, biologii*) scientist
naukowy *adj* **1** (*eksperyment*) scientific **2** (*dyskusja, referat*) scholarly; **przeprowadzać** (**przeprowadzić** *pf*) **badania naukowe** to (carry out) research; **pracownik ~** (*na uniwersytecie*) research worker; **pomoce naukowe** (*w szkole, na uniwersytecie*) teaching aids
naumyślnie *adv* deliberately
na|wa (**-wy, -wy**; *loc sg* **-wie**) *f*: **~ główna** (*w koście*) nave; **~ boczna** (*w kościele*) aisle
nawet *adv* even
nawia|s (**-su, -sy**; *loc sg* **-sie**) *m* bracket; **w ~ach kwadratowych** in square brackets; **w ~ach okrągłych** in round brackets; **w ~ach klamrowych** in curly brackets; **to słowo jest w ~ie** this word is in parentheses
nawierzch|nia (**-ni, -nie**; *gen pl* **-ni**) *f* (*drogi*) surface
nawilż|ać (**-am, -asz**; *pf* **-yć**) *vt* **1** (*ubranie*) dampen **2** (*twarz, ciało*) to moisturize
nawy|k (**-ku, -ki**; *inst sg* **-kiem**) *m* habit
nawzajem *adv* each other; **oni lubią się ~** they like each other; **Wesołych**

Świąt! N~! Merry Christmas! Same to you!

naz|wa (**-wy, -wy**; *dat sg* **-wie**) *f* name; **to jest restauracja tylko z nazwy** this is a restaurant in name only

naz|wać (**-wę, -wiesz**; *imp* **-wij**) *vb pf od* **nazywać**

nazwis|ko (**-ka, -ka**; *inst sg* **-kiem**) *nt* surname (*Brit*), last name (*US*); **~ panieńskie** maiden name; **wypisywać** (**wypisać** *pf*) **czek na czyjeś ~** to write (out) a cheque (*Brit*) *lub* check (*US*) in sb's name; **wyrobił sobie ~ w świecie sztuki** he made a name for himself in the art world

nazyw|ać (**-am, -asz**; *pf* **nazwać**) *vt* to call; **~ się** *vr* to be called; **musimy ~ rzeczy po imieniu** we need to call a spade a spade; **jak się pan/pani nazywa?** what's your name, please?; **to nazywa się marketing bezpośredni** this is known as direct marketing

n.e. *abbr* (*= naszej ery*) AD

negatywny *adj* negative

negocjacj|e (**-i**) *pl* (*pokojowe, biznesowe*) negotiations

negocj|ować (**-uję, -ujesz**) *vb* to negotiate

nekrolo|g (**-gu, -gi**; *inst sg* **-giem**) *m* obituary

ner|ka (**-ki, -ki**; *dat sg* **-ce**; *gen pl* **-ek**) *f* kidney

nerwic|a (**-y, -e**) *f* (*Med, Psych*) neurosis

nerwowy *adj* (*załamanie, zachowanie*) nervous; **tik ~** a nervous tic

netboo|k (**-ka, -ki**; *loc sg* **-ku**; *inst sg* **-kiem**) *m* (*Komput*) netbook

neurolo|g (**-ga, -dzy** *lub* **-gowie**) *m* neurologist

neutralny *adj* **1** neutral **2** (*polityk*) independent; (*kraj*) neutral

nędz|a (**-y, -e**) *f* misery

nędzarz (**-a, -e**; *gen pl* **-y**) *m* destitute person

nędzny *adj* (*ubogi, marny*) miserable

nia|nia (**-ni, -nie**; *gen pl* **-ń**) *f* nanny

nią *pron inst od* **ona**

nic *pron* **1** nothing **2** (*z innym wyrazem przeczącym*) anything; **~ dziwnego, że wygrał** no wonder he won; **~ z tego nie będzie** it's no use!; **to ~** (*nie ma sprawy*) never mind; **~ nie wie** he knows nothing

nicpo|ń (**-nia, -nie**; *gen pl* **-ni** *lub* **-niów**) *m* good-for-nothing

niczyj *adj* nobody's; **ziemia ~a** no-man's-land

ni|ć (**-ci, -ci**; *inst pl* **-ćmi**) *f* thread; **z interesu wyszły nici** the business came to nothing

nie *part* **1** no **2** (*z czasownikiem*) not; **~ ma jej tam** she's not there; **o ~!** oh no!; **~ ma na co czekać** it's no use waiting; **~ przejmuj się!** don't worry!

nieaktualny *adj* **1** (*wejściówka*) invalid **2** (*oferta handlowa*) unavailable **3** (*wiadomość*) out-of-date

niebezpieczeńst|wo (**-wa, -wa**; *loc sg* **-wie**) *nt* **1** (*zagrożenie*) danger **2** (*ryzyko*) risk

niebezpieczny *adj* **1** (*przestępca, miejsce*) dangerous **2** (*ruch*) risky **3** (*praca, wyprawa*) hazardous

niebieski *adj* **1** (*barwa*) blue **2** (*Astron*) celestial; **ciała ~e** (*Astron*) heavenly bodies; **królestwo ~e** (*Rel*) the kingdom of heaven; **~ ptak** free-loader

nie|bo (**-ba, -ba**; *loc sg* **-bie**; *gen pl* **-bios**; *dat pl* **-biosom**; *inst pl* **-biosami**; *loc pl* **-biosach**) *nt* **1** sky **2** (*królestwo boże lub niebieskie*) heaven; **gwiazdy na niebie** stars in the sky; **nie każdy anioł mieszka w niebie** not all angels dwell in heaven; **na wakacjach śpi pod gołym niebem** during the holidays (*Brit*) *lub* vacation (*US*) he sleeps outdoors; **ta potrawa to ~ w gębie!** (*pot*) this dish is divine!; **on jest o ~ lepszym uczniem** he is streets ahead of the other pupils

nieboszczy|k (**-ka, -cy** *lub* **-ki**; *inst sg* **-kiem**) *m* the deceased

niech *part*: **~ przyjdą** let them come; **~ się zastanowię** let me think *lub* see; **~ ci będzie** have it your way

niechcący *adv* (*nieumyślnie*) accidentally

niechę|ć (**-ci, -ci**) *f* dislike; **żywi ~ do niej od dawna** he has disliked her for a long time; **czuł ~ do swojej nudnej pracy** he had an aversion to his

boring job; **z niechęcią pomyślała o nim** she thought of him with distaste
niechętnie *adv* reluctantly
niechlujny *adj* (*zaniedbany*) slovenly
nieciekawy *adj* **1** boring **2** (*dzielnica*) unpleasant
niecierpliwy *adj* impatient
nieco *adv* somewhat; **~ mniejszy** somewhat smaller; **wiedział co ~ o niej** he knew a little bit about her
nieczynny *adj* **1** (*firma*) defunct **2** (*mechanizm*) non-functioning **3** (*wulkan*) extinct
nieczytelny *adj* **1** (*charakter pisma*) illegible **2** (*wiadomość*) unintelligible
niedaleko *adv* **1** (*w przestrzeni*) near (by) **2** (*w czasie*) soon
niedawno *adv* recently
niedawny *adj* recent; **studiował tu do niedawna** he studied here until recently; **studiuje tu od niedawna** he began studying here recently
niedługo *adv* **1** (*zaraz*) soon, before long **2** (*przez krótki czas*) briefly
niedobrany *adj* mismatched
niedobry *adj* **1** (*osoba*) bad **2** (*informacja*) bad **3** (*niesmaczny*) disgusting
niedobrze *adv* **1** (*czuć się, wyglądać*) unwell **2** (*w sposób niepożądany*) badly **3** (*z trudem*) not well; **~ mi** I feel sick; **zrobiło mi się ~** I started to feel sick; **z babcią bardzo ~, trzeba wezwać lekarza** grandma's really not doing well, we'll need to call the doctor; **żylaste mięso ~ się kroi** stringy meat doesn't cut well
niedojrzałoś|ć (**-ci**) *f* (*psychiczna, fizyczna*) immaturity
niedojrzały *adj* **1** (*osoba*) immature **2** (*warzywo, owoc*) unripe **3** (*wino, ser*) immature
niedokładny *adj* **1** (*osoba, praca*) careless **2** (*pomiar, dane*) imprecise
niedokonany *adj* (*w językoznawstwie*) imperfective
niedokończony *adj* (*praca, zdanie*) incomplete
niedopuszczalny *adj* (*zachowanie*) unacceptable
niedorozwinięty *adj*: **dzieci niedorozwinięte** children with learning difficulties
niedostępny *adj* inaccessible
niedrogi *adj* inexpensive
niedwuznaczny *adj* (*oczywisty*) unambiguous
niedziel|a (**-i, -e**) *f* Sunday; **~ Palmowa/Wielkanocna** Palm/ Easter Sunday
niedźwie|dź (**-dzia, -dzie**; *gen pl* **-dzi**) *m* bear
nieefektowny *adj* (*styl, wygląd*) unremarkable
nieformalny *adj* informal
niefortunny *adj* (*wypowiedź, wydarzenie*) unfortunate
niefrasobliwy *adj* (*człowiek, rozrywka*) light-hearted
niegazowany *adj* (*płyn*) still
niegrzeczny *adj* **1** (*niekulturalny*) impolite **2** (*źle wychowany: o dzieciach*) naughty
nieistotny *adj* **1** (*bez znaczenia*) unimportant **2** (*bez związku*) irrelevant
niej *pron gen, dat, loc od* **ona**
niejadalny *adj* inedible
niejaki *adj* (*pewien*) a (certain); **~ pan Smith** a (certain) Mr Smith
niejednoznaczny *adj* ambiguous
niekiedy *adv* sometimes
niekoleżeński *adj* (*relacja, osoba*) unfriendly
niekompetentny *adj* **1** (*bez odpowiednich kwalifikacji*) incompetent **2** (*bez uprawnień*) unauthorized
niekompletny *adj* incomplete
niektórzy (*f, nt* **niektóre**) *pron* some; **~ sądzą, że masz rację** some (people) say that you're right
nielegalny *adj* (*substancja, emigrant*) illegal
nieletni *adj* (*Jur: przestępca*) juvenile ▷ *m decl like adj* (*Jur*) minor; **sąd dla ~ch** juvenile court
nieła|d (**-du**; *loc sg* **-dzie**) *m* (*brak porządku*) disarray
niemal *adv* almost; **jestem ~ pewien, że wyszedł** I am almost certain that he has left; **~ mu się udało** he was very nearly successful
niemiecki *adj* German
Niemcy *pl* Germany

niemniej *adv* however; **tym ~** even so; **nie jest to krokodyl, ~ jednak jest niebezpieczny** it isn't a crocodile, but it is dangerous all the same
niemodny *adj* unfashionable
niemoralny *adj* immoral
niem|owa (**-owy, -owy**; *dat sg* **-owie**; *gen pl* **-ów**) *m/f decl like f in sg* (*osoba niema*) person unable to speak
niemowl|ę (**-ęcia, -ęta**; *gen pl* **-ąt**) *nt* infant
niemożliwy *adj* impossible; **~ do osiągnięcia** unachievable
niemy *adj* **1** (*o osobie*) without speech **2** (*kino, zgoda*) silent
nienaturalny *adj* unnatural
nienawi|dzić (**-dzę, -dzisz**; *imp* **-dź**) *vt +gen* to hate
nienawiś|ć (**-ci**) *f* hatred, hate
nieobecny *adj* (*w szkole, pracy*) absent; **był obecny ciałem, ale ~ duchem** (*przen*) he was physically present but his mind was elsewhere
nieoczekiwany *adj* (*efekt, wydarzenie*) unexpected
nieodpłatnie *adv* free of charge
nieodpłatny *adj* (*gratis*) free
nieodpowiedni *adj* (*strój, zachowanie*) inappropriate
nieodpowiedzialny *adj* irresponsible
nieoficjalny *adj* unofficial
nieograniczony *adj* unlimited
nieosiągalny *adj* (*cel, wynik*) unattainable
niepalący *adj* non-smoking ▷ *m decl like adj* non-smoker; **sala dla ~ch** non-smoking room
nieparzysty *adj* (*liczba, cyfra*) odd
niepełnoletni *adj* under-age
niepełnosprawny *adj* disabled
niepewny *adj* **1** (*przyszłość*) uncertain **2** (*niegodny zaufania*) unreliable **3** (*wahający się*) faltering
niepodległoś|ć (**-ci**) *f* independence
niepodległy *adj* independent
niepok|oić (**-oję, -oisz**; *imp* **-ój**; *pf* **za-**) *vt* **1** (*powodować zmartwienie*) to worry **2** (*nachodzić*) to bother; **~ się** *vr* to worry; **niepokoił się o swoją pracę** he was worried about his job
niepokojący *adj* disturbing
niepokonany *adj* invincible
nieporęczny *adj* (*pakunek, bagaż*) cumbersome
nieposłuszeńst|wo (**-wa**; *loc sg* **-wie**) *nt* disobedience
niepotrzebny *adj* **1** (*gest, wysiłek: niekonieczny*) unnecessary **2** (*niepożądany*) superfluous
nieprawdopodobny *adj* improbable, unlikely
nieprawdziwy *adj* **1** (*zmyślony, nierzeczywisty*) false **2** (*fałszywy*) artificial
nieprawidłowy *adj* (*niepoprawny, nie odpowiadający normom*) wrong
nieprzychylny *adj* **1** (*wrogo nastawiony*) disapproving **2** (*niepomyślny: wiatr*) unfavourable (*Brit*), unfavorable (*US*)
nieprzydatny *adj* (*bezużyteczny*) useless
nieprzyja|ciel (**-ciela, -ciele**; *gen pl* **-ciół**; *dat pl* **-ciołom**; *inst pl* **-ciółmi**; *loc pl* **-ciołach**) *m* (*wróg*) enemy
nieprzyjacielski *adj* enemy
nieprzyjazny *adj* hostile
nieprzyjemny *adj* unpleasant
nieprzytomny *adj* **1** (*bez świadomości*) unconscious **2** (*nieobecny: wzrok*) vacant **3** (*z nienawiści*) mad; (*ze strachu*) paralysed
nieprzyzwoity *adj* (*zachowanie, obraz*) indecent
niepunktualny *adj* unpunctual
nierealny *adj* **1** (*wymyślony*) unreal **2** (*niemożliwy do wykonania*) unrealistic
nieregularny *adj* irregular
nierentowny *adj* unprofitable
nierówny *adj* **1** (*podłoga, blat*) uneven, rough **2** (*ulica*) bumpy **3** (*tempo, oddech*) uneven **4** (*podzielony nierówno*) unequal **5** (*zmienny*) erratic
niesamowity *adj* **1** (*straszny*) uncanny **2** (*zachwycający*) extraordinary
niesiesz *itd. vb zob.* **nieść**
nieskomplikowany *adj* straightforward
niesmaczny *adj* tasteless
niespodzian|ka (**-ki, -ki**; *dat sg* **-ce**; *gen pl* **-ek**) *f* surprise; **zrobił mi**

niespodziankę z okazji urodzin he gave me a surprise for my birthday
niespokojny *adj* **1** restless **2** (*morze*) rough
niesprawiedliwoś|ć (**-ci, -ci**; *gen pl* **-ci**) *f* injustice
niesprawiedliwy *adj* (*krzywdzący*) unfair, unjust
niestety *adv* unfortunately
niestrawnoś|ć (**-ci**) *f* indigestion
niestrawny *adj* indigestible
niesumienny *adj* unreliable
nieszczeroś|ć (**-ci**) *f* insincerity
nieszczery *adj* insincere; **ma ~ uśmiech** she has an insincere smile
nieszczęś|cie (**-cia, -cia**; *gen pl* **-ć**) *nt* **1** (*pech*) misfortune **2** (*tragedia*) disaster; **nieszczęścia chodzą parami** misfortunes never come singly
nieszczęśliwy *adj* **1** unhappy **2** (*żałosny*) miserable **3** (*przypadek*) unfortunate
nieszkodliwy *adj* **1** (*niegroźny*) harmless **2** (*niewinny*) innocent
nieść (**niosę, niesiesz**; *imp* **nieś**; *pt* **niósł, niosła, nieśli**) *vt* **1** to carry **2** (*pf* **przy-**) (*unosić*) to bring **3** (*pf* **z-**) (*składać*: *jaja*) to lay; **~ radość/smutek** to bring joy/sorrow; **wieść niesie, że był dobrym szefem** it is said that he was a good boss
nieślubny *adj*: **nieślubne dziecko** child born out of wedlock; **żyć w ~m związku** to cohabit
nieśmiały *adj* shy, timid
nieświadomy *adj* unaware; **on jest ~ konsekwencji** he is unaware of the consequences
nieświeży *adj* **1** (*czerstwy*) stale **2** (*zapach, potrawa*) bad, off **3** (*ubranie*) dirty; **czuję się jakaś nieświeża** I feel a bit worn out
nietolerancj|a (**-i**) *f* intolerance
nietolerancyjny *adj* intolerant
nietoperz (**-a, -e**; *gen pl* **-y**) *m* bat
nietrzeźwy *adj* drunk; **kierowca znajdował się w stanie ~m** the driver was in a state of intoxication
nietypowy *adj* **1** (*niezwyczajny*) uncharacteristic **2** (*wielkość*) non-standard
nieuczciwoś|ć (**-ci, -ci**; *gen pl* **-ci**) *f* dishonesty
nieuczciwy *adj* dishonest
nieudany *adj* (*eksperyment, przedsięwzięcie*) unsuccessful
nieudolny *adj* **1** (*niezdarny*) clumsy **2** (*nieudany*) ineffectual
nieufnoś|ć (**-ci**) *f* distrust
nieuleczalnie *adv*: **~ chory** incurably ill
nieuleczalny *adj* (*choroba, ból*) incurable
nieustannie *adv* (*nieprzerwanie, trwale*) unceasingly, continuously
nieuważny *adj* **1** (*słuchacz*) inattentive **2** (*zachowanie*) careless
nieważny *adj* **1** (*fakt, osoba*) insignificant **2** (*bilet, dokument*) invalid
niewątpliwie *adv* undoubtedly
niewdzięcznoś|ć (**-ci**) *f* ingratitude
niewdzięczny *adj* **1** (*o osobie*) ungrateful **2** (*zadanie*) unrewarding
niewiarygodny *adj* **1** (*niegodny zaufania*) unreliable **2** (*nie do wiary*) incredible
niewidoczny *adj* invisible
niewidomy *adj* blind; **niewidomi** *pl decl like adj* the blind
niewiele *pron* **1** (*czasu*) not much **2** (*przedmiotów*) not many ▷ *adv* (*trochę*) little
niewielki *adj* little
niewielu *pron*: **~ ludzi** few people; *zob.* **niewiele**
niewiernoś|ć (**-ci, -ci**; *gen pl* **-ci**) *f* infidelity
niewierny *adj* (*partner*) unfaithful
niewierzący *adj* unbelieving ▷ *m decl like adj* non-believer
niewinny *adj* innocent; **sąd uznał go za niewinnego** the court found him innocent
niewol|a (**-i**) *f* imprisonment; **jest w niewoli pieniądza** he is a slave to money
niewolnict|wo (**-wa**; *loc sg* **-wie**) *nt* slavery
niewolni|k (**-ka, -cy**; *inst sg* **-kiem**) *m* slave
niewrażliwy *adj* insensitive; **jest całkiem ~ na ludzką biedę** he is absolutely insensitive to poverty

niewybaczalny *adj* (*błąd, czyn*) unforgivable
niewygodny *adj* **1** (*fotel, ubranie*) uncomfortable **2** (*sytuacja*) inconvenient
niewyraźny *adj* **1** (*trudny do usłyszenia, do zobaczenia*) indistinct **2** (*trudny do zrozumienia*) obscure **3** (*nieswój*) out of sorts **4** (*niegodny zaufania: postać, działanie*) suspicious
niezadowolony *adj* dissatisfied; **ona jest ciągle niezadowolona ze swojego wyglądu** she is always unhappy with her appearance
niezależnoś|ć (**-ci**) *f* independence
niezależny *adj* (*ocena, fachowiec*) independent; **mowa niezależna** (*w językoznawstwie*) direct speech; **on od lat jest ~ materialnie** he has been financially independent for years
niezamężna *adj*: **~ kobieta** (*panna*) single woman
niezaprzeczalny *adj* (*fakt*) incontrovertible
niezaradny *adj* useless
niezbędny *adj* indispensable
niezbyt *adv* not very; **~ wysoki** not very tall
niezgrabny *adj* **1** (*człowiek, nogi*) unshapely **2** (*ruch*) awkward
niezły *adj* pretty good
nieznajomoś|ć (**-ci**) *f*: **~ języka polskiego** ignorance of Polish; **zgubiła go ~ przepisów** he was undone by his ignorance of the rules
nieznajomy *adj* unknown, unfamiliar ▷ *m decl like adj* stranger
nieznany *adj* unknown
niezręczny *adj* awkward
niezwykły *adj* unusual
nieźle *adv* not bad
nieżonaty *adj* (*kawaler*) unmarried, single
nieżywy *adj* dead
nigdy *adv* **1** never **2** (*w pytaniach, po przeczeniu*) ever; **nie rób tego ~ więcej** don't ever do that again; **już ~ (więcej) tego nie powiem** I will never (ever) say that again; **~ nie wiadomo, kiedy przyjdzie** you never know when he'll come
nigdzie *adv* **1** nowhere **2** (*w pytaniach, po przeczeniu*) anywhere; **~ indziej nie czułem się lepiej** I never felt better anywhere else
nijaki *adj* (*osoba, propozycja*) unremarkable; **rodzaj ~** (*w językoznawstwie*) neuter
nikoty|na (**-ny**; *dat sg* **-nie**) *f* nicotine
nikt *pron* **1** nobody **2** (*w pytaniach, po przeczeniu*) anyone, anybody; **~ z nas go nie zna** none of us knows him
nim *pron loc, inst od* **on, ono**
nimi *pron inst od* **oni, one**
niosę *itd. vb zob.* **nieść**
niski *adj* **1** (*stół, budynek*) low **2** (*osoba*) short
nisko *adv* low
niszcz|eć (**-eję, -ejesz**) *vi* to deteriorate
niszcz|yć (**-ę, -ysz**; *pf* **z-**) *vt* to destroy
nit|ka (**-ki, -ki**; *dat sg* **-ce**; *gen pl* **-ek**) *f* thread; **nitki** *pl* (*Kulin: makaron*) vermicelli; **krytycy nie zostawili na filmie suchej nitki** the critics tore the film to pieces; **~ dentystyczna** dental floss
nizi|na (**-ny, -ny**; *dat sg* **-nie**) *f* lowland
nizinny *adj* **1** (*teren*) lowland **2** (*region*) low-lying
niż[1] (**-u, -e**) *m* **1** (*niskie ciśnienie atmosferyczne*) low **2** (*w geografii*) lowland
niż[2] *conj* than
niżej *adv comp od* **nisko**; **wykonawca musi umieścić w ofercie ~ wymieniony dokument** the contractor must submit the document mentioned below; **ja, ~ podpisany, oświadczam...** I, the undersigned, declare...
niższy *adj comp od* **niski 1** (*stół, dom*) lower **2** (*o osobie*) shorter **3** (*standard*) inferior **4** (*w hierarchii*) subordinate
no *part* **1**: **no, no!** (*wyrażający podziw, zdziwienie*) well, well!; (*uspokajający*) there, now! **2** (*twierdzący: pot*) yeah; **no to idź już stąd!** so go!; **no to co, że wyszedł?** so what, he left?
noc (**-y, -e**; *gen pl* **-y**) *f* night; **w ~y** at night; **śni o tym co ~** he dreams about this every night

nocle|g (**-gu, -gi**; *inst sg* **-giem**) *m* (*w hotelu*) accommodation, accommodations *pl* (*US*)
nocni|k (**-ka, -ki**; *inst sg* **-kiem**) *m* (*dla małych dzieci*) potty; **obudzić się z ręką w ~u** (*pot: przen*) to have been caught napping
nocny *adj* (*lot, autobus*) night
noc|ować (**-uję, -ujesz**; *pf* **prze-**) *vi* to stay overnight *lub* for the night
no|ga (**-gi, -gi**; *dat sg* **-dze**; *gen pl* **nóg**) *f* **1** (*Anat: kończyna*) leg **2** (*stopa*) foot **3** (*krzesła*) leg; **od rana jest na ~ch** he's been on his feet since the morning; **wywrócił wszystko do góry ~mi** he turned everything upside down
nominacj|a (**-i, -e**; *gen pl* **-i**) *f* **1** (*w pracy*) appointment **2** (*do odznaczenia*) nomination
nomin|ować (**-uję, -ujesz**) *vt* (*im*)*pf* **1** (*w pracy*) to appoint **2** (*do odznaczenia*) to nominate
nonsens (**-u, -y**) *m* nonsense
nor|ma (**-my, -my**; *dat sg* **-mie**) *f* norm
normalnie *adv* normally
normalny *adj* **1** normal **2** (*bilet*) full-fare
Norwegi|a (**-i**) *f* Norway
norweski *adj* Norwegian
no|s (**-sa, -sy**; *loc sg* **-sie**) *m* nose; **nie wtykaj ~a w nie swoje sprawy** (*przen*) don't stick your nose into other people's affairs; **on ma ~a do interesów** he's got a flair for business
nosi|ć (**-szę, -sisz**; *imp* **noś**) *vt* **1** (*przedmiot*) to carry **2** (*ubranie, krawat, brodę, perukę*) to wear **3** (*tytuł*) to bear **4** (*imię, nazwisko*) to use
nosoroż|ec (**-ca, -ce**) *m* rhinoceros
nostalgi|a (**-i**) *f* nostalgia
nostalgiczny *adj* (*atmosfera, utwór*) nostalgic
nosz|e (**-y**) *pl* stretcher *sg*
notariusz (**-a, -e**; *gen pl* **-y**) *m* notary (public)
notatk|a (**-i**) *f* note
notatni|k (**-ka, -ki**; *inst sg* **-kiem**) *m* notebook
noteboo|k (**-ka, -ki**; *loc sg* **-ku**: *inst sg* **-kiem**) *m* (*Komput*) notebook
note|s (**-su, -sy**; *loc sg* **-sie**) *m* notebook
not|ować (**-uję, -ujesz**; *pf* **za-**) *vt* to note
nowatorski *adj* (*pomysł, rozwiązanie*) innovative
Nowa Zelandia (**Nowej Zelandii**) *f* New Zealand
nowel|a (**-i, -e**) *f* short story
nowicjusz (**-a, -e**; *gen pl* **-y**) *m* novice
nowi|na (**-ny, -ny**; *dat sg* **-nie**) *f* (*wiadomość*) news
nowoczesnoś|ć (**-ci**) *f* modernity
nowoczesny *adj* (*sztuka, technologia*) modern
noworod|ek (**-ka, -ki**; *inst sg* **-kiem**) *m* newborn baby
nowoś|ć (**-ci, -ci**; *gen pl* **-ci**) *f* **1** (*wprowadzenie czegoś nowego*) novelty **2** (*wydawnicza*) new release
nowotw|ór (**-oru, -ory**; *loc sg* **-orze**) *m* (*w medycynie*) tumour (*Brit*), tumor (*US*)
nowy *adj* new; **samochód fabrycznie ~** a (brand) new car; **stół jak ~** the table is as good as new; **~ Rok** New Year
nożycz|ki (**-ek**) *pl* scissors; **~ do paznokci** nail scissors
nóż (**noża, noże**; *gen pl* **noży**) *m* knife; **jest zadłużony i ma ~ na gardle** he is in debt and in an impossible situation
np. *abbr* (= *na przykład*) e.g.
nr *abbr* (= *numer*) no.
nu|da (**-dy, -dy**; *dat sg* **-dzie**; *gen pl* **-dów**) *f* boredom
nudny *adj* (*nieciekawy*) boring
nudziarz (**-a, -e**; *gen pl* **-y**) *m* bore
nudz|ić (**-ę, -isz**; *pf* **za-**) to bore; **~ się** *vr* to be bored; **za~ kogoś na śmierć** to bore sb to death
nume|r (**-ru, -ry**; *loc sg* **-rze**) *m* **1** (*telefonu, pokoju*) number **2** (*ubrania*) size **3** (*w teatrze, kabarecie*) act **4** (*czasopisma*) issue; **sprzedają stary ~ „National Geographic"** they are selling old issues of the National Geographic; **~ rejestracyjny samochodu** registration number
nur|ek (**-ka**; *inst sg* **-kiem**) *m* **1** (*nom pl* **-kowie**) (*osoba*) diver **2** (*nom pl* **-ki**) (*skok do wody*) dive

nurk|ować (**-uję, -ujesz**; *pf* **za-**) *vi* **1** (*o osobie*) to dive **2** (*o samolocie*) to nosedive

nu|ta (**-ty, -ty**; *dat sg* **-cie**) *f* note; **nuty** *pl* score; **kłamie cały czas jak z nut** he lies through his teeth the whole time

nużący *adj* tiresome

SŁOWO KLUCZOWE

o *prep +loc* **1** (*na temat*) about, on; **książka o historii** a book about *lub* on history; **rozmawiać/myśleć/wiedzieć o czymś** to talk/think/know about sth
2 (*za pomocą*): **o własnych siłach** unaided; **o kulach** on crutches
3 (*czas*) at; **o (godzinie) ósmej** at eight (o'clock); **o świcie/zmierzchu/północy** at dawn/dusk/midnight
4 (*do opisania*) with; **dziewczyna o niebieskich oczach** a girl with blue eyes
▷ *prep +acc* **1** (*do porównania*) by; **o połowę niższy** (*o człowieku*) half the size; **starszy o dwa lata** two years older
2 (*z czasownikiem*): **martwić się o kogoś/coś** to worry about sb/sth; **prosić/pytać o coś** to ask about *lub* for sth; **kłócić się o coś** to argue about sth
3: **opiera się o ścianę** he is leaning against the wall
▷ *excl* oh

oa|za (**-zy, -zy**; *loc sg* **-zie**) *f* oasis; **~ spokoju** an oasis of calm

oba *num* both; **~ psy/przepisy** both dogs/recipes

obaj *num* both; **~ chłopcy** both boys

obal|ać (**-am, -asz**; *pf* **-ić**) *vt* **1** (*na ringu*) to knock down **2** (*płot*) to fell

3 (*rząd*) to overthrow 4 (*hipotezę*) to refute

oba|wa (**-wy, -wy**; *dat sg & loc sg* **-wie**) *f*: **~ (o kogoś/coś)** concern (for sb/sth); **wyraził obawę przed nią** he expressed his fear of her

obawi|ać się (**-am, -asz**) *vr*: **~ kogoś/czegoś** to fear sb/sth; **obawiam się, że nie masz racji** I am afraid (that) you're wrong

obca|s (**-sa, -sy**; *loc sg* **-sie**) *m* (*na butach*) heel

obc|iąć (**-etnę, -etniesz**; *imp* **-etnij**) *vb pf od* **obcinać**

obciąż|ać (**-am, -asz**; *pf* **-yć**) *vt* 1 (*pakunkami, towarem*) to weigh down 2 (*w balonach*) to ballast 3 (*pracą*) to burden, to saddle 4 (*umysł*) to burden; **~ kogoś winą za coś** to blame sb for sth

obcier|ać (**-am, -asz**; *pf* **obetrzeć**) *vt* 1 (*chusteczką*) to wipe 2 (*kaleczyć skórę*) to graze, to scrape 3 (*o butach*) to rub

obcin|ać (**-am, -asz**; *pf* **obciąć**) *vt* 1 (*włosy*) to cut 2 (*krzew*) to cut off 3 (*zmniejszyć*) to cut down on

obcisły *adj* (*o ubraniu*) tight

obco *adv*: **okolica wyglądała ~ i nieprzyjaźnie** the neighbourhood (*Brit*) *lub* neighborhood (*US*) looked strange and unfriendly

obcokrajo|wiec (**-wca, -wcy**; *voc sg* **-wcze** *lub* **-wcu**) *m* foreigner

obcy *adj* 1 (*należący do kogoś innego*) someone else's 2 (*nie stąd*) alien 3 (*zagraniczny*) foreign ▷ *m decl like adj* (*osoba nie stąd*) stranger; **„~m wstęp wzbroniony"** (*w terenie*) "no trespassing"; (*w biurze, sklepie*) "private"; (*w budynku strzeżonym*) "authorized personnel only"

obecnie *adv* at present, currently

obecnoś|ć (**-ci**) *f* 1 (*istnienie*) existence 2 (*w szkole, pracy*) attendance; **spotkanie odbyło się w obecności prezesa** the meeting took place in the chairman's presence

obecny *adj* present; **obecni** *pl* those present; **jest ~ na zajęciach** he attends lessons; **w chwili obecnej** at present; **~/obecna!** (*w szkole*) here!, present!

obejm|ować (**-uję, -ujesz**; *pf* **objąć**) *vt* 1 (*rękoma*) to hug 2 (*zawierać*) to include, to encompass; **~ się** *vr* to hug each other

obejrz|eć (**-ę, -ysz**; *imp* **-yj**) *vb pf od* **oglądać**

obel|ga (**-gi, -gi**; *dat sg & loc sg* **-dze**) *f* (*obraza*) insult

obfitoś|ć (**-ci**) *f* (*towarów*) abundance

obfity *adj* abundant; **mleko jest obfite w wapń** milk is rich in calcium; **kobieta o ~ch kształtach** a corpulent woman

obgad|ywać (**-uję, -ujesz**; *pf* **-ać**) (*pot*) *vt* 1 (*dyskutować*) to talk over *lub* about 2 (*oczerniać*) to backbite

obi|ad (**-adu, -ady**; *loc sg* **-edzie**) *m* 1 (*w południe*) lunch 2 (*wieczorem*) dinner; **jeść** (**zjeść** *pf*) **~** to have lunch/dinner; **~ proszony** dinner (party)

obiadowy *adj* (*zestaw, danie*) lunch, dinner

obie *num* both; **~ dziewczyny** both girls

obiec|ywać (**-uję, -ujesz**; *pf* **-ać**) *vi* to promise ▷ *vt*: **~ (komuś) coś** to promise (sb) sth; **~ gruszki na wierzbie** to make empty promises

obie|g (**-gu**; *inst* **-giem**) *m* (*krwi, informacji*) circulation

obiek|t (**-tu, -ty**; *loc sg* **-cie**) *m* 1 (*rzecz*) object 2 (*budowla*) structure, building; **była ~em ciągłej krytyki** she was the target of constant criticism

obiektywnie *adv* objectively

obiektywny *adj* objective

objaś|niać (**-niam, -niasz**; *pf* **-nić**) *vt* 1 (*zadanie, problem*) to explain 2 (*interpretować*) to interpret

objaśnie|nie (**-nia, -nia**; *gen pl* **-ń**) *nt* explanation

obja|w (**-wu, -wy**; *loc sg* **-wie**) *m* (*choroby, niechęci*) symptom

obj|azd (**-azdu, -azdy**; *loc sg* **-eździe**) *m* 1 (*droga dookoła*) tour 2 (*obwodnica: na stałe*) bypass 3 (*droga alternatywna*) (traffic) diversion (*Brit*), detour (*US*)

ob|jąć (**-ejmę, -ejmiesz**; *imp* **-ejmij**) *vb pf od* **obejmować**

objętoś|ć (**-ci**) *f* **1** (*słoja*) capacity **2** (*część*) part, measure **3** (*książki*) length **4** (*Mat*) (cubic) volume

oblew|ać (**-am, -asz**; *pf* **oblać**) *vt* **1** (*polewać: płynem*) to pour **2** (*pokryć warstwą czegoś*) to coat **3** (*pot: egzamin*) to fail (*Brit*), to flunk (*US*) **4** (*chrzciny*) to celebrate; **~** (**oblać** *pf*) **coś czymś** to spill sth on sth

oblicz|ać (**-am, -asz**; *pf* **-yć**) *vt* **1** (*finanse*) to count **2** (*wynik, szybkość*) to calculate **3** (*oceniać*) to estimate

oblicz|e (**-a, -a**; *gen pl* **-y**) *nt* **1** (*twarz*) face **2** (*cechy charakterystyczne*) facet; **w obliczu problemów/śmierci** in the face of troubles/death; **w obliczu prawa** in the eyes of the law

oblodzony *adj* (*stok, ulica*) icy

obłę|d (**-du, -dy**; *loc sg* **-dzie**) *m* **1** (*pomieszanie zmysłów*) insanity **2** (*nieporządek*) bedlam

obłędny *adj* (*pot: zachwycający*) wicked (*Brit*), bad (*US*)

obmac|ywać (**-uję, -ujesz**; *pf* **-ać**) *vt* **1** to finger **2** (*napastować kobietę: pej*) to fondle, to grope

obmyśl|ać (**-am, -asz**; *pf* **-ić**) *vt* (*plan*) to devise

obnaż|ać (**-am, -asz**; *pf* **-yć**) *vt* (*błędy, przewinienia*) to expose, to bare; **~ się** *vr* to expose o.s.

obniż|ać (**-am, -asz**; *pf* **-yć**) *vt* to lower; **~ się** *vr* to fall

obniż|ka (**-ki, -ki**; *dat sg & loc sg* **-ce**) *f* (*cen, kosztów*) cut

obojczy|k (**-ka, -ki**; *inst* **-kiem**) *m* (*w anatomii*) collarbone

oboje *num* both

obojętnie *adv* (*bez zainteresowania*) indifferently; **~ kto przyjdzie, będziemy zadowoleni** (*nieważne kto*) no matter who comes, we'll be satisfied; **~ kto wie, niech się przyzna** (*ktokolwiek wie, niech się przyzna*) whoever knows, (please) own up; **~ kiedy będzie spotkanie, przyjedziemy** whatever the time of the meeting, we'll be there

obojętnoś|ć (**-ci**) *f* indifference

obojętny *adj* (*nieczuły*) indifferent

obok *prep +gen* **1** (*niedaleko*) by, near, close to **2** (*poza*) beside ▷ *adv*: **(tuż) ~** nearby, (very) close; **przeszła ~ niego i nic nie powiedziała** she walked past him without saying a word; **usiedli ~ siebie** they sat down next to each other

obowiąz|ek (**-ku, -ki**; *inst* **-kiem**) *m* duty, obligation; **obowiązki** *pl* duties *pl*; **pełniący obowiązki dyrektora** acting chairman

obowiązkowo *adv* **1** (*pod przymusem*) obligatorily **2** (*pot: koniecznie*) whatever happens; **pasażerowie ~ muszą zapiąć** (*pf*) **pasy** passengers are required to wear seat belts; **musisz ~ ten spektakl obejrzeć** you just have to see this play

obowiązkowy *adj* **1** (*lekcje, zadania*) obligatory **2** (*uczeń*) conscientious

obowiązujący *adj* **1** (*rozkład jazdy*) (currently) valid, current **2** (*przepis*) (currently) in force, (legally) binding

obowiąz|ywać (**-uje**) *vi* to be in force; **na przyjęciu obowiązuje strój wieczorowy** it is a black tie event

ob|ój (**-oju, -oje**) *m* oboe

ob|óz (**-ozu, -ozy**; *loc sg* **-ozie**) *m* (*harcerski*) camp; **~ dla uchodźców** refugee camp; **~ koncentracyjny** concentration camp

obrab|ować (**-uję, -ujesz**) *vt pf* to rob

obrac|ać (**-am, -asz**) *vt* (*przekręcić*) to turn; **~ się** *vr* to whirl, to rotate; **obrócić wzrok na kogoś** to look at sb; **obrócić coś w żart** to turn sth into a joke; **Ziemia obraca się wokół Słońca** the Earth revolves around the Sun; **~ się w towarzystwie** (*przen*) to socialize with; **obrócić się przeciwko komuś** to turn against sb

obra|z (**-zu, -zy**; *loc sg* **-zie**) *m* **1** (*dzieło sztuki*) painting, picture **2** (*sceneria*) sight, scenery **3** (*rys: wydarzeń, historyczny*) picture **4** (*telewizyjny*) image, picture **5** (*film*) film **6** (*w fizyce, fotografii*) image

obraz|ek (**-ka, -ki**; *inst sg* **-kiem**) *m* picture

obraźliwy *adj* **1** (*uwaga, zachowanie*) offensive **2** (*łatwo obrażający się*) touchy

obraż|ać (**-am, -asz**; *pf* **obrazić**) *vt* to offend; **~ się** *vr*: **~ się na kogoś** to be offended by sb; **obraził się za**

jego słowa he took offence (*Brit*) *lub* offense (*US*) at his words; **nie obrażaj się** don't be offended

obrażony *adj* offended; **być ~m na** to be offended by

obrącz|ka (**-ki, -ki**; *dat sg & loc sg* **-ce**) *f* **1** (*ślubna*) wedding ring **2** (*dla zwierząt*) ring

obro|na (**-ny**; *dat sg & loc sg* **-nie**) *f* **1** (*reakcja na atak*) defence (*Brit*), defense (*US*) **2** (*zabezpieczenie*) protection; **zrobił to w obronie własnej** he did it in self-defence (*Brit*) *lub* self-defense (*US*)

OBRONA CZĘSTOCHOWY

Obrona Częstochowy is one of Poland's patriotic myths. The siege of the monastery of Jasna Góra in Częstochowa took place in the 17th century during the Polish-Swedish war. Over time this event became steeped in legend and became a symbol of the "nation's victorious spirit" and the "defence of the faith", with the phrase **Obrona Częstochowy** becoming part of everyday language.

obro|nić (**-nię, -nisz**; *imp* **-ń**) *vb pf od* **bronić**

obronny *adj* **1** (*działanie*) defensive **2** (*budowla*) fortified; **mury obronne** fortifications

obrońc|a (**-y, -y**) *m decl like f in sg* **1** (*kraju, poglądów*) defender **2** (*sprawy*) advocate **3** (*w prawie*) defence counsel (*Brit*), defense attorney (*US*)

obrotny *adj* resourceful; **on jest ~ w gębie** (*pot!*) he has the gift of the gab

obroż|a (**-y, -e**; *gen pl* **-y**) *f* collar

obró|cić (**-cę, -cisz**; *imp* **-ć**) *vb pf od* **obracać**

obru|s (**-sa** *lub* **-su, -sy**; *loc sg* **-sie**) *m* tablecloth

obrzę|k (**-ku, -ki**; *inst* **-kiem**) *m* (*gardła, nogi*) swelling

obrzu|cać (**-cam, -casz**; *pf* **-cić**) *vt*: **~ kogoś/coś czymś** to throw sth at sb/sth; **obrzucali go bezustannie błotem** they were constantly showering him with abuse

obrzydliwy *adj* (*człowiek, zapach*) disgusting

obserwacj|a (**-i, -e**; *gen pl* **-i**) *f* observation

obserwacyjny *adj* (*sprzęt*) observational; **punkt ~** vantage point

obserw|ować (**-uję, -ujesz**) *vt* (*uważnie przyglądać się*) to observe

obsesj|a (**-i, -e**; *gen pl* **-i**) *f* (*uporczywa myśl*) obsession

obsłu|ga (**-gi**; *dat sg & loc sg* **-dze**) *f* **1** (*urządzenia*) maintenance **2** (*klientów*) service **3** (*pracownicy usług*) staff; **instrukcja obsługi** instruction manual

obsłu|giwać (**-guję, -gujesz**; *pf* **-żyć**) *vt* **1** (*w restauracji*) to serve **2** (*urządzenie*) to operate ▷ *vi* (*obsługiwać do stołu*) to wait at table; **~ się** *vr*: **w tym domu obsługujesz się sam** you help yourself in this house

obsza|r (**-ru, -ry**; *loc sg* **-rze**) *m* **1** (*powierzchnia terenu*) area **2** (*wodny*) territory; **na ~ze całego kraju** all over the country/nationwide; **~ leśny/górzysty** forest/mountainous area

obszerny *adj* (*room*) spacious; **obszerne sprawozdanie** extensive report

obud|owa (**-owy, -owy**; *gen pl* **-ów**) *f* (*osłona*) casing

obu|dzić (**-dzę, -dzisz**; *imp* **-dź**) *vb pf od* **budzić**; **~ się** *vr* to wake up

oburz|ać (**-am, -asz**; *pf* **-yć**) *vt* (*denerwować*) to outrage; **~ się** *vr*: **~ się (na kogoś/coś)** to be outraged (at sb/sth)

oburzający *adj* (*uwaga, zachowanie*) outrageous

oburzeni|e (**-a**) *nt* indignation

oburzony *adj*: **~ (na kogoś/coś)** outraged (at sb/sth)

obustronny *adj* mutual

obuwi|e (**-a**) *nt* (*buty*) footwear

obwieszcze|nie (**-nia, -nia**; *gen pl* **-ń**) *nt* (*ogłoszenie*) announcement

obwi|niać (**-niam, -niasz**; *pf* **-nić**) *vt*: **~ kogoś (o coś)** to accuse sb (of sth)

obwodnic|a (**-y, -e**) *f* (*trasa okrążająca miasto*) bypass

obw|ód (**-odu, -ody**; *loc sg* **-odzie**) *m* **1** (*w geometrii: okręgu*) circumference

2 (*wielokąta*) perimeter **3** (*w elektronice*) circuit **4** (*jednostka podziału administracyjnego*) district
obyczaj (**-u, -e**) *m* **1** (*tradycja*) custom **2** (*codzienna czynność*) habit; **obyczaje** *pl* **1** (*zachowanie się*) manners **2** (*zasady moralne*) morals
obyczajowy *adj* (*skandal*) moral; **swoboda obyczajowa** moral freedom; **powieść obyczajowa** a novel of manners; **film ~** (film) drama
obydwa *num* both; *zob. też* **oba**
obydwaj *num* both; *zob. też* **obaj**
obydwie *num* both; *zob. też* **obie**
obydwoje *num* both; *zob. też* **oboje**
obywatel (**-a, -e**; *gen pl* **-i**) *m* (*mieszkaniec kraju*) citizen; **szary ~** the man in the street
obywatelst|wo (**-wa**; *loc sg* **-wie**) *nt* (*honorowe, podwójne*) citizenship
ocea|n (**-nu, -ny**; *loc sg* **-nie**) *m* ocean; **~ smutków** ocean of sorrows; **~ Atlantycki** the Atlantic (Ocean); **~ Indyjski** the Indian Ocean; **~ Spokojny** the Pacific (Ocean)
oce|na (**-ny, -ny**; *dat sg & loc sg* **-nie**) *f* **1** (*opinia*) assessment **2** (*w szkole: stopień*) mark (*Brit*), grade (*US*) **3** (*wycena*) estimation, evaluation
oce|niać (**-niam, -niasz**; *pf* **-nić**) *vt* **1** (*wydać sąd*) to judge **2** (*wyceniać*) to evaluate
oc|et (**-tu, -ty**; *loc sg* **-cie**) *m* (*w gotowaniu*) vinegar
ochładz|ać (**-am, -asz**; *pf* **ochłodzić**) *vt* **1** (*herbatę, płyn*) to cool **2** (*piwo*) to chill **3** (*odświeżać się*) to refresh; **~ się** *vr* **1** (*być chłodnym*) to cool **2** (*stawać się zimnym*) to cool (down) **3** (*orzeźwiać się*) to cool off **4** (*o relacjach międzyludzkich*) to chill; **wczoraj ochłodziło się** it got cooler yesterday
ochot|a (**-ty**; *dat sg & loc sg* **-cie**) *f* (*chęć*) willingness; **przyjdę z ochotą** I'll gladly come; **mam ochotę na coś do jedzenia** I feel like something to eat; **mam ochotę pojechać w góry** I feel like going to the mountains; **czy masz ochotę na lody?** do you fancy some ice cream?
ochotnicz|ka (**-ki, -ki**; *dat sg* **-ce**; *gen pl* **-ek**) *f* volunteer
ochotni|k (**-ka, -cy**; *inst sg* **-kiem**) *m* volunteer
ochrani|ać (**-am, -asz**; *pf* **ochronić**) *vt*: **~ kogoś/coś (od czegoś** *lub* **przed czymś)** to protect sb/sth (from sth); **~ się** *vr*: **~ się przed czymś** to protect o.s. from sth; **ochraniał go przed deszczem** he protected him from the rain
ochron|a (**-ny**; *dat sg & loc sg* **-nie**) *f* **1** (*przed chorobą, nieszczęściem*) protection **2** (*w klubie, rządu*) security; **~ środowiska naturalnego** environment(al) protection; **~ osobista** bodyguard
ochroniarz (**-a, -e**; *gen pl* **-y**) *m* (*pot*) security guard
ochronny *adj* (*ubranie, sprzęt*) protective; **szczepienie ochronne** vaccination
ociąg|ać się (**-am, -asz**) *vr*: **~ (z czymś)** to be reluctant (about sth); **nie ociągaj się z tą pracą** don't delay doing the work
ocze|kiwać (**-kuję, -kujesz**) *vt*: **~ kogoś/czegoś** to wait for sb/sth; (*być przygotowanym na coś*) to expect sb/sth
oczy *itd. n zob.* **oko**
oczyszcz|ać (**-am, -asz**; *pf* **oczyścić**) *vt* **1** (*skórę*) to clean **2** (*płyn z zanieczyszczeń*) to purify; **~ się** *vr* to clean *lub* cleanse o.s.
oczywisty *adj* obvious
oczywiście *adv* obviously; **~ masz rację!** of course you're right!

SŁOWO KLUCZOWE

od *prep +gen* **1** (*kierunek*) from; **od domu** from home *lub* from the house; **od wschodu** from the east; **na południe od Polski** to the south of Poland
2 (*czas trwania*) for; **od dwóch dni** for two days; **od bardzo dawna** for a very long time
3 since; **od środy** since Wednesday; **od rana do wieczora** from morning till night; **od wczoraj** since yesterday; **od jutra** as from tomorrow; **od poniedziałku do piątku** Monday to Friday (*Brit*), Monday through Friday (*US*)

4 (*odległość*) (away) from; **sto metrów od brzegu** a hundred metres (*Brit*) *lub* meters (*US*) away from the shore
5 (*dolna granica zakresu*) from; **od dwóch do sześciu razy w tygodniu** (from) two to six times a week
6 (*początkowa granica skali*) (starting) from; **od wierszy po powieści** from poems to novels
7 (*przyczyna*) with, from; **twarz mokra od deszczu** a face wet from the rain; **zamarzł od zimna** he froze from the cold
8 (*pochodzenie*) from; **prezent od mojej siostry** a present from my sister
9 (*przeznaczenie*): **klucze od mieszkania** house keys; **syrop od kaszlu** cough mixture; **pudełko od zapałek** matchbox; **ubezpieczenie od następstw nieszczęśliwych wypadków** accident insurance
10 (*specjalizacja*): **nauczyciel od polskiego** Polish teacher; **fachowiec od pralek** washing machine technician
11 (*przy porównaniach*) than; **ona jest młodsza od siostry** she is younger than her sister; **on jest grubszy od niej** he is fatter than her

odbi|cie (**-cia, -cia**; *gen pl* **-ć**) *nt* 1 (*w lustrze, tafli wody*) reflection 2 (*kopia*) image 3 (*w fizyce*) reflection 4 (*odcisk buta, dłoni*) print 5 (*ataku*) parry
odbier|ać (**-am, -asz**; *pf* **odebrać**) *vt* 1 (*należność*) to take back 2 (*otrzymywać*) to receive 3 (*walizkę, wezwanie*) to collect 4 (*dziecko ze szkoły*) to pick up 5 (*telefon*) to answer 6 (*pozbawiać*: *ochotę*) to deprive of 7 (*prawo, przywilej*) to withdraw 8 (*zabierać przy użyciu przemocy*) to confiscate 9 (*program radiowy, telewizyjny*) to receive 10 (*doświadczać uczucia*) to experience; **odebrał sobie życie** he took his own life
odbij|ać (**-am, -asz**; *pf* **odbić**) *vt* 1 (*odzwierciedlać*) to reflect 2 (*piłkę*) to return 3 (*o ziemię*) to bounce 4 (*pieczątkę*) to stamp 5 (*zostawiać ślady*) to leave 6 (*z niewoli*) to rescue ▷ *vi* (*odłączać się od grupy*) to break away; **~ się** *vr* 1 to be reflected 2 (*ślad*) to leave traces 3 (*piłka*) to bounce (off), to deflect; **~ od czegoś** (*odróżniać się*) to stand out against sth; **palenie papierosów odbiło się na jego zdrowiu** smoking affected his health; **odbiło mu się po posiłku** he belched after the meal
odbiorc|a (**-y, -y**) *m decl like f in sg* 1 (*danych, wiadomości*) recipient 2 (*listu*) addressee 3 (*prądu*) consumer; **~ audycji radiowej** listener; **~ programu telewizyjnego** viewer
odbudo|wa (**-wy**; *dat sg & loc sg* **-wie**) *f* (*zamku, miasta*) reconstruction
odby|t (**-tu, -ty**; *loc sg* **-cie**) *m* anus
odbyw|ać (**-am, -asz**; *pf* **odbyć**) *vt* 1 (*zajęcia*) to undergo 2 (*służbę wojskową*) to serve; **~ się** *vr* (*o wydarzeniu*) to take place; **odbywał praktykę w fabryce** he served his apprenticeship (in a factory); **~ praktykę nauczycielską** to do teaching practice
odchod|y (**-ów**) *pl* (*ludzkie, zwierzęce*) faeces (*Brit*), feces (*US*)
odcho|dzić (**-dzę, -dzisz**; *imp* **-dź**; *pf* **odejść**) *vi* 1 (*opuszczać*) to walk away 2 (*o pociągu, autobusie*) to depart 3 (*umierać*) to pass away 4 (*z pracy*) to leave 5 (*gałęzi*) to spread out 6 (*ulicy*) to diverge 7 (*odpryskiwać*) to peel (off)
odchu|dzać się (**-dzam, -dzasz**; *pf* **-dzić**) *vr* (*tracić na wadze*) to be on a diet
odchudzani|e (**-a**) *nt* dieting
odcie|ń (**-nia**) *m* 1 shade 2 (*głosu*) tone
odcin|ać (**-am, -asz**; *pf* **odciąć**) *vt* 1 to cut off 2 (*sznur*) to sever 3 (*amputować*) to amputate 4 (*wyjście*) to seal off; **~ się** *vr* (*ostro reagować na wypowiedź*): **~ się od** *+gen* (*zerwać się z*) to distance o.s. from; (*wyróżniać się*) to stand out against
odcin|ek (**-ka, -ki**; *inst sg* **-kiem**) *m* 1 (*trasy*) section 2 (*czas*) period 3 (*rachunek*) receipt 4 (*w radiu, telewizji*) episode 5 (*w matematyce*) segment 6 (*dziedzina, zakres*) area
odcis|k (**-ku, -ki**; *inst sg* **-kiem**) *m*

1 (*zostawiony ślad*) imprint **2** (*ślad stopy*) footprint **3** (*ślad palca*) fingerprint **4** (*zgrubienie naskórka na ręce, stopie*) corn

odd|ać (**-am, -asz**; *3 pl* **-adzą**) *vb pf od* **oddawać**

oddal|ać (**-am, -asz**; *pf* **-ić**) *vt* (*sprawę sądową*) to dismiss; **~ się** *vr* **1** (*odchodzić*) to walk away **2** (*odjeżdżać: o pojeździe*) to drive away **3** (*o koniu, rowerze*) to ride away **4** (*o samolocie*) to fly away **5** (*odpływać: o łodzi*) to sail away **6** (*o lądzie*) to vanish away

oddalony *adj* (*punkt, cel*) remote

oddany *adj* devoted

odd|awać (**-aję, -ajesz**; *imp* **-awaj**; *pf* **-ać**) *vt* **1** (*rzecz do wypożyczalni*) to return **2** (*wydawać resztę*) to give **3** (*pieniądze*) to pay back **4** (*zostawiać w zakładzie usługowym: buty, spodnie*) to leave **5** (*w przechowalni, sejfie: kosztowności, bagaż*) to deposit **6** (*pod opiekę: chorego, ucznia*) to send **7** (*głos, pierwszeństwo*) to give **8** (*majątek, bogactwo*) to renounce **9** (*odwzajemniać*) to return **10** (*uderzenie*) to hit back **11** (*miłość*) to reciprocate; **~ się** *vr* **1** (*poddawać się*) to surrender **2** (*ulegać*) to give o.s.; **~ komuś przysługę** to do sb a favour (*Brit*) *lub* favor (*US*); **oddaje się nałogowemu pijaństwu** he has surrendered to drink; **~ się czemuś** (*pracy, marzeniom*) to devote o.s. to sth; (*relaksowi*) to indulge in sth

oddech (**-u, -y**) *m* (*wdech i wydech*) breath; **wstrzymywać** (**wstrzymać** *pf*) **~** to hold one's breath

oddych|ać (**-am, -asz**) *vi* to breathe; **ulżyło mu i odetchnął pełną piersią** he felt relieved and breathed deeply

oddychani|e (**-a**) *nt* breathing; **sztuczne ~** artificial respiration

oddzia|ł (**-łu, -ły**; *loc sg* **-le**) *m* **1** (*w wojsku*) unit **2** (*w policji*) squad **3** (*ministerstwa*) department **4** (*banku, agencji*) branch **5** (*w szpitalu*) ward

oddział|ywać (**-uję, -ujesz**) *vi*: **~ na** (*na ludzi, zjawiska*) to influence

oddziaływani|e (**-a**) *nt* **1** (*wpływ na ludzi, zjawiska*) influence **2** (*działanie*) effect **3** (*wzajemne*) interaction

oddziel|ać (**-am, -asz**; *pf* **-ić**) *vt* to separate

oddzielnie *adv* (*mieszkać, pracować*) separately

oddzielny *adj* (*pomieszczenie*) separate

ode *prep* = **od**; **jest młodszy ~ mnie** he is younger than me

odebrać (**odbiorę, odbierzesz**; *imp* **odbierz**) *vb pf od* **odbierać**

odejm|ować (**-uję, -ujesz**; *pf* **odjąć**) *vt* **1** (*w matematyce*) to subtract **2** (*nadwyżkę*) to deduct **3** (*odbierać*) to take away

odejmowani|e (**-a**) *nt* (*działanie matematyczne*) subtraction

odejści|e (**-a**) *nt* (*pociągu, człowieka*) departure

odej|ść (**-dę, -dziesz**; *imp* **-dź**; *pt* **odszedł, odeszła, odeszli**) *vb pf od* **odchodzić**

oder|wać (**-wę, -wiesz**; *imp* **-wij**) *vb pf od* **odrywać**

odgło|s (**-su, -sy**; *loc sg* **-sie**) *m* (*dźwięk*) sound

odgraż|ać się (**-am, -asz**) *vr* to make threats; **odgrażał się, że go zwolni z pracy** he threatened to sack him

odj|azd (**-azdu, -azdy**; *loc sg* **-eździe**) *m* (*pociągu, autobusu*) departure; **~!** all aboard!

odjeżdż|ać (**-am, -asz**; *pf* **odjechać**) *vi* **1** (*o człowieku*) to leave **2** (*o pojeździe*) to depart, to leave **3** (*Mot*) to drive off **4** (*na rowerze*) to ride off; **nasz pociąg już odjechał** our train has already departed

odkaż|ać (**-am, -asz**; *pf* **odkazić**) *vt* **1** (*ranę*) to disinfect **2** (*o ziemi, wodzie*) to decontaminate

odkąd *pron* since; **~ go znasz?** how long have you known him?; **~ mamy zacząć czytać?** where shall we start reading from?; **~ wyjechała, on tęskni** he has missed her (ever) since she left; **~ pamiętam** for as long as I can remember

odkład|ać (**-am, -asz**; *pf* **odłożyć**) *vt* **1** (*na półkę*) to put away **2** (*przekładać, opóźniać*) to postpone **3** (*oszczędzać*) to put aside; **~ się** *vr* to accumulate; **nie odkładaj słuchawki!** don't hang up (the phone)!

odkręc|ać (**-am, -asz**; *pf* **odkręcić**) *vt* **1** (*śrubokrętem*) to unscrew **2** (*słoik*) to twist off *lub* open **3** (*wodę*) to turn on **4** (*przen*) to undo; **tego błędu nie da się już odkręcić** it is impossible to rectify the mistake now

odkry|cie (**-cia, -cia**; *gen pl* **-ć**) *nt* (*geograficzne, naukowe*) discovery

odkryty *adj* **1** (*bez dachu*) open **2** (*basen*) outdoor **3** (*pod gołym niebem: koncert, występ*) open-air

odkryw|ać (**-am, -asz**; *pf* **odkryć**) *vt* **1** (*zdejmować wierzchnie przykrycie*) to uncover **2** (*otwierać*) to open **3** (*ląd*) to discover **4** (*sekret, tajemnicę*) to uncover **5** (*wyjaśniać*) to reveal

odkrywc|a (**-y, -y**) *m decl like f in sg* **1** (*badacz*) discoverer **2** (*lądów, krajów*) explorer

odkurzacz (**-a, -e**; *gen pl* **-y**) *m* vacuum cleaner, Hoover® (*Brit*)

odkurz|ać (**-am, -asz**; *pf* **-yć**) *vt* **1** (*powierzchnię ścierką*) to dust **2** (*odkurzaczem*) to vacuum, to hoover (*Brit*)

odległoś|ć (**-ci, -ci**) *f* distance; **na ~ dwóch metrów** two metres (*Brit*) *lub* meters (*US*) apart; **w niewielkiej odległości od domu** not far away from the house

odludny *adj* (*budynek, teren*) deserted

odlu|dzie (**-dzia, -dzia**; *gen pl* **-dzi**) *nt* secluded spot; **dom na odludziu** a house in the middle of nowhere

odmawi|ać (**-am, -asz**; *pf* **odmówić**) *vi* (*odrzucać propozycję, plan*) to decline ▷ *vt* (*odwoływać wizytę, spotkanie*) to cancel; **~ modlitwę** to say one's prayers; **odmawiał mu pomocy** he refused to help him; **odmawia zjedzenia obiadu** he refuses to eat lunch/dinner; **ojciec odmawia zgody na małżeństwo** father refuses to grant his approval to the marriage

odmia|na (**-ny, -ny**; *dat sg & loc sg* **-nie**) *f* **1** (*przemiana*) change **2** (*wariant*) variety **3** (*gatunek, rodzaj*) strain, variety **4** (*w językoznawstwie*) inflection; **dla odmiany pójdę do kina** for a change I'll go to the cinema (*Brit*) *lub* movies (*US*)

odmie|niać (**-niam, -niasz**; *pf* **-nić**) *vt* **1** (*osobę*) to transform **2** (*w językoznawstwie*) to inflect; **~ się** *vr* (*o wyrazach*) to inflect

odmienny *adj* **1** (*odróżniający się*) different **2** (*swoisty*) distinct **3** (*w językoznawstwie*) inflected

odmierz|ać (**-am, -asz**; *pf* **-yć**) *vt* **1** (*ilość, objętość*) to measure **2** (*wydzielać*) to measure out; **~ takt** to beat time

odmo|wa (**-wy, -wy**; *dat sg & loc sg* **-wie**; *gen pl* **odmów**) *f* (*zapłaty, wykonania usługi*) refusal

odmraż|ać (**-am, -asz**; *pf* **odmrozić**) *vt* **1** (*mięso*) to defrost **2** (*samolot*) to de-ice; **tej zimy odmroziłem sobie ręce** my hands got frostbitten this winter

odmroże|nie (**-nia**) *nt* (*nom pl* **-nia**; *gen pl* **-ń**) **1** (*w medycynie*) frostbite **2** (*palców rąk lub nóg*) chilblains

odnajd|ować (**-uję, -ujesz**; *pf* **odnaleźć**) *vt* to find; **~ się** *vr* **1** (*pojawiać się ponownie*) to show up **2** (*w nowych okolicznościach życiowych*) to find one's feet

odnawi|ać (**-am, -asz**; *pf* **odnowić**) *vt* **1** (*pokój*) to renovate, to refurbish **2** (*zabytek*) to restore **3** (*znajomość*) to renew

odno|sić (**-szę, -sisz**; *imp* **-ś**; *pf* **odnieść**) *vt* **1** (*przynosić z powrotem*) to take (back) **2** (*sukces*) to achieve **3** (*porażkę*) to suffer **4** (*rany*) to sustain; **~ się** *vr*: **~ się do kogoś/czegoś** to treat sb/sth; (*ustosunkowywać się*) to feel about sb/sth; (*dotyczyć*) to relate to sb/sth; **interwencja odniosła oczekiwany skutek** the intervention brought the expected results

odn|owa (**-owy**) *f* revival

odosobniony *adj* **1** (*oddalony*) isolated **2** (*samotny*) secluded **3** (*pojedynczy: fakt, przypadek, zjawisko*) isolated

od|ór (**-oru, -ory**; *loc sg* **-orze**) *m* (*smród*) odour (*Brit*), odor (*US*)

odpad|ać (**-am, -asz**; *pf* **odpaść**) *vi* **1** to come off **2** (*nie wytrzymywać konkurencji*) to drop out **3** (*przegrywać w wyborach*) to be defeated

odpad|ki (**-ków**) *pl* waste
odpad|y (**-ów**) *pl* (*toksyczne, przemysłowe*) waste (material)
odpier|ać (**-am, -asz**; *pf* **odeprzeć**) *vt* **1** (*atak*) to fight off **2** (*walczyć z nieprzyjacielem*) to repel, to repulse **3** (*ciosy*) to fight off **4** (*argumenty w dyskusji*) to refute
odpin|ać (**-am, -asz**; *pf* **odpiąć**) *vt* **1** (*suwak*) to undo **2** (*kurtkę, bluzkę*) to unbutton **3** (*sprzączkę*) to unbuckle **4** (*broszkę*) to unclip; **~ się** *vr* to come undone
odpi|s (**-su, -sy**; *loc sg* **-sie**) *m* **1** (*duplikat dokumentu*) copy **2** (*od podatku*) deduction
odpis|ywać (**-uję, -ujesz**; *pf* **-ać**) *vt* **1** (*przepisywać*) to copy **2** (*w szkole: ściągać*) to copy **3** (*w księgowości*) to deduct ▷ *vi*: **~ (na list)** (*odpowiadać*) to reply (to a letter)
odplamiacz (**-a, -e**; *gen pl* **-y**) *m* (*do zaplamionych materiałów*) stain remover
odpła|cać (się) (**-cam, -casz**; *pf* **-cić**) *vb*: **~ komuś za coś (czymś)** to repay sb for sth (with sth)
odpłatnie *adv* (*wykonywać usługę*) for a fee
odpłatnoś|ć (**-ci**) *f* payment, charge
odpłatny *adj* paid
odpły|w (**-wu, -wy**; *loc sg* **-wie**) *m* **1** (*wody*) outflow **2** (*ludzi*) emigration **3** (*Geo*) low tide
odpływ|ać (**-am, -asz**; *pf* **odpłynąć**) *vi* **1** (*statek, łódź*) to sail away **2** (*ryba*) to swim away **3** (*o rzeczy*) to float away **4** (*o cieczy*) to flow away
odpoczyn|ek (**-ku**) *m* (*przerwa w pracy*) rest, break
odpoczyw|ać (**-am, -asz**; *pf* **odpocząć**) *vi* (*relaksować się*) to have a rest
odpornoś|ć (**-ci**) *f* resistance
odporny *adj*: **~ (na coś)** (*nie poddający się*) unaffected (by sth); (*wytrzymały*) resistant (to sth); (*w medycynie*) immune (to sth)
odpowiad|ać (**-am, -asz**; *pf* **odpowiedzieć**) *vi* **1** to answer, to reply **2** (*w szkole: no pf*) to answer **3** (*na coś*) to respond; **nie odpowiadał na jej zaczepki** he did not react to her taunts; **odpowiedział nauczycielowi na pytanie** he replied to the teacher's question; **~ na pukanie w drzwi** to answer the door; **odpowiada za bezpieczeństwo w pracy** (*być odpowiedzialnym*) he is responsible for safety at work; **w pełni odpowiada za wypadek** he is fully responsible for the accident
odpowiedni *adj* (*chwila, osoba*) suitable, right **1** (*miejsce*) appropriate **2** (*adekwatny*) right **3** (*doświadczenie, wykształcenie*) adequate **4** (*zachowanie, ubranie*) suitable
odpowiedzialnoś|ć (**-ci**) *f* responsibility; **spółka z ograniczoną odpowiedzialnością** (*Comm*) limited (liability) company; **ponosi ~ za straty** he bears responsibility for the losses
odpowiedzialny *adj* responsible
odpowie|dź (**-dzi, -dzi**; *gen pl* **-dzi**) *f* **1** (*na zadane pytanie*) answer, reply **2** (*na korespondencję*) answer **3** (*na krytyczną uwagę*) response **4** (*na prośbę*) reply **5** (*w szkole*) answer; **w odpowiedzi na Pański list z 12 stycznia** in reply to your letter dated 12th January
Od|ra (**-ry**; *dat sg* & *loc sg* **-rze**) *f* (*nazwa geograficzna*) the Oder (river)
odrabi|ać (**-am, -asz**; *pf* **odrobić**) *vt* **1** (*zaległą pracę*) to catch up on **2** (*straty*) to make up for; **~ pracę domową** to do homework
odracz|ać (**-am, -asz**; *pf* **odroczyć**) *vt* **1** (*odkładać na późniejszy termin*) to postpone **2** (*karę*) to reprieve **3** (*Wojsk*) to defer
odradz|ać (**-am, -asz**; *pf* **odradzić**) *vt*: **~ komuś coś** to advise sb against sth
odrębnoś|ć (**-ci, -ci**) *f* **1** (*autonomia*) autonomy, independence **2** (*cecha wyróżniająca*) difference
odrębny *adj* (*niezależny*) distinct
odręcznie *adv* **1** manually **2** (*od razu*) immediately
odróż|niać (**-niam, -niasz**; *pf* **-nić**) *vt* **1** (*widzieć różnicę*) to distinguish **2** (*wyróżniać*) to differentiate; **~ się** *vr* (*być innym*) to be distinct, to differ

odruch (**-u, -y**) *m* **1** (*w medycynie, psychologii*) reflex **2** (*automatyczna reakcja*) impulse
odruchowy *adj* **1** (*reakcja*) reflex, spontaneous **2** (*automatyczny*) involuntary
odryw|ać (**-am, -asz**; *pf* **oderwać**) *vt* (*kawałek materiału*) to tear off; **~ się** *vr* (*odłączyć się*) to come off; **nie mogłem się oderwać od pracy** I couldn't get away from my work
odstrasz|ać (**-am, -asz**; *pf* **-yć**) *vt* (*ptaki, złodziei*) to scare away; **~ kogoś (od czegoś)** (*zniechęcać*) to deter sb (from sth)
odstraszający *adj* **1** (*środek*) deterrent **2** (*wygląd*) scary; **środek ~ komary** mosquito repellent
odsuw|ać (**-am, -asz**) *vt* (*pf* **odsunąć**) **1** (*meble*) to move back **2** (*zasłonę, firankę*) to draw (back) **3** (*zasuwkę*) to pull back **4** (*natrętne myśli*) to put aside **5** (*zagrożenie*) to avert; **~ się** *vr* **1** (*cofać się*) to stand back **2** (*zostawiać wolne miejsce*) to step aside
odszkodowa|nie (**-nia, -nia**; *gen pl* **-ń**) *nt* **1** (*od firmy ubezpieczeniowej*) compensation **2** (*kara*) damages *pl*, compensation **3** (*rekompensata*) settlement
odśnieżać (**-am, -asz**; *pf* **-yć**) *vt* to clear (of snow)
odtąd *adv* **1** (*od tamtego czasu*) since then **2** (*od tej chwili*) from now on **3** (*poczynając od tamtego momentu*) from that time on, from then on **4** (*od tego miejsca*) (starting) from here
odtrą|cać (**-cam, -casz**; *pf* **-cić**) *vt* **1** (*rękę*) to push away **2** (*miłość, osobę*) to reject
odtrut|ka (**-ki, -ki**; *dat sg & loc sg* **-ce**; *gen pl* **-ek**) *f* (*antidotum*) antidote; **on jest odtrutką na złamane serce** he's the remedy for a broken heart
odtwarzacz (**-a, -e**; *gen pl* **-y**) *m* **1** (*magnetofon*) cassette player **2** (*magnetowid*) video (cassette) player **3** (*kompaktowy*) CD player
odwa|ga (**-gi**; *dat sg & loc sg* **-dze**) *f* courage; **miał odwagę się sprzeciwić** he had the courage to object; **dodawał jej odwagi przed egzaminem** he bolstered her courage before the exam; **zdobył się na odwagę i powiedział prawdę** he mustered up his courage and told the truth
odważny *adj* brave
odwie|dzać (**-dzam, -dzasz**; *pf* **-dzić**) *vt* to visit; **odwiedź mnie dzisiaj wieczorem** come and see me tonight
odwodnieni|e (**-a**) *nt* dehydration
odwoł|ywać (**-uję, -ujesz**; *pf* **-ać**) *vt* **1** (*pozbawiać stanowiska*) to dismiss **2** (*dyplomatę*) to recall **3** (*lekcję, samolot*) to cancel **4** (*obietnicę*) to retract, to withdraw; **~ się** *vr* (*w sądzie*) to appeal; **odwołał się od decyzji sądu** he appealed against the court's decision
odwrac|ać (**-am, -asz**; *pf* **odwrócić**) *vt* **1** (*wzrok*) to avert **2** (*głowę*) to turn away **3** (*zmieniać bieg rzeki*) to reverse; **~ się** *vr* to turn away
odwrotnie *adv* **1** (*przeciwnie*) conversely **2** (*na odwrót*) inversely, the other way around **3** (*do góry nogami*) upside down **4** (*na lewą stronę*) inside out; **~ niż sądził** contrary to his judgement
odwrotny *adj* (*przeciwny*) opposite
odwzajem|niać (**-niam, -niasz**; *pf* **-nić**) *vt* to return; **~ się** *vr* to return
odziedzicz|yć (**-ę, -ysz**) *vt pf od* **dziedziczyć**; (*majątek, dom*) to inherit
odzież (**-y**) *f* (*ubrania*) clothing; **~ ochronna** protective clothing
odzna|ka (**-ki, -ki**; *dat sg & loc sg* **-ce**) *f* **1** (*medal*) distinction, award **2** (*symbol przynależności*) badge
odzwierciedl|ać (**-am, -asz**; *pf* **-ić**) *vt* (*poglądy*) to mirror; **~ się** *vr* to be reflected
odżywczy *adj* **1** (*napój, posiłek*) nutritious **2** (*element*) nutritious **3** (*wartość*) nutritional **4** (*balsam*) nourishing
odży|wiać (**-wiam, -wiasz**; *pf* **-wić**) *vt* (*podawać jedzenie*) to nourish; **~ się** *vr* **1** (*o osobie*) to feed o.s. **2** (*o kocie, psie*) to feed
odżywiani|e (**-a**) *nt* nutrition
odżyw|ka (**-ki, -ki**; *dat sg & loc sg* **-ce**; *gen pl* **-ek**) *f* **1** (*jedzenie*) nutrient

2 (*dla niemowląt*) formula **3** (*do włosów*) conditioner
ofer|ma (**-my, -my**; *dat sg & loc sg* **-mie**) *f* (*pot*) wimp
ofer|ować (**-uję, -ujesz**; *pf* **za-**) *vt* (*proponować*) to offer
ofer|ta (**-ty, -ty**; *dat sg & loc sg* **-cie**) *f* (*handlowa*) offer; **~ matrymonialna** marriage proposal
ofi|ara (**-ary, -ary**; *dat sg & loc sg* **-erze**) *f* **1** (*datek*) gift, donation **2** (*pieniężna*) donation **3** (*w religii*) offering **4** (*poświęcenie*) sacrifice **5** (*wypadku, przestępstwa*) victim **6** (*pot: pechowiec*) sucker
ofice|r (**-ra, -rowie**; *loc sg* **-rze**) *m* officer
oficjalny *adj* formal
ogień (**ognia, ognie**; *gen pl* **ogni**) *m* **1** (*płomień*) fire **2** (*zapalniczka*) light **3** (*przen: zapał*) fervour (*Brit*), fervor (*US*) **4** (*gwałtowne uczucie*) passion; **zimne ognie** sparklers; **sztuczne ognie** fireworks
ogląd|ać (**-am, -asz**; *pf* **obejrzeć**) *vt* **1** (*ilustrację*) to look at **2** (*telewizję*) to watch **3** (*wystawę, zabytki*) to see; **~ się** *vr* **1** (*patrzeć na swoje odbicie*) to look at o.s. **2** (*spoglądać w tył*) to look back **3** (*rozglądać się*) to look around
ogłasz|ać (**-am, -asz**; *pf* **ogłosić**) *vt* **1** (*w gazecie*) to announce **2** (*program polityczny*) to issue **3** (*niepodległość*) to declare **4** (*konkurs*) to announce **5** (*w sądzie*) to publish **6** (*stan wyjątkowy*) to proclaim; **~ się** *vr* (*w gazecie*) to advertise
ogłosze|nie (**-nia, -nia**; *gen pl* **-ń**) *nt* **1** announcement **2** (*w prasie*) notice **3** (*informacja w gazecie*) announcement **4** (*reklama*) ad, advertisement
ognis|ko (**-ka, -ka**; *inst sg* **-kiem**) *nt* **1** (*ogień*) bonfire **2** (*impreza na powietrzu*) (camp)fire **3** (*centrum*) centre (*Brit*), center (*US*) **4** (*kółko hobbystyczne*) group **5** (*w fizyce, fotografii, medycynie*) focus
ogol|ić (**-ę, -isz**; *imp* **ogol** *lub* **ogól**) *vb pf od* **golić**
ogo|n (**-na, -ny**; *loc sg* **-nie**) *m* tail; **diabeł to ~em nakrył** it vanished into thin air
ogólnie *adv* generally; **~ biorąc należy się temu raz jeszcze przyjrzeć** it is necessary, on the whole, to have another look at this; **~ mówiąc wszystko się powiodło** generally speaking everything was successful
ogólnokrajowy *adj* nationwide
ogólnokształcący *adj* (*liceum*) secondary education
ogólnopolski *adj* all-Poland
ogólny *adj* **1** (*opinia*) general **2** (*powszechny*) common **3** (*bez szczegółów*) general **4** (*suma*) total
ogór|ek (**-ka, -ki**; *inst sg* **-kiem**) *m* cucumber
ogranicz|ać (**-am, -asz**; *pf* **-yć**) *vt* **1** (*teren*) to delimit **2** (*zakres działań*) to limit **3** (*swobodę*) to restrict **4** (*koszty*) to reduce **5** (*szybkość*) to limit; **~ się** *vr* to limit o.s.; **~ wydatki** to cut down on spending; **~ się do** *+gen* (*jednej kanapki*) to limit o.s. to; (*jednej sprawy*) to be restricted to; (*sprowadzać się do*) to boil down to
ogranicze|nie (**-nia, -nia**; *gen pl* **-ń**) *nt* **1** (*przepis*) restriction **2** (*głupota*) limitations *pl*; **~ prędkości do 50 km/h** 50 km/h speed limit
ogrodnict|wo (**-wa**; *loc sg* **-wie**) *nt* gardening
ogrodni|k (**-ka, -cy**; *inst sg* **-kiem**) *m* (*zawodowy, amator*) gardener
ogrodze|nie (**-nia, -nia**; *gen pl* **-ń**) *nt* fence; **~ murowane** wall; **~ z żywopłotu** hedge
ogromny *adj* **1** (*budynek*) huge **2** (*rozległy*) vast **3** (*uczucie*) immense
ogr|ód (**-odu, -ody**; *loc sg* **-odzie**) *m* garden; **~ zoologiczny** zoo, zoological garden(s *pl*); **~ botaniczny** botanical garden(s *pl*); **warzywa prosto z ogrodu** garden-fresh vegetables
ogród|ek (**-ka, -ki**; *inst sg* **-kiem**) *m* **1** (*niewielki ogród*) garden **2** (*przy restauracji*) open-air café; **~ działkowy** allotment
ogrzew|ać (**-am, -asz**; *pf* **ogrzać**) *vt* **1** (*mieszkanie*) to heat **2** (*dłonie*) to warm up; **~ się** *vr* to warm up; **pokój szybko się ogrzał** the room got warm quickly

ogrzewani|e (**-a**) *nt* heating; **centralne ~** central heating
ogumieni|e (**-a**) *nt* (*opony samochodowe*) tyres *pl* (*Brit*), tires *pl* (*US*)
ohydny *adj* (*obrzydliwy*) hideous
oj|ciec (**-ca, -cowie**; *dat sg & loc sg* **-cu**; *voc sg* **-cze**) *m* **1** father **2** (*założyciel instytucji*) (founding) father; **ojcowie** *pl* (*przodkowie*) forefathers, ancestors; **~ chrzestny** godfather; **~ Święty** (*papież*) the holy Father, the Pope
ojczy|m (**-ma, -mowie** *lub* **-mi**; *loc sg* **-mie**) *m* stepfather
ojczysty *adj* (*język, kraj*) native; **język ~** mother tongue
ojczy|zna (**-zny, -zny**; *dat sg & loc sg* **-źnie**) *f* **1** (*kraj rodzinny*) homeland **2** (*przen*: *kolebka*) cradle
ok. *abbr* (= *około*) about, ca.
okazj|a (**-i, -e**; *gen pl* **-i**) *f* **1** (*szansa*) opportunity **2** (*korzystnego zakupu*) bargain **3** (*sprzyjająca okoliczność*) occasion; **a przy okazji, wpadnij do nas jutro** if you get the chance, pay us a visit tomorrow; **wszystkiego najlepszego z okazji urodzin** happy birthday
okaz|ywać (**-uję, -ujesz**; *pf* **-ać**) *vt* **1** (*pokazywać*) to show **2** (*wyrażać uczucia*) to demonstrate **3** (*odwagę, zainteresowanie*) to demonstrate; **~ się** *vr* to turn out (to be); **okazało się, że wyszedł wcześniej** it turned out that he left earlier
okien|ko (**-ka, -ka**; *inst sg* **-kiem**; *gen pl* **-ek**) *nt* **1** *dimin od* **okno** **2** (*stanowisko w sklepie, urzędzie*) counter **3** (*w kopercie*) window **4** (*w szkole*: *wolna godzina*) free period
oklas|ki (**-ków**) *pl* applause *sg*
oklas|kiwać (**-kuję, -kujesz**) *vt* to applaud; **gorąco oklaskiwano jej występ** she received rapturous applause for her performance
okłam|ywać (**-uję, -ujesz**; *pf* **-ać**) *vt* to deceive; **nie okłamuj się** don't deceive yourself
okno (**okna, okna**; *loc sg* **oknie**; *gen pl* **okien**) *nt* window; **~ wystawowe** shop window
oko[1] (**oka, oczy**; *gen pl* **oczu**; *dat pl & loc sg* **oczom**; *inst pl* **oczami** *lub* **oczyma**) *nt* **1** (*Anat*) eye **2** (*zmysł*) (eye)sight; **na ~ sto metrów** roughly one hundred metres (*Brit*) *lub* meters (*US*); **na pierwszy rzut oka wygląda nieźle** at first glance it doesn't look too bad; **rozmawiali w cztery oczy** they spoke face to face; **od dawna ma ją na oku** he's had his eye on her for a long time; **ona nie spuszcza go z oczu** she never lets him out of her sight; **przymykała oczy na jego wady** she turned a blind eye to his faults; **ten wzór rzucał się w oczy** the design *lub* pattern stood out
oko[2] (**oka, oka**) *nt* **1** (*cyklonu*) eye **2** (*w sieci*) mesh **3** (*w rosole*) *drops of fat in a broth*
okolic|a (**-y, -e**) *f* **1** (*bliskie otoczenie*) neighbourhood (*Brit*), neighborhood (*US*) **2** (*region*) district
okolicznoś|ć (**-ci, -ci**) *f* **1** (*sposobność*) occasion **2** (*sytuacja*) circumstance; **okoliczności** *pl* circumstances
około *prep +gen* about
okrad|ać (**-am, -asz**; *pf* **okraść**) *vt*: **~ kogoś (z czegoś)** to rob sb (of sth)
okr|ąg (**-ęgu, -ęgi**; *inst sg* **-ęgiem**) *m* (*figura geometryczna*) circle
okrągły *adj* round
okre|s (**-su, -sy**; *loc sg* **-sie**) *m* **1** (*w życie*) period **2** (*czas*) time **3** (*faza*) stage **4** (*romantyzmu*) era **5** (*Szkol*) term, semester **6** (*menstruacja*) period **7** (*w astronomii, fizyce*) period
określe|nie (**-nie, -nia**; *gen pl* **-ń**) *nt* **1** (*epitet*) epithet, name **2** (*w językoznawstwie*) modifier **3** (*termin*) terminology
określony *adj* (*konkretny*) specific, definite
okręc|ać (**-am, -asz**; *pf* **okręcić**) *vt* **1** (*owijać wokół*) to wrap **2** (*w tańcu*) to spin; **~ się** *vr* **1** (*wokół palca*) to twist around **2** (*kręcić się wkoło*) to turn (round *lub* around), to spin (round *lub* around)
okrę|t (**-tu, -ty**; *loc sg* **-cie**) *m* **1** (*wojenny*) warship **2** (*pot*: *duży statek*) ship **3** (*podwodny*) submarine
okropny *adj* **1** (*widok, charakter*) horrible **2** (*osoba nie do zniesienia*) terrible **3** (*aura*) awful
okrucieńst|wo (**-wa**; *loc sg* **-wie**) *nt* cruelty; **okrucieństwa** *pl* atrocities

okrutny *adj* (*czyn, człowiek*) cruel
okryw|ać (**-am, -asz**; *pf* **okryć**) *vt* (*przykrywać*) to cover
okrzy|k (**-ku, -ki**; *inst sg* **-kiem**) *m* (*radości, bólu*) shout, cry
okular|y (**-ów**) *pl* **1** (*korekcyjne*) glasses, spectacles **2** ((*przeciw*) *słoneczne*) sunglasses **3** (*ochronne*) (safety) goggles; **patrzy na sytuację przez różowe ~** she sees things through rose-tinted spectacles
okuli|sta (**-sty, -ści**; *dat sg & loc sg* **-ście**) *m decl like f in sg* optician (*Brit*), optometrist (*US*)
oku|p (**-pu**; *loc sg* **-pie**) *m* ransom
okupacj|a (**-i, -e**; *gen pl* **-i**) *f* **1** (*wojskowa*) occupation **2** (*w prawie*) occupancy
okup|ować (**-uję, -ujesz**) *vt* (*zajmować*) to occupy
olbrzymi *adj* enormous
ole|j (**-ju, -je**; *gen pl* **-i** *lub* **-jów**) *m* oil; **obraz ~ny** oil painting; **~ słonecznikowy/rzepakowy** sunflower/rape-seed oil; **~ napędowy** diesel oil
olimpia|da (**-dy, -dy**; *dat sg & loc sg* **-dzie**) *f* **1** (*Sport*) the Olympics® *pl*, the Olympic Games® *pl* **2** (*zawody*) contest
olimpijski *adj* **1** (*związany z Olimpiadą*) Olympic® **2** (*postawa*) Olympian®
oli|wa (**-wy**; *dat sg & loc sg* **-wie**) *f* **1** (*z oliwek*) olive oil **2** (*Kulin*) (salad *lub* cooking) oil **3** (*mineralny*) oil (lubricant)
oliw|ka (**-ki, -ki**; *dat sg & loc sg* **-ce**; *gen pl* **-ek**) *f* **1** (*owoc*) olive **2** (*drzewo*) olive (tree)
oł|ów (**-owiu**) *m* lead; **benzyna bezołowiowa** unleaded fuel
ołów|ek (**-ka, -ki**; *inst sg* **-kiem**) *m* **1** pencil **2** (*automatyczny*) propelling *lub* mechanical pencil **3** (*do brwi*) eyebrow pencil
ołtarz (**-a, -e**; *gen pl* **-y**) *m* altar
omawi|ać (**-am, -asz**; *pf* **omówić**) *vt* (*problem, zagadnienie*) to discuss, to talk over
omij|ać (**-am, -asz**; *pf* **ominąć**) *vt* **1** (*wybierać okrężną drogę*) to go (a) round **2** (*unikać: problemów*) to avoid **3** (*łamać zakaz, prawo*) to dodge
omle|t (**-tu** *lub* **-ta, -ty**; *loc sg* **-cie**) *m* omelette (*Brit*), omelet (*US*)
on *pron* **1** (*o osobie: w pozycji podmiotu*) he **2** (*w innych pozycjach*) him **3** (*o zwierzęciu, rzeczy, pojęciu*) it; **to on!** that's him!
ona *pron* **1** (*o osobie: w pozycji podmiotu*) she **2** (*w innych pozycjach*) her **3** (*o zwierzęciu, rzeczy, pojęciu*) it; **to ~!** that's her!
onaniz|ować się (**-uję, -ujesz**) *vr* to masturbate
one *pron* **1** (*w pozycji podmiotu*) they **2** (*w innych pozycjach*) them
oni *pron* **1** (*w pozycji podmiotu*) they **2** (*w innych pozycjach*) them
onieśmiel|ać (**-am, -asz**; *pf* **-ić**) *vt* (*zawstydzać*) to intimidate
onieśmielony *adj* (*zawstydzony*) intimidated
onkologi|a (**-i**) *f* oncology
ono *pron* it
ONZ (**ONZ-etu**; *loc sg* **ONZ-ecie**) *m abbr* (= *Organizacja Narodów Zjednoczonych*) UN
opad|ać (**-am, -asz**; *pf* **opaść**) *vi* **1** (*liści*) to fall **2** (*mgła*) to descend **3** (*o zawiesinie*) to settle **4** (*o roślinach*) to die **5** (*o ciśnieniu*) to fall **6** (*obniżać się*) to descend, to subside **7** (*ustępować*) to subside
opak; **na ~** the wrong way round
opakowa|nie (**-nia, -nia**; *gen pl* **-ń**) *nt* **1** (*szklane, plastikowe*) packaging **2** (*z zawartością*) package
opal|ać (**-am, -asz**; *pf* **-ić**) *vt* (*dom*) to heat; **~ się** *vr*: **~ się na słońcu** to sunbathe
opalony *adj* (sun)tanned
oparze|nie (**-nia, -nia**; *gen pl* **-ń**) *nt* (*słoneczne, chemiczne*) burn
oparz|yć (**-ę, -ysz**) *vt pf* **1** (*płomieniem, gorącym metalem*) to burn **2** (*gorącą wodą*) to scald **3** (*chemicznie*) to burn; **~ się** *vr pf* to get burned; **~ się w rękę** to burn one's hand
opatrun|ek (**-ku, -ki**; *inst sg* **-kiem**) *m* (*plaster, bandaż*) dressing
opcj|a (**-i, -e**; *gen pl* **-i**) *f* (*możliwość*) option
ope|ra (**-ry, -ry**; *dat sg & loc sg* **-rze**) *f* **1** (*przedstawienie*) opera **2** (*budynek*) opera house

operacj|a (**-i, -e**; *gen pl* **-i**) *f* **1** (*zabieg chirurgiczny*) operation, surgery **2** (*finansowa*) transaction **3** (*wojskowa*) operation; **~ plastyczna** (*w medycynie*) cosmetic surgery

oper|ować (**-uję, -ujesz**) *vi* to operate ▷ *vt* (*pf* **z-**) (*zabieg chirurgiczny*) to operate on; **doskonale operował głosem** he used his voice brilliantly

opie|ka (**-ki**; *dat sg & loc sg* **-ce**) *f* **1** (*troska*) care, protection **2** (*dozór*) care, charge **3** (*pomoc: medyczna*) care, assistance **4** (*Jur*) protection **5** (*przyznawana przez sąd*) custody, guardianship; **~ społeczna** social welfare

opiek|ować się (**-uję, -ujesz**; *pf* **za-**) *vr*: **~ kimś/czymś** (*troszczyć się*) to look after sb/sth; (*zajmować się*) to take care of sb/sth

opieku|n (**-na, -nowie**; *loc sg* **-nie**) *m* **1** (*osób starych*) carer **2** (*przyznawany przez sąd*) guardian; **~ społeczny** social worker

opiekun|ka (**-ki, -ki**; *dat sg & loc sg* **-ce**; *gen pl* **-ek**) *f* carer; **~ do dziecka** (*niania*) childminder, babysitter

opier|ać (**-am, -asz**; *pf* **oprzeć**) *vt*: **~ coś o** to prop *lub* lean sth against; **~ coś na** *+loc* to rest sth against, to put sth on; (*przen*) to base sth on; **~ się** *vr*: **~ się komuś/czemuś** to resist sb/sth; **~ się o** to lean against; **~ się na** *+loc* (*o poglądach, opiniach*) to be based on; (*polegać na: bliskich, znajomych*) to rely on; **~ się na lasce** to lean on a walking stick

opini|a (**-i, -e**; *gen pl* **-i**) *f* **1** (*pogląd*) view, opinion **2** (*renoma*) opinion, reputation **3** (*ocena*) judgement; **badanie opinii publicznej** (public) opinion poll

opi|s (**-su, -sy**; *loc sg* **-sie**) *m* **1** description **2** (*relacja wydarzenia*) account

opis|ywać (**-uję, -ujesz**; *pf* **-ać**) *vt* to describe

opłac|ać (**-am, -asz**; *pf* **opłacić**) *vt* **1** (*czesne*) to pay **2** (*dawać łapówkę*) to bribe; **~ się** *vr* to pay; **nie opłaca się tego robić** it's not worth doing; **ta transakcja się nie opłaca** this deal isn't worth the trouble; **w końcu opłaciło mi się!** finally, it was worth my while!

opłacalny *adj* (*interes*) profitable

opła|ta (**-ty, -ty**; *dat sg & loc sg* **-cie**) *f* **1** (*za usługę*) payment **2** (*za naukę*) fee **3** (*za bilet*) fare **4** (*urzędowa*) payment

opodatkowani|e (**-a**) *nt* taxation

opo|na (**-ny, -ny**; *dat sg & loc sg* **-nie**) *f* (*ogumienie*) tyre (*Brit*), tire (*US*); **opony** *pl*: **zapalenie opon mózgowych** meningitis

opowiad|ać (**-am, -asz**; *pf* **opowiedzieć**) *vi*: **~** (**o** *+loc*) (*bajkę, wydarzenie*) to talk (about) ▷ *vt* to tell; **~ się** *vr*: **~ się za** *+inst* (*popierać*) to be in favour (*Brit*) *lub* favor (*US*) of

opowiada|nie (**-nia, -nia**; *gen pl* **-ń**) *nt* **1** (*historia*) story **2** (*krótki utwór literacki*) short story

opowieś|ć (**-ci, -ci**; *gen pl* **-ci**) *f* tale, story

opozycj|a (**-i, -e**; *gen pl* **-i**) *f* (*parlamentarna, polityczna*) opposition

opozycyjny *adj* **1** (*partia, stowarzyszenie*) opposition **2** (*postępowanie*) oppositional

op|ór (**-oru**; *loc sg* **-orze**) *m* (*sprzeciw*) resistance; **ruch oporu** resistance movement

opóźnie|nie (**-nia, -nia**; *gen pl* **-ń**) *nt* delay

opóźniony *adj* **1** (*samolot*) delayed **2** (*intelektualnie*) retarded (*offensive*)

oprocentowa|nie (**-nia, -nia**; *gen pl* **-ń**) *nt* interest (rate)

oprogramowa|nie (**-nia, -nia**; *loc sg* **-niu**; *gen pl* **-ń**) *nt* software

oprócz *prep +gen* **1** (*poza czymś*) apart from **2** (*z wyjątkiem*) except; **~ tego jest lekarzem** apart from that he is a doctor

optyczny *adj* (*urządzenie, złudzenie*) optical

opty|k (**-ka, -cy**; *inst sg* **-kiem**) *m* optician

optymalny *adj* optimal

optymi|sta (**-sty, -ści**; *loc sg* **-ście**) *m* *decl like f in sg* optimist

optymist|ka (**-ki, -ki**; *dat sg & loc sg* **-ce**) *f* optimist

optymistyczny *adj* (*wiadomość, stosunek*) optimistic

optymiz|m (**-mu**; *loc sg* **-mie**) *m* optimism
opuchli|zna (**-zny**; *dat sg & loc sg* **-źnie**) *f* (*narządów wewnętrznych, zewnętrznych*) swelling
opuchnięty *adj* (*noga*) swollen
opuszcz|ać (**-am, -asz**; *pf* **opuścić**) *vt* **1** (*obniżać*) to lower **2** (*Mot: szybę*) to wind down **3** (*porzucać rodzinę*) to abandon **4** (*dom, firmę*) to leave **5** (*lekcje, zajęcia*) to miss **6** (*pomijać*) to leave out; **~ się** *vr* **1** (*obniżać się*) to lower **2** (*na linie*) to let o.s. down; **nie opuściła go mimo kłopotów** in spite of the problems she stuck by him
oranguta|n (**-na, -ny**; *loc sg* **-nie**) *m* orang-utan(g)
oranża|da (**-dy, -dy**; *dat sg & loc sg* **-dzie**) *f* (*gazowany napój owocowy*) orangeade
oraz *conj* as well as
orga|n (**-nu, -ny**; *loc sg* **-nie**) *m* (*wewnętrzny w ciele, władzy*) organ; **organy** *pl* (*instrument muzyczny*) organ *sg*
organizacj|a (**-i, -e**; *gen pl* **-i**) *f* organization
organizato|r (**-ra, -rzy**; *loc sg* **-rze**) *m* organizer
organiz|m (**-mu, -my**; *loc sg* **-mie**) *m* organism; **~ człowieka** the human body
organiz|ować (**-uję, -ujesz**; *pf* **z-**) *vt* **1** (*wyjazd, zawody*) to organize **2** (*imprezę*) to arrange **3** (*stowarzyszenie*) to set up **4** (*pot: samochód*) to sort out; **~ się** *vr* to organize
orgaz|m (**-mu, -my**; *loc sg* **-mie**) *m* orgasm
orientalny *adj* (*kuchnia, styl*) oriental
orkiest|ra (**-ry, -ry**; *dat sg & loc sg* **-rze**) *f* **1** orchestra **2** (*na weselu*) band
ortografi|a (**-i, -e**; *gen pl* **-i**) *f* **1** (*zasady pisowni*) orthography **2** (*pisownia*) spelling
ortograficzny *adj*: **słownik/błąd ~** dictionary/spelling mistake
oryginalny *adj* **1** (*niepowtarzalny*) original **2** (*prawdziwy*) genuine **3** (*unikatowy*) unique
orygina|ł (**-łu, -ły**; *loc sg* **-le**) *m* **1** (*pisma, dzieła sztuki*) original **2** (*o osobie*) eccentric
orzech (**-a, -y**) *m* (*owoc*) nut; **~ ziemny** peanut; **~ laskowy** hazelnut; **~ włoski** walnut; **czekolada z ~ami** chocolate with nuts; **dziadek do ~ów** nutcracker
orzechowy *adj* (*barwa*) nut-brown; **masło orzechowe** peanut butter
orzeł (**orła, orły**; *loc sg* **orle**) *m* **1** eagle **2** (*przen: osoba pozytywnie wyróżniająca się*) high-flier; **~ czy reszka?** heads or tails?
orzeź|wiać (**-wiam, -wiasz**; *pf* **-wić**) *vt* to refresh; **~ się** *vr* (*odświeżać się*) to refresh o.s.
osa (**osy, osy**; *dat sg & loc sg* **osie**) *f* wasp
osiąg|ać (**-am, -asz**; *pf* **-nąć**) *vt* **1** (*efekt, cel*) to achieve, to accomplish **2** (*szczyt*) to reach
osiągalny *adj* (*możliwy do zrealizowania*) attainable
osiągnię|cie (**-cia, -cia**; *gen pl* **-ć**) *nt* achievement
osiedl|e (**-a, -a**; *gen pl* **-i**) *nt* **1** (*też*: **~ mieszkaniowe**) (housing) estate (*Brit*), housing development (*US*) **2** (*Hist*) settlement

OSIEDLE MIESZKANIOWE

Osiedle mieszkaniowe is a common feature in Polish cities. This is a small area with a large number of huge blocks of flats with thousands of residents. Residential areas such as these were built on a large scale in the 1970s and 1980s.

osiem *num* eight
osiemdziesiąt *num* eighty
osiemnasty *adj* eighteenth
osiemnaście *num* eighteen
osiemset *num* eight hundred
oskarż|ać (**-am, -asz**; *pf* **-yć**) *vt*: **~ kogoś (o coś)** to accuse sb (of sth); (*w sądzie*) to charge sb (with sth)
oskarże|nie (**-nia, -nia**; *gen pl* **-ń**) *nt* **1** (*zarzut*) accusation **2** (*w sądzie: strona oskarżająca*) prosecution; **akt oskarżenia** indictment
oskarżon|a (**-ej, -e**) *f decl like adj* (*w sądzie*) the accused, the defendant

oskarż|ony (**-onego, -eni**) *m decl like adj* (*w sądzie*) the accused, the defendant
oskarżyciel (**-a, -e**) *m* (*prokurator*) prosecutor
osłabiony *adj* (*psychicznie, fizycznie*) weak
os|oba (**-oby, -oby**; *dat sg & loc sg* **-obie**; *gen pl* **-ób**) *f* **1** (*człowiek*) person **2** (*w językoznawstwie*) person **3** (*w filmie*) character, protagonist; **namiot mieszczący cztery osoby** four-man tent; **~ fizyczna** private individual; **~ prawna** legal entity *lub* person; **~ trzecia** third party
osobistoś|ć (**-ci, -ci**; *gen pl* **-ci**) *f* **1** (*ważna osoba*) personage **2** (*sławna osoba*) celebrity, personality
osobisty *adj* (*bielizna, sukces*) personal; **dowód ~** ≈ identity card; **komputer ~** personal computer
osobiście *adv* (*we własnej osobie*) personally, in person
osobno *adv* (*oddzielnie*) separately
osobny *adj* (*pokój*) separate; **każdy z osobna** separately, individually
osobowoś|ć (**-ci, -ci**; *gen pl* **-ci**) *f* (*charakter*) personality
osobowy *adj* **1** (*dla pasażerów*) passenger **2** (*w językoznawstwie*) personal; **pociąg ~** passenger train
ostatecznie *adv* **1** (*zdecydować, zakończyć*) finally, ultimately **2** (*ewentualnie*) after all
ostateczny *adj* (*definitywny*) final
ostatni *adj* **1** (*końcowy*) last **2** (*najnowszy*) latest **3** (*finałowy*) final **4** (*pośród wymienionych*) (the) latter
ostatnio *adv* (*niedawno*) recently, lately
ostro *adv* sharply, harshly
ostrożnie *adv* carefully; **~!** watch out!; **„~"** (*poczta*) "(handle) with care"
ostry *adj* **1** sharp **2** (*mróz*) severe, hard **3** (*przyprawa*) spicy **4** (*Mat*) acute **5** (*ból*) acute
ostrz|e (**-a, -a**; *gen pl* **-y**) *nt* **1** (*noża*) blade, edge **2** (*ostre zakończenie*) point
ostrzeg|ać (**-am, -asz**; *pf* **ostrzec**) *vt*: **~ kogoś (o czymś)** to warn sb (of sth); **ostrzegł go przed niebezpieczeństwem** he warned him of the danger
ostrzegawczy *adj* (*sygnał, strzał*) warning
ostrzeże|nie (**-nia, -nia**; *gen pl* **-ń**) *nt* warning
ostrz|yć (**-ę, -ysz**; *pf* **na-**) *vt* (*nóż*) to sharpen
osusz|ać (**-am, -asz**; *pf* **-yć**) *vt* **1** (*wycierać z potu, łez*) to wipe, to dry **2** (*teren*) to drain
oszac|ować (**-uję, -ujesz**) *vb pf od* **szacować**
oszale|ć (**-ję, -jesz**) *vi pf* (*zwariować*) to go mad
oszczędnoś|ć (**-ci**) *f* **1** (*sposób postępowania*) thrift **2** (*wody, prądu*) economy; **oszczędności** *pl* savings
oszczędny *adj* **1** (*osoba*) thrifty **2** (*sposób działania*) economical **3** (*maszyna*) energy-efficient
oszczędz|ać (**-am, -asz**) *vt* **1** (*pieniądze*) to save **2** (*czas*) to save **3** (*prąd*) to conserve, to save **4** (*siły, osobę*) to spare ▷ *vi* **1** (*żyć oszczędnie*) to economize **2** (*oszczędzać pieniądze*) to save (up)
oszczę|dzić (**-dzę, -dzisz**; *imp* **-dź**) *vt pf*: **~ kogoś** (*chronić kogoś*) to spare sb; **tragedia nie oszczędziła nikogo** the catastrophe spared nobody; **chciał ~ sobie kłopotów** he wanted to spare himself the trouble
oszu|kiwać (**-kuję, -kujesz**; *pf* **-kać**) *vi* (*na egzaminie*) to cheat ▷ *vt* (*zdradzać*) to deceive
oszu|st (**-sta, -ści**; *loc sg* **-ście**) *m* cheat
oszust|ka (**-ki, -ki**; *dat sg & loc sg* **-ce**; *gen pl* **-ek**) *f* cheat
oszust|wo (**-wa, -wa**; *loc sg* **-wie**) *nt* (*finansowe, podatkowe*) fraud
ośmiel|ać (**-am, -asz**; *pf* **-ić**) *vt* (*dodawać odwagi*) to encourage; **~ się** *vr* **1** (*stać się śmiałym*) to gain confidence **2** (*mieć odwagę*) to dare **3** (*mieć czelność*) to dare
ośmiesz|ać (**-am, -asz**; *pf* **-yć**) *vt* (*wyśmiewać się*) to ridicule; **~ się** *vr* (*poniżać się*) to make a fool of o.s.
ośmioro *num* eight
ośrod|ek (**-ka, -ki**; *inst sg* **-kiem**) *m* (*centrum, instytucja*) centre (*Brit*), center (*US*); **~ zdrowia** health centre; **~ wypoczynkowy** resort, holiday camp

oświadcz|ać (**-am, -asz**; *pf* **-yć**) *vt* (*stwierdzać*) to declare; **~ się** *vr*: **~ się komuś** (*proponować małżeństwo*) to propose to sb
oświadcze|nie (**-nia, -nia**; *gen pl* **-ń**) *nt* (*deklaracja*) statement; **~ podatkowe** tax return
oświadczyn|y (-) *pl* marriage proposal
oświa|ta (**-ty**; *dat sg & loc sg* **-cie**) *f* (*nauka, edukacja*) education
oświetl|ać (**-am, -asz**; *pf* **-ić**) *vt* to illuminate
oświetleni|e (**-a**) *nt* lighting
Oświęci|m (**-mia**; *loc sg* **-miu**) *m* Auschwitz
otacz|ać (**-am, -asz**; *pf* **otoczyć**) *vt* **1** (*okrążać*) to surround **2** (*o ogrodzeniu*) to enclose; **~ się** *vr*: **~ się kimś/czymś** to surround o.s. with sb/sth
oto *part*: **~ nasz kot** that's our cat; **~ wszystko, co wiem** that's all I know; **~ jestem** here I am
otoczeni|e (**-a**) *nt* **1** (*okolica*) surroundings *pl* **2** (*środowisko naturalne*) environment
otru|ć (**-ję, -jesz**) *vt pf* (*podać truciznę*) to poison; **~ się** *vr pf* to poison o.s.
otrzym|ywać (**-uję, -ujesz**; *pf* **-ać**) *vt* (*list, wynagrodzenie*) to receive
otwarcie[1] *adv* (*szczerze*) openly
otwar|cie[2] (**-cia, -cia**; *gen pl* **-ć**) *nt* (*sklepu, firmy*) opening; **godziny otwarcia od 8:00 do 16:00** opening hours: 8 a.m. to 4 p.m.
otwarty *adj* (*sklep, człowiek*) open; **list ~** open letter; **grał z nimi w otwarte karty** (*przen*) he laid his cards on the table; **posiedzenie odbyło się przy drzwiach ~ch** it was an open meeting (attended by the media); **"u" otwarte** (*w językoznawstwie*) the letter "u"
otwieracz (**-a, -e**; *gen pl* **-y**) *m* opener; **~ do puszek** *lub* **konserw** tin-opener (*Brit*), can-opener (*US*); **~ do butelek** bottle-opener
otwier|ać (**-am, -asz**; *pf* **otworzyć**) *vt* **1** to open **2** (*zamek w drzwiach*) to unlock **3** (*odkręcać wodę, gaz*) to turn on; **~ się** *vr* **1** to open **2** (*widok*) to open up; **otworzył się przed nią** he opened up to her
otyłoś|ć (**-ci**) *f* obesity
otyły *adj* obese
owa|d (**-da, -dy**; *loc sg* **-dzie**) *m* insect
owadobójczy *adj*: **środek ~** insecticide
owca (**owcy, owce**; *gen pl* **owiec**) *f* sheep; **był czarną owcą w rodzinie** (*przen*) he was the black sheep of the family
owij|ać (**-am, -asz**; *pf* **owinąć**) *vt* **1** (*bandażem*) to wrap (around) **2** (*papierem, folią*) to wrap up **3** (*kołdrą, kocem*) to wrap (up); **był szczery i nie owijał w bawełnę** he was honest and didn't beat about the bush
owłosiony *adj* (*nogi*) hairy
owoc (**-u, -e**) *m* fruit; **owoce** *pl* fruit
owocowy *adj* (*napój, sad*) fruit
owsian|ka (**-ki, -ki**; *dat sg & loc sg* **-ce**) *f* porridge
ozdabi|ać (**-am, -asz**; *pf* **ozdobić**) *vt* (*pokój*) to decorate
ozdobny *adj* (*wazon, mebel*) decorative
oznacz|ać (**-am, -asz**) *vt* **1** (*znaczyć*) to mean **2** (*przedstawiać*) to represent, to signify **3** (*o wyrazie*) to stand for, to mean **4** (*pf* **-yć**) (*postawić znak*) to mark; **co to oznacza?** what does this mean?; **oznacza to, że wygrał** this means that he won
ozo|n (**-nu**; *loc sg* **-nie**) *m* (*gaz*) ozone

ó

ósem|ka (**-ki, -ki**; *dat sg & loc sg* **-ce**) *f* **1** eight **2** (*kształt*) figure of eight (*Brit*), figure eight (*US*) **3** (*w muzyce*) quaver (*Brit*), eighth note (*US*)

ósmy *adj* eighth; **jedna ósma** one eighth; **jest (godzina) ósma** it's eight o'clock

ówczesny *adj*: **~ premier** the then Prime Minister

p

p. *abbr* **1** (= *pan*) Mr **2** (= *pani*) Mrs

pa|cha (**-chy, -chy**; *dat sg & loc sg* **-sze**) *f* armpit

pach|nieć (**-nę, -niesz**; *imp* **-nij**) *vi* to smell (pleasant); **~ czymś** to smell (pleasantly) of sth

pacjen|t (**-ta, -ci**; *loc sg* **-cie**) *m* (*nowy, stały*) patient

pacjent|ka (**-ki, -ki**; *dat sg & loc sg* **-ce**; *gen pl* **-ek**) *f* (*szpitala, przychodni*) patient

Pacyfi|k (**-ku**; *inst sg* **-kiem**) *m* (*Ocean Spokojny*) the Pacific

pacyfi|sta (**-sty, -ści**; *dat sg & loc sg* **-ście**) *m decl like f in sg* (*zagorzały*) pacifist

pacz|ka (**-ki, -ki**; *dat sg* **-ce**; *gen pl* **-ek**) *f* **1** (*mała paka*) package **2** (*Poczta*) parcel **3** (*papierosów*) packet (*Brit*), pack(age) (*US*)

padacz|ka (**-ki**; *dat sg & loc sg* **-ce**) (*epilepsja*) *f* epilepsy; **cierpieć na padaczkę** to suffer from epilepsy; **atak padaczki** epileptic fit

pad|ać (**-am, -asz**; *pf* **paść**) *vi* to fall; **pada (deszcz)** it's raining; **pada śnieg/grad** it's snowing/hailing

pagór|ek (**-ka, -ki**; *inst sg* **-kiem**) *m* hillock

pają|k (**-ka, -ki**; *inst sg* **-kiem**) *m* spider

pak|ować (**-uję, -ujesz**) *vt* **1** (*pf* **s-** *lub* **za-**) (*walizkę*) to pack **2** (*pf* **o-**) (*prezent*) to wrap (up); **~ się** *vr* **1** (*pf* **s-** *lub* **za-**) to pack (up) **2** (*pf* **w-**) (*pot: pchać się*) to barge in

palący *adj* **1** (*słońce, ból*) blazing **2** (*przen: pytanie*) urgent ▷ *m decl like adj* (*ten, który pali*) smoker; **przedział/wagon dla ~ch** smoking compartment/carriage

pal|ec (**-ca, -ce**) *m* **1** (*u nogi*) toe **2** (*u ręki*) finger; **ten starszy człowiek jest sam jak ~** that elderly person is all alone; **maczać w czymś palce** (*przen*) to have a hand in sth; **mieć coś w małym palcu** (*przen*) to know sth inside out; **chodzić na palcach** to tiptoe

paleni|e (**-a**) *nt* **1** (*fajki, papierosów*) smoking **2** (*śmieci*) incineration; **~ wzbronione** no smoking; **~ szkodzi zdrowiu** smoking damages your health

Palesty|na (**-ny**; *dat sg* **-nie**) *f* Palestine

pal|ić (**-ę, -isz**) *vt* **1** (*świecę*) to burn **2** (*światła*) to keep on **3** (*papierosy*) to smoke **4** (*pf* **s-**) (*niszczyć ogniem*) to burn (down) ▷ *vi* (*palić papierosy*) to smoke; **~ się** *vr* **1** (*płonąć*) to burn **2** (*o domu*) to be on fire **3** (*o świetle*) to be on; **pali się!** fire!; **~ e-papierosa** to vape

palmto|p (**-pu, -py**; *loc sg* **-pie**) *m* palmtop

palny *adj* (*materiał, substancja, produkt*) flammable; **łatwo ~** (highly) flammable; **broń palna** firearms *pl*

pałac (**-u, -e**) *m* (*królewski, książęcy, wspaniały*) palace

pamiąt|ka (**-ki, -ki**; *dat sg & loc sg* **-ce**; *gen pl* **-ek**) *f* **1** (*z wakacji*) souvenir **2** (*symbol*) token; **sklep z ~mi** souvenir shop; **na pamiątkę (czegoś)** in memory (of sth); **nasze miejscowe muzeum gromadzi pamiątki z przeszłości miasta** our local museum collects mementos of the town's history

pamię|ć (**-ci**) *f* memory; **z pamięci** from memory; **uczyć (nauczyć** *pf*) **się czegoś na ~** to learn sth by heart

pamięt|ać (**-am, -asz**; *pf* **za-**) *vt* to remember ▷ *vi*: **~ o kimś/czymś** to keep sb/sth in mind; **~ coś zrobić** to remember to do sth

pamiętni|k (**-ka, -ki**; *inst sg* **-kiem**) *m* (*nastolatki: dziecięcy, sekretny*) diary; **pamiętniki** *pl* (*Lit: opasłe, wieloletnie*) memoirs *pl*

pa|n (**-na, -nowie**; *dat sg & loc sg* **-nu**; *voc sg* **-nie**) *m* **1** (*mężczyzna*) gentleman **2** (*zaimek*) you **3** (*Bóg*) Lord **4** (*arystokrata*) lord **5** (*właściciel psa*) master **6** (*pot: nauczyciel*) teacher; **P~ Kowalski** Mr Kowalski; **proszę P~a!** excuse me, sir!; **P~ Bóg** Lord God; **~ młody** (bride)groom

pa|ni (**-ni, -nie**; *acc sg* **-nią**; *gen pl* **-ń**) *f* **1** (*kobieta*) lady **2** (*przy zwracaniu się*) you **3** (*pot: nauczycielka*) teacher; **P~ Kowalska** Mrs Kowalski; **proszę P~!** excuse me, madam!

PAN/PANI

The polite form of address in Polish is expressed using **Pan** (gentleman) or **Pani** (lady) in the singular and **Panowie** (gentlemen), **Panie** (ladies) or **Państwo** (ladies and gentlemen) in the plural plus the verb in the third person. The polite form is very common and should be used when addressing someone you do not know well, or someone who is older or more senior than yourself. Unlike English, which commonly includes the surname in polite forms of address, e.g. Mr Brown, it is more common in Polish to address someone simply as **Pan** or **Pani**.

panieński *adj*: **nazwisko ~e** maiden name; **stan ~** unmarried

pani|ka (**-ki**; *dat sg & loc sg* **-ce**) *f* panic; **gdy wyłączono prąd, miasto ogarnęła ~** the town was in a state of panic when the power was cut

panik|ować (**-uję, -ujesz**; *pf* **s-**) *vi* (*pot*) to panic; **nie panikuj, wszystko będzie dobrze** don't panic, everything will be fine

pa|nna (**-nny, -nny**; *dat sg & loc sg* **-nnie**; *gen pl* **-nien**) *f* **1** (young) girl **2** (*stan cywilny*) unmarried woman **3** (*Astrol*): **P~** Virgo; **P~ Kowalska** Miss Kowalska; **~ młoda** bride; **stara ~** (*pej*) old maid

panora|ma (**-my, -my**; *dat sg & loc sg* **-mie**) *f* (*rozległy widok*) panorama
pan|ować (**-uję, -ujesz**) *vi* **1** (*długo, mądrze, sprawiedliwie*) to rule **2** (*pf* **za-**) (*hałas*) to reign **3** (*poglądy*) to prevail; **~ nad kimś/czymś** to be master of sb/sth; **~ nad sobą** to be in control of o.s.
państ|wo (**-wa**; *loc sg & dat sg* **-wie**) *nt* **1** (*pl* **-wa**) (*kraj: bogate, zasobne*) state **2** (*forma grzecznościowa*) you; **P~ Kowalscy** the Kowalskis; **proszę Państwa!** Ladies and Gentlemen!; **~ młodzi** the bride and bridegroom
państwowy *adj* **1** (*hymn, święto, obchody*) national **2** (*szkoła*) state-owned
papie|r (**-ru, -ry**; *loc sg* **-rze**) *m* (*elegancki, delikatny, do kaligrafii*) paper; **papiery** *pl* (*dokumenty*) papers *pl*; **arkusz ~u** a sheet of paper; **~ firmowy** letterhead; **ściana jest cienka jak z ~u, wszystko przez nią słychać** the wall is paper thin, you can hear everything through it; **~ toaletowy** toilet paper; **~y wartościowe** (*Fin*) securities *pl*; **komisja P~ów Wartościowych** (*Ekon*) *state organization set up to supervise trading in securities and give reliable information on stocks and shares*
papiero|s (**-sa, -sy**; *loc sg* **-sie**) *m* cigarette; **palić ~y** to smoke cigarettes; **zaciągać się ~em** to take a drag on a cigarette
papierowy *adj* (*opakowanie, osłona, kubek*) paper
papież (**-a, -e**; *gen pl* **-y**) *m* the Pope
papry|ka (**-ki, -ki**; *dat sg & loc sg* **-ce**) *f* (*suszona*) paprika; **~ zielona/czerwona** green/red pepper; **piekielnie ostra ~** devilishly hot pepper
pa|ra (**-ry**; *dat sg & loc sg* **-rze**) *f* **1** (*nom pl* **-ry**) (*rękawiczek*) pair **2** (*nom pl* **-ry**) (*dwoje ludzi*) couple **3** (*Fiz*) vapour (*Brit*), vapor (*US*); **nie puszczać (puścić** *pf*) **pary z ust** (*przen*) not to breathe a word; **młoda ~** (*w czasie ślubu*) the bride and groom; (*po ślubie*) the newlyweds; **~mi** (*siedzieć*) in pairs; **iść w parze z czymś** (*przen*) to go hand in hand with sth
paradok|s (**-su, -sy**; *loc sg* **-sie**) *m* paradox
paradoksalny *adj* (*przypadek, sytuacja, położenie*) paradoxical
parafi|a (**-i, -e**; *gen pl* **-i**) *f* parish
parago|n (**-nu, -ny**; *loc sg* **-nie**) *m* (*zakupu, nabycia towaru, VAT*) receipt
paragra|f (**-fu, -fy**; *loc sg* **-fie**) *m* **1** (*Jur*) article **2** (*akapit*) paragraph
paraliż|ować (**-uję, -ujesz**; *pf* **s-**) *vt* to paralyse (*Brit*), to paralyze (*US*); **~ ruch uliczny** (*przen*) to stop traffic
parapetów|ka (**-ki, -ki**; *dat sg* **-ce**; *gen pl* **-ek**) *f* housewarming
parasol (**-a, -e**; *gen pl* **-i**) *m* **1** (*od słońca*) parasol **2** (*od deszczu*) umbrella
parasol|ka (**-ki, -ki**; *dat sg & loc sg* **-ce**; *gen pl* **-ek**) *f* umbrella
parę *num* a few; **~ lat temu** a few years ago; **~ minut/godzin/dni** a few minutes/hours/days; **od paru minut/godzin/dni** for a few minutes/hours/days; **za ~ lat** in a few years
par|k (**-ku, -ki**; *inst sg* **-kiem**) *m* (*krajobrazowy, miejski*) park; **~ narodowy** national park
parkin|g (**-gu, -gi**; *inst sg* **-giem**) *m* (*wielopoziomowy, podziemny*) car park (*Brit*), parking lot (*US*); **~ strzeżony/niestrzeżony** attended/unattended car park; **~ płatny/bezpłatny** paid/free parking
parkomet|r (**-ru, -ry**; *loc sg* **-rze**) *m* parking meter
park|ować (**-uję, -ujesz**; *pf* **za-**) *vt, vi* to park; **~ nielegalnie** to park illegally
parkowani|e (**-a**) *nt* parking
parlamen|t (**-tu, -ty**; *loc sg* **-cie**) *m* parliament; **posiedzenie ~u** sitting of parliament
parlamentarny *adj* (*sesja parlamentarna*) parliamentary
parte|r (**-ru, -ry**; *loc sg* **-rze**) *m* (*najniższe piętro*) ground floor (*Brit*), first floor (*US*)
parterowy *adj*: **dom ~** (*budynek*) bungalow
parti|a (**-i, -e**; *gen pl* **-i**) *f* **1** (*Pol*) party **2** (*pewna ilość towaru*) batch **3** (*szachów*) game **4** (*Teatr*) part

partne|r (**-ra, -rzy**; *loc sg* **-rze**) *m* (*życiowy, lojalny*) (male) partner
partner|ka (**-ki, -ki**; *dat sg & loc sg* **-ce**; *gen pl* **-ek**) *f* (female) partner
partnerski *adj* (*układ, związek*) based on partnership
partnerst|wo (**-wa**; *loc sg & dat sg* **-wie**) *nt* partnership
party *nt inv* (*urodzinowe*) party
partyjny *adj* (*działacz, aktywista*) party
paryski *adj*: **bułka paryska** French bread
pas (**-a**) *m* belt; **~ zieleni** green belt; **~ jezdni** (motorway) lane
pasaż (**-u, -e**; *gen pl* **-y**) *m* passage
pasaże|r (**-ra, -rowie**; *loc sg* **-rze**) *m* passenger
pasażer|ka (**-ki, -ki**; *loc sg & dat sg* **-ce**; *gen pl* **-ek**) *f* (female) passenger
pasażerski *adj* (*statek, rejs*) passenger
pas|ek (**-ka, -ki**; *inst sg* **-kiem**) *m dimin od* **pas**; (*skórzany, damski, męski*) belt; **~ do zegarka** watch strap; **~ klinowy** (*Aut*) fan belt; **w paski** (*wzór*) striped
pasier|b (**-ba, -bowie**; *loc sg* **-bie**) *m* stepson
pasierbic|a (**-y, -e**) *f* stepdaughter
pasjon|ować (**-uję, -ujesz**) *vt* to fascinate; **~ się** *vr*: **~ się czymś** (*sztuką*) to be very keen on sth
pasjonujący *adj* (*książka, film, wykład*) fascinating
paskudny *adj* (*pogoda, nastrój, humor*) nasty
pa|sta (**-sty, -sty**; *dat sg & loc sg* **-ście**) *f*: **~ do zębów** toothpaste; **~ mięsna/pomidorowa** meat/tomato spread; **~ do butów** shoe polish
pastyl|ka (**-ki, -ki**; *dat sg & loc sg* **-ce**; *gen pl* **-ek**) *f* **1** (*Med*) pill **2** (*cukierek*) pastille
pasywny *adj* (*zachowanie*) passive
paszpor|t (**-tu, -ty**; *loc sg* **-cie**) *m* passport
paszportowy *adj* (*urząd, formularz*) passport; **kontrola paszportowa** passport control
paszte|t (**-tu, -ty**; *loc sg* **-cie**) *m* (*drobiowy, cielęcy*) pâté
pa|ść (**-dnę, -dniesz**; *imp* **-dnij**; *pt* **-dł**) *vb pf od* **padać**; **~ trupem** to drop dead
patel|nia (**-ni, -nie**; *gen pl* **-ni**) *f* (*teflonowa*) frying pan
patrio|ta (**-ty, -ci**; *dat sg & loc sg* **-cie**) *m decl like f in sg* (*zagorzały, prawdziwy, wielki*) patriot
patriotyczny *adj* (*pieśń, wiersz, przemowa*) patriotic
patriotyz|m (**-mu**; *loc sg & dat sg* **-mie**) *m* (*głęboki*) patriotism
patrol (**-u, -e**; *gen pl* **-i**) *m* (*policyjny, wojskowy, harcerski*) patrol
patrol|ować (**-uję, -ujesz**) *vt* to patrol
patro|n (**-na, -nowie** *lub* **-ni**; *loc sg* **-nie**) *m* **1** (*szkoły, kościoła, parafii: opiekun*) patron **2** (*Rel*) patron saint
patrz|eć (**-ę, -ysz**) *vi* to look; **~ na coś trzeźwo/optymistycznie** to look at sth objectively/optimistically; **~ na coś przez palce** (*przen*) to turn a blind eye to sth; **~ na kogoś z góry** (*przen*) to look down on sb
patrz|yć (**-ę, -ysz**) *vi* = **patrzeć**
pau|za (**-zy, -zy**; *dat sg & loc sg* **-zie**) *f* **1** (*przerwa*) pause **2** (*Szkol*) break
pa|w (**-wia, -wie**; *gen pl* **-wi**) *m* peacock; **dumny jak ~** (as) proud as a peacock
pazno|kieć (**-kcia, -kcie**; *gen pl* **-kci**) *m* **1** (*u nogi*) toenail **2** (*u ręki*) fingernail
październi|k (**-ka, -ki**; *inst sg* **-kiem**) *m* October
pącz|ek (**-ka, -ki**; *inst sg* **-kiem**) *m* **1** (*Bot*) bud **2** (*Kulin*) doughnut, donut (*US*); **żyć wygodnie jak ~ w maśle** to live in the lap of luxury
pch|ać (**-am, -asz**; *pf* **-nąć**) *vt* **1** (*gwałtownie, brutalnie*) to push **2** (*wpychać*) to thrust; **~ się** *vr* (*przez tłum*) to force one's way
pch|ła (**-ły, -ły**; *dat sg & loc sg* **-le**; *gen pl* **-eł**) *f* flea
pch|nąć (**-nę, -niesz**; *imp* **-nij**) *vt pf od* **pchać**; (*nożem*) to stab
pchnię|cie (**-cia, -cia**; *gen pl* **-ć**) *nt* (*nożem*) stab
pech (**-a**) *m* bad luck; **mieć ~a** to be unlucky
pecho|wiec (**-wca, -wcy**) *m* unlucky person

pechowy *adj* (*dzień, okres*) unlucky
pedago|g (**-ga, -gowie** *lub* **-dzy**; *inst sg* **-giem**) *m* (*lubiany, szanowany, szacowny*) educator
pedagogi|ka (**-ki**; *dat sg & loc sg* **-ce**) *f* pedagogy; **Wydział Pedagogiki** (*Uniw*) Department of Pedagogy
pediat|ra (**-ry, -rzy**; *dat sg & loc sg* **-rze**) *m decl like f in sg* paediatrician (*Brit*), pediatrician (*US*)
pełen *adj* = **pełny**
pełno *adv* (*wiele*) a lot of; **w autobusie było ~ ludzi** the bus was full; **w butelce jest ~ wody** the bottle is full of water
pełnoletni *adj* (*widz, pasażer, czytelnik*) of age
pełnomocnict|wo (**-wa, -wa**; *loc sg & dat sg* **-wie**) *nt* power of attorney
pełnomocni|k (**-ka, -cy**; *inst sg* **-kiem**) *m* proxy, plenipotentiary (*in foreign diplomacy*)
pełnopłatny *adj* (*bilet, wstęp, przejazd*) full-price
pełnotłusty *adj* (*mleko, śmietana, masło*) full-fat
pełnoziarnisty *adj* (*chleb, makaron*) wholemeal (*Brit*), wholewheat (*US*)
pełny *adj* (*kubek, worek, sala*) full; (*szczęście*) complete; **pełen entuzjazmu** full of enthusiasm; **pełen nadziei** hopeful; **pełne mleko** full-cream milk; **pełne morze** open sea; **do pełna proszę!** fill her up, please!
pendri|ve (**-ve'a, -ve'y**; *loc sg* **-vie**) *m* (*Komput*) pen drive
pendrive (**-'a, -'y**; *dat sg* **-owi**) *m* USB stick
penicyli|na (**-ny**; *dat sg & loc sg* **-nie**) *f* penicillin
peni|s (**-sa, -sy**; *loc sg* **-sie**) *m* penis
pen|s (**-sa, -sy**; *loc sg* **-sie**) *m* penny; **dziesięć ~ów** 10 pence
pensj|a (**-i, -e**; *gen pl* **-i**) *f* (*płaca: tygodniowa, miesięczna, stała*) salary
pensjona|t (**-tu, -ty**; *loc sg* **-cie**) *m* (*górski, nadmorski, rodzinny*) guesthouse
perfekcjoni|sta (**-sty, -ści**; *dat sg & loc sg* **-ście**) *m decl like f in sg* perfectionist; **on jest perfekcjonistą w każdym calu** he is a perfectionist about everything
perfekcyjny *adj* (*wykonanie, występ*) perfect
perfum|y (**-**) *pl* (*ekskluzywne, najnowsze, eleganckie*) perfume
periody|k (**-ku, -ki**; *inst sg* **-kiem**) *m* periodical
perkusj|a (**-i, -e**; *gen pl* **-i**) *f* drums *pl*; **grać na perkusji** to play the drums
per|ła (**-ły, -ły**; *dat sg & loc sg* **-le**; *gen pl* **-eł**) *f* (*rzadka, olbrzymia, bezcenna*) pearl
perłowy *adj* (*naszyjnik, bransoleta, kolczyki*) pearl; **masa perłowa** mother-of-pearl; **macica perłowa** mother-of-pearl
pero|n (**-nu, -ny**; *loc sg* **-nie**) *m* platform
perski *adj*: **Zatoka Perska** the (Persian) Gulf
personalny *adj* **1** (*dane, akta, dokumenty*) personal **2** (*dział*) personnel
personel (**-u**) *m* (*sklepu, firmy: uprzejmy*) personnel
pertrakt|ować (**-uję, -ujesz**) *vi* to negotiate; **~ z kimś** to negotiate with sb
peru|ka (**-ki, -ki**; *dat sg & loc sg* **-ce**) *f* wig; **nosić perukę** to wear a wig
peryferi|e (**-i**) *pl* **1** (*krańce miasta*) outskirts *pl* **2** (*zewnętrzne części*) periphery *sg*
pest|ka (**-ki, -ki**; *dat sg & loc sg* **-ce**; *gen pl* **-ek**) *f* **1** (*wiśni*) stone **2** (*pomarańczy*) pip **3** (*słonecznika*) seed; **to (dla mnie) ~** (*pot*) it's a piece of cake (for me)
pesymi|sta (**-sty, -ści**; *dat sg & loc sg* **-ście**) *m decl like f in sg* (*urodzony, zgorzkniały*) pessimist
pesymistyczny *adj* (*prognoza, przepowiednia, wróżba*) pessimistic
pesymiz|m (**-mu**; *loc sg* **-mie**) *m* pessimism
peten|t (**-ta, -ci**; *loc sg* **-cie**) *m* (*urzędu, administracji*) inquirer
petycj|a (**-i, -e**; *gen pl* **-i**) *f* petition; **podpisywać petycję** to sign a petition; **zbierać podpisy pod petycją** to collect signatures for a petition
pewien (*f* **pewna**; *nt* **pewne**) *adj* **1** (*jakiś*) a certain **2** (*pewny*) certain; **~ pan** a certain gentleman;

pewnego dnia one day; **pewnego razu** once (upon a time); **przez ~ czas** for some time; **w pewnym stopniu** to some extent; **w pewnym sensie** in a sense

pewnie *adv* **1** (*zdecydowanie*) firmly **2** (*sprawnie*) confidently **3** (*niezawodnie*) reliably **4** (*prawdopodobnie*) probably; **(no) ~!** (*pot*) you bet!

pewnoś|ć (**-ci**) *f* **1** (*przekonanie*: *niezachwiana, absolutna*) certainty **2** (*zdecydowanie*) firmness **3** (*sprawność*) confidence **4** (*niezawodność*) reliability; **dla pewności** to be on the safe side; **~ siebie** self-confidence; **z pewnością** surely; **mieć ~** to be sure

pewny *adj* **1** (*śmierć*) certain **2** (*wniosek*) unquestionable **3** (*krok*) firm **4** (*oko*) steady **5** (*człowiek*) reliable **6** (*bezpieczny*) secure; **być ~m czegoś** to be sure of sth; **~ siebie** self-confident; **on jest ~** *lub* **pewien, że...** he's sure (that)...

pęcherzy|k (**-ka, -ki**; *inst sg* **-kiem**) *m* **1** (*na skórze*) blister **2** (*mydło*) bubble; **~ żółciowy** gall bladder

pędz|el (**-la, -le**; *gen pl* **-li**) *m* **1** (*do golenia*) (shaving) brush **2** (*do malowania*) (paint)brush; **wystawa obrazów pędzla Rembrandta** exhibition of paintings by Rembrandt

pę|dzić (**-dzę, -dzisz**; *imp* **-dź**) *vt* (*bydło*) to drive ▷ *vi* (*pf* **po-**) to speed along; **~ na złamanie karku** to go at breakneck speed

pęk|ać (**-am, -asz**; *pf* **-nąć**) *vi* **1** (*szyba*) to crack **2** (*sznurek*) to burst **3** (*koszula*) to rip; **głowa mi pęka** (*przen*) my head is splitting; **nie pękaj, wytrzymaj jeszcze trochę** (*pot*) don't give up, hold on a bit longer; **~ ze śmiechu** (*przen*) to laugh one's head off

pęknię|cie (**-cia, -cia**; *gen pl* **-ć**) *nt* **1** (*kości, czaszki*) fracture **2** (*rysa*: *szyby*) crack

pęp|ek (**-ka, -ki**; *inst sg* **-kiem**) *m* navel, belly button (*pot*)

pępowi|na (**-ny, -ny**; *dat sg & loc sg* **-nie**) *f* umbilical cord

pia|na (**-ny**; *dat sg & loc sg* **-nie**) *f* **1** (*aromatyczna, obfita*) foam **2** (*szampon*) lather **3** (*na powierzchni piwa*) head

piani|no (**-na, -na**; *loc sg* **-nie**) *nt* piano

piani|sta (**-sty, -ści**; *dat sg & loc sg* **-ście**) *m decl like f in sg* pianist

pianist|ka (**-ki, -ki**; *dat sg & loc sg* **-ce**; *gen pl* **-ek**) *f* pianist

pian|ka (**-ki**; *dat sg & loc sg* **-ce**) *f dimin od* **piana**; **~ do włosów** styling mousse; **~ do golenia** shaving foam

pias|ek (**-ku, -ki**; *inst sg* **-kiem**) *m* (*miękki, złoty*) sand

piaskownic|a (**-y, -e**) *f* sandpit (*Brit*), sandbox (*US*)

piąć się (**pnę, pniesz**; *imp* **pnij**) *vr* to climb (up)

piąt|ek (**-ku, -ki**; *inst sg* **-kiem**) *m* Friday; **Wielki P~** Good Friday; **~ zły początek** (*przysł*) *popular Polish phrase meaning that it is not wise to start doing something new on a Friday*

piąt|ka (**-ki, -ki**; *dat sg & loc sg* **-ce**; *gen pl* **-ek**) *f* **1** five **2** (*Szkol*) ≈ A

piąty *num decl like adj* fifth

pi|cie (**-cia**) *nt* **1** (*czynność*) drinking **2** (*pot*: *napój*) drink; **ta woda jest do picia** this water is drinkable

pi|ć (**-ję, -jesz**) *vt* (*pf* **wy-**) (*łapczywie*) to drink ▷ *vi* to drink; **chce mi się ~** I'm thirsty

piec[1] (**-a, -e**) *m* **1** (*kuchenny*) stove **2** (*piekarniczy*) oven **3** (*hutniczy*) furnace

pie|c[2] (**-kę, -czesz**; *imp* **-cz**) *vt* **1** (*pf* **u-**) (*chleb*) to bake **2** (*pf* **u-**) (*wołowinę*) to roast ▷ *vi* (*o słońcu*) to beat down; **~ się** (*pf* **u-**) *vr* **1** (*o chlebie*) to bake **2** (*o wołowinie*) to roast

piecho|ta (**-ty**; *dat sg* **-cie**) *f* (*Wojsk*) infantry; **~ morska** Royal Marines *pl* (*Brit*), Marine Corps (*US*), Marines *pl* (*US*); **iść piechotą** *lub* **na piechotę** to walk

pieczar|ka (**-ki, -ki**; *dat sg & loc sg* **-ce**; *gen pl* **-ek**) *f* (field) mushroom

pieczęt|ka (**-ki, -ki**; *dat sg & loc sg* **-ce**; *gen pl* **-ek**) *f* stamp

piecze|ń (**-ni, -nie**; *gen pl* **-ni**) *f* (*smakowita, aromatyczna, chrupiąca*) roast; **~ wołowa** roast beef

pieczę|ć (**-ci, -cie**; *gen pl* **-ci**) *f* **1** (*urzędowa, oficjalna*) stamp **2** (*lakowa*) seal
pieczy|wo (**-wa**; *loc sg & dat sg* **-wie**) *nt* (*świeże, czerstwe*) bread
piegowaty *adj* (*twarz, nos, cera*) freckled
piekar|nia (**-ni, -nie**; *gen pl* **-ni**) *f* (*pomieszczenie*) bakery
piekarni|k (**-ka, -ki**; *inst sg* **-kiem**) *m* oven
piekarz (**-a, -e**; *gen pl* **-y**) *m* baker; **u ~a** at the baker's
piek|ło (**-ła**; *loc sg & dat sg* **-le**) *nt* hell
pielęgniar|ka (**-ki, -ki**; *dat sg & loc sg* **-ce**; *gen pl* **-ek**) *f* (*rejonowa, oddziałowa*) (female) nurse
pielęgniarz (**-a, -e**; *gen pl* **-y**) *m* (male) nurse
pielęgn|ować (**-uję, -ujesz**) *vt* **1** (*osobę*) to nurse **2** (*zwierzę*) to take care of **3** (*ogródek*) to tend **4** (*skóra*) to take care of **5** (*tradycje*) to foster
pielgrzy|m (**-ma, -mi**; *loc sg* **-mie**) *m* pilgrim
pielgrzym|ka (**-ki, -ki**; *dat sg & loc sg* **-ce**; *gen pl* **-ek**) *f* pilgrimage
pielu|cha (**-chy, -chy**; *dat sg & loc sg* **-sze**) *f* (*tetrowa, jednorazowa*) nappy (*Brit*), diaper (*US*)
pieni|ądz (**-ądza, -ądze**; *gen pl* **-ędzy**) *m* money; **pieniądze** *pl* money *sg*
pieprz (**-u**) *m* pepper
pierni|k (**-ka, -ki**; *inst sg* **-kiem**) *m* gingerbread
piero|gi (**-gów**) *pl* (*ruskie, nadziewane, z farszem*) *dumplings filled with meat, cheese or fruit*

PIEROGI

Pierogi is a popular dish in Central and Eastern European cuisine. **Pierogi** are small dumplings, made from dough which have been stuffed with various fillings, such as meat, cabbage with mushrooms or potato, cheese and onion and then boiled or fried in fat. **Pierogi** can also be served sweet with cottage cheese or fruit, and covered in thick cream.

pier|ś (**-si, -si**; *gen pl* **-si**) *f* **1** (*Anat*) chest **2** (*u kobiety*) breast; **karmić dziecko piersią** to breast-feed a child
pierścion|ek (**-ka, -ki**; *inst sg* **-kiem**) *m* ring
pierwszeńst|wo (**-wa**; *loc sg & dat sg* **-wie**) *nt* **1** (*prawo, przywilej*) precedence **2** (*Mot*): **~ przejazdu** right of way; **ustąpić** (*pf*) **pierwszeństwa** to give way
pierwszy *num decl like adj* first; **~ maja** the first of May; **pierwsze piętro** first floor (*Brit*), second floor (*US*); **pierwsza pomoc** first aid; **pierwsze danie** starter; **pierwsza litera** initial; **pierwsza wojna światowa** World War One; **pierwsza w prawo/lewo** the next on the right/left; **po pierwsze** firstly; **~ raz** *lub* **po raz ~** (for) the first time
pies (**psa, psy**; *loc sg & dat sg* **psie**) *m* dog; **pogoda pod psem** dreadful weather; **~ z rodowodem** pedigree dog
pieszo *adv* on foot; **iść** (**pójść** *pf*) **~** to go on foot
pieszy *adj* **1** (*żołnierz*) foot **2** (*oddział*) infantry ▷ *m decl like adj* pedestrian; **piesza wycieczka** hike; **~ turysta** hiker; **przejście dla ~ch** (pedestrian) crossing
pieś|ń (**-ni, -ni**; *gen pl* **-ni**) *f* (*religijna, wzniosła, uroczysta*) song
pietrusz|ka (**-ki, -ki**; *dat sg & loc sg* **-ce**; *gen pl* **-ek**) *f* **1** (*korzeń*) parsley-root **2** (*roślina*) parsley
pięć *num* five
pięćdziesiąt *num* fifty
pięćset *num* five hundred
pięknie *adv* beautifully; **~ wyglądać** to look beautiful; **no ~!** (*pot*) oh great!
pięk|no (**-na**; *loc sg & dat sg* **-nie**) *nt* (*wewnętrzne*) beauty
piękny *adj* beautiful; **literatura piękna** belles-lettres; **sztuki piękne** fine arts; **płeć piękna** the fair sex
pięś|ć (**-ci, -ci**; *gen pl* **-ci**) *f* (*żelazna*) fist
pię|ta (**-ty, -ty**; *dat sg & loc sg* **-cie**) *f* heel; **~ Achillesa** *lub* **achillesowa** Achilles heel
piętnasty *num decl like adj* fifteenth
piętnaście *num* fifteen; **za ~ czwarta** quarter to four

pięt|ro (**-ra, -ra**; *loc sg* **-rze**; *gen pl* **-er**) *nt* (*w budynku*) floor; **mieszkać na drugim piętrze** to live on the second (*Brit*) *lub* third (*US*) floor; **na piętrze** upstairs; **iść na ~** to go upstairs
piętrowy *adj*: **dom ~** house (*with more than one storey*); **łóżko piętrowe** bunk beds *pl*; **autobus ~** double-decker bus
pigułka (**-ki, -ki**; *dat sg & loc sg* **-ce**; *gen pl* **-ek**) *f* pill; **~ nasenna** sleeping pill; **~ antykoncepcyjna** the pill
pija|k (**-ka, -cy** *lub* **-ki**; *inst sg* **-kiem**) *m* drunk
pijany *adj* drunk(en) ▷ *m decl like adj* drunk; **on jest ~ w sztok** he is steaming (drunk); **jazda po pijanemu** drink driving (*Brit*), drunk driving (*US*)
pikantny *adj* **1** (*smak*) piquant **2** (*ostry*) hot **3** (*przen: historia*) juicy **4** (*anegdota*) bawdy
pikni|k (**-ku, -ki**; *inst sg* **-kiem**) *m* picnic
piln|ować (**-uję, -ujesz**) *vt +gen* **1** (*dziecka*) to look after **2** (*interesów*) to look after **3** (*pf* **przy-**) (*robotników*) to supervise **4** (*porządku*) to maintain; **~ się** *vr* to look after o.s.
pilny *adj* **1** (*student*) diligent **2** (*sprawa*) urgent
pilo|t (**-ta**; *loc sg* **-cie**) *m* **1** (*nom pl* **-ci**) (*samolot*) pilot **2** (*nom pl* **-ty**) (*do telewizora*) remote control **3** (*nom pl* **-ci**) (*wycieczek*) guide
piłka (**-ki, -ki**; *dat sg & loc sg* **-ce**; *gen pl* **-ek**) *f* **1** (*do zabaw*) ball **2** (*mała piła*) handsaw; **grać w piłkę** to play ball; **~ nożna** football (*Brit*), soccer (*US*); **~ ręczna** (*Sport*) handball
piłkarz (**-a, -e**; *gen pl* **-y**) *m* footballer (*Brit*), soccer player (*US*)
pingwi|n (**-na, -ny**; *loc sg* **-nie**) *m* penguin
pionie|r (**-ra, -rzy**; *loc sg* **-rze**) *m* pioneer
pionowo *adv* **1** vertically **2** (*w krzyżówce*) down
pionowy *adj* **1** vertical **2** (*w pozycji pionowej*) upright
pioru|n (**-na, -ny**; *loc sg* **-nie**) *m* thunder and lightning; **burza z ~ami** thunderstorm
piosen|ka (**-ki, -ki**; *dat sg & loc sg* **-ce**; *gen pl* **-ek**) *f* (*popularna, skoczna*) song
piosenkar|ka (**-ki, -ki**; *dat sg & loc sg* **-ce**; *gen pl* **-ek**) *f* singer
piosenkarz (**-a, -e**; *gen pl* **-y**) *m* singer
piórni|k (**-ka, -ki**; *inst sg* **-kiem**) *m* pencil case
pió|ro (**-ra, -ra**; *loc sg & dat sg* **-rze**) *nt* **1** (*ptaka*) feather **2** (*też*: **wieczne ~**) fountain pen **3** (*wycieraczki*) blade; **powieść pióra Prousta** a novel penned by Proust
Pirenej|e (**-ów**) *pl* the Pyrenees
pi|sać (**-szę, -szesz**; *pf* **na-**) *vi* to write ▷ *vi* to write; **~ się** *vr*: **jak to się pisze?** how do you spell it?; **~ na komputerze** to type
pisan|ka (**-ki, -ki**; *dat sg & loc sg* **-ce**; *gen pl* **-ek**) *f* Easter egg
pisar|ka (**-ki, -ki**; *dat sg & loc sg* **-ce**; *gen pl* **-ek**) *f* writer
pisarz (**-a, -e**; *gen pl* **-y**) *m* writer
pisemnie *adv* in writing
pisemny *adj* (*wniosek, egzamin, test*) written
pi|smo (**-sma**; *loc sg & dat sg* **-śmie**) *nt* **1** writing **2** (*litery*) alphabet **3** (*kreślenie liter*) hand(writing) **4** (*nom pl* **-sma**) (*czasopismo*) magazine **5** (*nom pl* **-sma**) (*dokument*) letter; **na piśmie** in writing; **P~ Święte** the (Holy) Scriptures; **~ pochyłe** italics
pisow|nia (**-ni, -nie**; *gen pl* **-ni**) *f* spelling
pistole|t (**-tu, -ty**; *loc sg* **-cie**) *m* gun; **~ maszynowy** submachine gun
PIT *nt* tax return
pitny *adj* (*woda*) drinking; **miód ~** mead
piwnic|a (**-y, -e**) *f* (*winna, zatęchła*) cellar
pi|wo (**-wa, -wa**; *dat sg* **-wu**; *loc sg* **-wie**) *nt* **1** (*napój*) beer **2** (*porcja*) pint
pizz|a (**-y, -e**) *f* pizza
piża|ma (**-my, -my**; *dat sg & loc sg* **-mie**) *f* (*flanelowa, ciepła, dziecięca*) pyjamas *pl* (*Brit*), pajamas *pl* (*US*)
PKP *abbr* (= *Polskie Koleje Państwowe*) Polish State Railways
PKS *abbr* (= *Państwowa Komunikacja Samochodowa*) National Transport Company

pkt *abbr* (= *punkt*) pt.
pl. *abbr* (= *plac*) sq.
plac (**-u, -e**) *m* square; **~ budowy** building site; **~ zabaw** playground
plac|ek (**-ka, -ki**; *inst sg* **-kiem**) *m* (*słodki*) cake; **placki kartoflane** potato pancakes; **~ drożdżowy** yeast cake; **masz babo ~!** damn and blast! (*pot*)
plaka|t (**-tu, -ty**; *loc sg* **-cie**) *m* (*filmowy, teatralny*) poster
pla|ma (**-my, -my**; *dat sg & loc sg* **-mie**) *f* stain; **tłusta ~** greasy spot
pla|mić (**-mię, -misz**) *vt* (*pf* **po-**) **1** (*robić plamy*) to stain **2** (*pf* **s-**) (*zniesławiać*) to tarnish; **~ się** *vr* **1** (*pf* **po-**) (*brudzić się*) to get dirty **2** (*pf* **s-**) (*przen*) to tarnish one's reputation
pla|n (**-nu, -ny**; *loc sg* **-nie**) *m* **1** (*zamierzenie*) plan **2** (*program*) schedule **3** (*inwestycyjny*) scheme **4** (*miasta*) street map **5** (*Teatr*) set; **mieć coś w ~ie** to plan sth; **~ zajęć** (*Szkol*) timetable; **według ~u** *lub* **zgodnie z ~em** according to plan
plane|ta (**-ty, -ty**; *dat sg & loc sg* **-cie**) *f* planet
plan|ować (**-uję, -ujesz**; *pf* **za-**) *vt* **1** (*wakacje*) to plan **2** (*zebranie*) to schedule
plast|er (**-ra, -ry**; *loc sg* **-rze**) *m* **1** (*Med*) (sticking) plaster (*Brit*), Bandaid® (*US*) **2** (*sera*) slice
plaster|ek (**-ka, -ki**; *inst sg* **-kiem**) *m* *dimin od* **plaster**
plastyczny *adj* **1** (*materiał*) plastic **2** (*sztuka*) artistic **3** (*opis*) vivid; **operacja plastyczna** (*zabieg chirurgiczny*) plastic surgery
plasty|k (**-ka, -cy**; *inst sg* **-kiem**) *m* artist
plaż|a (**-y, -e**) *f* beach; **~ dla nudystów** nudist beach
pleca|k (**-ka, -ki**; *inst sg* **-kiem**) *m* (*wodoodporny, górski*) rucksack, backpack (*US*)
plec|y (**-ów**) *pl* back
pl|eść (**-otę, -eciesz**; *imp* **-eć**; *pt* **plótł, plotła, pletli**) *vt* **1** (*pf* **s-** *lub* **za-**) (*wyplatać*) to plait **2** (*pf* **na-**) (*pot: bzdury*) to blabber; **~ trzy po trzy** to talk rubbish
pleś|ń (**-ni**) *f* mould (*Brit*), mold (*US*)
pli|k (**-ku, -ki**; *loc sg* **-ku**; *inst sg* **-kiem**) *m* **1** (*dokumentów, gazet, papierów*) bundle **2** (*Komput*) file
plom|ba (**-by, -by**; *dat sg & loc sg* **-bie**) *f* **1** (*przy drzwiach*) seal **2** (*u dentysty*) filling
plot|ka (**-ki, -ki**; *dat sg & loc sg* **-ce**; *gen pl* **-ek**) *f* rumour (*Brit*), rumor (*US*); **plotki** *pl* gossip *sg*; **wylęgarnia plotek** hotbed of gossip
plotk|ować (**-uję, -ujesz**) *vi* to gossip
plu|s (**-sa, -sy**; *loc sg* **-sie**) *m* **1** (*w matematyce*) plus **2** (*coś pozytywnego*) advantage; **~y i minusy** pros and cons; **~ minus** more or less
płac|a (**-y, -e**) *f* **1** (*ogólnie: tygodniowa, miesięczna, stała*) pay **2** (*dzienna, tygodniowa*) wages *pl*; (*roczna*) salary
pła|cić (**-cę, -cisz**; *imp* **-ć**; *pf* **za-**) *vt, vi* to pay; **~ za coś** to pay for sth; **on drogo za to zapłaci** (*przen*) he'll pay dearly for that
płacz (**-u, -e**) *m* (*rozpaczliwy*) crying
płaczliwy *adj* **1** (*człowiek*) tearful **2** (*smutny*) tearful **3** (*piosenka*) moving
pła|kać (**-czę, -czesz**) *vi* to cry
płaski *adj* flat; **~ talerz** dinner plate
płaszcz (**-a, -e**; *gen pl* **-y**) *m* (*okrycie: wełniany, ciepły*) (over)coat
płatni|k (**-ka, -cy**; *inst sg* **-kiem**) *m* payer
płatnoś|ć (**-ci, -ci**; *gen pl* **-ci**) *f* (*gotówką, kartą, przelewem*) payment
płatny *adj* paid; **dobrze/nisko ~** well-/low-paid; **parking ~** paid parking
płd. *abbr* (= *południowy*) S.
pł|eć (**-ci, -ci**; *gen pl* **-ci**) *f* sex
płn. *abbr* (= *północny*) N.
płodny *adj* **1** fertile **2** (*pisarz, rok, twórca*) prolific
płomie|ń (**-nia, -nie**; *gen pl* **-ni**) *m* **1** (*blask*) blaze **2** (*ogień*) flame **3** (*pasja*) flame
pło|nąć (**-nę, -niesz**; *imp* **-ń**) *vi* to burn
pło|t (**-tu, -ty**; *loc sg* **-cie**) *m* (*drewniany, druciany, stalowy*) fence
pł|ód (**-odu, -ody**; *loc sg* **-odzie**) *m* foetus (*Brit*), fetus (*US*); **płody** *pl* (*leśne*) produce *sg*

płuc|o (**-a, -a**) *nt* lung; **zapalenie płuc** pneumonia; **ten park to prawdziwe płuca miasta** (*przen*) the park is the lungs of the city
płu|kać (**-czę, -czesz**) *vt* (*pf* **wy-**) **1** (*tkaninę*) to rinse **2** (*pf* **o-** *lub* **wy-**) (*sałatę*) to rinse **3** (*pf* **wy-** *lub* **prze-**) (*usta*) to rinse; **~ gardło** to gargle
Płw. *abbr* (= *półwysep*) Pen.
pły|n (**-nu, -ny**; *loc sg* **-nie**) *m* liquid; **~ po goleniu** aftershave (lotion); **~ do mycia naczyń** washing-up liquid
pły|nąć (**-nę, -niesz**; *imp* **-ń**) *vi* **1** to flow **2** (*człowiek*) to swim **3** (*statkiem*) to sail
płynnie *adv* **1** (*mówić, czytać, recytować*) fluently **2** (*chodzić*) smoothly
płynny *adj* **1** (*miód*) liquid **2** (*ruch*) smooth **3** (*wymowa*) fluent
pły|ta (**-ty, -ty**; *dat sg & loc sg* **-cie**) *f* **1** (*z kamienia, metalu*) plate **2** (*Muz*) record; **~ kompaktowa** compact disc
pływacz|ka (**-ki, -ki**; *dat sg & loc sg* **-ce**; *gen pl* **-ek**) *f* swimmer
pływ|ać (**-am, -asz**) *vi* **1** (*człowiek*) to swim **2** (*statek*) to sail **3** (*korek*) to float
pływa|k (**-ka**; *inst sg* **-kiem**) *m* **1** (*nom pl* **-cy**) (*człowiek*) swimmer **2** (*nom pl* **-ki**) (*przyrząd*) float
pływal|nia (**-ni, -nie**; *gen pl* **-ni**) *f* (*publiczna, szkolna, kryta*) swimming pool
pływani|e (**-a**) *nt* swimming
p.n.e. *abbr* (= *przed naszą erą*) BC

SŁOWO KLUCZOWE

po *prep +loc* **1** (*czas*) after; **po kolacji** after dinner; **po chwili** after a while; **pięć po drugiej** five past *lub* after (*US*) two
2 (*kolejność*) after; **jeden po drugim** one after another; **butelka po piwie** beer bottle
3 (*na podstawie*) by; **rozpoznać kogoś po głosie** to recognize sb by his voice
4 (*dziedziczenie*) from; **ma urodę po babce** she gets her beauty from her grandmother; **spadek po ojcu** inheritance from one's father
5 (*hierarchia*) after; **po kapitanie** second to the captain; **pierwszy po Bogu** next to God
6: **chodzić po parku/górach** to walk in the park/mountains; **po niebie** in the sky; **chodzić po piasku/trawie** to walk on sand/grass; **jeździć po mieście/kraju** to travel around the town/country; **po szynach** on rails; **spacerować po korytarzu** to walk along the corridor; **po całym globie** all over the globe; **po lewej stronie** on the left side; **schodzić po drabinie/schodach** to go down the ladder/stairs; **głaskać kogoś po włosach** to stroke sb's hair
7: **po kawałku** piece by piece
▷ *prep +acc* **1** (*kres*) to; **wody było po kostki** the water was ankle-deep; **po brzegi** to the rim
2 (*cel*) for; **przychodzić** (**przyjść** *pf*) **po mleko** to come to get milk; **posłać** (**posyłać** *pf*) **po lekarza** to send for a doctor; **po co?** what for?; **po trzydzieści sztuk w paczce** thirty items per pack; **po cztery złote za sztukę** (at) four zlotys a piece
▷ *prep +dat*; **po cichu** (*bezgłośnie*) quietly; (*potajemnie*) on the quiet; **po trochu** bit by bit; **po polsku/angielsku** in Polish/English; **mówić po polsku/angielsku** to speak Polish/English

po|bić (**-biję, -bijesz**) *vt* **1** (*w walce*) to defeat **2** (*kogoś*) to beat up; **~ się** *vr pf* to have a fight; **~** (*pf*) **kogoś na kwaśne jabłko** (*pot*) to beat sb to a pulp
pobud|ka (**-ki, -ki**; *dat sg & loc sg* **-ce**; *gen pl* **-ek**) *f* (*sygnał*) alarm; **pobudki** *pl* (*powody: niskie, szlachetne*) motives
poby|t (**-tu, -ty**; *loc sg* **-cie**) *m* stay
pocał|ować (**-uję, -ujesz**) *vb pf od* **całować**
pocałun|ek (**-ku, -ki**; *inst sg* **-kiem**) *m* (*delikatny, płomienny*) kiss; **~ śmierci** (*przen*) kiss of death
pochmurno *adv*: **jest ~** it's cloudy
pochmurny *adj* **1** (*pogoda*) cloudy **2** (*twarz, wzrok, nastrój*) gloomy
pochodzeni|e (**-a**) *nt* origin; **on jest Szkotem z pochodzenia** he is of Scottish descent

pocho|dzić (**-dzę, -dzisz**) *vi*: **pochodzę z Anglii/biednej rodziny** I come from England/a poor family
poch|wa (**-wy, -wy**; *dat sg & loc sg* **-wie**; *gen pl* **-ew**) *f* **1** (*Anat*) vagina **2** (*futerał*) sheath
pochwal|ać (**-am, -asz**) *vt* (*zachowanie*) to approve of; **nie ~ czegoś** to disapprove of sth
pochwal|ić (**-ę, -isz**) *vb pf od* **chwalić**
pochwa|ła (**-ły, -ły**; *dat sg & loc sg* **-le**) *f* **1** (*wyraz uznania: pisemna, ustna*) praise **2** (*pisana*) citation
po|ciąć (**-tnę, -tniesz**; *imp* **-tnij**) *vt pf* to cut up; **~** *(pf)* **na kawałki** to cut into pieces
pocią|g (**-gu, -gi**; *inst sg* **-giem**) *m* **1** (*transport*) train **2** (*do ciastka*) attraction; **jechać ~iem** to go by train; **~ towarowy** goods (*Brit*) *lub* freight (*US*) train; **~ ekspresowy** express (train)
pociąg|ać (**-am, -asz**) *vt* to attract ▷ *vi*: **~** (**pociągnąć** *pf*) **za coś** to pull (at) sth; **~** (**pociągnąć** *pf*) **za sobą** to entail; **~** (**pociągnąć** *pf*) **nosem** to sniff
pociąg|nąć (**-nę, -niesz**; *imp* **-nij**) *vb pf od* **pociągać, ciągnąć**
po|cić się (**-cę, -cisz**; *imp* **-ć**) *vr* **1** (*pf* **s-**) (*stopy*) to sweat **2** (*pf* **za-**) (*okulary*) to steam up; **~ ze strachu** to sweat with fear
pociesz|ać (**-am, -asz**; *pf* **-yć**) *vt* to comfort; **~ się** *vr* to console o.s.
począt|ek (**-ku, -ki**; *inst sg* **-kiem**) *m* (*udany, dobry, obiecujący*) beginning; **na ~** for a start; **na początku** at the beginning; **od początku** from the beginning; **z początku** at first
początkowo *adv* initially
początkowy *adj* (*etap, plan, zamysł*) initial
początkujący *adj* (*pisarz*) novice ▷ *m decl like adj* beginner
poczekal|nia (**-ni, -nie**; *gen pl* **-ni**) *f* waiting room; **~ u lekarza** doctor's waiting room
pocz|ta (**-ty, -ty**; *dat sg & loc sg* **-cie**) *f* **1** (*urząd pocztowy: miejscowa, wiejska, główna*) post office **2** (*korespondencja*) post (*Brit*), mail (*US*); **pocztą lotniczą** (by) airmail; **~ elektroniczna** email
pocztowy *adj* postal; **kod ~** postcode (*Brit*), zip code (*US*); **urząd ~** post office; **znaczek ~** postage stamp; **skrzynka pocztowa** *lub* **na listy** letterbox (*Brit*), mailbox (*US*); **skrzynka pocztowa** (*na ulicy*) postbox (*Brit*), mailbox (*US*)
pocztów|ka (**-ki, -ki**; *dat sg & loc sg* **-ce**; *gen pl* **-ek**) *f* postcard
pocz|uć (**-uję, -ujesz**) *vb pf od* **czuć**

SŁOWO KLUCZOWE

pod *prep +inst* **1** (*poniżej*) under; **pod krzesłem** under the chair; **pod ziemią/wodą** underground/underwater; **pod spodem** underneath
2 (*obok*) by; **pod domem** by the house; **pod drzwiami** at the door
3 (*w pobliżu*) near; **wieś pod miastem** a village near the town; **bitwa pod Grunwaldem** the Battle of Grunwald
4 (*dla wyrażenia przyczyny*) under; **pod przymusem/wpływem** under pressure/the influence
▷ *prep +acc* **1** (*kierunek*) under; **mysz weszła pod łóżko** the mouse went under the bed; **biec** *(impf)* **pod prąd/wiatr** to run against the current/wind; **iść pod górę** to walk uphill; **wpaść** *(pf)* **pod autobus** to get run over by a bus
2 (*dla wyrażenia czasu*): **pod koniec/wieczór** towards the end/evening; **pod czyjąś nieobecność** in sb's absence
3: **pod kierunkiem matki** under mother's supervision; **pod czyjąś opieką** in sb's care; **pod nazwiskiem Kowalski** under the name of Kowalski; **pod warunkiem, że...** on condition (that)...; **książka pod tytułem...** a book entitled...

pod|ać (**-am, -asz**) *vb pf od* **podawać**
poda|nie (**-nia, -nia**; *gen pl* **-ń**) *nt* **1** (*wniosek: oficjalne, pisemne*) application **2** (*w piłce nożnej*) pass
podarty *adj* (*materiał, papier*) tattered
podat|ek (**-ku, -ki**; *inst sg* **-kiem**) *m* tax; **~ dochodowy** income tax;

~ od wartości dodanej value added tax, VAT
podatkowy *adj* (*system*) tax
podatni|k (**-ka, -cy**; *inst sg* **-kiem**) *m* taxpayer
pod|awać (**-aję, -ajesz**; *pf* **-ać**) *vt* **1** (*masło*) to pass **2** (*przykład*) to give **3** (*wiadomość*) to announce **4** (*lekarstwo*) to administer **5** (*w tenisie*) to serve **6** (*w piłce nożnej*) to pass; **~ się** *vr*: **~ się za kogoś** to pose as sb; **~** (**podać** *pf*) **komuś coś** to pass sb sth *lub* sth to sb; **~** (**podać** *pf*) **do stołu** to wait at table; **podać się do dymisji** to hand in one's resignation
podczas *prep +gen* during; **~ gdy** (*kiedy*) while; (*natomiast*) whereas
poddasz|e (**-a, -a**; *gen pl* **-y**) *nt* loft; **pokój na poddaszu** attic
podejm|ować (**-uję, -ujesz**; *pf* **podjąć**) *vt* **1** (*ryzyko*) to take **2** (*obowiązki*) to take up **3** (*walkę*) to put up **4** (*dyskusję*) to take up **5** (*gościć*) to receive **6** (*pieniądze*) to withdraw; **~ się** *vr*: **~ się czegoś/coś zrobić** to undertake sth/to do sth; **~** (**podjąć** *pf*) **decyzję** to make a decision
podejrzany *adj* (*zachowanie, typ, transakcja*) suspicious ▷ *m decl like adj* suspect
podejrzew|ać (**-am, -asz**) *vt* to suspect; **~ kogoś o coś** to suspect sb of sth
podejrzliwy *adj* suspicious
podeszły *adj*: **w ~m wieku** advanced in years; **osoby w ~m wieku** the aged
pod|jąć (**-ejmę, -ejmiesz**; *imp* **-ejmij**) *vb pf od* **podejmować**
podkoszul|ek (**-ka, -ki**; *inst sg* **-kiem**) *m* (*męski, bawełniany, ciepły*) vest (*Brit*), undershirt (*US*)
podleg|ać (**-am, -asz**) *vi*: **~ komuś/czemuś** (*kierownictwu*) to be subordinate to sb/sth; **~ czemuś** (*obowiązkowi*) to be subject to sth
podliz|ywać się (**-uję, -ujesz**; *pf* **-ać**) *vr*: **podlizywać** (**podlizać** *pf*) **się komuś** (*pot*) to suck up to sb
podłącz|ać (**-am, -asz**; *pf* **-yć**) *vt* (*kable, sieć, urządzenie*) to connect
podł|oga (**-ogi, -ogi**; *dat sg & loc sg* **-odze**; *gen pl* **-óg**) *f* floor
podły *adj* mean
podniecający *adj* (*perspektywa, pomysł, doznanie*) exciting
podniece|nie (**-nia**) *nt* **1** excitement **2** (*seksualne*) arousal
podniecony *adj* **1** (*ożywiony*) excited **2** (*pobudzony seksualnie*) aroused
pod|nieść (**-niosę, -niesiesz**; *imp* **-nieś**; *pt* **-niósł, -niosła, -nieśli**) *vb pf od* **podnosić**
podno|sić (**-szę, -sisz**; *imp* **-ś**; *pf* **podnieść**) *vt* **1** (*ręce*) to raise **2** (*kieliszek*) to lift **3** (*zbierać*) to pick up **4** (*pomagać wstać*) to lift **5** (*alarm*) to raise **6** (*kwestię*) to raise; **~ się** *vr* **1** (*z krzesła*) to lift o.s. **2** (*ceny*) to rise; **~ głos** to raise one's voice
podob|ać się (**-am, -asz**) *vr*: **ona mi się podoba** I like her; **to mi się nie podoba** I don't like it
podobieńst|wo (**-wa, -wa**; *dat sg* **-wu**; *loc sg* **-wie**) *nt* **1** similarity **2** (*jednakowy wygląd*) likeness; **rzeźba na ~ sławnego pisarza** a sculpture of a famous writer
podobnie *adv* **1** (*w podobny sposób*) similarly **2** (*równie*) as; **~ jak** like
podobno *adv* supposedly
podobny *adj* similar; **być ~m do kogoś/czegoś** to be similar to sb/sth; **i tym podobne** and the like
podpal|ać (**-am, -asz**; *pf* **-ić**) *vt*: **~** (**podpalić** *pf*) **coś** to set fire to sth
podpas|ka (**-ki, -ki**; *dat sg & loc sg* **-ce**; *gen pl* **-ek**) *f* (*też*: **~ higieniczna**) sanitary towel (*Brit*) *lub* napkin (*US*)
podpi|s (**-su, -sy**; *loc sg* **-sie**) *m* **1** (*czyjś: zamaszysty, nieczytelny, wyraźny*) signature **2** (*pod obrazem*) caption
podpis|ywać (**-uję, -ujesz**; *pf* **-ać**) *vt* (*dokument, traktat, książkę*) to sign; **~ się** *vr* to sign one's name
podręczni|k (**-ka, -ki**; *inst sg* **-kiem**) *m* (*szkolny, do matematyki, opasły*) textbook
podrób|ka (**-ki, -ki**; *dat sg* **-ce**; *gen pl* **-ek**) *f* fake
podróż (**-y, -e**; *gen pl* **-y**) *f* **1** (*wycieczka*) trip **2** (*długa*) journey; **podróże** *pl* travels; **biuro ~y** travel agency; **szczęśliwej ~y!** have a safe trip!
podróżni|k (**-ka, -cy**; *inst sg* **-kiem**) *m* traveller (*Brit*), traveler (*US*)

podróżny *adj*: **torba podróżna** travelling (*Brit*) *lub* traveling (*US*) bag; **czek ~** traveller's cheque (*Brit*), traveler's check (*US*) ▷ *m decl like adj* passenger

podróż|ować (**-uję, -ujesz**) *vi* to travel

podryw|ać (**-am, -asz**; *pf* **poderwać**) *vt* (*pot*) to pick up; **~ chłopców** to pick up boys

podstawowy *adj* (*kurs, zasada, wiedza*) basic; **szkoła podstawowa** primary (*Brit*) *lub* elementary (*US*) school

podusz|ka (**-ki, -ki**; *dat sg & loc sg* **-ce**; *gen pl* **-ek**) *f* (*puchowa, miękka, niewygodna*) pillow; **~ powietrzna** airbag

podwieczor|ek (**-ku, -ki**; *inst sg* **-kiem**) *m* tea (*meal*)

podwójnie *adv* doubly; **płacić/ kosztować ~** to pay/cost double

podwójny *adj* (*korzyść*) double

podwór|ko (**-ka, -ka**; *inst sg* **-kiem**; *gen pl* **-ek**) *nt* **1** yard **2** (*za domem*) backyard

podwyż|ka (**-ki, -ki**; *dat sg & loc sg* **-ce**; *gen pl* **-ek**) *f* **1** (*pensji, płac, emerytur*) rise (*Brit*), raise (*US*) **2** (*cen*) rise

podzia|ł (**-łu, -ły**; *loc sg* **-le**) *m* **1** division **2** (*Sci*) fission; **~ majątku** division of estate

podziel|ić (**-ę, -isz**) *vb pf od* **dzielić**

podziemny *adj* underground; **przejście podziemne** subway (*Brit*), underpass (*US*); **kolejka podziemna** underground (train)

podzięk|ować (**-uję, -ujesz**) *vb pf od* **dziękować**

podziękowa|nie (**-nia, -nia**; *gen pl* **-ń**) *nt* (*serdeczne, szczere, wylewne*) thanks *pl*

podziwi|ać (**-am, -asz**) *vt* to admire

poe|ta (**-ty, -ci**; *dat sg & loc sg* **-cie**) *m decl like f in sg* (*romantyczny, współczesny*) poet

poezj|a (**-i, -e**; *gen pl* **-i**) *f* poetry

pogański *adj* (*zwyczaj, wierzenie, bóstwo*) pagan

pogar|dzać (**-dzam, -dzasz**; *pf* **-dzić**) *vi*: **~ kimś/czymś** (*odnosić się z pogardą*) to hold sb/sth in contempt; (*brak szacunku*) to disdain sb/sth

poglą|d (**-du, -dy**; *loc sg* **-dzie**) *m* view

pogo|da (**-dy**; *dat sg & loc sg* **-dzie**) *f* **1** weather **2** (*ciepła pora*) sunny weather; **~ ducha** cheerfulness

pogodny *adj* **1** bright **2** (*niebo, dzień*) clear **3** (*humor, nastrój*) bright

pogotowi|e (**-a**) *nt* **1** (*stan*) alert **2** (*górskie*) emergency service **3** (*ambulans*) ambulance; **być w pogotowiu** to be on stand-by; **~ ratunkowe** ambulance service

pogrze|b (**-bu, -by**; *loc sg* **-bie**) *m* funeral

pogrzeb|ać (**-ię, -iesz**) *vt pf od* **grzebać**

poja|wiać się (**-wiam, -wiasz**; *pf* **-wić**) *vr* (*znienacka, regularnie*) to appear

poj|azd (**-azdu, -azdy**; *loc sg* **-eździe**) *m* vehicle

pojedynkę *inv*: **w ~** by oneself

pojemni|k (**-ka, -ki**; *inst sg* **-kiem**) *m* (*plastikowy, nierdzewny*) container; **~ na śmieci** rubbish bin (*Brit*), trash *lub* garbage can (*US*)

pojemnoś|ć (**-ci**) *f* capacity; **~ pamięci** (*Komput*) memory

pojemny *adj* spacious

poję|cie (**-cia, -cia**; *gen pl* **-ć**) *nt* **1** concept **2** (*pot*) idea; **nie mieć (zielonego** *lub* **najmniejszego) pojęcia o czymś** not to have a clue about sth

pojutrze *adv* the day after tomorrow

pokar|m (**-mu, -my**; *loc sg* **-mie**) *m* **1** (*jedzenie*) food **2** (*mleko matki*) breast milk

poka|z (**-zu, -zy**; *loc sg* **-zie**) *m* demonstration

poka|zać (**-żę, -żesz**) *vb pf od* **pokazywać**

pokaz|ywać (**-uję, -ujesz**; *pf* **-ać**) *vt* to show; **~ się** *vr* (*pojawiać się*) to turn up

pokłó|cić (**-cę, -cisz**; *imp* **-ć**) *vt pf*: **~ kogoś z kimś** to turn sb against sb; **~ się** *vr pf*: **~ się z kimś** to have a row with sb

pokoch|ać (**-am, -asz**) *vt pf* to fall in love with

pokojowy *adj* **1** (*rozmowa*) peaceful **2** (*traktat*) peace **3** (*o pokoju*) room

pokojów|ka (**-ki, -ki**; *dat sg & loc sg* **-ce**; *gen pl* **-ek**) *f* (chamber)maid
pokole|nie (**-nia, -nia**; *gen pl* **-ń**) *nt* (*młode, naszych rodziców*) generation
pok|ój (**-oju, -oje**; *gen pl* **-oi** *lub* **-ojów**) *m* **1** (*część mieszkania*) room **2** (*Pol*) peace; **~ gościnny** living room; **~ jadalny** dining room; **~ jednoosobowy/dwuosobowy** single/double room
pokrewieńst|wo (**-wa**; *loc sg & dat sg* **-wie**) *nt* **1** (*rodzina*) kinship **2** (*przen*) affinity **3** (*Bio*) affinity
Pola|k (**-ka, -cy**; *inst sg* **-kiem**) *m* Pole
pol|e (**-a, -a**; *gen pl* **pól**) *nt* **1** field **2** (*w matematyce*) area; **~ namiotowe** campsite (*Brit*), campground (*US*)
pole|cać (**-cam, -casz**; *pf* **-cić**) *vt* **1** (*film*) to recommend **2** (*powierzać*) to entrust **3** (*kazać*) to command
polepsz|ać (**-am, -asz**; *pf* **-yć**) *vt* to improve; **~ się** *vr* to improve
policj|a (**-i**) *f* police
policjan|t (**-ta, -ci**; *loc sg* **-cie**) *m* policeman, (police) officer
policjant|ka (**-ki, -ki**; *dat sg & loc sg* **-ce**; *gen pl* **-ek**) *f* policewoman, (police) officer
policyjny *adj* (*mundur, samochód, patrol*) police; **godzina policyjna** curfew
policz|ek (**-ka, -ki**; *inst sg* **-kiem**) *m* (*rumiany, pulchny, różowy*) cheek
politechni|ka (**-ki, -ki**; *dat sg & loc sg* **-ce**) *f* polytechnic
polity|k (**-ka, -cy**; *inst sg* **-kiem**) *m* politician
polity|ka (**-ka**; *dat sg & loc sg* **-ce**) *f* **1** politics **2** (*zagraniczna*) policy; **~ biurowa** office politics
Pol|ka (**-ki, -ki**; *dat sg & loc sg* **-ce**; *gen pl* **-ek**) *f* (*rodowita, z pochodzenia*) Polish woman
pol|ka (**-ki, -ki**; *dat sg & loc sg* **-ce**; *gen pl* **-ek**) *f* (*skoczna*) polka

POLONEZ

The **polonez** is a Polish national dance. It is a slow and dignified dance, often performed at the opening of grand balls. See also **studniówka**.

Poloni|a (**-i**) *f*: **~ Amerykańska** Polish Americans *pl*
polonisty|ka (**-ka, -ki**; *dat sg & loc sg* **-ce**) *f* **1** (*nauka*) Polish language and literature **2** (*Uniw*) Polish Department *lub* Faculty
pol|ować (**-uję, -ujesz**) *vi* to hunt
polowa|nie (**-nia**; *dat sg & loc sg* **-niu**; *gen pl* **-ń**) *nt* hunt
Pols|ka (**-ki**; *dat sg* **-ce**) *f* Poland

POLSKA WÓDKA

Polska wódka (Polish vodka) is usually drunk straight out of small shot glasses. **Polska wódka** has been made since medieval times and holds an important place in Polish culture and customs. There are also many flavoured vodkas in Poland, the most famous of which are **Żubrówka**, **Krupnik** and **Śliwowica**. See also **bruderszaft**.

polski *adj* Polish; **Rzeczpospolita Polska** the Republic of Poland
polu|bić (**-bię, -bisz**) *vt pf* to take (a liking) to; **~ się** *vr pf* to grow to like each other
połącze|nie (**-nia, -nia**; *gen pl* **-ń**) *nt* (*telefoniczne*) connection
połącz|yć (**-ę, -ysz**) *vt pf*: **~ kogoś z kimś** (*telefon*) to put sb through to sb; **~ się** *vr pf*: **~ się z kimś** (*telefon*) to get through to sb
połk|nąć (**-nę, -niesz**; *imp* **-nij**) *vb pf od* **połykać**
poło|wa (**-wy, -wy**; *dat sg & loc sg* **-wie**) *f* **1** (*rodzaju*) half **2** (*w połowie drogi*) middle; **na połowę** in half; **o połowę więcej** half as much again; **o połowę mniej** half as much; **do połowy pusty** half empty; **po połowie** fifty-fifty; **w połowie drogi** halfway; **w połowie czerwca** in mid-June; **za połowę ceny** half-price
położe|nie (**-nia**) *nt* **1** (*miejsce: dramatyczne, wygodne*) location **2** (*wygodne*) situation
położn|a (**-ej, -e**) *f decl like adj* midwife
położony *adj*: **wieś położona jest nad rzeką** the village is situated on the river

poł|ożyć (**-ożę, -ożysz**; *imp* **-óż**) *vb pf od* **kłaść**
połów|ka (**-ki, -ki**; *dat sg & loc sg* **-ce**; *gen pl* **-ek**) *f* (*jabłka, pomarańczy*) half
południ|e (**-a**) *nt* **1** (*godzina dwunasta*) midday **2** (*strona świata*) south **3** (*kraje południowe*) the South; **przed ~m** in the morning; **po południu** in the afternoon; **w ~** at midday; **na ~ od** *+gen* to the south of
połyk|ać (**-am, -asz**; *pf* **połknąć**) *vt* **1** to swallow **2** (*pot: książkę*) to devour
pomag|ać (**-am, -asz**; *pf* **pomóc**) *vi* to help; **~ komuś w czymś** to help sb with sth; **w czym mogę pomóc?** how can I help you?; **krzyk/płacz nic nie pomoże** shouting/crying won't help (you)
pomału *adv* slowly; **~!** slow down!
pomarańcz|a (**-y, -e**; *gen pl* **-y**) *f* (*soczysta*) orange
pomarańczowy *adj* orange
pomarszczony *adj* (*twarz, papier, bibułka*) wrinkled
pomido|r (**-ra, -ry**; *loc sg* **-rze**) *m* (*dojrzały, jędrny*) tomato
pomidorowy *adj* (*zupa, sok, przecier*) tomato
pomiędzy *prep +inst* = **między**
pomimo *prep +gen* in spite of; **~ że** even though; **~ to** *lub* **wszystko** nevertheless; *zob. też* **mimo**
pomni|k (**-ka, -ki**; *inst sg* **-kiem**) *m* monument
pomoc (**-y**) *f* **1** help **2** (*wsparcie*) aid; **na ~!** help!; **przy ~y** *+gen* with the help of; **za ~ą** *+gen* by means of; **~ drogowa** emergency road service; **~ domowa** home help; **pierwsza ~** first aid
Pomorz|e (**-a**) *nt* Pomerania (*region in north-western Poland*)
pom|óc (**-ogę, -ożesz**; *imp* **-óż**) *vb pf od* **pomagać**
pom|pa (**-py**; *dat sg & loc sg* **-pie**) *f* **1** (*nom pl* **-py**) (*urządzenie*) pump **2** (*wystawność*) pomp; **~ paliwowa** fuel pump
pomył|ka (**-ki, -ki**; *loc sg & dat sg* **-ce**; *gen pl* **-ek**) *f* **1** (*życiowa, drobna*) mistake **2** (*telefon*) wrong number; **przez pomyłkę** by mistake
pomy|sł (**-słu, -sły**; *loc sg* **-śle**) *m* idea
pomysłowy *adj* ingenious
pomyśl|eć (**-ę, -isz**) *vi pf*: **~ o** *+loc* (*problemach*) to think about; (*rodzinie*) to think of
ponad *prep +inst* (*dla oznaczenia miejsca*) above, over ▷ *prep +acc* **1** (*dla oznaczenia kierunku*) over **2** (*więcej niż*) above, over **3** (*dłużej niż*) over
ponadto *adv* (*książk*) further(more)
ponawi|ać (**-am, -asz**; *pf* **ponowić**) *vt* to renew; **~ (ponowić** *pf*) **prenumeratę** to renew a subscription
poniedział|ek (**-ku, -ki**; *inst sg* **-kiem**) *m* Monday
ponieważ *conj* because
poniż|ać (**-am, -asz**; *pf* **-yć**) *vt* to demean; **~ się** *vr* to demean o.s.
poniżej *prep +gen* below ▷ *adv* (*w tekście*) below; **osiem stopni ~ zera** eight degrees below zero
poniższy *adj*: **poniższe uwagi** the following remarks
ponownie *adv* again
ponury *adj* **1** (*wiadomość*) gloomy **2** (*widok*) bleak **3** (*pokój*) bleak **4** (*myśli, nastrój*) dismal
pończo|cha (**-chy, -chy**; *dat sg & loc sg* **-sze**) *f* stocking
poparze|nie (**-nia, -nia**; *gen pl* **-ń**) *nt* burn; **~ pierwszego stopnia** first degree burn
poparz|yć (**-ę, -ysz**) *vt pf* to burn; **~ się** *vr pf* to burn o.s.
popeł|niać (**-niam, -niasz**; *pf* **-nić**) *vt* **1** (*przestępstwo*) to commit **2** (*błąd, nietakt, gafę*) to make; **popełnić** (*pf*) **samobójstwo** to commit suicide
popielaty *adj* grey (*Brit*), gray (*US*)
Popiel|ec (**-ca**) *m* Ash Wednesday
popielnicz|ka (**-ki, -ki**; *dat sg & loc sg* **-ce**; *gen pl* **-ek**) *f* ashtray
popier|ać (**-am, -asz**; *pf* **poprzeć**) *vt* **1** to support **2** (*plan*) to second **3** (*ustnie*) to back **4** (*uzasadnić*) to support
popi|ół (**-ołu, -oły**; *loc sg* **-ele**) *m* (*z papierosa, z ogniska*) ash
popołudni|e (**-a, -a**) *nt* (*spokojne, upalne*) afternoon
popra|wiać (**-wiam, -wiasz**; *pf* **-wić**) *vt* **1** (*krawat*) to straighten **2** (*wynik*) to better **3** (*test*) to correct; **~ się** *vr*

1 (*wyrażać się inaczej*) to correct o.s. **2** (*polepszać się*) to improve
poprawnie *adv* correctly
poprawny *adj* **1** (*odpowiedź, wymowa*) correct **2** (*zachowanie*) proper
popro|sić (**-szę, -sisz**; *imp* **-ś**) *vb pf od* **prosić**
poprzedni *adj* **1** (*małżeństwo*) previous **2** (*miesiąc*) preceding
poprzednio *adv* previously
poprze|dzać (**-dzam, -dzasz**; *pf* **-dzić**) *vt* to precede
popularnoś|ć (**-ci**) *f* popularity
popularny *adj* popular
po|ra (**-ry, -ry**; *dat sg & loc sg* **-rze**; *gen pl* **pór**) *f* (*okres*) time; **od tej pory** from now on; **do tej pory** so far; **~ roku** season; **w (samą) porę** (just) in time; **uwaga/wizyta nie w porę** ill-timed remark/visit
porabi|ać (**-am, -asz**) *vi*: **co porabiasz?** what are you up to (these days)?
poradni|k (**-ka, -ki**; *inst sg* **-kiem**) *m* (*ogrodniczy, domowy, kucharski*) handbook
pora|dzić (**-dzę, -dzisz**; *imp* **-dź**) *vi pf*: **~ sobie z czymś** to manage sth; **nic na to nie poradzę** I can't help it
poran|ek (**-ka, -ki**; *inst sg* **-kiem**) *m* morning
poranny *adj* (*rytuał, gazeta, kawa*) morning
porаż|ka (**-ki, -ki**; *dat sg & loc sg* **-ce**; *gen pl* **-ek**) *f* **1** (*dotkliwa, nieoczekiwana*) defeat **2** (*brak powodzenia*) failure
porcela|na (**-ny**; *dat sg & loc sg* **-nie**) *f* (*delikatna, cienka, przezroczysta*) porcelain
porcj|a (**-i, -e**; *gen pl* **-i**) *f* portion
pornografi|a (**-i**) *f* pornography
pornograficzny *adj* (*film, magazyn*) pornographic
porodowy *adj*: **bóle porodowe** labour (*Brit*) *lub* labor (*US*) pains
poro|nić (**-nię, -nisz**; *imp* **-ń**) *vi pf* to miscarry
poronie|nie (**-nia, -nia**; *gen pl* **-ń**) *nt* **1** miscarriage **2** (*Med*) abortion
porozmawi|ać (**-am, -asz**; *imp* **-aj**) *vi pf*: **~ (z kimś o czymś)** to talk (to sb about sth)
porozumie|nie (**-nia, -nia**; *gen pl* **-ń**) *nt* agreement; **w porozumieniu z kimś** in consultation with sb
porozumiew|ać się (**-am, -asz**; *pf* **porozumieć**) *vr* **1** (*komunikować się*) to communicate **2** (*dogadywać się*) to reach an agreement
por|ód (**-odu, -ody**; *loc sg* **-odzie**) *m* (*naturalny, domowy*) (child)birth
porówna|nie (**-nia, -nia**; *gen pl* **-ń**) *nt* comparison; **w porównaniu z** *+inst* compared to
porówn|ywać (**-uję, -ujesz**; *pf* **-ać**) *vt* to compare; **~ kogoś/coś z** *+inst* to compare sb/sth to
por|t (**-tu, -ty**; *loc sg* **-cie**) *m* port, harbour (*Brit*), harbor (*US*); **~ lotniczy** airport; **zawijać (zawinąć** *pf*) **do ~u** to call at a port
portal (**-u, -e**; *gen pl* **-i**) *m* (*architektura*) portal
portfel (**-a, -e**; *gen pl* **-i**) *m* **1** wallet, billfold (*US*) **2** (*ekonomia*) portfolio
portie|r (**-ra, -rzy**; *loc sg* **-rze**) *m* **1** (*recepcjonista*) receptionist **2** (*przy wejściu*) porter
portre|t (**-tu, -ty**; *loc sg* **-cie**) *m* portrait
porwa|nie (**-nia, -nia**; *gen pl* **-ń**) *nt* **1** (*dziecko*) abduction **2** (*autobus*) hijacking
poryw|ać (**-am, -asz**; *pf* **porwać**) *vt* **1** (*dziecko*) to abduct **2** (*autobus*) to hijack **3** (*liście*) to sweep away **4** (*przen*) to carry away; **~ się** *vr*: **~ się na kogoś** to make an attempt on sb's life
porząd|ek (**-ku, -ki**; *inst sg* **-kiem**) *m* order; **porządki** *pl* (*sprzątanie*) cleaning *sg*; **w porządku!** all right!; **doprowadzać (doprowadzić** *pf*) **coś do porządku** to put sth in order; **~ dzienny/obrad** the agenda; **być na porządku dziennym** to be on the agenda
porządk|ować (**-uję, -ujesz**; *pf* **u-**) *vt* **1** (*układać*) to put in order **2** (*sprzątać*) to tidy
porządkowy *adj* **1** (*liczebnik*) ordinal **2** (*numer*) serial
porządny *adj* **1** (*w dobrym stanie*) tidy **2** (*solidny*) respectable **3** (*ogromny*) severe **4** (*pot: ulewa*) heavy **5** (*posiłek*)

square; **~ z niego facet** he's a sound bloke
porzecz|ka (**-ki, -ki**; *dat sg & loc sg* **-ce**; *gen pl* **-ek**) *f* currant; **czarna ~** blackcurrant; **czerwona ~** redcurrant
porzu|cać (**-cam, -casz**; *pf* **-cić**) *vt* **1** (*kraj*) to abandon **2** (*pracę*) to quit; **~ kogoś/coś na pastwę losu** to leave sb/sth to their/its own fate
posa|g (**-gu, -gi**; *inst sg* **-giem**) *m* dowry
po|seł (**-sła, -słowie**; *loc sg* **-śle**) *m* **1** (*członek parlamentu*) ≈ Member of Parliament (*Brit*), ≈ Representative (*US*) **2** (*wysłannik*) envoy
posiadacz (**-a, -e**; *gen pl* **-y**) *m* (*karty kredytowej, konta bankowego*) owner
posiad|ać (**-am, -asz**) *vt* **1** (*mieszkanie*) to own **2** (*umiejętności*) to possess
posiadłoś|ć (**-ci, -ci**; *gen pl* **-ci**) *f* property
posił|ek (**-ku, -ki**; *inst sg* **-kiem**) *m* (*wspólny, wieczorny, obfity*) meal; **posiłki** *pl* reinforcements
posła|niec (**-ńca, -ńcy**) *m* (*pocztowy*) messenger
posłu|giwać się (**-guję, -gujesz**; *pf* **posłużyć**) *vr*: **~ czymś/kimś** to use sth/sb
posmutni|eć (**-eję, -ejesz**) *vi pf* to become sad
pospieszny *itd. zob.* **pośpieszny**
pospolity *adj* (*wygląd, pogląd*) common; **rzeczownik ~** common noun
posta|ć (**-ci, -cie** *lub* **-ci**; *gen pl* **-ci**) *m* **1** (*kształt*) form **2** (*sylwetka*) figure **3** (*literacki*) character
postanawi|ać (**-am, -asz**; *pf* **postanowić**) *vt* to decide on ▷ *vi* to decide; **postanowić coś zrobić** to decide to do sth; **postanowić czegoś nie robić** to decide against doing sth; **postanowić, że...** to decide that...; (*Prawo*) to rule that...
postar|ać się (**-am, -asz**) *vb pf od* **starać się** ▷ *vr pf*: **~ o coś** (*zdobyć*) to obtain sth
posterun|ek (**-ku, -ki**; *inst sg* **-kiem**) *m* post; **~ straży pożarnej/policji** fire/police station; **być na posterunku** (*przen*) to be on duty
postę|p (**-pu**; *loc sg* **-pie**) *m* progress; **postępy** *pl* progress *sg*
postęp|ować (**-uję, -ujesz**; *pf* **postąpić**) *vi* **1** (*praca*) to proceed **2** (*choroba*) to progress **3** (*dobrze, uczciwie*) to behave
postępowy *adj* (*umysł*) progressive
postkomuni|sta (**-sty, -ści**; *dat sg* **-ście**) *m decl like f in sg* post-communist
postul|ować (**-uję, -ujesz**) *vt* to postulate
posuw|ać (**-am, -asz**; *pf* **posunąć**) *vt* to move forward; **~ się** *vr* to move forward; **~ się do desperackich czynów** to act in desperation; **~ się za daleko** (*przen*) to go too far
poszedł *itd. vb zob.* **pójść**
poszuk|ać (**-am, -asz**) *vt pf*: **~ kogoś/czegoś** to find sb/sth
poszu|kiwać (**-kuję, -kujesz**) *vt*: **~ kogoś/czegoś** to search for sb/sth
poszukiwany *adj* **1** (*ceniony*) sought-after **2** (*złodziej*) wanted
pościel (**-i, -e**; *gen pl* **-i**) *f* bedding
poślizg|nąć się (**-nę, -niesz**; *imp* **-nij**) *vr pf* to slip
poślu|bić (**-bię, -bisz**) *vt pf* to wed
pośpiech (**-u**) *m* hurry; **bez ~u** unhurried; **w ~u** hurriedly
pośpieszny *adj* hurried; **pociąg ~** fast train
pośredni|k (**-ka, -cy**; *inst sg* **-kiem**) *m* **1** mediator **2** (*Comm*) agent **3** (*też*: **~ handlu nieruchomościami**) (real) estate agent (*Brit*), realtor (*US*)
pośród *prep +gen* in the midst of
po|t (**-tu, -ty**; *loc sg* **-cie**) *m* sweat
potem *adv* **1** (*później*) later **2** (*następnie*) then; **na ~** for later
potę|ga (**-gi**; *dat sg & loc sg* **-dze**) *f* power; **cztery do potęgi trzeciej** four to the power of three
potężny *adj* **1** (*władca*) powerful **2** (*maszyna*) mighty
poto|k (**-ku, -ki**; *inst sg* **-kiem**) *m* stream
potom|ek (**-ka, -kowie**; *inst sg* **-kiem**) *m* descendant
potomst|wo (**-wo**; *loc sg* **-wie**) *nt* offspring

poto|p (**-pu**; *loc sg* **-pie**) *m* **1** deluge **2** (*Rel*) the Great Flood
potra|fić (**-fię, -fisz**) *vi*: **on potrafi to zrobić** (*jest zdolny*) he is capable of doing it; (*umie*) he can do it
potra|wa (**-wy, -wy**; *dat sg & loc sg* **-wie**) *f* (*danie*) dish; **spis potraw** menu
potrą|cać (**-cam, -casz**; *pf* **-cić**) *vt* **1** (*szturchać*) to jostle **2** (*odliczać*) to deduct
potrw|ać (**-a**) *vi pf* **1** (*podróż*) to take **2** (*zebranie*) to last; **jak długo to potrwa?** how long is it going to take?; **to nie potrwa długo** it won't take long
potrze|ba¹ (**-by, -by**; *dat sg* **-bie**) *f* need; **potrzeby** *pl* needs *pl*; **bez potrzeby** unnecessarily; **w razie potrzeby** if necessary; **nie ma potrzeby się spieszyć** there's no need to hurry; **w potrzebie** in need; **~ matką wynalazków** (*przysł*) necessity is the mother of invention
potrzeba² *inv*: **~ nam pieniędzy/ czasu** we need money/time; **czego ci ~?** what do you need?
potrzebny *adj* necessary; **to mi jest potrzebne** I need that; **jestem ci ~?** do you need me?; **to nie jest potrzebne** this isn't necessary
potrzeb|ować (**-uję, -ujesz**) *vt pf*: **~ czegoś** *lub* **coś** to need sth; **nie potrzebujesz tego robić** you don't need to do this
potwier|dzać (**-dzam, -dzasz**; *imp* **-dź**; *pf* **-dzić**) *vt* **1** to confirm **2** (*odbiór przesyłki*) to acknowledge; **~ się** *vr* to be confirmed
potw|ór (**-ora, -ory**; *loc sg* **-orze**) *m* monster
poważnie *adv* seriously; **wyglądać ~** to look serious; **~?** seriously?; **mówisz ~?** are you serious?
poważny *adj* **1** (*mina, strata*) serious **2** (*rola*) substantial **3** (*organizacja*) reputable; **muzyka poważna** classical music
powiadami|ać (**-am, -asz**; *pf* **powiadomić**) *vt*: **~ kogoś (o czymś)** to notify sb (of sth)
powi|at (**-atu, -aty**; *loc sg* **-ecie**) *m* *Polish administrative unit*
powiadomieni|e (**-a, -a**; *dat sg* **-u**) *nt* (*Komput*) notification
powi|edzieć (**-em, -esz**; *3 pl* **-edzą**; *imp* **-edz**) *vt pf*: **~ coś/, że...** to say sth/that... ▷ *vi pf* to say; **~ komuś coś/o czymś/, że...** to tell sb sth/ about sth/that...; **co chcesz przez to ~?** what do you mean by that?; **co powiesz na to?** what about that?
powierzch|nia (**-ni, -nie**; *gen pl* **-ni**) *f* **1** (*na zewnątrz*) surface **2** (*teren, Mat*) area
powie|sić (**-szę, -sisz**; *imp* **-ś**) *vt pf* to hang; **~ się** *vr pf* (*samobójstwo*) to hang o.s.
powieś|ć (**-ci, -ci**; *gen pl* **-ci**) *f* (*historyczna, dla dziewcząt*) novel
powietrz|e (**-a**) *nt* air; **na wolnym powietrzu** in the open air
powiększ|ać (**-am, -asz**; *pf* **-yć**) *vt* **1** (*teren*) to expand **2** (*ilość, deficyt*) to increase **3** (*organizację, Fot*) to enlarge; **~ się** *vr* **1** (*terytorium*) to expand **2** (*grupa*) to grow
powiększ|yć (**-ę, -ysz**) *vb pf od* **powiększać**
powinien (*f* **powinna**; *nt* **powinno**) *aux vb*: **powinna tam pójść** she should go there; **~eś mi pokazać** you should show me; **~em był zadzwonić** I should have phoned
powit|ać (**-am, -asz**) *vb pf od* **witać**
powita|nie (**-nia, -nia**; *gen pl* **-ń**) *nt* welcome
powod|ować (**-uję, -ujesz**; *pf* **s-**) *vt* to cause
powodze|nie (**-nia**) *nt* success; **powodzenia!** good luck!
powojenny *adj* postwar
powoli *adv* slowly
powolny *adj* slow
pow|ód (**-odu, -ody**; *loc sg* **-odzie**) *m* **1** (*przyczyna*) cause **2** (*uzasadnienie*) reason; **z powodu** *+gen* because of; **z tego powodu** for this reason
pow|ódź (**-odzi, -odzie**; *gen pl* **-odzi**) *f* flood
powrac|ać (**-am, -asz**; *pf* **powrócić**) *vi* to return
powrotny *adj*: **bilet ~** return (*Brit*) *lub* round-trip (*US*) ticket
powr|ót (**-otu, -oty**; *loc sg* **-ocie**) *m* return

powsta|nie (-nia) *nt* **1** (*utworzenie*) rise **2** (*nom pl* **-nia**; *gen pl* **-ń**) (*bunt*) uprising

powstrzym|ywać (-uję, -ujesz; *pf* **-ać**) *vt* **1** (*zatrzymać*) to restrain **2** (*łzy*) to hold back; **~ kogoś od robienia czegoś** to stop sb from doing sth

powszechny *adj* **1** (*opinia, pogląd*) common **2** (*wybory*) general **3** (*edukacja*) primary (*Brit*), elementary (*US*)

powtarz|ać (-am, -asz; *pf* **powtórzyć**) *vt* **1** to repeat **2** (*materiał*) to revise (*Brit*), to review (*US*); **~ się** *vr* **1** (*zdarzać się ponownie*) to recur **2** (*historia*) to repeat itself **3** (*osoba*) to repeat o.s.; **czy mógłby pan to powtórzyć?** could you say that again?

powtór|ka (-ki, -ki; *dat sg & loc sg* **-ce**; *gen pl* **-ek**) *f* **1** (*Szkol*) revision (*Brit*), review (*US*) **2** (*TV, Rad*) repeat

powtórnie *adv* again

powtórny *adj* second

powtórze|nie (-nia, -nia; *gen pl* **-ń**) *nt* **1** repetition **2** (*materiału*) revision (*Brit*), review (*US*) **3** (*TV, Rad*) repeat

powyżej *prep +gen* **1** (*wyżej*) above **2** (*ponad*) over ▷ *adv* above; **mam tego ~ uszu!** that really gets up my nose!

powyższy *adj* (*cytat*) aforementioned

po|za[1] **(-zy, -zy**; *dat sg & loc sg* **-zie**; *gen pl* **póz**) *f* pose

poza[2] *prep +acc* beyond ▷ *prep +inst* **1** (*na zewnątrz*) outside **2** (*z wyjątkiem*) apart from; **~ tym** (*zresztą*) apart from that; (*też*) also

pozdrawi|ać (-am, -asz; *pf* **pozdrowić**) *vt* to greet; **pozdrów ode mnie Mateusza** give my regards to Mateusz

pozio|m (-mu, -my; *loc sg* **-mie**) *m* **1** (*wysokość*) level **2** (*jakość*) standard **3** (*zawartość*) content

poziomo *adv* **1** (*ułożyć, ustawić*) horizontally **2** (*w krzyżówce*) across

poziomy *adj* horizontal

pozn|ać (-am, -asz) *vt pf od* **poznawać**; (*pierwszy raz*) to meet; **~ się** *vr pf* (*zawrzeć znajomość*) to meet; **~ kogoś z kimś drugim** to introduce sb to sb else; **miło mi pana/panią ~** pleased to meet you; **~ się bliżej** to get to know each other better

pozn|awać (-aję, -ajesz; *pf* **-ać**) *vt* **1** (*miasto*) to get to know **2** (*świat*) to see **3** (*język*) to learn **4** (*rozpoznać*) to recognize **5** (*doświadczać*) to experience **6** (*tajemnice*) to find out; **~ się** *vr* **1** (*rozpoznawać siebie*) to recognize o.s. **2** (*rozpoznawać jeden drugiego*) to recognize each other **3** (*dowiedzieć się o sobie*) to get to know each other

pozostały *adj* **1** remaining **2** (*drugi*) the other

pozost|awać (-aję, -ajesz; *imp* **-awaj**; *pf* **-ać**) *vi* **1** (*przebywać*) to stay **2** (*jeszcze być*) to remain; **~ wiernym** to remain faithful; **~ w tyle** to lag behind

pozosta|wiać (-wiam, -wiasz) *vt* (*pf* **-wić**) to leave

pozw|alać (-alam, -alasz; *pf* **pozwolić**) *vt* to allow

pozwole|nie (-nia, -nia; *gen pl* **-ń**) *nt* **1** (*zgoda*) permission **2** (*dokument*) permit

pozw|olić (-olę, -olisz; *imp* **-ól**) *vb pf od* **pozwalać**; **on pozwala sobie na zbyt dużo** he takes too many liberties

pozycj|a (-i, -e; *gen pl* **-i**) *f* **1** position **2** (*w kolekcji*) item; **nadużywać (nadużyć** *pf*) **swej pozycji** to abuse one's position

pozytywny *adj* **1** (*reakcja, komentarz*) positive **2** (*rezultaty*) favourable (*Brit*), favorable (*US*)

poża|r (-ru, -ry; *loc sg* **-rze**) *m* fire; **~ doszczętnie strawił budynek** fire completely destroyed the building

pożąd|ać (-am, -asz) *vt +gen* to covet

pożąda|nie (-nia) *nt* desire

pożegn|ać (-am, -asz) *vb pf od* **żegnać**; **~ się z kimś** to say goodbye to sb

pożegna|nie (-nia, -nia; *gen pl* **-ń**) *nt* farewell

pożyczać (-am, -asz) *vt* (*pieniądze, książkę*) to borrow; **~ coś od kogoś** to borrow sth from sb; **~ coś komuś** to lend sth to sb

pożycz|ka (**-ki, -ki**; *dat sg & loc sg* **-ce**; *gen pl* **-ek**) *f* (*długoterminowa, nieoprocentowana*) loan

pożywie|nie (**-nia**) *nt* food

pój|ść (**-dę, -dziesz**; *imp* **-dź**; *pt* **poszedł, poszła, poszli**) *vb pf od* **iść**; **~ do diabła** (*przen*) go to hell

CHODZIĆ/IŚĆ/PÓJŚĆ

Chodzić, **iść** and **pójść** are all verbs of motion meaning "to go" (on foot), but they have different implications. With the perfective verb – **pójść** – the emphasis is on the act of going to and arriving at the destination, whereas with the imperfective verbs – **chodzić** and **iść** – the focus is more on the act of going itself and it is not made clear whether the subject arrives at the destination or not. **Chodzić** is also used to describe habitual activities and **iść** is used to describe going to or from a particular point on one occasion.

pół *inv* half; **~ szklanki** half a glass; **~ godziny** half an hour; **trzy i ~** three and a half

półfina|ł (**-łu, -ły**; *loc sg* **-le**) *m* the semi-finals *pl*; **~ mistrzostw świata** world championships semi-final

pół|ka (**-ki, -ki**; *dat sg & loc sg* **-ce**; *gen pl* **-ek**) *f* **1** shelf **2** (*książek*) bookshelf **3** (*bagażu*) rack

północ (**-y**) *f* **1** (*godzina*) midnight **2** (*świata*) north; **na ~ od** *+gen* to the north of

północny *adj* **1** (*klimat*) northern **2** (*wiatr*) northerly; **~ zachód** north-west; **Ameryka Północna** North America; **Irlandia Północna** Northern Ireland

półtora *num* one and a half; **~ kilograma** one and a half kilogrammes; **półtorej godziny** an hour and a half; **on wygląda jak ~ nieszczęścia** (*przen*) he's got a face like a wet weekend

półwys|ep (**-pu, -py**; *loc sg* **-pie**) *m* peninsula

później *adv comp od* **późno** later; **trzy dni ~** three days later

późniejszy *adj comp od* **późny**; (*następny: termin*) subsequent; **~ prezydent** the future president

późno *adv* late; **za ~** too late; **lepiej ~ niż wcale** better late than never

późny *adj* late

prabab|ka (**-ki, -ki**; *dat sg & loc sg* **-ce**; *gen pl* **-ek**) *f* great-grandmother

prac|a (**-y, -e**) *f* work; **~ domowa** homework; **~ magisterska** MA thesis; **być w pracy** to be at work

pracodawc|a (**-y, -y**) *m decl like f in sg* employer

prac|ować (**-uję, -ujesz**) *vi* **1** (*robić pracę*) to work **2** (*mieć stanowisko*) to have a job **3** (*działać*) to work

pracowity *adj* **1** (*człowiek*) hard-working **2** (*dzień*) arduous

pracowni|k (**-ka, -cy**; *inst sg* **-kiem**) *m* (*solidny, lojalny, długoletni*) worker; **~ fizyczny** labourer (*Brit*), laborer (*US*); **~ umysłowy** office worker

prać (**piorę, pierzesz**) *vt* **1** (*pf* **wy-**) to wash **2** (*chemicznie*) to dry-clean **3** (*pf* **s-**) (*pot*: *bić*) to thrash ▷ *vi* to do the laundry; **~ się** (*pf* **wy-**) *vr* (*być pranym*) to wash; **~ publicznie swoje brudy** (*przen*) to wash one's dirty laundry in public

pradziad|ek (**-ka, -kowie**; *inst sg* **-kiem**) *m* great-grandfather

praktyczny *adj* practical

pral|ka (**-ki, -ki**; *dat sg & loc sg* **-ce**; *gen pl* **-ek**) *f* (*automatyczna*) washing machine

pral|nia (**-ni, -nie**; *gen pl* **-ni**) *f* **1** (*publiczna, ogólnodostępna*) laundry **2** (*chemiczna*) dry-cleaner's **3** (*samoobsługowa*) Launderette® (*Brit*), Laundromat® (*US*)

pra|nie (**-nia**) *nt* **1** (*czynność*) washing **2** (*nom pl* **-nia**; *gen pl* **-ń**) (*ubranie itd*) washing, laundry (*US*)

pra|sa (**-sy**; *dat sg & loc sg* **-sie**) *f* **1** (*kobieca, obcojęzyczna, fachowa*) press **2** (*dziennikarze*) the Press

pras|ować (**-uję, -ujesz**) *vt* (*pf* **wy-**) (*ubranie itd*) to iron

praw|da (**-dy, -dy**; *dat sg & loc sg* **-dzie**) *f* truth; **czy to ~?** is that true?; **(jest) zimno, ~?** (it's) cold, isn't it?; **lubisz ją, ~?** you like her, don't you?; **~ w oczy kole** (*przysł*) the truth hurts

prawdopodobnie *adv* (*może*) probably
prawdopodobny *adj* probable
prawdziwy *adj* **1** (*przyjemność*) real **2** (*skóra*) genuine **3** (*historia*) true **4** (*zdarzenie*) authentic
prawicowy *adj* (*partia, aktywista, polityk*) right-wing
prawidłowy *adj* **1** (*poprawny: odpowiedź*) correct **2** (*należyty: ubiór, zachowanie, maniery*) proper **3** (*normalny*) normal
prawie *adv* almost; **~ go nie znam** I hardly know him; **~ nic** hardly anything; **~ nigdy** hardly ever; **~ nikt** hardly anyone; **~ to zrobiłem** I've almost done it
prawni|k (**-ka, -cy**; *inst sg* **-kiem**) *m* lawyer
pra|wo[1] (**-wa**; *loc sg* **-wie**) *nt* **1** law **2** (*ustawa*) statute **3** (*nom pl* **-wa**) (*uprawnienie*) right **4** (*zasada*) principle; **~ cywilne** civil law; **~ jazdy** (*Mot*) driving licence (*Brit*), driver's license (*US*); **prawa człowieka** human rights; **mieć ~ do czegoś/coś zrobić** to have the right to sth/to do sth; **~ stoi po jego stronie** (*przen*) he has the law on his side
prawo[2] *adv*: **w ~** (*kręcić*) to the right; **na ~** (*w prawą stronę*) to the right; (*po prawej stronie*) on the right
prawosławny *adj* (*kościół, zwyczaj, pieśń*) Orthodox
prą|cie (**-cia, -cia**; *gen pl* **-ci**) *nt* penis
prą|d (**-du, -dy**; *loc sg* **-dzie**) *m* **1** (*elektryczny*) current **2** (*elektryczność*) electricity **3** (*kierunek*) trend; **iść pod ~** to go against the tide; **iść z ~em** to go with the flow
precyzyjny *adj* **1** (*definicja*) precise **2** (*instrument*) precision
prekurso|r (**-ra, -rzy**; *loc sg* **-rze**) *m* predecessor
premi|a (**-i, -e**; *gen pl* **-i**) *f* **1** (*dodatek do płacy: roczna, jednorazowa*) bonus **2** (*nagroda*) prize
premie|r (**-ra, -rzy**; *loc sg* **-rze**) *m* prime minister
premie|ra (**-ry, -ry**; *dat sg & loc sg* **-rze**) *f* première
prezen|t (**-tu, -ty**; *loc sg* **-cie**) *m* (*nieoczekiwany, niechciany*) present
prezentacj|a (**-i, -e**; *gen pl* **-i**) *f* **1** (*człowieka*) introduction **2** (*pokaz*) presentation
prezent|ować (**-uję, -ujesz**; *pf* **za-**) *vt* (*ludzi*) to introduce; **~ się** *vr*: **dobrze się ~** to look presentable; **~** (**za~** *pf*) **coś komuś** to show sth to sb
prezerwaty|wa (**-wy, -wy**; *dat sg* **-wie**) *f* condom
preze|s (**-sa, -si**; *loc sg* **-sie**) *m* chairman (*Brit*), president (*US*); **~ Rady Ministrów** Prime Minister
prezyden|t (**-ta, -ci**; *loc sg* **-cie**) *m* **1** (*kraju*) president **2** (*miasta*) mayor
prę|dko *adv* **1** (*szybko*) quickly **2** (*wkrótce*) soon
prędkoś|ć (**-ci**) *f* **1** (*pojazd*) speed **2** (*Fiz*) velocity
prima aprilis *m inv* April Fool's Day
PRL *abbr* (= *Polska Rzeczpospolita Ludowa*) (*Hist*) the People's Republic of Poland

PRL

PRL is the abbreviation of the **Polska Rzeczpospolita Ludowa** (the People's Republic of Poland). This is how the Polish state was referred to from the post-war era to the collapse of communism in 1989. Nowadays the word **PRL** is often used as a synonym for the numerous shortcomings of that period: aesthetic blandness, shortages and queues. See also **sklep monopolowy**, **bar mleczny**, **osiedle mieszkaniowe**.

proble|m (**-mu, -my**; *loc sg* **-mie**) *m* problem; **nie ma ~u** (*pot*) no problem
proc. *abbr* (= *procent*) percent
procen|t (**-tu, -ty**; *loc sg* **-cie**) *m* **1** (*setna część*) percent **2** (*odsetki*) interest; **duży ~** a high percentage
proce|s (**-su, -sy**; *loc sg* **-sie**) *m* **1** process **2** (*Prawo: sądowy, karny*) (law)suit
produkcj|a (**-i**) *f* production
produk|ować (**-uję, -ujesz**; *pf* **wy-**) *vt* to produce

produk|t (**-tu, -ty**; *loc sg* **-cie**) *m* product; **~y spożywcze** foodstuffs
produktywny *adj* (*pracownik*) productive
profeso|r (**-ra, -rowie**; *loc sg* **-rze**) *m* professor; **~ zwyczajny** professor
profil (**-u, -e**; *dat sg* **-owi**) *m* (online) profile
progno|za (**-zy, -zy**; *dat sg* **-zie**) *f* **1** (*przewidywanie*: *ponura, obiecująca, gospodarcza*) forecast **2** (*zapowiedź*) prognosis; **~ pogody** weather forecast
progra|m (**-mu, -my**; *loc sg* **-mie**) *m* **1** programme (*Brit*), program (*US*) **2** (*Pol*) manifesto **3** (*spotkania*) agenda **4** (*edukacja*) curriculum **5** (*Komput*) program
projekt|ować (**-uję, -ujesz**; *pf* **za-**) *vt* (*ubrania, urządzenia, wnętrza*) to design
prokurato|r (**-ra, -rzy**; *loc sg* **-rze**) *m* prosecutor
pro|m (**-mu, -my**; *loc sg* **-mie**) *m* ferry
promie|ń (**-nia, -nie**; *gen pl* **-ni**) *m* **1** (*światła, Roentgena*) ray **2** (*okręgu*) radius; **~ słońca** sunbeam; **w promieniu stu metrów od** *+gen* within 100 metres (*Brit*) *lub* meters (*US*) of
promocj|a (**-i, -e**; *gen pl* **-i**) *f* (*świąteczna*) promotion
prom|ować (**-uję, -ujesz**) *vt* **1** (*pf* **wy-**) to promote **2** (*przen*: *nagrodzić*) to reward
propag|ować (**-uję, -ujesz**; *pf* **roz-**) *vt* (*ideę, poglądy, zasady*) to propagate
propon|ować (**-uję, -ujesz**; *pf* **za-**) *vt* to suggest; **~ coś komuś** to offer sb sth
pro|sić (**-szę, -sisz**; *imp* **-ś**; *pf* **po-**) *vt*: **~ kogoś o coś/żeby coś zrobił** to ask sb for sth/to do sth; **proszę państwa** ladies and gentlemen; **proszę bardzo** (*odpowiedź na "dziękuję"*) you're welcome; (*podając coś*) here you are; **proszę wejść** come in
prosto *adv* **1** (*iść*) straight ahead **2** (*chodzić, stać*) upright **3** (*tłumaczyć*) clearly **4** (*bezpośrednio*) straight
prostoką|t (**-ta, -ty**; *loc sg* **-cie**) *m* rectangle
prostu *inv*: **po ~** (*zwyczajnie*) basically; (*wprost*) straight
prosty *adj* **1** (*włosy, droga*) straight **2** (*człowiek, maszyna, zdanie*) simple **3** (*wyprostowany*) erect; **kąt ~** right angle
prostytut|ka (**-ki, -ki**; *dat sg & loc sg* **-ce**; *gen pl* **-ek**) *f* prostitute
prosz|ek (**-ku, -ki**; *inst sg* **-kiem**) *m* **1** (*substancja*) powder **2** (*lekarstwo*) pill; **~ do prania** washing powder; **mleko w proszku** powdered milk; **~ do pieczenia** baking powder; **zmielić na ~** to grind to a powder
pr|ośba (**-ośby, -ośby**; *dat sg & loc sg* **-ośbie**; *gen pl* **-óśb**) *f* request; **mam do ciebie prośbę** I have a favour (*Brit*) *lub* favor (*US*) to ask of you; **chodzić po prośbie** to beg
prote|st (**-stu, -sty**; *loc sg* **-ście**) *m* protest
protestancki *adj* (*kościół, wyznanie, wiara*) Protestant
protestan|t (**-ta, -ci**; *loc sg* **-cie**) *m* Protestant
protestant|ka (**-ki, -ki**; *loc sg & dat sg* **-ce**; *gen pl* **-ek**) *f* Protestant
prowa|dzić (**-dzę, -dzisz**; *imp* **-dź**) *vt* **1** (*dziecko, życie*) to lead **2** (*samochód*) to drive **3** (*rozmowę*) to hold **4** (*badania*) to conduct **5** (*śledztwo*) to hold **6** (*zakład*) to run **7** (*interesy*) to do **8** (*wojnę*) to wage ▷ *vi* (*Sport*) to lead, to be in the lead; **~** (**do~** *pf*) **do czegoś** to lead (up) to sth
prowincjonalny *adj* (*pej*: *szkoła, pogląd, ubiór*) provincial
prowok|ować (**-uję, -ujesz**; *pf* **s-**) *vt* to provoke; **~** (**s~** *pf*) **kogoś do dyskusji/działania/bójki** to provoke sb into discussion/action/a fight
pró|ba (**-by, -by**; *loc sg & dat sg* **-bie**) *f* **1** (*wytrzymałości itp.*) test **2** (*w teatrze*) rehearsal; **~ (zrobienia czegoś)** attempt (at doing sth); **~ generalna** dress rehearsal
prób|ka (**-ki, -ki**; *dat sg & loc sg* **-ce**; *gen pl* **-ek**) *f* sample
prób|ować (**-uję, -ujesz**; *pf* **s-**) *vt* **1** (*jedzenie*) to taste **2** (*maszyny*) to test; **~** (**s~** *pf*) **coś zrobić** to try to do sth; **~** (**s~** *pf*) **sił w czymś** to try one's hand at sth

prymitywny *adj* (*człowiek, zachowanie, maniery*) primitive
prysznic (**-u, -e**) *m* shower; **brać (wziąć** *pf*) **~** to have a shower
prywat|ka (**-ki, -ki**; *dat sg & loc sg* **-ce**; *gen pl* **-ek**) *f* party
prywatny *adj* **1** private **2** (*szkoła*) private, public (*Brit*) **3** (*użytek, sprawa, problem*) personal
przebacz|ać (**-am, -asz**; *pf* **-yć**) *vt*: **przebaczyć** (*pf*) **coś komuś** to forgive sb sth
przebiegły *adj* cunning; **ależ z niego ~ lis!** well, he's a sly fox!
przebieral|nia (**-ni, -nie**; *gen pl* **-ni**) *f* (*damska, koedukacyjna*) changing room
przebłys|k (**-ku, -ki**; *inst sg* **-kiem**) *m* **1** (*światła*) glimmer **2**: **~ geniuszu** stroke of genius
przeb|ój (**-oju, -oje**) *m* **1** (*piosenka*) hit **2** (*sukces*) success; **lista przebojów** the charts *pl*
przebudow|ywać (**-uję, -ujesz**; *pf* **-ać**) *vt* **1** (*budynek*) to convert **2** (*ulicę*) to rebuild
przebu|dzić (**-dzę, -dzisz**; *imp* **-dź**) *vb pf* to awaken; **~ się** *vr* to awaken
przechadz|ać się (**-am, -asz**) *vr* to stroll
przecho|dzić (**-dzę, -dzisz**; *imp* **-dź**; *pf* **przejść**) *vt* **1** (*ulicę*) to cross **2** (*chorobę*) to suffer **3** (*doświadczyć*) to experience **4** (*operację*) to undergo ▷ *vi* **1** (*iść*) to move on **2** (*iść obok*) to pass by **3** (*ból*) to ease **4** (*czas*) to pass **5** (*zostawać zaakceptowanym*) to go through **6** (*ustawa*) to be passed **7** (*pomysł*) to be accepted
przecho|dzień (**-dnia, -dnie**) *m* passer-by
przechow|ywać (**-uję, -ujesz**; *pf* **-ać**) *vt* **1** (*żywność, ubrania, rzeczy osobiste*) to store **2** (*dokumenty*) to keep
prze|ciąć (**-tnę, -tniesz**; *imp* **-tnij**) *vb pf od* **ciąć, przecinać**; **~ więzy** to cut ties
przeciek|ać (**-a**; *pf* **przeciec**) *vi* **1** (*dachu*) to leak **2** (*pot: o informacjach*) to leak out
przecież *adv* but; **~ to prawda!** but it's true!; **~ znasz go?** you do know him, don't you?
przecin|ać (**-am, -asz**; *pf* **przeciąć**) *vt* **1** (*skórę*) to cut **2** (*dyskusję*) to cut short; **~ się** *vr* **1** (*o dwóch ulicach, liniach, drogach życiowych*) to cross **2** (*o ulicach, liniach*) to criss-cross
przeciw *prep +dat* against; **argumenty za i ~** pros and cons; **nie mam nic ~ko temu** I've got nothing against it
przeciw... *prefix* anti-, counter-
przeciwbólowy *adj* (*Med*): **środek ~** painkiller
przeciwdeszczowy *adj*: **płaszcz ~** raincoat
przeciwieńst|wo (**-wa, -wa**; *dat sg* **-wu**; *loc sg* **-wie**) *nt* **1** (*sprzeczność*) contrast **2** (*odwrotny*) opposite; **w przeciwieństwie do** *+gen* unlike
przeciwko *prep* = **przeciw**
przeciwni|k (**-ka, -cy**; *inst sg* **-kiem**) *m* **1** (*wróg*) enemy **2** (*rywal*) opponent
przeciwny *adj* **1** (*ściana*) opposite **2** (*poglądy*) contrary; **być ~m czemuś** to oppose sth
przeciwpożarowy *adj* (*schody, wyjście*) fire; **alarm ~** fire alarm
przeciwsłoneczny *adj*: **okulary przeciwsłoneczne** sunglasses
przecz|yć (**-ę, -ysz**; *pf* **za-**) *vi*: **~ czemuś** to deny sth
przeczyt|ać (**-am, -asz**) *vb pf od* **czytać**; **~ książkę od deski do deski** to read a book from cover to cover

SŁOWO KLUCZOWE

przed *prep +inst* **1** (*miejsce*) in front of; **przed szkołą** in front of the school **2** (*czas*) before; **przed śniadaniem** before breakfast **3** (*w obronie*): **przed zimnem** against the cold; **chronić się przed czymś** to shelter from sth **4** (*wobec*): **ukrywać coś przed kimś** to hide sth from sb ▷ *prep +acc* (*ruch*): **zajechać** (*pf*) **przed szkołę** to pull up in front of the school

przed... *prefix* pre...
przedawk|ować (**-uję, -ujesz**) *vt pf* (*lekarstwo, narkotyk*) to overdose on

przede *prep* = **przed**; **~ mną** (*w czasie*) before me; (*przestrzeń*) in front of me; **~ wszystkim** (*pierwszy*) first of all
przedłużacz (**-a, -e**; *gen pl* **-y**) *m* (*Elektr*) extension lead (*Brit*), extension cord (*US*)
przedłuż|ać (**-am, -asz**; *pf* **-yć**) *vt* to extend; **~ się** *vr* to overrun
przedmio|t (**-tu, -ty**; *loc sg* **-cie**) *m* **1** object **2** (*dyskusji*) topic **3** (*badań*) subject
przedostatni *adj* last but one (*Brit*), next to last (*US*)
przedpok|ój (**-oju, -oje**; *gen pl* **-oi** *lub* **-ojów**) *m* hall
przedpołud|nie (**-nia, -nia**; *gen pl* **-ni**) *nt* morning
przedsiębiorc|a (**-y, -y**) *m decl like adj in sg* entrepreneur; **~ pogrzebowy** undertaker (*Brit*), funeral director (*US*)
przedsiębiorst|wo (**-wa, -wa**; *loc sg & dat sg* **-wie**) *nt* (*usługowe, produkcyjne, zagraniczne*) enterprise
przedstawiciel (**-a, -e**; *gen pl* **-i**) *m* **1** representative **2** (*Prawo*) proxy **3** (*handlowy*) agent
przedstawicielst|wo (**-wa, -wa**; *gen pl* **-wie**) *nt* **1** (*handlowy*) agency **2** (*Pol*) diplomatic post
przedstawie|nie (**-nia, -nia**; *gen pl* **-ń**) *nt* (*widowisko: teatralne, cyrkowe*) show
przedszkol|e (**-a, -a**; *gen pl* **-i**) *nt* nursery school (*Brit*), kindergarten (*US*)
przedtem *adv* **1** (*wcześniej*) previously **2** (*dawniej*) formerly
przedwczoraj *adv* the day before yesterday
przedwojenny *adj* (*film, aktor*) pre-war
przedzia|ł (**-łu, -ły**; *loc sg* **-le**) *m* **1** (*w pociągu*) compartment **2** (*cenowy*) range
przega|pić (**-pię, -pisz**) *vt pf* (*pot: okazję*) to overlook
przeglą|d (**-du, -dy**; *loc sg* **-dzie**) *m* **1** (*kontrolny*) inspection **2** (*filmów*) review **3** (*wiadomości*) roundup; **dokonać** (*pf*) **~u samochodu** to service a car
przegląd|ać (**-am, -asz**; *pf* **przejrzeć**) *vt* to look through; **~ się** *vr*: **~ się w lustrze** to look at o.s. in the mirror
przeglądar|ka (**-ki, -ki**; *dat sg & loc sg* **-ce**; *gen pl* **-ek**) *f* (*Komput*) search engine
przegran|a (**-ej, -e**) *f decl like adj* **1** (*kwota, zakład*) loss **2** (*porażka*) defeat
przegryw|ać (**-am, -asz**; *pf* **przegrać**) *vt* **1** (*mecz, wybory*) to lose **2** (*CD, DVD*) to copy ▷ *vi* to lose
przej|azd (**-azdu, -azdy**; *loc sg* **-eździe**) *m* **1** (*samochodem*) drive **2** (*pociągiem*) ride **3** (*miejsce*) crossing; **opłata za ~** fare; **~ kolejowy** level (*Brit*) *lub* grade (*US*) crossing
przejażdż|ka (**-ki, -ki**; *dat sg & loc sg* **-ce**; *gen pl* **-ek**) *f* ride
przejeżdż|ać (**-am, -asz**; *pf* **przejechać**) *vt* **1** (*przekraczać*) to cross **2** (*mijać*) to pass; **przejechać przystanek** to miss one's stop
przejęzycz|ać się (**-am, -asz**; *pf* **-yć**) *vr* to slip up
przejm|ować (**-uję, -ujesz**; *pf* **przejąć**) *vt* **1** (*majątek, obowiązki*) to take over **2** (*list, transport*) to intercept **3** (*tradycje*) to adopt; **~ się** *vr*: **~ się czymś** to be concerned about sth; **nie przejmuj się** don't worry
przejrz|eć (**-ę, -ysz**; *imp* **-yj**) *vb pf od* **przeglądać** ▷ *vt* (*plany*) to see through
przejrzysty *adj* transparent
przejś|cie (**-cia, -cia**; *gen pl* **-ć**) *nt* (*miejsce*) passage; **~ dla pieszych** (pedestrian) crossing; **~ podziemne** subway (*Brit*), underpass (*US*); **~ graniczne** border checkpoint
przejściowy *adj* **1** (*krótkotrwały: etap, sytuacja*) transitory **2** (*pośredni*) transitional
przej|ść (**-dę, -dziesz**; *imp* **-dź**) *vb pf od* **przechodzić**; **~ się** *vr* to go for a walk
przekleńst|wo (**-wa, -wa**; *loc sg* **-wie**) *nt* (*wyraz*) swearword
przeklin|ać (**-am, -asz**; *pf* **przekląć**) *vt* to curse ▷ *vi* to swear
przekła|d (**-du, -dy**; *loc sg* **-dzie**) *m* (*wierny, solidny, dosłowny*) translation
przekon|ać (**-am, -asz**) *vb pf od* **przekonywać**; **~ się** *vr pf*: **~ się do kogoś/czegoś** to grow to like sb/sth

przekonany *adj*: **być ~m o czymś** to be convinced of sth
przekonujący *adj* (*argument, komentarz*) convincing
przekon|ywać (**-uję, -ujesz**; *pf* **-ać**) *vt* to convince; **~ się** *vr* to become convinced; **~ kogoś o czymś** to convince sb of sth
przekonywający *adj* = **przekonujący**
przekracz|ać (**-am, -asz**; *pf* **przekroczyć**) *vt* **1** (*granicę*) to cross **2** (*limit, wiek*) to exceed
przekraw|ać (**-am, -asz**; *pf* **przekroić**) *vt* (*materiał, ciasto*) to cut through
przekr|oić (**-oję, -oisz**; *imp* **-ój**) *vb pf od* **przekrawać**
przeku|pywać (**-puję, -pujesz**; *pf* **-pić**) *vt* (*urzędnika*) to bribe
przele|w (**-wu, -wy**; *loc sg* **-wie**) *m* (*Ekon*: *pieniędzy*) transfer
przelicz|ać (**-am, -asz**; *pf* **-yć**) *vt* **1** (*zamienić*) to convert **2** (*liczyć*) to count
przelicz|yć (**-ę, -ysz**) *vb pf od* **przeliczać**; **~ się** *vr* to miscalculate
przeło|m (**-mu, -my**; *loc sg* **-mie**) *m* **1** (*moment zmiany*) breakthrough **2** (*Geol*) gorge; **~ w sztuce** breakthrough in art; **na ~ie XIX wieku** at the turn of the nineteenth century
przełomowy *adj* **1** (*znaczenie*) crucial **2** (*utwór*) breakthrough
przeły|k (**-ku, -ki**; *inst sg* **-kiem**) *m* oesophagus (*Brit*), esophagus (*US*)
przemarz|ać (**-am, -asz**; *pf* **-nąć**) *vi* to freeze; **~ na kość/do szpiku kości** to freeze to the bone
przemarznięty *adj* frozen
przemawi|ać (**-am, -asz**; *pf* **przemówić**) *vi* **1** (*wygłosić mowę*) to make a speech **2** (*mówić*) to speak
przemęczony *adj* exhausted
przemia|na (**-ny, -ny**; *dat sg & loc sg* **-nie**) *f* transformation
przemoc (**-y**) *f* violence; **~ą** forcibly
przemó|wić (**-wię, -wisz**) *vb pf od* **przemawiać**
przemówie|nie (**-nia, -nia**; *gen pl* **-ń**) *nt* speech; **wygłaszać** (**wygłosić** *pf*) **~** to make a speech
przemy|cać (**-cam, -casz**; *pf* **-cić**) *vt* (*papierosy, alkohol, narkotyki*) to smuggle
przemy|sł (**-słu, -sły**; *loc sg* **-śle**) *m* industry
przemysłowy *adj* (*strefa, zakład*) industrial
przemy|t (**-tu**; *loc sg* **-cie**) *m* smuggling
przeno|sić (**-szę, -sisz**; *imp* **-ś**; *pf* **przenieść**) *vt* **1** (*zakupy, bagaż*) to carry **2** (*stolicę*) to move **3** (*chorobę*) to transmit; **~ się** *vr* **1** (*przeprowadzić się*) to move **2** (*ogień, wojnę*) to spread
przepadać (**-am, -asz**; *pf* **przepaść**) *vi* to disappear; **nie przepadam za wołowiną** I'm not keen on beef
przepaś|ć¹ (**-ci, -ci**; *gen pl* **-ci**) *f* precipice
przepa|ść² (**-dnę, -dniesz**; *imp* **-dnij**) *vb pf od* **przepadać**; **~ bez wieści/jak kamień w wodę** to disappear without a trace
przepełniony *adj* **1** (*ludźmi*: *autobus, biuro*) overcrowded **2** (*płynem*) overflowing
przepi|s (**-su, -sy**; *loc sg* **-sie**) *m* **1** (*Kulin*) recipe **2** (*Prawo*) regulation
przepis|ywać (**-uję, -ujesz**; *pf* **-ać**) *vt* **1** (*pisać ponownie*) to copy out **2** (*na komputerze*) to type out **3** (*lekarstwo*) to prescribe
przeprasz|ać (**-am, -asz**; *pf* **przeprosić**) *vt*: **~ kogoś/za coś** to apologize to sb/for sth; **przepraszam** excuse me; **przepraszam, gdzie jest najbliższy bank?** excuse me, where's the nearest bank?
przeprosi|ny (**-n**) *pl* apology
przeprowa|dzać (**-dzam, -dzasz**; *pf* **-dzić**) *vt* **1** to take **2** (*badanie*) to carry out; **~ się** *vr* (*do innego miasta itd.*) to move
przeprowadz|ka (**-ki, -ki**; *dat sg & loc sg* **-ce**; *gen pl* **-ek**) *f* move
przerażający *adj* horrifying
przer|wa (**-wy, -wy**; *dat sg & loc sg* **-wie**) *f* **1** (*pauza*) break **2** (*w szkole*) playtime (*Brit*), recess (*US*) **3** (*w teatrze*) interval; (*Sport*) half-time **4** (*szpara*) gap; **bez przerwy** without a break; **~ obiadowa** lunch break; **~ na kawę** coffee break

przeryw|ać (**-am, -asz**; *pf* **przerwać**) *vt* **1** (*front*) to break **2** (*rozmowę*) to interrupt **3** (*produkcję*) to discontinue ▷ *vi* (*podczas rozmowy*) to pause; **~ się** *vr* to break; **~ ciążę** to have an abortion

przesa|da (**-dy**; *dat sg & loc sg* **-dzie**) *f* exaggeration

przesadnie *adv* excessively

przesadny *adj* (*uprzejmość, agresja*) exaggerated

przesa|dzać (**-dzam, -dzasz**; *pf* **-dzić**) *vt* **1** (*kwiaty*) to transplant **2** (*widza*) to move seats ▷ *vi* to exaggerate

przesą|d (**-du, -dy**; *loc sg* **-dzie**) *m* **1** superstition **2** (*uprzedzenie*) prejudice

przesądny *adj* superstitious

przesiad|ka (**-ki, -ki**; *dat sg & loc sg* **-ce**; *gen pl* **-ek**) *f* change; **dojechać gdzieś bez przesiadki** to go somewhere direct

prze|słać (**-ślę, -ślesz**; *imp* **-ślij**) *vb pf od* **przesyłać**

przesłucha|nie (**-nia, -nia**; *gen pl* **-ń**) *nt* **1** (*świadka*) examination **2** (*zatrzymanego*) interrogation **3** (*aktora*) audition

przesłu|chiwać (**-chuję, -chujesz**; *pf* **-chać**) *vt* **1** (*świadka*) to examine **2** (*zatrzymanego*) to interrogate **3** (*aktora*) to audition

przest|awać (**-aję, -ajesz**; *imp* **-awaj**; *pf* **-ać**) *vi*: **~ coś robić** to stop doing sth; **przestań!** stop it!

przesta|wiać (**-wiam, -wiasz**; *pf* **-wić**) *vt* **1** (*książkę, wazon*) to move **2** (*meble*) to rearrange **3** (*zmienić kolejność*) to reorder

przestępc|a (**-y, -y**) *m decl like f in sg* criminal

przestępst|wo (**-wa, -wa**; *loc sg* **-wie**) *nt* crime; **popełniać** (**popełnić** *pf*) **~** to commit a crime

przestraszony *adj* frightened

przestrasz|yć (**-ę, -ysz**) *vt pf* to frighten; **~ się** *vr pf* to get scared

przestrzeg|ać (**-am, -asz**) *vi +gen* **1** (*regulaminów*) to obey **2** (*prawa*) to abide by **3** (*obyczaju*) to observe **4** (*pf* **przestrzec**) (*udzielać przestrogi*) to warn; **~** (**przestrzec** *pf*) **kogoś przed czymś** to warn sb about sth

przestrze|ń (**-ni, -nie**; *gen pl* **-ni**) *f* **1** (*obszar*) space **2** (*powierzchnia*) expanse; **~ kosmiczna** outer space

przesył|ać (**-am, -asz**; *pf* **przesłać**) *vt* to send; **~ komuś pozdrowienia** to give one's regards to sb

przesył|ka (**-ki, -ki**; *dat sg & loc sg* **-ce**; *gen pl* **-ek**) *f* (*pocztowa*) (piece of) post; **~ lotnicza** air mail

przeszk|oda (**-ody, -ody**; *dat sg & loc sg* **-odzie**; *gen pl* **-ód**) *f* **1** (*rzecz*) obstruction **2** (*kłopoty*) obstacle

przeszkol|ić (**-ę, -isz**) *vt pf* (*pracownika*) to train

przeszłoś|ć (**-ci**) *f* the past

przeszły *adj* past

prześcierad|ło (**-ła, -ła**; *loc sg* **-le**; *gen pl* **-eł**) *nt* sheet

prześlad|ować (**-uję, -ujesz**) *vt* **1** (*człowieka*) to persecute **2** (*dręczyć*) to pester **3** (*wspomnienia*) to haunt

przetłumacz|yć (**-ę, -ysz**) *vb pf od* **tłumaczyć**

przetrw|ać (**-am, -asz**) *vt, vi pf* to survive

przetwor|y (**-ów**) *pl* (Kulin) preserves

przewa|ga (**-gi**; *dat sg & loc sg* **-dze**) *f* **1** advantage **2** (*stopień*) superiority

przeważnie *adv* mostly

prze|wieźć (**-wiozę, -wieziesz**; *imp* **-wieź**) *vb pf od* **przewozić**

przewlekły *adj* chronic

przewodni|k (**-ka**; *inst sg* **-kiem**) *m* **1** (*nom pl* **-cy**) (*człowiek: górski, miejski*) guide **2** (*nom pl* **-ki**) (*książka*) guidebook; **~ wycieczek** tour guide

prze|wodzić (**-wodzę, -wodzisz**) *vi +dat* to lead; **~ zespołowi** to lead a team

prze|wozić (**-wożę, -wozisz**; *imp* **-woź**) *vt* (*towary, pasażerów*) to transport

przew|ód (**-odu, -ody**; *loc sg* **-odzie**) *m* **1** wire **2** (*gazowy*) pipe **3** (*oddechowy*) canal

SŁOWO KLUCZOWE

przez *prep +acc* **1** across; **przechodzić** (**przejść** *pf*) **przez ulicę** to cross the street
2 through; **przez ogród** across the garden

3 (*ponad*) over; **przeskakiwać (przeskoczyć** *pf*) **przez mur** to jump over a wall
4 (*za pomocą*): **przez telefon** over the phone; **to się pisze przez dwa „t"** it's spelt with a double "t"; **co przez to rozumiesz?** what do you mean by that?
5 (*czas*) for; **chorowałem przez miesiąc** I was ill for a month; **robić (zrobić** *pf*) **coś przez wakacje** to do something over the holidays
6 (*przyczyna*): **przez niego** because of him; **przez pomyłkę** by mistake
7 (*w konstrukcjach biernych*) by; **skomponowany przez Mozarta** composed by Mozart
8 (*Mat*): **mnożyć/dzielić przez 3** to multiply/divide by 3

przeze *prep* = **przez**
przezię|biać się (**-biam, -biasz**; *pf* **-bić**) *vr* to catch a cold
przeziębie|nie (**-nia, -nia**; *gen pl* **-ń**) *nt* cold
przeziębiony *adj*: **być ~m** to have a cold
przezroczysty *adj* transparent
przezwis|ko (**-ka, -ka**; *inst sg* **-kiem**) *nt* nickname
przeż|yć (**-yję, -yjesz**) *vt pf* 1 (*wojnę*) to survive 2 (*człowieka*) to outlive ▷ *vi* to survive
przeż|ywać (**-ywam, -ywasz**; *pf* **przeżyć**) *vt* to survive; **on bardzo mocno przeżył śmierć ojca** his father's death has affected him very deeply
przod|ek (**-ka, -kowie**; *inst sg* **-kiem**) *m* ancestor

SŁOWO KLUCZOWE

przy *prep +loc* 1 (*blisko*): **przy oknie** by the window; **przy stole** at the table; **nie mam przy sobie pieniędzy** I don't have any money on me
2 (*czas*): **przy pracy** at work; **przy kawie** over coffee
3 (*obecność*) in front of; **przy papieżu** in the presence of the Pope

przybieg|ać (**-am, -asz**; *pf* **-nąć** *lub* **przybiec**) *vi* to rush across
przybliżony *adj* (*data, godzina, moment*) approximate
przybrany *adj* 1 (*rodzina*) adoptive 2 (*nazwisko*) assumed
przychod|nia (**-ni, -nie**; *gen pl* **-ni**) *f* (*Med*) outpatients' clinic
przycho|dzić (**-dzę, -dzisz**; *imp* **-dź**; *pf* **przyjść**) *vi* 1 to come 2 (*list*) to arrive; **~ na świat** to be born
przyciąg|ać (**-am, -asz**; *pf* **-nąć**) *vt* to attract
przyczy|na (**-ny, -ny**; *dat sg & loc sg* **-nie**) *f* reason; **z tej przyczyny** for that reason
przydatny *adj* useful
przyd|awać się (**-aję, -ajesz**; *pf* **przydać**) *vr*: **~ komuś/czemuś (na coś)** to be useful to sb/sth (for sth)
przygląd|ać się (**-am, -asz**; *pf* **przyjrzeć**) *vr*: **~ komuś/czemuś** to watch sb/sth
przyg|oda (**-ody, -ody**; *dat sg & loc sg* **-odzie**; *gen pl* **-ód**) *f* adventure
przygodowy *adj* (*film, książka, powieść*) adventure
przygotowany *adj*: **~ (na coś/do czegoś)** prepared (for sth)
przyjaci|el (**-ela, -ele**; *gen pl* **-ół**; *dat pl* **-ołom**; *inst pl* **-ółmi**; *loc pl* **-ołach**) *m* (*długoletni, serdeczny*) friend
przyjacielski *adj* (*uśmiech, gest*) friendly
przyjaciół|ka (**-ki, -ki**; *dat sg & loc sg* **-ce**; *gen pl* **-ek**) *f* (girl)friend; **~ od serca** soul mate
przyj|azd (**-azdu, -azdy**; *loc sg* **-eździe**) *m* (*pociągu*) arrival
przyjazny *adj* friendly
przyjaź|nić się (**-nię, -nisz**; *imp* **-nij**) *vr* to be friends
przyjaźnie *adv* 1 (*powitać*) amicably 2 (*usposobiony*) favourably (*Brit*), favorably (*US*)
przyjaź|ń (**-ni, -nie**; *gen pl* **-ni**) *f* friendship
przyj|ąć (**-mę, -miesz**; *imp* **-mij**) *vb pf od* **przyjmować**
przyj|echać (**-adę, -edziesz**; *imp* **-edź**) *vb pf od* **przyjeżdżać**
przyjemnie *adv* pleasantly; **byłoby mu bardzo ~** he would be delighted
przyjemnoś|ć (**-ci, -ci**; *gen pl* **-ci**) *f* pleasure; **z przyjemnością** with pleasure

przyjemny *adj* (*zapach, melodia, głos*) pleasant
przyjeżdż|ać (**-am, -asz**; *pf* **przyjechać**) *vi* to arrive
przyję|cie (**-cia, -cia**; *gen pl* **-ć**) *nt* **1** (*impreza*) reception **2** (*prezentu*) acceptance **3** (*studenta*) admission
przyjm|ować (**-uję, -ujesz**; *pf* **przyjąć**) *vt* (*pacjentów, towar, gości*) to receive
przyjrz|eć się (**-ę, -ysz**; *imp* **-yj**) *vb pf od* **przyglądać się**
przyj|ść (**-dę, -dziesz**; *imp* **-dź**) *vb pf od* **przychodzić**
przykła|d (**-du, -dy**; *loc sg* **-dzie**) *m* example; **na ~** for example; **dawać** (**dać** *pf*) **dobry/zły ~** to set a good/bad example
przykr|ywać (**-ywam, -ywasz**; *pf* **przykryć**) *vt* to cover; **~ dziecko kołdrą** to cover the child with a quilt; **~ garnek pokrywką** to cover the pan with a lid
przykryw|ka (**-ki, -ki**; *dat sg & loc sg* **-ce**; *gen pl* **-ek**) *f* lid
przylo|t (**-tu, -ty**; *loc sg* **-cie**) *m* (*samolotu*) arrival; **~ opóźniony** delayed arrival
przymierz|ać (**-am, -asz**; *pf* **-yć**) *vt* (*sukienkę, naszyjnik, płaszcz*) to try on
przymierzal|nia (**-ni, -nie**; *gen pl* **-ni**) *f* fitting room
przymiotni|k (**-ka, -ki**; *inst sg* **-kiem**) *m* adjective
przymusowy *adj* **1** (*pobyt*) enforced **2** (*praca*) forced **3** (*bezrobocie*) compulsory
przynajmniej *adv* at least
przyni|eść (**-osę, -esiesz**; *imp* **-eś**; *pt* **-ósł, -osła, -eśli**) *vb pf od* **przynosić**
przyno|sić (**-szę, -sisz**; *imp* **-ś**; *pf* **przynieść**) *vt* (*zyski, dochód, sławę*) to bring
przyp|adać (**-adam, -adasz**; *pf* **przypaść**) *vi*: **Wielkanoc zawsze przypada w niedzielę i poniedziałek** Easter always falls on a Sunday and a Monday
przypad|ek (*inst sg* **-kiem**; *nom pl* **-ki**) *m* **1** (*gen sg* **-ku**) (*traf*) coincidence **2** (*gen sg* **-ku**) (*Med*) case **3** (*gen sg* **-ka**) (*Jęz*) case; **przypadkiem** *lub* **przez ~** by accident; **w przypadku** *+gen* in case of
przypadkowo *adv* accidentally
przypadkowy *adj* (*spotkanie*) accidental
przypomin|ać (**-am, -asz**; *pf* **przypomnieć**) *vt*: **~ kogoś/coś** to resemble sb/sth; **~ się** *vr*: **przypomniało mu się, że...** he remembered that...; **~ komuś coś** to make sb think of sth; **~ sobie** to recall; **przypomnieć komuś o czymś** to remind sb of sth
przypra|wa (**-wy, -wy**; *dat sg & loc sg* **-wie**) *f* (*ostra, egzotyczna, wonna*) seasoning
przyprowa|dzać (**-dzam, -dzasz**; *pf* **-dzić**) *vt* to bring
przypuszcz|ać (**-am, -asz**; *pf* **przypuścić**) *vi* **1** (*snuć domysły*) to suppose **2** (*zakładać*) to presume; **~ do egzaminu** to put o.s. forward for an examination
przyro|da (**-dy**; *dat sg & loc sg* **-dzie**) *f* nature
przyrodni *adj*: **~ brat** half-brother; **~a siostra** half-sister
przyro|st (**-stu, -sty**; *loc sg* **-ście**) *m* (*dochodów, płac*) increase; **~ naturalny** population growth rate
przysięg|ać (**-am, -asz**; *pf* **przysiąc**) *vt, vi* to swear
przy|słać (**-ślę, -ślesz**; *imp* **-ślij**) *vb pf od* **przysyłać**
przysł|owie (**-owia, -owia**; *gen pl* **-ów**) *nt* proverb
przysłów|ek (**-ka, -ki**; *inst sg* **-kiem**) *m* adverb
przysłu|ga (**-gi, -gi**; *dat sg & loc sg* **-dze**) *f* favour (*Brit*), favor (*US*); **wyświadczać** (**wyświadczyć** *pf*) **komuś przysługę** to do sb a favo(u)r
przysma|k (**-ku, -ki**; *inst sg* **-kiem**) *m* delicacy
przyspiesz|ać, przyśpiesz|ać (**-am, -asz**; *pf* **-yć**) *vt* **1** (*prędkość*) to speed up **2** (*wyjazd*) to advance ▷ *vi* (*zwiększać szybkość*) to speed up
przystan|ek (**-ku, -ki**; *inst sg* **-kiem**) *m*: **~ autobusowy/tramwajowy** bus/tram stop
przystojny *adj* handsome
przysył|ać (**-am, -asz**; *pf* **przysłać**) *vt* **1** (*wiadomość*) to send **2** (*katalog*) to mail **3** (*montera*) to send in

przyszłoś|ć (**-ci**) *f* (*przepowiadać*) future
przyszły *adj* **1** (*student*) prospective **2** (*czas*) future **3** (*miesiąc*) next; **w ~m tygodniu/roku** next week/year; **~ mąż** husband-to-be
przyta|kiwać (**-kuję, -kujesz**; *pf* **-knąć**) *vi* to nod
przytomnoś|ć (**-ci**) *f* consciousness; **tracić** (**stracić** *pf*) **~** to lose consciousness
przytomny *adj* **1** (*świadomy*) conscious **2** (*rozsądny*) astute
przytul|ać (**-am, -asz**; *pf* **-ić**) *vt* to hug; **~ się** *vr* to cuddle
przytulny *adj* (*dom, hotel, kąt*) cosy (*Brit*), cozy (*US*)
przywit|ać (**-am, -asz**) *vb pf od* **witać**
przywódc|a (**-y, -y**) *m decl like f in sg* leader
przyziemny *adj* (*zmartwienie, sprawy*) mundane
przyzn|awać (**-aję, -ajesz**; *pf* **-ać**) *vt*: **~ coś komuś** (*kredyt, obywatelstwo*) to grant sb sth; (*nagrodę*) to award sb sth ▷ *vi*: **~, że...** to grant that...; **~ się** *vr*: **~ się do** *+gen* to confess to
przyzwyczaj|ać (**-am, -asz**; *pf* **przyzwyczaić**) *vt*: **~ kogoś do czegoś** to accustom sb to sth; **~ się** *vr*: **~ się do czegoś** to get used to sth
przyzwyczaje|nie (**-nia, -nia**; *gen pl* **-ń**) *nt* habit; **robię to z przyzwyczajenia** I do it out of habit
PS *abbr* (= *postscriptum*) PS
pstrą|g (**-ga, -gi**; *inst sg* **-giem**) *m* trout
psu|ć (**-ję, -jesz**; *pf* **ze-** *lub* **po-**) *vt* **1** (*maszynę*) to break **2** (*zabawę*) to spoil **3** (*reputację*) to ruin; **~ się** *vr* **1** (*maszyna*) to break down **2** (*żywność*) to go bad **3** (*pogoda*) to deteriorate **4** (*stosunek*) to deteriorate
psycholo|g (**-ga, -dzy** *lub* **-gowie**; *inst sg* **-giem**) *m* psychologist
psychologi|a (**-i**) *f* psychology; **Wydział Psychologii** (*Uniw*) Psychology Department
pszcz|oła (**-oły, -oły**; *dat sg & loc sg* **-ole**; *gen pl* **-ół**) *f* bee
pta|k (**-ka, -ki**; *inst sg* **-kiem**) *m* bird
publicznoś|ć (**-ci**) *f* audience
publiczny *adj* (*występ, wróg*) public
publikacj|a (**-i, -e**; *gen pl* **-i**) *f* (*fachowa*) publication
publik|ować (**-uję, -ujesz**; *pf* **o-**) *vt* (*książkę, esej, czasopismo*) to publish
pucha|r (**-ru, -ry**; *loc sg* **-rze**) *m* cup; **~ świata** world cup
pudeł|ko (**-ka, -ka**; *inst sg* **-kiem**; *gen pl* **-ek**) *nt* box
pudł|ować (**-uję, -ujesz**; *pf* **s-**) *vi* (*pot*) to miss
puk|ać (**-am, -asz**; *pf* **-nąć**) *vi* to knock; **~ się** *vr*: **puknij się w czoło** *lub* **głowę!** (*pot*) you're nuts!; **~ do drzwi** to knock at the door
pulowe|r (**-ru** *lub* **-ra, -ry**; *loc sg* **-rze**) *m* pullover, jumper (*Brit*)
pulpi|t (**-tu, -ty**; *loc sg* **-cie**) *m* (*Komput*) desktop
pul|s (**-su, -sy**; *loc sg* **-sie**) *m* pulse
pułap|ka (**-ki, -ki**; *dat sg & loc sg* **-ce**; *gen pl* **-ek**) *f* trap; **~ na myszy** mousetrap
punk|t¹ (**-tu, -ty**; *loc sg* **-cie**) *m* **1** point **2** (*sprzedaży*) outlet **3** (*dokumentu*) item; **~ widzenia** point of view; **~ zwrotny** turning point
punkt² *adv* (*pot*): **~ druga** two o'clock sharp
punktualnie *adv* (*przybyć, nadjechać*) on time; **~ o drugiej** at two o'clock sharp
punktualny *adj* punctual
pu|pa (**-py, -py**; *dat sg & loc sg* **-pie**) *f* (*pot*) bum (*Brit*), butt (*US*)
purpurowy *adj* purple
pusto *adv*: **w sklepach jest ~** the shops are empty; **~ brzmiący** hollow
pusty *adj* **1** empty **2** (*przen*: *człowiek*) hollow; **~ w środku** hollow
pusty|nia (**-ni, -nie**; *gen pl* **-ń**) *f* desert
puszcz|ać (**-am, -asz**; *pf* **puścić**) *vt* **1** (*linę, rękę*) to let go of **2** (*więźnia*) to let go ▷ *vi* **1** (*CD, piosenkę*) to play **2** (*plama*) to come off **3** (*pot*: *o bluzce*) to bleed; **~ się** *vr* **1** (*nie trzymać*) to let go **2** (*pot*: *mieć dużo partnerów/partnerek*) to sleep around
py|ł (**-łu, -ły**; *loc sg* **-le**) *m* dust

pyt|ać (**-am, -asz**; *pf* **za-** *lub* **s-**) *vt, vi* to ask; **~ się** *vr* to ask; **~ kogoś o coś/czy...** to ask sb about sth/if...; **~ kogoś z chemii** to give sb an oral in chemistry

pyta|nie (**-nia, -nia**; *gen pl* **-ń**) *nt* question; **zadawać** (**zadać** *pf*) **~** to ask a question

qui|z (**-zu, -zy**; *loc sg* **-zie**) *m* (*telewizyjny*) quiz show

r. *abbr* y (= *year*)

raba|t (**-tu, -ty**; *loc sg* **-cie**) *m* (*zniżka*) discount; **udzielać** (**udzielić** *pf*) **~u** to give a discount

rab|ować (**-uję, -ujesz**) *vt* **1** (*pf* **z-**) (*kraść*) to steal **2** (*pf* **ob-**) (*człowieka, sklep: okradać*) to rob

rabun|ek (**-ku, -ki**; *inst sg* **-kiem**) *m* robbery

rachun|ek (**-ku, -ki**; *inst sg* **-kiem**) *m* **1** (*obliczenie*) calculation **2** (*bankowy*) account **3** (*należność*) bill (*Brit*), check (*US*); **robisz to na własny ~** you are doing this off your own bat; **~ bieżący** current account (*Brit*), checking account (*US*); **~ oszczędnościowo-rozliczeniowy** cheque account, interest-bearing current account

racj|a (**-i, -e**; *gen pl* **-i**) *f* **1** (*słuszność*) rightness **2** (*przyczyna*) reason **3** (*jedzenia*) ration; **racje** *pl* (*argumenty*) arguments; **mieć rację** to be right; **nie mieć racji** to be wrong; **wiem, że masz rację** I know you are right; **obawiam się, że nie masz racji** I'm afraid you are wrong; **~ stanu** raison d'État; **co ~ to ~** yes, indeed!

raczej *adv* rather; **wolałbym ~ zjeść coś innego** I'd rather have something else to eat

ra|da (**-dy, -dy**; *dat sg & loc sg* **-dzie**) *f* **1** (*w trudności*) tip **2** (*organ*) council; **nie ma rady, trzeba jej pomóc** there's nothing else we can do, we have to help her; **nie ma innej rady, tylko pojechać samochodem** there is no other solution but to go by car; **~ nadzorcza** supervisory board; **R~ Ministrów** the Cabinet; **~ gminy/miasta** local/municipal council

radi|o (**-a, -a**) *nt* radio; **słuchać radia** to listen to the radio; **w ~** *lub* **radiu** on the radio; **~ taxi** minicab

radioaktywny *adj* (*odpad, chmura*) radioactive

Radio i Telewizja: **sklep ~** electronics shop (*Brit*) *lub* store (*US*)

radiostacj|a (**-i, -e**; *gen pl* **-i**) *f* radio station

radiow|óz (**-ozu, -ozy**; *loc sg* **-ozie**) *m* police car

radosny *adj* (*osoba, atmosfera*) cheerful, happy

radoś|ć (**-ci**) *f* joy

ra|dzić (**-dzę, -dzisz**; *imp* **-dź**) *vt* (*pf* **po-**): **~ komuś** to advise sb ▷ *vi* (*debatować*) to debate; **nie radzę ci tego jeść** I wouldn't eat that (if I were you); **radzę sobie z tym bardzo dobrze** I'm coping with it very well; **~ się** *vr* to seek advice; **poradził się lekarza** he asked his doctor's advice

radziecki *adj* (*literatura, władza*) Soviet; **Związek R~** the Soviet Union

raj (**-u**) *m* paradise; **czuję się tu jak w ~u** this place feels like heaven to me

rajstop|y (**-**) *pl* tights (*Brit*), pantihose (*US*)

ra|k (**-ka, -ki**; *inst sg* **-kiem**) *m* **1** (*w biologii*) crayfish, crawfish (*US*) **2** (*choroba nowotworowa*) cancer **3**: **Rak** (*Astrol*) Cancer; **Zwrotnik R~a** Tropic of Cancer

rakie|ta (**-ty, -ty**; *dat sg & loc sg* **-cie**) *f* **1** (*kosmiczna, pocisk*) rocket **2** (*do tenisa*) racket

ra|ma (**-my, -my**; *dat sg & loc sg* **-mie**) *f* frame; **ramy** *pl* (*granice*) scope; **zrobił to w ~ch swoich obowiązków** he did it as part of his duties

ramiącz|ko (**-ka, -ka**; *inst sg* **-kiem**) *nt* **1** (*sukienki, bluzki*) (shoulder) strap **2** (*do wieszania*) (coat) hanger

ra|mię (**-mienia, -miona**; *gen pl* **-mion**) *nt* **1** arm **2** (*bark*) shoulder; **wzruszać** (**wzruszyć** *pf*) **ramionami** to shrug (one's shoulders);

wystąpił z ramienia organizacji młodzieżowej he acted on behalf of the youth organization

ram|ka (**-ki, -ki**; *dat sg & loc sg* **-ce**; *gen pl* **-ek**) *f* **1** frame **2** (*Druk: w tekście*) box; **oprawiać** (**oprawić** *pf*) **obraz w ramki** to frame a picture

ra|na (**-ny, -ny**; *dat sg & loc sg* **-nie**) *f* (*cięta, kłuta*) wound

rand|ka (**-ki, -ki**; *dat sg & loc sg* **-ce**; *gen pl* **-ek**) *f* (*spotkanie towarzyskie*) date; **mam dziś z nim randkę** I'm going on a date with him today; **~ w ciemno** blind date

ra|nić (**-nię, -nisz**; *imp* **-ń**; *pf* **z-**) *vt impf* **1** (*kaleczyć*) to wound **2** (*uczucia*) to hurt

ranny[1] *adj* (*osoba*) wounded ▷ *m decl like adj* casualty

ranny[2] *adj* (*pociąg, zajęcia*) morning

ra|no[1] (**-na**; *loc sg* **-nie**) *nt* morning; **co ~ je śniadanie** he eats breakfast every morning; **tańczyli do białego rana** they danced till dawn

rano[2] *adv* in the morning; **wczoraj/jutro ~** yesterday/tomorrow morning

rapor|t (**-tu, -ty**; *loc sg* **-cie**) *m* report; **on często staje do ~u przed szefem** he is often called to account by the boss

ra|sa (**-sy, -sy**; *dat sg & loc sg* **-sie**) *f* **1** (*ludzka*) race **2** (*kota, psa*) breed

rasi|sta (**-sty, -ści**; *dat sg & loc sg* **-ście**) *m decl like f in sg* racist

rasist|ka (**-ki, -ki**; *dat sg & loc sg* **-ce**; *gen pl* **-ek**) *f* racist

rasistowski *adj* (*pogląd, hasło*) racist

rasiz|m (**-mu**; *loc sg* **-mie**) *m* (*ideologia*) racism

ra|ta (**-ty, -ty**; *dat sg & loc sg* **-cie**) *f* instalment (*Brit*), installment (*US*); **kupił samochód na raty** he bought a car on hire purchase (*Brit*) *lub* on an installment plan (*US*); **zapłacił za to w ~ch** he paid for it in instalments

ratalny *adj*: **sprzedaż ratalna** hire purchase (*Brit*), installment plan (*US*); **spłata ratalna** repayment in instalments

rat|ować (**-uję, -ujesz**; *pf* **u-**) *vt* **1** to save **2** (*ofiarę wypadku*) to rescue **3** (*reanimować chorego*) to resuscitate **4** (*dobra materialne*) to salvage; **u~** (*pf*) **komuś życie** to save sb's life

ratowni|k (**-ka, -cy**; *inst sg* **-kiem**) *m* **1** (*na basenie*) lifeguard **2** (*w górach*) rescuer

ratun|ek (**-ku, -ki**; *inst sg* **-kiem**) *m* **1** (*w stanie zagrożenia*) rescue **2** (*zbawienie*) salvation; **ratunku!** help!; **był dla nas ostatnią deską ratunku** he was our last resort

ratunkowy *adj*: **pogotowie ratunkowe** ambulance service; **akcja ratunkowa** rescue operation; **kamizelka ratunkowa** life jacket; **koło ratunkowe** life belt; **łódź ratunkowa** lifeboat

ratusz (**-a, -e**; *gen pl* **-y** *lub* **-ów**) *m* (*siedziba władz miejskich*) town hall

ra|z (**-zu, -zy**; *loc sg* **-zie**) *m* (*określając wielokrotność, porównywanie*) time ▷ *num* one; **(jeden) ~ w tygodniu** once a week; **dwa ~y w miesiącu** twice a month; **dwa ~y więcej** (*uczniów, gazet*) twice as many; (*płynu, środków finansowych*) twice as much; **dwa ~y dwa jest cztery** two times two is four; **~ na miesiąc/rok** once a month/year; **ile ~y tu byłeś?** how many times have you been here?; **jeszcze ~ musiał to zrobić** he had to do it (once) again; **na ~ie mu się nie udało** (*do tej pory*) as yet he has not managed to do it; **na ~ie!** (*pot*) see you later!; **od ~u go zobaczyła** she spotted him straight away; **na ~** at a time; **pewnego ~u** (*w bajkach*) once upon a time; **po ~ drugi/szósty** for the second/sixth time; **tym/innym ~em** this/another time; **za każdym ~em ma rację** he's right each *lub* every time; **za jednym ~em** at a *lub* one time; **w ~ie potrzeby proszę dzwonić** should the need arise please call; **ta bluzka jest w sam ~** this top is just right; **na drugi ~ się lepiej przygotuj** next time prepare more thoroughly; **~, dwa, trzy...** one, two, three...

razem *adv* together

razow|iec (**-ca, -ce**) *m* (*rodzaj chleba*) wholemeal (*Brit*) *lub* wholewheat (*US*) bread

rdz|a (**-y**) *f* rust; **~ zżera karoserię samochodu** rust is eating away at the body of the car
reag|ować (**-uję, -ujesz**; *pf* **za-**) *vi*: **~ (na)** to respond (to); **czy miedź reaguje z wodą?** (*Chem*) does copper react with water?
reakcj|a (**-i, -e**; *gen pl* **-i**) *f* **1** response **2** (*w chemii*) reaction
realiz|m (**-mu**; *loc sg* **-mie**) *m* (*w sztuce*) realism
realny *adj* **1** (*prawdziwy*) real **2** (*możliwy*) feasible
recenzj|a (**-i, -e**; *gen pl* **-i**) *f* (*filmowa, literacka*) review
recepcj|a (**-i, -e**; *gen pl* **-i**) *f* (*w hotelu, w biurze*) reception (Brit), front desk (US)
recepcjoni|sta (**-sty, -ści**; *dat sg & loc sg* **-ście**) *m decl like f in sg* (*pracownik recepcji*) receptionist
recepcjonist|ka (**-ki, -ki**; *dat sg & loc sg* **-ce**; *gen pl* **-ek**) *f* (*pracownica recepcji*) receptionist
recep|ta (**-ty, -ty**; *dat sg & loc sg* **-cie**) *f* **1** (*na leki*) prescription **2** (*kulinarna*) recipe
recyklin|g (**-gu**; *inst sg* **-giem**) *m* recycling
redag|ować (**-uję, -ujesz**; *pf* **z-**) *vt* (*tekst, artykuł*) to edit
redakcj|a (**-i, -e**; *gen pl* **-i**) *f* **1** (*czynność*) editing **2** (*zespół redakcyjny*) editorial staff **3** (*pomieszczenie redakcyjne*) editorial office
redakcyjny *adj* (*zespół, spotkanie*) editorial
redakto|r (**-ra, -rzy**; *loc sg* **-rze**) *m* **1** editor **2** (*w radiu, telewizji*) newscaster **3** (*działu sportowego*) sports editor; **~ naczelny** editor-in-chief
redaktor|ka (**-ki, -ki**; *dat sg & loc sg* **-ce**; *gen pl* **-ek**) *f* editor
referencj|e (**-i**) *pl* references
refor|ma (**-my, -my**; *dat sg & loc sg* **-mie**) *f* (*zdrowia, rolna*) reform
rega|ł (**-łu, -ły**; *loc sg* **-le**) *m* bookshelf
regio|n (**-nu, -ny**; *loc sg* **-nie**) *m* (*terytorium*) region
regularny *adj* (*kształt, płatność*) regular
rejestracj|a (**-i, -e**; *gen pl* **-i**) *f* **1** (*spis*) registration **2** (*u lekarza*) registration **3** (*miejsce*) reception **4** (*nagranie dźwięku, obrazu*) recording **5** (*pot: tablica rejestracyjna pojazdu*) number plate (Brit), license plate (US)
rejo|n (**-nu, -ny**; *loc sg* **-nie**) *m* **1** (*podział administracyjny*) district, region **2** (*obszar*) area
rej|s (**-su, -sy**; *loc sg* **-sie**) *m* **1** (*na statku*) voyage **2** (*rekreacyjny*) cruise **3** (*Aviat*) flight
reki|n (**-na, -ny**) *m* shark
rekla|ma (**-my, -my**; *loc sg* **-mie**) *f* **1** (*produktu*) advertising **2** (*kampania promocyjna*) promotion **3** (*rozgłos*) publicity **4** (*informacja w radiu, telewizji*) commercial **5** (*ogłoszenie drukowane*) advertisement
reklamacj|a (**-i, -e**; *gen pl* **-i**) *f* (*wadliwego produktu*) complaint
reklam|ować (**-uję, -ujesz**; *pf* **za-**) *vt* **1** (*produkt klientom*) to promote **2** (*wadliwą rzecz*) to complain about
reklamów|ka (**-ki, -ki**; *dat sg & loc sg* **-ce**; *gen pl* **-ek**) *f* **1** (*pot: krótki film promocyjny*) commercial **2** (*torba*) carrier bag
rekor|d (**-du, -dy**; *loc sg* **-dzie**) *m* (*świata, kraju*) record; **jego płyta bije ~y popularności** his album is breaking all sales records
rekordowy *adj* record(-breaking); **osiągnął rekordowe zyski** he achieved record profits
rekordzi|sta (**-sty, -ści**; *dat sg & loc sg* **-ście**) *m decl like f in sg* record holder
rekordzist|ka (**-ki, -ki**; *dat sg & loc sg* **-ce**; *gen pl* **-ek**) *f* record holder
rekto|r (**-ra, -rzy**; *loc sg* **-rze**) *m* (*uniwersytetu*) ≈ vice chancellor (Brit), ≈ president (US)
relak|s (**-su**; *loc sg* **-sie**) *m* (*odpoczynek*) relaxation
relaks|ować się (**-uję, -ujesz**; *pf* **z-**) *vr* (*odpoczywać*) to relax
religi|a (**-i, -e**; *gen pl* **-i**) *f* **1** (*wiara*) religion **2** (*przedmiot w szkole*) religious education
religijny *adj* religious
remi|s (**-su, -sy**; *loc sg* **-sie**) *m* (*Sport*) draw

remis|ować (**-uję, -ujesz**; *pf* **z-**) *vi* (*Sport*) to draw

remon|t (**-tu, -ty**; *loc sg* **-cie**) *m* **1** (*domu, pokoju*) redecoration **2** (*samochodu*) repair

remont|ować (**-uję, -ujesz**; *pf* **wy-** *lub* **od-**) *vt* **1** (*dom, pokój*) to redecorate **2** (*samochód*) to repair

renci|sta (**-sty, -ści**; *dat sg & loc sg* **-ście**) *m decl like f in sg* pensioner

rencist|ka (**-ki, -ki**; *dat sg & loc sg* **-ce**; *gen pl* **-ek**) *f* pensioner

ren|ta (**-ty, -ty**; *dat sg & loc sg* **-cie**) *f* (*inwalidzka, emerytalna*) pension; **od dwóch lat jest na rencie** he's been drawing his pension for two years

rentgenowski *adj* (*prześwietlenie, promienie*) X-ray

reper|ować (**-uję, -ujesz**; *pf* **z-**) *vt* to repair

reportaż (**-u, -e**; *gen pl* **-y**) *m* (*w dziennikarstwie*) report

reporte|r (**-ra, -rzy**; *loc sg* **-rze**) *m* (*dziennikarz*) reporter

reporter|ka (**-ki, -ki**; *dat sg & loc sg* **-ce**; *gen pl* **-ek**) *f* (*dziennikarka*) reporter

reprezentacj|a (**-i, -e**; *gen pl* **-i**) *f* **1** (*przedstawiciele*) representation **2** (*w sporcie*): **~ kraju** national team *lub* squad

republi|ka (**-ki, -ki**; *dat sg & loc sg* **-ce**) *f* republic; **R~ Południowej Afryki** the Republic of South Africa

restauracj|a (**-i, -e**; *gen pl* **-i**) *f* **1** (*lokal gastronomiczny*) restaurant **2** (*domu, zamku*) restoration **3** (*okres w historii*) the Restoration

restauracyjny *adj*: **wagon ~** dining *lub* restaurant car

resz|ta (**-ty, -ty**; *dat sg & loc sg* **-cie**) *f* **1** (*jedzenia, pracy*) rest, remainder **2** (*pieniędzy*) change; **dziękuję, reszty nie trzeba!** keep the change!

reszt|ka (**-ki, -ki**; *dat sg & loc sg* **-ce**; *gen pl* **-ek**) *f* (*niewielka pozostałość*) remainder; **resztki jedzenia** *pl* leftovers

retoryczny *adj*: **pytanie retoryczne** rhetorical question

rewelacyjny *adj* (*niesamowity*) sensational

rewolucj|a (**-i, -e**; *gen pl* **-i**) *f* (*przewrót, zmiana*) revolution

rewolucyjny *adj* revolutionary

rezer|wa (**-wy, -wy**; *dat sg & loc sg* **-wie**) *f* reserve; **ona odnosi się do niego z rezerwą** she treats him with reserve

rezerwacj|a (**-i, -e**; *gen pl* **-i**) *f* (*pokoju, podróży*) reservation

rezerw|ować (**-uję, -ujesz**; *pf* **za-**) *vt* **1** (*miejsce w hotelu, restauracji*) to reserve **2** (*pieniądze*) to set aside

rezulta|t (**-tu, -ty**; *loc sg* **-cie**) *m* (*wynik*) result; **w rezultacie spóźniliśmy się** as a result we were late

rezygn|ować (**-uję, -ujesz**; *pf* **z-**) *vi* (*przestać podejmować wysiłki*) to give up; **rezygnuję z tej rezerwacji** I am cancelling this reservation; **rezygnował ze stanowiska w każdej firmie, w której pracował** he resigned from his job at every firm he ever worked for

reżi|m (**-mu, -my**; *loc sg* **-mie**) *m* (*wojskowy, w jedzeniu*) regime

reżyse|r (**-ra, -rzy**; *loc sg* **-rze**) *m* (*Kino*) director

reżyseri|a (**-i**) *f*: **„~: Andrzej Wajda"** "directed by Andrzej Wajda"; **w reżyserii Krzysztofa Kieślowskiego** directed by Krzysztof Kieślowski

reżyser|ka (**-ki, -ki**; *dat sg & loc sg* **-ce**; *gen pl* **-ek**) *f* (*Kino*) director

reżyser|ować (**-uję, -ujesz**; *pf* **wy-**) *vt* (*film, sztukę*) to direct

ręczni|k (**-ka, -ki**; *inst sg* **-kiem**) *m* (*kąpielowy, do rąk*) towel

ręczny *adj* hand; **piłka ręczna** (*Sport*) handball; **nie wiem, dlaczego nie działa ~ hamulec** I don't know why the handbrake (*Brit*) *lub* emergency brake (*US*) doesn't work; **pudełko ręcznej roboty** handmade box

rę|ka (**-ki, -ce**; *dat sg & loc sg* **-ce**; *gen pl* **rąk**; *inst pl* **-kami** *lub* **-koma**; *loc pl* **-kach**) *f* **1** (*dłoń*) hand **2** (*ramię*) arm; **do rąk własnych adresata** to be opened by addressee only; **załatwimy to od ręki** we'll sort it out while you wait; **zawsze mam to pod ręką** I always have it close at hand; **machała ~mi** she waved her arms about; **informacja z pierwszej**

ręki first-hand information; **uzyskać informację z pierwszej ręki** to hear it straight from the horse's mouth; **poszła mu na rękę w pracy** she helped him out at work; **przyszedł do niej z pustymi rękoma** he came to her empty-handed; **nic nie robi i siedzi z założonymi rękoma** he doesn't do anything and just sits on his hands; **ręce do góry!** hands up!; **szła pod rękę z Prezydentem** she walked arm in arm with the President; **prosić kogoś o rękę** (*zaręczyć się*) to propose to sb, to ask for sb's hand in marriage; **ręce przy sobie!** (keep your) hands to yourself!

ręka|w (**-wa, -wy**; *loc sg* **-wie**) *m* sleeve; **bluzka bez ~ów** sleeveless blouse *lub* top

rękawicz|ka (**-ki, -ki**; *dat sg & loc sg* **-ce**; *gen pl* **-ek**) *f* **1** glove **2** (*z jednym palcem*) mitten; **obchodzą się z nim w białych ~ch** they treat him with kid gloves

rękopi|s (**-su, -sy**; *loc sg* **-sie**) *m* manuscript

r.m. *abbr* (*= rodzaj męski*) m (*= masculine*)

r.n. *abbr* (*= rodzaj nijaki*) nt (*= neuter*)

roba|k (**-ka, -ki**; *inst sg* **-kiem**) *m* worm; **robaki** *pl* (*Med: pasożytnicze, inwazyjne*) worms *pl*

ro|bić (**-bię, -bisz**; *imp* **rób**; *pf* **z-**) *vt* **1** (*jedzenie, kawę*) to make **2** (*wykonywać*) to do **3** (*powodować*) to cause ▷ *vi* (*pot: wykonywać pracę*) to work; **co tu robisz?** what are you doing here?; **~ się** *vr* (*stawać się*) to become; **robi się ciemno/ciepło** it's getting dark/warm; **robi mi się niedobrze po jedzeniu** I'm starting to feel sick after eating

roboczy *adj* **1** (*wersja, strój*) working **2** (*służbowy*) business; **dzień ~** weekday; **ubrany po roboczemu** dressed in work clothes

rob|ota (**-oty, -oty**; *dat sg & loc sg* **-ocie**; *gen pl* **-ót**) *f* **1** (*robienie czegoś*) work **2** (*praca fizyczna, umysłowa*) work **3** (*pot: zawód*) job; **roboty** *pl*: **roboty drogowe** road works (*Brit*), roadwork (*US*); **ciasto własnej roboty** home-made cake

robotniczy *adj* (*klasa*) working

robotni|k (**-ka, -cy**; *inst sg* **-kiem**) *m* (*pracownik fizyczny*) worker; **~ rolny** farm worker

rocznic|a (**-y, -e**) *f* anniversary; **~ ślubu** wedding anniversary

roczni|k (**-ka, -ki**; *inst sg* **-kiem**) *m* **1** (*ogół urodzonych w tym samym roku*) year-mates group **2** (*w szkole*) class

roczny *adj* **1** (*trwający jeden rok*) year-long **2** (*mający rok*) year-old; **roczna prenumerata** annual subscription fee

rodacz|ka (**-ki, -ki**; *dat sg & loc sg* **-ce**; *gen pl* **-ek**) *f* (fellow) countrywoman

roda|k (**-ka, -cy**; *inst sg* **-kiem**) *m* (fellow) countryman

rodow|ód (**-odu, -ody**; *loc sg* **-odzie**) *m* **1** (*geneza*) origin **2** (*pochodzenie*) lineage **3** (*zwierzęcia*) pedigree

rodza|j (**-ju, -je**; *gen pl* **-jów**) *m* **1** (*gatunek*) kind **2** (*w językoznawstwie*): **~ gramatyczny** gender; **kupiła kozaki lub coś w tym ~u** she bought some knee-high boots or something of the sort

rodzeńst|wo (**-wa, -wa**; *loc sg* **-wie**) *nt* siblings *pl*; **ja też chcę mieć ~!** I want to have brothers and sisters, too!

rodzic|e (**-ów**) *pl* parents

ro|dzić (**-dzę, -dzisz**; *imp* **rodź** *lub* **ródź**) *vt* **1** (*pf* **u-**) (*wydawać na świat: dziecko*) to give birth to **2** (*płody rolne*) to bear **3** (*pf* **z-**) (*przen: wywoływać*) to give rise to; **~ się** *vr* **1** (*pf* **u-**) (*dosł*) to be born **2** (*pf* **z-**) (*przen: zaczynać istnieć: uczucia*) to arise

rodzi|na (**-ny, -ny**; *dat sg & loc sg* **-nie**) *f* family; **~ wielodzietna/zastępcza** a large/step-family

rodzinny *adj* **1** (*związany z miejscem urodzenia*) home **2** (*święto*) family

rodzony *adj*: **mój ~ brat** my own brother

rogali|k (**-ka, -ki**; *inst sg* **-kiem**) *m* croissant

ro|k (**-ku, lata**; *inst sg* **-kiem**) *m decl like nt in pl* year; **jeździ na wakacje co ~u** he goes on holiday every year; **w zeszłym/przyszłym ~u** last/next year; **w tym ~u kupimy samochód** we shall buy a car this year; **kolega**

z ~u a classmate from university; **Nowy R~** New Year
rol|a (**-i, -e**; *gen pl* **ról**) *f* (*w filmie, teatrze*) part; **pieniądze nie grają roli** money is no object
rolnict|wo (**-wa**; *loc sg* **-wie**) *nt* agriculture
rolniczy *adj* (*uczelnia, ciągnik*) agricultural
rolni|k (**-ka, -cy**; *inst sg* **-kiem**) *m* farmer
roman|s (**-su, -se**; *loc sg* **-sie**) *m* **1** (*gatunek literacki*) love story **2** (*przygoda miłosna*) (love) affair
romantyczny *adj* (*kolacja, wątek*) romantic
ron|do (**-da, -da**; *loc sg* **-dzie**) *nt* (*na ulicy*) roundabout (*Brit*), traffic circle (*US*)
ro|pa (**-py**; *dat sg & loc sg* **-pie**) *f* **1** (*w chemii*: *też*: **~ naftowa**) (crude) oil, petroleum **2** (*w medycynie*) pus
Rosj|a (**-i**) *f* Russia
ro|snąć (**-snę, -śniesz**; *imp* **-śnij**) *vi* **1** (*pf* **u-**) (*o zwierzętach, ludziach, roślinach*) to grow **2** (*pf* **wy-**) (*osiągnąć dojrzałość*) to grow up **3** (*pf* **wz-**) (*o kosztach*) to rise
ros|ół (**-ołu, -oły**; *loc sg* **-ole**) *m* broth
rosyjski *adj* Russian
rośli|na (**-ny, -ny**; *dat sg & loc sg* **-nie**) *f* plant
roślinny *adj* (*pochodzenia roślinnego*) vegetable, plant
rowe|r (**-ru, -ry**; *loc sg* **-rze**) *m* bicycle, bike; **jechać na ~ze** to cycle
rowerzy|sta (**-sty, -ści**; *loc sg* **-ście**) *m* cyclist
rowerzyst|ka (**-ki, -ki**; *dat sg & loc sg* **-ce**; *gen pl* **-ek**) *f* cyclist
rozbier|ać (**-am, -asz**; *pf* **rozebrać**) *vt* **1** (*osobę*) to undress **2** (*rzecz na części*) to take apart **3** (*budowlę*) to pull down; **~ się** *vr* to undress; **rozbiera mnie grypa** the flu is making me drowsy
rozbudow|ywać (**-uję, -ujesz**; *pf* **-ać**) *vt* **1** (*osiedle*) to extend **2** (*rozwijać*) to develop
rozchor|ować się (**-uję, -ujesz**) *vr pf* to fall ill
rozczarowa|nie (**-nia, -nia**; *gen pl* **-ń**) *nt* disappointment; **przeżył gorzkie ~** he was bitterly disappointed
rozczarowany *adj*: **była rozczarowana, że przegrała** she was disappointed that she lost
rozd|awać (**-aję, -ajesz**; *pf* **-ać**) *vt* **1** (*foldery, gazety, pieniądze*) to distribute **2** (*podczas gry w karty*) to deal
rozdzia|ł (**-łu, -ły**; *loc sg* **-le**) *m* **1** (*fragment książki*) chapter **2** (*podział*) partitioning **3** (*przydzielanie*) apportionment
rozdziel|ać (**-am, -asz**; *pf* **-ić**) *vt* **1** (*rozdawać*) to distribute **2** (*oddzielać*) to separate; **~ się** *vr* **1** (*o osobach*) to split up **2** (*o nurcie rzeki*) to fork, to branch
rozebrany *adj* undressed
roześmi|ać się (**-eję, -ejesz**) *vr pf* to laugh out loud; **roześmiał się mu prosto w twarz** he laughed right in his face
rozgląd|ać się (**-am, -asz**; *pf* **rozejrzeć**) *vr* to look around; **rozgląda się za lepszą posadą** he is looking around for a better job
rozgło|s (**-su**; *loc sg* **-sie**) *m* publicity
rozgniew|ać (**-am, -asz**) *vt pf*: **śmierć matki bardzo go rozgniewała** his mother's death greatly angered him; **~ się** *vr* to get angry
rozgo|ścić się (**-szczę, -ścisz**; *imp* **-ść**) *vr pf* to make o.s. comfortable; **każdy może się wygodnie rozgościć w fotelach** everybody can relax comfortably in the armchairs
rozka|z (**-zu, -zy**; *loc sg* **-zie**) *m* order; **wydał ~ do odwrotu** he ordered a retreat; **wykonać** (*pf*) **~** to obey an order
rozkła|d (**-du, -dy**; *loc sg* **-dzie**) *m* **1** (*jazdy, zajęć*) timetable **2** (*domu*) layout **3** (*w biologii*) decomposition; **~ jazdy pociągów/autobusów** railway/bus timetable (*Brit*) *lub* schedule (*US*)
rozkład|ać (**-am, -asz**; *pf* **rozłożyć**) *vt* **1** (*obrus na stole*) to spread **2** (*przedmioty*) to set out **3** (*parasol, wersalkę*) to unfold **4** (*urządzenie*) to dismantle

rozkosz (**-y, -e**; *gen pl* **-y**) *f* **1** (*przyjemność*) pleasure **2** (*szczęście*) delight
rozlew|ać (**-am, -asz**; *pf* **rozlać**) *vt* **1** (*płyn na podłogę*) to spill **2** (*płyn do butelki*) to pour (out); **~ się** *vr* to spill
rozmawi|ać (**-am, -asz**) *vi* to talk; **rozmawiał ze mną o pracy** he talked to me about work; **oni ze sobą nie rozmawiają od wielu lat** they have not been on speaking terms for years
rozmia|r (**-ru, -ry**; *loc sg* **-rze**) *m* **1** (*ubrania, butów*) size **2** (*zasięg*) extent
rozm|owa (**-owy, -owy**; *dat sg & loc sg* **-owie**; *gen pl* **-ów**) *f* **1** conversation **2** (*kwalifikacyjna w pracy*) interview; **rozmowy** *pl* negotiations *pl*; **odbyli długą rozmowę telefoniczną** they had a long telephone conversation
rozmowny *adj* talkative
rozmówc|a (**-y, -y**) *m decl like f in sg* interlocutor
rozmówczy|ni (**-ni, -nie**; *gen pl* **-ń**) *f* interlocutor
rozmów|ki (**-ek**) *pl* phrase book *sg*
rozmyśl|ić się (**-ę, -isz**) *vr pf* to change one's mind
rozpacz (**-y**) *f* despair; **to był z jego strony akt ~y** it was an act of desperation on his part
rozpacz|ać (**-am, -asz**) *vi* to despair
rozpad|ać się (**-am, -asz**; *pf* **rozpaść**) *vr* **1** (*o krześle*) to fall apart **2** (*o związku dwóch osób*) to disintegrate, to break up
rozpę|dzać (**-dzam, -dzasz**; *pf* **-dzić**) *vt* **1** (*samochód*) to speed up, to accelerate **2** (*demonstrację*) to disperse; **~ się** *vr* (*zwiększać szybkość*) to speed up
rozpieszczony *adj* (*dziecko, pies*) pampered, spoilt (*Brit*), spoiled (*US*)
rozpin|ać (**-am, -asz**; *pf* **rozpiąć**) *vt* (*bluzkę*) to undo
rozpoczęci|e (**-a**) *nt* (*uroczystości, roku szkolnego*) start
rozpoczyn|ać (**-am, -asz**; *pf* **rozpocząć**) *vt* to begin; **~ się** *vr* to begin
rozrast|ać się (**-am, -asz**; *pf* **rozrosnąć**) *vr* (*powiększać się*) to grow
rozróż|niać (**-niam, -niasz**; *pf* **-nić**) *vt* to distinguish
rozryw|ka (**-ki, -ki**; *dat sg & loc sg* **-ce**; *gen pl* **-ek**) *f* entertainment
rozrywkowy *adj*: **lokal ~** nightclub; **lektura rozrywkowa** light reading; **przemysł ~** entertainment industry
rozrzu|cać (**-cam, -casz**; *pf* **-cić**) *vt* **1** (*rzeczy*) to scatter **2** (*nasiona*) to spread
rozsąd|ek (**-ku**; *inst sg* **-kiem**) *m* good sense; **wykazał się zdrowym rozsądkiem** he demonstrated his common sense
rozsądny *adj* (*człowiek, propozycja*) reasonable
rozsyp|ywać (**-uję, -ujesz**; *pf* **-ać**) *vt* to spill; **~ się** *vr* **1** to spill **2** (*o osobie załamanej nerwowo*) to go to pieces
rozśmiesz|ać (**-am, -asz**; *pf* **-yć**) *vt*: **~ kogoś** to make sb laugh
roztargniony *adj* absent-minded
rozter|ka (**-ki, -ki**; *dat sg & loc sg* **-ce**; *gen pl* **-ek**) *f* dilemma; **przeżywał rozterki moralne** he faced moral dilemmas
roztropny *adj* prudent
rozu|m (**-mu, -my**; *loc sg* **-mie**) *m* reason; **na chłopski** *lub* **zdrowy ~, masz rację** common sense suggests that you're right; **jesteś niespełna ~u!** you're out of your mind!
rozumi|eć (**-em, -esz**; *pf* **z-**) *vt* to understand; **~ się** *vr*: **~ się (ze sobą)** to understand (each other); **rozumiem twój punkt widzenia** I see your point (of view); **co przez to rozumiesz?** what do you mean by that?; **to rozumiem!** now you're talking!; **~ po rosyjsku** to understand Russian; **rozumiem, że nie jesteś gotów** I understand you're not ready; **do wojska, ma się ~, nie poszliśmy!** naturally, we didn't join the army!
rozumny *adj* (*istota, propozycja*) rational
rozwa|ga (**-gi**; *dat sg & loc sg* **-dze**) *f* judiciousness; **powinniśmy wziąć to pod rozwagę** we should take that into consideration; **należy to robić**

z rozwagą it should be done with deliberation
rozwiąza|nie (**-nia, -nia**; *gen pl* **-ń**) *nt* **1** (*krzyżówki, zagadnienia*) solution **2** (*parlamentu, małżeństwa*) dissolution **3** (*urodzenie dziecka*) delivery
rozwiąz|ywać (**-uję, -ujesz**; *pf* **-ać**) *vt* **1** (*odplątać: supeł, paczkę, jeńca*) to untie **2** (*unieważnić: umowę, małżeństwo*) to annul **3** (*zamknąć: parlament*) to dissolve **4** (*znaleźć rozwiązanie: problem*) to solve
rozwiedziony *adj* divorced
rozwi|jać (**-jam, -jasz**; *pf* **-nąć**) *vt* **1** (*chodnik, śpiwór*) to unroll **2** (*rozpakowywać*) to unwrap **3** (*talent*) to develop **4** (*firmę*) to expand; **~ się** *vr* **1** (*rozprostować się: o drucie*) to uncoil **2** (*wydarzyć się: o fabule*) to unfold **3** (*ukształtować się*) to grow **4** (*osiągnąć wyższy poziom*) to develop
rozwodni|k (**-ka, -cy**; *inst sg* **-kiem**) *m* divorcee (*Brit*), divorcé (*US*)
roz|wodzić się (**-wodzę, -wodzisz**; *imp* **-wódź**; *pf* **-wieść**) *vr* to get divorced; **~ z mężem/żoną** to divorce one's husband/wife; **rozwodzi się nad swoim pechem** he's dwelling on his misfortune
rozwolnie|nie (**-nia**) *nt* (*biegunka*) diarrhoea (*Brit*), diarrhea (*US*)
rozw|ód (**-odu, -ody**; *loc sg* **-odzie**) *m* divorce; **brać** (**wziąć** *pf*) **~** to get a divorce
rozwód|ka (**-ki, -ki**; *dat sg & loc sg* **-ce**; *gen pl* **-ek**) *f* divorcee (*Brit*), divorcée (*US*)
rozw|ój (**-oju**) *m* **1** (*cywilizacji, człowieka*) development **2** (*zdarzeń*) progress
rób *itd. vb zob.* **robić**
róg (**rogu, rogi**; *inst sg* **rogiem**) *m* **1** (*u krowy*) horn **2** (*u jelenia*) antler **3** (*pokoju*) corner **4** (*ulicy*) corner **5** (*instrument muzyczny*) horn **6** (*w sporcie*) corner; **sklep jest na rogu** the shop is on the corner; **samochód stoi za rogiem** the car is parked round the corner; **zapędziła go w kozi ~** she forced him into a corner
rówieśni|k (**-ka, -cy**; *inst sg* **-kiem**) *m* peer
również *adv* also, as well; **psy jak ~ koty** dogs and also cats
równo *adv* **1** (*bez wypukłości*) evenly **2** (*w jednakowej ilości*) equally **3** (*dokładnie*) exactly
równocześnie *adv* at the same time
równoś|ć (**-ci**) *f* equality; **znak równości** equals sign
równowa|ga (**-gi**; *dat sg* **-dze**) *f* **1** balance **2** (*psychiczna*) balance, poise **3** (*w tenisie*) deuce; **zachowywać** (**zachować** *pf*) **równowagę** to keep one's balance
równy *adj* **1** (*płaski*) even **2** (*jednakowy*) equal **3** (*jednostajny*) steady
róż|a (**-y, -e**) *f* rose; **dzika ~** briar
róża|niec (**-ńca, -ńce**) *m* rosary
różnic|a (**-y, -e**) *f* difference; **bez różnicy** it makes no difference
róż|nić (**-nię, -nisz**; *imp* **-nij**) *vt*: **~ kogoś/coś od** *+gen* to make sb/sth different from; **~ się** *vr*: **~ się (od kogoś/czegoś)** to be different (from sb/sth); **różnimy się w poglądach na tę sprawę** our opinions differ on this matter
różnorodny *adj* (*rozmaity*) diverse
różny *adj* different
różowy *adj* **1** (*barwa*) pink **2** (*przen: o przyszłości*) rosy
RP *abbr*: **sklep ~** electronics shop (*Brit*) *lub* store (*US*)
RTV *abbr*: **sklep ~** electronics shop (*Brit*) *lub* store (*US*)
rubry|ka (**-ki, -ki**; *dat sg & loc sg* **-ce**) *f* **1** blank space **2** (*tekst w gazecie*) column
ruch (**-u, -y**) *m* **1** (*przesunięcie w innym kierunku*) movement **2** (*Fiz*) motion **3** (*aktywność fizyczna*) exercise **4** (*na ulicach*) traffic **5** (*pionkiem*) move **6** (*ożywienie gospodarcze*) boom **7** (*Hist: w sztuce, polityce, religii*) movement; **~ oporu** the Resistance; **zgodnie z ~em wskazówek zegara** clockwise; **odwrotnie do ~u wskazówek zegara** anticlockwise (*Brit*), counterclockwise (*US*)
ruchomy *adj* **1** (*element*) moving **2** (*majątek*) movable; **ruchome schody** escalator
rudowłosy *adj* redheaded
rudy *adj* **1** russet **2** (*włosy*) ginger
rugby *nt inv* rugby

rumie|nić (**-nię, -nisz**; *imp* **-ń**) *vt* (*pf* **przy-**) (*ciasto, pieczeń*) to brown; **~ się** (*pf* **za-**) *vr* (*na twarzy*) to blush
ru|nąć (**-nę, -niesz**; *imp* **-ń**) *vi pf* **1** (*o budowli, osobie*) to collapse **2** (*spaść w dół*) to plummet (down), to tumble (down) **3** (*przen: o pomysłach*) to collapse
ru|ra (**-ry, -ry**; *dat sg & loc sg* **-rze**) *f* (*kanalizacyjna*) pipe; **~ wydechowa** exhaust (pipe) (*Brit*), tailpipe (*US*)
ruski *adj* (*pot!*) Russian
rusz|ać (**-am, -asz**; *pf* **-yć**) *vt*: **~ czymś** to move sth ▷ *vi* **1** (*o pojeździe*) to move **2** (*w podróż*) to set off **3** (*o fabryce*) to start working
ry|ba (**-by, -by**; *dat sg & loc sg* **-bie**) *f* fish; **jesteś zdrów jak ~** you're as right as rain; **z niego jest prawdziwa gruba ~** (*przen*) he's a real big shot (*pot*); **iść na ryby** to go fishing; **Ryby** *pl* (*Astrol*) Pisces
rycerz (**-a, -e**; *gen pl* **-y**) *m* knight
rym (**-u, -y**) *m* rhyme
ryne|k (**-ku, -ki**; *inst sg* **-kiem**) *m* **1** (*główny plac*) market (square) **2** (*Fin: instytucja*) market; **czarny ~** black market; **wolny ~** free market
rys (**-u, -y**) *m* feature; **~y twarzy** facial features
rys|ować (**-uję, -ujesz**; *pf* **na-**) *vt* **1** to draw **2** (*przen: wizję przyszłości*) to picture **3** (*szkicować*) to sketch; **~ się** (*pf* **za-**) *vr* **1** (*uwidaczniać się*) to appear **2** (*karoserię, blat*) to have scratches
rysun|ek (**-ku, -ki**; *inst sg* **-kiem**) *m* drawing
rysunkowy *adj* drawing; **film ~** (*kreskówka*) cartoon
ryt|m (**-mu, -my**; *loc sg* **-mie**) *m* rhythm
rytua|ł (**-łu, -ły**; *loc sg* **-le**) *m* ritual; **piątkowe spotkania stały się ~em** the Friday meetings have become a ritual
ryzy|ko (**-ka**; *inst sg* **-kiem**) *nt* risk; **robisz to na własne ~** you're doing this at your own risk
ryż (**-u**) *m* rice
r.ż. *abbr* (= *rodzaj żeński*) f (= *feminine*)
rzadki *adj* **1** (*sos, zupa*) thin **2** (*spotkania*) rare
rzadko *adv* **1** (*nieczęsto*) seldom **2** (*w odstępach*) sparsely; **~ kto zdaje ten egzamin** hardly anyone passes this exam; **~ kiedy się spotykają** they hardly ever meet
rząd[1] (**rzędu, rzędy**; *loc sg* **rzędzie**) *m* **1** (*równy szereg*) row **2** (*w biologii*) order; **musimy to zrobić w pierwszym rzędzie** this is a matter of primary concern to us
rzą|d[2] (**-du, -dy**; *loc sg* **-dzie**) *m* (*Rada Ministrów*) government; **rządy** *pl* rule; **~y silnej ręki** strong government
rzą|dzić (**-dzę, -dzisz**; *imp* **-dź**) *vt*: **~** *+inst* to govern ▷ *vi* **1** (*mieć władzę*) to govern **2** (*dowodzić*) to be in charge; **~ się** *vr* to throw one's weight about; **młodość rządzi się swoimi prawami** youth has its own rules
rzecz (**-y, -y**; *gen pl* **-y**) *f* thing; **rzeczy** *pl* (*przedmioty*) things *pl*; **to nie ma nic do ~y** that's beside the point; **mówi od ~y** he talks nonsense; **kwesta na ~ szpitala** a collection in aid of the hospital; **ogólnie ~ biorąc to ma sens** on the whole this makes sense; **w gruncie ~y popełnił błąd** essentially he made a mistake
rzeczowni|k (**-ka, -ki**; *inst sg* **-kiem**) *m* noun

RZECZPOSPOLITA

Rzeczpospolita means 'republic', but in Poland the term is used exclusively to refer to the Polish state. The first **Rzeczpospolita** existed in the sixteenth and seventeenth centuries when Poland formed a union with Lithuania. The second **Rzeczpospolita** existed during the inter-war period, and the third **Rzeczpospolita** began after the collapse of the **PRL** in 1989.

Rzeczpospolit|a Polska (**-ej Polskiej, -e Polskie**) *f* Republic of Poland
rzeczywistoś|ć (**-ci**) *f* reality; **ten opis nie odpowiada rzeczywistości**

this description does not match the reality; **w rzeczywistości on wyglądał całkiem inaczej** in reality he looked completely different
rzeczywisty *adj* (*prawdziwy*) real
rzeczywiście *adv* really
rze|ka (**-ki, -ki**; *dat sg &loc sg* **-ce**) *f* river; **obóz nad rzeką** a camp on the river; **pływać** (**płynąć** *pf*) **w dół/górę rzeki** to swim down/up (the) river
rzetelny *adj* (*pracownik, sprawozdanie*) reliable, honest
rzeź|ba (**-by, -by**; *dat sg & loc sg* **-bie**) *f* sculpture
rze|źbić (**-źbię, -źbisz**; *imp* **-źb**; *pf* **wy-**) *vt* to sculpt
rzę|sa (**-sy, -sy**; *dat sg & loc sg* **-sie**) *f* (eye)lash
rzęsisty *adj* **1** (*ulewny*) torrential **2** (*w teatru: o oklaskach*) thunderous
rzodkiew|ka (**-ki, -ki**; *dat sg & loc sg* **-ce**; *gen pl* **-ek**) *f* radish
rzu|cać (**-cam, -casz**; *pf* **-cić**) *vt* **1** (*oszczepem, dyskiem*) to throw **2** (*cień*) to cast **3** (*męża, żonę*) to abandon **4** (*pot: chłopaka, dziewczynę*) to dump **5** (*nałóg*) to quit **6** (*komentarz*) to throw in ▷ *vi* (*o pojeździe*) to abandon
Rzymia|nin (**-nina, -nie**; *loc sg* **-ninie**; *gen pl* **-n**) *m* Roman
rzymski *adj* (*mitologia, obyczaje*) Roman; **pieczeń rzymska** meat loaf
rzymskokatolicki *adj* Roman Catholic

S

SA, S.A. *abbr* (*= spółka akcyjna*) (*firma*) Co.
sa|d (**-du, -dy**; *loc sg* **-dzie**) *m* (*wiśniowy, jabłkowy*) orchard
sal|a (**-i, -e**; *loc & dat sg, gen. pl* **-i**) *f* **1** (*większa*) hall **2** (*mniejsza*) room **3** (*przen: publika*) (the) audience; **~ wykładowa** lecture hall; **~ gimnastyczna** gymnasium; **~ operacyjna** operating theatre (*Brit*), operating room (*US*)
salami *nt inv* (*kiełbasa*) salami
salo|n (**-nu, -ny**; *loc sg* **-nie**) *m* **1** (*w mieszkaniu*) lounge **2** (*zakład usługowy, sklep*) salon **3** (*literacki, towarzyski*) salon
sała|ta (**-ty, -ty**; *dat & loc sg* **-cie**) *f* (*warzywo*) lettuce
sałat|ka (**-ki, -ki**; *dat & loc sg* **-ce**; *gen pl* **-ek**) *f* (*potrawa*) salad; **~ owocowa** fruit salad

SŁOWO KLUCZOWE

sam[1] *pron decl like adj* **1** (*bez niczyjej pomocy*): **sam to zrobił** he did it himself; **okno samo się otworzyło** the window opened by itself
2 (*bez nikogo*): **mieszka sama** she lives alone
3 (*uściślając lub podkreślając*): **na samym dole/początku** at the very bottom/beginning; **w samą porę** just in time
4 (*wyłącznie*): **same problemy** nothing but trouble; **same książki**

zajęły dużo miejsca w walizce the books alone took up a lot of room in the suitcase
5 (*wskazując na przyczynę*): **na samą myśl o czymś** at the mere thought of sth
6 (*o ważnej osobie*): **sam król tam był** the king himself was there
7 (*w wyrażeniach z: sobie, siebie, się*): **sam jest sobie winien** he has only himself to blame
8 (*w wyrażeniach z 'ten', 'taki'*): **taki sam** exact same; **taki sam samochód** the exact same car; **ma taką samą spódnicę** she has the exact same skirt

sa|m² (**-mu, -my**; *loc sg* **-mie**) *m* (*sklep spożywczy*) self-service shop
samo *pron decl like adj zob.* **sam** ▷ *pron inv*: **tak ~** (*identycznie*) in the same way
samobójc|a (**-y, -y**; *dat & loc sg* **-y**) *m* (*osoba, która odbiera sobie życie*) suicide (victim)
samobójst|wo (**-wa, -wa**; *loc sg* **-wie**) *nt* (*odebranie sobie życia*) suicide; **popełnić** (*pf*) **~** to commit suicide
samoch|ód (**-odu, -ody**; *loc sg* **-odzie**) *m* (*auto*) car; **~ ciężarowy** lorry (*Brit*), truck (*US*); **jeździć** (**jechać** *pf*) **samochodem** to go by car; **prowadzić ~** to drive (a car)
samodzielnie *adv* **1** (*samemu, w pojedynkę*) single-handed(ly) **2** (*niezależnie*) independently
samodzielny *adj* **1** (*zaradny*) independent **2** (*pracownik, decyzja*) independent **3** (*odrębny*) self-contained
samolo|t (**-tu, -ty**; *loc sg* **-cie**) *m* (*środek transportu*) aeroplane (*Brit*), airplane (*US*); **latać** (**lecieć** *pf*) **~em** to go by plane
samoobro|na (**-ny**; *dat & loc sg* **-nie**) *f* **1** (*pojedynczej osoby*) self-defence (*Brit*), self-defense (*US*) **2** (*kraju*) civil defence (*Brit*) *lub* defense (*US*)
samopoczuci|e (**-a**) *nt* (*fizyczne, psychiczne*) mood
samorzą|d (**-du, -dy**; *loc sg* **-dzie**) *m* (*Admin*): **~ miejski** town/city council; **~ terytorialny** local government
samotnoś|ć (**-ci**; *dat & loc sg* **-ci**) *f* **1** (*brak towarzystwa*) loneliness **2** (*bycie na odludziu*) solitude
samotny *adj* **1** (*sam, bez towarzystwa*) lonely **2** (*odosobniony*) solitary **3** (*rodzic*) single
samoucz|ek (**-ka, -ki**; *inst sg* **-kiem**) *m* (*podręcznik*): **~ języka polskiego** a "Teach Yourself Polish" book
samou|k (**-ka, -cy** *lub* **-ki**; *inst sg* **-kiem**) *m* (*osoba*): **być ~iem** to be self-taught
sanatori|um (**-um, -a**; *gen pl* **-ów**) *nt inv in sg* (*zakład leczniczy*) sanatorium
sandał (**-a, -y**) *m* (*but*) sandal; **sandały** *pl* sandals
saty|ra (**-ry, -ry**; *dat & loc sg* **-rze**) *f*: **~ na** (*Lit*) satire of
satysfakcj|a (**-i**; *dat & loc sg* **-i**) *f* (*zadowolenie*) satisfaction
są *vb zob.* **być**
są|d (**-du, -dy**; *loc sg* **-dzie**) *m* **1** (*urząd*) court of law **2** (*proces*) trial **3** (*książk: zdanie*) judgement
są|dzić (**-dzę, -dzisz**; *imp* **-dź**) *vt* (*pf* **o-**) (*przestępcę*) to try ▷ *vi* (*być zdania, uważać*) to think; **co o tym sądzicie?** what do you think of that?
sąsi|ad (**-ada, -edzi**) *m* (*osoba*) neighbour (*Brit*), neighbor (*US*)
sce|na (**-ny, -ny**; *dat & loc sg* **-nie**) *f* **1** (*wypadku, wydarzenia: w filmie*) scene **2** (*podium*) stage; **~ polityczna** political scene
scenariusz (**-a, -e**; *gen pl* **-y**) *m* **1** (*filmu*) screenplay **2** (*przedstawienia, słuchowiska*) script **3** (*przen: przebieg wydarzeń*) scenario
scenarzy|sta (**-sty, -ści**; *dat & loc sg* **-ście**) *m decl like f in sg* **1** (*filmowy*) screenwriter **2** (*teatralny*) scriptwriter
schabowy *adj*: **kotlet ~** (*Kulin*) pork chop
schema|t (**-tu, -ty**; *loc sg* **-cie**) *m* **1** (*zachowania, wydarzeń*) pattern **2** (*rysunek*) diagram
schłodzony *adj* chilled
sch|nąć (**-nę, -niesz**; *imp* **-nij**) *vi* to dry; **pranie schnie na słońcu** the laundry is drying in the sun
schod|y (**-ów**) *pl* (*Bud*) stairs *pl*; **ruchome ~** escalator

scho|dzić (**-dzę, -dzisz**; *imp* **-dź**; *pf* **zejść**) *vi* **1** (*po schodach*) to go down **2** (*zsiadać z konia, roweru*) to dismount **3** (*wstać z tapczanu*) to get off **4** (*dać się usunąć/ściągnąć*) to come off **5** (*o skórze* (*z nosa*), *tapecie*) to peel; **~ się** *vr* **1** (*zbierać się*) to gather **2** (*o ulicach*) to join
schow|ać (**-am, -asz**) *vb pf od* **chować**
schronis|ko (**-ka, -ka**; *inst sg* **-kiem**) *nt* **1** (*w górach*) chalet **2** (*hotel dla młodzieży*) hostel **3** (*dla bezdomnych*) shelter
schud|nąć (**-nę, -niesz**; *imp* **-nij**) *vb pf od* **chudnąć**
schwy|cić (**-cę, -cisz**; *imp* **-ć**) *vt pf* (*ująć*) to catch
schwyt|ać (**-am, -asz**) *vb pf od* **chwytać**
scyzory|k (**-ka, -ki**; *inst sg* **-kiem**) *m* (*nożyk*) penknife
sean|s (**-su, -se**; *loc sg* **-sie**) *m* (*filmowy*) show
sede|s (**-su, -sy**; *loc sg* **-sie**) *m* **1** (*o muszli klozetowej*) toilet bowl **2** (*o desce klozetowej*) toilet seat
sej|f (**-fu, -fy**; *loc sg* **-fie**) *m* (*na pieniądze, broń*) safe
sej|m (**-mu, -my**; *loc sg* **-mie**) *m* (*Pol*) the Sejm

SEJM

The Polish parliament consists of two houses: **Sejm** and **Senat**. The **Sejm** is made up of 460 members.

sekre|t (**-tu, -ty**; *loc sg* **-cie**) *m* (*tajemnica*) secret
sekretaria|t (**-tu, -ty**; *loc sg* **-cie**) *m* (secretary's) office
sekretar|ka (**-ki, -ki**; *dat & loc sg* **-ce**; *gen pl* **-ek**) *f* (*osoba*) office administrator; **automatyczna ~** answering machine
sekretarz (**-a, -e**; *gen pl* **-y**) *m* (*osoba*) office administrator
sek|s (**-su**; *loc sg* **-sie**) *m* (*aktywność płciowa*) sex
seksowny *adj* (*pot: głos, taniec, chód*) sexy
sekun|da (**-dy, -dy**; *dat & loc sg* **-dzie**) *f* second; **sekundę!** (*pot*) just a sec!
sele|r (**-ra, -ry**; *loc sg* **-rze**) *m* **1** (*korzeń*) celeriac **2** (*liście*) celery
selfie *nt* selfie
semest|r (**-ru, -ry**; *loc sg* **-rze**) *m* (*Szkol, Uniw*) semester
sen (**snu, sny**; *loc sg* **śnie**) *m* **1** (*spanie*) sleep **2** (*o marzeniu sennym*) dream; **mieć zły ~** to have a bad dream

SENAT

The Polish parliament consists of two houses: **Sejm** and **Senat**. The **Senat** is made up of one hundred senators, who are elected in general elections.

senato|r (**-ra, -rowie** *lub* **-rzy**; *loc sg* **-rze**) *m* (*Pol*) senator
senio|r (**-ra, -rzy**; *loc sg* **-rze**) *m* (*osoba najstarsza wiekiem*) senior
senny *adj* **1** (*śpiący, bez energii*) sleepy **2** (*usypiający*) drowsy
sen|s (**-su**; *loc sg* **-sie**) *m* **1** (*cel*) point **2** (*o znaczeniu*) sense; **bez ~u** pointless; **to nie ma ~u** that doesn't make sense
separacj|a (**-i**) *f* (*małżeńska*) separation; **być/żyć w separacji** to be separated
se|r (**-ra, -ry**; *loc sg* **-rze**) *m* (*Kulin*) cheese; **biały ~** cottage cheese; **żółty ~** hard cheese
Serbi|a (**-i**) *f* Serbia
serbski *adj* Serbian
serbsko-chorwacki *adj* Serbo-Croatian
serc|e (**-a, -a**; *nom pl* **-a**) *nt* (*Med*) heart; **jest bez serca** he is heartless; **życzenia płynące z głębi serca** best wishes from the bottom of one's heart
serdecznie *adv* **1** (*powitać, podziękować*) warmly **2** (*bardzo, naprawdę*) heartily; **pozdrawiam ~** (*na zakończenie listu*) kind regards
serdeczny *adj* **1** (*człowiek*) friendly **2** (*o przyjacielu*) bosom **3** (*uśmiech, gest*) warm **4** (*powitanie*) hearty; **~ palec** ring finger; **serdeczne pozdrowienia** heartfelt greetings

ser|ek (**-ka, -ki**; *inst sg* **-kiem**) *m dimin od* **ser** (*Kulin*) cheese; **~ topiony** processed cheese

seri|a (**-i, -e**; *gen pl, dat & loc sg* **-i**) *f* **1** (*zdarzeń*) series **2** (*antybiotyku, zabiegów*) course **3** (*kolekcja*) set **4** (*negocjacji*) round **5** (*wyrobów przemysłowych*) batch **6** (*kosmetyków*) line

serial (**-u, -e**; *gen pl* **-i**) *m* (*TV*) series

serni|k (**-ka, -ki**; *inst sg* **-kiem**) *m* (*Kulin*) cheesecake

serwe|r (**-ra, -ry**; *loc sg* **-rze**) *m* (*Komput*) server

sesj|a (**-i, -e**; *gen pl* **-i**) *f* **1** (*sejmu, nagraniowa*) session **2** (*na uniwersytecie*): **~ egzaminacyjna** end-of-term examinations *pl* **3** (*na giełdzie*) trading session **4** (*fotograficzna*) shoot

sę|dzia (**-dziego** *lub* **-dzi, -dziowie**) *m decl like adj lub f in sg* **1** (*Prawo*) judge **2** (*konkursowy*) juror **3** (*w piłce nożnej, koszykówce, boksie*) referee **4** (*w tenisie, siatkówce*) umpire

sędzi|ować (**-uję, -ujesz**) *vi* **1** (*prowadzić rozprawę*) to judge **2** (*w meczu piłki nożnej, koszykówki*) to referee **3** (*w meczu tenisowym, siatkówki*) to umpire

sfałsz|ować (**-uję, -ujesz**) *vb pf od* **fałszować**

sfe|ra (**-ry, -ry**; *dat & loc sg* **-rze**) *f* **1** (*szara; podbiegunowa*) zone **2** (*Astron*) sphere **3** (*wpływów, działań, gospodarcza*) sphere **4** (*klasa społeczna*) class

si|ać (**-eję, -ejesz**) *vt* to sow

siad|ać (**-am, -asz**; *imp* **-aj**) *vb impf* to sit; **mleko się zsiadło** the milk has gone off

siat|ka (**-ki, -ki**; *dat & loc sg* **-ce**; *gen pl* **-ek**) *f* **1** (*plecionka*) mesh, net **2** (*w ogrodzie*) wire fence **3** (*układ*) network **4** (*w tenisie, koszykówce*) net **5** (*przestępcza*) ring; **~ na zakupy** string bag

siatków|ka (**-ki**; *dat & loc sg* **-ce**) *f* **1** (*nom pl* **-ki**; *gen pl* **-ek**) (*oka*) retina **2** (*gra sportowa*) volleyball

sią|ść (**-dę, -dziesz**; *imp* **-dź**) *vb pf od* **siadać**

siebie *pron* **1** (*dotyczący siebie samego*) oneself **2** (*z wzajemnością*) each other; **przed ~** straight ahead; **być u ~** (*w domu*) to be at home; **czuj się jak u ~** make yourself at home; **oni są o ~ zazdrośni** they are jealous of one another; **siedzieliśmy obok ~** we sat next to each other

sie|ć (**-ci, -ci**; *gen pl, dat & loc sg* **-ci**) *f* **1** (*do łowienia ryb*) net **2** (*pajęcza*) (cob)web **3** (*elektryczna, internetowa*) network **4** (*barów, kin*) chain **5** (*przen: zasadzka*) trap

siedem *num* seven

siedemdziesiąt *num* seventy

siedemnasty *num decl like adj* seventeenth; **jest siedemnasta** it's 5 o'clock

siedemnaście *num* seventeen

siedemset *num* seven hundred

siedze|nie (**-nia, -nia**; *gen pl* **-ń**) *nt* **1** (*krzesło, fotel*) seat **2** (*pot: tyłek*) bum

siedzi|ba (**-by, -by**; *dat & loc sg* **-bie**) *f* (*instytucji*) base; **główna ~** headquarters *pl*; **firma ma swoją siedzibę w Poznaniu** the firm is based in Poznań

sie|dzieć (**-dzę, -dzisz**; *imp* **-dź**) *vi* **1** (*być w pozycji siedzącej*) to sit **2** (*pot: w domu, przed komputerem*) to stay **3** (*pot: odbywać karę więzienia*) to do time **4** (*powtarzać klasę w szkole*) to repeat

siero|ta (**-ty, -ty**; *dat sg* **-cie**) *m/f decl like f* **1** (*dziecko bez rodziców*) orphan **2** (*niezdarna, niezaradna osoba*) waif

sier|pień (**-pnia, -pnie**) *m* August

SŁOWO KLUCZOWE

się *pron inv* **1** (*odnoszący się do siebie samego*) oneself; **skompromitował się** he compromised himself **2** (*nawzajem*) each other; **spotykamy się regularnie** we meet up with each other regularly **3** (*przy tworzeniu strony zwrotnej czasownika*): **interesuję się historią** I'm interested in history; **myć** (**umyć** *pf*) **się** to wash oneself; **cieszę się, że tu jesteście** I'm pleased that you are here **4** (*jako odpowiednik strony biernej*): **tę koszulę dobrze się prasuje** this shirt irons well **5** (*bezosobowo*): **robi się późno** it's getting late

ik|ać (-am, -asz; *pf* **-nąć**) *vi* **1** (*pot: wytrysnąć strumieniem*) to squirt **2** (*pot: siusiać*) to pee
ilnie *adv* **1** (*uderzyć*) hard **2** (*intensywnie*) strongly; **~ przeżyła jego śmierć** she took his death badly
ilni|k (-ka, -ki; *inst sg* **-kiem**) *m* (*urządzenie*) engine; **~ elektryczny** electric motor
ilny *adj* **1** (*mężczyzna, wiatr, organizm*) strong **2** (*stres, ból*) intense **3** (*leki, szkła*) strong **4** (*akcent*) strong
i|ła (-ły, -ły; *dat & loc sg* **-le**) *f* **1** (*energia*) strength **2** (*natężenie*) intensity **3** (*w fizyce*) force; **siły** *pl* forces; **siłą** by force; **siły zbrojne** armed forces
iłow|nia (-ni, -nie; *gen & loc pl* **-ni**) *f* **1** (*klub sportowy*) body-building gym **2** (*energetyczna, wodna*) power plant
in|gel, sin|giel (-gla, -gle; *gen pl* **-gli**) *m* **1** (*Muz*) single **2** (*w sporcie*) singles *pl*
i|ostra (-ostry, -ostry; *dat & loc sg* **-ostrze**; *gen pl* **-óstr**) *f* **1** (*rodzeństwo*) sister **2** (*w szpitalu*) nurse; **~ oddziałowa** charge nurse; **~ zakonna** nun, sister
iostrzenic|a (-y, -e) *f* (*krewna*) niece
iostrze|niec (-ńca, -ńcy) *m* (*krewny*) nephew
iódmy *num decl like adj* seventh; **jest siódma** it's seven o'clock; **na stronie siódmej** on page seven
iwi|eć (-eję, -ejesz; *pf* **o-** *lub* **po-**) *vi* (*o włosach i o osobie*) to go grey (Brit) *lub* gray (US)
iwy *adj* (*o włosach i o osobie*) grey (Brit), gray (US)
ka|kać (-czę, -czesz; *pf* **skoczyć**) *vi* **1** (*wykonać podskok*) to jump **2** (*na skakance*) to skip **3** (*o wartości, akcjach*) to shoot up
kalecze|nie (-nia, -nia; *gen pl* **-ń**) *nt* (*mała rana*) cut
kalecz|yć (-ę, -ysz) *vt pf* (*zranić, uszkodzić*) to cut; **~ się** *vr pf* (*zranić się*) to cut o.s.
ka|ła (-ły, -ły; *dat & loc sg* **-le**) *f* (*Geol*) rock
kandal (-u, -e; *gen pl* **-i** *lub* **-ów**) *m* (*gorsząca sytuacja/atmosfera*) scandal
kandynawi|a (-i; *dat & loc sg* **-i**) *f* (*region*) Scandinavia
skandynawski *adj* (*dotyczący regionu*) Scandinavian; **półwysep S~** Scandinavian Peninsula
skanse|n (-nu, -ny; *loc sg* **-nie**) *m* (*muzeum etnograficzne*) heritage park
skar|b (-bu, -by; *loc sg* **-bie**) *m* (*coś drogocennego*) treasure; **~ państwa** (*Pol*) the treasury
skarbowy *adj* **1** (*przepis, bon, obligacja*) treasury **2** (*znaczek, opłata*) duty **3** (*kontrola*) treasury; **urząd ~** ≈ HM Revenue and Customs (Brit), ≈ Internal Revenue Service (US)
skar|ga (-gi, -gi; *dat & loc sg* **-dze**) *f* (*zażalenie*) complaint
skarpet|ka (-ki, -ki; *dat & loc sg* **-ce**; *gen pl* **-ek**) *f* (*ubranie*) sock
skarż|yć (-ę, -ysz) *vt*: **~ kogoś (do sądu)** (*pozwać do sądu*) to sue sb ▷ *vi*: **~ (na~** *pf*) **na kogoś** (*donosić*) to tell on sb; **~ się** (*pf* **po-**) *vr* **1** (*utyskiwać, narzekać*) to complain **2** (*mieć problem zdrowotny*): **~ się na coś** to complain of sth; **~ się na kogoś/coś** to complain about sb/sth
skazany *adj* **1** (*w sądzie*) convicted **2** (*przen*): **~ na coś** doomed to sth ▷ *m decl like adj* (*wyrokiem sądowym*) convict
skąd *pron* (*z jakiego miejsca/źródła*) where… from; **~ pan/pani jest?** where are you from?; **~ wiesz?** (*familiar sg*) how do you know?
ską|piec (-pca, -pcy) *m* (*sknera*) miser
skąpy *adj* **1** (*sknerowaty*) stingy **2** (*strój, posiłek, blask*) scant
sklej|ać (-am, -asz; *pf* **skleić**) *vt* (*połączyć klejem*) to glue together
skle|p (-pu, -py; *loc sg* **-pie**) *m* (*punkt sprzedaży towarów*) shop (Brit), store (US); **~ spożywczy** grocer's; **~ mięsny** butcher's

SKLEP MONOPOLOWY

Sklep monopolowy is a store which sells a wide selection of alcohol. Its name comes from the fact that during the **PRL** the state had a total monopoly on the production of alcohol.

skła|d (**-du, -dy**; *loc sg* **-dzie**) *m* **1** (*opału*) yard **2** (*budynek*) warehouse **3** (*składniki danego produktu*) composition **4** (*w chemii*) composition **5** (*tekstu w drukarni*) typesetting **6** (*sportowej grupy*) lineup **7** (*delegacji*) makeup; **wchodzić** (**wejść** *pf*) **w ~ czegoś** to be part of sth

skład|ać (**-am, -asz**; *pf* **złożyć**) *vt* **1** (*kartkę, wózek*) to fold **2** (*parasolkę*) to roll up **3** (*montować*) to assemble **4** (*przechowywać*) to store **5** (*podanie, wymówienie*) to hand in **6** (*o ofercie, obietnicy*) to make **7** (*o zażaleniu*) to file **8** (*gratulacje, wyrazy szacunku*) to express **9** (*o wizycie*) to pay; **~ się** *vr* **1** (*o meblu, wózeczku*) to fold up **2** (*pot: dawać pieniądze na wspólny cel*) to chip in **3** (*być elementem składowym*): **~ się z czegoś** to consist of sth

składni|k (**-ka, -ki**; *inst sg* **-kiem**) *m* **1** (*część składowa*) ingredient **2** (*w matematyce*) element

skła|mać (**-mię, -miesz**) *vb pf od* **kłamać**

skocz|yć (**-ę, -ysz**) *vb pf od* **skakać**

sko|k (**-ku, -ki**; *inst sg* **-kiem**) *m* **1** (*podskok*) jump **2** (*nagła zmiana: cen*) hike; **~ w dal/wzwyż** long/high jump

skomplikowany *adj* (*trudny*) complicated

skończ|yć (**-ę, -ysz**) *vb pf od* **kończyć**

skoro *conj* (*jeśli*) since, as; **~ tylko** as soon as

skorpio|n (**-na, -ny**; *loc sg* **-nie**) *m* **1** (*zwierzę*) scorpion **2** (*Astrol*): **S~** Scorpio

skowron|ek (**-ka, -ki**; *inst sg* **-kiem**) *m* (*ptak*) lark

skó|ra (**-ry, -ry**; *dat & loc sg* **-rze**) *f* **1** (*Anat*) skin **2** (*na zwierzętach gruboskórnych*) hide **3** (*surowiec na odzież*) leather; **buty ze skóry** leather shoes

skórzany *adj* (*rękawiczki, płaszcz, pasek*) leather

skrę|cać (**-cam, -casz**; *pf* **-cić**) *vt* **1** (*splatać*) to weave **2** (*zwijać np. papierosa*) to roll **3** (*wkrętami, śrubami*) to screw together **4** (*kostkę, nogę*) to twist ▷ *vi* (*o samochodzie, ulicy*) to turn; **~ w prawo/ulicę Prostą** to turn right/into Prosta street; **skręć w trzecią ulicę w lewo** take the third turning on the left

skrę|cić (**-cę, -cisz**; *imp* **-ć**) *vb pf od* **skręcać**

skromny *adj* (*człowiek, strój, posiłek*) modest

skrytyk|ować (**-uję, -ujesz**) *vb pf od* **krytykować**

skrzyd|ło (**-ła, -ła**; *loc sg* **-le**; *gen pl* **-eł**) *nt* **1** (*ptaka, samolotu*) wing **2** (*Tech*) blade **3** (*u okna*) sash

skrzy|nia (**-ni, -nie**; *dat & loc sg* **-ni**; *gen pl* **-ń**) *f* **1** (*kufer*) chest **2** (*pojemnik bez wieka na jedzenie*) crate **3** (*w tapczanie*) frame; **~ biegów** (*w samochodzie*) gearbox

skrzyn|ka (**-ki, -ki**; *dat & loc sg* **-ce**; *gen pl* **-ek**) *f dimin od* **skrzynia** **1** (*korytko na kwiaty*) window box **2** (*o obudowie*) case; **~ pocztowa** *lub* **na listy** (*w bloku mieszkalnym*) letterbox (*Brit*), mailbox (*US*); **~ pocztowa** (*do wysłania listu*) postbox (*Brit*), mailbox (*US*); **~ emailowa** (*Komput*) mailbox; **pczarna ~** (*w samolocie*) black box; **~ odbiorcza** inbox

skrzy|pce (**-piec**) *pl* (*instrument muzyczny*) violin *sg*

skrzyw|dzić (**-dzę, -dzisz**; *imp* **-dź**) *vb pf od* **krzywdzić**

skrzyżowa|nie (**-nia, -nia**; *gen pl* **-ń**) *nt* (*dróg*) crossroads

skuteczny *adj* (*lek, plan, pracownik*) effective

skut|ek (**-ku, -ki**; *inst sg* **-kiem**) *m* (*następstwo*) result; **aż do skutku** to the bitter end; **dojść** (*pf*) **do skutku** to come into effect; **na ~ czegoś** as a result of sth

slip|y (**-ów**) *pl* (*bielizna*) briefs

słab|nąć (**-nę, -niesz**; *imp* **-nij**; *pf* **o-**) *vi* **1** (*tracić energię*) to weaken **2** (*zainteresowanie*) to diminish **3** (*tracić intensywność*) to die down **4** (*o problemach, utrapieniach, bólu*) to ease off

słabo *adv* **1** (*bez energii, siły*) weakly **2** (*rozwinięty (kraj), zaludniony*) poorly **3** (*przygotowany, słyszący*) poorly; **~ mi** I feel faint

łaby *adj* **1** (*wątły, bez siły*) weak **2** (*marny*) poor

ła|wa (**-wy**; *dat & loc sg* **-wie**) *f* **1** (*popularność*) fame **2** (*opinia*) reputation **3** (*sławny człowiek*) famous person; **światowej sławy aktor** a world-famous actor

ławny *adj* (*znany*) famous

łodki *adj* (*uśmiech, smak, człowiek*) sweet; **słodka woda** fresh water

łodycz (**-y**) *f* (*smaku, uśmiechu*) sweetness; **słodycze** *pl* (*cukierki, czekolada*) sweets (Brit), candy *sg* (*US*)

ł|odzić (**-odzę, -odzisz**; *imp* **-ódź** *lub* **-odź**; *pf* **o-** *lub* **po-**) *vt* (*dodawać cukru*) to sweeten; **czy pan/pani słodzi?** do you take sugar?

łoi|k (**-ka, -ki**; *inst sg* **-kiem**) *m* (*dżemu, korniszonów*) jar

łom|ka (**-ki, -ki**; *dat & loc sg* **-ce**; *gen pl* **-ek**) *f* (*do napojów*) straw

łoneczny *adj* **1** (*niebo, mieszkanie*) sunny **2** (*o energii*) solar; **światło słoneczne** sunlight; **okulary słoneczne** sunglasses *pl*

łony *adj* **1** (*jedzenie*) salty **2** (*o wodzie*) salt **3** (*przen: wygórowany*) steep

ło|ń (**-nia, -nie**; *gen pl* **-ni**) *m* (*zwierzę*) elephant

łońc|e (**-a**; *nom pl* **-a**) *nt* **1** (*ciało niebieskie*) sun **2** (*o świetle słonecznym*) sunshine; **w** *lub* **na słońcu** in the sunshine

łowacj|a (**-i**) *f* Slovakia

łowacki *adj* Slovakian

łoweni|a (**-i**) *f* Slovenia

łoweński *adj* Slovenian

łownict|wo (**-wa**; *loc sg* **-wie**) *nt* vocabulary

łownicz|ek (**-ka, -ki**; *inst sg* **-kiem**) *m* **1** (*lista terminów/wyrazów*) glossary **2** (*mały słownik*) pocket dictionary

łowni|k (**-ka, -ki**; *inst sg* **-kiem**) *m* (*jednojęzyczny, dwujęzyczny*) dictionary

ł|owo (**-owa, -owa**; *loc sg* **-owie**; *gen pl* **-ów**) *nt* (*wyraz*) word; **słowa** *pl* (*w tekście piosenki*) lyrics *pl*; **innymi słowy** in other words; **~ w ~** word for word; **dawać (dać** *pf*) **~** to give one's word; **dotrzymywać (dotrzymać** *pf*) **słowa** to keep one's word

łuch (**-u**) *m* **1** (*o zmyśle*) hearing **2** (*Muz*) (an) ear for music; **słuchy** *pl* (*pogłoski*): **chodzą ~y, że pogoda będzie ładna** rumour (*Brit*) *lub* rumor (*US*) has it that the weather will be good

słuch|ać (**-am, -asz**) *vt +gen* (*muzyki, radia*) to listen to ▷ *vi* (*pf* **u-** *lub* **po-**) (*rodziców, nauczycieli*) to obey; **słucham?** (*halo?*) hello?; (*nie dosłyszałem*) pardon?

słuchaw|ka (**-ki, -ki**; *dat & loc sg* **-ce**; *gen pl* **-ek**) *f* (*w telefonie*) receiver; **słuchawki** *pl* **1** (*nakładane na głowę*) headphones **2** (*wkładane do ucha*) earphones

służ|ba (**-by, -by**; *dat sg* **-bie**) *f* **1** (*wojskowa, drogowa, dyplomatyczna, zdrowia*) service **2** (*godziny pracy milicjanta, żołnierza*) duty **3** (*osoby pełniące pracę służącego*) servants *pl*

służbowo *adv* (*odbywać podróż*) on business

służbowy *adj* **1** (*podróż, spotkanie*) business **2** (*obowiązek, funkcja*) official **3** (*samochód, telefon*) company

służ|yć (**-ę, -ysz**) *vi* **1** (*pełnić funkcję, usługiwać*) to serve **2** (*o psie*) to beg **3** (*być użytecznym*) to be useful; **do czego to służy?** what's this for?; **czym mogę ~?** can I help you?

słychać *vi* (*być słyszalnym*): **~ było hałas** there was noise; **~, że...** there's news that...; **nic nie ~** I can't hear a thing; **co ~?** how's it going? (Brit), what's up? (*US*)

słynny *adj* (*sławny, znany*) famous

słysz|eć (**-ę, -ysz**; *pf* **u-**) *vt* **1** (*dźwięki*) to hear **2** (*dowiadywać się*) to hear; **słyszysz mnie?** (*familiar sg*) can you hear me?; **nigdy nie słyszałam o tym aktorze** I've never heard of that actor

smaczny *adj* (*posiłek*) tasty; **smacznego!** enjoy your meal!

sma|k (**-ku**; *inst sg* **-kiem**) *m* **1** (*zmysł*) taste **2** (*nom pl* **-ki**) (*dania, napoju*) taste, flavour (Brit), flavor (US); **bez ~u** tasteless

smak|ować (**-uję, -ujesz**) *vt* (*pf* **po-**) (*kosztować*) to taste ▷ *vi* (*być smacznym*): **~ świetnie** to taste excellent; **jak panu/pani smakuje?** how does it taste to you?

smal|ec (**-cu**) *m* (*Kulin*) lard

smar|ować (**-uję, -ujesz**; *pf* **po-**) *vt* **1** (*kromkę masłem*) to butter **2** (*dżemem, serem*) to spread **3** (*pf* **na-**) (*smarem*) to grease

smartfon (**-u, -y**; *loc sg* **-ie**) *m* smart phone

smażony *adj* (*Kulin*) fried

smaż|yć (**-ę, -ysz**; *pf* **u-**) *vt* (*Kulin*) to fry

smo|k (**-ka, -ki**; *inst sg* **-kiem**) *m* (*z baśni*) dragon

smoothie *nt* smoothie

smr|ód (**-odu, -ody**; *loc sg* **-odzie**) *m* (*fetor*) stench

SMS (**SMS-a, SMS-y**; *loc sg* **SMS-ie**) *nt* text message

smukły *adj* (*wysoki i szczupły*) slender

smutno *adv* (*wyglądać, uśmiechać się*) sadly; **~ mi** I feel sad

smutny *adj* (*nieszczęśliwy, niewesoły*) sad

sobą *pron* **1** (*dotyczący siebie samego*) oneself **2** (*wzajemnie, razem*) each other; **być ~** to be oneself; **chodzili ze ~ przez trzy lata** they were together for three years; **mieszkać ze ~** to live together

sobie *pron* **1** (*dotyczący siebie samego*) oneself **2** (*nawzajem*) each other; **mieć coś na ~** (*ubranie*) to have sth on; **mówić o ~** to talk about oneself; **idź ~!** go away!; **ręce przy ~!** hands off!; **tak ~** (*pot*) so-so

sob|ota (**-oty, -oty**; *dat & loc sg* **-ocie**; *gen pl* **-ót**) *f* Saturday

socjalistyczny *adj* (*ruch, związek, partia*) socialist

socjologi|a (**-i**) *f* (*nauka*) sociology

so|fa (**-fy, -fy**; *dat & loc sg* **-fie**) *f* (*kanapa*) sofa

so|k (**-ku, -ki**; *inst sg* **-kiem**) *m* **1** (*Kulin*) juice **2** (*Bot*) sap

solenizan|t (**-ta, -ci**; *loc sg* **-cie**) *m* (*obchodzący urodziny/imieniny*) *person celebrating his birthday/nameday*

solidarnoś|ć (**-ci**) *f* (*poczucie wspólnoty*) solidarity

solidny *adj* **1** (*spolegliwy*) solid **2** (*budynek*) sturdy **3** (*mocny i trwały*) solid **4** (*gruntowny*) thorough **5** (*dużych rozmiarów*) substantial

solony *adj* (*popcorn, ryba*) salted

SOS *nt inv* (*sygnał wzywania pomocy*) SOS, distress signal

so|s (**-su, -sy**; *loc sg* **-sie**) *m* **1** (*pieczarkowy, czekoladowy*) sauce **2** (*własny z mięsa*) gravy **3** (*sałatkowy*) dressing

so|wa (**-wy, -wy**; *dat & loc sg* **-wie**; *gen pl* **sów**) *f* (*ptak*) owl

sól (**soli**) *f* (*przyprawa*) salt; **sole** *pl* (*mineralne, trzeźwiące*) salts

space|r (**-ru, -ry**; *loc sg* **-rze**) *m* (*przechadzka*) walk; **iść (pójść** *pf*) **na ~** to go for a walk

spacer|ować (**-uję, -ujesz**) *vi* (*przechadzać się*) to stroll

spać (**śpię, śpisz**; *imp* **śpij**) *vi* (*być w stanie snu*) to sleep; **on śpi/nie śpi** he's asleep/awake; **iść (pójść** *pf*) **~** to go to bed; **chce ci się ~?** are you sleepy?; **~ z kimś** to sleep with sb

spak|ować (**-uję, -ujesz**) *vb pf od* **pakować**

spal|ać (**-am, -asz**; *pf* **-ić**) *vt* **1** (*niszczyć ogniem/słońcem*) to burn **2** (*wysadzać bezpieczniki*) to blow; **~ się** *vr* (*zostać zniszczonym ogniem*) to burn

spal|ić (**-ę, -isz**) *vb pf od* **palić, spalać**

specjali|sta (**-sty, -ści**; *dat sg* **-ście**) *m decl like f in sg* **1** (*fachowiec*) expert **2** (*Med*) specialist

specjaliz|ować się (**-uję, -ujesz**; *pf* **wy-**) *vr* (*być fachowcem w jakiejś dziedzinie*): **~ w czymś** to specialize in sth

spektakl (**-u, -e**; *gen pl* **-i**) *m* (*przedstawienie*) performance

spinacz (**-a, -e**; *gen pl* **-y**) *m* (*biurowy*) paper clip

spirytu|s (**-su, -sy**; *loc sg* **-sie**) *m* (*mocny alkohol*) spirit

spi|s (**-su, -sy**; *loc sg* **-sie**) *m* (*rejestr*) list; **~ treści** table of contents

spis|ek (**-ku, -ki**; *inst sg* **-kiem**) *m* (*tajny plan*) conspiracy

spisk|ować (**-uję, -ujesz**) *vi* (*zawierać tajne porozumienie*) to conspire

spis|ywać (**-uję, -ujesz**; *pf* **-ać**) *vt* **1** (*sporządzać rejestr*) to make a list of **2** (*dokumenty*) to draw up **3** (*przepisywać skądś, zapisywać*) to copy **4** (*na egzaminie*) to copy; **~ się**

vr (*działać, postępować*): **dobrze/źle się ~** (*o osobie*) to do well/badly; (*o urządzeniu*) to run well/badly
pleśniały *adj* (*zepsute jedzenie/ubranie*) mouldy (*Brit*), moldy (*US*)
płu|kiwać (**-kuję, -kujesz**; *pf* **-kać**) *vt* (*pianę, szampon*) to rinse off
pod *prep +gen* (*stołu, biurka*) from under; **~ Krakowa** from somewhere around Cracow
pod|nie (**-ni**) *pl* (*ubranie*) trousers (*Brit*), pants (*US*)
podziew|ać się (**-am, -asz**) *vr* (*oczekiwać*): **~ kogoś/czegoś** to be expecting sb/sth
pogląd|ać (**-am, -asz**; *pf* **spojrzeć**) *vi* (*patrzeć*) to look
pojrz|eć (**-ę, -ysz**; *imp* **spójrz** *lub* **spojrzyj**) *vb pf od* **spoglądać**
pojrze|nie (**-nia, -nia**; *gen pl* **-ń**) *nt* (*wzrok*) look
poko *excl* **1** (*w porządku*) no problem! (*pot*) **2** (*nie denerwuj się*) cool it! (*pot*)
pokojnie *adv* **1** (*bez emocji*) calmly **2** (*wolno*) slowly **3** (*cicho*) quietly **4** (*niespiesznie*) leisurely **5** (*pewnie*) smoothly
pokojny *adj* **1** (*osoba, wody*) calm **2** (*usposobienie*) placid **3** (*barwa*) sober; **być ~m o kogoś/coś** to be confident about sb/sth
pok|ój (**-oju**) *m* **1** (*równowaga psychiczna*) peace **2** (*cisza, bezruch*) calm **3** (*bez konfliktów/wojny*) peace; **daj ~!** come off it! (*pot*); **dać** (*pf*) **komuś ~, zostawić** (*pf*) **kogoś w spokoju** to leave sb in peace; **proszę o ~!** quiet, please!
połeczeńst|wo (**-wa, -wa**; *loc sg* **-wie**) *nt* (*ogół ludzi danego kraju*) society; **~ polskie** (*ogół Polaków*) Polish society
połecznoś|ć (**-ci, -ci**; *gen pl, dat & loc sg* **-ci**) *f* (*grupa zawodowa/społeczna*) community
połeczny *adj* **1** (*dotyczący ogółu społeczeństwa*) social **2** (*należący do społeczeństwa*) public **3** (*służący społeczeństwu*) community; **klasa społeczna** social class; **praca społeczna** community service; **ubezpieczenie społeczne** national insurance (*Brit*), social security (*US*)
spontaniczny *adj* (*odruchowy*) spontaneous
spor|t (**-tu, -ty**; *loc sg* **-cie**) *m* (*ćwiczenia i gry*) sport(s *pl*); **uprawiać ~** to do sport
sporto|wiec (**-wca, -wcy**) *m* (*osoba uprawiająca sport*) athlete
sportowy *adj* **1** (*klub, auto, sprzęt*) sports **2** (*o zachowaniu*) sporting **3** (*styl ubierania się*) sporty
spos|ób (**-obu, -oby**; *loc sg* **-obie**) *m* **1** (*robienia czegoś*) manner **2** (*komunikacji, działania*) means; **w ten ~** in this way; **~ bycia** manners
spotka|nie (**-nia, -nia**; *gen pl* **-ń**) *nt* meeting
spotyk|ać (**-am, -asz**; *pf* **spotkać**) *vt* **1** (*nowych ludzi*) to meet **2** (*zobaczyć przez przypadek*) to come across **3** (*zdarzyć się*) to happen to; **~ się** *vr* (*schodzić się*) to meet
spożyw|ać (**-am, -asz**; *pf* **spożyć**) *vt* (*książk: jeść*) to consume
spożywczy *adj* (*dotyczący jedzenia*): **sklep ~** grocer's (*Brit*), grocery (*US*); **artykuły spożywcze** groceries
spódnic|a (**-y, -e**) *f* (*ubranie*) skirt
spół|ka (**-ki, -ki**; *dat sg* **-ce**; *gen pl* **-ek**) *f* (*rodzaj firmy*) company; **~ akcyjna** joint-stock company; **~ z ograniczoną odpowiedzialnością** limited (liability) company; **~ cywilna** civil partnership
spóź|niać się (**-niam, -niasz**; *pf* **-nić**) *vr* **1** (*przybyć za późno*) to be late **2** (*o zegarku*) to be slow **3** (*mieć miejsce z opóźnieniem*) to be (running) late; **spóźnić** (*pf*) **się na samolot** to miss one's plane; **spóźnić** (*pf*) **się do pracy** to be late for work
spóźniony *adj* **1** (*o pociągu/autobusie, osobie*) late **2** (*o przesyłce, samolocie*) delayed **3** (*o życzeniach*) belated
spragniony *adj* (*napoju*) thirsty
spra|wa (**-wy, -wy**; *dat & loc sg* **-wie**) *f* **1** (*fakt*) matter **2** (*rzecz do załatwienia*) business **3** (*w sądzie*) case; **to nie twoja ~** it's none of your business
sprawc|a (**-y, -y**) *m decl like f in sg* (*przestępstwa, wypadku*) perpetrator
spraw|dzać (**-dzam, -dzasz**; *pf* **-dzić**) *vt* **1** (*kontrolować*) to check **2** (*pisownię, znaczenie w słowniku*) to

look up; **~ się** *vr* **1** (*o przypuszczeniach, przepowiedniach*) to come true **2** (*okazać się użytecznym*) to turn out to be useful

spra|wiać (**-wiam, -wiasz**; *pf* **-wić**) *vt* **1** (*zadawać np. ból*) to inflict **2** (*przyjemność*) to give **3** (*problem*) to cause **4** (*być przyczyną czegoś*) to cause; **silny deszcz sprawił, że odwołano koncert** heavy rain meant that the concert was cancelled

sprawiedliwie *adv* (*oceniać, postępować*) fairly

sprawiedliwoś|ć (**-ci**) *f* **1** (*uczciwość*) fairness **2** (*Prawo*) justice system

sprawiedliwy *adj* (*słuszny*) fair

sprawny *adj* **1** (*fizycznie*) fit **2** (*manualnie*) adroit **3** (*wydajny: pracownik, instytucja, organizacja*) efficient **4** (*o urządzeniu, sprzęcie*) in working order

spróbo|wać (**-uję, -ujesz**) *vb pf od* **próbować**

sprytny *adj* **1** (*osoba*) shrewd **2** (*pomysł, plan*) clever

sprzątacz|ka (**-ki, -ki**; *dat & loc sg* **-ce**; *gen pl* **-ek**) *f* (*kobieta*) cleaning lady

sprząt|ać (**-am, -asz**; *pf* **-nąć**) *vt od* **posprzątać 1** (*umyć, odkurzyć: dom, pokój*) to clean **2** (*uporządkować: zabawki, zeszyty*) to clear

sprząt|nąć (**-nę, -niesz**; *imp* **-nij**) *vb pf od* **sprzątać**

sprzeci|wiać się (**-wiam, -wiasz**; *pf* **-wić**) *vr*: **~ komuś/czemuś** (*wystąpić przeciwko*) to oppose sb/sth; **~ czemuś** (*protestować*) to object to sth; (*być sprzecznym z czymś*) to be at odds with sth

sprzed *prep +gen* **1** (*miejsca: dworca, bloku*) from in front of **2** (*okresu: lat, wojny*): **budynki ~ rewolucji** pre-revolution buildings; **gazeta ~ miesiąca** a month-old newspaper

sprzed|ać (**-am, -asz**; *imp* **-aj**) *vb pf od* **sprzedawać**

sprzed|awać (**-aję, -ajesz**; *imp* **-awaj**; *pf* **-ać**) *vt* (*odstępować za pieniądze*) to sell; **~ się** *vr* **1** (*o produktach*) to sell **2** (*o osobie*) to sell out

sprzedawc|a (**-y, -y**) *m decl like f in sg* **1** (*w sklepie lub terenie*) salesman **2** (*w sklepie*) shop assistant (*Brit*), salesclerk (*US*)

sprzedawczy|ni (**-ni, -nie**; *gen pl* **-ń**) *f* **1** (*w sklepie lub terenie*) saleswoman **2** (*w sklepie*) shop assistant (*Brit*), salesclerk (*US*)

sprzedaż (**-y**) *f* (*towaru*) sale; **na ~** for sale

sprzę|t (**-tu**; *loc sg* **-cie**) *m* **1** (*wyposażenie*) equipment **2** (*nom pl* **-ty**) (*meble*) piece of furniture; **~ komputerowy** computer equipment; **~ sportowy** sports equipment

spuszcz|ać (**-am, -asz**; *pf* **spuścić**) *vt* **1** (*obniżać: cenę, oczy, głowę*) to lower **2** (*odprowadzić: ciecz, gaz*) to let out; **~ się** *vr* (*zsunąć się w dół*) to come down; **~ wodę** (*w ubikacji*) to flush (the toilet)

spyt|ać (**-am, -asz**) *vb pf od* **pytać**

srebrny *adj* (*pierścionek, medal*) silver

sreb|ro (**-ra, -ra**; *loc sg* **-rze**; *gen pl* **-er**) *nt* (*metal; kolor, medal sportowy*) silver

ssać (**ssę, ssiesz**; *imp* **ssij**) *vt* (*pierś, tabletkę*) to suck

ssa|k (**-ka, -ki**; *inst sg* **-kiem**) *m* (*zwierzę*) mammal

stabilny *adj* (*plan, związek, budynek*) stable

stacj|a (**-i, -e**; *gen pl, dat & loc sg* **-i**) *f* (*dworzec*) station; **~ kolejowa/autobusowa** railway (*Brit*) *lub* railroad (*US*)/bus station; **~ radiowa** radio station; **~ benzynowa** petrol (*Brit*) *lub* gas (*US*) station; **~ dysków** (*w komputerze*) disk drive

st|ać (**-oję, -oisz**; *imp* **-ój**; *pf* **-anąć**) *vi* **1** (*o meblach, budynkach*) to stand **2** (*o urządzeniu, przedsiębiorstwie*) to be at a standstill; **stój!** stop!; **~ w kolejce** to queue (up) (*Brit*), to line up (*US*)

stadio|n (**-nu, -ny**; *loc sg* **-nie**) *m* (*sportowy*) stadium

stały *adj* **1** (*nie w formie cieczy lub gazu*) solid **2** (*pracownik, zatrudnienie, zarobki, wystawa*) permanent **3** (*o kliencie*) regular **4** (*o komisji, zaproszeniu*) standing **5** (*w poglądach, uczuciach, usposobieniu*) constant

6 (*koszt, opłata, temperatura*) fixed **7** (*o postępie*) steady; **na stałe** permanently

sta|n (**-nu**; *loc sg* **-nie**) *m* **1** (*sytuacja, forma, nastrój*) state **2** (*nom pl* **-ny**) (*fizyczny, gospodarczy: zdrowia*) condition **3** (*nom pl* **-ny**) (*jednostka administracyjna*) state **4** (*Prawo*) status **5** (*umiejętność, zdolność*): **nie jest w ~ie tego zrozumieć** he is incapable of understanding this; **w dobrym/kiepskim ~ie** in good/ poor condition; **~ konta** bank balance; **~ cywilny** marital status; **~ wojenny** martial law

sta|nąć (**-nę, -niesz**; *imp* **-ń**) *vb pf od* **stać, stawać**

stani|k (**-ka, -ki**; *inst sg* **-kiem**) *m* (*bielizna*) bra

stanowczy *adj* (*zdecydowany*) firm

Stany Zjednoczone Ameryki (**Stanów Zjednoczonych Ameryki**) *pl* United States of America

star|ać się (**-am, -asz**; *pf* **po-**) *vr* (*usiłować coś zrobić*) to try; **~ o coś** (*o pracę, stypendium*) to try for sth; **staraj się pisać czytelnie** try to write legibly

staromodny *adj* (*niemodny, staroświecki*) old-fashioned

staroś|ć (**-ci**) *f* **1** (*ludzi*) old age **2** (*rzeczy*) age

starożytny *adj* (*literatura, sztuka*) ancient

starszy *adj comp od* **stary**; **starsza siostra** older sister

start (**-y, -y**) *m* **1** (*Sport*) start **2** (*Lot*) take off

start|ować (**-uję, -ujesz**; *pf* **wy-**) *vi* **1** (*Sport*) to start **2** (*o samolocie*) to take off

starusz|ek (**-ka, -kowie**; *inst sg* **-kiem**) *m* (*mężczyzna*) old man

starusz|ka (**-ki, -ki**; *dat & loc sg* **-ce**; *gen pl* **-ek**) *f* (*kobieta*) old lady

stary *adj* **1** (*nienowy, niemłody*) old **2** (*pieczywo*) stale ▷ *m* (*pot*) *decl like adj* **1** (*o koledze*) old boy (*pot*) **2** (*o szefie*) gaffer (*pot*) **3** (*o ojcu*) old man (*pot*)

starz|eć się (**-eję, -ejesz**; *pf* **ze-**) *vr* **1** (*człowiek*) to age **2** (*żywność*) to go stale **3** (*przen: o dziele, teorii*) to grow stale

stat|ek (**-ku, -ki**; *inst sg* **-kiem**) *m* (*w żegludze*) ship; **~ kosmiczny** spaceship

sta|w (**-wu, -wy**; *loc sg* **-wie**) *m* **1** (*akwen wodny*) pond **2** (*połączenie kości w ciele*) joint

sta|wać (**-ję, -jesz**; *imp* **-ń**; *pf* **-ć**) *vi impf* **1** (*z krzesła*) to stand up **2** (*zatrzymywać się*) to stop ▷ *vi pf* (*o pomniku, budynku*) to be erected

stawi|ać (**-am, -asz**; *imp* **-aj**; *pf* **postawić**) *vi impf* **1** (*kłaść*) to place **2** (*budynek*) to erect **3** (*oceny*) to make **4** (*kroki*) to make **5** (*pytanie*) to ask **6** (*diagnozę, wniosek*) to make **7** (*cele, zadanie*) to set **8** (*fundować*) to provide

stąd *adv* **1** (*o miejscu*) from here **2** (*z tej przyczyny*) hence; **nie jestem ~** I'm not from round here; **niedaleko ~** not far from here; **to daleko ~** it's far from here

stewarde|sa (**-sy, -sy**; *dat & loc sg* **-sie**) *f* **1** (*w samolocie*) flight attendant **2** (*na statku*) stewardess

stęsk|nić się (**-nię, -nisz**; *imp* **-nij**) *vr pf* (*odczuwać brak*): **~ za kimś/czymś** to miss sb/sth

stł|uc (**-ukę, -uczesz**) *vt* (*szkło, talerz, wazon*) to break

stłucz|ka (**-ki, -ki**; *dat & loc sg* **-ce**; *gen pl* **-ek**) *f* (*samochodowa*) bump

sto *num* hundred; **~ dwadzieścia** a hundred and twenty; **~ osób** a hundred people; **~ lat!** (*życzenia*) many happy returns; (*pieśń*) ≈ Happy Birthday

stocz|nia (**-ni, -nie**; *gen pl, dat & loc sg* **-ni**) *f* (*zakład produkcyjny*) shipyard

stois|ko (**-ka, -ka**; *inst sg* **-kiem**) *nt* **1** (*dział sklepu*) department **2** (*na kiermaszach, targach*) stall

stoję *vb zob.* **stać**

stokrot|ka (**-ki, -ki**; *dat & loc sg* **-ce**; *gen pl* **-ek**) *f* (*kwiat*) daisy

stolic|a (**-y, -e**) *f* (*główne miasto*) capital

stoli|k (**-ka, -ki**; *inst sg* **-kiem**) *m* **1** (*mały mebel*) (small) table **2** (*w restauracji*) table

stołów|ka (**-ki, -ki**; *dat & loc sg* **-ce**; *gen pl* **-ek**) *f* (*szkolna, zakładowa*) canteen

stomatolo|g (**-ga, -dzy** *lub* **-gowie**; *inst sg* **-giem**) *m* (*dentysta*) dentist
st|opa (**-opy, -opy**; *dat & loc sg* **-opie**; *gen pl* **-óp**) *f* **1** (*część nogi*) foot **2** (*standard, poziom*) level; **~ życiowa** standard of living
sto|pień (**-pnia, -pnie**; *gen pl* **-pni**) *m* **1** (*schody w budynku*) stair **2** (*schody przed budynkiem*) step **3** (*hierarchia*) rank **4** (*Szkol*) mark (*Brit*), grade (*US*) **5** (*o jednostce miary*) degree **6** (*o poziomie, intensywności*) degree; **uwaga ~!** mind the step; **~ naukowy** (university) degree; **10 stopni Celsjusza** 10 degrees centigrade; **do pewnego stopnia** to some degree
stos|ować (**-uję, -ujesz**; *pf* **za-**) *vt* **1** (*zasady, reguły, przemoc*) to apply **2** (*lekarstwa*) to administer; **~ się** *vr*: **~ się do** *+gen* (*być użytecznym*) to apply to; (*przepisów*) to comply with
stosun|ek (**-ku, -ki**; *inst sg* **-kiem**) *m* **1** (*relacja, proporcja, związek*) relation **2** (*nastawienie*) attitude **3** (*Mat*) ratio **4** (*płciowy*) intercourse; **w stosunku do** *+gen* (*porównanie*) in relation to; (*odniesienie*) with reference to
stowarzysze|nie (**-nia, -nia**; *gen pl* **-ń**) *nt* (*związek, organizacja*) association
st|ół (**-ołu, -oły**; *loc sg* **-ole**) *m* (*mebel*) table; **przy stole** at the table; **sprzątać** (**posprzątać** *pf*) **ze stołu** to clear the table
str. *abbr* (*= strona*) p.; (*= strony*) pp.
stra|ch (**-chu**) *m* (*uczucie niepokoju*) fear
stra|cić (**-cę, -cisz**; *imp* **-ć**) *vb pf od* **tracić**
straj|k (**-ku, -ki**; *inst sg* **-kiem**) *m* (*akcja protestacyjna*) strike
strajk|ować (**-uję, -ujesz**; *imp* **-uj**; *pf* **za-**) *vi* (*nie pracować*) to strike
strasznie *adv* **1** (*okropnie*) terribly **2** (*bardzo, niezmiernie*) awfully
straszny *adj* **1** (*budzący przerażenie*) scary **2** (*bardzo zły*) dreadful **3** (*ogromny*) tremendous
strasz|yć (**-ę, -ysz**; *imp* **-**; *pf* **prze-**) *vt* (*wzbudzać strach*) to scare ▷ *vi*: **w tym zamku straszy** this castle is haunted; **~** *+inst* (*grozić*) to threaten
straża|k (**-ka, -cy**; *inst sg* **-kiem**) *m* (*mężczyzna*) firefighter
strażni|k (**-ka, -cy**; *inst sg* **-kiem**) *m* **1** (*w firmie*) (security) guard **2** (*w więzieniu*) warder; **~ leśny** forest ranger
stream|ować (**-uje, -ujesz**) *vt* (*Komput*) to stream
stre|s (**-su, -sy**; *loc sg* **-sie**) *m* (*Psych*) stress; **być w ~ie** to be under stress
stresujący *adj* (*Psych*) stressful
stro|na (**-ny, -ny**; *dat & loc sg* **-nie**) *f* **1** (*bok, część*) side **2** (*książki*) page **3** (*o kierunku*) direction; **strony** *pl* (*rodzinne*) parts *pl*; **po prawej stronie** on the right-hand side; **z jednej strony..., z drugiej strony...** on the one hand..., on the other hand...; **bilet w jedną stronę/w obie strony** single/return ticket (*Brit*), one-way/ round-trip ticket (*US*); **to miło z twojej strony** that's nice of you
str|ój (**-oju, -oje**) *m* (*ubranie*) attire; **~ kąpielowy** swimming costume (*Brit*), swimsuit
strza|ł (**-łu, -ły**; *loc sg* **-le**) *m* (*z broni*) shot
strzał|ka (**-ki, -ki**; *dat & loc sg* **-ce**; *gen pl* **-ek**) *f* **1** (*symbol*) arrow **2** (*wskazówka w urządzeniu*) pointer
strzel|ać (**-am, -asz**; *pf* **-ić**) *vt* (*gola*) to shoot ▷ *vi* **1** (*z pistoletu*) to shoot **2** (*trzaskać palcami*) to snap
Strzelec *n* (*Astrol*) Sagittarius
strzykaw|ka (**-ki, -ki**; *dat & loc sg* **-ce**; *gen pl* **-ek**) *f* (*Med*) syringe
studencki *adj* student; **dom ~** hall of residence (*Brit*), dormitory (*US*)
studen|t (**-ta, -ci**; *loc sg* **-cie**) *m* (*Uniw*) student
student|ka (**-ki, -ki**; *dat & loc sg* **-ce**; *gen pl* **-ek**) *f* (*Uniw*) student
studi|a (**-ów**) *pl* **1** (*licencjackie, magisterskie*) studies **2** (*badania*) research *sg*
studi|ować (**-uję, -ujesz**) *vt* **1** (*Uniw*) to study **2** (*pf* **prze-**) (*plan miasta, książkę*) to study

STUDNIÓWKA

Studniówka is the ceremonial ball held for secondary school students, which takes place about one hundred days before their exams in May. Traditionally the ball opens with a dance called the **Polonez**. See also **matura**.

stule|cie (**-cia, -cia**; *gen pl* **-ci**) *nt* **1** (*sto lat*) century **2** (*rocznica, obchody*) centenary
stuletni *adj* **1** (*o człowieku*) hundred-year-old **2** (*o okresie, budynku*) hundred-year
stwier|dzać (**-dzam, -dzasz**; *pf* **-dzić**) *vt* (*ustalać, uznawać*) to affirm ▷ *vi* (*mówić*) to state
stwierdze|nie (**-nia, -nia**; *gen pl* **-ń**) *nt* **1** (*uznanie, ustalenie*) assertion **2** (*o wypowiedzi*) statement
stycz|eń (**-nia, -nie**) *m* January
styl (**-u, -e**) *m* **1** (*zachowania się, mówienia, malarstwa*) style **2** (*pływacki*) stroke; **~ życia** life style
stypendi|um (**-um, -a**; *gen pl* **-ów**) *nt inv in sg* scholarship
subiektywny *adj* (*osąd, zdanie*) subjective
subtelny *adj* (*wnikliwy, wyszukany*) subtle
suchy *adj* (*niemokry*) dry
sufi|t (**-tu, -ty**; *loc sg* **-cie**) *m* (*w pokoju*) ceiling
su|ka (**-ki, -ki**; *dat & loc sg* **-ce**) *f* (*pies*) bitch (*dog*)
sukce|s (**-su, -sy**; *loc sg* **-sie**) *m* (*powodzenie*) success; **odnieść** (*pf*) **~** to succeed
su|knia (**-kni, -knie**; *gen pl* **-kni** *lub* **-kien**) *f* (*odzież damska*) dress
su|ma (**-my, -my**; *dat & loc sg* **-mie**) *f* **1** (*wynik zadania*) sum **2** (*pieniędzy*) amount; **w sumie** all in all
sumie|nie (**-nia, -nia**; *gen pl* **-ń**) *nt* (*spokojne, czyste*) conscience
supermarke|t (**-tu, -ty**; *loc sg* **-cie**) *m* (*sklep*) supermarket
surowy *adj* **1** (*warzywa, ryba, ciasto*) raw **2** (*materiały budowlane*) unseasoned **3** (*wymagający*) strict **4** (*o krytyce, wyroku*) severe **5** (*bez ozdób, wygód*) austere **6** (*o klimacie, zimie*) harsh **7** (*o warunkach, życiu*) austere
surów|ka (**-ki, -ki**; *dat sg* **-ce**; *gen pl* **-ek**) *f* **1** (*potrawa*) salad **2** (*stop*) pig-iron
suszar|ka (**-ki, -ki**; *dat & loc sg* **-ce**; *gen pl* **-ek**) *f* (*urządzenie, konstrukcja*) dryer; **~ do włosów** hair dryer
susz|yć (**-ę, -ysz**) *vt* **1** (*pf* **wy-**) (*o włosach, praniu*) to dry **2** (*pf* **u-**) (*o kwiatach, grzybach*) to dry; **~ się** *vr* (*schnąć*) to get dry
swet|er (**-ra, -ry**; *loc sg* **-rze**) *m* (*ubranie*) sweater, jumper (*Brit*)
swobodnie *adv* **1** (*decydować, rozwijać się*) freely **2** (*poruszać się, rozmawiać*) freely **3** (*bez trudności, łatwo*) at ease **4** (*ubierać się*) casually
swobodny *adj* **1** (*o wyborze*) free **2** (*o rozwoju, poruszaniu się*) unconstrained **3** (*Jęz*) free **4** (*atmosfera*) informal **5** (*ubiór*) informal **6** (*przekład*) free
swoja *itd. pron zob.* **swój**
swój *od* **mój** *pron* **1** (*własny*) one's **2** (*mój*) my **3** (*twój*) your **4** (*jego*) his **5** (*jej*) her **6** (*nasz*) our **7** (*wasz*) your **8** (*ich*) their **9** (*pot: domowy*) home-made
sygna|ł (**-łu, -ły**; *loc sg* **-le**) *m* **1** (*znak*) signal **2** (*w telefonie*) tone **3** (*audycji*) signature tune
sylwest|er (**-ra, -ry**; *loc sg* **-rze**) *m* (*ostatni dzień roku*) New Year's Eve, Hogmanay (*Scottish*)
sylwet|ka (**-ki, -ki**; *dat & loc sg* **-ce**; *gen pl* **-ek**) *f* **1** (*postawa*) figure **2** (*kształt ciała*) silhouette **3** (*pisemna charakterystyka osoby*) profile
symbol (**-u, -e**) *m* (*znak*) symbol
symboliz|ować (**-uje**) *vt* (*oznaczać*) to symbolize
symfoni|a (**-i, -e**; *gen pl, dat & loc sg* **-i**) *f* (*Muz*) symphony
sympatyczny *adj* (*miły, życzliwy*) pleasant
sy|n (**-na, -nowie**; *loc sg* **-nu**) *m* (*dziecko*) son
synow|a (**-ej, -e**) *f decl like adj* (*żona syna*) daughter-in-law
sy|pać (**-pię, -piesz**; *pf* **-pnąć**) *vt* **1** (*proszek, sól*) to sprinkle **2** (*o śniegu*) to fall ▷ *vi* (*pot: donosić*): **~ kogoś/coś** to grass on sb/sth; **~ się** *vr* **1** (*o farbie, ścianie*) to fall off **2** (*o odpryskach*) to fly **3** (*o listkach*) to fall **4** (*o uderzeniach*) to rain down **5** (*pf* **roz-**) (*pot: ulegać zniszczeniu*) to fall apart

sypi|ać (**-am, -asz**) *vi* (*spać*) to sleep
sypial|nia (**-ni, -nie**; *gen pl* **-ni**) *f* (*pokój*) bedroom
syste|m (**-mu, -my**; *loc sg* **-mie**) *m* (*społeczny, operacyjny, planetarny*) system
systematyczny *adj* **1** (*planowy, metodyczny*) systematic **2** (*student, pracownik*) methodical
sytuacj|a (**-i, -e**; *gen pl* **-i**) *f* (*okoliczności, warunki*) situation
szach|y (**-ów**) *pl* **1** (*rodzaj gry*) chess **2** (*szachownica i komplet figur*) chess set
szacun|ek (**-ku**; *inst sg* **-kiem**) *m* **1** (*o poważaniu*) respect **2** (*określenie wartości*) assessment
sza|fa (**-fy, -fy**; *dat & loc sg* **-fie**) *f* **1** (*na odzież*) wardrobe **2** (*na dokumentację*) cabinet
szaf|ka (**-ki, -ki**; *dat & loc sg* **-ce**; *gen pl* **-ek**) *f* cabinet
szale|niec (**-ńca, -ńcy**) *m* (*wariat*) madman
szaleńst|wo (**-wa, -wa**; *loc sg* **-wie**) *nt* **1** (*szalony akt*) madness **2** (*ogólne zachowanie*) frenzy
szali|k (**-ka, -ki**; *inst sg* **-kiem**) *m* (*dodatek do ubrania*) scarf
szalony *adj* **1** (*osoba*) mad **2** (*plan, czyn*) crazy **3** (*o życiu, tańcu*) mad
szampa|n (**-na, -ny**; *loc sg* **-nie**) *m* (*Kulin*) champagne
szampo|n (**-nu, -ny**; *loc sg* **-nie**) *m* (*do włosów*) shampoo
szan|ować (**-uję, -ujesz**) *vt* **1** (*ludzi*) to respect **2** (*ubranie, meble, książki*) to take care of; **~ się** *vr* **1** (*mieć godność własną*) to have self-respect **2** (*poważać się nawzajem*) to respect one another
szanowny *adj* (*drogi*) honourable (*Brit*), honorable (*US*); **~ Panie!/ Szanowna Pani!** (*list*) dear Sir/ Madam,; **szanowni Państwo!** Ladies and Gentlemen!
szan|sa (**-sy, -se**; *dat & loc sg* **-sie**) *f* (*okazja*) chance
szantaż (**-u**) *m* (*wymuszenie*) blackmail
szantaż|ować (**-uję, -ujesz**) *vt* (*wymuszać*): **~ kogoś czymś** to blackmail sb with sth
szarlot|ka (**-ki, -ki**; *dat & loc sg* **-ce**; *gen pl* **-ek**) *f* (*ciasto*) apple pie
szary *adj* **1** (*o kolorze*) grey (*Brit*), gray (*US*) **2** (*o dniu, pogodzie*) gloomy **3** (*o papierze*) brown **4** (*o życiu*) ordinary
szaszły|k (**-ka, -ki**; *inst sg* **-kiem**) *m* (*Kulin*) shish kebab
szata|n (**-na, -ny** *lub* **-ni**; *loc sg* **-nie**) *m* **1** (*w religii*) satan **2** (*pot: człowiek zły, niesforny, podstępny*) devil **3** (*człowiek ruchliwy*) ball of fire
szat|nia (**-ni, -nie**; *gen pl* **-ni**) *f* **1** (*na basenie*) changing room **2** (*w restauracji*) cloakroom
szczególnie *adv* **1** (*specjalnie*) especially **2** (*w dziwaczny sposób*) peculiarly
szczegó|ł (**-łu, -ły**; *loc sg* **-le**) *m* (*drobny element*) detail; **szczegóły** *pl* (*wszystkie (małe) elementy*) details
szczegółowo *adv* (*dokładnie*) in detail
szczegółowy *adj* (*dokładny*) detailed
szczepion|ka (**-ki, -ki**; *dat & loc sg* **-ce**; *gen pl* **-ek**) *f* (*Med*) vaccine
szczery *adj* **1** (*osoba, śmiech, serce*) sincere **2** (*radość, żal*) genuine **3** (*o prawdzie*) plain **4** (*o złocie*) pure
szczerze *adv* (*prawdziwie*) sincerely; **~ mówiąc** frankly speaking
szczęści|e (**-a**) *nt* **1** (*powodzenie*) (good) luck **2** (*radość, zadowolenie*) happiness; **na ~** luckily; **mieć ~** to be lucky; **nie mieć szczęścia** to be unlucky
szczęśliwy *adj* **1** (*przynoszący powodzenie*) lucky **2** (*radosny*) happy; **szczęśliwego Nowego Roku!** Happy New Year!; **szczęśliwej podróży!** have a good trip!
szczotecz|ka (**-ki, -ki**; *dat & loc sg* **-ce**; *gen pl* **-ek**) *f* (*przedmiot*) brush; **~ do zębów** toothbrush
szczot|ka (**-ki, -ki**; *dat sg* **-ce**; *gen pl* **-ek**) *f* (*przedmiot*) brush; **~ do włosów** hairbrush; **~ do butów** shoebrush; **~ do zamiatania** broom
szczupły *adj* **1** (*niegruby*) slim **2** (*nieliczny, wątły*) slender
szczy|t (**-tu, -ty**; *loc sg* **-cie**) *m* **1** (*górski*) summit **2** (*u drzewa, schodów*) top **3** (*szczęścia, powodzenia, choroby, głupoty*) peak **4** (*Pol*) summit

5 (*intensywne obciążenie*) peak **6** (*u stołu*) head; **spotkanie na szczycie** summit; **godziny ~u** peak times

szedł *itd. vb zob.* **iść**

sze|f (**-fa, -fowie**; *loc sg* **-fie**) *m* (*zwierzchnik*) boss; **~ rządu** prime minister; **~ kuchni** chef

szep|tać (**-czę, -czesz**; *pf* **-nąć**) *vt* (*mówić bardzo cicho*) to whisper

szermier|ka (**-ki**; *dat & loc sg* **-ce**) *f* (*Sport*) fencing

szer|oki *adj* **1** (*rzeka, plaża, spódnica*) wide **2** (*droga, ruch, uśmiech*) broad **3** (*przen: pytanie, perspektywy, skala*) broad **4** (*publika, krąg odbiorców*) wide; **~ na 2 metry** 2 m wide

sze|roko *adv* **1** (*rozlegle na boki*) widely **2** (*rozlegle naokoło*) broadly **3** (*mówić, opisywać*) at length; **otworzyć** (*pf*) **~ usta** to open one's mouth wide

szerokoś|ć (**-ci, -ci**; *gen pl* **-ci**) *f* **1** (*wymiar materiału*) width **2** (*Geo*): **~ geograficzna** latitude; **mieć siedem metrów szerokości** to be 7 m wide

szesnasty *num decl like adj* sixteenth; **strona szesnasta** page sixteen; **godzina szesnasta** 4 o'clock

szesnaście *num* sixteen

sześć *num* six

sześćdziesiąt *num* sixty

sześćset *num* six hundred

szewc (**-a, -y**) *m* (*rzemieślnik*) cobbler

szklan|ka (**-ki, -ki**; *dat & loc sg* **-ce**; *gen pl* **-ek**) *f* **1** (*szklane naczynie*) glass **2** (*mąki, mleka*) ≈ cup

szklany *adj* (*ze szkła*) glass

sz|kło (**-kła**; *loc sg* **-kle**) *nt* **1** (*materiał*) glass **2** (*nom pl* **-kła**; *gen pl* **-kieł**) (*szklane produkty*) glass(ware); **szkła** *pl* (*okulary*) glasses; **szkła kontaktowe** contact lenses

Szkocj|a (**-i**) *f* Scotland

szkocki *adj* Scottish

szk|oda (**-ody, -ody**; *dat sg* **-odzie**; *gen pl* **-ód**) *f* (*strata materialna*) damage ▷ *adv* (*żal, przykro*) pity; **~, że...** it's a pity that...; **~!** what a pity!

szkodliwy *adj* (*niszczący*) harmful

szko|dzić (**-dzę, -dzisz**) *vi* (*zdrowiu, reputacji*): **~ komuś/czemuś** to be bad for sb/sth; **palenie szkodzi** smoking is bad for you; **nic nie szkodzi!** never mind!

szk|olić (**-olę, -olisz**; *imp* **-ol** *lub* **-ól**; *pf* **wy-**) *vt* (*kształcić, ćwiczyć*) to train

szkolnict|wo (**-wa**; *loc sg* **-wie**) *nt* (*wyższe, zawodowe*) education

szkolny *adj* (*rok, mundurek, boisko*) school

szk|oła (**-oły, -oły**; *dat & loc sg* **-ole**; *gen pl* **-ół**) *f* (*instytucja*) school; **~ podstawowa** primary (*Brit*) *lub* elementary (*US*) school; **~ średnia** secondary (*Brit*) *lub* high (*US*) school; **chodzić do szkoły** to go to school; **być w szkole** to be at school

Szko|t (**-ta, -ci**; *loc sg* **-cie**) *m* Scotsman

Szkot|ka (**-ki, -ki**; *dat sg* **-ce**; *gen pl* **-ek**) *f* Scotswoman

szlach|ta (**-ty**; *dat & loc sg* **-cie**) *f* (*stan społeczny*) nobility

szlafro|k (**-ka, -ki**; *inst sg* **-kiem**) *m* (*ubranie*) dressing gown (*Brit*), (bath) robe (*US*)

szmin|ka (**-ki, -ki**; *dat & loc sg* **-ce**; *gen pl* **-ek**) *f* (*pomadka: też:* **~ do ust**) lipstick

sznur|ek (**-ka, -ki**; *inst sg* **-kiem**) *m* (*cienki sznur*) string

szo|k (**-ku**; *inst sg* **-kiem**) *m* (*silny wstrząs emocjonalny*) shock

szokujący *adj* (*wywołujący silny wstrząs*) shocking

szósty *num decl like adj* sixth; **strona szósta** page six

szpie|g (**-ga, -dzy**; *inst sg* **-giem**) *m* (*tajny agent*) spy

szpital (**-a, -e**; *gen pl* **-i**) *m* (*zakład lecznictwa*) hospital; **być** *lub* **leżeć w ~u** to be in (the (*US*)) hospital; **zabrać** (*pf*) **kogoś do ~a** to take sb to (the (*US*)) hospital

sztuczny *adj* (*nienaturalny*) artificial; **sztuczne ognie** fireworks

sztućc|e (**-ów**) *pl* (*przybory do jedzenia*) cutlery

sztu|ka (**-ki, -ki**; *dat & loc sg* **-ce**) *f* **1** (*działalność artystyczna i jej wytwory, talent*) art **2** (*teatralna*) play **3** (*pojedynczy przedmiot*) piece; **~ ludowa** folk art; **sztuki piękne** the fine arts; **po dwa złote ~** *lub* **za sztukę** 2 zloty each

sztywny *adj* **1** (*o kołnierzyku, części ciała, ruchu*) stiff **2** (*o konstrukcji,* *przepisach*) rigid **3** (*o cenach*) fixed **4** (*o wyglądzie*) prim

szufla|da (**-dy, -dy**; *dat & loc sg* **-dzie**) *f* (*wysuwana część mebla*) drawer

szuk|ać (**-am, -asz**; *pf* **po-**) *vt +gen* **1** (*mieszkania, zatrudnienia, przestępcy, możliwości*) to look for **2** (*rozwiązania, pomocy, szczęścia*) to seek **3** (*wyrazu w słowniku*) to look up

szwa|gier (**-gra, -growie**; *loc sg* **-grze**) *m* (*członek rodziny*) brother-in-law

szwagier|ka (**-ki, -ki**; *dat & loc sg* **-ce**; *gen pl* **-ek**) *f* (*członek rodziny*) sister-in-law

Szwajcari|a (**-i**) *f* Switzerland

szwajcarski *adj* Swiss

Szwecj|a (**-i**) *f* Sweden

szwedzki *adj* Swedish

szy|ba (**-by, -by**; *dat & loc sg* **-bie**) *f* **1** (*o szklanej tafli*) (window) pane **2** (*o oknie*) window; **przednia ~** (*w samochodzie*) windscreen (*Brit*), windshield (*US*)

szyb|ki *adj* (*pociąg, samochód*) fast; (*odpowiedź, reakcja*) quick; **bar ~ej obsługi** fast-food restaurant

szyb|ko *adv* **1** (*jeździć, chodzić*) fast **2** (*zareagować, odpowiedzieć*) quickly; **~!** hurry up!

szy|ć (**-ję, -jesz**) *vt* **1** (*pf* **u-**) (*nowe ubranie*) to sew **2** (*pf* **z-**) (*rozprucie*) to stitch **3** (*pf* **z-**) (*ranę*) to suture; **~ na maszynie** to sew (*on a sewing machine*)

szy|ja (**-i, -je**; *dat & loc sg* **-i**) *f* (*Anat*) neck

szyn|ka (**-ki, -ki**; *dat & loc sg* **-ce**; *gen pl* **-ek**) *f* (*wędlina*) ham

Ś

ścia|na (**-ny, -ny**; *dat & loc sg* **-nie**) *f* (*część pokoju*) wall

ściąć (**zetnę, zetniesz**; *imp* **zetnij**) *vb pf od* **ścinać**

ściel|ić (**-ę, -isz**; *imp* **ściel**) *vt*: **~ łóżko** to make one's bed

ścin|ać (**-am, -asz**; *imp* **-aj**) *vt* **1** (*drzewo*) to chop down **2** (*włosy*) to cut; **~ się** *vr* **1** (*o mleku*) to turn **2** (*o krwi*) to curdle **3** (*o sosie*) to curdle

śla|d (**-du, -dy**; *loc sg* **-dzie**) *m* **1** (*stóp*) footprint **2** (*zwierza*) track **3** (*kopyt*) hoofprint; (*zaniepokojenia, radości*) trace

Śląs|k (**-ka**; *inst sg* **-kiem**) *m* (*Geo*) Silesia

śle|dzić (**-dzę, -dzisz**; *imp* **-dź**) *vt* **1** (*obserwować, szpiegować, Komput*) to follow **2** (*ruch armii*) to monitor **3** (*radarem*) to track

śledzt|wo (**-wa, -wa**; *loc sg* **-wie**) *nt* (*policyjne*) investigation

śle|dź (**-dzia, -dzie**; *gen pl* **-dzi**) *m* **1** (*ryba*) herring **2** (*przy namiocie*) tent peg

ślepy *adj* (*niewidzący*) blind; **ślepa ulica** dead end

ślisko *adv* (*o gładkiej powierzchni*): **na drogach jest ~** the roads are slippery

śliw|ka (**-ki, -ki**; *dat & loc sg* **-ce**; *gen pl* **-ek**) *f* **1** (*o owocu*) plum **2** (*o drzewie*) plum tree; **suszona ~** prune

ślu|b (**-bu, -by**; *loc sg* **-bie**) *m* (*zawarcie małżeństwa*) marriage, wedding; **~ kościelny** church wedding; **~ cywilny** civil marriage ceremony; **brać** (**wziąć** *pf*) ~ to get married

śmiać się (**śmieję, śmiejesz**; *pf* **za-**) *vr* (*głośno, do rozpuku*) to laugh; ~ **z kogoś/czegoś** to laugh at sb/sth

śmiały *adj* (*odważny*) bold

śmieć[1] (**śmiecia, śmieci** *lub* **śmiecie**) *m* (*o odpadku*) piece of litter; **śmieci** *pl* **1** (*do wyrzucenia*) rubbish *sg*, garbage *sg* (*US*) **2** (*na podwórku, skwerze*) litter *sg*

śmieć[2] (**śmiem, śmiesz**; *3 pl* **śmią** *lub* **śmieją**; *imp* **śmiej**) *vi* (*mieć czelność; odwagę*) to dare; **jak on śmie!** how dare he!

śmier|ć (**-ci**) *f* (*zgon*) death; **ponieść** (*pf*) ~ to die; **kara śmierci** the death penalty

śmierdzący *adj* (*cuchnący*) stinking

śmier|dzieć (**-dzę, -dzisz**; *imp* **-dź**) *vi* (*cuchnąć*): ~ **czymś** to stink of sth

śmiertelny *adj* **1** (*o dawce*) lethal **2** (*o truciźnie, grzybie*) deadly **3** (*o bladości, ciszy*) deathly **4** (*o chorobie*) terminal **5** (*stworzenie, cios, wróg*) mortal **6** (*zranienie*) fatal; **wypadek** ~ fatal accident; **grzech** ~ mortal sin

śmiesznie *adv* (*mówić, opowiadać*) in a comical manner; ~ **tani** ridiculously cheap

śmieszny *adj* **1** (*rozweselający*) funny **2** (*żałosny*) ridiculous

śmiesz|yć (**-ę, -ysz**; *pf* **rozśmieszyć**) *vt* (*rozweselać*) to amuse

śmietan|ka (**-ki**; *dat & loc sg* **-ce**; *gen pl* **-ek**) *f* (*Kulin*) cream

śmietni|k (**-ka, -ki**; *inst sg* **-kiem**) *m* **1** (*miejsce z pojemnikami na śmieci*) the bins *pl* **2** (*kosz na śmieci*) skip (*Brit*), Dumpster® (*US*)

ŚMIGUS-DYNGUS

Easter Monday, or **Śmigus-dyngus**, is also known as "wet Monday". Traditionally, young bachelors show their interest in girls by throwing water over them. Children often also join in. Some people are content with a symbolic sprinkling while others unscrupulously splash buckets of water over passers-by!

śniada|nie (**-nia, -nia**; *gen pl* **-ń**) *nt* (*posiłek*) breakfast; **jeść** ~ to have breakfast; **drugie** ~ (*o posiłku*) midmorning snack; (*kanapki*) packed lunch (*Brit*), box *lub* bag lunch (*US*)

śnie *n zob.* **sen**

śnie|g (**-gu, -gi**; *inst sg* **-giem**) *m* (*opady*) snow; **pada** ~ it's snowing; ~ **z deszczem** sleet

śpiesz|yć, spiesz|yć (**-ę, -ysz**; *pf* **po-**) *vi* (*być skorym do czegoś*): ~ **komuś z pomocą** to rush to help sb; ~ **się** *vr* **1** (*o osobie*) to (be in a) hurry **2** (*o zegarku*) to be fast; **śpieszy mi się** I'm in a hurry

śpiew|ać (**-am, -asz**; *pf* **za-**) *vt, vi* (*piosenkę*) to sing

śpiw|ór (**-ora, -ory**; *loc sg* **-orze**) *m* (*turystyczna pościel*) sleeping bag

średni *adj* **1** (*zwykły*) average **2** (*o rozmiarze*) medium; **~ego wzrostu** of average height; **w ~m wieku** middle-aged; **szkoła ~a** secondary (*Brit*) *lub* high (*US*) school

średniowiecz|e (**-a**) *nt* (*okres historii*) the Middle Ages

średniozaawansowany *adj* (*poziom*) intermediate

śr|oda (**-ody, -ody**; *dat & loc sg* **-odzie**; *gen pl* **-ód**) *f* (*dzień tygodnia*) Wednesday; ~ **popielcowa** Ash Wednesday

środ|ek (**-ka, -ki**; *inst sg* **-kiem**) *m* **1** (*miejsce w centrum*) middle **2** (*wewnętrzna część pomieszczenia*) inside **3** (*ułatwienie*) means **4** (*metoda*) measure **5** (*o preparacie chemicznym*) agent **6** (*przeciwbólowy, nasenny*) medication **7** (*zaradczy*) remedy; **środki** *pl* (*fundusze*) means *pl*; **w środku** (*w centralnym miejscu*) in the middle; **poprosić** (*pf*) **kogoś do środka** to ask sb in; ~ **transportu** means of transport (*Brit*) *lub* transportation (*US*)

środkowoeuropejski *adj* (*Geo*) Central European

środkowy *adj* (*centralny*) central

śródmieś|cie (**-cia, -cia**; *gen pl* **-ci**) *nt* (*centrum miasta*) city centre (*Brit*), downtown (*US*)

śródziemnomorski *adj* (*Geo*) Mediterranean

śru|ba (**-by, -by**; *dat & loc sg* **-bie**) *f* **1** (*do łączenia elementów*) screw **2** (*wkręt*) bolt

św. *abbr* (= *święty, święta*) St

świadect|wo (**-wa, -wa**; *loc sg* **-wie**) *nt* **1** (*urodzenia, zgonu*) certificate **2** (*udowodnienie*) testimony; **~ szkolne** report card; **~ dojrzałości** ≈ GCSE (*Brit*), ≈ High School Diploma (*US*)

świad|ek (**-ka, -kowie**; *inst sg* **-kiem**) *m* witness; **być świadkiem czegoś** to witness sth

świa|t (**-ta, -ty**; *loc sg* **świecie**) *m* (*planeta, środowisko*) world; **na całym świecie** all over the world

świat|ło (**-ła, -ła**; *loc sg* **świetle**; *gen pl* **-eł**) *nt* (*słoneczne, elektryczne*) light; **światła** *pl* (*pot: sygnalizacja świetlna*) traffic lights

światopoglą|d (**-du, -dy**; *loc sg* **-dzie**) *m* (*pogląd na świat i życie*) outlook

świąteczny *adj* **1** (*uroczysty, podniosły*) festive **2** (*związany z Bożym Narodzeniem*) Christmas **3** (*związany z Wielkanocą*) Easter

świąty|nia (**-ni, -nie**; *dat & loc sg* **-ni**; *gen pl* **-ń**) *f* (*kościół*) temple

świec|a (**-y, -e**; *dat & loc sg* **-y**) *f* **1** (*z wosku*) candle **2** (*w silniku*): **~ zapłonowa** spark plug

świe|cić (**-cę, -cisz**; *imp* **-ć**) *vi* **1** (*być źródłem światła: o żarówce, słońcu*) to shine **2** (*błyszczeć: o cerze*) to glow; **~ się** *vr* **1** (*o żarówce*) to be on **2** (*błyszczeć*) to shine

świecz|ka (**-ki, -ki**; *dat & loc sg* **-ce**; *gen pl* **-ek**) *f* (*z wosku*) candle

świeży *adj* (*owoce, warzywa, śnieg, pościel*) fresh; **na ~m powietrzu** in the fresh air

świę|to (**-ta, -ta**; *loc sg* **-cie**; *gen pl* **świąt**) *nt* (*dzień wolny*) holiday; **~ państwowe/kościelne** national/religious holiday; **święta** *pl*: **święta Bożego Narodzenia** Christmas; **Święta Wielkanocne** Easter; **Wesołych Świąt!** (*Bożego Narodzenia*) Merry Christmas!

ŚWIĘTO ODZYSKANIA NIEPODLEGŁOŚCI 11 LISTOPADA

Święto Odzyskania Niepodległości 11 Listopada is the most important Polish national holiday. It is celebrated on 11 November, the date Poland regained its independence in 1918, following 123 years of partitions between Russia, Austro-Hungary and Prussia.

święty *adj* **1** (*będący przedmiotem kultu religijnego*) holy **2** (*w połączeniu z imieniem*) saint **3** (*bardzo dobry, pokorny, życzliwy*) saintly **4** (*o prawie*) sacred ▷ *m decl like adj* (*osoba*) saint; **Pismo Święte** the Holy Scriptures; **Duch Ś~** Holy Spirit; **Ś~ Mikołaj** Father Christmas (*Brit*), Santa (Claus); **świętej pamięci pan Kowalski** the late Mr Kowalski

świ|nia (**-ni, -nie**; *gen pl* **-ń**) *f* **1** (*zwierzę*) pig **2** (*pot!: o osobie*) swine (*pot*)

świ|t (**-tu, -ty**; *loc sg* **-cie**) *m* (*początek dnia*) dawn

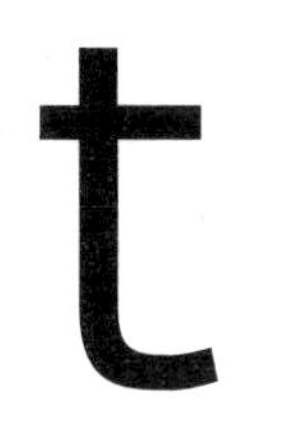

ta *pron fem* this; *od* **ten**
tabel|a (**-i, -e**; *dat sg & loc sg* **-i**) *f* (*rubryka*) table
tabel|ka (**-ki, -ki**; *dat sg & loc sg* **-ce**; *gen pl* **-ek**) *f dimin od* **tabela**
tablet (**-u, -y**; *dat sg* **-owi**) *m* (*Komput*) tablet
table|t (**-tu, -ty**; *loc sg* **-cie**) *m* touchpad
tablet|ka (**-ki, -ki**; *dat sg & loc sg* **-ce**; *gen pl* **-ek**) *f* tablet
tablic|a (**-y, -e**) *f* **1** (*w szkole*) blackboard **2** (*plansza*) chart; **~ z ogłoszeniami** noticeboard (*Brit*), bulletin board (*US*); **tablice rejestracyjne** number plates (*Brit*), license plates (*US*)
tabu *nt inv* taboo
tacy *pron decl like adj zob.* **taki**
tajemnic|a (**-y, -e**) *f* secret; **~ państwowa** state secret; **~ służbowa** confidential information; **tajemnice natury** mysteries of nature
tajemniczy *adj* (*zagadkowy*) mysterious; **zniknął w ~ sposób** he disappeared mysteriously
Tajlandi|a (**-i**) *f* Thailand
tajny *adj* **1** (*sekretny*) secret **2** (*ścisłego zarachowania*) classified **3** (*nielegalny*) underground; **ściśle tajne informacje** top secret information
Tajwa|n (**-nu**; *loc sg* **-nie**) *f* Taiwan

SŁOWO KLUCZOWE

tak *pron* (*twierdzący*) yes; **tak jest!** (*Wojsk: pot*) yes, sir!
▷ *adv* **1** (*w taki sposób*): **nie obrażaj się tak** don't take offence (*Brit*) *lub* offense (*US*) like that; **zrobił to tak, jak prosiliśmy** he did it as we requested; **zrobił to tak, jak uważał** he did it just as he liked; **i tak dalej** and so on; **tak zwany pomocnik** so-called assistant; **tak czy owak zrobimy to po swojemu** (*pot*) we'll do it our own way, in any case
2 (*nasilenie*): **tak mocno/mocny (, że...)** so hard/strong (that...); **tak sobie** (*pot*) so-so

SŁOWO KLUCZOWE

taki *pron decl like adj* **1** (*określonego rodzaju*) such; **taki sam jak ja** the same as me; **taki jak my** like us; **jest taki, jak prosiłeś** it's just what you asked for; **on już taki jest, że lubi pracować całe noce** that's the way he is, he likes to work all through the night; **o takiej a takiej godzinie** (*pot*) at such-and-such a time; **w takim razie pojedziemy razem** in that case, we'll go together
2 (*w połączeniach zdaniowych*): **był taki deszcz, że zalało piwnicę** it was so wet that our basement flooded
3 (*wzmacniająco*): **on jest taki stary** he is so old; **taki szanowany człowiek** such a well-respected man; **taka brzydka pogoda** such rotten weather

taksów|ka (**-ki, -ki**; *dat sg & loc sg* **-ce**; *gen pl* **-ek**) *f* (*osobowa*) taxi; **~ bagażowa** removal van
taksówkarz (**-a, -e**; *gen pl* **-y**) *m* (*kierowca taksówki*) taxi driver
także *adv* as well
talen|t (**-tu, -ty**; *loc sg* **-cie**) *m* talent
talerz (**-a, -e**; *gen pl* **-y**) *m* **1** plate **2** (*głęboki*) soup plate **3** (*płytki*) plate; **latający ~** (*UFO*) flying saucer
tam *adv* there; **tu i ~** here and there
tamci *pron* those
Tami|za (**-zy**; *dat sg & loc sg* **-zie**) *f* the Thames
tampo|n (**-nu, -ny**; *loc sg* **-nie**) *m* (*wata tamująca krew*) tampon
tamta *pron* that

tamte *pron* those
tamten *pron* that
tamtędy *adv* (down) that way; **pójdź ~** go that way
tancerz (**-a, -e**; *gen pl* **-y**) *m* (*zawodowiec, amator*) dancer
tani *adj* (*niedrogi*) cheap
ta|niec (**-ńca, -ńce**) *m* **1** (*czynność*) dancing **2** (*układ choreograficzny*) dance; **~ towarzyski** ballroom dancing
tanio *adv*: **kupuj ~, sprzedaj drogo** buy cheap, sell dear
tańcz|yć (**-ę, -ysz**; *pf* **za-**) *vt, vi* to dance; **~ twista/rumbę** to do the twist/the rumba
tańszy *itd. adj comp od* **tani**
tar|g (**-gu, -gi**; *inst sg* **-giem**) *m* (*plac handlowy*) market; **targi** *pl* (trade) fair; **dobił z nim ~u** he struck a bargain with him
ta|ta, ta|to (**-ty**; *dat sg & loc sg* **-cie**) *m decl like f* (*ojciec, teść*) dad
tatarski *adj* (*kulinaria*): **sos/befsztyk ~** tartare sauce/steak tartare
ta|to (**-ty, -towie**; *loc sg* **-cie**) *m* = **tata**
Tatr|y (-) *pl* the Tatra Mountains *pl*
tatuaż (**-u, -e**; *gen pl* **-y**) *m* tattoo
tą *pron instr od* **ta**
tchórz (**-a, -e**; *gen pl* **-y**) *m* **1** (*człowiek*) coward **2** (*zwierzę*) polecat; **widać, że ~ go obleciał** (*pot*) he must have got cold feet
te *pron* these; **te okna/koty** these windows/cats
teat|r (**-ru, -ry**; *loc sg* **-rze**) *m* theatre (*Brit*), theater (*US*); **~ lalkowy** puppet theatre
tecz|ka (**-ki, -ki**; *dat sg & loc sg* **-ce**; *gen pl* **-ek**) *f* **1** (*skórzana*) briefcase **2** (*papierowa*) folder
tego *pron gen, acc od* **ten, to**
tegoroczny *adj* (*plan, zima*) this year's
tej *pron gen, dat od* **ta**
tek|st (**-stu, -sty**; *loc sg* **-ście**) *m* (*książki, artykułu*) text; **znam na pamięć ~y piosenek** I know the lyrics by heart
tel. *abbr* (= *telefon*) tel.
telefo|n (**-nu, -ny**; *loc sg* **-nie**) *m* **1** (*rzecz*) telephone, phone **2** (*numer*) phone number **3** (*rozmowa*) phone call; **dał mi swój ~ domowy** he gave me his home number; **rozmawiał przez ~** he talked on the phone; **rozmawiał z nią przez ~** he talked to her on the phone; **~ komórkowy** mobile phone (*Brit*), cellphone (*US*); **~ zaufania działa już od 5 lat** the telephone helpline has been running for 5 years; **odbierać** (**odebrać** *pf*) **~** to answer the phone; **~ wewnętrzny** extension
telefon|ować (**-uję, -ujesz**; *pf* **za-**) *vi* (*dzwonić*) to call; **telefonował do mnie** he called me
telekomunikacj|a (**-i**) *f* (*gałąź nauki*) telecommunications
telenowel|a (**-i, -e**) *f* soap opera
telewizj|a (**-i, -e**; *gen pl* **-i**) *f* TV; **ogląda telewizję codziennie** he watches TV every day; **~ satelitarna** satellite TV; **~ kablowa** cable TV
telewizo|r (**-ra, -ry**; *loc sg* **-rze**) *m* (*urządzenie*) TV (set); **~ plazmowy** plasma screen TV
telewizyjny *adj* TV; (*program, serial*) television
tema|t (**-tu, -ty**; *loc sg* **-cie**) *m* (*myśl przewodnia*) subject
temp. *abbr* (= *temperature*) temp.
temperatu|ra (**-ry, -ry**; *dat sg & loc sg* **-rze**) *f* temperature; **~ wrzenia** boiling point; **mam temperaturę** (*w medycynie*) I've got a temperature
temu[1] *pron dat od* **ten, to**
temu[2] *adv*: **trzy lata ~** two years ago; **zdarzyło się to dawno ~** that happened a long time ago; **jak dawno ~ tam byłeś?** how long is it since you were there?; **parę miesięcy ~** a couple of months ago
ten *pron* **1** (*z rzeczownikiem*) this **2** (*bez rzeczownika*) this one **3** (*tamten*) that; **~ sam co wczoraj** the same as yesterday; **~ jest bardzo ładny** this one is very nice; **w ~ piątek** this Friday
teni|s (**-sa**; *loc sg* **-sie**) *m* (*dyscyplina sportu*) tennis
tenisi|sta (**-sty, -ści**; *dat sg & loc sg* **-ście**) *m decl like f in sg* tennis player
tenisist|ka (**-ki, -ki**; *dat sg & loc sg* **-ce**; *gen pl* **-ek**) *f* tennis player

tenisów|ki (**-ek**) *pl* (*buty sportowe*) plimsolls
teoretycznie *adv* in theory; **~ masz rację** in theory you are right
teori|a (**-i, -e**; *gen pl* **-i**) *f* theory; **~ względności** relativity theory
teraz *adv* now, nowadays
teraźniejszoś|ć (**-ci**) *f* the present
teraźniejszy *adj* (*obecny*) present, today's; **czas ~** (*w językoznawstwie*) present tense
tere|n (**-nu, -ny**; *loc sg* **-nie**) *m* **1** (*obszar*) terrain **2** (*ziemia*) land
termi|n (**-nu, -ny**; *loc sg* **-nie**) *m* **1** (*czas potrzebny do wykonania czegoś*) deadline **2** (*u lekarza*) appointment **3** (*wyrażenie*) term
terro|r (**-ru**; *loc sg* **-rze**) *m* (*strach, przemoc*) terror
terrory|sta (**-sty, -ści**; *loc sg* **-ście**) *m* *decl like f in sg* terrorist
terrorystyczny *adj* (*organizacja, zamach*) terrorist
terroryz|m (**-mu**; *loc sg* **-mie**) *m* terrorism
terroryz|ować (**-uję, -ujesz**; *pf* **s-**) *vt* (*zastraszać*) to terrorize
te|st (**-stu, -sty**; *loc sg* **-ście**) *m* test
testamen|t (**-tu, -ty**; *loc sg* **-cie**) *m* (*ostatnia wola*) will, testament; **Stary/Nowy T~** the Old/New Testament
teściow|a (**-ej, -e**) *f decl like adj* (*matka żony, matka męża*) mother-in-law
teś|ć (**-cia, -ciowie**) *m* (*ojciec żony, ojciec męża*) father-in-law; **teściowie** *pl* in-laws *pl*
też *adv* too; **on ~** him too; **ja ~ nie pójdę** I'm not going either; **to sport niebezpieczny, dlatego ~ nazywają go głupim** it is a dangerous sport, and that is why people call it stupid
tę *pron acc od* **ta**
tęcz|a (**-y, -e**) *f* rainbow
tędy *adv* this way; **idź ~** go this way
tępy *adj* **1** (*nieostry*) blunt **2** (*osoba*) dense **3** (*wzrok*) vacant **4** (*ból*) dull
tęsk|nić (**-nię, -nisz**; *impf* **-nij**; *pf* **za-**) *vi*: **~ za** *+inst* to miss; **tęsknię za ojczyzną** (*pragnąć*) I miss my own country
tęskno|ta (**-ty, -ty**; *dat sg & loc sg* **-cie**) *f* longing; **ogarnęła go ~ za domem** he longed to be home
tj. *abbr* (*= to jest*) i.e.
tkani|na (**-ny, -ny**; *dat sg & loc sg* **-nie**) *f* (*materiał*) fabric
tle|n (**-nu**; *loc sg* **-nie**) *m* oxygen
tło|k (*inst sg* **-kiem**) *m* **1** (*gen sg* **-ku**) (*tłum*) crowd **2** (*gen sg* **-ka**; *nom pl* **-ki**) (*w technologii*) piston
tłu|m (**-mu, -my**; *loc sg* **-mie**) *m* (*dużo ludzi*) crowd
tłumacz (**-a, -e**; *gen pl* **-y**) *m* **1** (*tekstów pisanych*) translator **2** (*ustny*) interpreter; **~ przysięgły** certified translator
tłumacze|nie (**-nia**) *nt* translation
tłumacz|yć (**-ę, -ysz**) *vt* (*pf* **wy-**) **1** (*wyjaśniać*) to explain **2** (*pf* **prze-**) (*przekładać: tekst*) to translate **3** (*rozmowę*) to interpret; **~ się** (*pf* **wy-**) *vr* (*usprawiedliwiać się*) to explain o.s.
tłusty *adj* **1** (*potrawa*) fatty **2** (*ubranie*) greasy **3** (*człowiek*) fat **4** (*druk, czcionka*) bold; **tłuste mleko** full-cream milk; **~ czwartek** *the last Thursday before Lent*

TŁUSTY CZWARTEK

Tłusty czwartek is the last Thursday before Lent, when traditionally a large number of doughnuts and **faworki** are consumed.

tłuszcz (**-u, -e**) *m* fat; **~e dzielimy na ~e roślinne i zwierzęce** we distinguish fats as vegetable and animal fats

 **SŁOWO KLUCZOWE**

to *pron* **1** (*zaimek wskazujący*) this; **to okno** this window
2 (*w funkcji podmiotu*): **to prawda** it's the truth; **to jest kot** this *lub* it is a cat; **co/kto to jest?** what's/who's this?; **czy to ona?** is that her?
3 (*w funkcji ekspresywnej*): **a to chuligan!** what a lout!
4: **jak to?** how so?, how come?; **no to**

co z tego? so what of it?; **otóż to!** exactly!
▷ *conj*: **jeśli chcesz, to przyjedź** come if you want; **nie chcesz, to nie** if you don't want to, you don't want to
▷ *inv* (*w funkcji łącznika*): **czas to pieniądz** time is money

toale|ta (**-ty, -ty**; *dat sg & loc sg* **-cie**) *f* **1** (*ubikacja*) toilet, rest room (*US*) **2** (*eleganckie ubranie damskie*) gown; **~ damska/męska** the ladies'/gents' (toilet) (*Brit*), women's/men's room (*US*)
toaletowy *adj* (*papier, przybory*) toilet
toa|st (**-stu, -sty**; *loc sg* **-ście**) *m* toast; **wzniósł ~ za zdrowie gospodarzy** he drank a toast to his host's health
tobie *pron zob.* **ty**
tolerancj|a (**-i**) *f* tolerance
tolerancyjny *adj* (*człowiek, stosunek*) tolerant
toler|ować (**-uję, -ujesz**) *vt* (*szanować poglądy*) to tolerate
to|pić (**-pię, -pisz**) *vt* **1** (*pf* **u-**) (*pozbawiać życia*) to drown **2** (*pf* **s-**) (*roztapiać*) to melt; **~ się** *vr* **1** (*pf* **u-**) (*osoba, zwierzę*) to drown **2** (*pf* **s-**) (*masło*) to melt
tor|ba (**-by, -by**; *dat sg & loc sg* **-bie**; *gen pl* **-eb**) *f* **1** bag **2** (*na podróż*) holdall
toreb|ka (**-ki, -ki**; *dat sg & loc sg* **-ce**; *gen pl* **-ek**) *f* **1** (*z papieru*) (paper) bag **2** (*damska*) handbag, purse (*US*)
tor|t (**-tu, -ty**; *loc sg* **-cie**) *m* cake (*Brit*), layer cake (*US*)
to|st (**-stu, -sty**; *loc sg* **-ście**) *m* slice of toast
towa|r (**-ru, -ry**; *loc sg* **-rze**) *m* **1** (*produkt*) commodity **2** (*dziewczyna*: *pot!*) babe; **~y konsumpcyjne** consumer goods
towarowy *adj*: **pociąg ~** goods (*Brit*) *lub* freight (*US*) train; **statek ~** cargo vessel; **bon ~** voucher
towarzyski *adj* **1** (*osoba*) sociable **2** (*impreza, zebranie*) social; **rozmowa towarzyska** small talk; **zaczęła pojawiać się w kronikach ~ch** she began to feature in the gossip columns
towarzyst|wo (**-wa**; *loc sg* **-wie**; *nom pl* **-wa**) *nt* **1** (*przebywanie*) company **2** (*grono przyjaciół*) company **3** (*organizacja*) society
towarzysz|yć (**-ę, -ysz**) *vi*: **~** *+dat* to accompany
tożsamoś|ć (**-ci**) *f* (*samoświadomość*) identity; **dowód tożsamości** ID
tra|cić (**-cę, -cisz**; *imp* **-ć**) *vt* **1** (*pf* **s-** *lub* **u-**) (*nie mieć*) to lose **2** (*pf* **s-**) (*marnować*: *okazję*) to miss **3** (*czas, środki finansowe*) to waste ▷ *vi* (*pf* **s-**) (*znaleźć się w sytuacji niekorzystnej*) to lose (out); **dokument traci ważność we wrześniu** the document expires in September
tradycj|a (**-i, -e**; *gen pl* **-i**) *f* (*obyczaj*) tradition
tradycyjny *adj* (*występujący od dawna*) traditional
tra|fiać (**-fiam, -fiasz**; *pf* **-fić**) *vt* to hit ▷ *vi* **1** (*nie chybiać*) to hit the target **2** (*znajdować właściwą drogę*) to get there; **~ się** *vr* to come up; **nie trafił do celu** he missed his target; **trafił na ostry dyżur** he landed up in casualty; **trafiła w dziesiątkę** she hit the bull's-eye; (*przen*) she was spot-on; **na chybił trafił** (*wybierać*) at random; **trafia się okazja!** opportunity knocks!
tragedi|a (**-i, -e**; *gen pl* **-i**) *f* tragedy
tragiczny *adj* **1** tragic **2** (*pot*: *wizerunek*) awful
trakt|ować (**-uję, -ujesz**) *vt* (*pf* **po-**) to treat ▷ *vi*: **~ o czymś** (*omawiać*) to discuss sth; **traktuje go źle** he treats him badly; **książka traktuje o miłości** the book deals with love
tramwa|j (**-ju, -je**; *gen pl* **-jów** *lub* **-i**) *m* tram (*Brit*), streetcar (*US*)
transatlantycki *adj* (*lot, rejs*) transatlantic
transpor|t (**-tu, -ty**; *loc sg* **-cie**) *m* **1** (*środek lokomocji*) transport (*Brit*), transportation (*US*) **2** (*towar*) shipment; **~ publiczny** public transport
tra|sa (**-sy, -sy**; *loc sg* **-sie**) *f* **1** (*droga*) route **2** (*wycieczki*) itinerary;

~ **maratonu** the marathon route; **jest w trasie od trzech dni** he has been on the road for three days

tra|wa (**-wy, -wy**; *loc sg* **-wie**) *f* **1** (*roślina*) grass **2** (*trawnik*) lawn; **mowa-~** clap-trap

tra|wić (**-wię, -wisz**) *vt* **1** (*pf* **s-**) (*jedzenie*) to digest **2** (*pf* **s-**) (*o bólu*) to consume **3** (*pf* **wy-**) (*Tech, Druk: metal, szkło*) to etch

trawie|nie (**-nia**) *nt* **1** (*system*) digestion **2** (*Chem, Druk: płytek drukowanych*) etching

trawni|k (**-ka, -ki**; *inst sg* **-kiem**) *m* lawn

trąb|ka (**-ki, -ki**; *dat sg & loc sg* **-ce**; *gen pl* **-ek**) *f* (*instrument muzyczny*) trumpet

trend|ować (**-uję, -ujesz**) *vi* to trend (*on social media*)

trene|r (**-ra, -rzy**; *loc sg* **-rze**) *m* coach

trenin|g (**-gu, -gi**; *inst sg* **-giem**) *m* (*fizyczny, intelektualny*) training

tren|ować (**-uję, -ujesz**; *pf* **wy-**) *vt, vi* (*sportowców*) to train

tres|ować (**-uję, -ujesz**; *pf* **wy-**) *vt* (*psa*) to train

treś|ć (**-ci, -ci**; *gen pl* **-ci**) *f* **1** (*przemówienia*) content **2** (*powieści*) plot **3** (*życia*) meaning; **spis treści** (table of) contents

trochę *adv* **1** a little, a bit **2** (*przez krótki czas*) (for) a while; **nie rozumiem ani ~** I don't begin to understand; **jedz po trochu** eat a little bit

trolejbu|s (**-su, -sy**; *loc sg* **-sie**) *m* trolley bus

tros|ka (**-ki, -ki**; *dat sg & loc sg* **-ce**) *f* **1** (*zmartwienie*) worry **2** (*opieka*) concern

troskliwie *adv* with care

troskliwoś|ć (**-ci**) *f* (*dbałość*) care

troskliwy *adj* caring

troszcz|yć się (**-ę, -ysz**) *vr*: **~ o kogoś/coś** (*zajmować się*) to take care of sb/sth; (*z niepokojem*) to worry about sb/sth

trójką|t (**-ta, -ty**; *loc sg* **-cie**) *m* (*figura geometryczna*) triangle; **~ odblaskowy** *lub* **ostrzegawczy** warning triangle; **jeszcze jedna historia ~a małżeńskiego** one more case of the marital triangle

truci|zna (**-zny, -zny**; *dat sg & loc sg* **-źnie**) *f* (*substancja szkodliwa*) poison

tr|uć (**-uję, -ujesz**; *pf* **o-**) *vt* to poison

trudno *adv* hard; **~ powiedzieć** it's hard to tell; **~ mu uwierzyć, że...** he finds it hard to believe that...

trudny *adj* (*skomplikowany*) difficult

tru|p (**-pa, -py**; *loc sg* **-pie**) *m* (*nieboszczyk*) dead body

truskaw|ka (**-ki, -ki**; *dat sg & loc sg* **-ce**; *gen pl* **-ek**) *f* strawberry

trw|ać (**-am, -asz**) *vt*: **~ minutę/rok** to last (for) a minute/a year ▷ *vi* **1** to last **2** (*o dyskusji, procesie*) to go on **3** (*pf* **wy-**) (*nie poddawać się*) to persist; **trwał w bezruchu kilka chwil** he kept still for a moment or two; **~ w milczeniu** to remain silent

trwały *adj* **1** (*wytrzymały*) durable **2** (*nieprzerwany*) lasting; **trwała ondulacja** perm

try|b (**-bu, -by**; *loc sg* **-bie**) *m* **1** mode **2** (*w językoznawstwie*) mood; **tryby** *pl* (*w technologii*) gears; **prowadzi siedzący ~ życia** he leads a sedentary life

trzeba *part inv* it is necessary to; **~ mu powiedzieć prawdę** he's got to be told the truth; **~ było go posłuchać** we should have listened to him; **~ przyznać, że jest bardzo ładna** admittedly she is very pretty; **jeśli ~, pomożemy mu** if necessary we will help him; **~ wam czegoś?** do you need anything?

trzeci *num* third; **jedna ~a** one third; **po ~e** third(ly); **co ~ miesiąc** every three months

trzeźwie|ć (**-ję, -jesz**; *pf* **wy-**) *vi* **1** (*odzyskiwać przytomność*) to come round **2** (*po alkoholu*) to sober up

trzeźwy *adj* (*nie pijany*) sober

trzy *num* three

trzydzieści *num* thirty

trzym|ać (**-am, -asz**) *vt* **1** (*w ramionach*) to hold **2** (*w lodówce, w więzieniu*) to keep ▷ *vi* (*konstrukcja, materiał*) to hold; **~ się** *vr +gen* **1** (*poręczy, gałęzi*) to hold on to **2** (*wytyczonej trasy*) to follow

3 (*prawa*) to adhere to; **nie trzymaj rąk w kieszeniach** don't put your hands in your pockets; **trzymali ją w niepewności** they kept her in suspense; **~ coś (przed kimś) w sekrecie** to keep sth secret (from sb); **on zawsze trzyma jej stronę** he always takes her side; **trzymała to w tajemnicy przed mężem** she kept it a secret from her husband; **trzymajcie się razem!** stick together!; **~ się kogoś/czegoś** to hang on to sb/sth; **trzymaj się prosto!** stand up straight!

trzynasty *num* thirteenth

trzynaście *num* thirteen

trzysta *num* three hundred

tu *adv* here; **tu (mówi) Kowalska** this is Kowalska (speaking)

tul|ić (**-ę, -isz**) *vt* (*w ramionach*) to hug; **~ się** (*pf* **przy-**) *vr*: **~ się do kogoś/czegoś** (*obejmować kogoś z czułością*) to snuggle up to sb/sth

tunel (**-u, -e**; *gen pl* **-i** *lub* **-ów**) *m* tunnel

Tunezj|a (**-i**) *f* Tunisia

tuńczy|k (**-ka, -ki**; *inst sg* **-kiem**) *m* tuna (fish)

Turcj|a (**-i**) *f* Turkey

tury|sta (**-sty, -ści**; *dat sg & loc sg* **-ście**) *m decl like f in sg* tourist

turysty|ka (**-ki**; *dat sg & loc sg* **-ce**) *f* (*hobby, sektor gospodarki*) tourism

tutaj *adv* here

tuzi|n (**-na, -ny**; *loc sg* **-nie**) *m* (*dwanaście*) dozen

tuż *adv* **1** (*nieopodal*) close by **2** (*niedługo*) close on; **wakacje ~, ~** the holidays are almost here; **sklep jest ~ za rogiem** the shop is just round the corner

TVP *abbr* (= *Telewizja Polska*) Polish Television

twardy *adj* **1** (*mebel*) hard **2** (*kawałek mięsa*) tough **3** (*zasady moralne*) harsh **4** (*przen: nieprzyjemny*) stern

twarz (**-y, -e**; *gen pl* **-y**) *f* face; **był zwrócony ~ą do mnie** he had his face turned towards me; **jest ci do ~y w tej sukience** this dress suits you; **nie jest ci do ~y w tym stroju** this outfit doesn't flatter you

twarzowy *adj* **1** (*strój*) becoming **2** (*nerw*) facial

tweet|ować (**-uję, -ujesz**) *vi* to tweet

twier|dzić (**-dzę, -dzisz**; *impf* **-dź**; *pf* **s-**) *vi* (*stanowczo, jednoznacznie*) to claim

twoja *itd. pron zob.* **twój**

tworz|yć (**-ę, -ysz**; *impf* **twórz**) *vt* **1** (*pf* **s-**) (*dzieło sztuki*) to create **2** (*pf* **u-** *lub* **s-**) (*gabinet polityczny*) to form **3** (*pf* **s-**) (*muzykę*) to produce **4** (*pf* **u-**) (*stanowić*) to form; **~ się** *vr* **1** (*powstawać*) to be formed **2** (*formować się*) to form; **tworzyły się podziemne organizacje wojskowe** underground military organizations were formed

twój *possessive pron* **1** (*przed rzeczownikiem*) your **2** (*bez rzeczownika*) yours; **czy to są twoje rzeczy?** are these your things?; **czy te rzeczy są twoje?** are these things yours?

twórc|a (**-y, -y**) *m decl like f in sg* **1** (*pisarz*) author **2** (*muzyk, aktor*) artist

ty *pron* you; **jestem z nim na „ty"** I am on first-name terms with him

tych *pron gen, loc od* **ci, te**

tyć (**tyję, tyjesz**; *pf* **u-**) *vi* (*przybierać na wadze*) to put on weight

ty|dzień (**-godnia, -godnie**; *gen pl* **-godni**) *m* week; **pływa co ~** he goes swimming every week; **przyjdzie za ~** she'll come in a week's time; **w przyszłym/zeszłym tygodniu** next/last week; **Wielki T~** Holy Week

tygodni|k (**-ka, -ki**; *inst sg* **-kiem**) *m* weekly

tygodniowo *adv* (*raz na tydzień*) weekly

tygodniowy *adj* **1** (*trwający tydzień*) week's **2** (*pensja*) weekly

tygry|s (**-sa, -sy**; *loc sg* **-sie**) *m* tiger

tyle *pron* **1** (*z rzeczownikiem: rzeczy, danych*) so many **2** (*z rzeczownikiem: nienawiści, wody*) so much **3** (*bez rzeczownika*) this many, this much; **straciłem z tobą ~ czasu** I wasted so much time with you; **tylu uczniów/zawodników** so many pupils/contestants; **mam ~ kłopotów co**

i ty I've got as many problems as you have; **ona już ~ przeżyła!** she has been through so much already!; **dwa razy ~ wina/kanapek** twice as much wine/as many sandwiches

tylko *part* only, just ▷ *conj*: **gdyby/ jeśli ~** if only; **posłuchaj ~, co mam ci do powiedzenia** just listen to what I have got to say to you; **~ nie ona!** anybody *lub* anyone but her!; **jak ~ zadzwonisz, wyjdę** as soon as you phone, I'll leave; **kiedy ~ miałem możliwość** whenever I had a chance; **kiedy ~ wyszedłem, on zadzwonił** as soon as I left, he called; **nie ~ ona, ale (również) jej dzieci** not only her, but her children too

ty|ł (**-łu, -ły**; *loc sg* **-le**) *m* back; **tyły** *pl* (*Wojsk*) rear *sg*; **stał ~em do ulicy** he stood with his back towards the street; **szedł ~em** he walked backwards; **jechać ~em** (*cofać*) to reverse; **z ~u sklepu** at the back of the shop; **zrobił krok do ~u i stanął** he took a step backwards and stopped

tym¹ *pron instr, loc od* **ten, to** ▷ *pron dat od* **ci, te**

tym² *part*: **im więcej, ~ lepiej** the more, the better; **~ bardziej, że nie przyszedł** all the more so as he didn't come; **~ lepiej/gorzej dla mnie** so much the better/worse for me

tymczasowy *adj* **1** (*dorywczy*) temporary **2** (*rząd*) interim **3** (*prowizoryczny*) provisional

ty|p (*loc sg* **-pie**; *nom pl* **-py**) *m* **1** (*gen sg* **-pu**) (*rodzaj*) type **2** (*gen sg* **-pa**) (*pej*: *osoba*) character; **on jest w jej ~ie** he is her type

typowy *adj* **1** (*charakterystyczny*) typical **2** (*często spotykany*) standard; **zachowanie typowe dla nich** typical behaviour (*Brit*) *lub* behavior (*US*) for them

tys. *abbr* (= *tysiące*) thousand

tysi|ąc (**-ąca, -ące**; *gen pl* **-ęcy**) *m* thousand

tytu|ł (**-łu, -ły**; *loc sg* **-le**) *m* (*powieści, artykułu*) title; **film pod ~em...** a film entitled...; **otrzymał ~ szlachecki** he got a knighthood; **~ profesora** professorship; **~ mistrzowski** the championship

tzn. *abbr* (= *to znaczy*) i.e.

tzw. *abbr* (= *tak zwany*) so-called

SŁOWO KLUCZOWE

u *prep +gen* **1** (*niedaleko*) at; **stać u okna** to stand by the window; **jest u władzy** he's in power; **szuka pomocy u rodziców** he's seeking help from his parents
2 (*część całości*): **palce u rąk/nóg** fingers/toes
3 (*dotyczące osoby, dzieła literackiego*): **zostawiłem klucze u portiera** I left the keys with the concierge; **u Mickiewicza** in Mickiewicz; **co u was słychać?** (*familiar pl*) how are things with you?
4 (*dla określenia miejsca*): **u Jana** at John's (place); **u moich przyjaciół** at my friends' (place); **czy szef jest u siebie** (*pot*) is the boss in?

ubezpiecze|nie (**-nia, -nia**; *gen pl* **-ń**) *nt* insurance; **~ od ognia/włamania** cover against fire/burglary; **obowiązkowe ~ odpowiedzialności cywilnej** compulsory insurance against civil liability; **~ międzynarodowe** (*samochodowe*) green card; **~ społeczne** national insurance (*Brit*), social security (*US*); **~ maszyn, urządzeń i aparatów technicznych od awarii** insurance of equipment against breakdown; **~ straty spowodowanej przestojem w działalności gospodarczej** loss-of-profits cover

ubiegły *adj* (*rok, miesiąc*) past, last; **w ~m roku/tygodniu** last year/week

ubier|ać (**-am, -asz**) *vt* (*pf* **ubrać**) **1** (*człowieka*) to dress **2** (*zakładać ubranie*) to put on **3** (*choinkę, ciasto*) to decorate; **~ się** (*pf* **ubrać**) *vr* (*włożyć na siebie ubranie*) to get dressed; **ubrał się starannie** he dressed with care

ubika|cja (**-cji, -cje**; *loc sg & dat sg* **-cji**) *f* toilet, restroom (*US*)

ubi|ór (**-oru, -ory**; *loc sg* **-orze**) *m* (*strój*) clothing

ubliż|ać (**-am, -asz**; *pf* **-yć**) *vi*: **~ komuś** to insult sb; **~ czemuś** to offend against sth

ubogi *adj* (*biedny*) poor

ubrać (**ubiorę, ubierzesz**; *imp* **ubierz**) *vb pf od* **ubierać**

ubra|nie (**-nia, -nia**; *gen pl* **-ń**) *nt* **1** (*strój*) clothing **2** (*garnitur*) suit; **~ ochronne** protective clothing

ubrany *adj* dressed; **być ~m w rzeczy codzienne** to be dressed in ordinary clothes

ucho[1] (**ucha, uszy**; *gen pl* **uszu**; *dat pl* **uszom**; *inst pl* **uszami**; *loc pl* **uszach**) *nt* ear; **mam powyżej uszu tej sytuacji** (*pot*) I've had it up to here with this

uch|o[2] (**-a, -a**) *nt* **1** (*dzbanka*) handle **2** (*igły*) eye

uciąć (**utnę, utniesz**; *imp* **utnij**; *pt* **uciął, ucięła, ucięli**) *vb pf od* **ucinać**

uciecz|ka (**-ki, -ki**; *dat sg & loc sg* **-ce**; *gen pl* **-ek**) *f* escape; **szuka ucieczki w alkoholu/narkotykach** he's seeking refuge in drink/drugs

uciek|ać (**-am, -asz**; *pf* **uciec**) *vi* to run away, to escape; **~ się** *vr*: **~ się do czegoś** to resort to sth; **uciekł mi pociąg** I missed my train; **uciekł się do podstępu** he resorted to deceit

ucin|ać (**-am, -asz**; *pf* **uciąć**) *vb* (*rozmowę, więzy, kontakt*) to cut off

uczciwie *adv* (*pracować, zeznawać*) honestly

uczciwoś|ć (**-ci**) *f* (*rzetelność, sumienność*) honesty

uczciwy *adj* honest

uczel|nia (**-ni, -nie**; *dat sg & loc sg* **-ni**; *gen pl* **-ni**) *f* (*szkoła wyższa*) university, college

uczennic|a (**-y, -e**; *dat sg & loc sg* **-y**) *f* (*w szkole, liceum*) schoolgirl, student
ucz|eń (**-nia, -niowie**; *loc sg* **-niu**) *m* (*w szkole, liceum*) schoolboy, student
ucze|sać (**-szę, -szesz**) *vb pf od* **czesać**
uczesa|nie (**-nia, -nia**; *gen pl* **-ń**) *nt* (*fryzura*) hairstyle
uczestnicz|yć (**-ę, -ysz**) *vi* (*brać udział*) to participate
uczestni|k (**-ka, -cy**; *inst sg* **-kiem**) *m* participant
uczu|cie (**-cia, -cia**; *gen pl* **-ć**) *nt* **1** (*emocja*) emotion **2** (*lęku*) feeling **3** (*gorąca, pragnienia*) sensation **4** (*miłość*) affection
uczule|nie (**-nia**) *nt*: **~ (na coś)** allergy (to sth); **ma ~ na pyłki** he has hay fever; **ma ~ na koty** he is allergic to cats
uczulony *adj*: **~ na coś** allergic to sth
ucz|yć (**-ę, -ysz**; *pf* **na-**) *vt* to teach ▷ *vi* to teach; **~ się** *vr* to study; **~ (kogoś) fizyki/polskiego** to teach (sb) physics/Polish; **Ewa uczy się dobrze/źle** Ewa is a good/bad student; **~ się do klasówki** to study *lub* revise (Brit) for a test
udawać (**udaję, udajesz**; *imp* **udawaj**; *pf* **udać**) *vt* **1** (*chorobę*) to fake, to feign **2** (*naśladować*) to imitate ▷ *vi*: **udawał, że śpi** he pretended he was sleeping; **~ się** *vr* (*okazać się sukcesem*) to be successful; **udawała, że nie wie, co on ma na myśli** she pretended not to know what he meant; **udało mi się dopełnić wszystkich formalności** I managed to comply with all the formalities
uderz|ać (**-am, -asz**; *pf* **-yć**) *vt*: **~ kogoś (w coś)** to hit sb (in *lub* on sth) ▷ *vi* **1** (*pięścią*) to punch **2** (*młotkiem*) to hit; **~ się** *vr* **1** (*samemu*) to hit o.s. **2** (*nawzajem*) to hit one another
udo (**uda, uda**; *loc sg* **udzie**) *nt* thigh
uf|ać (**-am, -asz**; *pf* **za-**) *vi*: **~ komuś/czemuś** to trust sb/sth; **ufam, że nie narobisz głupstw** I trust that you won't do anything stupid
ufny *adj* trusting
uga|sić (**-szę, -sisz**; *imp* **-ś**) *vb pf od* **gasić** ▷ *vt pf*: **ugasił pragnienie łykiem wina** he quenched his thirst with a gulp of wine; **powstanie zostało ugaszone** the uprising was quelled
ugot|ować (**-uję, -ujesz**) *vb pf od* **gotować**
ugry|źć (**-zę, -ziesz**; *imp* **-ź**) *vb pf od* **gryźć**; **~ się** *vr*: **~ się w język** (*przen*) to hold one's tongue
ujemny *adj* negative; **~ ładunek** negative charge
ujrz|eć (**-ę, -ysz**; *imp* **-yj**) *vt pf*: **jego dzieło ujrzało światło dzienne** his work saw the light of day
uka|rać (**-rzę, -rzesz**) *vb pf od* **karać**
ukło|nić się (**-nię, -nisz**; *imp* **-ń**) *vb pf od* **kłaniać się**
ukochan|a (**-ej, -e**) *f decl like adj* (*kobieta, którą się kocha*) sweetheart
ukochany *adj* (*mężczyzna, którego się kocha*) beloved ▷ *m decl like adj* sweetheart
ukończ|yć (**-ę, -ysz**) *vt pf* (*pracę, edukację*) to complete, to finish
ukra|ść (**-dnę, -dniesz**; *imp* **-dnij**; *pt* **-dł**) *vb pf od* **kraść**
ukry|ć (**-ję, -jesz**) *vb pf od* **ukrywać**
ukr|ywać (**-ywam, -ywasz**) *vb* to hide, to conceal; **nie da się ukryć, że...** there's no hiding that...
ul. *abbr* (*= ulica*) St
ul|egać (**-egam, -egasz**; *pf* **ulec, ulegnąć**) *vb* to surrender; **~ komuś** to surrender to sb
ule|wa (**-wy, -wy**; *loc sg* **-wie**) *f* (*rzęsisty deszcz*) downpour
ul|ga (**-gi**; *dat sg & loc sg* **-dze**) *f* **1** (*wrażenie*) relief **2** (*nom pl* **-gi**) (*zniżka*) concession, allowance; **~ podatkowa** tax relief
ulgowy *adj* **1** (*opłata*) reduced **2** (*traktowanie*) preferential; **opłata ulgowa** reduced fare, concessionary rate
ulic|a (**-y, -e**) *f* street; **na ulicy Mickiewicza** on Mickiewicz Street; **szliśmy/jechaliśmy ulicą** we walked/drove down the street; **przechodzić przez ulicę na światłach** to cross the street at the lights

ulot|ka (**-ki, -ki**; *dat sg & loc sg* **-ce**; *gen pl* **-ek**) *f* (*wyborcza, informacyjna*) leaflet, flyer
ulubienic|a (**-y, -e**) *f* favourite (*Brit*), favorite (*US*); **~ publiczności** the audience's favo(u)rite
ulubie|niec (**-ńca, -ńcy**) *m* favourite (*Brit*), favorite (*US*); **~ tłumów** the popular favo(u)rite
ulubiony *adj* (*napój, książka*) favourite (*Brit*), favorite (*US*)
ułat|wiać (**-wiam, -wiasz**; *pf* **-wić**) *vt* (*życie, pracę*) to make easier
ułoże|nie (**-nia**) *nt* **1** (*układ*) arrangement **2** (*psa: tresura*) training
umal|ować (**-uję, -ujesz**) *vt pf* **1** (*zrobić makijaż*) to make up **2** (*powieki, usta*) to apply (*make-up*); **~ się** *vr* to make (o.s.) up
um|awiać (**-awiam, -awiasz**) *vt* (*pf* **umówić**) to arrange; **~ się** *vr*: **~ się z kimś** to make an appointment with sb; **umówiłam się z chłopakiem** I have a date with a guy; **umówiłem się z nim na szóstą na Rynku** I've arranged to meet him at six on the Market Square; **~ spotkanie** to arrange a meeting; **~ kogoś z kimś** to make an appointment for sb with sb
umiarkowany *adj* moderate; **~ klimat/entuzjazm** moderate climate/enthusiasm
umieć (**umiem, umiesz**) *vi*: **~ coś robić** to know how *lub* be able to do sth; **nie umiem tańczyć/śpiewać** I can't dance/sing; **~ po angielsku** (*pot*) to have some English
umiejętnoś|ć (**-ci, -ci**; *gen pl* **-ci**) *f* **1** (*zdolność robienia czegoś*) ability **2** (*biegłość w czymś*) skill
umier|ać (**-am, -asz**; *pf* **umrzeć**) *vi* to die; **~ na gruźlicę** to die of tuberculosis; **~ z głodu** to die of starvation; **umierał z nudów na wykładzie** he was bored to death during the lecture
um|owa (**-owy, -owy**; *loc sg* **-owie**; *gen pl* **-ów**) *f* (*prawna, międzynarodowa*) agreement, contract; **zawierać** (**zawrzeć** *pf*) **umowę** to enter into an agreement *lub* a contract; **związany umową** bound by contract; **wczoraj podpisała umowę o pracę** yesterday she signed an employment contract
umożli|wiać (**-wiam, -wiasz**; *pf* **-wić**) *vt* (*czynić możliwym*) to make possible; **to umożliwi mu kupno domu** it'll enable him to buy a house
um|rzeć (**-rę, -rzesz**; *imp* **-rzyj**; *pt* **-arł**) *vb pf od* **umierać**
umy|ć (**-ję, -jesz**) *vb pf od* **myć**
umy|sł (**-słu, -sły**; *loc sg* **-śle**) *m* (*rozum*) mind, intellect; **ma bardzo przytomny ~** he has a highly astute mind
uni|a (**-i, -e**; *loc sg* **-i**) *f* union; **U~ Europejska** European Union
uniewin|niać (**-niam, -niasz**; *pf* **-nić**) *vt* (*w sądzie*) to acquit
uniewinnieni|e (**-a**) *nt* acquittal
unijny *adj* EU; **przepisy unijne** EU regulations
unik|ać (**-am, -asz**; *pf* **-nąć**) *vt* *+gen* **1** (*spotkania, rozmowy*) to avoid **2** (*uderzenia*) to dodge **3** (*kary*) to escape
uniwersalny *adj* (*ogólny*) universal; **klucz ~** master *lub* skeleton key
uniwersytecki *adj* university; **miasteczko ~e** campus
uniwersyte|t (**-tu, -ty**; *loc sg* **-cie**) *m* (*wyższa uczelnia*) university
uno|sić (**-szę, -sisz**; *imp* **-ś**; *pf* **unieść**) *vt* **1** (*podnosić: nogę*) to raise **2** (*przemieścić*) to sweep away; **~ się** *vr* **1** (*wisieć: nad powierzchnią ziemi*) to hover **2** (*zostać uniesionym: o mgle*) to rise **3** (*z krzesła*) to rise **4** (*denerwować się*) to get carried away
unowocześ|niać (**-niam, -niasz**; *pf* **-nić**) *vt* (*firmę, urządzenie*) to modernize
upad|ać (**-am, -asz**; *pf* **upaść**) *vi* (*przewracać się*) to fall (down); **upadł ze zmęczenia** he collapsed from exhaustion
upad|ek (**-ku, -ki**; *inst sg* **-kiem**) *m* **1** (*przewrócenie się*) fall **2** (*sztuki, obyczajów*) decay, decline **3** (*klęska*) downfall; **firma chyli się ku upadkowi** the firm is heading for collapse
upalny *adj* (*dzień, pogoda*) sweltering, (scorching) hot

upał (**-łu, -ły**; *loc sg* **-le**) *m* (*gorąco*) heat

upa|ść (**-dnę, -dniesz**; *imp* **-dnij**; *pt* **-dł**) *vi pf od* **upadać**; (*spaść*) to fall

upew|niać (**-niam, -niasz**; *pf* **-nić**) *vt*: **~ kogoś o czymś** to assure sb of sth; **~ się** *vr* to make sure

upie|c (**-kę, -czesz**; *pt* **-kł**) *vb pf od* **piec**

upier|ać się (**-am, -asz**; *pf* **uprzeć**) *vr* (*nalegać*) to insist; **upiera się przy spotkaniu z nimi** he insists on meeting them

upij|ać (**-am, -asz**) *vt* **1** (*napój*) to take a sip of **2** (*człowieka*) to make drunk; **~ się** *vr* to get drunk

upomin|ek (**-ku, -ki**; *inst sg* **-kiem**) *m* (*prezent*) gift

uporządkowany *adj* (*życie, pokój*) ordered, orderly

upowszech|niać (**-niam, -niasz**; *pf* **-nić**) *vt* (*wiedzę, opinie*) to disseminate; **~ się** *vr* to become widespread

up|ór (**-oru**; *loc sg* **-orze**) *m* stubbornness; **z uporem obstawał przy swoim** stubbornly he stuck to his guns

uprzejmy *adj* polite

ur. *abbr* (= *urodzony*) b.

Ural (**-u**) *m* the Ural Mountains *pl*

urat|ować (**-uję, -ujesz**) *vb pf od* **ratować**

ura|z (**-zu, -zy**; *loc sg* **-zie**) *m* **1** (*ciała*) injury **2** (*psychiczny*) trauma

uraż|ać (**-am, -asz**; *pf* **-zić**) *vt* to offend

urażony *adj* **1** (*osoba*) offended **2** (*uczucia*) hurt; **czuł się ~ jej zachowaniem** he felt hurt by her behaviour (*Brit*) *lub* behavior (*US*)

urlo|p (**-pu, -py**; *loc sg* **-pie**) *m* **1** (*wychowawczy, zdrowotny*) leave (of absence) **2** (*wakacje*) holiday (*Brit*), vacation (*esp US*); **być na ~ie** to be on holiday; **~ macierzyński** maternity leave; **~ zdrowotny** sick leave; **~ dziekański** sabbatical leave

uroczy *adj* (*człowiek, miejsce*) charming

uroczystoś|ć (**-ci, -ci**; *gen pl* **-ci**) *f* ceremony, celebration(s *pl*)

uroczysty *adj* (*podniosły*) solemn

uroczyście *adv* solemnly

uro|da (**-dy**; *dat sg & loc sg* **-dzie**) *f* (*atrakcyjny wygląd*) beauty, good looks; **ona urodą nie grzeszy** she's not too great in the looks department

uro|dzić (**-dzę, -dzisz**; *imp* **urodź** *lub* **uródź**) *vb pf od* **rodzić**

urodzin|y (-) *pl* birthday; **wszystkiego najlepszego w dniu urodzin!** happy birthday!

urodzony *adj* **1** born **2** (*rodowity*) born and bred; **jest ~m aktorem** he was born to be an actor

urojony *adj* (*choroba, dolegliwość*) imaginary

uro|k (**-ku, -ki**; *inst sg* **-kiem**) *m* (*wdzięk*) charm

urozmaicony *adj* (*różnorodny*) varied, diverse

urz|ąd (**-ędu, -ędy**; *loc sg* **-ędzie**) *m* **1** (*wojewódzki, pracy*) department **2** (*biuro*) office **3** (*miejsce pracy*) post; **~ Wojewódzki** ≈ county council (*Brit*); **~ Pracy** job centre (*Brit*) *lub* center (*US*); **~ pocztowy** post office; **U~ Miasta i Gminy** the Municipal Council; **~ Skarbowy** ≈ HM Revenue & Customs (*Brit*), ≈ the IRS (*US*); **U~ Rady Ministrów** Office of the Council of Ministers; **~ stanu cywilnego** registry (*Brit*) *lub* register (*US*) office

urzą|dzać (**-dzam, -dzasz**; *pf* **-dzić**) *vt* **1** (*dom*) to furnish **2** (*przedstawienie*) to organize; **~ się** *vr* (*w nowym domu itp.*) to settle down

urządze|nie (**-nia, -nia**; *gen pl* **-ń**) *nt* (*maszyna*) device, appliance; **urządzenia** *pl* equipment *sg*

urzędnicz|ka (**-ki, -ki**; *dat sg & loc sg* **-ce**; *gen pl* **-ek**) *f* (*pracownica urzędu*) office worker

urzędni|k (**-ka, -cy**; *inst sg* **-kiem**) *m* **1** (*pracownik urzędu*) office worker **2** (*wysoki rangą*) official

urzędowy *adj* **1** (*list, tajemnica*) official **2** (*czas*) standard **3** (*sztywny: styl, relacja*) official

usią|ść (**-dę, -dziesz**; *imp* **-dź**) *vb pf od* **siadać**

usłu|ga (**-gi, -gi**; *dat sg & loc sg* **-dze**) *f* (*uprzejmość*) favour (*Brit*), favor (*US*);

usługi *pl* (*szewskie, krawieckie*) services

usłysz|eć (**-ę, -ysz**) *vb pf od* **słyszeć** ▷ *vt*: **niedokładnie ~** to mishear; **~ przez przypadek** to overhear

usmaż|yć (**-ę, -ysz**) *vb pf od* **smażyć**

usnąć (**usnę, uśniesz**; *imp* **uśnij**) *vb pf od* **usypiać**

uspokaj|ać (**-am, -asz**; *pf* **uspokoić**) *vt* **1** to calm (down) **2** (*uciszyć*) to quieten (*Brit*) *lub* quiet (*US*) (down) **3** (*przestać się denerwować*) to calm (down); **~ się** *vr* **1** to calm down **2** (*uciszyć*) to quieten (*Brit*), to quiet (*US*) **3** (*o wichurze*) to calm, to subside

usprawiedli|wiać (**-wiam, -wiasz**; *pf* **-wić**) *vt* **1** (*tłumaczyć*) to excuse **2** (*uzasadniać*) to justify; **~ się** (*przed nauczycielem, pracodawcą*) *vr* to excuse o.s., to explain o.s.

usprawiedliwie|nie (**-nia, -nia**; *gen pl* **-ń**) *nt* **1** (*wymówka*) excuse **2** (*uzasadnienie*) justification **3** (*w szkole*) excuse note

ust|a (**-**; *gen pl* **-**) *pl* mouth *sg*; **zrobili mu oddychanie metodą ~-~** they gave him mouth-to-mouth resuscitation

ustal|ać (**-am, -asz**; *pf* **-ić**) *vt* **1** to establish **2** (*datę spotkania*) to fix; **~ się** *vr* **1** (*o obyczaju*) to become established **2** (*stabilizować się*) to settle

ustale|nie (**-nia, -nia**; *gen pl* **-ń**) *nt* (*decyzja*) decision; **ustalenia** *pl* **1** plan *sg*, arrangements **2** (*badanie*) findings

ustalony *adj* **1** (*data spotkania*) fixed **2** (*dane*) established **3** (*reguły*) set, established

ustaw|a (**-y, -y**) *f* law, act of Parliament

usta|wiać (**-wiam, -wiasz**; *pf* **-wić**) *vt* **1** (*meble, książki*) to put, to place **2** (*rozmieszczać*) to arrange **3** (*urządzać*) to put up, to set up **4** (*ostrość, wysokość*) to adjust; **~ się** *vr*: **~ się w kolejce** to line up; **ustawił się przodem do wyjścia** he stood facing the exit

ustawie|nie (**-nia, -nia**; *loc sg* **-niu**; *gen pl* **-ń**) *nt* setup

uster|ka (**-ki, -ki**; *dat sg & loc sg* **-ce**; *gen pl* **-ek**) *f* **1** (*w maszynie*) fault **2** (*w danych*) error

ustny *adj* **1** (*egzamin, tradycja*) oral **2** (*zgoda*) verbal; **jama ustna** (*Anat*) the mouth cavity; **harmonijka ustna** harmonica, mouth organ

ustr|ój (**-oju, -oje**) *m* (*Pol*) system

us|ypiać (**-ypiam, -ypiasz**) *vi* to fall asleep ▷ *vt*: **~** (**uśpić** *pf*) **psa** to put a dog down

uszkodzony *adj* (*popsuty*) damaged

uszy|ć (**-ję, -jesz**) *vb pf od* **szyć**

uścis|k (**-ku, -ki**; *inst sg* **-kiem**) *m* hug, embrace; **przywitał go ~iem dłoni** he greeted him with a handshake; **przesyłam wam serdeczne ~i** I send you my love

uści|snąć (**-snę, -śniesz**; *imp* **-śnij**) *vt* (*objąć ramionami*) to hug, to embrace; **uścisnął moją dłoń** he shook my hand

uściśl|ać (**-am, -asz**; *pf* **-ić**) *vt* **1** (*pojęcie*) to specify **2** (*słowa*) to qualify

uśmiech (**-u, -y**) *m* smile

uśmiech|ać się (**-am, -asz**; *pf* **-nąć**) *vr* to smile; **szczęście się do niego uśmiecha** Lady Luck is smiling on him

uśmiechnięty *adj* (*człowiek, twarz*) smiling

uśmierz|ać (**-am, -asz**; *pf* **-yć**) *vt* **1** (*koić*) to relieve, to soothe **2** (*tłumić*) to quell

utalentowany *adj* (*uzdolniony*) talented, gifted

uty|ć (**-ję, -jesz**) *vb pf od* **tyć**

uwa|ga (**-gi, -gi**; *dat sg & loc sg* **-dze**) *f* **1** (*koncentracja*) attention **2** (*spostrzeżenie*) remark **3** (*upomnienie*) reproof; **~!** (*rozważnie!*) be careful!; (*o nadciągającym niebezpieczeństwie*) look out!; **„U~! Niski strop!"** "Warning! Low ceiling!"; **„U~! Wysokie napięcie!"** "Danger! High voltage!"; **„U~! Gaz palny!"** "Danger! Inflammable gas!"; **„U~! Strefa zagrożona wybuchem"** "Explosion danger"; **brać** (**wziąć** *pf*) **coś pod uwagę** to take sth into consideration; **zwracać** (**zwrócić** *pf*) **uwagę na kogoś/coś** to pay attention to sb/sth

uważ|ać (**-am, -asz**) *vt*: **~ kogoś za wroga** to consider sb (to be) an enemy ▷ *vi* **1** (*być ostrożnym*) to be careful **2** (*wyrażać opinię*) to think; **~ się** *vr*: **on się uważa za zdolnego pianistę** he considers himself a gifted pianist; **uważaj na nich** keep an eye on them; **rób jak uważasz, ale będziesz żałował** do as you wish, but you'll regret it; **uważaj na siebie** take care (of yourself); **uważaj!** (*strzeż się!*) be careful!; (*o nadciągającym niebezpieczeństwie*) look out!

uważnie *adv* **1** (*rozglądać się*) attentively **2** (*czytać*) carefully

uważny *adj* **1** (*słuchacz*) attentive **2** (*spojrzenie*) careful

uwielbi|ać (**-am, -asz**) *vt* (*czcić*) to adore

uwierz|yć (**-ę, -ysz**) *vi pf* (*komuś, w coś*) to believe

uzależ|niać (**-niam, -niasz**; *pf* **-nić**) *vt*: **~ coś od czegoś** (*od okoliczności*) to make sth dependent on sth; **~ się** *vr*: **~ się od** *+gen* (*od osoby*) to become dependent on; **~ się od alkoholu** to become addicted to alcohol

uzależnieni|e (**-a**) *nt* addiction

uzależniony *adj*: **być ~m od kogoś/czegoś** to be dependent on sb/sth

uzasad|niać (**-niam, -niasz**; *pf* **-nić**) *vt* (*tłumaczyć*) to justify

uzasadnie|nie (**-nia, -nia**; *gen pl* **-ń**) *nt* (*podanie powodów*) justification

uzasadniony *adj* justified

uzdrowi|sko (**-ska, -ska**; *inst sg* **-skiem**) *nt* **1** health resort **2** (*z wodami mineralnymi*) spa

uzgad|niać (**-niam, -niasz**; *pf* **uzgodnić**) *vt* (*plan, umowę*) to negotiate, to agree

uzn|awać (**-aję, -ajesz**; *pf* **uznać**) *vb* to acknowledge, to recognize

użytkowni|k (**-ka, -cy**; *loc sg* **-ku**; *inst sg* **-kiem**) *m* user

używ|ać (**-am, -asz**) *vt* (*pf* **użyć**) **1** (*posługiwać się*) to use **2** (*przyjmować lekarstwa*) to take

używany *adj* (*samochód, ubranie*) used, secondhand

V

video *nt inv* = **wideo**

verte *excl* PTO

versus *conj* versus

vloger (**-a, -zy**; *dat sg* **-owi**) *m* vlogger

vloger|ka (**-ki, -ki**; *dat sg* **-ce**) *f* vlogger

vlog|ować (**-uję, -ujesz**) *vi* to vlog

SŁOWO KLUCZOWE

w *prep +loc* **1** (*wskazując na miejsce*) in; **pracuję w domu** I work at home; **w teatrze** at the theatre (*Brit*) *lub* theater (*US*); **grać w orkiestrze** to play in an orchestra
2 (*o ubiorze*): **pojawiła się starsza kobieta w czerni** an elderly woman in black appeared
3 (*wskazując na postać*): **sztuka w trzech aktach** a play in three acts; **mleko w proszku** powdered milk; **honorarium w gotówce** a cash fee
4 (*o czasie*): **w dniu 3 listopada 2005** on the 3rd November 2005; **w czwartek** on Thursday; **we wrześniu** in September
▷ *prep* (*wskazując na kierunek*) in(to); **spojrzeć w niebo** to gaze at the sky; **skręcać w lewo/prawo** to turn to the left/right; **iść w dół/górę** to go down/up

wa|da (**-dy, -dy**; *dat sg & loc sg* **-dzie**) *f* **1** (*ujemna cecha*) disadvantage **2** (*Med: nieprawidłowość*) defect **3** (*usterka*) fault
wa|ga (**-gi, -gi**; *dat sg & loc sg* **-dze**) *f* **1** (*przyrząd*) scales *pl* **2** (*znaczenie*) significance **3** (*Astrol*): **W~** Libra; **wydarzenie ogromnej wagi** an event of enormous significance
wago|n (**-nu, -ny**; *loc sg* **-nie**) *m* (*Rail*) **1** (*pasażerski*) carriage (*Brit*), car (*US*) **2** (*towarowy*) wagon (*Brit*), freight car (*US*)
wah|ać się (**-am, -asz**; *pf* **za-**) *vr* to hesitate
wakacj|e (**-i**) *pl* (*letnie, zimowe*) holiday(s *pl*) (*Brit*), vacation *sg* (*US*); **byłem na wakacjach w Polsce** I was on holiday *lub* vacation in Poland; **rodzina jeździła na ~** the family used to go on holiday *lub* vacation
walcz|yć (**-ę, -ysz**) *vi* to struggle; **musimy ~ o** *lub* **za prawa człowieka** we have to fight for human rights; **walczyła z chorobą** she struggled against illness
Wali|a (**-i**) *f* Wales
wal|ić (**-ę, -isz**; *pf* **-nąć**) *vt, vi* (*pot*) to thump; **~ się** *vr* (*mur, dom*) to collapse
Walijczy|k (**-ka, -cy**; *inst sg* **-kiem**) *m* Welshman
Walij|ka (**-ki, -ki**; *dat sg* **-ce**; *gen pl* **-ek**) *f* Welshwoman
walijski *adj* Welsh
waliz|ka (**-ki, -ki**; *dat sg & loc sg* **-ce**; *gen pl* **-ek**) *f* (*skórzana, podróżna*) (suit) case
wal|ka (**-ki, -ki**; *dat sg & loc sg* **-ce**; *gen pl* **-k**) *f* fight; **~ na śmierć i życie** battle of life and death
walu|ta (**-ty, -ty**; *dat sg & loc sg* **-cie**) *f* foreign currency; **silna/twarda ~** strong/hard currency
wam *pron dat od* **wy**
wampi|r (**-ra, -ry**; *loc sg* **-rze**) *m* vampire
wandal (**-a, -e**; *gen pl* **-i** *lub* **-ów**) *m* vandal
wanili|a (**-i**) *f* vanilla
waniliowy *adj* (*aromat do pieczenia*) vanilla
wan|na (**-ny, -ny**; *dat sg & loc sg* **-nie**) *f* bath(tub)
waria|t (**-ta, -ci**; *loc sg* **-cie**) *m* (*pot*) madman; **dom ~ów** (*pot*) madhouse
wari|ować (**-uję, -ujesz**; *pf* **z-**) *vi* (*pot*) to go crazy
warkocz (**-a, -e**; *gen pl* **-y**) *m* (*z włosów*) plait (*Brit*), braid (*US*)
Warsza|wa (**-wy**; *dat sg & loc sg* **-wie**) *f* Warsaw
wart *adj*: **~ pięć tysięcy złotych** worth 5,000 zlotys; **jeden jest ~**

drugiego each is as bad as the other; **~ jest każdej ceny** it's worth any amount of money; **bez miłości świat nic nie jest ~** without love, the world is worth nothing

warto *inv*: **~ zobaczyć** *(pf)*/**zrobić** *(pf)* it's worth seeing/doing

wartościowy *adj* *(książka, znajomość, człowiek)* valuable; **papiery wartościowe** (*Fin*) securities

wartoś|ć (**-ci**) *f* value, worth; **wartości** *pl* (*w filozofii*) values; **towar o wartości 1000 dolarów** 1,000 dollars' worth of goods; **fotka nie ma wartości artystycznej** the photo has no artistic value

warun|ek (**-ku, -ki**; *inst sg* **-kiem**) *m* condition; **warunki** *pl* conditions; **pod warunkiem, że...** on condition (that)...; **pod pewnymi warunkami** under certain conditions

warzywny *adj* vegetable; **bulion ~** vegetable broth; **stragan ~** vegetable stall

warzy|wo (**-wa, -wa**; *loc sg* **-wie**) *nt* (*smaczne, soczyste, zdrowe*) vegetable

was *pron gen, acc, loc od* **wy**

wasz *possessive pron* **1** (*z rzeczownikiem*) your **2** (*bez rzeczownika*) yours; **~ dom** your house

Watyka|n (**-nu**; *loc sg* **-nie**) *m* the Vatican

wazo|n (**-nu, -ny**; *loc sg* **-nie**) *m* (*szklany, kryształowy, ceramiczny*) vase

ważny *adj* **1** (*informacja, osoba*) important **2** (*dokument*) valid **3** (*pot: osoba: zarozumiały*) self-important

waż|yć (**-ę, -ysz**; *pf* **z-**) *vt* to weigh ▷ *vi*: **on waży 100 kg** he weighs 100 kg; **~ się** *vr* **1** (*dosł*) to weigh o.s. **2** (*wynik nieprzewidywalny*) to hang in the balance

wą|s (**-sa, -sy**; *loc sg* **-sie**) *m usu pl* moustache (*Brit*), mustache (*US*); **wąsy** *pl* **1** (*u mężczyzny*) moustache *sg* (*Brit*), mustache *sg* (*US*) **2** (*u kota*) whiskers

wąski *adj* narrow

wąt|ek (**-ku, -ki**; *inst sg* **-kiem**) *m* **1** (*powieści, Komput*) thread **2** (*wykładu, filmu, powieści*) theme; **chciałbym podjąć ~** I should like to pick up the theme

wąt|pić (**-pię, -pisz**) *vi* to doubt; **nikt nie wątpił w legalność jego majątku** nobody doubted that his wealth was legally come by; **wątpię w twoje zdolności** I am doubtful about your abilities; **wątpię** I doubt it

wątpliwoś|ć (**-ci, -ci**; *gen pl* **-ci**) *f* doubt; **istnieją wątpliwości co do jego uczciwości** doubts exist about his honesty; **nie ulega wątpliwości, że jest winny** there's no doubt that he is guilty

wątr|oba (**-oby, -oby**; *dat sg & loc sg* **-obie**; *gen pl* **-ób**) *f* liver

wąż (**węża, węże**; *gen pl* **węży** *lub* **wężów**) *m* **1** (*Zool*) snake **2** (*rura*) hose

wbrew *prep +dat* contrary to; **~ naturze** against nature; **~ zakazowi jej ojca** in defiance of her father

WC, w.c. *abbr* WC

wcale *adv* **1** (*w ogóle*) (not) at all **2** (*całkiem: pot*) quite; **~ nie!** not at all!; **~ często** quite often

wcho|dzić (**-dzę, -dzisz**; *imp* **-dź**; *pf* **wejść**) *vi +gen* **1** (*do budynku*) to enter **2** (*do samochodu*) to get in; **wejść do firmy** to join the firm; **weszła do Internetu** she went on (to) the internet; **klucz wchodził do zamka** the key went into the lock

wciąg|ać (**-am, -asz**; *pf* **-nąć**) *vt* **1** to pull (in) **2** (*powietrze*) to draw in **3** (*buty, spodnie*) to pull on

wciąż *adv* still

wczas|y (**-ów**) *pl* holiday *sg* (*Brit*), vacation *sg* (*US*); **pojechał na ~** he went on holiday (*Brit*) *lub* vacation (*US*)

wcze|sny *adj* **1** (*ranek, śnieg, godzina*) early **2** (*przedwczesny*) premature

wcześnia|k (**-ka, -ki**; *inst sg* **-kiem**) *m* premature baby

wcześnie *adv* early; **za ~ jeszcze wyrokować** it's still too early to say

wcześniej *adv comp od* **wcześnie**; (*zawczasu*) beforehand

wcześniejszy *adj comp od* **wczesny**; (*poprzedzający*) previous

wczoraj *adv* yesterday; **~ rano/wieczorem** yesterday morning/evening; **~ w nocy widziałem wilka** last night I saw a wolf

wczorajszy *adj* yesterday's
wd|owa (**-owy, -owy**; *dat sg & loc sg* **-owie**; *gen pl* **-ów**) *f* widow
wdo|wiec (**-wca, -wcy**) *m* widower
wdych|ać (**-am, -asz**) *vt* to breathe in
wdzięczny *adj* **1** grateful **2** (*uroczy: uśmiech, spojrzenie*) graceful **3** (*korzystny*) rewarding
we *prep* = **w**
według *prep +gen* according to; **~ mojej matki** according to my mother
weeken|d (**-du, -dy**; *loc sg* **-dzie**) *m* weekend
wegetariański *adj* (*danie, restauracja, dieta*) vegetarian
wejś|cie (**-cia**) *nt* **1** (*wstęp*) access **2** (*znajomości*) connections *pl* **3** (*nom pl* **-cia**; *gen pl* **-ć**) (*drzwi*) entrance; **„~"** "entrance"
wej|ść (**-dę, -dziesz**; *imp* **-dź**; *pt* **wszedł, weszła, weszli**) *vb pf od* **wchodzić**; **(proszę) ~!** come in!
weł|na (**-ny, -ny**; *dat sg & loc sg* **-nie**; *gen pl* **-en**) *f* wool
Wenezuel|a (**-i**) *f* Venezuela
werdyk|t (**-tu, -ty**; *loc sg* **-cie**) *m* (*ostateczny, sądowy*) verdict
wersal|ka (**-ki, -ki**; *dat sg & loc sg* **-ce**; *gen pl* **-ek**) *f* (*rozkładana, wygodna*) sofa bed
wersj|a (**-i, -e**; *gen pl* **-i**) *f* (*językowa, odmienna*) version
wesel|e (**-a, -a**) *nt* (*huczne, wystawne*) wedding
wes|oło *adv* happily; **było bardzo ~** it was great fun
wesoły *adj* cheerful; **wesołe miasteczko** funfair (*Brit*), amusement park (*US*); **W~ch Świąt!** (*na Boże Narodzenie*) Merry Christmas!; (*na Wielkanoc*) Happy Easter!
wewnątrz *prep +gen* inside ▷ *adv* inside; **pomieszczenie było zamknięte od** *lub* **z ~** the room was locked from the inside
wewnętrznie *adv* internally
wewnętrzny *adj* **1** internal **2** (*Bud: drzwi, ściany*) interior **3** (*Ekon: handel*) domestic **4** (*Psych: spokój, życie*) inner ▷ *m decl like adj* (*też:* **numer** *lub* **telefon ~**) extension; **Ministerstwo Spraw W~ch** Ministry of the Interior, ≈ Home Office (*Brit*)
węch (**-u**) *m* **1** (*zmysł: wyostrzony*) (sense of) smell **2** (*przen*) nose
węd|ka (**-ki, -ki**; *dat sg & loc sg* **-ce**; *gen pl* **-ek**) *f* fishing rod; **złapać na wędkę** to catch with a rod and line
wędli|na (**-ny, -ny**; *dat sg & loc sg* **-nie**) *f* smoked meat(s *pl*)
wędrów|ka (**-ki, -ki**; *dat sg & loc sg* **-ce**; *gen pl* **-ek**) *f* **1** (*podróż: daleka, górska*) trek **2** (*piesza*) walking tour
wę|giel (**-gla**) *m* **1** (*Geol*) coal **2** (*Chem*) carbon; **~ do rysowania** charcoal; **~ kamienny/brunatny** bituminous coal/brown coal
węgierski *adj* Hungarian
Wę|gry (**-gier**; *loc pl* **-grzech**) *pl* Hungary
węższy *adj comp od* **wąski**
WF, wf. *abbr* (= *wychowanie fizyczne*) PE
wg *abbr* (= *według*) according to
wiadomoś|ć (**-ci, -ci**; *gen pl* **-ci**) *f* **1** (*informacja*) message **2** (*Radio, TV*) news item; **wiadomości** *pl* (*wiedza*) **1** information **2** (*Radio, TV*) the news; **podawać coś do publicznej wiadomości** to make sth generally known; **nie przyjmuję tego do wiadomości** I don't accept that
wiad|ro (**-ra, -ra**; *loc sg* **-rze**; *gen pl* **-er**) *nt* bucket; **~ wody** bucket of water
wi|ara (**-ary**; *dat sg & loc sg* **-erze**) *f* faith; **~ w Boga** faith in God; **straciła wiarę w siebie** she has lost self-confidence; **wyznanie wiary** (*Rel*) the Creed
wiarygodny *adj* **1** (*wiadomość, człowiek*) credible **2** (*źródło historyczne*) reliable; **~ świadek** a credible witness
wi|atr (**-atru, -atry**; *loc sg* **-etrze**) *m* wind; **wiatry** *pl*: **puszczać ~y** to break wind; **pod ~** into the wind; **z ~em** with the wind; **kto sieje ~, zbiera burzę** sow the wind and reap the whirlwind; **biednemu zawsze ~ w oczy** things are always harder if you're poor

widel|ec (**-ca, -ce**) *m* fork
wideo *nt inv* video ▷ *adj*: **kamera ~** video camera
widny *adj* (*mieszkanie, pokój, pomieszczenie*) light
wido|k (**-ku, -ki**; *inst sg* **-kiem**) *m* **1** (*krajobraz*: *rozległy, zapierający dech w piersiach*) view **2** (*obraz*) sight; **widoki** *pl* (*perspektywy*) prospects
widoków|ka (**-ki, -ki**; *dat sg & loc sg* **-ce**; *gen pl* **-ek**) *f* postcard
widowis|ko (**-ka, -ka**; *inst sg* **-kiem**) *nt* (*teatralne, cyrkowe*) spectacle
widow|nia (**-ni, -nie**; *gen pl* **-ni**) *f* **1** (*widzowie*) audience **2** (*sala dla widzów*) auditorium; **siedzieć na widowni** to sit in the audience
widz (**-a, -owie**) *m* **1** (*TV*) viewer **2** (*Sport*) spectator **3** (*świadek*: *przygodny, przypadkowy*) bystander; **widzowie** *pl* (*publiczność, widownia*) audience
wi|dzieć (**-dzę, -dzisz**) *vt, vi* to see; **widzę Pałac Prezydencki** I (can) see the Presidential Palace; **widziała już tę sztukę** she has already seen this play; **widzę, że nie ma wszystkich** I can see that not everyone is here; **powinien ~ więcej niż swój nos!** he has to take a broader view here; **sam widzisz, że mamy ograniczone pole manewru** you can see for yourself we have limited room for manoeuvre; **widzimy się z nim jedynie w święta Bożego Narodzenia** we only see him at Christmas
wieczny *adj* eternal; **wieczne miasto Rzym** Rome, the eternal city
wieczorny *adj* **1** (*wczesnym wieczorem*: *pociąg, seans*) evening **2** (*późnym wieczorem*) night
wiecz|ór (**-oru, -ory**; *loc sg* **-orze**) *m* **1** (*część doby*) evening **2** (*impreza*: *literacki*) soirée; **~ autorski** a meet-the-author event; **dobry ~!** good evening!; **dzisiaj wieczorem** this evening; **wczoraj wieczorem** last night; **co ~** every evening
wiedz|a (**-y**) *f* knowledge; **posiada gruntowną wiedzę z tej dziedziny** she has a sound knowledge of the field; **bez wiedzy matki** without his mother's knowledge
wiedzieć (**wiem, wiesz**; *imp* **wiedz**) *vt* to know ▷ *vi*: **~ o rolnictwie** to know about agriculture; **wie to od mamy** she knows that from her mum; **wiesz co?** (*pot*) (do) you know what?; **wiem to z własnego doświadczenia** I know this from personal experience; **niewiele wiem na ten temat** I don't know much about that
wiejski *adj* **1** (*okolica*) country **2** (*ubranie*) farmer's **3** (*przemysł, życie*) rural
wie|k (**-ku, -ki**; *inst sg* **-kiem**) *m* **1** (*liczba lat*) age **2** (*stulecie*) century; **pod koniec XX ~u** towards the end of the 20th century; **~i średnie** the Middle Ages; **~ szkolny** school age; **~ emerytalny** retirement age; **jesteśmy w tym samym ~u** we are the same age
wiel|bić (**-bię, -bisz**) *vt* to worship
wielbłą|d (**-da, -dy**; *loc sg* **-dzie**) *m* (*dwugarbny*) camel
wiele *pron*: **~** (*+gen*) a lot (of) ▷ *adv* much, a lot; **na początku ~ kobiet to mówiło** that's what lots of women said, to begin with; **wydał ~ pieniędzy** he spent a lot of money; **podróż samolotem jest o ~ szybsza niż jazda pociągiem** air travel is a lot quicker than the train; **wielu studentów pojechało do Paryża** a lot of students went to Paris; **wyniki końcowe są o ~ lepsze** the final results are a lot better
Wielka Brytania (**Wielkiej Brytanii**) *f* Great Britain
Wielkanoc (**-y, -e**) *f* Easter
wielkanocny *adj* (*pisanka, obiad, nabożeństwo*) Easter
wielki *adj* **1** (*ogromny*) large **2** (*znaczny*) great; **W~ Tydzień** (*Rel*) Holy Week; **W~ Piątek** (*Rel*) Good Friday; **W~ Post** (*Rel*) Lent; **Aleksander W~** Alexander the Great; **miała ~e, ciemne oczy** she had big dark eyes; **~ mi ekspert!** what an idiot he is!; **wielka szkoda, że się nie zobaczymy!** too bad we won't be able to see each other!
Wielkopols|ka (**-ki**; *dat sg & loc sg* **-ce**) *f* Greater Poland, *a lowland area in*

Central Poland containing the ancient capital, Gniezno

wielokrotnie *pron* repeatedly

wieloznaczny *adj* (*komentarz, uśmiech*) ambiguous

wielu *pron zob.* **wiele**

wieprzowi|na (**-ny**; *dat sg & loc sg* **-nie**) *f* pork

wieprzowy *adj* (*kotlet*) pork

wiernie *adv* faithfully; **~ naśladować** to copy exactly

wiernoś|ć (**-ci**) *f* **1** faithfulness **2** (*Tech: w odtwarzaniu dźwięków*) fidelity

wierny *adj* faithful; **wierni** *pl* (*Rel*) the faithful; **~ jak pies** (*przen*) faithful as a dog

wiersz (**-a, -e**; *gen pl* **-y**) *m* **1** (*utwór*) poem **2** (*linijka wiersza*) line

wierz|yć (**-ę, -ysz**) *vi*: **czy wierzysz w niebo i piekło?** do you believe in heaven and hell?; **taka była wersja urzędowa, w którą oczywiście nikt nie wierzył** that was the official version, which obviously nobody believed; **~** (**u~** *pf*) **komuś** to believe sb; **teraz już mi wierzysz?** do you believe me now?

wiesz|ać (**-am, -asz**; *pf* **powiesić**) *vt* to hang; **~ się** *vr* to hang o.s.; **~ na kimś psy** (*przen*) to bad-mouth sb

wiesza|k (**-ka, -ki**; *inst sg* **-kiem**) *m* **1** (*do wieszania ubrań*) stand **2** (*kawałek druta*) loop

wieś (**wsi, wsie**; *gen pl* **wsi**) *f* **1** (*okolica: zapadła, głucha*) country **2** (*miejscowość*) village; **mieszkać na wsi** to live in the country

wi|eść (**-odę, -edziesz**; *imp* **-edź**; *pt* **-ódł, -odła, -edli**) *vt* **1** (*prowadzić: życie*) to lead **2** (*pf* **po-**) (*przewodzić*) to lead; **~ się** (*pf* **po-**) *vr*: **wiodło jej się nieźle** she was doing OK

Wietna|m (**-mu**; *loc sg* **-mie**) *m* Vietnam

wietrzny *adj* (*dzień, pogoda, klimat*) windy; **czy ma naprawdę ospę wietrzną?** has he really got chickenpox?

wiewiór|ka (**-ki, -ki**; *dat sg & loc sg* **-ce**; *gen pl* **-ek**) *f* squirrel

wi|eźć (**-ozę, -eziesz**; *imp* **-eź**; *pt* **-ózł, -ozła, -eźli**; *pf* **za-**) *vt* (*przewozić*) to carry

wież|a (**-y, -e**) *f* **1** (*Archit*) tower **2** (*w szachach*) castle; **~ Babel** the tower of Babel

więc *conj* so; **tak ~** thus; **zmęczyła się, ~ usiadła** she was tired, so she sat down; **wszystkie kraje europejskie, a ~ Francja, Niemcy,..** all the countries of Europe, that is France, Germany,...

więcej *adv comp od* **dużo, wiele** more; **nikt ~ nie jest zainteresowany** nobody else is interested; **nic ~ nie trzeba mówić** nothing more *lub* else need be said; **nigdy ~!** never again!; **coraz ~** more and more; **mniej ~** more or less; **zarabiasz ~ niż ja** you earn more than me

większoś|ć (**-ci**) *f* majority; **w większości przypadków miała rację** in most cases she was right

większy *adj comp od* **duży, wielki**

więzie|nie (**-nia**; *nom pl* **-nia**; *gen pl* **-ń**) *nt* prison; **dziesięć lat siedział w więzieniu** he did ten years in prison

wię|zień (**-źnia, -źniowie**) *m* prisoner

wigili|a (**-i, -e**; *gen pl* **-i**) *f* (*święto*): **W~** Christmas Eve

WIGILIA

Wieczór wigilijny (Christmas Eve) is the most important part of Christmas for Poles. After the first star appears in the sky, the family begins supper by breaking wafers together and exchanging good wishes. The supper should be made up of twelve dishes, such as: **barszcz z uszkami**, **pierogi z kapustą**, and the obligatory carp. After supper, the family sings Christmas carols and they give each other presents.

wigilijny *adj*: **wieczór ~** Christmas Eve; **kolacja wigilijna** Christmas Eve supper

wilgo|ć (**-ci**) *f* damp

wilgotny *adj* damp

wi|na (**-ny, -ny**; *dat sg & loc sg* **-nie**) *f* **1** (*przyczyna złego*) fault **2** (*za zły czyn*) blame; **nie poczuwa się do winy** he doesn't feel guilty; **czyja to ~?** whose fault is it?
win|da (**-dy, -dy**; *dat sg & loc sg* **-dzie**) *f* lift (*Brit*), elevator (*US*)
wi|nić (**-nię, -nisz**; *imp* **-ń**) *vt*: **~ kogoś za coś** to blame sb for sth
wi|no (**-na, -na**; *loc sg* **-nie**) *nt* (*wytrawne, półsłodkie, musujące*) wine
winogro|no (**-na, -na**; *loc sg* **-nie**) *nt* grape
wiosenny *adj* (*poranek, promocja, wyprzedaż*) spring
wio|sna (**-sny, -sny**; *dat sg & loc sg* **-śnie**; *gen pl* **-sen**) *f* spring; **wiosną** *lub* **na wiosnę** in the springtime
wiru|s (**-sa, -sy**; *loc sg* **-sie**) *m* virus; **~ grypy** flu virus
wi|sieć (**-szę, -sisz**; *imp* **-ś**) *vi* to hang; **jego życie wisi na włosku** (*przen*) his life is hanging by a thread
Wi|sła (**-sły**; *dat sg & loc sg* **-śle**) *f* the Vistula
wi|śnia (**-śni, -śnie**; *gen pl* **-śni** *lub* **-sien**) *f* **1** (*owoc: cierpka, dojrzała*) cherry **2** (*Bot: drzewo*) cherry (tree)
wit|ać (**-am, -asz**; *pf* **po-** *lub* **przy-**) *vt* to welcome; **witamy w Lublinie!** welcome to Lublin!; **~ się** (*pf* **przy-**) *vr*: **witała się z każdym** she greeted everyone
witami|na (**-ny, -ny**; *dat sg & loc sg* **-nie**) *f* vitamin; **~ B** vitamin B
wi|za (**-zy, -zy**; *dat sg & loc sg* **-zie**) *f* visa; **pańska ~ wygasła** your visa has expired
wizy|ta (**-ty, -ty**; *dat sg & loc sg* **-cie**) *f* **1** visit **2** (*u lekarza, dentysty itp.*) appointment; **następnego dnia złożyła mi wizytę** next day she paid me a visit
wizytów|ka (**-ki, -ki**; *dat sg & loc sg* **-ce**; *gen pl* **-ek**) *f* (business) card
wj|azd (**-azdu, -azdy**; *loc sg* **-eździe**) *m* **1** (*czynność*) entrance **2** (*brama*) access; **triumfalny ~ cesarza do miasta** the emperor's triumphal entry into the city; **~ dla wózków inwalidzkich** wheelchair access; **„zakaz ~u"** "no entry"
wj|echać (**-adę, -edziesz**; *imp* **-edź**) *vb pf od* **wjeżdżać**
wjeżdż|ać (**-am, -asz**; *pf* **wjechać**) *vi* **1** (*do wewnątrz*) to drive in **2** (*wyżej*) to go up **3** (*Rail: na stację*) to pull in; **ciężarówka wjechała w dom** the lorry ran into a house
wkładać (**-am, -asz**; *pf* **włożyć**) *vi* to put in; **włożyła list z powrotem do szuflady** she put the letter back into the drawer; **włóż płaszcz!** put on your coat!
wkoło *prep +gen* around
wkrótce *adv* soon
wlat|ywać (**-uję, -ujesz**; *pf* **wlecieć**) *vi* **1** (*o ptakach*) to fly in **2** (*o dymie, osobach*) to rush in
władz|a (**-y**) *f* power; **władze** *pl* (*państwowe, lokalne*) the authorities; **dojść do władzy** to come to power; **on ma nad nią tajemną władzę** he has a mysterious hold over her; **pacjent nie był w pełni władz umysłowych** the patient was not in full possession of his faculties
włama|nie (**-nia, -nia**; *gen pl* **-ń**) *nt* burglary; **dokonywać** (**dokonać** *pf*) **włamania do sejfu** to break in to a safe; **ślady włamania** signs of a break-in
włamywacz (**-a, -e**; *gen pl* **-y**) *m* burglar
włam|ywać się (**-uję, -ujesz**; *pf* **-ać**) *vr* to break in
własnoś|ć (**-ci**) *f* **1** (*majątek*) property **2** (*Jur*) ownership; **mieć coś na ~** to be the owner of sth
własny *adj*: **mój/jego/jej ~** my/his/her own; **mówić ~mi słowami** to speak in one's own words; **dbać o własną skórę** to look out for oneself; **każdy ma własne zdanie** everybody has their own opinion
właściciel (**-a, -e**; *gen pl* **-i**) *m* owner
właściciel|ka (**-ki, -ki**; *dat sg & loc sg* **-ce**; *gen pl* **-ek**) *f* owner
właściwie *adv* **1** (*należycie*) correctly **2** (*tak naprawdę*) actually
właśnie *adv*: **dlaczego ~ dziś wrócił?** why did he have to come back today (of all days)?; **to ~ mam zamiar powiedzieć** that's just what I plan to say; **~ idzie/przyjechał** he is just coming/has just arrived; **~ widzę,**

że pan jest zajęty as a matter of fact I can see that you are busy; **i o to ~ chodzi!** and that's what it's all about!; **(no) ~!** just so!

Wło|chy (**-ch**; *loc pl* **-szech**) *pl* Italy

wło|s (**-sa, -sy**; *loc sg* **-sie**) *m* hair; **włosy** *pl* (*blond, gęste*) hair *sg*

włoski *adj* Italian

wł|ożyć (**-ożę, -ożysz**; *imp* **-óż**) *vb pf od* **wkładać**

wnętrznośc|i (**-i**) *pl* entrails; **wypatroszyć ~** to gut

wni|eść (**-osę, -esiesz**; *imp* **-eś**; *pt* **-ósł, -osła, -eśli**) *vb pf od* **wnosić**

wnikliwy *adj* **1** (*badanie*) careful **2** (*zapach, dźwięk*) penetrating

wnios|ek (**-ku, -ki**; *inst sg* **-kiem**) *m* **1** (*propozycja*) proposal **2** (*wynik rozumowania*) conclusion **3** (*podanie*) application; **dojść do wniosku, że...** to reach the conclusion that...; **wyciągnęła ~, że...** she drew the conclusion that...

wno|sić (**-szę, -sisz**; *imp* **-ś**; *pf* **wnieść**) *vt* **1** (*umieścić we wnętrzu*) to carry in **2** (*przen: radość*) to bring **3** (*Fin: opłatę, składkę*) to pay **4** (*przedstawić: podanie*) to put in

WNP *abbr* (= *Wspólnota Niepodległych Państw*) CIS (= *Commonwealth of Independent States*)

wnucz|ek (**-ka, -kowie**; *inst sg* **-kiem**) *m* grandson

wnucz|ka (**-ki, -ki**; *dat sg & loc sg* **-ce**; *gen pl* **-ek**) *f* granddaughter

wnu|k (**-ka, -kowie** *lub* **-ki**; *inst sg* **-kiem**) *m* grandson; **wnuki** *pl* grandchildren

wo|da (**-dy, -dy**; *dat sg & loc sg* **-dzie**; *gen pl* **wód**) *f* water; **~ miękka/twarda** soft/hard water; **~ słodka/morska** fresh/salt water; **~ pitna** drinking water; **~ święcona** holy water; **~ powierzchniowa** surface water; **spuszczać (spuścić** *pf*) **wodę** to flush the toilet

Wodni|k (**-ka, -ki**; *inst sg* **-kiem**) *m* (*Astrol*) Aquarius

woj. *abbr* (= *województwo*): **~ lublińskie** the Lublin Province

województ|wo (**-wa, -wa**; *loc sg* **-wie**) *nt* province; **~ lublińskie** the Lublin Province

WOJEWÓDZTWO

Województwo is an administrative unit in Poland (the equivalent of English "regions"). The number of **województwa** has changed over the centuries and currently there are 16. **Województwa** also make up part of local government – many decisions concerning the life of the local community are made at this level.

woj|na (**-ny, -ny**; *dat sg & loc sg* **-nie**; *gen pl* **-en**) *f* war; **pierwsza/druga ~ światowa** the First/Second World War; **~ partyzancka** guerilla war; **~ domowa** civil war; **~ secesyjna** the American Civil War

wojs|ko (**-ka, -ka**; *inst sg* **-kiem**) *nt* army; **pójść do wojska** to join the army

wojskowy *adj* (*mundur, koszary*) military ▷ *m decl like adj* serviceman

wokali|sta (**-sty, -ści**; *dat sg & loc sg* **-ście**) *m decl like f in sg* singer

wokalist|ka (**-ki, -ki**; *dat sg & loc sg* **-ce**; *gen pl* **-ek**) *f* singer

wokoło, wokół *prep +gen* round ▷ *adv* all around

wol|a (**-i**) *f* will; **dobra ~** goodwill; **wolna ~** free will; **brak mu silnej woli, żeby rzucić palenie** he hasn't got the willpower to give up smoking; **ostatnia ~** (*testament*) will; **mimo woli** involuntarily; **jeść do woli** to eat one's fill

wol|eć (**-ę, -isz**) *vt, vi* to prefer; **wolę herbatę niż kawę** I prefer tea to coffee; **Spartanie woleli zginąć niż się poddać** the Spartans would rather die than surrender; **woli o tym nie mówić** he'd rather not talk about it; **wolę, jak drzwi są otwarte** I'd prefer the door open

wolno[1] *adv* **1** (*powoli*) slowly **2** (*swobodnie*) freely; **~ stojący budynek** a free-standing building

wolno[2] *inv*: **tu nie ~ palić** you can't smoke here; **nie ~ mi palić** I'm not allowed to smoke; **są sprawy, o których nie ~ nam nigdy zapomnieć** there are things that

we have no right ever to forget; **czy ~ o coś zapytać?** can I ask you something?
wolnoś|ć (**-ci**) *f* freedom
wolny *adj* **1** (*niezależny*) free **2** (*niezajęty*) free **3** (*nieżonaty/ niezamężna*) single; **3 maja jest dniem ~m od pracy** the third of May is a day off work; **czy pan dyrektor jest ~?** is the manager available?
woł|ać (**-am, -asz**; *pf* **za-**) *vt* to call ▷ *vi* to call
wołowi|na (**-ny**; *dat sg & loc sg* **-nie**) *f* beef
wołowy *adj*: **mięso wołowe** beef
wo|zić (**-żę, -zisz**; *imp* **woź** *lub* **wóź**) *vt* **1** (*towar*) to transport **2** (*samochodem*) to drive
wód|ka (**-ki, -ki**; *dat sg & loc sg* **-ce**; *gen pl* **-ek**) *f* vodka
wówczas *adv* then
wóz|ek (**-ka, -ki**; *inst sg* **-kiem**) *m* **1** pram (*Brit*), baby carriage (*US*) **2** (*spacerówka*) pushchair (*Brit*), stroller (*US*); **~ inwalidzki** wheelchair; **~ w supermarkecie/na lotnisku** shopping/baggage trolley
WP *abbr* **1** (= *Wielmożny Pan*) Mr **2** (= *Wielmożna Pani*) Mrs, Ms **3** (= *Wielmożni Państwo*) Mr and Mrs **4** (= *Wojsko Polskie*) Polish Army
wpad|ać (**-am, -asz**; *pf* **wpaść**) *vt* to fall; **~ w panikę** to fall into a panic; **~ w długi** to run into debt
wpa|ść (**-dnę, -dniesz**; *imp* **-dnij**; *pt* **-dł, -dła, -dli**) *vb pf od* **wpadać**; **samochód wpadł na drzewo/ wpadł w poślizg** the car ran into a tree/went into a skid; **mój ojciec wpadł pod pociąg** my father was hit by a train; **wpadła w rozpacz** she fell victim to despair; **~ w pułapkę** to fall into a trap; **może wpadnę dziś wieczorem** maybe I'll drop by tonight; **piłka wpadła do bramki** the ball went into the net
wpatr|ywać się (**-uję, -ujesz**; *pf* **wpatrzyć**) *vr*: **~ w** to stare at; **~ jak sroka w kość** (*przen*) to stare intently
wpi|s (**-su, -sy**; *loc sg* **-sie**) *m* (*w dokumentach*) entry; **~ do księgi zwiedzających** an entry in the visitors' book; **~ na blogu** blogpost
wpis|ywać (**-uję, -ujesz**; *pf* **-ać**) *vt* **1** to write down **2** (*do rejestru*) to add
wpła|cać (**-cam, -casz**; *pf* **-cić**) *vt* to pay (in); **~ składki członkowskie** to pay a membership fee
wpły|w (**-wu, -wy**; *loc sg* **-wie**) *m* influence; **wpływy** *pl* **1** (*Fin: przychody*) takings **2** (*Teatr: znajomości*) influential friends; **czy wierzysz we ~ gwiazd na los ludzki?** do you believe that the stars have an influence on human affairs?
wpływ|ać (**-am, -asz**; *pf* **wpłynąć**) *vi* to come in; **okręt wpływał do portu** the boat entered the harbour; **pieniądze wpłynęły na konto parafialne** money poured into the parish's account; **to może źle wpłynąć na pana zdrowie** that can have an adverse effect on your health
wpływowy *adj* (*znajomy, polityk*) influential
wrac|ać (**-am, -asz**; *pf* **wrócić**) *vi* to return; **kiedy pan wróci?** when will you be back?; **wróćmy do pierwszego pytania** let's return to the first question
wraz *adv*: **~ z matką zginęło w wypadku dwoje dzieci** the accident claimed the lives of two children along with their mother
wraże|nie (**-nia, -nia**; *gen pl* **-ń**) *nt* impression; **ulegam wrażeniu, że...** I have the feeling that...; **zrobiła na mnie złe ~** she made a bad impression on me
wrażliwoś|ć (**-ci**) *f* sensitivity
wrażliwy *adj* (*skóra, zmysł węchu*) sensitive; **był bardzo ~ na krzywdę zwierząt** he was very sensitive to animal cruelty; **czy jest pan ~ na ból?** are you sensitive to pain?; **testy są bardzo wrażliwe na zmiany temperatury** the tests are very sensitive to changes in temperature
wrób|el (**-la, -le**; *gen pl* **-li**) *m* sparrow
wró|cić (**-cę, -cisz**; *imp* **-ć**) *vb pf od* **wracać**
wr|óg (**-oga, -ogowie**; *inst sg* **-ogiem**) *m* **1** (*nieprzyjaciel*) enemy **2** (*przeciwnik*) opponent
wróż|yć (**-ę, -ysz**) *vt* **1** (*pf* **wy-**) (*osoba: przepowiadać*) to predict **2** (*zjawisko,*

zachowanie: *być zapowiedzią*) to foreshadow ▷ *vi*: **~ (po~** *pf*) **komuś z gwiazd** to tell sb's fortune from the stars; **moja matka wróżyła z fusów** my mother used to read fortunes in tea leaves

wrzeć (**wrę, wrzesz**; *3 sg* **wre** *lub* **wrze**; *imp* **wrzyj**) *vi* to boil

wrze|sień (**-śnia, -śnie**; *gen pl* **-śniów** *lub* **-śni**) *m* September

wrzuca|ć (**-m, -sz**) *vt* to upload

wschodni *adj* east; **wiatr ~** an east wind; **Europa W~a** Eastern Europe

wschodnioeuropejski *adj* Eastern European; **czas ~** Eastern European Time

wscho|dzić (**-dzi**; *pf* **wzejść**) *vi* **1** (*o ciałach niebieskich*) to rise **2** (*o roślinach*) to sprout

wsch|ód (**-odu**; *loc sg* **-odzie**) *m* **1** (*nom pl* **-ody**) sunrise **2** (*Geo*) (the) east; **wieje od wschodu** the wind is in the east; **W~** (*kraje wschodnie*) the East

wsiad|ać (**-am, -asz**; *pf* **wsiąść**) *vi*: **~ do autobusu/pociągu** to get on a bus/train; **~ do samochodu** to get in a car; **~ na statek** to board a ship

wskazów|ka (**-ki, -ki**; *dat sg & loc sg* **-ce**; *gen pl* **-ek**) *f* **1** (*zegara*) hand **2** (*przen*) indicator; **wskazówki dotyczące techniki jazdy** tips on driving technique; **zgodnie z ruchem wskazówek zegara** clockwise; **przeciwnie do ruchu wskazówek zegara** anticlockwise (*Brit*), counterclockwise (*US*)

wskaz|ywać (**-uję, -ujesz**; *pf* **-ać**) *vt, vi* to indicate; **czy mógłby pan wskazać powody takiej decyzji?** would you indicate the reasons for this decision?; **dziadek wskazał mnie jako wykonawcę testamentu** grandfather identified me as his executor; **wszystko wskazuje na pogarszanie się sytuacji** all signs point to the fact that the situation is getting worse

wspaniale *adv* magnificently; **to ~!** that's fantastic!

wspaniały *adj* **1** (*efektowny*) wonderful **2** (*strój, uroczystość*) magnificent; **to ~ pomysł!** that's a brilliant idea!

wspier|ać (**-am, -asz**; *pf* **wesprzeć**) *vt* to support; **~ się** *vr* (*podtrzymywać się*) to support one another; **wspierał się na lasce** he leant on his stick; **wspierali się wzajemnie w trudnych sytuacjach** they supported one another through difficult times

wspólnie *adv* together; **~ z kimś** together with sb

współczesnoś|ć (**-ci**) *f* the present day

współczesny *adj* contemporary; **sztuka współczesna** contemporary art

współczuci|e (**-a**) *nt* sympathy; **proszę przyjąć najszczersze wyrazy współczucia** may I offer my most sincere condolences

współcz|uć (**-uję, -ujesz**) *vi*: **~ komuś** to feel sorry for sb; **~ komuś (z powodu czegoś)** to offer sb one's sympathy (over sth)

współprac|ować (**-uję, -ujesz**) *vi* **1** to co-operate **2** (*o pisarzach*) to collaborate

wst|awać (**-aję, -ajesz**; *imp* **-awaj**; *pf* **-ać**) *vi* to get up; **wstawał bardzo późno** he used to rise very late; **odstawiła kubek herbaty i wstała z krzesła** she put down her tea and stood up

wsta|wiać (**-wiam, -wiasz**; *pf* **-wić**) *vt* to set; **~ się** *vr*: **zawsze wstawiała się za synem** she would always put in a good word for her son; **dentysta wstawił ząb** the dentist replaced the tooth; **wstawiłem wodę na herbatę** I put the kettle on for tea

wstecz *adv* (*ruszyć, spojrzeć*) backwards

wstę|p (**-pu, -py**; *loc sg* **-pie**) *m* **1** (*wejście*) entry **2** (*początek*: *w książce*) introduction; **na ~ie kilka refleksji ogólnych** to begin with, some general reflections

wstępny *adj* **1** (*początkowy*) preliminary **2** (*prowizoryczny*) provisional; **wstępna faza prac** the initial phase; **wstępne oględziny** a preliminary examination

wstręt (**-tu**; *loc sg* **-cie**) *m* revulsion; **czuła do niego ~** she found him repulsive
wstrętny *adj* revolting
wstyd (**-du**; *loc sg* **-dzie**) *m* shame; **czy ty zawsze musisz narobić mi ~u?** must you always make me ashamed of you?; **nie ~ ci, że zapomniałaś o ojcu?** don't you feel shame that you have forgotten your father?
wstydliwy *adj* bashful
wstydzić się (**-dzę, -dzisz**; *imp* **-dź**) *vr*: **wstydziłem się za zachowanie mojego ojca** I was embarrassed by my father's behaviour (*Brit*) *lub* behavior (*US*); **nie wstydzisz się, że kłamałaś?** aren't you ashamed that you were lying?; **czy wstydzi się własnej matki?** is he ashamed of his own mother?; **wstydziła się powiedzieć to rodzicom** she was embarrassed to tell her parents
wszedł *itd. vb zob.* **wejść**
wszędzie *adv* everywhere; **~ go pełno!** he gets everywhere!
wszyscy *pron decl like adj* all; **~ ludzie rodzą się równi** everybody is born equal; **~ wiedzą** everybody *lub* everyone knows; **wszystkich nie zadowolisz** you'll never please everybody; **~ razem!** all together!
wszystkie *pron decl like adj* all; **~ drużyny** all (the) teams; **na ~ sposoby** in every possible way
wszystko *pron decl like adj* everything; **mimo ~** in spite of everything; **przede wszystkim musisz mu o tym powiedzieć** first and foremost you have got to tell him about it; **zrobiłbym ~, żeby dostać tę pracę** I'd have done anything to get that job; **gdzie pan chce usiąść? – ~ jedno** where do you wish to sit? – I don't mind; **~ w porządku?** is everything OK?; **wszystkiego najlepszego!** all the best!; **to na dzisiaj ~** that's all for today; **kiedy pan się obudzi, będzie już po wszystkim** when you wake up it will all be over
wściekły *adj* **1** (*o zwierzętach: chory na wściekliznę*) rabid **2** (*o ludziach: zły*) furious
wśród *prep* among
wtedy *pron* then; **~, kiedy...** when...
wtorek (**-ku, -ki**; *inst sg* **-kiem**) *m* Tuesday
wuj (**-a, -owie**) *m* uncle
wujek (**-ka, -kowie**; *inst sg* **-kiem**) *m* uncle
ww. *abbr* (= *wyżej wymieniony*) above-mentioned
wy *pron* you
wybaczać (**-am, -asz**; *pf* **-yć**) *vt*: **~ (komuś) coś** to forgive (sb) sth
wybierać (**-am, -asz**; *pf* **wybrać**) *vt* **1** to choose **2** (*wodę ze studni*) to draw; **~ się** *vr*: **wybieram się do biura/do Warszawy** I'm going to the office/to Warsaw; **wybrała jego numer** she dialled his number; **wybrał sto funtów z konta** he withdrew a hundred pounds from his account; **wybiera się w podróż/na spacer** he's going away/for a walk
wybitny *adj* (*naukowiec, osiągnięcie, dzieło*) outstanding
wybór (**-oru, -ory**; *loc sg* **-orze**) *m* (*zawodu*) choice; **wybory** *pl* election(s *pl*); **nie miałem wyboru** I had no choice
wybrzeże (**-a, -a**; *gen pl* **-y**) *nt* coast
wybuch (**-u, -y**) *m* **1** (*eksplozja*) explosion **2** (*gwałtowny początek: paniki*) outbreak; **~ wulkanu** volcanic eruption
wybuchać (**-am, -asz**; *pf* **-nąć**) *vi* **1** (*bomba*) to explode **2** (*panika, epidemia*) to break out **3** (*Geol: wulkan*) to erupt; **wybuchnął płaczem/gniewem** he burst into tears/flared up angrily; **wybuchnęła śmiechem** she burst out laughing
wybuchowy *adj* **1** (*substancja*) explosive **2** (*charakter*) quick-tempered; **materiały wybuchowe** explosives
wychodzić (**-dzę, -dzisz**; *imp* **-dź**; *pf* **wyjść**) *vi* **1** (*opuścić miejsce*) to leave **2** (*stać się widocznym: słońce, inicjatywa, pismo*) to come out **3** (*udać się*) to work (out); **wyszedł z domu** he went out of the house; **zakładnik wyszedł z domu przed chwilą** a hostage came out of the house a little while ago; **wyjdź na spacer!**

go out for a walk!; **bardzo chciałbym ~ z długów** I would love to get out of debt; **właśnie wyszła za mąż** she has just got married; **moje okno wychodzi na zachód** my window looks west; **~ z mody** to go out of fashion

wychowawc|a (**-y, -y**) *m decl like f in sg* (*Szkol*) year-group tutor (*Brit*), home-room teacher (*US*)

wychowawczy|ni (**-ni, -nie**; *gen pl* **-ń**) *f* (*Szkol*) year-group tutor (*Brit*), home-room teacher (*US*)

wychow|ywać (**-uję, -ujesz**; *pf* **-ać**) *vt* **1** (*uczyć*) to bring up **2** (*wykształcić*) to educate; **~ się** *vr* to be brought up; **wychowywał się u dziadków** he was brought up by his grandparents

wyciecz|ka (**-ki, -ki**; *dat sg & loc sg* **-ce**; *gen pl* **-ek**) *f* trip, excursion; **~ piesza** a walking trip; **~ po mieście prowadzi za kościół** the city tour takes you behind the church

wycieńczony *adj* emaciated

wycierać (**-am, -asz**; *pf* **-trzeć**) *vt* to wipe up

wycof|ywać (**-uję, -ujesz**; *pf* **-ać**) *vt* to withdraw; **~ się** *vr* to withdraw; **sprawa została wycofana z sądu** the case was withdrawn

wyczerpujący *adj* **1** (*ćwiczenie fizyczne*) exhausting **2** (*odpowiedź*) exhaustive

wydajny *adj* efficient

wyda|nie (**-nia, -nia**; *gen pl* **-ń**) *nt* edition; **~ książki w miękkiej oprawie** paperback edition

wydarze|nie (**-nia, -nia**; *gen pl* **-ń**) *nt* event; **ostatnie wydarzenia budzą niepokój** recent events are worrying

wyd|awać (**-aję, -ajesz**; *pf* **-ać**) *vt* **1** (*zapłacić*) to spend **2** (*wystawić*) to issue **3** (*wydzielić*) to serve; **~ się** *vr* **1** (*wyglądać*) to seem **2** (*o tajemnicach*) to come out; **~ kogoś za mąż** to marry sb off (*woman to man*); **wydał opinię** he put forward his opinion; **stołówka wydaje obiady od 12:00** the canteen serves lunches from 12.00; **wydawał się zmęczony** he seemed exhausted; **wydało się prawdopodobne, że...** it seemed likely that...

wydawc|a (**-y, -y**) *m* publisher

wydawnict|wo (**-wa, -wa**; *loc sg* **-wie**) *nt* **1** (*o instytucji*) publishing house **2** (*o publikacji*) publication; **~ ciągłe** a periodical

wydech (**-u, -y**) *m* **1** exhalation **2** (*Tech*: *w samochodzie*) exhaust

wydobrz|eć (**-eję, -ejesz**) *vi pf* to get better

wydorośl|eć (**-eję, -ejesz**) *vi pf* to grow up

wydzia|ł (**-łu, -ły**; *loc sg* **-le**) *m* **1** (*w urzędzie*) department **2** (*na uniwersytecie*) faculty

wydźwię|k (**-ku**; *inst sg* **-kiem**) *m* overtones *pl*; **wystawa ma ~ polityczny** the exhibition has political overtones

wyelimin|ować (**-uję, -ujesz**) *vb pf od* **eliminować**

wyemigr|ować (**-uję, -ujesz**) *vb pf od* **emigrować**

wygani|ać (**-am, -asz**; *pf* **wygonić** *lub* **wygnać**) *vt* to drive (out); **~ na dwór** to chase outside

wygin|ać (**-am, -asz**; *pf* **wygiąć**) *vt* to bend; **~ się** *vr* to bend

wygi|nąć (**-nie**) *vi pf* to become extinct

wyglą|d (**-du**; *loc sg* **-dzie**) *m* appearance

wygląd|ać (**-am, -asz**; *pf* **wyjrzeć**) *vi* to look; **zawsze wygląda przez okno** she is always looking out of the window; **czy grubo w tym wyglądam?** does this make me look fat?; **wyglądasz bardzo ładnie w tej sukience** you look really nice in that dress; **nie wygląda na swoje lata** he doesn't look his age; **jak ona wygląda?** what does she look like?; **wygląda na to, że...** it looks as if...

wygłasz|ać (**-am, -asz**; *pf* **wygłosić**) *vt* (*przemówienie, kwestię*) to deliver (*a speech*)

wygłupi|ać się (**-am, -asz**) *vr* to fool about

wygłu|pić się (**-pię, -pisz**) *vr pf* to make a fool of o.s.

wyg|oda (**-ody, -ody**; *dat sg & loc sg* **-odzie**; *gen pl* **-ód**) *f* convenience; **wygody** *pl* amenities *pl*; **dom z wszelkimi ~mi** a house with all mod cons

wygodnie *adv* comfortably
wygodny *adj* **1** (*fotel*) comfortable **2** (*termin*) convenient **3** (*osoba*) comfort-loving
wygran|a (**-ej, -e**) *f decl like adj* win; **nigdy nie dawała za wygraną** she never gave up; **trafił główną wygraną** he hit the jackpot
wygryw|ać (**-am, -asz**; *pf* **wygrać**) *vt, vi* to win
wyjaś|niać (**-niam, -niasz**; *pf* **-nić**) *vt* to explain; **~ się** *vr* (*o sytuacji, sporze*) to become clear; **tajemnica się wyjaśniła** the mystery is solved
wyjaśnie|nie (**-nia, -nia**; *gen pl* **-ń**) *nt* explanation
wyj|azd (**-azdu, -azdy**; *loc sg* **-eździe**) *m* **1** (*odjazd*) departure **2** (*podróż*) journey **3** (*miejsce*) exit; **rodzinny ~ za miasto** a family trip out of town
wyjąt|ek (**-ku, -ki**; *inst sg* **-kiem**) *m* exception; **zrobiła dla mnie ~** she made an exception for me
wyjątkowo *adv* exceptionally; **~ pozwolę ci oglądać TV do późna** as an exception you can stay up late to watch TV
wyjątkowy *adj* (*uprzejmość, grzeczność*) exceptional; **stan ~** (*Pol*) state of emergency
wyj|echać (**-adę, -edziesz**; *imp* **-edź**) *vb pf od* **wyjeżdżać**
wyjeżdż|ać (**-am, -asz**; *pf* **wyjechać**) *vi* **1** (*opuścić miejsce*) to go out **2** (*w podróż*) to go away
wyjm|ować (**-uję, -ujesz**; *pf* **wyjąć**) *vt* to take out; **~ pieniądze z bankomatu** to take money out of a cash machine (*Brit*) *lub* ATM
wyjrz|eć (**-ę, -ysz**; *imp* **-yj**) *vb pf od* **wyglądać**
wyjś|cie (**-cia**) *nt* **1** (*czynność*) departure **2** (*nom pl* **-cia**; *gen pl* **-ć**) (*miejsce*) exit **3** (*nom pl* **-cia**; *gen pl* **-ć**) (*z trudnej sytuacji: rozwiązanie*) solution; **nie miała wyjścia, jak tylko to zrobić** she had no choice but to do it
wyj|ść (**-dę, -dziesz**; *imp* **-dź**; *pt* **wyszedł, wyszła, wyszli**) *vb pf od* **wychodzić**; **~ z siebie ze złości** to fly into a rage
wyka|z (**-zu, -zy**; *loc sg* **-zie**) *m* (*spis*) register
wyką|pać (**-pię, -piesz**) *vb pf od* **kąpać**
wyklucz|ać (**-am, -asz**; *pf* **-yć**) *vt* to rule out; **~ się** *vr* to be mutually exclusive
wykluczony *adj*: **to jest wykluczone** it's out of the question
wykła|d (**-du, -dy**; *loc sg* **-dzie**) *m* lecture
wykładowc|a (**-y, -y**) *m decl like f in sg* lecturer
wykonawc|a (**-y, -y**) *m decl like f in sg* **1** (*wytwórca*) contractor **2** (*realizator: testamentu*) executor **3** (*artysta*) performer
wykon|ywać (**-uję, -ujesz**; *pf* **-ać**) *vt* to carry out; **wykonać rozkaz** to carry out an order; **~ zawód stolarza** to work as a joiner
wykończony *adj* finished
wykre|s (**-su, -sy**; *loc sg* **-sie**) *m* (*rysunek*) chart
wykształ|cać (**-cam, -casz**; *impf* **-cić**) *vt pf* to educate
wykształceni|e (**-a**) *nt* education; **~ podstawowe** primary (*Brit*) *lub* elementary (*US*) education; **~ średnie** secondary education; **~ wyższe** higher education; **jest z wykształcenia ekonomistą** he is an economist by training
wykształ|cić (**-cę, -cisz**; *imp* **-ć**) *vb pf od* **kształcić, wykształcać**
wykształcony *adj* educated
wykwalifikowany *adj* (*położna, pomoc domowa*) qualified; **robotnik ~** skilled worker
wykwintny *adj* (*zapach, potrawa, strój*) (very) fine
wyląd|ować (**-uję, -ujesz**) *vb pf od* **lądować**
wylecz|yć (**-ę, -ysz**) *vb pf od* **leczyć**
wyle|w (**-wu, -wy**; *loc sg* **-wie**) *m*: **~ krwi do mózgu** stroke
wylew|ać (**-am, -asz**; *pf* **wylać**) *vt* **1** (*płyn*) to pour (out) **2** (*pot: pracownika*) to sack ▷ *vi* (*wystąpić z brzegów*) to overflow; **~ się** *vr* (*rozlewać się*) to spill; **zupa wylała się na stół** the soup spilled over the table

wylog|ować się (**-uję, -ujesz**) *vr pf* (*Komput*) to log out
wylo|t (**-tu, -ty**; *loc sg* **-cie**) *m* exit; **nigdy nie kieruj ~u lufy karabinu w kierunku ludzi** never point the muzzle of a rifle towards people; **przejrzałem go na ~** I saw right through him; **jesteśmy na wylocie** we are just about to leave
wyluz|ować się (**-uję, -ujesz**) *vr pf* to chill out
wyłącz|ać (**-am, -asz**; *pf* **-yć**) *vt* (*prąd, telewizor*) to turn off; **~ się** *vr* (*Tel*) to hang up; **~ kogoś/coś** (**z** *+gen*) to exclude sb/sth (from); **wyłączając tu obecnych** present company excepted; **czuł się wyłączony z rozmowy** he felt left out of the conversation; **wyłącz żelazko z sieci!** unplug the iron!
wyłącznie *adv* exclusively
wyłączony *adj* switched off
wymag|ać (**-am, -asz**) *vt +gen* to require; **ten projekt wymaga czasu** this project requires time
wymagający *adj* (*nauczyciel, rodzic*) demanding
wymaga|nia (**-ń**) *pl* demands
wymagany *adj* (*opłata, strój, dokument*) required
wymeldow|ywać się (**-uję, -ujesz**; *pf* **-ać**) *vr* to check out; **~ z hotelu** to check out of a hotel
wymia|na (**-ny, -ny**; *dat* **-nie**) *f* **1** exchange **2** (*części*) replacement; **kantor wymiany** bureau de change
wymie|niać (**-niam, -niasz**; *pf* **-nić**) *vt* **1** to exchange **2** (*w samochodzie: olej, opony*) to change **3** (*waluty obce*) to change **4** (*wyliczać*) to list; **wymienił dolary na funty** he changed dollars for pounds; **wymień pięć zwierząt żyjących w Afryce** name five animals living in Africa; **czy mogę to wymienić na rozmiar 12?** could I change this for a size 12?
wymienialny *adj* (*waluta, żeton, ubranie*) convertible
wymienny *adj* (*element*) replaceable; **handel ~** barter
wymiot|ować (**-uję, -ujesz**; *pf* **z-**) *vi* to vomit
wymiot|y (**-ów**) *pl* vomiting *sg*
wymo|wa (**-wy**; *dat sg & loc sg* **-wie**) *f* **1** (*Jęz*) pronunciation **2** (*znaczenie*) significance; **to wydarzenie o szczególnej wymowie** it's an event of great significance
wymówie|nie (**-nia, -nia**; *gen pl* **-ń**) *nt* (*zwolnienie*) notice; **dostali miesięczne ~** they got a month's notice; **już złożyła ~** she has already put in her notice
wymusz|ać (**-am, -asz**; *pf* **wymusić**) *vt* to extort; **wymuszono na niej przyznanie się do winy** they forced her into confessing her guilt
wymyśl|ać (**-am, -asz**) *vt* (*pf* **-ić**) to invent ▷ *vi*: **wymyślał mi** he hurled abuse at me
wynagradz|ać (**-am, -asz**; *pf* **wynagrodzić**) *vt*: **~ coś komuś** to make sth up to sb; **wynagrodzono mu straty** they made his losses up to him; **~ kogoś za poniesiony trud** to compensate sb for inconvenience
wynagrodze|nie (**-nia, -nia**; *gen pl* **-ń**) *nt* (*miesięczne, tygodniowe, sowite*) pay
wynajdywać (**-uję, -ujesz**; *pf* **wynaleźć**) *vt* to discover
wynaj|em (**-mu**; *loc sg* **-mie**) *m* **1** (*mieszkania*) renting **2** (*samochodu*) hiring
wynajęci|e (**-a**) *nt* = **wynajem**; **do wynajęcia** to let (*Brit*), for rent (*US*)
wynajm|ować (**-uję, -ujesz**; *pf* **wynająć**) *vt* **1** (*pracownika, samochód*) to hire **2** (*pokój*) to rent
wynalazc|a (**-y, -y**) *m decl like f in sg* inventor
wynalaz|ek (**-ku, -ki**; *inst sg* **-kiem**) *m* (*pożyteczny, pomysłowy, genialny*) invention
wyna|leźć (**-jdę, -jdziesz**; *imp* **-jdź**; *pt* **-lazł, -lazła, -leźli**) *vt pf od* **wynajdywać**
wyni|k (**-ku, -ki**; *inst sg* **-kiem**) *m* **1** (*doskonały, rekordowy, mierny*) result **2** (*rozmów*) outcome; **w ~u śledztwa aresztowano trzy osoby** as a result of the investigation three people have been arrested
wynik|ać (**-a**; *pf* **-nąć**) *vi* to arise; **z braku informacji wynikło wiele**

nieporozumień many misunderstandings arose from lack of information; **wynika z tego, że...** it follows that...
wynos *inv*: **danie na ~** a takeaway (*Brit*), a take-out (*US*)
wyno|sić (**-szę, -sisz**; *imp* **-ś**; *pf* **wynieść**) *vt* **1** to take away **2** (*usunąć*) to take out **3** (*awansować*) to elevate **4** (*Mat, Fin*) to amount to; **~ się** *vr* (*pot*: *odchodzić*) to clear out; **koszty wynoszą cztery miliony złotych** the costs will amount to four million zlotys; **wynoś się (stąd)!** get out (of here)!
wyobraź|nia (**-ni**) *f* (*chora, bujna*) imagination
wyobraż|ać (**-am, -asz**; *pf* **wyobrazić**) *vt* to represent; **wyobraź sobie, jak nam było wstyd** imagine our embarrassment; **co ty sobie wyobrażasz!** what are you thinking!
wyobraże|nie (**-nia, -nia**; *gen pl* **-ń**) *nt* (*pogląd*) idea
wypad|ać (**-am, -asz**; *pf* **wypaść**) *vi* **1** (*wylecieć*: *o włosach*) to fall out **2** (*wybiegać*): **pociąg wypadł z torów** the train jumped the track **3** (*wydarzyć się*): **Wielkanoc wypada często w marcu** Easter often falls in March **4** (*wynikać*): **wypada po dwa na każde gospodarstwo** it works out at two for each farm; **wszystko wypadło dobrze** all went well; **przyjdę, jeżeli nic nie wypadnie** I'll be there, if nothing happens to stop me; **spotkanie wypadło z planu** the meeting was cancelled
wypad|ek (**-ku, -ki**; *inst sg* **-kiem**) *m* **1** (*nieszczęśliwe wydarzenie*) accident **2** (*zdarzenie*) incident; **na ~ wojny/pożaru** in case of war/fire; **w nagłych wypadkach** in cases of emergency; **nie było wypadku** on no occasion; **w takim wypadku miał rację** in that case he was right; **na wszelki ~** just in case
wypakow|ywać (**-uję, -ujesz**; *pf* **-ać**) *vt* (*plecak, walizkę, siatkę*) to unpack
wypełniony *adj* full; **~ po brzegi** full to the brim
wy|pić (**-piję, -pijesz**) *vb pf od* **pić, wypijać**
wypijać (**-pijam, -pijasz**) *vb* to drain (*glass*)
wypis|ywać (**-uję, -ujesz**; *pf* **-ać**) *vt* **1** (*receptę*) to write out **2** (*formularz*) to fill out **3** (*zapisywać*) to write down; **~ się** *vr* (*atrament*) to run out; **kiedy wypiszą ją ze szpitala?** when are they going to discharge her?; **wypisał się z kościoła ewangelickiego** he left the evangelical church
wypła|cać (**-cam, -casz**; *pf* **-cić**) *vt*: **~ coś (komuś)** (*zaliczkę, prowizję*) to pay (sb) sth
wypłacalny *adj* solvent
wypła|ta (**-ty, -ty**; *dat sg & loc sg* **-cie**) *f* (*Fin*: *wypłacanie należności*) payment; **należność do wypłaty** amount payable
wypocz|ąć (**-nę, -niesz**; *imp* **-nij**) *vi pf* to get some rest
wypoczęty *adj* (*twarz, cera*) well-rested
wypoczyn|ek (**-ku**; *inst sg* **-kiem**) *m* (*letni, zimowy, aktywny*) rest
wypoczyw|ać (**-am, -asz**; *pf* **wypocząć**) *vi* to rest
wyposażony *adj*: **dobrze ~** well-equipped; **łódź została wyposażona w motor** the boat was fitted with a motor
wypowie|dź (**-dzi, -dzi**; *gen pl* **-dzi**) *f* statement
wypożycz|ać (**-am, -asz**; *pf* **-yć**) *vt*: **~ coś (komuś)** to lend sth (to sb); **~ coś (od kogoś)** to borrow sth (from sb)
wypożyczal|nia (**-ni, -nie**; *gen pl* **-ni**) *f* hire-shop; **~ strojów karnawałowych** carnival-costume depot; **~ samochodów** car hire (*Brit*), auto rental (*US*)
wy|prać (**-piorę, -pierzesz**) *vb pf od* **prać**
wypras|ować (**-uję, -ujesz**) *vb pf od* **prasować**
wypra|wa (**-wy, -wy**; *dat sg & loc sg* **-wie**) *f* (*ekspedycja*) expedition
wyproduk|ować (**-uję, -ujesz**) *vb pf od* **produkować**

wyprze|dzać (**-dzam, -dzasz**; *pf* **-dzić**) *vt* **1** (*na drodze*) to pass **2** (*być bardziej postępowym*) to be ahead of
wypyt|ywać (**-uję, -ujesz**; *pf* **-ać**) *vt*: **~ kogoś (o coś)** to question sb (about sth)
wyra|z (**-zu, -zy**; *loc sg* **-zie**) *m* **1** (*Ling*) word **2** (*objaw*) expression; **~ obcy** (*Ling*) a foreign expression; **podpisz tę petycję i daj ~ swojej złości!** sign this petition and give expression to your anger!; **~ wdzięczności** an expression of gratitude; **~y współczucia** my sympathies
wyrazisty *adj* **1** (*gest*) expressive **2** (*nos*) distinctive
wyraźnie *adv* **1** (*słyszeć*) distinctly **2** (*zdenerwowany*) evidently
wyraźny *adj* **1** (*pismo*) clear **2** (*zapach*) distinctive **3** (*rozkaz*) evident
wyraż|ać (**-am, -asz**; *pf* **wyrazić**) *vt* to express; **~ się** *vr* (*wysławiać się*) to express o.s.; **rodzice muszą wyrazić zgodę na adopcję** the parents must agree to the adoption; **napięcie prądu wyrażamy w woltach** e.m.f. is expressed in volts; **jak ty się wyrażasz do nauczyciela!** what kind of language is that to use to the teacher!
wyraże|nie (**-nia, -nia**; *gen pl* **-ń**) *nt* (*idiomatyczne*) expression
wyro|k (**-ku, -ki**; *inst sg* **-kiem**) *m* verdict; **~ już zapadł** the verdict has already been reached; **~ skazujący** guilty verdict
wyrost|ek (**-ka, -ki**; *inst sg* **-kiem**) *m* **1** (*też*: **~ robaczkowy**) appendix **2** (*osoba*) youngster
wyrozumiały *adj* understanding
wyrzą|dzać (**-dzam, -dzasz**; *pf* **-dzić**) *vt*: **~ komuś krzywdę/szkodę** to inflict harm/damage on sb
wyrzu|cać (**-cam, -casz**) *vt* (*pf* **-cić**) to throw away *lub* out; **~ coś komuś** to reproach sb for sth; **wyrzucić kogoś z pracy/ze szkoły** to sack sb/ to exclude sb from school
wysch|nąć (**-nę, -niesz**; *imp* **-nij**; *pt* **-nął** *lub* **wysechł, -ła, -li**) *vb pf od* **schnąć, wysychać**
wysiad|ać (**-am, -asz**; *pf* **wysiąść**) *vi* **1** (*z pojazdu*) to get off **2** (*z samochodu*) to get out **3** (*pot*: *psuć się*) to pack up
wysil|ać (**-am, -asz**; *pf* **-ić**) *vt*: **~ mózg/pamięć** to rack one's brains/ memory; **~ się** *vr* to exert o.s.; **~ słuch** to strain one's ears; **~ się, żeby wstać** to make an effort to get up; **~ się na grzeczność** to try hard to be polite
wysił|ek (**-ku, -ki**; *inst sg* **-kiem**) *m* (*fizyczny, umysłowy*) effort; **wysiłki** *pl* efforts; **bez (żadnego) wysiłku** effortlessly
wy|słać[1] (**-ślę, -ślesz**; *imp* **-ślij**) *vb pf od* **wysyłać**
wy|słać[2] (**-ścielę, -ścielisz**; *imp* **-ściel**) *vb pf od* **wyściełać**
wysłuch|ać (**-am, -asz**) *vt pf* (*koncertu, wykładu*) to listen to; **~ kogoś do końca** to give sb a hearing
wy|soki *adj* **1** (*półka*) high **2** (*budynek, drzewo, człowiek*) tall **3** (*urzędnik*) high(-ranking) **4** (*Fiz*: *głos*) high-pitched; **~ na 3 metry** 3 metres (*Brit*) *lub* meters (*US*) high
wy|soko *adv* high (up); **~ płatna praca** highly-paid work; **~ postawione osoby** highly placed people
wys|pa (**-py, -py**; *dat sg & loc sg* **-pie**) *f* island; **Wyspy Brytyjskie** the British Isles
wystarcz|ać (**-a**; *pf* **-yć**) *vi* to be enough; **godzina wystarczy na przygotowania** an hour will do for preparations; **trzy krzesła wystarczą** three chairs will be enough; **jego nazwisko wystarczyło za reklamę** his name was publicity enough; **czy to wystarczy?** will that do?
wystarczająco *adv*: **~ długi** long enough; **~ dużo** enough
wystarczający *adj* (*kwota, ilość*) sufficient
wystart|ować (**-uję, -ujesz**) *vb pf od* **startować**
wysta|wa (**-wy, -wy**; *dat sg & loc sg* **-wie**) *f* **1** (*malarstwa*) exhibition **2** (*zwierząt*) show **3** (*sklepowa*) window display
występ|p (**-pu, -py**; *loc sg* **-pie**) *m* **1** (*popis*) performance **2** (*udział*) appearance **3** (*wystająca część*) ledge; **występy** *pl* show *sg*

występ|ować (**-uję, -ujesz**; *pf* **wystąpić**) *vi* **1** to occur **2** (*w sądzie: zabierać głos*) to speak **3** (*Film, Teatr*) to appear **4** (*Sport*) to take part **5** (*Med: o objawach*) to appear; **~ w imieniu kogoś/czegoś** to appear in the interests of sb/sth; **wystąpiła z pomysłem** she came forward with the idea; **on występował w wielu filmach** he has appeared in many films

wysusz|yć (**-ę, -ysz**) *vb pf od* **suszyć**

wysych|ać (**-a**; *pf* **wyschnąć**) *vi* to dry up

wysył|ka (**-ki, -ki**; *dat sg & loc sg* **-ce**; *gen pl* **-ek**) *f* (*listu, paczki, towaru*) dispatch

wyszczupl|eć (**-eję, -ejesz**) *vi pf* to slim down

wyszkol|ić (**-ę, -isz**) *vb pf od* **szkolić**

wyściełać (**-ścielam, -ścielasz**; *imp* **-ściel**) *vt*: **~ pudełko materiałem** to line the box with fabric

wyści|g (**-gu, -gi**; *inst sg* **-giem**) *m* race; **~ szczurów** (*przen*) the rat race

wyśmienity *adj* **1** (*aktor*) splendid **2** (*potrawa*) delicious

wyświadcz|ać (**-am, -asz**; *pf* **-yć**) *vt*: **~ komuś grzeczność** *lub* **przysługę** to do sb a favour (*Brit*) *lub* favor (*US*)

wyświetl|ać (**-am, -asz**; *pf* **-ić**) *vt* **1** (*film*) to project **2** (*Komput: informację*) to display

wytłumaczeni|e (**-a**) *nt* (*proste, oczywiste*) explanation

wytłumacz|yć (**-ę, -ysz**) *vb pf od* **tłumaczyć**

wytrwały *adj* persistent

wyt|rzeć (**-rę, -rzesz**; *imp* **-rzyj**; *pt* **-arł**) *vb pf od* **wycierać**

wytrzeźwi|eć (**-eję, -ejesz**) *vb pf od* **trzeźwieć**

wytrzym|ać (**-am, -asz**) *vi pf*: **nie ~** (*o moście, budowli*) to give way; (*o człowieku*) to lose one's cool

wytrzym|ywać (**-uję, -ujesz**; *pf* **-ać**) *vt* to bear ▹ *vi* to hold on

wywia|d (**-du, -dy**; *loc sg* **-dzie**) *m* **1** (*rozmowa*) interview **2** (*Pol, Wojsk: instytucja*) intelligence service; **~y można przeprowadzać również przez telefon** interviews can also be done over the phone

wywiąz|ywać się (**-uję, -ujesz**; *pf* **-ać**) *vr* **1** (*powstawać: dyskusja, walka*) to develop **2** (*wypełnić rolę*) to fulfil (expectations); **wywiązywał się z obowiązków** he did his duty; **musisz ~ z obietnic** *lub* **obietnicy** (*przen*) you have got to deliver (the goods)

wyzn|ać (**-am, -asz**) *vt pf*: **~ coś (komuś)** (*uczucia, tajemnicę*) to confess sth (to sb)

wyzna|nie (**-nia, -nia**; *gen pl* **-ń**) *nt* **1** (*sekretu*) confession **2** (*religia*) religion; **~ wiary** (*Rel*) the Creed

wyżej *adv comp od* **wysoko** ▹ *adv* (*w tekście*) above

wyższoś|ć (**-ci**) *f* superiority; **patrzeć na kogoś z wyższością** to look down on sb

wyższy *adj comp od* **wysoki** ▹ *adj* **1** (*wykształcenie*) higher **2** (*urzędnik*) higher-ranking; **siła wyższa** force majeure

wyży|wić (**-wię, -wisz**) *vt pf* to feed; **~ się** *vr pf* to subsist

wyżywieni|e (**-a**) *nt* food; **pełne/niepełne ~** full/half board

wzajemnie *adv* mutually; **pomagajcie sobie ~!** help one another!; **dziękuję – ~!** thank you – the same to you!

wzajemnoś|ć (**-ci**) *f* mutuality

wzajemny *adj* (*pomoc, opieka, uczucie*) mutual

wzdłuż *prep +gen* along ▹ *adv* (*przeciąć*) lengthways; **~ i wszerz** every way

wzgórz|e (**-a, -a**) *nt* hill

wziąć (**wezmę, weźmiesz**; *imp* **weź**) *vb pf od* **brać**

wzmacni|ać (**-am, -asz**; *pf* **wzmocnić**) *vt* **1** (*siły*) to build up **2** (*ścianę*) to reinforce **3** (*sygnał*) to amplify; **~ się** *vr* (*nabierać sił*) to get stronger

wzno|sić (**-szę, -sisz**; *imp* **-ś**; *pf* **wznieść**) *vt* **1** (*podnosić: głowę, szablę*) to raise **2** (*postawić*) to erect; **~ się** *vr* **1** (*pf* **wznieść**) (*o ptaku*) to rise **2** (*piąć się w górę: o drodze*) to rise **3** (*wystawać: o górach*) to tower; **~ kielich za kogoś/coś** to propose a toast to sb/sth

wzorowy *adj* **1** model **2** (*uczeń*) exemplary; **wzorowe sprawowanie** (*Szkol*) good conduct

wz|ór (**-oru, -ory**; *loc sg* **-orze**) *m* **1** (*deseń*) pattern **2** (*konfekcji*) model; **~ taktu** a model of tact; **ta książka może służyć za ~ doskonałej pracy edytorskiej** this book can serve as a model of outstanding editorial work

wzro|k (**-ku**; *inst sg* **-kiem**) *m* **1** (*zmysł: doskonały, przenikliwy, sokoli*) (eye) sight **2** (*spojrzenie*) gaze

wzro|st (**-stu**; *loc sg* **-ście**) *m* **1** (*człowieka*) height **2** (*roślin*) growth; **być niskiego/średniego ~u** to be of short/medium height; **nie był wysokiego ~u** he wasn't tall; **miała prawie dwa metry ~u** she was almost two metres (*Brit*) *lub* meters (*US*) tall; **ile masz ~u?** how tall are you?; **~ gospodarczy** (*Ekon*) economic growth; **~ bezrobocia** (*Ekon*) a rise in unemployment

wzruszający *adj* (*film, opowieść, książka*) moving

wzrusze|nie (**-nia, -nia**; *gen pl* **-ń**) *nt* emotion

wzwyż *adv* up(wards); **skok ~** the high jump; **skoczek ~** a high jumper; **od 30 lat ~** 30 years and over

Z

SŁOWO KLUCZOWE

z[1], **ze** *prep +gen* **1** (*wyjść lub wracać skądś*) from; **z pracy/wakacji/kursu** from work/from holiday/from a course
2 (*pochodzący ze źródła*) from; **z artykułu/filmu/badań** from an article/a film/research
3 (*określając czas*) from; **z wtorku/wczoraj** from Tuesday/yesterday
4 (*część grupy*) from; **kolega ze studiów** a friend from university; **niektórzy z nas** some of us
5 (*powodu*) out of; **z bólu/szacunku** out of pain/respect
6 (*surowiec, tworzywo*): **dzbanek z porcelany** a porcelain jug; **zrobiony z plastiku/bawełny** made of plastic/cotton; **bukiet z tulipanów** a bunch of tulips
7 (*jakiejś dziedziny*): **on jest kiepski z fizyki** he is lousy at physics; **on jest z zawodu piekarzem** he is a baker by profession; **egzamin z historii** a history exam; **ćwiczenie z gramatyki** a grammar exercise

SŁOWO KLUCZOWE

z[2] *prep +instr* **1** (*razem z kimś*) with; **zatańcz ze mną!** dance with me!
2 (*z jakimś produktem*) with; **herbata z cytryną** tea with lemon; **kanapka z serem** bread and cheese;

z dokładnością with accuracy
3 (*zawierający coś*) of; **dzbanek z mlekiem** a jug of milk
4 (*określając rzeczownik*) with; **oczy z długimi rzęsami** eyes with long lashes; **sklep z butami** shoe shop

SŁOWO KLUCZOWE

za *prep +inst* **1** (*z tyłu, poza*) behind; **za drzwiami/domem** behind the door/house; **daleko za miastem** far out of town
2 (*w kolejności, następstwie*) after; **jeden za drugim** one after another
3 (*przyczyna czynności*) for; **tęsknić za czymś** to miss sth; **gonić za przygodą** to seek adventure
▷ *prep +acc* **1** (*na tył, poza*) behind; **schować walizkę za szafę** to stow the suitcase behind the wardrobe; **wyjeżdżać** (**wyjechać** *pf*) **za granicę** to go abroad
2: **chwytać** (**chwycić** *pf*) **kogoś za rękę** to grab sb's hand
3 (*cel działania*) for; **walczyć za równość** to fight for equality; **wznosić** (**wznieść** *pf*) **toast za czyjeś powodzenia** to drink (a toast) to sb's success
4 (*po jakimś czasie*) in; **za dwa tygodnie** in two weeks; **za rok** in a year's time; **jest za dziesięć szósta** it's ten to six
5 (*wymieniając na*) for; **kupiłem to za sześć złotych** I bought this for six zlotys; **za to, że dałaś mi wykształcenie** in return for giving me my education
6 (*zastępując*) in place of; **pracować za trzech** to do the work of three
▷ *adv* **1** (*zbytnio*) too; **za wcześnie/szybko** too early/quickly; **za dużo** too much/many; **on jest za mało doświadczony na to stanowisko** he's too inexperienced for the job
2 (*w formach wykrzyknikowych*): **co za film!** what a film!

zaadres|ować (**-uję, -ujesz**) *vb pf od* **adresować**
zaakcept|ować (**-uję, -ujesz**) *vb pf od* **akceptować**
zaareszt|ować (**-uję, -ujesz**) *vb pf od* **aresztować**
zaba|wa (**-wy, -wy**; *dat & loc sg* **-wie**) *f* **1** (*dzieci*) play **2** (*według reguł*) game **3** (*rozrywka*) game **4** (*taneczna*) party; **plac zabaw** playground; **dobrej zabawy!** have a good time!; **dla zabawy** for fun
zabaw|ka (**-ki, -ki**; *dat & loc sg* **-ce**; *gen pl* **-ek**) *f* (*dla dzieci*) toy
zabawny *adj* (*śmieszny*) funny
zabezpiecz|ać (**-am, -asz**; *pf* **-yć**) *vt* **1** (*stanowić ochronę*) to protect **2** (*finansowo*) to secure; **~ się** *vr* (*ochronić się*): **~** (**zabezpieczyć** *pf*) **się przed czymś** to protect o.s. against sth; **~** (**zabezpieczyć** *pf*) **coś przed czymś** to guard sth against sth
zabezpiecze|nie (**-nia, -nia**; *gen pl* **-ń**) *nt* (*ochrona*) protection
zabi|ć (**-ję, -jesz**) *vb pf od* **zabijać**; **~ się** *vr pf* **1** (*popełnić samobójstwo*) to kill o.s. **2** (*w wypadku*) to be killed
zabier|ać (**-am, -asz**; *pf* **zabrać**) *vt* to take; **~ kogoś ze sobą w podróż** to take sb along on a journey
zabij|ać (**-am, -asz**; *pf* **zabić**) *vt* (*odebrać życie*) to kill; **~ się** *vr* (*odbierać sobie życie*) to kill oneself; **~ czas** to kill time
zabity *adj* (*martwy*) killed; **spać jak ~** to sleep like a log
zabłą|dzić (**-dzę, -dzisz**; *imp* **-dź**) *vi pf* (*zgubić się*) to get lost
zabójc|a (**-y, -y**) *m decl like f in sg* **1** (*przestępca*) murderer **2** (*zamachowiec*) assassin
zabójczy *adj* **1** (*broń*) lethal; (*strzał*) fatal **2** (*tempo, pogoda, życie*) destructive
zabójst|wo (**-wa, -wa**; *loc sg* **-wie**) *nt* **1** (*morderstwo*) murder **2** (*zamach*) assassination
za|brać (**-biorę, -bierzesz**) *vb pf od* **zabierać 1** (*odbierać, wziąć ze sobą*) to take **2** (*czas*) to take (up); **~ się** *vr pf* (*pojechać z kimś*): **~ się z kimś** (*pot*) to tag along with sb
zabrak|nąć (*3rd pers sg* **-nie**; *pt* **-ło**) *vi pf*: **zabrakło nam czasu/sił** we ran out of time/energy
zabrani|ać (**-am, -asz**; *pf* **zabronić**) *vt* (*zakazywać*): **~ czegoś** to forbid sth;

~ komuś robić coś to forbid sb to do sth
zabroniony *adj* (*zakazany*) prohibited
zabyt|ek (**-ku, -ki**; *inst sg* **-kiem**) *m* (*kultury, sztuki*) (historic) monument; **zabytki przyrody** sites of scientific interest
zabytkowy *adj* **1** (*budowla*) historic **2** (*przedmiot*) antique
zach. *abbr* (= *zachodni*) W.
zachę|cać (**-cam, -casz**; *pf* **-cić**) *vt* (*motywować*): **~ kogoś do czegoś** to encourage sb to do sth
zachę|ta (**-ty, -ty**; *dat & loc sg* **-cie**) *f* **1** (*słowna*) encouragement **2** (*finansowa*) incentive
zachmurzeni|e (**-a**) *nt* (*Meteo*) clouds *pl*
zachmurzony *adj* (*Meteo*) cloudy
zachmurz|yć się (**-ę, -ysz**) *vr pf* **1** (*o niebie, czole, oczach*) to cloud over **2** (*posmutnieć*) to become gloomy
zachodni *adj* **1** (*strona świata*) west **2** (*o wietrze*) westerly **3** (*kraj, waluta, towar*) western; **Europa Z~a** western Europe; **~a Anglia** the west of England
zacho|dzić (**-dzę, -dzisz**; *imp* **-dź**; *pf* **zajść**) *vt* (*podchodzić niezauważonym*): **~ kogoś** to steal up on sb ▷ *vi* **1** (*słońce, księżyc*) to set **2** (*dojść*) to get **3** (*składać wizytę*) to drop in **4** (*o wydarzeniu, błędzie*) to occur; **zajść w ciążę** to become pregnant
zachor|ować (**-uję, -ujesz**) *vi pf* (*na grypę, anginę*) to be taken ill
zachowani|e (**-a**) *nt* **1** (*o sposobie bycia*) behaviour (Brit), behavior (*US*) **2** (*o manierach*) manners *pl* **3** (*o ochronie zabytków*) preservation
zachow|ywać (**-uję, -ujesz**; *pf* **-ać**) *vt* **1** (*wspomnienia, przedmioty*) to retain **2** (*energię, wdzięczność*) to retain **3** (*zwyczaje*) to maintain; **~ się** *vr* **1** (*grzecznie, agresywnie*) to behave **2** (*o danych, zwyczajach, historiach*) to survive
zach|ód (**-odu, -ody**; *loc sg* **-odzie**) *m* **1** (*zajście*): **~ słońca** sunset **2** (*o stronie świata*) west **3** (*o Europie Zachodniej*) the West; **na ~ od** *+gen* to the west of
zachwycający *adj* (*urzekający*) delightful
zachwycony *adj* (*urzeczony*) delighted; **jestem ~ widokiem** I am delighted with the view
zacofany *adj* (*zapóźniony*) backward
zacz|ąć (**-nę, -niesz**; *imp* **-nij**) *vb pf od* **zaczynać**
zaczek|ać (**-am, -asz**) *vb pf od* **czekać**
zaczyn|ać (**-am, -asz**; *pf* **zacząć**) *vt* (*nową pracę, projekt, wojnę*) to start; **~ się** *vr* (*o filmie, lekcji*) to begin; **~ (zacząć** *pf*) **coś robić** to start doing sth
zada|nie (**-nia, -nia**; *gen pl* **-ń**) *nt* **1** (*sprawa do wykonania*) task **2** (*ćwiczenie szkolne*) assignment **3** (*Mat, Fiz*) problem; **~ domowe** homework
zad|awać (**-aję, -ajesz**; *pf* **-ać**) *vt* **1** (*zadanie domowe, ćwiczenie*) to set **2** (*ciosy, uderzenia*) to deal; **~ się** *vr* (*pot: utrzymywać znajomość*): **~ się z kimś** to hang around with sb; **zadać** (*pf*) **komuś pytanie** to ask sb a question
zadbany *adj* **1** (*osoba*) well-groomed **2** (*strój, pokój*) neat, tidy
zadecyd|ować (**-uję, -ujesz**) *vb pf od* **decydować**
zademonstr|ować (**-uję, -ujesz**) *vb pf od* **demonstrować**
zadłuż|ać się (**-am, -asz**; *pf* **-yć**) *vr* (*zaciągać dług*) to get into debt
zadłużeni|e (**-a**) *nt* (*zagraniczne, krajowe*) debt
zadłużony *adj* (*szpital, firma*) indebted
zadowal|ać (**-am, -asz**; *pf* **zadowolić**) *vt* **1** (*spełniać potrzeby*) to satisfy **2** (*sprawiać przyjemność*) to please; **~ się** *vr* (*zaakceptować*): **~ się czymś** to settle for sth
zadowalający *adj* (*wynik, stopień*) satisfactory
zadowoleni|e (**-a**) *nt* (*z pracy, z rodziny*) satisfaction
zadowolony *adj* **1** (*uradowany*) pleased **2** (*ze spełnionych oczekiwań*) contented
Zadusz|ki (**-ek**) *pl* (*święto*) All Souls' Day *sg*

ZADUSZKI

Zaduszki (All Souls' Day), also known as **Święto Zmarłych**, is on 2 November, the day after **Wszystkich Świętych** (All Saints' Day). On this day, people visit the graves of their relatives and friends, where they light small candles to commemorate the dead.

zadział|ać (**-am, -asz**) *vb pf od* **działać**
zadzwon|ić (**-ię, -isz**) *vb pf od* **dzwonić**
zafascynowany *adj* (*bardzo zainteresowany*) fascinated
zagad|ka (**-ki, -ki**; *dat & loc sg* **-ce**; *gen pl* **-ek**) *f* **1** (*problem do rozwiązania*) riddle **2** (*coś tajemniczego*) mystery
zagadkowy *adj* (*tajemniczy*) enigmatic
zagadnie|nie (**-nia, -nia**; *gen pl* **-ń**) *nt* (*kwestia*) problem
zagi|nąć (**-nę, -niesz**; *imp* **-ń**) *vi pf* (*zniknąć*) to go missing; **ślad po niej zaginął** there is no trace of her
zaginiony *adj* (*żołnierz, dziecko*) missing ▷ *m decl like adj* (*człowiek poszukiwany*) missing person
zaglą|dać (**-am, -asz**; *pf* **zajrzeć**) *vi* **1** (*do pokoju*) to look in **2** (*do książki*) to look into
zag|oić (**-oję, -oisz**; *imp* **-ój**) *vb pf od* **goić**
zagorzały *adj* **1** (*wielbiciel*) ardent **2** (*opponent*) fervent **3** (*debata*) heated
zagot|ować (**-uję, -ujesz**) *vb pf od* **gotować**
zagranic|a (**-y**) *f* (*kraje obce*) foreign countries *pl*
zagraniczny *adj* (*obcy*) foreign; **handel ~** foreign trade; **ministerstwo Spraw Z~ch** Ministry of Foreign Affairs, ≈ Foreign Office (*Brit*), ≈ State Department (*US*)
zagraż|ać (**-am, -asz**; *pf* **zagrozić**) *vi* (*grozić*): **~ komuś** to threaten sb; **to zagraża jego zdrowiu** this threatens his health
zagroże|nie (**-nia, -nia**; *gen pl* **-ń**) *nt* (*pożarem, terroryzmem*) risk
zagu|bić (**-bię, -bisz**) *vt pf* (*utracić*) to lose; **~ się** *vr* (*zapodziać się*) to get lost
zainteresowany *adj* (*interesujący się czymś*): **być czymś ~m** to be interested in sth
zaj|ąć (**-mę, -miesz**; *imp* **-mij**) *vb pf od* **zajmować**; **~ się** *vr pf* (*czymś nowym*) to take up; **zajmiesz się tym?** will you see to that?; **~ się malarstwem/architekturą** to take up painting/architecture
zaję|cie (**-cia, -cia**; *gen pl* **-ć**) *nt* **1** (*o czynności*) occupation **2** (*o pracy*) job; **zajęcia** *pl* (*na uniwersytecie*) classes; **rozkład zajęć** timetable
zajęty *adj* **1** (*osoba*) busy **2** (*siedzenie*) taken **3** (*telefon*) busy; (*toaleta*) occupied; **jutro jestem ~** I'm busy tomorrow
zajm|ować (**-uję, -ujesz**; *pf* **zająć**) *vt* **1** (*przestrzeń*) to occupy **2** (*pomieszczenie*) to occupy **3** (*miejscowość, państwo*) to seize **4** (*zaciekawiać*) to engage **5** (*usiąść*) to take **6** (*czas*) to take; **~ się** *vr* **1** (*ogniem*) to catch fire **2** (*obowiązkami itp.*): **~ się czymś/robieniem czegoś** to busy o.s. with sth/doing sth; **zająć miejsce** to take one's seat; **zająć komuś miejsce** to save a seat for sb; **zajęło (nam) to godzinę** it took (us) an hour; **czym się zajmujesz?** (*familiar sg*) what do you do (for a living)?; **~ się kimś/czymś** (*zaopiekować się*) to look after sb/sth
zajmujący *adj* **1** (*historia, lektura*) engrossing **2** (*o pracy*) absorbing **3** (*osoba*) interesting
zajrz|eć (**-ę, -ysz**; *imp* **-yj**) *vb pf od* **zaglądać**
zakańcz|ać (**-am, -asz**) *vb* (*imp* **zakończyć**) to finish; **~ się** *vr* (*film, urlop*) to end
zaka|z (**-zu, -zy**; *loc sg* **-zie**) *m* (*parkowania, palenia*) prohibition; **„~ skrętu w lewo"** "no left turn"; **„~ wstępu"** "no entry"
zakaz|ywać (**-uję, -ujesz**; *pf* **-ać**) *vt* (*zabronić*): **~ komuś czegoś** to forbid sb to do sth
zakaźny *adj* (*Med*) infectious; **oddział ~** isolation ward

zakaż|ać (**-am, -asz**; *pf* **zakazić**) *vt* (*Med*) to infect
zakaże|nie (**-nia, -nia**; *gen pl* **-ń**) *nt* (*Med*) infection
zakła|d (**-du, -dy**; *loc sg* **-dzie**) *m* **1** (*o jakąś sumę*) bet **2** (*przedsiębiorstwo*) factory **3** (*Uniw*) department **4** (*instytucja wychowawcza lub lecznicza*) institution; **~ przemysłowy** industrial plant; **~ fryzjerski** (*damski*) hairdresser's; (*męski*) barber's; **~ badawczy** research institute; **~ poprawczy** Young Offender Institution (*Brit*), Juvenile Detention Center (*US*)
zakład|ka (**-ki, -ki**; *loc sg* **-ce**; *gen pl* **-ek**) *f* (*Komput: też:* **~ ulubione**) bookmark
zakłó|cać (**-cam, -casz**; *pf* **-cić**) *vt* **1** (*atmosferę, ład, porządek*) to disturb **2** (*pracę, funkcję*) to disrupt **3** (*odbiór, słyszalność*) to interfere with
zakłóce|nie (**-nia, -nia**; *gen pl* **-ń**) *nt* **1** (*w radio*) interference **2** (*w pracy, funkcji*) disruption
zakoch|ać się (**-am, -asz**) *vb pf od* **zakochiwać się**
zakochany *adj* (*darzący miłością, uwielbieniem*): **~ w kimś/czymś** in love with sb/sth ▷ *m decl like adj* (*mężczyzna*) lover
zakoch|iwać się (**-uję, -ujesz**; *pf* **zakochać**) *vr* (*darzyć miłością*): **~ (w kimś/czymś)** to fall in love (with sb/sth)
zakonnic|a (**-y, -e**) *f* (*siostra zakonna*) nun
zakończe|nie (**-nia, -nia**; *gen pl* **-ń**) *nt* **1** (*wykonywania pracy*) end **2** (*filmu, historii*) ending **3** (*artykułu, dysertacji*) conclusion
zakończ|yć (**-ę, -ysz**) *vb pf od* **kończyć, zakańczać**
zakrę|t (**-tu, -ty**; *loc sg* **-cie**) *m* (*ulicy*) bend; **~ w lewo/prawo** left/right bend
zaku|p (**-pu, -py**; *loc sg* **-pie**) *m* (*kupowanie*) purchase; **iść na ~y** to go shopping; **robić ~y** to shop
zaledwie *adv* (*tylko*) just ▷ *conj* (*tylko co*): **~ się obudził,...** no sooner had he woken up than...; **~ godzinę temu** just an hour ago
zale|ta (**-ty, -ty**; *dat & loc sg* **-cie**) *f* (*pozytywna cecha*) virtue
zależ|eć (**-y**) *vi* (*od sytuacji, kontekstu*): **~ od kogoś/czegoś** to depend on sb/sth; **bardzo mu na niej zależy** he cares deeply about her; **to zależy** it depends; **to zależy od was** it's up to you
zależnoś|ć (**-ci, -ci**; *gen pl* **-ci**) *f* **1** (*związek*) relationship **2** (*uzależnienie*): **~ od** *+gen* dependence on; **w zależności od czegoś** depending on sth
zależny *adj* **1** (*finansowo, emocjonalnie*) dependent **2** (*Jęz*): **mowa zależna** reported speech
zalicz|ać (**-am, -asz**; *pf* **-yć**) *vt* **1** (*egzamin na uniwersytecie*) to pass **2** (*kurs*) to complete successfully **3** (*zakwalifikować*): **~ kogoś/coś do** *+gen* to rate sb/sth among; **~ się** *vr* (*przynależeć*): **~ się do** *+gen* to rank among; **~ komuś coś** to give sb credit for sth
zalicz|ka (**-ki, -ki**; *dat & loc sg* **-ce**; *gen pl* **-ek**) *f* (*część wynagrodzenia*) advance
zalog|ować się (**-uję, -ujesz**) *pf vi* (*Komput*) to log in
załam|ywać (**-uję, -ujesz**; *pf* **-ać**) *vt* (*giąć*) to bend; **~ się** *vr* **1** (*giąć się*) to bend **2** (*o dachu, moście, lodzie*) to collapse **3** (*głos*) to break **4** (*być przygnębionym*) to break down
załat|wiać (**-wiam, -wiasz**; *pf* **-wić**) *vt* **1** (*sprawę*) to take care of **2** (*pot: obsługiwać*) to serve; **~ się** *vr* (*pot: wypróżnić się*) to relieve o.s.; **on to załatwi** he'll handle that
załat|wić (**-wię, -wisz**) *vb pf od* **załatwiać** ▷ *vt*: **~ kogoś** (*wykiwać*) to fix sb (*pot*); (*zamordować*) to dispose of sb
załącz|ać (**-am, -asz**; *pf* **-yć**) *vt* **1** (*w liście*) to enclose **2** (*w e-mailu*) to attach
załączni|k (**-ka, -ki**; *inst sg* **-kiem**) *m* **1** (*w liście*) enclosure **2** (*w e-mailu*) attachment
zał|oga (**-ogi, -ogi**; *dat & loc sg* **-odze**; *gen pl* **-óg**) *f* **1** (*na statku, w samolocie*) crew **2** (*zakładu pracy*) staff

założyciel (**-a, -e**; *gen pl* **-i**) *m* (*instytucji, firmy*) founder
zamach (**-u, -y**) *m* **1** (*o próbie zamordowania*) assassination attempt **2** (*o morderstwie*) assassination **3** (*zbrojny*) attack; **~ stanu** coup d'état
zamacho|wiec (**-wca, -wcy**) *m* **1** (*o zabójcy*) assassin **2** (*o napastniku*) assailant **3** (*osoba podkładająca bombę*) bomber
zamarz|ać (**-am, -asz**; *pf* **-nąć**) *vi* to freeze
zamarz|nąć (**-nę, -niesz**; *imp* **-nij**) *vi pf od* **marznąć, zamarzać**; **~ na śmierć** to freeze to death
zamarznięty *adj* (*pokryty lodem*) frozen
za|mawiać (**-wiam, -wiasz**; *pf* **zamówić**) *vt* **1** (*towar, usługę, posiłek*) to order **2** (*pokój, stolik*) to book
zam|ek (**-ku, -ki**; *inst sg* **-kiem**) *m* **1** (*królewski*) castle **2** (*urządzenie*) lock **3** (*w spodniach*) zip (Brit), zipper (US)
zamężna *adj* (*mężatka*) married
zamia|na (**-ny, -ny**; *dat & loc sg* **-nie**) *f* **1** (*o wymianie*) exchange **2** (*o przekształceniu*) conversion
zamia|r (**-ru, -ry**; *loc sg* **-rze**) *m* intention; **mieć ~ coś zrobić** to intend to do sth
zamiast *prep +gen* instead of; **~ marudzić...** instead of grumbling...; **~ chleba kupiła bułki** instead of a loaf she bought rolls; **~ tego** instead of this
zamiat|ać (**-am, -asz**; *pf* **zamieść**) *vt* (*podłogę*) to sweep
zamienny *adj*: **części zamienne** spare parts
zamiesz|ać (**-am, -asz**) *vb pf od* **mieszać**
zamieszcza|ć (**-m, -sz**) *vt* (*Komput*) to post
zamieszk|ać (**-am, -asz**) *vi pf* (*zacząć mieszkać*) to settle
zamieszkani|e (**-a**) *nt*: **miejsce zamieszkania** place of residence
zamk|nąć (**-nę, -niesz**; *imp* **-nij**) *vb pf od* **zamykać**
zamknię|cie (**-cia**) *nt* **1** (*na zawsze*) closure **2** (*sklepu itp. na noc*) closing time **3** (*nom pl* **-cia**; *gen pl* **-ć**) (*urządzenie*) lock; **w zamknięciu** under lock and key
zamknięty *adj* **1** (*książka, okno*) closed **2** (*na klucz*) locked **3** (*skryty: osoba*) self-contained; **„zamknięte"** "closed"
zamocow|ywać (**-uję, -ujesz**; *pf* **-ać**) *vt* (*przytwierdzić*) to attach
zamożny *adj* (*bogaty*) wealthy
zamó|wić (**-wię, -wisz**) *vb pf od* **zamawiać**
zamówie|nie (**-nia, -nia**; *gen pl* **-ń**) *nt* (*na towar, usługę*) order; **zrobiony na ~** custom-made
zamraż|ać (**-am, -asz**; *pf* **zamrozić**) *vt* (*żywność, ceny*) to freeze
zamrażalni|k (**-ka, -ki**; *inst sg* **-kiem**) *m* (*w lodówce*) freezer compartment
zamrażar|ka (**-ki, -ki**; *dat & loc sg* **-ce**; *gen pl* **-ek**) *f* (*urządzenie*) freezer
zamy|kać (**-kam, -kasz**; *imp* **-knij**; *pf* **zamknąć**) *vt* **1** (*książkę, okno, otwór, oczy*) to close **2** (*na klucz*) to lock **3** (*parasol*) to close **4** (*w sejfie*) to lock up **5** (*likwidować fabrykę itp.*) to close down **6** (*w więzieniu*) to lock up
zaniedbany *adj* **1** (*budynek*) run-down **2** (*wygląd, dziecko, obowiązek*) neglected
za|nieść (**-niosę, -niesiesz**) *vb impf od* **zanosić**
zanim *conj* (*przed*) before; **~ wyjdę/wyszłam z domu...** before I leave/left home...; **nie komentuj, ~ nie przeczytasz** don't comment before you read it through
zano|sić (**-szę, -sisz**; *imp* **-ś**; *pf* **zanieść**) *vt* (*dostarczać*) to take; **~ się** *vr* (*wyglądać na coś*): **zanosi się na deszcz** it looks like rain
zanot|ować (**-uję, -ujesz**) *vb pf od* **notować**
zaoczny *adj* **1** (*proces*) in absentia **2** (*student*) external
zaofer|ować (**-uję, -ujesz**) *vb pf od* **oferować**
zaopiek|ować się (**-uję, -ujesz**) *vb pf od* **opiekować się**
zaoszczę|dzić (**-dzę, -dzisz**; *imp* **-dź**) *vt pf* **1** (*fundusze, siły*) to save **2** (*czegoś przykrego*): **zaoszczędziło mu to kłopotów** it saved him some problems; **~ na jedzeniu/biletach** to save on food/tickets

zapach (**-u, -y**) *m* **1** (*woń*) smell **2** (*kwiatu; perfumy*) fragrance
zapaleni|e (**-a**) *nt* (*stan chorobowy*) inflammation; **~ płuc** pneumonia
zapalnicz|ka (**-ki, -ki**; *dat & loc sg* **-ce**; *gen pl* **-ek**) *f* (*do krzesania ognia*) lighter
zapał|ka (**-ki, -ki**; *dat & loc sg* **-ce**; *gen pl* **-ek**) *f* (*do krzesania ognia*) match
zapar|cie (**-cia, -cia**; *gen pl* **-ć**) *nt* **1** (*zatwardzenie*) constipation **2** (*poświęcenie*) determination; **z ~m** with determination
zapa|s (**-su, -sy**; *loc sg* **-sie**) *m* (*towaru, energii*) (spare) supply; **zapasy** *pl* **1** (*jedzenia*) provisions **2** (*dyscyplina sportowa*) wrestling *sg*; **mieć coś w ~ie** to have sth in reserve; **na ~** (*kupować, jeść*) ahead of time
zapasowy *adj* **1** (*o kole, części*) spare **2** (*o wyjściu, schodach*) emergency
za|piąć (**-pnę, -pniesz**; *imp* **-pnij**) *vb pf od* **zapinać**
zapin|ać (**-am, -asz**; *pf* **zapiąć**) *vt* **1** (*na pasek, rzepy*) to fasten **2** (*na guzik*) to button (up) **3** (*na zamek błyskawiczny*) to zip up **4** (*guzik, zamek błyskawiczny*) to do up; **~ się** (*pf* **zapiąć**) *vr* **1** (*na guzik*) to button up **2** (*na zamek błyskawiczny*) to zip up **3** (*mieć jakieś zapięcie*) to fasten
zapi|s (**-su, -sy**; *loc sg* **-sie**) *m* **1** (*rejestrowanie*) recording **2** (*o tekście, nagraniu, taśmie*) record **3** (*dźwięku*) recording **4** (*sposób zapisania*) notation **5** (*Prawo: testamentowy*) bequest; **zapisy** *pl* **1** (*na kurs*) registration *sg* **2** (*na zakup czegoś*) waiting list *sg*
zapła|ta (**-ty, -ty**; *dat & loc sg* **-cie**) *f* **1** (*za towar, usługę*) payment **2** (*za gościnność, trud*) reward
zapobieg|ać (**-am, -asz**; *pf* **zapobiec**) *vi* (*nie dopuszczać*): **~ czemuś** to prevent sth
zapomin|ać (**-am, -asz**; *pf* **zapomnieć**) *vt +gen* to forget ▷ *vi* (*nie pamiętać*): **~ (o** *+loc*) to forget (about); **~ się** *vr* (*źle się zachowywać*) to forget o.s.
zapom|nieć (**-nę, -nisz**; *imp* **-nij**) *vb pf od* **zapominać**
zaprasz|ać (**-am, -asz**; *pf* **zaprosić**) *vt* (*w odwiedziny, na kolację, spacer*): **~ kogoś na coś** to invite sb to sth; **~ się** *vr* **1** (*wprosić się*) to invite o.s. **2** (*jeden drugiego*) to exchange invitations
zapro|sić (**-szę, -sisz**; *imp* **-ś**) *vb pf od* **zapraszać**
zaprosze|nie (**-nia, -nia**; *gen pl* **-ń**) *nt* (*prośba o przyjście*) invitation; **na czyjeś ~** at sb's invitation
zaprzecz|ać (**-am, -asz**; *pf* **-yć**) *vi* **1** (*kwestionować*) to disagree **2** (*pogłoskom, pomówieniom*): **~ czemuś** to deny sth **3** (*pozostawać w sprzeczności*) to conflict with; **to zaprzecza faktom historycznym** this conflicts with the historical facts; **~ komuś** to contradict sb
zaprzyjaź|nić się (**-nię, -nisz**; *imp* **-nij**) *vr pf*: **~ z kimś** to make friends with sb
zapuk|ać (**-am, -asz**) *vb pf od* **pukać**
zapyt|ać (**-am, -asz**) *vb pf od* **pytać**
zapyta|nie (**-nia, -nia**; *gen pl* **-ń**) *nt* (*oficjalne pytanie*) inquiry; **znak zapytania** question mark
zarabi|ać (**-am, -asz**) *vt* (*pf* **zarobić**) (*pracować zarobkowo*) to earn ▷ *vi* (*osiągać zyski*) to make a profit; **~ na czymś** to make a profit on sth
zaradny *adj* (*pomysłowy*) resourceful
zaraz *adv* **1** (*od razu*) right away **2** (*za moment*) soon **3** (*niedaleko*) just; **~ za mostem/parkiem** just over the bridge/just the other side of the park; **~ po wakacjach** immediately after the holidays; **~ wracam** I'll be right back; **~, ~!** wait a minute!
zaraźliwy *adj* (*choroba, śmiech*) infectious
zaraż|ać (**-am, -asz**; *pf* **zarazić**) *vt* (*chorobą, entuzjazmem*) to infect; **~ się** *vr* (*chorobą*) to get infected; **zarazić się czymś od kogoś** to catch sth from sb
zarezerw|ować (**-uję, -ujesz**) *vb pf od* **rezerwować**
zaręcz|ać (**-am, -asz**; *pf* **-yć**) *vt* (*gwarantować*) to guarantee; **~ za kogoś** to vouch for sb; **zaręczam (wam), że...** I warrant (you) (that)...
zaręczyć się *vr pf*: **~ (z kimś)** to get engaged (to sb)
zaręczynowy *adj*: **pierścionek ~** engagement ring

zaręczyn|y (-) *pl* (*przyrzeczenie małżeństwa*) engagement *sg*
zarob|ek (**-ku, -ki**; *inst sg* **-kiem**) *m* **1** (*o wynagrodzeniu*) wage **2** (*o pracy*) job **3** (*o zysku*) profit; **zarobki** *pl* (*dochód*) earnings
zarobkowy *adj*: **praca zarobkowa** paid work
zarzu|t (**-tu, -ty**; *loc sg* **-cie**) *m* (*oskarżenie*) accusation; **bez ~u** beyond reproach
zasa|da (**-dy, -dy**; *dat & loc sg* **-dzie**) *f* **1** (*norma postępowania*) principle **2** (*związek chemiczny*) alkali; **dla zasady** on principle; **w zasadzie** in principle
zaska|kiwać (**-kuję, -kujesz**; *pf* **zaskoczyć**) *vt* (*zdarzyć się nieoczekiwanie*) to surprise ▷ *vi* **1** (*o mechanizmach*) to click **2** (*o silnikach*) to start
zaskakujący *adj* (*niespodziewany*) surprising
zaskoczeni|e (**-a**) *nt* (*niespodzianka*) surprise
zasłab|nąć (**-nę, -niesz**; *imp* **-nij**; *pt* **-ł** *lub* **-nął, -ła, -li**) *vi pf* (*zemdleć*) to collapse
zasło|na (**-ny, -ny**; *dat & loc sg* **-nie**) *f* (*w oknach*) curtain (*Brit*), drape (*US*); **zasuwać/rozsuwać zasłony** to draw/open the curtains
zasmu|cać (**-cam, -casz**; *pf* **-cić**) *vt* (*wywoływać smutek*) to sadden; **~ się** *vr* (*posmutnieć*) to be saddened
zasta|wa (**-wy, -wy**; *dat & loc sg* **-wie**) *f* (*komplet naczyń i sztućców*): **~ stołowa** tableware; **~ do herbaty** tea set
zastęp|ować (**-uję, -ujesz**; *pf* **zastąpić**) *vt* **1** (*wykonywać czyjeś obowiązki*): **~ kogoś** to stand in for sb **2** (*zamieniać*): **~ coś czymś innym** to replace sth with sth else **3** (*zagradzać*): **zastąpić komuś drogę** to bar sb's way
zastosow|ywać (**-uję, -ujesz**; *pf* **-ać**) *vt* (*regułę, technikę*) to apply; **~ się** *vr* (*do reguł, wymagań*): **~ się do czegoś** to comply with sth
zastrzy|k (**-ku, -ki**; *inst sg* **-kiem**) *m* injection; **~ gotówki** a cash injection; **~ energii** a shot in the arm
zaświadcze|nie (**-nia, -nia**; *gen pl* **-ń**) *nt* (*dokument*) certificate; **~ lekarskie** medical certificate
zatelefon|ować (**-uję, -ujesz**) *vb pf od* **telefonować**
zato|ka (**-ki, -ki**; *dat & loc sg* **-ce**) *f* **1** (*o części morza*) bay **2** (*o części jeziora*) bay **3** (*czołowa, szczękowa*) sinus **4** (*na jezdni*) lay-by
zatrzym|ywać (**-uję, -ujesz**; *pf* **-ać**) *vt* **1** (*człowieka, urządzenie, proces*) to stop **2** (*o policji: aresztować*) to arrest **3** (*pojazd*) to pull over **4** (*zachować*) to keep **5** (*opóźnić*) to detain; **~ się** (*pf* **-ać**) *vr* **1** (*o człowieku, pojeździe*) to stop **2** (*przestać działać*) to (come to a) stop **3** (*w hotelu, schronisku*) to stay
zauf|ać (**-am, -asz**) *vb pf od* **ufać**
zaufani|e (**-a**) *nt* (*wiara, pewność*) confidence; **mieć do kogoś ~** to have confidence in sb; **telefon zaufania** helpline
zauważ|ać (**-am, -asz**; *pf* **-yć**) *vt* (*zobaczyć*) to notice ▷ *vi* (*powiedzieć*) to observe
zawa|ł (**-łu, -ły**; *loc sg* **-le**) *m* (*Med*): **~ serca** heart attack
zawartoś|ć (**-ci**) *f* **1** (*kieszeni, książki*) contents *pl* **2** (*soli, witamin*) content; **produkty o niskiej zawartości tłuszczu** low-fat products
zawier|ać (**-am, -asz**; *pf* **zawrzeć**) *vt* **1** (*zawierać w sobie*) to include **2** (*zgodę*) to reach **3** (*kontrakt*) to enter (into)
zawiły *adj* (*zagmatwany*) complicated
zawodnicz|ka (**-ki, -ki**; *dat & loc sg* **-ce**; *gen pl* **-ek**) *f* **1** (*Sport*) competitor **2** (*w konkursie*) contestant
zawodni|k (**-ka, -cy**; *inst sg* **-kiem**) *m* **1** (*Sport*) competitor **2** (*w konkursie*) contestant
zawodo|wiec (**-wca, -wcy**) *m* (*profesjonalista*) professional
zawodowy *adj* (*profesjonalny*) professional; **szkoła zawodowa** vocational school; **związek ~** trade union (*Brit*), labor union (*US*)
zawod|y (**-ów**) *pl* (*sportowe*) competition; *zob. też* **zawód**
zaw|ód (**-odu, -ody**; *loc sg* **-odzie**) *m* **1** (*praca*) profession **2** (*przykre uczucie*) disappointment

zawsty|dzać (**-dzam, -dzasz**; *pf* **-dzić**) *vt* (*wzbudzać wstyd*) to shame; **~ się** *vr* (*odczuć wstyd*) to be ashamed
zawstydzony *adj* (*głos, wzrok*) embarrassed
zawsze *adv* (*ciągle*) always ▷ *part*: **ale ~** but still; **na ~** for ever; **tyle co ~** as much as usual; **~ gdy** whenever
zazdrosny *adj* **1** (*o osobę*): **~ o kogoś** jealous of sb **2** (*o dom, samochód*): **~ o coś** envious of sth
zazdro|ścić (**-szczę, -ścisz**; *imp* **-ść**) *vi* (*domu, samochodu*): **~ komuś/czegoś** to envy sb/sth
zazdroś|ć (**-ci**) *f* **1** (*o osobę*) jealousy **2** (*o dom, samochód*) envy
zazę|biać się (**-bia**; *pf* **-bić**) *vr* **1** (*o urządzeniu*) to mesh **2** (*przen*: *o datach, terminologii*) to be interconnected
zazię|biać się (**-biam, -biasz**; *pf* **-bić**) *vr* (*przeziębić się*) to catch a cold
zaziębie|nie (**-nia, -nia**; *gen pl* **-ń**) *nt* (*przeziębienie*) cold
zaziębiony *adj*: **jestem ~** I have got a cold
zaznacz|ać (**-am, -asz**; *pf* **-yć**) *vt* **1** (*kółkiem, krzyżykiem*) to mark **2** (*w wypowiedzi*) to stress ▷ *vi* (*podkreślać*): **~, że...** to stress that...; **~ się** *vr* (*wybijać się*) to be evident
ząb (**zęba, zęby**; *loc sg* **zębie**) *m* (*Anat*) tooth; **sztuczne zęby** false teeth; **boli mnie ~** I have got toothache
zbier|ać (**-am, -asz**; *pf* **zebrać**) *vt* **1** (*znaczki*) to collect **2** (*ludzi*) to gather **3** (*śmieci*) to gather **4** (*grzyby, poziomki*) to pick **5** (*nabierać wody*) to mop up; **~ się** *vr* **1** (*o ludziach*) to gather **2** (*przygotowywać się*): **~ się (do czegoś)** to brace o.s. (for sth)
zbieżnoś|ć (**-ci**; *gen pl* **-ci**) *f* **1** (*w poglądach*) concurrence **2** (*w działaniu*) coincidence
zbi|ór (**-oru, -ory**; *loc sg* **-orze**) *m* **1** (*opowiadań, płyt*) collection **2** (*zbóż, warzyw*) harvest **3** (*zespół liczb*) set; **zbiory** *pl* (*zebrane zboże, warzywa*) crop *sg*
zbliż|ać (**-am, -asz**; *pf* **-yć**) *vt* **1** (*przybliżyć*) to bring closer **2** (*przen*: *upodabniać*) to bring together; **~ się** *vr* **1** (*przybliżyć się*) to approach **2** (*przen*: *zacieśnić stosunki*) to become close **3** (*o dacie, porze roku*) to approach; **nie zbliżaj się!** keep away!
zbliże|nie (**-nia, -nia**; *gen pl* **-ń**) *nt* **1** (*bliskie kontakty*) close relations **2** (*zdjęcie*) close-up
zbliżony *adj* (*podobny*) similar
zbrod|nia (**-ni, -nie**; *gen pl* **-ni**) *f* (*przestępstwo*) crime
zbrodniarz (**-a, -e**; *gen pl* **-y**) *m* (*przestępca*) criminal
zby|t[1] (**-tu**; *loc sg* **-cie**) *m* **1** (*o popycie*) market **2** (*o sprzedaży*) sale(s *pl*); **cena ~u** selling price; **rynek ~u** market
zbyt[2] *adv* (*za bardzo*) too
zd|ać (**-am, -asz**) *vb pf od* **zdawać** ▷ *vt*: **~ egzamin** to pass an exam; **~ na uniwersytet** to get into university
zdarz|ać się (**-a**; *pf* **-yć**) *vr* (*stać się*) to happen, to occur
zda|wać (**-ję, -jesz**; *imp* **-waj**; *pf* **zdać**) *vt* **1**: **~ relację** to inform **2** (*butelki, makulaturę*) to return ▷ *vi* (*przystępować do egzaminu*): **~ (na uniwersytet)** to take (one's) entrance exams (to university); **~ się** *vr* **1** (*wywoływać wrażenie*) to seem **2** (*polegać*): **~ się na kogoś/coś** to depend on sb/sth; **~ sobie sprawę z czegoś** to be aware of sth; **zdaje (mi) się, że...** it seems (to me) that...
zdecyd|ować (**-uję, -ujesz**) *vb pf od* **decydować**
zdecydowani|e[1] (**-a**) *nt* (*pewność*) determination
zdecydowanie[2] *adv* **1** (*bez wahania*) decidedly **2** (*niewątpliwie*) definitely; **~ najgorszy** by far the worst
zdecydowany *adj* **1** (*osoba*) determined **2** (*stanowczy*) decisive **3** (*wyrazisty*) unquestionable; **~ na coś** determined about sth
zdejm|ować (**-uję, -ujesz**; *pf* **zdjąć**) *vt* **1** (*płaszcz, spodnie*) to take off **2** (*obraz ze ściany*) to take down
zdenerw|ować (**-uję, -ujesz**) *vb pf od* **denerwować**
zdenerwowany *adj* **1** (*przejęty lękiem*) nervous **2** (*rozdrażniony*): **~ czymś/na kogoś** angry *lub* annoyed at sth/with sb

zd|jąć (**-ejmę, -ejmiesz**; *imp* **-ejmij**) *vb pf od* **zdejmować**

zdję|cie (**-cia, -cia**; *gen pl* **-ć**) *nt* **1** (*Fot*) photograph **2** (*zabranie*) removal; **robić** (**zrobić** *pf*) **komuś ~** to take a photo of sb; **~ profilowe** profile picture

zdobyw|ać (**-am, -asz**; *pf* **zdobyć**) *vt* **1** (*kraj, zamek*) to capture **2** (*fortunę*) to gain **3** (*bilet, jedzenie*) to get **4** (*reputację, przychylność ludzi, nagrodę*) to win **5** (*Sport: gola*) to score

zdobywc|a (**-y, -y**) *m decl like f in sg* **1** (*kraju, zamku*) conqueror **2** (*nagród*) winner **3** (*gola*) scorer

zdolnoś|ć (**-ci, -ci**; *gen pl* **-ci**) *f* (*umiejętność*) ability; **zdolności** *pl* (*intelektualne, muzyczne*) gift *sg*

zdolny *adj* **1** (*utalentowany*) gifted **2** (*mający możliwości*): **~ do (zrobienia) czegoś** capable of (doing) sth

zdrowi|e (**-a**) *nt* (*fizyczne, psychiczne*) health; **ośrodek zdrowia** health centre (*Brit*) *lub* center (*US*); **na ~!** (*przy toaście*) cheers!; (*przy kichnięciu*) bless you!

zdrowo *adv* **1** (*jeść*) healthily **2** (*wyglądać, żyć*) healthy

zdrowotny *adj* (*o warunkach, klimacie*) healthy; **opieka zdrowotna** healthcare; **urlop ~** sick leave

zdrowy *adj* (*nie chory*) healthy; **~ rozsądek** common sense

ze *prep* = **z**

zebra|nie (**-nia, -nia**; *gen pl* **-ń**) *nt* (*spotkanie*) meeting

zega|r (**-ra, -ry**; *loc sg* **-rze**) *m* (*wiszący, stojący*) clock

zegar|ek (**-ka, -ki**; *inst sg* **-kiem**) *m* (*na rękę*) watch; **mój ~ się śpieszy** my watch is fast

zejś|cie (**-cia, -cia**; *gen pl* **-ć**) *nt* **1** (*droga w dół*) descent **2** (*zgon*) death; **~ na parter** stairs to the ground floor

zej|ść (**-dę, -dziesz**; *imp* **-dź**; *pt* **zszedł** *lub* **zeszedł, zeszła, zeszli**) *vb pf od* **schodzić**

zemdl|eć (**-eję, -ejesz**) *vb pf od* **mdleć**

zem|sta (**-sty**; *dat & loc sg* **-ście**) *f* (*odwet*) revenge

zepsu|ć (**-ję, -jesz**) *vb pf od* **psuć**

zepsuty *adj* **1** (*telewizor, samochód*) broken **2** (*osoba*) corrupt

ze|ro (**-ra, -ra**; *loc sg* **-rze**) *nt* **1** (*cyfra*) zero **2** (*przy podawaniu numerów*) zero **3** (*zupełny brak*) nought **4** (*w meczu piłkarskim*) nil (*Brit*), nothing (*US*); (*w meczu tenisowym*) love **5** (*przen: człowiek bez wartości*) nonentity

zesp|ół (**-ołu, -oły**; *loc pl* **-ole**) *m* **1** (*muzyczny*) group **2** (*profesjonalistów, sportowy*) team **3** (*Bud*) complex, set **4** (*teatralny*) company **5** (*Tech*) unit **6** (*Med*) syndrome; **~ jazzowy/rockowy** jazz band/rock group

zesta|w (**-wu, -wy**; *loc sg* **-wie**) *m* **1** (*komplet*) set **2** (*dobór np. barw*) combination **3** (*np. wypoczynkowy*) suite **4** (*urządzeń, maszyn*) kit

zestresowany *adj* (*osoba*) stressed

zewnątrz *adv*: **na ~** outside; **z** *lub* **od ~** from the outside

zewnętrzny *adj* **1** (*poza obrębem*) outside, exterior **2** (*o wyglądzie*) outward, external; **„do użytku zewnętrznego"** "for external use only"

zgadz|ać się (**-am, -asz**; *pf* **zgodzić**) *vr* **1** (*pozwalać*): **~ na coś** to agree to sth **2** (*podzielać poglądy*): **~ z kimś** to agree with sb **3** (*okazywać zgodność*): **~ (z czymś)** to tally (with sth)

zgo|da (**-dy**; *dat & loc sg* **-dzie**) *f* **1** (*harmonia*) harmony **2** (*zezwolenie*) consent **3** (*zgodność zdania*) consensus **4** (*porozumienie*) reconciliation

zgodnie *adv* **1** (*harmonijnie*) in harmony **2** (*według*) according to, in accordance with; **~ z przepisami** in accordance with the rules

zgrabny *adj* **1** (*figura*) shapely **2** (*zwinny*) deft **3** (*wypowiedź, utwór*) neat

ziar|no (**-na, -na**; *loc sg* **-nie**; *gen pl* **-en**) *nt* **1** (*zboża, prawdy, piasku*) grain **2** (*fasoli, kawy*) bean **3** (*do zasiania*) seed

zielony *adj* (*kolor*) green; **nie mam zielonego pojęcia** (*pot*) I haven't a clue *lub* the foggiest (idea)

zie|mia (**-mi**) *f* **1** (*Astron*): **Z~** Earth **2** (*pl* **-mie**) (*o glebie*) soil **3** (*o gruncie pod nogami*) ground **4** (*o podłodze*)

floor **5** (*pl* **-mie**) (*majątek ziemski, terytorium*) land; **do (samej) ziemi** (*firana, płaszcz*) full-length; **trzęsienie ziemi** earthquake
ziemnia|k (**-ka, -ki**; *inst sg* **-kiem**) *m* (*kartofel*) potato
zię|ć (**-cia, -ciowie**) *m* (*mąż córki*) son-in-law
zi|ma (**-my, -my**; *dat & loc sg* **-mie**) *f* (*pora roku*) winter; **zimą** *lub* **w zimie** in winter
zim|no[1] (**-na**; *loc sg* **-nie**) *nt* **1** (*niskie temperatury*) cold **2** (*opryszczka*) cold sore
zimno[2] *adv* **1** (*o niskiej temperaturze*) cold **2** (*przen: bez okazywania uczuć*) coldly; **~ mi** I am cold; **~ mi w ręce** my hands are cold
zimny *adj* (*o niskiej temperaturze, bez uczuć*) cold; **zimna wojna** (*historycznie*) the Cold War
zimowy *adj* (*dzień, urlop, pogoda*) winter
zi|oło (**-oła, -oła**; *loc sg* **-ole**; *gen pl* **-ół**) *nt* (*ziele*) herb
ziołowy *adj* (*herbata*) herbal
zj|eść (**-em, -esz**; *pt* **-adł, -adła, -edli**) *vb pf od* **jeść**
zjeżdż|ać (**-am, -asz**; *pf* **zjechać**) *vi* **1** (*dźwigiem*) to go down; (*na snowboardzie, saniach*) to go downhill; (*autem*) to drive downhill; (*rowerem*) to ride downhill **2** (*zbaczać z trasy*) to turn (off) **3** (*przybyć*) to arrive; **~ się** *vr* (*gromadzić się*) to arrive; **zjeżdżaj stąd!** (*pot*) get out of here!
zle|w (**-wu, -wy**; *loc sg* **-wie**) *m* (*kuchenny*) sink
zlikwid|ować (**-uję, -ujesz**) *vb pf od* **likwidować**
zł *abbr* (= *złoty: waluta*) zloty
zła|mać (**-mię, -miesz**) *vb pf od* **łamać**
złama|nie (**-nia, -nia**; *gen pl* **-ń**) *nt* (*kości*) fracture
złamany *adj* (*ręka, serce*) broken
zła|pać (**-pię, -piesz**) *vb pf od* **łapać**
zł|o (**-a**) *nt* (*odwrotność dobra*) evil
złocisty *adj* (*kolor*) golden
złocony *adj* **1** (*wazon*) gilded **2** (*pierścionek, sztućce*) gold-plated
złoczyńc|a (**-y, -y**) *m decl like f in sg* (*książk: przestępca*) villain
złodzie|j (**-ja, -je**; *gen pl* **-i**) *m* (*dokonujący kradzieży*) thief; **~ kieszonkowy** pickpocket
zło|m (**-mu**; *loc sg* **-mie**) *m* (*zużyte urządzenie*) scrap (metal)
zło|ścić (**-szczę, -ścisz**; *imp* **-ść**; *pf* **roz-** *lub* **ze-**) *vt* (*wywoływać złość*) to anger; **~ się** *vr* (*odczuwać/okazywać złość*): **~ się (na kogoś/o coś)** to be angry (with sb/about sth)
złoś|ć (**-ci**) *f* (*gniew*) anger; **na ~ komuś** to spite sb
złośliwy *adj* **1** (*przedmiot, człowiek*) malicious **2** (*nowotwór*) malignant
zło|to (**-ta**; *loc sg* **-cie**) *nt* (*Chem*) gold
złotów|ka (**-ki, -ki**; *dat & loc sg* **-ce**; *gen pl* **-ek**) *f* **1** (*waluta*) one zloty **2** (*o monecie*) one-zloty coin
złot|y[1] (**-ego, -e**) *m decl like adj* (*waluta*) zloty
złoty[2] *adj* gold; **złota rączka** handyman
zły *adj* **1** (*wynik, ocena, dzień, wiadomość*) bad **2** (*rozgniewany*) angry **3** (*nieetyczny, nieuczciwy*) evil, wicked **4** (*niepoprawny*) wrong **5** (*marnej jakości*) poor; **w ~m humorze** in a bad mood; **w ~m guście** in bad taste
zmarły *adj* (*nieżywy*) dead, deceased ▷ *m decl like adj* (*nieżyjący mężczyzna*) the deceased; **zmarli** *pl* (*nieżyjące osoby*) the dead; **~ pan Nowak** the late Mr Nowak
zmarn|ować (**-uję, -ujesz**) *vb pf od* **marnować**
zmarszcz|ka (**-ki, -ki**; *dat & loc sg* **-ce**; *gen pl* **-ek**) *f* **1** (*przy oczach*) wrinkle **2** (*na powierzchni wody*) ripple **3** (*na tkaninie*) crease
zmarszcz|yć (**-ę, -ysz**) *vb pf od* **marszczyć**
zmart|wić (**-wię, -wisz**) *vb pf od* **martwić**
zmartwie|nie (**-nia, -nia**; *gen pl* **-ń**) *nt* (*problem*) worry
zmartwiony *adj* (*przygnębiony*) worried
zmądrz|eć (**-eję, -ejesz**) *vb pf od* **mądrzeć**
zmęczeni|e (**-a**) *nt* (*znużenie, wyczerpanie*) tiredness
zmęczony *adj* (*znużony, wyczerpany*) tired

zmęcz|yć (**-ę, -ysz**) *vb pf od* **męczyć**
zmia|na (**-ny, -ny**; *dat & loc sg* **-nie**) *f* **1** (*odmiana*) change **2** (*w pracy*) shift; **~ na lepsze/gorsze** a change for the better/worse; **dzienna/nocna ~** day/night shift; **~ klimatyczna** climate change
zmie|niać (**-niam, -niasz**; *pf* **-nić**) *vt* (*przeobrażać*) to change; **~ się** *vr* **1** (*ulegać przeobrażeniu*) to change **2** (*między sobą*) to take turns; **~ (zmienić** *pf*) **zdanie** to change one's mind
zmienny *adj* (*niestały*) changeable; **prąd ~** alternating current
zmierz|ać (**-am, -asz**) *vi* (*książk*: *wybierać się*): **~ do** *+gen*/**w stronę** *+gen* to head for/towards; **do czego zmierzasz?** (*przen*) what are you driving at?
zmierzch (**-u, -y**) *m* **1** (*pora dnia*) dusk **2** (*przen*: *koniec, upadek*) twilight; **o ~u** at dusk
zmierz|yć (**-ę, -ysz**) *vb pf od* **mierzyć**
zmiesz|ać (**-am, -asz**) *vb pf od* **mieszać**
zmniejsz|ać (**-am, -asz**; *pf* **-yć**) *vt* (*wielkość, odległość*) to reduce; **~ się** *vr* (*o wielkości, odległości*) to reduce
zmocz|yć (**-ę, -ysz**) *vb pf od* **moczyć**
zmok|nąć (**-nę, -niesz**; *imp* **-nij**; *pt* **-nął** *lub* **zmókł, -ła, -li**) *vb pf od* **moknąć**
zmusz|ać (**-am, -asz**; *pf* **zmusić**) *vt* (*nakłaniać siłą/groźbami*) to force; **~ się** *vr* (*robić coś wbrew sobie*): **~ się do zrobienia czegoś** to force o.s. to do sth; **~ kogoś do zrobienia czegoś** to force sb to do sth
zm|yć (**-yję, -yjesz**) *vb pf od* **myć**; **~ komuś głowę** (*przen*) to give sb a dressing-down
zmy|sł (**-słu, -sły**; *loc sg* **-śle**) *m* **1** sense **2** (*predyspozycja*) aptitude; **~ artystyczny** artistic flair
zmyśl|ać (**-am, -asz**; *pf* **-ić**) *vt* (*mówić nieprawdę*) to make up
zmywar|ka (**-ki, -ki**; *dat & loc sg* **-ce**; *gen pl* **-ek**) *f* (*urządzenie*) dishwasher
znacz|ek (**-ka, -ki**; *inst sg* **-kiem**) *m* **1** *dimin od* **znak** **2** (*naklejka*: *pocztowy, skarbowy*) stamp **3** (*plakietka*) badge **4** (*graficzny*) mark; **~ pocztowy** (postage) stamp
znacze|nie (**-nia, -nia**; *gen pl* **-ń**) *nt* **1** (*treść*) meaning **2** (*waga*) significance; **to nie ma znaczenia** it doesn't matter; **to jest bez znaczenia** it is of no importance
zn|ać (**-am, -asz**) *vt* (*wiedzieć*) to know; **~ się** *vr* **1** (*samego siebie*) to know o.s. **2** (*z innymi*) to know each other **3** (*być obeznanym*): **~ się na czymś** to be knowledgeable about sth; **dawać** (**dać** *pf*) **komuś ~ (o czymś)** (*powiadomić*) to let sb know (about sth); **~ kogoś** to know sb
znad *prep +gen* **1** (*książki*) from above **2** (*morza*) from
znajd|ować (**-uję, -ujesz**; *pf* **znaleźć**) *vt* **1** (*odszukiwać, natrafiać*) to find **2** (*wsparcie, zrozumienie*) to meet with; **~ się** *vr* **1** (*być położonym*) to be situated **2** (*dać się odszukać*) to be found **3** (*pojawić się*) to turn up
znajomoś|ć (**-ci, -ci**) *f* **1** (*stosunki towarzyskie*) acquaintance **2** (*języka, matematyki*) knowledge; **zawierać (zawrzeć** *pf*) **z kimś ~** to make sb's acquaintance
znajomy *adj* (*teren, głos, piosenka*) familiar ▷ *m decl like adj* (*osoba*) acquaintance; **~ prawnik** a lawyer I know; **usunąć z listy ~ch** to unfriend (*on social media*)
zna|k (**-ku, -ki**; *inst sg* **-kiem**) *m* (*symbol, dowód*) sign; **~ drogowy** road sign; **~ zapytania** question mark; **~ Zodiaku** sign of the zodiac
znakomitoś|ć (**-ci, -ci**; *gen pl* **-ci**) *f* (*człowiek*) celebrity
znakomity *adj* (*doskonały*) superb
zna|leźć (**-jdę, -jdziesz**; *imp* **-jdź**; *pt* **-lazł, -lazła, -leźli**) *vb pf od* **znajdować**
znany *adj* **1** (*okolica, grupa*) well-known **2** (*artysta, naukowiec*) famous **3** (*kłamca, przestępca*) notorious
znawc|a (**-y, -y**) *m decl like f in sg* (*ekspert, koneser*): **~ (czegoś)** an expert (on sth)
znęc|ać się (**-am, -asz**) *vr* (*pastwić się*): **~ nad** *+inst* to abuse
znicz (**-a, -e**; *gen pl* **-y** *lub* **-ów**) *m* (*na grobie*) candle; **~ olimpijski** the Olympic® torch

zniechę|cać (**-cam, -casz**; *pf* **-cić**) *vt* (*zrazić*): **~ kogoś do czegoś** to discourage sb from sth; **~ się** *vr* (*zrazić się*) to become discouraged
zniechęceni|e (**-a**) *nt* (*brak chęci*) discouragement
zniecierpliwieni|e (**-a**) *nt* (*brak cierpliwości*) impatience
zniecierpliwiony *adj* (*pozbawiony cierpliwości*) impatient
znieczul|ać (**-am, -asz**; *pf* **-ić**) *vt* (*Med*) to anaesthetize (*Brit*), to anesthetize (*US*)
znieczulający *adj*: **środek ~** anaesthetic (*Brit*), anesthetic (*US*)
znieczule|nie (**-nia, -nia**; *gen pl* **-ń**) *nt* (*Med*) anaesthetic (*Brit*), anesthetic (*US*)
znik|ać (**-am, -asz**; *pf* **-nąć**) *vi* (*ginąć, wychodzić niepostrzeżenie*) to disappear
znikomy *adj* (*bardzo mały*) slight
zno|sić (**-szę, -sisz**; *imp* **-ś**; *pf* **znieść**) *vt* **1** (*na dół*) to carry down **2** (*zgromadzić*) to gather **3** (*o kurze: jajko*) to lay **4** (*o wodzie, powietrzu: zmienić kierunek*) to carry **5** (*bolączki, przykrości, trudy*) to endure **6** (*przepis, akt*) to abolish **7** (*zakaz, sankcje*) to lift **8** (*wytrzymywać, cierpieć*): **nie znoszę go** I can't stand him; **~ się** *vr* **1** (*wzajemnie usuwać swoje działanie*) to cancel each other out **2** (*wytrzymywać ze sobą wzajemnie*): **oni się nie znoszą** they hate each other
znowu *adv* (*ponownie*) again ▷ *part* (*konkretnie*) after all; **~ się spóźnił** he was late again
znużeni|e (**-a**) *nt* (*zmęczenie, znudzenie*) weariness
znużony *adj* (*zmęczony, znudzony*) weary
zob. *abbr* (= *zobacz*) see, cf.
zobacz|yć (**-ę, -ysz**) *vt pf* (*widzieć*) to see; **~ się** *vr* (*spotkać się*): **~ się z kimś** to see sb
zobowiąza|nie (**-nia, -nia**; *gen pl* **-ń**) *nt* (*obowiązek*) commitment
zodia|k (**-ku**; *inst sg* **-kiem**) *m* (*Astrol*) zodiac; **znak Z~u** sign of the zodiac
zoo *nt inv* (*ogród zoologiczny*) zoo
z o.o. *abbr* (*firma, spółka*) Ltd.
zorganizowany *adj* **1** (*drużyna*) organized **2** (*wyjazd*) guided
zr|obić (**-obię, -obisz**; *imp* **-ób**) *vb pf od* **robić**
zrozumi|eć (**-em, -esz**; *3 pl* **-eją**) *vb pf od* **rozumieć**
zrównoważony *adj* **1** (*o człowieku*) even-tempered **2** (*o charakterze*) level-headed **3** (*o budżecie*) balanced
zróżnicowany *adj* (*niejednolity*) diverse
zryw|ać (**-am, -asz**; *pf* **zerwać**) *vt* **1** (*jabłka, róże*) to pick **2** (*tapety, ogłoszenia*) to tear off **3** (*węzeł, sznur, pęta*) to break **4** (*kontrakt, zaręczyny*) to break off **5** (*znajomość, kontakty*) to break off ▷ *vi* (*o parze: przestać się spotykać*): **~ (z kimś)** to break up (with sb); **~ się** *vr* **1** (*o sznurze, niciach*) to break **2** (*o osobie: podskoczyć w pośpiechu*) to jump up **3** (*o wietrze, aplauzie*) to break out; **~ (zerwać** *pf*) **z nałogiem** to kick a habit
zszedł *itd. vb zob.* **schodzić**
zu|pa (**-py, -py**; *dat & loc sg* **-pie**) *f* (*potrawa*) soup; **~ z puszki** tinned soup
zupełnie *adv* (*całkowicie*) completely, utterly
zużyty *adj* used, worn out
zwalcz|ać (**-am, -asz**) *vt impf* (*pf* **-yć**) **1** (*przeciwników*) to fight **2** (*słabość, ból*) to overcome **3** (*insekty*) to exterminate; **~ się** *vr* (*wzajemnie*) to fight each other
zwalcz|yć (**-ę, -ysz**) *vt pf zob.* **zwalczać**
zwal|niać (**-niam, -niasz**; *imp* **-niaj**) *vt impf* **1** (*tempo*) to slow down **2** (*z pracy*) to make redundant **3** (*z obowiązku*) to exempt, to release
zwany *adj*: **tak ~** so-called
zwari|ować (**-uję, -ujesz**) *vi pf* (*pot: oszaleć*) to go mad
zwariowany *adj* (*pot: szalony*) mad
zwarz|yć się (**-ę, -ysz**) *vr pf* (*o mleku, śmietanie*) to go sour
zwąt|pić (**-pię, -pisz**) *vb pf od* **wątpić**
zwątpie|nie (**-nia, -nia**; *gen pl* **-ń**) *nt* (*brak pewności/wiary*) pessimism
zwęż|ać (**-am, -asz**; *pf* **zwęzić**) *vt* **1** (*drogę*) to narrow **2** (*ubranie*) to take in; **~ się** *vr* (*o drodze*) to narrow

zwęże|nie (**-nia, -nia**; *gen pl* **-ń**) *nt* (*drogi*) narrowing

związ|ywać (**-uję, -ujesz**; *pf* **-ać**) *vt* (*włosy, paczkę, ręce*) to tie (up)

zwie|dzać (**-dzam, -dzasz**; *pf* **-dzić**) *vt* (*muzeum, kraj*) to visit

zwierz|ę (**-ęcia, -ęta**; *gen pl* **-ąt**) *nt* animal; **~ domowe** pet

zwierzęcy *adj* (*folwark, tłuszcz, nawóz*) animal

zwinny *adj* (*szybki i zgrabny*) agile, nimble

zwłaszcza *adv* (*szczególnie*) especially

zwło|ka (**-ki**; *dat & loc sg* **-ce**) *f* (*opóźnienie*) delay; **grać na zwłokę** to play for time

zwolenni|k (**-ka, -cy**; *inst sg* **-kiem**) *m* **1** (*króla*) follower **2** (*partii, idei*) supporter

zwol|nić (**-nię, -nisz**; *imp* **-nij**) *vb pf od* **zwalniać**

zwolnie|nie (**-nia, -nia**; *gen pl* **-ń**) *nt* **1** (*z pracy*) dismissal **2** (*usprawiedliwienie*) sick note, doctor's note **3** (*ulga*) relief; **~ lekarskie** sick leave; **~ podatkowe** tax exemption

zwro|t (**-tu, -ty**; *loc sg* **-cie**) *m* **1** (*skręt, zmiana*) turn **2** (*długu, książki*) return **3** (*językowy*) expression; **w lewo ~!** left turn!

zwycięst|wo (**-wa, -wa**; *loc sg* **-wie**) *nt* (*wygrana*) victory; **odnieść** (*pf*) **~ (nad kimś/czymś)** to gain a victory (over sb/sth)

zwycięzc|a (**-y, -y**) *m decl like f in sg* (*konkursu, wojny*) winner

zwycięż|ać (**-am, -asz**; *pf* **-yć**) *vt* (*słabości, bolączki, nałóg*) to overcome ▷ *vi* (*w meczu, w walce, w wyborach*) to win

zwyczaj (**-u, -e**) *m* **1** (*tradycja*) custom **2** (*przyzwyczajenie*) habit

zwyczajnie *adv* **1** (*jak zwykle*) as usual **2** (*podkreślając oczywistość*) simply

zwyczajny *adj* **1** (*zwykły, przeciętny*) ordinary **2** (*typowy*) usual **3** (*częsty*) common **4** (*prosty*) common, simple **5** (*kłamca, naiwność*) downright

zwykle *adv* (*zazwyczaj*) usually; **jak ~** as usual

zwykły *adj* **1** (*przeciętny*) ordinary **2** (*typowy*) usual **3** (*regularny*) common **4** (*niewyszukany*) common, simple **5** (*naiwność, kłamca*) downright, sheer

zys|k (**-ku, -ki**; *inst sg* **-kiem**) *m* **1** (*dochód*) profit **2** (*pożytek*) gain

źle *adv* **1** (*błędnie odpowiadać*) wrongly **2** (*niestarannie*) poorly, badly; **~ dziś wyglądasz** you don't look well today; **~ się czuję** I don't feel well

źród|ło (**-ła, -ła**; *loc sg* **-le**; *gen pl* **-eł**) *nt* **1** (*wiadomości, mocy*) source **2** (*rzeki*) source **3** (*zdrój*) spring **4** (*powód*) source

ża|ba (**-by, -by**; *dat sg & loc sg* **-bie**) *f* frog; **będziesz musiał zjeść** *lub* **połknąć tę żabę** you'll just have to live with it

żaden (*f* **żadna**; *nt* **żadne**) *pron* **1** (*przed rzeczownikiem*) no **2** (*zamiast rzeczownika*) none **3** (*ani jeden, ani drugi*) neither **4** (*spośród dwóch*) neither (of them); **w ~ sposób tego nie można zrobić** there's no way at all to do this; **w żadnym razie** *lub* **wypadku nie pójdziemy tam jutro** under no circumstances will we go there tomorrow; **w żadnym wypadku!** no way!; **jego zasługi są żadne** he has no redeeming features; **~ z nich nie przyszedł** none *lub* not one of them came

żaglów|ka (**-ki, -ki**; *dat sg & loc sg* **-ce**; *gen pl* **-ek**) *f* sailing boat (*Brit*), sailboat (*US*)

żakie|t (**-tu, -ty**; *loc sg* **-cie**) *m* (*damska marynarka*) jacket

żal (**-u, -e**) *m* **1** (*uczucie smutku*) sorrow **2** (*skrucha*) regret **3** (*rozgoryczenie*) bitterness; **żale** *pl* complaints; **było mi jej ~** I felt sorry for her; **mam do ciebie ~ za twój uczynek** I have a grudge against you because of what you did

żal|ić się (**-ę, -isz**; *pf* **po-**) *vr* (*narzekać*) to complain

żało|ba (**-by**; *dat sg & loc sg* **-bie**) *f* (*smutek po śmierci kogoś, obyczaj*) mourning; **~ narodowa** national mourning

żałobny *adj* (*nabożeństwo*) funeral; **ubiór ~** mourning; **msza żałobna** memorial *lub* funeral service

żał|ować (**-uję, -ujesz**; *pf* **po-**) *vt*: **~ czegoś** to regret sth ▷ *vi* to regret; **żałował, że nie przyjechała** he felt sorry that she didn't come; **żałował jej ciastka** he begrudged her a biscuit; **żałuję, że nie wyjechałem** I wish I had left

żarów|ka (**-ki, -ki**; *dat sg & loc sg* **-ce**; *gen pl* **-ek**) *f* light bulb

żar|t (**-tu, -ty**; *loc sg* **-cie**) *m* joke; **zrobił to dla ~u** he did it as a joke; **~y ~ami** a joke's a joke; **robili sobie z niego ~y** they made fun of him

żart|ować (**-uję, -ujesz**; *pf* **za-**) *vi* (*dowcipkować*) to joke; **~ z** *+gen* to make fun of

żąd|ać (**-am, -asz**; *pf* **za-**) *vt*: **~ czegoś** (*wymagać*) to demand sth

żąda|nie (**-nia, -nia**; *gen pl* **-ń**) *nt* (*wymaganie*) demand; **przystanek autobusowy na ~** request stop (*Brit*), flag stop (*US*)

że *conj* that ▷ *part*: **(po)mimo że długo pracowali, nie zdążyli na czas** although they worked long hours they still missed the deadline; **dlatego że nie ma racji** because he's wrong; **był tak zmęczony, że zasnął w fotelu** he was so tired he fell asleep in his armchair; **jako że** since; **tyle że** but, only; **chyba że przyjdziecie wszyscy razem** unless you all come together

żebra|k (**-ka, -cy**; *inst sg* **-kiem**) *m* beggar

żeb|ro (**-ra, -ra**; *loc sg* **-rze**; *gen pl* **-er**) *nt* rib; **porachować komuś żebra** (*pot*) to beat sb up

żeby *conj* (*oznaczenie skutku*) in order to ▷ *part*: **~ tylko nam się udało** if only it all works out for us; **jest zbyt biedny, ~ kupić dom** he's too poor to buy a house; **~ nie przestraszyć kota** so as not to frighten the cat; **~ nie on, zwyciężyłaby** if it weren't for him she would have won; **nie chcę, ~ś tu mieszkał** I don't want you to live here

żeglarz (**-a, -e**; *gen pl* **-y**) *m* (*sportowiec*) yachtsman

żegl|ować (**-uję, -ujesz**) *vi* to sail

żegn|ać (**-am, -asz**; *pf* **po-**) *vt*: **~ kogoś** to say goodbye to sb; **~ się** *vr* **1** (*pf* **po-**) (*na do widzenia*) to say goodbye **2** (*pf* **prze-**) (*w kościele: kreślić znak krzyża*): **~ się** to cross o.s.; **żegnaj!** farewell!

żelaz|ko (**-ka, -ka**; *inst sg* **-kiem**; *gen pl* **-ek**) *nt* (*urządzenie do prasowania*) iron (*for pressing clothes*)

żelazny *adj* **1** (*zrobiony z żelaza*) iron **2** (*o zdrowiu*) robust; **masz żelazne nerwy** you have nerves of steel

żela|zo (**-za**; *loc sg* **-zie**) *nt* iron

że|nić (**-nię, -nisz**; *imp* **-ń**; *pf* **o-**) *vt* to marry (off); **~ się** *vr*: **~ się z** *+inst* (*o mężczyźnie*) to get married to

żeński *adj* **1** (*dla dziewcząt*) girls' **2** (*płeć*) female; **rodzaj ~** (*w językoznawstwie*) feminine (gender)

żeto|n (**-nu, -ny**; *loc sg* **-nie**) *m* **1** (*do telefonu*) token **2** (*do gier hazardowych*) chip

żłob|ek (**-ka, -ki**; *inst sg* **-kiem**) *m* (*miejsce opieki nad dziećmi*) crèche (*Brit*), daycare (*US*)

żmij|a (**-i, -e**; *gen pl* **-i**) *f* viper, adder; **hodować (wyhodować** *pf*) **żmiję na własnej piersi** to nurse a viper in one's bosom

żołąd|ek (**-ka, -ki**; *inst sg* **-kiem**) *m* stomach; **przez ~ do serca** the way to a man's heart is through his stomach

żołądkowy *adj* **1** stomach **2** (*soki*) gastric; **krople żołądkowe** ≈ bitters

żołnierz (**-a, -e**; *gen pl* **-y**) *m* (*wojskowy*) soldier

żo|na (**-ny, -ny**; *dat sg & loc sg* **-nie**) *f* (*małżonka*) wife

żonaty *adj* (*mężczyzna*) married

żółt|ko (**-ka, -ka**; *inst sg* **-kiem**; *gen pl* **-ek**) *nt* yolk

żółty *adj* (*barwa*) yellow; **~ ser** hard cheese

żół|w (**-wia, -wie**; *gen pl* **-wi**) *m* **1** (*lądowy*) tortoise, turtle (*US*) **2** (*morski*) turtle

żurawi|na (**-ny, -ny**; *dat sg & loc sg* **-nie**) *f* cranberry

żur|ek (**-ku, -ki**; *inst sg* **-kiem**) *m* (*Kulin*) *traditional Polish soup made from fermented rye, often with sausage or smoked bacon*

życi|e (**-a**) *nt* **1** life **2** (*pot*: *codzienne*) living (costs); **prowadzić zdrowy tryb życia** to lead a healthy lifestyle; **~ osobiste** private life; **ubezpieczenie na ~** life assurance; **wprowadzać** (**wprowadzić** *pf*) **coś w ~** to put sth into effect

życiory|s (**-su, -sy**; *loc sg* **-sie**) *m* **1** (*informacja dla pracodawcy*) CV, curriculum vitae (*Brit*), résumé (*US*) **2** (*biografia*) biography

życiowy *adj* **1** (*proces*) vital **2** (*doświadczenie*) practical **3** (*pot*: *stosunek do rzeczywistości*) realistic

życze|nie (**-nia, -nia**; *gen pl* **-ń**) *nt* (*pragnienie*) wish; **życzenia** *pl* (*świąteczne, imieninowe*) wishes; **usługa na ~** a request service; **składać komuś życzenia z okazji urodzin** to wish sb all the best on their birthday

życzliwoś|ć (**-ci**) *f* kindness

życzliwy *adj* (*człowiek, relacja*) kind

życz|yć (**-ę, -ysz**) *vt*: **~ komuś czegoś** to wish sb sth; **czego państwo sobie życzą?** can I help you?

ży|ć (**-ję, -jesz**) *vi* to live; **niech żyje król!** long live the king!; **~ z zapomogi** to live off benefit (*Brit*) *lub* social welfare (*US*)

Ży|d (**-da, -dzi**; *loc sg* **-dzie**) *m* Jew

Żydów|ka (**-ki, -ki**; *dat sg* **-ce**; *gen pl* **-ek**) *f* Jew

żydowski *adj* (*kultura, teatr*) Jewish

ży|ła (**-ły, -ły**; *loc sg* **-le**) *f* vein; **strach zmroził mu krew w ~ch** he felt a blood-curdling fear

żyra|fa (**-fy, -fy**; *loc sg* **-fie**) *f* giraffe

żytni *adj* (*chleb, mąka*) rye

żywio|ł (**-łu, -ły**; *loc sg* **-le**) *m* (*woda, ziemia, powietrze, ogień*) element; **być w swoim żywiole** to be in one's element

żywopło|t (**-tu, -ty**; *loc sg* **-cie**) *m* hedge

żywy *adj* **1** (*żyjący*) living **2** (*żywiołowy*) lively **3** (*wyrazisty*) vivid; **to ona, jak żywa** it's her down to a T; **na żywo** live; **mecz był transmitowany na żywo** the match was broadcast live

Polish Grammar

1 Nouns

1.1 Gender of nouns

Polish nouns take two numbers: singular and plural. In the singular, there are three genders, and in the plural there are two genders. Without exception, all nouns in Polish are allocated a grammatical gender.

Masculine nouns

- usually end in a consonant, e.g.

paszport	**komputer**	**samochód**	**Kraków**	**Lichtenstein**
passport	*computer*	*car*	*Cracow*	*Liechtenstein*

- end in the vowel **–a** when denoting a male family relation or an occupation, e.g.

tata	**kolega**	**dyplomata**	**artysta**	**ekonomista**
Dad	*friend*	*diplomat*	*artist*	*economist*

Feminine nouns

- usually end in **–a**, e.g.

kobieta	**dziewczyna**	**książka**	**Warszawa**	**Anglia**	**Europa**
woman	*young woman*	*book*	*Warsaw*	*England*	*Europe*

- can end in a soft consonant especially when referring to abstract ideas, e.g.

solidarność	**narodowość**	**powieść**	**noc**	**twarz**	**Białoruś**	**jesień**
solidarity	*nationality*	*novel*	*night*	*face*	*Bielarus*	*autumn*

- rarely end in **–i**, e.g.

Pani	**gospodyni**	**sprzedawczyni**	**bogini**
formal form of address; Ms	*hostess*	*female sales assistant*	*goddess*

There are some proper names, e.g. **Kowalska**, or words relating to female family members and occupations, e.g. **znajoma** acquaintance, **teściowa** mother-in-law, **księgowa** accountant, that end in **–ska** or **–owa**. This ending indicates that these words are likely to be adjectives and follow a declension pattern of adjectives.

Neuter nouns

- usually end in **–o** or **–e**, e.g.

słowo	**wino**	**kino**	**Gniezno**	**mieszkanie**	**zdjęcie**
word	*wine*	*cinema*	*(a Polish town)*	*flat*	*photo*

- end in **–ę** (these nouns tend to have an irregular plural ending), e.g.

imię	**zwierzę**	**niemowlę**
first name	*animal*	*infant*

- are foreign words that end in **–i** (they are non-declinable), e.g.

pepsi	**sushi**	**spaghetti**
pepsi	*sushi*	*spaghetti*

- are foreign words that end in **–um** (they retain the same form for all singular forms in all cases in the singular), e.g.

centrum	**stypendium**	**archiwum**	**akwarium**
centre	*scholarship*	*archives*	*fish tank, aquarium*

1.2 Plural

There are two genders in the plural: **masculine animate virile** (i.e. nouns denoting men or groups of people that include men) and the **non-masculine animate virile** group (i.e. masculine animate, masculine inanimate, feminine and neuter). There are two personal pronouns for **they** to denote the two groups:

oni (*they* for masculine animate virile), e.g.

Polacy	**studenci**	**ludzie**
Poles	*students*	*people*

one (*they* for all the other nouns), e.g.

filmy	**psy**	**dziewczyny**	**dzieci**	**zdjęcia**
films	*dogs*	*young women*	*children*	*photos*

The two plural forms require different endings, for example of adjectives or verbs. The pronouns are rarely used explicitly in sentences, however, they are evident in the choice of the verb or adjective ending.

Na premierę filmu przybyli aktorzy [=oni], którzy pozowali do zdjęć z fanami.
The first night was attended by actors who posed for pictures with their fans.

W naszym ogródku rosną truskawki [= one]. W tym roku zakwitły w maju.
There are strawberries in our garden. This year they bloomed in May.

1.3 Case system

The notion of case is crucial in Polish grammar. In a nutshell, it indicates the role nouns, adjectives and pronouns can play in a sentence. For example: **Adam mieszka z Anną**. (*Adam lives with Anna*) can be reordered to **Z Anną mieszka Adam**. (*With-Anna-lives-Adam*). The meaning of both sentences is the same. What differs is the focus, which is usually on the last item of the clause. The same word takes a different ending depending on its role in a given context/ sentence, for instance:

Adam lubi grać w piłkę.
Adam [nominative, subject] *likes playing football.*

Piłka nożna interesuje Adama.
Football interests Adam [accusative, direct object].

Wczoraj grałem z Adamem w piłkę.
Yesterday I played football with Adam [instrumental, prepositional phrase]

There are seven cases (nominative, genitive, dative, accusative, instrumental, locative and vocative) and two numbers (singular and plural) in the declension of Polish nouns. Since most endings are quite regular for each gender, they are not shown in this dictionary. However, each noun entry in the dictionary includes the genitive singular ending (or genitive plural for plural-only nouns), along with the nominative plural. These endings are given in brackets right after the headword and separated with a comma, for example:

pies (psa, psy) *dog*

kompute|r (–ra, –ry) *computer*

If a given word has no plural form, only the genitive singular ending is shown after the headword, e.g.

młodoś|ć (–ci) *youth*

Irregular forms are given in smaller print before the part of speech information or, when limited to a specific sense of the word, inside the entry:

ko|t (–ta, –ty) (*loc sg* **–cie)** *m cat*

1.4 Nominal phrase agreement

Adjectives, pronouns, numerals and other elements that describe a noun in a phrase have to agree with the noun in case, number and gender. This is called grammatical agreement and is an essential part of the Polish language.

Nominative

The nominative is the form of the noun you find when you look up a Polish word in the dictionary.

Słownik podaje wszystkie formy gramatyczne danego słowa.
The dictionary lists all grammatical forms of a given word.

Mój urlop zaczyna się w środę.
My holiday starts on Wednesday.

The plural form of the nominative is provided in the dictionary.

Genitive

The genitive is the most frequent case in Polish and it has a variety of functions.

Nie mam samochodu.
I do not have a car.

koniec filmu
the end of the film

kartka od Ani
a card from Ania

The dictionary will indicate when the genitive form is required by adding a note (+ *gen*).

The genitive singular form is given in the dictionary entry; the plural form for masculine nouns is usually **–ów** or, after semi soft consonants, **–i**, for feminine and neuter nouns the ending **–a**, **–e**, **–ę** or **–o** is dropped.

Dative

The dative case is mainly used with personal pronouns and after prepositions.

Czy ci się to podoba?
Do you like it?

To jest wbrew naszym przekonaniom.
This is against our convictions.

Accusative

The accusative is used for the direct object of the sentence, and after prepositions.

Lubię kawę.
I like coffee.

Dziękuję za prezent.
Thank you for your present.

Instrumental

The instrumental is used for the direct object or verb complement, and after prepositions.

> **Interesuję się sportem.**
> *I'm interested in sport.*
>
> **między nami mówiąc**
> *between you and me*

Locative

The locative case is only used after certain prepositions to say where an activity takes place, and in some cases, when it takes place.

> **Mieszkam w Polsce.**
> *I live in Poland.*
>
> **Po pracy często chodzę na siłownię.**
> *After work I often go to the gym.*

Vocative

The vocative is the least used case in Polish. Its main function is in forms of address such as at the beginning of a letter.

> **Tomku, podaj mi sól.**
> *Tomek, pass the salt please.*

The noun endings for each case are shown in the tables on the next page.

Overview of cases (nouns) – Singular

	Masculine			Feminine						Neuter	
	virile	animate	Inanimate	**–ka, –ga**	**–la, –ja**	**–ia** (Polish origin)	**–ia** (loan words)	Soft consonant	Hard consonant	**–o, –e, –ę**	**–um, –i**
Nominative	*Always shown in noun entry*										
Genitive	*Always shown in noun entry*										
Dative	**–u** *(monosyllabic) or* **–owi** *(longer words)*			*Change to* **–ce** *and* **–dze**	**–i**	**–i**	**–ii**	**–ii**	**–ie** *or consonant change*	**–u**	
Accusative	*–a*	*–a*	*As nominative*	**–ę**	**–ę**	**–ę**	**–ę**	*As nominative*	**–ę**	*As nominative*	
Instrumental	*–(i)em*			*–ą*						*–(i)em*	
Locative	*Always shown in noun entry*										
Vocative	*–e* or *–u*			*–o*				**–i**	*–o*	*As nominative*	

Overview of cases (nouns) – Plural

	Masculine			Feminine						Neuter	
	virile	animate	Inanimate	**–ka, –ga**	**–la, –ja**	**–ia** (Polish origin)	**–ia** (loan words)	Soft consonant	Hard consonant	**–o, –e, –ę**	**–um, –i**
Nominative	*Always shown in noun entry*										
Genitive	**–ów** *or* **–y**			*Dropped* **–a**				**–i**	*Dropped* **–a**	*Dropped* **–o** *and* **–e**	**–ów**
Dative	**–om**										
Accusative	**–ów**	*As nominative plural*									
Instrumental	**–ami**										
Locative	**–ach**										
Vocative	**–e**			**–ie**					**–y**	*As nominative*	

Tables showing the declension of nouns are given at the beginning of the dictionary, on pages xvi–xvii.

2 Pronouns

Pronouns are used instead of a noun, when you don't need or want to name someone or something directly. They help maintain the coherence of the text without unnecessary repetition. Just like nouns, pronouns are declined according to gender, case and number.

The pronouns in Polish in the nominative case are:

Singular Nominative

Ja *I*

Ty *you* (informal singular)

Pan *you* (masculine formal singular)

Pani *you* (feminine formal singular)

On *he, it* (replaces all masculine nouns in the singular)

Ona *she, it* (replaces all feminine nouns in the singular)

Ono *it* (replaces all neuter nouns in the singular)

Plural Nominative

My *we*

Wy *you* (informal plural)

Panowie *you* (masculine formal plural)

Panie *you* (feminine formal plural)

Państwo *you* (mixed gender formal plural)

Oni *they* (masculine virile animate)

One *they* (masculine animate non-virile, masculine inanimate, feminine and neuter)

Tables showing the declension of all other pronouns are given at the beginning of the dictionary, on pages xiv–xvi.

3 Adjectives

3.1 Agreement with nouns

When you look up a Polish adjective in the dictionary, you find the masculine singular nominative form. Adjectives need to agree with the noun or pronoun they are describing in gender, case and number. Therefore, just like nouns, adjectives take different endings, e.g.

nowy dom	**nowa książka**	**nowe ćwiczenie**	**nowi sąsiedzi**	**nowe okna**
a new house	*a new book*	*a new exercise*	*new neighbours*	*new windows*

To czarna kawa.
This is black coffee. (nominative feminine singular)

Lubię czarną kawę.
I like black coffee. (accusative feminine singular)

Londyn jest starym miastem.
London is an old town. (instrumental neuter singular)

Gniezno i Kraków są starymi miastami.
Gniezno and Kraków are old towns. (instrumental neuter plural)

Adjectives that end in **–ki** or **–gi** in the masculine form always retain **–i** before adding a suffix that starts in an **–e**.

To jest długi film.
This is a long film. (nominative masculine inanimate singular)

Byłam na długiej przerwie.
I was on a long break. (locative feminine singular)

Ten reżyser nigdy nie nakręcił tak długiego filmu.
This director has never directed such a long film. (genitive masculine inanimate singular)

There are some words with a stem that ends in **–n** or **–p** that also take the ending **–i**; they require it before all suffixes in all cases, genders and numbers. However, it is important to remember that these adjectives, although frequently used, are exceptions, e.g.

ostatni dzień	**ostatnia godzina**	**ostatnie spotkanie**	**ostatni dyrektor**
the last day	*the last hour*	*the last meeting*	*the last director*
średni uczeń	**średnia pensja**	**średni pracownicy**	**średnie frytki**
an average pupil	*average pay*	*average employees*	*medium fries*
głupi pomysł	**głupia uwaga**	**głupie zachowanie**	**głupi ludzie**
a silly idea	*a silly comment*	*foolish behaviour*	*stupid people*

Tables showing the declension of adjectives are given at the beginning of the dictionary, on pages xvii.

4 Verbs

4.1 The infinitive verb form

When you look up a verb in the dictionary, you find the infinitive form. This usually ends in **–ć**, or in rare cases, **–c**, e.g.

pisać	**mówić**	**grać**	**czytać**	**móc**	**biec**	**piec**
to write	*to speak*	*to play*	*to read*	*to be able to*	*to run*	*to bake*

4.2 Aspect of verbs – function

The Polish language has three tenses that indicate whether an action took place in the past, takes place in the present, or will take place in the future. To convey more complex nuances of time, such as the length of the activity, its regularity, continuity or completion, the aspects of verbs are applied. Most Polish verbs come in pairs, one of them in each aspect, i.e. **niedokonany** (imperfective), which is the one provided as the entry in the dictionary, and **dokonany** (perfective):

The imperfective aspect is used to:

- focus on the duration or length of an action (and not its outcome), irrespective of how long (or short) the action is, e.g.

  Czekaliśmy na autobus dwie godziny.
  We were waiting for the bus for two hours.

  Wczoraj wieczorem oglądałam wiadomości.
  Last night I was watching the news.

  Uczę się polskiego od miesiąca.
  I've been learning Polish for a month.

- highlight a routine or a repeated action

  Codziennie na śniadanie jem płatki z mlekiem.
  Everyday for breakfast I eat cereal with milk.

  Na wakacjach wstawaliśmy bardzo późno.
  On holiday we used to get up late.

- provide background to another activity

  Rozmawiałam przez telefon, gdy przyszedł listonosz.
  I was just talking on the phone when the postman arrived.

  Będzie pracował za granicą, kiedy skończy 40 lat.
  He'll be working abroad when he turns 40.

The perfective aspect is used to:

- focus on a single completed action, highlighting the outcome, result etc.

  Wczoraj wieczorem obejrzałem wiadomości.
  Last night I watched the news.

  Kto napisał ten raport?
  Who wrote this report?

- provide a list of activities that either were or will be completed

  Przyszedł do pracy, włączył komputer i zaczął czytać emaile.
  He arrived at work, turned his computer on and started reading his emails.

  Jutro spotkam się z szefem, przedstawię nowy projekt i poproszę o podwyżkę.
  Tomorrow I'll meet with my boss, present my new project and ask for a pay rise.

4.3 Aspect of verbs – form

The imperfective form is the form that you find when you look up a Polish verb in the dictionary i.e. it's the same as the infinitive. The perfective is given in the entry.

4.4 Expressing the present

In Polish, there is only one present tense and it is used to indicate what has been done, is done regularly, and is being done at the moment. Only the imperfective aspect is used in the present tense as the actions described are either repeated, habitual, or continuous.

Raz w tygodniu uczę się polskiego.
I learn Polish once a week.

Uczę się polskiego od roku.
I've been learning Polish for a year.

Właśnie uczę się polskiego, dlatego korzystam ze słownika.
I'm learning Polish right now, that is why I'm using the dictionary.

4.5 Expressing the past

In Polish, there is only one past tense but either of the aspects can be used to indicate difference in the time and completion of the activity. The imperfective aspect is used to focus on the regularity of the activity or on its length and duration, whereas the perfective aspect highlights the outcome of the activity. The verb aspect is chosen by the speaker to emphasise their intention.

Wczoraj wieczorem czytałam tę książkę.
Last night I was reading this book. (imperfective, focus on the activity, its duration)

Wczoraj wieczorem przeczytałam tę książkę.
Last night I read this book. (perfective, focus on the completion of the activity)

Na wakacjach codziennie jedliśmy lody.
On holiday, we ate ice-cream every day. (imperfective, regular activity)

Kto zjadł wszystkie jabłka?
Who ate all the apples? (perfective, focus on the outcome)

Na uniwersytecie często chodziłem na koncerty.
While at university, I often went to concerts. (imperfective, regular activity)

Spotkałem Adama, kiedy szedłem na koncert.
I met Adam when I was (going) on my way to the concert.
(imperfective, focus on the background activity)

W weekend poszedłem na koncert.
At the weekend I went to a concert. (perfective, a one-off activity in the past)

The past tense is formed by replacing the infinitive ending **–ć** or **–c** with the ending that indicates the person, number and also gender. Both perfective and imperfective verbs follow the same pattern, e.g.

Przed chwilą zadzwonił twój szef.
Your boss called a moment ago. (masculine animate virile singular)

W weekend zadzwonili do mnie moi rodzice.
My parents called at the weekend. (masculine animate virile plural)

Moja siostra kupiła nowe buty.
My sister bought new shoes. (feminine singular)

Moje koleżanki kupiły tanie bilety do kina.
My girlfriends bought cheap cinema tickets. (feminine plural)

4.6 Expressing the future

In Polish, the future can be expressed by using the present tense forms as well as future tense forms. There are two future tenses: imperfective and perfective. The imperfective future is used to focus on the regularity of the activity or on its length and duration, whereas the future perfective aspect highlights the outcome of an activity to be undertaken in the future. The verb aspect is chosen by the speaker to emphasise their intention.

Future imperfective

The future imperfective is the only descriptive tense in Polish, i.e. it requires two words to be formed: the verb **być** (to be) plus a verb in its imperfective aspect, either in the infinitive form or in the past tense form. The difference relates to the form only, there is no difference in the meaning.

Będę dzwonić / dzwonił(a) co tydzień.
I'll be calling every week.

W tym roku będę regularnie uprawiać / uprawiał(a) sport.
This year I will do sport regularly.

Future imperfective (with the infinitive)

grać *(to play)*

	Masculine		Feminine	Neuter
	Virile	Non-virile		
ja	będę grać			
ty	będziesz grać			
on, pan, ona, pani, ono	będzie grać			
my	będziemy grać			
wy	będziecie grać			
oni, panowie, państwo	będą grać			
one, panie	będą grać			

Future imperfective (with the past tense form)
grać *(to play)*

	Masculine		Feminine	Neuter
	Virile	Non-virile		
ja	będę grał		będę grała	
ty	będziesz grał		będziesz grała	
on, pan	będzie grał			
ona, pani			będzie grała	
ono				będzie grało
my	będziemy grali	będziemy grały		
wy	będziecie grali	będziecie grały		
oni, panowie, państwo	będą grali			
one, panie		będą grały		

Future perfective
The future perfective is formed by applying the present tense conjugation patterns to the perfective aspect of verbs. Thus, the future perfective tense is formed by replacing the infinitive ending **–ć** or **–c** with the ending that indicates the person and number. Depending on the last syllable of the verb, the verbs can follow one of several conjugation patterns.

> **Kiedy zrobisz to zadanie?**
> *When will you do this exercise?*
>
> **O której zacznie się film?**
> *What time will the film start?*
>
> **Jutro wstanę wcześnie rano.**
> *Tomorrow I will get up early.*
>
> **Czego się napijesz?**
> *What will you drink?*

	Verb endings			
	-ować	-ić	-yć	-ać
ja	-uję	-(i)ę	-ę	-am
ty	-ujesz	-isz	-ysz	-asz
on, pan, ona, pani, ono	-uje	-i	-y	-a
my	-ujemy	-imy	-ymy	-amy
wy	-ujecie	-icie	-ycie	-acie
oni, panowie, państwo, one, panie	-ują	-(i)ą	-ą	-ają

There are also a few irregular present tense conjugations:

	być (to be)	**zaczynać** (to start)	**wziąć** (to take)
ja	**będę**	**zacznę**	**wezmę**
ty	**będziesz**	**zaczniesz**	**weźmiesz**
on, pan, ona, pani, ono	**będzie**	**zacznie**	**weźmie**
my	**będziemy**	**zaczniemy**	**weźmiemy**
wy	**będziecie**	**zaczniecie**	**weźmiecie**
oni, panowie, państwo, one, panie	**będą**	**zaczną**	**wezmą**

4.7 Imperative mood

The imperative is used to ask people to do something in a more direct way. It can be formed by using both the imperfective and perfective aspect, depending on whether a continuous/regular or one-off action is required.

Formal imperative
The formal imperative can be formed by:

- using the infinitive form after the verb **proszę** *(I would like you to)*

  Proszę usiąść. *Please sit down.*
  Proszę poczekać. *Please wait.*
  Proszę uważać. *Be careful please.*

- using the particle **niech** (let) followed by the third person singular or plural. The formal form of address **pan** (sir), **pani** (madam) etc. is then explicitly used in the structure.

  Niech pan usiądzie. *Please sit down (sir).*
  Niech pani poczeka. *Please wait (madam).*
  Niech państwo uważają. *Be careful please (ladies and gentlemen).*
  Niech pan nie siada na tym krześle. *Do not sit on this chair (sir).*
  Niech pani nie czeka. *Do not wait (madam).*

4.8 Interrogative forms

Questions are usually formed by putting a question word at the beginning of the sentence. The pronoun **czy** (yes/no question pronoun) starts questions in all tenses.

Czy mówi pan po polsku?
Do you speak Polish?

Czy był pan kiedyś w Polsce?
Have you ever been to Poland?

Kiedy będą ogłoszone wyniki?
When will the results be announced?

If the main verb requires a preposition, questions are often formed by moving the preposition to the start of the sentence.

O czym myślisz?
What are you thinking about?

Tables showing the conjugation of verbs are given at the beginning of the dictionary, on pages xviii–xxi.

5 Prepositions

Prepositions indicate the location of an object or activity, or a direction in which a movement is taking place. In Polish, prepositions take different cases depending on the verbs that they follow.

5.1 Prepositions with verbs of movement

Verbs that indicate movement to or from a place are referred to as **czasowniki ruchu** (verbs of movement). Prepositions that follow them can take one of the following cases:

- the genitive case after the preposition **do** (*to*), **z** (*from a place*), **znad** (*from an area of water*), **od** (*from a person*) etc.

  Jadę do Polski.
  I'm going to Poland.

  Pochodzę z Anglii.
  I come from England.

  Przesyłam pozdrowienia znad Bałtyku.
  I'm sending greetings from the Baltic Sea.

- the accusative case after the preposition **na** (*to attend an activity, to a region or island*), **nad** (*to an area of water*), **w** (*to the mountain range*) etc.

  Jutro idę na koncert.
  Tomorrow I'm going to a concert.

  Chciałabym pojechać na Kubę.
  I'd like to travel to Cuba.

  Wyprowadzili się na Śląsk.
  They have moved to Silesia (region).

  W sobotę jedziemy nad jezioro.
  On Saturday we are going to the lakeside.

5.2 Prepositions with verbs of location/state

Verbs that indicate location are referred to as **czasowniki statyczne** (non-movement verbs). Prepositions that follow them can take one of the following cases:

- the locative case after the preposition **w** (*in, at a place*), **na** (*at an event, on an island, in a region*) etc.

  Wczoraj byliśmy w teatrze.
  We were at the theatre yesterday.

  Na wakacjach byliśmy w Polsce.
  We were in Poland on holiday.

- the genitive case after the preposition **u** (*at a person's home*), **obok** (*next to*) etc.

  W weekend byliśmy u rodziców.
  At the weekend we were at our parents'.

  Moje mieszkanie jest obok windy.
  My flat is next to the lift.

- the instrumental case after the preposition **nad** (*at an area of water*), **za** (*out of, outside, behind*) etc.

  Warszawa leży nad Wisłą.
  Warsaw is located on the Wisła river.

  Wakacje spędziliśmy nad morzem.
  We spent our holiday at the seaside.

  Mieszkamy za miastem.
  We live just out of town.

6 Numbers

Cardinal numbers

Cardinal numbers need to agree in gender, case and number with the nouns they modify.

jeden słownik
one dictionary
(masculine)

jedna kawa
one coffee
(feminine)

jedno piwo
one beer
(neuter)

dwa słowniki
two dictionaries
(masculine inanimate)

dwóch braci = dwaj bracia
two brothers
(masculine virile)

dwie kawy
two coffees (feminine)

dwa piwa
two beers (neuter)

dwoje dzieci
two children (group)

Ordinal numbers

Ordinal numbers need to agree in gender, case and number with the nouns they modify.

Pierwsza godzina pracy jest najgorsza.
The first hour of work is the worst.

To moje pierwsze piwo.
This is my first beer.

Ordinal numbers are used when, for instance, talking about the date or the time e.g.

Dzisiaj jest pierwszy kwietnia.
Today is the first of April.

Jest (godzina) ósma.
It is eight (o'clock).

Tables showing the declension of numerals are given at the beginning of the dictionary, on pages xii–xiv.

Gramatyka angielska

1 Rzeczowniki

1.1 Liczba pojedyncza i mnoga rzeczowników

Niektóre rzeczowniki w formie liczby pojedynczej odnoszą się do rzeczy, które są niepowtarzalne, jedyne w swoim rodzaju. Ponieważ są użyte w konkretnym znaczeniu, zwykle poprzedza je przedimek **the**.

The sun was shining.
Świeciło słońce.

I'm afraid of the dark.
Boję się ciemności.

Inne rzeczowniki w formie liczby pojedynczej są zwykle poprzedzone przedimkiem **a (an)**, ponieważ odnoszą się do rzeczy, o których mówimy po raz pierwszy w danej chwili.

I went upstairs and had a shower.
Poszedłem na górę i wziąłem prysznic.

I felt I had to give him a chance.
Czułem, że powinienem mu dać szansę.

Niektóre rzeczowniki w formie liczby mnogiej są używane tylko w jednym konkretnym znaczeniu.

His clothes looked terribly dirty.
Jego ubrania wyglądały na bardzo brudne.

Troops will be sent to Afghanistan.
Oddziały zostaną wysłane do Afganistanu.

Niektóre z tych rzeczowników są używane z określnikami.

I went to the pictures with Tina.
Poszłam do kina z Tiną.

You hurt his feelings.
Zraniłaś jego uczucia.

Inne są używane bez określników.

Refreshments are available inside.
Napoje i przekąski są dostępne wewnątrz.

Mała grupa rzeczowników w liczbie mnogiej odnosi się do pojedynczego przedmiotu składającego się z dwóch części.

She was wearing brown trousers.
Miała na sobie brązowe spodnie.

W przypadku rzeczowników, które odnoszą się do grupy osób lub rzeczy, ta sama forma rzeczownika może łączyć się z czasownikiem w formie liczby pojedynczej lub mnogiej. Te rzeczowniki często są określane mianem zbiorowych.

Our little group is complete.
Nasza mała grupa jest kompletna.

The largest group are the boys.
Największą grupę stanowią chłopcy.

2 Określniki

2.1 Przedimek określony

Wyraz **the** jest przedimkiem określonym. Używa się go, gdy osoba, z którą się rozmawia, zna osobę lub rzecz, o której mowa.

The man began to run towards the boy.
Mężczyzna zaczął biec w kierunku chłopca.

The girls were not at home.
Dziewczyn nie było w domu.

Przedimka **the** używa się, gdy odnosi się do rzeczy, która jest tylko jedna na świecie lub znajduje się w konkretnym miejscu.

They all sat in the sun.
Wszyscy siedzieli na słońcu.

The sky was a brilliant blue.
Niebo było olśniewająco niebieskie.

Przedimka **the** używa się, gdy chce się wypowiedzieć ogólnie na jakiś temat.

I don't like using the phone.
Nie lubię korzystać z telefonu.

Shirin plays the piano very well.
Shirin gra bardzo dobrze na fortepianie.

Przedimka **the** używa się przed niektórymi tytułami oraz nazwami organizacji, budynków, gazet czy dzieł sztuki.

...the Queen of England
...Królowa Anglii

...the Taj Mahal
...Tadź Mahal

...the Times
...Times (dziennik)

...the United Nations
...Narody Zjednoczone

Przedimka **the** używa się przed nazwami łańcuchów górskich i archipelagów.

...the Alps
...Alpy

...the Canary Islands
...Wyspy Kanaryjskie

Przedimka **the** używa się przed nazwami akwenów wodnych.

...the Bay of Biscay
...Zatoka Biskajska

...the Atlantic Ocean
...Ocean Atlantycki

Przedimka **the** używa się przed nazwami krajów, które zawierają słowa takie jak **kingdom** czy **states**, oraz przed nazwami krajów, które mają formę liczby mnogiej.

...the Netherlands
...Holandia

...the United Kingdom
...Zjednoczone Królestwo

Przedimka **the** nie używa się przed nazwami większości krajów, kontynentów, miast, ulic, adresów i jezior.

...Turkey
...Turcja

...Tokyo
...Tokio

...Asia
...Azja

...Oxford Street
...ulica Oxford

Przedimka **the** nie używa się przed nazwiskami i imionami ludzi lub przed tytułami, jeśli podane jest nazwisko.

...Queen Elizabeth *...Królowa Elżbieta*	**...President Obama** *...Prezydent Obama*
...Mr Brown *...Pan Brown*	**...Lord Olivier** *...Lord Olivier*

2.2 Przedimek nieokreślony

Wyrazy **a** i **an** to przedimki nieokreślone. Przedimka **a** używa się przed wyrazem rozpoczynającym się od głoski wymawianej jak spółgłoska, nawet jeśli pierwsza litera wyrazu to samogłoska, na przykład **a university**, **a European language**. Przedimka **an** używa się przed wyrazem rozpoczynającym się w wymowie od samogłoski, nawet jeśli pierwszą literą wyrazu jest spółgłoska, na przykład **an honest man**. Przedimka **a** (**an**) używa się, gdy wspomina się o osobie lub rzeczy po raz pierwszy.

She picked up a book.
Wzięła książkę.

He was eating an apple.
Jadł jabłko.

Gdy odnosi się do tej samej osoby lub rzeczy po raz drugi, wówczas używa się przedimka **the**.

She picked up a book. The book was lying on the table.
Wzięła książkę. Książka leżała na stole.

Po czasowniku **to be** lub innym czasowniku łącznikowym, można użyć przedimka **a** (**an**) przed przymiotnikiem i rzeczownikiem, aby podać więcej informacji na temat kogoś lub czegoś.

It was a really beautiful house.
To był naprawdę piękny dom.

Przedimka **a** (**an**) używa się po czasowniku **to be** lub innym czasowniku łącznikowym, kiedy podaje się nazwę zawodu.

He became a school teacher.
Został nauczycielem.

Przedimka **a** (**an**) używa się w znaczeniu wyrazu **one** z liczbami, ułamkami, pieniędzmi, określeniami miar i wag.

a hundred *sto*	**a quarter** *ćwierć*	**a pound** *funt*	**a kilo** *kilo*

Przedimka **a** czy **an** nie używa się przed rzeczownikami niepoliczalnymi ani przed formą liczby mnogiej rzeczowników policzalnych.

I love dogs.
Uwielbiam psy.

Many adults don't listen to children.
Wielu dorosłych nie słucha dzieci.

Money can't buy happiness.
Pieniądze szczęścia nie dają.

2.3 Wyrażanie ilości (1): much, little, many, few, more, less, fewer

Wyrazu **much** używa się do określenia dużej ilości czegoś, a wyrazu **little** – małej. Wyrazów **much** oraz little używa się tylko z niepoliczalnymi rzeczownikami.

I haven't got much time.
Nie mam dużo czasu.

We've made little progress.
Zrobiliśmy niewielki postęp.

Wyrazu **many** używa się do określenia dużej ilości ludzi lub rzeczy, a wyrazu **few** – małej. Wyrazów **many** oraz **few** używa się z liczbą mnogą rzeczowników policzalnych.

He wrote many novels.
Napisał wiele powieści.

There were few visitors to our house.
Mieliśmy niewielu gości w naszym domu.

Zwykle wyrazu **much** używa się w zaprzeczeniach i pytaniach.

He did not speak much English.
Nie mówił dobrze po angielsku.

Why haven't I given much attention to this problem?
Dlaczego nie poświęciłem więcej uwagi temu problemowi?

W zdaniach twierdzących zamiast wyrazu **much** używa się wyrażeń **a lot of**, **lots of**, czy **plenty of**. Można ich używać przed rzeczownikami niepoliczalnymi i przed formą liczby mnogiej.

I make a lot of mistakes.
Popełniam mnóstwo błędów.

They spend lots of time on the project.
Spędzają bardzo dużo czasu nad tym projektem.

I've got plenty of money.
Mam mnóstwo pieniędzy.

Wyrażeń **so much** oraz **too much** można używać w zdaniach twierdzących.

She spends so much time here.
Ona spędza tutaj tak dużo czasu.

Wyrazu **more** używa się z rzeczownikami niepoliczalnymi oraz formą liczby mnogiej rzeczowników policzalnych, gdy odnosi się do ilości czegoś lub liczby ludzi, która jest większa niż inna ilość lub liczba.

His visit might do more harm than good.
Jego wizyta może wyrządzić więcej złego niż dobrego.

He does more hours than I do.
On pracuje więcej godzin niż ja.

Wyrazu **less** używa się, gdy odnosi się do ilości, która jest mniejsza niż ilość czegoś innego.

This machinery uses less energy.
Ta maszyna zużywa mniej energii.

Wyrazu **fewer** używa się z formą liczby mnogiej, gdy odnosi się do liczby ludzi lub rzeczy, która jest mniejsza niż liczebność innej grupy.

There are fewer trees here.
Tutaj jest mniej drzew.

2.4 Wyrażanie ilości (2): some, any, another, other, each, every

Wyrazu **some** używa się przed niepoliczalnymi rzeczownikami i formą liczby mnogiej, gdy określa się ogólnie ilość czegoś lub liczbę ludzi czy rzeczy.

We have left some food for you in the fridge.
Zostawiliśmy ci w lodówce trochę jedzenia.

Some trains are running late.
Niektóre pociągi mają opóźnienia.

Wyrazu **some** używa się w pytaniach, jeśli oczekuje się odpowiedzi pozytywnej **yes**.

Would you like some coffee?
Czy chcesz trochę kawy?

Could you give me some examples?
Czy mógłby mi pan podać kilka przykładów?

Wyrazu **any** używa się przed rzeczownikami niepoliczalnymi lub formą liczby mnogiej, aby określić ilość czegoś, co istnieje lub nie. W pytaniach lub zaprzeczeniach zwykle wówczas używa się wyrazu **any**.

It hasn't made any difference.
T o nie zrobiło żadnej różnicy.

Wyrazu **another** używa się przed formą liczby pojedynczej, aby określić dodatkową osobę lub rzecz.

Could I have another cup of coffee?
Czy mogę poprosić o jeszcze jedną filiżankę kawy?

Wyrazu **another** można też użyć przed formą liczby mnogiej, by określić większą liczbę osób lub rzeczy.

Another four years passed before we met again.
Minęły kolejne cztery lata, zanim znowu się spotkaliśmy.

Wyrazu **other** używa się przed formą liczby mnogiej, a zwrotu **the other** albo przed formą liczby pojedynczej, albo mnogiej.

I've got other things to think about.
Mam inne rzeczy do przemyślenia.

The other man has gone.
Ten drugi mężczyzna już wyszedł.

Wyrazów **each** lub **every** używa się przed formą liczby pojedynczej, aby zaznaczyć wszystkich członków danej grupy. Wyrazu **each** używa się, gdy chce się zaznaczyć członków grupy jako pojedyncze osoby czy części składowe, a wyrazu **every**, kiedy wypowiada się ogólne twierdzenie na temat całej grupy.

Each county is subdivided into several districts.
Każde hrabstwo jest podzielone na kilka okręgów.

Wyraz **every** może być określony innymi przymiotnikami lub przysłówkami, natomiast wyraz **each** występuje tylko samodzielnie.

He spoke to them nearly every weekend.
Rozmawiał z nimi niemal co weekend.

Each of them wore a blue shirt.
Każdy z nich miał na sobie niebieską koszulę.

3 Przymiotniki

Stopniowanie przymiotników

W przypadku przymiotników jednosylabowych, formę wyższą przymiotnika tworzy się przez dodanie końcówki **–er**, a formę najwyższą przez dodanie końcówki **–est**. Jeśli w stopniu równym przymiotnik kończy się na **–e**, wówczas dodaje się odpowiednio **–r** i **–st**.

cheap	→	**cheaper**	→	**cheapest**
tani	→	*tańszy*	→	*najtańszy*
safe	→	**safer**	→	**safest**
bezpieczny	→	*bezpieczniejszy*	→	*najbezpieczniejszy*

Ben Nevis is the highest mountain in Britain.
Ben Nevis jest najwyższą górą w Wielkiej Brytanii.

I've found a nicer hotel.
Znalazłem sympatyczniejszy hotel.

Jeśli przymiotniki zakończone są na pojedynczą samogłoskę poprzedzającą pojedynczą spółgłoskę (za wyjątkiem spółgłoski **–w**), ostatnia spółgłoska zostaje podwojona.

big	→	**bigger**	→	**biggest**
duży	→	*większy*	→	*największy*
hot	→	**hotter**	→	**hottest**
gorący	→	*gorętszy*	→	*najgorętszy*

The day grew hotter.
Dzień robił się coraz gorętszy.

My piece of cake was the biggest.
Mój kawałek ciasta był największy.

Przymiotniki dwusylabowe zakończone na **–y** po spółgłosce zamieniają **–y** na **–i**, zanim dodana zostanie końcówka **–er** lub **–est**.

happy	→	**happier**	→	**happiest**
szczęśliwy	→	*szczęśliwszy*	→	*najszczęśliwszy*
dirty	→	**dirtier**	→	**dirtiest**
brudny	→	*brudniejszy*	→	*najbrudniejszy*

It couldn't be easier.
To nie mogło być prostsze.

That is the funniest bit of the film.
To jest najzabawniejszy kawałek filmu.

W przypadku większości przymiotników dwusylabowych oraz dłuższych przymiotników, formę wyższą tworzy się przez dodanie wyrazu **more**, a formę najwyższą przez dodanie wyrazu **most**. Zwykle dodaje się przedimek **the** przed formą najwyższą, gdy przymiotnik poprzedza rzeczownik. Jeśli przymiotnik użyty jest po czasowniku łącznikowym, wówczas można pominąć wyraz **the**.

careful	→	**more careful**	→	**most careful**
uważny	→	*bardziej uważny*	→	*najbardziej uważny*
beautiful	→	**more beautiful**	→	**most beautiful**
piękny	→	*piękniejszy*	→	*najpiękniejszy*

They are the most beautiful gardens in the world.
To są najpiękniejsze ogrody na świecie.

I was happiest when I was on my own.
Byłem najszczęśliwszy, kiedy byłem sam.

Dwusylabowe przymiotniki, które są często używane, mogą tworzyć stopień wyższy i najwyższy albo przez dodanie końcówek **–er** i **–est**, albo przez użycie wyrazów **more** i **most**. Wyrazy **clever** i **quiet** stopniowane są wyłącznie przez dodanie końcówek **–er** i **–est**.

It was quieter outside.
Na zewnątrz było ciszej.

He was the cleverest man I ever knew.
Był najmądrzejszym człowiekiem, jakiego znałem.

Niektóre często używane przymiotniki mają nieregularne formy.

good	→	**better**	→	**best**
dobry	→	*lepszy*	→	*najlepszy*
bad	→	**worse**	→	**worst**
zły	→	*gorszy*	→	*najgorszy*

There's nothing better than a cup of hot coffee.
Nie ma nic lepszego niż filiżanka gorącej kawy.

4 Czasowniki

4.1 Czasy

Czasowniki posiłkowe

Czasowniki posiłkowe to czasowniki **be**, **have** oraz **do**. Używane są wraz z czasownikiem głównym, przy tworzeniu czasów, zaprzeczeń i pytań.

He is planning to get married soon.
On planuje ożenić się wkrótce.

I haven't seen Peter since last night.
Nie widziałem Petera od wczoraj wieczorem.

Czasownik **be** jako czasownik posiłkowy jest używany przy tworzeniu formy **–ing** głównego czasownika w czasach ciągłych.

He is living in Germany.
On mieszka w Niemczech.

They were going to phone you.
Mieli do was zadzwonić.

Czasownik **be** jako czasownik posiłkowy jest używany również wraz z imiesłowem przeszłym (*past participle*) przy tworzeniu strony biernej.

These cars are made in Japan.
Te samochody są produkowane w Japonii.

The walls of her flat were covered with posters.
Ściany jej mieszkania były pokryte plakatami.

Czasownik **have** używany jest jako czasownik pomocniczy wraz z imiesłowem przeszłym przy tworzeniu czasów uprzednich (*perfect*).

I have changed my mind.
Zmieniłem zdanie.

I wish you had met Guy.
Szkoda, że nie poznałeś Guya.

Czas teraźniejszy uprzedni ciągły (*present perfect continuous*), przeszły uprzedni ciągły (*past perfect continuous*) oraz czasy uprzednie (*perfect*) w stronie biernej tworzone są przy użyciu zarówno czasownika **have** jak i czasownika **be**.

He has been working very hard recently.
Ostatnio pracuje bardzo ciężko.

They had been taught by a young teacher.
Uczył ich młody nauczyciel.

Czasowniki **be** oraz **have** są również używane przy tworzeniu zaprzeczeń oraz pytań w czasach ciągłych (*continuous*) oraz uprzednich (*perfect*), jak również w stronie biernej.

He isn't going.
On nie idzie.

Was it written in English?
Czy to było napisane po angielsku?

Czasownik **do** używany jest jako czasownik posiłkowy przy tworzeniu zaprzeczeń oraz pytań w czasie teraźniejszym prostym (*present simple*) i przeszłym prostym (*past simple*).

Do you like her new haircut?
Czy podoba ci się jej nowa fryzura?

She didn't buy the house.
Nie kupiła tego domu.

Czasy teraźniejsze

W języku angielskim wyróżnia się cztery czasy teraźniejsze: czas teraźniejszy prosty (*the present simple*), czas teraźniejszy ciągły (*the present continuous*), czas teraźniejszy uprzedni (*the present perfect*) oraz czas teraźniejszy uprzedni ciągły (*the present perfect continuous*).

Czas teraźniejszy prosty oraz teraźniejszy ciągły odnoszą się do czasu teraźniejszego. Czas teraźniejszy prosty określa generalnie teraźniejszość oraz regularne, powtarzalne wydarzenia i czynności.

George lives in Birmingham.
George mieszka w Birmingham.

They often phone my mother.
Często dzwonią do mojej matki.

Aby określić coś wydarzającego się właśnie teraz, w danej chwili, używa się czasu teraźniejszego ciągłego.

I'm cooking the dinner.
Gotuję obiad.

Czas teraźniejszy ciągły używany jest często w opisach tymczasowej sytuacji.

She's living in a small flat at present.
Obecnie mieszka w małym mieszkaniu.

Czasu teraźniejszego uprzedniego oraz teraźniejszego uprzedniego ciągłego używa się, gdy opisuje się obecne (teraźniejsze) rezultaty wydarzeń, które zdarzyły się w przeszłości lub gdy opisuje się wydarzenie, które rozpoczęło się w przeszłości, i trwa nadal.

Have you seen the film at the Odeon?
Czy widziałeś film w kinie Odeon?

We've been waiting here since two o'clock.
Czekamy tutaj od drugiej.

Czasu teraźniejszego prostego używa się również przy podawaniu informacji dotyczących wydarzenia zaplanowanego (przez instytucje itp.) na przyszłość i podanego na przykład w formie rozkładu jazdy.

The next train leaves at two fifteen in the morning.
Następny pociąg odjeżdża o drugiej piętnaście w nocy.

It's Tuesday tomorrow.
Jutro jest wtorek.

Czasu teraźniejszego ciągłego, niemal zawsze z okolicznikiem czasu, używa się, by zaznaczyć plany prywatne.

We're going on holiday with my parents this year.
W tym roku jedziemy na wakacje z moimi rodzicami.

Czas teraźniejszy prosty zwykle nie wymaga użycia czasownika posiłkowego w zdaniach twierdzących, ale przy zaprzeczeniach i pytaniach wykorzystuje czasownik posiłkowy **do**.

Do you live round here?
Czy mieszkasz gdzieś w okolicy?

She doesn't like being late if she can help it.
Ona nie lubi się spóźniać, jeśli może temu zaradzić.

Czasy przeszłe

W języku angielskim wyróżnia się cztery czasy przeszłe: czas przeszły prosty (*the past simple*), czas przeszły ciągły (*the past continuous*), czas przeszły uprzedni (*the past perfect*) oraz czas przeszły uprzedni ciągły (*the past perfect continuous*).

Czas przeszły prosty oraz przeszły ciągły odnoszą się do przeszłości. Czasu przeszłego prostego używa się przy opisywaniu wydarzeń, które odbyły się w przeszłości.

I woke up early and got out of bed.
Obudziłem się wcześnie i wstałem z łóżka.

Czas przeszły prosty stosowany jest również do mówienia ogólnie o przeszłości, o przeszłych zwyczajach i regularnie powtarzających się zdarzeniach.

She lived just outside London.
Mieszkała tuż pod Londynem.

We often saw his dog sitting outside his house.
Często widzieliśmy, jak jego pies siedział przed domem.

Czasu przeszłego ciągłego używa się, opisując wydarzenie, które odbywało się (działo się) przed i po pewnym punkcie w czasie.

They were sitting in the kitchen when they heard the explosion.
Siedzieli w kuchni, kiedy usłyszeli wybuch.

Jack arrived while the children were having their bath.
Jack przyjechał, kiedy dzieci brały kąpiel.

Czas przeszły ciągły opisuje również tymczasową sytuację.

He was working at home at the time.
W tym czasie pracował w domu.

Czasu przeszłego uprzedniego oraz przeszłego uprzedniego ciągłego używa się, gdy opisuje się wydarzenie, które miało miejsce przed innym wydarzeniem, lub rozpoczęło się wcześniej i trwało nadal.

I had heard it was a good film so we decided to go and see it.
Słyszałam, że to dobry film, więc zdecydowaliśmy się go zobaczyć.

It was getting late. I had been waiting there since two o'clock.
Robiło się późno. Czekałam tam już od drugiej.

Czasami wykorzystuje się czas przeszły zamiast czasu teraźniejszego, gdy chce się coś wyrazić w uprzejmy sposób.

Did you want to see me now?
Czy chciał pan ze mną porozmawiać teraz?

I was wondering if you could help me.
Zastanawiałem się, czy mogłaby pani mi pomóc.

Czasy ciągłe

Czasów ciągłych używa się do zaznaczenia czynności, która trwa pomiędzy dwoma punktami w czasie, bez przerwy. Czasu teraźniejszego ciągłego używa się do opisania czynności, które rozpoczęły się przed czasem wypowiedzi i trwają po nim.

I'm looking at the photographs my brother sent me.
Oglądam zdjęcia, które przysłał mi brat.

Kiedy opisuje się dwa wydarzenia odbywające się w teraźniejszości, czasu ciągłego używa się do opisania tej czynności, która tworzy tło innej czynności, tj. czynności, która przerywa trwanie tej pierwszej. Druga czynność wyrażona jest czasem teraźniejszym prostym.

The phone always rings when I'm having a bath.
Telefon dzwoni zawsze wtedy, kiedy biorę kąpiel.

Opisując przeszłość, używa się czasu przeszłego ciągłego do opisania czynności, która rozpoczęła się przed inną czynnością, i trwała nieprzerwanie po zakończeniu tej drugiej czynności, która odbyła się w konkretnym punkcie czasu. Dla opisania drugiej czynności używa się czasu przeszłego prostego.

He was watching television when the doorbell rang.
Oglądał telewizję, gdy zadzwonił dzwonek u drzwi.

UWAGA: Jeśli dwie czynności następują jedna po drugiej, wówczas obie opisane są w czasie przeszłym prostym.

As soon as he saw me, he waved.
Jak tylko mnie zobaczył, pomachał do mnie ręką.

Czasów ciągłych używa się, gdy chce się podkreślić okres trwania czynności i gdy chce się podkreślić, jak długo coś trwało.

We had been living in Athens for five years.
Mieszkaliśmy w Atenach pięć lat.

They'll be staying with us for a couple of weeks.
Zatrzymają się u nas na parę tygodni.

Jednak dla zaznaczenia okresu trwania jakiejś czynności, nie trzeba używać czasu ciągłego.

We had lived in Africa for five years.
Mieszkaliśmy w Afryce pięć lat.

He worked for us for ten years.
Pracował u nas dziesięć lat.

Czasu ciągłego używa się do opisania tymczasowego stanu lub tymczasowej sytuacji.

I'm living in London at the moment.
W tej chwili mieszkam w Londynie.

He'll be working nights next week.
W przyszłym tygodniu pracuje na nocki.

Czasów ciągłych używa się dla zaznaczenia zmian i rozwoju jakiegoś stanu.

Her English was improving.
Jej angielski się poprawiał.

The children are growing up quickly.
Dzieci rosną szybko.

4.2 Czasowniki modalne

Czasowniki modalne to następujące czasowniki: **can**, **could**, **may**, **might**, **must**, **ought**, **shall**, **should**, **will** oraz **would**.

Czasownik modalny jest czasownikiem pojawiającym się na pierwszej pozycji w grupie czasownikowej. Wszystkie czasowniki modalne za wyjątkiem **ought** wymagają formy czasownika w formie bezokolicznika bez wyznacznika **to**. **Ought** zawsze wymaga pełnej formy bezokolicznika (**to**-infinitive).

> **I must leave fairly soon.**
> *Muszę wyjść dość wcześnie.*
>
> **She ought to go straight back to England.**
> *Powinna od razu wrócić do Anglii.*

Czasowniki modalne mają tylko jedną formę. Nie ma formy zakończonej na **–s** oznaczającej trzecią osobę liczby pojedynczej czasu teraźniejszego, nie ma też form zakończonych na **–ing** czy **–ed**.

> **I'm sure he can do it.**
> *Jestem pewien, że potrafi to zrobić.*

Zaprzeczenia i pytania

Zaprzeczenia tworzone są przez dodanie odpowiedniego słowa zaraz po czasowniku.

> **You must not worry.**
> *Nie powinieneś się martwić.*
>
> **I can never remember his name.**
> *Nigdy nie mogę sobie przypomnieć jego imienia.*

Cannot jest zawsze pisane jako jeden wyraz:

> **I cannot go back.**
> *Nie mogę wrócić.*

W mówionym angielskim oraz w codziennym pisanym angielskim wyraz **not** często jest skracany do **n't**, który to skrót jest dołączany do czasownika modalnego.

could not	**couldn't**	**must not**	**mustn't**
should not	**shouldn't**	**would not**	**wouldn't**

> **We couldn't leave the farm.**
> *Nie mogliśmy wyjechać z gospodarstwa.*

Poniżej podane są formy nieregularne zaprzeczeń.

shall not	**shan't**	**cannot**	**can't**
will not	**won't**		

> **Won't you change your mind?**
> *Czy nie zmienisz zdania?*

Możliwość

Kiedy chcemy powiedzieć, że coś jest możliwe, używa się czasownika modalnego **can**.

> **Cooking can be a real pleasure.**
> *Gotowanie może być prawdziwą przyjemnością.*
>
> **In some cases this can cause difficulty.**
> *W niektórych przypadkach może to sprawiać trudność.*

Aby opisać coś jako niemożliwe, używa się **cannot** lub **can't**.

This cannot be the answer.
To nie może być właściwa odpowiedź.

You can't be serious.
Nie możesz tego chyba mówić poważnie.

Kiedy nie ma się pewności, czy dana rzecz jest możliwa, choć samemu tak się sądzi, używa się **could**, **might** czy **may**. **May** ma nieco bardziej formalne znaczenie.

That could be the reason.
To może być powodem.

He might come.
Może przyjdzie.

They may help us.
Może nam pomogą.

He might not be in England at all.
Może wcale nie jest w Anglii.

Prawdopodobieństwo i pewność

Kiedy chce się powiedzieć, że coś prawdopodobnie jest prawdziwe lub prawdopodobnie się zdarzy, używa się **should** lub **ought**.

We should arrive by dinner time.
Powinniśmy przyjechać przed obiadem.

She ought to know.
Powinna to wiedzieć.

Kiedy chce się powiedzieć, że coś prawdopodobnie nie jest prawdziwe lub się nie wydarzy, używa się wówczas **should not** lub **ought not**.

There shouldn't be any problem.
Nie powinno być żadnego problemu.

That ought not to be too difficult.
To nie powinno być zbyt trudne.

Umiejętność

Czasownik **can** używany jest w celu zaznaczenia, że ktoś posiada umiejętność wykonania czegoś.

Anybody can become a qualified teacher.
Każdy może zostać wykwalifikowanym nauczycielem.

Aby zaznaczyć, że ktoś nie posiada umiejętności wykonania jakiejś czynności, używa się **cannot** lub **can't**.

He can't dance.
On nie umie tańczyć.

Kiedy opisuje się umiejętność, którą ktoś posiadał (lub nie posiadał) w przeszłości, używa się czasowników **could**, **couldn't** lub **could not**.

He could run faster than anyone else.
Biegał szybciej niż ktokolwiek inny.

A lot of them couldn't read or write.
Wielu z nich nie potrafiło czytać ani pisać.

Zgoda

Czasownika **can** używa się, by prosić o udzielenie zgody lub gdy wyraża się zgodę.

> **She can go with you.**
> *Ona może pójść z tobą.*
>
> **Can I ask a question?**
> *Czy mogę zadać pytanie?*

Could jest bardziej uprzejme niż **can**.

> **Could I just interrupt a minute?**
> *Czy mógłbym na chwilę przerwać?*

May również jest stosowane przy udzielaniu zgody, ale jest znacznie bardziej formalne.

> **You may leave as soon as you have finished.**
> *Możecie wyjść, jak tylko skończycie.*

Zdania wyrażające odmowę udzielenia zgody zawierają **cannot** lub **can't**.

> **Can I have some sweets? No, you can't.**
> *Czy mogę się poczęstować cukierkami? Nie.*

Polecenia i żądania

Kiedy chce się kogoś poprosić o zrobienie czegoś, używa się wyrażeń **could you**, **will you** lub **would you**. **Could you** oraz **would you** są bardziej uprzejme.

> **Could you make out her bill, please?**
> *Czy mógłby pan wypisać jej rachunek?*
>
> **Would you tell her that Adrian phoned?**
> *Czy mógłbyś jej przekazać, że dzwonił Adrian?*
>
> **Will you please leave the room?**
> *Czy możecie wyjść z pokoju?*

Zwracając się do kogoś z prośbą o pomoc, używamy wyrażeń **can you**, **could you**, **will you** lub **would you**. **Could you** i **would you** są bardziej formalne i uprzejme.

> **Could you show me how to do this?**
> *Czy mogłabyś mi pokazać, jak to się robi?*
>
> **Would you do me a favour?**
> *Czy moglibyście mi oddać przysługę?*
>
> **Will you post this for me on your way to work?**
> *Czy mógłbyś to wysłać po drodze do pracy?*
>
> **Can you make me a copy of that?**
> *Czy mogłabyś mi to skopiować?*

Sugestie

Aby zaproponować zrobienie czegoś, używa się czasownika **could**.

> **We could go on Friday.**
> *Moglibyśmy pojechać w piątek.*

Wyrażenia **Shall we** używamy, gdy proponujemy zrobienie czegoś wspólnie z kimś, natomiast **Shall I** używamy, gdy proponujemy, że zrobimy to sami.

Shall we go and see a film?
Może pójdziemy na film?

Shall I contact the chairman?
Czy mam skontaktować się z przewodniczącym?

Propozycje i zaproszenia
Kiedy się coś komuś proponuje lub zaprasza na coś, używa się wyrażenia **Would you like**.

Would you like a drink?
Czy masz ochotę na coś do picia?

Można użyć wyrażenia **can I**, gdy oferuje się zrobienie czegoś za kogoś.

Can I help you with the dishes?
Czy mogę ci pomóc w zmywaniu naczyń?

Można również użyć wyrażenia **shall I**, zwłaszcza gdy jest się dość pewnym, z
e oferta pomocy zostanie przyjęta.

Shall I shut the door?
Czy mam zamknąć drzwi?

Zobowiązanie i konieczność
Kiedy chce się przekazać, że ktoś ma obowiązek coś zrobić lub że zrobienie czegoś jest konieczne, używa się czasowników **must** lub **have to**. Kiedy podaje się swoje prywatne zdanie, zwykle używa się czasownika **must**.

I must be very careful not to upset him.
Muszę bardzo uważać, by go nie urazić.

Kiedy przekazujemy informację o czymś, co ktoś inny uważa za obowiązek lub konieczność, zwykle używamy **have to**.

She has to go now.
Ona musi już iść.

Kiedy mówimy do konieczności wykonania czegoś, używamy **need to**.

You might need to see a doctor.
Możliwe, że będziesz musiał pójść do lekarza.

Kiedy nie istnieje żadne zobowiązanie lub konieczność zrobienia czegoś, używamy **don't have to**.

Some people don't have to work.
Niektórzy ludzie nie muszą pracować.

Angielsko – Polski

English – Polish

KEYWORD

a [eɪ, ə] (*before vowel or silent h*: **an**) *indef art* **1** (*article*) *there is no direct equivalent of the indefinite article in Polish*; **a man** mężczyzna; **a human being** człowiek; **a girl** dziewczyna; **an elephant** słoń; **she's a doctor** ona jest lekarzem; **they haven't got a television** oni nie mają telewizora **2** (*one*) *there is no direct equivalent in Polish*; **a year ago** rok temu; **a hundred/thousand/million pounds** sto/tysiąc/milion funtów **3** (*expressing ratios, prices etc*): **five hours a day/week** pięć godzin dziennie/tygodniowo; **100 km an hour** sto km na godzinę

A & E (*Brit*) *n abbr* (= *accident and emergency*) oddział pomocy doraźnej
abandon [ə'bændən] *vt* (*leave*: *person, family*) porzucać (porzucić *pf*)
abbey ['æbɪ] *n* opactwo
abbreviation [əbri:vɪ'eɪʃən] *n* skrót
ability [ə'bɪlɪtɪ] *n* **1** (*capacity*): **~ (to do sth)** umiejętność (zrobienia czegoś) **2** (*talent, skill*) zdolność
able ['eɪbl] *adj* **1**: **to be ~ to do sth** (*have skill, ability*) umieć coś zrobić; (*have opportunity*) być w stanie coś zrobić **2** (*clever*: *pupil, player*) uzdolniony; **you'll be ~ to read in peace here** będziesz tu mógł czytać w spokoju
abolish [ə'bɔlɪʃ] *vt* (*practice*) znosić (znieść *pf*); (*system*) obalać (obalić *pf*)
abortion [ə'bɔ:ʃən] (*Med*) *n* aborcja; **to have an ~** poddawać (poddać *pf*) się zabiegowi aborcji

KEYWORD

about [ə'baut] *prep* **1** (*relating to*) o; **a book about London** książka o Londynie; **what's it about?** o czym to jest?; **we talked about it** rozmawialiśmy o tym; **I am sorry about that!** przepraszam!; **I am sorry to hear about that** przykro mi to słyszeć; **to be pleased/angry about sth** być zadowolonym/złym z jakiegoś powodu; **what** *or* **how about eating out?** może pójdziemy coś zjeść?
2 (*place*) po; **he was wandering about the garden** błąkał się po ogrodzie
▷ *adv* **1** (*approximately*) mniej więcej; **about a hundred/thousand people** koło sto/tysiąc osób
2 (*place*) dookoła; **to leave things lying about** zostawiać (zostawić *pf*) wszystko porozrzucane dookoła; **to be about to do sth** właśnie mieć coś zrobić (*pf*)

above [ə'bʌv] *prep* **1** (*higher than*) nad; **~ the photograph** nad fotografią **2** (*in rank, authority*) nad +*inst* ▷ *adv* **1** (*in position*) (po)wyżej, u góry **2** (*in amount, number*) powyżej, więcej ▷ *adj*: **the ~ address** powyższy adres; **the temperature was ~ 30°C** temperatura była powyżej trzydziestu stopni Celsjusza; **~ all** przede wszystkim
abroad [ə'brɔ:d] *adv* **1** (*be*) za granicą **2** (*go*) za granicę
absence ['æbsəns] *n* **1** (*of person*) nieobecność **2** (*of thing*) brak
absent ['æbsənt] *adj* nieobecny; **to be ~** być nieobecnym
absent-minded [-'maɪndɪd] *adj* roztargniony
absolutely [æbsə'lu:tlɪ] *adv* (*utterly*) całkowicie

absorbent cotton [əbˈzɔːbənt-] (*US*) *n* wata higroskopijna
abuse [*n* əˈbjuːs, *vb* əˈbjuːz] *n* **1** (*insults*) obelgi *f pl* **2** (*ill-treatment: physical*) maltretowanie; (*sexual*) molestowanie **3** (*misuse: of power, alcohol, drug*) nadużywanie ▷ *vt* **1** (*ill-treat: physically*) znęcać się **2** (*sexually: child*) molestować
academic [ækəˈdɛmɪk] *adj* (*books*) naukowy; (*system*) akademicki; (*freedom*) akademicki ▷ *n* pracownik naukowy
academy [əˈkædəmɪ] *n* **1** (*organisation*) akademia **2** (*school, college*) szkoła
accelerate [ækˈsɛləreɪt] *vi* przyspieszać (przyspieszyć *pf*)
accelerator [ækˈsɛləreɪtəʳ] (*Aut*) *n* pedał gazu
accent [ˈæksɛnt] *n* (*pronunciation*) akcent; **to speak with an (Irish/ French) ~** mówić z (irlandzkim/ francuskim) akcentem
accept [əkˈsɛpt] *vt* **1** (*invitation, advice, credit cards etc*) przyjmować (przyjąć *pf*); (*responsibility*) brać (wziąć *pf*) na siebie **2** (*as true, valid: fact, view*) akceptować (zaakceptować *pf*)
acceptable [əkˈsɛptəbl] *adj* **1** (*permissible*) do przyjęcia **2** (*suitable*) właściwy
access [ˈæksɛs] *n* (*to building, room*) dojście; (*to information, papers*) dostęp ▷ *vt* (*Comput*) wchodzić (wejść *pf*); **to have ~ to sb** (*child*) mieć prawo do kontaktu z kimś
accessory [ækˈsɛsərɪ] *n* **1** (*for room, car*) wyposażenie dodatkowe **2** (*Clothing*) dodatek
accident [ˈæksɪdənt] *n* **1** (*involving vehicle*) wypadek **2** (*mishap*) wypadek **3** (*chance event*) przypadek; **to have an ~** mieć wypadek; **by ~** przez przypadek
accidental [æksɪˈdɛntl] *adj* przypadkowy
accident and emergency (*Brit*) *n* oddział pomocy doraźnej
accommodation [əkɔməˈdeɪʃən] *n* (*place to stay*) kwatera; **accommodations** (*US*) *n pl* = **accommodation**
accompany [əˈkʌmpənɪ] *vt* **1** (*formal: escort*) towarzyszyć **2** (*Mus*) akompaniować
according [əˈkɔːdɪŋ]: **~ to** *prep* według *+gen*
account [əˈkaunt] *n* **1** (*with bank, at shop*) konto **2** (*report*) relacja; **accounts** *n pl* (*Comm*) rozliczenie; **to take sth into ~, take ~ of sth** brać (wziąć *pf*) coś pod uwagę
▶ **account for** *vt fus* (*explain*) wyjaśniać (wyjaśnić *pf*)
accountant [əˈkauntənt] *n* księgowy(-wa) *m/f*
accuracy [ˈækjurəsɪ] *n* **1** (*of information, measurements*) dokładność **2** (*of person, device*) precyzja
accurate [ˈækjurɪt] *adj* **1** dokładny **2** (*weapon, throw*) celny
accurately [ˈækjurɪtlɪ] *adv* **1** (*measure, predict*) dokładnie **2** (*describe, assess, aim*) precyzyjnie; (*report*) dokładnie
accuse [əˈkjuːz] *vt* **1**: **to ~ sb of sth/ doing sth** (*of dishonesty, immorality*) oskarżać (oskarżyć *pf*) kogoś o coś/o zrobienie czegoś **2**: **to be ~d of sth** (*of crime*) być oskarżonym o coś
ace [eɪs] *n* as
ache [eɪk] *vi* (*part of body*) boleć ▷ *n* ból; **I've got (a) stomach ~** boli mnie brzuch
achieve [əˈtʃiːv] *vt* **1** (*aim*) osiągać (osiągnąć *pf*) **2** (*victory, success, result*) odnosić (odnieść *pf*)
achievement [əˈtʃiːvmənt] *n* **1** (*accomplishment: of person, organization*) osiągnięcie **2** (*fulfilment*) dokonanie
acid [ˈæsɪd] *n* (*Chem*) kwas ▷ *adj* **1** (*Chem: soil*) kwaśny **2** (*sharp: taste*) kwaśny
acne [ˈæknɪ] *n* trądzik
across [əˈkrɔs] *prep* **1** (*moving from one side to the other of*) przez **2** (*situated on the other side of*) po drugiej stronie *+gen* **3** (*extending from one side to the other of*) przez ▷ *adv* **1** (*from one side to the other*) na drugą stronę **2**: **~ from** (*opposite*) po drugiej stronie *+gen* **3** (*in width*) wszerz
act [ækt] *vi* **1** (*take action*) działać **2** (*behave*) zachowywać (zachować *pf*)

się **3** (*in play, film*) grać ▷ *n* **1** (*action*) akt **2** (*Theat: of play, opera*) akt; (*of performer*) numer; **~s of sabotage** akty sabotażu
▶ **act on** *vt fus* (*advice, information*) postępować (postąpić *pf*) zgodnie z +*inst*
action ['ækʃən] *n* **1** (*steps, measures*) działanie **2** (*deed*) czyn; **to take ~** podejmować (podjąć *pf*) działanie
active ['æktɪv] *adj* **1** (*person, life*) aktywny **2** (*volcano*) czynny
activity [æk'tɪvɪtɪ] *n* (*pastime*) zajęcie; **activities** *n pl* (*actions*) działania
actor ['æktə^r] *n* aktor
actress ['æktrɪs] *n* aktorka
actual ['æktjuəl] *adj* **1** (*real, genuine*) rzeczywisty **2** (*for emphasis*) faktyczny
actually ['æktjuəlɪ] *adv* **1** (*indicating or emphasizing truth*) w rzeczywistości **2** (*in fact*) właściwie; **~, we have the same opinion** właściwie mamy takie samo zdanie
AD *adv abbr* (= *Anno Domini*) A.D.
ad [æd] (*inf*) *n* (*advertisement*) reklama; (*classified ad in newspaper, magazine*) ogłoszenie
adapt [ə'dæpt] *vt* (*alter, change*) adaptować (zaadaptować *pf*) ▷ *vi*: **to ~ to sth** przystosowywać (przystosować *pf*) do czegoś
adaptor [ə'dæptə^r] (*Elec*) *n* rozgałęźnik
add [æd] *vt* **1** (*put in, put on*) dodawać (dodać *pf*) **2**: **to ~ (together)** (*calculate total of*) dodawać (dodać *pf*) ▷ *vi* (*calculate*) dodawać (dodać *pf*)
▶ **add up** *vi* (*accumulate*) powiększać (powiększyć *pf*) ▷ *vt* (*calculate total of*) zgadzać (zgodzić *pf*) się
addict ['ædɪkt] *n* osoba uzależniona; **drug ~** narkoman(ka) *m/f*
addicted [ə'dɪktɪd] *adj*: **to be ~ to sth** (*drugs, drink*) być uzależnionym od czegoś
addition [ə'dɪʃən] *n* (*Math*) dodawanie; **in ~** na dodatek
address [ə'drɛs] *n* (*postal address*) adres ▷ *vt* (*letter, parcel*) zaadresować; **to be ~ed to sb** (*letter, parcel*) być zaadresowanym do kogoś
adjective ['ædʒɛktɪv] *n* przymiotnik
adjust [ə'dʒʌst] *vt* (*device, position*) ustawiać (ustawić *pf*); (*setting*) regulować (*pf*) ▷ *vi* (*adapt: figures*) dostosowywać (dostosować *pf*); (*mechanism*) przystosowywać (przystosować *pf*)
adjustable [ə'dʒʌstəbl] *adj* regulowany
administration [ədmɪnɪs'treɪʃən] *n* (*organizing, supervising*) administracja
admiral ['ædmərəl] *n* admirał
admire [əd'maɪə^r] *vt* (*like, respect: person*) podziwiać
admission [əd'mɪʃən] *n* **1** (*admittance*) przyjęcie **2** (*also*: **~ charge**) opłata za wstęp **3** (*confession*) przyznanie się; **~ fee** opłata za wstęp
admit [əd'mɪt] *vt* **1** (*confess*) przyznawać (przyznać *pf*) się do +*gen* **2** (*accept: defeat*) przyznawać (przyznać *pf*) się do +*gen*; (*responsibility*) przyjmować (przyjąć *pf*) **3** (*to club, organization*) przyjmować (przyjąć *pf*); (*to place, area*) wpuszczać (wpuścić *pf*); **he ~s that...** przyznaje, że...; **to be ~ted to hospital** zostać przyjętym do szpitala
adolescent [ædəu'lɛsnt] *adj* młodzieńczy ▷ *n* (*teenager*) nastolatek(-ka) *m/f*
adopt [ə'dɔpt] *vt* **1** (*approach*) przyjmować (przyjąć *pf*); (*attitude*) przybierać (przybrać *pf*); (*plan*) powziąć **2** (*child*) adoptować
adopted [ə'dɔptɪd] *adj* (*child*) adoptowany
adoption [ə'dɔpʃən] *n* (*of child*) adopcja
adore [ə'dɔː^r] *vt* **1** (*person*) uwielbiać (uwielbić *pf*) **2** (*inf: film, activity, food etc*) uwielbiać
Adriatic [eɪdrɪ'ætɪk] *n* Adriatyk; **the ~ Sea** Morze Adriatyckie
adult ['ædʌlt] *n* (*person*) dorosły ▷ *adj* (*grown-up: life*) dorosły
advance [əd'vɑːns] *vi* **1** (*move forward*) posuwać (posunąć *pf*) się **2** (*make progress*) robić (zrobić *pf*) postępy ▷ *n* (*development*) postęp ▷ *adj* (*notice, warning*)

wcześniejszy; **in ~** (*book, prepare, plan*) z wyprzedzeniem
advanced [əd'vɑːnst] *adj* **1** (*highly developed: system, device*) zaawansowany; (*country*) rozwinięty **2** (*Scol*) zaawansowany
advantage [əd'vɑːntɪdʒ] *n* **1** (*benefit*) korzyść **2** (*favourable factor*) zaleta; **to take ~ of** (*person*) wykorzystywać (wykorzystać *pf*); (*opportunity*) korzystać (skorzystać *pf*)
adventure [əd'vɛntʃə^r] *n* (*exciting event*) przygoda
adverb ['ædvəːb] *n* przysłówek
advert ['ædvəːt] (*Brit*) *n* reklama; (*classified ad in newspaper, magazine*) ogłoszenie
advertise ['ædvətaɪz] *vi* (*in newspaper, on television etc*) reklamować (zareklamować *pf*) się ▷ *vt* **1** (*product, event*) promować (wypromować *pf*) **2** (*job*) zamieszczać (zamieścić *pf*) ofertę *+gen*
advertisement [əd'vəːtɪsmənt] (*Comm*) *n* (*in newspaper, on television*) reklama; (*classified ad in newspaper, magazines*) ogłoszenie; **to be an ~ for sth** (*esp Brit*) być reklamą czegoś
advertising ['ædvətaɪzɪŋ] *n* (*advertisements*) reklama
advice [əd'vaɪs] *n* rada; **a piece of ~** porada; **to ask (sb) for ~ (about/on sth)** prosić (poprosić *pf*) (kogoś) o radę (na temat czegoś)
advise [əd'vaɪz] *vt* (*tell*): **to ~ sb to do sth** radzić (poradzić *pf*) komuś coś zrobić
aerial ['ɛərɪəl] (*Brit*) *n* antena
aerobics [ɛə'rəubɪks] *n* aerobik ▷ *adj*: **~ instructor** instruktor aerobiku
aeroplane ['ɛərəpleɪn] (*Brit*) *n* samolot
aerosol ['ɛərəsɔl] *n* aerozol
affair [ə'fɛə^r] *n* **1** (*matter, business*) sprawa **2** (*romance*) romans; **affairs** *n pl* **1** (*matters*) sprawy **2** (*personal concerns*) sprawa; **to have an ~ (with sb)** mieć romans (z kimś)
affect [ə'fɛkt] *vt* (*influence: person, object*) wpływać (wpłynąć *pf*) na
affectionate [ə'fɛkʃənɪt] *adj* (*person, kiss*) serdeczny; (*animal*) przywiązany
afford [ə'fɔːd] *vt*: **to be able to ~ sth** móc sobie pozwolić na coś
afraid [ə'freɪd] *adj* (*frightened*) przestraszony; **to be ~ of sb/sth** bać się kogoś/czegoś; **to be ~ to do sth/of doing sth** bać się zrobić coś; **to be ~ that...** (*worry, fear*) bać się, że...; (*expressing apology, disagreement*) obawiać się, że...; **I'm ~ so/not** obawiam się, że tak/nie
Africa ['æfrɪkə] *n* Afryka
African ['æfrɪkən] *adj* afrykański ▷ *n* (*person*) Afrykanin(-nka) *m/f*
after ['ɑːftə^r] *prep* **1** (*in time*) po **2** (*in place, order*) po ▷ *adv* (*afterwards*) później ▷ *conj* (*once*) po; **the day ~ tomorrow** pojutrze; **it's ten ~ eight** (*US*) jest dziesięć po ósmej; **day ~ day/year ~ year** dzień po dniu/rok po roku; **~ all** mimo wszystko; **~ doing sth** po zrobieniu czegoś
afternoon ['ɑːftə'nuːn] *n* popołudnie; **this ~** dziś po południu; **tomorrow/yesterday ~** jutro/wczoraj po południu; **(good) ~!** (*goodbye*) do widzenia!; (*hello*) dzień dobry!
after-shave (lotion) ['ɑːftəʃeɪv-] *n* płyn po goleniu
afterwards ['ɑːftəwədz] (*US* **afterward** ['ɑːftəwəd]) *adv* później
again [ə'gɛn] *adv* (*a second or another time*) znów; **~ and ~** *or* **time and ~** raz za razem
against [ə'gɛnst] *prep* **1** (*leaning on, touching*) o **2** (*opposed to*) przeciwko **3** (*in game or competition*) przeciwko **4**: **to protect ~ sth** chronić przed czymś; **they'll be playing ~ Australia** oni zagrają przeciwko Australii; **~ the law/rules** wbrew prawu/zasadom; **~ one's will** wbrew czyjejś woli
age [eɪdʒ] *n* **1** (*of person, object*) wiek **2** (*being old*) starość **3** (*period in history*) epoka; **what ~ is he?** ile on ma lat?; **20 years of ~** dwadzieścia lat; **at the ~ of 20** w wieku dwudziestu lat; **an ~, ~s** (*inf*) wieki; **the Stone/Bronze/Iron A~** era kamienia/brązu/żelaza
aged[1] ['eɪdʒd] *adj*: **~ 10** w wieku dziesięciu lat

aged² ['eɪdʒɪd] *adj* (*elderly*) w podeszłym wieku ▷ *n pl*: **the ~** ludzie w podeszłym wieku
agenda [ə'dʒɛndə] *n* **1** (*of meeting*) porządek dzienny **2** (*political*) agenda
agent ['eɪdʒənt] *n* (*representative*) przedstawiciel(ka) *m/f*
aggressive [ə'grɛsɪv] *adj* (*belligerent*) agresywny
ago [ə'gəu] *adv*: **2 days ~** dwa dni temu; **long ~/a long time ~** dawno temu; **how long ~?** jak dawno temu?
agony ['ægənɪ] *n* męka
agree [ə'griː] *vi* **1** (*have same opinion*) zgadzać (zgodzić *pf*) się **2**: **to ~ to sth/to do sth** zgadzać (zgodzić *pf*) się na coś/coś zrobić **3**: **to ~ with sth** (*approve of*) aprobować coś; **to ~ with sb about sth** (*person*) zgadzać się z kimś w sprawie czegoś; **to ~ on sth** (*price, arrangement*) zgadzać (zgodzić *pf*) się co do czegoś; **to ~ that...** przyznawać (przyznać *pf*), że...
agreement [ə'griːmənt] *n* **1**: **an ~ (on sth)** (*decision, arrangement*) porozumienie (w sprawie czegoś) **2** (*consent*) zgoda; **to be in ~ (with sb/sth)** zgadzać się (z kimś/z czymś)
agricultural [ægrɪ'kʌltʃərəl] *adj* (*land, worker*) rolniczy
agriculture ['ægrɪkʌltʃəʳ] *n* rolnictwo
ahead [ə'hɛd] *adv* **1** (*in front*: *of place*) z przodu **2** (*in work, achievements*) do przodu **3**: **to be ~** (*in competition*) mieć przewagę **4** (*in the future*) do przodu; **the days/months ~** w następnych dniach/miesiącach; **~ of** (*in front of*) przed; (*in advance of*: *event*) wcześniej; **to be ~ of one's time** wyprzedzać (wyprzedzić *pf*) swoją epokę; **~ of time/schedule** przed czasem/terminem; **right** *or* **straight ~** (*direction*) prosto przed siebie; (*location*) na wprost; **go ~!** (*giving permission*) proszę bardzo!
aid [eɪd] *n* pomoc
AIDS [eɪdz] *n abbr* (= *acquired immune deficiency syndrome*) AIDS
aim [eɪm] *vt*: **to ~ sth (at sb/sth)** (*camera*) kierować (skierować *pf*) coś (na kogoś/na coś); (*gun*) celować (wycelować *pf*) coś (do kogoś/do czegoś); (*punch, kick*) wymierzać (wymierzyć *pf*) coś (komuś/czemuś) ▷ *vi* (*with weapon*) celować (wycelować *pf*) ▷ *n* cel; **to ~ at sth** (*with weapon*) celować (wycelować *pf*) w coś; **to ~ to do sth** (*inf*) zamierzać (zamierzyć *pf*) coś zrobić
air [ɛəʳ] *n* (*atmosphere*) powietrze ▷ *adj* (*travel, fare*) lotniczy; **in/into/through the ~** w powietrzu; **by ~** (*flying*) drogą lotniczą
air-conditioned ['ɛəkən'dɪʃənd] *adj* klimatyzowany
air conditioning [-kən'dɪʃənɪŋ] *n* klimatyzacja
air force *n* siły powietrzne; **the ~** siły powietrzne
air hostess (*Brit*) *n* stewardesa
airline ['ɛəlaɪn] *n* linia lotnicza
airmail ['ɛəmeɪl] *n*: **by ~** pocztą lotniczą
airplane ['ɛəpleɪn] (*US*) *n* samolot
airport ['ɛəpɔːt] *n* lotnisko
aisle [aɪl] *n* (*in church*) nawa; (*in theatre, supermarket, on plane*) przejście; **~ seat** (*on plane*) fotel od strony przejścia
alarm [ə'lɑːm] *n* **1** (*anxiety*) niepokój **2** (*warning device*: *in house, car etc*) alarm **3** (*on clock*) budzik ▷ *vt* (*person*) niepokoić (zaniepokoić *pf*)
alarm clock *n* budzik
Albania [æl'beɪnɪə] *n* Albania
album ['ælbəm] *n* album
alcohol ['ælkəhɔl] *n* alkohol
alcoholic [ælkə'hɔlɪk] *n* alkoholik(-iczka) *m/f* ▷ *adj* (*drink*) alkoholowy
alert [ə'ləːt] *adj* (*wide awake*) czujny ▷ *n* (*situation*): **a security ~** stan pogotowia ▷ *vt* (*authorities, police*) powiadamiać (powiadomić *pf*)
A level (*Brit*) *n* *egzamin kończący szkołę średnią*

A LEVELS

Licealiści w wieku 17 lub 18 lat podchodzą do egzaminów **A level** (odpowiednik polskiej matury) na koniec szkoły średniej. Wyniki egzaminów decydują o tym, czy zostaną przyjęci na studia.

Algeria [æl'dʒɪərɪə] *n* Algieria
alien ['eɪlɪən] *n* **1** (*foreigner*) cudzoziemiec(-mka) *m/f* **2** (*extra-terrestrial*) istota pozaziemska ▷ *adj* obcy
alike [ə'laɪk] *adj*: **to be/look ~** być podobnym; **they are all ~** oni wszyscy są do siebie podobni
alive [ə'laɪv] *adj* (*living*): **to be ~** być żywym; **to keep sb ~** utrzymywać kogoś przy życiu; **~ and well** cały i zdrowy

KEYWORD

all [ɔːl] *adj* cały; **all day/night** cały dzień/całą noc; **all big cities** wszystkie duże miasta; **all the time** cały czas; **all his life** całe swoje życie ▷ *pron* **1** (*of things, everything*) wszystko; (*of people*) wszyscy *vir pl*, wszystkie *non-vir pl*; **it's all settled** wszystko jest załatwione; **all I could do was apologize** wszystko co mogłem zrobić to przeprosić; **I ate it all, I ate all of it** wszystko zjadłem; **have you got it all?** masz wszystko?; **all of us** my wszyscy; **all of the books** wszystkie książki; **all of the boys** wszyscy chłopcy; **all of the women** wszystkie kobiety; **we all sat down** wszyscy usiedliśmy; **is that all?** (*anything else?*) to wszystko?; (*not more expensive?*) tylko tyle?
2 (*in expressions*): **after all** (*considering*) poza tym; (*regardless*) mimo wszystko; **in all** w sumie; **best of all** najlepszy ze wszystkich
▷ *adv* **1** (*emphatic*) zupełnie; **he was doing it all by himself** robił to zupełnie samodzielnie; **all alone** całkiem sam; **all around** dookoła
2 (*in scores*): **the score is 2 all** remis dwa do dwóch

allergic [ə'ləːdʒɪk] *adj* (*reaction, response*) alergiczny; **to be ~ to sth** (*peanuts, cats etc*) być uczulonym na coś
allergy ['ælədʒɪ] (*Med*) *n* alergia; **to have an ~ to sth** mieć alergię na coś
allow [ə'lau] *vt* **1** (*permit: practice, behaviour*) pozwalać (pozwolić *pf*) na **2** (*set aside: sum, time, amount*) przeznaczać (przeznaczyć *pf*) **3** (*claim, goal*) uznawać (uznać *pf*); **to ~ sb to do sth** (*give permission for sth*) pozwalać (pozwolić *pf*) komuś coś zrobić; **don't ~ the soil to dry out** nie pozwól, aby ziemia wyschła; **smoking is not ~ed** nie wolno palić
all right *adj* (*satisfactory*) niezły; (*well, safe*) dobrze ▷ *adv* **1** (*well: go, work out*) prawidłowo **2** (*properly: see, hear, work*) dobrze **3** (*as answer: okay*) w porządku; **it's** *or* **that's ~ by me** to mi pasuje
almond ['ɑːmənd] *n* **1** (*nut*) migdał **2** (*tree*) migdałowiec
almost ['ɔːlməust] *adv* prawie; **I spent ~ a month in China** spędziłem prawie miesiąc w Chinach
alone [ə'ləun] *adj* **1** (*not with other people*) sam **2** (*having no family or friends*) samotny **3**: **~ together** (*with no other people*) sami ▷ *adv* **1** (*unaided*) w pojedynkę **2**: **in Florida/France ~** (*merely: used for emphasis*) tylko na Florydzie/we Francji; **to leave sb/sth ~** (*undisturbed*) zostawiać (zostawić *pf*) kogoś/coś w spokoju; **leave it ~!** zostaw to!
along [ə'lɔŋ] *prep* wzdłuż *+gen* ▷ *adv* wzdłuż; **~ with** (*together with*) razem z *+inst*; **all ~** (*all the time*) przez cały czas
aloud [ə'laud] *adv* (*read*) na głos; (*speak*) głośno
alphabet ['ælfəbɛt] *n*: **the ~** alfabet
Alps [ælps] *n pl*: **the ~** Alpy
already [ɔːl'rɛdɪ] *adv* już; **I have ~ started making dinner** już zacząłem gotować obiad; **is it five o'clock ~?** (*expressing surprise*) czy już piąta?
also ['ɔːlsəu] *adv* **1** (*too*) też **2** (*moreover*) poza tym
alter ['ɔltə^r] *vt* zmieniać (zmienić *pf*) ▷ *vi* zmieniać (zmienić *pf*) się
alternate [*adj* ɔl'təːnɪt, *vb* 'ɔltəːneɪt] *adj* **1** (*successive: actions, events*) naprzemienny **2** (*US: alternative*) alternatywny ▷ *vi*: **to ~ (with/between)** zamieniać (zamienić *pf*) się (z *+inst*); **on ~ days/weeks** co drugi dzień/tydzień
alternative [ɔl'təːnətɪv] *adj* **1** (*Brit:*

plan, method, solution) alternatywny **2** (*technology, energy*) alternatywny ▷ *n*: **(an) ~ (to)** alternatywa (dla *+gen*); **to have no ~ (but to)** nie mieć innego wyjścia (niż)

alternatively [ɔl'tə:nətɪvlɪ] *adv* ewentualnie

although [ɔ:l'ðəu] *conj* **1** (*despite the fact that*) mimo że **2** (*but*) chociaż

altogether [ɔ:ltə'gɛðə^r] *adv* **1** (*completely*) całkowicie **2** (*in total*) razem; **how much is that ~?** ile to będzie razem?; **~ different/ stronger/better** całkiem inny/ silniejszy/lepszy

aluminium [ælju'mɪnɪəm] (*US* **aluminum** [ə'lu:mɪnəm]) *n* aluminium

always ['ɔ:lweɪz] *adv* zawsze; **he's ~ late** zawsze się spóźnia

am [æm] *vb see* **be**

a.m. *adv abbr* (= *ante meridiem*): **at 10 ~** o dziesiątej rano

amateur ['æmətə^r] *n* (*non-professional*) amator(ka) *m/f* ▷ *adj* amatorski

amaze [ə'meɪz] *vt* zdumiewać (zdumieć *pf*); **to be ~d (at** *or* **by sth)** być zdumionym (czymś)

amazing [ə'meɪzɪŋ] *adj* (*surprising, fantastic*) niesamowity

ambassador [æm'bæsədə^r] *n* ambasador

ambition [æm'bɪʃən] *n*: **an ~ (to do sth)** ambicja (zrobienia czegoś); **to achieve one's ~** realizować (zrealizować *pf*) czyjeś ambicje

ambitious [æm'bɪʃəs] *adj* ambitny

ambulance ['æmbjuləns] *n* karetka

America [ə'mɛrɪkə] *n* Ameryka

American [ə'mɛrɪkən] *adj* amerykański ▷ *n* (*person*) Amerykanin(-nka) *m/f*

among(st) [ə'mʌŋ(st)] *prep* **1** (*surrounded by, included in: group of people*) wśród *+gen* **2** (*share, distribute: between*) między *+inst*

amount [ə'maunt] *n* (*quantity*) ilość; (*of money*) suma; (*of work*) ilość

amp ['æmp] *n* amper; **a 13 ~ plug** wtyczka na trzynaście amperów

amphetamine [æm'fɛtəmi:n] *n* amfetamina

amplifier ['æmplɪfaɪə^r] *n* wzmacniacz

amuse [ə'mju:z] *vt* **1** (*make laugh*) rozśmieszać (rozśmieszyć *pf*) **2** (*entertain*) rozbawić (bawić *pf*); (*distract*) zabawiać (zabawić *pf*); **to ~ o.s.** zabawiać (zabawić *pf*) się; **to be ~d at** *or* **by sth** być rozbawionym czymś

amusement arcade [ə'mju:zmənt-ɑ:'keɪd] *n* salon gier automatycznych

an [æn, ən] *indef art see* **a**

anaesthetic [ænɪs'θɛtɪk] (*US* **anesthetic**) *n* środek znieczulający; **local ~** znieczulenie miejscowe; **general ~** znieczulenie ogólne; **under ~** pod narkozą

analyse ['ænəlaɪz] (*US* **analyze**) *vt* (*situation, information*) analizować (przeanalizować *pf*)

analysis [ə'næləsɪs] (*pl* **analyses**) *n* (*of situation, statistics*) analiza

analyze ['ænəlaɪz] (*US*) *vt* = **analyse**

ancestor ['ænsɪstə^r] *n* przodek

anchor ['æŋkə^r] *n* kotwica

ancient ['eɪnʃənt] *adj* **1** (*Greece, Rome, monument*) starożytny **2** (*very old*) pradawny

and [ænd] *conj* i; **men ~ women** kobiety i mężczyźni; **better ~ better** coraz lepiej; **to try ~ do sth** próbować (spróbować *pf*) coś zrobić

angel ['eɪndʒəl] *n* (*spirit*) anioł

anger ['æŋgə^r] *n* gniew

angle ['æŋgl] *n* **1** (*Math*) kąt **2** (*position, direction*) kąt; **at an ~** pod kątem; **an ~ of ninety/sixty degrees** pod kątem dziewięćdziesiąt/ sześćdziesiąt stopni

angry ['æŋgrɪ] *adj* (*person*) rozgniewany; (*response*) gniewny; **to be ~ with sb/about sth** złościć się na kogoś/o coś; **to make sb ~** złościć (rozzłościć *pf*) kogoś

animal ['ænɪməl] *n* **1** (*creature*) zwierzę **2** (*type of person*) zwierzę **3** (*pej: brute*) bydlę ▷ *adj* zwierzęcy

ankle ['æŋkl] (*Anat*) *n* kostka

anniversary [ænɪ'və:sərɪ] *n* **1**: **~ (of sth)** rocznica (czegoś) **2** (*also*: **wedding ~**) rocznica ślubu

announce [ə'nauns] *vt* ogłaszać (ogłosić *pf*); **the government has ~d that...** rząd ogłosił, że...
announcement [ə'naunsmənt] *n* **1** (*statement*) oświadczenie **2** (*notice*: *in newspaper*) ogłoszenie **3** (*at airport or station*) ogłoszenie; **to make an ~ (about sth)** obwieścić (coś)
annoy [ə'nɔɪ] *vt* denerwować (zdenerwować *pf*)
annoyed [ə'nɔɪd] *adj* zdenerwowany; **to be ~ at sth/with sb** być zdenerwowanym czymś/na kogoś
annoying [ə'nɔɪɪŋ] *adj* (*noise, habit, person*) denerwujący
annual ['ænjuəl] *adj* **1** (*once every year*) doroczny **2** (*during a year*) roczny
anorak ['ænəræk] *n* (*jacket*) anorak
anorexia [ænə'rɛksɪə] (*also*: **~ nervosa**: *Med*) *n* anoreksja
anorexic [ænə'rɛksɪk] *adj* anorektyczny
another [ə'nʌðə^r] *adj* **1** (*one more*) następny **2** (*a different one*) inny **3**: **~ 5 years/miles/kilos** kolejne pięć lat/mil/kilo ▷ *pron* **1** (*one more*) kolejny **2** (*a different one*) inny; **one ~** wzajemnie; **they like one ~** lubią się
answer ['ɑːnsə^r] *n* **1** (*reply*) odpowiedź **2** (*solution*) rozwiązanie ▷ *vi* (*reply*: *to question*) odpowiadać (odpowiedzieć *pf*); (*to telephone ringing*) odbierać (odebrać *pf*) (telefon); (*knock at door*) otwierać (otworzyć *pf*) drzwi ▷ *vt* (*reply to*: *person*) odpowiadać (odpowiedzieć *pf*) na; (*question*: *letter*) odpowiadać (odpowiedzieć *pf*)
answering machine ['ɑːnsərɪŋ-] *n* automatyczna sekretarka
ant [ænt] *n* mrówka
Antarctic [ænt'ɑːktɪk] *n*: **the ~** Antarktyka
anthem ['ænθəm] *n* hymn
antibiotic ['æntɪbaɪ'ɔtɪk] *n* antybiotyk
antique [æn'tiːk] *n* (*valuable old object*) antyk ▷ *adj* (*furniture, jewellery*) zabytkowy
antiseptic [æntɪ'sɛptɪk] *n* środek odkażający ▷ *adj* antyseptyczny
antivirus ['æntɪ'vaɪərəs] *adj* (*Comput*) antywirusowy
anxious ['æŋkʃəs] *adj* **1** (*worried*: *expression, person*) zatroskany **2** (*worrying*) niespokojny; **he was ~ for the game to start** pragnął, by gra się już rozpoczęła

 **KEYWORD**

any ['ɛnɪ] *adj* **1** (*in negatives*) żaden, ani trochę; **I haven't any chocolate/sweets** nie mam żadnej czekolady/żadnych słodyczy; **there was hardly any food** nie było ani trochę jedzenia; **have you got any chocolate/sweets?** masz jakąś czekoladę/jakieś słodycze?
2 (*in "if" clauses*) jakiś; **if there are any tickets left** jeśli są jeszcze jakieś bilety
3 (*no matter which*) którykolwiek; **take any card you like** weź którąkolwiek z kart
4 (*in expressions*): **any day now** niedługo; **(at) any moment** w każdej chwili; **any time** (*whenever*) zawsze gdy; (*also*: **at any time**) lada chwila; **at any rate** (*more precisely*) dokładniej; (*whatever the case*) w każdym razie
▷ *pron* **1** (*in negatives*) ani jednego; **I didn't eat any (of it)** nic nie zjadłem; **I haven't any (of them)** nie mam ani jednego (z nich)
2 (*in questions*) jakieś; **have you got any?** czy masz jakieś?
3 (*in "if" clauses*: *person*) ktokolwiek; (*object*) cokolwiek; **if any of you would like to take part,...** jeśli ktoś z was będzie chciał wziąć udział,...
4 (*no matter which ones*) którykolwiek; **help yourself to any of the books** weź którąkolwiek z książek
▷ *adv* **1** (*with negative*) już; **I don't play tennis any more** już nie gram w tenisa; **don't wait any longer** nie czekaj już dłużej
2 (*in questions*) trochę; **are you feeling any better?** czujesz się trochę lepiej?; **do you want any more soup/sandwiches?** chcesz jeszcze trochę zupy/kanapek?

3 (*in "if" clauses*) trochę; **if it had been any colder we would have frozen to death** jeśli byłoby trochę zimniej zamarzlibyśmy na śmierć

anybody ['ɛnɪbɔdɪ] *pron* = **anyone**
anyhow ['ɛnɪhau] *adv* **1** = **anyway** **2** (*Brit: inf: haphazardly*) byle jak
anyone ['ɛnɪwʌn] *pron* **1** (*in negatives, "if" clauses*) nikt **2** (*in questions*) ktoś **3** (*no matter who*) ktokolwiek; **I can't see ~** nikogo nie widzę; **did ~ see you?** czy ktoś cię widział?; **~ could do it** każdy mógłby to zrobić
anything ['ɛnɪθɪŋ] *pron* **1** (*in negatives, questions, "if" clauses*) nic **2** (*no matter what*) wszystko; **I will do ~ for you** zrobię dla ciebie wszystko; **I can't see ~** nic nie widzę; **hardly ~** prawie nic; **did you find ~?** znalazłeś coś?; **if ~ happens to me...** jeśli coś mi się stanie...; **you can say ~ you like** możesz powiedzieć co chcesz
anyway ['ɛnɪweɪ] *adv* **1** (*besides*) w każdym razie **2** (*all the same*) mimo wszystko **3** (*at least*) w każdym razie **4** (*in short*) więc **5** (*well*) i tak; **I shall go ~** pójdę i tak
anywhere ['ɛnɪwɛəʳ] *adv* **1** (*in negatives*) nigdzie; (*in questions*) gdzieś **2** (*no matter where*) gdziekolwiek; **I can't see him ~** nigdzie go nie widzę; **have you seen the scissors ~?** widziałeś gdzieś nożyczki?
apart [ə'pɑːt] *adv* **1** (*move, pull*) w oddaleniu **2**: **to sit ~ from the others** usiąść w oddaleniu od innych; **to take sth ~** rozkładać (rozłożyć *pf*) coś na części; **~ from** (*excepting*) oprócz; (*in addition to*) poza
apartment [ə'pɑːtmənt] *n* (*US*) mieszkanie
apologize [ə'pɔlədʒaɪz] *vi* przepraszać (przeprosić *pf*); **to ~ to sb (for sth)** przepraszać (przeprosić *pf*) kogoś (za coś)
apology [ə'pɔlədʒɪ] *n* przeprosiny; **to make (sb) an ~** przeprosić (kogoś)
apostrophe [ə'pɔstrəfɪ] *n* apostrof
app [æp] *n* apka
apparent [ə'pærənt] *adj* **1** (*seeming*) pozorny **2** (*obvious*) widoczny
apparently [ə'pærəntlɪ] *adv* najwidoczniej
appeal [ə'piːl] *vi* (*Law*) odwoływać (odwołać *pf*) się ▷ *vt* (*US: decision, verdict*) odwoływać (odwołać *pf*) ▷ *n* **1** (*request*) apel **2** (*for good cause*) apel **3** (*Law*) apelacja; **he ~ed for calm/silence** poprosił o spokój/ciszę; **it doesn't ~ to me** nie przemawia to do mnie
appear [ə'pɪəʳ] *vi* **1** (*seem*) wydawać **(***wydać pf*) się **2** (*come into view, begin to develop*) pojawiać (pojawić *pf*) się; **to ~ to be/have** wydawać (wydać *pf*) się być/mieć
appendicitis [əpɛndɪ'saɪtɪs] *n* zapalenie wyrostka robaczkowego
appetite ['æpɪtaɪt] *n* **1** (*desire to eat*) apetyt **2**: **an ~ for sth** (*desire*) chętka na coś
applaud [ə'plɔːd] *vi* (*clap*) bić brawo ▷ *vt* (*cheer*) oklaskiwać (*pf*)
applause [ə'plɔːz] *n* (*clapping*) oklaski
apple ['æpl] *n* jabłko
appliance [ə'plaɪəns] *n* (*device*) urządzenie
applicant ['æplɪkənt] *n* (*for job, place at college*) kandydat(ka) *m/f*
application [æplɪ'keɪʃən] *n* **1** (*for job, grant etc*) podanie **2** (*use: of knowledge, theory etc*) zastosowanie **3** (*Comput: program*) program użytkowy
application form *n* podanie
apply [ə'plaɪ] *vi* **1**: **to ~ (to sb)** (*be relevant*) dotyczyć (kogoś) **2** (*make application*) składać (złożyć *pf*) podanie; **to ~ for sth** (*job, grant, membership*) ubiegać się o coś; **to ~ to sb** (*council, governing body*) składać (złożyć *pf*) podanie do kogoś; **to ~ to do sth** zgłaszać (zgłosić *pf*) się do zrobienia czegoś
appointment [ə'pɔɪntmənt] *n* (*in business, politics*) spotkanie; (*with hairdresser, dentist, doctor*) wizyta; **to make an ~ (with sb)** (*in business, politics*) ustalać (ustalić *pf*) termin spotkania (z kimś); **to make an ~ with the hairdresser/dentist** mieć wizytę u fryzjera/dentysty

appreciate [əˈpriːʃɪeɪt] *vt* **1** (*like, value*) cenić (docenić *pf*) **2** (*be grateful for*) być wdzięcznym za; **I (really) ~ your help** (naprawdę) jestem ci wdzięczny za twoją pomoc

apprentice [əˈprɛntɪs] *n* praktykant(ka) *m/f*

approach [əˈprəutʃ] *vi* (*draw near: person*) podchodzić (podejść *pf*); (*car*) podjeżdżać (podjechać *pf*); (*event, time*) zbliżać (zbliżyć *pf*) się ▷ *vt* **1** (*draw near to: place, person*) zbliżać (zbliżyć *pf*) się **2** (*consult, speak to: person*) zwracać (zwrócić *pf*) się **3** (*deal with: situation, problem*) podchodzić (podejść *pf*) do *+gen* ▷ *n* (*to a problem, situation*) podejście

appropriate [əˈprəuprɪɪt] *adj* (*suitable: remarks, behaviour, clothing*) stosowny; (*person, authority*) właściwy; **it is/seems ~ to...** odpowiedni do...; **it is ~ to do sth** wypada coś zrobić

approval [əˈpruːvəl] *n* **1** (*permission*) zgoda **2** (*liking*) aprobata; **to meet with sb's ~** (*proposal etc*) uzyskać czyjąś aprobatę

approve [əˈpruːv] *vt* zatwierdzać (zatwierdzić *pf*) ▷ *vi* zgadzać (zgodzić *pf*) się; **to be ~d by sb** (*authorized*) uzyskać zgodę od kogoś
▸ **approve of** *vt fus* akceptować (zaakceptować *pf*)

approximate [əˈprɔksɪmɪt] *adj* (*amount, number, age*) przybliżony

apricot [ˈeɪprɪkɔt] *n* (*fruit*) morela

April [ˈeɪprəl] *n* kwiecień; *see also* **July**

apron [ˈeɪprən] *n* (*clothing*) fartuch

Aquarius [əˈkwɛərɪəs] *n* Wodnik

Arab [ˈærəb] *adj* arabski ▷ *n* Arab(ka) *m/f*

Arabic [ˈærəbɪk] *adj* arabski ▷ *n* arabski

arch [ɑːtʃ] *n* (*curved structure*) łuk ▷ *vt* (*one's back*) wyginać (wygiąć *pf*) w łuk

archaeology [ɑːkɪˈɔlədʒɪ] (*US* **archeology**) *n* archeologia

archbishop [ɑːtʃˈbɪʃəp] *n* arcybiskup

archeology [ɑːkɪˈɔlədʒɪ] *n* (*US*) = **archaeology**

architect [ˈɑːkɪtɛkt] *n* (*of building*) architekt

architecture [ˈɑːkɪtɛktʃəʳ] *n* architektura

Arctic [ˈɑːktɪk] *n*: **the ~** Arktyka ▷ *adj* (*ice, explorer etc*) arktyczny

are [ɑːʳ] *vb see* **be**

area [ˈɛərɪə] *n* **1** (*region, zone*) obszar **2** (*of room, building etc*) część **3** (*Math, Geom*) pole **4** (*part: of surface*) powierzchnia **5** (*aspect*) zakres; **in the London ~** w rejonie Londynu

area code (*esp US*) *n* numer kierunkowy

Argentina [ɑːdʒənˈtiːnə] *n* Argentyna

Argentinian [ɑːdʒənˈtɪnɪən] *adj* argentyński ▷ *n* (*person*) Argentyńczyk(-ynka) *m/f*

argue [ˈɑːgjuː] *vi* (*quarrel*): **to ~ (with sb) (about sth)** kłócić się (z kimś) (o coś) ▷ *vt* (*debate: case, point*) dyskutować

argument [ˈɑːgjumənt] *n* **1** (*quarrel*) kłótnia **2** (*reason*) argument; **an ~ for/against sth** argument za czymś/przeciwko czemuś

Aries [ˈɛərɪz] *n* Baran

arithmetic [əˈrɪθmətɪk] *n* (*Math*) arytmetyka

arm [ɑːm] *n* **1** (*of person*) ramię **2** (*of jacket, shirt etc*) rękaw **3** (*of chair*) poręcz **4** (*of organization etc*) filia ▷ *vt* (*person, nation*) uzbrajać (uzbroić *pf*); **arms** *n pl* (*weapons*) broń ▷ *adj*: **~s dealer/~s trade** handlarz bronią/handel bronią; **to twist sb's ~** (*inf*) przyprzeć kogoś do muru

armchair [ˈɑːmtʃɛəʳ] *n* fotel

armed [ɑːmd] *adj* **1** (*robber, police officer etc*) uzbrojony **2** (*conflict, attack etc*) zbrojny

army [ˈɑːmɪ] *n*: **the ~** armia, wojsko

around [əˈraund] *adv* (*about*) dookoła ▷ *prep* **1** (*encircling*) wokół *+gen* **2** (*near*) koło *+gen* **3** (*about, roughly*) około *+gen*

arrange [əˈreɪndʒ] *vt* **1** (*organize*) organizować (zorganizować *pf*) **2** (*put in order*) ustawiać (ustawić *pf*); (*flowers*) układać (ułożyć *pf*) ▷ *vi*: **to ~ to do sth** postanawiać (postanowić *pf*) coś zrobić

arrangement [əˈreɪndʒmənt] *n* **1** (*agreement*) umowa **2** (*grouping,* *layout*) ustawienie **3** (*display*: *of flowers*) kompozycja **4** (*of piece of music*) aranżacja; **arrangements** *n pl* (*preparations*) przygotowania; (*plans*) ustalenia

arrest [ə'rɛst] *vt* (*detain*) aresztować (zaaresztować *pf*); **to be under ~** być aresztowanym

arrival [ə'raɪvl] *n* **1** (*of person, vehicle*) przybycie; (*of vehicle*) przyjazd **2** (*product*) pojawienie się; (*of invention, idea*) nadejście

arrive [ə'raɪv] *vi* **1** (*person*) przybywać (przybyć *pf*); (*vehicle*) przyjeżdżać (przyjechać *pf*) **2** (*letter, meal*) nadchodzić (nadejść *pf*)

arrow ['ærəu] *n* **1** (*weapon*) strzała **2** (*sign*) strzałka

art [ɑːt] *n* sztuka ▷ *adj* (*exhibition, student*) sztuka; **~ collection** kolekcja dzieł sztuki; **arts** *n pl* **1**: **the ~s** (*creative activities*) sztuka **2** (*in education*) nauki humanistyczne ▷ *adj*: **~s** (*graduate, student, course*) nauk humanistycznych; **work of ~** dzieło sztuki

artery ['ɑːtərɪ] *n* **1** (*blood vessel*) tętnica **2** (*route*) arteria

art gallery *n* galeria sztuki

article ['ɑːtɪkl] *n* **1** (*formal*: *object, item*) przedmiot **2** (*in newspaper*) artykuł **3** (*Ling*) przedimek

artificial [ɑːtɪ'fɪʃəl] *adj* sztuczny

artist ['ɑːtɪst] *n* artysta(-tka) *m/f*

artistic [ɑː'tɪstɪk] *adj* **1** (*person*) uzdolniony artystycznie **2** (*tradition, freedom*) artystyczny **3** (*design, arrangement*) artystyczny

KEYWORD

as [æz, əz] *conj* **1** (*referring to time*) kiedy; **he came in as I was leaving** przyszedł kiedy wychodziłem **2** (*since, because*) ponieważ; **as you can't come, I'll go on my own** ponieważ nie możesz przyjść, pójdę bez ciebie **3** (*referring to manner, way*) jak; **as you can see** jak widać; **it's on the left as you go in** jest na lewo od wejścia ▷ *prep* **1** (*in the capacity of*) jako; **he works as a salesman** pracuje jako sprzedawca; **as a teacher, I am very aware that...** jako nauczyciel jestem świadom, że...; **to come as a surprise/shock** okazać się zaskoczeniem/szokiem **2** (*when*) jako; **he was very energetic as a child** był bardzo energiczny jako dziecko ▷ *adv* **1** (*in comparisons*): **as big/ good/easy as...** tak duży/dobry/ łatwy jak...; **you're as tall as he is** *or* **as him** jesteś tak wysoki jak on; **as much money/many books as...** tak dużo pieniędzy/książek jak...; **as soon as** tak szybko jak **2** (*in expressions*): **as if** *or* **though** jakby; **as from** *or* **of tomorrow** począwszy od jutra

ash [æʃ] *n* (*from fire, cigarette*) popiół; **ashes** *n pl* **1** (*of fire*) popiół **2** (*remains*) prochy

ashamed [ə'ʃeɪmd] *adj*: **to be/ feel ~** (*embarrassed, guilty*) być zawstydzonym; **to be ~ of sb/sth** wstydzić się kogoś/czegoś

ashtray ['æʃtreɪ] *n* popielniczka

Asia ['eɪʃə] *n* Azja

Asian ['eɪʃən] *adj* azjatycki ▷ *n* (*person*) Azjata(-tka) *m/f*

ask [ɑːsk] *vt* **1**: **to ~ (sb) a question** zadawać (zadać *pf*) (komuś) pytanie **2** (*invite*) zapraszać (zaprosić *pf*) ▷ *vi* pytać; **to ~ (sb) whether/why...** pytać (kogoś) czy...; **to ~ sb to do sth** prosić (poprosić *pf*) kogoś, żeby coś zrobił; **to ~ to do sth** prosić (poprosić *pf*) o pozwolenie na coś; **to ~ sb the time** zapytać kogoś o godzinę; **to ~ sb about sth** pytać (spytać *pf*) kogoś o coś; **I ~ed him his name** spytałem go jak ma na imię; **to ~ sb's opinion** pytać (zapytać *pf*) kogoś o jego zdanie; **to ~ sb out to dinner** zaprosić kogoś na obiad

▶ **ask after** *vt fus* (*person*) dopytywać się

▶ **ask for** *vt fus* **1** (*ask to have*: *thing*) prosić (poprosić *pf*) o **2** (*ask to see*: *person*) prosić o spotkanie z +*inst*

asleep [ə'sliːp] *adj* pogrążony we śnie; **to be ~** spać; **to fall ~** zasypiać (zasnąć *pf*)

asparagus [əs'pærəgəs] *n* szparag
aspirin ['æsprɪn] *n* **1** (*drug*) aspiryna **2** (*tablet*) tabletka aspiryny
assemble [ə'sɛmbl] *vt* **1** (*people, group*) gromadzić (zgromadzić *pf*) **2** (*machinery, object*) montować (zmontować *pf*) ▷ *vi* (*gather: people, crowd*) gromadzić (zgromadzić *pf*)
assembly [ə'sɛmblɪ] *n* **1** (*meeting*) zgromadzenie **2** (*construction: of vehicles etc*) montaż **3** (*in school*) apel
assignment [ə'saɪnmənt] *n* (*task*) zadanie; (*for student*) praca zadana
assistance [ə'sɪstəns] *n* pomoc
assistant [ə'sɪstənt] *n* **1** (*helper*) pomocnik(-ica) *m/f*; (*in office*) zastępca(-czyni) *m/f* **2** (*Brit: in shop*) ekspedient(ka) *m/f* ▷ *adj* zastępujący; **~ professor** docent
association [əsəusɪ'eɪʃən] *n* **1** (*group*) stowarzyszenie **2**: **to have ~s (with sth/for sb)** (*mental connection*) kojarzyć się (z czymś/z kimś) **3** (*involvement, link*): **~ (with sb/sth)** związek (z kimś/czymś)
assortment [ə'sɔːtmənt] *n* (*of shapes, colours*) asortyment; (*of objects, people*) mieszanka
assume [ə'sjuːm] *vt* **1** (*suppose*) przypuszczać (przypuścić *pf*) **2** (*responsibility, power*) przejmować (przejąć *pf*)
assure [ə'ʃuəʳ] *vt* zapewniać (zapewnić *pf*)
asterisk ['æstərɪsk] *n* gwiazdka (w tekście)
asthma ['æsmə] *n* astma
astonishing [ə'stɔnɪʃɪŋ] *adj* zadziwiający
astrology [əs'trɔlədʒɪ] *n* astrologia
astronaut ['æstrənɔːt] *n* astronauta(-tka) *m/f*
astronomy [əs'trɔnəmɪ] *n* astronomia

KEYWORD

at [æt] *prep* **1** (*position, time, age*) w; **we had dinner at a restaurant** zjedliśmy obiad w restauracji; **at home** w domu; **at work** (*not at home*) w pracy; **at my brother's** u mojego brata; **at the bus stop** na przystanku; **to be sitting at a table/desk** siedzieć przy stole/biurku; **there's someone at the door** ktoś jest pod drzwiami; (*towards*): **to throw sth at sb** rzucać (rzucić *pf*) czymś w kogoś; **at four o'clock** o czwartej; **at night** w nocy; **at Christmas** na Święta Bożego Narodzenia
2 (*referring to price*) po; (*referring to speed*) z; **apples at £2 a kilo** jabłka po dwa funty za kilo; **at 50 km/h** z prędkością pięćdziesiąt kilometrów na godzinę
3 (*referring to activity*) nad; **he's at work on a novel** pracuje nad powieścią; **to be good at sth/at doing sth** być dobrym w czymś/robieniu czegoś
4 (*in expressions*): **not at all** (*in answer to question*) wcale nie; (*in answer to thanks*) nie ma za co

ate [eɪt] *pt of* **eat**
Athens ['æθɪnz] *n* Ateny
athlete ['æθliːt] *n* sportowiec
athletic [æθ'lɛtɪk] *adj* **1** (*tradition, excellence etc*) sportowy **2** (*sporty: person*) wysportowany **3** (*muscular: build, frame*) atletyczny
athletics [æθ'lɛtɪks] *n* lekka atletyka
Atlantic [ət'læntɪk] *adj* atlantycki ▷ *n*: **the ~ (Ocean)** Atlantyk
atlas ['ætləs] *n* atlas
atmosphere ['ætməsfɪəʳ] *n* **1** (*of planet*) atmosfera **2** (*feel: of place*) nastrój **3** (*air*) powietrze
atom ['ætəm] (*Phys*) *n* atom
atomic [ə'tɔmɪk] *adj* atomowy
attach [ə'tætʃ] *vt* **1** (*fasten, join*) przymocowywać (przymocować *pf*) **2** (*importance, significance etc*) przywiązywać (przywiązać *pf*)
attachment [ə'tætʃmənt] *n* **1** (*affection*): **~ (to sb)** przywiązanie (do kogoś) **2** (*of tool*) nasadka **3** (*Comput*) załącznik
attack [ə'tæk] *vt* **1** (*assault: person*) napadać (napaść *pf*) **2** (*place, troops*) atakować (zaatakować *pf*) **3** (*criticise: person, idea*) atakować (zaatakować *pf*) **4** (*in sport*)

atakować (zaatakować *pf*) ▷ *vi* (*Mil, Sport*) atakować (zaatakować *pf*) ▷ *n* **1** (*on person*) napaść **2** (*military assault*) atak **3** (*criticism*) atak **4** (*of illness*) napad **5** (*in sport*) atak; **an ~ on sb** (*assault*) napad na kogoś; (*criticism*) atak krytyki na kogoś

attempt [ə'tɛmpt] *n* (*try*) próba ▷ *vt* (*try*) próbować (spróbować *pf*) ▷ *vi*: **to ~ to do sth** próbować (spróbować *pf*) coś zrobić; **an ~ to do sth** próba zrobienia czegoś

attend [ə'tɛnd] *vt* **1** (*be member of*) uczęszczać do *+gen* **2** (*take part in*) uczęszczać na

▶ **attend to** *vt fus* **1** (*needs, affairs*) zajmować (zająć *pf*) się **2** (*patient*) zajmować (zająć *pf*) się *+inst*; (*customer*) obsługiwać (obsłużyć *pf*)

attention [ə'tɛnʃən] *n* **1** (*concentration*) uwaga **2** (*care*) pomoc ▷ *excl* (*Mil*) baczność; **to draw sb's ~ to sth** zwracać (zwrócić *pf*) czyjąś uwagę na coś; **to pay ~ (to sth/sb)** uważać (na coś/kogoś)

attic ['ætɪk] *n* strych

attitude ['ætɪtju:d] *n* **1** (*mental view*) pogląd **2** (*behaviour*) postawa

attorney [ə'tə:nɪ] (*US*) *n* (*lawyer*) adwokat

attract [ə'trækt] *vt* **1** (*people, animals, metal*) przyciągać (przyciągnąć *pf*) **2** (*gain: support, publicity*) zyskiwać (zyskać *pf*); (*sb's attention*) przyciągać (przyciągnąć *pf*); (*sb's interest*) wzbudzać (wzbudzić *pf*)

attraction [ə'trækʃən] *n* (*of person*) urok; **attractions** *n pl* (*also*: **tourist ~s**: *amusements*) atrakcja

attractive [ə'træktɪv] *adj* **1** (*man, woman, place*) atrakcyjny; (*thing*) ładny **2** (*interesting: price, idea, offer*) atrakcyjny; **he was very ~ to women** był bardzo atrakcyjny dla kobiet

aubergine ['əubəʒi:n] (*Brit*) *n* (*vegetable*) bakłażan

auburn ['ɔ:bən] *adj* (*hair*) kasztanowy

auction ['ɔ:kʃən] *n* aukcja ▷ *vt* sprzedawać (sprzedać *pf*) na aukcji

▶ **auction off** *vt* sprzedawać (sprzedać *pf*) na aukcji

audience ['ɔ:dɪəns] *n* **1** (*in theatre etc*) widownia **2** (*Rad, TV*) widownia **3** (*public*) publiczność

August ['ɔ:gəst] *n* sierpień; *see also* **July**

aunt [ɑ:nt] *n* (*father's sister*) ciotka; (*father's brother's wife*) stryjenka; (*mother's sister*) ciotka; (*mother's brother's wife*) wujenka

auntie, aunty ['ɑ:ntɪ] (*inf*) *n* = **aunt**

au pair ['əu'pɛə^r] *n au pair*

Australia [ɔs'treɪlɪə] *n* Australia

Australian [ɔs'treɪlɪən] *adj* australijski ▷ *n* (*person*) Australijczyk(-jka) *m/f*

Austria ['ɔstrɪə] *n* Austria

Austrian ['ɔstrɪən] *adj* austriacki ▷ *n* (*person*) Austriak(-aczka) *m/f*

author ['ɔ:θə^r] *n* autor(ka) *m/f*

autobiography [ɔ:təbaɪ'ɔgrəfɪ] *n* autobiografia

autograph ['ɔ:təgrɑ:f] *n* autograf

automatic [ɔ:tə'mætɪk] *adj* automatyczny ▷ *n* (*car*) automatyczny

automatically [ɔ:tə'mætɪklɪ] *adv* **1** (*by itself*) automatycznie **2** (*without thinking*) odruchowo **3** (*as a matter of course*) automatycznie

automobile ['ɔ:təməbi:l] (*US*) *n* samochód

autumn ['ɔ:təm] (*Brit*) *n* jesień; **in (the) ~** jesienią

availability [əveɪlə'bɪlɪtɪ] *n* (*of goods*) dostępność; (*staff*) osiągalność

available [ə'veɪləbl] *adj* **1** (*obtainable: article, service*) dostępny **2** (*person: unoccupied*) wolny; **is the manager ~?** czy dyrektor jest wolny?; **to make sth ~ to sb** udostępniać (udostępnić *pf*) komuś coś

avalanche ['ævəlɑ:nʃ] *n* lawina

avenue ['ævənju:] *n* aleja

average ['ævərɪdʒ] *n* **1** (*Math: mean*) średnia **2**: **the ~ (for sth/sb)** średnia (dla czegoś/kogoś) ▷ *adj* **1** (*Math*) średni **2** (*ordinary*) zwyczajny **3** (*mediocre*) przeciętny; **on ~** przeciętnie; **above/below (the) ~** powyżej/poniżej średniej

▶ **average out** *vi*: **to ~ out at/to sth** wynosić (wynieść *pf*) przeciętnie

avocado [ævə'kɑːdəu] (*Brit*) *n* (*also*: **~ pear**) awokado
avoid [ə'vɔɪd] *vt* **1** (*person*) omijać (ominąć *pf*); (*obstacles*) unikać (uniknąć *pf*) *+gen* **2** (*prevent*: *trouble, danger*) unikać (uniknąć *pf*) *+gen* **3** (*evade, shun*) uchylać (uchylić *pf*) się od *+gen*; **to ~ doing sth** unikać (uniknąć *pf*) zrobienia czegoś
awake [ə'weɪk] (*pt* **awoke**, *pp* **awoken** *or* **awakened**) *adj*: **to be ~** nie spać
award [ə'wɔːd] *n* (*prize*) nagroda ▷ *vt* **1** (*prize*) przyznawać (przyznać *pf*) **2** (*penalty, free kick*) przyznawać (przyznać *pf*)
aware [ə'wɛə^r] *adj*: **politically/ socially ~** świadomy politycznie/ społecznie; **to be ~ of sth** (*know about*) być zorientowanym w czymś; (*be conscious of*) zdawać sobie sprawę z czegoś; **to be ~ that...** zdawać sobie sprawę, że...
away [ə'weɪ] *adv* **1** (*move, walk*) od **2** (*not present*) nieobecny **3**: **to put sth ~** odłożyć coś **4**: **to fade ~** zacierać (zatrzeć *pf*) się ▷ *adj* (*match, game*) wyjazdowy; **a week/month ~** za tydzień/miesiąc; **the exam is three weeks ~** egzamin będzie za trzy tygodnie; **two kilometres ~** dwa kilometry stąd; **it's two hours ~ by car** dwie godziny jazdy samochodem stąd; **~ from** z dala od
awful ['ɔːfəl] *adj* **1** (*frightful*) okropny **2** (*dreadful*: *shock, crime etc*) straszny **3**: **to look/feel ~** (*ill*) wyglądać/czuć się strasznie ▷ *adv* (*US*: *inf*: *very*) strasznie; **an ~ lot** strasznie dużo
awkward ['ɔːkwəd] *adj* **1** (*clumsy*) niezgrabny **2** (*inconvenient*) niedogodny **3** (*difficult to use, do, or carry*) niewygodny **4** (*deliberately difficult*: *person*) trudny
axe [æks] (*US* **ax**) *n* siekiera

b

baby ['beɪbɪ] *n* **1** (*infant*) niemowlę **2** (*esp US*: *inf*: *darling*) dzidziuś ▷ *adj* (*seal, elephant*) młody; **to have a ~** mieć dziecko
baby carriage (*US*) *n* wózek dziecięcy
babysit ['beɪbɪsɪt] (*pt, pp* **babysat**) *vi* opiekować się dzieckiem
babysitter ['beɪbɪsɪtə^r] *n* opiekun(ka) *m/f* do dziecka
bachelor ['bætʃələ^r] *n* **1** (*unmarried man*) kawaler **2**: **~ of Arts/Science** (*degree*) licencjat; (*Brit*: *person*) osoba z tytułem licencjata
back [bæk] *n* **1** (*of person*) plecy; (*of animal*) grzbiet **2** (*not front*: *of hand*) wierzch; (*of neck, legs*) tył; (*of house, door, book, car, train*) tył; (*of chair*) oparcie **3** (*Football*: *defender*) obrońca ▷ *vt* **1** (*support*: *candidate, plan*) popierać (poprzeć *pf*); (*financially*) wspierać (wesprzeć *pf*) **2** (*bet on*: *horse, team*) stawiać (postawić *pf*) na **3** (*reverse*: *car*) cofać (cofnąć *pf*) ▷ *vi* (*reverse*: *person, car etc*) cofać (cofnąć *pf*) się ▷ *adj* tylny ▷ *adv* **1** (*not forward*) do tyłu **2** (*returned*): **to be ~** z powrotem; **to do sth behind sb's ~** robić (zrobić *pf*) coś za plecami kogoś; **can I have it ~?** czy mogę prosić o zwrot?; **at the ~ (of)** (*of crowd, building*) na tyłach (*+gen*); **~ to front** (*esp Brit*) tył na przód
▸ **back down** *vi* ustępować (ustąpić *pf*)

▶ **back out** *vi* (*withdraw*) cofać (wycofać *pf*) się
▶ **back up** *vt* **1** (*support*: *statement, theory etc*) popierać (poprzeć *pf*) **2** (*Comput*: *disk*) robić (zrobić *pf*) kopia zapasowa *+gen*
backache ['bækeɪk] *n* ból pleców
backbone ['bækbəun] *n* kręgosłup
backfire [bæk'faɪə^r] *vi* (*plan*) przynosić (przynieść *pf*) odwrotny skutek
background ['bækgraund] *n* **1** (*of picture, scene, events*) tło **2** (*of person*: *origins*) pochodzenie; (*experience*) tło ▷ *adj* (*noise, music*) w tle; (*information*) wprowadzający; **in the ~** w tle
backing ['bækɪŋ] *n* (*support*) poparcie; (*financial*) wsparcie
backpack ['bækpæk] *n* plecak
backpacker ['bækpækə^r] *n* turysta(-tka) *m/f* podróżujący(-ca) z plecakiem
backstroke ['bækstrəuk] *n* (*also*: **the ~**) styl grzbietowy
backup ['bækʌp] *adj* **1** (*staff, services*) rezerwowy **2** (*Comput*) zapasowy ▷ *n* **1** (*support*) poparcie **2** (*reserve*) rezerwa
backward ['bækwəd] *adj* (*glance, movement*) do tyłu ▷ *adv* (*esp US*) = **backwards**
backwards ['bækwədz] *adv* **1** (*move, look*) w tył **2** (*in reverse*: *count, work*) wstecz **3** (*in time*) wstecz
bacon ['beɪkən] *n* bekon
bad [bæd] *adj* **1** (*not good*) zły **2** (*naughty*) niegrzeczny **3** (*serious*) poważny **4** (*injured*: *back, arm*) uszkodzony **5** (*rotten*: *fruit, meat etc*) zepsuty; **to be ~ for sth/sb** być niedobrym dla czegoś/kogoś; **to be ~ at sth/at doing sth** nie być dobrym w czymś/robieniu czegoś; **not ~** nieźle
badge [bædʒ] *n* (*Brit*) odznaka
badger ['bædʒə^r] *n* borsuk
badly ['bædlɪ] *adv* **1** (*poorly*) źle **2** (*seriously*) ciężko; **to want sth ~** bardzo czegoś chcieć
badminton ['bædmɪntən] *n* badminton
bad-tempered ['bæd'tɛmpəd] *adj* (*by nature*) wybuchowy; (*on one occasion*) zirytowany
bag [bæg] *n* **1** (*made of paper, plastic*) torebka **2** (*suitcase*) torba **3** (*handbag*) torebka; **to pack one's ~s** pakować (spakować *pf*) manatki
baggage ['bægɪdʒ] *n* bagaż
baggage (re)claim *n* odbiór bagażu
bagpipes ['bægpaɪps] *n pl* dudy
bake [beɪk] *vt* piec (upiec *pf*)
baker ['beɪkə^r] *n* (*shop*: *also*: **~'s**) piekarnia
bakery ['beɪkərɪ] *n* piekarnia
balance ['bæləns] *n* **1** (*equilibrium*) równowaga **2** (*in bank account*) saldo **3** (*remainder to be paid*) różnica ▷ *vt* (*object*) utrzymywać (utrzymać *pf*) w równowadze ▷ *vi* (*person, object*) balansować; **to keep/lose one's ~** utrzymywać (utrzymać *pf*)/tracić (stracić *pf*) równowagę
balanced ['bælənst] *adj* zrównoważony
balcony ['bælkənɪ] *n* (*of building*: *open*) balkon; (*covered*) loggia
bald [bɔːld] *adj* (*head, person*) łysy; **to go ~** łysieć (wyłysieć *pf*)
ball [bɔːl] *n* **1** (*football, golf ball etc*) piłka **2** (*of wool, string*) kłębek **3** (*sphere*) kula
ballet ['bæleɪ] (*US* [bæ'leɪ]) *n* balet
ballet dancer *n* tancerz(-rka) *m/f* baletowy(-a)
balloon [bə'luːn] *n* **1** (*child's*) balonik **2** (*also*: **hot-air ~**) balon
ballpoint (pen) ['bɔːlpɔɪnt(-)] *n* długopis
ban [bæn] *n* (*prohibition*) zakaz ▷ *vt* (*prohibit*) zakazywać (zakazywać *pf*) *+gen*
banana [bə'nɑːnə] *n* banan
band [bænd] *n* **1** (*group*) grupa **2** (*Mus*: *jazz, rock etc*) zespół
▶ **band together** *vi* skrzykiwać (skrzyknąć *pf*) się
bandage ['bændɪdʒ] *n* bandaż ▷ *vt* (*wound, leg*) bandażować (zabandażować *pf*)
Band-Aid® ['bændeɪd] (*US*) *n* plaster z opatrunkiem
bang [bæŋ] *n* **1** (*noise*: *of door*) trzask; (*of gun, exhaust*) huk **2** (*blow*) huk ▷ *excl* bum! ▷ *vt* **1** (*door*) trzaskać (trzasnąć *pf*) **2** (*also*: **~ on**: *wall, drum etc*) walić (walnąć *pf*) **3** (*one's head,*

elbow etc) walić (walnąć *pf*) ▷ *vi* **1** (*door*) trzaskać (trzasnąć *pf*) **2** (*firework, engine*) huknąć; **bangs** *n pl* (*US: fringe*) grzywka *sg*; **to ~ into sth/sb** wpadać (wpaść *pf*) na coś/kogoś

bank [bæŋk] *n* **1** (*Fin: building, institution*) bank **2** (*of river, lake*) brzeg **3** (*of earth*) wał

▸ **bank on** *vt fus* (*rely on*) liczyć na

bank account *n* konto bankowe

bank card *n* **1** (*Brit: for cash machine*) karta bankowa **2** (*US: credit card*) karta kredytowa

banker ['bæŋkəʳ] *n* bankier

bank holiday (*Brit*) *n* *dzień wolny od pracy*

BANK HOLIDAYS

Bank holidays są to w Wielkiej Brytanii dni (najczęściej poniedziałki), w których urzędy, firmy, sklepy, a przede wszystkim banki, są nieczynne. Nie muszą to być święta religijne.

banknote ['bæŋknəut] *n* banknot

bar [bɑːʳ] *n* **1** (*place for drinking*) bar **2** (*counter: in pub*) bar **3** (*rod: of metal etc*) pręt **4** (*on window, in prison*) krata **5** (*tablet: of soap*) kostka; (*of chocolate*) tabliczka ▷ *vt* **1** (*way, road*) blokować (zablokować *pf*) **2** (*door, window*) ryglować (zaryglować *pf*)

barbecue ['bɑːbɪkjuː] *n* **1** (*cooking device*) grill **2** (*meal, party*) barbecue

bare [bɛəʳ] *adj* **1** (*naked: body, feet*) nagi **2** (*not covered: rock, floor*) goły

barefoot(ed) ['bɛəfut(ɪd)] *adv* na bosaka

barely ['bɛəlɪ] *adv* (*scarcely*) ledwie

bargain ['bɑːgɪn] *n* **1** (*good buy*) okazja **2** (*deal, agreement*) umowa ▷ *vi* **1** (*negotiate*): **to ~ (with sb)** pertraktować (z kimś) **2** (*haggle*) targować się

▸ **bargain for, bargain on** *vt fus* spodziewać się +*gen*

barge [bɑːdʒ] *n* (*boat*) barka

▸ **barge in** (*inf*) *vi* (*enter*) wtargnąć

bark [bɑːk] *n* **1** (*of tree*) kora **2** (*of dog*) szczeknięcie ▷ *vi* (*dog*) szczekać (zaszczekać *pf*)

barmaid ['bɑːmeɪd] (*esp Brit*) *n* barmanka

barman ['bɑːmən] (*irreg*) *n* (*esp Brit*) barman

barn [bɑːn] *n* stodoła

barrel ['bærəl] *n* **1** (*of wine, beer*) beczka; (*of oil*) baryłka **2** (*of gun*) lufa

barrier ['bærɪəʳ] *n* bariera

bartender ['bɑːtɛndəʳ] (*US*) *n* barman(ka) *m/f*

base [beɪs] *n* **1** (*of post, tree*) podstawa **2** (*basis*) podstawa **3** (*centre: military*) baza; (*for individual, organization*) siedziba ▷ *vt*: **to ~ sth on** *or* **upon sth** opierać (oprzeć *pf*) coś na czymś; **to be ~d on sth** być opartym na czymś; **I'm ~d in London** mam siedzibę w Londynie

baseball ['beɪsbɔːl] *n* (*Sport*) baseball

basement ['beɪsmənt] *n* piwnica ▷ *adj* (*flat, apartment, kitchen etc*) w suterenie

bash [bæʃ] (*inf*) *vt* (*hit*) walić (walnąć *pf*) ▷ *vi* (*crash*): **to ~ into/against sth/sb** walić (walnąć *pf*) w coś/kogoś

basic ['beɪsɪk] *adj* **1** (*principle, rule, right*) podstawowy **2** (*facilities*) prymitywny; *see also* **basics**

basically ['beɪsɪklɪ] *adv* **1** (*fundamentally*) zasadniczo **2** (*in fact, put simply*) właściwie

basics ['beɪsɪks] *n pl*: **the ~** podstawy

basin ['beɪsn] *n* **1** (*bowl*) miska **2** (*also*: **wash ~**) umywalka **3** (*of river, lake*) dorzecze

basis ['beɪsɪs] (*pl* **bases**) *n* **1** (*starting point*) punkt wyjściowy **2** (*foundation*) podstawa; **on a regular ~** regularnie

basket ['bɑːskɪt] *n* kosz

basketball ['bɑːskɪtbɔːl] *n* (*Sport*) koszykówka

bass [beɪs] (*Mus*) *n* **1** (*singer*) bas **2** (*also*: **~ guitar**) gitara basowa **3** (*on radio, music system etc*) basy

bat [bæt] *n* **1** (*animal*) nietoperz **2** (*for cricket, baseball*) kij **3** (*Brit: for table tennis*) rakietka

bath [bɑːθ] *n* **1** (*Brit: bathtub*) wanna **2** (*act of bathing*) kąpiel ▷ *vt* (*Brit: baby, patient*) kąpać (wykąpać *pf*); **baths** *n pl* (*swimming pool*) basen *sg*;

to have *or* **take a ~** kąpać (wykąpać *pf*) się
bathe [beɪð] *vi* kąpać (wykąpać *pf*) się ▷ *vt* **1** (*wound*) przemywać (przemyć *pf*) **2** (*US: baby, patient*) kąpać (wykąpać *pf*)
bathroom [ˈbɑːθrum] *n* **1** (*in house*) łazienka **2** (*US: toilet*) toaleta; **to go to the ~** (*US*) iść (pójść *pf*) do toalety
bath towel *n* ręcznik kąpielowy
bathtub [ˈbɑːθtʌb] (*US*) *n* wanna
batter [ˈbætəʳ] *vt* (*wife*) maltretować ▷ *n* (*Culin*) rzadkie ciasto
battery [ˈbætərɪ] *n* **1** (*for torch, radio etc*) bateria **2** (*in car*) akumulator
battle [ˈbætl] *n* **1** (*Mil*) bitwa **2** (*fig: struggle*) walka ▷ *vi* **1** (*fight*) walczyć **2** (*struggle*): **to ~ for sth/to do sth** walczyć o coś/o zrobienie czegoś
bay [beɪ] *n* (*Geo*) zatoka
BC *adv abbr* (= *before Christ*) p.n.e.

KEYWORD

be [biː] (*pt* **was, were**, *pp* **been**) *vi*
1 (*with complement*) być; **I'm English** jestem Anglikiem; **she's tall/pretty** jest wysoka/ładna; **I'm tired/hot** jestem zmęczony/jest mi gorąco; **he's a doctor** jest lekarzem; **this is my mother** to jest moja matka; **who is it?** kto to jest?; **be careful/quiet!** bądź ostrożny/cicho!
2 (*referring to time, date*) być; **it's 5 o'clock** jest piąta; **it's the 28th of April, it's April 28th** jest dwudziestego ósmego kwietnia
3 (*describing weather*): **it's hot/cold** jest gorąco/zimno
4 (*talking about health*): **how are you?** jak się masz?
5 (*talking about age*) mieć; **how old are you?** ile masz lat?; **I'll be 18 on Friday** skończę osiemnaście lat w piątek
6 (*talking about place*) jest; **Madrid is in Spain** Madryt jest w Hiszpanii; **the supermarket isn't far from here** supermarket jest niedaleko stąd; **I won't be here tomorrow** nie będzie mnie tu jutro; **have you been to Warsaw?** byłeś w Warszawe?; **we've been here for ages** jesteśmy tu od wieków; **where have you been?** gdzie byłeś?; **the meeting will be in the canteen** spotkanie będzie w stołówce
7 (*referring to distance*) być; **it's 10 km to the village** jest dziesięć kilometrów do wioski
8 (*cost*) być; **how much was the meal?** ile kosztował posiłek?; **that'll be £5, please** to będzie pięć funtów, proszę
9 (*linking clauses*) być; **the problem is that...** problem jest w tym, że...
10 (*exist, occur etc*) być; **is there a God?** czy Bóg istnieje?
11 (*assessing a situation*): **it is likely that he'll resign** możliwe, że zrezygnuje; **it is difficult for me to complain** trudno jest mi narzekać
▷ *aux vb* **1** (*forming continuous tenses*): **what are you doing?** co robisz?; **they're coming tomorrow** przyjdą jutro
2 (*forming passives*): **to be murdered** zostać zamordowanym; **he was killed in a car crash** został zabity w wypadku samochodowym; **the box had been opened** pudełko zostało otwarte
3 (*with "to" infinitive*): **the house is to be sold** dom zostanie sprzedany; **these flowers are to be found all over the country** te kwiaty można znaleźć w całym kraju
4 (*in tag questions*): **it was fun, wasn't it?** było fajnie, prawda?; **he's good-looking, isn't he?** jest przystojny, prawda?
5 (*in short answers*): **"was the vase where I said?" — "yes, it was/no, it wasn't"** „czy wazon był tam, gdzie mówiłem?" — „tak, był/nie, nie było"

beach [biːtʃ] *n* plaża
bead [biːd] *n* (*glass, plastic etc*) koralik; **beads** *n pl* (*necklace*) korale
beak [biːk] *n* dziób
beam [biːm] *n* **1** (*of wood, metal*) belka **2** (*of light*) promień **3** (*Rad, Phys*) wiązka; **to drive on full** *or* **main** *or* (*US*) **high ~** jechać na długich światłach

bean [biːn] *n* fasola; **coffee/cocoa ~s** ziarna kawy/kakao

bear [bɛəʳ] (*pt* **bore**, *pp* **borne**) *n* (*animal*) niedźwiedź(-dzica) *m/f* ▷ *vt* **1** (*support: weight*) dźwigać (dźwignąć *pf*) **2** (*responsibility*) ponosić (ponieść *pf*) **3** (*tolerate*) znosić (znieść *pf*)

beard [bɪəd] *n* broda

bearded ['bɪədɪd] *adj* brodaty

beat [biːt] (*pt* **beat**, *pp* **beaten**) *n* **1** (*of heart*) bicie **2** (*Mus: rhythm*) rytm ▷ *vt* **1** (*strike: wife, child*) uderzać (uderzyć *pf*) **2** (*eggs, cream*) ubijać (ubić *pf*) **3** (*defeat: opponent, record*) pobić ▷ *vi* (*heart*) bić; **to ~ time** (*Mus: drum, percussion*) uderzać (uderzyć *pf*); (*rhythm*) wybijać (wybić *pf*)
▶ **beat up** *vt* (*person*) bić (pobić *pf*)

beautiful ['bjuːtɪful] *adj* **1** (*woman, day, place, weather*) piękny **2** (*shot, performance*) wspaniały

beautifully ['bjuːtɪflɪ] *adv* **1** (*play, sing etc*) świetnie **2** (*quiet, written etc*) idealnie

beauty ['bjuːtɪ] *n* (*quality*) piękno

became [bɪ'keɪm] *pt of* **become**

because [bɪ'kɔz] *conj* ponieważ, bo; **~ of** z powodu *+gen*

become [bɪ'kʌm] (*pt* **became**, *pp* **become**) *vi* stawać (stać *pf*) się; **what has ~ of him?** co się z nim stało?

bed [bɛd] *n* **1** (*piece of furniture*) łóżko **2** (*bottom: of river, sea*) dno **3** (*of flowers*) grządka; **to go to ~** iść do łóżka; **to go to ~ with sb** pójść z kimś do łóżka

bed and breakfast *n* **1** (*service*) zakwaterowanie ze śniadaniem **2** (*guest house*) pensjonat

BED AND BREAKFAST

Bed and breakfast – mały pensjonat z pokojami gościnnymi oraz śniadaniem wliczonym w cenę noclegu. Popularnie zwane **B&B** (skrót od **bed and breakfast**), oferują swoim gościom przystępne ceny.

bedclothes ['bɛdkləuðz] *n pl* pościel

bedding ['bɛdɪŋ] *n* pościel

bedroom ['bɛdrum] *n* sypialnia

bedspread ['bɛdsprɛd] *n* narzuta

bedtime ['bɛdtaɪm] *n* pora na sen; **at ~** przed snem

bee [biː] *n* pszczoła

beech [biːtʃ] *n* **1** (*tree*) buk **2** (*wood*) drewno bukowe

beef [biːf] *n* wołowina; **roast ~** pieczeń wołowa

beefburger ['biːfbəːgəʳ] (*Brit*) *n* hamburger z wołowiny

been [biːn] *pp of* **be**

beer [bɪəʳ] *n* (*substance*) piwo; **would you like a ~?** napijesz się piwa?

beet [biːt] *n* burak

beetle ['biːtl] *n* żuk

beetroot ['biːtruːt] (*Brit*) *n* burak

before [bɪ'fɔːʳ] *prep* (*in time*) przed *+inst* ▷ *conj* (*in time*) zanim ▷ *adv* (*time*) przedtem, wcześniej; **~ doing sth** przed zrobieniem czegoś; **I've never seen it ~** nigdy tego przedtem nie widziałem

beforehand [bɪ'fɔːhænd] *adv* zawczasu

beg [bɛg] *vi* (*beggar*) żebrać; **to ~ for sth** błagać o coś; **to ~ sb to do sth** błagać kogoś o zrobienie czegoś; **I ~ your pardon** (*apologizing*) przepraszam; (*not hearing*) słucham?

began [bɪ'gæn] *pt of* **begin**

beggar ['bɛgəʳ] *n* żebrak(-aczka) *m/f*

begin [bɪ'gɪn] (*pt* **began**, *pp* **begun**) *vt* zaczynać (zacząć *pf*) ▷ *vi* zaczynać (zacząć *pf*) się; **to ~ doing** *or* **to do sth** zaczynać (zacząć *pf*) coś robić; **to ~ with...** zaczynać (zacząć *pf*) się od *+gen*...

beginner [bɪ'gɪnəʳ] *n* początkujący

beginning [bɪ'gɪnɪŋ] *n* (*of event, period, book*) początek; **at the ~** na początku

begun [bɪ'gʌn] *pp of* **begin**

behalf [bɪ'hɑːf] *n*: **on ~ of,** (*US*) **in ~ of** (*as representative of*) w imieniu *+gen*; (*for benefit of*) na rzecz *+gen*; **on my/his ~** w moim/jego imieniu

behave [bɪ'heɪv] *vi* **1** (*person*) zachowywać (zachować *pf*) się **2** (*behave well*) zachowywać (zachować *pf*) się dobrze; **to ~ oneself** dobrze się zachowywać (zachować *pf*)

behaviour [bɪ'heɪvjə^r] (*US* **behavior**) *n* zachowanie
behind [bɪ'haɪnd] *prep* **1** (*at the back of*) za +*inst* **2** (*supporting*) za +*inst* **3** (*in race, career etc*) w tyle za +*inst* ▷ *adv* **1** (*at/towards the back*) z tyłu **2**: **Jane asked me to stay ~** Jane poprosiła, żebym został ▷ *n* (*inf*: *buttocks*) siedzenie; **to be ~ (schedule)** pozostawać (pozostać *pf*) w tyle; **to leave sth ~** (*forget*) pozostawiać (pozostawić *pf*) coś za sobą
beige [beɪʒ] *adj* beżowy
Belgian ['bɛldʒən] *adj* belgijski ▷ *n* (*person*) Belg(ijka) *m/f*
Belgium ['bɛldʒəm] *n* Belgia
believe [bɪ'li:v] *vt* (*person, story*) wierzyć (uwierzyć *pf*) +*dat* ▷ *vi*: **to ~ in** (*God, ghosts*) wierzyć (uwierzyć *pf*) w; **to ~ that...** wierzyć (uwierzyć *pf*), że...; **I don't ~ in corporal punishment** nie wierzę w kary cielesne
bell [bɛl] *n* **1** (*of church*) dzwon **2** (*also*: **hand~**) dzwonek **3** (*on door*) dzwonek
belong [bɪ'lɔŋ] *vi*: **to ~ to** należeć do +*gen*; **this book ~s here** ta książka powinna być tu
belongings [bɪ'lɔŋɪŋz] *n pl* dobytek *sg*
below [bɪ'ləu] *prep* **1** (*beneath*) pod +*inst* **2** (*less than*: *level, rate*) poniżej +*gen* ▷ *adv* **1** (*beneath*) niżej **2** (*less*) poniżej; **~ zero** poniżej zera; **temperatures ~ normal** *or* **average** temperatura poniżej normalnej
belt [bɛlt] *n* **1** (*clothing*) pasek **2** (*of land, sea, air*) pas **3** (*Tech*) taśma
bench [bɛntʃ] *n* **1** (*seat*) ławka **2** (*table*: *in factory, laboratory etc*) stół
bend [bɛnd] (*pt, pp* **bent**) *vt* (*leg, arm, bar, wire*) zginać (zgiąć *pf*) się ▷ *vi* **1** (*person*) pochylać (pochylić *pf*) się **2** (*leg, arm, bar, wire*) zginać (zgiąć *pf*) się **3** (*road, river*) zakręcać (zakręcić *pf*) się ▷ *n* (*in road, river*) zakręt
▶ **bend down** *vi* pochylać (pochylić *pf*) się
beneath [bɪ'ni:θ] *prep* **1** (*in position*) pod +*inst* **2** (*in status*): **~ him/her** poniżej niego/niej ▷ *adv* poniżej
benefit ['bɛnɪfɪt] *n* **1** (*advantage*) korzyść **2** (*money*) zysk ▷ *vt* przynosić (przynieść *pf*) korzyści +*dat* ▷ *vi*: **to ~ from sth** korzystać (skorzystać *pf*) z czegoś
bent [bɛnt] *pt, pp of* **bend** ▷ *adj* (*wire, pipe*) zgięty
beret ['bɛreɪ] *n* beret
berth [bə:θ] *n* (*bed*: *on boat*) koja; (*on train*) kuszetka
beside [bɪ'saɪd] *prep* (*next to*) obok +*gen*; *see also* **besides**
besides [bɪ'saɪdz] *adv* **1** (*also*: **beside**: *in addition*) ponadto **2** (*in any case*) poza tym ▷ *prep* (*also*: **beside**: *in addition to, as well as*) poza +*inst*
best [bɛst] *adj* najlepszy ▷ *adv* najlepiej ▷ *n* najlepszy; **the ~ thing to do is...** najlepsze co można zrobić, to...; **to do** *or* **try one's ~** starać się ze wszystkich sił
best man *n* drużba
bet [bɛt] (*pt, pp* **bet** *or* **betted**) *n* (*wager*) zakład ▷ *vt* **1** (*wager*): **to ~ sb £100 that...** zakładać (założyć *pf*) się o sto funtów, że... **2** (*expect, guess*): **to ~ (that)** założyć się (że) ▷ *vi* (*wager*): **to ~ on** (*horse, result*) robić (zrobić *pf*) zakłady na
better ['bɛtə^r] *adj* **1** lepszy **2** (*after an illness or injury*): **to feel ~** czuć (poczuć *pf*) się lepiej ▷ *adv* lepiej; **to get ~** polepszyć; **I'd ~ go** *or* **I had ~ go** lepiej już pójdę
between [bɪ'twi:n] *prep* między +*inst* ▷ *adv*: **in ~** pośrodku; **to choose ~** (*two things*) wybierać (wybrać *pf*) pomiędzy +*inst*; **to be shared/divided ~ people** być podzielonym między ludźmi; **~ you and me, ~ ourselves** między tobą a mną, między nami
beyond [bɪ'jɔnd] *prep* **1** (*on the other side of*) po drugiej stronie +*gen* **2** (*fig*) poza +*inst* **3** (*after*: *time, date, age*) po +*loc* ▷ *adv* dalej; **~ doubt** poza wszelką wątpliwością
Bible ['baɪbl] (*Rel*) *n*: **the ~** Biblia
bicycle ['baɪsɪkl] *n* rower; **to ride a ~** jeździć na rowerze
big [bɪg] *adj* **1** (*in size*: *man, country, object*) duży **2** (*inf*: *person*: *important*) ważny **3** (*major*: *change, increase,*

problem) duży; **~ brother/sister** starszy brat/starsza siostra; **in a ~ way** (*inf*) na wielką skalę
bigheaded ['bɪg'hɛdɪd] (*inf*) *adj* zarozumiały
bike [baɪk] *n* **1** (*bicycle*) rower **2** (*motorcycle*) motor
bikini [bɪ'kiːnɪ] *n* bikini
bilingual [baɪ'lɪŋgwəl] *adj* dwujęzyczny; **to be ~** być dwujęzycznym
bill [bɪl] *n* **1** (*requesting payment*) rachunek **2** (*Brit: in restaurant*) rachunek **3** (*US: banknote*) banknot
billfold ['bɪlfəuld] (*US*) *n* portfel
billiards ['bɪljədz] *n* bilard
billion ['bɪljən] *n* miliard
bin [bɪn] *n* **1** (*Brit: for rubbish*) kosz na śmieci **2** (*container*) pojemnik
binoculars [bɪ'nɔkjuləz] *n pl* lornetka *sg*
biochemistry [baɪə'kɛmɪstrɪ] *n* biochemia
biography [baɪ'ɔgrəfɪ] *n* biografia; **a ~ of Dylan Thomas** biografia Dylana Thomasa
biology [baɪ'ɔlədʒɪ] *n* biologia
bird [bəːd] *n* (*Zool*) ptak
bird-watching ['bəːdwɔtʃɪŋ] *n* ptasiarstwo
Biro® ['baɪərəu] (*Brit*) *n* długopis
birth [bəːθ] *n* narodziny; **to give ~ (to)** (*child, animal*) rodzić (urodzić *pf*)
birth certificate *n* metryka urodzenia
birth control *n* regulacja urodzeń
birthday ['bəːθdeɪ] *n* urodziny ▷ *adj* urodzinowy
biscuit ['bɪskɪt] *n* **1** (*Brit: cookie*) ciastko **2** (*US: cake*) ciasto
bisexual ['baɪ'sɛksjuəl] *adj* biseksualny ▷ *n* biseksualista(-tka) *m/f*
bishop ['bɪʃəp] *n* (*Rel*) biskup
bit [bɪt] *pt of* **bite** ▷ *n* **1** (*esp Brit: piece*) kawałek **2** (*esp Brit: part*) fragment **3** (*Comput*) bit **4** (*US: coin*) *moneta*; **a ~ of** trochę *+gen*; **a ~ mad/dangerous** trochę szalony/niebezpieczny; **~ by ~** stopniowo; **every ~ as good/interesting as** równie dobry/interesujący jak; **for a ~** (*inf*) na trochę; **quite a ~** sporo
bite [baɪt] (*pt* **bit**, *pp* **bitten** ['bɪtn]) *vt* (*person, dog, snake, mosquito*) gryźć (pogryźć *pf*) ▷ *vi* (*dog etc*) gryźć (pogryźć *pf*) ▷ *n* **1** (*mouthful*) kęs **2** (*from dog*) ugryzienie **3** (*from snake, mosquito*) ukąszenie; **to ~ one's nails** obgryzać paznokcie
bitter ['bɪtə^r] *adj* gorzki
black [blæk] *adj* **1** (*in colour: paint, jacket, cat*) czarny **2** (*person*) czarnoskóry **3** (*tea, coffee*) czarny ▷ *n* (*colour*) czerń **~ and blue** (*bruised*) posiniaczony
▸ **black out** *vi* (*faint*) tracić (stracić *pf*) przyjemność
blackberry ['blækbərɪ] *n* jeżyna
blackbird ['blækbəːd] *n* kos
blackboard ['blækbɔːd] *n* tablica
blackcurrant ['blæk'kʌrənt] (*Brit*) *n* czarna porzeczka
blackmail ['blækmeɪl] *n* szantaż ▷ *vt* szantażować (zaszantażować *pf*)
black pudding (*Brit*) *n* kaszanka
blade [bleɪd] *n* (*of knife, sword*) ostrze
blame [bleɪm] *n* wina ▷ *vt*: **to ~ sb for sth** winić kogoś za coś; **to be to ~ (for sth)** być winnym (czegoś); **to ~ sth on sb** obwiniać (obwinić *pf*) kogoś za coś; **you can't ~ him for trying** nie możesz winić go za to, że próbował
blank [blæŋk] *adj* (*paper, cassette*) czysty ▷ *n* (*on form*) puste miejsce; **my mind went ~** *or* **was a ~** miałem pustkę w głowie
blanket ['blæŋkɪt] *n* (*for bed*) koc ▷ *adj* (*comprehensive: ban, coverage*) całkowity
blast [blɑːst] *n* (*explosion*) wybuch ▷ *vt* **1** (*blow up*) wysadzać (wysadzić *pf*) **2** (*shoot*) strzelać (strzelić *pf*)
▸ **blast off** *vi* (*Space*) odpalać (odpalić *pf*)
blaze [bleɪz] *n* (*fire*) pożar ▷ *vi* (*fire*) płonąć (zapłonąć *pf*) ▷ *vt*: **to ~ a trail** przecierać (przetrzeć *pf*) szlaki; **in a ~ of publicity** w błysku reflektorów
blazer ['bleɪzə^r] *n* marynarka
bleach [bliːtʃ] *n* (*chemical*) wybielacz ▷ *vt* **1** (*fabric, foodstuff etc*) wybielać (wybielić *pf*) **2** (*hair*) utleniać (utlenić *pf*)

bleed [bli:d] (*pt, pp* **bled** [blɛd]) *vi* (*Med*) krwawić; **my nose is ~ing** leci mi krew z nosa
blender ['blɛndəʳ] *n* mikser
bless [blɛs] *vt* (*Rel*) błogosławić (pobłogosławić *pf*); **~ you!** (*after sneeze*) na zdrowie!; (*inf: expressing affection*) Bóg zapłać!
blew [blu:] *pt of* **blow**
blind [blaɪnd] *adj* (*Med*) niewidomy ▷ *n* (*for window*) roleta ▷ *vt* oślepiać (oślepić *pf*); **to go ~** oślepnąć; **to turn a ~ eye (to sth)** przymykać (przymknąć *pf*) oczy (na coś)
blink [blɪŋk] *vi* (*person, animal*) mrugać (mrugnąć *pf*) ▷ *vt*: **to ~ one's eyes** mrugać (mrugnąć *pf*) powiekami
blister ['blɪstəʳ] *n* (*on skin*) pęcherz ▷ *vi* (*skin*) pokrywać (pokryć *pf*) się pęcherzami
blizzard ['blɪzəd] *n* śnieżyca
block [blɔk] *n* **1** (*group of buildings*) blok **2** (*of stone, wood, ice*) blok ▷ *vt* **1** (*entrance, road*) blokować (zablokować *pf*) **2** (*view*) zasłaniać (zasłonić *pf*); **~ of flats** *or* (*US*) **apartment ~** blok mieszkalny; **3 ~s from here** trzy ulice stąd
▸ **block up** *vt* (*sink, pipe etc*) zatykać (zatkać *pf*) ▷ *vi* (*sink, pipe*) zatykać (zatkać *pf*) się
blog [blɔg] (*Comput*) *n* blog
blogger ['blɔgəʳ] *n* bloger(ka) *m/f*
blogpost ['blɔgpəust] *n* wpis na blogu
blond(e) [blɔnd] *adj* **1** (*hair*) blond **2** (*person*) jasnowłosy ▷ *n*: **blonde** (*woman*) blondynka
blood [blʌd] *n* (*Bio*) krew; **in cold ~** z zimną krwią
blood pressure *n* ciśnienie krwi; **to have high/low ~** mieć wysokie/niskie ciśnienie krwi; **to take sb's ~** mierzyć (zmierzyć *pf*) komuś ciśnienie krwi
blood test *n* badanie krwi
blouse [blauz] (*US* [blaus]) *n* (*woman's garment*) bluzka
blow [bləu] (*pt* **blew**, *pp* **blown**) *n* **1** (*punch*) uderzenie **2** (*fig: setback*) cios ▷ *vi* **1** (*wind, sand, dust etc*) wiać **2** (*person*) dmuchać (dmuchnąć *pf*) **3** (*whistle, horn*) dmuchać (dmuchnąć *pf*) ▷ *vt* **1** (*wind*) wiać **2** (*whistle, horn*) dmuchać (dmuchnąć *pf*); **to ~ one's nose** dmuchać (wydmuchać *pf*) nos
▸ **blow away** *vt* odfruwać (odfrunąć *pf*) ▷ *vi* odfruwać (odfrunąć *pf*)
▸ **blow down** *vt* (*tree, house*) przewracać (przewrócić *pf*)
▸ **blow out** *vt* (*flame, candle*) gasić (zgasić *pf*)
▸ **blow up** *vi* (*explode*) wybuchać (wybuchnąć *pf*) ▷ *vt* **1** (*destroy: bridge etc*) wysadzać (wysadzić *pf*) **2** (*inflate: balloon, tyre*) dmuchać (nadmuchać *pf*)
blow-dry ['bləudraɪ] *vt* (*hair*) suszyć (wysuszyć *pf*)
blown [bləun] *pp of* **blow**
blue [blu:] *adj* **1** (*in colour*) niebieski **2** (*inf: depressed*) smutny ▷ *n* błękit; **blues** *n pl* (*Mus*): **the ~s** blues; **out of the ~** ni z tego ni z owego
blunder ['blʌndəʳ] *n* gafa ▷ *vi* popełniać (popełnić *pf*) gafę
blunt [blʌnt] *adj* **1** (*pencil, knife*) tępy **2** (*person, remark*) szczery, bez ogródek; **to be ~...** mówiąc szczerze...
blush [blʌʃ] *vi* rumienić (zarumienić *pf*) się ▷ *n* rumieniec
board [bɔ:d] *n* **1** (*piece of wood*) deska **2** (*also:* **notice~**) tablica **3** (*also:* **black~**) tablica **4** (*for chess etc*) plansza **5** (*committee*) rada **6** (*at hotel*) wyżywienie ▷ *vt* (*formal: ship, train, plane*) wchodzić (wejść *pf*) na pokład *+gen* ▷ *vi* (*formal: on ship, train, plane*) wchodzić (wejść *pf*) na pokład; **~ and lodging** mieszkanie z wyżywieniem; **on ~** na pokładzie
▸ **board up** *vt* (*door, window*) zabijać (zabić *pf*) deskami
board game *n* gra planszowa
boarding card ['bɔ:dɪŋ-] *n* karta pokładowa
boarding school *n* szkoła z internatem
boast [bəust] *vi*: **to ~ (about** *or* **of sth)** przechwalać się (czymś) ▷ *n* przechwałka
boat [bəut] *n* **1** (*small vessel*) łódka **2** (*ship*) łódź; **to go by ~** pływać (płynąć *pf*) łódką

body ['bɔdɪ] *n* ciało
bodybuilding ['bɔdɪ'bɪldɪŋ] *n* kulturystyka
bodyguard ['bɔdɪgɑːd] *n* ochroniarz
boil [bɔɪl] *vt* **1** (*water*) gotować (zagotować *pf*) **2** (*eggs, potatoes etc*) gotować (ugotować *pf*) ▷ *vi* (*liquid*) gotować (zagotować *pf*) się ▷ *n* (*Med*) czyrak; **to ~ a kettle** gotować (zagotować *pf*) wodę w czajniku
boiled egg ['bɔɪld-] *n* jajko gotowane
boiler ['bɔɪləʳ] *n* (*device*) bojler
boiling (hot) ['bɔɪlɪŋ-] (*inf*) *adj*: **I'm ~** jest mi tak gorąco, że można się ugotować
bolt [bəult] *n* **1** (*to lock door*) rygiel **2** (*used with nut*) śruba ▷ *vt* (*door*) ryglować (zaryglować *pf*)
bomb [bɔm] *n* bomba ▷ *vt* bombardować (zbombardować *pf*)
bomber ['bɔməʳ] *n* **1** (*Aviat*) bombowiec **2** (*terrorist*) zamachowiec podkładający bomby
bombing ['bɔmɪŋ] *n* bombardowanie
bone [bəun] *n* **1** (*in human, animal*) kość **2** (*in fish*) ość
bonfire ['bɔnfaɪəʳ] *n* ognisko

BONFIRE NIGHT

Bonfire Night przypada na 5 listopada, kiedy to w Wielkiej Brytanii rozpalane są ogniska i puszczane sztuczne ognie w celu upamiętnienia spisku Guy Fawkesa, który w 1605 roku usiłował zabić króla poprzez wysadzenie w powietrze budynków parlamentu.

bonnet ['bɔnɪt] *n* (*Brit: of car*) maska
bonus ['bəunəs] *n* **1** (*extra payment*) premia **2** (*additional benefit*) dodatek
book [buk] *n* **1** (*novel etc*) książka **2** (*of stamps, tickets*) bloczek ▷ *vt* (*ticket, table, seat, room*) rezerwować (zarezerwować *pf*); **fully ~ed** wszystkie miejsca zarezerwowane
▸ **book in** (*Brit*) *vi* (*at hotel*) meldować (zameldować *pf*) się
▸ **book into** (*Brit*) *vt fus* (*hotel*) meldować (zameldować *pf*) się w +*loc*
bookcase ['bukkeɪs] *n* biblioteczka
booklet ['buklɪt] *n* broszurka
bookmark ['bukmɑːk] *n* **1** zakładka **2** (*Comput*) zakładka ulubione ▷ *vt* (*Comput*) dodawać (dodać *pf*) do zakładki ulubionych
bookshelf ['bukʃɛlf] *n* półka na książki
bookshop ['bukʃɔp] (*Brit*) *n* księgarnia
bookstore ['bukstɔːʳ] (*esp US*) *n* = **bookshop**
boot [buːt] *n* **1** (*footwear: for winter*) kozak; (*for football, walking etc*) but **2** (*Brit: of car*) bagażnik
▸ **boot up** (*Comput*) *vt* ładować (załadować *pf*) ▷ *vi* ładować (załadować *pf*) się
border ['bɔːdəʳ] *n* (*of country*) granica
bore [bɔːʳ] *pt of* **bear** ▷ *vt* **1** (*hole*) drążyć *pf* **2** (*oil well, tunnel*) wywiercać (wywiercić *pf*) **3** (*person*) zanudzać (zanudzić *pf*) ▷ *n*: **to be a ~** (*person*) być nudziarzem; (*situation*) być nudnym; **to be ~d (with sth)** być znudzonym (czymś)
boring ['bɔːrɪŋ] *adj* (*person, job, film*) nudny
born [bɔːn] *adj*: **to be ~** (*baby*) rodzić (urodzić *pf*) się
borrow ['bɔrəu] *vt* (*from sb, from library*) pożyczać (pożyczyć *pf*); **can I ~ a pen, please?** mogę pożyczyć długopis?
boss [bɔs] *n* szef
bossy ['bɔsɪ] *adj* apodyktyczny
both [bəuθ] *adj* obaj ▷ *pron* **1** (*things*) oba *m, nt*, obie *f* **2** (*people*) obaj ▷ *conj*: **~ A and B** zarówno A jak i B; **~ of us went** *or* **we ~ went** obaj poszliśmy
bother ['bɔðəʳ] *vt* **1** (*worry*) martwić (zmartwić *pf*) **2** (*disturb*) niepokoić (zaniepokoić *pf*) ▷ *vi* robić (zrobić *pf*) sobie kłopot ▷ *n* (*trouble*) kłopot; **to ~ doing sth** *or* **to do sth** zadawać (zadać *pf*) sobie trud, aby coś zrobić; **I can't be ~ed to go** nie chce mi się iść; **don't ~** nie kłopocz się
bottle ['bɔtl] *n* butelka ▷ *vt* (*beer, wine*) butelkować; **a ~ of wine/milk** butelka wina/mleka; **a wine/milk ~** butelka na wino/mleko

bottle bank (*Brit*) *n* pojemnik na szkło
bottle opener *n* otwieracz do butelek
bottom ['bɔtəm] *n* **1** (*of container, sea*) dno **2** (*of page, list*) dół **3** (*of class, league*) ostatnie miejsca **4** (*of hill, tree, stairs*) dół **5** (*buttocks*) pośladki **6** (*also*: **~s**: *of bikini, tracksuit*) dół ▷ *adj* (*lowest*) najniższy; **at the ~ of** na dole *+gen*
bought [bɔːt] *pt, pp of* **buy**
bounce [bauns] *vi* (*ball*) odbijać (odbić *pf*) się ▷ *vt* (*ball*) odbijać (odbić *pf*) ▷ *n* (*of ball*) odbicie
bouncer ['baunsəʳ] (*inf*) *n* (*at dance, club*) bramkarz
bound [baund] *pt, pp of* **bind** ▷ *vi* (*leap*) przeskakiwać (przeskoczyć *pf*) ▷ *adj*: **to be ~ to do sth** (*certain*) na pewno coś zrobić
boundary ['baundrɪ] *n* (*border, limit*) granica
bow¹ [bəu] *n* **1** (*knot*) kokarda **2** (*weapon*) łuk **3** (*Mus*) smyczek
bow² [bau] *vt* (*head*) skinąć *+inst*
bowl [bəul] *n* miska
bowling ['bəulɪŋ] *n* (*game*) kręgle; **to go ~** iść na kręgle
bow tie [bəu-] *n* muszka
box [bɔks] *n* **1** (*container*) pudło **2** (*contents*) pudło **3** (*also*: **cardboard ~**) pudło tekturowe **4** (*crate*) skrzynia ▷ *vi* (*Sport*) boksować
boxer ['bɔksəʳ] *n* (*person*) bokser
boxer shorts, boxers [-ʃɔːtz, 'bɔksəz] *n pl* bokserki
boxing ['bɔksɪŋ] (*Sport*) *n* boks
Boxing Day (*Brit*) *n drugi dzień Świąt Bożego Narodzenia*

BOXING DAY

Boxing Day – tak w kręgu kultury brytyjskiej nazywany jest drugi dzień świąt Bożego Narodzenia, który także jest dniem wolnym od pracy. Jego nazwa wywodzi się od dawnego zwyczaju obdarowywania prezentami (**Christmas boxes**) pracowników przez pracodawców.

boy [bɔɪ] *n* **1** (*male child*) chłopiec **2** (*young man*) chłopak
boyfriend ['bɔɪfrɛnd] *n* chłopak
bra [brɑː] *n* stanik
brace [breɪs] *n* (*on teeth*) aparat na zęby
bracelet ['breɪslɪt] *n* bransoletka
bracket ['brækɪt] *n* (*group, range*) przedział ▷ *vt* (*word, phrase*) brać (wziąć *pf*) w nawias; **in ~s** w nawiasie
braid [breɪd] *n* (*US*: *plait*) warkocz
brain [breɪn] *n* mózg; **brains** *n pl* (*intelligence*) mózg; **he's got ~s** ma głowę
brainy ['breɪnɪ] *adj* (*inf*) bystry
brake [breɪk] *n* (*Aut*) hamulec ▷ *vi* (*driver, vehicle*) hamować (zahamować *pf*)
branch [brɑːntʃ] *n* **1** (*of tree*) gałąź **2** (*of shop, bank etc*) oddział
brand [brænd] *n* (*make*) marka
brand-new ['brænd'njuː] *adj* nowiutki
brandy ['brændɪ] *n* brandy
brass [brɑːs] *n* (*metal*) mosiądz; **the ~ (section)** (*Mus*) instrumenty dęte blaszane
brass band *n* orkiestra dęta blaszana
brave [breɪv] *adj* **1** (*person*) dzielny **2** (*attempt, smile, action*) śmiały
Brazil [brə'zɪl] *n* Brazylia
bread [brɛd] *n* chleb
break [break] (*pt* **broke**, *pp* **broken**) *vt* **1** (*cup, window etc*) tłuc (stłuc *pf*) **2** (*leg, arm*) łamać (złamać *pf*) **3** (*contract*) zrywać (zerwać *pf*); (*promise*) łamać (złamać *pf*) **4** (*law, rule*) łamać (złamać *pf*) **5** (*record*) bić (pobić *pf*) **6** (*habit, pattern etc*) zrywać (zerwać *pf*) ▷ *vi* (*cup, window etc*) tłuc (stłuc *pf*) się ▷ *n* **1** (*rest*) przerwa **2** (*pause, interval*) przerwa **3** (*fracture*) pęknięcie **4** (*holiday*) przerwa; **to ~ the news to sb** przekazywać (przekazać *pf*) komuś wiadomości; **to take a ~** (*for a few minutes*) robić (zrobić *pf*) sobie przerwę; (*have a holiday*) mieć przerwę; **without a ~** bez przerwy
▸ **break down** *vi* (*machine, car*) psuć (zepsuć *pf*) się ▷ *vt* (*door etc*) wyważać (wyważyć *pf*)
▸ **break in** *vi* (*burglar*) włamywać (włamać *pf*) się

▸ **break into** *vt fus* (*house*) włamywać (włamać *pf*) się do *+gen*
▸ **break off** *vi* **1** (*branch*) odłamywać (odłamać *pf*) się **2** (*speaker*) przerywać (przerwać *pf*) ▹ *vt* **1** (*branch, piece of chocolate*) odłamywać (odłamać *pf*) **2** (*engagement, relationship*) zrywać (zerwać *pf*)
▸ **break out** *vi* **1** (*begin*) wybuchać (wybuchnąć *pf*) **2** (*escape*) uciekać (uciec *pf*); **to ~ out in spots/a rash** pokrywać (pokryć *pf*) się plamami/ wysypką; **to ~ out in a sweat** zalewać (zalać *pf*) się potem
▸ **break up** *vi* **1** (*couple, marriage*) zrywać (zerwać *pf*) ze sobą **2** (*meeting, party*) kończyć (skończyć *pf*) się **3** (*Brit: Scol*) kończyć (skończyć *pf*) się ▹ *vt* **1** (*fight etc*) przerywać (przerwać *pf*) **2** (*meeting, demonstration*) przerywać (przerwać *pf*); **to ~ up with sb** zrywać (zerwać *pf*) z kimś; **you're ~ing up** (*on mobile phone*) coś mi przerywa, nie słyszę pana

breakdown ['breɪkdaun] *n* **1** (*Aut*) awaria **2** (*of system, talks*) zerwanie **3** (*of marriage*) rozpad **4** (*Med: also:* **nervous ~**) załamanie nerwowe; **to have a ~** załamywać (załamać *pf*) się psychicznie

breakfast ['brɛkfəst] *n* śniadanie

break-in ['breɪkɪn] *n* włamanie

breast [brɛst] *n* pierś

breaststroke ['brɛststrəuk] *n* (*also:* **the ~**) żabka

breath [brɛθ] *n* **1** (*intake of air*) wdech **2** (*air from mouth*) wydech; **out of ~** bez tchu; **bad ~** nieświeży oddech; **to get one's ~ back** (*Brit*) łapać (złapać *pf*) oddech; **to hold one's ~** wstrzymywać (wstrzymać *pf*) oddech

breathe [bri:ð] *vt* (*air*) oddychać (odetchnąć *pf*) *+inst* ▹ *vi* oddychać (odetchnąć *pf*)
▸ **breathe in** *vi* robić (zrobić *pf*) wdech
▸ **breathe out** *vi* robić (zrobić *pf*) wydech

breed [bri:d] (*pt, pp* **bred** [brɛd]) *vt* (*animals*) hodować (wyhodować *pf*) ▹ *vi* (*Zool*) rozmnażać (rozmnożyć *pf*) się ▹ *n* (*Zool*) rasa

breeze [bri:z] *n* wiaterek

brewery ['bru:ərɪ] *n* browar

bribe [braɪb] *n* łapówka ▹ *vt* (*person, witness*) przekupywać (przekupić *pf*); **to ~ sb to do sth** proponować (zaproponować *pf*) komuś łapówkę za zrobienie czegoś

brick [brɪk] *n* (*for building*) cegła

bride [braɪd] *n* panna młoda

bridegroom ['braɪdgru:m] *n* pan młody

bridesmaid ['braɪdzmeɪd] *n* druhna

bridge [brɪdʒ] *n* **1** (*Archit*) most **2** (*Cards*) brydż

brief [bri:f] *adj* **1** (*period, visit, appearance*) krótki **2** (*description, speech*) zwięzły; **briefs** *n pl* **1** (*for men*) slipy **2** (*for women*) figi

briefcase ['bri:fkeɪs] *n* teczka

briefly ['bri:flɪ] *adv* (*smile*) przelotnie; (*talk, explain, say*) zwięźle

bright [braɪt] *adj* **1** (*light*) jasny **2** (*clever: person*) bystry; (*idea*) genialny **3** (*colour*) jasny

brilliant ['brɪljənt] *adj* **1** (*person, mind*) błyskotliwy **2** (*idea, performance*) znakomity **3** (*esp Brit: inf: wonderful*) fantastyczny

bring [brɪŋ] (*pt, pp* **brought**) *vt* (*thing, person: with you*) przenosić (przenieść *pf*); (*to sb*) przynosić (przynieść *pf*)
▸ **bring about** *vt* (*cause*) powodować (spowodować *pf*)
▸ **bring along** *vt* przyprowadzać (przyprowadzić *pf*) ze sobą
▸ **bring back** *vt* (*return*) przywozić (przywieźć *pf*)
▸ **bring forward** *vt* (*meeting*) przyspieszać (przyspieszyć *pf*)
▸ **bring round** *vt* (*unconscious person*) cucić (ocucić *pf*)
▸ **bring up** *vt* **1** (*rear: child*) wychowywać (wychować *pf*) **2** (*question, subject*) podnosić (podnieść *pf*); (*food*) wymiotować (zwymiotować *pf*)

Britain ['brɪtən] *n* (*also:* **Great ~**) Wielka Brytania; **in ~** w Wielkiej Brytanii

British ['brɪtɪʃ] *adj* brytyjski ▹ *n pl:* **the ~** Brytyjczycy

broad [brɔːd] *adj* (*street, shoulders*) szeroki; **in ~ daylight** w biały dzień
broadband ['brɔːdbænd] (*Comput*) *n* sztywne łącze
broad bean (*esp Brit*) *n* bób
broadcast ['brɔːdkɑːst] (*pt, pp* **broadcast**) *n* audycja ▷ *vt* nadawać (nadać *pf*) ▷ *vi* prowadzić program
broccoli ['brɔkəlɪ] *n* brokuły
brochure ['brəuʃjuə^r] (*US* [brəu'ʃʌr]) *n* (*booklet*) broszura
broil [brɔɪl] (*US*) *vt* opiekać (opiec *pf*)
broke [brəuk] *pt of* **break** ▷ *adj* (*inf: penniless*) spłukany
broken ['brəukn] *pp of* **break** ▷ *adj* **1** (*window, cup etc*) rozbity **2** (*machine*) zepsuty; **a ~ leg** złamana noga; **a ~ marriage** rozbite małżeństwo
bronchitis [brɔŋ'kaɪtɪs] *n* zapalenie oskrzeli
bronze [brɔnz] *n* **1** (*metal*) brąz **2** (*Sport: also:* **~ medal**) brąz ▷ *adj* (*in colour*) brąz
brooch [brəutʃ] *n* broszka
broom [brum] *n* (*for cleaning*) miotła
brother ['brʌðə^r] *n* brat
brother-in-law ['brʌðərɪnlɔː] *n* szwagier
brought [brɔːt] *pt, pp of* **bring**
brown [braun] *adj* **1** (*in colour: object*) brązowy; (*hair, eyes*) brązowy **2** (*tanned: skin, person*) opalony ▷ *n* (*colour*) brąz
browse [brauz] *vi* **1** (*Comput*) przeglądać (przejrzeć *pf*) **2** (*in shop*) szperać (wyszperać *pf*)
browser ['brauzə^r] (*Comput*) *n* przeglądarka
bruise [bruːz] *n* (*on face etc*) siniak ▷ *vt* posiniaczyć (posiniaczyć *pf*)
brush [brʌʃ] *n* (*for cleaning, for decorating*) miotła; (*for hair*) szczotka; (*artist's*) pędzel ▷ *vt* **1** (*carpet etc*) zmiatać (zmieść *pf*) **2** (*hair*) szczotkować (wyszczotkować *pf*); **to ~ one's teeth** myć (umyć *pf*) zęby
Brussels sprout ['brʌslz spraut] *n* brukselka
bubble ['bʌbl] *n* **1** (*in liquid*) pęcherzyk **2** (*also:* **soap ~**) bańka ▷ *vi* (*liquid*) bulgotać (zabulgotać *pf*)
bubble bath *n* (*liquid*) płyn do kąpieli
bubble gum *n* guma balonowa
bucket ['bʌkɪt] *n* wiadro
buckle ['bʌkl] *n* (*on shoe, belt*) klamra ▷ *vt* (*shoe, belt*) zapinać (zapiąć *pf*) na klamrę
Buddhism ['budɪzəm] *n* buddyzm
Buddhist ['budɪst] *adj* buddyjski ▷ *n* buddysta(-yjka) *m/f*
buffet ['bufeɪ] (*US* [bu'feɪ]) *n* bufet
bug [bʌg] *n* **1** (*esp US: insect*) robak **2** (*Comput*) błąd **3** (*inf: virus*) wirus
build [bɪld] (*pt, pp* **built**) *n* (*of person*) budowa ciała ▷ *vt* (*house, machine*) budować (zbudować *pf*)
▸ **build up** *vi* (*accumulate*) narastać
builder ['bɪldə^r] *n* (*worker*) robotnik budowlany
building ['bɪldɪŋ] *n* (*house, office etc*) budynek

BUILDING SOCIETY

Building societies – oszczędnościowe kasy mieszkaniowe, pierwotnie zakładane po to, aby udzielać kredytów na zakup mieszkań, obecnie zaś oferujące większy zakres usług finansowych.

built [bɪlt] *pt, pp of* **build** ▷ *adj*: **well-/heavily-~** (*person*) dobrze zbudowany
bulb [bʌlb] *n* **1** (*Elec*) żarówka **2** (*Bot*) cebulka
Bulgaria [bʌl'gɛərɪə] *n* Bułgaria
bull [bul] *n* (*Zool*) byk
bullet ['bulɪt] *n* pocisk
bulletin ['bulɪtɪn] *n* (*TV etc: news update*) biuletyn
bulletin board *n* **1** (*Comput*) tablica ogłoszeniowa **2** (*US: noticeboard*) tablica informacyjna
bullfighting ['bulfaɪtɪŋ] *n* walki *pl* byków
bully ['bulɪ] *n* łobuz ▷ *vt* zastraszać (zastraszyć *pf*)
bum [bʌm] (*inf*) *n* **1** (*Brit: backside*) tyłek **2** (*esp US: tramp*) menel
bump [bʌmp] *n* **1** (*swelling: on head*) guz **2** (*jolt*) wstrząs **3** (*on road*) wyboje ▷ *vt* (*strike*) uderzać (uderzyć *pf*)
▸ **bump into** *vt fus* **1** (*strike: obstacle, person*) uderzać (uderzyć *pf*) **2** (*inf: meet: person*) wpadać (wpaść *pf*) na

bumper ['bʌmpəʳ] *n* (*Aut*) zderzak
bumpy ['bʌmpɪ] *adj* (*road*) wyboisty
bun [bʌn] *n* (*Culin*) bułka
bunch [bʌntʃ] *n* **1** (*of flowers*) bukiet **2** (*of keys*) pęk; (*of bananas, grapes*) kiść; **bunches** *n pl* (*Brit: in hair*) kucyki
bungalow ['bʌŋgələu] *n* dom parterowy
bunk [bʌŋk] *n* (*bed*) łóżko piętrowe
burger ['bə:gəʳ] *n* hamburger
burglar ['bə:gləʳ] *n* włamywacz(ka) *m/f*
burglar alarm *n* alarm antywłamaniowy
burglary ['bə:glərɪ] *n* włamanie
burn [bə:n] (*pt, pp* **burned** *or* (*Brit*) **burnt**) *vt* **1** (*papers etc*) palić (spalić *pf*) **2** (*fuel*) spalać (spalić *pf*) **3** (*toast, rice*) przypalać (przypalić *pf*) ▹ *vi* **1** (*fire, flame*) palić się **2** (*house, car*) palić (spalić *pf*) się ▹ *n* oparzenie; **I've ~t myself!** oparzyłem się!
▸ **burn down** *vi* (*house etc*) palić (spalić *pf*) się
burst [bə:st] (*pt, pp* **burst**) *vt* (*bag, balloon etc*) przekłuwać (przekłuć *pf*) ▹ *vi* (*pipe, tyre*) pękać (pęknąć *pf*); **to ~ into flames** wybuchać (wybuchnąć *pf*) płomieniem; **to ~ into tears** wybuchać (wybuchnąć *pf*) płaczem; **to ~ out laughing** wybuchać (wybuchnąć *pf*) śmiechem
bury ['bɛrɪ] *vt* **1** (*in ground*) zakopywać (zakopać *pf*) **2** (*dead person*) chować (pochować *pf*)
bus [bʌs] *n* autobus
bus driver *n* kierowca autobusu
bush [buʃ] *n* (*plant*) krzak
business ['bɪznɪs] *n* biznes; **to be away on ~** być w podróży służbowej; **to do ~ with sb** robić (zrobić *pf*) z kimś interesy; **it's none of your ~** to nie twoja sprawa
businessman ['bɪznɪsmən] (*irreg*) *n* przedsiębiorca
businesswoman ['bɪznɪswumən] (*irreg*) *n* kobieta interesu
bus station *n* dworzec autobusowy
bus stop *n* przystanek autobusowy
bust [bʌst] *vt, n* (*breasts*) biust
busy ['bɪzɪ] *adj* **1** (*person*) zajęty **2** (*shop, street*) ruchliwy **3** (*schedule, time, day*) pracowity **4** (*esp US: Tel: line*) zajęty ▹ *vt*: **to ~ oneself (with sth)** zajmować (zająć *pf*) się (czymś); **I'm ~** jestem zajęty

KEYWORD

but [bʌt] *conj* **1** (*yet, however*) ale; **I'd love to come, but I'm busy** bardzo chciałbym przyjść, ale jestem zajęty; **not only... but also** nie tylko... ale także
2 (*showing disagreement, surprise etc*): **but that's far too expensive!** ale to jest za drogie!
▹ *prep* (*apart from, except*) poza +*inst*; **nothing but** nic poza +*inst*; **anything but** wszystko poza +*inst*; **they've got no-one but themselves to blame** nikogo nie mogą winić poza sobą
▹ *adv* **1** (*just, only*) tylko
2: **but for** (*without*) gdyby nie; (*except for*) gdyby nie; **but for his help/him, we wouldn't have finished the job** gdyby nie jego pomoc/on, nie skończylibyśmy pracy

butcher ['butʃəʳ] *n* **1** (*person*) rzeźnik(-iczka) *m/f* **2** (*shop: also*: **~'s**) sklep mięsny
butter ['bʌtəʳ] *n* masło
butterfly ['bʌtəflaɪ] *n* **1** (*insect*) motyl **2** (*also*: **the ~**: *in swimming*) motylek
button ['bʌtn] *n* **1** (*on clothes*) guzik **2** (*on machine*) przycisk **3** (*US: badge*) znaczek ▹ *vt* (*also*: **~ up**) zapinać (zapiać *pf*)
buy [baɪ] (*pt, pp* **bought**) *vt* kupować (kupić *pf*) ▹ *n* (*purchase*) zakup; **to ~ sb sth** kupować (kupić *pf*) coś komuś; **to ~ sth off** *or* **from sb** kupować (kupić *pf*) coś od kogoś
buzz [bʌz] *vi* (*insect*) bzyczeć (bzyknąć *pf*); (*machine*) brzęczeć (zabrzęczeć *pf*)

KEYWORD

by [baɪ] *prep* **1** (*referring to cause, agent*): **a painting by Picasso** obraz Picassa; **surrounded by a fence** otoczony ogrodzeniem

2 (*referring to method, manner, means*): **by bus/car/train** autobusem/ samochodem/pociągiem; **to pay by cheque** płacić (zapłacić *pf*) czekiem; **she grabbed him by the arm** chwyciła go za rękę; **by moonlight/ candlelight** przy świetle księżyca/ świecach
3 (*via, through*) przez; **he came in by the back door** wszedł przez tylne drzwi
4 (*close to, beside*) przy +*loc*; **he was standing by the door** stał przy drzwiach; **the house by the river** dom przy rzece
5 (*past*) obok +*gen*
6 (*with times, dates, years*) do +*gen*; **by 4 o'clock** do czwartej godziny; **by this time tomorrow** o tej porze jutro; **by the time I got here** zanim tu przyszedłem; **by now/then** już
7 (*during*): **by day/night** w ciągu dnia/nocy
8 (*specifying number, quantity, rate*) na +*acc*; **sold by the kilo/metre** sprzedawane na kilogramy/metry
9 (*specifying degree of change*) o; **crime has increased by 10 per cent** przestępczość wzrosła o dziesięć procent
10 (*in measurements*): **a room 3 metres by 4** pokój trzy metry na cztery
11 (*Math*): **to divide/multiply by 3** dzielić/mnożyć przez trzy
12 (*according to*): **by law** według prawa; **it's all right by me** nie mam nic przeciwko temu; **by profession/ birth/nature** z zawodu/urodzenia/ natury
13: **by myself/himself** *etc* (*unaided*) samemu; (*alone*) sam

bye(-bye) ['baɪ('baɪ)] (*inf*) *excl* pa, pa
bypass ['baɪpɑːs] *n* (*Aut*) obwodnica ▷ *vt* (*town*) omijać (ominąć *pf*)

cab [kæb] *n* (*taxi*) taksówka
cabbage ['kæbɪdʒ] *n* kapusta
cabin ['kæbɪn] *n* kabina
cable ['keɪbl] *n* **1** (*rope*) lina **2** (*Elec*) kabel **3** (*also*: **~ television**) kablówka
cable car *n* kolejka linowa
cable television *n* telewizja kablowa
cactus ['kæk] (*pl* **cactuses** *or* **cacti** ['kæktaɪ]) *n* kaktus
café ['kæfeɪ] *n* kawiarnia
cafeteria [kæfɪ'tɪərɪə] *n* buffet
cage [keɪdʒ] *n* klatka
cagoule [kə'guːl] *n* sztormiak
cake [keɪk] *n* (*large*) ciasto; (*small*) ciastko
calculate ['kælkjuleɪt] *vt* (*work out*) obliczać (obliczyć *pf*); **to ~ (that)...** (*using maths*) obliczać (obliczyć *pf*), (że)...
calculation [kælkju'leɪʃən] *n* (*Math*) obliczenie
calculator ['kælkjuleɪtəʳ] *n* kalkulator
calendar ['kæləndəʳ] *n* (*showing date*) kalendarz
calf [kɑːf] (*pl* **calves**) *n* **1** (*Zool*: *of cow*) cielę **2** (*Anat*) łydka
call [kɔːl] *vt* **1** (*name*) nazywać (nazwać *pf*) **2** (*address as*) zwracać (zwrócić *pf*) się **3** (*describe as*) nazywać (nazwać *pf*) **4** (*Tel*) dzwonić (zadzwonić *pf*) **5** (*summon*: *person*) wołać (zawołać *pf*) ▷ *vi* (*telephone*) dzwonić (zadzwonić *pf*) ▷ *n* **1** (*Tel*) telefon **2** (*demand*): **~ for sth** żądanie

czegoś **3** (*visit*) wizyta; **to be ~ed** nazywać się; **who's ~ing?** (*Tel*) kto mówi?; **to make a phone ~** dzwonić (zadzwonić *pf*); **to give sb a ~** zadzwonić do kogoś
▸ **call back** *vi* **1** (*return*) wracać (wrócić *pf*) **2** (*Tel*) oddzwonić ▹ *vt* (*Tel*) dzwonić (zadzwonić *pf*)
▸ **call for** *vt fus* (*fetch: person*) wstępować (wstąpić *pf*) po; (*parcel*) odbierać (odebrać *pf*)
▸ **call off** *vt* (*deal, event*) odwoływać (odwołać *pf*)
▸ **call out** *vi* wołać

callbox ['kɔːlbɔks] (*Brit: Tel*) *n* budka telefoniczna

call centre (*US* **call center**) *n* (*Tel*) call centre

calm [kɑːm] *adj* **1** (*person*) opanowany; (*voice*) cichy; (*place*) spokojny **2** (*not stormy: sea*) spokojny
▸ **calm down** *vt* (*person, animal*) uspokajać (uspokoić *pf*) ▹ *vi* (*person*) uspokajać (uspokoić *pf*) się

calorie ['kælərɪ] *n* kaloria

calves [kɑːvz] *n pl of* **calf**

camcorder ['kæmkɔːdə^r] *n* kamera wideo

came [keɪm] *pt of* **come**

camel ['kæməl] *n* wielbłąd(zica) *m/f*

camera ['kæmərə] *n* **1** (*Phot*) aparat fotograficzny **2** (*Cine, TV*) kamera

cameraman ['kæmərəmæn] (*irreg*) *n* operator

camera phone *n* telefon z aparatem (fotograficznym)

camp [kæmp] *n* **1** (*for refugees, prisoners, soldiers*) obóz **2** (*encampment*) obozowisko ▹ *vi* biwakować (*pf*)

campaign [kæm'peɪn] *n* (*for change*) kampania

camper ['kæmpə^r] *n* **1** (*person*) obozowicz(ka) *m/f* **2** (*also:* **~ van**) samochód kempingowy

camping ['kæmpɪŋ] *n* biwakowanie; **to go ~** jechać (pojechać *pf*) pod namiot *lub* na kemping

campsite ['kæmpsaɪt] *n* kemping

campus ['kæmpəs] *n* miasteczko uniwersyteckie

can[1] [kæn] *n* **1** (*for food, drinks*) puszka; (*for petrol, oil*) kanister **2** (*contents*) puszka

KEYWORD

can[2] [kæn] (*negative* **cannot, can't**, *conditional, pt* **could**) *aux vb* **1** (*be able to*) móc; **can I help you?** (*in shop*) w czym mogę panu/pani pomóc?; (*in general*) mogę jakoś pomóc?; **you can do it if you try** możesz to zrobić, jeśli spróbujesz; **I can't hear/see anything** nic nie słyszę/widzę; **she can't sleep** nie może spać; **I can't understand why...** nie mogę zrozumieć dlaczego...
2 (*know how to*) umieć; **I can swim/drive** umiem pływać/kierować (pojazdem)
3 (*permission, requests*) móc; **can I use your phone?** mogę skorzystać z twojego telefonu?; **can you help me?** możesz mi pomóc?
4 (*disbelief, puzzlement*): **it can't be true!** to nie może być prawda!; **you can't be serious!** nie mówisz poważnie!
5 (*possibility*) móc, potrafić; **he can be very unpleasant** potrafi być bardzo niemiły; **can she have finished already?** czy mogła już skończyć?

Canada ['kænədə] *n* Kanada

Canadian [kə'neɪdɪən] *adj* kanadyjski ▹ *n* (*person*) Kanadyjczyk(-jka) *m/f*

canal [kə'næl] *n* (*for ships, barges*) kanał

Canaries [kə'nɛərɪz] *n pl*: **the ~** Wyspy Kanaryjskie

canary [kə'nɛərɪ] *n* kanarek

cancel ['kænsəl] *vt* odwoływać (odwołać *pf*)

cancer ['kænsə^r] *n* **1** (*Med*) nowotwór **2** (*Astrol*): **C~** Rak

candidate ['kændɪdeɪt] *n* **1** (*for job*) kandydat(ka) *m/f* **2** (*in exam*) zdający(-ca) *m/f*

candle ['kændl] *n* świeca

candy ['kændɪ] (*US*) *n* słodycze; **piece of ~** cukierek

candyfloss ['kændɪflɔs] (*Brit*) *n* wata cukrowa

canned [kænd] *adj* (*fruit, vegetables*) w puszce
cannot ['kænɔt] = **can not**
canoe [kə'nuː] *n* kajak
canoeing [kə'nuːɪŋ] *n* kajakarstwo; **to go ~** pływać (płynąć *pf*) kajakiem
can opener *n* otwieracz do puszek
can't [kɑːnt] = **can not**
canteen [kæn'tiːn] *n* (*in workplace, school*) stołówka
canter ['kæntəʳ] *vi* (*horse*) biec krótkim galopem
canvas ['kænvəs] *n* (*fabric*) płótno
cap [kæp] *n* **1** (*hat*) czapka **2** (*top: of bottle*) nakrętka
capable ['keɪpəbl] *adj* (*able: person*) sprawny; **to be ~ of sth** (*speed, output*) potrafić coś; **to be ~ of doing sth** być w stanie coś zrobić
capacity [kə'pæsɪtɪ] *n* pojemność; **filled to ~** zapchany; **a ~ crowd** wypełniony do ostatniego miejsca; **~ for sth/to do sth** zdolność do czegoś/do zrobienia czegoś
capital ['kæpɪtl] *n* **1** (*city*) stolica **2** (*money*) fundusze, kapitał **3** (*also: ~ letter*) wielka litera; **in ~s** dużymi literami; **~ R/L** duże R/L
capitalism ['kæpɪtəlɪzəm] *n* kapitalizm
Capricorn ['kæprɪkɔːn] *n* (*Astrol*) Koziorożec
captain ['kæptɪn] *n* kapitan
capture ['kæptʃəʳ] *vt* (*catch: animal*) chwytać (schwytać *pf*); (*person*) pojmać (*pf*)
car [kɑːʳ] *n* **1** (*Aut*) samochód **2** (*US: Rail*) wagon; **by ~** samochodem
caramel ['kærəməl] (*Culin*) *n* karmel
caravan ['kærəvæn] *n* (*Brit: vehicle*) przyczepa kempingowa

CAR BOOT SALE

Car boot sale to brytyjska odmiana pchlego targu, gdzie sprzedaje się rzeczy używane. Wyprzedaże takie odbywają się na terenach otwartych, często np. parkingach. Sprzedawane dobra prezentowane są na rozkładanych stołach lub w otwartych bagażnikach samochodów.

card [kɑːd] *n* **1** (*record card, index card etc*) kartka **2** (*also:* **playing ~**) karta **3** (*greetings card*) kartka z życzeniami **4** (*also:* **business ~**) wizytówka **5** (*bank card, credit card etc*) karta; **to play ~s** grać w karty
cardboard ['kɑːdbɔːd] *n* karton
cardigan ['kɑːdɪgən] *n* sweter rozpinany
care [kɛəʳ] *n* (*attention*) ostrożność ▷ *vi* przejmować (przejąć *pf*) się; **with ~** ostrożnie; **take ~!** (*saying goodbye*) trzymaj się!; **to take ~ to do sth** starać (postarać *pf*) się coś zrobić; **to take ~ of sb** opiekować się kimś; **to take ~ of sth** (*possession, clothes*) dbać (zadbać *pf*) o coś; (*problem, situation*) zajmować (zająć *pf*) się czymś; **I don't ~** nie obchodzi mnie to
▶ **care about** *vt fus* (*person, thing, idea*) interesować się *+inst*
▶ **care for** *vt fus* (*look after*) opiekować (zaopiekować *pf*) się *+inst*
career [kə'rɪəʳ] *n* **1** (*job, profession*) zawód **2** (*working life*) kariera
careful ['kɛəful] *adj* **1** (*cautious*) ostrożny **2** (*thorough: work, thought, analysis*) staranny; **(be) ~!** uważaj!; **to be ~ with sth** (*money*) ostrożnie się z czymś obchodzić; (*fragile object*) ostrożnie się z czymś obchodzić; **to be ~ to do sth/not to do sth** uważać, żeby coś zrobić/czegoś nie zrobić
carefully ['kɛəfəlɪ] *adv* **1** (*cautiously*) ostrożnie **2** (*methodically*) skrupulatnie
careless ['kɛəlɪs] *adj* (*negligent: person, worker*) nieuważny; (*driving*) nieostrożny; (*mistake*) wynikający z nieuwagi; **to be ~ with sth** (*money, resources*) trwonić coś
caretaker ['kɛəteɪkəʳ] *n* (*Brit: of building*) dozorca(-czyni) *m/f*
car ferry *n* prom samochodowy
cargo ['kɑːgəu] (*pl* **cargoes**) *n* ładunek
car hire (*Brit*) *n* wynajem samochodów
Caribbean [kærɪ'biːən] *n*: **the ~ (Sea)** Morze Karaibskie ▷ *adj* karaibski
carnation [kɑː'neɪʃən] *n* goździk

carnival ['kɑːnɪvl] *n* **1** (*festival*) karnawał **2** (*US*) parada
carol ['kærəl] *n*: **(Christmas) ~** kolęda
car park (*Brit*) *n* parking
carpenter ['kɑːpɪntəʳ] *n* stolarz
carpentry ['kɑːpɪntrɪ] *n* stolarstwo
carpet ['kɑːpɪt] *n* (*fitted*) wykładzina; (*rug*) dywan
car rental [-'rɛntl] *n* wynajem samochodów
carriage ['kærɪdʒ] *n* (*Brit: Rail*) wagon
carrier bag ['kærɪəʳ-] (*Brit*) *n* reklamówka
carrot ['kærət] *n* marchewka
carry ['kærɪ] *vt* **1** (*person*) nieść (zanieść *pf*); (*by hand with the arm down*) przenosić (przenieść *pf*); (*on one's back*) przenosić (przenieść *pf*); (*by hand*) nosić (nieść *pf*) **2** (*transport: ship, plane*) przewozić (przewieźć *pf*)
▸ **carry on** *vi* (*continue*) kontynuować ▹ *vt* (*continue: work, tradition*): **to ~ on with sth** kontynuować coś; **to ~ on doing sth** kontynuować robienie czegoś
▸ **carry out** *vt* (*order, instruction*) realizować (zrealizować *pf*)
cart [kɑːt] *n* **1** (*for people, goods*) wóz **2** (*US: also*: **shopping ~**) wózek
carton ['kɑːtən] *n* karton
cartoon [kɑː'tuːn] *n* **1** (*drawing*) dowcip rysunkowy **2** (*Brit: comic strip*) komiks **3** (*animated*) kreskówka
cartridge ['kɑːtrɪdʒ] *n* **1** (*for gun*) nabój **2** (*of ink: for printer*) wkład drukujący **3** (*for camera*) rolka filmu
carve [kɑːv] *vt* **1** (*Culin: meat*) kroić (pokroić *pf*) **2** (*wood, stone, figure*) rzeźbić (wyrzeźbić *pf*)
case [keɪs] *n* **1** (*instance*) przypadek **2** (*container*) opakowanie **3** (*Brit: also*: **suit~**) walizka; **lower/upper ~** małe/duże litery; **in ~ of** (*fire, emergency*) w razie; **in ~ he comes** jeśli przyjdzie; **in any ~** w każdym przypadku; **just in ~** na wszelki wypadek; **in that ~** w takim razie
cash [kæʃ] *n* **1** (*notes and coins*) gotówka **2** (*money*) pieniądze ▹ *vt* (*cheque, money order*) realizować (zrealizować *pf*); **to pay (in) ~** płacić (zapłacić *pf*) gotówką
cash dispenser [-dɪs'pɛnsəʳ] (*Brit*) *n* bankomat
cashew [kæ'ʃuː] *n* (*also*: **~ nut**) nerkowiec
cashier [kæ'ʃɪəʳ] *n* (*in bank*) kasjer(ka) *m/f*
cashmere ['kæʃmɪəʳ] *n* kaszmir ▹ *adj* kaszmirowy
casino [kə'siːnəu] *n* kasyno
cassette [kæ'sɛt] *n* kaseta
cast [kɑːst] (*pt, pp* **cast**) *n* (*Theat*) obsada; **to ~ one's vote** oddawać (oddać *pf*) głos
castle ['kɑːsl] *n* zamek
casual ['kæʒjul] *adj* **1** (*chance: remark*) przypadkowy **2** (*unconcerned*) swobodny **3** (*informal: clothes*) swobodny
casualty ['kæʒjultɪ] *n* **1** (*of war, accident: injured*) ofiara; (*dead*) ofiara śmiertelna **2** (*Brit: in hospital*) ostry dyżur
cat [kæt] *n* kot
catalogue ['kætəlɔg] (*US* **catalog**) *n* katalog
catastrophe [kə'tæstrəfɪ] *n* katastrofa
catch [kætʃ] (*pt, pp* **caught**) *vt* **1** łapać (złapać *pf*) **2** (*discover: person*) przyłapać **3** (*flu, illness*) łapać (złapać *pf*) ▹ *n*: **to ~ sb doing sth** łapać (złapać *pf*) kogoś na robieniu czegoś; **to be** *or* **get caught in sth** (*storm*) być złapanym przez coś; (*traffic jam*) utkwić w czymś
▸ **catch up** *vi* (*walking, driving*) nadganiać (nadgonić *pf*)
▸ **catch up with** *vt fus* doganiać (dogonić *pf*)
category ['kætɪgərɪ] *n* kategoria
catering ['keɪtərɪŋ] *n* **1** (*industry*) gastronomia **2** (*for specific occasion*) catering
cathedral [kə'θiːdrəl] *n* katedra
Catholic ['kæθəlɪk] *adj* katolicki ▹ *n* katolik(-iczka) *m/f*
cattle ['kætl] *n pl* bydło
caught [kɔːt] *pt, pp of* **catch**
cauliflower ['kɔlɪflauəʳ] *n* kalafior
cause [kɔːz] *n* **1** (*of event*) przyczyna **2** (*reason*) powód ▹ *vt* (*produce, lead*

to) powodować (spowodować *pf*); **to ~ sb to do sth** skłonić kogoś do czegoś; **to ~ sth to happen** spowodować coś
cautious ['kɔːʃəs] *adj* ostrożny; **to be ~ about doing sth** robić (zrobić *pf*) coś ostrożnie
cave [keɪv] *n* jaskinia
CCTV *n abbr* (= *closed-circuit television*) telewizja przemysłowa
CD *n abbr* (= *compact disc*) płyta kompaktowa
CD player *n* odtwarzacz płyt kompaktowych
CD-ROM [siːdiː'rɔm] *n abbr* (= *compact disc read-only memory*) CD-ROM; **on ~** na CD-ROMie
ceiling ['siːlɪŋ] *n* (*in room*) sufit
celebrate ['sɛlɪbreɪt] *vt* **1** (*success, birthday*) świętować **2** (*Rel*: *mass*) celebrować ▷ *vi* świętować
celebrity [sɪ'lɛbrɪtɪ] *n* (*person*) znana osobistość
celery ['sɛlərɪ] *n* seler naciowy; **a stick of ~** łodyga selera naciowego
cell [sɛl] *n* **1** (*Bio*) komórka **2** (*in prison*) cela
cellar ['sɛlə^r] *n* piwnica
cello ['tʃɛləu] *n* wiolonczela
cellphone ['sɛlfəun] *n* (*US*) telefon komórkowy
cellular phone ['sɛljulə-] *n* (*US*) = **cellphone**
cement [sə'mɛnt] *n* **1** (*powder*) cement **2** (*concrete*) beton ▷ *vt* (*stick, glue*) cementować
cemetery ['sɛmɪtrɪ] *n* cmentarz
cent [sɛnt] *n* cent
centenary [sɛn'tiːnərɪ] (*Brit*) *n* stulecie
centennial [sɛn'tɛnɪəl] (*US*) *n* stulecie
center ['sɛntə^r] (*US*) *n* = **centre**
centigrade ['sɛntɪgreɪd] *adj* w skali Celsjusza
centimetre ['sɛntɪmiːtə^r] (*US* **centimeter**) *n* centymetr
central ['sɛntrəl] *adj* **1** (*in the centre*) centralny **2** (*most important*: *idea, figure*) główny
central heating *n* centralne ogrzewanie
centre ['sɛntə^r] (*US* **center**) *n* **1** (*of circle, line*) środek; (*of town, activity*) centrum **2** (*building*) ośrodek; **to be at the ~ of sth** być w centrum czegoś; **to be the ~ of attention/interest** być w centrum uwagi/zainteresowania; **to ~** *or* **be ~d on sth** (*focus on*) skupiać (skupić *pf*) się na czymś
century ['sɛntjurɪ] *n* (*period*) wiek; **in the twenty-first ~** w dwudziestym pierwszym wieku
cereal ['siːrɪəl] *n* **1** (*plant, crop*) zboże **2** (*also*: **breakfast ~**) płatki śniadaniowe
ceremony ['sɛrɪmənɪ] *n* (*event*) uroczystość; (*ritual*) ceremonia
certain ['səːtən] *adj* pewny; **to be ~ that...** (*person*) być pewnym, że...; **it is ~ that...** jest pewne, że...; **to make ~ that...** upewnić się, że...; **to be ~ of** być pewnym *+gen*; **a ~ amount of sth** pewna ilość czegoś; **to know sth for ~** wiedzieć coś na pewno
certainly ['səːtənlɪ] *adv* **1** (*undoubtedly*) z pewnością **2** (*of course*) oczywiście; **~ not** zdecydowanie nie
certificate [sə'tɪfɪkɪt] *n* **1** (*of birth, marriage etc*) świadectwo **2** (*diploma*) dyplom, certyfikat
chain [tʃeɪn] *n* **1** łańcuch **2** (*piece of jewellery*) łańcuszek ▷ *vt*: **to ~ sb/sth to sth** przykuć kogoś/coś łańcuchami do czegoś
chair [tʃɛə^r] *n* krzesło; (*armchair*) fotel
chair lift *n* wyciąg krzesełkowy
chairman ['tʃɛəmən] (*irreg*) *n* przewodniczący
chairwoman ['tʃɛəwumən] (*irreg*) *n* przewodnicząca
chalet ['ʃæleɪ] *n* drewniana chata
chalk [tʃɔːk] *n* kreda; **a piece of ~** (*for blackboard*) kawałek kredy
challenge ['tʃælɪndʒ] *n* **1** (*hard task*) wyzwanie **2** (*to authority, ideas*) podważenie; (*to rival, competitor*) wyzwanie ▷ *vt* (*authority, right, idea*) kwestionować (zakwestionować *pf*); (*rival, competitor*) rzucać (rzucić *pf*) wyzwanie *+dat*; **to ~ sb to do sth** rzucać (rzucić *pf*) komuś wyzwanie do zrobienia czegoś; **to ~ sb to a fight** wyzwać kogoś na pojedynek

champagne [ʃæm'peɪn] *n* szampan
champion ['tʃæmpɪən] *n* (*of league, contest*) mistrz(yni) *m/f*
championship ['tʃæmpɪənʃɪp] *n* (*contest*) mistrzostwa
chance [tʃɑːns] *n* **1** (*likelihood, possibility*) szansa **2** (*opportunity*) okazja **3** (*luck*) traf ▷ *adj* (*meeting, discovery*) przypadkowy; **he hasn't much ~ of winning** nie ma wielu szans na wygraną; **to stand a ~ of (doing) sth** mieć szansę na zrobienie czegoś; **the ~s are that...** są szanse, że...; **the ~ to do sth** okazja do zrobienia czegoś; **by ~** przypadkiem
change [tʃeɪndʒ] *vt* **1** (*alter*) zmieniać (zmienić *pf*) **2** (*replace: wheel, battery etc*) wymieniać (wymienić *pf*) **3** (*trains, buses etc*) przesiadać (przesiąść *pf*) się **4** (*clothes*) przebierać (przebrać *pf*) się **5** (*job, address*) zmieniać (zmienić *pf*) **6** (*put fresh nappy on: baby*) przewijać (przewinąć *pf*) **7** (*replace: nappy*) zmieniać (zmienić *pf*) **8** (*exchange: money*) wymieniać (wymienić *pf*) **9** (*transform*): **to ~ sb/sth into sth** zamieniać (zamienić *pf*) kogoś/coś w coś ▷ *vi* **1** (*alter*) zmieniać (zmienić *pf*) **2** (*change clothes*) zmieniać (zmienić *pf*) **3** (*traffic lights*) zmieniać (zmienić *pf*) **4** (*on bus, train etc*) przesiadać (przesiąść *pf*) się **5** (*be transformed*): **to ~ into sth** zmieniać (zmienić *pf*) w coś ▷ *n* **1** (*alteration*) zmiana **2** (*novelty*) odmiana **3** (*referring to money: coins*) drobne; (*money returned*) reszta; **to ~ sth for sth** zamieniać (zamienić *pf*) coś na coś; **to ~ one's mind** zmienić zdanie; **to ~ gear** (*Brit: Aut*) zmieniać (zmienić *pf*) bieg; **she ~d into an old skirt** przebrała się w starą spódnicę; **for a ~** dla odmiany; **a ~ of clothes/underwear** zmiana ubrania/bielizny; **small ~** drobne; **to give sb ~ for** *or* **of £10** rozmieniać (rozmienić *pf*) komuś dziesięć funtów; **keep the ~** reszty nie trzeba
changing room ['tʃeɪndʒɪŋ-] (*Brit*) *n* **1** (*in shop*) przymierzalnia **2** (*Sport*) szatnia
channel ['tʃænl] *n* **1** (*TV*) kanał **2** (*for water*) kanał; **the (English) C~** Kanał La Manche
chaos ['keɪɔs] *n* chaos
chapel ['tʃæpl] *n* **1** (*in church*) kaplica **2** (*in hospital, prison, school*) kaplica **3** (*non-conformist chapel*) kościół
chapter ['tʃæptə^r] *n* (*of book*) rozdział
character ['kærɪktə^r] *n* **1** (*nature: of person, place*) charakter **2** (*in novel, film*) postać **3** (*letter, symbol etc*) znak; **a strange/sad ~** (*inf*) dziwna/żałosna osoba
characteristic [kærɪktə'rɪstɪk] *adj* charakterystyczny ▷ *n* cecha charakterystyczna; **to be ~ of sb/sth** być charakterystycznym dla kogoś/czegoś
charcoal ['tʃɑːkəul] *n* (*for fuel*) węgiel drzewny; **a piece of ~** kawałek węgla
charge [tʃɑːdʒ] *n* **1** (*fee*) opłata **2** (*accusation*) oskarżenie ▷ *vt* **1** (*sum of money*) liczyć (policzyć *pf*); (*customer, client*) pobierać (pobrać *pf*) **2** (*also*: **~ up**: *battery*) ładować (naładować *pf*); **charges** *n pl* (*bank charges, telephone charges etc*) opłata; **there's no ~** nie ma opłat; **free of ~** bezpłatnie; **to take ~ of sth** obejmować (objąć *pf*) kierownictwo czegoś; **to be in ~ of sth/sb** (*of person, machine*) kierować czymś/kimś; **how much do you ~?** ile to będzie kosztować?; **to ~ sb £20 for sth** liczyć (policzyć *pf*) komuś dwadzieścia funtów za coś
charity ['tʃærɪtɪ] *n* (*organization*) organizacja dobroczynna; **to give money to ~** dawać (dać *pf*) pieniądze na cele dobroczynne

CHARITY SHOP

Charity shop – sklep prowadzony przez wolontariuszy, w którym sprzedawane są używane ubrania, książki oraz artykuły gospodarstwa domowego. Zyski ze sprzedaży przekazywane są organizacji dobroczynnej, którą wspiera sklep.

charm [tʃɑːm] *n* (*of place, thing*) czar; (*of person*) urok ▷ *vt* oczarowywać (oczarować *pf*)

charming ['tʃɑːmɪŋ] *adj* (*person*) czarujący; (*place, custom*) uroczy

chart [tʃɑːt] *n* (*graph, diagram*) wykres; **the charts** *n pl* (*Mus*) lista przebojów; **to be in the ~s** (*song, pop group*) być na liście przebojów

charter flight ['tʃɑːtə^r-] *n* lot czarterowy

chase [tʃeɪs] *vt* (*pursue*) gonić ▷ *n* (*pursuit*) pościg

chat [tʃæt] *vi* (*also*: **have a ~**) ucinać (uciąć *pf*) sobie pogawędkę ▷ *n* (*conversation*) pogawędka; (*Comput*) czat

▸ **chat up** (*Brit*: *inf*) *vt* przygadać (*pf*) sobie

chatroom ['tʃætrum] (*Comput*) *n* pokój czatowy

chat show (*Brit*) *n* talk show

chauvinist ['ʃəuvɪnɪst] *n* (*also*: **male ~**) męski szowinista

cheap [tʃiːp] *adj* **1** (*inexpensive*) tani **2** (*reduced*) zniżkowy

cheat [tʃiːt] *vi* (*in game, exam*) oszukiwać (oszukać *pf*) ▷ *vt* oszukiwać (oszukać *pf*) ▷ *n* (*in games, exams*) oszust(ka) *m/f*

▸ **cheat on** (*inf*) *vt fus* (*husband, girlfriend, etc*) zdradzać (zdradzić *pf*)

check [tʃɛk] *vt* (*examine, verify*) sprawdzać (sprawdzić *pf*); (*passport, ticket*) kontrolować (skontrolować *pf*) ▷ *vi* (*investigate*) sprawdzać (sprawdzić *pf*) ▷ *n* **1** (*inspection*) kontrola **2** (*US*: *in restaurant etc*) rachunek **3** (*US*: *Fin*) = **cheque** **4** (*pattern*: *gen pl*) kratka **5** (*US*: *mark*) ptaszek ▷ *adj* (*also*: **~ed**: *pattern, cloth*) w kratę; **to ~ that...** sprawdzać (sprawdzić *pf*), czy...; **to ~ sth against sth** sprawdzać (sprawdzić *pf*) coś z czymś; **to ~ on sb/sth** sprawdzać (sprawdzić *pf*) kogoś/coś; **to ~ with sb** pytać (zapytać *pf*) kogoś; **to keep a ~ on sb/sth** (*watch*) obserwować kogoś/coś

▸ **check in** *vi* (*at hotel*) meldować (zameldować *pf*) się; (*to clinic*) zgłaszać (zgłosić *pf*) się; (*at airport*) zgłaszać (zgłosić *pf*) się do odprawy ▷ *vt* sprawdzać (sprawdzić *pf*)

▸ **check into** *vt* (*hotel*) meldować (zameldować *pf*) się w; (*clinic*) zgłaszać (zgłosić *pf*) się do *+gen*

▸ **check out** *vi* (*of hotel*) wymeldowywać (wymeldować *pf*) się

▸ **check up** *vi* sprawdzać (sprawdzić *pf*)

checkbook ['tʃɛkbuk] (*US*) *n* = **cheque book**

checked [tʃɛkt] *adj see* **check**

checkers ['tʃɛkəz] (*US*) *n pl* warcaby

check-in ['tʃɛkɪn] (*also*: **~ desk**) *n* (*at airport*) stanowisko odprawy

checkout ['tʃɛkaut] *n* (*in shop*) kasa

check-up ['tʃɛkʌp] *n* (*by doctor*) badanie; (*by dentist*) kontrola; **to have a ~** (*by doctor*) mieć badanie lekarskie; (*by dentist*) mieć kontrolę u dentysty

cheek [tʃiːk] *n* **1** (*on face*) policzek **2** (*inf*: *impudence*) tupet; **to have the ~ to do sth** mieć czelność coś zrobić

cheeky ['tʃiːkɪ] (*esp Brit*) *adj* bezczelny

cheer [tʃɪə^r] *vt* (*team, speaker*) wiwatować ▷ *vi* wiwatować ▷ *n* wiwat; **~s!** (*esp Brit*: *toast*) na zdrowie!; (*Brit*: *inf*: *thanks*) dzięki!

▸ **cheer up** *vt* (*person*) rozweselać (rozweselić *pf*) ▷ *vi* (*person*) rozchmurzać (rozchmurzyć *pf*) się

cheerful ['tʃɪəful] *adj* **1** (*wave, smile, person*) pogodny **2** (*place, object*) wesoły

cheese [tʃiːz] *n* ser

chef [ʃɛf] *n* szef kuchni

chemical ['kɛmɪkl] *adj* (*reaction, composition*) chemiczny ▷ *n* substancja chemiczna

chemist ['kɛmɪst] *n* **1** (*Brit*: *also*: **~'s**) aptekarz(-rka) *m/f* **2** (*Brit*: *in shop*) aptekarz(-rka) *m/f* **3** (*scientist*) chemik

chemistry ['kɛmɪstrɪ] *n* chemia

cheque [tʃɛk] (*US* **check**) *n* czek; **to pay by ~** płacić (zapłacić *pf*) czekiem

cheque book (*US* **checkbook**) *n* książeczka czekowa

cherry ['tʃɛrɪ] *n* **1** (*fruit*) czereśnia **2** (*also*: **~ tree**) czereśnia

chess [tʃɛs] *n* szachy

chest [tʃɛst] *n* **1** (*part of body*) klatka piersiowa **2** (*box*) skrzynia
chestnut ['tʃɛsnʌt] *n* **1** (*nut*) kasztan **2** (*also*: **~ tree**) kasztan
chew [tʃuː] *vt* (*food, gum*) żuć; (*pen, fingernails*) obgryzać (obgryźć *pf*) ▷ *vi* żuć
chewing gum ['tʃuːɪŋ-] *n* guma do żucia
chick [tʃɪk] *n* (*young bird*) pisklę
chicken ['tʃɪkɪn] *n* **1** (*bird: young*) kurczak; (*grown*) kura **2** (*meat*) kurczak
chickenpox ['tʃɪkɪnpɔks] *n* ospa wietrzna
chickpea ['tʃɪkpiː] *n* ciecierzyca
chief [tʃiːf] *n* (*of organization, department*) szef ▷ *adj* główny
child [tʃaɪld] (*pl* **children**) *n* dziecko; **she's just had her second ~** właśnie urodziła drugie dziecko
childish ['tʃaɪldɪʃ] *adj* (*pej: person, behaviour*) dziecinny
child minder [tʃaɪld 'maɪndəʳ] (*Brit*) *n* opiekun(ka) *m/f* do dziecka
children ['tʃɪldrən] *n pl of* **child**
Chile ['tʃɪlɪ] *n* Chile
chill [tʃɪl] *vt* (*cool: food, drinks*) studzić (ostudzić *pf*); **to catch a ~** zaziębiać (zaziębić *pf*) się; **to serve ~ed** podawać schłodzone
chilli ['tʃɪlɪ] (*US* **chili**) *n* chili
chilly ['tʃɪlɪ] *adj* (*weather, day*) chłodny; **it's a bit ~ today** dzisiaj jest trochę chłodno
chimney ['tʃɪmnɪ] *n* komin
chin [tʃɪn] *n* broda
China ['tʃaɪnə] *n* Chiny
china ['tʃaɪnə] *n* (*crockery*) zastawa ▷ *adj* (*cup, plate*) porcelanowy
Chinese [tʃaɪ'niːz] (*pl* **Chinese**) *adj* chiński ▷ *n* (*language*) chiński
chip [tʃɪp] *n* **1** (*Brit*) frytka **2** (*US*) chips **3** (*Comput: also:* **micro~**) mikroprocesor

CHIP SHOP

Chip shops – zwane także **fish and chip shops** to popularne brytyjskie fast foody, sprzedające ryby z frytkami, jak również inne smażone potrawy kuchni angielskiej. Jedzenie zamawia się tam na miejscu, lub, zwyczajowo zawinięte w gazetę, zabiera na wynos.

chiropodist [kɪ'rɔpədɪst] (*Brit*) *n* podiatra
chives [tʃaɪvz] *n pl* szczypiorek *sg*
chocolate ['tʃɔklɪt] *n* czekolada ▷ *adj* (*cake, pudding, mousse*) czekoladowy; **bar of ~** tabliczka czekolady; **piece of ~** kostka czekolady
choice [tʃɔɪs] *n* wybór; **a wide ~** szeroki wybór; **to make a ~** dokonywać (dokonać *pf*) wyboru; **to have no/little ~** nie mieć wyboru
choir ['kwaɪəʳ] *n* chór
choke [tʃəuk] *vi* krztusić (zakrztusić *pf*) się; **to ~ on sth** dławić (zadławić *pf*) się czymś
choose [tʃuːz] (*pt* **chose**, *pp* **chosen**) *vt* (*clothes, profession, candidate etc*) wybierać (wybrać *pf*) ▷ *vi*: **to ~ between** wybierać (wybrać *pf*) pomiędzy *inst*; **to ~ to do sth** postanawiać (postanowić *pf*) coś zrobić
chop [tʃɔp] *vt* **1** (*wood*) rąbać (porąbać *pf*) **2** (*also*: **~ up**: *vegetables, fruit, meat*) kroić (pokroić *pf*) ▷ *n* (*Culin*) kotlet
▸ **chop down** *vt* (*tree*) ciąć (ściąć *pf*)
▸ **chop up** *vt* kroić (pokroić *pf*)
chopsticks ['tʃɔpstɪks] *n pl* pałeczki
chore [tʃɔːʳ] *n* (*unpleasant task*) obowiązek; **the chores** *n pl* obowiązki; **household ~s** obowiązki domowe
chose [tʃəuz] *pt of* **choose**
chosen ['tʃəuzn] *pp of* **choose**
Christ [kraɪst] *n* Chrystus
christening ['krɪsnɪŋ] *n* chrzest
Christian ['krɪstɪən] *adj* chrześcijański ▷ *n* chrześcijanin(-nka) *m/f*
Christian name *n* imię
Christmas ['krɪsməs] *n* **1** (*Rel: festival*) Boże Narodzenie **2** (*period*) Święta Bożego Narodzenia; **Happy** *or* **Merry ~!** Wesołych Świąt!; **at ~** na Boże Narodzenie; **for ~** na Święta Bożego Narodzenia

Christmas Eve *n* Wigilia Bożego Narodzenia

CHRISTMAS PUDDING

Christmas Pudding – świąteczny pudding – to gotowana na parze odmiana deseru, zawierająca dużą ilość suszonych owoców, tradycyjnie podawana w Boże Narodzenie.

Christmas tree *n* choinka
chunk [tʃʌŋk] *n* (*of ice, food etc*) kawał
church [tʃəːtʃ] *n* **1** (*building*) kościół **2** (*denomination*) wyznanie
cider ['saɪdə^r] *n* **1** (*Brit*: *alcoholic*) cydr **2** (*US*: *non-alcoholic*) jabłecznik
cigar [sɪ'gɑː^r] *n* cygaro
cigarette [sɪgə'rɛt] *n* papieros
cinema ['sɪnəmə] *n* (*Brit*: *place*) kino
cinnamon ['sɪnəmən] *n* cynamon
circle ['səːkl] *n* koło
circular ['səːkjulə^r] *adj* (*shape*) okrągły; (*movement, motion*) okrężny ▷ *n* (*letter*) okólnik
circumstances ['səːkəmstənsɪz] *n pl* **1** (*conditions, state of affairs*) położenie **2** (*of accident, death*) okoliczności; **in** *or* **under the ~** w tych okolicznościach
circus ['səːkəs] *n* (*show*) cyrk
citizen ['sɪtɪzn] *n* (*of country*) obywatel(ka) *m/f*; (*of town, area*) mieszkaniec(-nka) *m/f*
citizenship ['sɪtɪznʃɪp] *n* obywatelstwo
city ['sɪtɪ] *n* miasto; **the C~** (*Brit*: *Fin*) Londyńskie City
city centre (*esp Brit*) *n* centrum miasta
civilization [sɪvɪlaɪ'zeɪʃən] *n* (*society*) cywilizacja
civilized ['sɪvɪlaɪzd] *adj* **1** (*socially advanced*: *society, people*) cywilizowany **2** (*polite*: *person, behaviour*) kulturalny
civil partnership ['sɪvɪl 'pɑːtnəʃɪp] *n* zawarty zgodnie z prawem związek pary jednopłciowej (homoseksualnej) dający takie same prawa jak małżeństwo
civil servant ['sɪvɪl-] *n* urzędnik(-iczka) *m/f* służby cywilnej
civil war ['sɪvɪl-] *n* wojna domowa
claim [kleɪm] *vt* **1** (*demand*: *expenses*) występować (wystąpić *pf*) o; (*rights, inheritance*) domagać się *+gen* **2** (*compensation, damages, benefit*) występować (wystąpić *pf*) o ▷ *vi* (*for insurance*) występować (wystąpić *pf*) o odszkodowanie ▷ *n* (*application*) podanie; **to ~** *or* **make a ~ on one's insurance** składać(złożyć *pf*) wniosek o odszkodowanie; **insurance ~** roszczenie ubezpieczeniowe
clap [klæp] *vi* (*audience*) klaskać ▷ *n*: **to give sb a ~** bić komuś brawo
clarinet [klærɪ'nɛt] (*Mus*) *n* klarnet
clash [klæʃ] *vi* **1** konfrontować (skonfrontować *pf*) **2** (*colours, styles*) gryźć się **3** (*events, dates, appointments*) kolidować
clasp [klɑːsp] *vt* (*hold, embrace*) ściskać (ścisnąć *pf*)
class [klɑːs] *n* **1** (*Scol*: *group of pupils*) klasa; (*lesson*) lekcja **2** (*social*) klasa ▷ *adj* (*structure, conflict, struggle*) klasa ▷ *vt* (*categorize*): **to ~ sb/sth as** klasyfikować (zaklasyfikować *pf*) kogoś/coś jako; **in ~** (*Scol*) na lekcji
classic ['klæsɪk] *adj* **1** (*example*) typowy **2** (*film, work etc*) klasyczny ▷ *n* (*film, novel etc*) klasyka
classical ['klæsɪkl] *adj* klasyczny
classmate ['klɑːsmeɪt] *n* kolega(-eżanka) *m/f* z klasy
classroom ['klɑːsrum] *n* sala lekcyjna
claw [klɔː] *n* (*of cat, tiger*) pazur; (*of bird*) szpon
clay [kleɪ] *n* glina
clean [kliːn] *adj* czysty ▷ *vt* (*car, cooker etc*) myć (umyć *pf*); (*room*) czyścić (wyczyścić *pf*) ▷ *n*: **to give sth a ~** czyścić (wyczyścić *pf*) coś; **a ~ driving licence** *or* (*US*) **record** prawo jazdy bez punktów karnych; **to ~ one's teeth** (*Brit*) myć (umyć *pf*) zęby
▶ **clean up** *vt* (*room, place*) sprzątać (posprzątać *pf*); (*mess*) porządkować (uporządkować *pf*) ▷ *vi* sprzątać (sprzątnąć *pf*)

cleaner ['kli:nəʳ] *n* **1** (*person*) sprzątacz(ka) *m/f* **2** (*substance*) środek czyszczący
cleanser ['klɛnzəʳ] *n* (*for face*) środek do czyszczenia twarzy
clear [klɪəʳ] *adj* **1** (*explanation, account*) klarowny **2** (*footprint, photograph*) wyraźny **3** (*voice, echo*) wyraźny **4** (*obvious*) oczywisty **5** (*glass, plastic, water*) przezroczysty **6** (*road, way, floor etc*) wolny **7** (*day, sky*) jasny ▷ *vt* (*place, room*) opróżniać (opróżnić *pf*) ▷ *vi* (*weather, sky*) przejaśniać (przejaśnić *pf*) się; (*fog, smoke*) rozchodzić (rozejść *pf*) się ▷ *adv*: **~ of sth** (*place, ground*) z dala od czegoś; **to be ~ about sth** rozumieć (zrozumieć *pf*) coś; **to make o.s. ~** wyrażać (wyrazić *pf*) się jasno; **to make sth ~ to sb** wyjaśniać (wyjaśnić *pf*) coś komuś; **to ~ the table** sprzątać (sprzątnąć *pf*) ze stołu; **to ~ one's throat** odchrząkiwać (odchrząknąć *pf*)
▸ **clear away** *vt* (*plates etc*) sprzątać (posprzątać *pf*) ▷ *vi* (*remove plates etc*) sprzątać (posprzątać *pf*)
▸ **clear off** (*inf*) *vi* (*leave*) zmywać (zmyć *pf*) się
▸ **clear up** *vt* **1** (*room, mess*) sprzątać (posprzątać *pf*) **2** (*mystery, problem*) wyjaśniać (wyjaśnić *pf*) ▷ *vi* (*tidy up*) sprzątać (posprzątać *pf*)
clearly ['klɪəlɪ] *adv* **1** wyraźnie; (*think*) jasno **2** (*visible, audible*) dobrze **3** (*obviously*) najwyraźniej
clever ['klɛvəʳ] *adj* **1** (*intelligent*) zdolny **2** (*sly, crafty*) sprytny **3** (*ingenious: device, arrangement*) zmyślny
click [klɪk] *vi* **1** (*device, switch, camera*) pstrykać (pstryknąć *pf*) **2**: **to ~ (on sth)** (*Comput*) klikać (kliknąć *pf*) (na coś) ▷ *n* **1** (*sound*) pstryknięcie **2** (*Comput*): **with a ~ of one's mouse** po kliknięciu myszą
client ['klaɪənt] *n* klient(ka) *m/f*
cliff [klɪf] *n* klif
climate ['klaɪmɪt] *n* (*weather*) klimat
climate change *n* zmiana klimatyczna
climb [klaɪm] *vt* (*also*: **~ up**: *tree, hill etc*) wspinać (wspiąć *pf*) się na; (*stairs, steps*) wdrapywać (wdrapać *pf*) się po +*loc* ▷ *vi* **1** (*on frame, up mountain etc*) wspinać (wpiąć *pf*) się **2** (*move with effort*): **to ~ into a car** wsiadać (wsiąść *pf*) do samochodu ▷ *n* (*of mountain, hill*) wspinaczka; **to ~ into bed** kłaść (położyć *pf*) się do łóżka; **to ~ onto sth** (*roof, table*) wchodzić (wejść *pf*) na coś; **to ~ over sth** (*wall, fence*) przechodzić (przejść *pf*) przez coś
climber ['klaɪməʳ] *n* (*mountaineer*) alpinista(-tka) *m/f*
climbing ['klaɪmɪŋ] *n* wspinaczka; **to go ~** wspinać (wspiąć *pf*) się
clingfilm ['klɪŋfɪlm] (*Brit*) *n* folia
clinic ['klɪnɪk] (*Med*) *n* (*place*) przychodnia; (*session*) poradnia
clip [klɪp] *n* (*for papers etc*) spinacz; (*for hair*) spinka ▷ *vt* **1** (*fasten*) przypinać (przypiąć *pf*) **2** (*cut: hedge, nails*) obcinać (obciąć *pf*)
cloakroom ['kləukrum] *n* **1** (*for coats*) szatnia **2** (*Brit: bathroom*) toaleta publiczna
clock [klɔk] *n* zegar; **around the ~** (*work, guard*) dwadzieścia cztery godziny na dobę; **to turn** *or* **put the ~ back** (*fig*) cofać (cofnąć *pf*) czas
▸ **clock in** *vi* (*for work*) odbijać (odbić *pf*) kartę przychodząc do pracy
▸ **clock off** *vi* (*from work*) odbijać (odbić *pf*) kartę wychodząc z pracy
▸ **clock on** *vi* = **clock in**
▸ **clock out** *vi* = **clock off**
close¹ [kləus] *adj* **1** (*near*) bliski **2** (*relative*) bliski **3** (*contest*) wyrównany ▷ *adv* (*near*) blisko; **~ to** (*near*) w pobliżu; **a ~ friend** bliski przyjaciel; **to see sth ~ up** *or* **to** widzieć (zobaczyć *pf*) coś w zbliżeniu; **~ by, ~ at hand** w zasięgu ręki; **she was ~ to tears** była bliska łez
close² [kləuz] *vt* zamykać (zamknąć *pf*) ▷ *vi* zamykać (zamknąć *pf*) się
▸ **close down** *vi* (*factory, business*) zostać zamkniętym
closed [kləuzd] *adj* zamknięty
closely ['kləuslɪ] *adv* blisko
closet ['klɔzɪt] *n* (*US*) szafa
cloth [klɔθ] *n* **1** (*fabric*) tkanina **2** (*for cleaning, dusting*) ścierka **3** (*tablecloth*) obrus; **piece of ~** materiał

clothes [kləuðz] *n pl* ubranie; **to take one's ~ off** rozbierać (rozebrać *pf*) się
clothing ['kləuðɪŋ] *n* odzież; **an item** *or* **a piece of ~** sztuka odzieży
cloud [klaud] *n* chmura
▸ **cloud over** *vi* (*sky*) chmurzyć (zachmurzyć *pf*) się
cloudy ['klaudɪ] *adj* (*day, sky, weather*) pochmurny; **it's ~** jest pochmurno
clove [kləuv] *n* **1** (*spice*) goździk **2** (*of garlic*) ząbek
clown [klaun] *n* (*in circus*) klaun
club [klʌb] *n* **1** (*society, place*) klub **2** (*Sport*) klub **3** (*nightclub*) klub nocny **4** (*stick*: *also*: **golf ~**) kij golfowy ▷ *vi*: **to ~ together** (*Brit*: *for gift, card*) składać (złożyć *pf*) się; **clubs** *n pl* (*Cards*) trefl
clue [klu:] *n* wskazówka; **I haven't a ~** (*inf*) nie mam pojęcia
clumsy ['klʌmzɪ] *adj* (*person*) niezdarny
clutch [klʌtʃ] *vt* ściskać (ścisnąć *pf*) ▷ *n* (*Aut*) sprzęgło
clutter ['klʌtəʳ] *vt* (*also*: **~ up**) zagracać (zagracić *pf*) ▷ *n* rupiecie
coach [kəutʃ] *n* **1** (*Brit*) autokar **2** (*Brit*: *of train*) wagon **3** (*Sport*: *trainer*) trener(ka) *m/f* ▷ *vt* (*Sport*) trenować
coal [kəul] *n* (*substance*) węgiel
coarse [kɔ:s] *adj* **1** (*cloth, salt, sand*) szorstki **2** (*vulgar*: *person, remark*) ordynarny
coast [kəust] *n* wybrzeże
coastguard ['kəustgɑ:d] (*esp Brit*) *n* **1** (*person*) strażnik straży przybrzeżnej **2**: **the ~** (*service*) straż przybrzeżna
coat [kəut] *n* **1** (*overcoat*) płaszcz **2** (*of animal*) sierść **3** (*of paint, varnish*) warstwa
coat hanger *n* wieszak
cobweb ['kɔbwɛb] *n* pajęczyna
cocaine [kə'keɪn] *n* kokaina
cock [kɔk] *n* (*Brit*) kogut
cockerel ['kɔkərəl] (*esp Brit*) *n* kogucik
cocoa ['kəukəu] *n* kakao
coconut ['kəukənʌt] *n* kokos
cod [kɔd] (*pl* **cod** *or* **cods**) *n* **1** (*fish*) dorsz **2** (*as food*) dorsz
code [kəud] *n* **1** (*cipher*) szyfr **2** (*Tel*) numer kierunkowy **3** (*Comput, Sci*) kod
coffee ['kɔfɪ] *n* **1** kawa **2** (*cup of coffee*) filiżanka kawy; **black ~** czarna kawa; **white ~** kawa z mlekiem
coffee table *n* ława
coffin ['kɔfɪn] *n* trumna
coin [kɔɪn] *n* moneta
coincidence [kəu'ɪnsɪdəns] *n* zbieg okoliczności
Coke® [kəuk] *n* (*drink*) Coca Cola
colander ['kɔləndəʳ] *n* durszlak
cold [kəuld] *adj* zimny ▷ *n* **1** (*weather*): **the ~** zimno **2** (*illness*) przeziębienie; **it's ~** jest zimno; **I am/feel ~** (*person*) jest mi zimno; **to catch (a) ~** zaziębić się
coleslaw ['kəulslɔ:] (*Culin*) *n* surówka z białej kapusty
collapse [kə'læps] *vi* (*building, table*) walić (zawalić *pf*) się; (*person*) padać (paść *pf*)
collar ['kɔləʳ] *n* (*of coat, shirt*) kołnierz
collarbone ['kɔləbəun] *n* obojczyk
colleague ['kɔli:g] *n* kolega(-eżanka) *m/f*
collect [kə'lɛkt] *vt* **1** (*wood, litter etc*) zbierać (zebrać *pf*) **2** (*as hobby*) zbierać (zebrać *pf*) **3** (*Brit*: *fetch*) odbierać (odebrać *pf*) **4** (*money, donations*) zbierać (zebrać *pf*) ▷ *vi* (*for charity, gift*) kwestować; **to call ~, make a ~ call** (*US*: *Tel*) rozmawiać na koszt rozmówcy
collection [kə'lɛkʃən] *n* **1** (*of art, stamps etc*) kolekcja **2** (*of poems, stories etc*) antologia **3** (*for charity, gift*) zebrane pieniądze
collector [kə'lɛktəʳ] *n* (*of art, stamps etc*) kolekcjoner(ka) *m/f*
college ['kɔlɪdʒ] *n* **1** (*for further education*) szkoła wyższa **2** (*of university*) wydział; **to go to ~** studiować
collide [kə'laɪd] *vi* (*cars, people*) zderzać (zderzyć *pf*) się; **to ~ with sth/sb** zderzać (zderzyć *pf*) się z czymś/kimś
collision [kə'lɪʒən] *n* (*of vehicles*) kolizja
colon ['kəulən] *n* **1** (*punctuation mark*) dwukropek **2** (*Anat*) okrężnica

colonel ['kə:nl] *n* pułkownik
color *etc* ['kʌləʳ] (*US*) = **colour** *etc*
colour ['kʌləʳ] (*US* **color**) *n* kolor ▷ *vt* (*with paint, crayons, dye*) kolorować (pokolorować *pf*) ▷ *adj* (*film, photograph, television*) kolorowy; **in ~** (*film, illustrations*) barwny
colourful ['kʌləful] (*US* **colorful**) *adj* (*brightly coloured*) barwny
colour television (*US* **color television**) *n* telewizja kolorowa
column ['kɔləm] *n* **1** (*Archit*) kolumna **2** (*in newspaper etc*) rubryka
comb [kəum] *n* grzebień ▷ *vt* (*hair*) czesać (uczesać *pf*)
combination [kɔmbɪ'neɪʃən] *n* (*mixture*) połączenie
combine [kəm'baɪn] *vt*: **to ~ sth with sth** łączyć (połączyć *pf*) coś z czymś ▷ *vi* (*qualities, situations*) łączyć (połączyć *pf*); (*people, groups*) jednoczyć (zjednoczyć *pf*); **a ~d effort** wspólny wysiłek

 **KEYWORD**

come [kʌm] (*pt* **came**, *pp* **come**) *vi*
1 (*move towards, arrive*) przychodzić (przyjść *pf*); **come here!** chodź tutaj!; **can I come too?** czy też mogę przyjść?; **come with me** chodź ze mną; **a girl came into the room** dziewczyna weszła do pokoju; **why don't you come to lunch on Saturday?** może przyjdziesz na obiad w sobotę?; **he's come here to work** przyszedł tu pracować
2: **to come to** (*reach*) sięgać (sięgnąć *pf*) do *+gen*; (*amount to*) wynosić (wynieść *pf*); **to come to a decision** podejmować (podjąć *pf*) decyzję; **the bill came to £40** rachunek wyniósł czterdzieści funtów
3 (*be, become*): **to come first/ second/last** być pierwszym/ drugim/ostatnim
4 (*be available*): **it comes in blue or green** dostępne jest w kolorach niebieskim lub zielonym
▸ **come across** *vt fus* (*find*) spotykać (spotkać *pf*)
▸ **come apart** *vi* rozpadać (rozpaść *pf*) się
▸ **come back** *vi* (*return*) wracać (wrócić *pf*) do *+gen*; **I'm coming back to that** (*in discussion etc*) wrócę do tego
▸ **come down** *vi* **1** (*price*) spadać (spaść *pf*) **2** (*fall to ground: plane*) spadać (spaść *pf*) **3** (*descend*) schodzić (zejść *pf*)
▸ **come down with** *vt fus*: **to come down with sth** (*illness*) zachorować na coś
▸ **come forward** *vi* (*volunteer*) zgłaszać (zgłosić *pf*) się
▸ **come from** *vt fus* (*place, source*) pochodzić z *+gen*; **I come from London** pochodzę z Londynu; **where do you come from?** skąd pochodzisz?
▸ **come in** *vi* (*to room, house etc*) wchodzić (wejść *pf*); **come in!** wejdź!
▸ **come off** *vi* **1** (*button, handle*) urywać (urwać *pf*) się **2** (*succeed: event, attempt, plan*) dojść do skutku
▸ **come on** *vi* (*progress*) robić (zrobić *pf*) postępy; **come on!** (*giving encouragement*) no, spróbuj!; (*hurry up*) pospiesz się!
▸ **come out** *vi* **1** (*person: out of house, for evening etc*) wychodzić (wyjść *pf*) **2** (*appear: sun*) wyglądać (wyjrzeć *pf*) **3** (*become available: book*) pojawiać (pojawić *pf*) się; (*film*) wchodzić (wejść *pf*) na ekrany
▸ **come over** (*visit*) wpadać (wpaść *pf*); **I'll come over later** wpadnę później
▸ **come through** *vt fus* (*survive*) przechodzić (przejść *pf*)
▸ **come to** *vi* (*regain consciousness*) ocknąć się
▸ **come up** *vi* **1** (*approach*) podchodzić (podejść *pf*) **2** (*arise: problem, opportunity*) pojawiać (pojawić *pf*) się
▸ **come upon** *vt fus* (*find*) natknąć (*pf*) się na
▸ **come up to** *vt fus* **1** (*get on for*): **it's coming up to 11 o'clock** zbliża się jedenasta **2** (*approach*) zbliżać (zbliżyć *pf*) się do *+gen* **3** (*meet*): **the film didn't come up to our expectations** film nie spełnił naszych oczekiwań

comedian [kə'miːdɪən] (*Theat, TV*) *n* komik
comedy ['kɔmɪdɪ] *n* komedia
comfortable ['kʌmfətəbl] *adj* **1** (*person*): **to be ~** (*physically*) być odprężonym **2** (*furniture, room, clothes*) wygodny; **to make o.s. ~** siadać (usiąść *pf*) wygodnie
comic ['kɔmɪk] *adj* **1** (*also*: **~al**) komiczny **2** (*actor, opera*) komediowy ▷ *n* **1** (*comedian*) komik **2** (*Brit*: *magazine*) komiks
comic book (*US*) *n* komiks
comma ['kɔmə] *n* przecinek
command [kə'mɑːnd] *n* **1** (*order*) rozkaz **2** (*Comput*) polecenie
comment ['kɔmɛnt] *n* (*written, spoken*) komentarz ▷ *vi*: **to ~ (on sth)** komentować (skomentować *pf*) (coś); **"no ~"** „bez komentarza"; **to ~ that...** zauważać (zauważyć *pf*), że...
commentary ['kɔməntərɪ] *n* (*on match, proceedings*) komentarz
commentator ['kɔmənteɪtə^r] *n* (*describing match, proceedings*) komentator(ka) *m/f*
commercial [kə'məːʃəl] *adj* (*organization, activity*) handlowy; (*success, failure*) komercyjny; (*television, radio*) komercyjny ▷ *n* (*advertisement*) reklama
commit [kə'mɪt] *vt* (*crime, offence*) popełniać (popełnić *pf*); **to ~ suicide** popełnić samobójstwo
committee [kə'mɪtɪ] *n* komitet
common ['kɔmən] *adj* (*usual*) pospolity; **~ to** wspólny; **to have sth in ~** mieć coś wspólnego; **to have sth in ~ with sb/sth** mieć coś wspólnego z kimś/czymś
Commons ['kɔmənz] (*Brit*) *n*: **the (House of) ~** Izba Gmin

COMMONS

Commons – w Wielkiej Brytanii, Izba Gmin (**House of Commons**) jest jedną z dwóch izb parlamentu. Zasiada w niej 650 wybranych w wyborach powszechnych posłów (**Members of Parliament**), popularnie zwanych **MPs**.

common sense *n* zdrowy rozsądek
communicate [kə'mjuːnɪkeɪt] *vi* **1** (*by writing, speaking etc*) komunikować (skomunikować *pf*) się **2** (*talk openly*) porozumieć (porozumiewać *pf*) się ▷ *vt* (*idea, decision, feeling*) przekazywać (przekazać *pf*)
communication [kəmjuːnɪ'keɪʃən] *n* komunikacja; **communications** *n pl* łączność
communion [kə'mjuːnɪən] *n* (*also*: **Holy C~**) Komunia Święta
communism ['kɔmjunɪzəm] *n* komunizm
community [kə'mjuːnɪtɪ] *n* **1** (*neighbourhood*) społeczność **2**: **the business ~** świat biznesu; **the black/Jewish ~** czarna/żydowska społeczność
commute [kə'mjuːt] *vi* dojeżdżać do pracy; **to ~ to/from London/Brighton** dojeżdżać do/z Londynu/Brighton
compact disc ['kɔmpækt-] *n* płyta kompaktowa
company ['kʌmpənɪ] *n* **1** (*firm*) firma **2** (*companionship*) towarzystwo; **Smith and C~** Smith i wspólnicy; **to keep sb ~** dotrzymywać (dotrzymać *pf*) komuś towarzystwa
comparatively [kəm'pærətɪvlɪ] *adv* (*relatively*) stosunkowo
compare [kəm'pɛə^r] *vt* porównywać (porównać *pf*) ▷ *vi*: **to ~ favourably/unfavourably (with sth/sb)** prezentować (zaprezentować *pf*) się korzystnie/niekorzystnie (w porównaniu z czymś/kimś); **to ~ sb/sth to** (*liken to*) porównywać (porównać *pf*) kogoś/coś do *+gen*; **~d with** *or* **to** w porównaniu z *+inst*
comparison [kəm'pærɪsn] *n* porównanie; **in** *or* **by ~ (with)** w porównaniu (z *+inst*); **(there's) no ~** nie ma porównania
compartment [kəm'pɑːtmənt] *n* (*Rail*) przedział
compass ['kʌmpəs] *n* **1** (*for finding direction*) kompas **2** (*also*: **pair of ~es**: *for drawing circles*) cyrkiel
compatible [kəm'pætɪbl] *adj* (*people*) zgodny; (*Comput*)

kompatybilny; **to be ~ with sth** (*activity, idea*) być zgodnym z czymś; (*Comput*) być kompatybilnym z czymś

compensation [kɔmpən'seɪʃən] *n* (*money*) rekompensata; **~ for sth** (*money*) rekompensata za coś

compete [kəm'piːt] *vi* (*companies, rivals*) konkurować; (*in contest, game*) rywalizować; **to ~ for sth** (*companies, rivals*) konkurować o coś; (*in contest, game*) rywalizować o coś; **to ~ with sb/sth (for sth)** (*companies, rivals*) konkurować z kimś/czymś (o coś); (*in contest, game*) rywalizować z kimś/czymś (o coś)

competent ['kɔmpɪtənt] *adj* (*person*) kompetentny; (*piece of work*) zadowalający

competition [kɔmpɪ'tɪʃən] *n* **1** (*rivalry*) konkurencja **2** (*contest*) rywalizacja; **in ~ with** rywalizować z +*inst*

competitive [kəm'pɛtɪtɪv] *adj* **1** (*industry, society*) konkurencyjny **2** (*person*) ambitny

competitor [kəm'pɛtɪtəʳ] *n* **1** (*in business*) konkurent(ka) *m/f* **2** (*participant*) uczestnik(-iczka) *m/f*

complain [kəm'pleɪn] *vi*: **to ~ (about sth)** (*to relevant person*) składać (złożyć *pf*) skargę (na coś); (*grumble*) skarżyć (poskarżyć *pf*) się (na coś); **to ~ to sb (about sth)** skarżyć (poskarżyć *pf*) się komuś (na coś)

complaint [kəm'pleɪnt] *n* (*criticism*) skarga; **to make a ~ (to sb)** wnosić (wnieść *pf*) skargę (na ręce kogoś)

complete [kəm'pliːt] *adj* **1** (*total*) zupełny **2** (*whole*) całkowity **3** (*finished*) ukończony ▷ *vt* **1** (*finish*) kończyć (ukończyć *pf*) **2** (*fill in*) wypełniać (wypełnić *pf*); **~ with** wraz z +*inst*

completely [kəm'pliːtlɪ] *adv* (*different, satisfied, untrue etc*) całkowicie; (*forget, destroy etc*) zupełnie

complexion [kəm'plɛkʃən] *n* (*colouring*) karnacja

complicate ['kɔmplɪkeɪt] *vt* komplikować (skomplikować *pf*)

complicated ['kɔmplɪkeɪtɪd] *adj* skomplikowany

compliment [*n* 'kɔmplɪmənt, *vb* 'kɔmplɪmɛnt] *n* (*remark*) komplement ▷ *vt* chwalić (pochwalić *pf*); **to pay sb a ~** chwalić (pochwalić *pf*) kogoś; **to ~ sb on sth** gratulować (pogratulować *pf*) komuś czegoś

composer [kəm'pəuzəʳ] *n* kompozytor(ka) *m/f*

comprehension [kɔmprɪ'hɛnʃən] *n* **1** (*understanding*) zrozumienie **2** (*Scol*) ćwiczenia sprawdzające rozumienie

comprehensive [kɔmprɪ'hɛnsɪv] *adj* **1** (*review, list*) wyczerpujący **2** (*of insurance*) pełny ▷ *n* (*Brit*: *also*: **~ school**) szkoła średnia ogólna

COMPREHENSIVE SCHOOL

Comprehensive school to w Wielkiej Brytanii państwowa szkoła średnia dla uczniów w wieku 11 – 18 lat.

compulsory [kəm'pʌlsərɪ] *adj* obowiązkowy

computer [kəm'pjuːtəʳ] *n* komputer ▷ *adj* komputerowy

computer game *n* gra komputerowa

computer programmer *n* programista (-tka) *m/f*

computer science *n* informatyka

computing [kəm'pjuːtɪŋ] *n* (*also*: **~ studies**) informatyka

concentrate ['kɔnsəntreɪt] *vi* koncentrować (skoncentrować *pf*) się; **to ~ on sth** (*keep attention on*) koncentrować (skoncentrować *pf*) się na czymś; (*focus on*) skupiać (skupić *pf*) się na czymś

concentration [kɔnsən'treɪʃən] *n* **1** (*ability to concentrate*) koncentracja **2** (*focus*): **~ on sth/on doing sth** koncentracja na czymś/na robieniu czegoś

concern [kən'səːn] *n* **1** (*anxiety*) niepokój **2** (*affair*) sprawa ▷ *vt* (*worry*) martwić (zmartwić *pf*); **~ for sb** obawa o kogoś; **as far as I'm ~ed**

o ile mi wiadomo; **the people ~ed** zainteresowani

concerned [kən'sə:nd] *adj* (*worried*) zaniepokojony; **to be ~ about sb/sth** być zaniepokojonym o kogoś/coś; **we're ~ for her** niepokoimy się o nią

concerning [kən'sə:nɪŋ] *prep* odnośnie *+gen*

concert ['kɔnsət] *n* koncert

concert hall *n* sala koncertowa

conclusion [kən'klu:ʒən] *n* **1** (*end: of speech, chapter*) zakończenie **2** (*deduction*) wniosek; **to come to the ~ that...** dochodzić (dojść *pf*) do wniosku, że...

concrete ['kɔŋkri:t] *n* beton ▷ *adj* **1** (*lit: block, floor*) betonowy **2** (*fig: proposal, evidence*) konkretny

condemn [kən'dɛm] *vt* (*denounce*) potępiać (potępić *pf*)

condition [kən'dɪʃən] *n* **1** (*state*) stan **2** (*stipulation*) warunek; **conditions** *n pl* warunki; **in good/poor ~** w dobrym/złym stanie; **on ~ that...** pod warunkiem, że...; **weather ~s** warunki pogodowe

conditional [kən'dɪʃənl] *adj* warunkowy ▷ *n* (*Ling*): **the ~** tryb warunkowy

conditioner [kən'dɪʃənəʳ] *n* (*for hair*) odżywka

condom ['kɔndəm] *n* prezerwatywa

conduct [kən'dʌkt] *vt* (*orchestra, choir etc*) dyrygować

conductor [kən'dʌktəʳ] *n* **1** (*of orchestra*) dyrygent(ka) *m/f* **2** (*US: on train*) konduktor(ka) *m/f* **3** (*on bus*) konduktor(ka) *m/f*

cone [kəun] *n* **1** (*shape*) stożek **2** (*also:* **traffic ~**) pachołek **3** (*on tree*) szyszka **4** (*also:* **ice cream ~**) rożek

conference ['kɔnfərəns] *n* (*meeting*) konferencja

confess [kən'fɛs] *vi* (*to sin, crime*) przyznawać (przyznać *pf*) się; **to ~ to sth/to doing sth** przyznawać (przyznać *pf*) się do czegoś/zrobienia czegoś; **I must ~ that...** muszę przyznać, że...

confession [kən'fɛʃən] *n* **1** (*admission*) przyznanie się **2** (*written*) zeznanie **3** (*Rel*) spowiedź; **to make a ~** przyznawać (przyznać *pf*) się

confidence ['kɔnfɪdns] *n* **1** (*faith*) zaufanie **2** (*self-assurance*) pewność siebie; **in ~** (*speak, say, write etc*) w tajemnicy

confident ['kɔnfɪdənt] *adj* (*self-assured*) pewny siebie; **to be ~ that...** być pewnym, że...

confidential [kɔnfɪ'dɛnʃəl] *adj* (*report, information*) poufny

confirm [kən'fə:m] *vt* potwierdzać (potwierdzić *pf*); **to ~ that...** (*person, data*) potwierdzać (potwierdzić *pf*), że...

confiscate ['kɔnfɪskeɪt] *vt* konfiskować (skonfiskować *pf*); **to ~ sth from sb** konfiskować (skonfiskować *pf*) coś komuś

confuse [kən'fju:z] *vt* **1** (*perplex*) gmatwać (zagmatwać *pf*) **2** (*mix up*) mylić (pomylić *pf*)

confused [kən'fju:zd] *adj* (*bewildered*) zdezorientowany

confusing [kən'fju:zɪŋ] *adj* zagmatwany

confusion [kən'fju:ʒən] *n* **1** (*uncertainty*) zamieszanie **2** (*mix-up*) nieporozumienie

congratulate [kən'grætjuleɪt] *vt* gratulować (pogratulować *pf*); **to ~ sb on sth/on doing sth** gratulować (pogratulować *pf*) komuś z okazji czegoś/zrobienia czegoś

congratulations [kəngrætju'leɪʃənz] *n pl* gratulacje; **~ on your engagement!** gratulacje z okazji zaręczyn!

Congress ['kɔŋgrɛs] *n* (*US*) Kongres

congressman ['kɔŋgrɛsmən] (*irreg*) *n* (*US*) kongresman

congresswoman ['kɔŋgrɛswumən] (*irreg*) *n* (*US*) członkini Kongresu

conjunction [kən'dʒʌŋkʃən] (*Ling*) *n* spójnik

connection [kə'nɛkʃən] *n* **1** (*link*) związek **2** (*Elec*) podłączenie **3** (*train, plane etc*) połączenie; **what is the ~ between them?** jaki jest między nimi związek?

conscience ['kɔnʃəns] *n* (*sense of morality*) sumienie; **to have a guilty ~** mieć wyrzuty sumienia; **to have clear ~** mieć czyste sumienie

conscientious [kɔnʃɪ'ɛnʃəs] *adj* sumienny

conscious ['kɔnʃəs] *adj* **1** (*awake*) świadomy **2** (*deliberate*: *decision, effort*) świadomy; **to be ~ of sth** być świadomym czegoś; **to be ~ that...** być świadomym tego, że...

consciousness ['kɔnʃəsnɪs] *n* (*Med*) przytomność; **to lose ~** (*black out*) tracić (stracić *pf*) przytomność

consequence ['kɔnsɪkwəns] *n* (*result*) konsekwencja

consequently ['kɔnsɪkwəntlɪ] *adv* w konsekwencji

conservation [kɔnsə'veɪʃən] *n* (*of environment*) ochrona; (*of energy etc*) oszczędzanie

conservative [kən'səːvətɪv] *adj* **1** (*traditional*) konserwatywny **2** (*Brit*: *Pol*): **C~** konserwatywny ▷ *n* (*Brit*: *Pol*): **C~** konserwatysta(-tka) *m/f*

conservatory [kən'səːvətrɪ] *n* (*on house*) oszklona weranda

consider [kən'sɪdəʳ] *vt* **1** (*think about*) rozważać (rozważyć *pf*) **2** (*take into account*) rozpatrywać (rozpatrzyć *pf*) **3** (*believe*): **to ~ sb (to be) an idiot/a coward** uważać kogoś za idiotę/tchórza; **to ~ doing sth** zastanawiać (zastanowić *pf*) się nad zrobieniem czegoś; **all things ~ed** w sumie

considerate [kən'sɪdərɪt] *adj* taktowny

considering [kən'sɪdərɪŋ] *prep* zważywszy ▷ *conj*: **~ (that)...** zważywszy (że)...

consist [kən'sɪst] *vi*: **to ~ of** składać się z

consonant ['kɔnsənənt] *n* spółgłoska

constant ['kɔnstənt] *adj* **1** (*ever-present*) stały **2** (*repeated*) ciągły **3** (*fixed*) stały

constantly ['kɔnstəntlɪ] *adv* **1** (*repeatedly*) ciągle **2** (*uninterruptedly*) nieustannie

constipated ['kɔnstɪpeɪtɪd] *adj* cierpiący na zaparcie

construct [kən'strʌkt] *vt* budować (zbudować *pf*)

construction [kən'strʌkʃən] *n* **1** (*of building, road, machine*) budowa **2** (*structure*) konstrukcja

consult [kən'sʌlt] *vt* (*doctor, lawyer, friend*) radzić (poradzić *pf*) się *+gen*; (*book, map*) sprawdzać (sprawdzić *pf*)

consumer [kən'sjuːməʳ] *n* (*of goods, services*) konsument(ka) *m/f*; (*of resources*) odbiorca

contact ['kɔntækt] *n* kontakt ▷ *vt* kontaktować (skontaktować *pf*) się z *+inst*; **to be in ~ with sb** kontaktować (skontaktować *pf*) się z kimś

contact lenses [-lɛnzɪz] *n pl* szkła kontaktowe

contactless ['kɔntæktlɪs] *adj* bezprzewodowa

contain [kən'teɪn] *vt* zawierać (zawrzeć *pf*)

container [kən'teɪnəʳ] *n* **1** (*box, jar etc*) pojemnik **2** (*for transport*) kontener

content¹ ['kɔntɛnt] *n* (*of speech, book, film*) treść; **contents** *n pl* (*of bottle, packet*) zawartość

content² [kən'tɛnt] *adj* (*satisfied*) zadowolony

contest ['kɔntɛst] *n* (*competition*) konkurs

contestant [kən'tɛstənt] *n* zawodnik(-iczka) *m/f*

context ['kɔntɛkst] *n* kontekst

continent ['kɔntɪnənt] *n* kontynent; **on the C~** (*Brit*) na kontynencie europejskim

continental breakfast [kɔntɪ'nɛntl-] *n* śniadanie kontynentalne

continue [kən'tɪnjuː] *vi* **1** (*carry on uninterrupted*) kontynuować **2** (*after interruption*: *event*) wznawiać (wznowić *pf*); (*speaker*) mówić dalej ▷ *vt* **1** (*carry on uninterrupted*) trwać **2** (*after interruption*) wznawiać (wznowić *pf*); **to ~ to do sth** *or* **doing sth** robić coś dalej; **to ~ with sth** kontynuować coś

continuous [kən'tɪnjuəs] *adj* **1** (*process, growth etc*) stały **2** (*Ling*: *tense*) ciągły

contraception [kɔntrə'sɛpʃən] *n* antykoncepcja

contraceptive [kɔntrə'sɛptɪv] *n* (*drug*) tabletka antykoncepcyjna; (*device*) środek antykoncepcyjny

contract ['kɔntrækt] *n* umowa
contradict [kɔntrə'dɪkt] *vt* (*person, statement etc*) zaprzeczać (zaprzeczyć *pf*)
contradiction [kɔntrə'dɪkʃən] *n* sprzeczność
contrary ['kɔntrərɪ] *adj* (*opposite, different*) sprzeczny ▷ *n*: **the ~** przeciwieństwo; **on the ~** wręcz przeciwnie
contrast [*n* 'kɔntrɑːst, *vb* kən'trɑːst] *n* **1** kontrast **2**: **to be a ~ to sth** stanowić kontrast względem czegoś ▷ *vt* porównywać (porównać *pf*) ▷ *vi*: **to ~ with sth** zestawiać (zestawić *pf*) z czymś; **to ~ sth with sth** zestawiać (zestawić *pf*) coś z czymś
contribute [kən'trɪbjuːt] *vi* (*with money*) ofiarowywać (ofiarować *pf*) ▷ *vt*: **to ~ £10 (to sth)** przekazywać (przekazać *pf*) dziesięć funtów (na coś)
contribution [kɔntrɪ'bjuːʃən] *n* (*donation*) datek
control [kən'trəul] *vt* (*country, organization*) kierować; (*person, emotion, disease, fire*) kontrolować (skontrolować *pf*) ▷ *n* (*of country, organization*) władza; (*of people*) panowanie; (*of vehicle, machine*) kierowanie; **controls** *n pl* (*of vehicle, machine*) stery; (*of TV*) regulacja; **to ~ o.s.** panować nad sobą; **to lose ~ (of sth)** (*emotionally*) tracić (stracić *pf*) panowanie (nad czymś); (*in vehicle, on machine*) tracić (stracić *pf*) panowanie (nad czymś); **to be in ~ (of sth)** (*of situation, car etc*) kontrolować (skontrolować *pf*) (coś); **to have sth under ~** (*fire, situation*) panować nad czymś; **to be out of ~** (*fire, situation*) wymykać (wymknąć *pf*) się spod kontroli; **circumstances beyond our ~** okoliczności niezależne od nas
controversial [kɔntrə'vəːʃl] *adj* kontrowersyjny
convenient [kən'viːnɪənt] *adj* (*method, system, time*) praktyczny; (*place*) dogodny
conventional [kən'vɛnʃənl] *adj* konwencjonalny
conversation [kɔnvə'seɪʃən] *n* rozmowa; **to have a ~ (about sth/with sb)** rozmawiać (porozmawiać *pf*) (o czymś/z kimś)
convert [kən'vəːt] *vt* (*transform: substance*) przetwarzać (przetworzyć *pf*); (*building*) przerabiać (przerobić *pf*); **to ~ sth into sth** (*substance*) zmieniać (zmienić *pf*) coś w coś; (*building*) przerabiać (przerobić *pf*) coś na coś
convince [kən'vɪns] *vt* **1** (*cause to believe*) przekonywać (przekonać *pf*) **2** (*esp US: persuade*) namawiać (namówić *pf*); **to ~ sb that...** przekonywać (przekonać *pf*) kogoś, że...; **to ~ sb to do sth** (*esp US*) namawiać (namówić *pf*) kogoś do zrobienia czegoś
cook [kuk] *vt* (*food, meat, vegetables*) gotować (ugotować *pf*); (*meal*) przyrządzać (przyrządzić *pf*) ▷ *vi* **1** (*person*) gotować (ugotować *pf*) **2** (*food*) gotować (ugotować *pf*) się ▷ *n* kucharz(-rka) *m/f*; **he is a good ~** on dobrze gotuje
cooker ['kukə^r] (*Brit*) *n* kuchenka
cookery ['kukərɪ] *n* sztuka kulinarna
cookie ['kukɪ] *n* **1** (*US: for eating*) ciastko **2** (*Comput*) cookies
cooking ['kukɪŋ] *n* **1** (*activity*) gotowanie **2** (*food*) kuchnia ▷ *adj* (*apples, chocolate*) jadalny; (*utensils*) kuchenny
cool [kuːl] *adj* **1** (*water, breeze, evening, place*) chłodny **2** (*calm, unemotional*) spokojny **3** (*inf: good*) na luzie; (*fashionable*) cool, odjazdowy ▷ *vt* studzić (ostudzić *pf*) ▷ *vi* stygnąć (ostygnąć *pf*) ▷ *n*: **to keep one's ~** (*inf*) zachowywać (zachować *pf*) spokój; **to lose one's ~** (*inf*) tracić (stracić *pf*) głowę; **to keep sth ~** przechowywać (przechować *pf*) coś w chłodnym miejscu
▶ **cool down** *vi* (*become colder*) stygnąć (ostygnąć *pf*)
co-operate [kəu'ɔpəreɪt] *vi* **1** (*collaborate*) współpracować **2** (*be helpful*) współdziałać
cop [kɔp] (*inf*) *n* gliniarz
cope [kəup] *vi* radzić (poradzić *pf*) sobie; **to ~ with sth** (*problem, situation, task*) radzić (poradzić *pf*) sobie z czymś

copper ['kɔpəʳ] *n* (*metal*) miedź

copy ['kɔpɪ] *n* **1** (*duplicate*) kopia **2** (*issue*) egzemplarz ▷ *vt* **1** (*imitate: person, idea etc*) naśladować **2** (*also:* **~ out**) przepisywać (przepisać *pf*); **to make a ~ of sth** robić (zrobić *pf*) kopię czegoś

▸ **copy down** *vt* przepisywać (przepisać *pf*)

core [kɔːʳ] *n* (*of fruit*) gniazdo; (*of nuclear reactor*) rdzeń

cork [kɔːk] *n* korek

corkscrew ['kɔːkskruː] *n* korkociąg

corn [kɔːn] *n* **1** (*Brit: cereal crop*) zboże **2** (*US: maize*) kukurydza; **~ on the cob** kolba kukurydzy

corner ['kɔːnəʳ] *n* **1** kąt **2** (*of road*) róg; **to be (just) round** *or* **around the ~** (*fig*) być za rogiem

cornflakes ['kɔːnfleɪks] *n pl* płatki kukurydziane

corpse [kɔːps] *n* zwłoki

correct [kə'rɛkt] *adj* (*answer, details, amount, spelling*) poprawny; (*decision, means, procedure*) właściwy ▷ *vt* poprawiać (poprawić *pf*); **you are ~** masz rację

correction [kə'rɛkʃən] *n* korekta

corridor ['kɔrɪdɔːʳ] *n* korytarz

corruption [kə'rʌpʃən] *n* korupcja

cosmetics [kɔz'mɛtɪks] *n pl* (*beauty products*) kosmetyki

cosmetic surgery [kɔz'mɛtɪk 'səːdʒərɪ] *n* chirurgia plastyczna

cost [kɔst] (*pt, pp* **cost**) *n* koszt ▷ *vt* (*be priced at*) kosztować; **how much does it ~?** ile to kosztuje?; **it ~s 5 pounds/too much** kosztuje pięć funtów/zbyt dużo; **the ~ of living** koszty utrzymania

costume ['kɔstjuːm] *n* (*of actor, artist*) kostium

cosy ['kəuzɪ] (*US* **cozy**) *adj* (*room, house*) przytulny

cot [kɔt] *n* **1** (*Brit: child's*) łóżeczko dziecięce **2** (*US: bed*) łóżko polowe

cottage ['kɔtɪdʒ] *n* chata

cotton ['kɔtn] *n* **1** (*fabric*) bawełna **2** (*thread*) bawełna ▷ *adj* (*dress, sheets etc*) bawełniany

cotton candy (*US*) *n* wata cukrowa

cotton wool (*Brit*) *n* wata

couch [kautʃ] *n* kanapa

cough [kɔf] *vi* (*person*) kasłać (kaszlnąć *pf*) ▷ *n* (*noise, illness*) kaszel; **to have a ~** mieć kaszel

KEYWORD

could [kud] *aux vb* **1** (*referring to past*): **we couldn't go to the party** nie mogliśmy iść na przyjęcie; **he couldn't read or write** nie umiał ani czytać ani pisać; **we could hear him whistling** słyszeliśmy jak gwiżdże; **she said she couldn't hear me** powiedziała, że mnie nie słyszy

2 (*possibility*): **he could be in the library** może jest w bibliotece; **he could be released next year** może być zwolniony w przyszłym roku; **you could have been killed!** mogłeś zostać zabity!

3 (*in conditionals with "if"*): **if we had more time, I could finish this** jeśli mielibyśmy więcej czasu, mógłbym to skończyć; **we'd have a holiday, if we could afford it** pojechalibyśmy na wakacje, jeśli moglibyśmy sobie na to pozwolić

4 (*in offers, suggestions, requests*) móc; **I could call a doctor** mógłbym zadzwonić po lekarza; **couldn't she give him a call?** mogłaby do niego zadzwonić?; **could I borrow the car?** mógłbym pożyczyć samochód?; **if I could just interrupt you for a minute** mogę przerwać Ci na chwilę?; **he asked if he could make a phone call** zapytał, czy może zadzwonić

5 (*emphatic*): **he could at least be polite!** mógłby chociaż być miły!; **he could have told me!** mógłby mi powiedzieć!

council ['kaunsl] *n* (*of city, county*) rada

councillor ['kaunsləʳ] *n* radny(-na) *m/f*

count [kaunt] *vt* **1** (*also:* **~ up**) liczyć (policzyć *pf*) **2** (*include*) zaliczać (zaliczyć *pf*) ▷ *vi* **1** (*add*) liczyć (policzyć *pf*) **2** (*matter*) liczyć się; **to ~ (up) to 10** liczyć (policzyć *pf*) do

dziesięciu; **to keep/lose ~ of sth** tracić (stracić *pf*) rachubę czegoś
▸ **count on, count upon** *vt fus* liczyć na
counter ['kauntəʳ] *n* **1** (*desk: in shop, café*) lada; (*bank, post office*) okienko **2** (*in game*) pionek
country ['kʌntrɪ] *n* **1** (*nation*) kraj **2** (*population*) naród **3** (*native land*) ojczyzna **4** (*countryside*): **the ~** wieś
countryside ['kʌntrɪsaɪd] *n* wieś
county ['kauntɪ] *n* hrabstwo
couple ['kʌpl] *n* para; **a ~ of** (*two*) para +*gen*; (*a few*) parę +*gen*
courage ['kʌrɪdʒ] *n* odwaga
courageous [kə'reɪdʒəs] *adj* odważny
courgette [kuə'ʒɛt] (*Brit*) *n* cukinia
courier ['kurɪəʳ] *n* **1** (*messenger*) kurier **2** (*rep*) posłaniec
course [kɔːs] *n* **1** (*educational*) kurs **2** (*of meal*) danie **3** (*for golf*) pole; (*horse-racing*) tor; **of ~** (*naturally*) oczywiście; (*certainly*) naturalnie; **of ~!** oczywiście!; **of ~ not!** oczywiście, że nie!
court [kɔːt] *n* **1** (*Law: place*) sąd **2** (*for tennis, badminton etc*) kort **3** (*royal*) dwór; **to take sb to ~** pozywać (pozwać *pf*) kogoś do sądu
courthouse ['kɔːthaus] (*US*) *n* gmach sądu
courtyard ['kɔːtjɑːd] *n* dziedziniec
cousin ['kʌzn] *n* kuzyn(ka) *m/f*
cover ['kʌvəʳ] *vt* **1**: **to ~ sth (with sth)** przykrywać (przykryć *pf*) coś (czymś) **2** (*in insurance*): **to ~ sb (against sth)** ubezpieczać (ubezpieczyć *pf*) kogoś (na wypadek czegoś) **3** (*be sufficient money for*) pokrywać (pokryć *pf*) ▹ *n* **1** (*for furniture, machinery etc*) nakrycie **2** (*jacket: of book, magazine*) okładka **3** (*insurance*) ochrona; **covers** *n pl* (*on bed*) nakrycie; **to be ~ed in sth** (*mud, blood, dust etc*) być pokrytym czymś
▸ **cover up** *vt* (*facts, feelings, mistakes*) ukrywać (ukryć *pf*) ▹ *vi*: **to ~ up for sb** kryć kogoś
cow [kau] *n* (*farm animal*) krowa
coward ['kauəd] *n* tchórz
cowboy ['kaubɔɪ] *n* (*in US*) kowboj
cozy ['kəuzɪ] (*US*) *adj* = **cosy**
crab [kræb] *n* krab
crack [kræk] *n* **1** (*in bone, dish, glass, wall*) pęknięcie **2** (*gap*) szpara **3** (*inf: drug*) crack ▹ *vt* (*dish, glass, mirror*) zarysowywać (zarysować *pf*); (*nut, egg*) rozbijać (rozbić *pf*) ▹ *vi* (*dish, mirror, pipe*) pękać (pęknąć *pf*)
▸ **crack down on** *vt fus* (*drug dealers, crime etc*) rozprawiać (rozprawić *pf*) się z +*inst*
▸ **crack up** *vi* (*inf: mentally*) wariować (zwariować *pf*)
cracked [krækt] *adj* (*dish, glass, mirror*) popękany
cracker ['krækəʳ] *n* **1** (*biscuit*) krakers **2** (*also*: **Christmas ~**) zabawka bożonarodzeniowa z niespodzianką, wydająca dzwięk podobny do trzaśnięcia podczas otwierania
cradle ['kreɪdl] *n* (*baby's*) kołyska
craft [krɑːft] *n* **1** (*pl* **craft**) (*boat*) statek; (*plane*) samolot **2** (*weaving, pottery etc*) rzemiosło
cramp [kræmp] *n* skurcz
crane [kreɪn] *n* (*machine*) dźwig
crash [kræʃ] *n* **1** (*of car*) wypadek; (*of plane*) katastrofa **2** (*noise*) trzask ▹ *vt* (*car, plane etc*) rozbijać (rozbić *pf*) ▹ *vi* **1** rozbijać (rozbić *pf*) się **2** (*Comput*) zawieszać (zawiesić *pf*) się; **a car/plane ~** katastrofa samochodowa/lotnicza; **to ~ into sth** wpadać (wpaść *pf*) na coś
crawl [krɔːl] *vi* (*adult, child*) czołgać się; (*insect*) pełzać; (*vehicle*) wlec się ▹ *n* (*also*: **the ~**: *in swimming*) kraul; **to do the ~** pływać (płynąć *pf*) kraulem
crayon ['kreɪən] *n* kredka
crazy ['kreɪzɪ] (*inf*) *adj* (*mad*) szalony; **to be ~ about sth** szaleć za czymś; **to go ~** oszaleć
cream [kriːm] *n* **1** (*dairy cream*) śmietanka **2** (*for skin*) krem ▹ *adj* (*in colour*) kremowy
crease [kriːs] *n* (*in cloth, paper: fold*) zagięcie; (*wrinkle*) zmarszczka; (*in trousers*) kant ▹ *vt* (*wrinkle*) marszczyć (zmarszczyć *pf*)
create [kriː'eɪt] *vt* (*job, situation, wealth, problem etc*) stwarzać (stworzyć *pf*); (*feeling*) wywoływać (wywołać *pf*)

creative [kriːˈeɪtɪv] *adj (person)* twórczy
creature [ˈkriːtʃəʳ] *n (animal)* stworzenie
crèche [krɛʃ] *(Brit) n* żłobek
credit [ˈkrɛdɪt] *n* **1** *(financial)* kredyt **2** *(recognition)* uznanie **3** *(Scol, Univ)* punkty ▷ *vt*: **the money will be ~ed to your account** pieniądze zostaną zaksięgowane na pana/pani koncie; **credits** *n pl* napisy; **to be in ~** *(esp Brit: person, bank account)* mieć dodatnie saldo; **on ~** na kredyt
credit card *n* karta kredytowa
credit crunch [-krʌntʃ] *n* kryzys kredytowy
crew [kruː] *n* **1** *(of ship, aircraft, spacecraft)* załoga **2** *(TV)* ekipa
crib [krɪb] *n (US: for baby)* łóżeczko dziecięce
cricket [ˈkrɪkɪt] *n* **1** *(Sport)* krykiet **2** *(insect)* świerszcz
crime [kraɪm] *n* **1** *(illegal act)* przestępstwo **2** *(illegal activities)* przestępczość **3** *(fig)* zbrodnia
criminal [ˈkrɪmɪnl] *n* przestępca(-czyni) *m/f* ▷ *adj (Law)* przestępczy
crisis [ˈkraɪsɪs] *(pl* **crises** [ˈkraɪsiːz]) *n* kryzys
crisp [krɪsp] *adj (bacon, biscuit)* chrupiący; *(lettuce, apple)* kruchy ▷ *n (Brit)* chips
critical [ˈkrɪtɪkl] *adj* **1** *(crucial)* decydujący **2** *(serious)* krytyczny **3** *(seriously ill)* krytyczny
criticism [ˈkrɪtɪsɪzəm] *n* krytyka
criticize [ˈkrɪtɪsaɪz] *vt* krytykować (skrytykować *pf*)
Croatia [krəuˈeɪʃə] *n* Chorwacja
crochet [ˈkrəuʃeɪ] *n* szydełkowanie ▷ *vi, vt* szydełkować
crocodile [ˈkrɔkədaɪl] *n* krokodyl
crook [kruk] *n (inf: criminal)* oszust(ka) *m/f*
crooked [ˈkrukɪd] *adj* **1** *(twisted: nose, teeth)* krzywy; *(line)* zakrzywiony **2** *(off-centre: picture, tie)* przekrzywiony
crop [krɔp] *n* **1** *(plants)* uprawa **2** *(amount produced)* plon
cross [krɔs] *n* **1** *(x shape)* krzyżyk **2** *(crucifix shape)* krzyż **3** *(Rel)* krzyż **4** *(mixture)*: **a ~ between sth and sth** krzyżówka czegoś z czymś ▷ *vt* przechodzić (przejść *pf*) ▷ *vi (roads, lines)* krzyżować (skrzyżować *pf*) się ▷ *adj (angry)* rozgniewany; **to be/get ~ about sth** być złym z powodu czegoś
▶ **cross off** *vt (delete)* skreślać (skreślić *pf*)
▶ **cross out** *vt (delete)* skreślać (skreślić *pf*)
▶ **cross over** *vi (cross the street)* przechodzić (przejść *pf*) na drugą stronę
cross-country [krɔsˈkʌntrɪ] *n (running)* bieg przełajowy ▷ *adj (running, race, skier, journey etc)* przełajowy ▷ *adv*: **to go ~** biegać na przełaj
crossing [ˈkrɔsɪŋ] *n* **1** *(voyage)* przeprawa **2** *(Brit: also:* **pedestrian ~**) przejście dla pieszych
crossroads [ˈkrɔsrəudz] *(pl* **crossroads**) *n* skrzyżowanie
crosswalk [ˈkrɔswɔːk] *(US) n* przejście dla pieszych
crossword [ˈkrɔswəːd] *n (also:* **~ puzzle**) krzyżówka
crouch [krautʃ] *vi (also:* **~ down**) robić (zrobić *pf*) przysiad
crow [krəu] *n (bird)* wrona
crowd [kraud] *n (of people, fans etc)* tłum ▷ *vi (gather)*: **to ~ around sb/sth** gromadzić (zgromadzić *pf*) się wokół kogoś/czegoś; **~s of people** tłumy ludzi
crowded [ˈkraudɪd] *adj* **1** *(full: room, ship, train)* zatłoczony **2** *(densely populated: area)* przeludniony
crowdfunding [ˈkraudfʌndɪŋ] *n* crowdfunding
crown [kraun] *n (of monarch)* korona
crude [kruːd] *adj* **1** *(simple)* prymitywny **2** *(not processed)* surowy
cruel [ˈkruəl] *adj* okrutny; **to be ~ to sb** być okrutnym w stosunku do kogoś
cruelty [ˈkruəltɪ] *n (of person)* okrucieństwo
cruise [kruːz] *n* rejs ▷ *vi (go on cruise)* odbywać (odbyć *pf*) rejs; **to be/go on a ~** odbywać (odbyć *pf*) rejs

crumb [krʌm] *n* (*of bread, cake*) okruch
crunchy ['krʌntʃɪ] *adj* chrupiący
crush [krʌʃ] *vt* **1** (*tin, box*) zgniatać (zgnieść *pf*) **2** (*break up*: *garlic*) wyciskać (wycisnąć *pf*); (*ice*) kruszyć (rozkruszyć *pf*) **3** (*squeeze*: *person*) miażdżyć (zmiażdżyć *pf*)
crutch [krʌtʃ] *n* (*stick*) kula inwalidzka
cry [kraɪ] *vi* (*weep*) płakać ▷ *vt* (*also*: **~ out**) krzyczeć (krzyknąć *pf*) ▷ *n* krzyk; **what are you ~ing about?** dlaczego płaczesz?
crystal ['krɪstl] *n* kryształ
cub [kʌb] *n* **1** (*young lion, wolf, fox, bear*) młode **2** (*also*: **~ scout**) zuch; **the Cubs** *n pl* (*also*: **the C~ Scouts**) Zuchy
cube [kju:b] *n* **1** (*shape*) sześcian **2** (*Math*: *of number*) trzecia potęga
cuckoo ['kuku:] *n* kukułka
cucumber ['kju:kʌmbəʳ] *n* ogórek
cuddle ['kʌdl] *vt* przytulać (przytulić *pf*) ▷ *vi* przytulać (przytulić *pf*) się ▷ *n*: **to give sb a ~** przytulać (przytulić *pf*) kogoś
cue [kju:] *n* (*fig*): **a ~ for sth** znak do rozpoczęcia czegoś
cultural ['kʌltʃərəl] *adj* (*heritage, tradition, exchange*) kulturowy
culture ['kʌltʃəʳ] *n* kultura
cunning ['kʌnɪŋ] *adj* (*person, plan, idea*) przebiegły
cup [kʌp] *n* **1** (*for drinking*) filiżanka **2** (*trophy*) puchar **3** (*quantity*) szklanka; **a ~ of tea** filiżanka herbaty
cupboard ['kʌbəd] *n* szafka
curb [kə:b] *n* (*US*) = **kerb**
cure [kjuəʳ] *vt* leczyć (wyleczyć *pf*) ▷ *n* (*Med*) kuracja
curious ['kjuərɪəs] *adj* **1** (*inquisitive*) ciekawy **2** (*strange*): **to be ~ about sth** być ciekawym czegoś; **I'm ~ about her** ona mnie interesuje
curl [kə:l] *n* (*of hair*) lok ▷ *vi* (*hair*) kręcić (zakręcić *pf*) się
curly ['kə:lɪ] *adj* (*hair, tail*) kręcony; (*leaves*) poskręcany
currant ['kʌrnt] *n* (*dried grape*) porzeczka
currency ['kʌrnsɪ] *n* waluta
current ['kʌrnt] *n* prąd ▷ *adj* (*present*) obecny
current affairs *n pl* aktualne wydarzenia; **a ~ programme** aktualności *f pl*
curriculum [kə'rɪkjuləm] (*pl* **curriculums** *or* **curricula** [kə'rɪkjulə]) *n* program nauczania
curriculum vitae [-'vi:taɪ] (*esp Brit*) *n* CV
curry ['kʌrɪ] *n* (*dish*) curry
cursor ['kə:səʳ] (*Comput*) *n* kursor
curtain ['kə:tn] *n* (*esp Brit*: *at window*) zasłona; **to draw the ~s** (*together*) zasuwać (zasunąć *pf*) zasłony; (*apart*) rozsuwać (rozsunąć *pf*) zasłony
cushion ['kuʃən] *n* (*on sofa, chair*) poduszka
custard ['kʌstəd] *n* budyń
custody ['kʌstədɪ] *n* **1** (*of child*) opieka **2** (*for offenders*) areszt
custom ['kʌstəm] *n* **1** (*tradition*) obyczaj **2** (*convention*) zwyczaj; **customs** *n pl* odprawa celna; **to go through ~s** przechodzić (przejść *pf*) przez odprawę celną
customer ['kʌstəməʳ] *n* (*in shop*) klient(ka) *m/f*
customs officer ['kʌstəmz 'ɔfɪsəʳ] *n* celnik(-iczka) *m/f*
cut [kʌt] (*pt, pp* **cut**) *vt* **1** (*bread, meat*) kroić (pokroić *pf*) **2** (*injure*): **to ~ one's hand/knee** kaleczyć (skaleczyć *pf*) się w rękę/kolano **3** (*shorten*: *grass, hair, nails*) przycinać (przyciąć *pf*) **4** (*remove*: *scene, episode, paragraph*) wycinać (wyciąć *pf*) **5** (*reduce*: *prices, spending*) obniżać (obniżyć *pf*) ▷ *n* **1** (*injury*) skaleczenie **2** (*reduction*) cięcie; **to ~ sth in half** (*food, object*) przecinać (przeciąć *pf*) coś na pół; **to ~ o.s.** zaciąć się; **to get** *or* **have one's hair ~** ostrzyc się; **to make a ~ in sth** nacinać (naciąć *pf*) coś; **a ~ and blow-dry** strzyżenie i modelowanie
▸ **cut down** *vt* **1** (*tree*) ścinać (ściąć *pf*) **2** (*reduce*: *consumption etc*) obniżać (obniżyć *pf*)
▸ **cut down on** *vt fus* (*alcohol, coffee, cigarettes etc*) ograniczać (ograniczyć *pf*)
▸ **cut off** *vt* odcinać (odciąć *pf*)

▸ **cut out** *vt* (*coupon, newspaper article*) wycinać (wyciąć *pf*)
▸ **cut up** *vt* (*paper, food*) kroić (pokroić *pf*)
cute [kjuːt] *adj* **1** (*inf: sweet*) słodki **2** (*esp US: inf: attractive*) fajny
cutlery ['kʌtlərɪ] (*Brit*) *n* sztućce
CV *n abbr* (= *curriculum vitae*) CV
cyberbullying ['saɪbəbulɪɪŋ] *n* cyberprzemoc
cyberspace ['saɪbəspeɪs] *n* cyberprzestrzeń
cycle ['saɪkl] *n* (*bicycle*) rower ▹ *vi* jeździć na rowerze ▹ *adj* (*shop, helmet, ride*) rowerowy
cycle lane *n* ścieżka rowerowa
cycle path *n* ścieżka rowerowa
cycling ['saɪklɪŋ] *n*: **to go ~** jeździć na rowerze
cyclist ['saɪklɪst] *n* kolarz, rowerzysta(-tka) *m/f*
cylinder ['sɪlɪndə^r] *n* **1** (*shape*) walec **2** (*of gas*) butla
cynical ['sɪnɪkl] *adj* (*person, attitude*) cyniczny
Cyprus ['saɪprəs] *n* Cypr
Czech [tʃɛk] *adj* czeski ▹ *n* **1** (*person*) Czech(-eszka) *m/f* **2** (*language*) czeski
Czech Republic *n*: **the ~** Republika Czeska

d

dad [dæd] (*inf*) *n* tata
daffodil ['dæfədɪl] *n* żonkil
daft [dɑːft] (*Brit: inf*) *adj* głupi
daily ['deɪlɪ] *adj* codzienny ▹ *n* (*newspaper*) dziennik ▹ *adv* codziennie; **twice ~** dwa razy dziennie; **~ life** życie codzienne
daisy ['deɪzɪ] *n* stokrotka
dam [dæm] *n* (*on river*) tama ▹ *vt* (*river*) budować (wybudować *pf*) tamę na *+loc*
damage ['dæmɪdʒ] *n* **1** (*harm*) szkoda **2** (*dents, scratches etc*) uszkodzenie **3** (*to sb's reputation etc*) szkoda ▹ *vt* **1** (*object, building*) uszkadzać (uszkodzić *pf*) **2** (*reputation, economy*) szkodzić (zaszkodzić *pf*); **damages** *n pl* (*Law*) odszkodowanie *n sg*; **to pay £5,000 in ~s** płacić (zapłacić *pf*) pięć tysięcy funtów odszkodowania; **to cause/inflict ~ on** (*physically*) uszkadzać (uszkodzić *pf*); (*fig*) narażać (narazić *pf*) na szwank
damp [dæmp] *adj* wilgotny ▹ *n* (*in air, in walls*) wilgoć ▹ *vt* (*also*: **~en**: *cloth*) zwilżać (zwilżyć *pf*); (*enthusiasm, spirits etc*) studzić (ostudzić *pf*)
dance [dɑːns] *n* **1** (*waltz, tango*) taniec **2** (*social event*) tańce **3** (*dancing*) dancing ▹ *vi* tańczyć (zatańczyć *pf*); **to ~ the tango** tańczyć (zatańczyć *pf*) tango; **to ~ with sb** tańczyć (zatańczyć *pf*) z kimś

dancer ['dɑːnsəʳ] *n* tancerz(-rka) *m/f*; **to be a good/bad ~** być dobrym/złym tancerzem
dandruff ['dændrəf] *n* łupież
Dane [deɪn] *n* Duńczyk/Dunka *m/f*
danger ['deɪndʒəʳ] *n* niebezpieczeństwo; **there is a ~ of/that...** istnieje niebezpieczeństwo, że...; **"~!"** (*on sign*) „uwaga!"; **your life is in ~** pana/pani życie jest w niebezpieczeństwie; **out of ~** (*patient*) nie zagraża niebezpieczeństwo
dangerous ['deɪndʒrəs] *adj* niebezpieczny; **it's ~ to...** niebezpiecznie jest...
Danish ['deɪnɪʃ] *adj* duński ▷ *n* (*language*) duński
dare [dɛəʳ] *vt*: **to ~ sb to do sth** rzucać (rzucić *pf*) komuś wyzwanie, żeby coś zrobił ▷ *vi*: **to ~ (to) do sth** ośmielać (ośmielić *pf*) się coś zrobić ▷ *n* wyzwanie; **I ~n't tell him** (*Brit*) nie odważę się mu powiedzieć; **I ~ say** (*I suppose*) zapewne; **don't you ~** nie waż się; **how ~ you!** jak śmiesz!; **to do sth for a ~** robić (zrobić *pf*) coś w odpowiedzi na wyzwanie
daring ['dɛərɪŋ] *adj* **1** (*audacious*: *escape, rescue, person*) odważny **2** (*bold*: *film, question, artist*) śmiały
dark [dɑːk] *adj* **1** ciemny **2** (*time*: *look*) ponury; (*remark*) mroczny; (*rumour*) czarny ▷ *n*: **the ~** ciemno; **~ blue/green** ciemnoniebieski/ciemnozielony; **~ chocolate** gorzka czekolada; **it is ~** jest ciemno; **it is getting ~** ściemnia się; **after ~** po zmroku; **to be in the ~ about sth** nic nie wiedzieć o czymś
darkness ['dɑːknɪs] *n* ciemność
darling ['dɑːlɪŋ] *n* (*as address*: *dear*) kochanie ▷ *adj* kochany
dart [dɑːt] *vi* rzucać (rzucić *pf*) ▷ *n* **1** (*in game*) strzałka **2** (*weapon*) strzała; **darts** *n pl* gra w strzałki
dashcam ['dæʃkæm] *n* kamera samochodowa
data ['deɪtə] *n pl* dane
database ['deɪtəbeɪs] *n* baza danych
date [deɪt] *n* **1** (*particular day*) data **2** (*meeting with friend*) spotkanie **3** (*friend*) randka **4** (*fruit*) daktyl ▷ *vt* **1** (*establish date of*: *event*) ustalać (ustalić *pf*) datę +*gen*; (*object*) ustalać (ustalić *pf*) wiek +*gen* **2** (*letter, cheque*) pisać (napisać *pf*) datę na **3** (*go out with*: *person*) iść (pójść *pf*) na randkę z +*inst* ▷ *vi* (*become old-fashioned*) wychodzić (wyjść *pf*) z mody; **what's the ~ today?, what's today's ~?** którego dzisiaj mamy?; **~ of birth** data urodzenia; **to ~** (*until now*) do dzisiaj; **to be out of ~** (*old-fashioned*) być przestarzałym; (*expired*) być przeterminowanym; **to be up to ~** (*modern*) być nowoczesnym; **to bring sb up to ~** zapoznawać (zapoznać *pf*) kogoś z najnowszymi informacjami; **to keep up to ~** uaktualniać (uaktualnić *pf*) na bieżąco; **it was ~d 5th July** (*letter*) to było z datą piątego lipca
▸ **date from** *vi* datować się od +*gen*
daughter ['dɔːtəʳ] *n* córka
daughter-in-law ['dɔːtərɪnlɔː] (*pl* **daughters-in-law**) *n* synowa
dawn [dɔːn] *n* **1** (*of day*) świt **2**: **the ~ of sth** początek czegoś ▷ *vi* (*day*) świtać (zaświtać *pf*); **from ~ to dusk** od świtu do zmierzchu
▸ **dawn on, dawn upon** *vt fus*: **it ~ed on me/him that...** zaświtało mi/mu w głowie, że...
day [deɪ] *n* **1** (*period of 24 hours*) doba **2** (*daylight hours*) dzień **3** (*working day*) dzień **4** (*heyday*) okres rozkwitu; **the ~ after tomorrow** pojutrze; **the ~ before yesterday** przedwczoraj; **these ~s** (*nowadays*) dziś; **~ in, ~ out** dzień w dzień; **the following ~** następnego dnia; **the ~ that I...** w dniu, w którym ja...; **~ by ~/from ~ to ~** z dnia na dzień; **one ~ a week** jeden dzień w tygodniu; **one ~/some ~/one of these ~s** któregoś dnia; **the other ~** tamtego dnia; **by ~** w ciągu dnia; **all ~ (long)** przez cały dzień; **~ and night** dzień i noc; **to work an 8-hour ~** pracować osiem godzin dziennie
dead [dɛd] *adj* **1** (*person*) martwy; (*animal*) zdechły; (*plant*) zwiędły **2** (*phone, line*) nieczynny; (*battery*) wyładowany **3** (*total, absolute*): **~ centre** w samym środku; (*silence*) zupełny ▷ *adv* **1** (*inf*: *very*) zupełnie

2: **~ against** (*completely*) zdecydowanie przeciw ▷ *n pl*: **the ~** zmarli; **to drop (down) ~** paść martwym; **to stop ~** stawać (stanąć *pf*) jak wryty; **~ tired** śmiertelnie zmęczony; **~ on time** punktualny; **~ centre/in the middle** sam środek; **over my ~ body!** (*inf*) po moim trupie!; **at/in the ~ of night** w środku nocy

dead end *n* (*street*) ślepa uliczka

deadline ['dɛdlaɪn] *n* nieprzekraczalny termin; **to work to a ~** pracować do deadline'u; **to meet a ~** zdążać (zdążyć *pf*) przed deadline'm

deaf [dɛf] *adj* (*totally*) głuchy; (*partially*) niedosłyszący

deafening ['dɛfnɪŋ] *adj* (*noise*) ogłuszający

deal [diːl] (*pt, pp* **dealt**) *n* (*agreement*) umowa ▷ *vt* **1**: **to ~ (out)** (*cards*) rozdawać (rozdać *pf*) **2** (*sell*: *drugs*) handlować; **to do/make/strike a ~ with sb** robić (zrobić *pf*)/ubijać (ubić *pf*) z kimś interes; **it's a ~!** (*inf*) zgoda!; **a good/fair/bad ~** dobry/uczciwy/zły interes; **a good** *or* **great ~ (of)** duża ilość (+*gen*)
▸ **deal in** (*Comm*) *vt fus* handlować
▸ **deal with** *vt fus* **1** (*criminal etc*) uporać (*pf*) się z + *inst* **2** (*company*) robić interesy z +*inst* **3** (*problem*) radzić (poradzić *pf*) sobie z +*inst* **4** (*book, film*: *subject*) zajmować (zająć *pf*) się +*inst*

dealer ['diːləʳ] *n* **1** (*in goods, services*) handlowiec **2** (*in drugs*) diler **3** (*in card game*) rozdający

dealt [dɛlt] *pt, pp of* **deal**

dear [dɪəʳ] *adj* **1** (*friend, house, car*) drogi **2**: **to be ~ to sb** być drogim dla kogoś **3** (*esp Brit*: *expensive*) drogi ▷ *n*: **(my) ~** (mój) drogi ▷ *excl*: **oh ~/~ ~/~ me!** o jejku!; **~ Sir/Madam** (*in letter*) szanowny Panie/Szanowna Pani; **~ Mr Smith/Mrs Dmowska** szanowny Pan Smith/Szanowna Pani Dmowska; **~ Peter/Jane** drogi Piotrze/Droga Jane

death [dɛθ] *n* śmierć; **(a matter of) life and ~** (sprawa) życia i śmierci; **to stab/beat to ~** zadźgać/pobić na śmierć; **to scare/bore sb to ~** przestraszyć/zanudzać (zanudzić *pf*) na śmierć

debate [dɪ'beɪt] *n* debata ▷ *vt* **1** (*topic, issue, motion*) debatować nad +*inst* **2** (*course of action*) zastanawiać (zastanowić *pf*) się nad +*inst*

debt [dɛt] *n* dług; **to be in ~** mieć długi; **to get into ~** popadać (popaść *pf*) w długi; **to get out of ~** wydobywać (wydobyć *pf*) się z długów; **bad ~** nieściągalne długi *n pl*

decade ['dɛkeɪd] *n* dekada

decaffeinated [dɪ'kæfɪneɪtɪd] *adj* (*coffee*) bezkofeinowy

deceive [dɪ'siːv] *vt* (*fool*) oszukiwać (oszukać *pf*)

December [dɪ'sɛmbəʳ] *n* grudzień; *see also* **July**

decent ['diːsənt] *adj* przyzwoity; **that was very ~ of him** to było bardzo miło z jego strony; **are you ~?** (*inf*: *dressed*) jesteś ubrany?

decide [dɪ'saɪd] *vt* **1** (*question, argument*) rozstrzygać (rozstrzygnąć *pf*) **2** (*persuade*: *person*) przekonywać (przekonać *pf*) ▷ *vi* decydować (zdecydować *pf*); **to ~ to do sth** decydować (zdecydować *pf*) się coś zrobić; **to ~ on** *or* **upon sth** (*choose*) decydować (zdecydować *pf*) się na coś; **to ~ that...** decydować (zdecydować *pf*), że...; **I can't ~ whether...** nie mogę zdecydować, czy...

decimal ['dɛsɪməl] *adj* (*system, currency*) dziesiętny ▷ *n* ułamek dziesiętny; **to three ~ places** do trzech miejsc po przecinku

decision [dɪ'sɪʒən] *n* **1** (*choice*) decyzja **2** (*act of choosing*) decydowanie; **to make a ~** podejmować (podjąć *pf*) decyzję

deck [dɛk] *n* **1** (*on ship*: *floor*) pokład; (*top deck*) górny pokład **2** (*of bus*) piętro **3** (*also*: **tape ~, cassette ~**) magnetofon **4** (*esp US*: *of cards*) talia; **(to go up) on ~** (wyjść) na pokład; **below ~(s)** pod pokładem

deckchair ['dɛktʃɛəʳ] *n* leżak

declare [dɪ'klɛəʳ] *vt* **1** (*intention, attitude*) oznajmiać (oznajmić *pf*); (*support*) deklarować (zadeklarować *pf*)

2 (*at customs*) zgłaszać (zgłosić *pf*) ▷ *vi* opowiadać (opowiedzieć *pf*) się; **to ~ sb innocent/insane** uznawać (uznać *pf*) kogoś winnym/szalonym; **to ~ war** wypowiadać (wypowiedzieć *pf*) wojnę
decorate ['dɛkəreɪt] *vt* **1** (*adorn*): **to ~ (with sth)** dekorować (udekorować *pf*) (czymś) **2** (*paint etc*: *room, house*) dekorować (udekorować *pf*)
decrease [*n* 'diːkriːs, *vb* diː'kriːs] *n*: **~ (in sth)** spadek (czegoś) ▷ *vt, vi* spadać (spaść *pf*); **to be on the ~** obniżać (obniżyć *pf*) się
dedication [dɛdɪ'keɪʃən] *n* **1** (*devotion*) oddanie **2** (*in book*) dedykacja; (*on radio*) dedykacja
deduct [dɪ'dʌkt] *vt*: **to ~ sth (from sth)** dedukować (wydedukować *pf*) coś (z czegoś)
deep [diːp] *adj* **1** (*water, hole, cut, breath*) głęboki **2** (*voice, sound*) głęboki **3** (*sleep*) mocny **4** (*profound*: *person*) poważny; (*thoughts, ideas*) głęboki; (*love, sympathy etc*) głęboki **5** (*serious*: *trouble, concern*) poważny **6** (*colour*) ciemny ▷ *adv* głęboko; **it is 1 m ~** to ma jeden metr głębokości; **to take a ~ breath** brać (wziąć *pf*) głęboki oddech; **ankle-/knee-~ (in water)** po kostki/kolana (w wodzie)
deeply ['diːplɪ] *adv* **1** głęboko **2** (*sleep*) mocno
deer [dɪə^r] (*pl* **deer**) *n* jeleń; **red ~** jeleń szlachetny; **roe ~** sarna
defeat [dɪ'fiːt] *n* **1** (*of army*) klęska **2** (*of team*) porażka **3** (*failure*) porażka ▷ *vt* **1** (*enemy, opposition*) pokonywać (pokonać *pf*) **2** (*team*) zwyciężać (zwyciężyć *pf*) **3** (*plan, proposal etc*) odrzucać (odrzucić *pf*)
defect [*n* 'diːfɛkt, *vb* dɪ'fɛkt] *n* (*flaw*) wada ▷ *vi*: **to ~ (to/from)** uciekać (uciec *pf*) (do/z +*gen*); **hearing ~** wada słuchu
defence [dɪ'fɛns] (*US* **defense**) *n* obrona ▷ *adj* (*spending, cuts, minister*) obrony; **defences** *n pl* obrona *n sg*; **to come to sb's ~** stawać (stanąć *pf*) w czyjejś obronie; **in ~ of sth/sb** w obronie czegoś/kogoś; **the Ministry of D~, (US) the Department of Defense** Ministerstwo Obrony Narodowej; **witness for the ~** świadek obrony
defend [dɪ'fɛnd] *vt* bronić (obronić *pf*); **to ~ o.s.** bronić (obronić *pf*) się
defender [dɪ'fɛndə^r] *n* obrońca(-czyni) *m/f*
defense [dɪ'fɛns] (*US*) *n* = **defence**
define [dɪ'faɪn] *vt* **1** (*limits, boundaries, role*) określać (określić *pf*) **2** (*expression, word*) definiować (zdefiniować *pf*)
definite ['dɛfɪnɪt] *adj* **1** (*plan, answer, views*) wyraźny **2** (*improvement, possibility, advantage*) wyraźny **3** (*proof, evidence, information*) pewny; **is that ~?** czy to pewne?
definitely ['dɛfɪnɪtlɪ] *adv* z pewnością
definition [dɛfɪ'nɪʃən] *n* **1** (*of word*) definicja **2** (*of thought, expression*) sprecyzowanie **3** (*of photograph, features*) rozdzielczość; **by ~** z definicji
degree [dɪ'griː] *n* stopień; **to some ~/a certain ~** do pewnego stopnia; **10 ~s below (zero)** dziesięć stopni poniżej zera; **a ~ in maths** dyplom z matematyki; **by ~s** (*gradually*) stopniowo
delay [dɪ'leɪ] *vt* **1** (*postpone*: *decision, ceremony*) opóźniać (opóźnić *pf*) **2** (*make late*: *person*) zatrzymywać (zatrzymać *pf*) ▷ *n* opóźnienie; **to be ~ed** (*person, flight, departure etc*) spóźniać (spóźnić *pf*) się; **without ~** bez opóźnień
delete [dɪ'liːt] *vt* **1** (*cross out*) wykreślać (wykreślić *pf*) **2** (*Comput*) kasować (skasować *pf*)
deliberate [dɪ'lɪbərɪt] *adj* **1** (*intentional*) zamierzony **2** (*careful*) uważny; **it wasn't ~** to nie było naumyślnie
deliberately [dɪ'lɪbərɪtlɪ] *adv* **1** (*intentionally*) umyślnie **2** (*carefully*) rozważnie
delicate ['dɛlɪkɪt] *adj* delikatny
delicatessen [dɛlɪkə'tɛsn] *n* delikatesy
delicious [dɪ'lɪʃəs] *adj* (*food, smell*) pyszny
delight [dɪ'laɪt] *n* (*feeling*) zachwyt ▷ *vt* (*please*) zachwycać (zachwycić *pf*) ▷ *vi*: **to ~ in sth** czerpać radość

z czegoś; **to my ~...** ku memu zadowoleniu...

delighted [dɪ'laɪtɪd] *adj*: **~ (at** *or* **with sth)** zachwycony (czymś); **to be ~ to do sth** zrobić coś z przyjemnością; **I'd be ~** z przyjemnością

deliver [dɪ'lɪvəʳ] *vt* **1** (*bring*: *letter, parcel etc*) dostarczać (dostarczyć *pf*) **2** (*baby*) odbierać (odebrać *pf*) poród **3** (*speech, lecture etc*) wygłaszać (wygłosić *pf*) **4** (*formal*: *verdict, judgement*) ogłaszać (ogłosić *pf*)

delivery [dɪ'lɪvərɪ] *n* **1** (*distribution*: *of goods, mail*) dostawa **2** (*consignment*) dostawa **3** (*Med*) poród; **~ man** dostawca; **to take ~ of sth** dostawać (dostać *pf*) coś; **allow 3 days for ~** dostawa w ciągu trzech dni

demand [dɪ'mɑːnd] *vt* domagać się *+gen* ▷ *n* **1** (*request*) żądanie **2** (*for product*) popyt; **demands** *n pl* (*requirements*) wymogi; **to ~ to do sth** żądać zrobienia czegoś; **to be in ~** mieć wzięcie; **on ~** na żądanie

democracy [dɪ'mɔkrəsɪ] *n* **1** (*system*) demokracja **2** (*country*) państwo demokratyczne

democratic [dɛmə'krætɪk] *adj* demokratyczny

demolish [dɪ'mɔlɪʃ] *vt* **1** (*building*) burzyć (zburzyć *pf*) **2** (*argument*) obalać (obalić *pf*)

demonstrate ['dɛmənstreɪt] *vt* **1** (*make clear*: *theory*) demonstrować (zademonstrować *pf*) **2** (*show*: *skill, appliance*) wykazywać (wykazać *pf*) **3** (*prove*) dowodzić (dowieść *pf*) ▷ *vi*: **to ~ (for/against sth)** demonstrować (na rzecz czegoś/przeciw czemuś); **to ~ that...** dowodzić (dowieść *pf*), że...; **to ~ how to do sth** demonstrować (zademonstrować *pf*) jak coś zrobić

demonstration [dɛmən'streɪʃən] *n* **1** (*protest march*) demonstracja **2** (*proof*) dowód **3** (*of appliance, cooking etc*) pokaz; **to hold/stage a ~** przeprowadzać (przeprowadzić *pf*) demonstrację

demonstrator ['dɛmənstreɪtəʳ] *n* **1** (*protester*) demonstrant(ka) *m/f* **2** (*sales person*) demonstrator(ka) *m/f*

denim ['dɛnɪm] *n* (*fabric*) dżins; **denims** *n pl* (*jeans*) dżinsy

Denmark ['dɛnmɑːk] *n* Dania

dense [dɛns] *adj* **1** (*crowd, forest*) gęsty **2** (*smoke, fog*) gęsty **3** (*inf*: *stupid*) tępy

dent [dɛnt] *n* (*in metal, box*) wgniecenie ▷ *vt* **1** (*metal, box*) wgniatać (wgnieść *pf*) **2** (*pride, ego, confidence*) zadawać (zadać *pf*) cios *+dat*

dental ['dɛntl] *adj* (*treatment, hygiene etc*) dentystyczny

dentist ['dɛntɪst] *n* **1** (*person*) dentysta(-tka) *m/f* **2**: **the ~('s)** gabinet dentystyczny

deny [dɪ'naɪ] *vt* **1** (*charge, allegation, accusation*) zaprzeczać (zaprzeczyć *pf*) **2**: **to ~ sb sth** odmawiać (odmówić *pf*) komuś czegoś; **he denies having said it** zaprzecza że to powiedział; **to ~ that...** zaprzeczać (zaprzeczyć *pf*), że...

deodorant [diː'əudərənt] *n* dezodorant

depart [dɪ'pɑːt] *vi* **1**: **to ~ (from/for)** (*traveller, visitor*) wyruszać (wyruszyć *pf*) (z/do *+gen*); (*bus, train*) odjeżdżać (odjechać *pf*) (z/do *+gen*); (*plane*) odlatywać (odlecieć *pf*) (z/do *+gen*) **2**: **to ~ from sth** (*stray from*) odchodzić (odejść *pf*) od czegoś

department [dɪ'pɑːtmənt] *n* **1** (*in shop*) stoisko **2** (*in school or college*) wydział **3** (*in government*) ministerstwo; **that's not my ~** to nie moja działka; **D~ of State** (*US*) Departament Stanu; **D~ of Health/the Environment** (*Brit*) Ministerstwo Zdrowia/Ochrony Środowiska

department store *n* dom towarowy

departure [dɪ'pɑːtʃəʳ] *n* **1** (*of visitor, traveller*) wyjazd; (*plane*) odlot **2** (*scheduled journey*) odjazd **3** (*formal*: *of employee, colleague*) odejście **4**: **a ~ from sth** odstępstwo od czegoś; **a new ~** nowy kierunek

departure lounge *n* hala odlotów

depend [dɪ'pɛnd] *vi* **1**: **to ~ on sth** (*be decided by*) polegać na czymś **2**: **you can ~ on me/him** (*rely on, trust*) może pan/pani na mnie/nim polegać **3**: **to ~ on sb/sth** (*for survival*) być zależnym od kogoś/czegoś; **it (all) ~s** (wszystko) zależy; **~ing on the result...** w zależności od wyniku...

deposit [dɪ'pɔzɪt] *n* **1** (*money: in account*) wpłata; (*on goods*) kaucja; (*on house, bottle, when hiring*) zaliczka **2** (*residue*) osad ▷ *vt* **1** (*money*) wpłacać (wpłacić *pf*) **2** (*put, leave*) zdeponować (*pf*); **to put down a ~ of £50** dawać (dać *pf*) zaliczkę w wysokości pięćdziesięciu funtów

depressed [dɪ'prɛst] *adj* (*person*) przygnębiony; **to feel ~** być przygnębionym; **to get ~** wpadać (wpaść *pf*) w depresję

depressing [dɪ'prɛsɪŋ] *adj* (*place, situation etc*) przygnębiający

depth [dɛpθ] *n* **1** (*from top to bottom*) głębokość **2** (*from front to back*) głębokość **3** (*of emotion, feeling*) głębia **4** (*of knowledge*) głębia; (*of understanding etc*) głębia **5**: **the depths** (*liter: of ocean, earth*) czeluść; **at/to/from a ~ of 3 metres** na/do/od głębokości trzech metrów; **18 metres in ~** osiemnaście metrów głębokości; **to be/go out of one's ~** (*in water*) nie sięgać (sięgnąć *pf*) gruntu; **to be/feel out of one's ~** (*fig*) czuć (poczuć *pf*) się zagubionym; **to study/analyse sth in ~** studiować (przestudiować *pf*)/analizować (przeanalizować *pf*) coś dogłębnie; **in the ~s of despair/recession/winter** w otchłani rozpaczy/recesji/zimy

descend [dɪ'sɛnd] *vt* (*formal: stairs, hill*) schodzić (zejść *pf*) ▷ *vi* **1** (*formal: go down*) zejść (schodzić *pf*) **2**: **to ~ (on/upon)** (*visitors, tourists*) zwalać (zwalić *pf*) się (do *+gen*) (*inf*); **in ~ing order** w kolejności od największego

describe [dɪs'kraɪb] *vt* opisywać (opisać *pf*); **to ~ sb/sth to sb** opisywać (opisać *pf*) kogoś/coś komuś

description [dɪs'krɪpʃən] *n* opis

desert [*n* 'dɛzət, *vb* dɪ'zəːt] *n* pustynia ▷ *vt* opuszczać (opuścić *pf*) ▷ *vi* (*Mil*) dezerterować (zdezerterować *pf*)

deserve [dɪ'zəːv] *vt* zasługiwać (zasłużyć *pf*) na; **to ~ to do sth** zasługiwać (zasłużyć *pf*) na zrobienie czegoś

design [dɪ'zaɪn] *n* **1** (*art, process, layout, shape*) projekt **2** (*drawing*) projekt **3** (*pattern*) wzór ▷ *vt* projektować (zaprojektować *pf*); **to be ~ed for sb/to do sth** być zaprojektowanym dla kogoś/do zrobienia czegoś; **by ~** (*on purpose*) celowo

designer [dɪ'zaɪnə^r] *n* projektant(ka) *m/f* ▷ *adj* (*clothes, label, jeans etc*) markowy

desire [dɪ'zaɪə^r] *n* (*formal: urge*) ochota ▷ *vt* (*formal: want*) pragnąć (zapragnąć *pf*) *+gen*; **the ~d effect/result** pożądany efekt/wynik

desk [dɛsk] *n* **1** (*in office*) biurko **2** (*for pupil*) ławka **3** (*in hotel, at airport, hospital etc*) recepcja **4**: **news/fashion ~** (*department*) dział

desk clerk [-kləːrk] (*US*) *n* recepcjonista(-tka) *m/f*

desktop ['dɛsktɔp] *n* (*Comput*) pulpit

despair [dɪs'pɛə^r] *n* rozpacz ▷ *vi* rozpaczać; **in ~** w rozpaczy; **to ~ of doing sth** tracić (stracić *pf*) nadzieję na zrobienie czegoś

desperate ['dɛspərɪt] *adj* **1** (*person*) zdesperowany **2** (*attempt, effort*) rozpaczliwy **3** (*situation*) rozpaczliwy **4** (*criminal*) zdesperowany; **to be ~ for sth/to do sth** rozpaczliwie wyczekiwać czegoś/zrobienia czegoś

desperately ['dɛspərɪtlɪ] *adv* **1** (*struggle, shout etc*) rozpaczliwie **2** (*ill, unhappy etc*) strasznie; **he ~ needs help** rozpaczliwie potrzebuje pomocy

despise [dɪs'paɪz] *vt* gardzić (wzgardzić *pf*) *+loc*

despite [dɪs'paɪt] *prep* pomimo *+gen*

dessert [dɪ'zəːt] *n* deser

destination [dɛstɪ'neɪʃən] *n* (*of traveller*) cel

destroy [dɪs'trɔɪ] *vt* **1** (*building, object*) niszczyć (zniszczyć *pf*) **2** (*faith*) obalać (obalić *pf*); (*confidence*) niszczyć (zniszczyć *pf*) **3** (*animal*) uśmiercać (uśmiercić *pf*)

destruction [dɪs'trʌkʃən] *n* **1** (*act of destroying*) niszczenie **2** (*state of being destroyed*) zniszczenie
detail ['di:teɪl] *n* szczegół ▷ *vt* (*formal*: *list*) wyszczególniać (wyszczególnić *pf*); **details** *n pl* szczegóły; **in ~** w szczegółach; **to (not) go into ~s** (*usually negative*) (nie) wdawać (wdać *pf*) się w szczegóły
detailed ['di:teɪld] *adj* (*account, description*) szczegółowy
detective [dɪ'tɛktɪv] *n* (*in police*) oficer prowadzący dochodzenie; **~ inspector** komisarz; (*Brit*): **(private) ~** (prywatny) detektyw
detention [dɪ'tɛnʃən] *n* **1** (*arrest*) zatrzymanie **2** (*at school*) zatrzymanie po lekcjach za karę; **to be in ~** zostawać (zostać *pf*) po lekcjach za karę
detergent [dɪ'tə:dʒənt] *n* środek czyszczący
determined [dɪ'tə:mɪnd] *adj* **1** (*person*) zdecydowany **2** (*effort, attempt*) stanowczy
detour ['di:tuəʳ] *n* **1**: **to make a ~** jechać (pojechać *pf*) okrężną drogą **2** (*US*: *on road*) objazd
develop [dɪ'vɛləp] *vt* **1** (*change and improve*) rozwijać (rozwinąć *pf*); (*land*) zagospodarowywać (zagospodarować *pf*); (*resource*) wykorzystywać (wykorzystać *pf*) **2** (*produce*: *product, weapon*) pracować nad powstaniem *+gen* **3** (*Phot*) wywoływać (wywołać *pf*) **4** (*fault, engine trouble*) pojawiać (pojawić *pf*); (*disease*) złapać (*pf*) ▷ *vi* **1** (*evolve*: *person*) rozwijać (rozwinąć *pf*) się; (*country, situation, friendship, skill*) rozwijać (rozwinąć *pf*) **2** (*appear*) pojawiać (pojawić *pf*) się; **to ~ a taste for sth** polubić (*pf*) coś; **to ~ into sth** rozwijać (rozwinąć *pf*) się w coś
development [dɪ'vɛləpmənt] *n* **1** rozwój **2** (*building complex*) osiedle; **an unexpected ~** niespodziewane wydarzenie
devil ['dɛvl] *n* **1** (*evil spirit*) diabeł **2**: **poor ~** biedaczysko; **lucky ~** szczęściarz **3**: **the D~** szatan; **talk of the ~!** o wilku mowa!
devoted [dɪ'vəutɪd] *adj* oddany; **~ to sth** (*specialising in*) oddany czemuś; **to be ~ to sb** być oddanym komuś
diabetes [daɪə'bi:ti:z] *n* cukrzyca
diabetic [daɪə'bɛtɪk] *adj* **1** (*person, patient*) chory na cukrzycę **2** (*coma*) cukrzycowy **3** (*chocolate, jam*) dla diabetyków ▷ *n* cukrzyk
diagonal [daɪ'ægənl] *adj* (*line*) ukośny ▷ *n* **1** (*in geometry*) przekątna **2** (*in pattern or design*) linia ukośna
diagram ['daɪəgræm] *n* schemat
dial ['daɪəl] *n* **1** (*on clock or meter*) tarcza **2** (*on radio*) pokrętło **3** (*on telephone*) tarcza ▷ *vt* (*number*) wykręcać (wykręcić *pf*) ▷ *vi* wykręcać (wykręcić *pf*); **can I ~ London direct?** czy mogę zadzwonić bezpośrednio do Londynu?
dialling tone ['daɪəlɪŋ-] (*Brit*) *n* sygnał
dialogue ['daɪəlɔg] (*US* **dialog**) *n* dialog
dial tone (*US*) *n* = **dialling tone**
diamond ['daɪəmənd] *n* **1** (*gem*) diament **2** (*shape*) romb; **diamonds** *n pl* (*on playing cards*) karo; **the six/king of ~s** szóstka/król karo
diaper ['daɪəpəʳ] (*US*) *n* pieluszka
diarrhoea [daɪə'ri:ə] (*US* **diarrhea**) *n* biegunka; **to have ~** mieć biegunkę
diary ['daɪərɪ] *n* **1** (*engagements book*) terminarz **2** (*daily account*) dziennik; **to keep a ~** prowadzić dziennik; **video ~** pamiętnik video
dice [daɪs] (*pl* **dice**) *n* **1** (*in game*) kostka **2** (*game*) kości ▷ *vt* (*in cooking*) kroić (pokroić *pf*) w kostkę
dictation [dɪk'teɪʃən] *n* **1** (*of letter*) dyktowanie **2** (*at school, college*) dyktando
dictionary ['dɪkʃənrɪ] *n* słownik
did [dɪd] *pt of* **do**
die [daɪ] *vi* **1** (*person*) umierać (umrzeć *pf*); (*animal*) zdychać (zdechnąć *pf*); (*plant*) usychać (uschnąć *pf*) **2** (*love, hope*) umierać (umrzeć *pf*) ▷ *n* (*pl* **dice**) (*for games*) kostka *n sg*; **to ~ of** *or* **from sth** umierać (umrzeć *pf*) od czegoś; **to be dying** (*person*) być umierającym; (*plant*) usychać (uschnąć *pf*); (*animal*) zdychać (zdechnąć *pf*); **old habits ~ hard**

przyzwyczajenie drugą naturą człowieka; **I'm dying of thirst/ boredom** umieram z pragnienia/ nudów; **to be dying for sth/to do sth** marzyć o czymś/o zrobieniu czegoś
▶ **die down** *vi* **1** (*wind*) uspokajać (uspokoić *pf*) się **2** (*fire*) gasić (zgasić *pf*) **3** (*excitement, controversy, laughter*) gasić (zgasić *pf*)
▶ **die out** *vi* **1** (*custom, way of life*) zanikać (zaniknąć *pf*) **2** (*species*) wymierać (wymrzeć *pf*)

diesel ['di:zl] *n* **1** (*also*: **~ oil**) olej napędowy **2** (*vehicle*) diesel

diet ['daɪət] *n* **1** (*food intake*) odżywianie **2** (*restricted food*) dieta ▷ *vi* być na diecie ▷ *adj* dietetyczny; **to be on a ~** być na diecie; **to go on a ~** przechodzić (przejść *pf*) na dietę; **to live on a ~ of fish and rice** żywić się rybami i ryżem

difference ['dɪfrəns] *n* różnica; **the ~ in size/colour** różnica w rozmiarze/ kolorze; **to make a ~ (to sb/sth)** mieć znaczenie (dla kogoś/czegoś); **to make no ~ (to sb/sth)** nie mieć znaczenia (dla kogoś/czegoś); **I can't tell the ~ between them** nie widzę różnicy między nimi; **to settle/ resolve one's ~s** pogodzić (*pf*) się

different ['dɪfrənt] *adj* **1** (*not the same*) różny **2** (*unusual*) inny; **~ from** inny niż; **~ to** *or* (*US*) **than** inny niż

difficult ['dɪfɪkəlt] *adj* trudny; **I found it ~ to...** było mi trudno...; **it is ~ being a parent** trudno jest być rodzicem

difficulty ['dɪfɪkəltɪ] *n* trudność; **to have ~/difficulties** mieć trudność/ trudności; **to be in ~** mieć kłopot; **he stood up with ~** stał z trudnością

dig [dɪg] (*pt, pp* **dug**) *vt* **1** (*hole*) kopać **2** (*garden*) skopywać (skopać *pf*) ▷ *vi* (*with spade*) skopywać (skopać *pf*) ▷ *n* **1** (*prod*): **to give sb a ~ in the ribs** szturchać (szturchnąć *pf*) kogoś w żebra **2** (*also*: **archaeological ~**: *excavation*) wykopalisko **3** (*inf*): **to have/take a ~ at sb** (*criticism*) robić (zrobić *pf*) przytyk pod adresem kogoś
▶ **dig out** *vt* **1** (*survivors, car*) odkopywać (odkopać *pf*) **2** (*inf*: *find*) odgrzebywać (odgrzebać *pf*)
▶ **dig up** *vt* **1** (*plant, body*) wykopywać (wykopać *pf*) **2** (*land, area*) przekopywać (przekopać *pf*) **3** (*discover*: *information, evidence*) wydobywać (wydobyć *pf*) na jaw

digestion [dɪ'dʒɛstʃən] *n* trawienie

digital ['dɪdʒɪtl] *adj* cyfrowy

digital camera *n* aparat cyfrowy

digital radio *n* radio cyfrowe

digital television *n* telewizja cyfrowa

dim [dɪm] *adj* **1** (*not bright*: *light*) przyciemniony; (*room, place*) ciemny **2** (*unclear*: *outline, figure*) niewyraźny **3** (*faint*: *memory, sight*) mglisty **4** (*future, prospects*) ponury **5** (*inf*: *stupid*) tępy ▷ *vt* **1** (*light*) przyciemniać (przyciemnić *pf*) **2** (*US*: *Aut*): **to ~ one's lights** wyłączać (wyłączyć *pf*) światła mijania ▷ *vi* (*light*) ściemniać (ściemnić *pf*) się

dime [daɪm] (*US*) *n* dziesięciocentówka

dimension [daɪ'mɛnʃən] *n* wymiar; **dimensions** *n pl* wymiar

din [dɪn] *n* (*row, racket*) gwar

diner ['daɪnə^r] *n* **1** (*person*) gość **2** (*US*: *restaurant*) niedroga restauracja

dinghy ['dɪŋgɪ] *n* **1** (*inflatable*: *also*: **rubber ~**) jolka **2** (*also*: **sailing ~**) mała łódka

dining room ['daɪnɪŋ-] *n* **1** (*in house*) jadalnia **2** (*in hotel*) sala restauracyjna

dinner ['dɪnə^r] *n* **1** (*evening meal*: *small*) kolacja; (: *large*) obiad **2** (*lunch*: *large*) obiad **3** (*formal meal*) przyjęcie

dinner party *n* przyjęcie

dinner time *n* **1** (*in evening*) pora kolacji **2** (*at midday*) pora obiadowa

dinosaur ['daɪnəsɔː^r] *n* dinozaur

diploma [dɪ'pləumə] *n* dyplom

direct [daɪ'rɛkt] *adj* bezpośredni ▷ *vt* **1** (*show*) zaprowadzać (zaprowadzić *pf*) **2** (*send*: *letter*) kierować (skierować *pf*) **3** (*focus*: *attention, remark*) kierować (skierować *pf*) **4** (*manage*: *company, project etc*) kierować (pokierować *pf*) **5** (*play, film, programme*) reżyserować (wyreżyserować *pf*) ▷ *adv* (*go, write,*

fly) bezpośrednio; **to ~ one's attention to sth** kierować (skierować *pf*) czyjąś uwagę na coś
direction [dɪ'rɛkʃən] *n* **1** (*way*) kierunek **2** (*of film, play etc*) reżyseria; **directions** *n pl* wskazówki; **sense of ~** orientacja (w terenie); **in the ~ of** (*towards*) w kierunku *+gen*; **in all ~s** (*everywhere*) ze wszystkich stron; **to ask for ~s** pytać (zapytać *pf*) o drogę; **~s for use** instrukcja obsługi
director [dɪ'rɛktəʳ] *n* **1** (*of company*) dyrektor(ka) *m/f* **2** (*of organization, public authority*) kierownik(-iczka) *m/f* **3** (*of play, film etc*) reżyser(ka) *m/f*
directory [dɪ'rɛktərɪ] *n* **1** (*also*: **telephone ~**) książka telefoniczna **2** (*list of names, addresses etc*) spis **3** (*Comput*) katalog
dirt [dəːt] *n* **1** brud **2** (*earth*) ziemia; **to treat sb like ~** traktować (potraktować *pf*) kogoś jak szmatę
dirty ['dəːtɪ] *adj* **1** (*clothes, face etc*) brudny **2** (*joke, magazine*) nieprzyzwoity ▷ *vt* (*clothes, face etc*) brudzić (ubrudzić *pf*)
disabled [dɪs'eɪbld] *adj* **1** (*physically*) niepełnosprawny **2** (*mentally*) upośledzony
disadvantage [dɪsəd'vɑːntɪdʒ] *n* (*drawback*) wada; **to be** *or* **work to sb's ~** działać na czyjąś niekorzyść; **to be at a ~** być w niekorzystnej sytuacji
disagree [dɪsə'griː] *vi*: **to ~ (with sb)** nie zgadzać (zgodzić *pf*) się (z kimś); **to ~ (with sth)** nie zgadzać (zgodzić *pf*) się (z czymś); **to ~ with sth** (*oppose*) sprzeciwiać (sprzeciwić *pf*) się czemuś; **I ~ with you** nie zgadzam się z tobą; **garlic ~s with me** czosnek mi nie służy
disagreement [dɪsə'griːmənt] *n* niezgoda; **to have a ~ (with sb)** nie zgadzać (zgodzić *pf*) się (z kimś)
disappear [dɪsə'pɪəʳ] *vi* znikać (zniknąć *pf*); **to ~ from view** znikać (zniknąć *pf*) z oczu
disappearance [dɪsə'pɪərəns] *n* **1** (*of person*) zniknięcie **2** (*of vehicle, object*) zaginięcie **3** (*of custom, species*) zanik
disappointed [dɪsə'pɔɪntɪd] *adj* rozczarowany; **to be ~ in sb** być rozczarowanym kimś; **to be ~ that...** być rozczarowanym, że...
disappointment [dɪsə'pɔɪntmənt] *n* **1** (*emotion*) rozczarowanie **2** (*cause*) zawód; **to my ~** ku memu rozczarowaniu
disaster [dɪ'zɑːstəʳ] *n* **1** (*earthquake, flood etc*) klęska żywiołowa **2** (*accident, crash etc*) katastrofa **3** (*fiasco*) klęska **4** (*serious situation*) nieszczęście
disastrous [dɪ'zɑːstrəs] *adj* **1** (*catastrophic*) katastrofalny **2** (*unsuccessful*) nieudany
disc [dɪsk] *n* dysk; *see also* **disk**
discipline ['dɪsɪplɪn] *n* dyscyplina ▷ *vt* **1** (*train*): **to ~ o.s. (to do sth)** narzucać (narzucić *pf*) sobie dyscyplinę (żeby coś zrobić) **2** (*punish*) dyscyplinować (zdyscyplinować *pf*)
disco ['dɪskəu] *n* dyskoteka
disconnect [dɪskə'nɛkt] *vt* **1** (*pipe, tap, hose etc*) odłączać (odłączyć *pf*) **2** (*computer, cooker, TV etc*) wyłączać (wyłączyć *pf*)
discount [*n* 'dɪskaunt, *vb* dɪs'kaunt] *n* rabat, zniżka ▷ *vt* **1** (*goods*) obniżać (obniżyć *pf*) cenę *+gen* **2** (*ignore, reject*) pomijać (pominąć *pf*); **to give sb a ~ on sth** dawać (dać *pf*) komuś zniżkę na coś; **at a ~** (*cheaply*) ze zniżką
discourage [dɪs'kʌrɪdʒ] *vt* **1** (*dishearten*: *person*) zniechęcać (zniechęcić *pf*) **2** (*dissuade*): **to ~ sb from doing sth** odwodzić (odwieść *pf*) kogoś od zrobienia czegoś **3** (*activity*) zniechęcać (zniechęcić *pf*); **to be ~d** być zniechęconym
discover [dɪs'kʌvəʳ] *vt* odkrywać (odkryć *pf*); **to ~ that...** (*find out*) dowiadywać (dowiedzieć *pf*) się, że...; **to ~ how to do sth** dowiadywać (dowiedzieć *pf*) się, jak coś zrobić
discrimination [dɪskrɪmɪ'neɪʃən] *n* dyskryminacja; **racial/sexual ~** dyskryminacja rasowa/płci
discuss [dɪs'kʌs] *vt* **1** (*talk over*) dyskutować (przedyskutować *pf*) **2** (*analyse*) omawiać (omówić *pf*)
discussion [dɪs'kʌʃən] *n* **1** (*talk*) rozmowa **2** (*debate*: *in article, lecture*

etc) dyskusja; **the matter under ~** sprawa będąca przedmiotem dyskusji

disease [dɪ'zi:z] *n* choroba

disgraceful [dɪs'greɪsful] *adj* haniebny

disguise [dɪs'gaɪz] *n* (*make-up, costume*) przebranie ▷ *vt* **1**: **to be ~d (as sth/sb)** (*person*) przebierać (przebrać *pf*) się (za coś/kogoś) **2** (*fact, emotions*) ukrywać (ukryć *pf*) **3** (*voice*) zmieniać (zmienić *pf*); **in ~** w przebraniu; **to ~ o.s. (as sb)** przebierać (przebrać *pf*) się (za kogoś)

disgusted [dɪs'gʌstɪd] *adj* pełen obrzydzenia

disgusting [dɪs'gʌstɪŋ] *adj* **1** (*food, habit*) wstrętny **2** (*behaviour, situation*) odrażający

dish [dɪʃ] *n* **1** (*piece of crockery*: *for serving*) naczynie; (*for eating*) talerz **2** (*contents*) potrawa **3** (*recipe, food*) potrawa **4** (*also*: **satellite ~**) antena satelitarna; **dishes** *n pl* naczynia; **to do** *or* **wash the ~es** myć (umyć *pf*) naczynia

dishonest [dɪs'ɔnɪst] *adj* nieuczciwy

dishwasher ['dɪʃwɔʃəʳ] *n* zmywarka do naczyń

dishwashing liquid ['dɪʃwɔʃɪŋ-] (*US*) *n* płyn do mycia naczyń

disinfectant [dɪsɪn'fɛktənt] *n* środek dezynfekujący

disk [dɪsk] *n* (*Comput*: *hard*) dysk; (*floppy*) dyskietka

dismal ['dɪzml] *adj* **1** (*weather, place, mood*) ponury **2** (*prospects, record, failure*) czarny

dismiss [dɪs'mɪs] *vt* **1** (*worker*) zwalniać (zwolnić *pf*) **2** (*send away*) odprawiać (odprawić *pf*) **3** (*case, charge*) oddalać (oddalić *pf*) **4** (*possibility, problem, idea*) odrzucać (odrzucić *pf*)

disobedient [dɪsə'bi:dɪənt] *adj* nieposłuszny

display [dɪs'pleɪ] *n* **1** (*in shop, at exhibition*) wystawa **2** (*exhibition*) wystawa **3** (*show*: *of feeling*) przejaw **4** (*screen*) monitor ▷ *vt* **1** (*show*: *exhibits*) wystawiać (wystawić *pf*); (*feelings, courage*) okazywać (okazać *pf*) **2** (*results, information*) pokazać (pokazywać *pf*) **3** (*information on screen*) wyświetlać (wyświetlić *pf*); **on ~** (*exhibits, goods, work*) na wystawie

disposable [dɪs'pəuzəbl] *adj* jednorazowy; **~ income** dochód netto

disqualify [dɪs'kwɔlɪfaɪ] *vt* (*team, competitor*) dyskwalifikować (zdyskwalifikować *pf*); **to ~ sb from (doing) sth** pozbawiać (pozbawić *pf*) kogoś prawa robienia czegoś

disrupt [dɪs'rʌpt] *vt* **1** (*conversation, meeting*) przerywać (przerwać *pf*) **2** (*disturb*: *plan*) krzyżować (pokrzyżować *pf*); (*process*) przerywać (przerwać *pf*)

dissolve [dɪ'zɔlv] *vt* **1** (*in liquid*) rozpuszczać (rozpuścić *pf*) **2**: **to be ~d** (*organization, parliament*) rozwiązywać (rozwiązać *pf*) się; (*marriage*) unieważniać (unieważnić *pf*) ▷ *vi* (*material*) rozwiewać (rozwiać *pf*) się; **to ~ in(to) tears** zalewać (zalać *pf*) się łzami

distance ['dɪstns] *n* **1** (*between two places*) odległość **2** (*remoteness*) odległość **3** (*formal*: *reserve*) dystans ▷ *vt*: **to ~ o.s. (from sb/sth)** dystansować (zdystansować *pf*) się (od kogoś/czegoś); **in the ~** w dali; **from a ~** z daleka; **to be some ~/quite a ~ from sth** (*far*) być w jakiejś odległości/w sporej odległości od czegoś; **within walking ~** można tam dojść na piechotę; **(at) a ~ of 2 metres** w odległości dwóch metrów; **keep your ~!** trzymaj się z daleka!

distant ['dɪstnt] *adj* **1** (*place*) odległy **2** (*future*) daleki; (*past*) odległy **3** (*relative, cousin*) daleki **4** (*aloof*: *person, manner*) chłodny **5** (*absent*: *person, look*) nieobecny

distract [dɪs'trækt] *vt* (*person*) rozpraszać (rozproszyć *pf*); **to ~ sb's attention** odwracać (odwrócić *pf*) czyjąś uwagę

distribute [dɪs'trɪbju:t] *vt* **1** (*food, leaflets*) rozdawać (rozdać *pf*) **2** (*resources, profits, work etc*) rozdzielać (rozdzielić *pf*) **3** (*goods*: *to shops*) rozprowadzać (rozprowadzić *pf*)

district ['dɪstrɪkt] *n* **1** (*of country*) region; (*town*) dzielnica **2** (*official area*) okręg **3** (*in titles*) dystrykt
disturb [dɪs'tə:b] *vt* **1** (*interrupt*) zakłócać (zakłócić *pf*) **2** (*upset*) niepokoić (zaniepokoić *pf*); **sorry to ~ you** przepraszam, że przeszkadzam
ditch [dɪtʃ] *n* rów
dive [daɪv] *vi* **1** (*swimmer: into water*) skakać (skoczyć *pf*) do wody; (*under water*) nurkować (zanurkować *pf*) **2** (*bird*) spadać (spaść *pf*) lotem nurkowym ▷ *n* **1** (*into water*) skok do wody **2** (*underwater*) nurkowanie **3** (*inf, pej: place*) spelunka
diver ['daɪvəʳ] *n* (*deep sea*) nurek; (*from board*) skoczek
diversion [daɪ'və:ʃən] *n* **1** (*Brit: for traffic*) objazd **2** (*distraction*) rozrywka **3** (*of profits, funds*) przekazanie; **to create a ~** odwracać (odwrócić *pf*) uwagę
divide [dɪ'vaɪd] *vt* **1**: **to ~ (up)** (*separate*) dzielić (podzielić *pf*) **2** (*in maths*) dzielić (podzielić *pf*) **3**: **to ~ sth between/among sb/sth** (*share*) dzielić (podzielić *pf*) coś między kogoś/coś **4**: **to ~ sth (from sth)** (*keep separate*) oddzielać (oddzielić *pf*) coś (od czegoś) **5** (*split*) dzielić (podzielić *pf*) ▷ *vi* dzielić (podzielić *pf*) się ▷ *n* (*gulf, rift*) przepaść; **to ~ sth in half** dzielić (podzielić *pf*) coś na pół; **40 ~d by 5** czterdzieści podzielić przez pięć; **~ 7 into 35** podzielić siedem na trzydzieści pięć
diving ['daɪvɪŋ] *n* **1** (*underwater*) nurkowanie **2** (*from board*) skoki do wody
division [dɪ'vɪʒən] *n* **1** (*splitting up*) podział **2** (*Math*) dzielenie **3** (*of labour, resources*) podział **4** (*gulf*) przepaść **5** (*department*) wydział **6** (*military unit*) dywizja
divorce [dɪ'vɔ:s] *n* rozwód ▷ *vt* (*spouse*) rozwodzić (rozwieść *pf*) ▷ *vi* rozwodzić (rozwieść *pf*) się
divorced [dɪ'vɔ:st] *adj* rozwiedziony; **to get ~** brać (wziąć *pf*) rozwód
DIY (*Brit*) *n abbr* (= *do-it-yourself*) majsterkowanie; **to do ~** majsterkować
dizzy ['dɪzɪ] *adj* **1**: **to feel ~** kręcić się w głowie **2** (*woman, blonde*) zakręcony; **I had a ~ spell** zakręciło mi się w głowie; **to make sb ~** przyprawiać (przyprawić *pf*) kogoś o zawrót głowy
DJ *n abbr* **1** (= *disc jockey*) didżej **2** (*Brit:* = *dinner jacket*) smoking

 **KEYWORD**

do [du:] (*pt* **did**, *pp* **done**) *vt* **1** (*be engaged in, achieve*) robić (zrobić *pf*); **what are you doing?** co pan/pani robi?; **what is he doing here?** co on tu robi?; **are you doing anything tomorrow evening?** robi pan/pani coś jutro wieczorem?; **what you should do is...** to, co powinien pan/powinna pani zrobić, to...; **we must do everything possible to help them** musimy zrobić wszystko, aby im pomóc; **what did you do with the money?** (*how did you spend it?*) co pan zrobił/pani zrobiła z pieniędzmi?; (*where did you put it?*) gdzie pan położył/pani położyła pieniądze?; **what are you going to do about this?** co z tym pan/pani zrobi?
2 (*for a living*): **what do you do?** gdzie pan/pani pracuje?
3 (*with noun*): **to do the cooking** gotować (ugotować *pf*); **to do one's teeth** myć (umyć *pf*) zęby; **to do one's hair** układać (ułożyć *pf*) sobie włosy; **we're doing "Othello" at school** (*studying it*) czytamy „Othella" w szkole; (*performing it*) gramy w „Othellu" w szkole
4 (*referring to speed, distance*): **the car was doing 100** samochód jechał setką; **we've done 200 km already** zrobiliśmy już dwieście kilometrów
5 (*cause*): **the explosion did a lot of damage** eksplozja spowodowała wiele szkód; **a holiday will do you good** wakacje się panu/pani przydadzą
▷ *vi* **1** (*act, behave*) robić (zrobić *pf*); **do as I do** rób, co ja robię; **do as I tell you** rób, co ci mówię
2 (*get on*) radzić (poradzić *pf*) sobie; **he's doing well/badly at school**

radzi sobie w szkole dobrze/źle; **the firm is doing well** firma prosperuje dobrze; **"how do you do?" — "how do you do?"** „miło mi" — „miło mi"
3 (*suit*) nadawać się (*pf*); **will it do?** czy to się nada?
4 (*be sufficient*) wystarczać (wystarczyć *pf*); **will £15 do?** piętnaście funtów wystarczy?; **that'll do** to wystarczy; **that'll do!** (*in annoyance*) dosyć!
▷ *aux vb* **1** (*in negative constructions*): **I don't understand** nie rozumiem; **she doesn't want it** ona nie chce tego; **he didn't seem to care** wydawało się, że go to nie obchodzi; **don't be silly!** nie wygłupiaj się!
2 (*to form questions*): **do you like jazz?** lubisz jazz?; **what do you think?** jak myślisz?; **where does she live?** gdzie ona mieszka?; **didn't you know?** nie wiedziałeś?; **why didn't you come?** dlaczego nie przyszedłeś?
3 (*for emphasis, in polite expressions*): **people do make mistakes sometimes** ludzie istotnie czasami popełniają błędy; **she does seem rather late** ona się istotnie trochę spóźnia; **do sit down/help yourself** proszę, niech pan/pani usiądzie/poczęstuje się; **do take care!** uważaj na siebie!; **oh do shut up!** och, zamknij się!
4 (*used to avoid repeating vb*) *używany, by uniknąć powtarzania czasownika*; **I make more money than he does** zarabiam więcej pieniędzy niż on; **they say they don't care, but they do** mówią, że ich to nie obchodzi, a jednak tak jest; **he asked me to help him and I did** poprosił mnie o pomoc i tak zrobiłem; **(and) so do I** (i) ja też; **and neither did we** my też nie; **better than I do** lepiej niż ja; **"who made this mess?" — "I did"** „kto nabałaganił?" — „Ja"; **"do you have a metal detector?" — "no, I don't"** „czy ma pan/pani wykrywacz metali?" — „nie, nie mam"
5 (*in question tags*): **I don't know him, do I?** nie znam go, prawda?; **you like him, don't you?** (*familiar*) lubisz go, prawda?; **she lives in London, doesn't she?** mieszka w Londynie, prawda?
▷ *n* (*Brit*: *inf*: *party etc*) przyjęcie; **we're having a little do on Saturday** robimy małe przyjęcie w sobotę; **it was quite a do** to było niezłe przyjęcie
▸ **do away with** *vt fus* (*get rid of*) likwidować (zlikwidować *pf*)
▸ **do in** (*inf*) *vt* (*kill*) ukatrupiać (ukatrupić *pf*)
▸ **do out of** (*inf*) *vt* (*deprive of*) pozbawiać (pozbawić *pf*); **he did me out of my share** pozbawił mnie mojej doli
▸ **do up** *vt fus* **1** (*fasten*) zapinać (zapiąć *pf*) **2** (*esp Brit*: *renovate*: *room, house*) odnawiać (odnowić *pf*)
▸ **do with** *vt fus* **1** (*need*): **I could do with a drink** napiłbym się czegoś; **I could do with some help** przydałaby mi się pomoc **2** (*be connected*): **to have to do with** mieć związek z +*inst*; **what has it got to do with you?** jaki to ma związek z tobą?; **I won't have anything to do with it** nie będę mieć z tym nic wspólnego; **it has to do with money** ma to związek z pieniędzmi; **it was something to do with football** to miało jakiś związek z futbolem
▸ **do without** *vt fus* obywać (obyć *pf*) się bez +*gen*
▷ *vi* robić (zrobić *pf*)

doctor ['dɔktəʳ] *n* **1** (*medic*) lekarz(-rka) *m/f* **2**: **the ~'s** gabinet lekarski **3** (*PhD etc*) doktor ▷ *vt* (*food, drink*) zatruwać (zatruć *pf*); (*figures, photograph*) fałszować (sfałszować *pf*); **~'s office** (*US*) przychodnia
document ['dɔkjumənt] *n* dokument
documentary [dɔkju'mɛntərɪ] *n* film dokumentalny ▷ *adj* (*evidence*) dokumentalny
dodge [dɔdʒ] *vt* **1** (*blow, ball, car*) uchylać (uchylić *pf*) się od +*gen* **2** (*tax, military service*) unikać (uniknąć *pf*) +*gen* **3** (*question, issue etc*) unikać (uniknąć *pf*) +*gen*
does [dʌz] *vb see* **do**
doesn't ['dʌznt] = **does not**

dog [dɔg] *n* **1** pies **2** (*male*) samiec ▷ *vt* (*problems, injuries*) utrudniać (utrudnić *pf*); **to go to the ~s** schodzić (zejść *pf*) na psy

do-it-yourself ['du:ɪtjɔ:'sɛlf] *n* majsterkowanie ▷ *adj* (*store*) dla majsterkowiczów

dole [dəul] (*inf*) *n* (*Brit*): **(the) ~** (*payment*) zasiłek; **(to be) on the ~** (*Brit*) (być) na zasiłku
▸ **dole out** *vt* rozdzielać (rozdzielić *pf*)

doll [dɔl] *n* (*toy*) lalka

dollar ['dɔlə^r] *n* dolar

dolphin ['dɔlfɪn] *n* delfin

dominoes ['dɔmɪnəuz] *n* domino

donate [də'neɪt] *vt* **1**: **to ~ (to sb)** (*money, clothes*) ofiarowywać (ofiarować *pf*) (komuś) **2** (*blood, organs*) oddawać (oddać *pf*)

done [dʌn] *pp of* **do**

donkey ['dɔŋkɪ] *n* osioł

don't [dəunt] = **do not**

donut ['dəunʌt] (*US*) *n* = **doughnut**

door [dɔ:^r] *n* **1** (*of house, room, etc*) drzwi *n pl* **2** (*doorway*) wejście; **to answer the ~** otwierać (otworzyć *pf*) drzwi; **out of ~s** na dworze; **to go from ~ to ~** chodzić od domu do domu

doorbell ['dɔ:bɛl] *n* dzwonek do drzwi

doorstep ['dɔ:stɛp] *n* próg; **on one's ~** za progiem

dormitory ['dɔ:mɪtrɪ] *n* **1** (*room*) sala **2** (*US: building*) akademik

dot [dɔt] *n* **1** (*small round mark*) kropka **2** (*in the distance*) punkt ▷ *vt*: **~ted with** usiany kropkami; **on the ~** (*punctually*) co do minuty

dot-com [dɔt'kɔm] *n* firma internetowa

double ['dʌbl] *adj* **1** podwójny **2** (*for two: room, sheet*) dwuosobowy ▷ *n* **1**: **to be sb's ~** być czyimś sobowtórem **2** (*drink*) setka ▷ *vt* (*offer, size*) podwajać (podwoić *pf*) ▷ *vi* (*population, size*) podwajać (podwoić *pf*) się; **~ five two six** (*Brit*: 5526) pięćdziesiąt pięć, dwadzieścia sześć; **it's spelt with a ~ "M"** pisze się przez dwa „M"; **~ the size/number (of sth)** podwójny rozmiar/podwójna liczba (czegoś); **~ in size/weight** podwójny rozmiar/waga; **to ~ as sth** służyć również jako coś
▸ **double back** *vi* (*person*) zawracać (zawrócić *pf*)
▸ **double up** *vi* (*bend over*) skręcać (skręcić *pf*) się; **to be ~d up with pain** skręcać się z bólu; **to be ~d up with laughter** pokładać się ze śmiechu

double bass *n* kontrabas

double-click ['dʌbl'klɪk] *vi*: **to ~ on sth** klikać (kliknąć *pf*) dwa razy na coś

double glazing [-'gleɪzɪŋ] (*Brit*) *n* podwójne szyby

doubles ['dʌblz] *n* (*Tennis*) debel

doubt [daut] *n* (*uncertainty*) wątpliwość ▷ *vt* wątpić (zwątpić *pf*) w; **without (a) ~** bez wątpienia; **to be in ~** mieć wątpliwości; **beyond ~** ponad wszelką wątpliwośc; **no ~** bez wątpienia; **to ~ if** *or* **whether...** wątpić (zwątpić *pf*) czy...; **I ~ it (very much)** (bardzo) w to wątpię; **I don't ~ that...** nie mam wątpliwości, że...

doubtful ['dautful] *adj* **1** (*questionable*): **it is ~ that/whether...** nie jest pewne, czy... **2** (*unconvinced: person*): **to be ~ about sth** mieć wątpliwości co do czegoś; **I'm a bit ~** mam pewne wątpliwości

dough [dəu] *n* **1** (*Culin*) ciasto **2** (*inf: money*) szmal

doughnut ['dəunʌt] (*US* **donut**) *n* pączek

down [daun] *n* (*soft feathers*) puch ▷ *adv* **1** (*downwards*) w dół **2** (*in a lower place*) na dole **3** (*in the south*) na południu; (*towards the south*) na południe ▷ *prep* **1** (*towards lower level*) w dół **2** (*at lower part of*) dalej **3** (*along*) wzdłuż ▷ *vt* (*inf: drink*) wypić (*pf*) jednym haustem; **~ there** tam na/w dole; **~ here** tu na/w dole; **the price of meat is ~** (*lower*) cena mięsa spadła; **I've got it ~ in my diary** (*written*) zapisałem to w kalendarzu; **to pay 5 pounds ~** (*esp US*) płacić (wpłacić *pf*) pięć funtów zaliczki; **England are two goals ~** (*behind*) Anglia przegrywa dwoma golami; **I'm ~ to my last five pounds** zostało mi ostatnie pięć funtów; **five ~, two**

to go mamy już pięć, dwa zostały; **to be ~ for sth** zapisywać (zapisać *pf*) się na coś; **it's all ~ to hard work** wszystko jest wynikiem ciężkiej pracy

DOWNING STREET

Downing Street to ulica znajdująca się w dzielnicy Westminster w Londynie, przy której mieszkają sprawujący urząd Premier Wielkiej Brytanii oraz Minister Skarbu. Termin **Downing Street** jest często używany w odniesieniu do rządu brytyjskiego w ogóle.

download ['daunləud] *vt* ściągać (ściągnąć *pf*) ▷ *n* dane *pl* ściągnięte z serwera
downstairs ['daun'stɛəz] *adv* **1** (*to floor below*) na dół; (*on floor below*) na dole **2** (*to ground floor*) na dół; (*on ground floor*) na dole ▷ *adj* na dole
downtown ['daun'taun] (*US*) *adv* centrum ▷ *adj*: **~ Chicago** centrum Chicago
doze [dəuz] *vi* drzemać (zdrzemnąć *pf*) się ▷ *n*: **to have a ~** ucinać (uciąć *pf*) sobie drzemkę
▸ **doze off** *vi* drzemać (zdrzemnąć sie *pf*)
dozen ['dʌzn] *n* tuzin; **a ~ books** tuzin książek; **two ~ eggs** dwa tuziny jajek; **~s of** tuziny *+gen*
draft [drɑːft] *n* **1** (*first version*) szkic **2** (*of bill*) projekt **3** (*also*: **bank ~**) przekaz **4**: **the ~** (*US*: *Mil*) pobór ▷ *vt* **1** (*letter, book, speech*) pisać (napisać *pf*) roboczą wersję *+gen* **2** (*Mil*): **to be ~ed** być powołanym; *see also* **draught**
drag [dræg] *vt* **1** (*pull*: *large object, body*) ciągnąć **2** (*force*): **to ~ sb out of a car** wyciągać (wyciągnąć *pf*) kogoś z samochodu **3** (*fig*): **it's impossible to ~ him out of bed** nie można go wyciągnąć z łóżka **4** (*search*: *river, lake*) przeszukiwać (przeszukać *pf*) ▷ *vi* (*time, film*) dłużyć się ▷ *n* **1** (*inf*): **a ~** (*person*) nudziarz(-ra) *m/f*; (*situation*) nuda **2** (*women's clothing*): **in ~** w damskim przebraniu; **to ~ sth out of sb** wyciągać (wyciągnąć *pf*) coś z kogoś
▸ **drag away** *vt*: **to ~ sb away (from sth)** odciągać (odciągnąć *pf*) kogoś (od czegoś); **to ~ o.s. away (from sth)** wyrywać (wyrwać *pf*) się (z czegoś)
▸ **drag on** *vi* (*meeting, concert*) dłużyć się; (*war*) ciągnąć się
▸ **drag out** *vt* (*prolong*) przeciągać (przeciągnąć *pf*)
dragon ['drægn] *n* smok
drain [dreɪn] *n* **1** (*in street*) studzienka ściekowa **2**: **to be a ~ on sth** (*resources, funds*) pochłaniać coś ▷ *vt* **1** (*land, marsh, pond*) osuszać (osuszyć *pf*) **2** (*vegetables*) odsączać (odsączyć *pf*) **3** (*liquid*) spuszczać (spuścić *pf*) **4** (*glass, cup*) wypić do dna *pf* **5** (*exhaust*: *person*) wyczerpywać (wyczerpać *pf*) ▷ *vi* (*liquid*) wyciekać (wyciec *pf*); **to go down the ~** (*inf*) marnować (zmarnować *pf*) się
drama ['drɑːmə] *n* **1** (*theatre*) dramat **2** (*play*) sztuka **3** (*excitement*) dramat
dramatic [drə'mætɪk] *adj* dramatyczny ▷ *adj* (*society, group*) dramatyczny
drank [dræŋk] *pt of* **drink**
drapes [dreɪps] (*US*) *n pl* zasłony
draught [drɑːft] (*US* **draft**) *n* (*of air*) przeciąg ▷ *adj* (*beer, bitter etc*) beczkowy; **on ~** (*beer*) z beczki
draughts [drɑːfts] (*Brit*) *n* warcaby
draw [drɔː] (*pt* **drew**, *pp* **drawn**) *vt* **1** (*picture, map*) rysować (narysować *pf*) **2** (*pull*: *cart*) ciągnąć (pociągnąć *pf*) **3** (*curtains, blinds*: *close*) zasuwać (zasunąć *pf*); (*open*) odsuwać (odsunąć *pf*) **4** (*take out*: *gun, knife, sword*) wyciągać (wyciągnąć *pf*) **5**: **to ~ (out) money from a bank/an account** wypłacać (wypłacić *pf*) pieniądze z banku/z konta **6**: **to ~ a conclusion (from sth)** wyciągać (wyciągnąć *pf*) wnioski (z czegoś) ▷ *vi* **1** (*with pen, pencil etc*) rysować (narysować *pf*) **2**: **to ~ near** (*move*) zbliżać (zbliżyć *pf*) się; **to ~ away** oddalać (oddalić *pf*) się **3** (*esp Brit*: *Sport*) remisować (zremisować *pf*) ▷ *n* **1** (*esp Brit*: *Sport*) remis **2** (*lottery*) los; **to ~ (sb's) attention (to sth)**

kierować (skierować *pf*) (czyjąś) uwagę (na coś); **to ~ near** *or* **close** (*approach*) zbliżać (zbliżyć *pf*) się; **to ~ to a close** dobiegać (dobiec *pf*) końca
▸ **draw in** *vi* (*Brit*: *nights*) stawać (stać *pf*) się krótszym ▷ *vt* (*also*: **~ into**: *involve*) wciągać (wciągnąć *pf*)
▸ **draw on** *vt fus* (*also*: **~ upon**) wykorzystywać (wykorzystać *pf*)
▸ **draw up** *vi* (*stop*: *car, bus etc*) ruszać (ruszyć *pf*) ze stacji ▷ *vt* **1** (*document, plan*) sporządzać (sporządzić *pf*) **2** (*chair etc*) przysuwać (przysunąć *pf*)

drawback ['drɔːbæk] *n* cecha ujemna

drawer [drɔːʳ] *n* (*of desk etc*) szuflada

drawing ['drɔːɪŋ] *n* rysunek

drawing pin (*Brit*) *n* pinezka

drawn [drɔːn] *pp of* **draw** ▷ *adj* (*haggard*) mizerny

dreadful ['drɛdful] *adj* okropny; **I feel ~!** (*ill*) okropnie się czuję!; (*ashamed*) czuję się głupio!

dream [driːm] (*pt, pp* **dreamed** *or* **dreamt**) *n* **1** (*when asleep*) sen **2** (*ambition*) marzenie ▷ *vi*: **to ~ about** (*when asleep*) śnić o; **I dreamt that...** śniło mi się, że...; **to have a ~ about sb/sth** (*when asleep*) śnić o kimś/czymś; **sweet ~s!** (*sleep well!*) miłych snów!; **to ~ that...** (*when asleep*) śnić, że...; (*when wishing for sth*) marzyć, że...; **I wouldn't ~ of...** nie śmiałbym marzyć o *+loc*...
▸ **dream up** *vt* (*plan, idea etc*) wymyślać (wymyślić *pf*)

drench [drɛntʃ] *vt* (*soak*) zamakać (zamoknąć *pf*); **~ed to the skin** przemoczony do suchej nitki

dress [drɛs] *n* **1** (*frock*) sukienka **2** (*clothing*) ubranie ▷ *vt* **1** (*child*) ubierać (ubrać *pf*) **2** (*wound*) opatrywać (opatrzyć *pf*) **3** (*salad*) przyprawiać (przyprawić *pf*) ▷ *vi* ubierać (ubrać *pf*) się; **to ~ o.s., get ~ed** ubierać (ubrać *pf*) się; **she ~es in jeans** ubiera się w dżinsy
▸ **dress down** *vi* ubierać (ubrać *pf*) się na luzie
▸ **dress up** *vi* **1** (*wear best clothes*) stroić (wystroić *pf*) się **2**: **to ~ up as** (*in fancy dress*) przebierać (przebrać *pf*) za

dresser ['drɛsəʳ] *n* **1** (*Brit*: *cupboard*) kredens **2** (*US*: *chest of drawers*) szafka

dressing gown ['drɛsɪŋ-] *n* szlafrok

dressing table *n* toaletka

drew [druː] *pt of* **draw**

dried [draɪd] *adj* (*fruit, herbs*) suszony; **~ milk/eggs** mleko/jajka w proszku

drier ['draɪəʳ] *n* = **dryer**

drift [drɪft] *vi* **1** (*boat*) dryfować (podryfować *pf*) **2** (*sand, snow*) tworzyć (utworzyć *pf*) zaspy ▷ *n* (*snow*) zaspa; **to ~ away** (*crowd, people*) rozchodzić (rozejść *pf*); **to ~ apart** (*friends, couple*) oddalać (oddalić *pf*) się; **to get** *or* **follow sb's ~** rozumieć (zrozumieć *pf*) o co komuś chodzi
▸ **drift off** *vi*: **to ~ off (to sleep)** zapadać (zapaść *pf*) w sen

drill [drɪl] *n* **1** (*for DIY etc*) wiertarka; (*of dentist*) wiertło; (*for mining etc*) świder **2** (*for fire, air raid*) próbny alarm ▷ *vt* (*hole*) wiercić (wywiercić *pf*) ▷ *vi* **1**: **to ~ (into sth)** (*wall, floor etc*) wiercić (w czymś) **2**: **to ~ (for sth)** (*oil, water, gas*) wiercić (w poszukiwaniu czegoś)

drink [drɪŋk] (*pt* **drank**, *pp* **drunk**) *n* **1** (*tea, water etc*) napój **2** (*alcohol*) drink ▷ *vt* pić (wypić *pf*) ▷ *vi* (*drink alcohol*) pić (wypić *pf*); **to have a ~** napić (*pf*) się; **a ~ of water** łyk wody; **would you like something to ~?** czy chciałby pan/chciałaby pani się czegoś napić?
▸ **drink to** *vt fus* pić (wypić *pf*) za
▸ **drink up** *vt, vi* pić (wypić *pf*) do dna

drive [draɪv] (*pt* **drove**, *pp* **driven**) *n* **1** (*journey*) jazda **2** (*also*: **~way**) droga dojazdowa **3** (*energy*) zapał **4** (*campaign*) działania **5** (*also*: **CD-ROM/disk ~**) stacja dysków ▷ *vt* **1** (*vehicle*) kierować *+inst* **2**: **to ~ sb to the station/airport** podwozić (podwieźć *pf*) kogoś na stację/lotnisko **3** (*run*: *machine, motor, wheel*) kierować *+inst* **4** (*nail, stake etc*): **to ~ sth into sth** wbijać (wbić *pf*) coś w coś **5** ▷ *vi* **1** (*at controls of vehicle*) prowadzić **2** (*travel*) jechać (pojechać *pf*); **to go for a ~** jechać na przejażdżkę; **it's a 3-hour ~ from**

London to jest trzy godziny jazdy z Londynu; **left-/right-hand ~ car** samochód z kierownicą po lewej/prawej stronie; **front-/rear-wheel ~** samochód z napędem przednim/tylnim; **he ~s a taxi/lorry** jest kierowcą taksówki/ciężarówki; **to ~ sb mad/to desperation** doprowadzać (doprowadzić *pf*) kogoś do szaleństwa/rozpaczy; **to ~ sb to (do) sth** doprowadzać (doprowadzić *pf*) kogoś do (zrobienia) czegoś; **to ~ at 50 km an hour** jechać z prędkością pięćdziesiąt kilometrów na godzinę
▸ **drive away** *vt* zniechęcać (zniechęcić *pf*)
▸ **drive off** *vi* (*car, driver*) odjeżdżać (odjechać *pf*)
▸ **drive out** *vt* (*force to leave*) wypędzać (wypędzić *pf*)

driver ['draɪvəʳ] *n* **1** kierowca **2** (*chauffeur*) szofer

driver's license ['draɪvəz-] (*US*) *n* prawo jazdy

driving instructor ['draɪvɪŋ-] *n* instruktor(ka) *m/f* jazdy

driving lesson *n* lekcja jazdy

driving licence (*Brit*) *n* prawo jazdy

driving test *n* egzamin na prawo jazdy

drop [drɔp] *n* **1** (*of liquid*) kropla **2** (*reduction*): **a ~ in sth** spadek czegoś **3** (*vertical distance*): **a 300m ~, a ~ of 300m** trzystumetrowy spadek ▷ *vt* **1** (*accidentally*) upuszczać (upuścić *pf*); (*deliberately*) zrzucać (zrzucić *pf*) **2** (*lower*: *arm, leg, hand etc*) opuszczać (opuścić *pf*) **3** (*reduce*: *price*) zniżać (zniżyć *pf*) **4** (*abandon*: *idea, case etc*) porzucać (porzucić *pf*) **5** (*from team*) odpadać (odpaść *pf*) ▷ *vi* **1** (*fall*) spadać (spaść *pf*) **2** (*die down*: *wind*) przycichać (przycichnąć *pf*) **3** (*fall*: *voice*) zniżać (zniżyć *pf*); **drops** *n pl* (*medicine*) krople; **a ~ of ten percent** spadek o dziesięć procent; **chocolate/fruit ~s** dropsy czekoladowe/owocowe; **to ~ sb a line** skrobnąć do kogoś parę słów; **to ~ a hint** robić (zrobić *pf*) aluzję
▸ **drop by** *vi* (*inf*: *visit*) wpadać (wpaść *pf*)
▸ **drop in** (*inf*) *vi* (*visit*): **to ~ in (on sb)** wpadać (wpaść *pf*) (do kogoś)
▸ **drop off** *vi* (*fall asleep*) zasypiać (zasnąć *pf*) ▷ *vt* (*passenger*) podrzucać (podrzucić *pf*)
▸ **drop out** *vi* **1** (*withdraw*) wycofywać (wycofać *pf*) się **2** (*of college, university etc*) porzucać (porzucić *pf*)

drought [draut] *n* susza

drove [drəuv] *pt of* **drive**

drown [draun] *vt* **1** (*person, animal*) topić (utopić *pf*) **2** (*also*: **~ out**: *sound, voice*) zagłuszać (zagłuszyć *pf*) ▷ *vi* (*person, animal*) tonąć (utonąć *pf*)

drug [drʌg] *n* **1** (*prescribed*) lekarstwo **2** (*recreational*) narkotyk ▷ *vt* (*sedate*: *person, animal*) podawać (podać *pf*) środki nasenne +*dat*; **to be on ~s** zażywać (zażyć *pf*) leki; **to take ~s** brać leki; **hard/soft ~s** twarde/miękkie narkotyki

druggist ['drʌgɪst] (*US*) *n* **1** (*person*) aptekarz(-rka) *m/f* **2**: **~('s)** (*shop*) apteka

drugstore ['drʌgstɔːʳ] (*US*) *n* apteka

DRUGSTORE

W USA **drugstore** to drogeria pełniąca także funkcje kawiarenki. Poza lekarstwami i kosmetykami można tam również zamówić napoje i drobne przekąski.

drum [drʌm] *n* **1** (*instrument*) bęben **2** (*container*) beczka ▷ *vi* **1** (*rain*) dudnić **2** (*with fingers*) bębnić ▷ *vt* (*fingers*) bębnić; **drums** *n pl* (*kit*) perkusja
▸ **drum up** *vt* (*enthusiasm, support*) pozyskiwać (pozyskać *pf*)

drummer ['drʌməʳ] *n* perkusista

drunk [drʌŋk] *pp of* **drink** ▷ *adj* pijany ▷ *n* (*drunkard*) pijak; **to get ~** upijać (upić *pf*) się

dry [draɪ] *adj* **1** suchy **2** (*empty*: *lake, riverbed, well*) wyschnięty **3** (*wine, sherry*) wytrawny **4** (*humour, account*) ironiczny **5** (*uninteresting*: *lecture, style*) nudny ▷ *vt* (*clothes, hair*) wysychać (wyschnąć *pf*) ▷ *vi* (*paint, washing*) wysychać (wyschnąć *pf*);

on ~ land na suchym lądzie; **to ~ (up) the dishes** wycierać (wytrzeć *pf*) naczynia; **to ~ one's hands/hair** suszyć (wysuszyć *pf*) ręce/włosy; **to ~ one's eyes** ocierać (otrzeć *pf*) łzy
▶ **dry off** *vi* wysychać (wyschnąć *pf*) ▷ *vt* suszyć (wysuszyć *pf*)
▶ **dry out** *vi* wysychać (wyschnąć *pf*)
▶ **dry up** *vi* **1** (*river, well*) wysychać (wyschnąć *pf*) **2** (*supply, flow etc*) wyczerpywać (wyczerpać *pf*) się

dry-cleaner ['draɪ'kliːnəʳ] *n* (*also*: **dry cleaner's**) pralnia chemiczna

dryer ['draɪəʳ] *n* suszarka

dub [dʌb] *vt* **1** (*film, TV programme*) dubbingować (zdubbingować *pf*) **2** (*nickname*): **a man ~bed "the terminator"** człowiek zwany „terminator"; **~bed into Spanish/French** z hiszpańskim/francuskim dubbingiem

duck [dʌk] *n* kaczka ▷ *vi* (*also*: **~ down**) schylać (schylić *pf*) się ▷ *vt* (*blow*) uchylać (uchylić *pf*) się przed *+inst*

due [djuː] *adj* **1** (*person, train, bus*) planowy przyjazd **2**: **to be ~** (*baby*) mieć termin porodu **3** (*rent, payment*) należny **4**: **to be ~ to sb** (*owed*) należeć się komuś **5** (*proper*: *consideration*) stosowny ▷ *n*: **to give sb his/her ~** oddawać (oddać *pf*) mu/jej sprawiedliwość ▷ *adv*: **~ north/south** dokładnie na północ/południe; **dues** *n pl* (*for club, union*) składki; **~ to...** (*because of*) z powodu *+gen*...; **to be ~ to sth/sb** przysługiwać czemuś/komuś; **in ~ course** (*eventually*) we właściwym czasie

dug [dʌg] *pt, pp of* **dig**

dull [dʌl] *adj* **1** (*weather, day*) pochmurny; (*light, colour*) mroczny **2** (*boring*) nudny **3** (*sound, pain*) tępy ▷ *vt* **1** (*pain, grief*) uśmierzać (uśmierzyć *pf*) **2** (*mind, senses*) przytępiać (przytępić *pf*)

dumb [dʌm] *adj* **1** (*silent*) niemy **2** (*pej*: *stupid, foolish*) tępy **3** (*US*: *inf*: *silly, annoying*) głupi; **to be struck ~** oniemieć (*pf*)

dummy ['dʌmɪ] *n* **1** (*Brit*: *for baby*) smoczek **2** (*mannequin*) manekin

dump [dʌmp] *n* **1** (*tip*: *for rubbish*) wysypisko **2** (*inf*: *pigsty, tip*) nora **3** (*store*: *for ammunition, arms*) skład ▷ *vt* **1** (*put down*) rzucać (rzucić *pf*) **2** (*get rid of*) wyrzucać (wyrzucić *pf*) **3** (*computer data*) zrzucać (zrzucić *pf*); **to be down in the ~s** (*inf*) być w dołku; **"no ~ing"** „zakaz wysypywania śmieci"

Dumpster® ['dʌmpstəʳ] (*US*) *n* kontener

dungarees [dʌŋgə'riːz] *n pl* (*for work*) kombinezon *n sg*; (*for child, woman*) ogrodniczki

dungeon ['dʌndʒən] *n* loch

during ['djuərɪŋ] *prep* **1** (*throughout*) podczas *+gen* **2** (*at some point in*) w trakcie *+gen*

dusk [dʌsk] *n* zmierzch; **at ~** o zmierzchu

dust [dʌst] *n* (*dirt*: *outdoors*) pył; (*indoors*) kurz ▷ *vt* **1** (*furniture*) odkurzać (odkurzyć *pf*) **2**: **to ~ sth with sth** (*cake*: *with flour, sugar*) posypywać (posypać *pf*) coś czymś

dustbin ['dʌstbɪn] (*Brit*) *n* kosz na śmieci

dustman ['dʌstmən] (*irreg*) *n* (*Brit*) śmieciarz

dusty ['dʌstɪ] *adj* zakurzony

Dutch [dʌtʃ] *adj* holenderski ▷ *n* (*language*) holenderski; **the Dutch** *n pl* (*people*) Holendrzy

duty ['djuːtɪ] *n* **1** (*responsibility*) obowiązek **2** (*tax*) cło; **duties** *n pl* (*tasks*) obowiązki; **it is my ~ to...** to mój obowiązek, aby...; **to pay ~ on sth** płacić (zapłacić *pf*) cło za coś; **to report for ~** meldować (zameldować *pf*) się na stanowisku pracy; **to be on/off ~** (*police officer, nurse*) być na/po służbie; **~ chemist/officer/doctor** dyżurny aptekarz/policjant/lekarz

duty-free ['djuːtɪ'friː] *adj* (*drink, cigarettes*) wolnocłowy; **~ shop** sklep wolnocłowy

duvet ['duːveɪ] (*Brit*) *n* kołdra

DVD *n* DVD

DVD player *n* odtwarzacz DVD

dwarf [dwɔːf] (*pl* **dwarves** [dwɔːvz]) *n* (*in stories*) krasnoludek ▷ *adj* (*shrub, plant etc*) karłowaty

dying ['daɪɪŋ] *adj* **1** (*person, animal*) umierający **2** (*final*) ostatni ▷ *n pl*: **the ~** umierający

dynamic [daɪ'næmɪk] *adj* dynamiczny

dyslexia [dɪs'lɛksɪə] *n* dysleksja

dyslexic [dɪs'lɛksɪk] *adj*: **a ~ child** dziecko z dysleksją

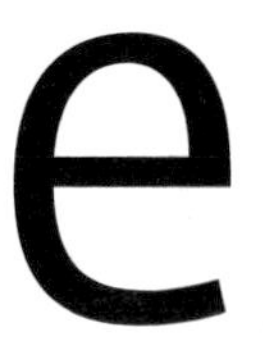

each [iːtʃ] *adj* (*thing, person, idea*) każdy ▷ *pron* (*each one*) każdy; **~ one of them** każdy z nich; **~ other** nawzajem; **they have two books ~** mają po dwie książki każdy; **they cost five pounds ~** kosztują (po) pięć funtów za sztukę; **~ of us** każdy z nas

eagle ['iːgl] *n* orzeł

ear [ɪə^r] *n* (*Anat*) ucho

earlier ['əːlɪə^r] *adj* wcześniejszy ▷ *adv* (*leave, go etc*) wcześniej; **~ this year** wcześniej w tym roku; **she left ~ than us** wyszła wcześniej niż my; **I can't come any ~** nie mogę przyjść wcześniej

early ['əːlɪ] *adv* wcześnie ▷ *adj* **1** (*near the beginning*: *stage, career*) wczesny **2** (*in history*) pierwszy **3** (*premature*: *death, departure*) przedwczesny **4** (*quick*: *reply*) szybki; **~ in the morning** wcześnie rano; **~ in the spring** wczesną wiosną; **in the ~ 80s** we wczesnych latach osiemdziesiątych; **in the ~ 19th century** na początku dziewiętnastego wieku; **she's in her ~ forties** jest po czterdziestce; **you're ~!** jesteś wcześnie!

earn [əːn] *vt* **1** (*salary, money*) zarabiać (zarobić *pf*) **2** (*Comm*: *interest*) przynosić (przynieść *pf*) **3** (*praise, reputation*) zyskiwać (zyskać *pf*); **to ~ one's** *or* **a living** zarabiać (zarobić *pf*) na życie

earnings ['əːnɪŋz] *n pl* zarobki

earring ['ɪərɪŋ] *n* kolczyk

earth [əːθ] *n* **1** (*also*: **the E~**: *planet*) Ziemia **2** (*land surface*) ziemia **3** (*soil*) ziemia

earthquake ['əːθkweɪk] *n* trzęsienie ziemi

easily ['iːzɪlɪ] *adv* **1** (*without difficulty*) łatwo **2** (*for emphasis*) bez wątpienia **3** (*quickly*) łatwo **4** (*in a relaxed way*) swobodnie

east [iːst] *n* **1** wschód **2**: **the E~** (*the Orient*) wschód ▷ *adj* wschodni ▷ *adv* na wschód; **the ~ of Spain** wschodnia część Hiszpanii; **to the ~** na wschód; **the ~ wind** wschodni wiatr; **~ of** na wschód od *+gen*

Easter ['iːstə^r] *n* Wielkanoc; **the ~ holidays** Święta Wielkanocne; **happy ~!** wesołych Świąt Wielkanocnych!

Easter egg *n* pisanka

eastern ['iːstən] *adj* **1** (*Geo*) wschodni **2**: **E~** (*oriental*) dalekowschodni; **~ Europe** Europa Wschodnia

easy ['iːzɪ] *adj* **1** (*simple*) łatwy **2** (*relaxed*) spokojny **3** (*comfortable*: *life, time*) łatwy **4** (*target, prey*) łatwy ▷ *adv*: **to take it** *or* **things ~** nie przejmować się; **it's ~ for sb to do sth** łatwo komuś coś zrobić; **to make life easier** ułatwiać (ułatwić *pf*) życie

eat [iːt] (*pt* **ate**, *pp* **eaten** ['iːtn]) *vt* (*food, breakfast, lunch, etc*) jeść (zjeść *pf*) ▷ *vi* **1** (*consume food*) jeść (zjeść *pf*) **2** (*have a meal*) jeść (zjeść *pf*) posiłek

e-book ['iːbuk] *n* książka elektroniczna

e-card ['iːkɑːd] *n* kartka elektroniczna

echo ['ɛkəu] (*pl* **echoes**) *n* **1** (*of sound*) echo **2** (*of opinion, attitude*) odbicie echem ▷ *vt* (*fig*: *repeat*) powtarzać (powtórzyć *pf*) ▷ *vi* **1** (*sound*) odbijać (odbić *pf*) się echem **2** (*cave, room*) rozbrzmiewać (rozbrzmieć *pf*)

e-cigarette ['iːsɪgə'rɛt] *n* e-papieros

eco-friendly ['iːkəu'frɛndlɪ] *adj* przyjazny dla środowiska

ecological [iːkə'lɔdʒɪkəl] *adj* ekologiczny

ecology [ɪ'kɔlədʒɪ] *n* **1** (*environment*) ekosystem **2** (*subject*) ekologia

economic [iːkə'nɔmɪk] *adj* **1** (*system, history, reform*) gospodarczy **2** (*profitable*: *business etc*) rentowny

economical [iːkə'nɔmɪkl] *adj* **1** (*system, car, machine*) ekonomiczny **2** (*person*) oszczędny

economics [iːkə'nɔmɪks] *n* **1** (*Scol, Univ*) ekonomia *f sg* **2** (*of project, situation*) ekonomika *f sg*

economy [ɪ'kɔnəmɪ] *n* **1** (*of country*) gospodarka **2** (*thrift*) oszczędność

edge [ɛdʒ] *n* **1** (*border*: *of road, town*) granica; (*of lake*) brzeg **2** (*of table, chair etc*) krawędź **3** (*of knife, sword etc*) ostrze ▷ *vi*: **to ~ forward** posuwać (posunąć *pf*) się do przodu; **to be on ~** (*nervous*) być spiętym

edible ['ɛdɪbl] *adj* jadalny

editor ['ɛdɪtə^r] *n* **1** (*of newspaper, magazine, book*) redaktor(ka) *m/f* **2** (*of text, report*) redaktor(ka) *m/f* **3** (*Rad, TV*) montażysta(-tka) *m/f*

education [ɛdju'keɪʃən] *n* (*schooling, teaching*) edukacja

educational [ɛdju'keɪʃənl] *adj* **1** (*institution, policy, needs*) oświatowy **2** (*instructive*: *experience*) pouczający

educator ['ɛdjukeɪtə^r] (*esp US*) *n* wychowawca(-czyni) *m/f*

effect [ɪ'fɛkt] *n* **1** (*result, consequence*) skutek **2** (*impression*) wrażenie; **effects** *n pl* **1** (*formal*: *belongings*) rzeczy osobiste **2** (*Cine*) efekty specjalne; **to come into** *or* **take ~** (*law*) wchodzić (wejść *pf*) w życie; **to take ~** (*drug*) zaczynać (zacząć *pf*) działać; **to put** *or* **bring** *or* **carry sth into ~** wprowadzać (wprowadzić *pf*) coś w życie; **to have an ~ on sb/sth** mieć wpływ na kogoś/coś; **in ~** w praktyce

effective [ɪ'fɛktɪv] *adj* **1** (*successful*) skuteczny **2** (*actual*: *leader, command*) faktyczny; **to become ~** (*Law*) wchodzić (wejść *pf*) w życie

effectively [ɪ'fɛktɪvlɪ] *adv* **1** (*successfully*) skutecznie **2** (*in reality*) faktycznie

efficient [ɪ'fɪʃənt] *adj* (*person*) sprawny; (*organization, system*) wydajny

effort ['ɛfət] *n* **1** (*energy*) wysiłek **2** (*attempt*) próba **3** (*physical/mental

exertion) trud; **to make an ~ to do sth** dokładać (dołożyć *pf*) starań, aby coś zrobić
e.g. *adv abbr* (= *exempli gratia*) np.
egg [ɛg] *n* **1** (*of bird, turtle etc*) jajo **2** (*for eating*) jajko **3** (*Bio*) jajo
eggplant ['ɛgplɑːnt] (*US*) *n* bakłażan
Egypt ['iːdʒɪpt] *n* Egipt
eight [eɪt] *num* osiem; *see also* **five**
eighteen [eɪ'tiːn] *num* osiemnaście; *see also* **fifteen**
eighteenth [eɪ'tiːnθ] *num* osiemnasty; *see also* **fifth**
eighth [eɪtθ] *num* **1** ósmy **2** (*fraction*) ósma część; *see also* **fifth**
eighty ['eɪtɪ] *num* osiemdziesiąt; *see also* **fifty**
Eire ['ɛərə] *n* Irlandia
either ['aɪðə^r] *adj* **1** (*one or other*) obojętnie który **2** (*both, each*) i jeden i drugi ▷ *pron* **1** (*after negative*) ani jeden ani drugi **2** (*after interrogative*) którykolwiek ▷ *adv* (*in negative statements*) też (nie) ▷ *conj*: **~... or...** albo...albo; **on ~ side** po obu stronach; **I don't like ~ of them** nie lubię ani jednego ani drugiego; **no, I don't ~** nie, ja też nie; **I haven't seen ~ one or the other** nie widziałem ani jednego ani drugiego
elastic [ɪ'læstɪk] *n* (*material*) elastik ▷ *adj* (*stretchy*) rozciągliwy
elastic band (*Brit*) *n* gumka
elbow ['ɛlbəu] *n* (*Anat*) łokieć ▷ *vt*: **to ~ one's way through the crowd** przepychać (przepchnąć *pf*) się przez tłum
elder ['ɛldə^r] *adj* (*brother, sister etc*) starszy ▷ *n* (*formal*: *older person*) osoba w podeszłym wieku; (*in tribe etc*): **~s** starszyzna
elderly ['ɛldəlɪ] *adj* (*old*) starszy
eldest ['ɛldɪst] *adj* (*child, daughter*) najstarszy ▷ *n* najstarszy
elect [ɪ'lɛkt] *vt* (*government, councillor, spokesman etc*) wybierać (wybrać *pf*); **to ~ to do sth** (*formal*: *choose*) postanawiać (postanowić *pf*) coś zrobić
election [ɪ'lɛkʃən] *n* wybory *m pl*; **to hold an ~** przeprowadzać (przeprowadzić *pf*) wybory
electric [ɪ'lɛktrɪk] *adj* **1** (*appliance*) elektryczny **2** (*fig*: *mood, atmosphere*) naelektryzowany
electrical [ɪ'lɛktrɪkl] *adj* elektryczny
electrician [ɪlɛk'trɪʃən] *n* elektryk
electricity [ɪlɛk'trɪsɪtɪ] *n* **1** (*energy*) elektryczność **2** (*supply*) prąd ▷ *adj* (*bill, meter*) rachunek za prąd
electronic [ɪlɛk'trɔnɪk] *adj* elektroniczny
electronics [ɪlɛk'trɔnɪks] *n* (*technology*) elektronika *f sg*
elegant ['ɛlɪgənt] *adj* **1** (*person, building*) elegancki **2** (*idea, prose*) zgrabny
elementary school [ɛlɪ'mɛntərɪ-] (*US*) *n* szkoła podstawowa
elephant ['ɛlɪfənt] *n* słoń
elevator ['ɛlɪveɪtə^r] (*US*) *n* winda
eleven [ɪ'lɛvn] *num* jedenaście; *see also* **five**
eleventh [ɪ'lɛvnθ] *num* jedenasty; *see also* **fifth**
else [ɛls] *adv*: **or ~** (*otherwise*) bo inaczej; (*threatening*) bo jak nie; **something ~, anything ~** coś innego; **where ~?** gdzie jeszcze?; **what ~?** co jeszcze?; **somewhere ~** gdzie indziej; **everywhere ~** wszędzie indziej; **everyone ~** wszyscy inni; **nobody ~** nikt inny; **if nothing ~** przynajmniej
email ['iːmeɪl] *n* email ▷ *vt* **1** (*person*) wysyłać (wysłać *pf*) emaila *+dat* **2** (*file, document*) wysyłać (wysłać *pf*)
email address *n* adres emailowy
embarrassed [ɪm'bærəst] *adj* (*laugh, silence*) pełen zażenowania; **to be ~** być zażenowanym
embarrassing [ɪm'bærəsɪŋ] *adj* **1** (*statement, situation*) żenujący **2** (*to politician, government*) kłopotliwy
embassy ['ɛmbəsɪ] *n* ambasada
emergency [ɪ'məːdʒənsɪ] *n* (*crisis*) nagły wypadek ▷ *adj* (*repair, talks, supplies, aid*) nadzwyczajny; **in an ~** w razie potrzeby
emigrate ['ɛmɪgreɪt] *vi* emigrować (wyemigrować *pf*)
emoji [ɪ'məudʒɪ] *n* emotikon
emotion [ɪ'məuʃən] *n* (*feeling*) uczucie
emotional [ɪ'məuʃənl] *adj* **1** (*support, problems*) emocjonalny

2 (*person*) uczuciowy **3** (*speech, plea*) wzruszający; **to get ~** wzruszać (wzruszyć *pf*) się
emperor ['ɛmpərəʳ] *n* cesarz
emphasize ['ɛmfəsaɪz] *vt* **1** (*word, point*) podkreślać (podkreślić *pf*) **2** (*make conspicuous*) uwydatniać (uwydatnić *pf*); **I must ~ that...** muszę podkreślić, że...
empire ['ɛmpaɪəʳ] *n* imperium; **a business/publishing ~** imperium biznesowe/wydawnicze
employ [ɪm'plɔɪ] *vt* **1** (*person, workforce*) zatrudniać (zatrudnić *pf*) **2** (*use: methods, materials*) stosować (zastosować *pf*); **he was ~ed as a technician** był zatrudniony jako technik
employee [ɪmplɔɪ'iː] *n* pracownik(-ica) *m/f*
employer [ɪm'plɔɪəʳ] *n* pracodawca(-czyni) *m/f*
employment [ɪm'plɔɪmənt] *n* (*work*) praca; **to find ~** znajdować (znaleźć *pf*) pracę; **to be in ~** mieć pracę
empty ['ɛmptɪ] *adj* **1** (*glass, container*) pusty **2** (*place, street*) wyludniony **3** (*house, room*) niezamieszkany **4** (*threat, gesture*) pusty ▷ *vt* **1** (*bin, ashtray*) opróżniać (opróżnić *pf*) **2** (*room, house etc*) opróżniać (opróżnić *pf*) ▷ *vi* (*room, building*) opróżniać (opróżnić *pf*) się; **to ~ sth into sth** (*pour out*) wylewać (wylać *pf*) coś z czegoś
enclose [ɪn'kləuz] *vt* **1** (*garden, space*) otaczać (otoczyć *pf*) **2** (*object in wrapping etc*) zamykać (zamknąć *pf*) **3** (*in letter: cheque*) załączać (załączyć *pf*); **please find ~d** w załączeniu przesyłam
encourage [ɪn'kʌrɪdʒ] *vt* **1** (*person*) zachęcać (zachęcić *pf*) **2** (*activity, attitude*) sprzyjać **3** (*growth, industry*) zachęcać (zachęcić *pf*); **to ~ sb to do sth** zachęcać (zachęcić *pf*) kogoś do zrobienia czegoś; **to be ~d by sth** być zachęconym przez coś
encouragement [ɪn'kʌrɪdʒmənt] *n* (*support*) zachęta
end [ɛnd] *n* **1** (*of period, event*) koniec **2** (*of film, book*) zakończenie **3** (*of street, queue, rope, table*) koniec **4** (*of town*) kraniec **5** (*of pencil, finger etc*) końcówka **6** (*purpose*) cel ▷ *vt* (*fighting, strike*) kończyć (skończyć *pf*) ▷ *vi* kończyć (skończyć *pf*) się; **at the ~ of the day** (*fig*) koniec końców; **to come to an ~** kończyć (skończyć *pf*) się; **to be at an ~** kończyć się; **in the ~** w końcu; **for hours on ~** całymi godzinami; **to bring sth to an ~, put an ~ to sth** zakończyć (*pf*) coś; **to make ~s meet** wiązać koniec z końcem; **to ~ (up) in tragedy/disaster** skończyć (*pf*) się tragedią/katastrofą
▶ **end up** *vi*: **to ~ up in** (*place*) znaleźć (*pf*) się w +*loc*; **he ~ed up buying it himself** skończyło się tak, że sam to kupił
ending ['ɛndɪŋ] *n* (*of book, film, play etc*) zakończenie; **a happy ~** szczęśliwe zakończenie
endless ['ɛndlɪs] *adj* **1** (*drought, war, speech*) niekończący się **2** (*arguments, meetings*) niekończący się **3** (*forest, beach*) bezkresny **4** (*possibilities*) nieskończony
enemy ['ɛnəmɪ] *n* **1** (*opponent*) przeciwnik(-iczka) *m/f* **2**: **the ~** (*Mil*) wróg ▷ *adj* (*forces, strategy, aircraft*) nieprzyjacielski
energetic [ɛnə'dʒɛtɪk] *adj* **1** (*person*) energiczny **2** (*activity*) dynamiczny
energy ['ɛnədʒɪ] *n* **1** (*strength*) siła **2** (*power*) energia
engaged [ɪn'geɪdʒd] *adj* **1** (*to be married*) zaręczony **2** (*Brit: Tel*) zajęty **3** (*Brit: toilet*) zajęty; **to get ~ (to sb)** zaręczać (zaręczyć *pf*) się (z kimś)
engagement [ɪn'geɪdʒmənt] *n* **1** (*formal: appointment*) spotkanie **2** (*to marry*) zaręczyny *f pl*
engine ['ɛndʒɪn] *n* **1** (*Aut*) silnik **2** (*Rail*) lokomotywa
engineer [ɛndʒɪ'nɪəʳ] *n* **1** (*who designs machines, bridges etc*) inżynier **2** (*who repairs machines, phones etc*) mechanik **3** (*US: train driver*) maszynista(-tka) *m/f*
engineering [ɛndʒɪ'nɪərɪŋ] *n* **1** (*of roads, bridges, machinery*) konstrukcja **2** (*science*) inżynieria
England ['ɪŋglənd] *n* Anglia

English ['ɪŋglɪʃ] *adj* angielski ▷ *n* (*language*) angielski; **the English** *n pl* (*people*) Anglicy; **an ~ speaker** osoba mówiąca po angielsku
Englishman ['ɪŋglɪʃmən] (*irreg*) *n* Anglik
Englishwoman ['ɪŋglɪʃwumən] (*irreg*) *n* Angielka
enjoy [ɪn'dʒɔɪ] *vt* **1** (*take pleasure in*) lubić **2** (*formal*: *have benefit of*) cieszyć się *+inst*; **to ~ doing sth** (*like doing*) lubić coś robić; **to ~ o.s.** dobrze się bawić; **~ your meal!** smacznego!
enjoyable [ɪn'dʒɔɪəbl] *adj* przyjemny
enormous [ɪ'nɔːməs] *adj* **1** (*in size or amount*) olbrzymi **2** (*in degree or extent*) ogromny
enough [ɪ'nʌf] *adj* (*time, books, people*) dość *+gen* ▷ *pron* wystarczająco dużo ▷ *adv* **1**: **big/old/tall ~** wystarczająco duży/stary/wysoki **2** (*reasonably*): **it's nice/interesting ~** to dość miłe/ciekawe; **~ time/money to do sth** dość czasu/pieniędzy, aby coś zrobić; **he has not worked ~** nie pracował wystarczająco dużo; **have you got ~?** wystarczy?; **~ to eat** dość do jedzenia; **will 5 be ~?** czy pięć wystarczy?; **I've had ~!** mam dość!; **he was kind ~ to lend me the money** był tak miły i pożyczył mi pieniądze; **(that's) ~!** wystarczy!; **I've had ~ of him** mam go dość; **that's ~, thanks** wystarczy, dziękuję
enter ['ɛntə[r]] *vt* **1** (*formal*: *room, building*) wchodzić (wejść *pf*) do *+gen* **2** (*army, profession*) wstępować (wstąpić *pf*) do *+gen* **3** (*race, competition*) zgłaszać (zgłosić *pf*) się do *+gen* **4** (*new phase, period*) zaczynać (zacząć *pf*) **5** (*Comput*: *data*) wprowadzać (wprowadzić *pf*) do *+gen* ▷ *vi* (*formal*: *come or go in*) wchodzić (wejść *pf*); **to ~ sb for sth** (*for competition, race*) zgłaszać (zgłosić *pf*) kogoś do czegoś
▸ **enter into** (*formal*) *vt fus* (*agreement, talks*) podejmować (podjąć *pf*)
entertain [ɛntə'teɪn] *vt* **1** (*amuse*) zabawiać (zabawić *pf*) **2** (*invite*: *guest*) podejmować (podjąć *pf*) **3** (*formal*: *consider idea, suggestion*) rozważać (rozważyć *pf*) ▷ *vi* zabawiać (zabawić *pf*) się
enthusiasm [ɪn'θuːzɪæzəm] *n* (*eagerness*) entuzjazm; **~ for sth** zapał do czegoś
enthusiastic [ɪnθuːzɪ'æstɪk] *adj* (*excited, eager*: *person*) zapalony; (*response, reception*) entuzjastyczny; **to be ~ about sth** odnosić (odnieść *pf*) się do czegoś z entuzjazmem
entire [ɪn'taɪə[r]] *adj* cały
entirely [ɪn'taɪəlɪ] *adv* całkowicie
entrance ['ɛntrns] *n* wejście; **the ~ to sth** wejście do czegoś; **to gain ~ to** zostać przyjętym do *+gen*
entry ['ɛntrɪ] *n* **1** (*way in*) wejście **2** (*in competition*) przystąpienie **3** (*item*: *in diary*) notatka; (*in reference book*) hasło; (*Comput*) wprowadzenie; **"no ~"** wstęp wzbroniony; (*Aut*) wjazd
envelope ['ɛnvələup] *n* koperta
environment [ɪn'vaɪərnmənt] *n* (*surroundings*) otoczenie; **the ~** (*natural world*) środowisko naturalne
environmental [ɪnvaɪərn'mɛntl] *adj* **1** (*of the natural world*) ekologiczny **2** (*of surroundings*) środowiskowy
envy ['ɛnvɪ] *n* (*jealousy*) zazdrość ▷ *vt* (*be jealous of*) być zazdrosnym o; **to ~ sb sth** zazdrościć komuś czegoś
episode ['ɛpɪsəud] *n* **1** (*period, event*) wydarzenie **2** (*Rad, TV*: *instalment*) odcinek
equal ['iːkwl] *adj* **1** (*size, number, amount*) równy **2** (*intensity, importance*) jednakowy ▷ *n* (*peer*) równy ▷ *vt* **1** (*number, amount*) równać się **2** (*match, rival*) dorównywać (dorównać *pf*) *+dat*; **they are roughly ~ in size** są mniej więcej tego samego rozmiaru; **to be ~ to** (*the same*) być równym *+dat*; **79 minus 14 ~s 65** siedemdziesiąt dziewięć odjąć czternaście równa się sześćdziesiąt pięć
equality [iː'kwɔlɪtɪ] *n* równość
equipment [ɪ'kwɪpmənt] *n* sprzęt
e-reader ['iːriːdə[r]] *n* czytnik e-booków
error ['ɛrə[r]] *n* błąd; **to make an ~** robić (zrobić *pf*) błąd; **typing ~**

literówka; **mathematical ~** błąd rachunkowy
escalator ['ɛskəleɪtəʳ] *n* schody ruchome
escape [ɪs'keɪp] *n* **1** ucieczka **2** (*from accident*): **to have a narrow** *or* **lucky ~** o włos uniknąć (*pf*) nieszczęścia ▷ *vi* **1** (*get away*) uciekać (uciec *pf*) **2** (*from jail*) uciekać (uciec *pf*) **3** (*from accident*): **to ~ unhurt** wyjść (*pf*) cało **4** (*leak*: *liquid*) wyciekać (wyciec *pf*); (*gas*) ulatniać (ulotnić *pf*) się; (*heat*) uciekać (uciec *pf*) ▷ *vt* (*injury*) unikać (uniknąć *pf*) +*gen*; **to ~ from** (*place*) uciekać (uciec *pf*) do +*gen*
escort [*n* 'ɛskɔːt, *vb* ɪs'kɔːt] *n* **1** (*Mil*) eskorta **2** (*companion*) osoba towarzysząca ▷ *vt* (*person*) towarzyszyć +*dat*; **to ~ sb to the door** odprowadzać (odprowadzić *pf*) kogoś do drzwi
especially [ɪs'pɛʃlɪ] *adv* **1** (*particularly*) zwłaszcza **2** (*happy, gifted, fond of sb*) szczególnie
essay ['ɛseɪ] *n* **1** (*Scol*) wypracowanie **2** (*paper, discussion*) praca
essential [ɪ'sɛnʃl] *adj* **1** (*necessary, vital*) niezbędny **2** (*basic*) podstawowy; **essentials** *n pl* (*necessities*) rzeczy niezbędne; **it is ~ that...** musimy...; **it is ~ to...** należy koniecznie...
estate [ɪs'teɪt] *n* **1** (*land*) posiadłość **2** (*Brit*: *also*: **housing ~**) osiedle mieszkaniowe **3** (*Law*) majątek
estate agent (*Brit*) *n* pośrednik(-iczka) *m/f* w handlu nieruchomościami
estimate [*n* 'ɛstɪmət, *vb* 'ɛstɪmeɪt] *n* **1** (*calculation*) obliczenie **2** (*assessment*) ocena **3** (*Comm*: *of price*) wycena ▷ *vt* (*reckon, calculate*) szacować (oszacować *pf*); **the damage was ~d at 300 million pounds** szkody oszacowano na trzysta milionów funtów; **I ~ that...** oceniam, że...
etc (*esp US* **etc.**) *abbr* (= *et cetera*) itd., itp.
ethnic ['ɛθnɪk] *adj* etniczny
EU *n abbr* (= *European Union*): **the EU** UE
euro ['juərəu] *n* euro
Europe ['juərəp] *n* Europa
European [juərə'piːən] *adj* europejski ▷ *n* (*person*) Europejczyk(-jka) *m/f*
European Union *n*: **the ~** Unia Europejska
eve [iːv] *n*: **on the ~ of** w przeddzień +*gen*
even ['iːvn] *adv* nawet ▷ *adj* **1** (*flat*) równy **2** (*constant*: *temperature, rate*) stały **3** (*equal*) równy **4** (*number*) parzysty; **~ more** nawet więcej; **~ better/faster** jeszcze lepiej/ szybciej; **~ if** nawet jeśli; **~ though** mimo że; **~ so** mimo wszystko; **not ~** nawet nie; **~ he was there** nawet on tam był; **~ on Sundays** nawet w niedziele; **to break ~** wychodzić (wyjść *pf*) na zero; **to get ~ with sb** (*inf*) policzyć (*pf*) się z kimś
evening ['iːvnɪŋ] *n* wieczór; **in the ~** wieczorem; **this ~** dziś wieczorem; **tomorrow/yesterday ~** jutro/ wczoraj wieczorem
evening class *n* kurs wieczorowy
event [ɪ'vɛnt] *n* **1** (*occurrence*) zdarzenie **2** (*Sport*) konkurencja; **in the ~ of...** w razie +*gen*...
eventual [ɪ'vɛntʃuəl] *adj* (*outcome, aim*) ostateczny
eventually [ɪ'vɛntʃuəlɪ] *adv* **1** (*finally*) ostatecznie **2** (*ultimately*) w końcu
ever ['ɛvəʳ] *adv* **1** (*at any time*) kiedykolwiek **2** (*always*) zawsze; **have you ~ seen it/been there?** czy kiedykolwiek to widziałeś/tam byłeś?; **~ since** (*adv*) od tego czasu; (*conj*) od kiedy; **why ~ not?** ależ dlaczego nie?; **who ~ would do such a thing?** kto zrobiłby coś takiego?; **the best ~** najlepszy; **hardly ~** prawie nigdy; **better than ~** lepszy niż kiedykolwiek; **as ~** jak zawsze

KEYWORD

every ['ɛvrɪ] *adj* **1** (*each*) każdy; **every village should have a post office** w każdej wiosce powinna być poczta; **every one of them** (*people*) każdy z nich; (*objects*) każdy z nich **2** (*all possible*) każdy; **there is every**

…zelkie szanse, … **occasion** … ię … ; **every** … dnia/każdego … **every Sunday** w każdą niedzielę; **every other week** co drugi tydzień; **every other/third day** co drugi/trzeci dzień; **every few days/ minutes** co kilka dni/minut; **every now and then** *or* **again** od czasu do czasu
4 (*statistics*): **one in every five people** co piąta osoba

everybody ['ɛvrɪbɔdɪ] *pron* wszyscy; **~ knows about it** wszyscy o tym wiedzą; **~ else** wszyscy inni
everyone ['ɛvrɪwʌn] *pron* = **everybody**
everything ['ɛvrɪθɪŋ] *pron* wszystko; **is ~ OK?** czy wszystko w porządku?; **~ is ready** wszystko gotowe; **he did ~ possible** zrobił wszystko, co było można
everywhere ['ɛvrɪwɛəʳ] *adv* wszędzie ▷ *pron* wszędzie; **there's rubbish ~** wszędzie są śmieci; **~ you go** gdziekolwiek pójdziesz
evil ['iːvl] *adj* (*person, system*) zły ▷ *n* (*wickedness*) zło
exact [ɪg'zækt] *adj* **1** (*time, number, word etc*) dokładny **2** (*person, worker*) dokładny **3** (*used for emphasis*) dokładnie
exactly [ɪg'zæktlɪ] *adv* **1** (*precisely*) dokładnie **2** (*indicating emphasis*) właśnie **3** (*indicating agreement*) właśnie tak; **at 5 o'clock ~** punktualnie o piątej; **not ~** (*indicating disagreement*) niezupełnie; **he's not ~ rich/poor** właściwie nie jest bogaty/ biedny
exaggerate [ɪg'zædʒəreɪt] *vi* przesadzać (przesadzić *pf*) ▷ *vt* **1** (*situation, effects*) wyolbrzymiać (wyolbrzymić *pf*) **2** (*feature, quality*) popadać (popaść *pf*) w przesadę
exam [ɪg'zæm] *n* (*Scol, Univ*) egzamin
examination [ɪgzæmɪ'neɪʃən] *n* **1** (*inspection*) kontrola **2** (*formal*: *Scol, Univ*) egzamin **3** (*Med*) badanie
examine [ɪg'zæmɪn] *vt* **1** (*inspect*) sprawdzać (sprawdzić *pf*) **2** (*Scol, Univ*) egzaminować (przeegzaminować *pf*) **3** (*Med*) badać (zbadać *pf*)
example [ɪg'zɑːmpl] *n* przykład; **for ~** na przykład; **an ~ of sth** przykład czegoś; **to set an ~** dawać (dać *pf*) przykład; **to follow sb's ~** iść (pójść *pf*) za przykładem kogoś
excellent ['ɛksələnt] *adj* doskonały ▷ *excl*: **~!** doskonale!
except [ɪk'sɛpt] *prep* (*apart from*) poza *+inst*; **~ for** poza *+inst*; **~ that…** tyle tylko, że…; **~ if/when** chyba że
exception [ɪk'sɛpʃən] *n* (*special case*) wyjątek; **to make an ~** robić (zrobić *pf*) wyjątek; **with the ~ of** z wyjątkiem *+gen*; **to take ~ (to sth)** czuć (poczuć *pf*) się dotkniętym (czymś)
exchange [ɪks'tʃeɪndʒ] *vt* **1** wymieniać (wymienić *pf*) **2**: **to ~ sth (for sth)** (*goods*) zamieniać (zamienić *pf*) coś (na coś) ▷ *n* wymiana; **in ~ (for)** w zamian (za)
exchange rate *n* kurs wymiany walut
excited [ɪk'saɪtɪd] *adj* podekscytowany; **to be ~ about sth/about doing sth** być podekscytowanym czymś/z powodu robienia czegoś; **to get ~** zachwycać (zachwycić *pf*) się
excitement [ɪk'saɪtmənt] *n* (*exhilaration*) podekscytowanie
exciting [ɪk'saɪtɪŋ] *adj* (*time, event, place*) ekscytujący
exclamation mark [ɛksklə'meɪʃən-] (*US* **exclamation point**) *n* wykrzyknik
excuse [*n* ɪks'kjuːs, *vb* ɪks'kjuːz] *n* (*justification*) usprawiedliwienie ▷ *vt* **1** (*justify*: *person, behaviour*) usprawiedliwiać (usprawiedliwić *pf*) **2** (*forgive*: *person, behaviour*) wybaczać (wybaczyć *pf*); **an ~ to do/not to do sth** wymówka do zrobienia/do niezrobienia czegoś; **to make an ~** znajdować (znaleźć *pf*) wymówkę; **to make ~s for sb** tłumaczyć (wytłumaczyć *pf*) się za kogoś; **there's no ~ for such behaviour**

nie ma usprawiedliwienia dla takiego zachowania; **to be ~d from (doing) sth** zostawać (zostać *pf*) zwolnionym z (robienia) czegoś; **to ~ sb for sth/for doing sth** przepraszać (przeprosić *pf*) kogoś za coś/za zrobienie czegoś; **~ me!** (*attracting attention*) przepraszam!; (*as apology*) przepraszam; **~ me, please** przepraszam; **~ me?** (*US*) słucham?

exercise ['ɛksəsaɪz] *n* **1** (*physical exertion*) ćwiczenie **2** (*series of movements*) gimnastyka **3** (*Scol, Mus*) ćwiczenie **4** (*Mil*) musztra ▷ *vt* **1** (*use*) wykazywać (wykazać *pf*) się **2** (*muscles, mind*) ćwiczyć ▷ *vi* (*person*) ćwiczyć; **to take** *or* **get ~** ćwiczyć; **to do ~s** (*Sport*) gimnastykować się; **to ~ one's right to do sth** korzystać (wykorzystać *pf*) prawo do zrobienia czegoś

exhausted [ɪg'zɔːstɪd] *adj* (*tired*) wyczerpany

exhibition [ɛksɪ'bɪʃən] *n* **1** (*of paintings etc*) wystawa **2** (*display: of skill, talent etc*) pokaz

exist [ɪg'zɪst] *vi* **1** (*be present*) istnieć **2** (*live, subsist*) egzystować; **to ~ on sth** żywić się czymś

exit ['ɛksɪt] *n* **1** (*from room, building, motorway etc*) wyjście **2** (*departure*): **to make a hasty** *or* **quick ~** ulatniać (ulotnić *pf*) się ▷ *vt* **1** (*formal: room, building*) wychodzić (wyjść *pf*) z *+gen* **2** (*Comput*) wychodzić (wyjść *pf*) z *+gen*

expect [ɪks'pɛkt] *vt* **1** (*anticipate*) oczekiwać *+gen* **2** (*await*) spodziewać się *+gen* **3** (*baby*) spodziewać się *+gen* **4** (*require*) oczekiwać *+gen* **5** (*suppose*) przypuszczać ▷ *vi*: **to be ~ing** (*be pregnant*) spodziewać się dziecka; **to ~ sth to happen** spodziewać się czegoś; **to ~ sb to do sth** (*anticipate*) spodziewać się, że ktoś coś zrobi; **to ~ to do sth** planować coś; **I ~ so** sądzę, że tak; **as ~ed** jak się spodziewano

expedition [ɛkspə'dɪʃən] *n* wyprawa

expel [ɪks'pɛl] *vt* **1** (*child: from school*) wydalać (wydalić *pf*) z *+gen* **2** (*person: from place*) usuwać (usunąć *pf*) z *+gen*

expensive [ɪks'pɛnsɪv] *ad*[...] drogi **2** (*mistake*) kosztowny[...] drogi

experience [ɪks'pɪərɪəns] *n* doświadczenie ▷ *vt* (*feeling, proble*[...]) doświadczać (doświadczyć *pf*) *+gen*

experienced [ɪks'pɪərɪənst] *adj* doświadczony

experiment [*n* ɪks'pɛrɪmənt, *vb* ɪks'pɛrɪmɛnt] *n* **1** (*Sci*) eksperyment **2** (*trial*) doświadczenie ▷ *vi* **1**: **to ~ (with/on)** (*Sci*) przeprowadzać (przeprowadzić *pf*) eksperyment (z *+inst*/na *+loc*) **2** (*fig*) próbować (spróbować *pf*); **to perform** *or* **conduct** *or* **carry out an ~** przeprowadzać (przeprowadzić *pf*) eksperyment

expert ['ɛkspəːt] *n* (*specialist*) specjalista(-tka) *m/f* ▷ *adj* (*help, advice*) fachowy; **an ~ on sth** specjalista od czegoś; **to be ~ in** *or* **at doing sth** radzić sobie doskonale z robieniem czegoś

expire [ɪks'paɪə^r] *vi* (*passport, licence etc*) tracić (stracić *pf*) ważność

explain [ɪks'pleɪn] *vt* **1** (*clarify*) tłumaczyć (wytłumaczyć *pf*) **2** (*give reasons for*) wyjaśniać (wyjaśnić *pf*); **to ~ why/how** wyjaśniać (wyjaśnić *pf*) dlaczego/jak; **to ~ sth to sb** wyjaśniać (wyjaśnić *pf*) coś komuś; **to ~ that...** wyjaśniać (wyjaśnić *pf*), że...

explanation [ɛksplə'neɪʃən] *n* **1** (*reason*): **~ (for sth)** wyjaśnienie (czegoś) **2** (*description*): **~ (of sth)** wytłumaczenie (czegoś)

explode [ɪks'pləud] *vi* **1** (*bomb*) wybuchać (wybuchnąć *pf*) **2** (*population*) gwałtownie wzrastać (wzrosnąć *pf*) **3** (*person: with rage etc*) wybuchać (wybuchnąć *pf*) ▷ *vt* **1** (*bomb, tank*) eksplodować **2** (*myth, theory*) obalać (obalić *pf*)

explore [ɪks'plɔː^r] *vt* **1** (*place, space*) penetrować (spenetrować *pf*) **2** (*with hands*) badać (zbadać *pf*) **3** (*idea, suggestion*) zgłębiać (zgłębić *pf*) ▷ *vi* (*look around*) prowadzić (przeprowadzić *pf*) poszukiwania

explosion [ɪks'pləuʒən] *n* **1** (*of bomb*) wybuch **2** (*increase: of population*) gwałtowny wzrost **3** (*outburst*: *of rage, laughter etc*) wybuch

export [*vb* ɛks'pɔːt, *n*, *adj* 'ɛkspɔːt] *vt* eksportować (wyeksportować *pf*) ▷ *n* **1** (*process*) eksport **2** (*product*) towar eksportowy ▷ *adj* (*duty, permit, licence*) eksportowy

express [ɪks'prɛs] *vt* **1** (*idea, view, concern*) wyrażać (wyrazić *pf*) **2** (*formal*: *quantity, number*): **~ed as a percentage/fraction** wyrażone w procentach/ułamkach ▷ *adj* **1** (*command, wishes etc*) wyraźny **2** (*purpose, intention*) wyraźny **3** (*service, mail*) ekspresowy ▷ *n* (*train, coach*) ekspres ▷ *adv* (*send*) ekspresowo; **to ~ o.s.** wyrażać (wyrazić *pf*) się

expression [ɪks'prɛʃən] *n* **1** (*word, phrase*) wyrażenie **2** (*on face*) wyraz **3** (*of idea, emotion*) wyraz **4** (*feeling*: *of actor, singer etc*) ekspresja

extension [ɪks'tɛnʃən] *n* **1** (*of building*) przybudówka **2** (*of contract, visa*) przedłużenie **3** (*of rights, campaign, idea*) rozszerzenie **4** (*Elec*) przedłużacz **5** (*of road, railway*) przedłużenie **6** (*Tel*) numer wewnętrzny; **~ 3718** (*Tel*) numer wewnętrzny trzydzieści siedem osiemnaście

extent [ɪks'tɛnt] *n* **1** (*of area, land etc*) rozmiar **2** (*of problem, damage etc*) zakres; **to a certain ~** w pewnym stopniu; **to a large ~** w znacznym stopniu; **to some ~** do pewnego stopnia; **to what ~?** do jakiego stopnia?

extinct [ɪks'tɪŋkt] *adj* (*animal, plant*) wymarły

extra ['ɛkstrə] *adj* (*thing, person, amount*) dodatkowy ▷ *adv* **1** (*in addition*) dodatkowo **2** (*inf*: *particularly*) szczególnie ▷ *n* **1** (*luxury*) dodatek **2** (*surcharge*) dodatek **3** (*Cine, Theat*) statysta(-tka) *m/f*; **wine will cost ~** za wino trzeba zapłacić osobno

extraordinary [ɪks'trɔːdnrɪ] *adj* **1** (*exceptional*) niezwykły **2** (*formal*: *meeting*) nadzwyczajny

extreme [ɪks'triːm] *adj* **1** (*poverty, caution*) skrajny **2** (*opinions, methods etc*) ekstremalny **3** (*point, edge*) skrajny

extremely [ɪks'triːmlɪ] *adv* wyjątkowo

extremist [ɪks'triːmɪst] *n* ekstremista(-tka) *m/f* ▷ *adj* (*views, group, actions*) ekstremistyczny

eye [aɪ] *n* (*Anat*) oko; **to keep an ~ on sb/sth** pilnować kogoś/czegoś; **to catch sb's ~** (*action, movement*) zwracać (zwrócić *pf*) czyjąś uwagę; (*person*: *deliberately*) ściągać (ściągnąć *pf*) kogoś wzrokiem; **to have one's ~ on sth** (*inf*: *want*) mieć na coś oko; **to keep an ~ out for sb/sth** (*look out for*) rozglądać (rozejrzeć *pf*) się za kimś/czymś; **to look sb in the ~** *or* **to meet sb's ~s** patrzeć (popatrzeć *pf*) komuś w oczy

eyebrow ['aɪbrau] *n* brew

eyelash ['aɪlæʃ] *n* rzęsa

eyelid ['aɪlɪd] *n* powieka

eyesight ['aɪsaɪt] *n* wzrok

fabric ['fæbrɪk] *n* (*cloth*) tkanina
fabulous ['fæbjuləs] *adj* **1** (*inf*: *fantastic*) wspaniały **2** (*extraordinary*) bajeczny
face [feɪs] *n* **1** (*Anat*) twarz **2** (*expression*) mina **3** (*of clock*) tarcza ▷ *vt* **1** (*direction*: *person*) patrzeć (popatrzeć *pf*) na **2** (*confront*: *unpleasant situation*) stawać (stanąć *pf*) w obliczu *+gen* **3** ▷ *vi*: **to stand facing sth** (*person*) stać (stanąć *pf*) przodem do czegoś; **to ~ towards sth** (*building, seat, car*) wychodzić na coś; **I can't** *or* **couldn't ~ it** nie mogę stawić temu czoła; **to come ~ to ~ with sb** stawać (stanąć *pf*) oko w oko z kimś; **to come ~ to ~ with sth** stawać (stanąć *pf*) oko w oko z czymś
▸ **face up to** *vt fus* **1** (*truth, facts*) godzić (pogodzić *pf*) się z *+inst* **2** (*responsibilities, duties*) sprostać (*pf*) *+dat*
face cloth (*Brit*) *n* myjka do twarzy
facility [fə'sɪlɪtɪ] *n* (*service*) udogodnienie
fact [fækt] *n* fakt; **in (actual) ~** *or* **as a matter of ~** (*for emphasis*) faktycznie; (*when disagreeing*) tak naprawdę; (*when qualifying statement*) rzeczywiście; **~s and figures** fakty i cyfry
factory ['fæktərɪ] *n* fabryka
fail [feɪl] *vt* (*exam, test*) nie zdać (*pf*) *+gen* ▷ *vi* **1** (*candidate*) nie zdać (*pf*) **2** (*attempt, plan, remedy*) nie powieść (*pf*) się; **to ~ to do sth** (*not succeed*) nie zdołać *pf* czegoś zrobić; **without ~** (*definitely*) z całą pewnością; (*without exception*) niezawodnie
failure ['feɪljə^r] *n* **1** (*lack of success*) niepowodzenie **2** (*person*) nieudacznik(-ica) *m/f*; **~ in sth** niezrobienie czegoś
faint [feɪnt] *adj* **1** (*sound, light, smell, hope*) słaby **2** (*mark, trace*) niewyraźny ▷ *vi* (*Med*) zasłabnąć (*pf*); **to feel ~** czuć (poczuć *pf*) się słabo
fair [fɛə^r] *adj* **1** (*person, decision, trial*) sprawiedliwy **2** (*size, number, distance*) spory **3** (*chance, guess, idea*) niezły **4** (*skin, complexion*) jasny; (*hair*) blond ▷ *n* **1** (*trade fair*) targi *m pl* **2** (*Brit*: *also*: **fun~**) wesołe miasteczko; **it's not ~!** to niesprawiedliwe!
fairground ['fɛəgraund] *n* wesołe miasteczko
fairly ['fɛəlɪ] *adv* **1** (*justly*: *share, distribute*) sprawiedliwie **2** (*quite*: *heavy, fast, good*) dość
fairy ['fɛərɪ] *n* wróżka
fairy tale *n* bajka
faith [feɪθ] *n* wiara; **to have ~ in sb/sth** ufać (zaufać *pf*) komuś/czemuś
faithful ['feɪθful] *adj* wierny
faithfully ['feɪθfəlɪ] *adv* wiernie; **yours ~** (*Brit*) z wyrazami szacunku
fake [feɪk] *n* (*painting, antique, document*) imitacja ▷ *adj* (*painting, document*) fałszywy
fall [fɔːl] (*pt* **fell**, *pp* **fallen**) *vi* **1** (*person, object*) spadać (spaść *pf*) **2** (*fall over*: *person, building*) upadać (upaść *pf*) **3** (*snow, rain*) padać (spaść *pf*) **4** (*price, temperature, currency*) spadać (spaść *pf*) ▷ *n* **1** (*of person*) upadek **2** (*in price, temperature*) spadek **3** (*US*: *autumn*) jesień; **to ~ in love (with sb/sth)** zakochiwać (zakochać *pf*) się (w kimś/czymś)
▸ **fall down** *vi* **1** (*person*) upadać (upaść *pf*) **2** (*building*) upadać (upaść *pf*)
▸ **fall for** *vt fus* **1** (*trick, story, lie*) dawać (dać *pf*) się nabrać na **2** (*person*) zakochiwać (zakochać *pf*) się w *+loc*
▸ **fall off** *vi* (*person, object*) odpadać (odpaść *pf*)

▸ **fall out** *vi* (*friends*) kłócić (pokłócić *pf*) się; **to ~ out with sb** kłócić (pokłócić *pf*) się z kimś
▸ **fall over** *vi* (*person, object*) przewracać (przewrócić *pf*) się
▸ **fall through** *vi* (*plan*) nie udać (*pf*) się
fallen ['fɔ:lən] *pp of* **fall**
false [fɔ:ls] *adj* **1** (*artificial*) sztuczny **2** (*untrue*) fałszywy
fame [feɪm] *n* sława
familiar [fə'mɪlɪəʳ] *adj* (*well-known*) znajomy; **to be ~ with** (*subject*) znać
family ['fæmɪlɪ] *n* rodzina
famine ['fæmɪn] *n* głód
famous ['feɪməs] *adj* znany
fan [fæn] *n* **1** (*admirer*) fan(ka) *m/f* **2** (*Elec*) wentylator **3** (*folding*) wachlarz
fanatic [fə'nætɪk] *n* fanatyk(-yczka) *m/f*
fancy ['fænsɪ] *vt* **1** (*esp Brit: inf: feel like, want*) mieć ochotę na **2** (*inf: person*): **she really fancies him** on bardzo jej się podoba; **~ seeing you here!** ty tutaj?
fancy dress *n* kostium
fancy-dress party ['fænsɪdrɛs-] *n* bal przebierańców
fantastic [fæn'tæstɪk] *adj* **1** (*wonderful*) fantastyczny **2** (*enormous*) niesamowity
FAQ *n abbr* (= *frequently asked questions*) FAQ (*często zadawane pytania*)
far [fɑ:ʳ] *adj* **1** (*distant*) daleki **2** (*extreme*): **the ~ end/side** drugi koniec ▹ *adv* **1** (*a long way*) daleko **2** (*much, greatly*) o wiele; **as ~ as I know** o ile wiem; **by ~** zdecydowanie; **so ~** jak do tej pory; **is it ~ to London?** czy daleko jest stąd do Londynu?; **it's not ~ from here** to niedaleko stąd; **how ~?** (*in distance*) jak daleko?; (*in degree*) jak bardzo?; (*in progress*) jak daleko?; **~ away** daleko; **~ better** znacznie lepiej
fare [fɛəʳ] *n* (*price*) opłata za przejazd; **half ~/full ~** opłata ze zniżką/pełna opłata
Far East *n*: **the ~** Daleki Wschód
farm [fɑ:m] *n* gospodarstwo rolne
farmer ['fɑ:məʳ] *n* rolnik
farmhouse ['fɑ:mhaus] *n* dom wiejski
farming ['fɑ:mɪŋ] *n* rolnictwo
fascinating ['fæsɪneɪtɪŋ] *adj* fascynujący
fashion ['fæʃən] *n* moda; **in ~** w modzie
fashionable ['fæʃnəbl] *adj* modny
fast [fɑ:st] *adj* szybki ▹ *adv* (*run, act, think*) szybko; **my watch is 5 minutes ~** mój zegarek spieszy się o pięć minut; **~ asleep** pogrążony w głębokim śnie; **as ~ as I can** najszybciej, jak mogę
fast food *n* (*burger etc*) fast food
fat [fæt] *adj* gruby ▹ *n* tłuszcz
fatal ['feɪtl] *adj* **1** (*accident, injury, illness*) śmiertelny **2** (*fig: mistake*) fatalny
father ['fɑ:ðəʳ] *n* **1** (*parent*) ojciec **2** (*Rel*) ksiądz
Father Christmas (*Brit*) *n* Święty Mikołaj
father-in-law ['fɑ:ðərənlɔ:] (*pl* **fathers-in-law**) *n* teść
faucet ['fɔ:sɪt] (*US*) *n* kran
fault [fɔ:lt] *n* **1** (*mistake*) błąd **2** (*defect: in person*) wada; (*in machine*) usterka; **it's my ~** to moja wina
fava bean ['fɑ:və-] (*US*) *n* bób
favour ['feɪvəʳ] (*US* **favor**) *n* (*approval*) przychylność; (*act of kindness*) przysługa; **to ask a ~ of sb** prosić (poprosić *pf*) kogoś o przysługę; **to do sb a ~** wyświadczać (wyświadczyć *pf*) komuś przysługę; **to be in ~ of sth/doing sth** być za czymś/zrobieniem czegoś
favourite ['feɪvrɪt] (*US* **favorite**) *adj* ulubiony ▹ *n* **1** (*person*) ulubieniec(-ica) *m/f* **2** (*in race*) faworyt(ka) *m/f*
fax [fæks] *n* **1** (*document*) faks **2** (*also:* **~ machine**) faks ▹ *vt* (*document*) faksować (przefaksować *pf*)
fear [fɪəʳ] *n* **1** (*terror*) strach **2** (*anxiety*) lęk ▹ *vt* (*be scared of*) bać się *+gen*; **to ~ that...** bać się, że...
feather ['fɛðəʳ] *n* (*of bird*) pióro
feature ['fi:tʃəʳ] *n* (*characteristic*) cecha
February ['fɛbruərɪ] *n* luty; *see also* **July**

fed [fɛd] *pt, pp of* **feed**
fed up (*inf*) *adj*: **to be ~ with sth** mieć czegoś dosyć
fee [fiː] *n* opłata
feeble ['fiːbl] *adj* **1** (*person, animal, voice*) słaby **2** (*attempt, excuse, argument*) nieprzekonujący
feed [fiːd] (*pt, pp* **fed**) *vt* **1** (*baby, invalid, dog*) karmić (nakarmić *pf*) **2** (*family*) żywić (wyżywić *pf*) ▷ *n* (*Comput*) zawartość kanału informacyjnego
feel [fiːl] (*pt, pp* **felt**) *vt* **1** (*touch: object, face*) dotykać (dotknąć *pf*) *+gen* **2** (*experience*) czuć (poczuć *pf*) **3** (*think, believe*) sądzić; **to ~ that...** czuć (poczuć *pf*), że...; **to ~ hungry** być głodnym; **to ~ cold** odczuwać (odczuć *pf*) zimno; **to ~ lonely/better** czuć się samotnym/lepszym; **I don't ~ well** nie czuję się dobrze; **to ~ sorry for sb** współczuć komuś; **it ~s colder here** tu jest zimniej; **to ~ like** (*want*) mieć ochotę na; **it ~s like** *or* **it ~s as if...** wygląda na to, że...
feeling ['fiːlɪŋ] *n* **1** (*emotion*) uczucie **2** (*physical sensation*) uczucie **3** (*impression*) wrażenie; **feelings** *n pl* **1** (*attitude*) opinia *f sg* **2** (*emotions*) uczucia; **what are your ~s about the matter?** jaka jest twoja opinia o tej sprawie?; **I have a ~ that...** mam wrażenie, że...; **to hurt sb's ~s** ranić (zranić *pf*) czyjeś uczucia
feet [fiːt] *n pl of* **foot**
fell [fɛl] *pt of* **fall**
felt [fɛlt] *pt, pp of* **feel** ▷ *n* (*fabric*) filc
felt-tip pen, felt-tip ['fɛlttɪp-] *n* flamaster
female ['fiːmeɪl] *n* **1** (*Zool*) samica **2** (*woman*) kobieta ▷ *adj* **1** (*Zool*) żeński **2** (*sex, character, child*) żeński **3** (*relating to women*) kobiecy; **male and ~ students** studenci i studentki
feminine ['fɛmɪnɪn] *adj* **1** (*clothing, behaviour*) kobiecy **2** (*Ling*) w rodzaju żeńskim
feminist ['fɛmɪnɪst] *n* feminista(-tka) *m/f*
fence [fɛns] *n* (*barrier*) ogrodzenie
fencing ['fɛnsɪŋ] *n* (*Sport*) szermierka
fern [fəːn] *n* paproć
ferry ['fɛrɪ] *n* (*also*: **~boat**) prom
festival ['fɛstɪvəl] *n* **1** (*Rel*) święto **2** (*Theat, Mus*) festiwal
fetch [fɛtʃ] *vt* (*bring*) przynosić (przynieść *pf*); **to ~ sth for sb, ~ sb sth** przynosić (przynieść *pf*) coś komuś
fever ['fiːvər] *n* (*Med*) gorączka
few [fjuː] *adj* **1** (*not many: vir*) niewielu *+gen*; (*non-vir*) niewiele *+gen* **2**: **a ~** (*some: vir*) kilku *+gen*; (*non-vir*) kilka *+gen* ▷ *pron* **1**: **a ~ Poles/Americans** (*some*) kilku Polaków/Amerykanów; (*not many*) niewielu Polaków/Amerykanów **2**: **in the next ~ days** w ciągu kilku następnych dni; **in the past ~ days** w ciągu kilku ostatnich dni; **a ~ of us/them** kilku z nas/z nich; **a ~ more times** jeszcze kilka razy; **very ~ survive** niewielu przeżywa
fewer ['fjuːər] *adj* mniej; **no ~ than** nie mniej niż
fiancé [fɪ'ɔnseɪ] *n* narzeczony
fiancée [fɪ'ɔnseɪ] *n* narzeczona
fiction ['fɪkʃən] *n* (*novels, stories*) literatura piękna
field [fiːld] *n* **1** (*grassland*) łąka **2** (*cultivated*) pole **3** (*Sport: pitch*) boisko **4** (*subject, area of interest*) dziedzina **5** (*Comput*) pole
fierce [fɪəs] *adj* **1** (*animal*) groźny; (*battle*) zażarty **2** (*loyalty, resistance, competition*) bezwzględny
fifteen [fɪf'tiːn] *num* piętnaście; **that will be ~ pounds, please** piętnaście funtów, proszę; **she's ~ (years old)** ma piętnaście lat; **there are ~ of us** jest nas piętnaście osób
fifteenth [fɪf'tiːnθ] *num* piętnasty; *see also* **fifth**
fifth [fɪfθ] *num* **1** (*in series*) piąty **2** (*fraction*) piąta część ▷ *adv*: **to come ~** (*in race, competition*) zająć piąte miejsce; **on July ~, on the ~ of July** piątego lipca
fifty ['fɪftɪ] *num* pięćdziesiąt; **he's in his fifties** ma pięćdziesiąt kilka lat
fight [faɪt] (*pt, pp* **fought**) *n* walka ▷ *vt* walczyć z *+inst* ▷ *vi* walczyć; **to ~ with sb** walczyć z kimś; **to ~ for/against sth** walczyć za czymś/przeciwko czemuś

figure ['fɪgəʳ] *n* **1** (*number, statistic*) liczba **2** (*digit*) cyfra **3** (*body, shape*) figura ▷ *vt* (*esp US: inf: reckon*) myśleć (pomyśleć *pf*), że; **that ~s** (*inf*) to jasne
▸ **figure out** (*inf*) *vt* (*work out*) rozgryźć (*pf*)

file [faɪl] *n* **1** (*dossier*) akta *nt pl* **2** (*folder*) teczka **3** (*Comput*) plik **4** (*tool*) pilnik ▷ *vt* **1** (*also*: **~ away**: *papers, document*) katalogować (skatalogować *pf*) **2** (*wood, metal, fingernails*) piłować (opiłować *pf*)

fill [fɪl] *vt* **1** (*container*) napełniać (napełnić *pf*) **2** (*space, area*) wypełniać (wypełnić *pf*) **3** (*tooth*) plombować (zaplombować *pf*); **to ~ sth with sth** wypełniać (wypełnić *pf*) coś czymś
▸ **fill in** *vt* (*esp Brit: form*) wypełniać (wypełnić *pf*); (*name*) wpisywać (wpisać *pf*)
▸ **fill out** *vt* (*form*) wypełniać (wypełnić *pf*)
▸ **fill up** *vt* (*cup, saucepan*) napełniać (napełnić *pf*); **~ it** *or* **her up, please** (*Aut*) do pełna, proszę! ▷ *vi* (*room, stadium*) wypełniać (wypełnić *pf*) się

filling ['fɪlɪŋ] *n* **1** (*in tooth*) wypełnienie **2** (*of cake, pie, sandwich*) nadzienie

film [fɪlm] *n* **1** (*esp Brit: TV*) film **2** (*Phot*) film ▷ *vt* (*scene, person, book*) filmować (sfilmować *pf*)

film star *n* (*esp Brit*) gwiazda filmowa

filthy ['fɪlθɪ] *adj* (*dirty*) brudny

final ['faɪnl] *adj* **1** (*last*) ostatni **2** (*definitive*) ostateczny ▷ *n* (*Sport*) finał; **finals** *n pl* (*Sport*) finał *m sg*

finally ['faɪnəlɪ] *adv* **1** (*eventually*) w końcu **2** (*lastly*) na koniec **3** (*definitively*) ostatecznie

find [faɪnd] (*pt, pp* **found**) *vt* **1** (*locate: person, object, exit*) znajdować (znaleźć *pf*) **2** (*discover: answer, solution*) odkrywać (odkryć *pf*) **3** (*get: work, money, time*) znajdować (znaleźć *pf*) ▷ *n* (*discovery*) odkrycie; **to ~ sb guilty/not guilty** uznawać (uznać *pf*) kogoś za winnego/niewinnego; **to ~ one's way (to)** trafiać (trafić *pf*) (do +*gen*); **to ~ sth easy/difficult** uważać, że coś jest łatwe/trudne
▸ **find out** *vt* (*fact, truth*) dowiadywać (dowiedzieć *pf*) się o +*loc* ▷ *vi*: **to ~ out about sth** dowiadywać (dowiedzieć *pf*) się o czymś

fine [faɪn] *adj* **1** (*satisfactory*) dobry **2** (*excellent: object, person*) świetny **3** (*in texture*) cienki **4** (*pleasant: weather, day*) piękny ▷ *adv* (*well*) świetnie ▷ *n* (*Law*) grzywna ▷ *vt* (*Law*) karać (ukarać *pf*) grzywną; **(I'm) ~** czuję się dobrze; **(that's) ~** dobrze; **you're doing ~** idzie ci dobrze

finger ['fɪŋgəʳ] *n* (*Anat*) palec; **to keep one's ~s crossed** (*fig*) trzymać kciuki

fingernail ['fɪŋgəneɪl] *n* paznokieć u ręki

finish ['fɪnɪʃ] *n* **1** (*end*) koniec **2** (*Sport*) finisz ▷ *vt* kończyć (skończyć *pf*) ▷ *vi* kończyć (skończyć *pf*); **to ~ doing sth** kończyć (skończyć *pf*) coś robić

Finland ['fɪnlənd] *n* Finlandia

Finnish ['fɪnɪʃ] *adj* fiński ▷ *n* (*language*) fiński

fir [fəːʳ] *n* (*also*: **~ tree**) jodła

fire ['faɪəʳ] *n* ogień ▷ *vt* **1** (*shoot*) strzelać (strzelić *pf*) **2** (*inf: dismiss*) zwalniać (zwolnić *pf*) ▷ *vi* (*shoot*) wystrzeliwać (wystrzelić *pf*); **on ~** w ogniu; **electric/gas ~** (*esp Brit*) grzejnik elektryczny/gazowy; **to catch ~** zapalić się *pf*

fire alarm *n* alarm pożarowy

fire brigade [-brɪgeɪd] *n* straż pożarna

fire engine (*Brit*) *n* wóz strażacki

firefighter ['faɪəfaɪtəʳ] *n* strażak

fireman ['faɪəmən] (*irreg*) *n* strażak

fireplace ['faɪəpleɪs] *n* kominek

fire station *n* remiza strażacka

fire truck (*US*) *n* wóz strażacki

firework ['faɪəwəːk] *n* (*explosive*) fajerwerk; **fireworks** *n pl* (*display*) pokaz *m sg* sztucznych ogni

firm [fəːm] *adj* **1** (*mattress, ground*) twardy **2** (*person*) stanowczy ▷ *n* (*company*) firma; **to be ~ with sb** być stanowczy wobec kogoś

first [fəːst] *adj* pierwszy ▷ *adv* **1** (*before anyone else*) jako pierwszy **2** (*before other things*) najpierw

3 (*when listing reasons*) najpierw
4 (*for the first time*) po raz pierwszy
5 (*in race, competition*): **to come ~** zajmować (zająć *pf*) pierwsze miejsce ▷ *n* (*Aut*: *also*: **~ gear**) pierwszy bieg; **at ~** na początku; **the ~ of January** pierwszy stycznia; **to put sb/sth ~** stawiać (postawić *pf*) kogoś/coś na pierwszym miejscu

first aid *n* pierwsza pomoc

first-class [fəːst'klɑːs] *adj*
1 (*excellent*) pierwszorzędny
2 (*carriage, ticket*) pierwszej klasy; (*letter, stamp*) priorytetowy ▷ *adv* (*travel*) pierwszą klasą; (*send*) ekspresem

firstly ['fəːstlɪ] *adv* po pierwsze

first name *n* imię

fish [fɪʃ] *n* ryba ▷ *vi* (*commercially*) łowić (złowić *pf*); (*as sport, hobby*) łowić; **to go ~ing** iść (pójść *pf*) na ryby

fisherman ['fɪʃəmən] (*irreg*) *n* rybak; (*angler*) wędkarz

fishing ['fɪʃɪŋ] *n* rybołówstwo

fishing boat *n* kuter rybacki

fishing rod *n* wędka

fist [fɪst] *n* pięść

fit [fɪt] *adj* (*healthy*) w dobrej formie ▷ *vt* (*clothes, shoes*) pasować na ▷ *vi* **1** (*clothes, shoes*) pasować **2** (*in space, gap*) mieścić (zmieścić *pf*) się; **to keep ~** utrzymywać (utrzymać *pf*) kondycję; **a ~ of giggles** atak śmiechu; **to have a ~** (*Med*) mieć atak; (*inf*: *fig*) dostać (*pf*) szału; **to be a good ~** dobrze leżeć
▶ **fit in** *vi* **1** (*lit*: *person, object*) mieścić (zmieścić *pf*) się **2** (*fig*: *person*) pasować ▷ *vt* (*fig*: *appointment*) znajdować (znaleźć *pf*) czas na; (*visitor*) znajdować (znaleźć *pf*) czas dla *+gen*

fitness ['fɪtnɪs] *n* (*Med*) sprawność fizyczna

five [faɪv] *num* pięć; **that will be ~ pounds, please** pięć funtów, proszę; **she's ~ (years old)** ma pięć lat; **it's ~ o'clock** jest piąta; **there are ~ of us** jest nas pięć osób

fix [fɪks] *vt* **1** (*date, price, meeting*) ustalać (ustalić *pf*) **2** (*machine, leak, fault*) naprawiać (naprawić *pf*)
3 (*problem*) rozwiązywać (rozwiązać *pf*); **to ~ sth to/on sth** (*attach*) przymocowywać (przymocować *pf*) coś do czegoś
▶ **fix up** *vt* (*arrange*) organizować (zorganizować *pf*)

fizzy ['fɪzɪ] (*Brit*) *adj* (*drink*) gazowany

flag [flæg] *n* flaga

flame [fleɪm] *n* (*of fire*) płomień; **to burst into ~s** stanąć w płomieniach; **in ~s** w płomieniach

flan [flæn] *n* tarta

flap [flæp] *vt* (*arms, wings*) machać (machnąć *pf*) *+inst*

flash [flæʃ] *vi* (*lightning, light*) błyskać (błysnąć *pf*) ▷ *n* **1** (*of light, lightning*) błysk **2** (*Phot*) flesz **3** (*US*: *inf*: *also*: **~light**) latarka; **in a ~** w okamgnieniu; **quick as a ~** w okamgnieniu; **to ~ one's headlights** dawać (dać *pf*) sygnał światłami; **to ~ by** *or* **past** przemykać (przemknąć *pf*)

flashlight ['flæʃlaɪt] (*esp US*) *n* latarka

flask [flɑːsk] *n* (*also*: **vacuum ~**) termos

flat [flæt] *adj* **1** (*level*: *ground, surface*) płaski **2** (*tyre, ball*) flakowaty **3** (*Brit*: *battery*) rozładowany ▷ *n* (*Brit*: *in building*) mieszkanie ▷ *adv* (*lie*) płasko; **in 10 minutes ~** równo w dziesięć minut

flatscreen ['flætskriːn] *n* (*also*: **~ TV**) telewizor z płaskim ekranem

flatter ['flætə^r] *vt* **1** (*praise*) pochlebiać **2**: **this hairstyle doesn't ~ her** nie do twarzy jej w tej fryzurze

flavour ['fleɪvə^r] (*US* **flavor**) *n* (*of food, drink*) smak ▷ *vt* (*food, drink*) przyprawiać (przyprawić *pf*); **strawberry-~ed** o smaku truskawkowym

flea [fliː] *n* pchła

flew [fluː] *pt of* **fly**

flexible ['flɛksəbl] *adj* elastyczny

flick [flɪk] *vt* pstrykać (pstryknąć *pf*) *+inst*
▶ **flick through** *vt fus* (*book, pages*) przeglądać (przejrzeć *pf*)

flight [flaɪt] *n* **1** (*Aviat*) lot **2** (*also*: **~ of stairs, ~ of steps**) schody *m pl*

flight attendant [-ətɛndənt] *n* steward(esa) *m/f*

fling [flɪŋ] (*pt, pp* **flung**) *vt* (*ball, stone, hat*) ciskać (cisnąć *pf*); (*one's arms*) zarzucić (*pf*)
flipper ['flɪpəʳ] *n* płetwa
float [fləut] *vi* **1** (*on water: object*) płynąć **2** (*stay afloat: swimmer, object*) unosić się na wodzie
flock [flɔk] *n* (*of sheep, birds*) stado
flood [flʌd] *n* **1** (*of water*) powódź **2** (*of letters, requests, imports*) zalew ▷ *vt* zalewać (zalać *pf*)
floor [flɔːʳ] *n* **1** (*of room*) podłoga **2** (*storey*) piętro; **on the ~** na podłodze; **ground ~** (*Brit*) parter; **first ~** (*Brit*) pierwsze piętro; (*US*) parter
floppy ['flɔpɪ] *n* (*also:* **~ disk**) dyskietka
florist ['flɔrɪst] *n* **1** (*shopkeeper*) kwiaciarz(-rka) *m/f* **2** (*also:* **~'s**) kwiaciarnia
flour ['flauəʳ] *n* mąka
flow [fləu] *vi* **1** (*liquid, gas, electricity*) płynąć **2** (*traffic, people*) napływać (napłynąć *pf*) ▷ *n* **1** (*of liquid, gas*) przepływ; (*electricity*) prąd **2** (*of traffic*) przepływ
flower ['flauəʳ] *n* kwiat ▷ *vi* (*plant, tree*) zakwitać (zakwitnąć *pf*); **in ~** w rozkwicie
flown [fləun] *pp of* **fly**
flu [fluː] *n* grypa
fluent ['fluːənt] *adj* biegły; **to speak ~ French, be ~ in French** mówić biegle po francusku
flung [flʌŋ] *pt, pp of* **fling**
flush [flʌʃ] *n* (*of toilet*) spłuczka ▷ *vt*: **to ~ the toilet** spuszczać (spuścić *pf*) wodę
flute [fluːt] *n* flet
fly [flaɪ] (*pt* **flew**, *pp* **flown**) *vt* **1** (*plane*) latać +*inst* **2** (*distance*) lecieć (przelecieć *pf*) **3** (*kite*) puszczać (puścić *pf*) ▷ *vi* latać ▷ *n* (*insect*) mucha; **to ~ into a rage** wpaść we wściekłość
▸ **fly away** *vi* (*bird, insect*) odlatywać (odlecieć *pf*)
focus ['fəukəs] (*pl* **focuses**) *n* **1** (*Phot*) ostrość **2** (*fig: subject*) nacisk ▷ *vi*: **to ~ (on)** (*with camera*) ustawiać (ustawić *pf*) ostrość (na); (*fig: concentrate on*) skupiać (skupić *pf*) się (na +*loc*); **in ~/out of ~** ostry/nieostry; **to be the ~ of attention** być w centrum zainteresowania; **to ~ (one's) attention on sb/sth** skupiać (skupić *pf*) (swoją) uwagę na kimś/czymś
fog [fɔg] *n* mgła
foggy ['fɔgɪ] *adj* (*day, climate*) mglisty; **it's ~** jest mgła
foil [fɔɪl] *n* (*also:* **kitchen ~**) folia aluminiowa
fold [fəuld] *n* (*in paper*) zagięcie; (*in cloth*) fałda ▷ *vt* **1** (*also:* **~ up**: *cloth, clothes, paper*) składać (złożyć *pf*) **2** (*one's arms, hands*) splatać (spleść *pf*)
folder ['fəuldəʳ] *n* (*for papers*) teczka
follow ['fɔləu] *vt* **1** (*person: go behind*) chodzić/iść (pójść *pf*) za +*inst*; (*car*) jechać (pojechać *pf*) za +*inst* **2** (*take heed of*) postępować (postąpić *pf*) zgodnie z +*inst* **3** (*trace: route, path*) biec (pobiec *pf*) wzdłuż +*gen* **4** (*understand: event, story*) nadążać (nadążyć *pf*) za +*inst* **5** (*on social media*) śledzić; **I don't quite ~ you** nie bardzo pana/pani rozumiem; **as ~s** (*when listing*) następujący; (*in this way*) następująco
following ['fɔləuɪŋ] *prep* (*after*) po +*loc* ▷ *adj* **1** (*next: day, week*) następny **2** (*next-mentioned: way, list etc*) następny
fond [fɔnd] *adj*: **to be ~ of sb** lubić kogoś; **to be ~ of doing sth** (*eating, walking*) lubić coś robić
food [fuːd] *n* jedzenie
food poisoning [-pɔɪzənɪŋ] *n* zatrucie pokarmowe
fool [fuːl] *n* (*idiot*) głupiec ▷ *vt* (*deceive*) oszukiwać (oszukać *pf*); **you can't ~ me** nie oszukasz mnie
▸ **fool about, fool around** (*pej*) *vi* (*behave foolishly*) wygłupiać się
foot [fut] (*pl* **feet**) *n* **1** (*measure*) stopa **2** (*of person*) stopa **3** (*of animal*) łapa; **on ~** pieszo; **to put one's ~ down** (*in car: accelerate*) wciskać (wcisnąć *pf*) gaz; (*say no*) postawić (*pf*) się; **to put one's feet up** (*relax*) kłaść (położyć *pf*) się wygodnie
football ['futbɔːl] *n* **1** (*ball*) piłka nożna **2** (*sport: Brit*) piłka nożna; (*US*) futbol amerykański

footballer ['futbɔːləʳ] (*Brit*) *n* piłkarz(-rka) *m/f*
footpath ['futpɑːθ] *n* ścieżka
footprint ['futprɪnt] *n* (*of person, animal*) ślad
footstep ['futstɛp] *n* (*sound*) krok

KEYWORD

for [fɔːʳ] *prep* **1** (*recipient*) dla *+gen*; **is this for me?** czy to dla mnie?; **a table for two** stolik dla dwóch osób
2 (*purpose*) do *+gen*; **what's it for?** do czego to służy?; **it's time for lunch** czas na lunch; **what for?** po co?; **a knife for chopping vegetables** nóż do krojenia warzyw
3 (*time*): **he was away for two years** nie było go przez dwa lata; **she will be away for a month** nie będzie jej przez miesiąc; **it hasn't rained for three weeks** nie padało od trzech tygodni; **the trip is scheduled for June 5** podróż jest zaplanowana na piątego czerwca
4 (*in exchange for*): **I sold it for £50** sprzedałem to za pięćdziesiąt funtów; **to pay 50 pence for a ticket** zapłacić pięćdziesiąt pensów za bilet
5 (*reason*) z powodu *+gen*; **for this reason** z tego powodu; **our reasons for doing this** nasze powody dla zrobienia czegoś
6 (*on behalf of, representing*) dla *+gen*; **he works for a local firm** pracuje dla miejscowej firmy; **g for George** g jak George
7 (*destination*) do *+gen*; **he left for Rome** wyjechał do Rzymu
8 (*with infinitive clause*): **it is not for me to decide** nie ode mnie to zależy; **there is still time for you to do it** nadal ma pan/pani czas na zrobienie tego
9 (*to get*): **for further information, see...** więcej informacji znajdzie pan/pani w...
10 (*with regard to*) jak na; **it's cold for July** jest zimno jak na lipiec; **for scientists, this is less important** dla naukowców to jest mniej ważne; **another word for this is...** inne słowo na określenie tego to...
11 (*in favour of*) za *+inst*
12 (*referring to distance*) na przestrzeni; **there are roadworks for 50 km** roboty drogowe są na przestrzeni pięćdziesięciu kilometrów
13 (*with "if"*): **I wouldn't be alive today, if it weren't for him** nie byłbym dziś żywy, gdyby nie on

forbid [fə'bɪd] (*pt* **forbade**, *pp* **forbidden**) *vt* zakazywać (zakazać *pf*) *+gen*; **to ~ sb to do sth** zakazywać (zakazać *pf*) komuś robienia czegoś
forbidden [fə'bɪdn] *pp of* **forbid**
force [fɔːs] *n* siła ▷ *vt* (*drive, compel*) zmuszać (zmusić *pf*); **forces** *n pl* (*Mil*): **the F~s** (*Brit*) siły zbrojne; **to be in ~** (*law, system*) obowiązywać; **a ~ 5 gale** sztorm o sile pięciu stopni w skali Beauforta; **to ~ o.s. to do sth** zmuszać (zmusić *pf*) się do zrobienia czegoś; **to ~ sb to do sth** zmuszać (zmusić *pf*) kogoś do zrobienia czegoś
forecast ['fɔːkɑːst] (*pt, pp* **forecast** *or* **forecasted**) *n* (*of weather*) prognoza ▷ *vt* (*predict*) przepowiadać (przepowiedzieć *pf*)
forehead ['fɔrɪd] *n* czoło
foreign ['fɔrɪn] *adj* (*country, language*) obcy; (*holiday*) zagraniczny
foreigner ['fɔrɪnəʳ] *n* cudzoziemiec(-mka) *m/f*
forest ['fɔrɪst] *n* las
forever [fə'rɛvəʳ] *adv* **1** (*permanently*) wiecznie **2** (*always*) zawsze; **it has gone ~** minęło bezpowrotnie
forgave [fə'geɪv] *pt of* **forgive**
forge [fɔːdʒ] *vt* (*signature, banknote*) podrabiać (podrobić *pf*)
forget [fə'gɛt] (*pt* **forgot**, *pp* **forgotten**) *vt* **1** (*not remember*) zapominać (zapomnieć *pf*) o *+loc* **2** (*leave behind: object*) zapominać (zapomnieć *pf*) *+gen* **3** (*put out of mind: quarrel, person*) zapominać (zapomnieć *pf*) o *+loc* ▷ *vi* (*fail to remember*) zapominać (zapomnieć *pf*); **to ~ to do sth** zapominać (zapomnieć *pf*) coś zrobić; **to ~ how to do sth** zapominać (zapomnieć *pf*), jak coś się robi; **to ~ that...** zapominać (zapomnieć *pf*), że...

forgive [fə'gɪv] (*pt* **forgave**, *pp* **forgiven** [fə'gɪvn)] *vt* (*pardon*) wybaczać (wybaczyć *pf*) +*dat*; **to ~ sb for sth** wybaczać (wybaczyć *pf*) komuś coś
forgot [fə'gɔt] *pt of* **forget**
forgotten [fə'gɔtn] *pp of* **forget**
fork [fɔːk] *n* **1** (*for eating*) widelec **2** (*for gardening*) widły **3** (*in road, river, railway*) rozwidlenie
form [fɔːm] *n* **1** (*type*) forma **2** (*manner*) sposób **3** (*Brit: Scol: class*) klasa **4** (*document*) formularz **5** (*Sport*) forma ▷ *vt* **1** (*make: shape, queue, object*) tworzyć (stworzyć *pf*) **2** (*create: group, organization, company*) stwarzać (stworzyć *pf*); **in the ~ of** w postaci +*gen*; **to be in good** *or* **top ~** (*Brit*) być w dobrej formie
formal ['fɔːməl] *adj* oficjalny
former ['fɔːmə^r] *adj* **1** (*no longer: husband, president*) były **2** (*earlier: power, authority*) dawny ▷ *pron*: **the ~** pierwszy; **in ~ times/years** w poprzednich latach
fortnight ['fɔːtnaɪt] (*Brit*) *n* dwa tygodnie; **it's a ~ since...** minęły dwa tygodnie, odkąd...
fortunate ['fɔːtʃənɪt] *adj* szczęśliwy; **he was ~ to survive** miał szczęście, że przeżył
fortunately ['fɔːtʃənɪtlɪ] *adv* na szczęście
fortune ['fɔːtʃən] *n* (*wealth*) fortuna; **to make a ~** zbijać (zbić *pf*) fortunę; **to tell sb's ~** wróżyć (powróżyć *pf*) komuś
forty ['fɔːtɪ] *num* czterdzieści; *see also* **fifty**
forum ['fɔːrəm] *n* (*Comput*) forum
forward ['fɔːwəd] *adj* **1** (*in position*) z przodu **2** (*in movement*) do przodu ▷ *n* (*Sport*) napastnik ▷ *adv* = **forwards**
forwards ['fɔːwədz] *adv* (*in space, time*) do przodu
foster ['fɔstə^r] *vt* (*child*) wychowywać (wychować *pf*) ▷ *adj* (*parent, mother, child*) przybrany
fought [fɔːt] *pt, pp of* **fight**
foul [faul] *adj* **1** (*filthy*) obrzydliwy **2** (*dreadful: temper, mood*) paskudny; (*day, time, luck*) ohydny; (*weather*) paskudny ▷ *n* (*Sport*) faul
found [faund] *pt, pp of* **find** ▷ *vt* (*organization, company*) zakładać (założyć *pf*)
fountain ['fauntɪn] *n* (*lit*) fontanna
fountain pen *n* wieczne pióro
four [fɔː^r] *num* cztery; *see also* **five**
fourteen ['fɔː'tiːn] *num* czternaście; *see also* **fifteen**
fourteenth ['fɔː'tiːnθ] *num* czternasty; *see also* **fifth**
fourth ['fɔːθ] *num* **1** czwarty **2** (*US: quarter*) czwarta część ▷ *n* (*Aut: also:* **~ gear**) czwarty bieg; *see also* **fifth**
fox [fɔks] *n* lis
fragile ['frædʒaɪl] *adj* **1** (*object, structure*) kruchy **2** (*delicate*) delikatny
frame [freɪm] *n* **1** (*of picture, mirror, door, window*) rama **2** (*also:* **~s**: *of spectacles*) ramka *f sg*
France [frɑːns] *n* Francja
frantic ['fræntɪk] *adj* **1** (*person*) oszalały **2** (*rush, pace, search*) gorączkowy
fraud [frɔːd] *n* **1** (*crime*) oszustwo **2** (*person*) oszust(ka) *m/f*
freckle ['frɛkl] *n* pieg
free [friː] *adj* **1** (*costing nothing*) darmowy **2** (*available*) wolny ▷ *vt* (*release: prisoner, slave*) uwalniać (uwolnić *pf*); **~ (of charge)** *or* **for ~** za darmo; **admission ~** wstęp wolny; **to be ~ of** *or* **from sth** być wolnym od czegoś; **to be ~ to do sth** mieć możliwość zrobienia czegoś
freedom ['friːdəm] *n* wolność
freeway ['friːweɪ] (*US*) *n* autostrada
freeze [friːz] (*pt* **froze**, *pp* **frozen**) *vi* **1** (*liquid, weather*) zamarzać (zamarznąć *pf*) **2** (*pipe*) zamarzać (zamarznąć *pf*) **3** (*person: with cold*) przemarzać (przemarznąć *pf*) ▷ *vt* **1** (*water, lake*) skuwać (skuć *pf*) lodem **2** (*food*) zamrażać (zamrozić *pf*); **it may ~ tonight** wieczorem może być mróz
freezer ['friːzə^r] *n* zamrażarka
freezing ['friːzɪŋ] *adj* (*also:* **~ cold**: *day, weather*) mroźny; (*person, hands*) przemarznięty; **I'm ~** jestem przemarznięty; **3 degrees below ~** trzy stopnie poniżej zera

French [frɛntʃ] *adj* francuski ▷ *n* (*language*) francuski; **the French** *n pl* (*people*) Francuzi
French bean (*Brit*) *n* fasolka
French fries [-fraɪz] (*esp US*) *n pl* frytki
frequent ['fri:kwənt] *adj* (*occurrence, visitor*) częsty
fresh [frɛʃ] *adj* świeży; **~ air** świeże powietrze; **to make a ~ start** zaczynać (zacząć *pf*) od nowa
Friday ['fraɪdɪ] *n* piątek; *see also* **Tuesday**
fridge [frɪdʒ] (*Brit*) *n* lodówka
fried [fraɪd] *pt, pp of* **fry** ▷ *adj* (*food*) smażony
friend [frɛnd] *n* przyjaciel(-iółka) *m/f* ▷ *vt* (*on social media*) dodać do znajomych; **to be ~s with sb** przyjaźnić się z kimś; **to make ~s with sb** zaprzyjaźniać (zaprzyjaźnić *pf*) się z kimś
friendly ['frɛndlɪ] *adj* **1** (*amicable*) przyjazny **2** (*Brit: Sport*) towarzyski; **to be ~ with** przyjaźnić się z *+inst*
friendship ['frɛndʃɪp] *n* (*relationship*) przyjaźń
fright [fraɪt] *n* **1** (*terror*) przerażenie **2** (*shock*) szok; **to give sb a ~** przestraszyć (*pf*) kogoś
frighten ['fraɪtn] *vt* przerażać (przerazić *pf*)
frightened ['fraɪtnd] *adj* (*person, animal*): **to be ~** bać się *+gen*; **to be ~ of sth/of doing sth** *or* **to do sth** bać się czegoś/zrobić coś
frightening ['fraɪtnɪŋ] *adj* (*experience, prospect*) przerażający
fringe [frɪndʒ] *n* (*Brit: hair*) grzywka
frog [frɔg] (*Zool*) *n* żaba

KEYWORD

from [frɔm] *prep* **1** (*indicating starting place*) z *+gen*; **where are you from?** skąd pan/pani pochodzi?; **from London to Glasgow** z Londynu do Glasgow
2 (*indicating origin*) z *+gen*; **a present/letter from sb** prezent/list od kogoś
3 (*with time, distance, price, numbers*) od *+gen*; **from one o'clock to** *or* **until two** od pierwszej do drugiej; **it's 1 km from the beach** to jest jeden kilometr od plaży; **unemployment has fallen from 7.5% to 7.2%** bezrobocie spadło z siedmiu i pół procenta do siedmiu i dwóch dziesiątych procenta
4 (*because of, on the basis of*) z *+gen*; **from what he says** z tego, co mówi
5 (*out of*): **made from** z *+gen*

front [frʌnt] *n* (*of house*) front; (*of dress*) przód; (*of coach, train, car*) przód ▷ *adj* (*garden, entrance etc*) frontowy; (*seat*) przedni; **in ~** z przodu; **in ~ of** (*facing*) przed *+inst*; (*in the presence of*) przy *+loc*
front door *n* drzwi frontowe
frontier ['frʌntɪə^r] (*Brit*) *n* granica
frost [frɔst] *n* **1** (*weather*) mróz **2** (*icy covering*) szron
frosty ['frɔstɪ] *adj* (*day, night, weather*) mroźny; (*grass, window*) oszroniony
frown [fraun] *n* zmarszczenie brwi ▷ *vi* marszczyć (zmarszczyć *pf*) brwi
froze [frəuz] *pt of* **freeze**
frozen ['frəuzn] *pp of* **freeze** ▷ *adj* **1** (*food*) mrożony; (*ground, lake*) zamarznięty **2** (*person, fingers*) przemarznięty
fruit [fru:t] (*pl* **fruit** *or* **fruits**) *n* owoc
fruit machine (*Brit*) *n* automat do gry
frustrated [frʌs'treɪtɪd] *adj* sfrustrowany
fry [fraɪ] (*pt, pp* **fried**) *vt* (*Culin*) smażyć (usmażyć *pf*); **fries** *n pl* (*Culin*) = **French fries**
frying pan ['fraɪɪŋ-] *n* patelnia
fuel ['fjuəl] *n* (*for heating etc*) paliwo
full [ful] *adj* pełny; **I'm ~ (up)** najadłem się; **~ marks** (*Brit: Scol*) maksymalny wynik; **at ~ speed** pełnym gazem; **~ of** pełny *+gen*; **to write one's name in ~** pisać (napisać *pf*) pełne imię i nazwisko
full stop (*Brit*) *n* kropka; **to come to a ~** (*fig*) utknąć w martwym punkcie
full-time ['ful'taɪm] *adj* (*work*) na pełnym etacie; (*study*) w pełnym wymiarze godzin; (*student*) dzienny; (*staff*) pełnoetatowy ▷ *adv* (*work, study*) na pełnym etacie

fully ['fulɪ] *adv* **1** (*completely*) w pełni **2** (*in full*) dokładnie
fumes [fjuːmz] *n pl* (*of fire, fuel, car*) opary
fun [fʌn] *n* zabawa; **to have ~** bawić się; **he's good ~** jest fajnym gościem; **it's not much ~** to nie jest zabawne; **to do sth for ~** robić (zrobić *pf*) coś dla przyjemności; **to make ~ of sb/sth** nabijać się z kogoś/czegoś
fund [fʌnd] *n* (*of money*) fundusz; **the disaster ~** fundusz pomocy ofiarom katastrof; **funds** *n pl* (*money*) fundusze
funeral ['fjuːnərəl] *n* pogrzeb
funfair ['fʌnfɛəʳ] (*Brit*) *n* wesołe miasteczko
funny ['fʌnɪ] *adj* **1** (*amusing*) śmieszny **2** (*strange*) dziwny
fur [fəːʳ] *n* (*of animal*) futro
furious ['fjuərɪəs] *adj* **1** (*person*) wściekły **2** (*row, argument*) zażarty; **to be ~ with sb** być wściekłym na kogoś
furniture ['fəːnɪtʃəʳ] *n* meble *m pl*; **a piece of ~** mebel
further ['fəːðəʳ] *adv* (*farther*: *in distance, time*) dalej; **how much ~ is it?** o ile to jest dalej?
further education *n* doskonalenie zawodowe
fuse [fjuːz] (*US* **fuze**) *n* **1** (*Elec*: *in plug, circuit*) bezpiecznik **2** (*for bomb, firework*) zapalnik; **a ~ has blown** bezpiecznik się przepalił
fuss [fʌs] *n* **1** (*bother*) kłopot **2** (*disturbance*) awantura; **to make** *or* **kick up a ~ (about sth)** (*inf*) robić (zrobić *pf*) zamieszanie (wokół czegoś)
fussy ['fʌsɪ] *adj* (*person*) grymaśny
future ['fjuːtʃəʳ] *adj* przyszły ▷ *n* **1** (*time to come*): **the ~** przyszłość **2** (*prospects*) przyszłość **3** (*Ling*: *also*: **~ tense**): **the ~** czas przyszły; **in (the) ~** (*from now on*) w przyszłości; **in the near ~** w najbliższej przyszłości
fuze [fjuːz] (*US*) *n* = **fuse**

g

gadget ['gædʒɪt] *n* gadżet
gain [geɪn] *vt* **1** (*speed, weight, confidence*) nabierać (nabrać *pf*) +*gen* **2** (*obtain*) zyskiwać (zyskać *pf*) ▷ *n* (*increase, improvement*) zysk; **to ~ in value/popularity** zyskiwać (zyskać *pf*) wartość/popularność; **to ~ from sth** (*money*) zyskiwać (zyskać *pf*) na czymś
gallery ['gælərɪ] *n* (*also*: **art ~**) galeria
gamble ['gæmbl] *vi* **1** (*bet*) uprawiać hazard **2** (*take a risk*) ryzykować (zaryzykować *pf*) ▷ *n* (*risk*) ryzyko; **to ~ on sth** stawiać (postawić *pf*) na coś; (*success, outcome*) postawić (*pf*) na coś
gambling ['gæmblɪŋ] *n* hazard
game [geɪm] *n* **1** (*sport*) gra **2** (*activity*: *children's*) zabawa **3** (*also*: **board ~**) gra planszowa; (*also*: **computer ~**) gra komputerowa **4** (*match*) mecz **5**: **a ~ of football/tennis** mecz piłki nożnej/tenisa
gang [gæŋ] *n* (*of criminals, hooligans*) banda
gangster ['gæŋstəʳ] *n* gangster
gap [gæp] *n* (*space*) odstęp
gap year (*Brit*) *n* *rok przerwy między ukończeniem szkoły średniej a podjęciem studiów, podczas którego młodzi ludzie pracują zawodowo, jako wolontariusze lub podróżują*
garage ['gærɑːʒ] *n* **1** (*of private house*) garaż **2** (*for car repairs*) warsztat samochodowy **3** (*Brit*: *petrol station*) stacja benzynowa

garbage ['gɑːbɪdʒ] *n* **1** (*esp US: rubbish*) śmieci *m pl* **2** (*nonsense*) bzdury *f pl*
garbage can (*US*) *n* pojemnik na śmieci
garbage man (*irreg*) *n* (*US*) śmieciarz
garden ['gɑːdn] *n* ogród ▷ *vi* pracować w ogrodzie
gardener ['gɑːdnəʳ] *n* ogrodnik(-iczka) *m/f*
gardening ['gɑːdnɪŋ] *n* (*non-professional*) uprawianie ogródka
garlic ['gɑːlɪk] *n* czosnek
garment ['gɑːmənt] *n* część garderoby
gas [gæs] *n* **1** (*Chem*) gaz **2** (*for cooking, heating*) gaz **3** (*US: inf: also:* **gasoline**) benzyna
gasoline ['gæsəliːn] (*US*) *n* benzyna
gas station (*US*) *n* stacja benzynowa
gate [geɪt] *n* **1** (*of garden, field*) furtka; (*of building*) brama **2** (*at airport*) wyjście
gather ['gæðəʳ] *vt* (*understand*): **to ~ (that)...** rozumieć (zrozumieć *pf*), (że)... ▷ *vi*: **to ~ speed** nabierać (nabrać *pf*) prędkości
gave [geɪv] *pt of* **give**
gay [geɪ] *adj* (*homosexual*) homoseksualny ▷ *n* (*homosexual*) gej
GCSE (*Brit*) *n abbr* (= *General Certificate of Secondary Education*)

GCSE

GCSE to egzaminy, do których przystępują piętnastoletni i szesnastoletni uczniowie na zakończenie szkoły średniej w Anglii, Walii i Irlandii Północnej. Niektóre przedmioty są obowiązkowe, inne do wyboru przez ucznia.

gear [gɪəʳ] *n* **1** (*Tech: of car, bicycle*) bieg **2** (*equipment*) sprzęt **3** (*clothing*) strój; **to change** *or* (*US*) **shift ~** zmieniać (zmienić *pf*) bieg
gear lever, gear stick (*Brit*) *n* dźwignia zmiany biegów
gearshift ['gɪəʃɪft] (*US*) *n* dźwignia zmiany biegów
geese [giːs] *n pl of* **goose**
gel [dʒɛl] *n* (*for hair, washing, shaving*) żel; **bath/shower ~** żel do kąpieli/pod prysznic
Gemini ['dʒɛmɪnaɪ] *n* (*Astrol*) Bliźnięta
gender ['dʒɛndəʳ] *n* **1** (*sex*) płeć **2** (*Ling*) rodzaj
general ['dʒɛnərl] *adj* **1** (*overall: situation*) ogólny; (*decline, standard*) powszechny **2** (*non-specific: terms, outline, idea*) ogólny ▷ *n* (*Mil*) generał; **in ~** (*as a whole*) ogólnie; (*on the whole*) generalnie
general election *n* (*in Britain, United States*) wybory powszechne *m pl*
generally ['dʒɛnrəlɪ] *adv* **1** (*on the whole*) ogólnie **2** (*usually*) na ogół
generation [dʒɛnə'reɪʃən] *n* (*of people, family*) pokolenie
generous ['dʒɛnərəs] *adj* **1** (*person*) hojny **2** (*sizeable: measure, gift*) pokaźny
genetically modified [dʒɪ'nɛtɪklɪ'mɔdɪfaɪd] *adj* modyfikowany genetycznie
genetics [dʒɪ'nɛtɪks] *n* (*science*) genetyka *f sg*
genius ['dʒiːnɪəs] *n* (*person*) geniusz
gentle ['dʒɛntl] *adj* **1** (*person, nature*) łagodny **2** (*light: movement, breeze, shake*) delikatny **3** (*Culin: heat*) mały
gentleman ['dʒɛntlmən] (*irreg*) *n* **1** (*man*) pan **2** (*well-mannered man*) dżentelmen
gently ['dʒɛntlɪ] *adv* **1** (*touch, move*) delikatnie **2** (*Culin: cook, heat*) na małym ogniu
gents [dʒɛnts] *n*: **the ~** (*Brit: inf*) toaleta męska
genuine ['dʒɛnjuɪn] *adj* **1** (*real*) prawdziwy **2** (*sincere: person*) szczery; (*emotion, interest*) autentyczny
geography [dʒɪ'ɔgrəfɪ] *n* geografia
geometry [dʒɪ'ɔmətrɪ] *n* (*science*) geometria
germ [dʒəːm] (*Bio*) *n* zarazek
German ['dʒəːmən] *adj* niemiecki ▷ *n* **1** (*person*) Niemiec(-mka) *m/f* **2** (*language*) niemiecki
Germany ['dʒəːmənɪ] *n* Niemcy

KEYWORD

get [gɛt] (*pt, pp* **got**, (*US*) *pp* **gotten**) *vt* **1**: **to have got**; *see* **have, got** **2** (*money, permission, information*) otrzymywać (otrzymać *pf*); (*job,

flat, room) dostawać (dostać *pf*); **he got a job in London** dostał pracę w Londynie; **we can get something to eat on the train** możemy dostać coś do jedzenia w pociągu
3 (*fetch*) sprowadzać (sprowadzić *pf*); **to get sth for sb** przynosić (przynieść *pf*) coś komuś; **can I get you a coffee?** czy przynieść panu/pani kawę?; **I'll come and get you** przyjadę (*or* przyjdę) po pana/panią
4 (*receive*) otrzymywać (otrzymać *pf*); **what did she get for her birthday?** co dostała na urodziny?; **he gets a lot of pleasure from music** czerpie z muzyki wiele przyjemności
5 (*board*): **to get a plane/bus** wchodzić (wejść *pf*) na pokład samolotu/do autobusu; **I'll get the bus** pojadę autobusem
6 (*cause to be/become*): **to get sth/sb ready** przygotowywać (przygotować *pf*) coś/kogoś; **did you get the answer right?** czy udzieliłeś właściwej odpowiedzi?
7 (*seize, catch*) łapać (złapać *pf*); **the police will get him eventually** policja w końcu go złapie
8 (*hit*: *target etc*) trafiać (trafić *pf*) do *+gen*
9 (*take, move*) zawozić (zawieźć *pf*) do *+gen*; **we must get him to hospital** musimy zawieźć go do szpitala
10 (*buy*) dostawać (dostać *pf*); (*regularly*) kupować (kupić *pf*); **I'll get some milk from the supermarket** kupię mleko w supermarkecie; **let me get you a drink** pozwól mi postawić ci drinka
11 (*be infected by*) chorować (zachorować *pf*); **you'll get a cold** przeziębisz się
12 (*understand*: *joke, point*) rozumieć (zrozumieć *pf*)
13 (*hear*) słyszeć (usłyszeć *pf*)
14 (*have*: *time, opportunity*) mieć; **I got a shock when I saw him** doznałem szoku, kiedy go zobaczyłem
15: **to get sth done** (*do oneself*) zrobić (*pf*) coś; (*have done*) oddawać (oddać *pf*) do zrobienia czegoś; **to get one's hair cut** obcinać (obciąć *pf*) włosy; **to get sb to do sth** nakłaniać (nakłonić *pf*) kogoś, by coś zrobił
16 (*inf*: *annoy*) złościć (zezłościć *pf*); **what gets me is his attitude** to, co mnie złości, to jego postawa
▷ *vi* **1** (*become, be*: *adj*) stawać (stać *pf*) się *+inst*; **to get old/tired/cold/dirty** stawać (stać *pf*) się starym/zmęczonym/zimnym/brudnym; **to get drunk** upijać (upić *pf*) się
2 (*go*): **to get to work/the airport** dostawać (dostać *pf*) się do pracy/na lotnisko; **how did he get here?** jak się tu dostał?; **he didn't get home till 10 p.m.** wrócił do domu dopiero o 22; **the talks are getting nowhere** te rozmowy prowadzą donikąd
3 (*begin*): **to get to know sb** poznawać (poznać *pf*) kogoś; **let's get going/started!** chodźmy/zaczynajmy!
4 (*manage*): **how often do you get to see him?** jak często udaje się panu/pani z nim widzieć?
▷ *aux vb* **1**: **to have got to**; *see* **have, got**
2 (*passive use*): **to get killed** zostać (*pf*) zabitym
▸ **get around to** *vt fus*: **to get around to sth/to doing sth** zabierać (zabrać *pf*) się za coś/za robienie czegoś
▸ **get away** *vi* (*leave*) odjeżdżać (odjechać *pf*); (*on holiday*) wyjeżdżać (wyjechać *pf*); (*escape*) uciekać (uciec *pf*)
▸ **get away with** *vt fus*: **to get away with sth** unikać (uniknąć *pf*) kary za coś; **he'll never get away with it!** nie ujdzie mu to na sucho!
▸ **get back** *vi* (*return*) wracać (wrócić *pf*)
▷ *vt* (*reclaim*) odzyskiwać (odzyskać *pf*)
▸ **get back to** *vt fus* (*return to*) powracać (powrócić *pf*) do *+gen*; **to get back to sleep** zasypiać (zasnąć *pf*) ponownie
▸ **get in** *vi* **1** (*arrive*: *train, bus*) przyjeżdżać (przyjechać *pf*); (*plane*) przylatywać (przylecieć *pf*) **2** (*arrive home*) wchodzić (wejść *pf*)
▸ **get into** *vt fus* **1**: **to get into university** dostać (*pf*) się na uniwersytet **2** (*vehicle*) wsiadać

(wsiąść *pf*) do *+gen* **3** (*in expressions*): **to get into bed** chodzić/iść (pójść *pf*) do łóżka
▸ **get off** *vi* (*from train, bus*) wysiadać (wysiąść *pf*)
▹ *vt* (*as holiday*): **we get three days off at Christmas** na Boże Narodzenie mamy trzy dni wolnego
▹ *vt fus* (*leave*: *train, bus*) wysiadać (wysiąść *pf*) do *+gen*
▸ **get on** *vi* **1** (*be friends*): **to get on well with sb** być z kimś w dobrych stosunkach **2** (*progress*): **how are you getting on?** jak ci idzie?
▹ *vt fus* (*bus, train*) wsiadać (wsiąść *pf*) do *+gen*
▸ **get on with** *vt fus* **1** (*be friends with*: *person*) być w dobrych stosunkach z *+inst* **2** (*continue, start*) kontynuować
▸ **get out** *vi*: **to get out (of)** (*person*: *of place*) wychodzić (wyjść *pf*) (z *+gen*); (*of vehicle*) wysiadać (wysiąść *pf*) (z *+gen*)
▹ *vt* (*take out*: *book, object etc*) wyciągać (wyciągnąć *pf*) z *+gen*
▸ **get out of** *vt fus* (*vehicle*) wysiadać (wysiąść *pf*) z *+gen*
▸ **get over** *vt fus* (*illness, shock*) wychodzić (wyjść *pf*) z *+gen*
▸ **get through** *vi* (*Tel*) dodzwonić (*pf*) się
▹ *vt fus* (*finish*) kończyć (skończyć *pf*)
▸ **get together** *vi* (*people*) gromadzić (zgromadzić *pf*) się
▸ **get up** *vi* (*rise*: *from chair, sofa*) podnosić (podnieść *pf*) się; (*out of bed*) wstawać (wstać *pf*)

ghost [gəust] *n* (*spirit*) duch
giant ['dʒaɪənt] *n* (*in stories*) olbrzym
▹ *adj* (*huge*) olbrzymi
gift [gɪft] *n* **1** (*present*) prezent **2** talent; **to have a ~ for sth** (*talent*) mieć do czegoś talent
gin [dʒɪn] *n* (*alcohol*) dżin
ginger ['dʒɪndʒəʳ] *n* (*spice*) imbir
▹ *adj* (*colour*) rudy
giraffe [dʒɪ'rɑːf] *n* żyrafa
girl [gəːl] *n* (*child*) dziewczynka; (*young woman*) dziewczyna
girlfriend ['gəːlfrɛnd] *n* **1** (*female friend*) przyjaciółka **2** (*partner*) dziewczyna

Girl Scout (*US*) *n* **1**: **the ~s** (*organization*) harcerstwo dziewcząt **2** (*person*) harcerka

 **KEYWORD**

give [gɪv] (*pt* **gave**, *pp* **given**) *vt*
1 (*hand over*): **to give sb sth, give sth to sb** dawać (dać *pf*) komuś coś; (*as gift*) darować (podarować *pf*) komuś coś; **I gave David the book, I gave the book to David** podarowałem Dawidowi książkę; **give it to him** daj mu to
2 (*provide*) dawać (dać *pf*); **to give sb sth** (*opportunity, surprise, job*) dawać (dać *pf*) coś komuś; **I gave him the chance to deny it** dałem mu szansę zaprzeczenia temu
3 (*deliver*): **to give a speech/a lecture** wygłaszać (wygłosić *pf*) przemówienie/wykład
4 (*organize*): **to give a party/dinner party** organizować (zorganizować *pf*) przyjęcie/proszony obiad
▸ **give back** *vt* (*money, book etc*) oddawać (oddać *pf*); **to give sth back to sb** oddawać (oddać *pf*) coś komuś
▸ **give in** *vi* (*yield*) ustępować (ustąpić *pf*)
▹ *vt* (*essay etc*) składać (złożyć *pf*)
▸ **give out** *vt* (*distribute*) rozdawać (rozdać *pf*)
▸ **give up** *vi* (*stop trying*) poddawać (poddać *pf*) się; **to give up smoking** rzucać (rzucić *pf*) palenie

glad [glæd] *adj* (*happy, pleased*) zadowolony; **to be ~ that...** być zadowolonym, że...; **I'd be ~ to help you** z przyjemnością panu/pani pomogę
glamorous ['glæmərəs] *adj* olśniewający
glass [glɑːs] *n* **1** (*substance*) szkło **2** (*container*) szklanka **3** (*glassful*) kieliszek; **glasses** *n pl* (*spectacles*) okulary; **a pair of ~es** para okularów
glider ['glaɪdəʳ] *n* szybowiec
global ['gləubl] *adj* globalny
global warming [-'wɔːmɪŋ] *n* globalne ocieplenie

globe [gləub] *n* **1**: **the ~** (*the world*) kula ziemska **2** (*model*) globus; **around the ~** dookoła świata
gloomy ['glu:mɪ] *adj* **1** (*dark*) posępny **2** (*sad*) ponury
glorious ['glɔ:rɪəs] *adj* **1** (*sunshine, day, weather*) cudowny **2** (*victory, occasion, career*) wspaniały
glove [glʌv] *n* rękawiczka; **a pair of ~s** para rękawiczek
glow [gləu] *vi* (*face, skin, cheeks*) czerwienić (zaczerwienić *pf*) się
glue [glu:] *n* klej ▷ *vt* kleić (skleić *pf*)
GM *adj abbr* (= *genetically modified*) modyfikowany genetycznie

KEYWORD

go [gəu] (*pt* **went**, *pp* **gone**) *vi*
1 (*travel, move: on foot*) iść (pójść *pf*); (*on foot, attend habitually*) chodzić; (*by transport*) jechać (pojechać *pf*); (*: habitually*) jeździć; (*by plane*) lecieć (polecieć *pf*); (*: habitually*) latać; (*by boat*) płynąć (popłynąć *pf*); (*: habitually*) pływać; **he's going to New York** on jedzie do Nowego Jorku; **where's he gone?** gdzie on poszedł?; (*by car, bike, bus, train etc*) gdzie on pojechał?; **shall we go by car or train?** pojedziemy samochodem czy pociągiem?; **to go to do sth, go and do sth** (*Brit*) chodzić/iść (pójść *pf*) coś zrobić
2 (*depart: on foot*) chodzić/iść (pójść *pf*); (*by transport*) wyjeżdżać (wyjechać *pf*); **let's go** chodźmy; **I must be going** muszę iść; **our plane goes at 11 p.m.** nasz samolot odlatuje o 23
3 (*disappear*) znikać (zniknąć *pf*); **all her jewellery had gone** zniknęła jej cała biżuteria
4 (*attend*): **to go to school/ university** (*habitually*) chodzić do szkoły/na uniwersytet
5 (*with activity*): **to go for a walk** iść (pójść *pf*) na spacer; (*habitually*) chodzić na spacer; **to go on a trip** chodzić/iść (pójść *pf*) na wycieczkę; (*by transport*) jechać (pojechać *pf*) na wycieczkę
6 (*work: clock, video etc*) działać
7 (*become*): **to go pale/mouldy/bald** blednąć (zblednąć *pf*)/pleśnieć (spleśnieć *pf*)/łysieć (wyłysieć *pf*)
8 (*be about to, intend to*): **are you going to come?** zamierzasz przyjść?; (*formal*) czy zamierza pan/pani przyjść?; **I think it's going to rain** myślę, że będzie padać
9 (*progress*) mijać (minąć *pf*); **time went very slowly/quickly** czas mijał bardzo powoli/szybko; **how did it go?** jak było?
10 (*be placed*): **where does this cup go?** gdzie ma stać ta filiżanka?
11 (*lead*) prowadzić (poprowadzić *pf*)
12 (*US: to take away*): **a hamburger and fries to go** hamburger i frytki na wynos
13 (*in other expressions*): **there's still a week to go before the exams** jest jeszcze tydzień do egzaminów; **to keep going** iść (pójść *pf*) dalej; (*by transport*) jechać (pojechać *pf*) dalej
▷ *n* (*pl* **goes**) **1** (*try*) próba; **to have a go (at doing sth)** próbować (spróbować *pf*) (coś robić)
2 (*turn*) kolej; **whose go is it?** czyja teraz kolej?
▸ **go after** *vt fus* **1** (*pursue: person*) ruszać (ruszyć *pf*) w pogoń za +*inst* **2** (*try to get: job*) szukać (*pf*) +*gen*
▸ **go ahead** *vi* **1** (*take place: event*) odbywać (odbyć *pf*) się **2** (*press on*): **to go ahead with sth** przystępować (przystąpić *pf*) do czegoś; **go ahead!** (*encouraging*) proszę bardzo!
▸ **go around** *vi* (*circulate: news, rumour*) krążyć
▸ **go away** *vi* **1** (*leave*) odchodzić (odejść *pf*) **2** (*on holiday*) wyjeżdżać (wyjechać *pf*)
▸ **go back** *vi* (*return*) wracać (wrócić *pf*)
▸ **go back to** *vt fus* (*activity, work, school*) wracać (wrócić *pf*) do +*gen*
▸ **go by** *vi* (*vehicle, years, time*) mijać (minąć *pf*)
▸ **go down** *vi* **1** (*fall: price, level, amount*) obniżać (obniżyć *pf*) **2** (*set: sun*) zachodzić (zajść *pf*) **3** (*crash: computer*) psuć (zepsuć *pf*) się
▷ *vt fus* (*stairs, ladder*) schodzić (zejść *pf*)

▸ **go for** *vt fus* (*fetch*) chodzić/iść (pójść *pf*) po +*loc*
▸ **go in** *vi* (*enter*) wchodzić (wejść *pf*)
▸ **go in for** *vt fus* (*competition*) startować (wystartować *pf*) w +*loc*
▸ **go into** *vt fus* (*enter: building, room*) wchodzić (wejść *pf*) do +*gen*
▸ **go off** *vi* **1** (*leave*) wychodzić (wyjść *pf*); **he's gone off to work** wyszedł do pracy **2** (*explode*) eksplodować **3** (*sound: alarm*) włączać (włączyć *pf*) się **4** (*switch off*) wyłączać (wyłączyć *pf*) się
▸ **go on** *vi* **1** (*continue*) iść (pójść *pf*) dalej; **to go on with one's work** pracować dalej; **to go on doing sth** robić coś dalej **2** (*happen*) dziać się; **what's going on here?** co się tu dzieje? **3** (*lights etc*) zapalać (zapalić *pf*) się
▸ **go on about** *vt fus*: **to go on about sth** ciągle o czymś mówić
▸ **go out** *vi* **1** (*person*) wychodzić (wyjść *pf*); **we are going out for a drink tonight** wychodzimy dziś wieczorem na drinka **2** (*couple*) chodzić ze sobą; **they've been going out for 3 years** chodzą ze sobą od trzech lat; **to go out with sb** chodzić z kimś **3** (*be extinguished*) gasnąć (zgasnąć *pf*)
▸ **go over** *vt* (*check*) sprawdzać (sprawdzić *pf*)
▸ **go round** *vi* = **go around**
▸ **go through** *vt fus* **1** (*place, town*) przechodzić (przejść *pf*) przez **2** (*undergo*) przechodzić (przejść *pf*) przez; **he's going through a difficult time** przechodzi teraz trudny okres
▸ **go together** *vi* (*colours, clothes, foods*) pasować do siebie
▸ **go up** *vi* **1** (*rise: price, level, value*) wzrastać (wzrosnąć *pf*) **2** (*go upstairs*) chodzić/iść (pójść *pf*) na górę
▸ **go up to** *vt fus* podchodzić/podejść (pójść *pf*) do +*gen*
▸ **go with** *vt fus* **1** (*combine well with*) pasować do +*gen* **2** (*accompany*) towarzyszyć
▸ **go without** *vt fus* (*food, treats*) nie mieć

goal [gəul] *n* **1** (*Sport*) gol; (*on pitch*) bramka **2** (*aim*) cel; **to score a ~** strzelać (strzelić *pf*) gola

goalie [gəuli] *n* (*inf*) bramkarz(-arka) *m/f*

goalkeeper ['gəulki:pə^r] *n* bramkarz(-arka) *m/f*

goat [gəut] *n* kozioł

God [gɔd] *n* Bóg

god [gɔd] *n* bóg

goddaughter ['gɔddɔ:tə^r] *n* chrześniaczka

godfather ['gɔdfɑ:ðə^r] *n* ojciec chrzestny

godmother ['gɔdmʌðə^r] *n* matka chrzestna

godson ['gɔdsʌn] *n* chrześniak

goggles ['gɔglz] *n pl* gogle

gold [gəuld] *n* **1** (*metal*) złoto **2** (*Sport: inf: also:* **~ medal**) złoty medal ▹ *adj* (*ring, watch, tooth*) złoty

goldfish ['gəuldfɪʃ] (*pl* **goldfish**) *n* złota rybka

golf [gɔlf] *n* golf; **to play ~** grać w golfa

golf course *n* pole golfowe

gone [gɔn] *pp of* **go** ▹ *adj* miniony; **the food's all ~** nie ma już jedzenia

good [gud] *adj* **1** dobry **2** (*well-behaved*) grzeczny ▹ *n* (*right*) dobro; **~!** dobrze!; **to be ~ at sth** być dobrym w czymś; **to be no ~ at sth** być kiepskim w czymś; **it didn't do any ~** to było do niczego; **it's ~ for him** to jest dla niego dobre; **to be ~ with people/with figures** dobrze sobie radzić z ludźmi/z liczbami; **it's ~ to see you** miło pana/panią widzieć; **it's a ~ thing he was there** (*Brit*) dobrze, że tam był; **that's very ~ of you** to bardzo miło z pana/pani strony; **~ morning/afternoon!** dzień dobry!; **~ evening!** dobry wieczór!; **~ night!** (*before going home*) dobrej nocy!; (*before going to bed*) dobranoc!; **to take a ~ look** dobrze się przyglądać (przyjrzeć *pf*); **for ~** (*forever*) na zawsze; **to do sb ~** robić (zrobić *pf*) komuś dobrze; *see also* **goods**

goodbye [gud'baɪ] *excl* do widzenia; **to say ~** żegnać (pożegnać *pf*) się

Good Friday *n* Wielki Piątek

good-looking ['gud'lukɪŋ] *adj* atrakcyjny

goods ['gudz] *n pl* **1** (*Comm*) towary **2** (*possessions*) dobytek *m sg*

goose [gu:s] (*pl* **geese**) *n* gęś
gorgeous ['gɔ:dʒəs] *adj* **1** (*necklace, dress*) cudowny; (*weather, day*) wspaniały **2** (*person*) cudowny
gorilla [gə'rɪlə] *n* (*animal*) goryl
gossip ['gɔsɪp] *n* **1** (*rumours*) plotka **2** (*chat*) plotkowanie ▷ *vi* (*chat*) plotkować (poplotkować *pf*); **to ~ with sb** plotkować (poplotkować *pf*) z kimś
got [gɔt] *pt, pp of* **get**; **have you ~ an umbrella?** czy ma pan/pani parasol?; **he has ~ to accept the situation** musi zaakceptować tę sytuację
gotten ['gɔtn] (*US*) *pp of* **get**
government ['gʌvnmənt] *n* (*institution*) rząd
GP *n abbr* (= *general practitioner*) lekarz rodzinny *m*, lekarka rodzinna *f*
grab [græb] *vt* **1** (*seize*) chwytać (chwycić *pf*) **2** (*chance, opportunity*) korzystać (skorzystać *pf*) z +*gen*
graceful ['greɪsful] *adj* pełen wdzięku
grade [greɪd] *n* **1** (*school mark*) ocena **2** (*US: school class*) klasa
grade crossing (*US*) *n* przejazd kolejowy
grade school (*US*) *n* szkoła podstawowa
gradual ['grædjuəl] *adj* (*change, process, improvement*) stopniowy
gradually ['grædjuəlɪ] *adv* stopniowo
graffiti [grə'fi:tɪ] *n* graffiti
grain [greɪn] *n* **1** (*of wheat, rice*) ziarno **2** (*cereals*) zboże **3** (*US: corn*) zboże **4** (*of sand, salt, sugar*) ziarenko **5**: **the ~** (*of wood*) słój; **it goes against the ~** to kłóci się z zasadami; **a ~ of truth** ziarno prawdy
gram [græm] *n* gram
grammar ['græmə^r] *n* gramatyka
grammar school (*Brit*) *n liceum ogólnokształcące*

GRAMMAR SCHOOL

W Wielkiej Brytanii **grammar school** jest to szkoła średnia, prowadząca własny nabór, niezależny od systemu rekrutacji do szkół państwowych (**comprehensive schools**). Obecnie niewiele jest takich szkół. W USA terminem tym określa się szkołę podstawową.

gramme [græm] (*Brit*) *n* = **gram**
grand [grænd] *adj* (*impressive*) okazały
grandad, granddad ['grændæd] *n* dziadek
grandchild ['græntʃaɪld] (*pl* **grandchildren**) *n* (*male*) wnuk; (*female*) wnuczka
granddaughter ['grændɔ:tə^r] *n* wnuczka
grandfather ['grændfɑ:ðə^r] *n* dziadek
grandma ['grænmɑ:] *n* babcia
grandmother ['grænmʌðə^r] *n* babcia
grandpa ['grænpɑ:] *n* dziadziuś
grandparents ['grændpɛərənts] *n pl* dziadkowie
grandson ['grænsʌn] *n* wnuk
granny, grannie ['grænɪ] *n* (*inf*) babunia
grape [greɪp] *n* winogrono; **a bunch of ~s** kiść winogron
grapefruit ['greɪpfru:t] (*pl* **grapefruit**) *n* grejpfrut
graph [grɑ:f] *n* wykres
graphics ['græfɪks] *n* (*design*) grafika *f sg* ▷ *n pl* (*images*) grafiki
grass [grɑ:s] *n* (*Bot*) trawa; **the ~** (*the lawn*) trawnik
grasshopper ['grɑ:shɔpə^r] *n* konik polny
grate [greɪt] *vt* (*food*) ucierać (utrzeć *pf*)
grateful ['greɪtful] *adj* (*person*) wdzięczny; **to be ~ for** (*help, opportunity*) być wdzięcznym za; **to be ~ to sb for sth** być wdzięcznym komuś za coś
grave [greɪv] *n* (*tomb*) grób
gravel ['grævl] *n* żwir
graveyard ['greɪvjɑ:d] *n* cmentarz
gravy ['greɪvɪ] *n* (*sauce*) sos
gray [greɪ] (*US*) *adj* = **grey**
grease [gri:s] *n* (*lubricant*) smar ▷ *vt* **1** (*lubricate*) smarować (nasmarować *pf*) **2** (*cooking dish*) smarować (posmarować *pf*) tłuszczem

greasy ['gri:sɪ] *adj* **1** (*tools, hands*) natłuszczony **2** (*food*) tłusty **3** (*skin, hair*) przetłuszczający się
great [greɪt] *adj* **1** (*large*) wielki **2** (*success, achievement*) wspaniały; (*pleasure, difficulty, value*) wielki; (*risk*) ogromny **3** (*important, famous*) znaczący **4** (*terrific: person, place*) wspaniały; (*idea*) świetny ▷ *excl*: **~!** (*enthusiastically*) świetnie!; **we had a ~ time** świetnie się bawiliśmy
Great Britain *n* Wielka Brytania

GREAT BRITAIN

Great Britain – wyspa Wielka Brytania obejmuje Anglię, Szkocję i Walię. Kraje te, wspólnie z Irlandią Północną (częścią wyspy Irlandia), tworzą Zjednoczone Królestwo Wielkiej Brytanii i Irlandii Północnej (po polsku najczęściej nazywane po prostu Wielką Brytanią).

great-grandfather [greɪt'grænfɑ:ðəʳ] *n* pradziadek
great-grandmother [greɪt'grænmʌðəʳ] *n* prababcia
Greece [gri:s] *n* Grecja
greedy ['gri:dɪ] *adj* chciwy
Greek [gri:k] *adj* grecki ▷ *n* **1** (*person*) Grek(-eczynka) *m/f* **2** (*modern language*) współczesna greka **3** (*also*: **ancient ~**) starożytna greka
green [gri:n] *adj* **1** (*colour*) zielony **2** (*environmental*) proekologiczny ▷ *n* **1** (*colour*) zieleń **2** (*Pol*): **the G~s** zieloni
greengrocer ['gri:ngrəusəʳ] (*esp Brit*) *n* (*shop*: *also*: **~'s**) warzywniak
greenhouse ['gri:nhaus] *n* szklarnia ▷ *adj* (*gas, emissions*) cieplarniany
Greenland ['gri:nlənd] *n* Grenlandia
greetings card ['gri:tɪŋz-] *n* kartka z życzeniami
grew [gru:] *pt of* **grow**
grey [greɪ] (*US* **gray**) *adj* **1** (*colour*) szary; (*hair*) siwy **2** (*dull*: *weather, day*) szary ▷ *n* (*colour*) szarość
grey-haired [greɪ'hɛəd] *adj* siwowłosy
grid [grɪd] *n* **1** (*pattern*) krata **2** (*cover for drain*) kratka ściekowa
grief [gri:f] *n* zmartwienie
grill [grɪl] *n* (*Brit*: *on cooker*) ruszt ▷ *vt* (*Brit*: *food*) piec (upiec *pf*) na ruszcie
grin [grɪn] *n* (*smile*) szeroki uśmiech ▷ *vi* uśmiechać (uśmiechnąć *pf*) się szeroko
grip [grɪp] *vt* (*object*) chwytać (chwycić *pf*)
grit [grɪt] *n* (*sand, gravel*) grys
groan [grəun] *n* (*of pain*) jęk; (*of unhappiness*) pomruk ▷ *vi* (*in pain*) jęczeć (jęknąć *pf*)
grocer ['grəusəʳ] *n* (*shop*: *also*: **~'s**) sklep spożywczy
grocery ['grəusərɪ] *n* sklep spożywczy; **groceries** *n pl* (*provisions*) artykuły spożywcze
groom [gru:m] *n* (*also*: **bride~**) pan młody
gross [grəus] *adj* **1** (*misconduct, indecency, negligence*) rażący **2** (*horrible*) obrzydliwy
ground [graund] *pt, pp of* **grind** ▷ *n* **1** (*floor*): **the ~** podłoga **2** (*earth, soil, land*): **the ~** ziemia **3** (*Sport*) boisko ▷ *adj* mielony; **on the ~** na ziemi; **below/above ~** pod/nad ziemią; **~s for** (*optimism, hope, concern*) podstawy do *+gen*; (*divorce, appeal, complaint*) przyczyny *+gen*; **on the ~s that...** z powodu tego, że...; **on medical/humanitarian ~s** z przyczyn medycznych/humanitarnych
ground floor *n* parter
group [gru:p] *n* **1** (*of people, buildings etc*) grupa **2** (*also*: **pop ~, rock ~**) zespół ▷ *vt* (*organize, arrange*) grupować (zgrupować *pf*); **in ~s** w grupach; **age/income ~** grupa wiekowa/zarobkowa
grow [grəu] (*pt* **grew**, *pp* **grown**) *vi* **1** (*plant, tree*) rosnąć (wyrosnąć *pf*); (*person, animal*) rosnąć (urosnąć *pf*) **2** (*increase*: *amount, feeling, problem*) rosnąć (wzrosnąć *pf*) ▷ *vt* (*flowers, vegetables*) hodować (wyhodować *pf*); (*beard, hair*) zapuszczać (zapuścić *pf*); **to ~ by 10%** wzrastać (wzrosnąć *pf*) o dziesięć procent; **to ~ rich/old** bogacić (wzbogacić *pf*)/starzeć (zestarzeć *pf*) się

▸ **grow out of** *vt fus* (*clothes*) wyrastać (wyrosnąć *pf*) z +*gen*
▸ **grow up** *vi* (*be brought up*) wychowywać (wychować *pf*) się; (*be mature*) dojrzewać (dojrzeć *pf*)

growl [graul] *vi* (*dog, bear, lion*) warczeć (warknąć *pf*) ▹ *n* (*of dog, bear, lion*) warknięcie

grown [grəun] *pp of* **grow**

grown-up [grəun'ʌp] *n* (*adult*) dorosły

growth [grəuθ] *n* wzrost; **a ~ in sth** przyrost czegoś

grudge [grʌdʒ] *n* (*grievance*) uraza; **to have** *or* **bear a ~ (against sb)** żywić (do kogoś) urazę

gruesome ['gru:səm] *adj* (*murder, discovery, details*) makabryczny

grumble ['grʌmbl] *vi* (*complain*) zrzędzić

guarantee [gærən'ti:] *n* **1** (*assurance*) zapewnienie **2** (*Comm*) gwarancja ▹ *vt* **1** (*promise*) gwarantować (zagwarantować *pf*) **2** (*ensure*) zapewniać (zapewnić *pf*); **a/no ~ that...** pewność/nie ma pewności, że...; **to ~ (that)...** gwarantować (zagwarantować *pf*), (że)...

guard [gɑ:d] *n* **1** (*sentry*) strażnik(-iczka) *m/f* **2** (*Brit: Rail*) konduktor(ka) *m/f* ▹ *vt* (*building, entrance, door*) strzec +*gen*; (*person*) ochraniać (ochronić *pf*); **to be on one's ~ (against)** mieć się na baczności (przed +*inst*); **to be on ~** stać na warcie
▸ **guard against** *vt fus* (*disease, damage*) chronić (uchronić *pf*) się przed +*inst*

guess [gɛs] *vt, vi* **1** (*conjecture*) zgadywać (zgadnąć *pf*) **2** (*work out*) odgadywać (odgadnąć *pf*) ▹ *n* przypuszczenie; **I ~ so** myślę, że tak; **to ~ (that)...** (*conjecture*) zgadywać (zgadnąć *pf*), (że)...; (*work out*) zastanawiać (zastanowić *pf*) się, (że)...; (*suppose*) zastanawiać (zastanowić *pf*) się, (że)...; **~ what I did last night** zgadnij co zrobiłem wczoraj w nocy; **you're right, I ~** chyba masz rację; **my ~ is that...** przypuszczam, że...; **to take** *or* **have a ~** próbować (spróbować *pf*) zgadnąć

guest [gɛst] *n* gość ▹ *adj* (*speaker, appearance*) gościnny

guesthouse ['gɛsthaus] (*Brit*) *n* pensjonat

guide [gaɪd] *n* **1** (*tour guide*) przewodnik(-iczka) *m/f* **2** (*local guide*) miejscowy(-owa) przewodnik(-iczka) *m/f* **3** (*also*: **~ book**) przewodnik **4**: **G~** (*Brit*: *group member*) harcerka *f*; **Guides** *n pl* (*Brit*: *youth group*) harcerki *f* ▹ *vt* **1** (*round city, museum etc*) oprowadzać (oprowadzić *pf*) **2** (*lead*) prowadzić (poprowadzić *pf*)

guidebook ['gaɪdbuk] *n* przewodnik

guide dog (*Brit*) *n* pies przewodnik

guided tour ['gaɪdɪd-] *n* zwiedzanie z przewodnikiem

guilty ['gɪltɪ] *adj* **1** (*remorseful*) winny **2** (*secret, conscience*) nieczysty **3** (*responsible*) odpowiedzialny **4** (*Law*) winny; **~ of murder/manslaughter** winny morderstwa/zabójstwa

guinea pig ['gɪnɪ-] *n* (*animal*) świnka morska

guitar [gɪ'tɑ:ʳ] *n* gitara

gum [gʌm] *n* **1** (*Anat*) dziąsło **2** (*also*: **chewing ~**) guma do żucia

gun [gʌn] *n* (*small, medium-sized*) pistolet; (*large*) strzelba

gunpoint ['gʌnpɔɪnt] *n*: **at ~** na muszce

guy [gaɪ] *n* (*man*) facet; **(you) ~s** wy

gym [dʒɪm] *n* (*also*: **~nasium**) sala gimnastyczna

gymnast ['dʒɪmnæst] *n* gimnastyk(-yczka) *m/f*

gymnastics [dʒɪm'næstɪks] *n* gimnastyka *f sg*

gypsy ['dʒɪpsɪ] *n* Cygan(ka) *m/f*

habit ['hæbɪt] *n* (*custom, practice*) zwyczaj; **to be in the ~ of doing sth** mieć w zwyczaju robić coś; **to get out of the ~ of doing sth** odzwyczajać (odzwyczaić *pf*) się od robienia czegoś; **to get into the ~ of doing sth** przyzwyczajać (przyzwyczaić *pf*) się do robienia czegoś; **a bad ~** zły nawyk
had [hæd] *pt, pp of* **have**
hadn't ['hædnt] = **had not**
hail [heɪl] *n* grad
hair [hɛəʳ] *n* (*human: on head*) włosy *m pl*; (*single strand*) włos; **to do one's ~** układać (ułożyć *pf*) sobie fryzurę; **to have** *or* **get one's ~ cut** strzyc (ostrzyc *pf*) się
hairbrush ['hɛəbrʌʃ] *n* szczotka do włosów
haircut ['hɛəkʌt] *n* **1** (*at hairdresser's etc*) strzyżenie **2** (*hairstyle*) fryzura; **to have** *or* **get a ~** strzyc (ostrzyc *pf*) się
hairdresser ['hɛədrɛsəʳ] *n* **1** (*person*) fryzjer(ka) *m/f* **2** (*also*: **~'s**) salon fryzjerski
hairdryer ['hɛədraɪəʳ] *n* suszarka do włosów
hair gel *n* żel do włosów
hairspray ['hɛəspreɪ] *n* lakier do włosów
hairstyle ['hɛəstaɪl] *n* fryzura
half [hɑːf] (*pl* **halves**) *n, pron* **1** (*of amount, object*) połowa **2** (*Brit: child's ticket*) *bilet ze zniżką pięćdziesięciu procent* ▷ *adj* (*bottle*) pół +*gen* ▷ *adv* (*inf: empty, closed, open, asleep*) do połowy; **the first/second ~** (*Sport*) pierwsza/druga połowa; **to cut sth in ~** przecinać (przeciąć *pf*) coś na pół; **two/three and a ~** dwa/trzy i pół; **~ a pound/kilo/mile** pół funta/kilo/mili; **a day/week/pound and a ~** półtora dnia/tygodnia/funta; **~ an hour** pół godziny; **~ past four/five** wpół do piątej/szóstej; **to be ~ German/Irish** być w połowie Niemcem/Irlandczykiem; **to go halves (with sb)** dzielić (podzielić się *pf*) (z kimś) po połowie; **she's ~ his age** ona jest od niego o połowę młodsza
half-brother ['hɑːfbrʌðəʳ] *n* brat przyrodni
half-hour [hɑːf'auəʳ] *n* pół godziny
half price *adj* o połowę tańszy ▷ *adv* za pół ceny
half-sister ['hɑːfsɪstəʳ] *n* siostra przyrodnia
half-term [hɑːf'təːm] (*Brit: Scol*) *n* przerwa semestralna; **at ~** w czasie przerwy semestralnej

HALF-TERM

Half-term – W Wielkiej Brytanii mianem **half-term** nazywa się kilka dni wolnych od zajęć szkolnych w połowie każdego z trzech semestrów.

half-time [hɑːf'taɪm] (*Sport*) *n* przerwa; **at ~** w przerwie
halfway ['hɑːf'weɪ] *adv* (*between two points*) w połowie drogi; **~ through sth** w połowie czegoś
hall [hɔːl] *n* **1** (*esp Brit: entrance*) hol **2** (*room*) przedpokój
Halloween ['hæləu'iːn] *n* wigilia Wszystkich Świętych

HALLOWEEN

Noc **Halloween** przypada na 31 października. Według tradycji jest to święto wiedźm i duchów. Dzieci przebierają się i z wydrążonych dyń robią lampiony-strachy. Chodzą też po domach, proponując gospodarzom **trick or treat** (psikus albo poczęstunek): jeżeli ci nie wykupią się słodyczami, dzieci robią im psikusa.

hallway ['hɔːlweɪ] (*Brit*) *n* (*vestibule*) przedpokój
ham [hæm] *n* (*meat, joint*) szynka ▷ *adj* (*sandwich, roll, salad*) z szynką
hamburger ['hæmbəːgəʳ] *n* hamburger
hammer ['hæməʳ] *n* (*tool*) młotek
hamster ['hæmstəʳ] *n* chomik
hand [hænd] *n* **1** (*Anat*) ręka **2** (*of clock*) wskazówka **3** (*of cards*) karty *f pl* ▷ *vt* (*pass, give*) podawać (podać *pf*) +*dat*; **to do sth by ~** robić (zrobić *pf*) coś ręcznie; **~ in ~** (*holding hands*) trzymając się za ręce; **to give** *or* **lend sb a ~ (with sth)** pomagać (pomóc *pf*) komuś (w czymś); **on the one ~..., on the other ~...** z jednej strony..., z drugiej strony...
▸ **hand in** *vt* (*submit*) składać (złożyć *pf*); (*homework*) oddawać (oddać *pf*)
▸ **hand out** *vt* rozdawać (rozdać *pf*)
▸ **hand over** *vt* (*object, present, letter*) przekazywać (przekazać *pf*)
handbag ['hændbæg] (*Brit*) *n* torebka
handcuffs ['hændkʌfs] *n pl* kajdanki; **in ~** w kajdankach
handkerchief ['hæŋkətʃɪf] *n* chusteczka
handle ['hændl] *n* (*of bag*) rączka; (*of knife, paintbrush, broom, spade*) trzonek; (*of cup*) ucho; (*of door, window*) klamka ▷ *vt* (*deal with: problem, job, responsibility*) zajmować (zająć *pf*) się +*inst*; (*people*) radzić (poradzić *pf*) sobie z +*inst*; **"~ with care"** „ostrożnie"
handlebars ['hændlbɑːz] *n pl* kierownica roweru
handmade ['hænd'meɪd] *adj* wykonany ręcznie
handset [hændsɛt] *n* (*Tel*) słuchawka
hands-free kit ['hændz'friː-] *n* samochodowy zestaw głośnomówiący
handsome ['hænsəm] *adj* przystojny
handwriting ['hændraɪtɪŋ] *n* charakter pisma
handy ['hændɪ] *adj* **1** (*useful*) przydatny **2** (*close at hand*) pod ręką
hang [hæŋ] (*pt, pp* **hung**) *vt* (*clothes, light, picture*) wieszać (powiesić *pf*) ▷ *vi* (*be suspended*) wisieć (zawisnąć *pf*) ▷ *n*: **to get the ~ of sth** (*inf*) chwytać (chwycić *pf*) o co w czymś chodzi; **I've got the ~ of it now** teraz juz chwyciłem o co w tym chodzi
▸ **hang about** *vi* = **hang around**
▸ **hang around** (*inf*) *vi* (*wait*) pałętać się
▸ **hang on** *vi* (*wait*) czekać (poczekać *pf*)
▸ **hang onto, hang on to** *vt fus* **1** (*grasp*) kurczowo trzymać się +*gen* **2** (*inf: fig: keep*) trzymać się +*gen*
▸ **hang round** (*Brit*) *vi* = **hang around**
▸ **hang up** *vi* (*Tel*) odkładać (odłożyć *pf*) słuchawkę ▷ *vt* (*coat, hat, clothes*) wieszać (powiesić *pf*)
hanger ['hæŋəʳ] *n* (*also*: **coat ~**) wieszak
hangover ['hæŋəuvəʳ] *n* (*after drinking*) kac
happen ['hæpən] *vi* (*occur, result: incident, accident*) wydarzać (wydarzyć *pf*) się; **what will ~ if...?** co się stanie jeśli...?; **tell me what ~ed** powiedz mi co się stało; **to ~ to do sth** przypadkowo coś robić (zrobić *pf*)
happily ['hæpɪlɪ] *adv* (*cheerfully*) radośnie; **~ married** szczęśliwie zaślubiony
happiness ['hæpɪnɪs] *n* (*joy*) szczęście
happy ['hæpɪ] *adj* szczęśliwy; **to be ~ with sth** (*satisfied*) być z czegoś zadowolonym; **to be ~ to do sth** (*willing*) robić (zrobić *pf*) coś chętnie; **~ birthday!** wszystkiego najlepszego z okazji urodzin!; **~ Christmas!** Wesołych Świąt!
harassment ['hærəsmənt] *n* nękanie
harbour ['hɑːbəʳ] (*US* **harbor**) *n* (*Naut*) przystań
hard [hɑːd] *adj* **1** (*not soft: surface, object*) twardy **2** (*not easy: question, problem*) trudny; (*work*) ciężki

3 (*violent: push, punch, kick*) silny ▷ *adv* **1** (*work*) ciężko; (*try*) bardzo; (*think*) usilnie **2** (*laugh*) głośno; (*rain, snow*) mocno **3** (*violently: hit, punch, kick*) mocno; **it's ~ to tell** *or* **say** trudno powiedzieć; **such events are ~ to understand** trudno jest zrozumieć takie rzeczy; **it's ~ work serving in a shop** obsługiwanie w sklepie to ciężka praca; **to try ~** bardzo się starać (postarać *pf*)

hard disk (*Comput*) *n* twardy dysk

hardly ['hɑːdlɪ] *adv* **1** (*scarcely*) ledwo **2** (*no sooner*): **he had ~ sat down when the door burst open** ledwie usiadł, drzwi otworzyły się z hukiem; **~ ever/any/anyone** prawie nigdy/żaden/nikt; **I can ~ believe it** prawie nie mogę w to uwierzyć

hard up (*inf*) *adj* spłukany

hardware ['hɑːdwɛəʳ] *n* (*Comput*) sprzęt komputerowy

hardworking [hɑːd'wəːkɪŋ] *adj* pracowity

hare [hɛəʳ] *n* (*animal*) zając

harm [hɑːm] *vt* **1** (*damage*) krzywdzić (skrzywdzić *pf*) **2** (*injure*) uszkadzać (uszkodzić *pf*)

harmful ['hɑːmful] *adj* szkodliwy

harmless ['hɑːmlɪs] *adj* (*safe*) niegroźny

harp [hɑːp] *n* (*Mus*) harfa

harvest ['hɑːvɪst] *n* **1** (*harvest time*) żniwa **2** (*crop*) zbiory

has [hæz] *vb see* **have**

hasn't ['hæznt] = **has not**

hat [hæt] *n* kapelusz

hate [heɪt] *vt* (*person*) nienawidzić (znienawidzić *pf*); (*food, activity, sensation*) nie znosić (*pf*); **to ~ doing sth** nie znosić (*pf*) robienia czegoś

hatred ['heɪtrɪd] *n* (*of person*) nienawiść

haunted ['hɔːntɪd] *adj* (*house, building*) nawiedzony

KEYWORD

have [hæv] (*pt, pp* **had**) *vt* **1** (*possess*) mieć; **he has** *or* **he has got blue eyes/dark hair** on ma niebieskie oczy/ciemne włosy; **do you have** *or* **have you got a car/phone?** masz samochód/telefon?; **to have** *or* **have got sth to do** mieć coś do zrobienia; **she had her eyes closed** miała zamknięte oczy

2 (*with meals, drinks*): **to have breakfast** zjeść śniadanie; **to have a drink/a cigarette** napić się/zapalić papierosa

3 (*with activity*): **to have a swim/bath** popływać/wykąpać się; **to have a meeting/party** mieć spotkanie/przyjęcie

4 (*receive, obtain*) dostawać (dostać *pf*); **can I have your address?** czy może mi pan/pani podać swój adres?; **you can have it for £5** możesz to dostać za pięć funtów

5 (*give birth to*): **to have a baby** rodzić (urodzić *pf*) dziecko

6: **to have one's hair cut** obciąć (*pf*) sobie włosy (u fryzjera)

7 (*experience, suffer*): **to have a headache** mieć ból głowy; **to have an operation** mieć operację; **she had her bag stolen** ukradziono jej torbę; **she had her arm broken** złamała sobie rękę

▷ *aux vb* **1**: **she has arrived** przyjechała; **has he told you?** powiedział panu/pani?; **when she had dressed, she went downstairs** kiedy się ubrała, zeszła na dół; **I haven't seen him for ages/since July** nie widziałem go od dawna/od lipca

2 (*in tag questions*): **he's done it, hasn't he?** zrobił to, prawda?

3 (*in short answers and questions*): **yes, I have** tak, zrobiłem (to); **no I haven't** nie, nie zrobiłem (tego); **so have I!** ja też!; **neither have I** ja też nie; **I've finished, have you?** ja już skończyłem, a ty?

4 (*be obliged*): **to have (got) to do sth** mieć coś do zrobienia; **she has (got) to do it** ona musi to zrobić; **this has (got) to be a mistake** to musi być jakaś pomyłka

▶ **have on** *vt* (*clothes*) mieć na sobie; **he didn't have anything on** nie miał nic na sobie; **I don't have any money on me** nie mam przy sobie żadnych pieniędzy

haven't ['hævnt] = **have not**
hay [heɪ] *n* siano
hay fever *n* katar sienny
hazel ['heɪzl] *adj* (*eyes*) orzechowy
hazelnut ['heɪzlnʌt] *n* orzech laskowy
he [hiː] *pron* (*man, boy*) on
head [hɛd] *n* **1** (*Anat*) głowa **2** (*mind*) głowa **3** (*of company, organization, department*) dyrektor(ka) *m/f* **4** (*Brit*: *head teacher*) dyrektor(ka) *m/f* ▷ *vt* **1** (*list, group*) być na początku +*gen* **2** (*Football*: *ball*) grać (zagrać *pf*) główką; **10 pounds a** *or* **per ~** dziesięć funtów na głowę; **it went to his ~** (*alcohol*) poszło mu do głowy; (*success, power*) uderzył mu do głowy; **to lose one's ~** tracić (stracić *pf*) głowę; **I can't make ~ or** *or* **nor tail of this** (*inf*) nic z tego nie rozumiem; **from ~ to foot** *or* **toe** od stóp do głów; **~s or tails?** orzeł czy reszka?
▸ **head for** *vt fus* (*place*) zmierzać do +*gen*; **to be ~ing** *or* **~ed for Glasgow** zmierzać w stronę Glasgow
▸ **head off** *vi* (*leave*) wyjeżdżać (wyjechać *pf*)
headache ['hɛdeɪk] *n* **1** (*pain*) ból głowy **2** (*problem*) utrapienie; **to have a ~** cierpieć na ból głowy
headlamp ['hɛdlæmp] (*Brit*) *n* = **headlight**
headlight ['hɛdlaɪt] *n* reflektor
headline ['hɛdlaɪn] *n* nagłówek; **the ~s** (*Publishing*) nagłówki; (*TV, Rad*) skrót najważniejszych wiadomości
headmaster [hɛd'mɑːstəʳ] (*Brit*) *n* dyrektor szkoły
headmistress [hɛd'mɪstrɪs] (*Brit*) *n* dyrektorka szkoły
headphones ['hɛdfəunz] *n pl* słuchawki
headquarters ['hɛdkwɔːtəz] *n pl* (*of company, organization*) siedziba główna
head teacher (*Brit*) *n* dyrektor(ka) *m/f* szkoły
heal [hiːl] *vi* (*physically*) goić (zagoić *pf*) się
health [hɛlθ] *n* zdrowie; **to be good for one's ~** służyć czyjemuś zdrowiu; **to be bad for one's ~** szkodzić (zaszkodzić *pf*) czyjemuś zdrowiu; **to drink (to) sb's ~** pić (wypić *pf*) czyjeś zdrowie
healthy ['hɛlθɪ] *adj* zdrowy
heap [hiːp] *n* (*pile*: *of clothes, papers*) sterta; **~s** *or* **a ~ of** (*inf*) kupa +*gen*
hear [hɪəʳ] (*pt, pp* **heard** [həːd]) *vt* **1** (*sound, voice, music*) słyszeć (usłyszeć *pf*) **2** (*news, lecture, concert*) słuchać (posłuchać *pf*) +*gen*; **to ~ sb doing sth** słyszeć (usłyszeć *pf*) jak ktoś coś robi; **to ~ that...** słyszeć (usłyszeć *pf*), że...; **to ~ about sth/sb** słyszeć (usłyszeć *pf*) o czymś/kimś; **to ~ from sb** dostawać (dostać *pf*) wiadomość od kogoś; **I've never ~d of him** nigdy o nim nie słyszałem
heart [hɑːt] *n* serce; **hearts** *n pl* (*Cards*) kier *sg*; **to learn sth (off) by ~** uczyć (nauczyć *pf*) się czegoś na pamięć; **to know sth (off) by ~** znać coś na pamięć; **the ~ of London** serce Londynu; **to lose ~** tracić (stracić *pf*) ducha; **to break sb's ~** łamać (złamać *pf*) komuś serce; **my ~ sank** straciłem zapał; **to one's ~'s content** ile dusza zapragnie
heart attack *n* atak serca; **to have a ~** mieć atak serca
heartbroken ['hɑːtbrəukən] *adj* zrozpaczony
heat [hiːt] *n* **1** (*warmth*) ciepło **2** (*temperature*) ciepło **3** (*hob, flame etc*) temperatura **4** (*Sport*: *also*: **qualifying ~**) zawody eliminacyjne *pl* ▷ *vt* (*water, food*) podgrzewać (podgrzać *pf*); (*room, house*) ogrzewać (ogrzać *pf*); **I find the ~ unbearable** ten upał jest nie do wytrzymania
▸ **heat up** *vt* (*food*) podgrzewać (podgrzać *pf*)
heater ['hiːtəʳ] *n* (*electric heater, gas heater*) grzejnik; (*in car*) ogrzewanie
heather ['hɛðəʳ] *n* wrzos
heating ['hiːtɪŋ] *n* (*system*) ogrzewanie
heatwave ['hiːtweɪv] *n* fala upałów
heaven ['hɛvn] *n* niebo
heavy ['hɛvɪ] *adj* **1** (*in weight*) ciężki **2** (*well-built*: *person*) dobrze zbudowany **3** (*thick*: *material, door etc*) gruby **4** (*traffic*) duży; (*fine, penalty, sentence*) ciężki; (*drinking, smoking,*

gambling) nałogowy; (*rain, snow*) obfity; **how ~ are you/is it?** ile pan/pani/to waży?; **a ~ drinker/smoker** osoba która dużo pije/pali

he'd [hi:d] = **he would, he had**

hedge [hɛdʒ] *n* żywopłot

hedgehog ['hɛdʒhɔg] *n* jeż

heel [hi:l] *n* **1** (*of foot*) pięta **2** (*of shoe*) obcas; **heels** *n pl* (*also*: **high ~s**) wysokie obcasy

height [haɪt] *n* **1** (*of person, tree, building*) wysokość **2** (*altitude*) wysokość; **of average** *or* **medium ~** średniego wzrostu; **what ~ are you?** ile ma pan/pani wzrostu?; **to gain ~** nabierać (nabrać *pf*) wysokości; **to lose ~** tracić (stracić *pf*) wysokość; **at knee/waist/shoulder ~** na wysokości kolana/talii/ramion; **it is the ~ of fashion/good taste** to jest szczyt mody/dobrego gustu

held [hɛld] *pt, pp of* **hold**

helicopter ['hɛlɪkɔptəʳ] *n* helikopter

hell [hɛl] *n* (*Rel*) piekło ▷ *excl* (*inf!*) piekło; **a** *or* **one ~ of a lot of** (*inf*) piekielnie dużo +*gen*; **to go to ~** (*Rel*) iść (pójść *pf*) do piekła; **go to ~!** (*fig: inf!*) idź do diabła!; **it was ~** (*inf*) to był koszmar; **oh, to ~ with it!** (*inf*) ech, mam to gdzieś!

he'll [hi:l] = **he will, he shall**

hello [hə'ləu] *excl* (*as greeting*) cześć; (*Tel*) halo; (*to attract attention*) halo

helmet ['hɛlmɪt] *n* (*of motorcyclist, cyclist, astronaut*) kask; (*of soldier, police officer, fireman*) hełm

help [hɛlp] *n* pomoc; (*when in danger*) ratunek ▷ *vt* (*person*) pomagać (pomóc *pf*) +*dat* ▷ *vi* **1** (*assist*) pomagać (pomóc *pf*) **2** (*be useful*) przydawać (przydać *pf*) się; **she needs ~ to get up the stairs** ona potrzebuje pomocy żeby wyjść po schodach; **he's been a great ~** bardzo mi pomógł; **with the ~ of sb/sth** z pomocą kogoś/czegoś; **I ~ed him (to) fix his car** pomogłem mu naprawić jego samochód; **~!** ratunku!; **can I ~ you?** (*in shop*) czym mogę panu/pani służyć?; **to ~ o.s. to sth** (*serve oneself*) częstować (poczęstować *pf*) się czymś; (*inf: steal*) podkradać (podkraść *pf*) coś; **he can't ~ it** nie może nic na to poradzić; **I can't ~ feeling sorry for him** jakoś mi go szkoda; **it can't be ~ed** nic się na to nie poradzi

helpful ['hɛlpful] *adj* (*person*) pomocny; (*advice, suggestion*) przydatny

helping ['hɛlpɪŋ] *n* (*of food*) porcja

helpless ['hɛlplɪs] *adj* (*defenceless*) bezbronny

hen [hɛn] *n* kura

her [hə:ʳ] *pron* (*acc*) ją; (*gen, dat*) jej; (*inst*) nią; (*loc*) niej ▷ *adj* jej; (*referring to subject of sentence*) swój; **~ face was very red** jej twarz była bardzo zaczerwieniona

herb [hə:b] (*US* [ə:rb]) *n* ziele

herd [hə:d] *n* stado

here [hɪəʳ] *adv* **1** (*in/to this place*) tutaj **2** (*near me*) tutaj; **"~!"** (*present*) „jestem!"; **~'s my phone number** oto mój numer telefonu; **~ he is** (*he's just arrived*) oto i on; **~ you are** (*take this*) proszę; **~ we are!** (*found it!*) jest!; (*we've arrived!*) jesteśmy na miejscu!; **~ and there** tu i tam; **I'm ~ to help you** jestem tutaj, żeby panu/pani pomóc

hero ['hɪərəu] (*pl* **heroes**) *n* bohater

heroin ['hɛrəuɪn] *n* heroina

heroine ['hɛrəuɪn] *n* bohaterka

hers [hə:z] *pron* **1** (*of woman, girl*) jej **2** (*of female animal*) jej; **this is ~** to jest jej; **a friend of ~** jej znajomy

herself [hə:'sɛlf] *pron* **1** (*gen, acc*) siebie; (*dat, loc*) sobie; (*inst*) sobą; (*reflexive pronoun*) się **2** (*emphatic*) sama; **she hurt ~** zrobiła sobie krzywdę; **she lives by ~** mieszka sama

he's [hi:z] = **he is, he has**

hesitate ['hɛzɪteɪt] *vi* wahać (zawahać *pf*) się; **he did not ~ to take action** nie zawahał się przed podjęciem działań; **don't ~ to contact me** proszę się ze mną kontaktować bez wahania

heterosexual ['hɛtərəu'sɛksjuəl] *adj* heteroseksualny ▷ *n* osoba heteroseksualna

hi [haɪ] *excl* cześć

hiccup ['hɪkʌp] *n*: **to have/get (the) ~s** mieć czkawkę/dostawać (dostać *pf*) czkawki

hide [haɪd] (*pt* **hid**, *pp* **hidden**) *vt* ukrywać (ukryć *pf*) ▷ *vi* chować (schować *pf*) się; **to ~ from sb** chować (schować *pf*) się przed kimś; **to ~ sth from sb** (*lit*) chować (schować *pf*) coś przed kimś; (*fig*) ukrywać (ukryć *pf*) coś przed kimś

hi-fi ['haɪfaɪ] *n* zestaw hi-fi

high [haɪ] *adj* wysoki ▷ *adv* wysoko; **it is 20m ~** to jest wysokie na dwadzieścia metrów; **foods that are ~ in fat** produkty spożywcze o wysokiej zawartości tłuszczu; **the temperature was in the ~ eighties** temperatura sięgnęła blisko dziewięćdziesięciu stopni; **safety has always been our ~est priority** zawsze stawialiśmy bezpieczeństwo na pierwszym miejscu; **~ up** (*above the ground*) wysoko w górze; **to search** *or* **look ~ and low for sth** szukać czegoś wszędzie

higher education ['haɪəʳ-] *n* wyższe wykształcenie

high heels *n pl* wysokie obcasy

high jump *n* (*Sport*): **the ~** skok wzwyż

high-rise ['haɪraɪz] *n* wieżowiec, w wieżowcu

high school *n* **1** (*Brit*: *for students aged 11-18*) szkoła ogólnokształcąca **2** (*US*: *for students aged 14-18*) liceum

HIGH SCHOOL

High school – W Wielkiej Brytanii uczniowie uczęszczają do szkoły średniej (**high school**) pomiędzy 11 a 18 rokiem życia. W USA wcześniej jeszcze jest **junior high school**, do **high school** uczęszcza się pomiędzy 14 a 18 rokiem życia.

hijack ['haɪdʒæk] *vt* (*plane*) porywać (porwać *pf*); (*idea, event*) przejmować (przejąć *pf*) ▷ *n* porwanie

hijacker ['haɪdʒækəʳ] *n* porywacz(ka) *m/f*

hike [haɪk] *vi* (*go walking*) wędrować (powędrować *pf*) ▷ *n* (*walk*) wędrówka

hiking ['haɪkɪŋ] *n* piesze wycieczki *pl*; **to go ~** iść/chodzić (pójść *pf*) na pieszą wędrówkę

hilarious [hɪ'lɛərɪəs] *adj* (*account, adventure*) komiczny

hill [hɪl] *n* (*hillock*) wzgórze; (*slope*) wzniesienie

hill-walking ['hɪlwɔːkɪŋ] *n* turystyka górska

him [hɪm] *pron* (*acc, gen*) jego, go; (*dat*) jemu, mu; (*inst, loc*) nim; **I haven't seen ~** nie widziałem go; **they gave ~ the job** dali mu tę pracę

himself [hɪm'sɛlf] *pron* **1** (*gen, acc*) siebie; (*dat, loc*) sobie; (*inst*) sobą; (*reflexive pronoun*) się **2** (*emphatic*) sam; **he hurt ~** skaleczył się; **he prepared the supper ~** sam przygotował kolację; **he lives by ~** mieszka sam

Hindu ['hɪnduː] *n* Hindus ▷ *adj* hinduski

hip [hɪp] *n* (*Anat*) biodro

hippie ['hɪpɪ] *n* hipis(ka) *m/f*

hippopotamus [hɪpə'pɔtəməs] (*pl* **hippopotamuses** *or* **hippopotami** [hɪpə'pɔtəmaɪ]) *n* hipopotam

hire ['haɪəʳ] *vt* (*esp Brit*: *car, equipment, hall*) wynajmować (wynająć *pf*); (*worker*) zatrudniać (zatrudnić *pf*) ▷ *n* (*Brit*: *of car, hall etc*) wynajem; **for ~** (*esp Brit*: *car, boat, building*) do wynajęcia; (*taxi*) wolny

his [hɪz] *adj* **1** (*of man, boy*) jego **2** (*of animal*) jego; (*referring to subject of sentence*) swój ▷ *pron* jego; **~ face was very red** jego twarz była bardzo czerwona; **these are ~** te są jego; **a friend of ~** jego przyjaciel

history ['hɪstərɪ] *n* historia; **to make ~** przechodzić (przejść *pf*) do historii

hit [hɪt] (*pt, pp* **hit**) *vt* **1** (*strike*) uderzać (uderzyć *pf*) **2** (*collide with*) uderzać (uderzyć *pf*) **3** (*target*: *bomb, bullet*) trafiać (trafić *pf*) ▷ *n* **1** uderzenie **2** (*on website*) trafienie **3** (*hit song*) przebój; **to be/become a ~** (*song, film, play*) być/stawać (stać *pf*) się przebojem

▶ **hit off** *vt*: **to ~ it off (with sb)** (*inf*) zaprzyjaźniać (zaprzyjaźnić *pf*) się (z kimś)

hitch [hɪtʃ] *n* (*difficulty*) szkopuł; **technical ~** drobny problem techniczny

hitchhike ['hɪtʃhaɪk] *vi* jeździć (pojechać *pf*) autostopem
hitchhiker ['hɪtʃhaɪkəʳ] *n* autostopowicz(ka) *m/f*
hitchhiking ['hɪtʃhaɪkɪŋ] *n* autostop
HIV *n abbr* (= *human immunodeficiency virus*) wirus HIV; **to be ~ positive/negative** być seropozytywnym/seronegatywnym
hoarse [hɔːs] *adj* (*voice etc*) zachrypnięty
hobby ['hɔbɪ] *n* hobby
hockey ['hɔkɪ] *n* **1** (*Brit*: *on grass*) hokej na trawie **2** (*US*: *on ice*) hokej

HOGMANAY

Hogmanay – tak w Szkocji nazywana jest wigilia Nowego Roku (31 grudnia). Według tradycji tuż po północy odwiedza się rodzinę i przyjaciół obnosząc ze sobą whisky oraz kawałek węgla, co ma przynieść szczęście w nowym roku. Zwyczaj ten nazywany jest **first footing** – pierwsza osoba przekraczająca próg domu ma ponoć wpływ na powodzenie jego gospodarzy w nadchodzącym roku.

hold [həuld] (*pt, pp* **held**) *vt* **1** (*grip*) trzymać **2** (*contain*) zawierać (zawrzeć *pf*) ▷ *vi* (*Tel*) czekać (poczekać *pf*) ▷ *n* **1** (*grasp*) uścisk **2** (*of ship, plane*) ładownia; **to ~ sb responsible** obarczać (obarczyć *pf*) kogoś odpowiedzialnością; **~ the line!** (*Tel*) proszę czekać!; **to ~ sb prisoner/hostage** przetrzymywać (przetrzymać *pf*) kogoś jako więźnia/zakładnika; **~ it!** chwileczkę!; **to get** *or* **grab ~ of sb/sth** chwytać (chwycić *pf*) kogoś/coś; **I need to get ~ of Bob** muszę złapać Boba
▸ **hold against** *vt*: **to ~ sth against sb** mieć coś komuś za złe
▸ **hold on** *vi* **1** (*keep hold*) nie puszczać (puścić *pf*) **2** (*inf*: *wait*) czekać (poczekać *pf*)
▸ **hold on to** *vt fus* (*grasp*) łapać (złapać *pf*) się *+gen*
▸ **hold up** *vt* **1** (*lift up*) unosić (unieść *pf*) **2** (*delay*) zatrzymywać (zatrzymać *pf*) **3** (*rob*: *person, bank*) napadać (napaść *pf*) na
hold-up ['həuldʌp] *n* **1** (*robbery*) napad z bronią w ręku **2** (*delay*) opóźnienie; (*in traffic*) korek
hole [həul] *n* dziura
holiday ['hɔlɪdeɪ] (*Brit*) *n* wakacje *f pl*; **public ~** dzień wolny od pracy; **the school/summer ~s** (*Brit*: *Scol*) wakacje szkolne/letnie; **the Christmas ~s** ferie świąteczne; **to be on ~** być na wakacjach
Holland ['hɔlənd] *n* Holandia
hollow ['hɔləu] *adj* pusty
holly ['hɔlɪ] *n* ostrokrzew
holy ['həulɪ] *adj* święty
home [həum] *n* **1** (*house*) dom **2** (*country, area*) ojczyzna **3** (*institution*) dom ▷ *adj* (*Sport*: *team*) miejscowy; (*game*) na własnym boisku ▷ *adv* (*be*) w domu; (*go*) do domu; **at ~** (*in house*) w domu; (*comfortable*) jak w domu; **make yourself at ~** czuj się jak u siebie w domu
homeland ['həumlænd] *n* kraj rodzinny
homeless ['həumlɪs] *adj* (*family, refugee*) bezdomny ▷ *n pl*: **the ~** bezdomni
homepage ['həumpeɪdʒ] (*Comput*) *n* strona główna
homesick ['həumsɪk] *adj* tęskniący za domem; **to be ~** tęsknić (zatęsknić *pf*) za domem
homework ['həumwəːk] *n* zadanie domowe; **to do one's ~** (*lit*) odrabiać (odrobić *pf*) zadanie domowe
homophobia [həuməfəubɪə] *n* homofobia
homosexual [hɔməu'sɛksjuəl] *adj* homoseksualny ▷ *n* homoseksualista(-tka) *m/f*
honest ['ɔnɪst] *adj* **1** (*truthful*) uczciwy **2** (*trustworthy*) godny zaufania; **to be ~,...** mówiąc szczerze,...
honestly ['ɔnɪstlɪ] *adv* **1** (*with integrity*) uczciwie **2** (*bluntly*) szczerze **3** (*emphasizing sth*) serio
honesty ['ɔnɪstɪ] *n* uczciwość
honey ['hʌnɪ] *n* **1** (*food*) miód **2** (*esp US*: *inf*: *darling*) kochanie

honeymoon ['hʌnɪmu:n] *n* (*lit, fig*) miesiąc miodowy; **to be on (one's) ~** być w podróży poślubnej
Hong Kong ['hɔŋ'kɔŋ] *n* Hong Kong
honour ['ɔnə^r] (*US* **honor**) *n* **1** (*pride, self-respect*) honor **2** (*tribute*) zaszczyt; **the ~ of hosting the Olympic Games®** zaszczyt bycia gospodarzem Igrzysk Olimpijskich
hood [hud] *n* **1** (*of coat etc*) kaptur **2** (*US: Aut*) maska
hoof [hu:f] (*pl* **hooves** [hu:vz]) *n* kopyto
hook [huk] *n* hak; **to take the phone off the ~** zdejmować (zdjąć *pf*) słuchawkę z widełek
hooligan ['hu:lɪgən] *n* chuligan
hooray [hu:'reɪ] *excl* hura
Hoover® ['hu:və^r] (*Brit*) *n* odkurzacz ▷ *vt* **to hoover** (*carpet*) odkurzać (odkurzyć *pf*)
hooves [hu:vz] *n pl of* **hoof**
hop [hɔp] *vi* (*jump: person*) skakać (skoczyć *pf*); (*bird*) podskakiwać (podskoczyć *pf*)
hope [həup] *vt* mieć nadzieję ▷ *vi* mieć nadzieję ▷ *n* nadzieja; **I ~ so/not** mam nadzieję/mam nadzieję, że nie; **to ~ to do sth** mieć nadzieję, że coś się zrobi; **to have no ~ of sth/doing sth** nie mieć szans na coś/na zrobienie czegoś; **in the ~ of/that...** w nadziei na/że...
hopefully ['həupfulɪ] *adv* (*expectantly*) z nadzieją; **~,...** przy odrobinie szczęścia,...
hopeless ['həuplɪs] *adj* beznadziejny; **I'm ~ at cooking** jestem beznadziejny w gotowaniu
horizon [hə'raɪzn] *n* (*skyline*): **the ~** horyzont; **on the ~** (*fig*) na horyzoncie
horizontal [hɔrɪ'zɔntl] *adj* poziomy
horn [hɔ:n] *n* **1** (*of animal*) róg **2** (*Mus*) róg **3** (*Aut*) klakson
horoscope ['hɔrəskəup] *n* horoskop
horrible ['hɔrɪbl] *adj* (*colour, food, mess*) okropny; (*accident, crime*) straszny; (*experience, situation, dream*) straszny
horrifying ['hɔrɪfaɪɪŋ] *adj* przerażający
horror ['hɔrə^r] *n* (*alarm*) przerażenie
horror film *n* horror
horse [hɔ:s] *n* koń
horse racing *n* wyścigi konne *pl*
horse riding *n* jazda konna
hose [həuz] *n* (*also*: **~pipe**) wąż
hospital ['hɔspɪtl] *n* szpital; **to be in ~** *or* (*US*) **in the ~** być w szpitalu
hospitality [hɔspɪ'tælɪtɪ] *n* gościnność
host [həust] *n* gospodarz
hostage ['hɔstɪdʒ] *n* (*prisoner*) zakładnik(-iczka) *m/f*; **to be taken/held ~** być wziętym/przetrzymywanym jako zakładnik
hostel ['hɔstl] (*esp Brit*) *n* (*for homeless etc*) schronisko
hostess ['həustɪs] *n* gospodyni
hot [hɔt] *adj* **1** (*very warm*) gorący **2** (*spicy: food*) ostry
hot dog *n* hot dog
hotel [həu'tɛl] *n* hotel; **to stay at a ~** zatrzymywać (zatrzymać *pf*) się w hotelu
hot spot *n* (*Comput*) punkt ogólnego dostępu do internetu
hour ['auə^r] *n* godzina; **hours** *n pl* (*ages*) całe godziny; **the buses leave on the ~** autobusy odjeżdżają o równych godzinach; **for three/four ~s** przez trzy/cztery godziny; **(at) 60 kilometres/miles an** *or* **per ~** z prędkością sześćdziesięciu kilometrów/mil na godzinę; **to pay sb by the ~** płacić (zapłacić *pf*) komuś od godziny; **lunch ~** pora lunchu
hourly ['auəlɪ] *adv* (*once each hour*) co godzinę ▷ *adj* **1** (*once each hour*) cogodzinny **2** (*per hour: rate, income*) od godziny
house [haus] *n* (*home*) dom; **at my ~/to my ~** w moim domu/do mojego domu

HOUSES OF PARLIAMENT

Houses of Parliament – w Wielkiej Brytanii parlament składa się z dwóch Izb: Izby Gmin i Izby Lordów.

housewife ['hauswaɪf] (*pl* **housewives**) *n* gospodyni domowa
housework ['hauswə:k] *n* prace domowe *pl*

housing estate ['hauzıŋ-] (*Brit*) *n* osiedle mieszkaniowe
hovercraft ['hɔvəkrɑːft] (*pl* **hovercraft**) *n* poduszkowiec

KEYWORD

how [hau] *adv* **1** (*in questions*) jak; **how did you do it?** jak to pan zrobił/pani zrobiła?; **how are you?** jak się pan/pani miewa?; **"how do you do?" — "how do you do?"** „miło mi!" — „miło mi!"; **how long have you lived here?** jak długo pan/pani tutaj mieszka?; **how much milk/how many people?** ile mleka/ilu ludzi?; **how old are you?** ile ma pan/pani lat?; **how tall is he?** jakiego on jest wzrostu?
2 (*in exclamations*): **how lovely/awful!** to wspaniale/okropne!
3 (*in suggestions*): **how about a cup of tea/a walk?** co powie pan/pani na filiżankę herbaty/spacer?; **how about going to the cinema?** co powie pan/pani na kino?
4 (*avoiding repetition*): **how about you?** a pan/pani?
▷ *conj* jak; **I know how she did it** wiem jak ona to zrobiła; **to know how to do sth** wiedzieć jak coś zrobić

however [hau'ɛvəʳ] *adv* **1** (*but*) jednak **2** (*with adj, adv*) bez względu na to jak **3** (*in questions*) jakim cudem
hug [hʌg] *vt* (*person*) przytulać (przytulić *pf*) ▷ *n* uścisk; **to give sb a ~** przytulać (przytulić *pf*) kogoś
huge [hjuːdʒ] *adj* (*enormous*) ogromny
hum [hʌm] *vt* (*tune, song*) nucić (zanucić *pf*) ▷ *vi* (*person*) nucić; (*machine*) buczeć (zabuczeć *pf*); (*buzz: insect*) brzęczeć (zabrzęczeć *pf*)
human ['hjuːmən] *adj* ludzki ▷ *n* (*also*: **~ being**) człowiek; **the ~ race** rasa ludzka; **~ nature** natura ludzka
humour ['hjuːməʳ] (*US* **humor**) *n* humor; **sense of ~** poczucie humoru
hundred ['hʌndrəd] *num* sto; **hundreds** *n pl* setki; **a** *or* **one ~ books/dollars** sto książek/dolarów; **a** *or* **one ~ people** stu ludzi
hung [hʌŋ] *pt, pp of* **hang**
Hungarian [hʌŋ'gɛərıən] *adj* węgierski ▷ *n* **1** (*person*) Węgier(ka) *m/f* **2** (*language*) węgierski
Hungary ['hʌŋgərı] *n* Węgry *f pl*
hunger ['hʌŋgəʳ] *n* głód
hungry ['hʌŋgrı] *adj* głodny; **to be ~** być głodnym
hunt [hʌnt] *vt* **1** (*for food, sport*) polować (zapolować *pf*) na **2** (*criminal, fugitive*) poszukiwać *+gen* ▷ *vi* polować (zapolować *pf*) ▷ *n* **1** (*for food, sport*) polowanie **2** (*for missing person*) poszukiwania *nt pl*; **detectives are ~ing for clues** policja poszukuje tropów
hunting ['hʌntıŋ] *n* polowanie; **job/house ~** polowanie na pracę/dom
hurdle ['həːdl] *n* (*difficulty*) przeszkoda; **hurdles** *n pl* (*Sport*) płotki
hurricane ['hʌrıkən] *n* huragan; **~ Charley/Tessa** huragan Charley/Tessa
hurry ['hʌrı] *vi* śpieszyć (pośpieszyć *pf*) się ▷ *n*: **to be in a ~ (to do sth)** śpieszyć się (żeby coś zrobić); **to ~ home** śpieszyć (pośpieszyć *pf*) się do domu; **to do sth in a ~** robić (zrobić *pf*) coś w pośpiechu; **there's** *or* **I'm in no ~** nie ma pośpiechu; **what's the ~?** po co ten pośpiech?
▶ **hurry up** *vi* śpieszyć (pośpieszyć *pf*) się ▷ *vt* popędzać (popędzić *pf*)
hurt [həːt] (*pt, pp* **hurt**) *vt* **1** (*cause pain to*) sprawiać (sprawić *pf*) *+dat* ból **2** (*injure*) ranić (zranić *pf*) **3** (*emotionally*) ranić (zranić *pf*) ▷ *vi* (*be painful*) boleć (zaboleć *pf*) ▷ *adj* **1** (*injured*) zraniony **2** (*emotionally*) urażony; **to ~ o.s.** ranić (zranić *pf*) się; **I didn't want to ~ your feelings** nie chciałem zranić twoich uczuć; **where does it ~?** gdzie boli?
husband ['hʌzbənd] *n* mąż
hut [hʌt] *n* **1** (*house*) chata **2** (*shed*) szopa
hymn [hım] *n* hymn
hyperlink ['haıpəlıŋk] *n* hiperłącze
hyphen ['haıfn] *n* łącznik

I

I [aɪ] *pron* ja
ice [aɪs] *n* lód
iceberg ['aɪsbəːg] *n* góra lodowa; **the tip of the ~** (*fig*) wierzchołek góry lodowej
ice cream *n* lody *m pl*
ice cube *n* kostka lodu
ice hockey (*esp Brit*) *n* hokej
Iceland ['aɪslənd] *n* Islandia
ice rink [-rɪŋk] *n* lodowisko
ice-skating ['aɪsskeɪtɪŋ] *n* łyżwiarstwo; (*figure skating*) łyżwiarstwo figurowe
icing ['aɪsɪŋ] *n* (*Culin*) lukier
icon ['aɪkɔn] *n* ikona
ICT (*Brit*) *n abbr* (= *Information and Communication Technology*) ICT
icy ['aɪsɪ] *adj* (*air, water, temperature*) lodowaty; (*road*) oblodzony
ID *n abbr* (= *identification*) dowód osobisty
I'd [aɪd] = **I would, I had**
idea [aɪ'dɪə] *n* **1** (*scheme*) pomysł **2** (*opinion, theory*) opinia **3** (*notion*) wyobrażenie; **(what a) good ~!** (cóż za) dobry pomysł!; **I haven't the slightest** *or* **faintest ~** nie mam zielonego pojęcia
ideal [aɪ'dɪəl] *adj* (*person, world*) idealny
identical [aɪ'dɛntɪkl] *adj* identyczny; **~ to** dokładnie taki sam jak
identification [aɪdɛntɪfɪ'keɪʃən] *n* identyfikacja
identify [aɪ'dɛntɪfaɪ] *vt* (*recognize*) rozpoznawać (rozpoznać *pf*)
identity card [aɪ'dɛntɪtɪ-] *n* dowód osobisty
identity theft *n* kradzież tożsamości
idiot ['ɪdɪət] *n* idiota(-tka) *m/f*
i.e. *abbr* (= *id est*) tj.

KEYWORD

if [ɪf] *conj* **1** (*conditional use*) jeśli; **I'll go if you come with me** pójdę jeśli pójdzie pan/pani ze mną; **if anyone comes in...** jeśli ktoś wejdzie...; **if I were you** gdybym był tobą; **if necessary** jeśli to konieczne; **if so** jeśli tak; **if not** jeśli nie
2 (*whenever*) kiedy; **if we are in Hong Kong, we always go to see her** kiedy jesteśmy w Hong Kongu, zawsze jedziemy ją odwiedzić
3 (*whether*) czy; **I don't know if he's in** nie wiem, czy jest w domu; **ask him if he can come** zapytaj, czy może przyjść
4 (*in expressions*): **if ever** jeśli; **if only we had more time!** gdybyśmy mieli więcej czasu!

ignore [ɪg'nɔːʳ] *vt* ignorować (zignorować *pf*)
I'll [aɪl] = **I will, I shall**
ill [ɪl] *adj* (*sick*) chory; **the ill** *n pl*: **the mentally/terminally ~** umysłowo/śmiertelnie chorzy; **to fall** *or* **be taken ~** zachorować (*pf*)
illegal [ɪ'liːgl] *adj* nielegalny
illness ['ɪlnɪs] *n* choroba
illusion [ɪ'luːʒən] *n* **1** (*false idea*) iluzja **2** (*false appearance*) złudzenie
illustration [ɪlə'streɪʃən] *n* (*picture*) ilustracja
image ['ɪmɪdʒ] *n* **1** (*mental picture*) wyobrażenie **2** (*public face*) wizerunek
imagination [ɪmædʒɪ'neɪʃən] *n* wyobraźnia
imagine [ɪ'mædʒɪn] *vt* **1** (*envisage*) wyobrażać (wyobrazić *pf*) sobie **2** (*dream*) wyobrażać (wyobrazić *pf*) sobie **3** (*suppose*) przypuszczać
imitate ['ɪmɪteɪt] *vt* **1** (*copy*) imitować **2** (*mimic*) naśladować
imitation [ɪmɪ'teɪʃən] *n* (*copy*) imitacja ▷ *adj* sztuczny

immediate [ɪ'miːdɪət] *adj* natychmiastowy
immediately [ɪ'miːdɪətlɪ] *adv* **1** (*at once*) natychmiast **2** (*apparent, obvious*) bezpośrednio ▷ *conj*: **~ after he had said it, he regretted it** jak tylko to powiedział, pożałował; **~ before/after** zaraz przed *+inst*/po *+loc*
immigrant ['ɪmɪgrənt] *n* imigrant(ka) *m/f*
immigration [ɪmɪ'greɪʃən] *n* **1** (*process*) imigracja **2** (*also*: **~ control**: *at airport, port, border*) kontrola paszportowa ▷ *adj* (*policy, controls, officer*) imigracyjny
impatience [ɪm'peɪʃəns] *n* niecierpliwość
impatient [ɪm'peɪʃənt] *adj* (*at waiting*) niecierpliwy; **to get ~ (at** *or* **with sth)** niecierpliwić (zniecierpliwić *pf*) się (czymś)
impolite [ɪmpə'laɪt] *adj* niegrzeczny
import [ɪm'pɔːt] *vt* (*goods*) importować (zaimportować *pf*)
importance [ɪm'pɔːtns] *n* **1** (*significance*) znaczenie **2** (*influence*) waga
important [ɪm'pɔːtənt] *adj* ważny; **it is ~ to eat sensibly** ważne, żeby jeść rozsądnie; **it is ~ for them to understand that...** ważne, żeby zrozumieli, że...; **it's not ~** to nie jest ważne
impossible [ɪm'pɔsɪbl] *adj* **1** (*task, demand*) niewykonalny **2** (*situation, position*) niemożliwy; **it is ~ to understand what's going on** nie można zrozumieć o co chodzi; **it's ~ for me to leave now** nie mogę teraz wyjść
impress [ɪm'prɛs] *vt* (*person*) robić (zrobić *pf*) wrażenie na *+loc*; **to be ~ed by** *or* **with sb/sth** być pod wrażeniem kogoś/czegoś
impression [ɪm'prɛʃən] *n* **1** (*of place, situation, person*) wrażenie **2** (*imitation*) udawanie; **to be under the ~ that...** mieć wrażenie, że...; **to make** *or* **create a good/bad ~** robić (zrobić *pf*) dobre/złe wrażenie
impressive [ɪm'prɛsɪv] *adj* imponujący
improve [ɪm'pruːv] *vt* poprawiać (poprawić *pf*) ▷ *vi* poprawiać (poprawić *pf*) się
improvement [ɪm'pruːvmənt] *n* poprawa; **~ in** postęp w *+loc*

 **KEYWORD**

in [ɪn] *prep* **1** (*indicating place, position*) w *+loc*; **it's in the house/garden/box** to jest w domu/ogrodzie/pudełku; **put it in the house/garden/box** połóż to w domu/ogrodzie/pudełku; **in here/there** tu/tam
2 (*with place names*) w *+loc*; **in London/England** w Londynie/Anglii
3 (*time: during*) w ciągu *+gen*; (*within: referring to future*) w *+loc*; (*referring to past*) w *+loc*; **in 1988/in May** w roku tysiąc dziewięćset osiemdziesiątym ósmym/w maju; **in spring/summer** wiosną/latem; **in the morning/afternoon** rano/po południu; **I'll see you in two weeks' time** *or* **in two weeks** zobaczymy się za dwa tygodnie; **I did it in three hours/days** zrobiłem to w ciągu trzech godzin/dni
4 (*indicating manner, style etc*) w *+loc*; **in pencil/ink** ołówkiem/atramentem; **the boy in the blue shirt** chłopiec w niebieskiej bluzce; **in the sun/rain** w słońcu/deszczu
5 (*with languages*) po *+loc*; **in English/French** po angielsku/francusku
6 (*with ratios, numbers*) na; **one in ten people** jedna na dziesięć osób; **they lined up in twos** ustawili się po dwóch
7 (*in book, film, activity*) w *+loc*; **I read it in a newspaper** czytałem o tym w gazecie
8 (*amongst*) w *+loc*; **the best athlete in the team** najlepszy sportowiec w drużynie
▷ *adv* **1**: **to be in** (*at home*) być w domu; (*at work*) być obecnym; **is Harry in?** czy jest Harry?; **to ask sb in** zapraszać (zaprosić *pf*) kogoś do środka
2 (*shock, surprise*): **he is in for a surprise** czeka go niespodzianka

inbox ['ɪnbɔks] *n* skrzynka odbiorcza
inch [ɪntʃ] *n* cal
include [ɪn'klu:d] *vt* zawierać (zawrzeć *pf*)
including [ɪn'klu:dɪŋ] *prep* w tym; **it costs £15, ~ postage and packing** kosztuje piętnaście funtów, w tym wysyłka i pakowanie; **nine people were injured, ~ two Britons** dziewięć osób zostało rannych, w tym dwoje Brytyjczyków
income ['ɪnkʌm] *n* dochód
income tax *n* podatek dochodowy
inconsistent [ɪnkən'sɪstnt] *adj* niekonsekwentny
inconvenient [ɪnkən'vi:njənt] *adj* (*time, moment*) niewygodny; **that's very ~ for me** to dla mnie bardzo kłopotliwe
incorrect [ɪnkə'rɛkt] *adj* (*information, answer*) błędny
increase [*n* 'ɪnkri:s, *vb* ɪn'kri:s] *n* wzrost ▷ *vi* (*price, level, productivity*) rosnąć (urosnąć *pf*) ▷ *vt* (*price, number, level*) podnosić (podnieść *pf*); **a 5% ~, an ~ of 5%** pięcioprocentowy wzrost; **to be on the ~** wzrastać (wzrosnąć *pf*)
incredible [ɪn'krɛdɪbl] *adj* **1** (*amazing, wonderful*) niesamowity **2** (*unbelievable*) niewiarygodny
indeed [ɪn'di:d] *adv* (*certainly*) rzeczywiście; **yes ~!** tak, oczywiście!
independence [ɪndɪ'pɛndns] *n* niepodległość; **to declare ~** ogłaszać (ogłosić *pf*) niepodległość; **~ of mind/spirit** niezależność myśli/ducha

INDEPENDENCE DAY

Independence Day – Dzień Niepodległości przypada 4 lipca. W USA jest to święto narodowe, upamiętniające podpisanie w 1776 roku Deklaracji Niepodległości głoszącej niezależność 13 kolonii amerykańskich od Wielkiej Brytanii.

independent [ɪndɪ'pɛndnt] *adj* (*person, inquiry, organization*) niezależny; (*country*) niepodległy; **financially ~** niezależny finansowo
index ['ɪndɛks] (*pl* **indexes**) *n* (*in book*) indeks; (*library etc*) katalog
India ['ɪndɪə] *n* Indie *f pl*
Indian ['ɪndɪən] *adj* indyjski ▷ *n* (*person from India*) Hindus(ka) *m/f*
indicate ['ɪndɪkeɪt] *vt* **1** (*show*) pokazywać (pokazać *pf*) **2** (*point to*) wskazywać (wskazać *pf*)
indicator ['ɪndɪkeɪtə[r]] *n* (*Brit: on car*) kierunkowskaz
indifferent [ɪn'dɪfrənt] *adj* **1** (*uninterested*) obojętny **2** (*mediocre*) przeciętny
indigestion [ɪndɪ'dʒɛstʃən] *n* niestrawność
individual [ɪndɪ'vɪdjuəl] *n* (*single person*) jednostka ▷ *adj* **1** (*personal*) osobisty **2** (*particular*) indywidualny
indoor ['ɪndɔ:[r]] *adj* we wnętrzach
indoors [ɪn'dɔ:z] *adv* wewnątrz
industrial [ɪn'dʌstrɪəl] *adj* (*equipment, production, waste*) przemysłowy; (*accident*) w miejscu pracy
industrial estate (*Brit*) *n* strefa przemysłowa
industrial park (*US*) *n* strefa przemysłowa
industry ['ɪndəstrɪ] *n* przemysł
inevitable [ɪn'ɛvɪtəbl] *adj* nieunikniony ▷ *n*: **the ~** to, co nieuniknione
inexperienced [ɪnɪk'spɪərɪənst] *adj* niedoświadczony

INFANT SCHOOL

Brytyjskie **infant schools** (szkoły dla najmłodszych) to odpowiedniki przedszkoli. Chodzą do nich, obowiązkowo, dzieci w wieku od lat pięciu (czasem czterech) do lat siedmiu.

infection [ɪn'fɛkʃən] *n* **1** (*disease*) infekcja **2** (*contagion*) zakażenie; **to have an ear/throat ~** mieć zapalenie ucha/gardła
infectious [ɪn'fɛkʃəs] *adj* (*disease*) zakaźny
inflation [ɪn'fleɪʃən] *n* inflacja
influence ['ɪnfluəns] *n* wpływ ▷ *vt* (*person, situation, choice*) wpływać

(wpłynąć *pf*) na; **to be a good/bad ~ on sb** mieć dobry/zły wpływ na kogoś
inform [ɪn'fɔːm] *vt* (*tell*) powiadamiać (powiadomić *pf*); **to ~ sb that...** informować (poinformować *pf*) kogoś, że...
informal [ɪn'fɔːml] *adj* **1** (*person, speech, behaviour*) bezpośredni **2** (*clothes, party*) swobodny **3** (*unofficial*) nieformalny
information [ɪnfə'meɪʃən] *n* informacja; **a piece of ~** informacja; **for your ~** do twojej wiadomości
information technology *n* technologia informacyjna
infuriating [ɪn'fjuərɪeɪtɪŋ] *adj* irytujący
ingredient [ɪn'griːdɪənt] *n* (*in food*) składnik
inhabitant [ɪn'hæbɪtnt] *n* mieszkaniec(-nka) *m/f*
inherit [ɪn'hɛrɪt] *vt* (*property, money*) dziedziczyć (odziedziczyć *pf*)
initial [ɪ'nɪʃl] *n* (*letter*) pierwsza litera; **initials** *n pl* (*of name*) inicjały
injection [ɪn'dʒɛkʃən] *n* (*Med*) zastrzyk; **to give sb an ~** robić (zrobić *pf*) komuś zastrzyk
injure ['ɪndʒə^r] *vt* (*person*) ranić (zranić *pf*); **he was badly ~d in the attack** został poważnie ranny podczas ataku
injured ['ɪndʒəd] *adj* (*person, part of body*) ranny ▷ *n pl*: **the ~** ranni
injury ['ɪndʒərɪ] *n* (*wound*) rana; **to escape without ~** uciec bez szwanku
ink [ɪŋk] *n* (*in pen*) atrament
in-laws ['ɪnlɔːz] *n pl* teściowie
innocent ['ɪnəsnt] *adj* (*not guilty*) niewinny; **to be ~ of a crime** nie być winnym zbrodni
insane [ɪn'seɪn] *adj* **1** (*clinically: person*) obłąkany **2** (*foolish: idea, scheme*) szalony
insect ['ɪnsɛkt] *n* owad
insect repellent [-rɪ'pɛlənt] *n* środek odstraszający owady
insert [ɪn'səːt] *vt* (*object: into sth*) wstawiać (wstawić *pf*)
inside ['ɪn'saɪd] *n* wnętrze ▷ *adj* (*wall, surface*) wewnętrzny ▷ *adv* **1** (*go*) do środka; (*be*) wewnątrz **2** (*indoors*) wewnątrz ▷ *prep* (*place, container*) wewnątrz *+gen*
inside out *adv* na lewą stronę
insist [ɪn'sɪst] *vi, vt* nalegać; **to ~ on sth/doing sth** nalegać na coś/na zrobienie czegoś
inspector [ɪn'spɛktə^r] *n* **1** (*official*) inspektor(ka) *m/f* **2** (*Brit: Police*) inspektor(ka) *m/f* **3** (*Brit: also:* **ticket ~**) kontroler(ka) *m/f*
install, instal [ɪn'stɔːl] *vt* instalować (zainstalować *pf*)
instalment [ɪn'stɔːlmənt] (*US* **installment**) *n* **1** (*payment*) rata **2** (*of story, TV serial*) odcinek
instance ['ɪnstəns] *n* (*example*) przykład; **for ~** na przykład
instant ['ɪnstənt] *n* (*moment*) chwila ▷ *adj* **1** (*reaction, success*) natychmiastowy **2** (*coffee*) rozpuszczalny; (*soup, noodles*) błyskawiczny; **for an ~** przez chwilę
instantly ['ɪnstəntlɪ] *adv* od razu
instead [ɪn'stɛd] *adv* natomiast; **~ of** zamiast *+gen*
instinct ['ɪnstɪŋkt] *n* instynkt
instruct [ɪn'strʌkt] *vt* (*tell*): **to ~ sb to do sth** instruować (poinstruować *pf*) kogoś, aby coś zrobił
instruction [ɪn'strʌkʃən] *adj* instrukcyjny; **~ manual** *or* **leaflet** instrukcja; **instructions** *n pl* instrukcja *f sg*
instructor [ɪn'strʌktə^r] *n* instruktor(ka) *m/f*
instrument ['ɪnstrumənt] *n* **1** (*tool, device*) przyrząd **2** (*Mus*) instrument
insulin ['ɪnsjulɪn] *n* insulina
insult [*n* 'ɪnsʌlt, *vb* ɪn'sʌlt] *n* obelga ▷ *vt* obrażać (obrazić *pf*)
insurance [ɪn'ʃuərəns] *n* ubezpieczenie; **life ~** ubezpieczenie na życie; **health ~** ubezpieczenie zdrowotne
insure [ɪn'ʃuə^r] *vt* (*house, car*) ubezpieczać (ubezpieczyć *pf*)
intelligent [ɪn'tɛlɪdʒənt] *adj* (*person*) inteligentny
intend [ɪn'tɛnd] *vt*: **to ~ to do sth** zamierzać coś zrobić; **to be ~ed for sb/sth** (*gift, money*) być przeznaczonym dla kogoś/czegoś

intense [ɪn'tɛns] *adj* **1** (*great: heat, pain*) intensywny; (*competition*) zacięty **2** (*person*) zasadniczy
intensive [ɪn'tɛnsɪv] *adj* intensywny
intensive care *n*: **to be in ~** być leczonym na oddziale intensywnej opieki medycznej
intention [ɪn'tɛnʃən] *n* zamiar; **to have no/every ~ of doing sth** nie mieć zamiaru/mieć zamiar coś zrobić
interest ['ɪntrɪst] *n* **1** (*in subject, idea, person*) zainteresowanie **2** (*pastime, hobby*) zainteresowanie **3** (*on loan, savings*) odsetki *m pl* ▷ *vt* (*work, subject, idea*) interesować (zainteresować *pf*); **to take an ~ in sth/sb** interesować (zainteresować *pf*) się czymś/kimś; **to lose ~ (in sth/sb)** tracić (stracić *pf*) zainteresowanie (czymś/kimś); **to be in sb's ~s** być w czyimś interesie
interested ['ɪntrɪstɪd] *adj*: **to be ~ (in sth/doing sth)** interesować (zainteresować *pf*) się (czymś/ robieniem czegoś)
interesting ['ɪntrɪstɪŋ] *adj* (*idea, place, person*) interesujący; **it will be ~ to see how he reacts** ciekawie będzie zobaczyć, jak on zareaguje
interfere [ɪntə'fɪə^r] *vi* (*meddle*) ingerować; **to ~ with sth** (*plans, career, duty*) kolidować z czymś
interior [ɪn'tɪərɪə^r] *n* (*of building, car, box*) wnętrze ▷ *adj* (*door, window, room*) wewnętrzny
international [ɪntə'næʃənl] *adj* międzynarodowy
internet ['ɪntənɛt] *n*: **the ~** internet
internet café *n* kawiarenka internetowa
interpreter [ɪn'tə:prɪtə^r] *n* tłumacz(ka) *m/f*
interrupt [ɪntə'rʌpt] *vt* **1** (*speaker, conversation*) przerywać (przerwać *pf*) +*dat* **2** (*activity*) przerywać (przerwać *pf*) ▷ *vi* (*in conversation*) przerywać (przerwać *pf*)
interruption [ɪntə'rʌpʃən] *n* przerwa
interval ['ɪntəvl] *n* **1** (*break, pause*) przerwa **2** (*Brit: Theat*) antrakt; (*Mus*) interwał; (*Sport*) przerwa
interview ['ɪntəvju:] *n* **1** (*for job*) rozmowa kwalifikacyjna **2** (*Publishing, Rad, TV*) wywiad ▷ *vt* **1** (*for job*) przeprowadzać (przeprowadzić *pf*) rozmowę kwalifikacyjną z +*inst* **2** (*Publishing, Rad, TV*) przeprowadzać (przeprowadzić *pf*) wywiad z +*inst*; **to go for/have an ~** iść na/mieć rozmowę kwalifikacyjną
interviewer ['ɪntəvjuə^r] *n* (*Rad, TV*) dziennikarz(-rka) *m/f* przeprowadzający(-ca) wywiad
intimidate [ɪn'tɪmɪdeɪt] *vt* zastraszać (zastraszyć *pf*)
into ['ɪntu] *prep* (*indicating motion, direction*) do +*gen*; **to come ~ the house/garden** wchodzić (wejść *pf*) do domu/ogrodu; **to get ~ the car** wsiadać (wsiąść *pf*) do samochodu; **he threw some socks ~ his case** wrzucił skarpetki do walizki; **let's go ~ town** chodźmy do miasta; **to translate sth from English ~ French** tłumaczyć (przetłumaczyć *pf*) coś z angielskiego na francuski; **research ~ cancer** badania nad rakiem; **he worked late ~ the night** pracował do późnej nocy; **they got ~ trouble** wpakowali się w kłopoty; **I'd like to change some zlotys ~ pounds** chciałbym wymienić trochę złotych na funty
introduce [ɪntrə'dju:s] *vt* **1** (*new idea, measure, technology*) przedstawiać (przedstawić *pf*) **2** (*speaker, TV show, radio programme*) poprzedzać (poprzedzić *pf*) słowem wstępnym **3**: **to ~ sb (to sb)** przedstawiać (przedstawić *pf*) kogoś (komuś) **4**: **to ~ sb to sth** (*pastime, technique*) prezentować (zaprezentować *pf*) komuś coś
introduction [ɪntrə'dʌkʃən] *n* **1** (*of new idea etc*) prezentacja **2** (*of person*) przedstawienie **3** (*beginning: of book, talk*) wstęp
invade [ɪn'veɪd] *vt* (*Mil*) atakować (zaatakować *pf*)
invalid ['ɪnvəlɪd] *n* inwalida(-dka) *m/f*
invent [ɪn'vɛnt] *vt* wynaleźć (*pf*)
invention [ɪn'vɛnʃən] *n* wynalazek

investigate [ɪn'vɛstɪgeɪt] *vi* przeprowadzać (przeprowadzić *pf*) dochodzenie
investigation [ɪnvɛstɪ'geɪʃən] *n* dochodzenie
invisible [ɪn'vɪzɪbl] *adj* niewidoczny
invitation [ɪnvɪ'teɪʃən] *n* zaproszenie
invite [ɪn'vaɪt] *vt* zapraszać (zaprosić *pf*); **to ~ sb to do sth** zapraszać (zaprosić *pf*) kogoś do zrobienia czegoś; **to ~ sb to dinner** zapraszać (zaprosić *pf*) kogoś na obiad
involve [ɪn'vɔlv] *vt* **1** (*entail*) wymagać *+gen* **2** (*concern, affect*) dotyczyć (*pf*) *+gen*; **to ~ sb (in sth)** włączać (włączyć *pf*) kogoś (w coś)
iPod® ['aɪpɔd] *n* iPod®
Iran [ɪ'rɑːn] *n* Iran
Iraq [ɪ'rɑːk] *n* Irak
Ireland ['aɪələnd] *n* Irlandia; **the Republic of ~** Republika Irlandii
Irish ['aɪrɪʃ] *adj* irlandzki ▷ (*language*) irlandzki; **the Irish** *n pl* Irlandczycy
Irishman ['aɪrɪʃmən] (*irreg*) *n* Irlandczyk
Irishwoman ['aɪrɪʃwumən] (*irreg*) *n* Irlandka
iron ['aɪən] *n* **1** (*metal*) żelazo **2** (*for clothes*) żelazko ▷ *adj* (*bar, railings*) żelazny ▷ *vt* (*clothes*) prasować (wyprasować *pf*)
ironing ['aɪənɪŋ] *n* prasowanie; **to do the ~** prasować (wyprasować *pf*)
ironing board *n* deska do prasowania
irresponsible [ɪrɪ'spɔnsɪbl] *adj* nieodpowiedzialny; **it is ~ to drive when tired** prowadzenie pojazdu w razie zmęczenia to przejaw nieodpowiedzialności
irritating ['ɪrɪteɪtɪŋ] *adj* irytujący
is [ɪz] *vb see* **be**
Islam ['ɪzlɑːm] *n* islam
Islamic [ɪz'læmɪk] *adj* (*law, faith*) islamski; (*country*) islamski
island ['aɪlənd] *n* (*Geo*) wyspa
isle [aɪl] *n* wyspa
isolated ['aɪsəleɪtɪd] *adj* **1** (*place*) odosobniony **2** (*person*) samotny **3** (*incident, case, example*) pojedynczy
Israel ['ɪzreɪl] *n* Izrael
issue ['ɪʃjuː] *n* (*problem, subject*) kwestia ▷ *vt*: **to ~ sb with sth** wydawać (wydać *pf*) komuś coś
IT *n abbr* (*= information technology*) IT
it [ɪt] *pron* **1** (*object or animal*) to; (*referring to baby*) ono **2** (*impersonal*): **I can't find it** nie mogę tego znaleźć; **it's raining** pada; **it doesn't matter** to nie ma znaczenia; **what is it?** (*thing*) co to jest?; (*what's the matter?*) o co chodzi?; **"who is it?" — "it's me"** „kto tam?" — „to ja"
Italian [ɪ'tæljən] *adj* włoski ▷ *n* **1** (*person*) Włoch(-oszka) *m/f* **2** (*language*) włoski
Italy ['ɪtəlɪ] *n* Włochy
itch [ɪtʃ] *vi* (*person, part of body*) swędzić (zaswędzić *pf*)
itchy ['ɪtʃɪ] *adj* (*skin, nose, eyes, scalp etc*) swędzący; (*piece of clothing*) drapiący
it'd ['ɪtd] = **it would, it had**
item ['aɪtəm] *n* **1** (*on list, agenda*) rzecz; (*on bill*) pozycja; (*in collection*) przedmiot **2** (*in newspaper, on TV*) artykuł; **~s of clothing** odzież *f sg*
it'll ['ɪtl] = **it will**
its [ɪts] *adj* **1** (*m, nt*) jego; (*f*) jej; (*referring to subject of sentence*) swój **2** (*of baby*) swój
it's [ɪts] = **it is, it has**
itself [ɪt'sɛlf] *pron* **1** (*reflexive*) się **2** (*after preposition*: *gen, acc*) siebie; (*dat, loc*) sobie; (*inst*) sobą **3** (*emphatic*) sam; **it switches ~ on automatically** to włącza się automatycznie; **the cat managed to climb down the tree by ~** kot był w stanie sam zejść z drzewa
I've [aɪv] = **I have**

jack [dʒæk] *n* **1** (*Aut*) lewarek **2** (*Cards*) walet
jacket ['dʒækɪt] *n* **1** (*garment*) marynarka **2** (*esp US*: *also*: **dust ~**) obwoluta; **~ potatoes** (*Brit*) ziemniaki w mundurkach
jail [dʒeɪl] *n* więzienie ▷ *vt* więzić (uwięzić *pf*); **in ~** w więzieniu
jam [dʒæm] *n* **1** (*Brit*: *preserve*) dżem **2** (*also*: **traffic ~**) korek
jammed [dʒæmd] *adj* **1** (*roads*) zapchany **2** (*mechanism, machine*) unieruchomiony
janitor ['dʒænɪtə^r] *n* dozorca(-czyni) *m/f*
January ['dʒænjuərɪ] *n* styczeń; *see also* **July**
Japan [dʒə'pæn] *n* Japonia
Japanese [dʒæpə'ni:z] (*pl* **Japanese**) *adj* japoński ▷ *n* (*language*) japoński
jar [dʒɑ:^r] *n* słoik
javelin ['dʒævlɪn] *n*: **the ~** rzut oszczepem
jaw [dʒɔ:] (*Anat*) *n* szczęka; **jaws** *n pl* szczęki
jazz [dʒæz] *n* (*Mus*) jazz
jealous ['dʒɛləs] *adj* zazdrosny; **to be ~ of sb/sth** być zazdrosnym o kogoś/coś
jeans [dʒi:nz] *n pl* dżins; **a pair of ~** dżinsy
Jell-O® ['dʒɛləu] (*US*) *n* galaretka
jelly ['dʒɛlɪ] *n* **1** (*Brit*: *dessert*) galaretka **2** (*US*: *preserve*) dżem
jellyfish ['dʒɛlɪfɪʃ] (*pl* **jellyfish**) *n* meduza
jersey ['dʒə:zɪ] *n* (*pullover*) sweter
Jesus ['dʒi:zəs] *n* (*Rel*) Jezus; **~ Christ** Jezus Chrystus
jet [dʒɛt] *n* (*aeroplane*) odrzutowiec
jet lag [-læg] *n zmęczenie po długiej podróży samolotem związane ze zmianą stref czasowych*
Jew [dʒu:] *n* żyd(ówka) *m/f*
jewel ['dʒu:əl] *n* (*gem*) klejnot
jeweller ['dʒu:ələ^r] (*US* **jeweler**) *n* **1** (*person*) jubiler **2** (*also*: **~'s**) sklep jubilerski
jewellery ['dʒu:əlrɪ] (*US* **jewelry**) *n* biżuteria
Jewish ['dʒu:ɪʃ] *adj* żydowski
jigsaw ['dʒɪgsɔ:] *n* (*also*: **~ puzzle**) układanka
job [dʒɔb] *n* **1** (*position*) praca **2** (*task*) zadanie **3** (*function*) zadanie; **Anne got a ~ as a secretary** Anne dostała pracę sekretarki; **it's a good ~ that…** dobrze, że…; **I had a ~ finding it** nie było łatwo to znaleźć; **a part-time/full-time ~** praca na pół etatu/na cały etat
jobless ['dʒɔblɪs] *adj* bezrobotny ▷ *n pl*: **the ~** bezrobotni
jockey ['dʒɔkɪ] *n* (*Sport*) dżokej(ka) *m/f*
jog [dʒɔg] *vi* biegać ▷ *n*: **to go for a ~** iść (pójść *pf*) pobiegać
jogging ['dʒɔgɪŋ] *n* jogging; **to go ~** biegać
join [dʒɔɪn] *vt* **1** (*become member of*) wstępować (wstąpić *pf*) do *+gen* **2** (*meet*: *person*) dołączać (dołączyć *pf*) do *+gen*; **will you ~ us for dinner?** zjesz z nami obiad?; **I'll ~ you later** dołączę do was później
▶ **join in** *vi* przyłączać (przyłączyć *pf*) się ▷ *vt fus* (*work, discussion etc*) przyłączać (przyłączyć *pf*) się do *+gen*
joiner ['dʒɔɪnə^r] (*Brit*) *n* stolarz
joint [dʒɔɪnt] *n* (*Anat*) staw; (*Brit*: *Culin*) mięso na pieczeń
joke [dʒəuk] *n* (*funny story*) żart ▷ *vi* żartować (zażartować *pf*); **it's no ~** (*inf*) to nie jest zabawne; **you must be joking!** (*inf*) chyba kpisz!
journalism ['dʒə:nəlɪzəm] *n* (*profession*) dziennikarstwo
journalist ['dʒə:nəlɪst] *n* dziennikarz(-rka) *m/f*

journey ['dʒəːnɪ] *n* podróż; **a 5-hour ~** 5-godzinna podróż; **to go on a ~** udawać (udać *pf*) się w podróż
joy [dʒɔɪ] *n* **1** (*happiness*) radość **2** (*delight*) zadowolenie
joystick ['dʒɔɪstɪk] *n* (*Comput*) joystick
judge [dʒʌdʒ] *n* **1** (*Law*) sędzia **2** (*in competition*) juror(ka) *m/f* ▷ *vt* **1** (*exhibits, competition etc*) sędziować **2** (*estimate: age, weight, size*) oceniać (ocenić *pf*)
judo ['dʒuːdəu] *n* judo
jug [dʒʌg] *n* dzbanek
juggler ['dʒʌglə^r] *n* żongler(ka) *m/f*
juice [dʒuːs] *n* (*from fruit*) sok
July [dʒuː'laɪ] *n* lipiec; **the first of ~** pierwszy lipca; **at the beginning/ end of ~** na początku/końcu lipca; **during ~** w lipcu; **each** *or* **every ~** zawsze w lipcu
jumble sale ['dʒʌmbl-] (*Brit*) *n* wyprzedaż rzeczy używanych

JUMBLE SALE

Jumble sale to wyprzedaż różnego rodzaju używanych artykułów i ubrań, odbywająca się zazwyczaj w miejscach takich, jak kościoły bądź szkolne hole. Często urządzana w celu zgromadzenia pieniędzy na cele dobroczynne.

jump [dʒʌmp] *vi* (*into air*) skakać (skoczyć *pf*) ▷ *vt* (*fence, stream*) przeskakiwać (przeskoczyć *pf*) ▷ *n* (*leap*) skok; **to ~ over sth** przeskakiwać (przeskoczyć *pf*) przez coś; **to ~ out of a window** wyskakiwać (wyskoczyć *pf*) przez okno; **to ~ on sth** wskakiwać (wskoczyć *pf*) na coś; **to ~ off sth** zeskakiwać (zeskoczyć *pf*) z czegoś; **to ~ the queue** (*Brit*) wpychać (wepchnąć *pf*) się poza kolejnością
jumper ['dʒʌmpə^r] *n* (*Brit: sweater*) pulower
junction ['dʒʌŋkʃən] (*Brit*) *n* **1** (*of roads*) skrzyżowanie **2** (*Rail*) węzeł kolejowy; **motorway ~** zjazd
June [dʒuːn] *n* czerwiec; *see also* **July**
jungle ['dʒʌŋgl] *n* dżungla
junior ['dʒuːnɪə^r] *adj* młody ▷ *n* (*Brit: Scol*) uczeń(-ennica) *m/f* szkoły podstawowej; **George Bush J~** (*US*) George Bush Junior
junior high (*US: also:* **~ school**) *n* gimnazjum
junior school (*Brit*) *n* szkoła podstawowa
junk [dʒʌŋk] *n* (*inf: rubbish*) grat
jury ['dʒuərɪ] *n* **1** (*Law*) sąd **2** (*in competition*) jury
just [dʒʌst] *adj* (*decision, punishment, reward*) sprawiedliwy; (*society, cause*) słuszny ▷ *adv* **1** (*exactly*) dokładnie **2** (*merely*) zaledwie **3** (*for emphasis*) po prostu **4** (*in instructions, requests: only*) tylko; **it's ~ right** właśnie tak; **I'm ~ finishing this** już kończę; **we were ~ going** właśnie wychodziliśmy; **I was ~ about to phone** *or* **I was ~ going to phone** właśnie miałem dzwonić; **~ now** (*a moment ago*) przed chwilą; (*at the present time*) właśnie teraz; **~ about everything/everyone** to już wszystko/wszyscy; **~ as he was leaving** w momencie, gdy wychodził; **~ before/after...** tuż przed/po *+inst*...; **~ enough time/ money** dokładnie tyle czasu/ pieniędzy; **he ~ missed** (*failed to hit target*) ledwo spudłował; **not ~ now** nie tylko teraz; **~ a minute, ~ one moment** (*asking someone to wait*) chwilę; (*interrupting*) chwileczkę!
justice ['dʒʌstɪs] *n* **1** (*Law*) sprawiedliwość **2** (*legitimacy: of cause, complaint*) zasadność

K *abbr* **1** (*inf*: = *thousands*) tys. **2** (*Comput*: = *kilobytes*) kB
kabob [kə'bɔb] (*US*) *n* = **kebab**
kangaroo [kæŋgə'ru:] *n* kangur(zyca) *m/f*
karaoke [kɑ:rə'əukɪ] *n* karaoke
karate [kə'rɑ:tɪ] *n* karate
kebab [kə'bæb] *n* kebab
keen [ki:n] *adj* **1** (*enthusiastic*) chętny **2** (*competition*) zagorzały; **to be ~ to do sth** być chętnym do zrobienia czegoś; **to be ~ on sth** uwielbiać coś; **to be ~ on doing sth** (*eager to do*) chcieć coś zrobić
keep [ki:p] (*pt, pp* **kept**) *vt* **1** (*retain*) zachowywać (zachować *pf*) **2** (*store*) trzymać **3** (*detain*) zatrzymywać (zatrzymać *pf*) **4** (*support: family*) utrzymywać (utrzymać *pf*) ▷ *vi* (*stay*) utrzymywać (utrzymać *pf*); **to ~ doing sth** (*repeatedly*) robić (zrobić *pf*) coś raz za razem; (*continuously*) robić coś ciągle; **to ~ sb waiting** kazać komuś czekać; **to ~ the room tidy** utrzymywać (utrzymać *pf*) pokój w czystości; **to ~ a promise** dotrzymywać (dotrzymać *pf*) obietnicy; **can you ~ a secret?** możesz dotrzymać tajemnicy?; **to ~ a record (of sth)** notować (zanotować *pf*) (coś); **what kept you?** co cię zatrzymało?; **how are you ~ing?** (*inf*) jak się trzymasz?
▸ **keep away** *vi*: **to ~ away (from sth)** trzymać się z dala (od czegoś)
▸ **keep back** *vt* (*information*) zatajać (zataić *pf*)
▸ **keep off** *vt fus*: **~ off the grass!** nie deptać trawników!
▸ **keep on** *vi*: **to ~ on doing sth** nie przestawać (przestać *pf*) coś robić
▸ **keep up** *vi*: **to ~ up** kontynuować; **to ~ up with sb** (*walking, moving*) dotrzymywać (dotrzymać *pf*) kroku komuś; (*in work*) nadążać (nadążyć *pf*) za kimś
keep-fit [ki:p'fɪt] *adj* (*class, session, course*) gimnastyczny
kept [kɛpt] *pt, pp of* **keep**
kerb [kə:b] (*US* **curb**) *n* krawężnik
ketchup ['kɛtʃəp] *n* keczup
kettle ['kɛtl] *n* czajnik; **the ~'s boiling** woda się gotuje
key [ki:] *n* **1** (*for lock*) klucz **2** (*of computer, piano*) klawisz
keyboard ['ki:bɔ:d] *n* klawiatura; **keyboards** *n pl* syntezator *n sg*
keyhole ['ki:həul] *n* dziurka od klucza
kick [kɪk] *vt* (*person, ball*) kopać (kopnąć *pf*) ▷ *n* **1** (*blow from person, animal*) kopniak **2** (*Sport*) kopnięcie; **to give sb a ~** kopać (kopnąć *pf*) kogoś
▸ **kick off** *vi* (*Sport*) rozpoczynać (rozpocząć *pf*) mecz
kick-off ['kɪkɔf] (*Sport*) *n* rozpoczęcie meczu
kid [kɪd] *n* **1** (*inf: child*) dziecko; (*teenager*) dzieciak **2** (*goat*) koźlę ▷ *vi* (*inf: joke*) stroić sobie żarty; **you're ~ding!** żartujesz!
kidnap ['kɪdnæp] *vt* porywać (porwać *pf*)
kidney ['kɪdnɪ] *n* **1** (*Anat*) nerka **2** (*Culin*) cynaderka
kill [kɪl] *vt* zabijać (zabić *pf*); **my back's ~ing me** (*inf*) okropnie bolą mnie plecy
killer ['kɪlə^r] *n* **1** (*murderer*) zabójca(-czyni) *m/f* **2** (*disease, activity*) zabójczy
kilo ['ki:ləu] *n* kilo
kilometre ['kɪləmi:tə^r] (*US* **kilometer**) *n* kilometr
kilt [kɪlt] *n* kilt
kind [kaɪnd] *adj* życzliwy ▷ *n* (*type, sort*) rodzaj; **an opportunity to meet all ~s of people** możliwość

spotkania bardzo różnych ludzi; **it was ~ of them to help** miło z ich strony, że pomogli
kindness ['kaındnıs] *n* (*quality*) życzliwość
king [kıŋ] *n* król
kingdom ['kıŋdəm] *n* królestwo; **the animal/plant ~** królestwo zwierząt/roślin
kiosk ['ki:ɔsk] *n* (*shop*) kiosk
kiss [kıs] *n* pocałunek ▷ *vt* całować (pocałować *pf*) ▷ *vi* całować (pocałować *pf*) się; **to give sb a ~** całować (pocałować *pf*) kogoś; **to ~ sb goodbye/goodnight** całować (pocałować *pf*) kogoś na do widzenia/dobranoc
kit [kıt] *n* (*esp Brit: equipment*) zestaw; (*clothing*) strój
kitchen ['kıtʃın] *n* kuchnia
kite [kaıt] *n* (*toy*) latawiec
kitten ['kıtn] *n* kociak
kiwi fruit ['ki:wi:-] *n* kiwi
knee [ni:] *n* kolano; **to be on one's ~s** klęczeć
kneel [ni:l] (*pt, pp* **knelt**) *vi* (*also*: **~ down**) klękać (klęknąć *pf*); **to be ~ing** klęczący
knew [nju:] *pt of* **know**
knickers ['nıkəz] (*Brit*) *n pl* majtki; **a pair of ~** para majtek
knife [naıf] (*pl* **knives**) *n* nóż; **~ and fork** nóż i widelec
knit [nıt] *vt* (*garment*) robić (zrobić *pf*) na drutach ▷ *vi* (*with wool*) robić (zrobić *pf*) na drutach
knitting ['nıtıŋ] *n* (*activity*) robienie na drutach
knives [naıvz] *n pl of* **knife**
knob [nɔb] *n* (*on door*) gałka
knock [nɔk] *vt* (*strike*) stukać (stuknąć *pf*) ▷ *vi* (*on door, window*) pukać (zapukać *pf*) ▷ *n* **1** (*blow, bump*) uderzenie **2** (*on door*) pukanie; **to ~ sb unconscious** ogłuszać (ogłuszyć *pf*) kogoś; **he ~ed on** *or* **at the door** zapukał do drzwi
▸ **knock down** *vt* **1** (*run over*) przewracać (przewrócić *pf*) **2** (*demolish*) rozbierać (rozebrać *pf*)
▸ **knock out** *vt* **1** (*make unconscious*) ogłuszać (ogłuszyć *pf*) **2** (*eliminate*) eliminować (wyeliminować *pf*)
▸ **knock over** *vt* przewracać (przewrócić *pf*)
knot [nɔt] *n* (*in rope, string*) węzeł; **to tie a ~** wiązać (zawiązać *pf*) węzeł
know [nəu] (*pt* **knew**, *pp* **known**) *vt* **1** (*facts, dates etc*) wiedzieć **2** (*language*) znać **3** (*person, place, subject*) znać; **to ~ that...** wiedzieć, że...; **to ~ where/when** wiedzieć gdzie/kiedy; **do you ~ how to swim?** umiesz pływać?; **to get to ~ sb** poznawać (poznać *pf*) kogoś; **to ~ sth about sb/sth** wiedzieć coś o kimś/czymś; **to ~ about sth** wiedzieć o czymś; **I don't ~ about that** nic o tym nie wiem; **yes, I ~** tak, wiem; **you never ~** nigdy nie wiadomo; **you ~** (*used for emphasis*) wiesz
knowledge ['nɔlıdʒ] *n* wiedza; **to (the best of) my ~** o ile wiem
known [nəun] *pp of* **know**
Koran [kɔ'ra:n] *n*: **the ~** Koran
Korea [kə'rıə] *n see* **North Korea, South Korea**
kosher ['kəuʃə^r] *adj* (*meat, restaurant*) koszerny

l

lab [læb] (*inf*) *n* (*laboratory*) laboratorium
label ['leɪbl] *n* (*on clothing*) metka; (*on bottle, tin*) nalepka; (*on suitcase*) przywieszka ▷ *vt* (*object*) oznakowywać (oznakować *pf*)
labor ['leɪbəʳ] (*US*) *n* = **labour**
laboratory [lə'bɔrətərɪ] *n* laboratorium

LABOR DAY

Labor Day – Święto Pracy jest obchodzone w USA oraz w Kanadzie w pierwszy poniedziałek września. Pierwotnie jego obchody miały charakter polityczny, obecnie święto traktowane jest po prostu jako okazja do odpoczynku w długi weekend.

labor union (*US*) *n* związek zawodowy
labour ['leɪbəʳ] (*US* **labor**) *n* **1** (*manpower*) siła robocza **2** (*Med*) poród **3**: **L~** (*also*: **L~ Party**) Partia Pracy ▷ *vt*: **to be in ~** (*Med*) rodzić; **to vote L~** głosować (zagłosować *pf*) na Partię Pracy
lace [leɪs] *n* **1** (*fabric*) koronka **2** (*of shoe etc*) sznurowadło ▷ *vt* (*also*: **~ up**: *shoe etc*) sznurować (zasznurować *pf*)
lack [læk] *n* (*absence*) brak ▷ *vt* brakować; **to be ~ing in sth** przejawiać (przejawić *pf*) brak czegoś
lad [læd] (*inf*) *n* (*boy*) chłopiec; (*young man*) chłopak
ladder ['lædəʳ] *n* drabina
lady ['leɪdɪ] *n* (*woman*) pani; **ladies and gentlemen...** panie i panowie...; **young ~** młoda kobieta; **the ladies'** (*Brit*) *or* **the ladies' room** (*US*) toaleta damska
ladybird ['leɪdɪbə:d] (*Brit*) *n* biedronka
ladybug ['leɪdɪbʌg] (*US*) *n* biedronka
lager ['lɑ:gəʳ] (*Brit*) *n* piwo pełne jasne
laid [leɪd] *pt, pp of* **lay**
laid-back [leɪd'bæk] (*inf*) *adj* wyluzowany
lain [leɪn] *pp of* **lie**
lake [leɪk] *n* jezioro
lamb [læm] *n* **1** (*animal*) jagnię **2** (*meat*) jagnięcina
lamp [læmp] *n* lampa
lamp-post ['læmppəust] (*Brit*) *n* latarnia
lampshade ['læmpʃeɪd] *n* abażur
land [lænd] *n* **1** (*area of open ground*) teren **2** (*not sea*) ląd ▷ *vi* lądować (wylądować *pf*); **to go/travel by ~** podróżować drogą lądową; **on dry ~** na stałym lądzie
landing ['lændɪŋ] *n* **1** (*on stairs*) podest **2** (*Aviat*) lądowanie
landlady ['lændleɪdɪ] *n* właścicielka
landlord ['lændlɔ:d] *n* właściciel
landscape ['lændskeɪp] *n* krajobraz
lane [leɪn] *n* **1** (*in country*) wąska droga **2** (*Aut: of road*) pas
language ['læŋgwɪdʒ] *n* **1** (*English, Polish etc*) język **2** (*speech*) mowa
language laboratory *n* laboratorium językowe
lap [læp] *n* **1** (*of person*) kolana **2** (*in race*) okrążenie
laptop ['læptɔp] *n* (*also*: **~ computer**) laptop
large [lɑ:dʒ] *adj* duży
laser ['leɪzəʳ] *n* laser
last [lɑ:st] *adj* **1** (*most recent*) ostatni; (*Monday, July, weekend etc*) zeszły **2** (*final*) ostatni ▷ *pron* ostatni ▷ *adv* **1** (*most recently*) ostatnio **2** (*at the end*) na końcu **3** (*in final position*) na końcu ▷ *vi* (*continue*) trwać; **~ week** zeszły tydzień; **~ night** (*yesterday evening*)

wczorajsza noc; (*during the night*) zeszłej nocy; **the ~ time** (*the previous time*) ostatni raz; **at (long) ~** (*finally*) wreszcie; **our house is the ~ but one** nasz dom jest przedostatni; **it ~s (for) 2 hours** to trwa 2 godziny
lastly ['lɑːstlɪ] *adv* wreszcie
late [leɪt] *adj* późny ▷ *adv* późno; **we're ~** spóźniliśmy się; **sorry I'm ~** przepraszam za spóźnienie; **to be ten minutes ~** spóźniać (spóźnić *pf*) się dziesięć minut; **it's ~** jest późno; **to be in one's ~ thirties/forties** zbliżać (zbliżyć *pf*) się do czterdziestki/pięćdziesiątki; **to work ~** pracować do późna; **in ~ May** pod koniec maja
lately ['leɪtlɪ] *adv* (*recently*) ostatnio
later ['leɪtəʳ] *adv* później; **some time ~** jakiś czas później; **some weeks/years ~** kilka tygodni/lat później; **~ on** później
latest ['leɪtɪst] *adj* **1** (*book, film, news etc*) ostatni **2** (*fashion*) najnowszy; **at the ~** najpóźniej
Latin ['lætɪn] *n* (*language*) łacina
Latin America *n* Ameryka łacińska
latter ['lætəʳ] *n*: **the ~** ostatni z wymienionych
laugh [lɑːf] *n* śmiech ▷ *vi* śmiać się
▸ **laugh at** *vt fus* **1** (*lit*) śmiać się z *+gen* **2** (*fig: mock*) wyśmiewać się z *+gen*
launch [lɔːntʃ] *vt* **1** (*Space*) wystrzeliwać (wystrzelić *pf*) **2** (*fig: product, publication*) wprowadzać (wprowadzić *pf*) na rynek
Launderette® [lɔːn'drɛt] (*Brit*) *n* pralnia samoobsługowa
Laundromat® ['lɔːndrəmæt] (*US*) *n* pralnia samoobsługowa
laundry ['lɔːndrɪ] *n* pranie; **to do the ~** robić (zrobić *pf*) pranie
laundry detergent (*US*) *n* proszek do prania
lavatory ['lævətərɪ] (*Brit*) *n* toaleta
lavender ['lævəndəʳ] *n* (*plant*) lawenda
law [lɔː] *n* prawo; **against the ~** niezgodnie z prawem; **to break the ~** łamać (złamać *pf*) prawo; **by ~** zgodnie z prawem; **to study ~** studiować prawo; **~ and order** prawo i porządek
lawn [lɔːn] *n* trawnik
lawnmower ['lɔːnməuəʳ] *n* kosiarka do trawy
lawyer ['lɔːjəʳ] *n* prawnik(-iczka) *m/f*
lay [leɪ] (*pt, pp* **laid**) *pt of* **lie** ▷ *vt* **1** (*put*) kłaść (położyć *pf*) **2** (*egg*) znosić (znieść *pf*); **to ~ the table** nakrywać (nakryć *pf*) do stołu
▸ **lay down** *vt* (*put down*) kłaść (położyć *pf*); **to ~ down the law** ustanawiać (ustanowić *pf*) prawo
lay-by ['leɪbaɪ] (*Brit*) *n* zatoczka
layer ['leɪəʳ] *n* (*of substance, material*) warstwa
layout ['leɪaut] *n* rozkład
lazy ['leɪzɪ] *adj* (*person*) leniwy
lead[1] [liːd] (*pt, pp* **led**) *n* **1** (*esp Brit: for dog*) smycz **2** (*Elec*) kabel ▷ *vt* **1** (*guide*) prowadzić (zaprowadzić *pf*) **2** (*be at the head of*) prowadzić (poprowadzić *pf*) ▷ *vi* (*in race, competition*) prowadzić; **to be in the ~** (*in race, competition, poll*) prowadzić; **to ~ an active life** prowadzić aktywne życie; **to ~ the way** wskazywać (wskazać *pf*) drogę
▸ **lead away** *vt* (*prisoner etc*) odprowadzać (odprowadzić *pf*)
▸ **lead to** *vt fus* (*result in*) prowadzić do *+gen*
lead[2] [lɛd] *n* (*metal*) ołów
leader ['liːdəʳ] *n* (*of group, organization*) lider(ka) *m/f*
lead-free ['lɛdfriː] *adj* (*petrol, paint*) bezołowiowy
lead singer [liːd-] *n* solista(-tka) *m/f*
leaf [liːf] (*pl* **leaves**) *n* (*Bot*) liść
leaflet ['liːflɪt] *n* ulotka
league [liːg] *n* (*Sport*) liga
leak [liːk] *n* **1** (*of liquid, gas*) wyciek **2** (*hole: in roof, pipe etc*) pęknięcie ▷ *vi* przeciekać
lean [liːn] (*pt, pp* **leaned** *or* **leant** [lɛnt]) *vt*: **to ~ sth on/against sth** opierać (oprzeć *pf*) coś o coś ▷ *adj* (*meat*) chudy; **to ~ against sth** (*person*) opierać (oprzeć *pf*) się o coś; **to ~ forward/back** pochylać (pochylić *pf*) się do przodu/tyłu
▸ **lean on** *vt fus* (*rest against*) wspierać (wesprzeć *pf*) się na *+inst*
leap [liːp] (*pt, pp* **leaped** *or* **leapt** [lɛpt]) *vi* **1** (*jump*) skakać (skoczyć *pf*)

2: **to ~ into/onto sth** wskakiwać (wskoczyć *pf*) do czegoś/na coś

leap year *n* rok przestępny

learn [lə:n] (*pt, pp* **learned** *or* **learnt**) *vt* uczyć (nauczyć *pf*)się *+gen* ▷ *vi* uczyć (nauczyć *pf*) się; **to ~ about sth** (*study*) uczyć (nauczyć *pf*) się czegoś; **to ~ how to do sth** uczyć (nauczyć *pf*) się jak coś robić

learner ['lə:nə^r] *n* **1** (*student*) uczący się **2** (*Brit*: *also*: **~ driver**) zdający na prawo jazdy

learnt [lə:nt] *pt, pp of* **learn**

least [li:st] *adj* najmniejszy ▷ *adv* **1** (*with adjective*): **the ~ expensive/attractive/interesting** najmniej drogi/atrakcyjny/interesujący **2** (*with verb*) najmniej ▷ *pron*: **the ~** najmniej; **at ~** (*in comparisons*) najmniej; (*still*) przynajmniej

leather ['lɛðə^r] *n* skóra ▷ *adj* (*jacket, shoes, chair*) skórzany

leave [li:v] (*pt, pp* **left**) *vt* **1** (*depart from*) opuszczać (opuścić *pf*) **2** (*give up*: *school, job*) porzucać (porzucić *pf*) **3** (*leave behind*) zostawiać (zostawić *pf*) **4** (*message*) zostawiać (zostawić *pf*) ▷ *vi* **1** (*depart*: *person*) odchodzić (odejść *pf*); (*bus, train*) odjeżdżać (odjechać *pf*) **2** (*give up school*) rzucać (rzucić *pf*); (*give up job*) odchodzić (odejść *pf*) ▷ *n* (*time off*) urlop; (*Mil*) przepustka; **to ~ sth to sb** (*money, property etc*) zostawiać (zostawić *pf*) coś dla kogoś; **to ~ sb/sth alone** zostawiać (zostawić *pf*) kogoś/coś w spokoju; **to ~ for** (*destination*) jechać (pojechać *pf*) do *+gen*

▶ **leave behind** *vt* (*forget*) zostawiać (zostawić *pf*)

▶ **leave on** *vt* (*light, heating*) zostawiać (zostawić *pf*) włączone

▶ **leave out** *vt* pomijać (pominąć *pf*); **to ~ sb/sth out of sth** pomijać (pominąć *pf*) kogoś podczas czegoś

leaves [li:vz] *n pl of* **leaf**

lecture ['lɛktʃə^r] *n* (*talk*) wykład; **to give a ~ (on sth)** wygłaszać (wygłosić *pf*) wykład (na jakiś temat)

lecturer ['lɛktʃərə^r] *n* wykładowca

led [lɛd] *pt, pp of* **lead¹**

leek [li:k] *n* por

left¹ [lɛft] *adj* (*not right*) lewy ▷ *n*: **the ~** lewica ▷ *adv* (*turn, go, look*) w lewo; **on the ~** na lewo; **to the ~** na lewo

left² [lɛft] *pt, pp of* **leave** ▷ *adj*: **to be ~ over** (*food, money etc*) zostawać (zostać *pf*)

left-hand ['lɛfthænd] *adj* (*side, corner*) lewy

left-handed [lɛft'hændɪd] *adj* leworęczny

left-luggage [lɛft'lʌgɪdʒ] (*Brit*) *n*: **~ locker** przechowalnia bagażu

leg [lɛg] *n* **1** (*of person, table, chair*) noga; (*of bird*) udko **2** (*Culin*) noga

legal ['li:gl] *adj* **1** (*relating to law*: *system, requirement*) prawny **2** (*allowed by law*: *action, situation*) legalny

legal holiday (*US*) *n* dzień ustawowo wolny od pracy

leggings ['lɛgɪŋz] *n pl* (*woman's*) legginsy

leisure ['lɛʒə^r, *US* 'li:ʒə^r] *n* (*free time*) wypoczynek

leisure centre (*Brit*) *n* centrum rekreacji

lemon ['lɛmən] *n* cytryna

lemonade [lɛmə'neɪd] *n* lemoniada

lend [lɛnd] (*pt, pp* **lent**) *vt* **1**: **to ~ sth to sb** pożyczać (pożyczyć *pf*) coś komuś **2** (*loan*: *bank etc*) pożyczać (pożyczyć *pf*)

length [lɛŋθ] *n* długość; **it is 10 metres in ~** to ma 10 metrów długości

lens [lɛnz] *n* (*of spectacles*) soczewka; (*of telescope, camera*) obiektyw

Lent [lɛnt] *n* Wielki Post

lent [lɛnt] *pt, pp of* **lend**

lentil ['lɛntɪl] *n* soczewica

Leo ['li:əu] *n* (*Astrol*) Lew

leopard ['lɛpəd] *n* lampart

leotard ['li:ətɑ:d] *n* (*for dancing etc*) trykot

lesbian ['lɛzbɪən] *adj* lesbijski ▷ *n* lesbijka

less [lɛs] *adj* mniej ▷ *adv* **1** (*with adjective/adverb*) mniej **2** (*with verb*) rzadziej ▷ *pron* mniej ▷ *prep*: **~ tax/10% discount** minus podatek/10% zniżki; **~ money/time** mniej pieniędzy/czasu; **~ than half** mniej niż połowa; **~ and ~** (*as adj*) coraz mniej; (*as adv*) coraz mniej

lesson ['lɛsn] *n* (*class*) lekcja

let [lɛt] (*pt, pp* **let**) *vt* **1**: **to ~ sb do sth** (*give permission*) pozwalać (pozwolić *pf*) komuś coś robić (zrobić *pf*) **2**: **to ~ sth happen** pozwalać (pozwolić *pf*) na coś; **to ~ sb know that...** powiedzieć komuś, że...; **to ~ sb in/out** wpuszczać (wpuścić *pf*)/wypuszczać (wypuścić *pf*) kogoś; **~'s go/eat** chodźmy/zjedzmy; **"to ~"** „do wynajęcia"; **to ~ go** (*release one's grip*) puszczać (puścić *pf*); **to ~ sb/sth go** (*release*) wypuszczać (wypuścić *pf*) kogoś/coś
▸ **let down** *vt* (*fail: person*) zawodzić (zawieść *pf*)
▸ **let in** *vt* wpuszczać (wpuścić *pf*)
▸ **let out** *vt* (*scream, cry*) wydawać (wydać *pf*)

letter ['lɛtə^r] *n* **1** (*piece of writing*) list **2** (*of alphabet*) litera

letterbox ['lɛtəbɔks] (*Brit*) *n* (*in door*) skrzynka pocztowa

LETTERBOX

Letterbox, czyli skrzynka na listy, ma bardzo często w Wielkiej Brytanii formę podłużnego prostokątnego wycięcia w drzwiach domu, przez które listonosz dostarcza listy na podany adres.

lettuce ['lɛtɪs] *n* sałata

leukaemia [lu:'ki:mɪə] (*US* **leukemia**) *n* białaczka

level ['lɛvl] *adj* równy ▹ *adv*: **to draw ~ with** (*esp Brit*) zrównywać (zrównać *pf*) się z *+inst* ▹ *n* poziom; **to ~ the score** (*Sport*) wyrównywać (wyrównać *pf*) wynik

level crossing (*Brit*) *n* przejazd kolejowy

lever ['li:və^r, *US* 'lɛvə^r] *n* (*to operate machine*) dźwignia

liar ['laɪə^r] *n* kłamca

liberal ['lɪbərl] *adj* (*tolerant*) liberalny ▹ *n* (*Pol*): **L~** liberał

Libra ['li:brə] *n* (*Astrol*) Waga

librarian [laɪ'brɛərɪən] *n* bibliotekarz(-rka) *m/f*

library ['laɪbrərɪ] *n* biblioteka

licence ['laɪsns] (*US* **license**) *n* **1** (*permit*) zezwolenie **2** (*also*: **driving ~**) prawo jazdy

license plate (*US*) *n* tablica rejestracyjna

lick [lɪk] *vt* lizać (polizać *pf*)

lid [lɪd] *n* **1** (*of box, case*) wieko; (*of pan*) pokrywka **2** (*eyelid*) powieka

lie¹ [laɪ] (*pt* **lay**, *pp* **lain**) *vi* leżeć
▸ **lie about** (*Brit*) *vi* = **lie around**
▸ **lie around** *vi* (*things*) poniewierać się
▸ **lie down** *vi* (*person*) kłaść się (położyć się *pf*)

lie² [laɪ] *vi* kłamać (skłamać *pf*) ▹ *n* kłamstwo; **to tell ~s** kłamać (skłamać *pf*)

lie-in ['laɪɪn] (*Brit: inf*) *n*: **to have a ~** poleżeć sobie

lieutenant [lɛf'tɛnənt, *US* lu:'tɛnənt] *n* porucznik

life [laɪf] (*pl* **lives**) *n* życie; **his personal/working ~** jego życie osobiste/zawodowe

lifebelt ['laɪfbɛlt] *n* pas ratunkowy

lifeboat ['laɪfbəut] *n* łódź ratunkowa

lifeguard ['laɪfgɑ:d] *n* ratownik(-iczka) *m/f*

life jacket *n* kamizelka ratunkowa

life preserver [-prɪ'zə:və^r] (*US*) *n* (*lifebelt*) pas ratunkowy; (*life jacket*) kamizelka ratunkowa

lifestyle ['laɪfstaɪl] *n* styl życia

lift [lɪft] *vt* podnosić (podnieść *pf*) ▹ *n* (*Brit*) winda; **to give sb a ~** (*esp Brit: Aut*) podwozić (podwieźć *pf*) kogoś
▸ **lift up** *vt* (*person, thing*) podnosić (podnieść *pf*)

light [laɪt] (*pt, pp* **lit**) *n* **1** (*from sun, moon, lamp, fire*) światło **2** (*for cigarette etc*) ogień ▹ *vt* (*candle, fire, cigarette*) zapalać (zapalić *pf*) ▹ *adj* **1** (*pale: colour*) jasny **2** (*not heavy: object*) lekki; **lights** *n pl* (*Aut: also:* **traffic ~s**) światła uliczne; **to turn** *or* **switch the ~ on/off** włączać (włączyć *pf*)/wyłączać (wyłączyć *pf*) światło

light bulb *n* żarówka

lighter ['laɪtə^r] *n* (*also*: **cigarette ~**) zapalniczka

lighthouse ['laɪthaus] *n* latarnia morska

lightning ['laɪtnɪŋ] *n* piorun

like¹ [laɪk] *prep* **1** (*similar to*) taki jak **2** (*in comparisons*) jak **3** (*such as*) taki jak; **a house ~ ours** dom taki jak nasz; **to be ~ sth/sb** być jak coś/ktoś; **what's he ~?** jaki on jest?; **what's the weather ~?** jaka jest pogoda?; **to look ~** wyglądać jak; **what does it look/sound/taste ~?** jak to wygląda/brzmi/smakuje?; **~ this** jak to

like² [laɪk] *vt* lubić ▷ *n*: **his ~s and dislikes** to, co lubi i czego nie lubi; **to ~ doing sth** lubić coś robić; **I would** *or* **I'd ~ an ice cream/to go for a walk** chciałbym loda/iść na spacer; **would you ~ a coffee?** chciałby pan/chciałaby pani kawy?; **if you ~** (*in offers, suggestions*) jak wolisz

likely ['laɪklɪ] *adj* **1** (*probable*) prawdopodobny **2** (*person, place, thing*) odpowiedni; **it is ~ that...** jest prawdopodobne, że...; **to be ~ to do sth** prawdopodobnie coś zrobić

lime [laɪm] *n* (*fruit*) limonka

limit ['lɪmɪt] *n* **1** (*maximum point*) kres **2** (*restriction*) ograniczenie

limp [lɪmp] *n*: **he walks with a ~** on kuleje ▷ *vi* (*person, animal*) kuleć

line [laɪn] *n* **1** (*long thin mark*) linia **2** (*of people, things*) rząd **3** (*of words*) linijka **4** (*also*: **washing ~**) sznur **5** (*Tel*) linia **6** (*railway track*) linia; **hold the ~ please!** (*Tel*) proszę nie odkładać słuchawki; **to stand/wait in ~** (*esp US*) stać/czekać w kolejce; **on the right ~s** w dobrym kierunku; **to draw the ~ at doing sth** odmawiać (odmówić *pf*) robienia (zrobienia *pf*) czegoś

linen ['lɪnɪn] *n* **1** (*cloth*) płótno **2** (*tablecloths*) bielizna stołowa; (*sheets*) bielizna pościelowa ▷ *adj* (*jacket, sheets, etc*) lniany

lining ['laɪnɪŋ] *n* (*of garment*) podszewka

link [lɪŋk] *n* **1** (*connection*) związek **2** (*Comput*: *also*: **hyper~**) link ▷ *vt* łączyć (połączyć *pf*)

lion ['laɪən] *n* lew

lip [lɪp] *n* (*Anat*) warga

lip-read ['lɪpriːd] *vi* czytać z ruchu warg

lipstick ['lɪpstɪk] *n* szminka

liquid ['lɪkwɪd] *n* płyn

liquidizer ['lɪkwɪdaɪzə^r] (*esp Brit*: *Culin*) *n* mikser

liquor ['lɪkə^r] (*US*) *n* alkohol wysokoprocentowy

list [lɪst] *n* lista ▷ *vt* (*record*: *person*) spisywać (spisać *pf*)

listen ['lɪsn] *vi* słuchać; **to ~ to sb** słuchać kogoś; **to ~ to sth** słuchać czegoś; **~!** słuchaj!

lit [lɪt] *pt, pp of* **light**

liter ['liːtə^r] (*US*) *n* = **litre**

literature ['lɪtrɪtʃə^r] *n* literatura

litre ['liːtə^r] (*US* **liter**) *n* litr

litter ['lɪtə^r] *n* (*rubbish*) śmieć

litter bin (*Brit*) *n* kosz na śmieci

little ['lɪtl] *adj* **1** (*small*: *thing, person*) mały **2** (*young*: *child*) mały **3** (*younger*): **~ brother/sister** młodszy brat/młodsza siostra **4** (*quantifier*): **to have ~ time/money** mieć mało czasu/pieniędzy ▷ *adv* mało; **a ~** mało *+gen*; **a ~ boy of eight** ośmioletni chłopiec; **a ~ bit of** trochę *+gen*; **~ by ~** po trochu

live¹ [lɪv] *vi* **1** (*reside*) mieszkać **2** (*lead one's life*) żyć ▷ *vt* (*life*) żyć

▸ **live on** *vt fus* (*money*) przeżyć

▸ **live together** *vi* mieszkać razem

▸ **live with** *vt fus* (*partner*) mieszkać z *+inst*

live² [laɪv] *adj* (*animal, plant*) żywy ▷ *adv* (*broadcast*) na żywo

lively ['laɪvlɪ] *adj* (*person*) żwawy; (*place, event*) wesoły; (*discussion*) ożywiony

liver ['lɪvə^r] *n* **1** (*Anat*) wątroba **2** (*Culin*) wątróbka

lives [laɪvz] *n pl of* **life**

living ['lɪvɪŋ] *n* (*life*) życie; **for a ~** na życie; **to earn** *or* **make a ~** zarabiać (zarobić *pf*) na życie

living room *n* pokój dzienny

lizard ['lɪzəd] *n* jaszczurka

load [ləud] *n* ładunek ▷ *vt* **1** (*also*: **~ up**: *vehicle, ship etc*) ładować (załadować *pf*) **2** (*Comput*) wgrywać (wgrać *pf*); **~s of** *or* **a ~ of money/people** (*inf*) wiele pieniędzy/ludzi

loaf [ləuf] (*pl* **loaves**) *n*: **a ~ (of bread)** bochenek (chleba)

loan [ləun] *n* (*sum of money*) pożyczka ▷ *vt*: **to ~ sth (out) to sb** (*money, thing*) pożyczać (pożyczyć *pf*) coś komuś

loaves [ləuvz] *n pl of* **loaf**
lobster ['lɔbstəʳ] *n* homar
local ['ləukl] *adj* **1** (*council, newspaper, library*) lokalny; (*residents*) miejscowy **2** (*Tel: call*) miejscowy
location [ləu'keɪʃən] *n* (*place*) położenie
loch [lɔx] *n* (*Scottish*) jezioro
lock [lɔk] *n* (*of door, drawer etc*) zamek ▷ *vt* **1** (*door, drawer etc*) zamykać (zamknąć *pf*) **2** (*Comput: screen*) blokować (zablokować *pf*)
▸ **lock in** *vt* (*person, object*) zamykać (zamknąć *pf*) w +*loc*
▸ **lock out** *vt*: **to ~ o.s. out** zatrzaskiwać (zatrzasnąć *pf*) się
▸ **lock up** *vt* zamykać (zamknąć *pf*)
locker ['lɔkəʳ] *n* szafka
lodger ['lɔdʒəʳ] *n* lokator(ka) *m/f*
loft [lɔft] *n* (*attic*) strych
log [lɔg] *n* (*from tree: trunk*) kłoda; (*for fuel etc*) bierwiono
▸ **log in, log on** (*Comput*) *vi* logować (zalogować *pf*) się
▸ **log into** (*Comput*) *vt fus* logować (zalogować *pf*) się do +*gen*
▸ **log out, log off** (*Comput*) *vi* wylogować się
logical ['lɔdʒɪkl] *adj* logiczny
login ['lɔgɪn] *n* (*Comput*) logowanie (się)
lollipop ['lɔlɪpɔp] *n* lizak
London ['lʌndən] *n* Londyn
Londoner ['lʌndənəʳ] *n* londyńczyk(-ynka) *m/f*
loneliness ['ləunlɪnɪs] *n* samotność
lonely ['ləunlɪ] *adj* **1** (*sad: person*) samotny **2** (*unfrequented: place*) odludny
long [lɔŋ] *adj* długi ▷ *adv* (*time*) długo ▷ *vi*: **to ~ for sth/to do sth** tęsknić (zatęsknić *pf*) za czymś/za robieniem (zrobieniem *pf*) czegoś; **how ~ is the lesson?** jak długo trwa lekcja?; **six metres ~** sześć metrów długości; **so** *or* **as ~ as** tak długo jak; **~ ago** dawno temu; **it won't take ~** to nie potrwa długo; **a ~ way** daleko
long jump (*Sport*) *n*: **the ~** skok w dal
loo [lu:] (*Brit: inf*) *n* ubikacja
look [luk] *vi* **1** (*glance, gaze*) spoglądać (spojrzeć *pf*) **2** (*seem, appear*) wyglądać ▷ *n* (*expression*) wyraz; **to ~ out of the window** wyglądać (wyjrzeć *pf*) z okna; **~ out!** uważaj!; **to ~ like sb/sth** wyglądać jak ktoś/coś; **it ~s as if...** wygląda na to, że...; **to have** *or* **take a ~ at** (*examine*) przyglądać (przyjrzeć *pf*) się +*dat*
▸ **look after** *vt fus* (*care for*) opiekować (zaopiekować *pf*) się +*inst*
▸ **look at** *vt fus* (*gaze at*) spoglądać (spojrzeć *pf*)
▸ **look for** *vt fus* szukać +*gen*
▸ **look forward to** *vt fus* cieszyć się na; **to ~ forward to doing sth** cieszyć się na robienie czegoś; **we ~ forward to hearing from you** czekamy na twoją odpowiedź
▸ **look into** *vt fus* (*investigate*) badać (zbadać *pf*)
▸ **look round, look around** *vi* rozglądać (rozejrzeć *pf*) się ▷ *vt fus* (*place, building*) rozglądać (rozejrzeć *pf*) się za +*inst*
▸ **look through** *vt fus* (*book, magazine, papers*) przeglądać (przejrzeć *pf*)
▸ **look up** *vt* (*information, meaning etc*) sprawdzać (sprawdzić *pf*)
loose [lu:s] *adj* **1** (*screw, connection, tooth*) luźny **2** (*hair*) rozpuszczony **3** (*clothes, trousers etc*) luźny
lord [lɔ:d] (*Brit*) *n* (*peer*) lord

LORDS

Izba Lordów (**House of Lords**) jest jedną z dwóch izb parlamentu brytyjskiego.

lorry ['lɔrɪ] (*Brit*) *n* ciężarówka
lorry driver (*Brit*) *n* kierowca ciężarówki
lose [lu:z] (*pt, pp* **lost**) *vt* **1** (*mislay: keys, pen etc*) gubić (zgubić *pf*) **2** (*contest, fight, argument*) przegrywać (przegrać *pf*) **3** (*relative, wife etc*) tracić (stracić *pf*) ▷ *vi* (*in competition, argument*) przegrywać (przegrać *pf*); **to ~ weight** tracić (stracić *pf*) na wadze
loser ['lu:zəʳ] *n* **1** (*in game, contest*) przegrywający **2** (*inf: failure*) nieudacznik(-ica) *m/f*; **to be a good/bad ~** umieć/nie umieć przegrywać

loss [lɔs] *n* strata
lost [lɔst] *pt, pp of* **lose** ▷ *adj* (*object*) zagubiony; (*person, animal*) zaginiony; **to get ~** (*lose one's way*) gubić (zgubić *pf*) się
lost and found (*US*) *n* = **lost property**
lost property *n* **1** (*things*) rzeczy znalezione **2** (*Brit: office*) biuro rzeczy znalezionych
lot [lɔt] *n*: **a ~** dużo; **a ~ of** dużo +*gen*; **~s of** (*things, people*) dużo +*gen*; **he reads/smokes a ~** on dużo czyta/pali
lottery ['lɔtərɪ] *n* (*game*) loteria
loud [laud] *adj* głośny ▷ *adv* (*speak etc*) głośno
loudly ['laudlɪ] *adv* głośno
loudspeaker [laud'spiːkə[r]] *n* głośnik
lounge [laundʒ] *n* **1** (*in hotel*) hol **2** (*at airport, station*) poczekalnia **3** (*esp Brit: in house*) salon
love [lʌv] *n* miłość ▷ *vt* (*partner, child, pet*) kochać; **I ~ you** kocham cię; (*thing, food, activity*) uwielbiać; **to be in ~ (with sb)** być zakochanym (w kimś); **to fall in ~ (with sb)** zakochiwać (zakochać *pf*) się (w kimś); **to make ~** kochać się; **~ (from) Anne** (*on letter*) pozdrowienia (od) Anne; **to ~ doing/to do sth** uwielbiać coś robić; **I'd ~ to come** przyjdę z chęcią
lovely ['lʌvlɪ] (*esp Brit*) *adj* **1** (*beautiful*) uroczy **2** (*delightful: holiday, meal, present*) cudowny; (*person*) śliczny; **how ~ to see you!** miło cię widzieć!
lover ['lʌvə[r]] *n* (*sexual partner*) kochanek(-nka) *m/f*; **an art ~** miłośnik sztuki
low [ləu] *adj* niski ▷ *adv* (*fly*) nisko; **~ in calories/salt/fat** o niskiej zawartości kalorii/soli/tłuszczu
lower ['ləuə[r]] *vt* obniżać (obniżyć *pf*)

LOWER SIXTH

Lower sixth to pierwszy z dwóch ostatnich lat szkoły średniej (**secondary school**), kiedy to uczniowie przygotowują się do egzaminów **A levels**.

loyal ['lɔɪəl] *adj* lojalny
loyalty ['lɔɪəltɪ] *n* lojalność

L-PLATES

L-plates to tablice „nauki jazdy", umieszczane na tyle i przedzie samochodu prowadzonego przez uczącego się kierowcę. W Wielkiej Brytanii są one białego koloru z czerwoną literą L.

luck [lʌk] *n* szczęście; **good ~** szczęście; **good ~!** *or* **best of ~!** powodzenia!; **bad ~** pech; **bad** *or* **hard** *or* **tough ~!** (*showing sympathy*) pech!
luckily ['lʌkɪlɪ] *adv* na szczęście; **~ for me/us** szczęśliwie dla mnie/nas
lucky ['lʌkɪ] *adj* (*person*) szczęśliwy; **to be ~** (*person*) mieć szczęście; **I'm ~ to be alive** mam szczęście, że żyję; **it is ~ that...** szczęście, że...; **to have a ~ escape** cudem ujść cało; **you'll be ~!** (*inf*) ale byś miał szczęście!
luggage ['lʌgɪdʒ] *n* bagaż; **piece of ~** bagaż
lump [lʌmp] *n* **1** (*piece: of clay*) bryła; (*of butter*) kawałek; (*of wood, sugar*) kostka **2** (*on body*) guz
lunch [lʌntʃ] *n* **1** (*meal*) lunch; (*large*) obiad **2** (*lunchtime*) pora lunchu; **to have ~ (with sb)** jeść (zjeść *pf*) (z kimś) lunch; **to have sth for ~** jeść (zjeść *pf*) coś na lunch
lung [lʌŋ] *n* płuco
Luxembourg ['lʌksəmbəːg] *n* Luksemburg
luxurious [lʌg'zjuərɪəs] *adj* luksusowy
luxury ['lʌkʃərɪ] *n* **1** (*comfort*) luksus **2** (*extra*) zbytek ▷ *adj* (*hotel, car, goods etc*) luksusowy
lying ['laɪɪŋ] *vb see* **lie**[1]; **lie**[2] ▷ *n* kłamstwo
lyrics ['lɪrɪks] *n pl* (*of song*) tekst *sg*

mac [mæk] (*Brit: inf*) *n* płaszcz przeciwdeszczowy
macaroni [mækəˈrəunɪ] *n* makaron rurki
machine [məˈʃiːn] *n* maszyna
machine gun *n* karabin maszynowy
machinery [məˈʃiːnərɪ] *n* mechanizm
mad [mæd] *adj* **1** (*insane*) szalony **2** (*inf: angry*) zły; **to go ~** (*inf: go insane*) oszaleć (*pf*); (*get angry*) złościć (zezłościć *pf*) się; **to be ~ about sth** (*inf*) szaleć (oszaleć *pf*) na punkcie czegoś; **to be ~ about sb** (*inf*) szaleć na punkcie kogoś
madam [ˈmædəm] *n* (*form of address*) pani; **Dear M~** Szanowna Pani
made [meɪd] *pt, pp of* **make**
madness [ˈmædnɪs] *n* **1** (*insanity*) szaleństwo **2** (*foolishness*) głupota
magazine [mægəˈziːn] *n* czasopismo
maggot [ˈmægət] *n* robak
magic [ˈmædʒɪk] *n* **1** (*supernatural power*) magia **2** (*conjuring*) sztuczki magiczne ▷ *adj* magiczny
magician [məˈdʒɪʃən] *n* (*wizard*) czarownik; (*conjurer*) magik
magnet [ˈmægnɪt] *n* magnes
magnifying glass [ˈmægnɪfaɪɪŋ-] *n* szkło powiększające
maid [meɪd] *n* (*servant*) pokojówka
maiden name [ˈmeɪdn-] *n* nazwisko panieńskie
mail [meɪl] *n* poczta ▷ *vt* (*letter etc*) wysyłać (wysłać *pf*); **by ~** (*email*) emailem; (*post*) pocztą
mailbox [ˈmeɪlbɔks] *n* **1** (*US*) skrzynka na listy **2** (*Comput*) skrzynka odbiorcza
mailman [ˈmeɪlmæn] (*irreg*) *n* (*US*) listonosz
mailwoman [ˈmeɪlwumən] (*irreg*) *n* (*US*) listonoszka
main [meɪn] *adj* główny
main course *n* danie główne
mainly [ˈmeɪnlɪ] *adv* głównie
main road *n* główna droga
majesty [ˈmædʒɪstɪ] *n* (*title*): **Your/His/Her M~** Wasza/Jego/Jej Królewska Mość
major [ˈmeɪdʒəʳ] *adj* ważny ▷ *n* **1** (*Mil*) major **2** (*US: Scol*) specjalizacja
majority [məˈdʒɔrɪtɪ] *n* (*of people, things*) większość
make [meɪk] (*pt, pp* **made**) *vt* **1** (*object, clothes, cake*) robić (zrobić *pf*); (*noise*) robić (narobić *pf*); (*mistake*) popełniać (popełnić *pf*) **2** (*manufacture: goods*) produkować (wyprodukować *pf*) **3** (*cause to be*): **to ~ sb sad** zasmucać (zasmucić *pf*) kogoś **4** (*force*): **to ~ sb do sth** zmuszać (zmusić *pf*) kogoś do zrobienia czegoś **5** (*earn: money*) zarabiać (zarobić *pf*) **6** (*equal*): **two and two ~ four** dwa plus dwa równa się cztery ▷ *n* (*brand*) marka; **to ~ a profit** zarabiać (zarobić *pf*); **to ~ a loss** tracić (stracić *pf*); **what time do you ~ it?** która jest godzina?; **to ~ do with sth** zadowalać (zadowolić *pf*) się czymś; **it's made (out) of glass** jest zrobiony ze szkła
▶ **make out** *vt* (*write: cheque*) wypisywać (wypisać *pf*)
▶ **make up** *vt* (*invent: story, excuse*) wymyślać (wymyślić *pf*) ▷ *vi* (*after quarrel*) godzić (pogodzić *pf*) się; **to ~ up one's mind** podejmować (podjąć *pf*) decyzję; **to ~ o.s. up** malować (umalować *pf*) się
make-up [ˈmeɪkʌp] *n* (*cosmetics*) kosmetyki *pl*
male [meɪl] *adj* (*employee, child, friend etc*) płci męskiej; (*animal, insect, plant, tree etc*) męski
malicious [məˈlɪʃəs] *adj* (*person, gossip*) złośliwy

mall [mɔːl] *n* (*also*: **shopping ~**) centrum handlowe
mammal ['mæml] *n* ssak
man [mæn] (*pl* **men**) *n* **1** (*person*) mężczyzna **2** (*mankind*) człowiek
manage ['mænɪdʒ] *vt* zarządzać ▷ *vi* (*cope*) radzić (poradzić *pf*) sobie; **to ~ to do sth** radzić (poradzić *pf*) sobie ze zrobieniem czegoś
management ['mænɪdʒmənt] *n* **1** (*managing*) zarządzanie **2** (*managers*) kierownictwo
manager ['mænɪdʒəʳ] *n* **1** (*of business, department etc*) kierownik(-iczka) *m/f* **2** (*Sport*) manager
manageress [mænɪdʒə'rɛs] *n* kierowniczka
mandarin ['mændərɪn] *n* **1**: **M~ (Chinese)** dialekt mandaryński **2** (*also*: **~ orange**) mandarynka
mango ['mæŋgəu] (*pl* **mangoes**) *n* (*fruit*) mango
mania ['meɪnɪə] *n* (*craze*) mania
maniac ['meɪnɪæk] *n* **1** (*lunatic*) maniak(-aczka) *m/f* **2** (*idiot*) wariat(ka) *m/f*
mankind [mæn'kaɪnd] *n* (*human beings*) ludzkość
manner ['mænəʳ] *n* (*way*) sposób; **manners** *n pl* (*polite behaviour*) maniery; **bad ~s** złe maniery
mansion ['mænʃən] *n* rezydencja
mantelpiece ['mæntlpiːs] *n* gzyms kominka
manual ['mænjuəl] *n* (*handbook*) podręcznik
manufacture [mænju'fæktʃəʳ] *vt* (*goods*) produkować (wyprodukować *pf*)
manufacturer [mænju'fæktʃərəʳ] *n* producent(ka) *m/f*
many ['mɛnɪ] *adj* (*a lot of*) wiele *+gen* ▷ *pron* wiele; **how ~** (*direct question*) ile *+gen*; **twice as ~ as** (*comparison*) dwa razy tyle *+gen*
map [mæp] *n* mapa
marathon ['mærəθən] *n* (*race*) maraton
marble ['mɑːbl] *n* (*stone*) marmur; **marbles** *n pl* (*game*) kulki
March [mɑːtʃ] *n* marzec; *see also* **July**
march [mɑːtʃ] *vi* maszerować ▷ *n* marsz
mare [mɛəʳ] *n* klacz
margarine [mɑːdʒə'riːn] *n* margaryna
margin ['mɑːdʒɪn] *n* (*on page*) margines
marijuana [mærɪ'wɑːnə] *n* marihuana
mark [mɑːk] *n* **1** (*cross, tick etc*) znak **2** (*stain*) plama **3** (*Brit*: *grade, score*) ocena ▷ *vt* **1** (*indicate*: *place*) oznaczać (oznaczyć *pf*) **2** (*Brit*: *Scol*) oceniać (ocenić *pf*)
marker ['mɑːkəʳ] *n* (*also*: **~ pen**) flamaster
market ['mɑːkɪt] *n* (*in town, village etc*: *place*) rynek; (*event*) targ
marketing ['mɑːkɪtɪŋ] *n* marketing
marmalade ['mɑːməleɪd] *n* marmolada
marriage ['mærɪdʒ] *n* **1** (*relationship, institution*) małżeństwo **2** (*wedding*) ślub
married ['mærɪd] *adj* (*man*) żonaty; (*woman*) zamężna; **to be ~ to sb** (*to a woman*) żonaty z kimś; **to be ~ to sb** (*to a man*) zamężna z kimś; **to get ~** pobierać (pobrać *pf*) się
marry ['mærɪ] *vt* (*man, woman*) poślubiać (poślubić *pf*)
marsh [mɑːʃ] *n* (*bog*) bagno
marvellous ['mɑːvləs] (*US* **marvelous**) *adj* cudowny
marzipan ['mɑːzɪpæn] *n* marcepan
mascara [mæs'kɑːrə] *n* tusz do rzęs
masculine ['mæskjulɪn] *adj* męski; (*Ling*) rodzaj męski
mashed potato [mæʃt-] *n* puree ziemniaczane
mask [mɑːsk] *n* maska
mass [mæs] *n* (*large amount, number*) masa; **~es of** (*inf*) masy *+gen*
massage ['mæsɑːʒ] *n* masaż
massive ['mæsɪv] *adj* (*enormous*) ogromny
master ['mɑːstəʳ] *vt* (*learn*: *skill, language*) doskonalić
masterpiece ['mɑːstəpiːs] *n* (*great work*) arcydzieło
mat [mæt] *n* **1** (*on floor*) dywanik **2** (*also*: **door~**) wycieraczka **3** (*also*: **table ~**) podstawka

match [mætʃ] *n* **1** (*game*) mecz **2** (*for lighting fire etc*) zapałka ▷ *vt* (*go well with*) pasować do +*gen* ▷ *vi* (*go together*) pasować
mate [meɪt] *n* **1** (*Brit: inf: friend*) kumpel(ka) *m/f* **2** (*animal*) partner
material [mə'tɪərɪəl] *n* materiał; **materials** *n pl* (*equipment*) materiały
math [mæθ] (*US*) *n* = **maths**
mathematics [mæθə'mætɪks] (*formal*) *n* matematyka
maths [mæθs] (*Brit*) *n* matematyka
matter ['mætə^r] *n* (*affair, situation, problem*) sprawa ▷ *vi* (*be important*) mieć znaczenie; **what's the ~ (with...)?** co się dzieje (z +*inst*...)?; **as a ~ of fact** w istocie; **it doesn't ~** to nie ma znaczenia
mattress ['mætrɪs] *n* materac
mature [mə'tjuə^r] *adj* (*not childlike*) dojrzały
maximum ['mæksɪməm] *adj* maksymalny ▷ *n* maksimum
May [meɪ] *n* maj; *see also* **July**

 **KEYWORD**

may [meɪ] *aux vb* **1** (*possibility*): **it may rain later** może później będzie padać; **we may not be able to come** może nie uda nam się przyjść; **he may have hurt himself** może się zranił
2 (*permission*): **may I come in?** mogę wejść?; **you may go now** możesz teraz iść

maybe ['meɪbi:] *adv* może; **~ so/not** może tak/nie
mayonnaise [meɪə'neɪz] *n* majonez
mayor [mɛə^r] *n* burmistrz
me [mi:] *pron* (*nom*) ja; (*gen, acc, loc*) mnie; (*dat*) mi; (*inst*) mną; **he loves me** on mnie kocha; **it's me** to ja
meal [mi:l] *n* posiłek; **to go out for a ~** chodzić (pójść *pf*) do restauracji
mean [mi:n] (*pt, pp* **meant**) *vt* **1** (*signify*) znaczyć **2** (*refer to*) mieć na myśli **3** (*involve*) oznaczać **4** (*intend*): **to ~ to do sth** mieć zamiar coś robić (zrobić *pf*) ▷ *adj* **1** (*not generous*) skąpy **2** (*unkind: person*) niemiły; **what does "imperialism" ~?** co znaczy „imperialism"?; **what do you ~?** co masz na myśli?; **to be ~ to sb** (*unkind*) być niemiłym wobec kogoś; *see also* **means**
meaning ['mi:nɪŋ] *n* znaczenie
means [mi:nz] (*pl* **means**) *n* (*method*) sposób *sg*
meant [mɛnt] *pt, pp of* **mean**
meanwhile ['mi:nwaɪl] *adv* tymczasem
measles ['mi:zlz] *n* odra
measure ['mɛʒə^r] *vt* mierzyć (zmierzyć *pf*) ▷ *vi* (*room, person, object*) mierzyć (zmierzyć *pf*)
measurement ['mɛʒəmənt] *n*: **~s** (*of person*) wymiary
meat [mi:t] *n* mięso
Mecca ['mɛkə] *n* Mekka
mechanic [mɪ'kænɪk] *n* mechanik
medal ['mɛdl] *n* (*award*) medal
media ['mi:dɪə] *pl of* **medium** ▷ *n pl*: **the ~** media
medical ['mɛdɪkl] *adj* (*treatment, care*) medyczny ▷ *n* (*examination*) badania
medicine ['mɛdsɪn] *n* **1** (*science*) medycyna **2** (*medication*) lek
Mediterranean [mɛdɪtə'reɪnɪən] *n*: **the ~** (*sea*) Morze Śródziemne; (*region*) region Morza Śródziemnego
medium ['mi:dɪəm] *adj* średni
medium-sized ['mi:dɪəm'saɪzd] *adj* w średnim rozmiarze
meet [mi:t] (*pt, pp* **met**) *vt* **1** (*friend: accidentally*) spotykać (spotkać *pf*); (*by arrangement*) spotykać (spotkać *pf*) się z +*inst* **2** (*stranger: for the first time*) spotykać (spotkać *pf*); (*be introduced to*) poznawać (poznać *pf*) **3** (*go and fetch*) witać (przywitać *pf*) ▷ *vi* spotykać (spotkać *pf*) się; **pleased to ~ you** miło pana/panią poznać
▸ **meet up** *vi* spotykać (spotkać *pf*) się
meeting ['mi:tɪŋ] *n* spotkanie
megabyte ['mɛgəbaɪt] *n* megabajt
melon ['mɛlən] *n* melon
melt [mɛlt] *vi* topić (stopić *pf*) się ▷ *vt* topić (stopić *pf*)
member ['mɛmbə^r] *n* członek(-nkini) *m/f*
meme [mi:m] *n* mem

memorial [mɪ'mɔːrɪəl] *n* pomnik
memorize ['mɛməraɪz] *vt*: **to ~ sth** uczyć (nauczyć *pf*) się czegoś na pamięć
memory ['mɛmərɪ] *n* **1** (*ability to remember*) pamięć **2** (*thing remembered*) wspomnienie **3** (*Comput*) pamięć; **to have a good/bad ~ (for sth)** mieć dobrą/ złą pamięć (do czegoś)
memory card *n* (*Comput*) karta pamięci
memory stick *n* (*Comput*) karta pamięci
men [mɛn] *n pl of* **man**
mend [mɛnd] *vt* (*repair: object*) naprawiać (naprawić *pf*)
mental ['mɛntl] *adj* **1** (*ability, effort, development*) umysłowy **2** (*illness*) umysłowy; (*health*) psychiczny
mention ['mɛnʃən] *vt* wspominać (wspomnieć *pf*) o *+loc*; **don't ~ it!** nie ma za co!
menu ['mɛnjuː] *n* menu
meringue [mə'ræŋ] *n* beza
merry ['mɛrɪ] *adj*: **M~ Christmas!** Wesołych Świąt!
merry-go-round ['mɛrɪgəuraund] *n* karuzela
mess [mɛs] *n* bałagan; **to be in a ~** (*room*) mieć bałagan
▸ **mess about, mess around** (*inf*) *vi* tracić (stracić *pf*) czas
▸ **mess up** (*inf*) *vt* (*make untidy*) robić (zrobić *pf*) bałagan w *+loc*
message ['mɛsɪdʒ] *n* (*to sb*) wiadomość; **to leave (sb) a ~** zostawiać (zostawić *pf*) (komuś) wiadomość
messenger ['mɛsɪndʒəʳ] *n* posłaniec
messy ['mɛsɪ] *adj* (*untidy: person, activity*) niechlujny; (*thing, place*) nieuporządkowany
met [mɛt] *pt, pp of* **meet**
metal ['mɛtl] *n* metal
meter ['miːtəʳ] *n* **1** (*for gas, water, electricity*) licznik; (*also*: **parking ~**) parkomat **2** (*US: unit*) = **metre**
method ['mɛθəd] *n* (*way*) metoda, sposób
metre ['miːtəʳ] (*US* **meter**) *n* (*unit*) metr
metric ['mɛtrɪk] *adj* metryczny
Mexico ['mɛksɪkəu] *n* Meksyk
mice [maɪs] *n pl of* **mouse**
microchip ['maɪkrəutʃɪp] *n* mikrochip
microphone ['maɪkrəfəun] *n* mikrofon
microscope ['maɪkrəskəup] *n* mikroskop
microwave ['maɪkrəuweɪv] *n* (*also*: **~ oven**) mikrofalówka
midday [mɪd'deɪ] *n* (*noon*) południe; **at ~** w południe
middle ['mɪdl] *n* **1** (*centre*) środek **2** (*half-way point*): **in the ~ of the night** w środku nocy ▷ *adj* (*position, event, period*) środkowy
middle-aged [mɪdl'eɪdʒd] *adj* w średnim wieku
middle class *adj*: **~ values** zasady typowe dla klasy średniej
Middle East *n*: **the ~** Bliski Wschód
middle name *n* drugie imię
midge [mɪdʒ] *n* muszka
midnight ['mɪdnaɪt] *n* północ; **at ~** o północy
midwife ['mɪdwaɪf] (*pl* **midwives**) *n* położna
might [maɪt] *aux vb* **1** (*possibility*): **I ~ get home late** może będę w domu późno **2** (*suggestions*): **you ~ try the bookshop** może spróbuje pan/ pani w księgarni; **it ~ have been an accident** to mógł być wypadek
migraine ['miːgreɪn] *n* migrena
mike [maɪk] (*inf*) *n* (*microphone*) mikrofon
mild [maɪld] *adj* lekki
mile [maɪl] *n* mila; **miles** *n pl* (*inf: a long way*) bardzo daleko; **70 ~s per** *or* **an hour** siedemdziesiąt mil na godzinę
military ['mɪlɪtərɪ] *adj* (*leader, action*) wojskowy
milk [mɪlk] *n* mleko
milk chocolate *n* czekolada mleczna
milkman ['mɪlkmən] (*irreg*) *n* mleczarz
milkshake ['mɪlkʃeɪk] *n* koktajl mleczny
millennium [mɪ'lɛnɪəm] (*pl* **millenniums** *or* **millennia** [mɪ'lɛnɪə]) *n* (*1000 years*) tysiąclecie

millimetre ['mɪlɪmiːtəʳ] (*US* **millimeter**) *n* milimetr
million ['mɪljən] *num* milion; **millions** *n pl* miliony; **a** *or* **one ~ books/people/dollars** milion książek/ludzi/dolarów
millionaire [mɪljə'nɛəʳ] *n* milioner(ka) *m/f*
mince [mɪns] *n* (*Brit*: *Culin*) mięso mielone
mind [maɪnd] *n* (*intellect*) umysł ▷ *vt* **1** (*Brit*: *look after*) zajmować (zająć *pf*) się *+inst* **2** (*be careful of*) uważać na **3** (*object to*): **would you ~ (if...)?** ma pan/pani coś przeciwko temu, (żeby...)? **4** (*have a preference*): **I don't ~ (what/who...)** jest mi wszystko jedno, (co/kto...) **5**: **to make up one's ~** *or* **make one's ~ up** podejmować (podjąć *pf*) decyzję; **to change one's ~** zmieniać (zmienić *pf*) zdanie; **never ~** nieważne; **I wouldn't ~ a coffee** z chęcią napiję się kawy; **~ the step** uwaga na stopień
mine[1] [maɪn] *pron* (*m sg*) mój; (*f sg*) moja; (*nt sg*) moje; (*pl*) moje; (*pl vir*) moi; **a friend of ~** mój przyjaciel; **this is ~** to jest moje; **these are ~** te są moje
mine[2] [maɪn] *n* (*for coal, gold etc*) kopalnia
miner ['maɪnəʳ] *n* górnik
mineral water ['mɪnərəl-] *n* woda mineralna
miniature ['mɪnətʃəʳ] *adj* miniaturowy ▷ *n* miniatura
minibus ['mɪnɪbʌs] *n* mikrobus
Minidisc® ['mɪnɪdɪsk] *n* minidisc
minimum ['mɪnɪməm] *adj* (*lowest, smallest*) minimalny ▷ *n* minimum
miniskirt ['mɪnɪskəːt] *n* spódnica mini
minister ['mɪnɪstəʳ] *n* **1** (*Brit*: *Pol*) minister **2** (*Rel*) pastor
minor ['maɪnəʳ] *adj* drobny
minority [maɪ'nɔrɪtɪ] *n* mniejszość
mint [mɪnt] *n* **1** (*plant*) mięta **2** (*sweet*) miętówka
minus ['maɪnəs] *prep* (*inf*: *without*) minus; **12 ~ 3 (is** *or* **equals 9)** dwanaście minus trzy (równa się dziewięć); **~ 24 (degrees)** (*temperature*) minus dwadzieścia cztery (stopnie)
minute[1] [maɪ'njuːt] *adj* (*amount*) drobny
minute[2] ['mɪnɪt] *n* **1** (*unit*) minuta **2** (*fig*: *short time*) chwila; **wait** *or* **just a ~!** chwileczkę!
miracle ['mɪrəkl] *n* cud
mirror ['mɪrəʳ] *n* lustro; (*in car*) lusterko
misbehave [mɪsbɪ'heɪv] *vi* źle się zachowywać (zachować *pf*)
miscellaneous [mɪsɪ'leɪnɪəs] *adj* (*people, objects*) różny
mischief ['mɪstʃɪf] *n* (*playfulness, fun*) psoty
mischievous ['mɪstʃɪvəs] *adj* (*playful, fun-loving*) figlarny
miser ['maɪzəʳ] (*pej*) *n* skąpiec
miserable ['mɪzərəbl] *adj* **1** (*unhappy*: *person*) nieszczęsny **2** (*unpleasant*: *weather, day*) ponury; **to feel ~** czuć (poczuć *pf*) się okropnie
misery ['mɪzərɪ] *n* nieszczęście
Miss [mɪs] *n* **1** (*before surname*) panna **2** (*esp Brit*: *as form of address*) panna; **Dear ~ Lily Smith** Droga Pani Lily Smith
miss [mɪs] *vt* **1** (*fail to hit*) chybiać (chybić *pf*) **2** (*Sport*: *shot, penalty*) nie trafiać (trafić *pf*) **3** (*train, bus, plane*) nie zdążać (zdążyć *pf*) **4** (*feel the absence of*): **I ~ my mum** tęsknię za mamą **5** (*chance, opportunity*) tracić (stracić *pf*) ▷ *vi* (*fail to hit*: *person*) chybiać (chybić *pf*); **you can't ~ it** nie może pan/pani tego przeoczyć
missing ['mɪsɪŋ] *adj* (*absent, lost*: *person*) zaginiony; (*object*) brakujący
mist [mɪst] *n* mgła
mistake [mɪs'teɪk] (*pt* **mistook**, *pp* **mistaken**) *n* błąd; **to make a ~** popełniać (popełnić *pf*) błąd; **to do sth by ~** robić (zrobić *pf*) coś przez pomyłkę
mistaken [mɪs'teɪkən] *pp of* **mistake** ▷ *adj*: **if I'm not** *or* **unless I'm ~** jeśli się nie mylę
mistletoe ['mɪsltəu] *n* jemioła
mistook [mɪs'tuk] *pt of* **mistake**
misty ['mɪstɪ] *adj* (*day, weather*) mglisty; **it's ~** jest mgliście
misunderstand [mɪsʌndə'stænd] (*pt, pp* **misunderstood**) *vt, vi* źle rozumieć (zrozumieć *pf*)

misunderstanding ['mɪsʌndə'stændɪŋ] *n* nieporozumienie
misunderstood [mɪsʌndə'stud] *pt, pp of* **misunderstand**
mix [mɪks] *vt* (*liquids, ingredients, colours*) mieszać (zmieszać *pf*) ▷ *vi* (*socially*): **to ~ (with sb)** zadawać (zadać *pf*) się (z kimś) ▷ *n* (*combination*) mieszanina; **to ~ sth with sth** (*activities*) mieszać (zmieszać *pf*) coś z czymś
▶ **mix up** *vt* mylić (pomylić *pf*)
mixed [mɪkst] *adj* **1** (*salad, herbs*) mieszany **2** (*diverse*: *group, community*) zróżnicowany **3** (*school, education*) koedukacyjny
mixer ['mɪksəʳ] *n* **1** (*also*: **food ~**) mikser **2** (*person*): **to be a good ~** łatwo nawiązywać (nawiązać *pf*) kontakty
mixture ['mɪkstʃəʳ] *n* mieszanina
mix-up ['mɪksʌp] (*inf*) *n* nieporozumienie
moan [məun] *vi* (*inf*: *complain*): **to ~ (about sth)** narzekać (na coś)
mobile ['məubaɪl] *n* (*Brit*: *also*: **~ phone**) telefon komórkowy
mobile home *n* mieszkalna przyczepa kempingowa
mobile phone (*Brit*) *n* telefon komórkowy
mock [mɔk] *vt* (*ridicule*) wyśmiewać się *+gen*
model ['mɔdl] *n* **1** (*of boat, building etc*) model **2** (*fashion model*) model(ka) *m/f* ▷ *adj* **1** (*exemplary*) modelowy **2** (*miniature*): **~ aircraft/train** model samolotu/pociągu ▷ *vt* (*clothes*) prezentować (zaprezentować *pf*)
modem ['məudɛm] *n* modem
moderate ['mɔdərət] *adj* (*views, people*) umiarkowany
modern ['mɔdən] *adj* **1** (*present-day*) współczesny **2** (*up-to-date*) nowoczesny
modernize ['mɔdənaɪz] *vt* modernizować (zmodernizować *pf*)
modern languages [-'læŋgwɪdʒɪz] *n pl* języki nowożytne
modest ['mɔdɪst] *adj* (*not boastful*: *person*) skromny
moisturizer ['mɔɪstʃəraɪzəʳ] *n* krem nawilżający
moldy ['məuldɪ] (*US*) *adj* = **mouldy**
mole [məul] *n* **1** (*on skin*) pieprzyk **2** (*animal*) kret
moment ['məumənt] *n* chwila; **at the/this (present) ~** w tej chwili; **(at) any ~ (now)** w każdej chwili; **at the last ~** w ostatniej chwili
monarchy ['mɔnəkɪ] *n* monarchia
Monday ['mʌndɪ] *n* poniedziałek; *see also* **Tuesday**
money ['mʌnɪ] *n* pieniądze; **to make ~** (*person, business*) zarabiać (zarobić *pf*)
mongrel ['mʌŋgrəl] *n* kundel
monitor ['mɔnɪtəʳ] *n* monitor
monkey ['mʌŋkɪ] *n* (*Zool*) małpa
monotonous [mə'nɔtənəs] *adj* monotonny
monster ['mɔnstəʳ] *n* (*imaginary creature*) potwór
month [mʌnθ] *n* (*calendar month*) miesiąc; **every ~** co miesiąc
monthly ['mʌnθlɪ] *adj* miesięczny ▷ *adv* miesięcznie
monument ['mɔnjumənt] *n* (*memorial*) pomnik
mood [mu:d] *n* (*of person*) nastrój; **to be in a good/bad/awkward ~** być w dobrym/złym/dziwnym nastroju
moody ['mu:dɪ] *adj* humorzasty
moon [mu:n] *n*: **the ~** księżyc
moonlight ['mu:nlaɪt] *n* światło księżyca
moped ['məupɛd] *n* motorower
moral ['mɔrl] *adj* moralny ▷ *n* (*of story*) morał

KEYWORD

more [mɔ:ʳ] *adj* **1** (*in comparisons with uncount noun, plural noun*) więcej *+gen*; **I get more money/holidays than you do** mam więcej pieniędzy/wakacji niż ty
2 (*additional*: *with uncount noun, plural noun*) jeszcze; **would you like some more tea/peanuts?** chce pan/pani jeszcze herbaty/orzeszków?; **is there any more wine?** czy jest jeszcze wino?; **a few more weeks** kilka tygodni dłużej

▷ *pron* **1** (*in comparisons: more in quantity, number*) więcej; **there's/there are more than I thought** jest więcej, niż myślałem; **more than 20** więcej niż dwadzieścia; **she's got more than me** ona ma więcej niż ja **2** (*further, additional: in quantity*) jeszcze; **is there/are there any more?** czy jest/są jeszcze?; **have you got any more of it?** czy pan/pani ma to jeszcze?; **a little/a few more** trochę więcej; **much/many more** wiele więcej
▷ *adv* **1** (*to form comparative*) bardziej; **more dangerous/difficult (than)** bardziej niebezpieczny/trudny (niż); **more easily/quickly (than)** łatwiej/szybciej (niż)
2 (*in expressions*): **more and more** coraz więcej; **more or less** (*adj, adv*) mniej więcej; **more than ever** więcej niż kiedykolwiek; **once more** raz jeszcze

morning ['mɔːnɪŋ] *n* (*early in the morning*) wcześnie rano; (*later in the morning*) późnym rankiem; **good ~!** dzień dobry!; **at three o'clock/seven o'clock in the ~** o trzeciej nad ranem/siódmej rano; **this ~** tego ranka; **on Monday ~** w poniedziałek rano

mortgage ['mɔːgɪdʒ] *n* hipoteka ▷ *vt* (*house, property*) obciążać (obciążyć *pf*) hipotekę; **to take out a ~** zaciągać (zaciągnąć *pf*) kredyt hipoteczny

Moslem ['mɔzləm] *adj, n* = **Muslim**

mosque [mɔsk] *n* meczet

mosquito [mɔs'kiːtəu] (*pl* **mosquitoes**) *n* komar

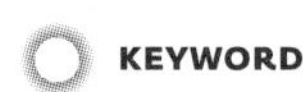
KEYWORD

most [məust] *adj* **1** (*almost all: with uncount noun, plural noun*) większość *+gen*; **most people** większość ludzi
2 (*in comparisons*): **(the) most** (*with uncount noun, plural noun*) najwięcej *+gen*; **who won the most money/prizes?** kto wygrał najwięcej pieniędzy/nagród?
▷ *pron* większość; **most of it/them** większość z tego/nich; **I paid the most** zapłaciłem większość; **to make the most of sth** wykorzystywać (wykorzystać *pf*) maksymalnie coś; **at the (very) most** co najwyżej
▷ *adv* (*superlative*) **1** (*with verb*): **(the) most** najbardziej; **what I miss (the) most is...** najbardziej brakuje mi...
2 (*with adj*): **the most comfortable/expensive sofa in the shop** najbardziej wygodna/najdroższa sofa w sklepie
3 (*with adv*): **most efficiently/effectively** najwydajniej/najefektywniej; **most of all** przede wszystkim

moth [mɔθ] *n* ćma

mother ['mʌðə^r^] *n* (*parent*) matka

mother-in-law ['mʌðərɪnlɔː] (*pl* **mothers-in-law**) *n* teściowa

Mother's Day (*Brit*) *n* Dzień Matki

motivated ['məutɪveɪtɪd] *adj* zmotywowany

motivation [məutɪ'veɪʃən] *n* (*motive*) motywacja

motor ['məutə^r^] *n* (*of machine, vehicle*) silnik

motorbike ['məutəbaɪk] *n* motocykl

motorboat ['məutəbəut] *n* motorówka

motorcycle ['məutəsaɪkl] *n* motocykl

motorcyclist ['məutəsaɪklɪst] *n* motocyklista(-tka) *m/f*

motorist ['məutərɪst] (*esp Brit*) *n* kierowca

motor racing (*Brit*) *n* wyścigi samochodowe

motorway ['məutəweɪ] (*Brit*) *n* autostrada

mouldy ['məuldɪ] (*US* **moldy**) *adj* (*bread, cheese*) spleśniały

mount [maunt] *vt* (*organize*) organizować (zorganizować *pf*) ▷ *vi* (*increase*) gromadzić (zgromadzić *pf*) się

mountain ['mauntɪn] *n* góra

mountain bike *n* rower górski

mountaineer [mauntɪ'nɪə^r^] *n* alpinista(-tka) *m/f*

mountaineering [mauntɪ'nɪərɪŋ] *n* wspinaczka wysokogórska; **to go ~** wspinać się

mountainous ['mauntɪnəs] *adj* (*country, area*) górzysty
mouse [maus] (*pl* **mice**) *n* **1** (*Zool*) mysz **2** (*Comput*) myszka
mouse mat *n* podkładka pod myszkę
mousse [mu:s] *n* mus
moustache [məs'tɑ:ʃ] (*US* **mustache**) *n* wąsy *pl*
mouth [mauθ] *n* **1** (*of person, animal*) usta **2** (*of river*) ujście
mouthful ['mauθful] *n* (*of food*) kęs
mouth organ (*esp Brit*) *n* harmonijka ustna
move [mu:v] *vi* **1** (*change position*) ruszać (ruszyć *pf*) się **2** (*relocate*) przeprowadzać (przeprowadzić *pf*) się; (*from activity*) przenosić (przenieść *pf*) się ▷ *vt* **1** (*change position of*) przestawiać (przestawić *pf*) **2** (*affect emotionally*) wzruszać (wzruszyć *pf*) ▷ *n* **1** (*change*: *of house*) przeprowadzka **2** (*in game*: *go, turn*) ruch; **to ~ house** przeprowadzać (przeprowadzić *pf*) się; **to ~ jobs/offices** zmieniać (zmienić *pf*) pracę/biuro; **to get a ~ on** (*inf*) pospieszyć (*pf*) się
▸ **move away** *vi* (*from town, area*) wyprowadzać (wyprowadzić *pf*) się; (*from window, door*) odsuwać (odsunąć *pf*) się
▸ **move back** *vi* **1** (*return*: *to town, area*) wracać (wrócić *pf*) **2** (*backwards*: *person, troops, vehicle*) cofać (cofnąć *pf*)
▸ **move forward** *vi* (*person, troops, vehicle*) posuwać (posunąć *pf*) się do przodu
▸ **move in** *vi* (*into house*) wprowadzać (wprowadzić *pf*) się
▸ **move into** *vt fus* (*house, area*) wprowadzać (wprowadzić *pf*) się do
▸ **move out** *vi* (*of house*) wyprowadzać (wyprowadzić *pf*) się
▸ **move over** *vi* (*to make room*) przesuwać (przesunąć *pf*) się
movement ['mu:vmənt] *n* ruch
movie ['mu:vɪ] (*US*) *n* film; **the movies** *n pl* kino
movie theater (*US*) *n* kino
moving ['mu:vɪŋ] *adj* **1** (*emotionally*) poruszający **2** (*not static*) ruchomy

MP *n abbr* (*Brit*: = *Member of Parliament*) poseł/posłanka *m/f*
MP3 [ɛmpi:'θri:] *n* MP3; **~ player** odtwarzacz MP3
mph *abbr* (= *miles per hour*) mil na godzinę
Mr ['mɪstə^r] (*US* **Mr.**) *n*: **Mr Edward Smith** pan Edward Smith

MR/MRS/MISS/MS

Grzecznościowe formy w języku angielskim to **Mr/Mrs/Miss/Ms**, co odpowiada polskim zwrotom: pan/pani/panna/pani. W języku angielskim nazwisko poprzedzone jest właśnie jedną z tych form, na przykład: Mr. Smith. Tych form grzecznościowych używa się w oficjalnych sytuacjach, zwracając się do osób, których dobrze nie znamy, lub osób starszych. Inaczej niż w języku polskim, formy **Mr/Mrs/Miss/Ms** nie mogą być używane bez nazwiska.

Mrs ['mɪsɪz] (*US* **Mrs.**) ▷ *n*: **~ Anna Smith** pani Anna Smith
Ms [mɪz] (*US* **Ms.**) *n* (*Miss or Mrs*): **Ms Tracey Smith** pani Tracey Smith

KEYWORD

much [mʌtʃ] *adj* dużo +*gen*; **we haven't got much time/money** nie mamy dużo czasu/pieniędzy
▷ *pron* dużo; **there isn't much left** nie zostało dużo; **he doesn't do much at the weekends** nie robi zbyt dużo podczas weekendu
▷ *adv* **1** (*a great deal*) bardzo; **he hasn't changed much** bardzo się nie zmienił; **"did you like her?" — "not much"** „lubiłeś ją?" — „nie bardzo"
2 (*far*) wiele; **I'm much better now** teraz czuję się o wiele lepiej; **those trousers are much too big for you** te spodnie są na ciebie o wiele za duże
3 (*often*) często; **do you go out much?** często gdzieś wychodzisz?

mud [mʌd] *n* błoto

muddle ['mʌdl] *n* bałagan ▷ *vt* (*also*: **~ up**) mieszać (wymieszać *pf*); **to be in a ~** mieć mętlik w głowie
muddy ['mʌdɪ] *adj* zabłocony
muesli ['mjuːzlɪ] *n* muesli
mug [mʌg] *n* **1** (*large cup*: *for drinks*) kubek; (*for beer*) kufel **2** (*contents*) kubek ▷ *vt* (*rob*) okradać (okraść *pf*)
mugging ['mʌgɪŋ] *n* (*assault*) kradzież (*na ulicy*)
multiplication [mʌltɪplɪ'keɪʃən] *n* (*Math*) mnożenie
multiply ['mʌltɪplaɪ] *vt* (*Math*): **to ~ sth (by sth)** mnożyć (pomnożyć *pf*) coś (przez coś) ▷ *vi* (*increase*) mnożyć (pomnożyć *pf*) się
mum [mʌm] *n* (*Brit*: *inf*) mama
mummy ['mʌmɪ] *n* (*Brit*: *inf*) mamusia
mumps [mʌmps] *n* świnka
murder ['məːdə^r] *n* (*killing*) morderstwo ▷ *vt* (*kill*) mordować (zamordować *pf*)
murderer ['məːdərə^r] *n* morderca(-rczyni) *m/f*
muscle ['mʌsl] *n* (*Anat*) mięsień
museum [mjuː'zɪəm] *n* muzeum
mushroom ['mʌʃrum] *n* grzyb
music ['mjuːzɪk] *n* muzyka
musical ['mjuːzɪkl] *adj* **1** (*career, skills*) muzyczny **2** (*musically gifted*: *person*) muzykalny
musical instrument *n* instrument muzyczny
musician [mjuː'zɪʃən] *n* muzyk
Muslim, Moslem ['muzlɪm] *n* muzułmanin(-nka) *m/f* ▷ *adj* muzułmański
mussel ['mʌsl] *n* małż
must [mʌst] *aux vb* musieć; **you ~ be joking** chyba żartujesz; **the doctor ~ allow the patient to decide** lekarz musi pozwolić pacjentowi podjąć decyzję; **I really ~ be getting back** naprawdę muszę wracać
mustard ['mʌstəd] *n* musztarda
mustn't ['mʌsnt] = **must not**
mutton ['mʌtn] *n* baranina
my [maɪ] *adj* (*m sg*) mój; (*f sg*) moja; (*nt sg*) moje; (*pl*) moje; (*pl vir*) moi; (*referring to subject of sentence*) swój; **my parents** moi rodzice
myself [maɪ'sɛlf] *pron* **1** (*gen, acc*) siebie; (*dat, loc*) sobie; (*inst*) sobą; (*reflexive pronoun*) się **2** (*emphatic*: *m sg*) sam; (*f sg*) sama **3** (*me*) ja; **a complete beginner like ~** zupełnie początkujący tak jak ja; **I hurt ~** skaleczyłem się; **by ~** (*unaided, alone*) sam
mysterious [mɪs'tɪərɪəs] *adj* (*strange*) tajemniczy
mystery ['mɪstərɪ] *n* tajemnica
myth [mɪθ] *n* mit

nag [næg] *vt* naprzykrzać się *+dat*
nail [neɪl] *n* **1** (*of finger, toe*) paznokieć **2** (*for hammering*) gwóźdź ▷ *vt* (*attach*): **to ~ sth to/on sth** przybijać (przybić *pf*) coś do czegoś
nail file *n* pilnik do paznokci
nail polish *n* lakier do paznokci
nail varnish (*Brit*) *n* = **nail polish**
naked ['neɪkɪd] *adj* (*person, body*) nagi
name [neɪm] *n* (*of person: forename*) imię; (*surname*) nazwisko; (*of thing*) nazwa ▷ *vt* **1** (*give name to: child*) dawać (dać *pf*) na imię *+dat*; (*ship, street*) nazywać (nazwać *pf*) **2** (*identify*) wymieniać (wymienić *pf*) z nazwiska; **what's your ~?** (*surname*) jak się pan/pani nazywa?; (*forename*) jak pan/pani ma na imię?; **my ~ is Peter** mam na imię Peter; **to give one's ~ and address** podawać (podać *pf*) swoje nazwisko i adres
nanny ['nænɪ] *n* opiekunka do dziecka
napkin ['næpkɪn] *n* serwetka
nappy ['næpɪ] (*Brit*) *n* pielucha
narrow ['nærəu] *adj* (*road, ledge, feet*) wąski ▷ *vi* (*road, river*) zwężać (zwęzić *pf*) się
nasty ['nɑːstɪ] *adj* **1** (*bad, obnoxious*) wstrętny **2** (*serious*) poważny; **to be ~ to sb** być złośliwym dla kogoś
nation ['neɪʃən] *n* (*country*) państwo; (*people*) naród
national ['næʃənl] *adj* (*election*) powszechny; (*newspaper*) ogólnokrajowy; (*interest*) krajowy ▷ *n* (*citizen*) obywatel(ka) *m/f*
national anthem *n* hymn państwowy
national holiday (*US*) *n* święto państwowe
nationality [næʃə'nælɪtɪ] *n* narodowość
national park *n* park narodowy

NATIONAL TRUST

National Trust to brytyjska organizacja, która została powołana, aby chronić budowle, monumenty oraz wszelkie miejsca upamiętniające historię i kulturę, jak również pominiki przyrody.

native ['neɪtɪv] *adj* ojczysty
natural ['nætʃrəl] *adj* **1** (*normal*) naturalny **2** (*innate: flair, aptitude*) wrodzony **3** (*not man-made*) naturalny
naturally ['nætʃrəlɪ] *adv* **1** (*unsurprisingly*) oczywiście **2** (*occur, happen*) w sposób naturalny
nature ['neɪtʃə^r] *n* **1** (*also*: **N~**) natura **2** (*of person*) charakter
naughty ['nɔːtɪ] *adj* (*disobedient: child*) niegrzeczny
navy ['neɪvɪ] *n*: **the ~** marynarka wojenna ▷ *adj* (*also*: **~-blue**) granatowy
near [nɪə^r] *adj* (*physically, in time*) bliski ▷ *adv* (*close*) blisko ▷ *prep* (*also*: **~ to**) **1** (*physically*) blisko *+gen* **2**: **~ the end of the year** niedługo przed końcem roku; **~ the beginning of the game** niedługo po rozpoczęciu meczu; **the ~est shops are 5 km away** najbliższe sklepy są pięć kilometrów stąd; **my office is quite ~** moje biuro jest dosyć blisko; **in the ~ future** w niedalekiej przyszłości
nearby [nɪə'baɪ] *adj* pobliski ▷ *adv* w pobliżu
nearly ['nɪəlɪ] *adv* prawie; **he's ~ as tall as I am** jest prawie tak samo wysoki jak ja; **I (very) ~ fell over** prawie się przewróciłem; **~ always** prawie zawsze

near-sighted [nɪə'saɪtɪd] (*US*) *adj* (*short-sighted: person*) krótkowzroczny

neat [niːt] *adj* **1** (*tidy: house, desk*) uporządkowany; (*pile*) równy; (*clothes*) porządny; (*handwriting*) staranny **2** (*US: inf: great*) świetny

neatly ['niːtlɪ] *adv* (*tidily*) starannie

necessarily ['nɛsɪsrɪlɪ] *adv* (*inevitably*) koniecznie

necessary ['nɛsɪsrɪ] *adj* konieczny; **if/when/where ~** jeśli/kiedy/gdzie to konieczne; **it may be ~ (for us) to buy a new cooker** kupno nowej kuchenki może się okazać (dla nas) konieczne

neck [nɛk] *n* **1** (*Anat*) szyja **2** (*of shirt, dress, jumper*) kołnierz

necklace ['nɛklɪs] *n* naszyjnik

necktie ['nɛktaɪ] (*US*) *n* krawat

nectarine ['nɛktərɪn] *n* (*fruit*) nektarynka

need [niːd] *vt* **1** (*require*) potrzebować *+gen* **2** (*want*): **I ~ a cigarette** muszę zapalić ▷ *n* (*necessity*) potrzeba; **I ~ a haircut/bath/wash** muszę obciąć włosy/wziąć kąpiel/umyć się; **I ~ a holiday** przydałby mi się urlop; **to ~ to do sth** musieć coś zrobić; **the car ~s servicing** samochód wymaga przeglądu; **there's no ~ to shout** (*please don't*) nie ma powodu do krzyku

needle ['niːdl] *n* **1** (*for sewing*) igła **2** (*for knitting*) drut **3** (*for injections*) igła do zastrzyków

negative ['nɛgətɪv] *adj* **1** negatywny **2** (*Math*) ujemny ▷ *n* (*Ling*) przeczenie

neglected [nɪ'glɛktɪd] *adj* zaniedbany

negotiate [nɪ'gəuʃɪeɪt] *vi* negocjować (wynegocjować *pf*) ▷ *vt* (*treaty, contract*) negocjować (wynegocjować *pf*)

neighbour ['neɪbə^r] (*US* **neighbor**) *n* sąsiad(ka) *m/f*

neighbourhood ['neɪbəhud] (*US* **neighborhood**) *n* (*place*) okolica

neither ['naɪðə^r] *pron* (*person, thing*) żaden ▷ *conj*: **I didn't move and ~ did John** ani ja się nie ruszyłem, ani John; **~ do I** ja też nie; **~ of us went** żaden z nas nie poszedł; **~...nor...** ani...ani...

nephew ['nɛvjuː] *n* (*brother's son*) bratanek; (*sister's son*) siostrzeniec

nerve [nəːv] *n* **1** (*Anat*) nerw **2** (*courage*) odwaga; **nerves** *n pl* (*anxiety*) nerwy; **to lose one's ~** tracić (stracić *pf*) zimną krew; **to get on sb's ~s** działać (podziałać *pf*) komuś na nerwy

nervous ['nəːvəs] *adj* **1** (*worried*) zdenerwowany **2** (*by nature*) nerwowy; **to be ~ about sth/about doing sth** obawiać się czegoś/zrobienia czegoś

nest [nɛst] *n* (*of bird*) gniazdo

net [nɛt] *n* **1** (*for fishing, trapping, in games*) sieć **2** (*Comput*): **the N~** internet ▷ *adj* **1** (*also*: **nett**: *assets, income, profit*) netto **2** (*final: result, effect*) końcowy; **an income/profit of 10,000 pounds ~** dochód/zysk dziesięciu tysięcy funtów netto

netball ['nɛtbɔːl] *n* netball

Netherlands ['nɛðələndz] *n pl*: **the ~** Holandia

network ['nɛtwəːk] *n* sieć

neutral ['njuːtrəl] *adj* (*Elec: wire*) zerowy

never ['nɛvə^r] *adv* nigdy; **I ~ met him** nigdy go nie poznałem; **we ~ saw him again** nigdy więcej go nie widzieliśmy

new [njuː] *adj* **1** nowy **2** (*inexperienced: mother, member*) młody; **I'm ~ here** jestem tutaj nowy

news [njuːz] *n* wiadomości *f pl*; **a piece of ~** wiadomość; **good/bad ~** dobre/złe wiadomości; **the ~** (*TV, Rad*) wiadomości

newsagent ['njuːzeɪdʒənt] (*Brit*) *n* (*also*: **~'s**) kiosk

newscaster ['njuːzkaːstə^r] (*US*) *n* prezenter(ka) *m/f*

newspaper ['njuːzpeɪpə^r] *n* gazeta

newsreader ['njuːzriːdə^r] (*Brit*) *n* prezenter(ka) *m/f*

New Year *n*: **(the) ~** nowy Rok; **in the ~** w Nowym Roku; **Happy ~!** Szczęśliwego Nowego Roku!; **to wish sb a Happy ~** życzyć komuś Szczęśliwego Nowego Roku

New Year's Day (*US* **New Year's**) *n* Nowy Rok

New Year's Eve (*US* **New Year's**) *n* sylwester
New Zealand [-ˈziːlənd] *n* Nowa Zelandia
next [nɛkst] *adj* **1** (*next in time*) następny; (*next week, month*) przyszły **2** (*adjacent: house, street, room*) przyległy **3** (*in queue, series, list*) następny ▷ *adv* następnie ▷ *pron* następny; **the ~ day/morning** następnego dnia/poranka; **the ~ five years/weeks will be very important** następne pięć lat/tygodni będzie bardzo ważnych; **the ~ flight/prime minister** następny lot/premier; **~ time, be a bit more careful** następnym razem bądź trochę bardziej ostrożny; **who's ~?** kto następny?; **the week after ~** za dwa tygodnie; **~ to** (*beside*) obok *+gen*
next door *adv* w sąsiedztwie ▷ *adj* (*building, house, flat, room*) sąsiedni; **my mother lives ~ to her** moja matka mieszka w jej sąsiedztwie; **my ~ neighbour** mój sąsiad obok
NHS (*Brit*) *n abbr* (= *National Health Service*): **the ~** *państwowa służba zdrowia*
nice [naɪs] *adj* **1** (*good: time, holiday*) przyjemny; (*meal*) smaczny; (*weather*) ładny **2** (*person: likeable, friendly*) miły **3** (*lovely*) miły; **to look ~** (*person, place*) wyglądać ładnie; **it's ~ to see you** miło pana/panią widzieć
nickname [ˈnɪkneɪm] *n* przezwisko
niece [niːs] *n* (*brother's daughter*) bratanica; (*sister's daughter*) siostrzenica
night [naɪt] *n* **1** (*period of darkness*) noc **2** (*evening*) wieczór; **at ~** w nocy; (*in the evening*) wieczorem; **from nine o'clock at ~ until nine in the morning** od dziewiątej wieczorem do dziewiątej rano; **by ~** nocą; **in the middle of the ~** w środku nocy; **the ~ before sth** wieczór przed czymś; **the ~ before** poprzedniego wieczoru
nightclub [ˈnaɪtklʌb] *n* klub nocny
nightie [ˈnaɪtɪ] *n* koszula nocna
nightmare [ˈnaɪtmɛəʳ] *n* koszmar; **to have a ~** mieć zły sen; **the bus journey was a ~** podróż autobusem była koszmarem
nil [nɪl] *n* (*Brit: Sport*) zero; **they lost two ~ to Italy** przegrali dwa do zera z Włochami; **their chances of survival are ~** mają zerowe szanse na przetrwanie
nine [naɪn] *num* dziewięć; *see also* **five**
nineteen [ˈnaɪnˈtiːn] *num* dziewiętnaście; *see also* **fifteen**
nineteenth [naɪnˈtiːnθ] *num* dziewiętnasty; *see also* **fifth**
ninety [ˈnaɪntɪ] *num* dziewięćdziesiąt; *see also* **fifty**
ninth [naɪnθ] *num* **1** (*in series*) dziewiąty **2** (*fraction*) dziewiąta; *see also* **fifth**

KEYWORD

no [nəu] *adv* (*opposite of "yes"*) nie; **"did she see it?" — "no (she didn't)"** „widziała to?" — „nie (nie widziała tego)"; **no thank you, no thanks** nie, dziękuję
▷ *adj* (*not any*): **I have no milk/books** nie mam mleka/książek; **there's no other solution** nie ma innego rozwiązania; **"no smoking"** „zakaz palenia"; **no way!** nie ma mowy!

nobody [ˈnəubədɪ] *pron* nikt
nod [nɔd] *vi* (*to show agreement*) kiwać (kiwnąć *pf*) głową; **to ~ agreement to** przytakiwać (przytaknąć *pf*) *+dat*
▸ **nod off** (*inf*) *vi* przysypiać (przysnąć *pf*)
noise [nɔɪz] *n* **1** (*sound*) dźwięk **2** (*din*) hałas; **to make a ~** hałasować
noisy [ˈnɔɪzɪ] *adj* (*people, machine*) głośny; (*place*) hałaśliwy
nominate [ˈnɔmɪneɪt] *vt* (*propose: for job, award*) nominować; **to ~ sb/sth for sth** (*award, prize*) nominować kogoś/coś do czegoś
none [nʌn] *pron*: **~ of us/them** nikt z nas/nich; **I've ~ left** (*not any*) nic mi nie zostało; **there's ~ left** nic nie zostało; **~ at all** (*not any*) żaden
nonsense [ˈnɔnsəns] *n* (*rubbish*) nonsens
non-smoking [ˈnɔnˈsməukɪŋ] *adj* (*area, carriage*) dla niepalących

non-stop ['nɔn'stɔp] *adj* (*activity, music*) bez przerwy; (*flight*) bez międzylądowania ▷ *adv* **1** (*ceaselessly*) nieustannie **2** (*fly, drive*) bez przerwy
noodles ['nu:dlz] *n pl* kluski
noon [nu:n] *n* południe ▷ *adj* południowy; **at ~** w południe
no-one ['nəuwʌn] *pron* = **nobody**
nor [nɔ:ʳ] *conj* ani; **~ me!** ani ja!; *see also* **neither**
normal ['nɔ:məl] *adj* normalny; **to get back** *or* **return to ~** wracać (wrócić *pf*) do normy; **higher/worse than ~** powyżej normy/gorzej niż zwykle
normally ['nɔ:məlɪ] *adv* **1** (*usually*) zwykle **2** (*conventionally: act, behave*) normalnie; **to be working ~** pracować normalnie
north [nɔ:θ] *n* północ ▷ *adj* północny ▷ *adv* (*movement*) na północ; (*location*) na północy; **the ~ of France** północ Francji; **to the ~ of** na północ od *+gen*; **it's 15 miles or so ~ of Oxford** to jest około piętnaście mil na północ od Oksfordu
North America *n* Ameryka Północna
north-east [nɔ:θ'i:st] *n* północny wschód ▷ *adj* północno-wschodni ▷ *adv* (*movement*) na północny wschód; (*location*) na połnocnym wschodzie
northern ['nɔ:ðən] *adj* północny; **the ~ hemisphere** północna półkula
Northern Ireland *n* Irlandia Północna
North Korea *n* Korea Północna
North Pole *n*: **the ~** biegun północny
North Sea *n*: **the ~** Morze Północne
north-west [nɔ:θ'wɛst] *n* północny zachód ▷ *adj* północno-zachodni ▷ *adv* (*movement*) na północny zachód; (*location*) na północnym zachodzie
Norway ['nɔ:weɪ] *n* Norwegia
Norwegian [nɔ:'wi:dʒən] *adj* norweski ▷ *n* **1** (*person*) Norweg(-eżka) *m/f* **2** (*language*) norweski
nose [nəuz] *n* (*on face*) nos; **to poke** *or* **stick one's ~ into sth** (*inf*) wtrącać (wtrącić *pf*) się do czegoś
nosebleed ['nəuzbli:d] *n* krwawienie z nosa; **I often have ~s** często leci mi krew z nosa
nosy ['nəuzɪ] (*inf*) *adj* wścibski
not [nɔt] *adv* nie; **he is ~** *or* **isn't here** jego tu nie ma; **I do ~** *or* **don't want to go out tonight** nie chcę nigdzie wychodzić dziś wieczorem; **it's too late, isn't it?** jest za późno, prawda?; **he asked me ~ to do it** poprosił mnie, żebym tego nie robił; **are you coming or ~?** idzie pan/pani, czy nie?; **~ at all** (*in answer to question*) wcale nie; (*in answer to thanks*) nie ma za co; **~ yet** jeszcze nie; **~ now** nie teraz; **~ really** raczej nie
note [nəut] *n* **1** (*message, reminder*) notatka **2** (*Brit: banknote*) banknot **3** (*Mus: sound*) nuta ▷ *vt* (*observe*) zauważać (zauważyć *pf*); **notes** *n pl* (*from lecture*) notatki; **to make a ~ of sth** notować (zanotować *pf*) coś; **to take ~s** robić (zrobić *pf*) notatki; **to take ~ (of sth)** zauważać (zauważyć *pf*) (coś); **please ~ that...** proszę zauważyć, że...
notebook ['nəutbuk] *n* **1** notes **2** (*Comput*) notatnik
notepad ['nəutpæd] *n* notes
nothing ['nʌθɪŋ] *pron* (*not anything*) nic; **I pressed the button but ~ happened** nacisnąłem przycisk, ale nic się nie stało; **~ new/serious** nic nowego/poważnego; **there's ~ to worry about** nie ma się czym martwić; **~ much** nic takiego; **~ else** nic innego; **for ~** (*free*) za nic; (*in vain*) na próżno; **~ at all** absolutnie nic; **~ but** nic oprócz *+gen*
notice ['nəutɪs] *vt* (*observe*) zauważać (zauważyć *pf*) ▷ *n* **1** (*sign*) ogłoszenie **2** (*warning*) zawiadomienie; **to ~ that...** zauważać (zauważyć *pf*), że...; **to bring sth to sb's ~** zwracać (zwrócić *pf*) czyjąś uwagę na coś; **to take no ~ of sb/sth** nie zwracać (zwrócić *pf*) na kogoś/coś uwagi; **to give sb ~ of sth** zawiadamiać (zawiadomić *pf*) kogoś o czymś; **without ~** bez uprzedzenia; **at short ~** z krótkim wyprzedzeniem; **to hand in** *or* **give in one's ~** składać (złożyć *pf*) wymówienie

noticeboard ['nəutɪsbɔːd] (*Brit*) *n* tablica ogłoszeniowa; **on the ~** na tablicy ogłoszeniowej
notification [nəutɪfɪ'keɪʃən] *n* (*Comput*) powiadomienie
nought [nɔːt] (*esp Brit*) *num* zero
noun [naun] *n* rzeczownik
novel ['nɔvl] *n* powieść
novelist ['nɔvəlɪst] *n* powieściopisarz(-rka) *m/f*
November [nəu'vɛmbəʳ] *n* listopad; *see also* **July**
now [nau] *adv* **1** (*at the present time*) teraz **2** (*these days*) obecnie **3** (*under the circumstances*) teraz **4** (*specifying length of time*): **it has been five weeks ~ since I saw him** minęło już pięć tygodni, od kiedy go ostatnio widziałem ▷ *conj*: **~ (that)** skoro już; **right ~** w tej chwili; **by ~** do tej pory; **just ~** (*at the moment*) w tej chwili; **from ~ on** od tej chwili; **in 3 days from ~** za trzy dni; **between ~ and Monday** do poniedziałku; **that's all for ~** to by było na tyle; **any day/time ~** lada dzień/chwila
nowhere ['nəuwɛəʳ] *adv* (*no place: emphatic*) nigdzie; **~ else** (*no place else: emphatic*) nigdzie indziej; **this is getting us ~** to nigdzie nas nie zaprowadzi
nuclear ['njuːklɪəʳ] *adj* nuklearny
nuisance ['njuːsns] *n* (*person*) uciążliwa osoba; **to be a ~** (*thing*) być uciążliwym
numb [nʌm] *adj* zdrętwiały
number ['nʌmbəʳ] *n* **1** (*Math*) liczba **2** (*telephone number*) numer telefonu **3** (*of house, bank account, bus*) numer **4** (*quantity: of things, people*) ilość ▷ *vt* (*pages*) numerować (ponumerować *pf*); **a ~ of** (*several*) kilka *+gen*; **a large/small ~ of** duża/mała ilość *+gen*
number plate (*Brit*) *n* tablica rejestracyjna
Number Ten (*Brit*) *n* (*10 Downing Street*) *Downing Street numer 10 (siedziba premiera Wielkiej Brytanii)*
nun [nʌn] *n* zakonnica
nurse [nəːs] *n* (*in hospital*) pielęgniarz(-ka) *m/f* ▷ *vt* (*patient*) opiekować (zaopiekować *pf*) się *+inst*
nursery ['nəːsərɪ] *n* **1** (*kindergarten*) przedszkole **2** (*garden centre*) szkółka
nursery school *n* przedszkole
nut [nʌt] *n* **1** (*Bot, Culin*) orzech **2** (*Tech*) nakrętka
nylon ['naɪlɔn] *n* nylon ▷ *adj* (*shirt, sheets*) nylonowy

oak [əuk] *n* dąb
oar [ɔːʳ] *n* wiosło
oats [əuts] *n pl* owies *m sg*
obedient [əˈbiːdɪənt] *adj* (*child, dog*) posłuszny
obese [əˈbiːs] *adj* otyły
obey [əˈbeɪ] *vt* (*person*) być posłusznym *+dat*; (*orders*) wykonywać (wykonać *pf*); (*law, regulations*) przestrzegać *+gen* ▷ *vi* podporządkowywać (podporządkować *pf*) się
object [*n* ˈɔbdʒɛkt, *vb* əbˈdʒɛkt] *n* **1** (*thing*) przedmiot **2** (*aim, purpose*) cel **3** (*Ling*) dopełnienie ▷ *vi* sprzeciwiać (sprzeciwić *pf*) się *+dat*
objection [əbˈdʒɛkʃən] *n* sprzeciw
oblige [əˈblaɪdʒ] *vt* (*compel*): **to ~ sb to do sth** zobowiązywać (zobowiązać *pf*) kogoś do zrobienia czegoś
oboe [ˈəubəu] *n* obój
obsess [əbˈsɛs] *vt*: **to be ~ed by** *or* **with sb/sth** mieć obsesję na punkcie kogoś/czegoś
obsession [əbˈsɛʃən] *n* obsesja
obtain [əbˈteɪn] (*formal*) *vt* (*information, degree etc*) uzyskiwać (uzyskać *pf*); (*book*) otrzymywać (otrzymać *pf*)
obvious [ˈɔbvɪəs] *adj* oczywisty
obviously [ˈɔbvɪəslɪ] *adv* **1** (*of course*) oczywiście **2** (*noticeably*) wyraźnie
occasion [əˈkeɪʒən] *n* **1** (*point in time*) okazja **2** (*event, celebration*) wydarzenie **3** (*opportunity*): **an ~ for sth/for doing sth** okazja do czegoś/do zrobienia czegoś
occasionally [əˈkeɪʒənəlɪ] *adv* czasami
occupation [ɔkjuˈpeɪʃən] *n* (*job*) zawód
occupy [ˈɔkjupaɪ] *vt* **1** (*inhabit*) zajmować (zająć *pf*) **2**: **to be occupied** (*seat, place etc*) być zajętym **3** (*take possession of*) okupować **4** (*take up*) zajmować (zająć *pf*) **5** (*fill: time*) zajmować (zająć *pf*)
occur [əˈkəːʳ] *vi* (*happen*) zdarzać (zdarzyć *pf*) się; **to ~ to sb** wydarzać (wydarzyć *pf*) się komuś
ocean [ˈəuʃən] *n* ocean
o'clock [əˈklɔk] *adv*: **six ~** godzina szósta; **it is nine o'clock** jest (godzina) dziewiąta
October [ɔkˈtəubəʳ] *n* październik; *see also* **July**
octopus [ˈɔktəpəs] *n* ośmiornica
odd [ɔd] *adj* **1** (*strange*) dziwny **2** (*not paired*): **he was wearing ~ socks** miał skarpetki nie do pary **3** (*number*) nieparzysty; *see also* **odds**
odour [ˈəudəʳ] (*US* **odor**) *n* zapach

 **KEYWORD**

of [ɔv, əv] *prep* **1** od *+gen*, ode *+gen*, z *+gen*, ze *+gen*; **that was nice of him!** to było miłe z jego strony!; **the history of China** historia Chin; **at the end of the street** na końcu ulicy; **the city of New York** miasto Nowy Jork
2 (*expressing quantity, amount*): **a kilo of flour** kilogram mąki; **a cup of tea/vase of flowers** filiżanka herbaty/wazon kwiatów; **there were three of them** było ich trzech; **can one of you help?** ktoś z was może pomóc?; **an annual income of less than 30,000 pounds** roczny dochód poniżej 30.000 funtów
3 (*made of*) z *+gen*, ze *+gen*; **made of wood** zrobiony z drewna
4 (*in dates*): **the 5th of July** piąty lipca
5 (*US*: *in times*): **at quarter of three** za kwadrans trzecia

KEYWORD

off [ɔf] *adj* **1** (*not turned on*) wyłączony **2** (*cancelled*) odwołany
▷ *adv* **1** (*away*): **I must be off** muszę iść; **where are you off to?** dokąd pan/pani idzie?; **it's a long way off** (*in distance*) to daleko stąd; **my holiday is a long way off** do moich wakacji jest jeszcze daleko
2 (*not at work*): **to be off** (*on holiday*) mieć wolne; (*due to illness*) być na zwolnieniu; **to have a day off** (*as holiday*) mieć dzień wolnego; (*because ill*) być na zwolnieniu jeden dzień
3 (*Comm*): **10% off** zniżka dziesięć procent
▷ *prep* **1** (*indicating motion, removal etc*): **to take a picture off the wall** zdejmować (zdjąć *pf*) obraz ze ściany
2 (*distant from*): **it's just off the motorway** tuż przy autostradzie

offence [ə'fɛns] (*US* **offense**) *n* (*crime*) przestępstwo
offend [ə'fɛnd] *vt* (*upset*) obrażać (obrazić *pf*)
offense [ə'fɛns] (*US*) *n* = **offence**
offer ['ɔfəʳ] *vt* **1** (*product, making invitation*) oferować (zaoferować *pf*); (*seat, cigarette etc*) proponować (zaproponować *pf*) **2** (*bid: money*) oferować (zaoferować *pf*) ▷ *n* **1** (*proposal*) oferta **2** (*special deal*) promocja
office ['ɔfɪs] *n* **1** (*room*) biuro **2** (*department*): **the Foreign O~** Ministerstwo Spraw Zagranicznych **3** (*US: of doctor, dentist*) gabinet
office block *n* biurowiec
officer ['ɔfɪsəʳ] *n* **1** (*Mil*) oficer **2** (*also*: **police ~**) policjant(ka) *m/f*
office worker *n* urzędnik(-iczka) *m/f*
official [ə'fɪʃl] *adj* oficjalny
off-licence ['ɔflaɪsns] (*Brit*) *n* (*shop*) monopolowy
offside ['ɔf'saɪd] *adj*: **to be ~** (*Sport*) być na spalonym
often ['ɔfn] *adv* (*frequently*) często; **how ~ do you wash the car?** jak często pan/pani myje samochód?; **I wash up twice as ~ as them** *or* **as they do** zmywam dwa razy częściej niż oni *lub* od nich
oil [ɔɪl] *n* (*in cooking*) olej; (*petroleum*) ropa ▷ *vt* (*engine, machine*) oliwić (naoliwić *pf*)
oil rig *n* (*on land*) szyb naftowy; (*at sea*) platforma wiertnicza
ointment ['ɔɪntmənt] *n* maść
okay [əu'keɪ] (*inf*) *adj* **1** (*acceptable*) do przyjęcia **2** (*safe and well*) w porządku ▷ *adv* (*acceptably*) w porządku ▷ *excl* zgoda; **are you ~?** (*familiar*) wszystko u ciebie w porządku?; (*polite*) wszystko u pana/pani w porządku?; **it's ~ with** *or* **by me** pasuje mi
old [əuld] *adj* **1** stary **2** (*long-standing*) dawny; **how ~ are you?** ile ma pan/pani lat?; **he's 8 years ~** on ma osiem lat; **~er brother/~er sister** starszy brat/starsza siostra
old age pensioner (*Brit*) *n* (*senior citizen*) emeryt(ka) *m/f*
old-fashioned ['əuld'fæʃnd] *adj* (*object*) staromodny; (*custom, idea*) staroświecki; (*person*) starej daty
olive ['ɔlɪv] *n* (*fruit*) oliwka ▷ *adj* (*also*: **~-green**) oliwkowy
olive oil *n* oliwa z oliwek
Olympic® [əu'lɪmpɪk] *adj* olimpijski; **the Olympics**® *n pl* igrzyska olimpijskie
omelette ['ɔmlɪt] (*US* **omelet**) *n* omlet

KEYWORD

on [ɔn] *prep* **1** (*indicating position*) na *+loc*; **it's on the table/wall** jest na stole/na ścianie; **the house is on the main road** dom stoi przy głównej ulicy; **on the left/right** na lewo/prawo; **on the top floor** na najwyższym piętrze
2 (*indicating means, method, condition etc*): **on foot** pieszo; **I'm on the train/bus** jestem w pociągu/autobusie; **on the television/radio** w telewizji/radio; **on the internet** w internecie; **to be on antibiotics** brać antybiotyki
3 (*referring to time*) w; **on Friday** w piątek; **on Fridays** w piątki; **on Friday, June 20th** w piątek 20 czerwca

4 (*about, concerning*) o +*loc*, na temat +*gen*; **information on train services** informacje na temat połączeń kolejowych
▷ *adv* **1** (*clothes*): **to have one's coat on** mieć na sobie płaszcz; **what's she got on?** co ona ma na sobie?
2 (*covering, lid etc*): **screw the lid on tightly** dokręcić mocno wieczko
▷ *adj* **1** (*turned on*) włączony
2 (*happening*): **is the meeting still on?** czy spotkanie się odbędzie?; **there's a good film on at the cinema** w kinie grają dobry film

once [wʌns] *adv* **1** (*one time only*) raz **2** (*at one time*) kiedyś **3** (*on one occasion*) jeden raz ▷ *conj* (*as soon as*) zaraz po tym jak; **at ~** (*immediately*) natychmiast; **~ a** *or* **every month** raz na miesiąc; **~ upon a time** (*in stories*) dawno dawno temu; (*in the past*) pewnego razu; **~ in a while** raz na jakiś czas; **~ or twice** (*a few times*) raz czy dwa

KEYWORD

one [wʌn] *adj* **1** (*number*) jeden; **he's one year old** on ma rok; **it's one o'clock** jest pierwsza godzina; **one hundred/thousand children** sto/tysiąc dzieci; **there will be one or two changes** będzie jedna lub dwie zmiany
2 (*same*) jeden; **shall I put it all on the one plate?** czy mam to wszystko położyć na jeden talerz?
▷ *pron* **1** (*number*) jeden; **I've already got one** już mam jeden; **one of them** jeden z nich; **one of the chairs** jedno z krzeseł; **one by one** pojedynczo
2 (*with adj*): **I've already got a red one** mam już czerwony
3 (*in generalizations*): **what can one do?** co można zrobić?; **to cut one's finger** kaleczyć (skaleczyć *pf*) się w palec; **to cut one's hair** obcinać (obciąć *pf*) sobie włosy; **this one** ten; **that one** tamten; **one another** nawzajem; **they love one another** kochają się; **one never knows** nigdy nie wiadomo
▷ *n* (*numeral*) jeden

oneself *pron* (*gen, acc*) siebie; (*dat, loc*) sobie; (*inst*) sobą; (*reflexive pronoun*) się; **to talk to ~** mówić do siebie; **to hurt ~** kaleczyć (skaleczyć *pf*) się; **by ~** (*alone*) sam

one-way ['wʌnweɪ] *adj* **1** (*street, traffic*) jednokierunkowy **2** (*ticket, trip*) w jedną stronę

onion ['ʌnjən] *n* cebula

online, on-line ['ɔnlaɪn] (*Comput*) *adj* (*person, computer*) online ▷ *adv* online, w sieci; **to go ~** (*person*) podłączyć się do sieci

only ['əunlɪ] *adv* tylko ▷ *adj* (*sole*) jedyny ▷ *conj* (*but*) tylko; **I was ~ joking** tylko żartowałem; **I saw her ~ last week** widziałem ją zaledwie w zeszłym tygodniu; **not ~... but (also)...** nie tylko... ale również...; **an ~ child** jedynak(-aczka) *m/f*

onto, on to ['ɔntu] *prep* na +*loc*, do +*gen*; **he put the book ~ the shelf** położył książkę na półce; **to get ~ a bus/train/plane** wsiadać (wsiąść *pf*) do autobusu/pociągu/samolotu

onwards ['ɔnwədz] *adv* dalej; **from that time ~** od tamtego czasu

open ['əupn] *adj* otwarty ▷ *vt* (*door, book, eyes*) otwierać (otworzyć *pf*) ▷ *vi* (*door, lid*) otwierać (otworzyć *pf*) się; **in the ~ air** na świeżym powietrzu

opener ['əupnə^r] *n* (*also*: **bottle ~**) otwieracz

opening hours ['əupnɪŋ-] *n pl* godziny otwarcia

open-minded [əupn'maɪndɪd] *adj* bez uprzedzeń

OPEN UNIVERSITY

Open University – Uniwersytet Otwarty został założony w 1969 roku. Jego specyfika polega na studiowaniu drogą korespondencyjną. Nauczanie odbywa się za pomocą książek materiałów audio, płyt DVD oraz internetu, organizowane są również szkoły letnie.

opera ['ɔpərə] *n* opera

operate ['ɔpəreɪt] *vt* (*machine, vehicle, system*) obsługiwać;

(*company, organization*) prowadzić (poprowadzić *pf*) ▷ *vi* **1** (*machine, vehicle, system*) działać; (*company, organization*) prowadzić (poprowadzić *pf*) działalność **2** (*Med*) operować (zoperować *pf*); **to ~ on sb** (*Med*) operować (zoperować *pf*) kogoś
operation [ɔpə'reɪʃən] *n* operacja; **to have an ~** (*Med*) mieć operację
operator ['ɔpəreɪtəʳ] *n* (*Tel*) telefonista(-ka) *m/f*
opinion [ə'pɪnjən] *n* opinia; **in my/her ~** moim/jej zdaniem
opinion poll *n* badanie opinii publicznej
opponent [ə'pəunənt] *n* przeciwnik(-iczka) *m/f*
opportunity [ɔpə'tju:nɪtɪ] *n* okazja; **to take the ~ of doing sth** *or* **to do sth** korzystać (skorzystać *pf*) z okazji, żeby coś zrobić
oppose [ə'pəuz] *vt* (*person, idea*) sprzeciwiać (sprzeciwić *pf*) się *+dat*; **to be ~d to sth** być przeciwko czemuś
opposite ['ɔpəzɪt] *adj* **1** (*facing: side, house*) przeciwny **2** (*farthest: end, corner*) przeciwległy **3** (*contrary: meaning, direction*) przeciwny ▷ *adv* (*live, work, sit*) naprzeciwko ▷ *prep* (*across from*) naprzeciw *+gen* ▷ *n*: **the ~** przeciwieństwo; **the ~ sex** płeć przeciwna
opposition [ɔpə'zɪʃən] *n* (*resistance: military*) opór; (*objection, lack of agreement*) sprzeciw
optician [ɔp'tɪʃən] *n* **1** (*person*) optyk(-yczka) *m/f* **2** (*also*: **~'s**) zakład optyczny
optimistic [ɔptɪ'mɪstɪk] *adj* optymistyczny
option ['ɔpʃən] *n* **1** (*choice*) opcja; (*possibility*) możliwość **2** (*Scol, Univ*) przedmiot nadobowiązkowy
or [ɔ:ʳ] *conj* **1** (*linking alternatives*) albo **2** (*also*: **or else**) bo inaczej
oral ['ɔ:rəl] *adj* (*test, report*) ustny ▷ *n* (*spoken examination*) egzamin ustny
orange ['ɔrɪndʒ] *n* (*fruit*) pomarańcza ▷ *adj* (*in colour*) pomarańczowy
orange juice ['ɔrɪndʒdʒu:s] *n* sok pomarańczowy
orchard ['ɔ:tʃəd] *n* sad
orchestra ['ɔ:kɪstrə] *n* orkiestra
order ['ɔ:dəʳ] *n* **1** (*command*) rozkaz **2** (*in restaurant*) zamówienie **3** (*sequence*) porządek ▷ *vt* **1** (*command*) kazać (rozkazać *pf*) *+dat* **2** (*in restaurant, shop*) zamawiać (zamówić *pf*) ▷ *vi* (*in restaurant*) składać (złożyć *pf*) zamówienie; **in alphabetical ~** w kolejności alfabetycznej; **out of ~** (*not working*) awaria; **in ~ to do sth** żeby coś robić (zrobić *pf*); **to ~ sb to do sth** rozkazywać (rozkazać *pf*) komuś, żeby coś zrobił
▶ **order around, order about** *vt* dyrygować *+inst*
ordinary ['ɔ:dnrɪ] *adj* (*everyday*) zwykły
organ ['ɔ:gən] *n* **1** (*Anat*) organ **2** (*Mus*) organy *m pl*
organic [ɔ:'gænɪk] *adj* **1** (*food, farming*) naturalny **2** (*substance*) organiczny
organization [ɔ:gənaɪ'zeɪʃən] *n* organizacja
organize ['ɔ:gənaɪz] *vt* organizować (zorganizować *pf*)
original [ə'rɪdʒɪnl] *adj* **1** (*first, earliest*) pierwotny **2** (*authentic*) oryginalny **3** (*imaginative*) oryginalny
originally [ə'rɪdʒɪnəlɪ] *adv* (*at first*) początkowo
ornament ['ɔ:nəmənt] *n* ozdoba
orphan ['ɔ:fn] *n* sierota
other ['ʌðəʳ] *adj* **1** (*additional*) jeszcze jeden **2** (*not this one*) inny **3**: **the ~...** (*of two things or people*) ten drugi... **4** (*apart from oneself*) inny ▷ *pron* **1** (*additional one, different one*) drugi **2** (*of two things or people*): **the ~** ten drugi; **the ~ day** (*inf: recently*) wczoraj; **the ~ week** tydzień temu
otherwise ['ʌðəwaɪz] *adv* **1** (*if not*) w przeciwnym razie **2** (*apart from that*) poza tym
otter ['ɔtəʳ] *n* wydra
ought [ɔ:t] (*pt* **ought**) *aux vb* **1** (*indicating advisability*): **she ~ to see a doctor** powinna pójść do lekarza **2** (*indicating likelihood*): **he ~ to be there now** powinien tam teraz być

our ['auə^{r}] *adj* (*m sg*) nasz; (*f sg*) nasza; (*nt sg*) nasze; (*pl vir*) nasi; (*pl non-vir*) nasze; (*referring to subject of sentence*) swój; **~ apartment** nasze mieszkanie

ours [auəz] *pron*: **a friend of ~** nasz przyjaciel; **that book is ~** ta książka jest nasza ; **this is ~** to jest nasze

ourselves [auə'sɛlvz] *pl pron* (*gen, acc*) siebie; (*dat, loc*) sobie; (*inst*) sobą; (*reflexive pronoun*) się; **we didn't hurt ~** nie skaleczyliśmy się; **by ~** (*unaided, alone*: *vir*) sami; (*non-vir*) same; **we were left by ~** zostawiono nas samych

KEYWORD

out [aut] *adv* **1** (*outside*) na zewnątrz; **out here/there** tutaj/tam
2 (*absent, not in*) nie ma *+gen*; **Mr Green is out at the moment** Pana Greena nie ma w tej chwili; **to have a day/night out** spędzać (spędzić *pf*) dzień/wieczór poza domem; **the ball was out** piłka była na aucie
▷ *adj*: **to be out** (*out of game*) być wyeliminowanym; (*extinguished*) być zgaszonym
▷ *prep*: **out of 1** (*outside*: *with movement*) z *+gen*, ze *+gen*; (*beyond*) poza; **to go/come out of the house** wychodzić (wyjść *pf*) z domu
2 (*from among*: *ratio*) na; **one out of every three smokers** jeden na trzech palaczy
3 (*without*): **we are out of milk/petrol** nie mamy mleka/benzyny

outdoor [aut'dɔː^{r}] *adj* na powietrzu

outdoors [aut'dɔːz] *adv* na dworze

outer space *n* przestrzeń kosmiczna

outfit ['autfɪt] *n* strój

outing ['autɪŋ] *n* (*excursion*) wycieczka

outlet ['autlɛt] *n* **1** (*hole, pipe*) odpływ **2** (*US*: *Elec*) gniazdko

outline ['autlaɪn] *n* zarys

outside [aut'saɪd] *n* (*exterior*) na zewnątrz ▷ *adj* (*exterior*) zewnętrzny ▷ *adv* na zewnątrz ▷ *prep* **1** (*on the outside of*) na zewnątrz *+gen*; (*from outside of*) z zewnątrz *+gen* **2** (*near to*: *larger place*) koło *+gen*

outskirts ['autskəːts] *n pl*: **the ~** peryferie; **on the ~ of...** na peryferiach *+gen*...

outstanding [aut'stændɪŋ] *adj* **1** (*excellent*) wybitny **2** (*obvious*: *example*) znakomity

oval ['əuvl] *adj* owalny

oven ['ʌvn] *n* piekarnik

over ['əuvə^{r}] *adj* (*finished*) zakończony
▷ *prep* **1** (*more than*) ponad *+inst*; **over 200 people came** przyszło ponad dwieście osób
2 (*indicating position*: *above, on top of*) nad *+inst*; (*spanning*) ponad *+inst*; (*across*) ponad *+inst*; (*on the other side of*) po drugiej stronie *+gen*; **a bridge over the river** most nad rzeką
3 (*during*) podczas *+gen*; **we talked about it over dinner** rozmawialiśmy o tym podczas obiadu
4 (*recovered from*: *illness, shock, trauma*) po *+loc*; **he's returned to work and is over his illness** wrócił do pracy i jest już po chorobie
5: **all over the town/house** po całym mieście/mieszkaniu
▷ *adv* **1** (*across*) przez; **over here/there** tutaj/tam
2 (*more, above*): **people aged 65 and over** osoby w wieku lat sześćdziesięciu pięciu i starsze
3 (*in expressions*): **all over** (*everywhere*) wszędzie

overcast ['əuvəkɑːst] *adj* zachmurzony

overdose ['əuvədəus] *n* nadmierna dawka

overdraft ['əuvədrɑːft] *n* debet

overseas [əuvə'siːz] *adv* za granicą ▷ *adj* (*foreign*) zagraniczny

overtake [əuvə'teɪk] (*pt* **overtook**, *pp* **overtaken**) *vt* (*esp Brit*: *Aut*) wyprzedzać (wyprzedzić *pf*)

overtime ['əuvətaɪm] *n* nadgodziny *f pl*

overtook [əuvə'tuk] *pt of* **overtake**

overweight [əuvə'weɪt] *adj* (*person*) z nadwagą

owe [əu] *vt*: **to ~ sb sth** być winnym komuś coś
owing to ['əuɪŋ-] *prep* (*because of*) z powodu *+gen*
owl [aul] *n* sowa
own [əun] *adj* własny ▷ *vt* (*possess*) posiadać; **a room of my ~** mój własny pokój; **on one's ~** sam; **she lived on her ~** mieszkała sama
▶ **own up** *vi* (*confess*) przyznawać (przyznać *pf*) się
owner ['əunə^r] *n* właściciel(ka) *m/f*
ox [ɔks] (*pl* **oxen**) *n* wół
oxygen ['ɔksɪdʒən] *n* tlen
oyster ['ɔɪstə^r] *n* ostryga
ozone layer *n* warstwa ozonowa

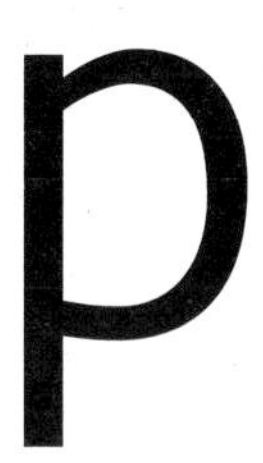

Pacific [pə'sɪfɪk] *n*: **the ~ (Ocean)** Pacyfik
pacifier ['pæsɪfaɪə^r] (*US*) *n* (*for sucking*) smoczek
pack [pæk] *vt* pakować (spakować *pf*) ▷ *vi* pakować (spakować *pf*) się ▷ *n* (*of cards*) talia; **~ it in!** (*stop it!*) przestań!
▶ **pack up** *vi* (*Brit*: *put things away*) pakować (spakować *pf*) się
package ['pækɪdʒ] *n* **1** (*parcel*) paczka **2** (*Comput*) pakiet
packed [pækt] *adj* (*crowded*) zatłoczony
packed lunch (*Brit*) *n* drugie śniadanie
packet ['pækɪt] *n* paczka
pad [pæd] *n* (*of paper*) blok
paddle ['pædl] *n* **1** (*for canoe*) wiosło **2** (*US*: *for table tennis*) rakietka ▷ *vt* (*boat, canoe*) wiosłować *+inst*
padlock ['pædlɔk] *n* kłódka
paedophile ['pi:dəufaɪl] (*US* **pedophile**) *n* pedofil(ka) *m/f*
page [peɪdʒ] *n* (*of book etc*) strona
pain [peɪn] *n* **1** (*physical*) ból **2** (*inf*: *nuisance*): **to be a ~ (in the neck)** sprawiać (sprawić *pf*) kłopot; **to have a ~ in one's chest/arm** odczuwać ból w klatce piersiowej/w ręce; **to be in ~** odczuwać ból; **what a ~!** (*inf*) co za cholerstwo!
painful ['peɪnful] *adj* bolesny
painkiller ['peɪnkɪlə^r] *n* środek przeciwbólowy

paint [peɪnt] *n* farba ▹ *vt* **1** (*decorate*) malować (pomalować *pf*) **2** (*portray*) malować (namalować *pf*) **3** (*create: picture, portrait*) malować (namalować *pf*) ▹ *vi* (*creatively*) malować (namalować *pf*); **a tin of ~** puszka farby; **to ~ sth blue/white** malować (pomalować *pf*) coś na niebiesko/na biało

paintbrush ['peɪntbrʌʃ] *n* pędzel

painter ['peɪntəʳ] *n* malarz(-rka) *m/f*

painting ['peɪntɪŋ] *n* **1** (*activity: artistic*) malarstwo; (*decorating walls, doors*) malowanie **2** (*picture*) obraz

pair [pɛəʳ] *n* para; **a ~ of scissors** nożyczki *m pl*; **a ~ of trousers** para spodni; **in ~s** w parach

pajamas [pə'dʒɑːməz] (*US*) *n pl* = **pyjamas**

Pakistan [pɑːkɪ'stɑːn] *n* Pakistan

Pakistani [pɑːkɪ'stɑːnɪ] *adj* pakistański ▹ *n* Pakistańczyk(-anka) *m/f*

palace ['pæləs] *n* pałac

pale [peɪl] *adj* **1** (*colour*) jasny **2** (*fair: skin, complexion*) jasny **3** (*from sickness, fear*) blady; **~ blue/pink** jasnoniebieski/jasnoróżowy

Palestine ['pælɪstaɪn] *n* Palestyna

palm [pɑːm] *n* **1** (*also:* **~ tree**) palma **2** (*of hand*) dłoń

pan [pæn] *n* **1** (*also:* **sauce~**) garnek **2** (*US: for baking*) forma

pancake ['pænkeɪk] *n* naleśnik

panda ['pændə] *n* panda

panic ['pænɪk] *n* **1** (*anxiety*) lęk **2** (*scare*) panika ▹ *vi* (*person, crowd*) wpadać (wpaść *pf*) w panikę

panther ['pænθəʳ] *n* pantera

PANTOMIME

Pantomime – W Wielkiej Brytanii mianem pantomimy (**pantomime**) określa się komedie teatralne z muzyką, oparte na popularnych bajkach, takich jak Kopciuszek albo Kot w butach. Adresowane głównie do dzieci, pantomimy wystawiane są w teatrach w okresie świąt Bożego Narodzenia.

pants [pænts] *n pl* **1** (*Brit: underwear*) majtki **2** (*US: trousers*) spodnie

pantyhose ['pæntɪhəuz] (*US*) *n pl* rajstopy; **a pair of ~** para rajstop

paper ['peɪpəʳ] *n* **1** papier **2** (*also:* **news~**) gazeta **3** (*wallpaper*) tapeta; **a piece of ~** (*odd bit*) kawałek papieru; (*sheet*) kartka papieru

paperback ['peɪpəbæk] *n* książka w miękkiej oprawie

paper clip *n* spinacz

parachute ['pærəʃuːt] *n* spadochron

parade [pə'reɪd] *n* parada

paradise ['pærədaɪs] *n* raj

paragraph ['pærəgrɑːf] *n* akapit

parallel ['pærəlɛl] *adj* równoległy

paralysed ['pærəlaɪzd] (*US* **paralyzed**) *adj* (*Med*) sparaliżowany

paramedic [pærə'mɛdɪk] *n* ratownik(-iczka) *m/f* medyczny(-na)

parcel ['pɑːsl] *n* (*package*) paczka

pardon ['pɑːdn] *n*: **(I beg your) ~?**, **~ me?** (*US: what did you say?*) przepraszam, niedosłyszałem?

parent ['pɛərənt] *n* rodzic; **parents** *n pl* rodzice

park [pɑːk] *n* (*public garden*) park ▹ *vt* parkować (zaparkować *pf*) ▹ *vi* parkować (zaparkować *pf*)

parking ['pɑːkɪŋ] *n* parkowanie; **"no ~"** „zakaz parkowania"

parking lot (*US*) *n* parking

parking meter *n* parkomat

parking ticket *n* mandat za nieprawidłowe parkowanie

parliament ['pɑːləmənt] (*Brit*) *n* parlament

parole [pə'rəul] *n* zwolnienie warunkowe

parrot ['pærət] *n* papuga

parsley ['pɑːslɪ] *n* natka pietruszki

part [pɑːt] *n* **1** (*section, division*) część **2** (*of machine, vehicle*) część **3** (*role*) rola; **to take ~ in** (*participate in*) brać (wziąć *pf*) udział w *+loc*

▸ **part with** *vt fus* oddawać (oddać *pf*)

participate [pɑː'tɪsɪpeɪt] *vi* brać (wziąć *pf*) udział; **to ~ in sth** (*activity, discussion*) brać (wziąć *pf*) udział w czymś

particular [pə'tɪkjuləʳ] *adj* **1** (*specific*) konkretny **2** (*great*)

szczególny; **particulars** *n pl* (*details*) szczegóły; (*name, address etc*) szczegółowe dane
particularly [pə'tɪkjuləlɪ] *adv* (*difficult, good, badly*) szczególnie; (*like, dislike, want*) wyjątkowo
partly ['pɑːtlɪ] *adv* (*to some extent*) częściowo
partner ['pɑːtnəʳ] *n* partner(ka) *m/f* ▷ *vt* (*person: at dance*) partnerować *+dat*
part-time ['pɑːt'taɪm] *adj* (*work, course*) w niepełnym wymiarze godzin; (*staff*) zatrudniony w niepełnym wymiarze godzin ▷ *adv* (*work, study*) na pół etatu; **~ student** student(ka) *m/f* zaoczny(-na)
party ['pɑːtɪ] *n* **1** (*Pol*) partia **2** (*social event*) przyjęcie; **birthday ~** przyjęcie urodzinowe
pass [pɑːs] *vt* **1** (*hand*): **to ~ sb sth** podawać (podać *pf*) coś komuś **2** (*go past: place, person*) mijać (minąć *pf*) **3** (*exam, test*) zdać (*pf*) **4** (*Sport*): **to ~ sb the ball** podawać (podać *pf*) komuś piłkę ▷ *vi* **1** (*go past: vehicles, people*) mijać (minąć *pf*) się **2** (*in exam*) zdać (*pf*); **to get a ~ (in sth)** (*Scol, Univ*) zdać (*pf*) egzamin z (czegoś)
▸ **pass away** *vi* (*die*) umrzeć (*pf*)
▸ **pass on** *vt*: **to ~ sth on (to sb)** (*news, information, message*) przekazywać (przekazać *pf*) coś (komuś)
▸ **pass out** *vi* (*faint*) mdleć (zemdleć *pf*)
passage ['pæsɪdʒ] *n* **1** (*corridor*) korytarz **2** (*in book, speech, piece of music*) ustęp
passenger ['pæsɪndʒəʳ] *n* pasażer(ka) *m/f*
passion ['pæʃən] *n* namiętność
passive ['pæsɪv] *adj* (*person, attitude*) bierny ▷ *n*: **the ~** (*Ling*) strona bierna
passport ['pɑːspɔːt] *n* **1** paszport **2** (*fig*): **a** *or* **the ~ to** klucz do *+gen*
password ['pɑːswəːd] *n* hasło
past [pɑːst] *prep* (*in front of*) obok *+gen*; (*beyond*) za *+inst*; (*later than*) po *+loc* ▷ *adv* (*by*): **to go/walk ~** przechodzić (przejść *pf*) ▷ *adj* (*previous*) poprzedni; (*week, month, year*) zeszły ▷ *n*: **the ~** przeszłość; (*tense*) czas przeszły; **it's ~ midnight** jest po północy; **ten/(a) quarter ~ eight** dziesięć/kwadrans po ósmej; **for the ~ few/3 days** przez ostatnie kilka/trzy dni; **the ~ tense** czas przeszły; **in the ~** (*before now*) w przeszłości; (*in the past tense*) w czasie przeszłym
pasta ['pæstə] *n* makaron
pasteurized ['pæstʃəraɪzd] *adj* pasteryzowany
pastry ['peɪstrɪ] *n* **1** (*dough*) ciasto **2** (*cake*) ciastko
patch [pætʃ] *n* **1** (*piece of material*) łata **2** (*area*) płat
path [pɑːθ] *n* (*track*) droga; (*in garden*) ścieżka
pathetic [pə'θɛtɪk] *adj* (*excuse, effort, attempt*) żałosny
patience ['peɪʃns] *n* cierpliwość
patient ['peɪʃnt] *n* (*Med*) pacjent(ka) *m/f* ▷ *adj* (*person*) cierpliwy
patio ['pætɪəu] *n* patio
patrol [pə'trəul] *vt* (*city, streets, area*) patrolować (spatrolować *pf*); **to be on ~** pójść na patrol
pattern ['pætən] *n* wzór
pause [pɔːz] *n* (*temporary halt*) przerwa ▷ *vi* robić (zrobić *pf*) przerwę
pavement ['peɪvmənt] *n* (*Brit*) chodnik
paw [pɔː] *n* łapa
pay [peɪ] (*pt, pp* **paid**) *n* (*wage, salary*) pensja ▷ *vt* **1** (*debt, bill, tax*) płacić (zapłacić *pf*) **2** (*person: as wage, salary*) płacić (zapłacić *pf*) *+dat* **3**: **to ~ sb sth** płacić (zapłacić *pf*) komuś coś; **to get paid** otrzymywać (otrzymać *pf*) wynagrodzenie; **how much did you ~ for it?** ile za to pan zapłacił/pani zapłaciła?
▸ **pay back** *vt* spłacać (spłacić *pf*)
▸ **pay for** *vt fus* (*purchases*) płacić (zapłacić *pf*) za
payment ['peɪmənt] *n* (*sum of money*) opłata
payphone ['peɪfəun] *n* automat telefoniczny
PC *n abbr* (*= personal computer*) komputer osobisty
PDA *n abbr* (*= personal digital assistant*) palmtop

PE (*Scol*) *n abbr* (= *physical education*) WF
pea [piː] *n* groszek
peace [piːs] *n* **1** (*not war*) pokój **2** (*calm*) spokój; (*inner, personal*) wyciszenie
peaceful ['piːsful] *adj* spokojny
peach [piːtʃ] *n* brzoskwinia
peacock ['piːkɔk] *n* paw
peak [piːk] *n* (*of mountain*) szczyt ▷ *adj* (*level*) górny; **at ~ times** w okresach szczytowego zapotrzebowania
peanut ['piːnʌt] *n* orzeszek ziemny
peanut butter *n* masło orzechowe
pear [pɛəʳ] *n* gruszka
pearl [pəːl] *n* perła
pebble ['pɛbl] *n* kamyk
peculiar [pɪ'kjuːlɪəʳ] *adj* (*strange*) dziwny
pedal ['pɛdl] *n* pedał ▷ *vi* pedałować
pedestrian [pɪ'dɛstrɪən] *n* pieszy(-za) *m/f*
pedestrian crossing (*Brit*) *n* przejście dla pieszych
pedophile ['piːdəufaɪl] (*US*) *n* = **paedophile**
pee [piː] (*inf*) *vi* siusiać (wysiusiać *pf*) się ▷ *n*: **to have a ~** robić (zrobić *pf*) siusiu
peel [piːl] *n* (*of orange, potato*) skórka ▷ *vt* (*vegetables, fruit*) obierać (obrać *pf*)
peg [pɛg] *n* **1** (*for coat, hat, bag*) wieszak **2** (*Brit*: *also*: **clothes ~**) klamerka
pelvis ['pɛlvɪs] *n* miednica
pen [pɛn] *n* (*for writing*) pióro; (*also*: **fountain ~**) pióro wieczne; (*also*: **ballpoint ~**) długopis
penalty ['pɛnltɪ] *n* **1** (*punishment, fine*) grzywna **2** (*Football, Rugby*) rzut karny
pence [pɛns] (*Brit*) *n pl of* **penny**
pencil ['pɛnsl] *n* ołówek
pencil case *n* piórnik
pencil sharpener *n* temperówka
pendant ['pɛndnt] *n* wisiorek
pen drive *n* (*Comput*) pendrive
penfriend ['pɛnfrɛnd] (*Brit*) *n* korespondencyjny(-na) przyjaciel(-iółka) *m/f*
penguin ['pɛŋgwɪn] *n* pingwin
penicillin [pɛnɪ'sɪlɪn] *n* penicylina
penis ['piːnɪs] *n* penis
penknife ['pɛnnaɪf] (*pl* **penknives**) *n* scyzoryk
penny ['pɛnɪ] (*pl* **pennies** *or* **pence**) *n* **1** (*Brit*) pens **2** (*US*: *inf*) cent
pen pal [-pæl] *n* korespondencyjny(-na) przyjaciel(-iółka) *m/f*
pension ['pɛnʃən] *n* emerytura
pensioner ['pɛnʃənəʳ] (*Brit*) *n* emeryt(ka) *m/f*
Pentagon ['pɛntəgən] (*US*) *n*: **the ~** Pentagon

PENTAGON

Pentagon to budynek w Arlington w stanie Virginia, siedziba Departamentu Obrony USA.

people ['piːpl] *n pl* ludzie; **old ~** starzy ludzie; **many ~** wielu ludzi; **~ say that...** mówi się, że...
pepper ['pɛpəʳ] *n* **1** (*spice*) pieprz **2** (*vegetable*) papryka
peppermint ['pɛpəmɪnt] *n* (*sweet, candy*) miętówka
per [pəːʳ] *prep* na; **~ day** na dzień; **~ person** na osobę; **~ hour** na godzinę; **~ annum** na rok
per cent, percent [pə'sɛnt] (*pl* **per cent**) *n* procent; **by 15 ~** o piętnaście procent
percentage [pə'sɛntɪdʒ] *n* (*amount*) procent
percussion [pə'kʌʃən] *n* perkusja
perfect ['pəːfɪkt] *adj* doskonały ▷ *n*: **the ~ (tense)** (czas) przeszły dokonany
perfectly ['pəːfɪktlɪ] *adv* **1** (*perform, work, do, speak*) doskonale **2** (*emphatic*) całkowicie
perform [pə'fɔːm] *vt* (*piece of music, dance*) wykonywać (wykonać *pf*); (*play*) wystawiać (wystawić *pf*) ▷ *vi* (*actor, singer, dancer*) występować (wystąpić *pf*)
performance [pə'fɔːməns] *n* **1** (*Theat*) przedstawienie **2** (*of employee, athlete, team*) wynik
perfume ['pəːfjuːm] *n* **1** perfumy *f pl* **2** (*of flowers, spices*) zapach

perhaps [pə'hæps] *adv* może; **~ not** może nie
period ['pɪərɪəd] *n* **1** (*interval, stretch*) okres **2** (*time*) okres **3** (*era*) epoka **4** (*Scol*) godzina lekcyjna **5** (*esp US: punctuation mark*) kropka **6** (*also*: **menstrual ~**) okres; **to have one's ~** mieć okres
perm [pə:m] (*Brit*) *n* trwała
permanent ['pə:mənənt] *adj* trwały ▷ *n* (*US*) = **perm**
permission [pə'mɪʃən] *n* **1** (*consent*) pozwolenie **2** (*official authorization*) zezwolenie
permit ['pə:mɪt] *n* (*authorization*) zezwolenie; **fishing ~** karta wędkarska
persecute ['pə:sɪkju:t] *vt* prześladować (*pf*)
person ['pə:sn] (*pl* **people**) *n* osoba; **in ~** osobiście; **first/second/third ~** pierwsza/druga/trzecia osoba
personal ['pə:snl] *adj* **1** (*opinion, habits*) własny; (*care, contact, appearance, appeal*) osobisty **2** (*life, matter, relationship*) prywatny; **nothing ~!** bez urazy!
personality [pə:sə'nælɪtɪ] *n* **1** (*character*) osobowość **2** (*famous person*) osobistość
personally ['pə:snəlɪ] *adv* (*for my part*) osobiście
personal stereo *n* odtwarzacz osobisty
perspiration [pə:spɪ'reɪʃən] *n* pot
persuade [pə'sweɪd] *vt*: **to ~ sb to do sth** przekonywać (przekonać *pf*) kogoś do zrobienia czegoś
pessimistic [pɛsɪ'mɪstɪk] *adj* pesymistyczny
pest [pɛst] *n* **1** (*insect*) szkodnik **2** (*fig: inf: person*) utrapieniec
pester ['pɛstə^r] *vt* dokuczać (dokuczyć *pf*) +*dat*
pet [pɛt] *n* zwierzę
petrol ['pɛtrəl] (*Brit*) *n* benzyna
petrol station (*Brit*) *n* stacja benzynowa
pharmacy ['fɑ:məsɪ] *n* **1** (*shop*) apteka **2** (*science*) farmacja
pheasant ['fɛznt] *n* bażant
philosophy [fɪ'lɔsəfɪ] *n* filozofia
phobia ['fəubjə] *n* fobia
phone [fəun] *n* telefon ▷ *vt* (*person, organization*) dzwonić (zadzwonić *pf*) do +*gen* ▷ *vi* dzwonić (zadzwonić *pf*); **to be on the ~** rozmawiać (porozmawiać *pf*) przez telefon; **by ~** przez telefon
▸ **phone back** *vt* **1** (*return call of*) oddzwaniać (oddzwonić *pf*) do +*gen* **2** (*call again*): **to ~ sb back** dzwonić (zadzwonić *pf*) do kogoś później ▷ *vi* **1** (*return call*) oddzwaniać (oddzwonić *pf*) **2** (*call again*) dzwonić (zadzwonić *pf*) później
phone bill *n* rachunek telefoniczny
phone book *n* książka telefoniczna
phone booth [-bu:ð] (*US*) *n* budka telefoniczna
phone box (*Brit*) *n* budka telefoniczna
phone call *n* rozmowa telefoniczna; **to make a ~** dzwonić (zadzwonić *pf*)
phonecard ['fəunkɑ:d] *n* karta telefoniczna
phone number *n* numer telefonu
photo ['fəutəu] (*inf*) *n* zdjęcie; **to take a ~ (of sb/sth)** robić (zrobić *pf*) zdjęcie (komuś/czemuś)
photobomb ['fəutəubɔm] *vt* celowo wejść w kadr
photocopier ['fəutəukɔpɪə^r] *n* kserokopiarka
photocopy ['fəutəukɔpɪ] *n* kserokopia ▷ *vt* (*document, picture*) robić (zrobić *pf*) kserokopię +*gen*
photograph ['fəutəgræf] *n* zdjęcie ▷ *vt* (*person, object, place*) robić (zrobić *pf*) zdjęcie +*dat*; **to take a ~ of sb/sth** robić (zrobić *pf*) zdjęcie komuś/czemuś
photographer [fə'tɔgrəfə^r] *n* fotograf(ka) *m/f*
photography [fə'tɔgrəfɪ] *n* fotografia
phrase [freɪz] *n* wyrażenie
phrase book *n* rozmówki
physical ['fɪzɪkl] *adj* (*not mental*) fizyczny
physical education *n* wychowanie fizyczne
physician [fɪ'zɪʃən] (*US*) *n* lekarz(-rka) *m/f*
physicist ['fɪzɪsɪst] *n* fizyk

physics ['fɪzɪks] *n* fizyka
physiotherapist [fɪzɪəu'θɛrəpɪst] *n* fizjoterapeuta(-tka) *m/f*
physiotherapy [fɪzɪəu'θɛrəpɪ] *n* fizjoterapia
pianist ['pi:ənɪst] *n* pianista(-tka) *m/f*
piano [pɪ'ænəu] *n* fortepian
pick [pɪk] *vt* **1** (*choose*) wybierać (wybrać *pf*) **2** (*gather: fruit, flowers*) zbierać (zebrać *pf*) **3** (*remove, take*): **to ~ sth out of** *or* **from sth** wybierać (wybrać *pf*) coś spośród czegoś; **take your ~** proszę wybrać
▸ **pick on** (*inf*) *vt fus* (*person*) czepiać się *+gen*
▸ **pick out** *vt* **1** (*recognise, identify: person, thing*) rozpoznawać (rozpoznać *pf*) **2** (*select: person, thing*) wybierać (wybrać *pf*)
▸ **pick up** *vt* **1** (*object*) podnosić (podnieść *pf*) **2** (*collect: person, parcel*) zbierać (zebrać *pf*) **3** (*inf: learn*) uczyć (nauczyć *pf*) się *+gen*
pickpocket ['pɪkpɔkɪt] *n* kieszonkowiec
picnic ['pɪknɪk] *n* (*meal*) piknik ▷ *vi* urządzać (urządzić *pf*) piknik
picture ['pɪktʃə[r]] *n* **1** (*painting, drawing, print*) obraz **2** (*photograph*) zdjęcie **3** (*film, movie*) film ▷ *vt* (*imagine*) wyobrażać (wyobrazić *pf*) sobie; **the pictures** *n pl* (*Brit: inf*) kino *sg*
picture message *n* wiadomość graficzna
pie [paɪ] *n* pasztecik
piece [pi:s] *n* kawałek; **a ~ of paper** kartka papieru; **a 10p ~** (*Brit*) moneta dziesięciopensowa
pier [pɪə[r]] *n* molo
pierce [pɪəs] *vt* (*surface, material, skin*) przekłuwać (przekłuć *pf*); **to have one's ears ~d** przekłuwać (przekłuć *pf*) sobie uszy
pierced [pɪəst] *adj* (*ears, nose, lip*) przekłuty
piercing ['pɪəsɪŋ] *n* piercing
pig [pɪg] *n* **1** świnia **2** (*inf: person: unkind*) świnia; (*greedy*) żarłok
pigeon ['pɪdʒən] *n* gołąb
piggy bank ['pɪgɪ-] *n* skarbonka
pigtail ['pɪgteɪl] *n* warkocz
pile [paɪl] *n* sterta ▷ *vt* (*objects*) układać (ułożyć *pf*) w stos; **piles** *n pl* (*haemorrhoids*) hemoroidy; **~s of** *or* **a ~ of sth** (*inf*) sterta *f sg* czegoś
pill [pɪl] *n* pigułka; **the ~** (*contraceptive pill*) pigułka antykoncepcyjna; **to be on the ~** brać (wziąć *pf*) pigułki antykoncepcyjne
pillow ['pɪləu] *n* poduszka
pilot ['paɪlət] *n* (*Aviat*) pilot ▷ *vt* (*aircraft*) pilotować
pimple ['pɪmpl] *n* pryszcz
PIN [pɪn] *n abbr* (= *personal identification number*) (*also:* **~ number**) numer PIN
pin [pɪn] *n* (*used in sewing*) szpilka ▷ *vt* (*on wall, door, board*) przypinać (przypiąć *pf*); **~s and needles** mrowienie *nt sg*
pinch [pɪntʃ] *vt* **1** (*person*) szczypać (szczypnąć *pf*) **2** (*inf: steal*) kraść (ukraść *pf*)
pine [paɪn] *n* **1** (*also:* **~ tree**) sosna **2** (*wood*) drewno sosnowe
pineapple ['paɪnæpl] *n* ananas
pink [pɪŋk] *adj* różowy ▷ *n* róż
pint [paɪnt] *n* (*measure: Brit*) *jednostka miary objętości, ok. pół litra (568 ml)*; (*US*) *jednostka miary objętości, ok. pół litra (473 ml)*
pipe [paɪp] *n* **1** (*for water, gas*) rura **2** (*for smoking*) fajka
pirate ['paɪərət] *n* pirat
pirated ['paɪərətɪd] *adj* (*video, CD, software etc*) piracki
Pisces ['paɪsi:z] *n* (*Astrol*) Ryby
pistol ['pɪstl] *n* pistolet
pitch [pɪtʃ] *n* (*Brit: Sport: field*) boisko ▷ *vt* (*tent*) rozbijać (rozbić *pf*)
pity ['pɪtɪ] *n* **1** (*compassion*) litość **2** (*misfortune*): **it is a ~ that...** szkoda, że... ▷ *vt* (*person*) litować (zlitować *pf*) się nad *+inst*; **what a ~!** szkoda!
pizza ['pi:tsə] *n* pizza
place [pleɪs] *n* miejsce ▷ *vt* (*put: object*) kłaść (położyć *pf*); **in ~s** w niektórych miejscach; **to change ~s with sb** (*fig*) zamieniać (zamienić *pf*) się miejscami z kimś; **at sb's ~** (*home*) u kogoś w domu; **to sb's ~** do czyjegoś domu; **to take sb's/sth's ~** zajmować (zająć *pf*) miejsce kogoś/

czyjeś; **to take ~** (*happen*) wydarzyć (*pf*) się; **some ~** (*US*: *inf*) gdzieś; **any ~** (*US*: *inf*) gdziekolwiek

placement ['pleɪsmənt] *n* (*job*) staż

plain [pleɪn] *adj* **1** (*not patterned*) gładki **2** (*simple*) prosty **3** (*clear, easily understood*) jasny ▷ *n* (*area of land*) równina

plain chocolate (*Brit*) *n* gorzka czekolada

plait [plæt] *n* (*of hair*) warkocz ▷ *vt* (*hair, rope, leather*) pleść (zapleść *pf*)

plan [plæn] *n* **1** (*scheme, project*) plan **2** (*drawing*) plan ▷ *vt* (*crime, holiday, future etc*) planować (zaplanować *pf*) ▷ *vi* (*think ahead*) snuć plany; **plans** *n pl* (*intentions*) plany; **to ~ to do sth** planować (zaplanować *pf*) zrobienie czegoś

plane [pleɪn] *n* samolot

planet ['plænɪt] *n* planeta

plant [plɑːnt] *n* **1** roślina **2** (*factory, power station*) zakład ▷ *vt* (*flower, tree, crop etc*) sadzić (zasadzić *pf*)

plasma screen ['plæzmə-] *n*: **a ~ TV** telewizor z ekranem plazmowym

plaster ['plɑːstəʳ] *n* (*for walls, ceilings*) tynk; (*Brit*: *also*: **sticking ~**) plaster; **in ~** (*Brit*) w gipsie

plastic ['plæstɪk] *n* plastik ▷ *adj* plastikowy

plastic wrap (*US*) *n* folia

plate [pleɪt] *n* (*dish*) talerz; (*for serving*) talerz

platform ['plætfɔːm] *n* **1** (*stage*) estrada **2** (*Rail*) peron; **the train leaves from ~ 7** pociąg odjeżdża z peronu siódmego

play [pleɪ] *n* (*Theat, TV, Rad*) sztuka ▷ *vt* **1** (*game, chess*) grać (zagrać *pf*) w **2** (*compete against*: *team, opponent*) grać (zagrać *pf*) z +*inst* **3** (*in play, film*) grać (zagrać *pf*) **4** (*Mus*: *instrument*) grać (zagrać *pf*) na +*loc*; (*piece of music*) grać (zagrać *pf*) **5** (*listen to*: *CD, tape*) słuchać (wysłuchać *pf*) ▷ *vi* **1** (*children*) bawić (pobawić *pf*) się **2** (*orchestra, band*) grać (zagrać *pf*) **3** (*CD, tape, radio*) grać; **to ~ cards** grać (zagrać *pf*) w karty; **to ~ a part** *or* **role in sth** (*fig*) odgrywać (odegrać *pf*) jakąś rolę w czymś

▸ **play back** *vt* (*message, video*) puszczać (puścić *pf*)

▸ **play down** *vt* pomniejszać (pomniejszyć *pf*)

player ['pleɪəʳ] *n* **1** (*Sport*) gracz **2** (*Mus*): **a piano ~** pianista(-tka) *m/f*

playground ['pleɪgraund] *n* (*at school*) boisko do zabaw; (*in park*) plac zabaw

playing card ['pleɪɪŋ-] *n* karta do gry

playing field ['pleɪɪŋ-] *n* boisko sportowe; **a level ~** (*fig*) równe szanse

playtime ['pleɪtaɪm] *n* przerwa w szkole

pleasant ['plɛznt] *adj* **1** (*agreeable*) miły **2** (*friendly*) sympatyczny

please [pliːz] *excl* **1** (*in polite requests, written instructions*) proszę **2** (*accepting sth*) poproszę ▷ *vt* (*satisfy*) zadowalać (zadowolić *pf*); **yes, ~** tak, poproszę; **~ don't cry!** proszę, nie płacz!

pleased [pliːzd] *adj* (*happy, satisfied*) zadowolony; **to be ~ that…** być zadowolonym, że…; **~ to meet you** miło mi pana/panią poznać; **~ with sth** zadowolony z czegoś

pleasure ['plɛʒəʳ] *n* **1** (*happiness, satisfaction*) zadowolenie **2** (*fun*) przyjemność **3** (*enjoyable experience*) przyjemność; **"it's a ~", "my ~"** „cała przyjemność po mojej stronie"

plenty ['plɛntɪ] *pron* **1** (*lots*) dużo **2** (*sufficient*) wiele; **~ of** (*food, money, time*) dużo +*gen*; (*jobs, people, houses*) wiele +*gen*; **we've got ~ of time to get there** mamy dużo czasu, żeby tam dotrzeć

pliers ['plaɪəz] *n pl* szczypce

plot [plɔt] *n* **1** (*secret plan*): **a ~ (to do sth)** intryga (w celu zrobienia czegoś) **2** (*of story, play, film*) fabuła ▷ *vi* (*conspire*) spiskować; **to ~ to do sth** knuć plany zrobienia czegoś

plough [plau] (*US* **plow**) *n* pług

plug [plʌg] *n* **1** (*Elec*: *on appliance*) wtyczka; (*inf*: *socket*) gniazdko **2** (*in sink, bath*) korek

▸ **plug in** (*Elec*) *vt* włączać (włączyć *pf*)

plum [plʌm] *n* (*fruit*) śliwka
plumber ['plʌməʳ] *n* hydraulik
plump [plʌmp] *adj* pulchny
plural ['pluərl] *adj* zróżnicowany ▷ *n* liczba mnoga
plus [plʌs] *conj* plus ▷ *adv* (*additionally*) dodatkowo ▷ *n* (*inf*): **it's a ~** to jest plus
p.m. *adv abbr* (= *post meridiem*) po południu
pneumonia [nju:'məunɪə] *n* zapalenie płuc
poached [pəutʃt] *adj* (*egg*) gotowany w koszulce
pocket ['pɔkɪt] *n* kieszeń
pocketbook ['pɔkɪtbuk] *n* **1** (*US: wallet*) portfel **2** (*US: handbag*) torebka
pocket money (*esp Brit*) *n* kieszonkowe
poem ['pəuɪm] *n* wiersz
poet ['pəuɪt] *n* poeta(-tka) *m/f*
poetry ['pəuɪtrɪ] *n* poezja
point [pɔɪnt] *n* **1** (*in report, lecture, interview*) punkt **2** (*of argument, discussion*) sedno **3** (*purpose: of action*) cel **4** (*place*) miejsce **5** (*moment*) moment **6** (*of needle, knife, instrument*) czubek **7** (*in score, competition, game*) punkt **8** (*also*: **decimal ~**) przecinek ▷ *vi*: **to ~ at sth/sb** (*with finger, stick*) wskazywać (wskazać *pf*) na coś/kogoś ▷ *vt*: **to ~ sth at sb** (*gun, finger, stick*) wskazywać (wskazać *pf*) czymś na kogoś; **the research made some valid ~s** badania naukowe wskazały na kilka ważnych kwestii; **there's no ~ (in doing that)** nie ma sensu (tego robić); **at that ~** w tym momencie; **two ~ five** (2.5) dwa przecinek pięć; **the ~s of the compass** kierunki na kompasie
▸ **point out** *vt* (*person, place, mistake, fact*) wskazywać (wskazać *pf*) na; **to ~ out that...** wskazywać (wskazać *pf*) na to, że...
pointless ['pɔɪntlɪs] *adj* bezcelowy; **it is ~ to complain** nie ma sensu narzekać
poison ['pɔɪzn] *n* trucizna ▷ *vt* (*person, animal*) truć (otruć *pf*)
poisonous ['pɔɪznəs] *adj* trujący
poke [pəuk] *vt* (*jab: with finger, stick*) szturchać (szturchnąć *pf*); **to ~ one's head out of the window** wystawiać (wystawić *pf*) głowę za okno
poker ['pəukəʳ] *n* (*Cards*) poker
Poland ['pəulənd] *n* Polska
polar bear ['pəuləʳ-] *n* niedźwiedź polarny
Pole [pəul] *n* Polak(-lka) *m/f*
pole [pəul] *n* **1** (*stick*) kij **2** (*Geo*) biegun
police [pə'li:s] *n pl* (*organization*) policja *sg*
policeman [pə'li:smən] (*irreg*) *n* policjant
police officer *n* policjant(ka) *m/f*
police station *n* posterunek policji
policewoman [pə'li:swumən] (*irreg*) *n* policjantka
Polish ['pəulɪʃ] *adj* polski ▷ *n* (*language*) polski
polish ['pɔlɪʃ] *n* **1** (*substance: for shoes, furniture, floor*) pasta **2** (*shine: on shoes, furniture, floor*) połysk ▷ *vt* (*shoes*) pastować (wypastować *pf*); (*furniture, floor*) polerować (wypolerować *pf*)
polite [pə'laɪt] *adj* grzeczny
political [pə'lɪtɪkl] *adj* polityczny
politician [pɔlɪ'tɪʃən] *n* polityk
politics ['pɔlɪtɪks] *n* **1** (*activity*) polityka **2** (*subject*) nauki *pl* polityczne
pollute [pə'lu:t] *vt* zanieczyszczać (zanieczyścić *pf*)
polluted [pə'lu:tɪd] *adj* zanieczyszczony
pollution [pə'lu:ʃən] *n* zanieczyszczenie
polythene bag ['pɔlɪθi:n-] *n* torebka plastikowa
pond [pɔnd] *n* staw
pony ['pəunɪ] *n* kucyk
ponytail ['pəunɪteɪl] *n* koński ogon
pony trekking [-trɛkɪŋ] (*Brit*) *n* jazda konna; **to go ~** jeździć konno
poodle ['pu:dl] *n* pudel
pool [pu:l] *n* **1** (*pond*) staw **2** (*also*: **swimming ~**) basen **3** (*game*) pul ▷ *vt* (*money, resources, ideas*) gromadzić (zgromadzić *pf*); **pools** *n pl* (*Brit*: *also*: **football ~s**) totalizator piłkarski *m sg*; **to do the (football)**

~s grać (zagrać *pf*) w totalizatora piłkarskiego

poor [puəʳ] *adj* **1** (*not rich*) biedny **2** (*bad*: *quality, performance*) słaby; (*wages, conditions, results*) marny ▷ *n pl*: **the ~** biedni

pop [pɔp] *n* **1** (*Mus*) muzyka pop **2** (*US*: *inf*: *father*) tata ▷ *vi* (*balloon, cork*) pękać (pęknąć *pf*) z hukiem

▸ **pop in** (*inf*) *vi* wpadać (wpaść *pf*)

▸ **pop out** (*inf*) *vi* wyskakiwać (wyskoczyć *pf*)

popcorn ['pɔpkɔːn] *n* popcorn

pope [pəup] *n* papież

poppy ['pɔpɪ] *n* mak

popular ['pɔpjuləʳ] *adj* popularny; **to be ~ with sb** (*food, activity etc*) cieszyć (*pf*) się popularnością wśród kogoś

population [pɔpju'leɪʃən] *n* **1** (*inhabitants*) ludność **2**: **the male/civilian/elephant ~** populacja osobników męskich/cywilna/słoni

porch [pɔːtʃ] *n* **1** (*entrance*) ganek **2** (*US*: *veranda*) weranda

pork [pɔːk] *n* wieprzowina

porridge ['pɔrɪdʒ] *n* owsianka

port [pɔːt] *n* **1** (*harbour*) port **2** (*town*) miasto portowe

portable ['pɔːtəbl] *adj* przenośny

porter ['pɔːtəʳ] *n* **1** (*Brit*: *doorkeeper*) portier **2** (*US*: *on train*) tragarz

portion ['pɔːʃən] *n* (*helping of food*) porcja

portrait ['pɔːtreɪt] *n* (*picture*) portret

Portugal ['pɔːtjugəl] *n* Portugalia

Portuguese [pɔːtju'giːz] (*pl* **Portuguese**) *adj* portugalski ▷ *n* (*language*) portugalski

posh [pɔʃ] (*inf*) *adj* **1** (*smart*) ekskluzywny **2** (*upper-class*: *person*) elegancki; (*voice*) wyniosły

position [pə'zɪʃən] *n* **1** (*place*) pozycja **2** (*posture*) postawa **3** (*in race, competition*) pozycja

positive ['pɔzɪtɪv] *adj* **1** (*good*: *situation, experience*) pozytywny **2** (*affirmative*: *test, result*) twierdzący **3** (*sure*): **to be ~ (about sth)** być pewnym (czegoś); **to be ~ that...** (*sure*) być pewnym, że...

possession [pə'zɛʃən] *n* (*act, state*) posiadanie; **possessions** *n pl* majątek *m sg*

possibility [pɔsɪ'bɪlɪtɪ] *n* **1** (*chance*: *that sth is true*) możliwość; (*of sth happening*) szansa **2** (*option*) możliwość

possible ['pɔsɪbl] *adj* (*conceivable*) możliwy; **it's ~ (that...)** możliwe (że...); **if ~** jeśli to możliwe; **as soon as ~** jak najszybciej; **as much as ~** jak najwięcej

possibly ['pɔsɪblɪ] *adv* być może; **if you ~ can** jeśli tylko pan/pani może

post [pəust] *n* **1** (*Brit*): **the ~** (*service, system*) poczta; (*letters, delivery*) poczta **2** (*pole*) słup **3** (*job*) posada ▷ *vt* (*Brit*: *letter*) wysyłać (wysłać *pf*); (*Comput*) zamieszczać; **by ~** (*Brit*) pocztą

postbox ['pəustbɔks] (*Brit*) *n* (*in street*) skrzynka na listy

postcard ['pəustkaːd] *n* pocztówka

postcode ['pəustkəud] (*Brit*) *n* kod pocztowy

poster ['pəustəʳ] *n* plakat

postman ['pəustmən] (*irreg*) *n* (*Brit*) listonosz

post office *n* (*building*) poczta

postpone [pəus'pəun] *vt* odkładać (odłożyć *pf*)

postwoman ['pəustwumən] (*irreg*) *n* (*Brit*) listonoszka

pot [pɔt] *n* **1** (*for cooking*) garnek **2** (*also*: **tea~**) dzbanek **3** (*also*: **coffee~**) dzbanek na kawę **4** (*for paint, jam etc*) słoik **5** (*also*: **flower~**) doniczka

potato [pə'teɪtəu] (*pl* **potatoes**) *n* ziemniak

potato chips [-tʃɪps] (*US*) *n pl* czipsy

pottery ['pɔtərɪ] *n* **1** (*work, hobby*) garncarstwo **2** (*factory, workshop*) garncarnia

pound [paund] *n* **1** (*unit of money*) funt **2** (*unit of weight*) funt; **a ~ coin** moneta jednofuntowa; **a five-~ note** pięciofuntowy banknot; **half a ~ (of sth)** pół funta (czegoś)

pour [pɔːʳ] *vt*: **to ~ sth (into/onto sth)** (*liquid*) wlewać (wlać *pf*) coś (do czegoś); **it is ~ing (with rain)** leje (deszcz)

▸ **pour out** *vt* (*tea, wine etc*) wylewać (wylać *pf*)

poverty ['pɔvətɪ] *n* bieda

powder ['paudəʳ] *n* puder
power ['pauəʳ] *n* **1** (*control*) władza **2** (*electricity*) energia
powerful ['pauəful] *adj* **1** (*influential*) potężny **2** (*physically strong*) silny
practical ['præktɪkl] *adj* praktyczny
practically ['præktɪklɪ] *adv* (*almost*) niemal
practice ['præktɪs] *n* praktyka ▷ *vt, vi* (*US*) = **practise**; **it's normal** *or* **standard ~** taka jest praktyka; **in ~** (*in reality*) w praktyce; **2 hours' piano ~** dwie godziny ćwiczeń na pianinie
practise ['præktɪs] (*US* **practice**) *vt* (*sport, technique, piece of music*) ćwiczyć (przećwiczyć *pf*); (*musical instrument*) ćwiczyć na *+loc* ▷ *vi* (*in music, theatre, sport*) ćwiczyć
praise [preɪz] *vt* chwalić (pochwalić *pf*); **to ~ sb for doing sth** chwalić (pochwalić *pf*) kogoś za zrobienie czegoś
pram [præm] (*Brit*) *n* wózek dziecięcy
prawn [prɔːn] (*Brit*) *n* krewetka
pray [preɪ] *vi* modlić (pomodlić *pf*) się; **to ~ for/that** (*Rel*) modlić (pomodlić *pf*) się o/żeby
prayer [prɛəʳ] (*Rel*) *n* modlitwa
precaution [prɪ'kɔːʃən] *n* zabezpieczenie
precious ['prɛʃəs] *adj* cenny
precise [prɪ'saɪs] *adj* **1** dokładny **2** (*detailed*) precyzyjny; **to be ~** (*in fact*) dokładnie mówiąc
precisely [prɪ'saɪslɪ] *adv* dokładnie; **~!** dokładnie!
predict [prɪ'dɪkt] *vt* (*event, death etc*) przewidywać (przewidzieć *pf*); **to ~ that...** przewidywać (przewidzieć *pf*), że...
prediction [prɪ'dɪkʃən] *n* przepowiednia
prefect ['priːfɛkt] (*Brit*) *n* (*in school*) *starszy uczeń w szkole odpowiedzialny za innych uczniów*
prefer [prɪ'fəːʳ] *vt* woleć; **to ~ coffee to tea** woleć kawę od herbaty; **to ~ doing sth** woleć coś robić; **I'd ~ to go by train** wolałbym jechać pociągiem
pregnant ['prɛgnənt] *adj* (*woman, animal*) w ciąży; **3 months ~** w trzecim miesiącu ciąży; **to get ~** zajść (*pf*) w ciążę
prejudice ['prɛdʒudɪs] *n* (*bias*) uprzedzenie
prejudiced ['prɛdʒudɪst] *adj* (*biased: person*) uprzedzony
premature ['prɛmətʃuəʳ] *adj* przedwczesny; **~ baby** wcześniak
Premier League ['prɛmɪəʳ-] (*Brit: Football*) *n*: **the ~** *angielska ekstraklasa piłkarska*
prep [prɛp] *n* (*Brit: homework*) zadanie domowe
preparation [prɛpə'reɪʃən] *n* (*activity*) przygotowanie; **preparations** *n pl* (*arrangements*): **~s (for sth)** przygotowania (do czegoś); **in ~ for sth** w przygotowaniu na coś
prepare [prɪ'pɛəʳ] *vt* przygotowywać (przygotować *pf*) ▷ *vi*: **to ~ (for sth)** przygotowywać (przygotować *pf*) się (do czegoś); **to ~ to do sth** (*get ready*) przygotowywać (przygotować *pf*) się do czegoś
prepared [prɪ'pɛəd] *adj*: **to be ~ to do sth** (*willing*) być gotowym coś zrobić; **~ (for sth)** (*ready*) przygotowany (do czegoś)
prep school *n* **1** (*Brit*) *prywatna szkoła podstawowa dla dzieci w wieku 6-13 lat przygotowująca do nauki w szkole prywatnej* **2** (*US*) *prywatna szkoła ponadpodstawowa przygotowująca młodzież do nauki w szkole wyższej*
prescribe [prɪ'skraɪb] *vt* (*Med*) przepisywać (przepisać *pf*); **to ~ sth for sb/sth** zapisywać (zapisać *pf*) coś komuś/na coś
prescription [prɪ'skrɪpʃən] *n* (*Med: slip of paper*) recepta; (*medicine*) przepisane lekarstwo; **to give sb a ~ for sth** zapisywać (zapisać *pf*) komuś lekarstwo na coś
present [*adj, n* 'prɛznt, *vb* prɪ'zɛnt] *adj* **1** (*current*) teraźniejszy **2** (*in attendance*) obecny ▷ *n* **1** (*not past*): **the ~** teraźniejszość **2** (*gift*) prezent **3**: **the ~** (*also*: **~ tense**) czas teraźniejszy ▷ *vt* **1** (*give*): **to ~ sth (to sb)** (*prize, award*) wręczać (wręczyć *pf*) coś (komuś) **2** (*difficulty, problem, threat*) stanowić **3** (*Rad, TV: programme*) prowadzić (poprowadzić *pf*); **to be ~ at sth** być obecnym na czymś; **at ~** obecnie; **to give sb a ~**

dawać (dać *pf*) komuś prezent; **to ~ sb with sth** (*prize, award*) wręczać (wręczyć *pf*) coś komuś

presenter [prɪ'zɛntəʳ] *n* (*on radio, TV*) prezenter

president ['prɛzɪdənt] *n* (*Pol*) prezydent

press [prɛs] *n* (*newspapers, journalists*): **the ~** prasa ▷ *vt* **1** (*button, switch, bell*) naciskać (nacisnąć *pf*); (*accelerator*) wciskać (wcisnąć *pf*) **2** (*iron*) prasować (wyprasować *pf*); **to be ~ed for time/money** mieć mało czasu/pieniędzy; **to ~ (down) on sth** naciskać (nacisnąć *pf*) coś

press-up ['prɛsʌp] (*Brit*) *n* (*exercise*) pompka; **to do ~s** robić (zrobić *pf*) pompki

pressure ['prɛʃəʳ] *n* **1** (*physical force*) nacisk **2** (*fig: coercion*): **~ (to do sth)** przymus (zrobienia czegoś) **3** (*stress*) napięcie; **high/low ~** wysokie/niskie ciśnienie; **to put ~ on sb (to do sth)** wywierać (wywrzeć *pf*) presję na kogoś (by coś zrobił); **to be under ~ to do sth** być pod presją zrobienia czegoś; **to ~ sb into doing sth** zmuszać (zmusić *pf*) kogoś do zrobienia czegoś

presume [prɪ'zjuːm] *vt* (*assume*): **to ~ (that...)** przypuszczać (przypuścić *pf*), (że...); **I ~ so** przypuszczam, że tak

pretend [prɪ'tɛnd] *vt*: **to ~ that...** (*make believe*) udawać (udać *pf*), że...

pretty ['prɪtɪ] *adj* ładny ▷ *adv* (*inf: quite*) całkiem; **~ much** *or* **well** (*inf: more or less*) prawie

prevent [prɪ'vɛnt] *vt* (*war, disease, situation*) zapobiegać (zapobiec *pf*) +*dat*; **to ~ sb (from) doing sth** przeszkadzać (przeszkodzić *pf*) komuś w zrobieniu czegoś; **to ~ sth (from) happening** zapobiegać (zapobiec *pf*) czemuś

previous ['priːvɪəs] *adj* poprzedni

previously ['priːvɪəslɪ] *adv* wcześniej; **10 days ~** dziesięć dni wcześniej

price [praɪs] *n* cena

price list *n* cennik

prick [prɪk] *n* (*sting*) ukłucie ▷ *vt* (*scratch*) kłuć (ukłuć *pf*)

pride [praɪd] *n* **1** (*satisfaction, dignity, self-respect*) duma **2** (*arrogance*) arogancja; **to take (a) ~ in sb/sth** być dumnym z kogoś/czegoś

priest [priːst] *n* ksiądz

primarily ['praɪmərɪlɪ] *adv* głównie

primary ['praɪmərɪ] *adj* **1** (*reason, aim, cause*) główny **2** (*Brit: education, teacher*) podstawowy

primary school (*Brit*) *n* szkoła podstawowa

Prime Minister [praɪm-] *n* (*of Poland*) Prezes Rady Ministrów; (*of other countries*) premier

prince [prɪns] *n* książę

princess [prɪn'sɛs] *n* księżniczka

principal ['prɪnsɪpl] *adj* (*main*) główny ▷ *n* (*head teacher: of school, college*) dyrektor(ka) *m/f*

principle ['prɪnsɪpl] *n* (*moral belief*) zasada; **in ~** (*in theory*) w zasadzie; **on ~** dla zasady

print [prɪnt] *n* **1** (*type*) druk **2** (*picture*) rycina **3** (*photograph*) odbitka ▷ *vt* **1** (*publish: story, article*) drukować (wydrukować *pf*) **2** (*stamp: word, number, pattern*) wytłaczać (wytłoczyć *pf*) **3** (*write*) pisać (napisać *pf*) drukowanymi literami **4** (*Comput*) drukować (wydrukować *pf*); **prints** *n pl* (*fingerprints*) odciski (palców)
▶ **print out** *vt* (*Comput: document, file*) drukować (wydrukować *pf*)

printer ['prɪntəʳ] *n* **1** (*machine*) drukarka **2** (*firm: also:* **~'s**) drukarnia

printout ['prɪntaut] *n* wydruk

priority [praɪ'ɔrɪtɪ] *n* (*concern*) sprawa nadrzędna; **priorities** *n pl* priorytety; **to give ~ to sth/sb** dawać (dać *pf*) pierwszeństwo czemuś/komuś

prison ['prɪzn] *n* **1** (*institution*) więzienie **2** (*imprisonment*) kara więzienia; **in ~** w więzieniu

prisoner ['prɪznəʳ] *n* więzień; (*during war*) jeniec

private ['praɪvɪt] *adj* **1** (*property, land, plane*) prywatny; (*performance, ceremony*) *niedostępny dla osób postronnych* **2** (*not state-owned*) prywatny **3** (*confidential*) poufny **4** (*personal*) osobisty; **in ~** na osobności

prize [praɪz] *n* nagroda
prize-giving ['praɪzgɪvɪŋ] *n* rozdanie nagród
prizewinner ['praɪzwɪnəʳ] *n* **1** (*in competition*) zdobywca(-czyni) *m/f* nagrody **2** (*Scol, Univ*) laureat(ka) *m/f*
pro [prəu] *n* (*professional*) zawodowiec; **the ~s and cons (of doing sth)** zalety i wady (robienia czegoś) ▷ *prep* (*in favour of*) za +*inst*
probability [prɔbə'bɪlɪtɪ] *n*: **~ (of sth/that...)** prawdopodobieństwo (czegoś/że...); **the ~ of sth happening** prawdopodobieństwo, że coś się zdarzy
probable ['prɔbəbl] *adj* prawdopodobny; **it is/seems ~ that...** jest/wydaje się prawdopodobne, że...
probably ['prɔbəblɪ] *adv* prawdopodobnie; **~!/~ not!** prawdopodobnie!/prawdopodobnie nie!
problem ['prɔbləm] *n* **1** (*difficulty*) problem **2** (*puzzle*) zagadka; **what's the ~?** w czym problem?; **I had no ~ finding her** znalazłem ją bez problemu; **no ~!** (*inf*) nie ma sprawy!
process ['prəusɛs] *n* (*procedure*) proces ▷ *vt* (*Comput: data*) przetwarzać (przetworzyć *pf*); **to be in the ~ of doing sth** być w trakcie robienia czegoś
procession [prə'sɛʃən] *n* pochód
produce [prə'dju:s] *vt* **1** (*effect, result etc*) przynosić (przynieść *pf*) **2** (*goods, commodity*) produkować (wyprodukować *pf*) **3** (*play, film, programme*) produkować (wyprodukować *pf*)
producer [prə'dju:səʳ] *n* **1** (*Theat, Cine, Mus*) producent(ka) *m/f* **2** (*of food, material: country*) producent; (*company*) producent
product ['prɔdʌkt] *n* produkt
production [prə'dʌkʃən] *n* **1** (*process*) produkcja; (*amount produced, amount grown*) produkcja **2** (*play, show*) wystawienie
profession [prə'fɛʃən] *n* (*job*) zawód
professional [prə'fɛʃənl] *adj* **1** (*work-related: activity, context, capacity*) zawodowy **2** (*not amateur*) zawodowy; (*advice, help*) fachowy **3** (*skilful*) profesjonalny ▷ *n* (*Sport*) zawodowiec
professor [prə'fɛsəʳ] *n* **1** (*Brit*) profesor **2** (*US*) nauczyciel akademicki
profile ['prəufaɪl] *n* (*on social media*) profil; **~ picture** zdjęcie profilowe
profit ['prɔfɪt] *n* zysk; **to make a ~** osiągać (osiągnąć *pf*) zysk
profitable ['prɔfɪtəbl] *adj* korzystny
program ['prəugræm] *n* **1** (*also*: **computer ~**) program **2** (*US*) = **programme** ▷ *vt* **1** (*Comput*): **to ~ sth (to do sth)** programować (zaprogramować *pf*) coś (do zrobienia czegoś) **2** (*US*) = **programme**
programme ['prəugræm] (*US* **program**) *n* program ▷ *vt*: **to ~ sth (to do sth)** (*machine, system*) programować (zaprogramować *pf*) coś (do zrobienia czegoś); *see also* **program**
programmer ['prəugræməʳ] (*Comput*) *n* programista(-tka) *m/f*
progress ['prəugrɛs] *n* postęp; **to make ~ (with sth)** robić (zrobić *pf*) postępy (w czymś)
prohibit [prə'hɪbɪt] (*formal*) *vt* zakazywać (zakazać *pf*); **"smoking ~ed"** „palenie zabronione"
project ['prɔdʒɛkt] *n* **1** (*plan, scheme*) projekt **2** (*Scol, Univ*) referat
projector [prə'dʒɛktəʳ] *n* rzutnik
prom [prɔm] *n* (*Brit: by sea*) promenada

PROM

Prom – w Wielkiej Brytanii **prom** (skrót od **promenade** – przechadzać się, spacerować) to określenie letnich koncertów muzyki klasycznej, z których najsłynniejsze odbywają się w Londynie, w sali koncertowej Royal Albert Hall. W USA zaś **prom** oznacza bal maturalny.

promise ['prɔmɪs] *n* obietnica ▷ *vi* obiecywać (obiecać *pf*) ▷ *vt*: **to ~ sb sth, ~ sth to sb** obiecywać (obiecać *pf*) coś komuś; **to make a ~ (to do sth)** składać (złożyć *pf*) obietnicę (zrobienia czegoś); **to break a ~ (to do sth)** łamać (złamać *pf*) obietnicę (zrobienia czegoś); **to keep a ~ (to do sth)** dotrzymywać (dotrzymać *pf*) obietnicy (zrobienia czegoś); **to ~ (sb) that...** obiecywać (obiecać *pf*) (komuś), że...; **to ~ to do sth** obiecywać (obiecać *pf*) coś zrobić

promote [prə'məut] *vt* (*employee*) awansować; **the team was ~d to the first division** (*Brit*: *Sport*) drużyna awansowała do pierwszej ligi

promotion [prə'məuʃən] *n* **1** (*at work*) awans **2** (*Brit*: *Sport*) awans

prompt [prɔmpt] *adj* **1** (*on time*) punktualny **2** (*rapid*) natychmiastowy ▷ *n* (*Comput*) znak zachęty systemu; **at 8 o'clock ~** punktualnie o godzinie ósmej

pronoun ['prəunaun] *n* zaimek

pronounce [prə'nauns] *vt* (*word, name*) wymawiać (wymówić *pf*)

pronunciation [prənʌnsɪ'eɪʃən] *n* wymowa

proof [pru:f] *n* dowód

proper ['prɔpə[r]] *adj* **1** (*genuine*: *job, meal etc*) porządny **2** (*correct*: *procedure, place, word*) właściwy **3** (*socially acceptable*) stosowny

properly ['prɔpəlɪ] *adv* **1** (*adequately*) odpowiednio **2** (*decently*) stosownie

property ['prɔpətɪ] *n* **1** (*possessions*) mienie **2** (*buildings and land*) nieruchomość

propose [prə'pəuz] *vt* (*plan, idea*) proponować (zaproponować *pf*) ▷ *vi* (*offer marriage*) oświadczać (oświadczyć *pf*) się; **to ~ to do** *or* **doing sth** (*intend*) zamierzać coś robić; **to ~ a toast** wznosić (wznieść *pf*) toast

prosecute ['prɔsɪkju:t] *vt*: **to ~ sb (for sth/for doing sth)** oskarżać (oskarżyć *pf*) kogoś (o coś/o zrobienie czegoś)

prostitute ['prɔstɪtju:t] *n* (*female*) prostytutka; **a male ~** męska prostytutka

protect [prə'tɛkt] *vt* (*person, floor, rights, freedom*) chronić; **to ~ sb/sth from** *or* **against sth** chronić kogoś/coś przed czymś

protection [prə'tɛkʃən] *n*: **~ (from** *or* **against sth)** ochrona (przed czymś)

protein ['prəuti:n] *n* białko

protest [*n* 'prəutɛst, *vb* prə'tɛst] *n* protest ▷ *vi*: **to ~ about** *or* **against** *or* **at sth** (*Brit*) protestować (zaprotestować *pf*) przeciwko czemuś ▷ *vt* (*US*: *voice opposition to*) zgłaszać (zgłosić *pf*) sprzeciw wobec *+gen*

Protestant ['prɔtɪstənt] *n* protestant(ka) *m/f* ▷ *adj* protestancki

protester [prə'tɛstə[r]] *n* protestujący(-ca) *m/f*

proud [praud] *adj* **1** (*parents, owner*) dumny **2** (*arrogant*) pyszny **3** (*dignified*) dostojny; **to be ~ of sb/sth** być dumnym z kogoś/czegoś

prove [pru:v] *vt* (*idea, theory*) udowadniać (udowodnić *pf*) ▷ *vi*: **to ~ that...** udowadniać (udowodnić *pf*), że...; **to ~ sb right/wrong** udowadniać (udowodnić *pf*), że ktoś ma rację/nie ma racji

proverb ['prɔvə:b] *n* przysłowie

provide [prə'vaɪd] *vt* (*food, money, shelter*) zapewniać (zapewnić *pf*); (*answer, opportunity, details*) dostarczać (dostarczyć *pf*); **to ~ sb with sth** (*food, job, resources*) zaopatrywać (zaopatrzyć *pf*) kogoś w coś

▸ **provide for** *vt fus* (*person*) zapewniać (zapewnić *pf*) *+dat*

provided (that) [prə'vaɪdɪd-] *conj* pod warunkiem, że

prune [pru:n] *n* suszona śliwka

PS *abbr* (= *postscript*) postscriptum

psychiatrist [saɪ'kaɪətrɪst] *n* psychiatra

psychological [saɪkə'lɔdʒɪkl] *adj* (*effect, problem, disorder*) psychologiczny

psychologist [saɪ'kɔlədʒɪst] *n* psycholog

psychology [saɪ'kɔlədʒɪ] *n* (*science*) psychologia

PTO *abbr* (= *please turn over*) verte, proszę odwrócić

pub [pʌb] (*Brit*) *n* piwiarnia

public ['pʌblɪk] *adj* **1** (*from people: support, opinion, interest*) społeczny **2** (*for people: building, service, library*) publiczny **3** (*not private*) publiczny ▷ *n*: **the (general) ~** społeczeństwo; **in ~** (*speak, smoke, drink*) publicznie
public holiday *n* święto państwowe
publicity [pʌb'lɪsɪtɪ] *n* **1** (*information, advertising*) reklama **2** (*attention*) rozgłos
public school *n* **1** (*Brit*) szkoła prywatna **2** (*US*) szkoła państwowa
public transport *n* komunikacja publiczna
publish ['pʌblɪʃ] *vt* **1** (*book, magazine*) wydawać (wydać *pf*) **2** (*letter, article*) publikować (opublikować *pf*)
publisher ['pʌblɪʃəʳ] *n* wydawca
pudding ['pudɪŋ] *n* (*Brit: dessert in general*) deser; **rice ~** deser ryżowy; **black ~**, (*US*) **blood ~** kaszanka
puddle ['pʌdl] *n* (*of rain*) kałuża
puff pastry ['pʌf-] *n* ciasto francuskie
pull [pul] *vt* **1** (*rope, hair*) ciągnąć (pociągnąć *pf*) za; (*handle, door, cart, carriage*) pociągać (pociągnąć *pf*) **2** (*curtain, blind*) zaciągać (zaciągnąć *pf*) **3** (*trigger*) naciskać (nacisnąć *pf*) ▷ *n* (*tug*): **to give sth a ~** pociągnąć (*pf*) za coś; **to ~ a muscle** naciągnąć (*pf*) mięsień; **to ~ a face** robić (zrobić *pf*) minę; **to ~ sb's leg** (*fig*) nabierać (nabrać *pf*) kogoś
▸ **pull down** *vt* (*building*) rozbierać (rozebrać *pf*)
▸ **pull in** *vi* (*at the kerb*) zatrzymywać (zatrzymać *pf*) się
▸ **pull out** *vi* **1** (*Aut: from kerb*) odjeżdżać (odjechać *pf*); (*when overtaking*) zmieniać (zmienić *pf*) pas ruchu **2** (*withdraw: from agreement, contest*) wycofywać (wycofać *pf*) się
▸ **pull through** *vi* (*from illness*) wyzdrowieć; (*from difficulties*) wydobywać (wydobyć *pf*) się (z kłopotów)
▸ **pull up** *vi* (*stop: driver, vehicle*) zatrzymywać (zatrzymać *pf*) się ▷ *vt* **1** (*raise: socks, trousers*) podciągać (podciągnąć *pf*) **2** (*uproot: plant, weed*) wyrywać (wyrwać *pf*)
pullover ['puləuvəʳ] *n* pulower
pulse [pʌls] *n* (*Anat*) tętno; **pulses** *n pl* (*Culin*) *jadalne nasiona roślin strączkowych*; **to take** *or* **feel sb's ~** mierzyć (zmierzyć *pf*) komuś tętno
pump [pʌmp] *n* pompa
▸ **pump up** *vt* (*inflate*) pompować (napompować *pf*)
pumpkin ['pʌmpkɪn] *n* dynia
punch [pʌntʃ] *n* (*blow*) uderzenie pięścią ▷ *vt* **1** (*hit*) uderzać (uderzyć *pf*) pięścią **2** (*button, keyboard*) naciskać **3** (*make a hole in: ticket, paper*) dziurkować (przedziurkować *pf*); **to ~ sb on the nose/in the eye** uderzać (uderzyć *pf*) kogoś pięścią w nos/oko
punctual ['pʌŋktjuəl] *adj* punktualny
punctuation [pʌŋktju'eɪʃən] *n* interpunkcja
puncture ['pʌŋktʃəʳ] *n* przebicie dętki ▷ *vt* (*tyre, lung*) przebijać (przebić *pf*); **to have a ~** złapać (*pf*) gumę
punish ['pʌnɪʃ] *vt* (*person*) karać (ukarać *pf*); **to ~ sb for sth/for doing sth** karać (ukarać *pf*) kogoś za coś/za zrobienie czegoś
punishment ['pʌnɪʃmənt] *n* kara
punk [pʌŋk] *n* **1** (*also*: **~ rocker**) punk **2** (*also*: **~ rock**) punk rock **3** (*US: inf*) chuligan
pupil ['pju:pl] *n* (*student*) uczeń(-ennica) *m/f*
puppet ['pʌpɪt] *n* **1** (*on strings*) marionetka **2** (*also*: **glove ~**) pacynka
puppy ['pʌpɪ] *n* szczeniak
purchase ['pə:tʃɪs] *vt* nabywać (nabyć *pf*) ▷ *n* **1** (*act of buying*) kupno **2** (*item bought*) nabytek
pure [pjuəʳ] *adj* **1** (*silk, gold, wool*) czysty **2** (*clean: water, air*) czysty **3** (*theoretical*) teoretyczny; **a ~ wool jumper** sweter z czystej wełny
purple ['pə:pl] *adj* fioletowy ▷ *n* fiolet
purpose ['pə:pəs] *n* cel; **on ~** celowo
purr [pə:ʳ] *vi* mruczeć (zamruczeć *pf*)
purse [pə:s] *n* **1** (*Brit*) portmonetka **2** (*US*) torebka
pursue [pə'sju:] (*formal*) *vt* ścigać

push [puʃ] *n* naciśnięcie ▹ *vt* **1** (*press: button*) naciskać (nacisnąć *pf*) **2** (*shove: car, door, person*) popychać (popchnąć *pf*) ▹ *vi* **1** (*press*) naciskać (nacisnąć *pf*) **2** (*shove*) popychać (popchnąć *pf*); **to give sth/sb a ~** (*with hand*) popychać (popchnąć *pf*) coś/kogoś; **to ~ one's way through the crowd** przepychać (przepchnąć *pf*) się przez tłum; **to ~ sth/sb out of the way** spychać (zepchnąć *pf*) coś/kogoś z drogi; **to ~ a door open/shut** otwierać (otworzyć *pf*)/zamykać (zamknąć *pf*) drzwi; **"~"** (*on door*) „pchać"; **to ~ sb to do sth** nakłaniać (nakłonić *pf*) kogoś do zrobienia czegoś; **to be ~ed for time/money** (*inf*) mieć mało czasu/pieniędzy; **to ~ forward** posuwać (posunąć *pf*) się naprzód; **to ~ through the crowd** przepychać (przepchnąć *pf*) się przez tłum

▸ **push around** (*inf*) *vt* (*bully*) pomiatać *+inst*

▸ **push in** *vi* (*in queue*) wpychać (wepchnąć *pf*) się

▸ **push over** *vt* (*person, object*) przewracać (przewrócić *pf*)

▸ **push through** *vt* (*measure, scheme*) przeprowadzać (przeprowadzić *pf*)

▸ **push up** *vt* (*total, prices*) podnosić (podnieść *pf*)

pushchair ['puʃtʃɛəʳ] (*Brit*) *n* spacerówka

pusher ['puʃəʳ] (*inf*) *n* (*drug dealer*) handlarz narkotykami

push-up ['puʃʌp] (*US*) *n* pompka; **to do ~s** robić (zrobić *pf*) pompki

put [put] (*pt, pp* **put**) *vt* **1** (*place: thing*) kłaść (położyć *pf*); (*person: in institution*) umieszczać (umieścić *pf*) **2** (*confidence, trust, faith: in person, thing*) pokładać **3** (*write, type: word, information*) zapisywać (zapisać *pf*); **to ~ a lot of time/energy into doing sth** włożyć dużo czasu/energii w zrobienie czegoś; **how shall I ~ it?** jak by to powiedzieć?

▸ **put across, put over** *vt* (*ideas, argument*) wyjaśniać (wyjaśnić *pf*)

▸ **put aside** *vt* odkładać (odłożyć *pf*)

▸ **put away** *vt* (*store, unpack*) chować (schować *pf*)

▸ **put back** *vt* **1** (*replace*) odkładać (odłożyć *pf*) **2** (*watch, clock*) cofać (cofnąć *pf*)

▸ **put down** *vt* **1** (*on floor, table*) odstawiać (odstawić *pf*) **2** (*in writing*) zapisywać (zapisać *pf*) **3** (*put to sleep: animal*) usypiać (uśpić *pf*)

▸ **put forward** *vt* **1** (*ideas, proposal, name*) wysuwać (wysunąć *pf*) **2** (*watch, clock*) przesuwać (przesunąć *pf*) do przodu

▸ **put in** *vt* **1** (*request, complaint, application*) składać (złożyć *pf*) **2** (*gas, electricity, sink*) instalować (zainstalować *pf*)

▸ **put off** *vt* **1** (*delay*) odkładać (odłożyć *pf*) **2** (*Brit: distract*) rozpraszać (rozproszyć *pf*) **3** (*discourage*) zniechęcać (zniechęcić *pf*); **to ~ off doing sth** (*postpone*) odkładać (odłożyć *pf*) robienie (zrobienie *pf*) czegoś; **to ~ sb off doing sth** odwodzić (odwieść *pf*) kogoś od zrobienia czegoś

▸ **put on** *vt* **1** (*clothes, make-up, glasses*) zakładać (założyć *pf*) **2** (*switch on*) włączać (włączyć *pf*); (*kettle*) wstawiać (wstawić *pf*) **3** (*organize: play, exhibition*) wystawiać (wystawić *pf*); **to ~ on weight/three kilos** przybierać (przybrać *pf*) na wadze/trzy kilo

▸ **put out** *vt* **1** (*candle, cigarette*) gasić (zgasić *pf*); (*fire, blaze*) gasić (ugasić *pf*) **2** (*electric light*) wyłączać (wyłączyć *pf*) **3** (*inf: inconvenience: person*) fatygować (pofatygować *pf*); **to ~ out one's tongue** wystawiać (wystawić *pf*) język

▸ **put over** *vt* = **put across**

▸ **put through** *vt* (*Tel: person, phone call*) łączyć (połączyć *pf*)

▸ **put up** *vt* **1** (*fence, building, tent*) stawiać (postawić *pf*); (*poster, sign*) wywieszać (wywiesić *pf*) **2** (*umbrella, hood*) rozkładać (rozłożyć *pf*) **3** (*increase: price, cost*) podnosić (podnieść *pf*) **4** (*accommodate*) przenocowywać (przenocować *pf*); **to ~ up one's hand** podnosić (podnieść *pf*) rękę

▸ **put up with** *vt fus* godzić (pogodzić *pf*) się z *+inst*

puzzle ['pʌzl] *n* zagadka; (*jigsaw*) układanka; (*mystery*) zagadka
puzzled ['pʌzld] *adj* zaintrygowany; **to be ~ by** *or* **about sth** głowić się nad czymś
pyjamas [pə'dʒɑːməz] (*US* **pajamas**) *n pl* piżama *f sg*; **a pair of ~** piżama
pylon ['paɪlən] *n* słup sieci wysokiego napięcia
pyramid ['pɪrəmɪd] *n* piramida

q

qualification [kwɔlɪfɪ'keɪʃən] *n* kwalifikacje *n pl*
qualified ['kwɔlɪfaɪd] *adj* (*trained*) dyplomowany; **fully ~** wykwalifikowany
qualify ['kwɔlɪfaɪ] *vi* **1** (*pass examinations*) zdobywać (zdobyć *pf*) kwalifikacje **2** (*in competition*) zakwalifikować się; **to ~ as an engineer/a nurse** zdobywać (zdobyć *pf*) dyplom inżyniera/pielęgniarki
quality ['kwɔlɪtɪ] *n* **1** (*standard*) jakość **2** (*characteristic: of person*) cecha; **~ of life** jakość życia
quantity ['kwɔntɪtɪ] *n* ilość; **in large/small quantities** w dużych/małych ilościach
quarantine ['kwɔrəntiːn] *n* kwarantanna; **in ~** w kwarantannie
quarrel ['kwɔrəl] *n* kłótnia ▷ *vi* kłócić (pokłócić *pf*) się
quarry ['kwɔrɪ] *n* (*for stone, minerals*) kopalnia
quarter ['kwɔːtə^r] *n* **1** (*fourth part*) ćwierć **2** (*three months*) kwartał **3** (*US: coin*) dwadzieścia pięć centów; **to cut/divide sth into ~s** ciąć (pociąć *pf*)/dzielić (podzielić *pf*) coś na ćwiartki; **a ~ of an hour** kwadrans; **it's a ~ to three** *or* (*US*) **of three** jest za kwadrans trzecia; **it's a ~ past three** *or* (*US*) **after three** jest kwadrans po trzeciej
quarter-final ['kwɔːtə'faɪnl] *n* ćwierć finał

quartet [kwɔːˈtɛt] *n* kwartet
quay [kiː] *n* nabrzeże
queen [kwiːn] *n* królowa
query [ˈkwɪərɪ] *n* (*question*) pytanie ▷ *vt* (*check*) sprawdzać (sprawdzić *pf*)
question [ˈkwɛstʃən] *n* **1** (*query*) pytanie **2** (*issue*) zagadnienie **3** (*in written exam*) pytanie ▷ *vt* (*interrogate*) pytać (zapytać *pf*); **to ask sb a ~, to put a ~ to sb** zadawać (zadać *pf*) komuś pytanie; **to be out of the ~** nie podlegać dyskusji
question mark *n* znak zapytania
questionnaire [kwɛstʃəˈnɛəʳ] *n* kwestionariusz
queue [kjuː] (*esp Brit*) *n* kolejka ▷ *vi* (*also*: **~ up**) ustawiać (ustawić *pf*) się w kolejce; **to ~ for sth** stawać (stać *pf*) w kolejce po coś
quick [kwɪk] *adj* **1** (*fast*) szybki **2** (*brief*) krótki ▷ *adv* (*inf*: *quickly*) szybko; **be ~!** szybko!
quickly [ˈkwɪklɪ] *adv* szybko
quiet [ˈkwaɪət] *adj* cichy; **be ~!** ucisz się!
quietly [ˈkwaɪətlɪ] *adv* cicho
quilt [kwɪlt] *n* **1** (*covering*) narzuta **2** (*Brit*: *duvet*) kołdra
quit [kwɪt] (*pt, pp* **quit** *or* **quitted**) *vt* **1** (*esp US*: *give up*) przestawać (przestać *pf*) **2** (*inf*: *leave*: *job*) rzucać (rzucić *pf*) ▷ *vi* **1** (*give up*) przestawać (przestać *pf*) **2** (*resign*) rezygnować (zrezygnować *pf*)
quite [kwaɪt] *adv* **1** (*rather*) dość **2** (*completely*) całkiem; **I see them ~ a lot** widuję ich dość często; **it costs ~ a lot to go to the States** wyjazd do Stanów sporo kosztuje; **~ a lot of money** całkiem sporo pieniędzy; **~ a few** całkiem sporo; **it's not ~ finished** to jest nie całkiem skończone; **there aren't ~ enough glasses** nie ma wystarczającej ilości szklanek; **I can't ~ remember** nie całkiem pamiętam; **~ (so)!** właśnie!; **it was ~ a sight** to był niezły widok
quiz [kwɪz] *n* (*game*) quiz
quotation [kwəuˈteɪʃən] *n* **1** (*from book, play etc*) cytat **2** (*estimate*) wycena
quote [kwəut] *vt* cytować (zacytować *pf*) ▷ *n* (*from book, play, person*) cytat; **quotes** *n pl* (*inf*: *quotation marks*) cudzysłów; **in ~s** w cudzysłowie

r

rabbi ['ræbaɪ] *n* rabin
rabbit ['ræbɪt] *n* królik
rabies ['reɪbiːz] *n* wścieklizna
race [reɪs] *n* **1** (*speed contest*) wyścig **2** (*ethnic group*) rasa ▷ *vi* **1** (*compete in races*) ścigać się **2** (*hurry*) śpieszyć (*pf*) się ▷ *vt* (*person*) ścigać się z *+inst*; **a ~ against time** wyścig z czasem
race car (*US*) *n* = **racing car**
racecourse ['reɪskɔːs] (*Brit*) *n* tor wyścigowy
racehorse ['reɪshɔːs] *n* koń wyścigowy
racetrack ['reɪstræk] *n* (*for cars*) tor wyścigowy; (*US: for horses*) tor wyścigów konnych
racial ['reɪʃl] *adj* rasowy
racing car ['reɪsɪŋ-] (*Brit*) *n* samochód wyścigowy
racing driver ['reɪsɪŋ-] (*Brit*) *n* kierowca wyścigowy
racism ['reɪsɪzəm] *n* rasizm
racist ['reɪsɪst] *adj* rasistowski ▷ *n* rasista(-tka) *m/f*
rack [ræk] *n* **1** (*also*: **luggage ~**) półka na bagaż **2** (*for hanging clothes, dishes*) wieszak
racket ['rækɪt] *n* **1** (*for tennis, squash etc*) rakieta **2** (*noise*: *inf*) hałas
racquet ['rækɪt] *n* rakieta
radar ['reɪdɑːʳ] *n* radar
radiation [reɪdɪ'eɪʃən] *n* (*radioactivity*) promieniowanie
radiator ['reɪdɪeɪtəʳ] *n* (*on wall*) kaloryfer
radio ['reɪdɪəu] *n* radio; **on the ~** w radiu
radioactive ['reɪdɪəu'æktɪv] *adj* radioaktywny
radio station *n* stacja radiowa
radish ['rædɪʃ] *n* rzodkiew
RAF (*Brit*) *n abbr* (= *Royal Air Force*): **the ~** Królewskie Siły Powietrzne
raffle ['ræfl] *n* loteria
raft [rɑːft] *n* (*also*: **life ~**) tratwa
rag [ræg] *n* szmata
rage [reɪdʒ] *n* wściekłość
raid [reɪd] *vt* (*soldiers, police*) atakować (zaatakować *pf*); (*criminal*) napadać (napaść *pf*) na
rail [reɪl] *n* **1** (*for safety on stairs*) poręcz; (*on bridge, balcony*) barierka **2** (*for hanging clothes*) drążek **3** (*for trains*) szyny *f pl*; **by ~** (*by train*) koleją
railcard ['reɪlkɑːd] (*Brit*) *n* zniżkowa karta kolejowa
railroad ['reɪlrəud] (*US*) *n* = **railway**
railway ['reɪlweɪ] (*Brit*) *n* (*system*) kolej
railway line (*Brit*) *n* linia kolejowa
railway station (*Brit*) *n* (*large*) dworzec kolejowy; (*small*) stacja kolejowa
rain [reɪn] *n* deszcz ▷ *vi* padać; **in the ~** w deszczu; (*stand*) na deszczu; (*walk*) po deszczu; **it's ~ing** pada (deszcz)
rainbow ['reɪnbəu] *n* tęcza
raincoat ['reɪnkəut] *n* płaszcz przeciwdeszczowy
rainforest ['reɪnfɔrɪst] *n* las deszczowy
rainy ['reɪnɪ] *adj* deszczowy
raise [reɪz] *vt* **1** (*lift*: *hand, glass*) podnosić (podnieść *pf*) **2** (*salary, rate, morale, standards*) podnosić (podnieść *pf*); (*speed limit*) zwiększać (zwiększyć *pf*) **3** (*child, family*) wychowywać (wychować *pf*) ▷ *n* (*US: pay rise*) podwyżka
raisin ['reɪzn] *n* rodzynek
rake [reɪk] *n* (*tool*) grabie
rally ['rælɪ] *n* **1** (*public meeting*) wiec **2** (*Aut*) rajd **3** (*Tennis*) wymiana
rambler ['ræmbləʳ] *n* (*Brit*: *walker*) wędrowiec(-wczyni) *m/f*
ramp [ræmp] *n* podjazd
ran [ræn] *pt of* **run**

random ['rændəm] *adj* **1** (*arrangement, selection*) losowy **2** (*haphazard*) przypadkowy ▷ *n*: **at ~** na chybił trafił
rang [ræŋ] *pt of* **ring**
range [reɪndʒ] *n* **1** (*of ages, prices*) rozpiętość; (*of subjects, possibilities, responsibilities*) zakres; (*products in a shop*) asortyment **2** (*also*: **mountain ~**) pasmo górskie ▷ *vt* (*place in a line*) ustawiać (ustawić *pf*); **to ~ from... to...** wahać się od +*gen*... do +*gen*...
rap [ræp] *n* (*also*: **~ music**) rap
rape [reɪp] *n* (*crime*) gwałt ▷ *vt* gwałcić (zgwałcić *pf*)
rapids ['ræpɪdz] *n pl* bystrza
rare [rɛəʳ] *adj* **1** (*uncommon*) rzadki **2** (*lightly cooked*) krwisty
rarely ['rɛəlɪ] *adv* rzadko
rasher ['ræʃəʳ] (*Brit*) *n* plasterek
raspberry ['rɑːzbərɪ] *n* (*fruit*) malina
rat [ræt] *n* (*Zool*) szczur
rate [reɪt] *n* (*speed*): **at a ~ of 60 kph** z prędkością sześćdziesiąt kilometrów na godzinę ▷ *vt* (*estimate*) oceniać (ocenić *pf*); **at this/that ~** w tym tempie; **at any ~** (*at least*) w każdym razie
rather ['rɑːðəʳ] *adv* (*somewhat*) raczej; **~ a lot** dość dużo; **I would ~ go than stay** wolałbym iść niż zostać; **I'd ~ not say** wolałbym nie mówić; **~ than** (*instead of*) zamiast +*gen*
rave [reɪv] *n* (*Brit*: *inf*: *dance*) rave
▶ **rave about** *vt fus* (*inf*) zachwycać (zachwycić *pf*) się +*inst*
raw [rɔː] *adj* surowy
raw materials *n pl* surowce
razor ['reɪzəʳ] *n* **1** (*also*: **safety ~**) maszynka do golenia **2** (*also*: **electric ~**) golarka
razor blade *n* żyletka
RE (*Brit*: *Scol*) *n abbr* (= *religious education*) religia
reach [riːtʃ] *vt* **1** (*arrive at*: *place, destination*) docierać (dotrzeć *pf*) do +*gen*; (*conclusion*) dochodzić (dojść *pf*) do +*gen*; (*agreement*) osiągać (osiągnąć *pf*); (*decision*) podejmować (podjąć *pf*); (*stage, level, age*) osiągać (osiągnąć *pf*) **2** (*be able to touch*) sięgać (sięgnąć *pf*) +*gen*; **within ~ of** w zasięgu +*gen*; **out of ~ of** poza zasięgiem +*gen*; **within easy ~ of...** w pobliżu +*gen*...
react [riː'ækt] *vi* (*respond*) reagować (zareagować *pf*)
reaction [riː'ækʃən] *n* (*response*) reakcja
reactor [riː'æktəʳ] *n* reaktor
read [riːd] (*pt, pp* **read** [rɛd]) *vi* (*person*) czytać (przeczytać *pf*) ▷ *vt* **1** (*book, newspaper etc*) czytać (przeczytać *pf*) **2** (*study at university*: *Brit*) studiować
▶ **read out** *vt* odczytywać (odczytać *pf*)
▶ **read through** *vt* czytać (przeczytać *pf*)
reading ['riːdɪŋ] *n* (*activity*) czytanie
ready ['rɛdɪ] *adj* (*prepared, available*) gotowy; **to get ~** (*prepare o.s.*) przygotowywać (przygotować *pf*) się; **to get sb/sth ~** przygotowywać (przygotować *pf*) kogoś/coś; **to be ~ to do sth** (*prepared*) być gotowym do zrobienia czegoś; (*willing*) być chętnym do zrobienia czegoś
real [rɪəl] *adj* prawdziwy; **in ~ life** w rzeczywistości
realistic [rɪə'lɪstɪk] *adj* realistyczny
reality [riː'ælɪtɪ] *n* (*real things*) rzeczywistość; **in ~** w rzeczywistości
realize ['rɪəlaɪz] *vt* (*understand*) zdawać (zdać *pf*) sobie sprawę z +*gen*; **to ~ that...** zdawać (zdać *pf*) sobie sprawę, że...
really ['rɪəlɪ] *adv* **1** (*very*): **~ good/delighted** naprawdę dobry/zadowolony **2** (*genuinely*) naprawdę **3** (*after negative*) naprawdę; **~?** (*indicating surprise, interest*) naprawdę?
realtor ['rɪəltɔːʳ] (*US*) *n* pośrednik w handlu nieruchomościami
rear [rɪəʳ] *n* (*back*) tył ▷ *vt* (*raise*: *cattle, chickens*: *esp Brit*) hodować (wyhodować *pf*); (*family, children*) wychowywać (wychować *pf*)
reason ['riːzn] *n* (*cause*) powód; **the ~ for sth** powód czegoś; **the ~ why** powód, dla którego
reasonable ['riːznəbl] *adj* **1** (*person, decision*) rozsądny **2** (*not bad*) znośny; **be ~!** bądź rozsądny!

reasonably ['ri:znəblɪ] *adv* rozsądnie
reassure [ri:ə'ʃuəʳ] *vt* uspokajać (uspokoić *pf*)
rebellious [rɪ'bɛljəs] *adj* buntowniczy
receipt [rɪ'si:t] *n* (*for purchases*) paragon
receive [rɪ'si:v] *vt* otrzymywać (otrzymać *pf*)
receiver [rɪ'si:vəʳ] *n* (*of telephone*) słuchawka
recent ['ri:snt] *adj* niedawny
recently ['ri:sntlɪ] *adv* ostatnio; **until ~** do niedawna
reception [rɪ'sɛpʃən] *n* **1** (*in public building*) recepcja **2** (*party*) przyjęcie **3** (*welcome*) przyjęcie
receptionist [rɪ'sɛpʃənɪst] (*esp Brit*) *n* recepcjonista(-tka) *m/f*
recipe ['rɛsɪpɪ] (*Culin*) *n* przepis
reckon ['rɛkən] *vt* **1** (*consider*) uważać **2** (*calculate*) szacować (oszacować *pf*); **I ~ that...** (*think*: *inf*) myślę, że...
recognize ['rɛkəgnaɪz] *vt* rozpoznawać (rozpoznać *pf*)
recommend [rɛkə'mɛnd] *vt*: **to ~ sth to sb** polecać (polecić *pf*) coś komuś
reconsider [ri:kən'sɪdəʳ] *vt* rozważać (rozważyć *pf*) ponownie ▷ *vi* zastanawiać (zastanowić *pf*) się jeszcze raz
record [*n, adj* 'rɛkɔ:d, *vb* rɪ'kɔ:d] *n* **1** (*sound-recording*) płyta **2** (*unbeaten statistic*) rekord ▷ *vt* (*make recording of*) nagrywać (nagrać *pf*) ▷ *adj* (*sales, profits, levels*) rekordowy; **records** *n pl* akta *m pl*; **in ~ time** w rekordowym czasie; **to keep a ~ of sth** zapisywać (zapisać *pf*) coś
recorded delivery [rɪ'kɔ:dɪd-] (*Brit*) *n* poczta polecona
recorder [rɪ'kɔ:dəʳ] *n* (*Mus*) flet
recording [rɪ'kɔ:dɪŋ] *n* nagranie
record player *n* adapter
recover [rɪ'kʌvəʳ] *vi* zdrowieć (wyzdrowieć *pf*)
recovery [rɪ'kʌvərɪ] *n* (*from illness, operation*) wyzdrowienie
rectangle ['rɛktæŋgl] *n* prostokąt
rectangular [rɛk'tæŋgjuləʳ] *adj* prostokątny
recycle [ri:'saɪkl] *vt* przetwarzać (przetworzyć *pf*)
recycling [ri:'saɪklɪŋ] *n* recykling
red [rɛd] *adj* **1** czerwony **2** (*hair*) rudy ▷ *n* czerwień
Red Cross *n*: **the ~** czerwony Krzyż
redcurrant ['rɛdkʌrənt] (*Brit*) *n* czerwona porzeczka
red-haired [rɛd'hɛəd] *adj* rudowłosy
redo [ri:'du:] *vt* (*pt* **redid**, *pp* **redone**) przerabiać (przerobić *pf*)
reduce [rɪ'dju:s] *vt* zmniejszać (zmniejszyć *pf*); **to ~ sth by** zmniejszać (zmniejszyć *pf*) coś o; **"~ speed now"** (*Aut*) „zwolnij"
reduction [rɪ'dʌkʃən] *n* **1** (*decrease*) obniżenie **2** (*discount*) obniżka
redundant [rɪ'dʌndnt] (*Brit*) *adj* (*unemployed*) bezrobotny; **to be made ~** (*worker*) zostać *pf* zwolnionym z pracy
refer [rɪ'fə:ʳ]
▸ **refer to** *vt fus* **1** (*mention*) wspominać (wspomnieć *pf*) o *+loc* **2** (*relate to*) nawiązywać (nawiązać *pf*) do *+gen* **3** (*mean*) oznaczać
referee [rɛfə'ri:] *n* (*Sport*) sędzia(-ina) *m/f*
reference ['rɛfrəns] *n* **1** (*mention*) wzmianka **2** (*for job application*: *letter*) referencje *f pl*
refill [ri:'fɪl] *vt* napełniać (napełnić *pf*) ponownie
reflect [rɪ'flɛkt] *vt* (*image, light, heat*) odbijać (odbić *pf*)
reflection [rɪ'flɛkʃən] *n* **1** (*image*) odbicie **2** (*thought*) refleksja
reflex ['ri:flɛks] *n* (*Physiol*) odruch
refreshing [rɪ'frɛʃɪŋ] *adj* orzeźwiający
refreshments [rɪ'frɛʃmənts] *n pl* napoje
refrigerator [rɪ'frɪdʒəreɪtəʳ] *n* lodówka
refuge ['rɛfju:dʒ] *n* (*safe house*) schronienie
refugee [rɛfju'dʒi:] *n* uchodźca(-źczyni) *m/f*
refund [*n* 'ri:fʌnd, *vb* rɪ'fʌnd] *n* zwrot pieniędzy ▷ *vt* (*money*) refundować (zrefundować *pf*)
refuse[1] [rɪ'fju:z] *vt* odmawiać (odmówić *pf*) *+gen*; **to ~ to do sth**

odmawiać (odmówić *pf*) zrobienia czegoś; **to ~ sb permission** odmawiać (odmówić *pf*) komuś pozwolenia
refuse² ['rɛfju:s] *n* śmieci *m pl*
regain [rɪ'geɪn] *vt* odzyskiwać (odzyskać *pf*)
regard [rɪ'gɑ:d] *vt* (*consider, view*) uważać ▷ *n* (*esteem*) szacunek; **to give one's ~s to sb** pozdrawiać (pozdrowić *pf*) kogoś
regime [reɪ'ʒi:m] *n* (*system of government*) reżim
regiment ['rɛdʒɪmənt] *n* (*Mil*) pułk
region ['ri:dʒən] *n* (*area*) region
regional ['ri:dʒənl] *adj* regionalny
register ['rɛdʒɪstə^r] *n* (*in school*) lista obecności
registered ['rɛdʒɪstəd] *adj* (*letter, mail*) polecony
registration [rɛdʒɪs'treɪʃən] *n* (*of birth, death, students etc*) rejestracja
regret [rɪ'grɛt] *n* żal ▷ *vt* (*one's action*) żałować (pożałować *pf*) +*gen*; **to have no ~s** w ogóle nie żałować; **to ~ that...** żałować (pożałować *pf*), że...
regular ['rɛgjulə^r] *adj* **1** (*even*) regularny **2** (*frequent*) regularny; (*visitor*) stały **3** (*normal*) normalny
regularly ['rɛgjuləlɪ] *adv* regularnie
regulation [rɛgju'leɪʃən] *n* (*rule*) przepis
rehab ['ri:hæb] (*inf*) *n* odwyk
rehearsal [rɪ'hə:səl] *n* próba
rehearse [rɪ'hə:s] *vt* robić (zrobić *pf*) próbę +*gen* ▷ *vi* robić (zrobić *pf*) próbę
rein [reɪn] *n*: **~s** (*for horse*) lejce
reindeer ['reɪndɪə^r] (*pl* **reindeer**) *n* renifer
reject [rɪ'dʒɛkt] *vt* odrzucać (odrzucić *pf*)
related [rɪ'leɪtɪd] *adj* (*people*) spokrewniony; **to be ~ to sb** być z kimś spokrewnionym
relation [rɪ'leɪʃən] *n* **1** (*relative*) krewny(-na) *m/f* **2** (*connection*) relacja; **in ~ to** w odniesieniu do +*gen*
relationship [rɪ'leɪʃənʃɪp] *n* **1** (*connection*) związek **2** (*between two people, countries*) stosunki *m pl* **3** (*affair*) związek; **to have a good ~** mieć dobre stosunki
relative ['rɛlətɪv] *n* (*member of family*) krewny(-na) *m/f*
relatively ['rɛlətɪvlɪ] *adv* stosunkowo
relax [rɪ'læks] *vi* (*person: unwind*) odprężać (odprężyć *pf*) się
relaxation [ri:læk'seɪʃən] *n* (*rest*) relaks
relaxed [rɪ'lækst] *adj* (*person*) odprężony; (*discussion, atmosphere*) spokojny
relaxing [rɪ'læksɪŋ] *adj* odprężający
relay ['ri:leɪ] *n* (*also*: **~ race**) sztafeta
release [rɪ'li:s] *n* (*of prisoner*) zwolnienie ▷ *vt* **1** (*person*) zwalniać (zwolnić *pf*) **2** (*record*) wydawać (wydać *pf*); (*film*) wypuszczać (wypuścić *pf*)
relevant ['rɛləvənt] *adj* **1** (*fact, information, question*) istotny **2** (*chapter, area*) odnośny; **~ to** mający związek z +*inst*
reliable [rɪ'laɪəbl] *adj* (*person, news, information*) pewny; (*method, machine*) niezawodny
relief [rɪ'li:f] *n* (*gladness*) ulga
relieved [rɪ'li:vd] *adj* odczuwający ulgę; **to be ~ that...** odczuwać (odczuć *pf*) ulgę, że...
religion [rɪ'lɪdʒən] *n* **1** (*belief*) wyznanie **2** (*set of beliefs*) religia
religious [rɪ'lɪdʒəs] *adj* religijny
religious education *n* wychowanie religijne
reluctant [rɪ'lʌktənt] *adj* niechętny; **to be ~ to do sth** nie mieć ochoty zrobić czegoś
reluctantly [rɪ'lʌktəntlɪ] *adv* niechętnie
rely on [rɪ'laɪ-] *vt fus* **1** (*be dependent on*) zależeć od +*gen* **2** (*trust*) polegać na +*loc*
remain [rɪ'meɪn] *vi* **1** (*continue to be*) pozostawać (pozostać *pf*) **2** (*stay*) zostawać (zostać *pf*); **to ~ silent** zachowywać (zachować *pf*) milczenie
remaining [rɪ'meɪnɪŋ] *adj* pozostały
remark [rɪ'mɑ:k] *n* uwaga

remarkable [rɪ'mɑːkəbl] *adj* nadzwyczajny
remarkably [rɪ'mɑːkəblɪ] *adv* nadzwyczajnie
remember [rɪ'mɛmbəʳ] *vt* **1** (*still have in mind*) pamiętać **2** (*bring back to mind*) przypominać (przypomnieć *pf*) sobie **3** (*bear in mind*) pamiętać (zapamiętać *pf*); **she ~ed to do it** pamiętała, żeby to zrobić

REMEMBRANCE DAY

Remembrance Day – Dzień Pamięci obchodzony jest w Wielkiej Brytanii co roku w niedzielę najbliższą 11 Listopada. Święto to upamiętnia poległych w obu wojnach światowych. W powszechnym zwyczaju jest noszenie w ten dzień w klapach marynarek i płaszczy sztucznych kwiatów maku.

remind [rɪ'maɪnd] *vt* przypominać (przypomnieć *pf*) *+dat*; **to ~ sb to do sth** przypominać (przypomnieć *pf*) komuś, by coś zrobił; **to ~ sb of sb/sth** (*be reminiscent of*) przypominać (przypomnieć *pf*) komuś kogoś/coś
remote [rɪ'məut] *adj* (*place*) odległy
remote control *n* (*device: for TV etc*) pilot
remotely [rɪ'məutlɪ] *adv* (*at all*) w ogóle
remove [rɪ'muːv] *vt* **1** (*object, organ*) usuwać (usunąć *pf*) **2** (*clothing, bandage etc*) zdejmować (zdjąć *pf*) **3** (*stain*) usuwać (usunąć *pf*)
renew [rɪ'njuː] *vt* (*loan, contract*) odnawiać (odnowić *pf*)
renovate ['rɛnəveɪt] *vt* odnawiać (odnowić *pf*)
rent [rɛnt] *n* (*for building, room, land*) czynsz ▷ *vt* **1** (*hire*) dzierżawić (wydzierżawić *pf*) **2** (*also*: **~ out**: *house, room*) wynajmować (wynająć *pf*)
reorganize [riː'ɔːgənaɪz] *vt* reorganizować (zreorganizować *pf*)
rep [rɛp] *n* (*representative: for group*) przedstawiciel(ka) *m/f*; (*also*: **sales ~**) przedstawiciel(ka) *m/f* handlowy(-wa)
repair [rɪ'pɛəʳ] *n* naprawa ▷ *vt* **1** (*object, building*) remontować (wyremontować *pf*) **2** (*damage*) naprawiać (naprawić *pf*)
repay [riː'peɪ] (*pt, pp* **repaid**) *vt* (*loan, debt, person*) spłacać (spłacić *pf*)
repeat [rɪ'piːt] *vt* **1** (*statement, question*) powtarzać (powtórzyć *pf*) **2** (*action, mistake*) ponawiać (ponowić *pf*) ▷ *vi*: **I ~** powtarzam ▷ *n* (*Rad, TV*) powtórka
repeatedly [rɪ'piːtɪdlɪ] *adv* wielokrotnie
repetitive [rɪ'pɛtɪtɪv] *adj* powtarzający się
replace [rɪ'pleɪs] *vt* **1** (*put back*) odkładać (odłożyć *pf*) **2** (*take the place of*) zastępować (zastąpić *pf*)
replay [*n* 'riːpleɪ, *vb* riː'pleɪ] *n* **1** (*TV: repeat showing*) powtórka **2** (*of match*) powtórnie rozegrany mecz ▷ *vt* (*on CD*) odtwarzać (odtworzyć *pf*) ponownie; **to ~ a match** ponownie rozgrywać (rozegrać *pf*) mecz
reply [rɪ'plaɪ] *n* (*answer*) odpowiedź ▷ *vi* (*to question, letter*) odpowiadać (odpowiedzieć *pf*); **there's no ~** (*Tel*) nikt nie odpowiada
report [rɪ'pɔːt] *n* **1** (*account*) sprawozdanie **2** (*bulletin*) relacja **3** (*Brit*: *also*: **school ~**) świadectwo szkolne ▷ *vt* (*theft, accident, death*) zgłaszać (zgłosić *pf*); (*person*) donosić (donieść *pf*) na
report card *n* świadectwo szkolne
reporter [rɪ'pɔːtəʳ] *n* reporter(ka) *m/f*
represent [rɛprɪ'zɛnt] *vt* (*act on behalf of*) reprezentować
representative [rɛprɪ'zɛntətɪv] *n* przedstawiciel(ka) *m/f*
reptile ['rɛptaɪl] *n* gad
republic [rɪ'pʌblɪk] *n* republika
reputation [rɛpju'teɪʃən] *n* reputacja
request [rɪ'kwɛst] *n* (*polite demand*) prośba ▷ *vt* prosić (poprosić *pf*) o
require [rɪ'kwaɪəʳ] *vt* **1** (*need*) potrzebować *+gen* **2** (*demand*) wymagać *+gen*; **to be ~d** (*approval, permission*) być wymaganym
rescue ['rɛskjuː] *n* ratunek ▷ *vt* ratować (uratować *pf*); **to go/come**

to sb's ~ iść/przychodzić (przyjść *pf*) komuś na ratunek
research [rɪ'sə:tʃ] *n* badanie; **to do ~** prowadzić badania
resemblance [rɪ'zɛmbləns] *n* podobieństwo
resemble [rɪ'zɛmbl] *vt* być podobnym do *+gen*
resent [rɪ'zɛnt] *vt* (*attitude, treatment*) czuć (poczuć *pf*) się urażonym *+inst*; (*person*) odczuwać (odczuć *pf*) urazę do *+gen*
resentful [rɪ'zɛntful] *adj* urażony
reservation [rɛzə'veɪʃən] *n* (*booking*) rezerwacja; **to make a ~** robić (zrobić *pf*) rezerwację
reservation desk (*US*) *n* (*in hotel*) recepcja
reserve [rɪ'zə:v] *vt* (*seat, table, ticket etc*) rezerwować (zarezerwować *pf*) ▷ *n* (*Brit: Sport*) rezerwowy(-wa) *m/f*
reserved [rɪ'zə:vd] *adj* **1** (*unavailable: seat*) zarezerwowany **2** (*restrained*) powściągliwy
residence permit ['rɛzɪdəns-] (*Brit*) *n* pozwolenie na pobyt
resident ['rɛzɪdənt] *n* mieszkaniec(-nka) *m/f*
residential [rɛzɪ'dɛnʃəl] *adj* (*area*) mieszkaniowy
resign [rɪ'zaɪn] *vi* ustępować (ustąpić *pf*)
resist [rɪ'zɪst] *vt* (*temptation, urge*) opierać (oprzeć *pf*) się *+dat*
resit [ri:'sɪt] (*Brit*) *vt* (*exam*) przystępować (przystąpić *pf*) ponownie do *+gen* ▷ *n* powtórka egzaminu pisemnego
resolution [rɛzə'lu:ʃən] *n* zdecydowanie; **to make a ~** zrobić (*pf*) postanowienie; **New Year's ~** noworoczne postanowienie
resort [rɪ'zɔ:t] *n* **1** (*also*: **holiday ~**) miejscowość wypoczynkowa **2** (*recourse*): **without ~ to** bez uciekania się do *+gen* ▷ *vi*: **to ~ to sth** uciekać (uciec *pf*) się do czegoś; **a seaside ~** kurort nadmorski; **winter sports ~** ośrodek sportów zimowych; **as a last ~** w ostateczności
resources [rɪ'zɔ:səz] *n pl* **1** (*coal, iron, oil*) zasoby **2** (*money*) środki pieniężne; **natural ~** bogactwa naturalne
respect [rɪs'pɛkt] *n* szacunek ▷ *vt* (*person*) szanować (uszanować *pf*); **to have ~ for sb/sth** mieć szacunek dla kogoś/czegoś
respectable [rɪs'pɛktəbl] *adj* **1** (*area, background*) przyzwoity **2** (*person*) porządny **3** (*standard, mark*) przyzwoity
responsibility [rɪspɔnsɪ'bɪlɪtɪ] *n* obowiązek; **responsibilities** *n pl* obowiązki
responsible [rɪs'pɔnsɪbl] *adj* odpowiedzialny
rest [rɛst] *n* **1** (*relaxation*) relaks **2** (*break*) odpoczynek **3** (*remainder*) reszta ▷ *vi* **1** (*relax*) odpoczywać (odpocząć *pf*) **2** (*be supported*): **to ~ on/against sth** opierać (oprzeć *pf*) się na czymś/o coś ▷ *vt* (*relax: eyes, legs, muscles*) dawać (dać *pf*) odpocząć *+dat*; **to ~ sth on sth** (*lean*) opierać (oprzeć *pf*) coś na czymś; **the ~ (of them)** reszta
rest area (*US*) *n* *miejsce odpoczynku przy drodze*
restaurant ['rɛstərɔŋ] *n* restauracja
restless ['rɛstlɪs] *adj* **1** (*dissatisfied*) niezadowolony **2** (*fidgety*) niespokojny
restore [rɪ'stɔ:ʳ] *vt* (*painting, building etc*) odrestaurowywać (odrestaurować *pf*)
restrict [rɪs'trɪkt] *vt* ograniczać (ograniczyć *pf*)
rest room (*US*) *n* toaleta
result [rɪ'zʌlt] *n* (*of event, action*) skutek; (*of match, election, exam, competition*) rezultat; (*of calculation*) wynik ▷ *vi*: **to ~ in** prowadzić (doprowadzić *pf*) do *+gen*; **as a ~ of** w wyniku *+gen*; **to ~ from** wynikać (wyniknąć *pf*) z *+gen*; **as a ~ it is...** w rezultacie to jest...
resume [rɪ'zju:m] *vt* (*work, journey*) podejmować (podjąć *pf*) na nowo
résumé ['reɪzju:meɪ] *n* (*US: CV*) życiorys
retire [rɪ'taɪəʳ] *vi* (*give up work*) przechodzić (przejść *pf*) na emeryturę
retired [rɪ'taɪəd] *adj* emerytowany

retiree [rɪtaɪə'riː] (*US*) *n* emeryt(ka) *m/f*
retirement [rɪ'taɪəmənt] *n* emerytura
return [rɪ'təːn] *vi* (*person*) wracać (wrócić *pf*); (*situation, symptom*) powracać (powrócić *pf*) ▷ *vt* (*something borrowed or stolen*) zwracać (zwrócić *pf*) ▷ *n* **1** (*of person*) powrót **2** (*of something borrowed or stolen*) zwrot **3** (*Comput*: *key*) klawisz powrotu ▷ *adj* **1** (*Brit*: *journey, ticket*) powrotny **2** (*Brit*: *match*) rewanżowy; **in ~ for** w zamian za; **many happy ~s (of the day)!** wszystkiego najlepszego (z okazji urodzin)!
reunion [riː'juːnɪən] *n* zjazd
reveal [rɪ'viːl] *vt* (*make known*) ujawniać (ujawnić *pf*)
revenge [rɪ'vɛndʒ] *n* zemsta; **to take (one's) ~ (on sb)** dokonywać (dokonać *pf*) (na kimś) zemsty
reverse [rɪ'vəːs] *adj* (*process, effect*) przeciwny ▷ *vt* (*car*: *esp Brit*) cofać (cofnąć *pf*) ▷ *vi* (*esp Brit*: *Aut*) cofać (cofnąć *pf*) się; **in ~ order** w odwrotnej kolejności
reverse-charge call [rɪ'vəːstʃɑːdʒ-] (*Brit*) *n* rozmowa na koszt rozmówcy
review [rɪ'vjuː] *n* (*of book, film etc*) recenzja
revise [rɪ'vaɪz] *vt* (*Brit*: *study*) powtarzać (powtórzyć *pf*) ▷ *vi* (*Brit*) powtarzać (powtórzyć *pf*)
revision [rɪ'vɪʒən] *n* (*Brit*: *studying*) powtórka
revolting [rɪ'vəultɪŋ] *adj* odrażający
revolution [rɛvə'luːʃən] *n* rewolucja
reward [rɪ'wɔːd] *n* (*for service, merit, work*) nagroda ▷ *vt* (*person*) nagradzać (nagrodzić *pf*)
rewarding [rɪ'wɔːdɪŋ] *adj* cenny
rewind [riː'waɪnd] (*pt, pp* **rewound**) *vt* (*wool, tape*) przewijać (przewinąć *pf*)
rhinoceros [raɪ'nɔsərəs] *n* nosorożec
rhubarb ['ruːbɑːb] *n* rabarbar
rhythm ['rɪðm] *n* rytm
rib [rɪb] *n* (*Anat*) żebro
ribbon ['rɪbən] *n* wstążka
rice [raɪs] *n* ryż
rich [rɪtʃ] *adj* (*person, country*) bogaty ▷ *n pl*: **the ~** bogaci
rid [rɪd] (*pt, pp* **rid**) *vt*: **to ~ sb/sth of sth** uwalniać (uwolnić *pf*) kogoś/coś od czegoś; **to get ~ of sth/sb** pozbywać (pozbyć *pf*) się czegoś/kogoś
ride [raɪd] (*pt* **rode**, *pp* **ridden** ['rɪdn]) *vi* **1** (*travel*: *on bicycle, on horse*) jechać (pojechać *pf*) **2** (*in car, on bus, on train*: *US*) jechać (pojechać *pf*) ▷ *vt* **1** (*horse, bicycle, motorcycle*: *habitually*) jeździć na *+loc* **2** (*traverse distance*: *on horseback*) przemierzać (przemierzyć *pf*) konno; **to go for a ~** jechać (pojechać *pf*) na przejażdżkę; **to give sb a ~** (*US*) podwozić (podwieźć *pf*) kogoś
rider ['raɪdə[r]] *n* (*on horse*) jeździec/amazonka *m/f*; (*on bicycle*) rowerzysta(-tka) *m/f*; (*on motorcycle*) motocyklista(-tka) *m/f*
ridiculous [rɪ'dɪkjuləs] *adj* śmieszny
riding ['raɪdɪŋ] *n* jazda konna; **to go ~** jeździć konno
rifle ['raɪfl] *n* karabin
right [raɪt] *adj* **1** (*not left*) prawy **2** (*correct*: *answer, size, person*) właściwy; (*appropriate*: *person, place, clothes*) odpowiedni; (*decision, direction, time*) właściwy ▷ *n* **1** (*not left*) prawa strona **2** (*entitlement*) prawo ▷ *adv* **1** (*correctly*) poprawnie **2** (*properly, fairly*) słusznie **3** (*not to/on the left*) po prawej stronie ▷ *excl* dobra jest!; **do you have the ~ time?** masz dokładną godzinę?; **to be ~** (*person*) mieć rację; (*answer, fact*) zgadzać (zgodzić *pf*) się; (*clock*) dobrze chodzić; **you did the ~ thing** postąpił pan/postąpiła pani słusznie; **~ ahead** prosto; **to** *or* **on the ~** (*position*) po prawo stronie; **to the ~** (*movement*) na prawo
right-hand drive ['raɪthænd-] *adj* (*vehicle*) z kierownicą po prawej stronie
right-handed [raɪt'hændɪd] *adj* praworęczny
rightly ['raɪtlɪ] *adv* (*with reason*) słusznie; **if I remember ~** (*Brit*) jeśli dobrze pamiętam

ring [rɪŋ] (*pt* **rang**, *pp* **rung**) *n* (*on finger*) pierścionek ▷ *vi* dzwonić (zadzwonić *pf*) ▷ *vt* **1** (*bell, doorbell*) dzwonić (zadzwonić *pf*) +*inst* **2** (*Brit: Tel*) dzwonić (zadzwonić *pf*) do +*gen*; **there was a ~ at the door, the doorbell rang** ktoś zadzwonił do drzwi; **to give sb a ~** (*Brit: Tel*) dzwonić (zadzwonić *pf*) do kogoś
▸ **ring back** (*Brit: Tel*) *vt* oddzwaniać (oddzwonić *pf*) do +*gen* ▷ *vi* oddzwaniać (oddzwonić *pf*)
▸ **ring up** (*Brit: Tel*) *vt* dzwonić (zadzwonić *pf*) do +*gen*

rinse [rɪns] *vt* płukać (spłukać *pf*); (*also*: **~ out**: *mouth*) płukać (wypłukać *pf*)

riot ['raɪət] *n* (*disturbance*) zamieszki *m pl* ▷ *vi* buntować (zbuntować *pf*) się

rip [rɪp] *vt* rozdzierać (rozedrzeć *pf*) ▷ *vi* drzeć (podrzeć *pf*) się
▸ **rip off** *vt* (*inf: swindle*) zdzierać (zedrzeć *pf*) z +*gen*

ripe [raɪp] *adj* (*fruit, corn*) dojrzały

rip-off ['rɪpɔf] (*inf*) *n* zdzierstwo

rise [raɪz] (*pt* **rose**, *pp* **risen** [rɪzn]) *n* **1** (*Brit: salary increase*) podwyżka **2** (*in prices, temperature, crime rate*) podwyżka ▷ *vi* **1** (*move upwards*) podnosić (podnieść *pf*) się **2** (*prices, numbers*) wzrastać (wzrosnąć *pf*) **3** (*sun, moon*) wschodzić (wzejść *pf*) **4** (*from chair*) wstawać (wstać *pf*)

risk [rɪsk] *n* (*danger, possibility, chance*) ryzyko ▷ *vt* (*take the chance of*) ryzykować (zaryzykować *pf*); **to take a ~** ryzykować (zaryzykować *pf*); **at one's own ~** na własne ryzyko; **to ~ it** (*inf*) ryzykować (zaryzykować *pf*)

rival ['raɪvl] *n* rywal(ka) *m/f* ▷ *adj* przeciwny

river ['rɪvə^r] *n* rzeka

river bank *n* brzeg rzeki

road [rəud] *n* **1** (*in country*) droga **2** (*in town*) ulica **3** (*fig*) droga; **it takes four hours by ~** podróż samochodem trwa cztery godziny

road map *n* mapa samochodowa

road rage *n* agresja na drodze

road sign *n* znak drogowy

roadworks ['rəudwə:ks] *n pl* roboty drogowe

roast [rəust] *vt* (*food*) piec (upiec *pf*)

rob [rɔb] *vt* okradać (okraść *pf*); **to ~ sb of sth** okradać (okraść *pf*) kogoś z czegoś

robber ['rɔbə^r] *n* złodziej

robbery ['rɔbərɪ] *n* rabunek

robin ['rɔbɪn] *n* rudzik

robot ['rəubɔt] *n* robot

rock [rɔk] *n* **1** (*boulder*) skała **2** (*esp US: small stone*) kamień **3** (*Mus: also*: **~ music**) rock ▷ *vt* **1** (*swing gently: child*) kołysać (ukołysać *pf*) **2** (*shake: explosion*) trząść (zatrząść *pf*) +*inst*

rock climbing *n* wspinaczka

rocket ['rɔkɪt] *n* **1** (*Space*) rakieta **2** (*firework*) raca

rocking horse ['rɔkɪŋ-] *n* koń na biegunach

rod [rɔd] *n* **1** (*pole*) pręt **2** (*also*: **fishing ~**) wędka

rode [rəud] *pt of* **ride**

role [rəul] *n* rola

roll [rəul] *n* **1** (*of paper, cloth, film*) rolka **2** (*also*: **bread ~**) bułka ▷ *vt* **1** (*ball, stone, dice etc*) toczyć (potoczyć *pf*) **2** (*also*: **~ out**: *pastry*) wałkować (rozwałkować *pf*) ▷ *vi* (*ball, stone etc*) toczyć (potoczyć *pf*) się; **cheese/ham ~** bułka z serem/szynką
▸ **roll about, roll around** *vi* (*inf*) turlać (poturlać *pf*) się

Rollerblades® ['rəuləbleɪdz] *n pl* łyżworolki®

roller coaster ['rəulə^r'kəustə^r] *n* kolejka górska

roller skates ['rəulə^r-] *n pl* wrotki

roller skating *n* jazda na wrotkach

Roman ['rəumən] *adj* rzymski

Roman Catholic *adj* rzymskokatolicki ▷ *n* katolik(-iczka) *m/f*

romance [rə'mæns] *n* **1** (*affair*) romans **2** (*charm, excitement*) romantyczność

Romania [rə'meɪnɪə] *n* Rumunia

romantic [rə'mæntɪk] *adj* romantyczny

roof [ru:f] *n* dach

roof rack *n* (*Brit: Aut*) bagażnik dachowy

room [ru:m] *n* **1** (*in house*) pokój **2** (*also*: **bed~**) sypialnia **3** (*space*) miejsce; **single/double ~** pokój jednoosobowy/dwuosobowy

root [ruːt] *n* (*Bot*) korzeń
rope [rəup] *n* lina
▸ **rope in** *vt* (*inf*: *person*) ściągać (ściągnąć *pf*) do pomocy
rose [rəuz] *pt of* **rise** ▷ *n* (*flower*) róża
rosy ['rəuzɪ] *adj* (*complexion*) różowy
rot [rɔt] *vt* (*cause to decay*) niszczyć (zniszczyć *pf*) ▷ *vi* (*decay*: *teeth*) psuć (popsuć *pf*) się; (*wood, fruit etc*) gnić (zgnić *pf*)
rotten ['rɔtn] *adj* **1** (*decayed*: *food*) zepsuty **2** (*inf*: *awful*) okropny; **to feel ~** (*ill*: *inf*) czuć się okropnie
rough [rʌf] *adj* **1** (*skin, surface, cloth*) szorstki **2** (*terrain*) nierówny **3** (*sea*) wzburzony; (*crossing*) ciężki **4** (*violent*: *person*) brutalny; (*town, area*) niebezpieczny **5** (*hard*: *life, conditions, journey*) ciężki **6** (*approximate*: *outline, plan, idea*) roboczy; **to feel ~** (*Brit*: *inf*) czuć się źle
roughly ['rʌflɪ] *adv* **1** (*violently*) brutalnie **2** (*approximately*) mniej więcej; **~ speaking** mniej więcej
round [raund] *adj* **1** (*circular*) okrągły **2** (*spherical*) okrągły **3** (*approximate*: *figure, sum*) przybliżony ▷ *n* **1** (*in competition*) runda **2** (*of drinks*) kolejka **3** (*Golf*) partia **4** (*Boxing*) runda ▷ *prep* **1** (*surrounding*) naokoło *+gen* **2** (*near*) blisko *+gen* **3**: **~ the corner** za rogiem **4** (*indicating circular movement*): **to move ~ the room/sail ~ the world** chodzić wokół pokoju/ żeglować dookoła świata; **all ~** generalnie; **to go ~ sth** wić się wokół czegoś; **to go ~ to sb's house** chodzić (pójść *pf*) do czyjegoś domu; **all (the) year ~** przez cały rok; **to ask sb ~** zapraszać (zaprosić *pf*) kogoś do siebie; **I'll be ~ at 6 o'clock** przyjdę na szóstą; **~ about** (*esp Brit*: *approximately*) w przybliżeniu; **~ the clock** (*inf*) całą dobę; **a ~ of applause** burza oklasków; **a ~ of toast/ sandwiches** (*Brit*) grzanka/kanapka
▸ **round off** *vt* (*meal, evening etc*) kończyć (zakończyć *pf*)
▸ **round up** *vt* **1** (*cattle, sheep*) spędzać (spędzić *pf*) **2** (*people*) gromadzić (zgromadzić *pf*) **3** (*price, figure*) zaokrąglać (zaokrąglić *pf*) w górę
roundabout ['raundəbaut] *n* (*Brit*) **1** (*Aut*) rondo **2** (*at funfair*) karuzela
round trip *n* podróż w obie strony ▷ *adj* (*also*: **round-trip**: *US*) w obie strony
route [ruːt] *n* **1** (*path, journey*) droga **2** (*of bus, train*) trasa
routine [ruː'tiːn] *n* (*procedure*) ustalony porządek
row¹ [rəu] *n* rząd ▷ *vi* (*in boat*) wiosłować (powiosłować *pf*) ▷ *vt* (*boat*) płynąć (popłynąć *pf*) *+inst*; **in a ~** w rzędzie
row² [rau] *n* **1** (*noise*: *Brit*: *inf*) hałas **2** (*noisy quarrel*) kłótnia
rowboat ['rəubəut] (*US*) *n* łódź wiosłowa
rowing ['rəuɪŋ] *n* (*Sport*) wioślarstwo
rowing boat (*Brit*) *n* łódź wiosłowa
royal ['rɔɪəl] *adj* królewski; **the ~ family** rodzina królewska
RSI (*Med*) *n abbr* (= *repetitive strain injury*) zespół RSI
rub [rʌb] *vt* (*with hand, fingers*) trzeć (potrzeć *pf*); (*with cloth, substance*) przecierać (przetrzeć *pf*)
▸ **rub out** *vt* (*erase*) wymazywać (wymazać *pf*)
rubber ['rʌbəʳ] *n* **1** (*substance*) guma **2** (*Brit*) gumka do wycierania
rubber boot (*US*) *n* kalosz
rubbish ['rʌbɪʃ] (*Brit*) *n* **1** (*refuse*) śmieci *m pl* **2** (*inferior material*) tandeta **3** (*nonsense*) bzdury *f pl* ▷ *adj* (*Brit*: *inf*): **I'm ~ at golf** jestem słaby w grze w golfa
rubbish bin (*Brit*) *n* kosz na śmieci
rucksack ['rʌksæk] *n* plecak
rude [ruːd] *adj* **1** (*person, behaviour, remark*) niegrzeczny **2** (*vulgar*: *word, joke*) wulgarny; (*noise*) nieprzyzwoity; **to be ~ to sb** być niegrzecznym wobec kogoś
rug [rʌg] *n* **1** (*carpet*) chodnik **2** (*Brit*: *blanket*) koc
rugby ['rʌgbɪ] *n* (*also*: **~ football**) rugby
ruin ['ruːɪn] *n* (*destruction*: *of building*) ruina ▷ *vt* (*spoil*: *clothes, carpet etc*) niszczyć (zniszczyć *pf*); (*plans, prospects etc*) rujnować (zrujnować *pf*); **ruins** *n pl* (*of building, castle etc*)

ruiny; **to be in ~s** (*building, town*) lec w gruzach

rule [ru:l] *n* **1** (*regulation*) reguła **2** (*of language*) zasada; **it's against the ~s** to niezgodne z przepisami; **as a ~** z reguły

▸ **rule out** *vt* (*idea, possibility etc*) wykluczać (wykluczyć *pf*)

ruler ['ru:ləʳ] *n* (*for measuring*) linijka

rum [rʌm] *n* rum

rumour ['ru:məʳ] (*US* **rumor**) *n* plotka

run [rʌn] (*pt* **ran**, *pp* **run**) *n* **1** (*as exercise, sport*) bieg **2** (*Cricket, Baseball*) punkt ▷ *vt* **1** (*race, distance*) przebiegać (przebiec *pf*) **2** (*operate: business, shop, country*) prowadzić (poprowadzić *pf*) **3** (*water, bath*) puszczać (puścić *pf*) **4** (*perform: program, test*) przeprowadzać (przeprowadzić *pf*) ▷ *vi* **1** (*person, animal*) biec (pobiec *pf*) **2** (*flee*) uciekać (uciec *pf*) **3** (*bus, train: operate*) jeździć; **to go for a ~** (*as exercise*) biegać (pobiegać *pf*); **in the long ~** na dłuższą metę; **I'll ~ you to the station** podwiozę pana/panią na dworzec; **to ~ on** *or* **off petrol/batteries** działać na benzynę/baterie

▸ **run after** *vt fus* (*chase*) ganiać (gonić *pf*)

▸ **run away** *vi* (*from home, situation*) uciekać (uciec *pf*)

▸ **run into** *vt fus* (*meet: person*) wpadać (wpaść *pf*) na; (*trouble, problems*) popadać (popaść *pf*) w

▸ **run off** *vi* (*person, animal*) uciekać (uciec *pf*); **to ~ off with sb** uciekać (uciec *pf*) z kimś

▸ **run out** *vi* **1** (*time, money, luck*) kończyć (skończyć *pf*) się **2** (*lease, passport*) wygasać (wygasnąć *pf*)

▸ **run out of** *vt fus* nie mieć już *+gen*

▸ **run over** *vt* (*Aut: person*) potrącać (potrącić *pf*)

rung [rʌŋ] *pp of* **ring**

runner ['rʌnəʳ] *n* (*in race*) biegacz(ka) *m/f*

runner-up [rʌnər'ʌp] *n* zdobywca(-czyni) *m/f* drugiego miejsca

running ['rʌnɪŋ] *n* (*sport*) biegi *m pl*; **6 days ~** sześć dni z rzędu

run-up ['rʌnʌp] *n*: **the ~ to...** (*election*) okres poprzedzający...

runway ['rʌnweɪ] *n* (*Aviat*) pas startowy

rush [rʌʃ] *n* (*hurry*) pośpiech ▷ *vi* (*person*) śpieszyć (pośpieszyć *pf*) się; **to be in a ~ (to do sth)** śpieszyć (pośpieszyć *pf*) się (ze zrobieniem czegoś)

▸ **rush through** *vt* (*order, application*) wykonywać (wykonać *pf*) w pośpiechu

rush hour *n* godziny szczytu

Russia ['rʌʃə] *n* Rosja

Russian ['rʌʃən] *adj* rosyjski ▷ *n* **1** (*person*) Rosjanin(ka) *m/f* **2** (*language*) rosyjski

rust [rʌst] *n* rdza

rusty ['rʌstɪ] *adj* **1** (*surface, object*) zardzewiały **2** (*skill*) przykurzony

RV (*US*) *n abbr* (= *recreational vehicle*) pojazd rekreacyjny

rye [raɪ] *n* (*cereal*) żyto

S

Sabbath ['sæbəθ] *n* szabat
sack [sæk] *n* worek ▷ *vt* wyrzucać (wyrzucić *pf*) z pracy; **to get the ~** zostać *(pf)* wyrzuconym z pracy
sacred ['seɪkrɪd] *adj* (*holy*) święty
sacrifice ['sækrɪfaɪs] *n* (*fig*) poświęcenie
sad [sæd] *adj* **1** (*unhappy*) smutny **2** (*distressing*) przykry **3** (*regrettable*) godny ubolewania; **he was ~ to see her go** było mu smutno, że odeszła
saddle ['sædl] *n* (*for horse*) siodło; (*on bike, motorbike*) siodełko
safe [seɪf] *adj* bezpieczny ▷ *n* sejf
safety ['seɪftɪ] *n* bezpieczeństwo
Sagittarius [sædʒɪ'tɛərɪəs] *n* (*Astrol*) Strzelec
said [sɛd] *pt, pp of* **say**
sail [seɪl] *n* (*of boat, yacht*) żagiel ▷ *vi* płynąć (popłynąć *pf*)
sailing ['seɪlɪŋ] *n* żeglarstwo; **to go ~** wybierać (wybrać *pf*) się na żagle
sailor ['seɪləʳ] *n* (*for pleasure*) żeglarz(-rka) *m/f*; (*seaman*) marynarz
saint [seɪnt] *n* święty(-ta) *m/f*
sake [seɪk] *n*: **for the ~ of** (*health, career, person*) ze względu na
salad ['sæləd] *n* sałatka
salami [sə'lɑːmɪ] *n* salami
salary ['sælərɪ] *n* pensja
sale [seɪl] *n* **1** (*selling*) sprzedaż **2** (*with reductions*) wyprzedaż; **sales** *n pl* (*quantity sold*) sprzedaż *f sg*; **to be (up) for ~** być wystawionym na sprzedaż; **to be on ~** (*Brit*) być w sprzedaży
sales assistant ['seɪlz-] (*Brit*) *n* sprzedawca(-czyni) *m/f*
sales clerk ['seɪlzkləːrk] (*US*) *n* sprzedawca(-czyni) *m/f*
salesman ['seɪlzmən] (*irreg*) *n* akwizytor
saleswoman ['seɪlzwumən] (*irreg*) *n* (*representative*) akwizytorka
salmon ['sæmən] (*pl* **salmon**) *n* łosoś
salon ['sælɔn] *n* (*hairdresser's shop*) salon fryzjerski
salt [sɔːlt] *n* sól
salty ['sɔːltɪ] *adj* (*food*) słony
same [seɪm] *adj* **1** (*similar*) taki sam **2** (*also*: **very ~**: *identical*) ten sam ▷ *pron*: **the ~** (*similar*) to samo; **the ~ as** taki sam jak; **the ~ book/ place as** taka sama książka/takie samo miejsce jak; **at the ~ time** (*simultaneously*) w tym samym czasie; **all** *or* **just the ~** mimo to
sample ['sɑːmpl] *n* próbka
sand [sænd] *n* piasek
sandal ['sændl] *n* sandał
sand castle *n* zamek z piasku
sandwich ['sændwɪtʃ] *n* kanapka; **a cheese/ham/jam ~** kanapka z serem/szynką/dżemem
sang [sæŋ] *pt of* **sing**
sanitary napkin ['sænɪtərɪ-] (*US*) *n* podpaska
sanitary towel ['sænɪtərɪ-] (*Brit*) *n* podpaska
sank [sæŋk] *pt of* **sink**
Santa (Claus) ['sæntə('klɔːz)] *n* Święty Mikołaj
sarcastic [sɑː'kæstɪk] *adj* sarkastyczny
sardine [sɑː'diːn] *n* sardynka
SAT *n abbr* (*US*: = *Scholastic Aptitude Test*) *egzamin sprawdzający zdolności naukowe kandydata na studia wyższe*
sat [sæt] *pt, pp of* **sit**
satchel ['sætʃl] *n* torba na ramię
satellite ['sætəlaɪt] *n* satelita
satellite television *n* telewizja satelitarna
satisfactory [sætɪs'fæktərɪ] *adj* zadowalający
satisfied ['sætɪsfaɪd] *adj* zadowolony; **to be ~ with sth** być zadowolonym z czegoś

Saturday ['sætədɪ] *n* sobota; *see also* **Tuesday**
sauce [sɔːs] *n* (*savoury*) sos; (*sweet*) polewa
saucepan ['sɔːspən] *n* rondel
saucer ['sɔːsə^r] *n* spodek
sausage ['sɔsɪdʒ] *n* kiełbasa
save [seɪv] *vt* **1** (*person*) ratować (uratować *pf*) **2** (*also*: **~ up**) oszczędzać (oszczędzić *pf*) **3** (*economize on*: *money, time*) oszczędzać (oszczędzić *pf*) **4** (*Comput*) zapisywać (zapisać *pf*) ▷ *vi* (*also*: **~ up**) oszczędzać (oszczędzić *pf*); **to ~ sb's life** ratować (uratować *pf*) komuś życie
▶ **save up** *vi* oszczędzać (zaoszczędzić *pf*)
saving ['seɪvɪŋ] *n* (*of time, money*) oszczędność; **savings** *n pl* (*money*) oszczędności
savoury ['seɪvərɪ] (*US* **savory**) *adj* pikantny
saw[1] [sɔː] *pt of* **see**
saw[2] [sɔː] (*pt* **sawed**, *pp* **sawed** *or* **sawn**) *vt* piłować (spiłować *pf*) ▷ *n* piła
saxophone ['sæksəfəun] *n* saksofon
say [seɪ] (*pt, pp* **said**) *vt* **1** (*utter*) mówić (powiedzieć *pf*) **2** (*indicate*) wskazywać (wskazać *pf*); **to ~ that...** (*verbally*) mówić (powiedzieć *pf*), że...; (*in writing*) twierdzić (stwierdzić *pf*), że...; **to ~ sth to sb** mówić (powiedzieć *pf*) coś komuś; **to ~ yes/no** zgadzać (zgodzić *pf*) się/nie zgadzać (zgodzić *pf*) się; **to ~ goodbye (to sb)** żegnać (pożegnać *pf*) się (z kimś); **to ~ sorry to sb** przepraszać (przeprosić *pf*) kogoś; **I must ~ that...** muszę powiedzieć, że...
saying ['seɪɪŋ] *n* powiedzenie
scale [skeɪl] *n* **1** (*size, extent*) skala **2** (*of map, model*) skala **3** (*Mus*) gama; **scales** *n pl* (*for weighing*) waga; **on a large/small ~** na dużą/na małą skalę
scampi ['skæmpɪ] (*Brit*) *n pl* panierowane krewetki
scandal ['skændl] *n* **1** (*shocking event*) skandal **2** (*gossip*) plotki *f pl*
Scandinavia [skændɪ'neɪvɪə] *n* Skandynawia
scanner ['skænə^r] *n* (*Comput*) skaner
scar [skɑː] *n* blizna
scarce [skɛəs] *adj* rzadki
scarcely ['skɛəslɪ] *adv* ledwo; **~ anybody** prawie nikt
scare [skɛə^r] *vt* przestraszać (przestraszyć *pf*) ▷ *n* (*public panic*) panika; **a security ~** zagrożenie bezpieczeństwa
scarecrow ['skɛəkrəu] *n* strach na wróble
scared ['skɛəd] *adj*: **to be ~ of sb/sth** bać się kogoś/czegoś; **to be ~ stiff** *or* **~ to death** śmiertelnie bać się
scarf [skɑːf] (*pl* **scarfs** *or* **scarves**) *n* (*long*) szalik; (*square*) chusta
scary ['skɛərɪ] (*inf*) *adj* straszny
scene [siːn] *n* (*of crime, accident*) miejsce; **to make a ~** robić (zrobić *pf*) scenę
scenery ['siːnərɪ] *n* krajobraz
schedule ['ʃɛdjuːl, *US* 'skɛdjuːl] *n* **1** (*agenda*) harmonogram **2** (*US*: *of trains, buses*) rozkład jazdy; **on ~** według planu; **to be ahead of ~** być przed czasem; **to be behind ~** mieć opóźnienie
scheduled flight ['ʃɛdjuːld-, *US* 'skɛdjuːld-] *n* lot rejsowy
scheme [skiːm] *n* **1** (*esp Brit*) program **2** (*plan*) plan
scholarship ['skɔləʃɪp] *n* stypendium
school [skuːl] *n* **1** szkoła **2** (*US*: *university*) uniwersytet ▷ *adj* (*uniform, shoes, year*) szkolny; **to go to ~** (*child*) iść/chodzić (pójść *pf*) do szkoły; (*US*: *adult*) uczęszczać do szkoły; **to go to law/medical ~** pójść *pf* na wydział prawa/medycyny
schoolboy ['skuːlbɔɪ] *n* uczeń
schoolchildren ['skuːltʃɪldrən] *n pl* uczniowie
schoolgirl ['skuːlgəːl] *n* uczennica
science ['saɪəns] *n* **1** (*scientific study*) nauka **2** (*school subject*) przedmioty *m pl* ścisłe; (*branch of science*) nauki *f pl* ścisłe; **the ~s** nauki ścisłe
science fiction *n* fantastyka naukowa
scientific [saɪən'tɪfɪk] *adj* naukowy

scientist ['saɪəntɪst] *n* naukowiec
scissors ['sɪzəz] *n pl* nożyce; **a pair of ~** nożyczki
scooter ['sku:tə^r] *n* **1** (*also*: **motor ~**) skuter **2** (*child's*) hulajnoga
score [skɔ:^r] *n* wynik ▷ *vt* (*goal, point*) zdobywać (zdobyć *pf*) ▷ *vi* (*in game, sport*) zdobywać (zdobyć *pf*) punkt
Scorpio ['skɔ:pɪəu] *n* (*Astrol*) Skorpion
Scot [skɔt] *n* Szkot(ka) *m/f*
Scotch tape® ['skɔtʃ-] (*US*) *n* taśma klejąca
Scotland ['skɔtlənd] *n* Szkocja
Scots [skɔts] *adj* szkocki
Scotsman ['skɔtsmən] (*irreg*) *n* Szkot
Scotswoman ['skɔtswumən] (*irreg*) *n* Szkotka
Scottish ['skɔtɪʃ] *adj* szkocki
scout [skaut] *n* (*also*: **boy ~**) harcerz
scrambled egg ['skræmbld-] *n* jajecznica
scrap [skræp] *n* **1** (*of paper, cloth*) skrawek **2** (*inf*: *fight*) bójka ▷ *vt* **1** (*car, ship*) przeznaczać (przeznaczyć *pf*) na złom **2** (*project, system, tax*) rezygnować (zrezygnować *pf*) z *+gen*
scrapbook ['skræpbuk] *n* album z wycinkami
scratch [skrætʃ] *n* **1** (*on car, furniture*) rysa **2** (*on body*) zadrapanie ▷ *vt* **1** (*damage*) rysować (porysować *pf*) **2** (*because of itch*) drapać (podrapać *pf*) **3** (*cat etc*) drapać (podrapać *pf*) ▷ *vi* drapać (podrapać *pf*) się; **to do sth from ~** robić (zrobić *pf*) coś od zera
scream [skri:m] *n* krzyk ▷ *vi* krzyczeć (krzyknąć *pf*) ▷ *vt*: **to ~ sth** krzyczeć (krzyknąć *pf*) coś; **to ~ at sb** krzyczeć (krzyknąć *pf*) na kogoś
screen [skri:n] *n* ekran
screensaver ['skri:nseɪvə^r] *n* wygaszacz ekranu
screw [skru:] *n* śruba
screwdriver ['skru:draɪvə^r] *n* śrubokręt
scribble ['skrɪbl] *vt* (*note*) gryzmolić (nagryzmolić *pf*) ▷ *vi* (*write quickly*) pisać (napisać *pf*) pośpiesznie
scroll [skrəul] *vi*: **to ~ up/down** przewinąć w górę/w dół
scrub [skrʌb] *vt* szorować (wyszorować *pf*)
sculpture ['skʌlptʃə^r] *n* **1** (*art*) rzeźbiarstwo **2** (*object*) rzeźba
sea [si:] *n* **1**: **the ~** morze **2** (*in names*): **the North/Irish/Dead S~** Morze Północne/Irlandzkie/Martwe; **beside** *or* **by the ~** nad morzem; **by ~** morzem
seafood ['si:fu:d] *n* owoce morza *m pl*
seagull ['si:gʌl] *n* mewa
seal [si:l] *n* **1** (*animal*) foka **2** (*official stamp*) pieczęć ▷ *vt* (*envelope*) zaklejać (zakleić *pf*)
search [sə:tʃ] *n* **1** (*for missing person*) poszukiwania *nt pl* **2** (*of place*) przeszukanie **3** (*Comput*) wyszukiwanie ▷ *vt* (*place, person*) przeszukiwać (przeszukać *pf*) ▷ *vi*: **to ~ for sb/sth** poszukiwać kogoś/czegoś; **a ~ for** (*object, person*) poszukiwanie *+gen*
▸ **search for** poszukiwać (poszukać *pf*) *+gen*
search engine (*Comput*) *n* wyszukiwarka
search party *n* ekipa poszukiwawcza
seashore ['si:ʃɔ:^r] *n* brzeg morza; **on the ~** nad brzegiem morza
seasick ['si:sɪk] *adj*: **to be** *or* **feel ~** cierpieć na chorobę morską
seaside ['si:saɪd] (*Brit*) *n*: **the ~** wybrzeże; **at the ~** nad morzem
season ['si:zn] *n* **1** (*of year*) pora roku **2** (*for activity*) sezon; **the football ~** sezon piłkarski; **raspberries are in ~/out of ~** jest sezon/nie ma sezonu na maliny
seat [si:t] *n* **1** (*chair*) siedzenie; (*in car, theatre, cinema*) miejsce **2** (*place*: *in theatre, bus, train*) miejsce; **are there any ~s left?** czy są jakieś wolne miejsca?; **to take a** *or* **one's ~** zajmować (zająć *pf*) (swoje) miejsce; **to be ~ed** (*be sitting*) siedzieć
seat belt *n* pas bezpieczeństwa
seaweed ['si:wi:d] *n* wodorosty *m pl*
second ['sɛkənd] *adj* drugi ▷ *adv* **1** (*come, finish*) jako drugi **2** (*secondly*) po drugie ▷ *n* (*unit of time*) sekunda; **~ floor** (*Brit*) drugie piętro; (*US*) pierwsze piętro; **just a ~!** chwileczkę!

secondary school ['sɛkəndərɪ-] *n* szkoła średnia
second-class ['sɛkənd'klɑːs] *adj* **1** (*letter, stamp*) zwykły **2** (*ticket, carriage*) drugiej klasy ▷ *adv* **1** (*travel*) drugą klasą **2** (*send, post*): **to send sth ~** wysyłać (wysłać *pf*) coś jako zwykły list
second-hand ['sɛkənd'hænd] *adj* używany; **to buy sth ~** kupować (kupić *pf*) coś używanego
secondly ['sɛkəndlɪ] *adv* po drugie
secret ['siːkrɪt] *adj* tajny ▷ *n* sekret; **to keep sth ~ (from sb)** trzymać coś (przed kimś) w tajemnicy; **can he keep a ~?** czy potrafi dochować tajemnicy?; **in ~** potajemnie
secretary ['sɛkrətərɪ] *n* (*in office*) sekretarz(-rka) *m/f*
secretly ['siːkrɪtlɪ] *adv* potajemnie
section ['sɛkʃən] *n* **1** (*part*) część **2** (*department*) dział
security [sɪ'kjuərɪtɪ] *n* **1** (*precautions*) środki bezpieczeństwa **2** (*of country, building, person*) bezpieczeństwo **3** (*of job*) bezpieczeństwo; **to increase** *or* **tighten ~** wzmacniać (wzmocnić *pf*) środki bezpieczeństwa
security guard *n* (*at building*) strażnik(-iczka) *m/f*; (*transporting money*) konwojent(ka) *m/f*
see [siː] (*pt* **saw**, *pp* **seen**) *vt* **1** widzieć (zobaczyć *pf*) **2** (*meet*) widywać (widzieć *pf*) się z +*inst* **3** (*film, play etc*) oglądać (obejrzeć *pf*) **4** (*understand*) rozumieć (zrozumieć *pf*) **5** (*notice*) zauważać (zauważyć *pf*) ▷ *vi* widzieć; **I can ~ something** widzę coś; **to ~ sb doing** *or* **do sth** widzieć, że ktoś coś robi; **have you ~n my glasses?** (*familiar*) czy widziałeś moje okulary?; **to go and ~ sb** odwiedzać (odwiedzić *pf*) kogoś; **to ~ that...** (*realize, notice*) zauważać (zauważyć *pf*), że...; **to ~ if** (*find out if*) zobaczyć, czy; **~ you (soon)!** (*inf*) do zobaczenia (wkrótce)!; **~ you later!** do zobaczenia!; **I'll ~ what I can do** zobaczę, co mogę zrobić; **let me ~, let's ~** (*let me think*) niech pomyślę; **I ~** rozumiem; **you ~** (*in explanations*) otóż; **as far as I can ~** o ile się orientuję
▸ **see to** *vt fus* zajmować (zająć *pf*) się +*inst*
seed [siːd] *n* nasienie
seeing-eye dog [siːɪŋ'aɪ-] (*US*) *n* pies przewodnik
seek [siːk] (*pt, pp* **sought**) *vt* szukać +*gen*; **to ~ advice/help from sb** szukać rady/pomocy u kogoś
seem [siːm] *vi* wydawać (wydać *pf*) się; **it ~s like...** wydaje się, że...; **to ~ (to be) happy/interested** wydawać (wydać *pf*) się szczęśliwym/zainteresowanym; **there ~s to be...** zdaje się, że jest...
seen [siːn] *pp of* **see**
seesaw ['siːsɔː] *n* huśtawka
seldom ['sɛldəm] *adv* rzadko
select [sɪ'lɛkt] *vt* wybierać (wybrać *pf*)
selection [sɪ'lɛkʃən] *n* wybór
self-catering [sɛlf'keɪtərɪŋ] (*Brit*) *adj* z wyżywieniem we własnym zakresie
self-confidence [sɛlf'kɔnfɪdns] *n* wiara w siebie
self-conscious [sɛlf'kɔnʃəs] *adj* skrępowany; **to be ~ about sth** być czymś skrępowanym
self-defence [sɛlfdɪ'fɛns] (*US* **self-defense**) *n* samoobrona; **in ~** w samoobronie
self-employed [sɛlfɪm'plɔɪd] *adj* pracujący na własny rachunek
selfie ['sɛlfɪ] *n* selfie
selfish ['sɛlfɪʃ] *adj* samolubny
self-service [sɛlf'səːvɪs] *adj* samoobsługowy
sell [sɛl] (*pt, pp* **sold**) *vt* sprzedawać (sprzedać *pf*); **to ~ sb sth, ~ sth to sb** sprzedawać (sprzedać *pf*) coś komuś
▸ **sell off** *vt* wyprzedawać (wyprzedać *pf*)
▸ **sell out** *vi* (*shop*) zostać (*pf*) wyprzedanym
sell-by date ['sɛlbaɪ-] (*Brit*) *n* data ważności
Sellotape® ['sɛləuteɪp] (*Brit*) *n* taśma klejąca
semicircle ['sɛmɪsəːkl] *n* półkole
semi-colon [sɛmɪ'kəulən] *n* średnik
semi-final [sɛmɪ'faɪnl] *n* półfinał
semi-skimmed (milk) [sɛmɪ-'skɪmd(-)] (*Brit*) *n* półtłusty

send [sɛnd] (*pt, pp* **sent**) *vt*: **to ~ sth (to sb)** (*letter, money*) wysyłać (wysłać *pf*) coś (komuś); **to ~ sth by post** *or* (*US*) **mail** wysyłać (wysłać *pf*) coś pocztą
▸ **send away for** *vt fus* zamawiać (zamówić *pf*) pocztą
▸ **send back** *vt* (*goods*) odsyłać (odesłać *pf*)
▸ **send off** *vt*: **to ~ sth off (to sb)** (*goods, parcel*) wysyłać (wysłać *pf*) coś (komuś)
▸ **send out** *vt* (*invitation, leaflet*) wysyłać (wysłać *pf*)
senior ['si:nɪəʳ] *adj* (*staff, manager, officer*) wyższy rangą; (*job, position*) wysoki
senior citizen *n* emeryt(ka) *m/f*
senior high (*US*) *n* (*also*: **~ school**) *wyższe klasy szkoły średniej*
sensational [sɛn'seɪʃənl] *adj* **1** (*wonderful*) wspaniały **2** (*event*) sensacyjny
sense [sɛns] *n* **1** (*of smell, taste*) zmysł **2** (*good sense*) rozsądek **3** (*meaning*) sens; **a keen ~ of smell** dobry węch; **it makes ~** (*can be understood*) to ma sens; (*is sensible*) to jest rozsądne
sensible ['sɛnsɪbl] *adj* rozsądny; (*shoes, clothes*) praktyczny
sensitive ['sɛnsɪtɪv] *adj* wrażliwy; **to be ~ to sth** (*sb's feelings*) być wyczulonym na coś
sent [sɛnt] *pt, pp of* **send**
sentence ['sɛntns] *n* **1** (*Ling*) zdanie **2** (*Law*) wyrok ▷ *vt*: **to ~ sb to death/to 5 years in prison** skazywać (skazać *pf*) kogoś na śmierć/na pięć lat więzienia
sentimental [sɛntɪ'mɛntl] *adj* (*person*) sentymentalny
separate [*adj* 'sɛprɪt, *vb* 'sɛpəreɪt] *adj* osobny ▷ *vt* (*split up*) rozdzielać (rozdzielić *pf*) ▷ *vi* **1** (*objects, groups*) rozdzielać (rozdzielić *pf*) się **2** (*parents, couple*) rozchodzić (rozejść *pf*) się; **to keep sth ~ from** trzymać coś oddzielnie od *+gen*; **to ~ from** (*husband, wife*) odchodzić (odejść *pf*) od *+gen*; **to be ~d** (*couple*) być w separacji
separated ['sɛpəreɪtɪd] *adj* (*not divorced*) w separacji
separately ['sɛprɪtlɪ] *adv* osobno
separation [sɛpə'reɪʃən] *n* **1** (*of things, groups*) oddzielenie **2** (*from loved ones*) rozłąka **3** (*of couple*) separacja
September [sɛp'tɛmbəʳ] *n* wrzesień; *see also* **July**
sequel ['si:kwl] *n* dalszy ciąg
sergeant ['sɑ:dʒənt] *n* sierżant
serial ['sɪərɪəl] *n* (*on TV, radio*) serial; (*in magazine*) powieść w odcinkach
series ['sɪərɪz] (*pl* **series**) *n* seria
serious ['sɪərɪəs] *adj* poważny; **are you ~?** czy pan/pani mówi poważnie?
seriously ['sɪərɪəslɪ] *adv* poważnie; **to take sb/sth ~** brać (wziąć *pf*) kogoś/coś poważnie
servant ['sə:vənt] *n* służący(-ca) *m/f*
serve [sə:v] *vt* **1** (*in shop, bar*) obsługiwać (obsłużyć *pf*) **2** (*food, drink, meal*) podawać (podać *pf*) **3** (*prison term*) odbywać (odbyć *pf*) ▷ *vi* **1** (*at table*) podawać (podać *pf*) **2** (*Tennis*) serwować (zaserwować *pf*); **it ~s you right** dobrze ci tak
service ['sə:vɪs] *n* **1** (*facility*) usługa **2** (*in hotel, restaurant*) obsługa **3** (*train/bus service*) połączenie **4** (*Rel*) nabożeństwo **5** (*Aut*) przegląd ▷ *vt* (*vehicle, machine*) dokonywać (dokonać *pf*) przeglądu *+gen*; **military** *or* (*esp Brit*) **national ~** służba wojskowa; **~ included/not included** (*on menu*) obsługa wliczona/nie wliczona w cenę; **to have one's car ~d** oddawać (oddać *pf*) samochód do przeglądu
service charge *n* (*restaurant*) opłata za obsługę; (*bank*) prowizja
service station *n* stacja obsługi
serviette [sə:vɪ'ɛt] (*Brit*) *n* serwetka
session ['sɛʃən] *n* sesja
set [sɛt] (*pt, pp* **set**) *n* **1** (*of cutlery, saucepans etc*) komplet; (*of golf clubs, spanners*) zestaw **2** (*TV, Rad*) telewizor, radio **3** (*Tennis*) set ▷ *adj* (*routine, time, price*) ustalony ▷ *vt* **1** (*put*) umieszczać (umieścić *pf*) **2** (*table*) przygotowywać (przygotować *pf*) **3** (*time, price, rules etc*) ustalać (ustalić *pf*) **4** (*record*) ustanawiać (ustanowić

pf) **5** (*adjust*) nastawiać (nastawić *pf*) ▷ *vi* (*sun*) zachodzić (zajść *pf*); **a ~ of dining-room furniture** komplet mebli stołowych; **a chess ~** szachy; **all ~ to do sth** (*ready*) w pełni gotowy coś zrobić; **a novel ~ in Rome** powieść, której akcja rozgrywa się w Rzymie; **to ~ sb free** uwalniać (uwolnić *pf*) kogoś
▸ **set off** *vi* (*depart*): **to ~ off (for)** wyruszać (wyruszyć *pf*) (do +*gen*) ▷ *vt* (*alarm*) uruchamiać (uruchomić *pf*)
▸ **set out** *vi* (*depart*) wyruszać (wyruszyć *pf*)
▸ **set up** *vt* **1** (*organization, service*) zakładać (założyć *pf*) **2** (*roadblock*) wznosić (wznieść *pf*) ▷ *vi*: **to ~ up in business** zakładać (założyć *pf*) firmę

settee [sɛ'ti:] *n* sofa

settle ['sɛtl] *vt* **1** (*argument, question*) rozstrzygać (rozstrzygnąć *pf*) **2** (*bill, account, debt*) regulować (uregulować *pf*); **that's ~d then!** no to załatwione!
▸ **settle down** *vi* **1** (*live stable life*) osiedlać (osiedlić *pf*) się **2** (*become calm*) uspokajać (uspokoić *pf*) się
▸ **settle in** *vi* przyzwyczajać (przyzwyczaić *pf*) się
▸ **settle on** *vt fus* decydować (zdecydować *pf*) się na

seven ['sɛvn] *num* siedem; *see also* **five**

seventeen [sɛvn'ti:n] *num* siedemnaście; *see also* **fifteen**

seventeenth [sɛvn'ti:nθ] *num* siedemnasty; *see also* **fifth**

seventh ['sɛvnθ] *num* siódmy; *see also* **fifth**

seventy ['sɛvntɪ] *num* siedemdziesiąt; *see also* **fifty**

several ['sɛvərl] *adj, pron* kilka; **~ times** kilka razy

severe [sɪ'vɪə^r] *adj* **1** (*pain*) ostry; (*damage, shortage*) poważny **2** (*punishment, criticism*) srogi; (*winter, climate*) surowy **3** (*person, expression*) surowy

sew [səu] (*pt* **sewed**, *pp* **sewn**) *vi, vt* szyć (uszyć *pf*); **to ~ sth together** zszywać (zszyć *pf*) coś
▸ **sew up** *vt* zszywać (zszyć *pf*)

sewing ['səuɪŋ] *n* szycie

sewing machine *n* maszyna do szycia

sewn [səun] *pp of* **sew**

sex [sɛks] *n* **1** (*gender*) płeć **2** (*lovemaking*) seks; **to have ~ with sb** uprawiać z kimś seks

sexism ['sɛksɪzəm] *n* seksizm

sexist ['sɛksɪst] *adj* seksistowski

sexual ['sɛksjuəl] *adj* (*attraction, relationship, health*) seksualny; (*differences, discrimination*) płciowy

sexuality [sɛksju'ælɪtɪ] *n* seksualność

sexy ['sɛksɪ] *adj* seksowny

shabby ['ʃæbɪ] *adj* (*clothes, place*) zaniedbany; (*person*) obdarty

shade [ʃeɪd] *n* **1** (*shelter*) cień **2** (*of colour*) odcień **3** (*also*: **lamp~**) abażur **4** (*US: on window*) roleta; **in the ~** w cieniu

shadow ['ʃædəu] *n* cień; **in the ~ of sth** w cieniu czegoś

shake [ʃeɪk] (*pt* **shook**, *pp* **shaken** ['ʃeɪkn]) *vt* (*dice, rug, person*) potrząsać (potrząsnąć *pf*) +*inst*; (*bottle, cocktail, medicine*) wstrząsać (wstrząsnąć *pf*) +*inst*; (*buildings, ground*) trząść (zatrząść *pf*) +*inst* ▷ *vi* (*person, part of the body*) drżeć (zadrżeć *pf*); (*building, table, ground*) trząść (zatrząść *pf*) się; **to ~ one's head** kręcić (pokręcić *pf*) głową; **to ~ one's fist (at sb)** wygrażać (komuś) pięścią; **to ~ hands (with sb)** uścisnąć (*pf*) (komuś) dłoń

shall [ʃæl] *aux vb* **1** (*indicating future in 1st person*): **I ~ go** pójdę **2** (*in 1st person questions*): **~ I/we open the door?** czy mam/mamy otworzyć drzwi? **3** (*in 1st person tag questions*): **I'll get some, ~ I?** przyniosę trochę, dobrze?

shallow ['ʃæləu] *adj* płytki

shambles ['ʃæmblz] *n* bałagan

shame [ʃeɪm] *n* wstyd; **it is a ~ that...** szkoda, że...; **it would be a ~ to waste this** szkoda byłoby to zmarnować; **what a ~!** jaka szkoda!

shampoo [ʃæm'pu:] *n* szampon

shandy ['ʃændɪ] (*Brit*) *n* *piwo z lemoniadą*

shape [ʃeɪp] *n* kształt ▷ *vt* kształtować (ukształtować *pf*); **in the ~ of a heart** w kształcie serca

share [ʃɛəʳ] *n* **1** (*part*) część **2** (*Comm, Fin*) udział ▷ *vt* **1** (*room, bed, taxi*) dzielić **2** (*job, cooking, task*) dzielić (podzielić *pf*) **3** (*divide*): **to ~ sth among/between** dzielić (podzielić *pf*) coś pomiędzy; **to ~ sth with sb** (*room, bed, taxi*) dzielić coś z kimś; **to ~ in** (*success, profits, benefits*) mieć swój udział w *+loc*
▸ **share out** *vt* rozdzielać (rozdzielić *pf*)
shareholder [ˈʃɛəhəuldəʳ] *n* akcjonariusz(ka) *m/f*
shark [ʃɑːk] *n* rekin
sharp [ʃɑːp] *adj* **1** (*not blunt*) ostry **2** (*abrupt: increase, change*) nagły; (*curve, bend*) ostry ▷ *adv* (*precisely*): **at 2 o'clock ~** punktualnie o godzinie drugiej; **C ~/F ~** cis/fis
sharpener [ˈʃɑːpnəʳ] *n* (*also*: **pencil ~**) temperówka
shave [ʃeɪv] *vt* golić (ogolić *pf*) ▷ *vi* golić (ogolić *pf*) się
▸ **shave off** *vt* (*beard*) golić (zgolić *pf*)
shaver [ˈʃeɪvəʳ] *n* (*also*: **electric ~**) golarka
shaving cream [ˈʃeɪvɪŋ-] *n* krem do golenia
shaving foam [ˈʃeɪvɪŋ-] *n* pianka do golenia
she [ʃiː] *pron* (*woman, girl*) ona
shed [ʃɛd] *n* szopa
she'd [ʃiːd] = **she had, she would**
sheep [ʃiːp] (*pl* **sheep**) *n* owca
sheepdog [ˈʃiːpdɔg] *n* owczarek
sheer [ʃɪəʳ] *adj* czysty; **it was ~ luck** to było czyste szczęście
sheet [ʃiːt] *n* **1** (*on bed*) prześcieradło **2** (*of paper*) kartka; (*of glass, metal, ice*) tafla
shelf [ʃɛlf] (*pl* **shelves**) *n* półka
shell [ʃɛl] *n* **1** (*on beach*) muszla **2** (*of tortoise, snail, crab*) skorupa **3** (*explosive*) pocisk
she'll [ʃiːl] = **she will**
shellfish [ˈʃɛlfɪʃ] *n* skorupiak
shelter [ˈʃɛltəʳ] *n* **1** (*building*) schronienie **2** (*protection*) osłona ▷ *vi* chronić (schronić *pf*) się; **to take ~ (from sth)** znajdować (znaleźć *pf*) schronienie (przed czymś)
shelves [ʃɛlvz] *n pl of* **shelf**
shepherd [ˈʃɛpəd] *n* pasterz(-rka) *m/f*
sheriff [ˈʃɛrɪf] (*US*) *n* szeryf
sherry [ˈʃɛrɪ] *n* sherry
she's [ʃiːz] = **she is, she has**
shift [ʃɪft] *n* zmiana ▷ *vt* przesuwać (przesunąć *pf*)
shin [ʃɪn] *n* goleń
shine [ʃaɪn] (*pt, pp* **shone**) *vi* świecić (zaświecić *pf*) ▷ *vt* (*torch, light*) świecić (zaświecić *pf*) *+inst*
shiny [ˈʃaɪnɪ] *adj* błyszczący
ship [ʃɪp] *n* statek
shirt [ʃəːt] *n* koszula
shiver [ˈʃɪvəʳ] *n* drżenie ▷ *vi* drżeć (zadrżeć *pf*)
shock [ʃɔk] *n* **1** szok **2** (*also*: **electric ~**) porażenie ▷ *vt* (*offend, scandalize*) szokować (zszokować *pf*); **to be in ~** (*Med*) być w szoku
shocked [ʃɔkt] *adj* zszokowany; **I was ~ to learn that...** byłem zszokowany, gdy dowiedziałem się, że...
shocking [ˈʃɔkɪŋ] *adj* (*outrageous*) szokujący
shoe [ʃuː] *n* but; **a pair of ~s** para butów
shoelace [ˈʃuːleɪs] *n* sznurowadło
shoe polish *n* pasta do butów
shoe shop *n* sklep obuwniczy
shone [ʃɔn] *pt, pp of* **shine**
shook [ʃuk] *pt of* **shake**
shoot [ʃuːt] (*pt, pp* **shot**) *vt* **1** (*kill: person, animal*) zastrzelić (*pf*) **2** (*Brit: hunt*) polować na **3** (*film*) kręcić (nakręcić *pf*) ▷ *vi* **1** (*with gun, bow*): **to ~ at sb/sth** strzelać (strzelić *pf*) do kogoś/czegoś **2** (*Football etc*) strzelać (strzelić *pf*); **to ~ sb in the back/leg** postrzelić *pf* kogoś w plecy/w nogę
shooting [ˈʃuːtɪŋ] *n* **1** (*attack, murder, shots*) strzelanina **2** (*Brit: hunting*) polowanie
shop [ʃɔp] *n* (*esp Brit*) sklep ▷ *vi* robić (zrobić *pf*) zakupy
shop assistant (*Brit*) *n* sprzedawca(-czyni) *m/f*
shopkeeper [ˈʃɔpkiːpəʳ] (*Brit*) *n* sklepikarz(-rka) *m/f*
shoplifting [ˈʃɔplɪftɪŋ] *n* kradzież sklepowa

shopping ['ʃɔpɪŋ] *n* zakupy *m pl*; **to do the ~** robić (zrobić *pf*) zakupy; **to go ~** iść/chodzić (pójść *pf*) na zakupy
shopping cart (*US*) *n* wózek sklepowy
shopping centre (*US* **shopping center**) *n* centrum handlowe
shopping mall *n* centrum handlowe
shopping trolley (*Brit*) *n* wózek sklepowy
shop window *n* wystawa sklepowa
shore [ʃɔːʳ] *n* brzeg; **on ~** na lądzie
short [ʃɔːt] *adj* **1** (*in time*) krótki **2** (*in length*) krótki **3** (*not tall*) niski; **shorts** *n pl* **1** (*short trousers*) szorty **2** (*esp US: underpants*) bokserki; **at ~ notice** z krótkim wyprzedzeniem; **to be ~ of sth** nie mieć czegoś; **a pair of ~s** para szortów
shortage ['ʃɔːtɪdʒ] *n* niedobór
short cut *n* skrót
shortly ['ʃɔːtlɪ] *adv* wkrótce; **~ after/before** krótko po *+loc*/krótko przed *+inst*
short-sighted [ʃɔːt'saɪtɪd] (*Brit*) *adj* krótkowzroczny
shot [ʃɔt] *pt, pp of* **shoot** ▷ *n* **1** (*from gun*) wystrzał **2** (*Football*) strzał **3** (*injection*) zastrzyk **4** (*Cine, Phot*) ujęcie; **to fire a ~ at sb/sth** strzelać (strzelić *pf*) do kogoś/czegoś
shotgun ['ʃɔtgʌn] *n* śrutówka
should [ʃud] *aux vb* **1** (*indicating advisability*): **I ~ go now** powinienem już iść **2** (*indicating obligation*): **he ~ listen to me** powinien mnie posłuchać **3** (*indicating likelihood*): **she ~ be there by now** powinna tam już być **4** (*after "that"*): **it's not right that we ~ be fined** nie powinniśmy być ukarani mandatem; **she ~ have been more careful** powinna była być bardziej ostrożna; **he ~ have arrived by now** już powinien przyjechać; **I ~ go if I were you** na pana/pani miejscu poszedłbym
shoulder ['ʃəuldəʳ] *n* bark
shouldn't ['ʃudnt] = **should not**
shout [ʃaut] *n* krzyk ▷ *vt* (*also*: **~ out**) krzyczeć (krzyknąć *pf*) ▷ *vi* (*also*: **~ out**) krzyczeć (krzyknąć *pf*)
shovel ['ʃʌvl] *n* łopata
show [ʃəu] (*pt* **showed**, *pp* **shown**) *n* **1** (*exhibition*) pokaz **2** (*Theat*) przedstawienie **3** (*TV, Rad*) program ▷ *vt* **1** pokazywać (pokazać *pf*) **2** (*illustrate, depict*) przedstawiać (przedstawić *pf*) ▷ *vi* (*be visible*) być widocznym; **on ~** (*exhibits*) wystawiany; **to ~ sb sth** *or* **to ~ sth to sb** pokazywać (pokazać *pf*) coś komuś; **to ~ that...** pokazywać (pokazać *pf*), że...; **to ~ sb how to do sth** pokazywać (pokazać *pf*) komuś, jak coś zrobić
▸ **show around** *vt* oprowadzać (oprowadzić *pf*)
▸ **show off** *vi* popisywać (popisać *pf*) się ▷ *vt* popisywać (popisać *pf*) się *+inst*
▸ **show up** *vi* **1** (*be visible, noticeable*) ukazywać (ukazać *pf*) się **2** (*arrive, appear*) pojawiać (pojawić *pf*) się
shower ['ʃauəʳ] *n* **1** (*rain*) przelotny deszcz **2** (*for washing*) prysznic ▷ *vi* brać (wziąć *pf*) prysznic; **to have** *or* **take a ~** brać (wziąć *pf*) prysznic
show jumping [-dʒʌmpɪŋ] *n* konkurs hipiczny
shown [ʃəun] *pp of* **show**
show-off ['ʃəuɔf] *n* pozer(ka) *m/f*
shrank [ʃræŋk] *pt of* **shrink**
shriek [ʃriːk] *vi* wrzeszczeć (wrzasnąć *pf*) ▷ *n* wrzask
shrimp [ʃrɪmp] *n* krewetka
shrink [ʃrɪŋk] (*pt* **shrank**, *pp* **shrunk**) *vi* kurczyć (skurczyć *pf*) się

SHROVE TUESDAY

Shrove Tuesday (polskie Ostatki) to dzień poprzedzający Środę Popielcową i początek Wielkiego Postu. Ponieważ tradycyjnie w Wielkiej Brytanii je się wtedy naleśniki (**pancakes**), dzień ten również nazywany jest **Pancake Day** (dniem naleśników).

shrug [ʃrʌg] *vi* wzruszać (wzruszyć *pf*) ramionami ▷ *vt*: **to ~ one's shoulders** wzruszać (wzruszyć *pf*) ramionami
shrunk [ʃrʌŋk] *pp of* **shrink**

shuffle ['ʃʌfl] *vi*: **to ~ along** przechodzić (przejść *pf*) powłócząc nogami ▷ *vt* (*cards*) tasować (potasować *pf*)
shut [ʃʌt] (*pt, pp* **shut**) *vt* zamykać (zamknąć *pf*) ▷ *vi* zamykać (zamknąć *pf*) się ▷ *adj* zamknięty
▶ **shut down** *vt* (*factory*) zamykać (zamknąć *pf*) ▷ *vi* (*factory*) zamykać (zamknąć *pf*) się
▶ **shut out** *vt* nie wpuszczać (wpuścić *pf*) *+gen* do środka
▶ **shut up** *vi* (*inf*) zamykać (zamknąć *pf*) się ▷ *vt* (*inf*: *person*) uciszać (uciszyć *pf*); **~ up!** (*inf*) zamknij się!
shuttle ['ʃʌtl] *n* (*plane, bus etc*) transport wahadłowy
shuttlecock ['ʃʌtlkɔk] *n* lotka
shy [ʃaɪ] *adj* (*person*) nieśmiały; (*animal*) płochliwy
sick [sɪk] *adj* **1** chory **2** (*vomit*): **to be ~** wymiotować (zwymiotować *pf*); **to feel ~** źle się czuć (poczuć *pf*); **to be ~ of sth/of doing sth** (*inf*) mieć dość czegoś/robienia czegoś
sickness ['sɪknɪs] *n* **1** (*illness*) choroba **2** (*vomiting*) wymioty *m pl*
side [saɪd] *n* **1** strona **2** (*of building, vehicle*) bok; (*of body*) bok **3** (*of paper, face*) strona; (*of tape*) strona **4** (*of road, bed*) strona **5** (*of hill, valley*) zbocze **6** (*aspect*) strona **7** (*Brit*: *team*) drużyna **8** (*in conflict, contest*) strona ▷ *adj* (*door, entrance*) boczny; **on the other ~ of sth** po drugiej stronie czegoś; **the right/wrong ~ of sth** właściwa/niewłaściwa strona czegoś; **by the ~ of** przy *+loc*; **~ by ~** tuż obok siebie; **they are on our ~** oni są po naszej stronie; **to take sb's ~** opowiadać (opowiedzieć *pf*) się po czyjejś stronie
sideboard ['saɪdbɔːd] *n* kredens
side-effect ['saɪdɪfɛkt] *n* skutek uboczny
sidewalk ['saɪdwɔːk] (*US*) *n* chodnik
sideways ['saɪdweɪz] *adv* w bok
sieve [sɪv] *n* sito ▷ *vt* przesiewać (przesiać *pf*)
sigh [saɪ] *n* westchnienie ▷ *vi* wzdychać (westchnąć *pf*)
sight [saɪt] *n* **1** (*faculty*) wzrok **2** (*spectacle*) widok; **sights** *n pl*: **the ~s** atrakcje turystyczne; **out of ~** niewidoczny; **I know her by ~** znam ją z widzenia
sightseeing ['saɪtsiːɪŋ] *n* zwiedzanie; **to go ~** zwiedzać (zwiedzić *pf*)
sign [saɪn] *n* znak ▷ *vt* (*document*) podpisywać (podpisać *pf*); **a plus/minus ~** znak plus/minus; **he was showing ~s of improvement** wykazywał oznaki poprawy; **it's a good/bad ~** to dobry/zły znak
▶ **sign on** (*Brit*) *vi* (*as unemployed*) zgłaszać (zgłosić *pf*) się (jako bezrobotny); **to ~ on for sth** (*course*) zapisywać (zapisać *pf*) się na coś
▶ **sign up** *vi*: **to ~ up for** (*course, trip*) zapisywać (zapisać *pf*) się na
signal ['sɪgnl] *n* **1** (*to do sth*) sygnał **2** (*indication*) znak **3** (*Rail*) sygnał **4** (*Elec, Tel*) sygnał ▷ *vi* **1** (*with gesture, sound*): **to ~ (to sb)** dawać (dać *pf*) (komuś) znak **2** (*Aut*: *with indicator*) sygnalizować (zasygnalizować *pf*)
signature ['sɪgnətʃəʳ] *n* podpis
significance [sɪg'nɪfɪkəns] *n* znaczenie
significant [sɪg'nɪfɪkənt] *adj* **1** (*important*) ważny **2** (*considerable*) znaczny
sign language *n* język migowy
signpost ['saɪnpəust] *n* znak drogowy
silence ['saɪləns] *n* cisza; **in ~** w ciszy
silent ['saɪlənt] *adj* (*person*) cichy
silk [sɪlk] *n* jedwab ▷ *adj* (*scarf, shirt*) jedwabny
silky ['sɪlkɪ] *adj* jedwabisty
silly ['sɪlɪ] *adj* głupi
silver ['sɪlvəʳ] *n* srebro ▷ *adj* **1** (*hair*) siwy **2** (*spoon, necklace*) srebrny
SIM card ['sɪm-] *n* karta SIM
similar ['sɪmɪləʳ] *adj* podobny; **to be ~ to sth** być podobnym do czegoś
simple ['sɪmpl] *adj* **1** (*easy*) prosty **2** (*basic*) zwyczajny **3** (*mere*) prosty **4** (*Ling*: *tense*) prosty; **it would be ~r to move house** łatwiej byłoby przeprowadzić się
simply ['sɪmplɪ] *adv* po prostu
sin [sɪn] *n* grzech
since [sɪns] *adv* (*from then onwards*) od tego czasu ▷ *prep* **1** (*from*) od

+*gen* **2** (*after*) po +*loc* ▷ *conj* **1** (*from when*) odkąd **2** (*after*) od kiedy **3** (*as*) ponieważ; **~ then** *or* **ever ~** od tej pory; **I've been here ~ the end of June** jestem tu od końca czerwca; **~ it was Saturday, he stayed in bed** ponieważ to była sobota, został w łóżku
sincere [sɪn'sɪəʳ] *adj* szczery
sincerely [sɪn'sɪəlɪ] *adv* szczerze; **yours ~** *or* (*US*) **S~ yours** z wyrazami szacunku
sing [sɪŋ] (*pt* **sang**, *pp* **sung**) *vi* śpiewać (zaśpiewać *pf*) ▷ *vt* (*song*) śpiewać (zaśpiewać *pf*)
singer ['sɪŋəʳ] *n* śpiewak(-aczka) *m/f*
singing ['sɪŋɪŋ] *n* (*activity*) śpiewanie; (*sounds*) śpiew
single ['sɪŋgl] *adj* **1** (*solitary*) jeden **2** (*unmarried*) stanu wolnego ▷ *n* (*Brit*: *also*: **~ ticket**) bilet w jedną stronę; **every ~ day** codziennie
single bed *n* łóżko jednoosobowe
single parent *n* rodzic samotnie wychowujący dziecko
singular ['sɪŋgjuləʳ] *adj* pojedynczy ▷ *n*: **the ~** liczba pojedyncza; **in the ~** w liczbie pojedynczej
sink [sɪŋk] (*pt* **sank**, *pp* **sunk**) *n* zlew ▷ *vi* (*ship*) tonąć (zatonąć *pf*); **my heart sank** podupadłem na duchu
sir [səʳ] *n* pan; **yes, ~** tak, proszę pana; **dear S~** szanowny Panie; **dear S~ or Madam** szanowni Państwo; **~ John Smith** sir John Smith (*tytuł szlachecki*)
siren ['saɪərn] *n* syrena
sister ['sɪstəʳ] *n* siostra; **my brothers and ~s** moi bracia i siostry
sister-in-law ['sɪstərɪnlɔː] (*pl* **sisters-in-law**) *n* (*husband or wife's sister*) szwagierka; (*brother's wife*) bratowa
sit [sɪt] (*pt*, *pp* **sat**) *vi* **1** (*also*: **~ down**) siadać (usiąść *pf*) **2** (*be sitting*) siedzieć ▷ *vt* (*Brit*: *exam*) podchodzić (podejść *pf*) do +*gen*
▸ **sit down** *vi* siadać (usiąść *pf*); **to be ~ting down** siedzieć
▸ **sit up** *vi* siadać (usiąść *pf*) z pozycji leżącej
site [saɪt] *n* **1** (*of event*) miejsce **2** (*building site*) plac budowy **3** (*also*: **web~**) witryna internetowa
sitting room ['sɪtɪŋ-] (*Brit*) *n* salon
situated ['sɪtjueɪtɪd] *adj*: **to be ~ in/on/near sth** być usytuowanym w/na czymś/obok czegoś
situation [sɪtju'eɪʃən] *n* sytuacja
six [sɪks] *num* sześć; *see also* **five**
sixteen [sɪks'tiːn] *num* szesnaście; *see also* **fifteen**
sixteenth [sɪks'tiːnθ] *num* szesnasty; *see also* **fifth**
sixth [sɪksθ] *num* **1** (*in series*) szósty **2** (*fraction*) szósta część; **the upper/lower ~** (*Brit*: *Scol*) *ostatnia/przedostatnia klasa w szkole brytyjskiej*; *see also* **fifth**

SIXTH FORM

Sixth form – w szkołach brytyjskich są to dwa lata nauki po ukończeniu obowiązkowej edukacji w wieku 16 lat. Uczniowie przygotowują się wtedy do egzaminów **A levels**.

sixty ['sɪkstɪ] *num* sześćdziesiąt; *see also* **fifty**
size [saɪz] *n* wielkość; (*of clothing, shoes*) rozmiar; **what ~ shoes do you take?** jaki ma pan/pani rozmiar butów?
skate [skeɪt] *n* **1** (*ice skate*) łyżwa **2** (*roller skate*) wrotka ▷ *vi* **1** (*ice skate*) jeździć na łyżwach **2** (*roller skate*) jeździć na wrotkach
skateboard ['skeɪtbɔːd] *n* deskorolka
skateboarding ['skeɪtbɔːdɪŋ] *n* jazda na deskorolce
skating ['skeɪtɪŋ] *n* (*ice-skating*) łyżwiarstwo; **to go ~** (*on ice skates*) jeździć na łyżwach; (*on roller skates*) jeździć na wrotkach
skating rink *n* lodowisko
skeleton ['skɛlɪtn] *n* szkielet
sketch [skɛtʃ] *n* **1** (*drawing*) szkic **2** (*outline*) zarys ▷ *vt* szkicować (naszkicować *pf*)
ski [skiː] *n* narta ▷ *vi* jeździć na nartach
skid [skɪd] *vi* (*car, driver*) wpadać (wpaść *pf*) w poślizg
skier ['skiːəʳ] *n* narciarz(-rka) *m/f*

skiing ['skiːɪŋ] *n* narciarstwo; **to go ~** jeździć na nartach
skilful ['skɪlful] (*US* **skillful**) *adj* (*person, player*) zręczny; (*use, choice, management*) sprawny
skill [skɪl] *n* umiejętność
skilled [skɪld] *adj* (*person*) wykwalifikowany; (*work*) wymagający kwalifikacji
skillful ['skɪlful] (*US*) *adj* = **skilful**
skimmed milk [skɪmd-] (*Brit*) *n* mleko odtłuszczone
skim milk [skɪm-] (*US*) *n* mleko odtłuszczone
skin [skɪn] *n* **1** (*of person*) skóra; (*of animal*) skóra; (*complexion*) cera **2** (*of fruit, vegetable*) skórka
skinhead ['skɪnhɛd] (*Brit*) *n* skin
skinny ['skɪnɪ] (*inf*) *adj* chudy
skip [skɪp] *vi* (*hop*) podskakiwać (podskoczyć *pf*) ▷ *vt* (*miss*) opuszczać (opuścić *pf*) ▷ *n* (*Brit: container*) kontener
skirt [skəːt] *n* spódnica
skive [skaɪv] (*Brit: inf*) *vi* wymigiwać (wymigać *pf*) się
▶ **skive off** (*Brit: inf*) *vt fus* (*school, work*) urywać (urwać *pf*) się z +*gen* ▷ *vi* wymigiwać (wymigać *pf*) się
skull [skʌl] *n* czaszka
sky [skaɪ] *n* niebo
skyscraper ['skaɪskreɪpəʳ] *n* drapacz chmur
slam [slæm] *vt* trzaskać (trzasnąć *pf*) +*inst* ▷ *vi* zatrzaskiwać (zatrzasnąć *pf*) się
slang [slæŋ] *n* slang
slap [slæp] *n* klepnięcie ▷ *vt* uderzać (uderzyć *pf*); **to give sb a ~** uderzyć (*pf*) kogoś
slate [sleɪt] *n* (*on roof*) dachówka łupkowa
slave [sleɪv] *n* niewolnik(-ica) *m/f*
sled [slɛd] (*US*) *n* sanie ▷ *vi*: **to go ~ding** jeździć na saniach
sledge [slɛdʒ] (*Brit*) *n* sanie ▷ *vi*: **to go sledging** jeździć na saniach
sleep [sliːp] (*pt, pp* **slept**) *n* **1** sen **2** (*nap*) drzemka ▷ *vi* (*be asleep*) spać; (*spend the night*) zatrzymywać (zatrzymać *pf*) się na noc; **to go to ~** zasypiać (zasnąć *pf*); **to have a good night's ~** dobrze się wyspać; **to put a cat/dog to ~** usypiać (uśpić *pf*) kota/psa
▶ **sleep around** (*inf*) *vi* puszczać się
▶ **sleep in** (*Brit*) *vi* zasypiać (zaspać *pf*)
▶ **sleep with** *vt fus* sypiać (spać *pf*) z +*inst*
sleeping bag ['sliːpɪŋ-] *n* śpiwór
sleeping pill *n* tabletka nasenna
sleepy ['sliːpɪ] *adj* śpiący
sleet [sliːt] *n* deszcz ze śniegiem
sleeve [sliːv] *n* rękaw; **with long/short ~s** z długim/krótkim rękawem
slept [slɛpt] *pt, pp of* **sleep**
slice [slaɪs] *n* (*of meat, lemon*) plasterek; (*of bread*) kromka ▷ *vt* kroić (pokroić *pf*); **~d bread** pokrojony chleb
slide [slaɪd] (*pt, pp* **slid**) *n* **1** (*in playground*) zjeżdżalnia **2** (*Phot*) slajd **3** (*Brit: also:* **hair ~**) wsuwka do włosów ▷ *vi*: **to ~ down sth** zjeżdżać (zjechać *pf*) w dół po czymś; **to ~ off sth** zsuwać (zsunąć *pf*) się z czegoś
slight [slaɪt] *adj* niewielki; **the ~est noise/problem** najmniejszy hałas/problem
slightly ['slaɪtlɪ] *adv* nieco
slim [slɪm] *adj* szczupły ▷ *vi* (*lose weight*) chudnąć (schudnąć *pf*)
sling [slɪŋ] *n* temblak; **to have one's arm in a ~** mieć rękę na temblaku
slip [slɪp] *vi* (*person*) pośliznąć (*pf*) się; (*object*) zsuwać (zsunąć *pf*) się ▷ *n* (*mistake*) pomyłka; **to ~ sth on/off** wkładać (włożyć *pf*)/zdejmować (zdjąć *pf*) coś; **a ~ of the tongue** przejęzyczenie
▶ **slip up** *vi* (*make mistake*) mylić (pomylić *pf*) się
slipper ['slɪpəʳ] *n* kapeć
slippery ['slɪpərɪ] *adj* śliski
slope [sləup] *n* **1** (*gentle hill*) zbocze **2** (*ski slope*) stok narciarski ▷ *vi*: **to ~ down** opadać (opaść *pf*)
slot [slɔt] *n* **1** (*in machine*) otwór **2** (*fig: in timetable*) okienko
slot machine *n* (*for drinks etc*) automat z napojami; (*for gambling*) automat do gier
slow [sləu] *adj* powolny ▷ *adv* (*inf*) wolno; **my watch is 20 minutes ~** mój zegarek spóźnia się o dwadzieścia minut

▸ **slow down** *vi* (*become less active*) zwalniać (zwolnić *pf*) tempo życia
slowly ['sləulɪ] *adv* powoli
slug [slʌg] *n* ślimak
slum [slʌm] *n* (*area*) slums
sly [slaɪ] *adj* (*smile*) chytry; (*expression, remark*) fałszywy; (*person*) przebiegły
smack [smæk] *n* uderzenie ▷ *vt* (*as punishment*) dawać (dać *pf*) klapsa *+dat*
small [smɔ:l] *adj* mały; **to get** *or* **grow ~er** (*thing*) maleć (zmaleć *pf*)
smart [smɑ:t] *adj* **1** (*esp Brit: neat, tidy*) elegancki **2** (*fashionable*) elegancki **3** (*clever*) bystry
smart card *n* karta chipowa
smart phone *n* smartfon
smash [smæʃ] *vt* tłuc (stłuc *pf*) ▷ *vi* (*break*) tłuc (stłuc *pf*) się
▸ **smash up** *vt* demolować (zdemolować *pf*)
smashing ['smæʃɪŋ] (*Brit: inf*) *adj* fantastyczny
smell [smɛl] (*pt, pp* **smelled** *or* **smelt**) *n* zapach ▷ *vt* czuć (poczuć *pf*) ▷ *vi* (*have unpleasant odour*) śmierdzieć; **to ~ nice/delicious/spicy** pachnieć ładnie/cudownie/pikantnymi przyprawami; **sense of ~** węch; **to ~ of** pachnieć *+inst*
smelly ['smɛlɪ] (*pej*) *adj* śmierdzący
smelt [smɛlt] *pt, pp of* **smell**
smile [smaɪl] *n* uśmiech ▷ *vi*: **to ~ (at sb)** uśmiechać (uśmiechnąć *pf*) się (do kogoś)
smoke [sməuk] *n* dym ▷ *vi* **1** (*use tobacco*) palić (wypalić *pf*) **2** (*chimney*) dymić się ▷ *vt* **1** (*cigarette, cigar, pipe*) palić (zapalić *pf*) **2** (*fish, meat*) wędzić (uwędzić *pf*); **do you ~?** czy pan/pani pali?
smoke alarm *n* czujnik dymu
smoker ['sməukəʳ] *n* (*person*) palacz(ka) *m/f*
smoking ['sməukɪŋ] *n* palenie; **"no ~"** „zakaz palenia"
smooth [smu:ð] *adj* **1** (*not rough*) gładki **2** (*successful*) płynny
smoothie ['smu:ðɪ] *n* smoothie
smother ['smʌðəʳ] *vt* dusić (udusić *pf*)
SMS *n abbr* (*= short message service*) sms
smudge [smʌdʒ] *n* plama ▷ *vt* rozmazywać (rozmazać *pf*)
smuggle ['smʌgl] *vt* przemycać (przemycić *pf*); **to ~ sth in/out** przemycać (przemycić *pf*) coś do środka/na zewnątrz
smuggler ['smʌgləʳ] *n* przemytnik(-iczka) *m/f*
smuggling ['smʌglɪŋ] *n* przemyt
snack [snæk] *n* przekąska; **to have a ~** przekąsić (*pf*) coś
snack bar *n* bar szybkiej obsługi
snail [sneɪl] *n* ślimak
snake [sneɪk] *n* wąż
snap [snæp] *vt* łamać (złamać *pf*) ▷ *vi* (*rope, stick*) pękać (pęknąć *pf*); **to ~ one's fingers** (*lit*) pstrykać (pstryknąć *pf*) palcami
snapshot ['snæpʃɔt] *n* zdjęcie
snatch [snætʃ] *vt* **1** (*grab*) chwytać (chwycić *pf*) **2** (*steal: handbag*) wyrywać (wyrwać *pf*)
sneak [sni:k] (*pt, pp* **sneaked** *or* (*US*) **snuck**) *vi*: **to ~ out/in** wymykać (wymknąć *pf*) się/wślizgać (wśliznąć *pf*) się ▷ *vt*: **to ~ a look at sth** zerkać (zerknąć *pf*) na coś
sneakers ['sni:kəz] (*US*) *n pl* tenisówki
sneeze [sni:z] *vi* kichać (kichnąć *pf*)
sniff [snɪf] *vi* pociągać (pociągnąć *pf*) nosem ▷ *vt* wąchać (powąchać *pf*)
snob [snɔb] (*pej*) *n* snob(ka) *m/f*
snooker ['snu:kəʳ] *n* (*Sport*) snooker
snooze [snu:z] (*inf*) *n* drzemka ▷ *vi* drzemać; **to have a ~** zdrzemnąć (*pf*) się
snore [snɔ:ʳ] *vi* chrapać (chrapnąć *pf*)
snow [snəu] *n* śnieg; **it's ~ing** pada śnieg
snowball ['snəubɔ:l] *n* śnieżka
snuck [snʌk] (*US*) *pt, pp of* **sneak**

KEYWORD

so [səu] *adv* **1** (*thus, likewise*) tak; **they do so because...** robią tak, ponieważ...; **if you don't want to go, say so** jeśli pan/pani nie chce iść, proszę powiedzieć; **if so** jeśli tak; **"it's five o'clock" — "so it is!"**

„jest piąta" — „rzeczywiście!"; **I hope/ think so** mam nadzieję/myślę, że tak; **so far** do tej pory; **and so on** i tak dalej
2 (*also*): **so do I/so am I** ja też
3 (*to such a degree*) do takiego stopnia; **so quickly/big (that)** tak szybko/ duży, (że); **not so clever (as)** nie tak mądry, (jak)
4 (*very*) tak; **we were so worried** tak się martwiliśmy; **so much** tak bardzo; **there's so much work to do** jest tak dużo pracy do zrobienia; **I love you so much** tak bardzo cię kocham; **so many** tak wiele; **I've got so many things to do** mam tyle rzeczy do zrobienia
5 (*linking events*) tak więc; **so I was right after all** tak więc miałem rację; **so how was your day?** więc jak minął panu/pani dzień?
6 (*in approximations*): **ten or so** w przybliżeniu dziesięć
▷ *conj* **1** (*expressing purpose*): **so (that)** aby; **I brought it so (that) she could see it** przyniosłem to, żeby mogła zobaczyć; **so as to** aby
2 (*expressing result*) więc; **he didn't come so I left** nie przyszedł, więc wyszedłem

soak [səuk] *vt* **1** (*drench*) moczyć (zmoczyć *pf*) **2** (*leave in water*) namaczać (namoczyć *pf*)
soaking ['səukɪŋ] *adj* (*also*: **~ wet**) przemoczony
soap [səup] *n* **1** mydło **2** (*also*: **~ opera**) opera mydlana
soap opera *n* opera mydlana
soap powder *n* proszek do prania
sob [sɔb] *vi* szlochać (zaszlochać *pf*)
sober ['səubə^r] *adj* trzeźwy
▸ **sober up** *vi* trzeźwieć (wytrzeźwieć *pf*)
soccer ['sɔkə^r] *n* piłka nożna
social ['səuʃl] *adj* **1** (*problems, change etc*) społeczny **2** (*event, function*) towarzyski
socialism ['səuʃəlɪzəm] *n* socjalizm
socialist ['səuʃəlɪst] *adj* socjalistyczny ▷ *n* socjalista(-tka) *m/f*
social media *n* media społecznościowe
social security (*Brit*) *n* zasiłek; **to be on ~** być na zasiłku
social worker *n* pracownik(-ica) *m/f* opieki społecznej
society [sə'saɪətɪ] *n* **1** (*people in general*) społeczeństwo **2** (*community*) towarzystwo
sociology [səusɪ'ɔlədʒɪ] *n* socjologia
sock [sɔk] *n* skarpeta
socket ['sɔkɪt] (*Brit*) *n* gniazdko elektryczne
sofa ['səufə] *n* sofa
soft [sɔft] *adj* (*towel, bed*) miękki; (*skin*) delikatny
soft drink *n* napój bezalkoholowy
software ['sɔftwɛə^r] *n* oprogramowanie
soil [sɔɪl] *n* gleba
solar ['səulə^r] *adj* słoneczny
solar power *n* energia słoneczna
sold [səuld] *pt, pp of* **sell**
soldier ['səuldʒə^r] *n* żołnierz
sole [səul] *n* podeszwa
solicitor [sə'lɪsɪtə^r] (*Brit*) *n* adwokat
solid ['sɔlɪd] *adj* **1** (*not soft*) twardy **2** (*without gaps*) jednolity **3** (*not liquid*) stały **4** (*pure: gold, oak*) lity
solo ['səuləu] *n* solo
solution [sə'lu:ʃən] *n* rozwiązanie
solve [sɔlv] *vt* **1** (*mystery, case*) wyjaśniać (wyjaśnić *pf*) **2** (*problem*) rozwiązywać (rozwiązać *pf*)

some [sʌm] *adj* **1** (*a little, a few*) trochę *+gen*; **some milk/books** trochę mleka/książek; **would you like some wine?** może trochę wina?
2 (*certain, in contrasts: vir*) niektórzy; (*non-vir*) niektóre; **some people say that...** niektórzy ludzie mówią, że...
3 (*unspecified*): **some (or other)** jakiś; **we'll meet again some day** pewnego dnia znowu się spotkamy
▷ *pron* (*a certain amount, certain number*) kilka; **I've got some (books)** mam kilka (książek); **I've got some (milk)** mam trochę (mleka); **there was/were some left** trochę zostało; **some of them** (*vir*) niektórzy z nich; (*non-vir*) niektóre z nich; **could I have**

some of that cheese? czy mogę prosić trochę tego sera?

somebody ['sʌmbədɪ] *pron* = **someone**
somehow ['sʌmhau] *adv* jakoś
someone ['sʌmwʌn] *pron* ktoś; **there's ~ coming** ktoś idzie; **I saw ~ in the garden** widziałem kogoś w ogrodzie; **~ else** ktoś inny
someplace ['sʌmpleɪs] (*US*) *adv* = **somewhere**
something ['sʌmθɪŋ] *pron* coś; **there was obviously ~ wrong** najwidoczniej coś było nie tak; **~ else** coś innego; **would you like a sandwich or ~?** chciałbyś kanapkę albo coś takiego?
sometime ['sʌmtaɪm] *adv* kiedyś
sometimes ['sʌmtaɪmz] *adv* czasami
somewhere ['sʌmwɛəʳ] *adv* gdzieś; **I need ~ to live** potrzebne mi miejsce zamieszkania; **I must have lost it ~** musiałem to gdzieś zgubić; **let's go ~ quiet** chodźmy w jakieś ciche miejsce; **~ else** gdzie indziej
son [sʌn] *n* syn
song [sɔŋ] *n* **1** piosenka **2** (*of bird*) śpiew
son-in-law ['sʌnɪnlɔː] (*pl* **sons-in-law**) *n* zięć
soon [suːn] *adv* **1** (*in a short time*) wkrótce **2** (*a short time later*) niedługo potem **3** (*early*) wcześnie; **~ afterwards** wkrótce potem; **as ~ as** jak tylko; **quite ~** za niedługo; **how ~?** kiedy?; **see you ~!** do zobaczenia wkrótce!
sooner ['suːnəʳ] *adv*: **I would ~...** wolałbym raczej...; **~ or later** prędzej czy później; **the ~ the better** im szybciej, tym lepiej
sophomore ['sɔfəmɔːʳ] (*US*) *n* student(ka) *m/f* drugiego roku
soprano [sə'prɑːnəu] *n* (*woman, girl*) sopranistka; (*boy*) sopran
sore [sɔːʳ] *adj* **1** (*painful*) obolały **2** (*US: inf: angry*) urażony ▷ *n* rana; **to be ~ about sth** (*US: inf*) być urażonym czymś
sorry ['sɔrɪ] *adj*: **(I'm) ~!** (*apology*) przepraszam!; **~?** (*pardon?*) słucham?; **to feel ~ for sb** współczuć komuś; **to be ~ about sth** żałować czegoś; **I'm ~ to hear that** przykro mi to słyszeć
sort [sɔːt] *n* rodzaj ▷ *vt* sortować (posortować *pf*); **~ of** (*inf*) w pewnym sensie; **all ~s of books/devices** wszelkiego rodzaju książki/urządzenia
▸ **sort out** *vt* **1** (*separate*) porządkować (uporządkować *pf*) **2** (*solve*) rozwiązywać (rozwiązać *pf*)
sought [sɔːt] *pt, pp of* **seek**
soul [səul] *n* dusza
sound [saund] *adj* **1** (*advice*) rozsądny **2** (*reliable, thorough*) solidny ▷ *adv*: **he is ~ asleep** śpi mocno ▷ *n* dźwięk ▷ *vt* (*alarm*) włączać (włączyć *pf*); (*bell*) dzwonić (zadzwonić *pf*) +*inst* ▷ *vi* **1** (*alarm, bell*) dzwonić (zadzwonić *pf*) **2** (*seem*) brzmieć (zabrzmieć *pf*); **to make a ~** brzmieć (zabrzmieć *pf*); **that ~s like an explosion** brzmi to jak wybuch; **that ~s like a great idea** to świetny pomysł; **it ~s as if...** (*fig*) wygląda na to, że...
soundtrack ['saundtræk] *n* ścieżka dźwiękowa
soup [suːp] *n* zupa
sour ['sauəʳ] *adj* kwaśny; **to go** *or* **turn ~** (*milk, wine*) kwaśnieć (skwaśnieć *pf*)
south [sauθ] *n* południe ▷ *adj* południowy ▷ *adv* na południe; **in the ~** na południu; **to the ~** na południe; **the ~ of France** południe Francji; **~ of...** na południe od +*gen*...
South Africa *n* Afryka Południowa
South America *n* Ameryka Południowa
south-east [sauθ'iːst] *n* południowy wschód ▷ *adj* południowo-wschodni ▷ *adv* na południowy wschód; **in the ~** na południowym wschodzie
southern ['sʌðən] *adj* południowy; **the ~ hemisphere** południowa półkula
South Korea *n* Korea Południowa
South Pole *n*: **the ~** biegun południowy
south-west [sauθ'wɛst] *n* południowy zachód ▷ *adj* południowo-zachodni ▷ *adv* na

południowy zachód; **in the ~** na południowym zachodzie
souvenir [suːvəˈnɪəʳ] *n* pamiątka
soy [sɔɪ] (*US*) *n* soja
soya [ˈsɔɪə] (*Brit*) *n* soja
soy sauce *n* sos sojowy
space [speɪs] *n* **1** (*gap, place*) miejsce **2** (*beyond Earth*) kosmos; **to clear a ~ for sth** robić (zrobić *pf*) miejsce dla czegoś
spacecraft [ˈspeɪskrɑːft] (*pl* **spacecraft**) *n* statek kosmiczny
spade [speɪd] *n* **1** (*tool*) łopata **2** (*child's*) łopatka; **spades** *n pl* (*Cards*) piki
spaghetti [spəˈgɛtɪ] *n* spaghetti
Spain [speɪn] *n* Hiszpania
spam [spæm] (*Comput*) *n* spam
Spanish [ˈspænɪʃ] *adj* hiszpański ▷ *n* (*language*) hiszpański; **the Spanish** *n pl* Hiszpanie
spanner [ˈspænəʳ] (*Brit*) *n* klucz do nakrętek
spare [spɛəʳ] *adj* **1** (*free*) wolny **2** (*extra*) dodatkowy ▷ *n* (*also*: **~ part**) część zamienna ▷ *vt* (*afford to give*) mieć na zbyciu
spare part *n* część zamienna
spare time *n* wolny czas
sparrow [ˈspærəu] *n* wróbel
spat [spæt] *pt, pp of* **spit**
speak [spiːk] (*pt* **spoke**, *pp* **spoken**) *vt* (*language*) mówić po +*dat* ▷ *vi* mówić; **to ~ to sb about sth** rozmawiać (porozmawiać *pf*) z kimś o czymś; **generally ~ing** ogólnie mówiąc; **technically ~ing** z technicznego punktu widzenia
▶ **speak up** *vi*: **~ up!** proszę mówić głośniej!
speaker [ˈspiːkəʳ] *n* **1** (*in debate*) mówca(-czyni) *m/f* **2** (*also*: **loud~**) głośnik; **a French/Russian ~** osoba znająca francuski/rosyjski
special [ˈspɛʃl] *adj* **1** (*important*) specjalny **2** (*particular*) szczególny; **we only use these plates on ~ occasions** używamy tych talerzy tylko przy specjalnych okazjach; **to take ~ care** zachowywać (zachować *pf*) szczególne środki ostrożności; **it's nothing ~** to nic szczególnego
specialist [ˈspɛʃəlɪst] *n* (*Med*) lekarz specjalista
speciality [spɛʃɪˈælɪtɪ] (*US* **specialty**) [ˈspɛʃəltɪ] *n* **1** (*food*) specjalność **2** (*subject area*) specjalizacja
specialize [ˈspɛʃəlaɪz] *vi*: **to ~ in** specjalizować (wyspecjalizować *pf*) się w +*loc*
specially [ˈspɛʃlɪ] *adv* **1** (*specifically*) specjalnie **2** (*inf*: *particularly*) szczególnie
special needs *n pl*: **children with ~** (*Brit*) dzieci specjalnej troski
specialty [ˈspɛʃəltɪ] (*US*) *n* = **speciality**
species [ˈspiːʃiːz] *n* gatunek
specific [spəˈsɪfɪk] *adj* **1** (*fixed*) określony **2** (*exact*) dokładny
spectacle [ˈspɛktəkl] *n* widowisko; **spectacles** *n pl* (*glasses*) okulary
spectacular [spɛkˈtækjuləʳ] *adj* spektakularny
spectator [spɛkˈteɪtəʳ] *n* widz
speech [spiːtʃ] *n* (*talk, lecture*) przemówienie
speechless [ˈspiːtʃlɪs] *adj* oniemiały
speed [spiːd] *n* **1** (*rate, promptness*) prędkość **2** (*fast movement*) szybkość **3** (*rapidity*) szybkość ▷ *vi* (*drive too fast*) przekraczać (przekroczyć *pf*) dozwoloną prędkość; **at full** *or* **top ~** z maksymalną prędkością; **at a ~ of 70km/h** z prędkością siedemdziesięciu kilometrów na godzinę
▶ **speed up** (*pt, pp* **speeded up**) *vi* **1** (*car, runner etc*) przyśpieszać (przyśpieszyć *pf*) **2** (*process*) nabierać (nabrać *pf*) tempa
speedboat [ˈspiːdbəut] *n* wyścigowa łódź motorowa
speeding [ˈspiːdɪŋ] (*Law*) *n* przekroczenie dozwolonej prędkości
speed limit (*Law*) *n* ograniczenie prędkości
spell [spɛl] (*pt, pp* **spelled** *or* **spelt**) *n* **1** (*period*) okres **2** (*also*: **magic ~**) zaklęcie ▷ *vt* literować (przeliterować *pf*); **to cast a ~ on sb** rzucać (rzucić *pf*) na kogoś urok; **he can't ~** on robi błędy ortograficzne

spelling ['spɛlɪŋ] *n* (*of word*) pisownia; **~ mistake** błąd ortograficzny
spelt [spɛlt] *pt, pp of* **spell**
spend [spɛnd] (*pt, pp* **spent**) *vt* **1** (*money*) wydawać (wydać *pf*) **2** (*time, life*) spędzać (spędzić *pf*); **to ~ time/energy doing sth** spędzać (spędzić *pf*) czas/zużywać (zużyć *pf*) siły na robienie czegoś; **to ~ the night in a hotel** spędzić (*pf*) noc w hotelu
spent [spɛnt] *pt, pp of* **spend**
spice [spaɪs] *n* przyprawa
spicy ['spaɪsɪ] *adj* pikantny
spider ['spaɪdəʳ] *n* pająk; **~'s web** pajęczyna
spill [spɪl] (*pt, pp* **spilt** *or* **spilled**) *vt* rozlewać (rozlać *pf*) ▷ *vi* rozlewać (rozlać *pf*) się; **to ~ sth on/over sth** rozlewać (rozlać *pf*) coś na coś
spinach ['spɪnɪtʃ] *n* szpinak
spine [spaɪn] *n* kręgosłup
spire ['spaɪəʳ] *n* iglica
spirit ['spɪrɪt] *n* **1** (*soul*) duch **2** (*ghost*) duch **3** (*energy, courage*) odwaga; **spirits** *n pl* **1** (*Brit: whisky etc*) alkohol *m sg* wysokoprocentowy **2** (*frame of mind*): **in good ~s** w dobrym nastroju
spiritual ['spɪrɪtjuəl] *adj* **1** (*of the spirit*) duchowy **2** (*religious*) religijny
spit [spɪt] (*pt, pp* **spat**) *vi* spluwać (splunąć *pf*)
▸ **spit out** *vt* wypluwać (wypluć *pf*)
spite [spaɪt] *n* złośliwość; **in ~ of** pomimo +*gen*
spiteful ['spaɪtful] *adj* złośliwy
splash [splæʃ] *n* **1** (*sound*) plusk **2** (*of liquid*) plama **3** (*of colour*) plama ▷ *vt* ochlapywać (ochlapać *pf*)
splendid ['splɛndɪd] *adj* wspaniały
splinter ['splɪntəʳ] *n* drzazga
split [splɪt] (*pt, pp* **split**) *vt* **1** (*divide*) dzielić (podzielić *pf*) **2** (*share equally*) dzielić (podzielić *pf*) się +*inst* ▷ *vi* (*party, group*) dzielić (podzielić *pf*) się
▸ **split up** *vi* rozchodzić (rozejść *pf*) się
spoil [spɔɪl] (*pt, pp* **spoiled** *or* **spoilt**) *vt* **1** (*damage*) psuć (popsuć *pf*) **2** (*child*) rozpieszczać (rozpieścić *pf*)
spoilt [spɔɪlt] *pt, pp of* **spoil** ▷ *adj* rozpieszczony
spoke [spəuk] *pt of* **speak**
spoken ['spəukn] *pp of* **speak**
spokesman ['spəuksmən] (*irreg*) *n* rzecznik
spokeswoman ['spəukswumən] (*irreg*) *n* rzeczniczka
sponge [spʌndʒ] *n* **1** (*material*) gąbka **2** (*for washing*) gąbka **3** (*also:* **~ cake**) biszkopt
sponsor ['spɔnsəʳ] *n* sponsor ▷ *vt* **1** (*player, event*) sponsorować **2** (*Brit: for charity*) wspomagać (wspomóc *pf*)
spontaneous [spɔn'teɪnɪəs] *adj* spontaniczny
spooky ['spu:kɪ] (*inf*) *adj* straszny
spoon [spu:n] *n* łyżka
sport [spɔ:t] *n* sport
sportsman ['spɔ:tsmən] (*irreg*) *n* sportowiec
sportswear ['spɔ:tswɛəʳ] *n* ubranie sportowe
sportswoman ['spɔ:tswumən] (*irreg*) *n* sportsmenka
sporty ['spɔ:tɪ] *adj* wysportowany
spot [spɔt] *n* **1** (*mark*) plama **2** (*dot*) kropka **3** (*pimple*) pryszcz **4** (*place*) miejsce ▷ *vt* (*notice*) zauważać (zauważyć *pf*); **on the ~** (*in that place*) na miejscu; (*immediately*) w tej samej chwili
spotless ['spɔtlɪs] *adj* bez skazy
spotlight ['spɔtlaɪt] *n* **1** (*on stage*) reflektor **2** (*in room*) światło punktowe
sprain [spreɪn] *vt*: **to ~ one's ankle/wrist** skręcać (skręcić *pf*) sobie kostkę/nadgarstek
spray [spreɪ] *n* (*in can*) spray ▷ *vt* **1** (*liquid*) rozpryskiwać (rozpryskać *pf*) **2** (*crops*) opryskiwać (opryskać *pf*) **3** (*with paint*) pryskać (prysnąć *pf*)
spread [sprɛd] (*pt, pp* **spread**) *n* (*on bread*) pasta ▷ *vt* **1**: **to ~ sth on/over** rozprowadzać (rozprowadzić *pf*) coś na +*loc* **2** (*butter, jam*) smarować (posmarować *pf*) +*inst* **3** (*disease*) roznosić (roznieść *pf*) ▷ *vi* (*news*) rozchodzić (rozejść *pf*) się; (*disease*) rozprzestrzeniać (rozprzestrzenić *pf*) się
▸ **spread out** *vi* rozpraszać (rozproszyć *pf*) się

spreadsheet ['sprɛdʃi:t] *n* arkusz kalkulacyjny

spring [sprɪŋ] *n* **1** (*season*) wiosna **2** (*wire coil*) sprężyna **3** (*of water*) źródło; **in (the) ~** wiosną

sprinkle ['sprɪŋkl] *vt* **1** (*with liquid*) kropić (pokropić *pf*) **2** (*with powder*) posypywać (posypać *pf*)

sprint [sprɪnt] *n* sprint ▷ *vi* biegać (pobiec *pf*) sprintem

spy [spaɪ] *n* szpieg ▷ *vi*: **to ~ on sb** (*watch*) szpiegować kogoś

spying ['spaɪɪŋ] *n* szpiegostwo

square [skwɛəʳ] *n* **1** kwadrat **2** (*in town*) plac ▷ *adj* (*in shape*) kwadratowy; **2 metres ~** w kształcie kwadratu o bokach o długości dwóch metrów; **2 ~ metres** dwa metry kwadratowe

squash [skwɔʃ] *n* **1** (*Brit*): **orange ~** sok pomarańczowy **2** (*US*: *vegetable*) kabaczek **3** (*Sport*) squash ▷ *vt* zgniatać (zgnieść *pf*)

squeak [skwi:k] *vi* **1** (*door*) skrzypieć (skrzypnąć *pf*) **2** (*mouse*) piszczeć (zapiszczeć *pf*)

squeeze [skwi:z] *vt* ściskać (ścisnąć *pf*)
▸ **squeeze out** *vt* wyciskać (wycisnąć *pf*)

squirrel ['skwɪrəl] *n* wiewiórka

stab [stæb] *vt* (*person*) pchnąć (*pf*) nożem

stable ['steɪbl] *adj* stały ▷ *n* (*for horse*) stajnia

stack [stæk] *n* sterta

stadium ['steɪdɪəm] (*pl* **stadiums** *or* **stadia** ['steɪdɪə]) *n* stadion

staff [stɑ:f] *n* personel

stage [steɪdʒ] *n* **1** (*in theatre*) scena **2** (*platform*) estrada; **to do sth in ~s** robić coś stopniowo; **in the early/final ~s** we wczesnym/końcowym stadium

stain [steɪn] *n* plama ▷ *vt* plamić (zaplamić *pf*)

stainless steel ['steɪnlɪs-] *n* stal nierdzewna

stair [stɛəʳ] *n* (*step*) stopień; **stairs** *n pl* (*flight of steps*) schody

staircase ['stɛəkeɪs] *n* klatka schodowa

stale [steɪl] *adj* czerstwy; (*cheese*) wyschnięty

stall [stɔ:l] *n* stragan ▷ *vi* (*engine, car*) gasnąć (zgasnąć *pf*); **the stalls** *n pl* (*Brit*) parter *m sg*

stammer ['stæməʳ] *vi* jąkać się

stamp [stæmp] *n* **1** (*for letter*) znaczek **2** (*in passport etc*) pieczątka ▷ *vi* (*with foot*) tupać (tupnąć *pf*) ▷ *vt* (*passport, visa*) stemplować (podstemplować *pf*); **to ~ one's foot** tupać (tupnąć *pf*) nogą

stand [stænd] (*pt, pp* **stood**) *n* (*Brit*: *podium*) trybuna ▷ *vi* **1** (*be upright*) stać **2** (*rise*) wstawać (wstać *pf*) **3**: **to ~ aside** schodzić (zejść *pf*) na bok ▷ *vt* (*bear*): **I can't ~ him/it** nie znoszę go/tego; **to ~ back** odsuwać (odsunąć *pf*) się do tyłu
▸ **stand for** *vt fus* **1** (*abbreviation*) oznaczać **2** (*tolerate*): **I will not ~ for it** nie pozwolę na to
▸ **stand in for** *vt fus* (*teacher*) zastępować (zastąpić *pf*)
▸ **stand out** *vi* wyróżniać (wyróżnić *pf*) się
▸ **stand up** *vi* **1** (*rise*) wstawać (wstać *pf*) **2** (*be on one's feet*) wstawać (wstać *pf*)
▸ **stand up for** *vt fus* stawać (stanąć *pf*) w obronie *+gen*

standard ['stændəd] *n* **1** (*level, quality*) poziom **2** (*norm, criterion*) standard ▷ *adj* **1** (*size*) standardowy **2** (*procedure, practice*) normalny **3** (*model, feature*) standardowy

stank [stæŋk] *pt of* **stink**

staple ['steɪpl] *n* (*for paper*) zszywka ▷ *vt* (*fasten*) zszywać (zszyć *pf*)

star [stɑ:ʳ] *n* gwiazda ▷ *vi*: **to ~ (in)** (*play, film*) grać (zagrać *pf*) główną rolę (w *+loc*); **the stars** *n pl* (*horoscope*) horoskop *m sg*; **a 4-~ hotel** hotel czterogwiazdkowy

stare [stɛəʳ] *vi*: **to ~ (at sb/sth)** wpatrywać się (w kogoś/coś)

star sign *n* znak zodiaku

start [stɑ:t] *n* początek ▷ *vt* **1** (*begin*) zaczynać (zacząć *pf*) **2** (*cause*: *fire, panic*) powodować (spowodować *pf*) **3** (*business*) zakładać (założyć *pf*) **4** (*engine, car*) uruchamiać (uruchomić *pf*) ▷ *vi* **1** (*begin*) zaczynać (zacząć *pf*) się **2** (*engine, car*) zapalać (zapalić *pf*); **to ~ doing** *or* **to do sth**

zaczynać (zacząć *pf*) coś robić
▸ **start off** *vi* (*begin moving*) ruszać (ruszyć *pf*) się
▸ **start out** *vi* (*begin*) zaczynać (zacząć *pf*) się
▸ **start up** *vt* zakładać (założyć *pf*)

starter ['stɑːtəʳ] (*Brit*) *n* przystawka

starve [stɑːv] *vi* **1** (*be very hungry*) głodować **2** (*die from hunger*) umierać (umrzeć *pf*) z głodu; **I'm starving!** (*inf*) umieram z głodu!

state [steɪt] *n* **1** (*condition*) stan **2** (*country*) państwo **3** (*part of country*) stan ▹ *vt* (*say, declare*) oświadczać (oświadczyć *pf*); **the States** *n pl* (*inf*) Stany Zjednoczone; **~ of affairs** stan rzeczy

statement ['steɪtmənt] *n* oświadczenie

station ['steɪʃən] *n* **1** (*railway station*) dworzec **2** (*on radio*) stacja

stationary ['steɪʃnərɪ] *adj* nieruchomy

stationery ['steɪʃnərɪ] *n* materiały biurowe *m pl*

statue ['stætjuː] *n* posąg

stay [steɪ] *n* pobyt ▹ *vi* **1** (*in place, position*) zostawać (zostać *pf*) **2** (*in town, hotel etc*) zatrzymywać (zatrzymać *pf*) się **3** (*in state, situation*) pozostawać (pozostać *pf*) ▹ *vt*: **to ~ the night** zatrzymywać (zatrzymać *pf*) się na noc; **to ~ with sb** zatrzymywać (zatrzymać *pf*) się u kogoś
▸ **stay in** *vi* zostawać (zostać *pf*) w domu
▸ **stay up** *vi* nie kłaść (położyć *pf*) się do łóżka

steady ['stɛdɪ] *adj* **1** (*progress, increase, fall*) ciągły **2** (*job, income*) stały **3** (*reliable*) solidny **4** (*object, hand*) pewny **5** (*look, voice*) spokojny

steak [steɪk] *n* stek

steal [stiːl] (*pt* **stole**, *pp* **stolen**) *vt* kraść (ukraść *pf*) ▹ *vi* (*be a thief*) kraść (ukraść *pf*); **he stole it from me** on mi to ukradł

steam [stiːm] *n* para ▹ *vt* gotować (ugotować *pf*) na parze

steel [stiːl] *n* stal ▹ *adj* stalowy

steep [stiːp] *adj* **1** (*hill, staircase*) stromy **2** (*increase, rise*) gwałtowny

steeple ['stiːpl] *n* wieża strzelista

steering wheel ['stɪərɪŋ-] *n* kierownica

step [stɛp] *n* **1** (*footstep*) krok **2** (*stage*) krok **3** (*of stairs*) stopień ▹ *vi*: **to ~ forward/backward** robić (zrobić *pf*) krok do przodu/do tyłu
▸ **step aside** *vi* = **step down**
▸ **step back** *vi*: **to ~ back (from sth)** (*fig*) nabierać (nabrać *pf*) dystansu (do czegoś)
▸ **step down, step aside** *vi* odsuwać (odsunąć *pf*) się na bok

stepbrother ['stɛpbrʌðəʳ] *n* przyrodni brat

stepdaughter ['stɛpdɔːtəʳ] *n* pasierbica

stepfather ['stɛpfɑːðəʳ] *n* ojczym

stepladder ['stɛplædəʳ] *n* drabina

stepmother ['stɛpmʌðəʳ] *n* macocha

stepsister ['stɛpsɪstəʳ] *n* przyrodnia siostra

stepson ['stɛpsʌn] *n* pasierb

stereo ['stɛrɪəu] *n* zestaw stereo

sterling ['stəːlɪŋ] *n* funt szterling; **one pound ~** jeden funt szterling

stew [stjuː] *n* potrawka

steward ['stjuːəd] *n* steward

stewardess ['stjuədɛs] *n* stewardesa

stick [stɪk] (*pt, pp* **stuck**) *n* **1** (*of wood*) kij **2** (*walking stick*) laska ▹ *vt*: **to ~ sth on/to sth** (*with glue etc*) przyklejać (przykleić *pf*) coś na czymś/do czegoś ▹ *vi*: **to ~ (to sth)** (*stamp, sticker*) przyklejać (przykleić *pf*) się (do czegoś)
▸ **stick out** *vi* wystawać ▹ *vt* (*tongue, hand*) wystawiać (wystawić *pf*)
▸ **stick up for** *vt fus* bronić (obronić *pf*)
▸ **stick with** *vt fus* trzymać się *+gen*

sticker ['stɪkəʳ] *n* naklejka

sticky ['stɪkɪ] *adj* **1** (*substance*) lepki **2** (*tape, paper*) samoprzylepny

stiff [stɪf] *adj* **1** (*with aching muscles*) zesztywniały **2** (*competition*) ostry ▹ *adv*: **to be bored ~** nudzić się śmiertelnie; **to be scared ~** być śmiertelnie przerażonym

still [stɪl] *adj* **1** (*person, hands*) nieruchomy **2** (*Brit: not fizzy*) niegazowany ▷ *adv* **1** (*up to the present*) ciągle **2** (*possibly*) jeszcze **3** (*even*) jeszcze **4** (*yet*) jeszcze **5** (*nonetheless*) mimo to; **to stand ~** stać nieruchomo; **to keep ~** być nieruchomym; **he ~ hasn't arrived** on jeszcze nie przyjechał; **better ~** jeszcze lepiej

sting [stɪŋ] (*pt, pp* **stung**) *n* użądlenie ▷ *vt* (*insect*) żądlić (użądlić *pf*); (*nettle*) parzyć (oparzyć *pf*) ▷ *vi* (*ointment, eye, cut*) szczypać (zaszczypać *pf*)

stink [stɪŋk] (*pt* **stank**, *pp* **stunk**) *n* smród ▷ *vi* śmierdzieć

stir [stəːʳ] *vt* mieszać (zamieszać *pf*)

stitch [stɪtʃ] *n* **1** (*in sewing*) ścieg **2** (*Med*) szew ▷ *vt*: **to ~ sth to sth** przyszywać (przyszyć *pf*) coś do czegoś

stock [stɔk] *n* **1** (*supply*) zapas **2** (*in shop*) towar **3** (*gravy*) wywar ▷ *vt* (*goods*) prowadzić sprzedaż +*gen*; **in ~** w sprzedaży; **out of ~** wyprzedany ▶ **stock up** *vi*: **to ~ up (on** *or* **with sth)** zaopatrywać (zaopatrzyć *pf*) się (w coś)

stockbroker ['stɔkbrəukəʳ] *n* makler giełdowy

stock exchange *n* giełda papierów wartościowych

stockholder ['stɔkhəuldəʳ] (*US*) *n* akcjonariusz(ka) *m/f*

stocking ['stɔkɪŋ] *n* pończocha

stole [stəul] *pt of* **steal**

stolen ['stəuln] *pp of* **steal**

stomach ['stʌmək] *n* **1** (*organ*) żołądek **2** (*abdomen*) brzuch

stomach ache *n* ból brzucha; **I've got ~** boli mnie brzuch

stone [stəun] *n* **1** kamień **2** (*pebble*) kamyk **3** (*Brit*: *in fruit*) pestka **4** (*Brit*: *weight*) *jednostka wagi, równa sześć i trzydzieści pięć setnych kilograma*

stood [stud] *pt, pp of* **stand**

stool [stuːl] *n* stołek

stop [stɔp] *vt* **1** zatrzymywać (zatrzymać *pf*) **2** (*prevent*) powstrzymywać (powstrzymać *pf*) ▷ *vi* **1** (*person, vehicle*) zatrzymywać (zatrzymać *pf*) się **2** (*rain, noise, activity*) ustawać (ustać *pf*) ▷ *n* (*for bus*) przystanek; (*for train*) stacja; **to ~ doing sth** przestawać (przestać *pf*) coś robić; **to ~ sb (from) doing sth** powstrzymywać (powstrzymać *pf*) kogoś przed zrobieniem czegoś; **~ it!** przestań!

stoplight ['stɔplaɪt] (*US*) *n* **1** (*in road*) czerwone światło **2** (*on vehicle*) światło stopu

store [stɔːʳ] *n* **1** (*of food*) zapas **2** (*Brit*: *large shop*) sklep **3** (*US*: *shop*) sklep ▷ *vt* (*information*) przechowywać (przechować *pf*)

storekeeper ['stɔːkiːpəʳ] (*US*) *n* właściciel(ka) *m/f* sklepu

storey ['stɔːrɪ] (*US* **story**) *n* piętro

storm [stɔːm] *n* burza

stormy ['stɔːmɪ] *adj* burzowy

story ['stɔːrɪ] *n* **1** (*account*) opowieść **2** (*tale*) historia **3** (*in news*) artykuł **4** (*US*: *of building*) = **storey**

stove [stəuv] *n* **1** (*for cooking*) kuchnia **2** (*for heating*) piecyk

straight [streɪt] *adj* **1** (*not curving*) prosty **2** (*hair*) prosty **3** (*inf*: *heterosexual*) heteroseksualny ▷ *adv* **1** (*walk, stand, look*) prosto **2** (*immediately*) zaraz; **~ away, ~ off** natychmiast

straightforward [streɪt'fɔːwəd] *adj* prosty

strain [streɪn] *n* **1** (*pressure*) obciążenie **2**: **back/muscle ~** nadwyrężenie pleców/mięśnia ▷ *vt* (*back, muscle*) naprężać (naprężyć *pf*)

strange [streɪndʒ] *adj* **1** (*odd*) dziwny **2** (*unfamiliar*) obcy

stranger ['streɪndʒəʳ] *n* obcy(-ca) *m/f*

strangle ['stræŋgl] *vt* dusić (udusić *pf*)

strap [stræp] *n* pasek

straw [strɔː] *n* **1** słoma **2** (*drinking straw*) słomka

strawberry ['strɔːbərɪ] *n* truskawka

stray [streɪ] *adj* bezpański

stream [striːm] *n* strumień ▷ *vt* (*Comput*) streamować

street [striːt] *n* ulica

streetcar ['striːtkɑːʳ] (*US*) *n* tramwaj

strength [strɛŋθ] *n* **1** siła **2** (*of object, material*) wytrzymałość

stress [strɛs] *n* stres ▷ *vt* podkreślać (podkreślić *pf*)

stressful ['strɛsful] *adj* (*job, situation*) stresujący
stretch [strɛtʃ] *vi* **1** (*person, animal*) przeciągać (przeciągnąć *pf*) się **2** (*elastic, garment*) rozciągać (rozciągnąć *pf*) się ▷ *vt* **1** (*arm, leg*) wyciągać (wyciągnąć *pf*) **2** (*elastic, garment*) naciągać (naciągnąć *pf*)
▸ **stretch out** *vt* (*arm, leg*) wyciągać (wyciągnąć *pf*)
stretcher ['strɛtʃəʳ] *n* nosze *m pl*
strict [strɪkt] *adj* **1** (*rule, instruction*) ścisły **2** (*person*) surowy
strike [straɪk] (*pt, pp* **struck**) *n* strajk ▷ *vt* **1** (*hit: person, thing*) uderzać (uderzyć *pf*) **2** (*match*) zapalać (zapalić *pf*) ▷ *vi* **1** (*workers*) strajkować (zastrajkować *pf*) **2** (*clock*) bić (wybić *pf*); **to be/go on ~** strajkować (zastrajkować *pf*); **the clock struck nine** zegar wybił dziewiątą
striker ['straɪkəʳ] *n* **1** (*person on strike*) strajkujący(-ca) *m/f* **2** (*Football*) napastnik(-iczka) *m/f*
string [strɪŋ] *n* **1** sznurek **2** (*Mus*) struna
string bean (*US*) *n* fasolka szparagowa
strip [strɪp] *n* (*of paper, cloth*) pasek ▷ *vi* (*undress*) rozbierać (rozebrać *pf*) się
stripe [straɪp] *n* pas
striped [straɪpt] *adj* w pasy
stroke [strəuk] *n* (*Med*) udar ▷ *vt* (*person, animal*) głaskać (pogłaskać *pf*); **a ~ of luck** łut szczęścia
stroll [strəul] *n* spacer; **to go for a ~** chodzić/iść (pójść *pf*) na spacer
stroller ['strəuləʳ] (*US*) *n* wózek spacerowy
strong [strɔŋ] *adj* **1** (*person, arms, grip*) silny **2** (*object, material*) mocny **3** (*wind, current*) silny
strongly ['strɔŋlɪ] *adv* **1** (*made, built*) porządnie **2** (*defend, advise, argue*) mocno; **I feel ~ about it** jest to dla mnie bardzo ważne
struck [strʌk] *pt, pp of* **strike**
struggle ['strʌgl] *n* walka ▷ *vi* **1** (*try hard*) walczyć **2** (*fight*) bić (pobić *pf*) się
stubborn ['stʌbən] *adj* uparty
stuck [stʌk] *pt, pp of* **stick** ▷ *adj*: **to be ~** (*object*) być zablokowanym; (*person*) nie móc się ruszyć (poruszyć *pf*)
stud [stʌd] *n* **1** (*on clothing*) ćwiek **2** (*earring*) kolczyk **3** (*Brit: on soles of boots*) kołek
student ['stju:dənt] *n* **1** (*at university*) student(ka) *m/f* **2** (*at school*) uczeń(-ennica) *m/f*; **a law/medical ~** student(ka) *m/f* prawa/medycyny
student driver (*US*) *n* uczestnik(-iczka) *m/f* kursu prawa jazdy
studio ['stju:dɪəu] *n* **1** (*TV, Rad, Mus*) studio **2** (*of artist*) pracownia; (*of photographer*) studio
study ['stʌdɪ] *n* (*room*) gabinet ▷ *vt* studiować ▷ *vi* uczyć się
stuff [stʌf] *n* **1** (*things*) rzeczy *f pl* **2** (*substance*) coś ▷ *vt* (*Culin*) nadziewać (nadziać *pf*)
stuffing ['stʌfɪŋ] *n* (*in sofa*) wypełnienie; (*in chicken*) nadzienie
stuffy ['stʌfɪ] *adj* duszny
stumble ['stʌmbl] *vi* potykać (potknąć *pf*) się
stung [stʌŋ] *pt, pp of* **sting**
stunk [stʌŋk] *pp of* **stink**
stunned [stʌnd] *adj* (*shocked*) zaszokowany; **a ~ silence** grobowa cisza
stunning ['stʌnɪŋ] *adj* **1** (*impressive*) imponujący **2** (*beautiful*) olśniewający
stunt [stʌnt] *n* wyczyn kaskaderski
stupid ['stju:pɪd] *adj* głupi
stutter ['stʌtəʳ] *vi* jąkać się
style [staɪl] *n* **1** (*type*) styl **2** (*elegance*) styl **3** (*design*) fason
stylish ['staɪlɪʃ] *adj* elegancki
subject [*n* 'sʌbdʒɪkt] *n* **1** (*matter*) temat **2** (*Scol*) przedmiot **3** (*Ling*) podmiot
submarine [sʌbmə'ri:n] *n* łódź podwodna
subscription [səb'skrɪpʃən] *n* prenumerata
subsidy ['sʌbsɪdɪ] *n* dotacja
substance ['sʌbstəns] *n* substancja
substitute ['sʌbstɪtju:t] *n* **1** (*person*) osoba w zastępstwie **2** (*thing*) substytut **3** (*Football*) zawodnik

rezerwowy ▷ *vt*: **to ~ sth (for sth)** zastępować (zastąpić *pf*) coś (czymś)
subtitles ['sʌbtaɪtlz] *n pl* napisy
subtle ['sʌtl] *adj* subtelny
subtract [səb'trækt] *vt*: **to ~ sth (from sth)** odejmować (odjąć *pf*) coś (od czegoś)
suburb ['sʌbəːb] *n* przedmieście; **the suburbs** *n pl* przedmieścia
subway ['sʌbweɪ] *n* **1** (*US: underground railway*) metro **2** (*Brit: underpass*) przejście podziemne
succeed [sək'siːd] *vi* (*plan*) powieść (*pf*) się; (*person*) odnosić (odnieść *pf*) sukces; **to ~ in doing sth** odnosić (odnieść *pf*) sukces w robieniu czegoś
success [sək'sɛs] *n* sukces; **without ~** bez powodzenia
successful [sək'sɛsful] *adj* **1** (*attempt*) pomyślny; (*film, product*) odnoszący sukcesy **2** (*writer*) słynny
successfully [sək'sɛsfəlɪ] *adv* z powodzeniem
such [sʌtʃ] *adj* **1** (*of this kind*) taki **2** (*so much*) tak; **~ was his anger, that...** był tak zły, że...; **~ a(n)** taki; **~ a lot of** tak dużo *+gen*; **~ as** (*like*) taki jak; **as ~** (*on its own*) sam
such-and-such ['sʌtʃənsʌtʃ] *adj* taki a taki
suck [sʌk] *vt* ssać
sudden ['sʌdn] *adj* nagły; **all of a ~** nagle
suddenly ['sʌdnlɪ] *adv* nagle
suede [sweɪd] *n* zamsz ▷ *adj* (*shoes, handbag*) zamszowy
suffer ['sʌfəʳ] *vi* **1** (*be in pain*) cierpieć (wycierpieć *pf*) **2** (*be badly affected*) cierpieć (ucierpieć *pf*)
suffocate ['sʌfəkeɪt] *vi* (*die*) dusić (udusić *pf*) się
sugar ['ʃugəʳ] *n* cukier
suggest [sə'dʒɛst] *vt* sugerować (zasugerować *pf*); **to ~ that...** sugerować (zasugerować *pf*), że...
suggestion [sə'dʒɛstʃən] *n* sugestia; **to make a ~** sugerować (zasugerować *pf*)
suicide ['suɪsaɪd] *n* samobójstwo; **a ~ bomber** zamachowiec samobójca; **to commit ~** popełnić (*pf*) samobójstwo
suit [suːt] *n* (*man's*) garnitur; (*woman's*) kostium ▷ *vt* pasować *+dat*
suitable ['suːtəbl] *adj* **1** (*time, place*) dogodny **2** (*person, clothes*) odpowiedni
suitcase ['suːtkeɪs] *n* walizka
suite [swiːt] *n* apartament
sulk [sʌlk] *vi* dąsać się
sultana [sʌl'tɑːnə] (*Brit*) *n* sułtanka
sum [sʌm] *n* suma; **to do a ~** robić (zrobić *pf*) rachunki
▸ **sum up** *vt* sumować (podsumować *pf*) ▷ *vi* reasumować (zreasumować *pf*)
summarize ['sʌməraɪz] *vt* streszczać (streścić *pf*)
summary ['sʌmərɪ] *n* streszczenie
summer ['sʌməʳ] *n* lato ▷ *adj* letni; **in (the) ~** latem
summertime ['sʌmətaɪm] *n* lato
summit ['sʌmɪt] *n* szczyt
sun [sʌn] *n* słońce
sunbathe ['sʌnbeɪð] *vi* opalać (opalić *pf*) się
sunburn ['sʌnbəːn] *n* oparzenie słoneczne
sunburned ['sʌnbəːnd], **sunburnt** *adj* poparzony przez słońce
sun cream *n* krem z filtrem przeciwsłonecznym
Sunday ['sʌndɪ] *n* niedziela; *see also* **Tuesday**
sunflower ['sʌnflauəʳ] *n* słonecznik
sung [sʌŋ] *pp of* **sing**
sunglasses ['sʌnglɑːsɪz] *n pl* okulary przeciwsłoneczne
sunk [sʌŋk] *pp of* **sink**
sunlight ['sʌnlaɪt] *n* światło słoneczne
sunny ['sʌnɪ] *adj* słoneczny; **it is ~** jest słoneczna pogoda
sunrise ['sʌnraɪz] *n* wschód słońca; **at ~** o wschodzie słońca
sun roof *n* (*on car*) szyberdach
sunset ['sʌnsɛt] *n* zachód słońca; **at ~** o zachodzie słońca
sunshine ['sʌnʃaɪn] *n* słońce
suntan ['sʌntæn] *n* opalenizna ▷ *adj* (*lotion, cream*) do opalania; **to get a ~** opalić (*pf*) się
super ['suːpəʳ] (*Brit: inf*) *adj* świetny
supermarket ['suːpəmɑːkɪt] *n* supermarket

supernatural [su:pəˈnætʃərəl] *adj* nadprzyrodzony
superstitious [su:pəˈstɪʃəs] *adj* przesądny
supervise [ˈsu:pəvaɪz] *vt* nadzorować
supervisor [ˈsu:pəvaɪzə^r] *n* **1** (*of workers*) nadzorca(-czyni) *m/f* **2** (*of student*) promotor(ka) *m/f*
supper [ˈsʌpə^r] *n* kolacja; **to have ~** jeść (zjeść *pf*) kolację
supplement [ˈsʌplɪmənt] *n* (*additional amount*) suplement
supply [səˈplaɪ] *vt* dostarczać (dostarczyć *pf*) ▷ *n* zapas; **supplies** *n pl* zapasy; **to ~ sb/sth with sth** zaopatrywać (zaopatrzyć *pf*) kogoś/coś w coś
support [səˈpɔ:t] *n* **1** (*moral*) wsparcie **2** (*for object, structure*) podpora ▷ *vt* **1** (*morally*) wspierać (wesprzeć *pf*) **2** (*financially*) utrzymywać (utrzymać *pf*) **3** (*football team*) kibicować *+dat*
supporter [səˈpɔ:tə^r] *n* **1** (*of politician, policy*) zwolennik(-iczka) *m/f* **2** (*of team*) kibic
suppose [səˈpəuz] *vt* przypuszczać; **I ~** przypuszczam; **he's about sixty, I ~** przypuszczam, że on ma około sześćdziesiątki; **I ~ so/not** przypuszczam, że tak/nie; **he's ~d to be an expert** on ma być ekspertem
supposing [səˈpəuzɪŋ] *conj* przypuśćmy, że
sure [ʃuə^r] *adj* **1** pewny **2** (*certain*): **she's ~ to do it** ona na pewno to zrobi; **to make ~ that…** (*take action*) upewniać (upewnić *pf*) się, że…; **~!** (*inf: of course*) jasne!; **I'm ~ of it** jestem tego pewien; **I'm not ~ how/why/when** nie jestem pewien jak/dlaczego/kiedy
surely [ˈʃuəlɪ] *adv* na pewno; **~ you don't mean that!** z pewnością o to ci chodzi!
surf [sə:f] *vi* surfować ▷ *vt*: **to ~ the internet** surfować po internecie
surface [ˈsə:fɪs] *n* powierzchnia; **on the ~** na powierzchni
surfboard [ˈsə:fbɔ:d] *n* deska surfingowa
surfing [ˈsə:fɪŋ] *n* surfing; **to go ~** surfować
surgeon [ˈsə:dʒən] *n* chirurg
surgery [ˈsə:dʒərɪ] *n* **1** (*treatment*) operacja **2** (*Brit: of doctor, dentist*) przychodnia
surname [ˈsə:neɪm] *n* nazwisko
surprise [səˈpraɪz] *n* **1** (*unexpected event*) niespodzianka **2** (*astonishment*) zaskoczenie ▷ *vt* dziwić (zdziwić *pf*); **to my (great) ~** ku memu (wielkiemu) zdziwieniu
surprised [səˈpraɪzd] *adj* zdziwiony; **to be ~ to find/see sth** ze zdziwieniem znaleźć/zobaczyć coś
surprising [səˈpraɪzɪŋ] *adj* zaskakujący
surrender [səˈrɛndə^r] *vi* poddawać (poddać *pf*) się
surround [səˈraund] *vt* otaczać (otoczyć *pf*)
surroundings [səˈraundɪŋz] *n pl* otoczenie *nt sg*
survey [ˈsə:veɪ] *n* sondaż
survive [səˈvaɪv] *vi* przeżyć *pf* ▷ *vt* (*accident, illness*) przeżyć (*pf*)
survivor [səˈvaɪvə^r] *n* ocalały
suspect [*n* ˈsʌspɛkt, *vb* səsˈpɛkt] *n* podejrzany ▷ *vt* **1** (*person*) podejrzewać **2** (*sb's motives*) wątpić w; **to ~ that…** podejrzewać, że…
suspend [səsˈpɛnd] *vt* zawieszać (zawiesić *pf*)
suspense [səsˈpɛns] *n* **1** (*uncertainty*) stan niepewności **2** (*in novel, film*) napięcie
suspicious [səsˈpɪʃəs] *adj* **1** (*showing suspicion*) podejrzliwy **2** (*arousing suspicion*) podejrzany
swallow [ˈswɔləu] *vt* połykać (połknąć *pf*) ▷ *vi* przełykać (przełknąć *pf*)
swam [swæm] *pt of* **swim**
swan [swɔn] *n* łabędź
swap [swɔp] *vt*: **to ~ sth (for)** (*exchange for*) zamieniać (zamienić *pf*) coś (na); (*replace with*) wymieniać (wymienić *pf*) coś (na); **to ~ places (with sb)** zamieniać (zamienić *pf*) się miejscami (z kimś)
swear [swɛə^r] (*pt* **swore**, *pp* **sworn**) *vi* (*curse*) przeklinać (przekląć *pf*) ▷ *vt* (*promise*) przysięgać (przysiąc *pf*); **to ~ that…** (*promise*) przysięgać (przysiąc *pf*), że…

swear word *n* przekleństwo
sweat [swɛt] *n* pot ▷ *vi* pocić (spocić *pf*) się
sweater ['swɛtəʳ] *n* sweter
sweatshirt ['swɛtʃə:t] *n* bluza sportowa
Sweden ['swi:dn] *n* Szwecja
Swedish ['swi:dɪʃ] *adj* szwedzki ▷ *n* (*language*) szwedzki
sweep [swi:p] (*pt, pp* **swept**) *vt* zamiatać (zamieść *pf*)
sweet [swi:t] *n* (*Brit*) **1** (*chocolate, mint*) cukierek **2** (*pudding*) deser ▷ *adj* **1** słodki **2** (*cute*) uroczy; **~ and sour** słodko-kwaśny
sweetcorn ['swi:tkɔ:n] *n* kukurydza
swept [swɛpt] *pt, pp of* **sweep**
swerve [swə:v] *vi* gwałtownie skręcać (skręcić *pf*)
swim [swɪm] (*pt* **swam**, *pp* **swum**) *vi* płynąć (popłynąć *pf*) ▷ *vt* (*distance*) przepływać (przepłynąć *pf*) ▷ *n*: **to go for a ~** chodzić/iść (pójść *pf*) popływać
swimmer ['swɪməʳ] *n* pływak(-aczka) *m/f*; **he's a good ~** jest dobrym pływakiem
swimming ['swɪmɪŋ] *n* pływanie; **to go ~** pływać
swimming pool *n* basen
swimsuit ['swɪmsu:t] *n* kostium kąpielowy
swing [swɪŋ] (*pt, pp* **swung**) *n* (*in playground*) huśtawka ▷ *vt* machać (machnąć *pf*) +*inst* ▷ *vi* **1** (*pendulum*) wahać się **2** (*door*) chwiać (zachwiać *pf*) się
Swiss [swɪs] *adj* szwajcarski
switch [swɪtʃ] *n* (*"on" switch*) włącznik; (*"off" switch*) wyłącznik ▷ *vt* (*change*) zmieniać (zmienić *pf*)
▸ **switch off** *vt* wyłączać (wyłączyć *pf*)
▸ **switch on** *vt* włączać (włączyć *pf*)
Switzerland ['swɪtsələnd] *n* Szwajcaria
swollen ['swəulən] *adj* spuchnięty
swop [swɔp] *n, vt* = **swap**
sword [sɔ:d] *n* szpada
swore [swɔ:ʳ] *pt of* **swear**
sworn [swɔ:n] *pp of* **swear**
swum [swʌm] *pp of* **swim**
swung [swʌŋ] *pt, pp of* **swing**
syllabus ['sɪləbəs] (*esp Brit*) *n* program nauczania; **on the ~** w programie nauczania
symbol ['sɪmbl] *n* symbol
sympathetic [sɪmpə'θɛtɪk] *adj* **1** (*understanding*) współczujący **2** (*supportive*) przychylny
sympathize ['sɪmpəθaɪz] *vi*: **to ~ with sb** współczuć komuś
sympathy ['sɪmpəθɪ] *n* współczucie; **"with deepest ~"** „z wyrazami najgłębszego współczucia"
symptom ['sɪmptəm] *n* objaw
synagogue ['sɪnəgɔg] *n* synagoga
syringe [sɪ'rɪndʒ] *n* strzykawka
system ['sɪstəm] *n* system

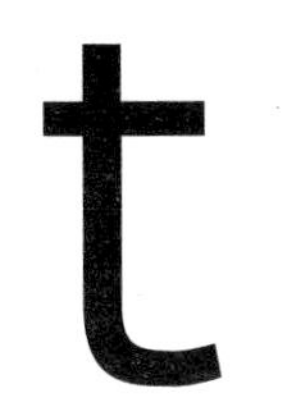

table ['teɪbl] *n* (*piece of furniture*) stół; **to lay** *or* **set the ~** nakrywać (nakryć *pf*) do stołu; **to clear the ~** sprzątać (sprzątnąć *pf*) ze stołu
tablecloth ['teɪblklɔθ] *n* obrus
tablespoon ['teɪblspuːn] *n* łyżka stołowa
tablet ['tæblɪt] *n* (*Med*) tabletka; (*Comput*) tablet
table tennis (*Sport*) *n* ping-pong

TABLOID

Tabloids – Tabloidy to popularne dzienniki z dużą ilością zdjęć. Inaczej po polsku zwane brukowcami, szczególnym zainteresowaniem gazety te darzą sensację, sport oraz życie gwiazd show biznesu. Angielskie słowo **tabloid** oznacza przede wszystkim mniejszy, poręczniejszy format, w jakim ukazują się tego typu gazety.

tact [tækt] *n* takt
tactful ['tæktful] *adj* (*diplomatic*) taktowny
tactics ['tæktɪks] *n pl* (*strategy*) taktyka *f sg*
tadpole ['tædpəul] *n* kijanka
taffy ['tæfɪ] (*US*) *n* toffi
tag [tæg] *n* (*label*) metka
tail [teɪl] *n* (*of animal*) ogon; **"heads or ~s?" — "~s"** „orzeł czy reszka?" — „reszka"
tailor ['teɪlə^r] *n* (*person*) krawiec
take [teɪk] (*pt* **took**, *pp* **taken**) *vt* **1** (*holiday, vacation*) robić (zrobić *pf*) sobie; (*shower, bath*) brać (wziąć *pf*); (*decision*) podejmować (podjąć *pf*) **2** (*take hold of*: *sb's arm*) brać (wziąć *pf*) za **3** (*steal*) zabierać (zabrać *pf*) **4** (*accompany*: *person*) zabierać (zabrać *pf*) **5** (*carry, bring*: *handbag, camera*) zabierać (zabrać *pf*) **6** (*travel along*: *road*) jechać (pojechać *pf*) +*inst* **7** (*car, train etc*) jechać (pojechać *pf*) +*inst* **8** (*size*) mieć **9** (*time*) zabierać (zabrać *pf*) **10** (*exam, test*) zdawać **11** (*drug, pill etc*) brać (wziąć *pf*); **don't forget to ~ your umbrella** nie zapomnij zabrać parasolki; **she's not yet ~n her driving test** jeszcze nie zdawała egzaminu na prawo jazdy
▸ **take after** *vt fus* (*resemble*) przypominać
▸ **take apart** *vt* (*dismantle*) rozbierać (rozebrać *pf*)
▸ **take away** *vt* zabierać (zabrać *pf*)
▸ **take back** *vt* (*return*: *goods*) zwracać (zwrócić *pf*)
▸ **take down** *vt* (*write down*) notować (zanotować *pf*)
▸ **take in** *vt* **1** (*deceive*: *person*) omamiać (omamić *pf*) **2** (*understand*) pojmować (pojąć *pf*)
▸ **take off** *vi* (*aircraft*) startować (wystartować *pf*) ▷ *vt* **1** (*time from work*): **to ~ two days off work** brać (wziąć *pf*) dwa dni wolnego **2** (*clothes, glasses, make-up*) zdejmować (zdjąć *pf*)
▸ **take out** *vt* **1** (*invite*: *person*) zabierać (zabrać *pf*) **2** (*remove*: *tooth*) wyrywać (wyrwać *pf*)
▸ **take over** *vi*: **to ~ over from sb** przejmować (przejąć *pf*) coś od kogoś
▸ **take up** *vt* **1** (*start*: *hobby, sport*) zaczynać (zacząć *pf*) **2** (*occupy*: *time, space*) zajmować (zająć *pf*)
takeaway ['teɪkəweɪ] (*Brit*) *n* **1** (*shop, restaurant*) *restauracja z jedzeniem na wynos* **2** (*food*) jedzenie na wynos
taken ['teɪkən] *pp of* **take**
takeoff ['teɪkɔf] *n* (*of plane*) start
takeout ['teɪkaut] (*US*) *n* **1** (*shop, restaurant*) *restauracja z jedzeniem na wynos* **2** (*food*) jedzenie na wynos

tale [teɪl] *n* (*story*) opowieść
talent ['tælnt] *n* (*gift*) talent; **to have a ~ for sth** mieć talent do czegoś
talented ['tæləntɪd] *adj* (*person, actor etc*) utalentowany
talk [tɔːk] *n* **1** (*prepared speech*) wystąpienie **2** (*conversation*) rozmowa **3** (*gossip*) pogłoska **4** (*discussion*) rozmowa ▷ *vi* **1** (*speak*) rozmawiać (porozmawiać *pf*) **2** (*chat*) rozmawiać (porozmawiać *pf*) **3** (*gossip*) gadać; **to give a ~** przemawiać (przemówić *pf*); (*politician*) przemawiać (przemówić *pf*); **to ~ to** *or* **with sb** rozmawiać (porozmawiać *pf*) z kimś; **to ~ about sth** rozmawiać (porozmawiać *pf*) o czymś
▸ **talk over, talk through** *vt* (*problem*) przedyskutowywać (przedyskutować *pf*)
talkative ['tɔːkətɪv] *adj* gadatliwy
talk show (*TV, Rad*) *n* talk show
tall [tɔːl] *adj* wysoki; **how ~ are you?** ile ma pan/pani wzrostu?; **he's two metres ~** ma dwa metry wzrostu
tame [teɪm] *adj* (*animal, bird*) oswojony
tampon ['tæmpɔn] *n* tampon
tan [tæn] *n* (*also*: **sun~**) opalenizna ▷ *vi* (*person*) opalać (opalić *pf*) się; **to get a ~** opalić (*pf*) się
tangerine [tændʒə'riːn] *n* (*fruit*) mandarynka
tangle ['tæŋgl] *n* (*of branches, knots, wire*) plątanina
tank [tæŋk] *n* **1** (*Mil*) czołg **2** (*for petrol, water*) zbiornik **3** (*also*: **fish ~**) akwarium
tanker ['tæŋkəʳ] *n* **1** (*ship*) tankowiec **2** (*truck*) cysterna
tanned [tænd] *adj* (*skin, person*) opalony
tap [tæp] *n* **1** (*esp Brit*: *on sink, pipe etc*) kran **2** (*gentle blow*) stuknięcie
tap-dancing ['tæpdɑːnsɪŋ] *n* stepowanie
tape [teɪp] *n* **1** (*cassette*) taśma **2** (*adhesive*) taśma ▷ *vt* **1** (*record*) nagrywać (nagrać *pf*) **2** (*attach*) przyklejać (przykleić *pf*)
tape measure *n* centymetr
tape recorder *n* magnetofon
tar [tɑːʳ] *n* (*on road etc*) smoła
target ['tɑːgɪt] *n* cel
tart [tɑːt] *n* (*cake*) tarta
tartan ['tɑːtn] *n* szkocka krata ▷ *adj* (*rug, scarf etc*) w szkocką kratę
task [tɑːsk] *n* zadanie
taste [teɪst] *n* **1** smak **2** (*choice, liking*) gust ▷ *vt* **1** (*get flavour of*) smakować (posmakować *pf*) +*gen* **2** (*test, detect*) czuć (poczuć *pf*) smak +*gen* ▷ *vi*: **to ~ of** *or* **like sth** smakować jak coś
tasty ['teɪstɪ] *adj* (*food*) smaczny
tattoo [tə'tuː] *n* (*on skin*) tatuaż
taught [tɔːt] *pt, pp of* **teach**
Taurus ['tɔːrəs] *n* (*Astrol*) Byk
tax [tæks] *n* (*Comm*) podatek
taxi ['tæksɪ] *n* taksówka
taxi rank [-ræŋk] (*Brit*) *n* postój taksówek
taxi stand (*US*) *n* postój taksówek
TB *n abbr* (= *tuberculosis*) gruźlica
tea [tiː] *n* **1** (*drink*) herbata **2** (*Brit*: *evening meal*) kolacja
teach [tiːtʃ] (*pt, pp* **taught**) *vt*: **to ~ sb sth, ~ sth to sb** uczyć (nauczyć *pf*) kogoś czegoś ▷ *vi* (*be a teacher*) uczyć (nauczyć *pf*); **to ~ sb how to do sth** uczyć (nauczyć *pf*) kogoś, jak coś się robi
teacher ['tiːtʃəʳ] *n* nauczyciel(ka) *m/f*
teaching ['tiːtʃɪŋ] *n* (*job*) nauczanie
team [tiːm] *n* **1** (*of people, experts*) grupa **2** (*Sport*) drużyna
teapot ['tiːpɔt] *n* imbryczek do herbaty
tear[1] [tɛəʳ] (*pt* **tore**, *pp* **torn**) *n* (*rip, hole*) dziura ▷ *vt* (*rip*) drzeć (podrzeć *pf*)
▸ **tear up** *vt* (*sheet of paper, cheque*) drzeć (podrzeć *pf*)
tear[2] [tɪəʳ] *n* (*when crying*) łza; **to burst into ~s** zalewać (zalać *pf*) się łzami
tease [tiːz] *vt* drażnić
teaspoon ['tiːspuːn] *n* (*spoon, amount*) łyżeczka
teatime ['tiːtaɪm] (*Brit*) *n* pora podwieczorku
tea towel (*Brit*) *n* ścierka do naczyń
technical ['tɛknɪkl] *adj* techniczny
technician [tɛk'nɪʃən] *n* technik

technological [tɛknəˈlɔdʒɪkl] *adj* technologiczny
technology [tɛkˈnɔlədʒɪ] *n* technologia
teddy (bear) [ˈtɛdɪ(-)] *n* miś pluszowy
teenage [ˈtiːneɪdʒ] *adj* (*children, fashions etc*) młodzieżowy
teenager [ˈtiːneɪdʒə^r] *n* nastolatek(-tka) *m/f*
teens [tiːnz] *n pl*: **to be in one's ~** mieć naście lat
tee-shirt [ˈtiːʃəːt] *n* = **T-shirt**
teeth [tiːθ] *n pl of* **tooth**
telephone [ˈtɛlɪfəun] *n* telefon
telephone book, telephone directory *n* książka telefoniczna
telescope [ˈtɛlɪskəup] *n* teleskop
television [ˈtɛlɪvɪʒən] *n* **1** (*also*: **~ set**) telewizor **2** (*system*) telewizja **3** (*business*) telewizja
tell [tɛl] (*pt, pp* **told**) *vt* **1** (*inform*): **to ~ sb sth** powiedzieć *pf* komuś coś **2** (*relate*: *story, joke*) opowiadać (opowiedzieć *pf*) **3** (*distinguish*): **to ~ sth from sth** odróżniać (odróżnić *pf*) coś od czegoś; **to ~ sb to do sth** powiedzieć komuś, żeby coś zrobił; **to ~ sb that...** powiedzieć komuś, że...
▸ **tell off** *vt*: **to ~ sb off** karcić (skarcić *pf*) kogoś
teller [ˈtɛlə^r] (*US*) *n* (*in bank*) kasjer(ka) *m/f*
telly [ˈtɛlɪ] (*Brit*: *inf*) *n* telewizja; **on ~** w telewizji
temper [ˈtɛmpə^r] *n* charakter; **to lose one's ~** tracić (stracić *pf*) panowanie nad sobą
temperature [ˈtɛmprətʃə^r] *n* temperatura; **to have** *or* **be running a ~** mieć temperaturę
temple [ˈtɛmpl] *n* (*building*) świątynia
temporary [ˈtɛmpərərɪ] *adj* chwilowy
temptation [tɛmpˈteɪʃən] *n* pokusa
tempting [ˈtɛmptɪŋ] *adj* kuszący
ten [tɛn] *num* dziesięć; *see also* **five**
tend [tɛnd] *vi*: **to ~ to do sth** zwykle coś robić
tennis [ˈtɛnɪs] *n* tenis
tennis court *n* kort tenisowy
tennis player *n* tenisista(-tka) *m/f*
tenor [ˈtɛnə^r] *n* (*Mus*) tenor
tenpin bowling [ˈtɛnpɪn-] (*esp Brit*) *n* kręgle *pl*
tense [tɛns] *adj* spięty ▹ *n* (*Ling*) czas
tension [ˈtɛnʃən] *n* napięcie
tent [tɛnt] *n* namiot
tenth [tɛnθ] *num* **1** (*in series*) dziesiąty **2** (*fraction*) dziesiąta część; *see also* **fifth**
term [təːm] *n* (*at school, university*) trymestr; (*at university*) semestr; **in the short/long ~** w krótkim/długim czasie; **to be on good ~s with sb** być z kimś w dobrych relacjach; **to come to ~s with sth** godzić (pogodzić *pf*) się z czymś
terminal [ˈtəːmɪnl] *adj* (*disease, patient*) śmiertelny ▹ *n* **1** (*Comput*) terminal **2** (*at airport*) terminal
terminally [ˈtəːmɪnlɪ] *adv*: **~ ill** śmiertelnie chory
terrace [ˈtɛrəs] *n* **1** (*Brit*: *row of houses*) szeregowiec **2** (*patio*) taras
terraced [ˈtɛrəst] *adj* (*house*) szeregowy
terrible [ˈtɛrɪbl] *adj* **1** (*accident, winter*) okropny **2** (*very poor*) nędzny **3** (*awful*) straszny
terribly [ˈtɛrɪblɪ] *adv* **1** (*very*) okropnie **2** (*very badly*) strasznie
terrific [təˈrɪfɪk] *adj* (*wonderful*) świetny
terrified [ˈtɛrɪfaɪd] *adj* przerażony
terror [ˈtɛrə^r] *n* przerażenie
terrorism [ˈtɛrərɪzəm] *n* terroryzm
terrorist [ˈtɛrərɪst] *n* terrorysta(-tka) *m/f* ▹ *adj* terrorystyczny
test [tɛst] *n* **1** (*trial, check*) test **2** (*Med*) badanie **3** (*Scol*) test **4** (*also*: **driving ~**) egzamin (na prawo jazdy) ▹ *vt* **1** (*try out*) testować (przetestować *pf*) **2** (*Med*) badać (zbadać *pf*) **3** (*Scol*) sprawdzać (sprawdzić *pf*)
test tube *n* probówka
text [tɛkst] *n* **1** (*written material*) tekst **2** (*book*) tekst **3** (*also*: **~ message**) sms ▹ *vt*: **to ~ sb** (*on mobile phone*) wysyłać (wysłać *pf*) komuś smsa
textbook [ˈtɛkstbuk] *n* podręcznik
text message *n* sms

than [ðæn, ðən] *prep* (*in comparisons*) od +*gen* ▷ *conj* niż; **it's smaller ~ a matchbox** jest mniejszy niż pudełko od zapałek; **more/less ~ Paul** bardziej/mniej niż Paul; **more ~ 20** więcej niż dwadzieścia; **she's older ~ you think** jest starsza, niż się panu/pani wydaje

thank [θæŋk] *vt* (*person*) dziękować (podziękować *pf*) +*dat*; **~ you (very much)** dziękuję (bardzo); **no, ~ you** nie, dziękuję; **to ~ sb for sth/for doing sth** dziękować (podziękować *pf*) komuś za coś/za zrobienie czegoś

thanks [θæŋks] *n pl* podziękowania ▷ *excl* (*inf*) dzięki; **many ~, ~ a lot** dziękuję bardzo; **no, ~** nie, dziękuję; **~ to sb/sth** dzięki komuś/czemuś

Thanksgiving (Day) ['θæŋksgɪvɪŋ(-)] (*US*) *n* Święto Dziękczynienia

THANKSGIVING DAY

Thanksgiving Day – Święto Dziękczynienia przypada w USA na czwarty czwartek listopada, a w Kanadzie na drugi poniedziałek października. Według tradycji w ten dzień ludzie składają Bogu podziękowania za wszystko, co mają. Tradycyjnym daniem podczas obchodów Święta Dziękczynienia jest indyk.

that [ðæt] (*pl* **those**) *adj* (*m*) ten; (*f*) ta; (*nt*) to; **that man/woman/book** ten mężczyzna/ta kobieta/ta książka; **that one** ten
▷ *pron* **1** (*demonstrative*) to; **who's/what's that?** kto/co to?; **is that you?** czy to ty?; **will he eat all that?** czy zje to wszystko?; **that's my house** to mój dom; **that's it** (*finished*) to tyle; (*exactly*) właśnie
2 (*relative*: *m*) który; (*f*) która; (*nt*) które; **the girl that came in** dziewczyna, która weszła; **the man that I saw** mężczyzna, którego widziałem; **the woman that he spoke to** kobieta, z którą rozmawiał
▷ *conj* że; **he thought that I was ill** myślał, że jestem chory
▷ *adv* (*so*) tak; **that much/bad/high** tak dużo/źle/wysoko

the [ði:, ðə] *def art* **1**: **the man/girl/house/book** mężczyzna/dziewczyna/dom/książka; **the men/women/houses/books** mężczyźni/kobiety/domy/książki; **the best solution** najlepsze rozwiązanie; **I'm going to the butcher's/the cinema** idę do rzeźnika/kina
2 (*in dates, decades*): **the fifth of March** piąty marca; **the nineties** lata dziewięćdziesiąte
3 (*in titles*): **Peter the Great** Piotr Wielki
4 (*in comparisons*): **the faster he works, the more mistakes he makes** im szybciej pracuje, tym więcej robi błędów

theatre ['θɪətə^r] (*US* **theater**) *n* **1** (*building*) teatr **2** (*entertainment*) teatr **3** (*Med*: *also*: **operating ~**) sala operacyjna **4** (*US*: *also*: **movie theater**) kino

theft [θɛft] *n* kradzież

their [ðɛə^r] *adj* ich; (*after prepositions*) nich; (*referring to subject of sentence*) swój

theirs [ðɛəz] *pron* ich; (*referring to subject of sentence*) swój; **a friend of ~** ich przyjaciel

them [ðɛm, ðəm] *pron* **1** (*direct object*: *vir*) ich; (*non-vir*) je; (*after preposition*: *vir*) nich **2** (*indirect object*) im; (*after preposition*) nim

theme park ['θi:m-] *n* park rozrywki

themselves [ðəm'sɛlvz] *pl pron* **1** (*gen, acc*) siebie; (*dat, loc*) sobie; (*inst*) sobą; (*reflexive pronoun*) się
2 (*emphatic*: *vir*) sami; (*non-vir*) same; **they enjoyed ~** dobrze się bawili; **by ~** (*unaided*) sami; (*alone*) sami

then [ðɛn] *adv* **1** (*at that time*: *past*) wtedy; (*future*) wtedy **2** (*after that*) później **3** (*therefore*) toteż; **by ~** wtedy; **before ~** wcześniej; **until ~**

do tego czasu; **since ~** od tego czasu; **well, OK ~** no to dobrze

there [ðɛəʳ] *adv* (*referring to place, pointing, indicating*) tam; **they've lived ~ for 30 years** mieszkają tam od trzydziestu lat; **is Shirley ~ please?** (*on telephone*) czy jest Shirley?; **it's over ~** jest tam; **~ he is!** tam jest!; **~ you are** (*offering something*) proszę; **~ is/~ are** jest/są; **~ has been an accident** był wypadek; **~ are 3 of them** jest ich troje/trzy/trzech

therefore ['ðɛəfɔːʳ] *adv* dlatego

there's ['ðɛəz] = **there is, there has**

thermometer [θə'mɔmɪtəʳ] *n* termometr

these [ðiːz] *pl adj* (*demonstrative*: *vir*) ci; (*non-vir*) te ▷ *pl pron* (*vir*) ci; (*non-vir*) te; **~ days** te dni

they [ðeɪ] *pl pron* **1** (*vir*) oni; (*non-vir*) one **2** (*in generalizations*) oni

they'd [ðeɪd] = **they had, they would**

they'll [ðeɪl] = **they shall, they will**

they're [ðɛəʳ] = **they are**

they've [ðeɪv] = **they have**

thick [θɪk] *adj* **1** (*slice, line, book, clothes etc*) gruby **2** (*sauce, mud, fog*) gęsty; **it's 20 cm ~** ma dwadzieścia centymetrów grubości

thief [θiːf] (*pl* **thieves** [θiːvz]) *n* złodziej(ka) *m/f*

thigh [θaɪ] *n* udo

thin [θɪn] *adj* **1** (*slice, line, book, material etc*) cienki **2** (*person, animal*) chudy

thing [θɪŋ] *n* **1** rzecz **2** (*matter, subject*) sprawa; **things** *n pl* (*belongings*) rzeczy; **a strange ~ happened** zdarzyła się dziwna rzecz; **how are ~s going?** jak sprawy?; **the ~ is...** chodzi o to, że...; **for one ~** po pierwsze; **the best ~ would be to...** najlepiej byłoby...; **first ~ (in the morning)** zaraz (rano); **last ~ (at night)** tuż przed położeniem się spać

think [θɪŋk] (*pt, pp* **thought**) *vi* myśleć (pomyśleć *pf*) ▷ *vt* myśleć (pomyśleć *pf*); **what do you ~ of...?** co pan/pani myśli o *+loc*...?; **to ~ about sth/sb** myśleć (pomyśleć *pf*) o czymś/kimś; **to ~ of doing sth** zastanawiać (zastanowić *pf*) się nad zrobieniem czegoś; **I ~ so/not** myślę, że tak/nie

▸ **think over** *vt* (*consider*) przemyśleć (*pf*)

third [θəːd] *num* **1** (*in series*) trzeci **2** (*fraction*) trzecia część; **a ~ of sth** jedna trzecia czegoś; *see also* **fifth**

thirdly ['θəːdlɪ] *adv* po trzecie

Third World *n*: **the ~** trzeci Świat ▷ *adj* trzeciego świata

thirst [θəːst] *n* pragnienie

thirsty ['θəːstɪ] *adj* spragniony; **I'm ~** pić mi się chce

thirteen [θəː'tiːn] *num* trzynaście; *see also* **fifteen**

thirteenth [θəː'tiːnθ] *num* trzynasty; *see also* **fifth**

thirty ['θəːtɪ] *num* trzydzieści; *see also* **fifty**

KEYWORD

this [ðɪs] (*pl* **these**) *adj* **1** (*demonstrative*: *m*) ten; (*f*) ta; (*nt*) to; **this man** ten człowiek; **this house** ten dom; **this one is better than that one** ten jest lepszy niż tamten **2** (*with days, months, years*): **this Sunday/month/year** ta niedziela/ten miesiąc/ten rok

▷ *pron* to; **who's/what's this?** kto/co to?; **this is Janet** (*in introduction*) to jest Janet; (*on telephone*) tu Janet; **like this** w ten sposób

▷ *adv* (*demonstrative*): **this much/high/long** tak dużo/wysoko/długo

thistle ['θɪsl] *n* oset

thorn [θɔːn] *n* cierń

thorough ['θʌrə] *adj* **1** (*search, investigation etc*) wnikliwy **2** (*methodical*: *person*) dokładny **3** (*complete*) całościowy

those [ðəuz] *pl adj* (*vir*) ci; (*non-vir*) te ▷ *pl pron* (*vir*) ci; (*non-vir*) te; **~ people/books** ci ludzie/te książki; **THOSE boots!** TE buty! ; **are ~ yours?** czy tamte należą do pana/pani?

though [ðəu] *conj* (*although*) chociaż ▷ *adv* (*however*) jednak; **even ~** mimo że

thought [θɔːt] *pt, pp of* **think** ▷ *n* (*idea*) myśl

thoughtful ['θɔ:tful] *adj* **1** (*deep in thought*) zamyślony **2** (*considerate*) troskliwy
thoughtless ['θɔ:tlɪs] *adj* bezmyślny
thousand ['θauzənd] *num*: **a** *or* **one ~** tysiąc; **~s of sth** tysiące czegoś
thousandth ['θauzəntθ] *num* (*in series*) tysięczny
thread [θrɛd] *n* (*yarn*) nić; (*in email*) wątek
threat [θrɛt] *n* groźba
threaten ['θrɛtn] *vi* (*storm, danger*) grozić (zagrozić *pf*) ▷ *vt* grozić (zagrozić *pf*) +*dat*; **to ~ to do sth** grozić (zagrozić *pf*), że coś się zrobi
three [θri:] *num* trzy; *see also* **five**
three-quarters [θri:'kwɔ:təz] *n pl* trzy czwarte ▷ *adv*: **~ full/empty** w trzech czwartych pełny/pusty ▷ *pron* trzy czwarte; **~ of an hour** trzy kwadranse
threw [θru:] *pt of* **throw**
thriller ['θrɪlə^r] *n* dreszczowiec
thrilling ['θrɪlɪŋ] *adj* (*performance, news etc*) pasjonujący
throat [θrəut] *n* gardło; **to have a sore ~** mieć ból gardła
through [θru:] *prep* przez ▷ *adj* (*ticket, train*) bezpośredni; **(from) Monday ~ Friday** (*US*) (od) poniedziałku do piątku
throughout [θru:'aut] *prep* przez ▷ *adv* **1** (*everywhere*) wszędzie **2** (*the whole time*) przez cały czas
throw [θrəu] (*pt* **threw**, *pp* **thrown** [θrəun]) *vt* **1** rzucać (rzucić *pf*) **2** (*fig*: *confuse*) zaskakiwać (zaskoczyć *pf*)
▸ **throw away** *vt* **1** (*rubbish*) wyrzucać (wyrzucić *pf*) **2** (*opportunity*) marnować (zmarnować *pf*)
▸ **throw out** *vt* wyrzucać (wyrzucić *pf*)
▸ **throw up** (*inf*) *vi* (*vomit*) wymiotować (zwymiotować *pf*)
thru [θru:] (*US*) = **through**
thumb [θʌm] *n* (*on hand*) kciuk
thumbtack ['θʌmtæk] (*US*) *n* pinezka
thump [θʌmp] *vt* (*hit*) walić (walnąć *pf*)
thunder ['θʌndə^r] *n* (*in sky*) grzmot
thunderstorm ['θʌndəstɔ:m] *n* burza
Thursday ['θə:zdɪ] *n* czwartek; *see also* **Tuesday**
tick [tɪk] *n* **1** (*esp Brit*: *mark*) ptaszek **2** (*Brit*: *inf*: *moment*) sekunda ▷ *vi* (*clock, watch*) tykać ▷ *vt* (*esp Brit*: *item on list*) odhaczać (odhaczyć *pf*)
▸ **tick off** *vt* (*esp Brit*: *item on list*) odhaczać (odhaczyć *pf*)
ticket ['tɪkɪt] *n* **1** bilet **2** (*Aut*: *also*: **parking ~**) mandat za złe parkowanie
ticket inspector *n* (*on train, bus*) konduktor(ka) *m/f*
ticket office *n* kasa biletowa
tickle ['tɪkl] *vt* (*person*) łaskotać (połaskotać *pf*)
tide [taɪd] *n* (*incoming tide*) przypływ; (*outgoing tide*) odpływ; **high/low ~** przypływ/odpływ
tidy ['taɪdɪ] *adj* uporządkowany ▷ *vt* (*also*: **~ up**) sprzątać (posprzątać *pf*)
▸ **tidy up** *vt, vi* sprzątać (posprzątać *pf*)
tie [taɪ] *n* **1** (*clothing*) krawat **2** (*esp Brit*: *Sport*: *match*) spotkanie **3** (*draw*: *in competition*) remis ▷ *vt* (*also*: **~ up**: *shoelaces etc*) wiązać (zawiązać *pf*)
▸ **tie up** *vt* **1** (*parcel etc*) wiązać (zawiązać *pf*) **2** (*dog*) uwiązywać (uwiązać *pf*) **3** (*person*) przywiązywać (przywiązać *pf*)
tiger ['taɪgə^r] *n* tygrys
tight [taɪt] *adj* **1** (*shoes, clothes*) ciasny **2** (*budget, schedule*) napięty; (*security, controls*) surowy ▷ *adv* (*firmly*: *hold, squeeze, shut*) mocno
tighten ['taɪtn] *vt* **1** (*rope, strap*) dociskać (docisnąć *pf*) **2** (*screw, bolt*) dokręcać (dokręcić *pf*)
tightly ['taɪtlɪ] *adv* (*firmly*: *hold, shut, squeeze*) mocno
tights [taɪts] (*Brit*) *n pl* rajstopy
tile [taɪl] *n* **1** (*on roof*) dachówka **2** (*on floor, wall*) płytka
till [tɪl] *n* (*Brit*: *in shop etc*) kasa ▷ *prep, conj* = **until**
timber ['tɪmbə^r] (*Brit*: *wood*) *n* drewno
time [taɪm] *n* **1** czas **2** (*period*) czas **3** (*by clock*) pora **4** (*occasion*) raz; **to have a good/bad ~** dobrze/źle się bawić; **to spend one's ~ doing sth** spędzać (spędzić *pf*) czas coś robiąc; **three ~s a day** trzy razy dziennie;

three ~s the size of sth trzy razy większy niż coś; **all the ~** przez cały czas; **from ~ to ~** od czasu do czasu; **at the same ~** (*nevertheless*) o tej samej porze; (*simultaneously*) równolegle; **at ~s** (*sometimes*) czasami; **she arrived in ~ for the start** zdążyła w sam raz na początek; **in a week's/month's ~** za tydzień/miesiąc; **any ~** kiedykolwiek; **on ~** na czas; **5 ~s 5 is 25** pięć razy pięć jest dwadzieścia pięć; **what ~ is it?, what's the ~?** która godzina?; **~ off** (*from work*) czas wolny; **to take ~** zabierać (zabrać *pf*) sporo czasu

timetable ['taɪmteɪbl] *n* **1** (*Brit: Rail etc*) rozkład jazdy **2** (*Brit: Scol*) plan lekcji **3** (*programme of events*) harmonogram

tin [tɪn] *n* **1** (*metal*) cyna **2** (*Brit: can*) puszka **3** (*for biscuits, tobacco etc*) pudełko

tin opener (*Brit*) *n* otwieracz do puszek

tiny ['taɪnɪ] *adj* mały

tip [tɪp] *n* **1** (*of branch, paintbrush etc*) czubek **2** (*to waiter*) napiwek **3** (*Brit: for rubbish*) wysypisko **4** (*advice*) porada ▷ *vt* **1** (*waiter*) dawać (dać *pf*) napiwek +*dat* **2** (*pour*) wylewać (wylać *pf*)

tiptoe ['tɪptəu] *vi* chodzić na palcach; **on ~** (*walk, run*) na paluszkach

tire ['taɪə[r]] (*US*) *n* = **tyre**

tired ['taɪəd] *adj* zmęczony; **to be ~ of doing sth** być zmęczonym robieniem czegoś

tiring ['taɪərɪŋ] *adj* męczący

tissue ['tɪʃuː] *n* chusteczka

title ['taɪtl] *n* tytuł

KEYWORD

to [tuː, tə] *prep* **1** (*direction*) do +*gen*; **to France/London/school** do Francji/Londynu/szkoły; **to the station** na stację

2 (*as far as*): **from here to London** stąd do Londynu

3 (*position, direction*) na; **to the left/right** na lewo/prawo

4 (*in time expressions*): **it's five/ten/a quarter to five** jest za pięć/dziesięć/kwadrans piąta

5 (*for, of*) do +*gen*; **a letter to his wife** list do jego żony

6 (*indirect object*): **to give sth to sb** dawać (dać *pf*) coś komuś; **to talk to sb** mówić do kogoś; **it was clear to me that...** było dla mnie jasne, że...; **damage to sth** zniszczenie czegoś; **a danger to sb** niebezpieczeństwo dla kogoś

7 (*towards*): **to be friendly/kind/loyal to sb** być przyjacielskim/miłym/lojalnym wobec kogoś

8 (*in relation to*): **30 miles to the gallon** trzydzieści mil na galon; **three goals to two** trzy gole do dwóch

9 (*purpose, result*): **to come to sb's aid** pomagać (pomóc *pf*) komuś

10 (*indicating range, extent*): **from... to...** od +*gen*... do +*gen*...; **from May to September** od maja do września

▷ *with vb* **1** (*simple infinitive*) *forma bezokolniczkowa*; **to go/eat** iść/jeść

2 (*with vb omitted*): **I don't want to** nie chcę

3 (*in order to*) aby; **I did it to help you** zrobiłem to, aby panu/pani pomóc

4 (*equivalent to relative clause*): **I have things to do** mam coś do roboty

5 (*after adjective*): **to be ready to go** być gotowym do wyjścia; **too old/young to do sth** zbyt stary/młody, aby coś zrobić

6 (*and*): **he awoke/arrived to find that everyone had gone** obudził się/przyjechał i dowiedział się, że wszyscy już poszli; **to and fro** tam i z powrotem

toad [təud] *n* ropucha

toast [təust] *n* **1** (*Culin*) tost **2** (*drink*) toast; **a piece** *or* **slice of ~** kromka chleba tostowego; **to drink a ~ to sb** pić (wypić *pf*) toast za kogoś

toaster ['təustə[r]] *n* toster

tobacco [tə'bækəu] *n* tytoń

tobacconist's (shop) [tə'bækənɪsts-] *n* sklep tytoniowy

today [tə'deɪ] *adv* dzisiaj ▷ *n* dziś; **what day is it ~?** który jest dzisiaj?; **~ is the 4th of March** dziś jest czwarty marca

toddler ['tɔdləʳ] *n* dziecko raczkujące
toe [təu] *n* **1** (*of foot*) palec **2** (*of shoe*) nosek; (*of sock*) palec; **big/little ~** duży/mały palec
toffee ['tɔfɪ] *n* toffi
together [tə'gɛðəʳ] *adv* razem; **~ with** razem z *+inst*
toilet ['tɔɪlət] *n* toaleta; **to go to the ~** (*esp Brit*) iść (pójść *pf*) do toalety
toilet paper *n* papier toaletowy
toiletries ['tɔɪlətrɪz] *n pl* przybory toaletowe
toilet roll *n* rolka papieru toaletowego
told [təuld] *pt, pp of* **tell**
toll [təul] *n* **1** (*of casualties, accidents*) liczba **2** (*on road, bridge*) opłata
tomato [tə'mɑːtəu] (*pl* **tomatoes**) *n* pomidor
tomorrow [tə'mɔrəu] *adv* jutro ▷ *n* jutro; **the day after ~** pojutrze; **~ morning** jutro rano
ton [tʌn] *n* **1** (*Brit*) tona **2** (*US*: *also*: **short ~**) tona
tongue [tʌŋ] *n* (*Anat*) język
tonic ['tɔnɪk] *n* (*also*: **~ water**) tonik
tonight [tə'naɪt] *adv* dziś wieczorem
tonsil ['tɔnsl] *n* migdałek
tonsillitis [tɔnsɪ'laɪtɪs] *n* zapalenie migdałków
too [tuː] *adv* **1** (*excessively*) za **2** (*also*) też; **you're from Brooklyn? Me ~!** pan/pani jest z Brooklynu? Ja też!; **~ bad!** bardzo niedobrze!
took [tuk] *pt of* **take**
tool [tuːl] *n* (*implement*) narzędzie
toolbar ['tuːlbɑːʳ] *n* (*Comput*) pasek narzędzi
tooth [tuːθ] (*pl* **teeth**) *n* (*Anat*) ząb
toothache ['tuːθeɪk] *n* ból zęba; **to have ~** mieć ból zęba
toothbrush ['tuːθbrʌʃ] *n* szczoteczka do zębów
toothpaste ['tuːθpeɪst] *n* pasta do zębów
top [tɔp] *n* **1** (*of mountain*) szczyt; (*of building, tree, stairs*) góra **2** (*of page*) góra **3** (*of surface, table*) góra **4** (*lid*: *of box, jar, bottle*) przykrywka **5** (*blouse*) bluzka ▷ *adj* **1** (*shelf, step, storey, marks*) najwyższy **2** (*executive, golfer*) najlepszy; **~ speed** największa prędkość; **at the ~ of the stairs/page** na górze schodów/strony; **at the ~ of the street** na końcu ulicy; **on ~ of** (*in addition to*) w dodatku do *+gen*; **from ~ to bottom** od góry do dołu; **to be** *or* **come ~** być najlepszym
▸ **top up** *vi* (*mobile phone*) zasilać (zasilić *pf*) konto
topic ['tɔpɪk] *n* temat
top-up ['tɔpʌp] *n* (*for mobile phone*) zasilenie konta
torch [tɔːtʃ] (*Brit*) *n* latarka
tore [tɔːʳ] *pt of* **tear¹**
torn [tɔːn] *pp of* **tear¹**
tortoise ['tɔːtəs] *n* żółw
torture ['tɔːtʃəʳ] *n* tortura ▷ *vt* torturować
total ['təutl] *adj* całkowity ▷ *n* suma; **in ~** w sumie
totally ['təutəlɪ] *adv* (*completely*) całkowicie
touch [tʌtʃ] *n* (*contact*) dotyk ▷ *vt* **1** (*with hand, foot*) dotykać (dotknąć *pf*) *+gen* **2** (*tamper with*) majstrować przy *+loc* **3** (*move*: *emotionally*) poruszać (poruszyć *pf*) ▷ *vi* (*be in contact*) dotykać (dotknąć *pf*); **to be/keep in ~ (with sb)** pozostawać (pozostać *pf*) w kontakcie (z kimś); **to get in ~ with sb** kontaktować (skontaktować *pf*) się z kimś; **to lose ~ (with sb)** tracić (stracić *pf*) kontakt (z kimś)
▸ **touch down** *vi* (*aircraft*) lądować (wylądować *pf*)
tough [tʌf] *adj* **1** (*material*) mocny **2** (*meat*) twardy **3** (*person, animal*) mocny **4** (*difficult*) ciężki **5** (*rough*) niebezpieczny
tour ['tuəʳ] *n* **1** (*journey*) wycieczka **2** (*of town, factory, museum*) wycieczka **3** (*by pop group, sports team etc*) trasa ▷ *vt* (*country, city etc*) zwiedzać (zwiedzić *pf*); **to go on a ~ of** (*region*) zwiedzać (zwiedzić *pf*)
tourism ['tuərɪzm] *n* turystyka
tourist ['tuərɪst] *n* turysta(-tka) *m/f* ▷ *adj* (*season, attraction*) turystyczny
tow [təu] *vt* (*vehicle, trailer*) holować (odholować *pf*)
▸ **tow away** *vt* (*vehicle*) odholować (*pf*)

toward(s) [tə'wɔːd(z)] *prep* **1** (*in direction of: lit*) do *+gen* **2** (*near*) w pobliżu *+gen* **3** (*as contribution to*) na rzecz *+gen*
towel ['tauəl] *n* ręcznik
tower ['tauəʳ] *n* wieża
tower block (*Brit*) *n* wieżowiec
town [taun] *n* miasto
town hall (*Brit*) *n* ratusz
tow truck (*US*) *n* (*breakdown lorry*) samochód pomocy drogowej
toy [tɔɪ] *n* zabawka ▷ *adj* (*train, car etc*) zabawkowy
trace [treɪs] *n* ślad ▷ *vt* (*draw: picture*) kalkować (przekalkować *pf*)
track [træk] *n* **1** (*path*) ścieżka **2** (*Rail*) tor **3** (*Mus*) ścieżka **4** (*Sport*) tor
▸ **track down** *vt* (*prey, criminal*) śledzić (wyśledzić *pf*)
tracksuit ['træksuːt] (*Brit*) *n* dres
tractor ['træktəʳ] *n* traktor
trade [treɪd] *n* **1** (*buying and selling*) handel **2** (*skill, job*) branża ▷ *vt* (*exchange*): **to ~ sth (for sth)** (*esp US*) wymieniać (wymienić *pf*) coś (na coś)
trademark ['treɪdmɑːk] *n* znak firmowy
trade union (*esp Brit*) *n* związek zawodowy
tradition [trə'dɪʃən] *n* tradycja
traditional [trə'dɪʃənl] *adj* tradycyjny
traffic ['træfɪk] *n* (*vehicles*) ruch
traffic circle (*US*) *n* rondo
traffic jam *n* korek
traffic lights *n pl* światła uliczne
traffic warden [-wɔːdn] (*esp Brit*) *n* funkcjonariusz(ka) *m/f* kontrolujący(-ca) prawidłowość parkowania
tragedy ['trædʒədɪ] *n* tragedia
tragic ['trædʒɪk] *adj* tragiczny
trailer ['treɪləʳ] *n* **1** (*Aut*) przyczepa **2** (*US: caravan*) przyczepa kempingowa **3** (*Cine, TV*) zwiastun
train [treɪn] *n* (*Rail*) pociąg ▷ *vt* **1** (*teach skills to*) uczyć (nauczyć *pf*) **2** (*athlete*) trenować (wytrenować *pf*) ▷ *vi* **1** (*learn a skill*) uczyć (nauczyć *pf*) się **2** (*Sport*) trenować (wytrenować *pf*)
trained [treɪnd] *adj* (*worker, teacher*) wykwalifikowany
trainee [treɪ'niː] *n* praktykant(ka) *m/f*
trainer ['treɪnəʳ] *n* **1** (*Sport*) trener(ka) *m/f* **2** (*Brit: shoe*) tenisówka
training ['treɪnɪŋ] *n* **1** (*for occupation*) szkolenie **2** (*Sport*) trening
training course *n* kurs szkoleniowy
tram [træm] (*Brit*) *n* (*also:* **~car**) tramwaj
tramp [træmp] *n* kloszard
trampoline ['træmpəliːn] *n* trampolina
transfer ['trænsfəʳ] *n* **1** (*flow: of information*) przepływ; (*of money*) przelew **2** (*Sport*) transfer **3** (*Brit: picture, design*) nadruk
transit ['trænzɪt] *n* **1**: **in ~** (*people*) w drodze **2** (*US*) transport
translate [trænz'leɪt] *vt* (*word, book etc*) tłumaczyć (przetłumaczyć *pf*)
translation [trænz'leɪʃən] *n* tłumaczenie
translator [trænz'leɪtəʳ] *n* tłumacz(ka) *m/f*
transparent [træns'pærnt] *adj* przezroczysty
transplant [*vb* træns'plɑːnt, *n* 'trænsplɑːnt] *vt* (*Med: organ*) przeszczepiać (przeszczepić *pf*) ▷ *n* (*Med: operation*) przeszczep
transport [*n* 'trænspɔːt, *vb* træns'pɔːt] *n* (*transportation*) transport ▷ *vt* (*move*) transportować (przetransportować *pf*); **public ~** (*esp Brit*) transport publiczny
transportation ['trænspɔː'teɪʃən] *n* (*US: transport*) transport
trap [træp] *n* (*for animals*) pułapka ▷ *vt* **1** (*animal*) łapać (złapać *pf*) **2** (*in building*) zatrzymywać (zatrzymać *pf*)
trash [træʃ] *n* **1** (*US*) śmieć **2** (*pej: tasteless stuff*) szmira
trash can (*US*) *n* kosz na śmieci
travel ['trævl] *n* (*travelling*) podróż ▷ *vi* (*person*) podróżować ▷ *vt* (*distance*) przemierzać (przemierzyć *pf*)
travel agency [-eɪdʒənsɪ] *n* biuro podróży
travel agent *n* **1** (*shop, office*) biuro podróży **2** (*person*) pracownik(-ica) *m/f* biura podróży

traveller ['trævləʳ] (*US* **traveler**) *n* podróżnik(-iczka) *m/f*
traveller's cheque ['trævləz-] (*US* **traveler's check**) *n* czek podróżny
travelling ['trævlɪŋ] (*US* **traveling**) *n* podróżowanie
travel sickness *n* choroba lokomocyjna
tray [treɪ] *n* taca
tread [trɛd] (*pt* **trod**, *pp* **trodden**) *vi* stąpać (stąpnąć *pf*)
▸ **tread on** *vt fus* stąpać (stąpnąć *pf*) po *+loc*
treasure ['trɛʒəʳ] *n* (*gold, jewels etc*) skarb
treat [tri:t] *n* przyjemność ▷ *vt* **1** (*behave towards: person, object*) traktować (potraktować *pf*) **2** (*Med: patient, illness*) leczyć (wyleczyć *pf*); **to ~ sb to sth** fundować (zafundować *pf*) komuś coś
treatment ['tri:tmənt] *n* (*Med*) leczenie
treble ['trɛbl] *vi* potrajać (potroić *pf*) się
tree [tri:] *n* drzewo
tremble ['trɛmbl] *vi* drżeć (zadrżeć *pf*)
tremendous [trɪ'mɛndəs] *adj* **1** (*enormous*) ogromny **2** (*excellent*) wspaniały
trend [trɛnd] *n* **1** (*tendency*) tendencja **2** (*fashion*) trend ▷ *vi* (*on social media*) trendować
trendy ['trɛndɪ] (*inf*) *adj* (*fashionable*) modny
trial ['traɪəl] *n* (*Law*) proces; **on ~** (*Law*) sądzony; (*on approval*) testowany
triangle ['traɪæŋgl] *n* (*Math*) trójkąt
tribe [traɪb] *n* plemię
trick [trɪk] *n* **1** (*by conjuror*) sztuczka **2** (*deception*) podstęp **3** (*skill, knack*) trik ▷ *vt* (*deceive*) oszukiwać (oszukać *pf*); **to play a ~ on sb** oszukiwać (oszukać *pf*) kogoś
tricky ['trɪkɪ] *adj* (*job, problem*) trudny
tricycle ['traɪsɪkl] *n* rower na trzech kółkach
trim [trɪm] *vt* (*cut: hair, beard*) przycinać (przyciąć *pf*)
trip [trɪp] *n* **1** (*journey*) podróż **2** (*outing*) wycieczka ▷ *vi* (*also:* **~ up**: *stumble*) potykać (potknąć *pf*) się; **to go on a ~** wybierać (wybrać *pf*) się na wycieczkę
triple ['trɪpl] *adj* potrójny ▷ *vi* potrajać (potroić *pf*) się
triplets ['trɪplɪts] *n pl* trojaczki
triumph ['traɪʌmf] *n* triumf
trivial ['trɪvɪəl] *adj* (*unimportant*) trywialny
trod [trɔd] *pt of* **tread**
trodden [trɔdn] *pp of* **tread**
trolley ['trɔlɪ] *n* **1** (*Brit: for luggage, in supermarket*) wózek **2** (*US: vehicle*) tramwaj
trombone [trɔm'bəun] *n* (*Mus*) puzon
troop [tru:p] *n* (*of people, animals*) grupa; **troops** *n pl* (*Mil*) wojska
trophy ['trəufɪ] *n* trofeum
tropical ['trɔpɪkl] *adj* tropikalny
trouble ['trʌbl] *n* kłopot; **to be in ~** (*with police, authorities*) mieć kłopoty; (*ship, climber etc*) mieć problemy; **the ~ is...** problem w tym, że...; **stomach/back ~** kłopoty z żołądkiem/kręgosłupem
troublemaker ['trʌblmeɪkəʳ] *n* osoba siejąca zamęt
trousers ['trauzəz] (*Brit*) *n pl* spodnie; **a pair of ~** para spodni
trout [traut] *n* pstrąg
truant ['truənt] *n*: **to play ~** chodzić (pójść *pf*) na wagary
truck [trʌk] *n* (*esp US*) ciężarówka
truck driver (*esp US*) *n* kierowca ciężarówki
true [tru:] *adj* (*story, motive, feelings*) prawdziwy; **to come ~** stawać (stać *pf*) się prawdą
truly ['tru:lɪ] *adv* **1** (*genuinely*) prawdziwie **2** (*for emphasis*) naprawdę **3** (*truthfully*) naprawdę; **yours ~** (*in letter*) z poważaniem
trumpet ['trʌmpɪt] *n* (*Mus*) trąbka
trunk [trʌŋk] *n* **1** (*of tree*) pień **2** (*of elephant*) trąba **3** (*case*) kufer **4** (*US: of car*) bagażnik; **trunks** *n pl* (*also:* **swimming ~s**) kąpielówki
trust [trʌst] *vt* ufać (zaufać *pf*) *+dat*
truth [tru:θ] (*pl* **truths** [tru:ðz]) *n* prawda

try [traɪ] *n* próba ▷ *vt* próbować (spróbować *pf*) +*gen* ▷ *vi* (*make effort*) próbować (spróbować *pf*); **to have a ~ at sth, give sth a ~** próbować (spróbować *pf*) czegoś; **to ~ to do sth, ~ doing sth** próbować (spróbować *pf*) coś zrobić
▸ **try on** *vt* (*dress, hat, shoes*) mierzyć (przymierzyć *pf*)
▸ **try out** *vt* (*test*) wypróbowywać (wypróbować *pf*)
T-shirt ['ti:ʃə:t] *n* T-shirt
tub [tʌb] *n* **1** (*container*) kadź **2** (*US*) wanna
tube [tju:b] *n* **1** (*pipe*) rura **2** (*container*) tubka **3** (*Brit*): **the ~** (*underground*) metro
tuberculosis [tjubə:kju'ləusɪs] *n* gruźlica
Tuesday ['tju:zdɪ] *n* wtorek; **it is ~ 23rd March** jest wtorek dwudziesty trzeci marca; **on ~** we wtorek; **on ~s** we wtorki; **every ~** co wtorek; **last/ next ~** w zeszły/następny wtorek; **on ~ morning/afternoon/evening** we wtorek rano/po południu/ wieczorem
tuition [tju:'ɪʃən] *n* **1** nauka **2** (*fees*) czesne
tulip ['tju:lɪp] *n* tulipan
tumble dryer ['tʌmbl-] (*Brit*) *n* suszarka do ubrań
tummy ['tʌmɪ] (*inf*) *n* brzuszek
tuna ['tju:nə] *n* (*also*: **~ fish**) tuńczyk
tune [tju:n] *n* (*melody*) melodia; **to be in ~** (*instrument*) być nastrojonym; (*singer*) śpiewać (zaśpiewać *pf*) czysto; **to be out of ~** (*instrument*) nie być nastrojonym; (*singer*) fałszować (sfałszować *pf*)
Tunisia [tju:'nɪzɪə] *n* Tunezja
tunnel ['tʌnl] *n* tunel
Turkey ['tə:kɪ] *n* Turcja
turkey ['tə:kɪ] *n* indyk
Turkish ['tə:kɪʃ] *adj* turecki ▷ *n* (*language*) turecki
turn [tə:n] *n* **1** (*in road*) zakręt **2** (*in game, queue, series*) kolej ▷ *vt* **1** (*part of body*) przekręcać (przekręcić *pf*) **2** (*object*) obracać (obrócić *pf*) **3** (*handle, key*) przekręcać (przekręcić *pf*) **4** (*page*) przewracać (przewrócić *pf*) ▷ *vi* **1** (*rotate*: *object, wheel*) obracać (obrócić *pf*) się **2** (*change direction*) skręcać (skręcić *pf*); **it's my ~ to...** moja kolej, aby...; **to take it in ~s to do sth** robić (zrobić *pf*) coś po kolei
▸ **turn around** *vi* = **turn round**
▸ **turn back** *vi* zawracać (zawrócić *pf*)
▸ **turn down** *vt* **1** (*request, offer*) odrzucać (odrzucić *pf*) **2** (*heat, sound*) przykręcać (przykręcić *pf*)
▸ **turn into** *vt fus* zmieniać (zmienić *pf*) w
▸ **turn off** *vt* **1** (*light, radio*) wyłączać (wyłączyć *pf*); (*tap*) zakręcać (zakręcić *pf*) **2** (*engine*) gasić (zgasić *pf*)
▸ **turn on** *vt* **1** (*light, radio*) włączać (włączyć *pf*); (*tap*) odkręcać (odkręcić *pf*) **2** (*engine*) zapalać (zapalić *pf*)
▸ **turn out** *vt* (*light, gas*) wyłączać (wyłączyć *pf*); **to ~ out to be** (*prove to be*) okazywać (okazać *pf*) się
▸ **turn round, turn around** *vi* **1** (*person, vehicle*) zawracać (zawrócić *pf*) **2** (*rotate*) obracać (obrócić *pf*) się ▷ *vt* (*person, vehicle*) zawracać (zawrócić *pf*)
▸ **turn up** *vi* **1** (*arrive*: *person*) przychodzić (przyjść *pf*) **2** (*be found*: *lost object*) znajdować (znaleźć *pf*) się ▷ *vt* (*radio, heater etc*) podkręcać (podkręcić *pf*)
turning ['tə:nɪŋ] *n* (*in road*) zakręt
turnip ['tə:nɪp] *n* rzepa
turn signal (*US*) *n* kierunkowskaz
turquoise ['tə:kwɔɪz] *n* (*stone*) turkus ▷ *adj* (*colour*) turkusowy
turtle ['tə:tl] (*Brit*) *n* żółw
tutor ['tju:tə^r] *n* **1** (*Brit*: *Scol*) nauczyciel(ka) *m/f* **2** (*private tutor*) korepetytor(ka) *m/f* ▷ *vt* (*teach*) uczyć (nauczyć *pf*); **she ~s adults in arithmetic** uczy dorosłych arytmetyki
tuxedo [tʌk'si:dəu] (*US*) *n* smoking
TV *n abbr* (= *television*) TV
tweet [twi:t] *vt* (*on Twitter*) tweetować
tweezers ['twi:zəz] *n pl* pęseta *f sg*; **a pair of ~** pęseta
twelfth [twɛlfθ] *num* **1** (*in series*) dwunasty **2** (*fraction*) dwunasta część; *see also* **fifth**

twelve [twɛlv] *num* dwanaście; **at ~ (o'clock)** (*midday*) o dwunastej w południe; (*midnight*) o dwunastej w nocy; *see also* **five**
twentieth ['twɛntɪɪθ] *num* dwudziesty; *see also* **fifth**
twenty ['twɛntɪ] *num* dwadzieścia; **~-one** dwadzieścia jeden; *see also* **fifty**
twice [twaɪs] *adv* dwa razy; **~ as much/long as** dwa razy więcej/dłużej niż
twin [twɪn] *adj* (*sister, brother*) bliźniaczy ▷ *n* **1** (*person*) bliźnię **2** (*also*: **~ room**) pokój dwuosobowy z dwoma łóżkami
twist [twɪst] *vt* **1** (*turn*) przekręcać (przekręcić *pf*) **2** (*injure*: *ankle etc*) skręcać (skręcić *pf*) **3** (*fig*: *meaning, words*) przekręcać (przekręcić *pf*)
two [tuː] *num* dwa; *see also* **five**
two-percent milk [tuːpə'sɛnt-] (*US*) *n* mleko o dwóch procentach zawartości tłuszczu
type [taɪp] *n* **1** (*category, example*) typ **2** (*sort, kind*) typ **3** (*Typ*) czcionka ▷ *vt, vi* (*on computer*) pisać (napisać *pf*) na komputerze
typewriter ['taɪpraɪtə^r] *n* maszyna do pisania
typical ['tɪpɪkl] *adj* (*behaviour, weather etc*) typowy
typist ['taɪpɪst] *n* maszynistka
tyre ['taɪə^r] (*US* **tire**) *n* opona
tyre pressure (*US* **tire pressure**) *n* ciśnienie w oponach

UFO *n abbr* (= *unidentified flying object*) UFO
ugly ['ʌglɪ] *adj* **1** (*person, dress, building*) brzydki **2** (*situation, incident*) paskudny
UK *n abbr* (= *United Kingdom*): **the UK** Zjednoczone Królestwo Wielkiej Brytanii i Irlandii Północnej
ulcer ['ʌlsə^r] *n* wrzód
umbrella [ʌm'brɛlə] *n* parasol
umpire ['ʌmpaɪə^r] *n* arbiter
UN *n abbr* (= *United Nations*): **the UN** ONZ
unable [ʌn'eɪbl] *adj*: **to be ~ to do sth** nie być w stanie czegoś zrobić
unanimous [juː'nænɪməs] *adj* (*decision*) jednomyślny
unavoidable [ʌnə'vɔɪdəbl] *adj* (*delay, job losses etc*) nieunikniony
unbearable [ʌn'bɛərəbl] *adj* (*heat, pain*) nie do wytrzymania
unbelievable [ʌnbɪ'liːvəbl] *adj* **1** (*implausible*) niewiarygodny **2** (*amazing*) niesamowity
unbreakable [ʌn'breɪkəbl] *adj* niezniszczalny
uncertain [ʌn'səːtn] *adj* (*future, outcome*) niepewny; **to be ~ about sth** być niepewnym czegoś
uncle ['ʌŋkl] *n* wujek
uncomfortable [ʌn'kʌmfətəbl] *adj* niewygodny
unconscious [ʌn'kɔnʃəs] *adj* (*not awake*) nieprzytomny
uncontrollable [ʌnkən'trəuləbl] *adj* **1** (*person*) nieokiełznany **2** (*temper, laughter*) niepohamowany

under [ˈʌndəʳ] *prep* **1** (*beneath*) pod *+inst* **2** (*less than*: *age, price*) poniżej *+gen* ▷ *adv*: **children aged 12 and ~** dzieci w wieku lat dwunastu i młodsze
under-age [ʌndərˈeɪdʒ] *adj* (*person*) niepełnoletni
underground [ˈʌndəgraund] *n*: **the ~** (*Brit*: *railway*) metro ▷ *adj* podziemny
underline [ʌndəˈlaɪn] (*Brit*) *vt* podkreślać (podkreślić *pf*)
underneath [ʌndəˈniːθ] *adv* (*below*) pod spodem ▷ *prep* pod *+inst*
underpants [ˈʌndəpænts] *n pl* slipy
underpass [ˈʌndəpɑːs] *n* (*for pedestrians*) przejście podziemne
undershirt [ˈʌndəʃəːt] (*US*) *n* podkoszulek
understand [ʌndəˈstænd] (*pt, pp* **understood**) *vt* rozumieć (zrozumieć *pf*)
understanding [ʌndəˈstændɪŋ] *adj* wyrozumiały
understood [ʌndəˈstud] *pt, pp of* **understand**
undertaker [ˈʌndəteɪkəʳ] (*Brit*) *n* przedsiębiorca pogrzebowy
underwater [ˈʌndəˈwɔːtəʳ] *adv* (*swim etc*) pod wodą
underwear [ˈʌndəwɛəʳ] *n* bielizna
undo [ʌnˈduː] (*pt* **undid**, *pp* **undone**) *vt* (*shoelaces, knot*) rozwiązywać (rozwiązać *pf*); (*buttons, trousers*) rozpinać (rozpiąć *pf*)
undress [ʌnˈdrɛs] *vi* rozbierać (rozebrać *pf*) się ▷ *vt* rozbierać (rozebrać *pf*)
uneasy [ʌnˈiːzɪ] *adj* (*worried*) niepewny; **to be ~ about sth** być niepewnym czegoś
unemployed [ʌnɪmˈplɔɪd] *adj* (*person*) bezrobotny ▷ *n pl*: **the ~** bezrobotni
unemployment [ʌnɪmˈplɔɪmənt] *n* bezrobocie
unexpected [ʌnɪksˈpɛktɪd] *adj* nieoczekiwany
unexpectedly [ʌnɪksˈpɛktɪdlɪ] *adv* nieoczekiwanie
unfair [ʌnˈfɛəʳ] *adj* niesprawiedliwy; **to be ~ to sb** być niesprawiedliwym dla kogoś
unfamiliar [ʌnfəˈmɪlɪəʳ] *adj* (*place, person, subject*) nieznany
unfashionable [ʌnˈfæʃnəbl] *adj* (*clothes, ideas, place*) niemodny
unfit [ʌnˈfɪt] *adj* (*physically*) nie w formie; **to be ~ for sth/to do sth** być niezdolnym do czegoś/do zrobienia czegoś; **~ for work** niezdolny do pracy; **~ for human consumption** nienadający się do spożycia przez ludzi
unfold [ʌnˈfəuld] *vt* (*sheet, map*) rozkładać (rozłożyć *pf*)
unfollow [ʌnˈfɔləu] *vt* przestać obserwować
unforgettable [ʌnfəˈgɛtəbl] *adj* niezapomniany
unfortunately [ʌnˈfɔːtʃənətlɪ] *adv* niestety
unfriend [ʌnˈfrɛnd] *vt* usunąć z listy znajomych
unfriendly [ʌnˈfrɛndlɪ] *adj* (*person*) nieprzyjazny
ungrateful [ʌnˈgreɪtful] *adj* niewdzięczny
unhappy [ʌnˈhæpɪ] *adj* nieszczęśliwy
unhealthy [ʌnˈhɛlθɪ] *adj* niezdrowy
uniform [ˈjuːnɪfɔːm] *n* mundur; **in ~** w mundurze
uninhabited [ʌnɪnˈhæbɪtɪd] *adj* niezamieszkany
union [ˈjuːnjən] *n* (*also*: **trade ~**) związek zawodowy
Union Jack *n flaga brytyjska*
unique [juːˈniːk] *adj* **1** (*individual*: *number, pattern etc*) jedyny w swoim rodzaju **2** (*distinctive*: *ability, skill, performance*) wyjątkowy
unit [ˈjuːnɪt] *n* **1** (*single whole*) jedność **2** (*group, centre*) sekcja **3** (*measurement*) jednostka **4** (*in course book*) część
United Kingdom [juːˈnaɪtɪd-] *n*: **the ~** Zjednoczone Królestwo Wielkiej Brytanii i Irlandii Północnej
United Nations *n*: **the ~** Organizacja Narodów Zjednoczonych
United States (of America) *n*: **the ~** Stany Zjednoczone (Ameryki Północnej)
universe [ˈjuːnɪvəːs] *n* wszechświat

university [ju:nɪ'və:sɪtɪ] *n* uniwersytet ▷ *adj* uniwersytecki; **to go to ~** chodzić na studia
unkind [ʌn'kaɪnd] *adj* niemiły; **to be ~ to sb** być niemiłym dla kogoś
unknown [ʌn'nəun] *adj* nieznany
unleaded [ʌn'lɛdɪd] *adj* bezołowiowy ▷ *n* paliwo bezołowiowe
unless [ʌn'lɛs] *conj* chyba, że
unlikely [ʌn'laɪklɪ] *adj* mało prawdopodobny; **he is ~ to win** jest mało prawdopodobne, że on wygra
unload [ʌn'ləud] *vt* rozładowywać (rozładować *pf*)
unlock [ʌn'lɔk] *vt* (*door, car, suitcase*) otwierać (otworzyć *pf*)
unlucky [ʌn'lʌkɪ] *adj* **1** (*person*) mający pecha **2** (*object, number*) pechowy
unmarried [ʌn'mærɪd] *adj* (*woman*) niezamężna; (*man*) nieżonaty
unnatural [ʌn'nætʃrəl] *adj* (*not normal*) nienaturalny
unnecessary [ʌn'nɛsəsərɪ] *adj* niekonieczny
unpack [ʌn'pæk] *vi* rozpakowywać (rozpakować *pf*) się ▷ *vt* (*suitcase, bag*) rozpakowywać (rozpakować *pf*)
unpleasant [ʌn'plɛznt] *adj* (*experience, task, situation*) nieprzyjemny; (*person, manner*) niemiły
unplug [ʌn'plʌg] *vt* wyłączać (wyłączyć *pf*) z sieci
unpopular [ʌn'pɔpjuləʳ] *adj* (*person, decision*) niepopularny
unrealistic ['ʌnrɪə'lɪstɪk] *adj* nierealny; **it is ~ to expect that...** nie można oczekiwać, że...
unreasonable [ʌn'ri:znəbl] *adj* **1** (*person, attitude*) niedorzeczny **2** (*decision*) nierozsądny **3** (*price, amount*) wygórowany
unreliable [ʌnrɪ'laɪəbl] *adj* **1** (*person, firm*) niesolidny **2** (*machine, method*) zawodny
unroll [ʌn'rəul] *vt* rozwijać (rozwinąć *pf*)
unscrew [ʌn'skru:] *vt* (*lid, cap*) odkręcać (odkręcić *pf*)
unsuccessful [ʌnsək'sɛsful] *adj* **1** (*attempt*) nieudany; (*application*) odrzucony **2** (*person, applicant*) odrzucony
unsuitable [ʌn'su:təbl] *adj* **1** (*place, time, clothes*) nieodpowiedni **2** (*candidate, applicant*) niewłaściwy; **to be ~ for sth** nie nadawać (nadać *pf*) się do czegoś
untidy [ʌn'taɪdɪ] *adj* **1** (*room*) nieporządny **2** (*person, appearance*) niechlujny
untie [ʌn'taɪ] *vt* rozwiązywać (rozwiązać *pf*)
until [ən'tɪl] *prep* do *+gen* ▷ *conj* aż; **~ now** aż do teraz; **~ then** aż do tego czasu
unusual [ʌn'ju:ʒuəl] *adj* **1** (*strange*) niezwykły **2** (*distinctive*) nadzwyczajny
unwilling [ʌn'wɪlɪŋ] *adj*: **to be ~ to do sth** być niechętnym do zrobienia czegoś
unwrap [ʌn'ræp] *vt* rozpakowywać (rozpakować *pf*)

KEYWORD

up [ʌp] *prep* **1** (*to higher point on*) na; **he went up the stairs/the hill/the ladder** wszedł na schody/wzgórze/drabinę
2 (*along: road, river*) wzdłuż *+gen*
3 (*at higher point on*) na górze; **up the road** trochę dalej; **they live further up the street** mieszkają trochę dalej przy tej ulicy
▷ *adv* **1** (*towards higher point*) na/w górę; **the lift only goes up to the twelfth floor** winda dojeżdża tylko do dwunastego piętra
2 (*at higher point*) na górze; **up here/there** tutaj/tam
3: **to be up** (*be out of bed*) wstawać (wstać *pf*)
4 (*to/in the north*) do *+gen*, na *+acc*; **he often comes up to Scotland** on często przyjeżdża do Szkocji
5 (*approaching*): **to go/come up (to sb)** podchodzić (podejść *pf*) (do kogoś); **to run up (to sb)** podbiegać (podbiec *pf*) (do kogoś)
6: **up to** do *+gen*; **I can spend up to £100** mogę wydać do stu funtów; **up to 100 people** do stu osób

7: **up to** *or* **until** aż do *+gen*; **I'll be here up to** *or* **until 5.30 pm** będę tu do siedemnastej trzydzieści; **up to now** do chwili obecnej
8: **it is up to you** to zależy od pana/pani
9: **to feel up to doing sth** czuć się na siłach coś zrobić
10 (*in other expressions*): **to be up against sth/sb** napotykać (napotkać *pf*) coś/kogoś

upcycle ['ʌpsaɪkl] *vt* przeznaczyć na upcykling
update [*vb* ʌp'deɪt, *n* 'ʌpdeɪt] *vt* aktualizować (zaktualizować *pf*) ▷ *n* aktualizacja
uphill ['ʌp'hɪl] *adv* w górę
upload [ʌp'ləud] *vt* wrzucać
upper ['ʌpəʳ] *adj* górny

UPPER SIXTH

Upper sixth to drugi z dwóch ostatnich lat szkoły średniej (**secondary school**), kiedy to uczniowie przygotowują się do egzaminów **A levels**.

upright ['ʌpraɪt] *adv* prosto
upset [*vb*, *adj* ʌp'sɛt, *n* 'ʌpsɛt] (*pt*, *pp* **upset**) *vt* (*make unhappy*: *person*) zasmucać (zasmucić *pf*) ▷ *adj* **1** (*unhappy*) zasmucony **2** (*stomach*) chory ▷ *n*: **to have a stomach ~** (*Brit*: *feel sick*) mieć rozstrój żołądka; **to be ~ about sth** martwić (zmartwić *pf*) się czymś
upside down [ʌpsaɪd-] *adv* (*hang*, *hold*, *turn*) do góry nogami
upstairs [ʌp'stɛəz] *adv* **1** (*be*) na górze **2** (*go*) na górę
up-to-date ['ʌptə'deɪt] *adj* (*modern*) aktualny
upwards ['ʌpwədz] *adv* w górę
urgent ['ə:dʒənt] *adj* (*letter*, *message etc*) pilny
US *n abbr* (= *United States*): **the US** USA
us [ʌs] *pron* (*gen*, *acc*, *loc*) nas; (*dat*) nam; (*inst*) nami
USA *n abbr* (= *United States of America*): **the ~** USA
USB stick [ju: ɛs bi:-] *n* pendrive
use [*n* ju:s, *vb* ju:z] *n* (*purpose*) zastosowanie ▷ *vt* **1** (*object*, *tool*) używać (użyć *pf*) *+gen* **2** (*word*, *phrase*) używać (użyć *pf*) *+gen*; **to make ~ of sth** używać (użyć *pf*) czegoś; **it's no ~** to na nic; **it's no ~ crying/arguing** nie ma co płakać/się kłócić; **to be no ~ (to sb)** być nieprzydatnym (dla kogoś); **to have a ~ for sth** mieć dla czegoś zastosowanie; **she ~d to do it** dawniej to robiła; **I didn't ~ to** *or* **I ~d not to worry so much** dawniej nie martwiłem się tak; **to be ~d to sth/to doing sth** być przyzwyczajonym do czegoś/do robienia czegoś; **to get ~d to sth/to doing sth** przyzwyczajać (przyzwyczaić *pf*) się do czegoś/do robienia czegoś
▸ **use up** *vt* (*finish*) zużywać (zużyć *pf*)
used [ju:zd] *adj* (*car*) używany
useful ['ju:sful] *adj* przydatny; **to be ~ for sth/doing sth** być przydatnym do czegoś/do zrobienia czegoś; **it's ~ to keep a diary** warto prowadzić dziennik; **to come in ~** przydawać (przydać *pf*) się
useless ['ju:slɪs] *adj* **1** (*unusable*) bezużyteczny **2** (*pointless*) bezcelowy **3** (*inf*: *hopeless*) beznadziejny; **to be ~ at sth/at doing sth** (*inf*) być beznadziejnym w czymś/w robieniu czegoś
user ['ju:zəʳ] *n* (*of product*, *service*) użytkownik(-iczka) *m/f*
user-friendly ['ju:zə'frɛndlɪ] *adj* przyjazny dla użytkownika
username ['ju:zəneɪm] *n* (*Comput*) nazwa użytkownika
usual ['ju:ʒuəl] *adj* (*time*, *place etc*) zwykły; **as ~** jak zwykle; **warmer/colder than ~** cieplej/zimniej niż zwykle
usually ['ju:ʒuəlɪ] *adv* zazwyczaj

V

vacancy ['veɪkənsɪ] *n* (*job*) wakat; (*hotel room*) wolny pokój; **"no vacancies"** „nie ma wolnych miejsc"
vacant ['veɪkənt] *adj* (*seat, bathroom*) wolny
vacation [və'keɪʃən] *n* **1** (*esp US*) urlop **2** (*at university etc*) wakacje *pl*; **to take a ~** brać (wziąć *pf*) urlop; **to be on ~** być na wakacjach; **to go on ~** jechać (pojechać *pf*) na wakacje
vaccinate ['væksɪneɪt] *vt*: **to ~ sb (against sth)** szczepić (zaszczepić *pf*) kogoś (przeciwko czemuś)
vacuum ['vækjum] *vt* (*room, carpet etc*) odkurzać (odkurzyć *pf*)
vacuum cleaner *n* (*also*: **vacuum**) odkurzacz
vagina [və'dʒaɪnə] *n* pochwa
vague [veɪg] *adj* niejasny
vain [veɪn] *adj* (*conceited*: *person*) próżny; **in ~** na próżno
Valentine's Day ['væləntaɪnz-] *n* dzień Świętego Walentego
valid ['vælɪd] *adj* **1** (*ticket, document*) ważny **2** (*argument, reason*) uzasadniony
valley ['vælɪ] *n* dolina
valuable ['væljuəbl] *adj* cenny
value ['vælju:] *n* **1** (*financial worth*) wartość **2** (*importance*) waga
van [væn] *n* (*Aut*) furgonetka
vandal ['vændl] *n* wandal
vandalism ['vændəlɪzəm] *n* wandalizm
vandalize ['vændəlaɪz] *vt* dewastować (zdewastować *pf*)
vanilla [və'nɪlə] *n* wanilia
vanish ['vænɪʃ] *vi* znikać (zniknąć *pf*)
vape [veɪp] *vi* palić e-papierosa
variety [və'raɪətɪ] *n* **1** (*diversity*) różnorodność **2** (*range*) wybór
various ['vɛərɪəs] *adj* (*several*) różny
vary ['vɛərɪ] *vt* (*make changes to*) urozmaicać (urozmaicić *pf*) ▷ *vi* (*be different*) różnić się *+inst*
vase [vɑ:z, *US* veɪs] *n* wazon
VAT [vi:eɪ'ti:, væt] (*Brit*) *n abbr* (= *value added tax*) VAT
VCR *n abbr* (= *video cassette recorder*) magnetowid
VDT (*US*) *n abbr* (= *visual display terminal*) monitor
VDU (*Brit*) *n abbr* (= *visual display unit*) monitor
veal [vi:l] *n* cielęcina
vegan ['vi:gən] *n* weganin(ka) *m/f*
vegetable ['vɛdʒtəbl] *n* warzywo
vegetarian [vɛdʒɪ'tɛərɪən] *n* wegetarianin(-anka) *m/f* ▷ *adj* wegetariański
vehicle ['vi:ɪkl] *n* pojazd
vein [veɪn] *n* (*in body*) żyła
velvet ['vɛlvɪt] *n* aksamit
vending machine ['vɛndɪŋ-] *n* automat (*z napojami, słodyczami itd*)
verb [və:b] *n* czasownik
verdict ['və:dɪkt] *n* **1** (*Law*) orzeczenie **2** (*opinion*) opinia
versus ['və:səs] *prep* przeciwko *+dat*
vertical ['və:tɪkl] *adj* pionowy
very ['vɛrɪ] *adv* bardzo; **at the ~ end/beginning** na samym końcu/początku; **~ much so** zdecydowanie tak; **~ little** bardzo mało; **there isn't ~ much (of...)** jest niezbyt dużo (*+gen...*); **I like him ~ much** bardzo go lubię
vest [vɛst] *n* **1** (*Brit*: *underwear*) podkoszulek **2** (*US*: *waistcoat*) kamizelka
vet [vɛt] *n* **1** (*esp Brit*: *veterinary surgeon*) weterynarz **2** (*US*: *inf*: *veteran*) kombatant(ka) *m/f*
veterinarian [vɛtrɪ'nɛərɪən] (*US*) *n* weterynarz
veterinary surgeon ['vɛtrɪnərɪ-] (*formal*: *Brit*) *n* weterynarz
via ['vaɪə] *prep* przez
vicar ['vɪkə^r] *n* pastor

vicious ['vɪʃəs] *adj* **1** (*attack, blow*) wściekły **2** (*person, dog*) zły
victim ['vɪktɪm] *n* ofiara; **to be the ~ of** być ofiarą *+gen*
victory ['vɪktərɪ] *n* zwycięstwo
video ['vɪdɪəu] *n* (*film*) wideo ▷ *vt* (*esp Brit*) nagrywać (nagrać *pf*) na wideo
video camera *n* kamera wideo
video game *n* gra wideo
Vietnam ['vjɛt'næm] *n* Wietnam
view [vju:] *n* **1** (*from window, hilltop etc*) widok **2** (*opinion*) pogląd
viewer ['vju:ə^r] *n* (*of TV*) widz
viewpoint ['vju:pɔɪnt] *n* **1** (*attitude*) punkt widzenia **2** (*place*) punkt obserwacyjny
vile [vaɪl] *adj* okropny
villa ['vɪlə] *n* **1** (*in countryside*) rezydencja **2** (*in town*) willa
village ['vɪlɪdʒ] *n* wioska
vine [vaɪn] *n* winorośl
vinegar ['vɪnɪgə^r] *n* ocet
vineyard ['vɪnjɑ:d] *n* winnica
viola [vɪ'əulə] *n* altówka
violence ['vaɪələns] *n* przemoc
violent ['vaɪələnt] *adj* (*person*) agresywny; (*crime*) brutalny
violin [vaɪə'lɪn] *n* skrzypce
violinist [vaɪə'lɪnɪst] *n* skrzypek(-paczka) *m/f*
virgin ['və:dʒɪn] *n* dziewica
Virgo ['və:gəu] *n* (*Astrol*) Panna
virtual reality ['və:tjuəl-] *n* rzeczywistość wirtualna
virus ['vaɪərəs] (*Med, Comput*) *n* wirus
visa ['vi:zə] *n* wiza
visible ['vɪzəbl] *adj* **1** (*able to be seen*) widoczny **2** (*fig: noticeable*) wyraźny
visit ['vɪzɪt] *n* **1** (*to person*) wizyta **2** (*to place*) pobyt ▷ *vt* **1** (*person*) odwiedzać (odwiedzić *pf*) **2** (*place*) zwiedzać (zwiedzić *pf*)
▶ **visit with** (*US*) *vt fus* odwiedzać (odwiedzić *pf*)
visitor ['vɪzɪtə^r] *n* **1** (*to city, country*) osoba przyjezdna **2** (*to person, house*) gość
visual ['vɪzjuəl] *adj* wizualny
vital ['vaɪtl] *adj* (*essential*) niezbędny
vitamin ['vɪtəmɪn, *US* vaɪtəmɪn] *n* witamina
vivid ['vɪvɪd] *adj* **1** (*description, memory*) żywy **2** (*colour, light*) jaskrawy
vlog [vlɔg] *vi* vlogować
vlogger ['vlɔgə^r] *n* vloger(ka) *m/f*
vocabulary [vəu'kæbjulərɪ] *n* **1** (*of person*) zasób słów **2** (*of language*) słownictwo
vocational [vəu'keɪʃənl] *adj* zawodowy
vodka ['vɔdkə] *n* wódka
voice [vɔɪs] *n* głos
voice mail *n* poczta głosowa
volcano [vɔl'keɪnəu] (*pl* **volcanoes**) *n* wulkan
volleyball ['vɔlɪbɔ:l] *n* siatkówka
volume ['vɔlju:m] *n* (*sound level*) głośność; **~ one/two** (*of book*) tom pierwszy/drugi
voluntary ['vɔləntərɪ] *adj* **1** (*not compulsory*) dobrowolny **2** (*work, worker*) ochotniczy **3** (*organization*) społeczny
volunteer [vɔlən'tɪə^r] *n* ochotnik(-iczka) *m/f*; **to ~ to do sth** zgłaszać (zgłosić *pf*) się na ochotnika do robienia (zrobienia *pf*) czegoś
vomit ['vɔmɪt] *n* wymiociny *pl* ▷ *vt* (*blood etc*) wymiotować (zwymiotować *pf*) *+inst* ▷ *vi* wymiotować (zwymiotować *pf*)
vote [vəut] *n* głos ▷ *vt*: **to ~ Labour/Green** głosować (zagłosować *pf*) na Partię Pracy/Zielonych ▷ *vi* głosować (zagłosować *pf*); **to ~ to do sth** głosować (zagłosować *pf*) za zrobieniem czegoś; **to ~ for sb** głosować (zagłosować *pf*) na kogoś; **to ~ for sth** głosować (zagłosować *pf*) za czymś; **to ~ against sth** głosować (zagłosować *pf*) przeciwko czemuś
voucher ['vautʃə^r] *n* kupon
vowel ['vauəl] *n* samogłoska
vulgar ['vʌlgə^r] *adj* (*rude: person, joke, gesture*) wulgarny

wage [weɪdʒ] *n* (*also*: **~s**) zarobki *m pl*
waist [weɪst] *n* **1** pas **2** (*of clothing*) talia
waistcoat ['weɪskəut] (*Brit*) *n* kamizelka
wait [weɪt] *vi* czekać (poczekać *pf*) ▷ *n* (*interval*) okres oczekiwania; **to ~ for sb/sth** czekać (poczekać *pf*) na kogoś/coś; **I can't ~** *or* **I can hardly ~ to tell her** nie mogę się doczekać, żeby jej powiedzieć; **~ a minute!** poczekaj chwilę!; **to keep sb ~ing** kazać komuś czekać
▸ **wait up** *vi* nie kłaść (położyć *pf*) się spać
waiter ['weɪtəʳ] *n* kelner
waiting list ['weɪtɪŋ-] *n* lista oczekujących
waiting room ['weɪtɪŋ-] *n* poczekalnia
waitress ['weɪtrɪs] *n* kelnerka
wake [weɪk] (*pt* **woke**, *pp* **woken**)
▸ **wake up** *vt* budzić (obudzić *pf*) ▷ *vi* budzić (obudzić *pf*) się
Wales [weɪlz] *n* Walia; **the Prince of ~** książę Walii
walk [wɔːk] *n* spacer ▷ *vi* chodzić/iść (pójść *pf*) ▷ *vt* (*distance*) przechodzić (przejść *pf*); **to go for a ~** chodzić/iść (pójść *pf*) na spacer; **to take the dog for a ~** wyprowadzać (wyprowadzić *pf*) psa na spacer; **it's 10 minutes' ~ from here** stąd idzie się dziesięć minut
walking ['wɔːkɪŋ] *n* spacerowanie
walking stick *n* laska
Walkman® ['wɔːkmən] *n* walkman
wall [wɔːl] *n* **1** (*of building, room*) ściana **2** (*around garden, field*) mur
wallet ['wɔlɪt] *n* portfel
wallpaper ['wɔːlpeɪpəʳ] *n* (*also Comput*) tapeta ▷ *vt* tapetować (wytapetować *pf*)
walnut ['wɔːlnʌt] *n* orzech włoski
wander ['wɔndəʳ] *vi* (*roam*) przechadzać się
want [wɔnt] *vt* **1** (*wish for*) chcieć *+gen* **2** (*inf: need*) potrzebować *+gen*; **to ~ to do sth** chcieć coś robić (zrobić *pf*); **to ~ sb to do sth** chcieć, aby ktoś coś zrobił
war [wɔːʳ] *n* wojna
ward [wɔːd] *n* (*in hospital*) oddział
wardrobe ['wɔːdrəub] *n* szafa
warehouse ['wɛəhaus] *n* magazyn
warm [wɔːm] *adj* ciepły; **it's ~** jest ciepło; **are you ~ enough?** czy jest panu/pani wystarczająco ciepło?
▸ **warm up** *vi* (*athlete, pianist etc*) rozgrzewać (rozgrzać *pf*) się ▷ *vt* **1** (*food*) podgrzewać (podgrzać *pf*) **2** (*person*) ogrzewać (ogrzać *pf*)
warn [wɔːn] *vt*: **to ~ sb that** ostrzegać (ostrzec *pf*) kogoś, że; **to ~ sb not to do sth** ostrzegać (ostrzec *pf*) kogoś przed zrobieniem czegoś
warning ['wɔːnɪŋ] *n* **1** (*action, words, sign*) ostrzeżenie **2** (*notice*) zapowiedź
wart [wɔːt] *n* brodawka
was [wɔz] *pt of* **be**
wash [wɔʃ] *vt* **1** (*clothes*) prać (uprać *pf*) **2** (*dishes, paintbrush*) myć (umyć *pf*) ▷ *vi* (*person*) myć (umyć *pf*) się ▷ *n* (*clean*) mycie; **to ~ one's face/hands/hair** myć (umyć *pf*) twarz/ręce/włosy; **to have a ~** myć (umyć *pf*) się
▸ **wash up** *vi* **1** (*Brit: wash dishes*) zmywać (pozmywać *pf*) **2** (*US: have a wash*) myć (umyć *pf*) się
washbasin ['wɔʃbeɪsn] *n* umywalka
washcloth ['wɔʃklɔθ] (*US*) *n* myjka (do twarzy)
washing ['wɔʃɪŋ] *n* **1** (*dirty*) rzeczy do prania **2** (*clean*) pranie; **to do the ~** robić (zrobić *pf*) pranie

washing machine *n* pralka
washing powder (*Brit*) *n* proszek do prania
washing-up [wɔʃɪŋ'ʌp] (*Brit*) *n* brudne naczynia *pl*; **to do the ~** zmywać (pozmywać *pf*) naczynia
washing-up liquid (*Brit*) *n* płyn do zmywania naczyń
wasn't ['wɔznt] = **was not**
wasp [wɔsp] *n* osa
waste [weɪst] *n* **1** (*of resources, food, money*) marnowanie **2** (*rubbish*) śmieci *m pl* ▷ *vt* (*money, energy, time, opportunity*) marnować (zmarnować *pf*); **it's a ~ of time** to strata czasu
wastepaper basket ['weɪstpeɪpə-] (*Brit*) *n* kosz na śmieci
watch [wɔtʃ] *n* (*wristwatch*) zegarek ▷ *vt* **1** (*look at: people, objects*) patrzeć (popatrzeć *pf*) na **2** (*match, programme, TV*) oglądać (obejrzeć *pf*) **3** (*pay attention to*) uważać na ▷ *vi* patrzeć (popatrzeć *pf*); **to ~ sb do/doing sth** patrzeć (popatrzeć *pf*), jak ktoś coś robi
▸ **watch out** *vi* uważać; **~ out!** (*inf*) uważaj!
water ['wɔːtə^r] *n* woda ▷ *vt* (*plant*) podlewać (podlać *pf*); **a drink of ~** szklanka wody
waterfall ['wɔːtəfɔːl] *n* wodospad
watering can ['wɔːtərɪŋ-] *n* konewka
watermelon ['wɔːtəmɛlən] *n* arbuz
waterproof ['wɔːtəpruːf] *adj* wodoodporny
water-skiing ['wɔːtəskiːɪŋ] *n*: **to go ~** jeździć na nartach wodnych
wave [weɪv] *n* **1** (*of hand*) machnięcie **2** (*on water*) fala ▷ *vi* (*gesture*) machać (pomachać *pf*) ▷ *vt* (*motion with: hand*) machać (pomachać *pf*) +*inst*; **to give sb a ~** machać (pomachać *pf*) do kogoś; **to ~ goodbye to sb, ~ sb goodbye** machać (pomachać *pf*) komuś na pożegnanie
wax [wæks] *n* wosk
way [weɪ] *n* **1** (*route*) droga **2** (*path, access*) ścieżka **3** (*distance*) odległość **4** (*direction*) kierunek **5** (*manner, method*) sposób ▷ *adv* (*far, a lot*) dużo; **ways** *n pl* (*habits*) nawyki; **"which ~?" — "this ~"** „którędy?" — „tędy"; **on the ~** w drodze; **it's a long ~ away** to daleko stąd; **to lose one's ~** gubić (zgubić *pf*) drogę; **the ~ back** droga powrotna; **to give ~** (*break, collapse*) upadać (upaść *pf*); (*stop resisting*) poddawać (poddać *pf*) się; **the wrong ~ round** (*Brit*) tyłem do przodu; **in a ~** w pewnym sensie; **by the ~** a propos; **"~ in"** (*Brit*) „wejście"; **"~ out"** (*Brit*) „wyjście"; **~ of life** sposób życia; **do it this ~** zrób to w ten sposób
we [wiː] *pl pron* my
weak [wiːk] *adj* słaby
wealthy ['wɛlθɪ] *adj* bogaty
weapon ['wɛpən] *n* (*lit*) broń
wear [wɛə^r] (*pt* **wore**, *pp* **worn**) *vt* nosić; **I can't decide what to ~** nie mogę się zdecydować, w co się ubrać
▸ **wear out** *vi* przecierać (przetrzeć *pf*) się
weather ['wɛðə^r] *n* pogoda; **what's the ~ like?** jaka jest pogoda?
weather forecast *n* prognoza pogody
web [wɛb] *n* **1** (*spider's*) pajęczyna **2**: **the W~** internet; **on the W~** w internecie
web page *n* strona internetowa
website ['wɛbsaɪt] *n* witryna internetowa
we'd [wiːd] = **we had, we would**
wedding ['wɛdɪŋ] *n* (*ceremony*) ślub; (*reception*) wesele
Wednesday ['wɛdnzdɪ] *n* środa; *see also* **Tuesday**
weed [wiːd] *n* chwast
week [wiːk] *n* tydzień; **this/next/last ~** w tym/przyszłym/zeszłym tygodniu; **once/twice a ~** raz/dwa razy w tygodniu; **in two ~s' time** za dwa tygodnie
weekday ['wiːkdeɪ] *n* dzień powszedni; **on ~s** w dni powszednie
weekend [wiːk'ɛnd] *n* weekend; **at the ~** w weekend; **this/next/last ~** w ten/następny/poprzedni weekend
weigh [weɪ] *vt* ważyć (zważyć *pf*) ▷ *vi*: **she ~s 50kg** ona waży pięćdziesiąt kg
weight [weɪt] *n* **1** waga **2** (*heavy object*) ciężarek; **weights** *n pl* (*in*

gym) ciężarki; **to lose ~** tracić (stracić *pf*) na wadze; **to put on ~** przybierać (przybrać *pf*) na wadze
weightlifting ['weɪtlɪftɪŋ] *n* podnoszenie ciężarów
weird [wɪəd] *adj* dziwny
welcome ['wɛlkəm] *n* powitanie ▷ *vt* **1** (*visitor, speaker etc*) witać (powitać *pf*) **2** (*news, change etc*) witać (powitać *pf*) z entuzjazmem; **~ to Beijing!** witamy w Pekinie!; **"thank you" — "you're ~!"** „dziękuję" — „proszę bardzo!"; **to give sb a warm ~** witać (przywitać *pf*) kogoś ciepło
welfare ['wɛlfɛə^r] *n* (*US: social aid*) opieka społeczna
well [wɛl] *n* (*for water*) studnia ▷ *adv* **1** (*to a high standard*) dobrze **2** (*completely*) dobrze **3** (*emphatic with adv, adj, phrase*) naprawdę ▷ *adj* (*healthy*) zdrowy ▷ *excl* no cóż; **to do ~** (*person*) dobrze radzić (poradzić *pf*) sobie; (*business*) dobrze wypadać (wypaść *pf*) finansowo; **~ done!** brawo!; **as ~** (*in addition*) również; **I don't feel ~** nie czuję się dobrze; **get ~ soon!** szybkiego powrotu do zdrowia!; **~, as I was saying...** a więc, jak mówiłem...
we'll [wi:l] = **we will, we shall**
well-behaved ['wɛlbɪ'heɪvd] *adj* grzeczny
wellington ['wɛlɪŋtən] (*esp Brit*) *n* (*also*: **~ boot**) kalosz
well-known ['wɛl'nəun] *adj* (*person*) słynny; (*fact, brand*) znany
well-off ['wɛl'ɔf] *adj* zamożny
Welsh [wɛlʃ] *adj* walijski ▷ *n* (*language*) język walijski ▷ *n pl*: **the ~** Walijczycy
Welshman ['wɛlʃmən] (*irreg*) *n* Walijczyk
Welshwoman ['wɛlʃwumən] (*irreg*) *n* Walijka
went [wɛnt] *pt of* **go**
were [wə:^{r}] *pt of* **be**
we're [wɪə^r] = **we are**
weren't [wə:nt] = **were not**
west [wɛst] *n* **1** (*direction*) zachód **2**: **the W~** (*Pol*) Zachód ▷ *adj* zachodni ▷ *adv* na zachód; **in the ~ (of Ireland)** na zachodzie (Irlandii); **to the ~** na zachód; **~ of** na zachód od +*gen*
western ['wɛstən] *adj* zachodni ▷ *n* (*film*) western
wet [wɛt] *adj* **1** (*person, clothes, paint, cement*) mokry **2** (*rainy: weather, day*) deszczowy; **to get ~** moknąć (zmoknąć *pf*)
wet suit *n* (*Sport*) strój do nurkowania
we've [wi:v] = **we have**
whale [weɪl] *n* wieloryb

KEYWORD

what [wɔt] *pron* **1** (*interrogative subject, object, object of prep*) co; **what is happening?** co się dzieje?; **what is this?** co to jest?; **what are you doing?** co robisz?; **what?, what did you say?** co?, co powiedziałeś?
2 (*in indirect questions*) co; **do you know what's happening?** czy pan/pani wie, co się dzieje?
3 (*relative*) co; **I saw what was on the table** widziałem, co było na stole
▷ *adj* **1** (*in direct/indirect questions*) który; **what time is it?** która godzina?; **tell me, what size is this shirt?** proszę mi powiedzieć, jaki rozmiar ma ta koszula?
2 (*in exclamations*) cóż za; **what a mess!** co za bałagan; **what a lovely day!** jaki ładny dzień!
▷ *excl* (*disbelieving*) co!; **what, there's no coffee!** co, nie ma kawy?

whatever [wɔt'ɛvə^r] *conj* (*no matter what*) cokolwiek ▷ *adv* (*whatsoever*) cokolwiek ▷ *pron*: **do ~ is necessary/you want** zrób, co tylko jest konieczne/co chcesz
wheat [wi:t] *n* pszenica
wheel [wi:l] *n* **1** koło **2** (*also*: **steering ~**) kierownica
wheelbarrow ['wi:lbærəu] *n* taczka
wheelchair ['wi:ltʃɛə^r] *n* wózek inwalidzki

KEYWORD

when [wɛn] *adv* (*interrogative*) kiedy; **when did it happen?** kiedy to się stało?

▷ *pron* (*relative*): **the day when** w dniu, kiedy
▷ *conj* (*in time clauses*) kiedy; **be careful when you cross the road** uważaj, kiedy przechodzisz przez jezdnię; **she was reading when I came in** czytała, kiedy wszedłem; **I know when it happened** wiem, kiedy to się wydarzyło

where [wɛəʳ] *adv* (*in or to what place*) gdzie; (*to what place*) dokąd ▷ *conj* (*the place in which*) tam, gdzie; **~ are you from?** skąd pan/pani pochodzi?
whether ['wɛðəʳ] *conj* czy; **I don't know ~ to accept it or not** nie wiem, czy mam to przyjąć, czy nie

KEYWORD

which [wɪtʃ] *adj* **1** (*interrogative*: *m sg*) który; (*f sg*) która; (*nt sg*) które; (*vir pl*) którzy; (*non-vir pl*) które; **which picture do you want?** który chcesz obraz?
2 (*in indirect questions*: *m sg*) który; (*f sg*) która; (*nt sg*) które; (*vir pl*) którzy; (*non-vir pl*) które; **he asked which book I wanted** zapytał, którą chcę książkę
▷ *pron* **1** (*interrogative subject, object*: *m sg*) który; (*f sg*) która; (*nt sg*) które; (*vir pl*) którzy; (*non-vir pl*) które; **which of these is yours?** który z nich jest pana/pani?
2 (*in indirect questions subject, object*) który; **ask him which of the models is the best** zapytaj go, który z modeli jest najlepszy
3 (*relative subject, object, referring to noun*: *m sg*) który; (*f sg*) która; (*nt sg*) które; (*vir pl*) którzy; (*non-vir pl*) które; **the book which he read/ which is very good** książka, którą czytał/która jest bardzo dobra
4 (*referring to clause*) co; **she said it was an accident, which was true** powiedziała, że to był wypadek, co było prawdą

while [waɪl] *n* chwila ▷ *conj* **1** (*at the same time as*) podczas **2** (*during the time that*) podczas gdy **3** (*although*) chociaż; **for a ~** na jakiś czas
whip [wɪp] *n* bat ▷ *vt* **1** (*hit*: *person, animal*) chłostać (wychłostać *pf*) **2** (*beat*: *cream, eggs*) ubijać (ubić *pf*)
whipped cream [wɪpt-] *n* bita śmietana
whiskers ['wɪskəz] *n pl* (*of animal*) wąsy; (*of man*) zarost *sg*
whisky ['wɪskɪ] (*US* **whiskey**) *n* whisky
whisper ['wɪspəʳ] *n* szept ▷ *vi* szeptać (szepnąć *pf*) ▷ *vt* szeptać (szepnąć *pf*)
whistle ['wɪsl] *vi* (*person*: *melodiously*) gwizdać (gwizdnąć *pf*) ▷ *vt* (*tune*) gwizdać (zagwizdać *pf*) ▷ *n* **1** (*device*) gwizdek **2** (*sound*) gwizd
white [waɪt] *adj* **1** biały **2** (*with milk*: *coffee*) z mlekiem **3** (*person*) biały ▷ *n* (*colour*) biel

KEYWORD

who [hu:] *pron* **1** (*interrogative subject, object, object of prep*) kto; **who is it?** kto to jest?; **who did you discuss it with?** (*polite m sg*) z kim pan o tym rozmawiał?
2 (*in indirect questions subject, object, after preposition*) kogo; **I told her who I was** powiedziałem jej, kim jestem; **I don't know who he gave it to** nie wiem, komu on to dał
3 (*relative subject, object*) który; **the girl who came in** dziewczyna, która weszła; **the man who we met in Sydney** mężczyzna, którego poznaliśmy w Sydney

whole [həul] *adj* cały ▷ *n* całość; **the ~ of sth** całość czegoś; **the ~ (of the) time** cały czas; **on the ~** ogólnie
wholemeal ['həulmi:l] (*Brit*) *adj* pełnoziarnisty
wholewheat ['həulwi:t] *adj* = **wholemeal**

KEYWORD

whom [hu:m] (*formal*) *pron* **1** (*interrogative*) kogo; (*to whom?*) komu; **whom did you see?** kogo

widziałeś?; **to whom did she give it?** komu to dała?
2 (*relative*): **the man whom I saw** mężczyzna, którego widziałem; **the man to whom I spoke** mężczyzna, z którym rozmawiałem

whose [hu:z] *adj* **1** (*interrogative*) czyj **2** (*relative*) którego ▷ *pron* (*m sg*) czyj; (*f sg*) czyja; (*nt sg*) czyje; (*vir pl*) czyi; (*non-vir pl*) czyje; **~ is this?** czyje to jest?; **~ book is this?** czyja to książka?; **~ coats are these?** czyje są te płaszcze?; **the woman ~ car was stolen** kobieta, której samochód został skradziony

KEYWORD

why [waɪ] *adv* dlaczego; **why is he always late?** dlaczego on zawsze się spóźnia?; **why not?** dlaczego nie?; **I don't know why** nie wiem, dlaczego
▷ *conj* dlaczego; **I wonder why he said that** zastanawiam się, dlaczego on to powiedział; **the reason why he did it** zrobił to dlatego

wicked ['wɪkɪd] *adj* (*evil: person*) podły; (*act, crime*) ohydny
wide [waɪd] *adj* szeroki ▷ *adv* szeroko
widow ['wɪdəu] *n* wdowa
widower ['wɪdəuəʳ] *n* wdowiec
width [wɪdθ] *n* szerokość; **to swim a ~** przepływać (przepłynąć *pf*) szerokość basenu
wife [waɪf] (*pl* **wives**) *n* żona
Wi-Fi ['waɪfaɪ] *n* (*Comput*) bezprzewodowa sieć komputerowa
wig [wɪg] *n* peruka
wild [waɪld] *adj* **1** (*animal, plant*) dziki **2** (*person, behaviour*) szalony
wildlife ['waɪldlaɪf] *n* natura

KEYWORD

will [wɪl] *aux vb* **1** (*forming future tense*): **I will call you tonight** zadzwonię do ciebie dziś wieczorem; **what will you do next?** co potem zrobisz?
2 (*in conjectures, predictions*): **he'll be there by now** pewnie jest już na miejscu
3 (*in commands, requests, offers*): **will you be quiet!** bądź cicho!
4 (*be prepared to*): **I won't put up with it!** nie będę tego znosił!
▷ *n* **1** (*volition*) wola; **against his will** wbrew jego woli
2 (*testament*) testament; **to make a will** spisywać (spisać *pf*) testament

willing ['wɪlɪŋ] *adj*: **to be ~ to do sth** być chętnym do robienia (zrobienia *pf*) czegoś
win [wɪn] (*pt, pp* **won**) *n* zwycięstwo ▷ *vt* wygrywać (wygrać *pf*) ▷ *vi* odnosić (odnieść *pf*) zwycięstwo
wind [wɪnd] *n* wiatr
window ['wɪndəu] *n* **1** (*in house, building*) okno; (*in shop*) witryna; (*in car, train*) okno **2** (*pane*) szyba **3** (*Comput*) okno
windscreen ['wɪndskri:n] (*Brit*) *n* szyba przednia
windscreen wiper [-waɪpəʳ] (*Brit*) *n* wycieraczka
windshield ['wɪndʃi:ld] (*US*) *n* szyba przednia
windshield wiper [-waɪpəʳ] (*US*) *n* wycieraczka
windsurfing ['wɪndsə:fɪŋ] *n* windsurfing
windy ['wɪndɪ] *adj* wietrzny; **it's ~** wieje wiatr
wine [waɪn] *n* wino
wing [wɪŋ] *n* skrzydło
wink [wɪŋk] *vi* mrugać (mrugnąć *pf*); **to ~ at sb** mrugać (mrugnąć *pf*) do kogoś
winner ['wɪnəʳ] *n* zwycięzca(-czyni) *m/f*
winning ['wɪnɪŋ] *adj* zwycięski
winter ['wɪntəʳ] *n* zima; **in (the) ~** zimą
wipe [waɪp] *vt* wycierać (wytrzeć *pf*); **to ~ one's nose** wycierać (wytrzeć *pf*) nos
▸ **wipe up** *vt* wycierać (wytrzeć *pf*)
wire ['waɪəʳ] *n* **1** (*metal*) drut **2** (*Elec: uninsulated*) przewód; (*insulated*) kabel

wireless ['waɪəlɪs] *adj* (*Comput: connection*) bezprzewodowy
wisdom ['wɪzdəm] *n* (*of person*) mądrość; (*of action, remark*) trafność
wisdom tooth (*pl* **wisdom teeth**) *n* ząb mądrości
wise [waɪz] *adj* (*person*) mądry
wish [wɪʃ] *n* życzenie ▷ *vt* życzyć sobie *+gen*; **best ~es** najlepsze życzenia; **with best ~es** (*in letter*) z najlepszymi życzeniami; **give her my best ~es** przekaż jej moje najserdeczniejsze życzenia; **to ~ to do sth** chcieć coś robić (zrobić *pf*)
wit [wɪt] *n* (*wittiness*) dowcip
witch [wɪtʃ] *n* wiedźma

KEYWORD

with [wɪð, wɪθ] *prep* **1** (*together with, at the house of*) z *+inst*; **I was with him** byłam z nim; **I'll be with you in a minute** przyjdę do ciebie za chwilkę; **we stayed with friends** zatrzymaliśmy się u znajomych
2 (*indicating feature, possession*) z *+inst*; **the man with the grey hat** mężczyzna w szarym kapeluszu; **the man with blue eyes** mężczyzna z niebieskimi oczami
3 (*indicating manner*) z *+inst*; **with a sigh/laugh** z westchnieniem/ze śmiechem
4 (*indicating means, substance*) *Polish uses the instrumental case*; **to walk with a stick** chodzić/iść (pójść *pf*) o lasce; **to fill sth with water** napełniać (napełnić *pf*) coś wodą
5 (*indicating cause*) z *+gen*; **red with anger** czerwony ze złości

without [wɪð'aut] *prep* bez *+gen*; **~ a coat** bez płaszcza; **~ speaking** bez słów
witness ['wɪtnɪs] *n* świadek
witty ['wɪtɪ] *adj* dowcipny
wives [waɪvz] *n pl of* **wife**
wizard ['wɪzəd] *n* czarodziej
woke [wəuk] *pt of* **wake**
woken ['wəukn] *pp of* **wake**
wolf [wulf] (*pl* **wolves** [wulvz]) *n* wilk
woman ['wumən] (*pl* **women** ['wɪmɪn]) *n* kobieta
won [wʌn] *pt, pp of* **win**
wonder ['wʌndə^r] *vt*: **to ~ whether/why** zastanawiać (zastanowić *pf*) się, czy/dlaczego ▷ *vi* zastanawiać (zastanowić *pf*) się
wonderful ['wʌndəful] *adj* cudowny
won't [wəunt] = **will not**
wood [wud] *n* **1** drewno **2** (*forest*) las
wooden ['wudn] *adj* (*object*) drewniany
woodwork ['wudwəːk] *n* (*craft*) stolarka
wool [wul] *n* wełna
word [wəːd] *n* słowo; **what's the ~ for "pen" in French?** jak jest „długopis" po francusku?; **in other ~s** innymi słowy
word processing [-'prəusɛsɪŋ] *n* przetwarzanie tekstów
word processor [-prəusɛsə^r] *n* (*machine*) procesor tekstów
wore [wɔː^r] *pt of* **wear**
work [wəːk] *n* praca ▷ *vi* **1** (*have job, do tasks*) pracować **2** (*function: mechanism, machine*) działać (zadziałać *pf*) **3** (*be successful: idea, method*) sprawdzać (sprawdzić *pf*) się; **to go to ~** chodzić/iść (pójść *pf*) do pracy; **to be out of ~** być bez pracy; **to ~ hard** pracować ciężko
▶ **work on** *vt fus* (*busy o.s. with*) pracować nad *+inst*
▶ **work out** *vi* (*Sport*) ćwiczyć ▷ *vt* (*answer, solution*) rozwiązywać (rozwiązać *pf*); (*plan, details*) rozpracowywać (rozpracować *pf*); **it ~s out at 100 pounds** wychodzi sto funtów; **I can't ~ out why...** nie mogę pojąć, dlaczego...
worker ['wəːkə^r] *n* (*employed person*) pracownik(-ica) *m/f*; **a hard/good ~** dobry(-ra) pracownik(-ica) *m/f*
work experience *n* doświadczenie zawodowe
working-class *adj* robotniczy
workman ['wəːkmən] (*irreg*) *n* robotnik
worksheet ['wəːkʃiːt] *n* **1** (*in school*) *spis zadań na kartce na lekcji szkolnej* **2** (*on computer*) arkusz kalkulacyjny

workshop ['wəːkʃɔp] *n* warsztat
workstation ['wəːksteɪʃən] *n* **1** (*desk*) stanowisko pracy **2** (*computer*) stacja robocza
world [wəːld] *n* (*earth*): **the ~** świat ▷ *adj* światowy; **all over the ~** na całym świecie
World Cup *n* (*Football*): **the ~** mistrzostwa świata *n pl* w piłce nożnej
World-Wide Web [wəːld'waɪd-] *n*: **the ~** internet
worm [wəːm] *n* (*also*: **earth~**) robak
worn [wɔːn] *pp of* **wear** ▷ *adj* wytarty
worried ['wʌrɪd] *adj* zmartwiony; **to be ~ about sth/sb** martwić (zmartwić *pf*) się o coś/o kogoś
worry ['wʌrɪ] *n* **1** (*feeling of anxiety*) niepokój **2** (*cause of anxiety*) zmartwienie ▷ *vt* martwić (zmartwić *pf*) ▷ *vi* martwić (zmartwić *pf*) się
worse [wəːs] *adj* gorszy ▷ *adv* gorzej; **to get ~** pogarszać (pogorszyć *pf*) się
worst [wəːst] *adj* najgorszy ▷ *adv* najgorzej ▷ *n* najgorszy; **at ~** w najgorszym przypadku
worth [wəːθ] *n* wartość ▷ *adj*: **to be ~ £50** być wartym pięćdziesiąt funtów; **it's ~ it** warto (to) zrobić; **400 dollars' ~ of damage** wartość szkody wynosi czterysta dolarów; **it would be (well) ~ doing...** (naprawdę) warto by zrobić...

KEYWORD

would [wud] *aux vb* **1** (*conditional mood*): **I would love to go to Italy** chciałbym bardzo pojechać do Włoch; **I'm sure he wouldn't do that** jestem pewien, że on tego by nie zrobił; **if she asked him he would do it** gdyby go poprosiła, zrobiłby to
2 (*in offers, invitations, requests*): **would you like a biscuit?** może ciastko?; **would you ask him to come in?** poprosiłby go pan/poprosiłaby go pani, żeby wszedł?
3 (*be willing to*): **she wouldn't help me** ona nie chciała mi pomóc; **the door wouldn't open** drzwi nie chciały się otworzyć
4 (*in indirect speech*): **he said he would be at home later** powiedział, że będzie w domu później
5 (*used to*): **he would spend every day on the beach** spędzał każdy dzień na plaży

wouldn't ['wudnt] = **would not**
wrap [ræp] *vt* zawijać (zawinąć *pf*); **to ~ sth around sth/sb** zawijać (zawinąć *pf*) coś wokół czegoś/kogoś
▶ **wrap up** *vt* (*pack*) owijać (owinąć *pf*)
wrapping paper ['ræpɪŋ-] *n* (*gift wrap*) papier do pakowania
wreck [rɛk] *n* **1** (*wreckage*) wrak **2** (*US: accident*) wypadek **3** (*inf: person*) wrak człowieka ▷ *vt* (*equipment, room etc*) niszczyć (zniszczyć *pf*); (*life, chances, marriage*) rujnować (zrujnować *pf*)
wrestler ['rɛsləʳ] *n* zapaśnik(-iczka) *m/f*
wrestling ['rɛslɪŋ] *n* zapasy *pl*
wrinkled ['rɪŋkld] *adj* (*skin, face*) pomarszczony
wrist [rɪst] *n* nadgarstek
write [raɪt] (*pt* **wrote**, *pp* **written**) *vt* **1** (*note down*) pisać (zapisać *pf*) **2** (*compose: letter, note*) pisać (napisać *pf*) **3** (*create: novel, music etc*) pisać (napisać *pf*) **4** (*also*: **~ out**: *cheque, receipt, prescription*) wypisywać (wypisać *pf*) ▷ *vi* pisać (napisać *pf*); **to ~ to sb** pisać (napisać *pf*) do kogoś
▶ **write down** *vt* zapisywać (zapisać *pf*)
writer ['raɪtəʳ] *n* (*author*) pisarz(-rka) *m/f*
writing ['raɪtɪŋ] *n* **1** (*sth written*) pismo **2** (*handwriting*) charakter pisma; **in ~** na piśmie
written ['rɪtn] *pp of* **write**
wrong [rɔŋ] *adj* **1** (*inappropriate*) nieodpowiedni **2** (*incorrect*) błędny **3** (*morally bad*) zły ▷ *adv* (*incorrectly*) źle; **to be ~** być w błędzie; **to be ~ (about sth)** (*person*) mylić (pomylić *pf*) się (w stosunku do czegoś); **what's ~?** co jest nie w porządku?; **what's ~ with you?** co ci dolega?;

there's nothing ~ nic złego się nie dzieje; **to go ~** (*plan*) nie udawać (udać *pf*) się; (*machine*) psuć (popsuć *pf*) się
wrote [rəut] *pt of* **write**
www (*Comput*) *n abbr* (= *World-Wide Web*) www

xenophobia [zɛnəˈfəubɪə] *n* ksenofobia
Xmas [ˈɛksməs] *n abbr* (= *Christmas*) Boże Narodzenie
X-ray [ˈɛksreɪ] *n* (*photo*) prześwietlenie ▷ *vt* robić (zrobić *pf*) prześwietlenie +*gen*; **to have an ~** robić (zrobić *pf*) sobie prześwietlenie
xylophone [ˈzaɪləfəun] *n* ksylofon

yacht [jɔt] *n* **1** (*sailing boat*) żaglówka **2** (*luxury craft*) jacht
yard [jɑːd] *n* (*US*: *garden*) ogród
yawn [jɔːn] *vi* ziewać (ziewnąć *pf*) ▷ *n* ziewanie
year [jɪəʳ] *n* rok; (*m pl*) lat, lata; **he's 8 ~s old** on ma osiem lat; **we lived there for 2 ~s** mieszkaliśmy tam przez dwa lata; **every ~** co roku; **this ~** w tym roku; **last ~** w zeszłym roku; **a** *or* **per ~** rocznie
yell [jɛl] *vi* krzyczeć (krzyknąć *pf*)
yellow ['jɛləu] *adj* żółty ▷ *n* żółty
yes [jɛs] *adv* (*replying to question*) tak ▷ *n* (*answer*) tak
yesterday ['jɛstədɪ] *adv* wczoraj ▷ *n* wczoraj; **the day before ~** przedwczoraj
yet [jɛt] *adv* **1** (*up to now*) jak dotąd; (*with negative*) jeszcze nie; (*in questions*) już **2** (*now*: *in negatives*) jeszcze ▷ *conj* mimo to; **they haven't finished ~** jeszcze nie skończyli; **~ again** znów
yog(h)urt ['jəugət] *n* jogurt
yolk [jəuk] *n* żółtko

KEYWORD

you [juː] *pron* **1** (*familiar sg*) ty; (*familiar pl*) wy; (*m sg polite*) pan; (*f sg polite*) pani; (*polite vir m pl*) panowie; (*polite non-vir f pl*) panie; (*polite vir m/f pl*) państwo; **do you know her?** (*polite m/f sg*) czy zna ją pan/pani?; **I like you** (*familiar sg*) lubię cię; **I'll send you the photos when I've got them** (*familiar sg*) wyślę ci zdjęcia, jak je dostanę; **I gave it to you** (*familiar sg*) dałem ci to; **it's for you** (*familiar sg*) to dla ciebie
2 (*in generalizations*: *one*): **you can't put metal dishes in a microwave** nie wkłada się metalowych naczyń do kuchenki mikrofalowej; **you never know** nigdy nie wiadomo

young [jʌŋ] *adj* młody; **my ~er brother** mój młodszy brat; **my ~er sister** moja młodsza siostra
your [jɔːʳ] *adj* (*familiar m sg*) twój; (*familiar f sg*) twoja; (*familiar nt sg*) twoje; (*familiar pl*) wasz; (*polite m sg*) pana; (*polite f sg*) pani; (*polite vir m pl*) panów; (*polite non-vir f pl*) pań; (*polite vir m/f pl*) państwa; (*referring to subject of sentence*) swój; **~ house** (*polite m/f sg*) pana/pani dom; **have you cleaned ~ teeth?** (*familiar sg*) umyłeś zęby?
yours [jɔːz] *pron* (*familiar sg*) twój; (*familiar pl*) wasz; (*polite m sg*) pana; (*polite f sg*) pani; (*polite vir m pl*) panów; (*polite non-vir f pl*) pań; (*polite vir m/f pl*) państwa; **is this ~?** (*familiar sg*) czy to twoje?; (*polite m/f sg*) czy to jest pana/pani?; **~ sincerely/faithfully** z wyrazami szacunku

KEYWORD

yourself [jɔː'sɛlf] *pron* **1** (*gen, acc*) siebie; (*dat, loc*) sobie; (*inst*) sobą; (*reflexive pronoun*) się; **have you hurt yourself?** (*familiar*) skaleczyłeś się?
2 (*emphatic*: *m*) sam; (*f*) sama; **did you paint the room yourself?** (*polite m*) czy sam pomalował pan ten pokój?; (*polite f*) czy sama pani pomalowała ten pokój?
3 (*you*: *familiar*) ty; (*polite m*) pan; (*polite f*) pani; **an intelligent person like yourself** (*polite m/f*) taka inteligentna osoba jak pan/pani; **by yourself** (*unaided, alone*) sam

KEYWORD

yourselves [jɔː'sɛlvz] *pl pron* **1** (*gen, acc*) siebie; (*dat, loc*) sobie;

(*inst*) sobą; (*reflexive pronoun*) się; **buy yourselves something nice** (*familiar*) kupcie sobie coś ładnego **2** (*emphatic*: *vir*) sami; (*non-vir*) same; **did you paint the house yourselves?** (*polite non-vir*) czy panie same pomalowały dom? **3** (*you*: *familiar*) wy; (*polite m vir*) panowie; (*polite f non-vir*) panie; (*polite m/f vir*) państwo; **intelligent people like yourselves** (*polite vir*) tacy inteligentni ludzie jak panowie; **by yourselves** (*unaided, alone*: *vir*) sami; (*non-vir*) same

youth [ju:θ] *n* młodość; (*young person*) młodzieniec; **in my ~** w czasach mojej młodości
youth club *n* klub młodzieżowy
youth hostel *n* schronisko młodzieżowe

Z

zebra ['zi:brə] *n* zebra
zebra crossing (*Brit*) *n* przejście dla pieszych
zero ['zɪərəu] (*pl* **zero** *or* **zeroes**) *n* zero; **5 degrees below ~** pięć stopni poniżej zera
zigzag ['zɪgzæg] *vi* iść zygzakiem
zip [zɪp] *n* (*Brit*: *fastener*) suwak ▷ *vt* (*also*: **~ up**) zapinać (zapiąć *pf*)
zip code (*US*) *n* kod pocztowy
zipper ['zɪpə^r] (*US*) *n* suwak
zodiac ['zəudɪæk] *n*: **the ~** zodiak
zone [zəun] *n* (*area*) strefa
zoo [zu:] *n* zoo
zucchini [zu:'ki:nɪ] ((*US*) *pl* **zucchini** *or* **zucchinis**) *n* cukinia